THE
PUBLIC GENERAL ACTS
AND GENERAL SYNOD MEASURES
1988

[IN FIVE PARTS]

PART I

(Chapters 1, 2)

with

Lists of the Public General Acts
Local Acts and an Index

LONDON: HMSO

1990

£310·00 net

HMSO
£310 set
7-90

HMSO publications are available from:

HMSO Publications Centre
(Mail and telephone orders only)
PO Box 276, London SW8 5DT
Telephone orders (01) 873 9090
General enquiries (01) 873 0011
(queuing system in operation for both numbers)

HMSO Bookshops
49 High Holborn, London WC1V 6HB   (01) 873 0011 (Counter service only)
258 Broad Street, Birmingham B1 2HE   (021) 643 3740
Southey House, 33 Wine Street, Bristol BS1 2BQ   (0272) 264306
9–21 Princess Street, Manchester M60 8AS   (061) 834 7201
80 Chichester Street, Belfast BT1 4JY   (0232) 238451
71 Lothian Road, Edinburgh EH3 9AZ   (031) 228 4181

HMSO's Accredited Agents
(see Yellow Pages)

and through good booksellers

From 6 May 1990 the London telephone numbers above carry the prefix
'071' instead of '01'.

ISBN 0 11 840290 0

THIS PUBLICATION
relates to
the Public General Acts
and General Synod Measures
which received the Royal Assent in 1988
in which year ended the THIRTY-SIXTH
and began the THIRTY-SEVENTH YEAR
of the Reign of HER MAJESTY
QUEEN ELIZABETH THE SECOND
and
ended the First session
and began the Second session
of the Fiftieth Parliament of the
United Kingdom of Great Britain
and Northern Ireland.

d

PRINTED IN THE UNITED KINGDOM BY PAUL FREEMAN
Controller and Chief Executive of HMSO and
Queen's Printer of Acts of Parliament

e

CONTENTS

PART I

TABLE I
Alphabetical List of
the Public General Acts of 1988

TABLE II

Chronological List of the
Public General Acts of 1988

Consolidation Act

2nd Session of 50th Parliament

*Consolidation Act

TABLE III

Alphabetical List of
the Local and Personal Acts of 1988

TABLE IV
Chronological List of
the General Synod Measures of 1988

Measures passed by the General Synod of the Church of England which received the Royal Assent during the year 1988.

Income and Corporation Taxes Act 1988

1988 CHAPTER 1

An Act to consolidate certain of the enactments relating to income tax and corporation tax, including certain enactments relating also to capital gains tax; and to repeal as obsolete section 339(1) of the Income and Corporation Taxes Act 1970 and paragraphs 3 and 4 of Schedule 11 to the Finance Act 1980.

[9th February 1988]

BE IT ENACTED by the Queen's most Excellent Majesty, by and with the advice and consent of the Lords Spiritual and Temporal, and Commons, in this present Parliament assembled, and by the authority of the same, as follows:—

PART I

THE CHARGE TO TAX

Income tax

1.—(1) Income tax shall be charged in accordance with the provisions of the Income Tax Acts in respect of all property, profits or gains respectively described or comprised in the Schedules, A, B, C, D, E and F, set out in sections 15 to 20 or which in accordance with the Income Tax Acts are to be brought into charge to tax under any of those Schedules or otherwise.

The charge to income tax.

(2) Where any Act enacts that income tax shall be charged for any year, income tax shall be charged for that year—

    (a) in respect of any income which does not fall within paragraph (b) below, at such rate as Parliament may determine to be the basic rate for that year;

    (b) in respect of so much of an individual's total income as exceeds £17,900, at such higher rates respectively as Parliament may determine in relation to the first £2,500, the next £5,000, the next £7,900, the next £7,900 and the remainder;

but this subsection has effect subject to any provision of the Income Tax Acts providing for income tax to be charged at a different rate in certain cases.

A

(3) The amount up to which an individual's income is by virtue of subsection (2) above chargeable for any year at the basic rate shall be known as the basic rate limit; and the parts of income in excess of the basic rate limit which are specified in paragraph (b) of that subsection shall be known respectively as the first, second, third, fourth and fifth higher rate bands.

(4) If the retail prices index for the month of December preceding a year of assessment is higher than it was for the previous December, then, unless Parliament otherwise determines, subsection (2) above shall apply for that year as if for each of the amounts specified in that subsection as it applied for the previous year (whether by virtue of this subsection or otherwise) there were substituted an amount arrived at by increasing the amount for the previous year by the same percentage as the percentage increase in the retail prices index and, if the result is not a multiple of £100, rounding it up to the nearest amount which is such a multiple.

(5) Subsection (4) above shall not require any change to be made in the amounts deductible or repayable under section 203 between the beginning of a year of assessment and 5th May in that year.

(6) The Treasury shall before each year of assessment make an order specifying the amounts which by virtue of subsection (4) above will be treated as specified for that year in subsection (2) above.

(7) Part VII contains general provisions relating to the taxation of income of individuals.

Fractions of a pound, and yearly assessments.

2.—(1) The due proportion of income tax shall be charged for every fractional part of one pound.

(2) Every assessment and charge to income tax shall be made for a year commencing on the 6th April and ending on the following 5th April.

Certain income charged at basic rate.

3. Where a person is required to be assessed and charged with income tax in respect of any property, profits or gains out of which he makes any payment in respect of—

    (a) any annuity or other annual payment (not being interest); or

    (b) any royalty or other sum in respect of the user of a patent; or

    (c) any rent, royalty or other payment which is declared by section 119 or 120 to be subject to deduction of tax under section 348 or 349 as if it were a royalty or other sum paid in respect of a patent;

he shall, in respect of so much of the property, profits or gains as is equal to the payment and may be deducted in computing his total income, be charged at the basic rate.

Construction of references in Income Tax Acts to deduction of tax.

4.—(1) Any provision of the Income Tax Acts requiring, permitting or assuming the deduction of income tax from any amount (otherwise than in pursuance of section 203) or treating income tax as having been deducted from or paid on any amount, shall, subject to any provision to the contrary, be construed as referring to deduction or payment of income tax at the basic rate in force for the relevant year of assessment.

(2) For the purposes of subsection (1) above, the relevant year of assessment shall be taken to be (except where otherwise provided)—

(a) if the amount is an amount payable wholly out of profits or gains brought into charge to tax, the year in which the amount becomes due;

(b) in any other case, the year in which the amount is paid.

5.—(1) Subject to the provisions of the Income Tax Acts and in particular to subsection (2) below and section 203, income tax contained in an assessment for any year shall be payable on or before the 1st January in that year, or at the expiration of a period of 30 days beginning with the date of the issue of the notice of assessment, whichever is the later.

(2) Subject to subsection (3) below, income tax under Schedule D charged for any year on any individual or firm in respect of the profits or gains of any trade, profession or vocation and contained in an assessment for that year shall, instead of being payable in accordance with subsection (1) above, be payable in two equal instalments, the first on or before the 1st January in that year or at the expiration of the period referred to in subsection (1) above, and the second on or before the following 1st July; and the provisions of the Income Tax Acts as to the recovery of income tax shall apply to each instalment of the tax in the same manner as they apply to the whole amount of the tax.

(3) Where the date of the issue of the notice of assessment is later than the 1st June following the end of the year of assessment, subsection (2) above shall not have effect, and the tax shall be due and payable as provided in subsection (1) above.

(4) Except as otherwise provided by the Income Tax Acts, any income tax charged at a rate other than the basic rate on—

(a) income from which income tax has been deducted (otherwise than under section 203); or

(b) income from or on which income tax is treated as having been deducted or paid; or

(c) income chargeable under Schedule F;

shall be due and payable on or before 1st December following the end of the year for which it is assessed, or at the expiration of a period of 30 days beginning with the date of the issue of the notice of assessment, whichever is the later.

Corporation tax

6.—(1) Corporation tax shall be charged on profits of companies, and the Corporation Tax Acts shall apply, for any financial year for which Parliament so determines, and where an Act charges corporation tax for any financial year the Corporation Tax Acts apply, without any express provision, for that year accordingly.

(2) The provisions of the Income Tax Acts relating to the charge of income tax shall not apply to income of a company (not arising to it in a fiduciary or representative capacity) if—

(a) the company is resident in the United Kingdom, or

(b) the income is, in the case of a company not so resident, within the chargeable profits of the company as defined for the purposes of corporation tax by section 11(2).

(3) A company shall not be chargeable to capital gains tax in respect of gains accruing to it so that it is chargeable in respect of them to corporation tax or would be so chargeable but for an exemption from corporation tax.

(4) In this section, sections 7 to 12, 114, 115 (but subject to subsection (7)), 242, 243, 247 and 248, Part VIII, Chapter IV of Part X and Part XI, except in so far as the context otherwise requires—

(a) "profits" means income and chargeable gains; and

(b) "trade" includes "vocation", and also includes an office or employment or the occupation of woodlands in any context in which the expression is applied to that in the Income Tax Acts.

(5) Part VIII contains general provisions relating to the taxation of profits of companies.

Treatment of certain payments and repayment of income tax.

7.—(1) No payment made by a company resident in the United Kingdom shall be treated for any purpose of the Income Tax Acts as paid out of profits or gains brought into charge to income tax; nor shall any right or obligation under the Income Tax Acts to deduct income tax from any payment be affected by the fact that the recipient is a company not chargeable to income tax in respect of the payment.

(2) Subject to the provisions of the Corporation Tax Acts, where a company resident in the United Kingdom receives any payment on which it bears income tax by deduction, the income tax thereon shall be set off against any corporation tax assessable on the company by an assessment made for the accounting period in which that payment falls to be taken into account for corporation tax (or would fall to be taken into account but for any exemption from corporation tax); and accordingly in respect of that payment the company, unless wholly exempt from corporation tax, shall not be entitled to a repayment of income tax before the assessment for that accounting period is finally determined and it appears that a repayment is due.

(3) Subsection (2) above does not apply to a payment of relevant loan interest to which section 369 applies.

(4) References in this section to payments received by a company apply to any received by another person on behalf of or in trust for the company, but not to any received by the company on behalf of or in trust for another person.

(5) Effect shall be given to section 6(2), to that section as modified by subsection (2) above and by section 11(3) and, so far as exemptions from income tax conferred by the Corporation Tax Acts call for repayment of tax, to those exemptions by means of a claim.

General scheme of corporation tax.

8.—(1) Subject to any exceptions provided for by the Corporation Tax Acts, a company shall be chargeable to corporation tax on all its profits wherever arising.

(2) A company shall be chargeable to corporation tax on profits accruing for its benefit under any trust, or arising under any partnership, in any case in which it would be so chargeable if the profits accrued to it directly; and a company shall be chargeable to corporation tax on profits

arising in the winding up of the company, but shall not otherwise be chargeable to corporation tax on profits accruing to it in a fiduciary or representative capacity except as respects its own beneficial interest (if any) in those profits.

(3) Corporation tax for any financial year shall be charged on profits arising in that year; but assessments to corporation tax shall be made on a company by reference to accounting periods, and the amount chargeable (after making all proper deductions) of the profits arising in an accounting period shall, where necessary, be apportioned between the financial years in which the accounting period falls.

In relation to accounting periods ending after such day, not being earlier than 31st March 1992, as the Treasury may by order appoint for the purposes of this subsection, this subsection shall have effect with the substitution for "assessments to corporation tax shall be made on a company" of "corporation tax shall be computed and chargeable (and any assessments shall accordingly be made)".

(4) In any financial year assessments for accounting periods falling wholly or partly in that year or (subject to subsection (5) below) in the preceding year may, notwithstanding that corporation tax has not at the time been charged for the year in question, charge tax for so much of the period as falls within that year according to the rate of tax and the other rates and the fractions last fixed, but any such charge shall be subject to later adjustment, if need be, by discharge or repayment of tax or by a further assessment if for that year corporation tax is not charged by an Act of Parliament passed not later than 5th August next after the end of the year or is charged otherwise than as it has been assessed.

(5) Where the House of Commons passes a resolution for fixing the rate of corporation tax for any financial year or for altering the tax for any financial year, then any assessment to tax afterwards made by virtue of subsection (4) above may be made in accordance with the resolution; but no assessment made by virtue of that subsection later than 5th May next after the end of any financial year shall charge tax for that year, unless a resolution for charging corporation tax for that year has been so passed, nor shall any assessment be made by virtue of any such resolution later than the prescribed period from the date on which the resolution is passed.

(6) In subsection (5) above "the prescribed period" means—

(a) as respects a resolution passed in March or April in any year, a period beginning with the passing of the resolution and ending with 5th August in the same calendar year,

(b) as respects any other resolution, four months after the date on which the resolution is passed.

9.—(1) Except as otherwise provided by the Tax Acts, the amount of any income shall for purposes of corporation tax be computed in accordance with income tax principles, all questions as to the amounts which are or are not to be taken into account as income, or in computing income, or charged to tax as a person's income, or as to the time when any such amount is to be treated as arising, being determined in accordance with income tax law and practice as if accounting periods were years of assessment.

Computation of income: application of income tax principles.

PART I

(2) For the purposes of this section "income tax law" means, in relation to any accounting period, the law applying, for the year of assessment in which the period ends, to the charge on individuals of income tax, except that it does not include such of the enactments of the Income Tax Acts as make special provision for individuals in relation to matters referred to in subsection (1) above.

(3) Accordingly, for purposes of corporation tax, income shall be computed, and the assessment shall be made, under the like Schedules and Cases as apply for purposes of income tax, and in accordance with the provisions applicable to those Schedules and Cases, but (subject to the provisions of the Corporation Tax Acts) the amounts so computed for the several sources of income, if more than one, together with any amount to be included in respect of chargeable gains, shall be aggregated to arrive at the total profits.

(4) Without prejudice to the generality of subsection (1) above, any provision of the Income Tax Acts which confers an exemption from income tax, or which provides for a person to be charged to income tax on any amount (whether expressed to be income or not, and whether an actual amount or not), shall, except as otherwise provided, have the like effect for purposes of corporation tax.

(5) Where, by virtue of this section or otherwise, any enactment applies both to income tax and to corporation tax—

(a) it shall not be affected in its operation by the fact that they are distinct taxes but, so far as is consistent with the Corporation Tax Acts, shall apply in relation to income tax and corporation tax as if they were one tax, so that, in particular, a matter which in a case involving two individuals is relevant for both of them in relation to income tax shall in a like case involving an individual and a company be relevant for him in relation to that tax and for it in relation to corporation tax; and

(b) for that purpose references in any such enactment to a relief from or charge to income tax, or to a specified provision of the Income Tax Acts shall, in the absence of or subject to any express adaptation, be construed as being or including a reference to any corresponding relief from or charge to corporation tax, or to any corresponding provision of the Corporation Tax Acts.

(6) The provisions of the Income Tax Acts applied by this section do not include sections 1 to 5, 60 to 69, Part VII or sections 348 to 350 of this Act; and nothing in this section shall be taken to mean that income arising in any period is to be computed by reference to any other period (except in so far as this results from apportioning to different parts of a period income of the whole period).

Time for payment of tax.

10.—(1) Except as provided by section 478—

(a) corporation tax for an accounting period ending after such day or days (not being earlier than 31st March 1992) as the Treasury may by order appoint for the purposes of this section shall be due and payable on the day following the expiry of nine months from the end of that period; and

(b) corporation tax assessed for any other accounting period shall be paid within nine months from the end of that period or, if it is later, within 30 days from the date of the issue of the notice of assessment.

(2) Notwithstanding that, by virtue of subsection (1)(a) above or section 419(1), any corporation tax (or any amount payable as if it were corporation tax) is due without the making of an assessment, no proceedings for collecting that tax (or other amount) shall be instituted—

(a) unless it has been assessed; and

(b) until the expiry of the period of 30 days beginning on the date on which the notice of assessment is issued;

and the reference in this subsection to proceedings for.collecting tax or any other amount includes a reference to proceedings by way of distraint or poinding for that tax or other amount.

(3) If, with respect to any accounting period—

(a) a company has paid an amount of corporation tax without the making of an assessment; and

(b) at any time before an assessment to corporation tax for the period becomes final, the company has grounds for believing that, by reason of a change in the circumstances of the case since the tax was paid, the amount paid exceeds the company's probable liability for corporation tax,

the company may, by notice given to the inspector on or after the date which, under section 826, is the material date in relation to that tax, make a claim for the repayment to the company of the amount of that excess; and a notice under this subsection shall state the amount which the company considers should be repaid and the grounds referred to in paragraph (b) above.

(4) If, apart from this subsection, a claim would fall to be made under subsection (3) above at a time when the company concerned has appealed against such an assessment as is referred to in paragraph (b) of that subsection but that appeal has not been finally determined, that subsection shall have effect as if, for the words from "make a claim" to "excess", there were substituted "apply to the Commissioners to whom the appeal stands referred for a determination of the amount which should be repaid to the company pending a determination of the company's liability for the accounting period in question"; and such an application shall be determined in the same way as the appeal.

(5) Where on an appeal against an assessment to corporation tax a company makes an application under section 55(3) or (4) of the Management Act (postponement of tax charged but not paid etc.), that application may be combined with an application under subsections (3) and (4) above (relating to tax which was paid prior to the assessment).

11.—(1) A company not resident in the United Kingdom shall not be within the charge to corporation tax unless it carries on a trade in the United Kingdom through a branch or agency but, if it does so, it shall, subject to any exceptions provided for by the Corporation Tax Acts, be chargeable to corporation tax on all its chargeable profits wherever arising.

Companies not resident in United Kingdom.

(2) For purposes of corporation tax the chargeable profits of a company not resident in the United Kingdom but carrying on a trade there through a branch or agency shall be—

  (a) any trading income arising directly or indirectly through or from the branch or agency, and any income from property or rights used by, or held by or for, the branch or agency (but so that this paragraph shall not include distributions received from companies resident in the United Kingdom); and

  (b) such chargeable gains accruing on the disposal of assets situated in the United Kingdom as are by section 12 of the 1979 Act made chargeable to capital gains tax in the case of an individual not resident or ordinarily resident in the United Kingdom.

(3) Subject to section 447, where a company not resident in the United Kingdom receives any payment on which it bears income tax by deduction, and the payment forms part of, or is to be taken into account in computing, the company's income chargeable to corporation tax, the income tax thereon shall be set off against any corporation tax assessable on that income by an assessment made for the accounting period in which the payment falls to be taken into account for corporation tax; and accordingly in respect of that payment the company shall not be entitled to a repayment of income tax before the assessment for that accounting period is finally determined and it appears that a repayment is due.

(4) Subsection (3) above does not apply to a payment of relevant loan interest to which section 369 applies.

Basis of, and periods for, assessment.

12.—(1) Except as otherwise provided by the Corporation Tax Acts, corporation tax shall be assessed and charged for any accounting period of a company on the full amount of the profits arising in the period (whether or not received in or transmitted to the United Kingdom) without any other deduction than is authorised by those Acts.

(2) An accounting period of a company shall begin for purposes of corporation tax whenever—

  (a) the company, not then being within the charge to corporation tax, comes within it, whether by the company becoming resident in the United Kingdom or acquiring a source of income, or otherwise; or

  (b) an accounting period of the company ends without the company then ceasing to be within the charge to corporation tax.

(3) An accounting period of a company shall end for purposes of corporation tax on the first occurrence of any of the following—

  (a) the expiration of 12 months from the beginning of the accounting period;

  (b) an accounting date of the company or, if there is a period for which the company does not make up accounts, the end of that period;

  (c) the company beginning or ceasing to trade or to be, in respect of the trade or (if more than one) of all the trades carried on by it, within the charge to corporation tax;

(d) the company beginning or ceasing to be resident in the United Kingdom;

(e) the company ceasing to be within the charge to corporation tax.

(4) For the purposes of this section a company resident in the United Kingdom, if not otherwise within the charge to corporation tax, shall be treated as coming within the charge to corporation tax at the time when it commences to carry on business.

(5) If a company carrying on more than one trade makes up accounts of any of them to different dates, and does not make up general accounts for the whole of the company's activities, subsection (3)(b) above shall apply with reference to the accounting date of such one of the trades as the Board may determine.

(6) If a chargeable gain or allowable loss accrues to a company at a time not otherwise within an accounting period of the company, an accounting period of the company shall then begin for the purposes of corporation tax, and the gain or loss shall accrue in that accounting period.

(7) Notwithstanding anything in subsections (1) to (6) above, where a company is wound up, an accounting period shall end and a new one begin with the commencement of the winding up, and thereafter, subject to section 342(6), an accounting period shall not end otherwise than by the expiration of 12 months from its beginning or by the completion of the winding up.

For this purpose a winding up is to be taken to commence on the passing by the company of a resolution for the winding up of the company, or on the presentation of a winding up petition if no such resolution has previously been passed and a winding up order is made on the petition, or on the doing of any other act for a like purpose in the case of a winding up otherwise than under the Insolvency Act 1986.

1986 c. 45.

(8) Where it appears to the inspector that the beginning or end of any accounting period of a company is uncertain, he may make an assessment on the company for such period, not exceeding 12 months, as appears to him appropriate, and that period shall be treated for all purposes as an accounting period of the company unless either—

(a) the inspector on further facts coming to his knowledge sees fit to revise it; or

(b) on an appeal against the assessment in respect of some other matter the company shows the true accounting periods;

and if on an appeal against an assessment made by virtue of this subsection the company shows the true accounting periods, the assessment appealed against shall, as regards the period to which it relates, have effect as an assessment or assessments for the true accounting periods, and there may be made such other assessments for any such periods or any of them as might have been made at the time when the assessment appealed against was made.

Small companies' rate

13.—(1) Where in any accounting period the profits of a company resident in the United Kingdom do not exceed the lower relevant

Small companies' relief.

maximum amount, the company may claim that the corporation tax charged on its basic profits for that period shall be calculated as if the rate of corporation tax (instead of being the rate fixed for companies generally) were such lower rate (to be known as the "small companies' rate") as Parliament may from time to time determine.

(2) Where in any accounting period the profits of any such company exceed the lower relevant maximum amount but do not exceed the upper relevant maximum amount, the company may claim that the corporation tax charged on its basic profits for that period shall be reduced by a sum equal to such fraction as Parliament may from time to time determine of the following amount—

$$(M - P) \times \frac{I}{P}$$

where—

M is the upper relevant maximum amount;

P is the amount of the profits; and

I is the amount of the basic profits.

(3) The lower and upper relevant maximum amounts mentioned above shall be determined as follows—

(a) where the company has no associated company in the accounting period, those amounts are £100,000 and £500,000 respectively;

(b) where the company has one or more associated companies in the accounting period, the lower relevant maximum amount is £100,000 divided by one plus the number of those associated companies, and the upper relevant maximum amount is £500,000 divided by one plus the number of those associated companies.

(4) In applying subsection (3) above to any accounting period of a company, an associated company which has not carried on any trade or business at any time in that accounting period (or, if an associated company during part only of that accounting period, at any time in that part of that accounting period) shall be disregarded and for the purposes of this section a company is to be treated as an "associated company" of another at a given time if at that time one of the two has control of the other or both are under the control of the same person or persons.

In this subsection "control" shall be construed in accordance with section 416.

(5) In determining how many associated companies a company has got in an accounting period or whether a company has an associated company in an accounting period, an associated company shall be counted even if it was an associated company for part only of the accounting period, and two or more associated companies shall be counted even if they were associated companies for different parts of the accounting period.

(6) For an accounting period of less than 12 months the relevant maximum amounts determined in accordance with subsection (3) above shall be proportionately reduced.

(7) For the purposes of this section the profits (but not the basic profits) of a company for an accounting period shall be taken to be the amount of its profits for that period on which corporation tax falls finally to be borne, with the addition of franked investment income other than franked investment income which the company (if a member of a group) receives from companies within the group; and for this purpose distributions received by the company from another are to be treated as coming from within the company's group if, but only if, dividends so received are group income or would be group income if the companies so elected.

(8) For the purposes of this section the basic profits of a company for an accounting period shall be taken to be the amount of its profits for that period on which corporation tax falls finally to be borne.

(9) Any power which the inspector may exercise under paragraph 17 of Schedule 19 may be exercised by him for the purposes of this section.

Advance corporation tax

14.—(1) Subject to section 247, where a company resident in the United Kingdom makes a qualifying distribution it shall be liable to pay an amount of corporation tax ("advance corporation tax") in accordance with subsection (3) below.

Advance corporation tax and qualifying distributions.

(2) In this Act "qualifying distribution" means any distribution other than—

(a) a distribution which, in relation to the company making it, is a distribution by virtue only of section 209(2)(c); or

(b) a distribution consisting of any share capital or security which the company making the distribution has directly or indirectly received from the company by which the share capital or security was issued and which, in relation to the latter company, is a distribution by virtue only of section 209(2)(c).

(3) Subject to section 241, for the financial year 1988 and any subsequent financial year advance corporation tax shall be payable on an amount equal to the amount or value of the distribution, and shall be so payable at a rate which shall be fixed by the fraction—

$$\frac{I}{100 - I}$$

where I is the percentage at which income tax at the basic rate is charged for the year of assessment which begins on 6th April in that financial year.

(4) The provisions of this Act as to the charge, calculation and payment of corporation tax (including provisions conferring any exemption) shall not be construed as affecting the charge, calculation or payment of advance corporation tax, and the Corporation Tax Acts shall apply for the purposes of advance corporation tax whether or not they are for the time being applicable for the purposes of corporation tax other than advance corporation tax.

(5) Part VI contains further provisions relating to advance corporation tax and company distributions.

The six Schedules

Schedule A.   **15.**—(1) The Schedule referred to as Schedule A is as follows:—

SCHEDULE A

1. Tax under this Schedule shall be charged on the annual profits or gains arising in respect of any such rents or receipts as follows, that is to say—

    (a) rents under leases of land in the United Kingdom;

    (b) rentcharges, ground annuals and feuduties, and any other annual payments reserved in respect of, or charged on or issuing out of, such land;

    (c) other receipts arising to a person from or by virtue of his ownership of an estate or interest in or right over such land or any incorporeal hereditament or incorporeal heritable subject in the United Kingdom.

2. Tax under this Schedule shall be charged by reference to the rents or receipts to which a person becomes entitled in the chargeable period.

Exceptions

3. Paragraph 1 above does not apply—

    (a) to any yearly interest, or

    (b) to any profits or gains charged to tax under Schedule D by virtue of section 55, or

    (c) to any payment so charged by virtue of section 119 or 120;

and has effect subject also to the provisions of section 98 with respect to tied premises.

4. Where rent is payable under a lease under which the tenant is entitled to the use of furniture and tax in respect of the payment for its use is chargeable under Case VI of Schedule D, tax in respect of the rent shall be charged under that Case instead of under this Schedule unless the landlord elects that this paragraph shall not apply.

(2) An election that paragraph 4 of Schedule A shall not apply shall be made by notice to the inspector given within two years after the end of the chargeable period; and where such notice is given, any adjustment of the liability to tax of the person giving it which is required in consequence thereof may be made by an assessment or by repayment or otherwise as the case may require.

(3) Profits or gains arising in any chargeable period from payments for any easement over or right to use any land made to the person who occupies the land shall not be excluded from the charge to tax under Schedule A by reason only that he is chargeable with respect to the land under Schedule B, but shall be treated for the purposes of Schedule A as limited to the amount (if any) by which they exceed the assessable value for the purposes of Schedule B of his occupation of the land in that period.

(4) Part II contains further provisions relating to the charge to tax under Schedule A.

16.—(1) The Schedule referred to as Schedule B is as follows:— Schedule B.

SCHEDULE B

1. Tax under this Schedule shall be charged in respect of the occupation of woodlands in the United Kingdom managed on a commercial basis and with a view to the realisation of profits.

2. Paragraph 1 above has effect subject to the right given by section 54 to elect for assessment under Schedule D.

(2) Tax under Schedule B shall be charged on the occupier of the woodlands on the assessable value of his occupation in the chargeable period, and the amount on which he is chargeable shall be deemed for all tax purposes to be income arising from that occupation.

(3) For the purposes of tax under Schedule B—

(a) the assessable value of a person's occupation of woodlands is an amount equal to one-third of the woodlands' annual value, or a proportionate part of that amount if the period in respect of which he is chargeable is less than one year, and

(b) the annual value of any woodlands shall be determined in accordance with section 837, but as if the land, instead of being woodlands, were let in its natural and unimproved state.

(4) For the purposes of Schedule B and subsections (2) and (3) above, every person having the use of lands shall be deemed to be the occupier thereof, and references to occupation shall be construed accordingly.

(5) A person who, in connection with any trade carried on by him, has the use of any woodlands wholly or mainly for the purpose of—

(a) felling, processing or removing timber; or

(b) clearing or otherwise preparing the lands, or any part of them, for replanting;

shall not be treated as an occupier of the lands for the purposes of Schedule B and subsections (2) and (3) above.

(6) Subsection (5) above shall not apply where the use in question began before 14th March 1984.

17.—(1) The Schedule referred to as Schedule C is as follows:— Schedule C.

SCHEDULE C

1. Tax under this Schedule shall be charged in respect of all profits arising from public revenue dividends payable in the United Kingdom in any chargeable period.

2. Tax under this Schedule shall also be charged in respect of profits arising from public revenue dividends payable in the Republic of Ireland in any chargeable period, being dividends on securities of the United Kingdom government entered in the register of the Bank of Ireland in Dublin.

3. Where a banker or any other person in the United Kingdom obtains payment of any overseas public revenue dividends by means of coupons received from any other person or otherwise on his behalf, tax under this Schedule shall be charged in respect of the dividends.

4. Where—

(a) any banker in the United Kingdom sells or otherwise realises coupons for any overseas public revenue dividends and pays over the proceeds to any person or carries them to his account, or

(b) any dealer in coupons in the United Kingdom purchases any such coupons otherwise than from a banker or another dealer in coupons,

tax under this Schedule shall be charged in respect of the proceeds of the sale or other realisation.

5. Notwithstanding anything in paragraphs 1 to 4 above but subject to paragraph 6 below, where any half-yearly payment in respect of any dividend entrusted to the Bank of England or the Bank of Ireland for payment and distribution or which is payable by the National Debt Commissioners or of which they have the distribution does not exceed £2.50, it shall not be charged under this Schedule, but shall be assessed and charged under Case III of Schedule D.

6. Paragraph 5 above does not apply to any payment obtained by means of a coupon in respect of a bond to bearer or stock certificate.

(2) Part III contains further provisions relating to the charge to tax under Schedule C and to government securities; and section 45 shall apply for the interpretation of Schedule C.

Schedule D.   **18.**—(1) The Schedule referred to as Schedule D is as follows:—

SCHEDULE D

Tax under this Schedule shall be charged in respect of—

(a) the annual profits or gains arising or accruing—

(i) to any person residing in the United Kingdom from any kind of property whatever, whether situated in the United Kingdom or elsewhere, and

(ii) to any person residing in the United Kingdom from any trade, profession or vocation, whether carried on in the United Kingdom or elsewhere, and

(iii) to any person, whether a Commonwealth citizen or not, although not resident in the United Kingdom from any property whatever in the United Kingdom or from any trade, profession or vocation exercised within the United Kingdom, and

(b) all interest of money, annuities and other annual profits or gains not charged under Schedule A, B, C or E, and not specially exempted from tax.

(2) Tax under Schedule D shall be charged under the Cases set out in subsection (3) below, and subject to and in accordance with the provisions of the Tax Acts applicable to those Cases respectively.

(3) The Cases are—

Case I:	tax in respect of any trade carried on in the United Kingdom or elsewhere;
Case II:	tax in respect of any profession or vocation not contained in any other Schedule;
Case III:	tax in respect of— (a) any interest of money, whether yearly or otherwise, or any annuity or other annual payment, whether such payment is payable within or out of the United Kingdom, either as a charge on any property of the person paying the same by virtue of any deed or will or otherwise, or as a reservation out of it, or as a personal debt or obligation by virtue of any contract, or whether the same is received and payable half-yearly or at any shorter or more distant periods, but not including any payment chargeable under Schedule A, and (b) all discounts, and (c) income, except income charged under Schedule C, from securities bearing interest payable out of the public revenue;
Case IV:	tax in respect of income arising from securities out of the United Kingdom except such income as is charged under Schedule C;
Case V:	tax in respect of income arising from possessions out of the United Kingdom not being income consisting of emoluments of any office or employment;

PART I

Case VI: tax in respect of any annual profits or gains not falling under any other Case of Schedule D and not charged by virtue of Schedule A, B, C or E.

(4) The provisions of Schedule D and of subsection (2) above are without prejudice to any other provision of the Tax Acts directing tax to be charged under Schedule D or under one or other of the Cases set out in subsection (3) above, and tax directed to be so charged shall be charged accordingly.

(5) Part IV contains further provisions relating to the charge to tax under Schedule D.

Schedule E.

19.—(1) The Schedule referred to as Schedule E is as follows:—

SCHEDULE E

1. Tax under this Schedule shall be charged in respect of any office or employment on emoluments therefrom which fall under one or more than one of the following Cases—

Case I: where the person holding the office or employment is resident and ordinarily resident in the United Kingdom, any emoluments for the chargeable period, subject however to section 192 if the emoluments are foreign emoluments (within the meaning of that section) and to section 193(1) if in the chargeable period he performs the duties of the office or employment wholly or partly outside the United Kingdom and subject also to section 170;

Case II: where that person is not resident or, if resident, then not ordinarily resident in the United Kingdom, any emoluments for the chargeable period in respect of duties performed in the United Kingdom, subject however to section 192 if the emoluments are foreign emoluments (within the meaning of that section) and subject also to section 170;

Case III: where that person is resident in the United Kingdom (whether or not ordinarily resident there), any emoluments received in the United Kingdom in the chargeable period being emoluments either for that period or for an earlier period in which he has been resident there and any emoluments for that period received in the United Kingdom in an earlier period;

and tax shall not be chargeable in respect of emoluments of an office or employment under any other paragraph of this Schedule.

2. Tax under this Schedule shall be charged in respect of every annuity, pension or stipend payable by the Crown or out of the public revenue of the United Kingdom or of Northern Ireland, other than annuities charged under Schedule C.

3. Tax under this Schedule shall also be charged in respect of any pension which is paid otherwise than by or on behalf of a person outside the United Kingdom.

4. Where—

(a) any pension or annuity is payable in the United Kingdom by or through any public department, officer or agent of a government of a territory to which this paragraph applies (but otherwise than out of the public revenue of the United Kingdom or of Northern Ireland) to a person who has been employed in relevant service outside the United Kingdom in respect of that service, or

(b) any pension or annuity is so payable to the widow, child, relative or dependant of any such person as is mentioned above,

and the person in receipt of the pension or annuity is chargeable to tax as a person resident in the United Kingdom, the pension or annuity shall be chargeable to tax under this Schedule.

The territories to which this paragraph applies are—

(i) any country forming part of Her Majesty's dominions,

(ii) any other country for the time being mentioned in Schedule 3 to the British Nationality Act 1981, and

1981 c. 61.

(iii) any territory under Her Majesty's protection;

and in this paragraph "relevant service" means the service of the Crown or service under the government of a territory to which this paragraph applies.

5. The preceding provisions of this Schedule are without prejudice to any other provision of the Tax Acts directing tax to be charged under this Schedule and tax so directed to be charged shall be charged accordingly.

(2) References in the Tax Acts to Cases I, II and III of Schedule E shall be taken as referring to the Cases under which tax is chargeable under paragraph 1 of that Schedule.

(3) Part V contains further provisions relating to the charge to tax under Schedule E.

20.—(1) The Schedule referred to as Schedule F is as follows:—   Schedule F.

PART I

SCHEDULE F

1. Subject to section 95(1)(a), income tax under this Schedule shall be chargeable for any year of assessment in respect of all dividends and other distributions in that year of a company resident in the United Kingdom which are not specially excluded from income tax, and for the purposes of income tax all such distributions shall be regarded as income however they fall to be dealt with in the hands of the recipient.

2. For the purposes of this Schedule and all other purposes of the Tax Acts any such distribution in respect of which a person is entitled to a tax credit shall be treated as representing income equal to the aggregate of the amount or value of that distribution and the amount of that credit, and income tax under this Schedule shall accordingly be charged on that aggregate.

(2) No distribution which is chargeable under Schedule F shall be chargeable under any other provision of the Income Tax Acts.

(3) Part VI contains further provisions relating to company distributions and tax credits.

PART II

PROVISIONS RELATING TO THE SCHEDULE A CHARGE AND THE ASSOCIATED SCHEDULE D CHARGES

General

21.—(1) Income tax under Schedule A shall be charged on and paid by the persons receiving or entitled to the profits or gains in respect of which tax under that Schedule is directed by the Income Tax Acts to be charged.

Persons chargeable.

(2) Subsection (1) above does not apply for the purposes of the Corporation Tax Acts.

22.—(1) The profits or gains arising to a person for any chargeable period which are assessable to tax under Schedule A may, if they arise from more than one source, be assessed in one or more assessments, and in the latter case, each assessment may relate to profits or gains from one or more sources.

Assessments.

(2) Subject to subsection (3) below, where an assessment to income tax under Schedule A for any year of assessment is made in that year—

(a) it shall be made on the basis that all sources of income and all amounts relevant in computing profits or gains are the same as for the last preceding year of assessment, and

(b) tax shall be leviable accordingly, but any necessary adjustments shall be made after the end of the year, whether by way of assessment, repayment of tax or otherwise, to secure that tax is charged by reference to the rents or receipts to which the person assessed becomes entitled in the year of assessment.

(3) If before the 1st January in any year a person delivers a statement in writing to the inspector—

(a) showing that since the beginning of the last preceding year of assessment he has ceased to possess one or more sources of income chargeable under Schedule A, and

(b) giving the aggregate of the rents and receipts relevant for the purposes of Schedule A to which he has become or is likely to become entitled in the current year ("the current aggregate"), and

(c) showing that the current aggregate is less than the aggregate of such rents and receipts to which he became entitled in the last preceding year ("the previous aggregate"), and that it would not have been less if he had not ceased to possess the said source or sources,

then, if the inspector is satisfied as to the correctness of the statement, an assessment made on that person in the current year shall be made on an amount which bears to the amount arrived at under subsection (2)(a) above the same proportion as the current aggregate bears to the previous aggregate, and subsection (2)(b) above shall apply accordingly.

23.—(1) In any case where—

(a) any tax under Schedule A is charged in respect of profits or gains arising from any land to a person who is not the occupier of the land, and

(b) the tax is not paid by that person ("the person in default"),

the tax may be recovered in accordance with the following provisions of this section.

(2) Subject to subsection (3) below, the collector may from time to time, by notice in such form as may be prescribed by the Board, require any lessee of the land or any part thereof whose interest is derived, directly or indirectly, from that held by the person in default, (a "derivative lessee"), to pay to him, on the date or dates specified in the notice, such sum or sums as may be required to satisfy the tax.

(3) The sum demanded from a derivative lessee to be paid during any period shall not exceed the amount of the rent or other payments arising out of the land which becomes due from him at the end of the period and payable to the person in default or to another derivative lessee.

(4) In default of payment by a derivative lessee of any amount duly demanded of him under subsection (2) above, that amount may be recovered from him in like manner as if he had been charged with tax of that amount.

(5) Where any sum on account of tax has been collected from a derivative lessee in pursuance of this section, he may deduct that sum from any subsequent payment arising and payable as mentioned in subsection (3) above, and shall be acquitted and discharged of the amount so deducted.

(6) Where under subsection (5) above, or under that subsection as applied by this subsection, a sum is deducted from an amount payable to another derivative lessee—

(a) that subsection shall apply as if the sum had been collected from him under a demand made under subsection (2) above by the collector; and

(b) where the amounts from which he is entitled, under subsection (5) above, to make deductions during the following 12 months are less than that sum, he shall be entitled to recover from the Board an amount equal to the difference, which shall be treated as reducing the tax recovered under the preceding provisions of this section.

(7) In any case where—

(a) rents or receipts from land are received by any person ("the agent") on behalf of another ("the principal"), and

(b) any tax under Schedule A charged on the principal has not been paid,

the collector may by notice, in such form as may be prescribed by the Board, require the agent to pay to the collector in or towards the satisfaction of the tax any sums from time to time received by the agent on behalf of the principal on account of rents or receipts from any land (including any sums so received which are in his hands when the notice is given) until the liability in respect of the tax has been satisfied; and the agent shall pay all such sums over to the collector accordingly, and the payment shall acquit and discharge him as against the person on whose behalf he received them.

(8) If the agent fails to comply with the requirements of a notice duly served on him, he shall be liable to a penalty not exceeding £50 for each failure, and non-compliance as respects sums in his hands when the notice is given, or as respects any one payment subsequently received by him, shall be treated as a separate failure.

24.—(1) In this Part, except where the context otherwise requires—

Construction of
Part II.

"lease" includes an agreement for a lease, and any tenancy, but does not include a mortgage or heritable security, and "lessee", "lessor" and "letting" shall be construed accordingly;

"lessee" and "lessor" include respectively the successors in title of a lessee or a lessor;

"premises" includes any land; and

"premium" includes any like sum, whether payable to the immediate or a superior landlord or to a person connected (within the meaning of section 839) with the immediate or a superior landlord.

(2) For the purposes of this Part, any sum (other than rent) paid on or in connection with the granting of a tenancy shall be presumed to have been paid by way of premium except in so far as other sufficient consideration for the payment is shown to have been given.

(3) Where paragraph (c) of section 38(1) applies, the premium, or an appropriate part of the premium, payable for or in connection with either lease mentioned in that paragraph may be treated as having been required under the other.

(4) References in this section to a sum shall be construed as including the value of any consideration, and references to a sum paid or payable or to the payment of a sum shall be construed accordingly.

(5) In the application of this Part to Scotland—

"assignment" means an assignation;

"intermediate landlord" means, where an occupying lessee is a sub-lessee, any person for the time being holding the interest of landlord under a sub-lease which comprises the property of which the occupying lessee is sub-lessee, but does not include the immediate landlord;

"premium" includes in particular a grassum payable to any landlord or intermediate landlord on the creation of a sub-lease; and

"reversion" means the interest of the landlord in the property subject to the lease.

(6) In Schedule A and in sections 25 to 31—

PART II

(a) references to a lease extend only to a lease conferring a right, as against the person whose interest is subject to the lease, to the possession of the premises;

(b) "rent" includes a payment by the tenant to defray the cost of work of maintenance of, or repairs to, the demised premises, not being work required by the lease to be carried out by the tenant; and

(c) "tenant's repairing lease" means a lease where the tenant is under an obligation to maintain and repair the whole or substantially the whole of the premises comprised in the lease.

(7) For the purposes of Schedule A and sections 25 to 31, a lease shall be taken to be at a full rent if the rent reserved under the lease (including an appropriate sum in respect of any premium under the lease) is sufficient, taking one year with another, to defray the cost to the lessor of fulfilling his obligations under the lease and of meeting any expenses of maintenance, repairs, insurance and management of the premises subject to the lease which fall to be borne by him.

Deductions and other allowances

Deductions from rent: general rules.

25.—(1) In computing for the purposes of Schedule A the profits or gains arising to a person (the "person chargeable") in any chargeable period, the amounts of any permitted deductions shall be deducted from rent to which he becomes entitled under a lease in that period.

(2) In this section—

"permitted deductions" means any payments, except any payment of interest, made by the person chargeable in respect of any of the following matters—

(a) maintenance, repairs, insurance or management;

(b) any services provided by him otherwise than by way of maintenance or repairs, being services which he was obliged to provide but in respect of which he received no separate consideration;

(c) rates or other charges on the occupier which the person chargeable was obliged to defray;

(d) any rent, rentcharge, ground annual, feuduty or other periodical payment reserved in respect of, or charged on or issuing out of, land;

being payments which are deductible in accordance with subsections (3) to (9) below and section 26; and

"void period" means a period during which the person chargeable was not in occupation of the premises or any part thereof but was entitled to possession thereof.

(3) There may be deducted from rent to which the person chargeable becomes entitled in a chargeable period the amount of any permitted deduction which became due in that period, or at an earlier time falling within the currency of the lease, in so far as the payment—

(a) was made in respect of the premises comprised in the lease, and

(b) in the case of a payment for maintenance or repairs, was incurred by reason of dilapidation attributable to a period falling within the currency of the lease or, in the case of any other payment, was incurred in respect of such a period.

(4) Where the person chargeable became the landlord after the lease began, references in subsection (3) above to the currency of the lease shall not include any time before he became the landlord.

(5) In the case of a lease at a full rent, subsection (3) above shall have effect as if references to the currency of the lease included any period ("a previous qualifying period")—

(a) during which the person chargeable was the landlord in relation to a previous lease of the premises, being a lease at a full rent; or

(b) which was a void period beginning either with the termination of an earlier lease at a full rent of the premises or with the acquisition by the person chargeable of the interest in the premises giving him the right to possession thereof;

but a period shall not be a previous qualifying period if it preceded a period ending before the beginning of the lease which was not itself a previous qualifying period.

(6) Where during any period the conditions necessary for the period to be a previous qualifying period were fulfilled as respects part of the premises, but not the whole, the period shall be treated as a previous qualifying period as respects that part of the premises only, and subsection (5) above shall have effect accordingly, any necessary apportionment being made of rent, payments or other matters.

(7) In the case of a lease at a full rent, not being a tenant's repairing lease, there may also be deducted the amount of any payment made in respect of other premises by the person chargeable—

(a) in so far as that amount could be deducted under subsections (3) and (5) above from rent to which he became entitled in the chargeable period under a lease of those other premises, being a lease at a full rent, or could be so deducted if that rent were not insufficient, or

(b) if any part of the chargeable period is, in respect of those other premises, a void period beginning with the termination of a lease at a full rent, in so far as the amount could be so deducted if the lease had continued until the end of the period.

(8) Where by reason of any change of circumstances a lease ceases to be, or becomes, a tenant's repairing lease, or ceases to be, or becomes, a lease at a full rent, subsections (5) and (7) above shall apply in relation to the lease as it subsists after the change of circumstances as if it were a new lease granted when the change occurred.

(9) Where the person chargeable retains possession of a part of the premises and that part is used in common by persons respectively occupying other parts of the premises, this section shall apply as if a payment made in respect of the part used in common had been made in respect of those other parts.

26.—(1) Where this section applies to an estate for a chargeable period, the owner shall be treated—

    (a) in relation to a part of the estate which for any portion of that period is not comprised in a lease under which he is the landlord, as if he were entitled under a lease of that part at a full rent (not being a tenant's repairing lease) to rent for that portion, becoming due from day to day, at a rate per annum equal to the relevant annual value, and

    (b) in relation to a part of the estate which for any portion of that period is comprised in a lease under which he is the landlord, not being a lease at a full rent, as if the lease were at a full rent, and as if the rent so far as it relates to that part were at a rate per annum not less than the relevant annual value;

and section 25 shall apply accordingly.

(2) In any case where subsection (1) above applies—

    (a) a payment relating to premises comprised in the estate shall not be deductible from rent in respect of premises not so comprised; and

    (b) paragraph (a) of that subsection shall not apply to premises occupied by the owner wholly and exclusively for purposes connected with the management of the estate or for the purposes of a trade, profession or vocation.

(3) This section shall apply to an estate if, at the end of the year 1962-63, the land comprised in the estate was managed as one estate and the owner for the time being of the estate by notice to the inspector so elects; but such an election—

    (a) must be made within 12 months after the end of the first chargeable period for which the person making it became entitled to make it or such further time as the Board may allow;

    (b) except in the case of the first election that can be made under this subsection or the first election made under section 73(2) of the 1970 Act, shall not have effect unless an election under this section has had effect as respects the immediately preceding ownership;

    (c) shall apply in relation to the estate throughout the ownership of the person making it.

(4) Where in any chargeable period the estate comprises premises not included in it at the end of the year 1962-63, subsection (1) above (but not subsection (2)) shall apply in relation to the chargeable period as if the premises were not included in the estate in that period.

(5) Subsection (4) above shall not have effect in relation to any premises if—

    (a) at the end of the year 1962-63 the owner of the remainder of the estate as then subsisting was entitled under trusts arising under a settlement or on an intestacy, or in Scotland, under a disposition by way of liferent and fee, to an interest such that, on the occurrence of some future event or events, he might become the owner of the premises in question, and

(b) before the end of that year, the premises and the remainder of the estate, as then subsisting, were together managed as one estate.

(6) In this section—

"estate" means land in one ownership managed as one estate (but without prejudice to section 27); and

"relevant annual value", in relation to any part of an estate, means the annual value of that part ascertained in accordance with section 837.

27.—(1) Where a building or land which is qualifying property for the purposes of paragraph 3(1) of Schedule 4 to the Inheritance Tax Act 1984 (maintenance funds for historic buildings) forms part of an estate in relation to which an election has effect under section 26—

Deductions from rent: maintenance funds for historic buildings.
1984 c.51.

(a) the election shall not cease to have effect by reason only of another part of the estate becoming comprised in, and managed by the trustees of, a settlement in relation to which the Treasury give a direction under paragraph 1 of that Schedule, and

(b) while such a direction has effect that other part shall be treated as continuing to form part of the estate to which the election relates.

(2) In any case where—

(a) a person becomes the owner of any such building or land as is mentioned in subsection (1) above, and

(b) that building or land, in the immediately preceding ownership, formed part of an estate in relation to which an election under section 26 had effect,

any other part of that estate which continues to be or becomes comprised in a settlement of the kind mentioned in subsection (1) above shall, while such a direction as is mentioned in that subsection has effect, be treated as part of the estate in relation to which an election under section 26 may be made by him.

(3) Where by virtue of this section an election has effect in relation to an estate part of which is comprised in a settlement—

(a) there may be treated as deductible from the rents arising from that part—

(i) any payments which are made in respect of the other part of the estate by the trustees of the settlement and which would be so deductible under section 25 if that part were also comprised in the settlement; and

(ii) any payments made in respect of the other part of the estate by its owner to the extent to which they cannot be deducted by him under that section in the chargeable period in which they become due because of an insufficiency of the rents arising in that period from that part; and

(b) any relief available to the trustees under section 33 in respect of the part of the estate comprised in the settlement shall instead be available to the owner of the other part of the estate.

(4) Where by virtue of this section an election has effect in relation to an estate part of which is comprised in a settlement, the election shall not cease to have effect in relation to any of that part by reason of its ceasing to be comprised in that settlement if either—

(a) it becomes comprised in another settlement in circumstances such that by virtue of paragraph 9(1) of Schedule 4 to the Inheritance Tax Act 1984 there is (or would but for paragraph 9(4) be) no charge to inheritance tax in respect of the property so ceasing; or

(b) both immediately before and immediately after its so ceasing it is property in respect of which a direction has effect under paragraph 1 of that Schedule.

(5) The inclusion by virtue of this section in an estate of property comprised in a settlement shall not be construed as requiring it to be treated as the property of the person who owns the remainder of the estate or as affecting any question as to the person entitled to the income arising from that property.

Deductions from receipts other than rent.

28. Subject to section 122, where a person becomes entitled in a chargeable period to a sum other than rent payable under a lease, then in computing for the purposes of Schedule A the profits or gains arising to that person in that period, there shall be deducted from that sum—

(a) so much of any payment made by that person as was made in respect of maintenance, repairs, insurance or management of premises to which the sum relates and constituted an expense of the transaction under which he became entitled to that sum;

(b) so much of any rent, rentcharge, ground annual, feuduty or other periodical payment made by that person as was reserved in respect of, or was charged upon or issued out of, premises to which the sum relates and constituted an expense of that transaction;

(c) so much of any other payment made by that person as constituted an expense of that transaction, not being an expense of a capital nature; and

(d) where, in or before the chargeable period, that person entered into any like transaction, any amount which, under paragraphs (a) to (c) above, is deductible from a sum to which he is entitled under that like transaction in the period, or was deductible from a sum to which he was so entitled in a previous chargeable period but has not been deducted.

Sporting rights.

29.—(1) Subject to subsection (2) below, in any case where the person entitled to possession of any land ("the person chargeable")—

(a) is in the practice of granting sporting rights over the land for payment, but

(b) in any year of assessment, such rights are for any reason not granted by him,

the aggregate of any amounts paid by him which, if such rights had been granted in that year (the "relevant year"), would have been deductible under section 28 from payments receivable by him in respect of the grant shall be treated for the purposes of section 25(7) as a deduction which, by virtue of section 25(3), might have been made by him from rent to which he was entitled for that year under a lease of the land, being a lease at a full rent.

(2) If in the relevant year sporting rights over the land are exercised—

(a) by the person chargeable, or

(b) by any other person at his invitation, or

(c) where the person chargeable is a close company, by a person who is, within the meaning of Part XI, a director of, or a participator in, that company,

the aggregate referred to in subsection (1) above shall be treated as reduced by an amount equal to the price which might reasonably be expected to have been paid for that exercise of the rights if the person exercising them had had to give full consideration therefor.

(3) For the purposes of subsection (2) above, an exercise of sporting rights shall be disregarded if it gives rise to a charge to tax under Schedule E by virtue of section 154.

(4) Where the person chargeable is a company, section 9(1) shall not have effect so as to require references in that subsection to a year of assessment to be read as references to an accounting period, but any deduction thereby authorised shall be apportioned between the accounting periods (if more than one) comprising the year of assessment.

(5) In this section, "sporting rights" means rights of fowling, shooting or fishing, or of taking or killing game, deer or rabbits.

30.—(1) Where in any year of assessment the owner or tenant of any premises incurs any expenditure in the making of any sea wall or other embankment necessary for the preservation or protection of the premises against the encroachment or overflowing of the sea or any tidal river, he shall be treated for the purposes of sections 25, 28 and 31 as making in that year of assessment and in each of the succeeding 20 years of assessment a payment in relation to the premises preserved or protected by the embankment of an amount equal to a twenty-first part of the expenditure and incurred in respect of dilapidation attributable to the year.

(2) Where the whole of that person's interest in the premises or any part thereof is transferred (whether by operation of law or otherwise) to some other person—

(a) the amount of the payment which he would be so treated as making for the year of assessment in which the transfer takes place shall be treated as being made partly by the transferor and partly by the transferee, as may be just; and

(b) the transferee shall, to the exclusion of the transferor, be treated in any subsequent year—

(i) where the interest transferred is in the whole of the premises, as having made the whole of the payment for that year, and

(ii) where the interest transferred is in part only of the premises, as having made so much of the payment as is properly referable to that part of the premises.

(3) For the purposes of subsection (2) above, where an interest in any premises is a lease and that lease comes to an end, that interest shall be deemed to have been transferred—

(a) if an incoming lessee makes any payment to the outgoing lessee in respect of the embankment in question, to the incoming lessee, and

(b) in any other case, to the owner of the interest in immediate reversion on the lease and, in relation to Scotland, the expression "the owner of the interest in immediate reversion on the lease" shall be construed as a reference to the landlord.

(4) In relation to a company, section 9(1) shall not have effect so as to require references in this section to a year of assessment to be read as references to an accounting period, but any deduction authorised by this section shall be apportioned between the accounting periods (if more than one) comprising the year of assessment, other than any such period ended before the expenditure is incurred, or transfer takes place, by virtue of which the company is entitled to the deduction.

(5) This section shall not apply in relation to any expenditure in respect of which a capital allowance has been made.

Provisions supplementary to sections 25 to 30.

31.—(1) Schedule 1, which makes provision in relation to certain expenditure incurred before the beginning of the year 1963-64, shall have effect (and the preceding provisions of this Part shall have effect subject to that Schedule).

(2) Any reference in this section to a deduction is a reference to a sum which is deductible under any of the provisions of sections 25 to 30 and Schedule 1, and any reference to a sum which can be deducted or which is deductible shall be construed accordingly.

(3) Subject to subsections (4) to (7) below, where a sum or part of a sum can be deducted for the chargeable period in which it is paid, it shall be so deducted, and, where it cannot, it shall be deducted for the earliest chargeable period for which it can be deducted.

(4) Where for any chargeable period the amount from which deductions can be made is sufficient to allow the deduction from that amount of some, but not all, of different sums or parts of sums which are deductible, the sum or parts to be deducted for that period shall in the aggregate be equal to that amount, and, subject to that requirement, shall be such as the person whose liability to tax is in question may choose.

(5) No deduction shall be made in respect of—

(a) a payment made by any person to the extent that the payment has been or will be—

(i) balanced by the receipt of insurance moneys, or

(ii) recovered from, or in any other manner borne by, some other person, otherwise than by means of an amount on the profits or gains arising from which the first-mentioned person would be chargeable under Schedule A, or

(b) a payment made by a person other than a company, if payable under deduction of income tax.

(6) An amount, or part of an amount, shall not be deducted more than once from any sum, or from more than one sum, and shall not in any case be deducted if it has otherwise been allowed as a deduction in computing the income of any person for tax purposes.

(7) Where, on account of a payment made in any chargeable period, a deduction falls to be made from any rents or receipts to which the person making the payment became entitled in a previous period, all such adjustments of liability to tax shall be made, by repayment or otherwise, as may be necessary to give effect to the deduction.

32.—(1) Subject to the provisions of this section, Chapter II of Part I of the 1968 Act and Chapter I of Part III of the Finance Act 1971, and such other provisions of the Tax Acts as relate to allowances or charges under those Chapters, shall apply with any necessary adaptations in relation to machinery or plant provided for use or used by a person entitled to rents or receipts falling within Schedule A for the maintenance, repair or management of premises in respect of which those rents or receipts arise as they apply in relation to machinery or plant provided for use or used for the purposes of a trade.

(2) Except as provided by subsection (3) below, the Tax Acts shall apply in relation to any allowances or balancing charges which fall to be made by virtue of this section as if they were to be made in taxing a trade.

(3) Allowances and balancing charges which by virtue of this section fall to be made to or on a person for any chargeable period shall be made by—

(a) adding the amount of any such allowances to the expenditure on maintenance, repair or management of the premises which is deductible under sections 25 or 28 in computing his profits or gains for the purposes of Schedule A; and

(b) deducting the amount on which any such charge is to be made from that expenditure (or from the sum of that expenditure and any addition made to it under this subsection);

and sections 46 of the 1968 Act and 48 of the Finance Act 1971 (manner of making allowances or charges) shall not apply.

(4) Any charge falling to be made under this section shall, in so far as a deduction cannot be made for it under subsection (3)(b) above, be made under Case VI of Schedule D.

(5) No allowance or balancing charge shall be made by virtue of this section for any chargeable period in respect of expenditure incurred by any person on machinery or plant, except in pursuance of an election made by him for that period; but an election for any chargeable period shall have effect as an election for that and all subsequent chargeable periods.

(6) Any such election shall be made by notice to the inspector either for all machinery or plant provided for use or used for the maintenance, repair or management of the relevant premises or for any class of machinery or plant so provided or used; but an election for machinery or plant of any class shall not be made for any chargeable period after

PART II

1971 c. 68.

payments made in that or a subsequent chargeable period for the maintenance, repair or management of the relevant premises have been taken into account in an assessment or claim for repayment of tax which has been finally determined.

(7) Corresponding allowances or charges in the case of the same machinery or plant shall not be made under Chapter II of Part I of the 1968 Act or Chapter I of Part III of the Finance Act 1971 (whether for the same or different chargeable periods) both in computing profits or gains for the purposes of Schedule A and in some other way; and, on any assessment to tax, expenditure to which an election under this section applies shall not be taken into account otherwise than under those Chapters.

(8) The Tax Acts shall have effect as if this section were contained in Chapter II of Part I of the 1968 Act or Chapter I of Part III of the Finance Act 1971, as the case may require.

Agricultural land: allowance for excess expenditure on maintenance.

33.—(1) Where in the case of an estate which consists of or includes agricultural land—

(a) provision is made in sections 25 to 32 for the deduction of a sum in respect of payments in a chargeable period for maintenance, repairs, insurance or management of the estate, or in respect of allowances for machinery or plant provided for use or used on the estate, and

(b) owing to the insufficiency of rents and receipts to which the owner of the estate becomes entitled in that period, whether from the estate or from other property, the sum in question cannot be deducted (other amounts deductible under Schedule A being treated as deductible in priority thereto),

then, subject to subsection (2) below, the sum in question shall be treated as if it were the amount of an allowance falling to be made under the 1968 Act by way of discharge or repayment of tax, and available primarily against agricultural income as defined in section 69 of that Act.

(2) The sum in question shall not exceed the sum which would have fallen to be so treated if—

(a) the estate had not included such parts thereof as were used wholly for purposes other than purposes of husbandry, and

(b) payments or allowances in respect of parts thereof which were used partly for purposes of husbandry and partly for other purposes were reduced to an extent corresponding to the extent to which those parts were used for other purposes.

(3) In this section—

"agricultural land" means land, houses or other buildings in the United Kingdom occupied wholly or mainly for the purposes of husbandry; and

"estate" means any land (including any houses or other buildings) managed as one estate.

(4) Sections 71 and 74 of the 1968 Act shall apply as if this section were contained in Part I of that Act.

67.—(1) Subject to the provisions of this section, if in any year of assessment a person charged or chargeable to income tax in respect of any income chargeable under Case III, IV or V of Schedule D ceases to possess any particular source of any such income or any part of any such source, the following provisions shall apply to the tax in respect of the income from that source or part—

PART IV

Special rules where source of income disposed of or yield ceases.

    (a) notwithstanding section 73, the tax shall for that year, and (if necessary) for the preceding year, be computed separately;

    (b) subject to paragraph (c) below, the tax shall for that year be computed on the amount of the income arising within the year (instead of the income arising within the preceding year), and shall for that preceding year also be computed on the amount of the income arising within it if greater than the amount on which tax is to be computed for that preceding year apart from this provision; and

    (c) if no income arose within those two years and the person charged or chargeable makes a claim under this section not later than two years after the end of them, then, subject to subsection (4) below—

        (i) paragraphs (a) and (b) above shall apply to the year of assessment in which income did last arise and the year preceding it as, apart from this paragraph, they would apply to the year in which he ceases to possess the source or part and the year preceding it, and

        (ii) tax for the year of assessment following that in which income did last arise shall not be chargeable on the amount of the income so arising.

(2) For the purposes of the charge under Case III, if at any time interest on a debt begins to be payable subject to deduction of income tax, subsection (1) above shall apply as if the debt were a source of income which the creditor ceased to possess at that time.

(3) Where income in respect of which a person has previously been charged or chargeable to income tax under Case IV or V of Schedule D becomes at any time chargeable to income tax by deduction under the provisions of section 123, subsection (1) above shall apply as if the security or possession in question were a source of income which he ceased to possess at that time.

(4) Without prejudice to subsection (5) below, a person shall not be entitled by virtue of subsection (1)(c) above to make a claim under this section in respect of any source of income or any part of such a source more than eight years after the end of the year of assessment in which income last arose from that source.

(5) A person possessing a source of income chargeable to income tax under Case III, IV or V of Schedule D and having possessed it for six consecutive years of assessment without any income arising from it, shall be entitled, if income did arise from it in the year preceding those six years, to make a claim under this section not later than two years after the end of those six years; and if he does so—

(a) subsection (1) above shall apply as if he had ceased to possess the source of income immediately before the end of those six years; and

(b) section 66(3) shall apply in relation to later years of assessment as if he had acquired the source as a new source immediately after the end of those six years.

(6) References in this section to income arising shall, in cases where tax under Case IV or V is to be computed by reference to the amount of income received in the United Kingdom, be construed as references to income being so received.

(7) There shall be made all such adjustments, whether by way of repayment of tax, assessment or otherwise, as may be necessary to give effect to this section.

(8) A person's executors or administrators may make any claim under this section which he might have made, if he had not died, in respect of any source of income, or part of such a source, which he ceased to possess before his death, and may also make a claim under this section in respect of sources of income which he ceased to possess by dying; and after a person's death—

(a) any tax paid by him and repayable by virtue of a claim under this section (whether made by him or by his executors or administrators) shall be repaid to his executors or administrators, and

(b) any additional tax chargeable by virtue of such a claim shall be assessed and charged on his executors or administrators, and shall be a debt due from and payable out of his estate.

Special rules where property etc. situated in Republic of Ireland.

68.—(1) Notwithstanding anything in sections 65 or 66, but subject to the provisions of this section, income tax chargeable under Case IV or V of Schedule D shall, in the case of property situated and profits or gains arising in the Republic of Ireland, be computed on the full amount of the income arising in the year of assessment, whether the income has been or will be received in the United Kingdom or not, subject in the case of income not received in the United Kingdom—

(a) to the same deductions and allowances as if it had been so received; and

(b) to a deduction on account of any annuity or other annual payment (not being interest) payable out of the income to a person not resident in the United Kingdom.

(2) Subsection (1) above shall not apply—

(a) to any income which is immediately derived by a person from the carrying on by him of any trade, profession or vocation, either solely or in partnership; or

(b) to any income which arises from any pension.

(3) The tax in respect of any such income as is mentioned in subsection (2) above arising in the Republic of Ireland shall be computed either—

(a) on the full amount thereof arising in the year of assessment; or

(b) on the full amount thereof on an average of such period as the case may require and as may be directed by the inspector;

so that, according to the nature of the income, the tax may be computed on the same basis as that on which it would have been computed if the income had arisen in the United Kingdom, and subject in either case to a deduction on account of any annuity or other annual payment (not being interest) payable out of the income to a person not resident in the United Kingdom; and the person chargeable and assessable shall be entitled to the same allowances, deductions and reliefs as if the income had arisen in the United Kingdom.

The jurisdiction of the General or Special Commissioners on any appeal shall include jurisdiction to review the inspector's decision under this subsection.

(4) In charging any income which is excluded from subsection (1) above by subsection (2)(a) above there shall be the same limitation on reliefs as under section 391(2) in the case of income computed by virtue of section 65(3) in accordance with the rules applicable to Cases I and II of Schedule D.

(5) In charging income arising from a pension under subsection (3) above, a deduction of one-tenth shall be allowed unless it is the income of a person falling within section 65(4).

Case VI

69.—(1) Income tax under Case VI of Schedule D shall be computed either on the full amount of the profits or gains arising in the year of assessment or according to an average of such period, not being greater than one year, as the case may require and as may be directed by the inspector. *[margin: Assessment on current year basis unless otherwise directed.]*

(2) On an appeal to the General or Special Commissioners, the Commissioners shall have jurisdiction to review the inspector's decision under this section.

CHAPTER III

CORPORATION TAX: BASIS OF ASSESSMENT ETC

70.—(1) In accordance with sections 6 to 12 and 337 to 344, for the purposes of corporation tax for any accounting period income shall be computed under Cases I to VI of Schedule D on the full amount of the profits or gains or income arising in the period (whether or not received in or transmitted to the United Kingdom), without any other deduction than is authorised by the Corporation Tax Acts. *[margin: Basis of assessment etc.]*

(2) Where a company is chargeable to corporation tax in respect of a trade or vocation under Case V of Schedule D, the income from the trade or vocation shall be computed in accordance with the rules applicable to Case I of Schedule D.

(3) Cases IV and V of Schedule D shall for the purposes of corporation tax extend to companies not resident in the United Kingdom, so far as those companies are chargeable to tax on income of descriptions which, in the case of companies resident in the United Kingdom, fall within those

PART IV   Cases (but without prejudice to any provision of the Tax Acts specially exempting non-residents from tax on any particular description of income).

CHAPTER IV

PROVISIONS SUPPLEMENTARY TO CHAPTERS II AND III

Computation of income tax where no profits in year of assessment.

71. Where it is provided by the Income Tax Acts that income tax under Schedule D in respect of profits or gains or income from any source is to be computed by reference to the amount of the profits or gains or income of some period preceding the year of assessment, tax as so computed shall be charged for that year of assessment notwithstanding that no profits or gains or income arise from that source for or within that year.

Apportionments etc. for purposes of Cases I, II and VI.

72.—(1) Where in the case of any profits or gains chargeable under Case I, II or VI of Schedule D it is necessary in order to arrive for the purposes of income tax or corporation tax at the profits or gains or losses of any year of assessment, accounting period or other period, to divide and apportion to specific periods the profits or gains or losses for any period for which the accounts have been made up, or to aggregate any such profits, gains or losses or any apportioned parts thereof, it shall be lawful to make such a division and apportionment or aggregation.

(2) Any apportionment under this section shall be made in proportion to the number of months, or fractions of months, in the respective periods.

Single assessments for purposes of Cases III, IV and V.

73. Except as otherwise provided by the Tax Acts all income in respect of which a person is chargeable to tax under Case III, IV or V of Schedule D may respectively be assessed and charged in one sum.

CHAPTER V

COMPUTATIONAL PROVISIONS

Deductions

General rules as to deductions not allowable.

74. Subject to the provisions of the Tax Acts, in computing the amount of the profits or gains to be charged under Case I or Case II of Schedule D, no sum shall be deducted in respect of—

(a) any disbursements or expenses, not being money wholly and exclusively laid out or expended for the purposes of the trade, profession or vocation;

(b) any disbursements or expenses of maintenance of the parties, their families or establishments, or any sums expended for any other domestic or private purposes distinct from the purposes of the trade, profession or vocation;

(c) the rent of the whole or any part of any dwelling-house or domestic offices, except any such part as is used for the purposes of the trade, profession or vocation, and where any such part is so used, the sum so deducted shall not, unless in any particular case it appears that having regard to all the circumstances some greater sum ought to be deducted, exceed two-thirds of the rent bona fide paid for that dwelling-house or those offices;

(d) any sum expended for repairs of premises occupied, or for the supply, repairs or alterations of any implements, utensils or articles employed, for the purposes of the trade, profession or vocation, beyond the sum actually expended for those purposes;

(e) any loss not connected with or arising out of the trade, profession or vocation;

(f) any capital withdrawn from, or any sum employed or intended to be employed as capital in, the trade, profession or vocation, but so that this paragraph shall not be treated as disallowing the deduction of any interest;

(g) any capital employed in improvements of premises occupied for the purposes of the trade, profession or vocation;

(h) any interest which might have been made if any such sums as aforesaid had been laid out at interest;

(j) any debts, except bad debts proved to be such, and doubtful debts to the extent that they are respectively estimated to be bad, and in the case of the bankruptcy or insolvency of a debtor the amount which may reasonably be expected to be received on any such debt shall be deemed to be the value thereof;

(k) any average loss beyond the actual amount of loss after adjustment;

(l) any sum recoverable under an insurance or contract of indemnity;

(m) any annuity or other annual payment (other than interest) payable out of the profits or gains;

(n) any interest paid to a person not resident in the United Kingdom if and so far as it is interest at more than a reasonable commercial rate;

(o) any relevant loan interest within the meaning of section 369, other than interest to which section 375(2) applies;

(p) any royalty or other sum paid in respect of the user of a patent;

(q) any rent, royalty or other payment which is by section 119 or 120 declared to be subject to deduction of tax under section 348 or 349 as if it were a royalty or other sum paid in respect of the user of a patent.

75.—(1) In computing for the purposes of corporation tax the total profits for any accounting period of an investment company resident in the United Kingdom there shall be deducted any sums disbursed as expenses of management (including commissions) for that period, except any such expenses as are deductible in computing profits apart from this section.

Expenses of management: investment companies.

(2) For the purposes of subsection (1) above there shall be deducted from the amount treated as expenses of management the amount of any income derived from sources not charged to tax, other than franked

investment income, group income and any regional development grant. In this subsection "regional development grant" means a payment by way of grant under Part II of the Industrial Development Act 1982.

(3) Where in any accounting period of an investment company the expenses of management deductible under subsection (1) above, together with any charges on income paid in the accounting period wholly and exclusively for purposes of the company's business, exceed the amount of the profits from which they are deductible—

>   (a) the excess shall be carried forward to the succeeding accounting period; and

>   (b) the amount so carried forward to the succeeding accounting period shall be treated for the purposes of this section, including any further application of this subsection, as if it had been disbursed as expenses of management for that accounting period.

(4) For the purposes of this section there shall be added to a company's expenses of management in any accounting period the amount of any allowances falling to be made to the company for that period by virtue of section 306 of the 1970 Act (capital allowances for machinery and plant) in so far as effect cannot be given to them under subsection (2) of that section.

(5) Where an appeal against an assessment to corporation tax or against a decision on a claim under section 242 relates exclusively to the relief to be given under subsection (1) above, the appeal shall lie to the Special Commissioners, and if and so far as the question in dispute on any such appeal which does not lie to the Special Commissioners relates to that relief, that question shall, instead of being determined on the appeal, be referred to and determined by the Special Commissioners, and the Management Act shall apply as if that reference were an appeal.

Expenses of management: insurance companies.

76.—(1) Subject to the provisions of this section and of section 432, section 75 shall apply for computing the profits of a company carrying on life assurance business, whether mutual or proprietary, (and not charged to corporation tax in respect of it under Case I of Schedule D), whether or not the company is resident in the United Kingdom, as that section applies in relation to an investment company except that—

>   (a) there shall be deducted from the amount treated as the expenses of management for any accounting period the amount of any fines, fees or profits arising from reversions, and

>   (b) no deduction shall be made under section 75(2).

(2) Relief in respect of management expenses shall not be given to any such company, whether under section 242 or subsection (1) above, so far as it would, if given in addition to all other reliefs to which the company is entitled, reduce the corporation tax borne by the company on the income and gains of its life assurance business for any accounting period to less than would have been paid if the company had been charged to tax in respect of that business under Case I of Schedule D.

In this subsection the references to reliefs do not include references to any set-off under section 239.

(3) For the purposes of subsection (2) above—

(a) any tax credit to which the company is entitled in respect of a distribution received by it shall be treated as an equivalent amount of corporation tax borne or paid in respect of that distribution; and

(b) any payment in respect of that credit under section 242 shall be treated as reducing the tax so treated as borne or paid.

(4) In applying subsection (2) above to an accounting period in which a company—

(a) carries on any business in addition to life assurance business, or

(b) carries on both ordinary life assurance business and industrial life assurance business,

the tax that would have been paid if the company had been charged under Case I of Schedule D in respect of its life assurance business, or its life assurance business of either of those classes, shall be calculated as if any advance corporation tax set against the company's liability to corporation tax for that accounting period were apportioned to the corporation tax attributable to each business in proportion to the profits of that business charged to corporation tax for that accounting period.

(5) Where relief has been withheld in respect of any accounting period by virtue of subsection (2) above, the excess to be carried forward by virtue of section 75(3) shall be increased accordingly.

(6) The relief under this section available to an overseas life insurance company (within the meaning of section 431) in respect of its expenses of management shall be limited to expenses attributable to the life assurance business carried on by the company at or through its branch or agency in the United Kingdom.

(7) For the purposes of this section any sums paid by a company under a long term business levy imposed by virtue of the Policyholders Protection Act 1975 shall be treated as part of its expenses of management.

1975 c. 75.

(8) In subsections (2) and (6) above "life assurance business" includes the business of granting annuities on human life.

77.—(1) Subject to subsection (5) below, in computing the profits or gains to be charged under Case I or II of Schedule D there may be deducted the incidental costs of obtaining finance by means of a qualifying loan or the issue of qualifying loan stock or a qualifying security; and the incidental costs of obtaining finance by those means shall be treated for the purposes of section 75 as expenses of management.

Incidental costs of obtaining loan finance.

(2) Subject to subsections (3) and (4) below, in this section—

(a) "a qualifying loan" and "qualifying loan stock" mean a loan or loan stock the interest on which is deductible—

(i) in computing for tax purposes the profits or gains of the person by whom the incidental costs in question are incurred; or

(ii) under section 338 against his total profits; and

(b) "qualifying security" means any deep discount security, as defined by paragraph 1 of Schedule 4, in respect of which the income elements, as defined by paragraph 4 of that Schedule, are deductible under paragraph 5(1) of that Schedule in computing the total profits of the company by which the incidental costs in question are incurred.

(3) Except as provided by subsection (4) below, a loan or loan stock which carries the right of conversion into or to the acquisition of—

    (a) shares, or

    (b) other securities not being a qualifying loan or qualifying loan stock,

is not a qualifying loan or qualifying loan stock if that right is exercisable before the expiry of the period of three years from the date when the loan was obtained or the stock issued.

(4) A loan or loan stock—

    (a) which carries such a right as is referred to in subsection (3) above, and

    (b) which by virtue of that subsection is not a qualifying loan or qualifying loan stock,

shall nevertheless be regarded as a qualifying loan or qualifying loan stock, as the case may be, if the right is not, or is not wholly, exercised before the expiry of the period of three years from the date when the loan was obtained or the stock was issued.

(5) For the purposes of the application of subsection (1) above in relation to a loan or loan stock which is a qualifying loan or qualifying loan stock by virtue of subsection (4) above—

    (a) if the right referred to in subsection (4)(a) above is exercised as to part of the loan or stock within the period referred to in that subsection, only that proportion of the incidental costs of obtaining finance which corresponds to the proportion of the stock in respect of which the right is not exercised within that period shall be taken into account; and

    (b) in so far as any of the incidental costs of obtaining finance are incurred before the expiry of the period referred to in subsection (4) above they shall be treated as incurred immediately after that period expires.

(6) In this section "the incidental costs of obtaining finance" means expenditure on fees, commissions, advertising, printing and other incidental matters (but not including stamp duty), being expenditure wholly and exclusively incurred for the purpose of obtaining the finance (whether or not it is in fact obtained), or of providing security for it or of repaying it.

(7) This section shall not be construed as affording relief—

    (a) for any sums paid in consequence of, or for obtaining protection against, losses resulting from changes in the rate of exchange between different currencies; or

(b) for the cost of repaying a loan or loan stock or a qualifying security so far as attributable to its being repayable at a premium or to its having been obtained or issued at a discount.

78.—(1) This section applies in any case where—

(a) a bill of exchange drawn by a company is or was accepted by a bank and discounted by that or any other bank or by a discount house; and

(b) the bill becomes or became payable on or after 1st April 1983; and

(c) the discount suffered by the company is not (apart from this section) deductible in computing the company's profits or any description of those profits for purposes of corporation tax.

(2) Subject to subsection (3) below, in computing, in a case where this section applies, the corporation tax chargeable for the accounting period of the company in which the bill of exchange is paid, an amount equal to the discount referred to in subsection (1)(c) above shall be allowed as a deduction against the total profits for the period as reduced by any relief other than group relief and, except for the purposes of an allowance under section 338(1), that amount shall be treated for the purposes of the Corporation Tax Acts as a charge on income.

(3) Subsection (2) above shall not apply if the discount is not ultimately suffered by the company and shall not apply unless—

(a) the company exists wholly or mainly for the purposes of carrying on a trade; or

(b) the bill is drawn to obtain funds which are wholly and exclusively expended for the purposes of a trade carried on by the company; or

(c) the company is an investment company.

(4) Where an amount falls to be allowed as mentioned in subsection (2) above, there may be deducted, in computing the profits or gains of the company to be charged under Case I of Schedule D, the incidental costs incurred on or after 1st April 1983 in securing the acceptance of the bill by the bank; and those incidental costs shall be treated for the purposes of section 75 as expenses of management.

(5) For the purposes of subsection (4) above "incidental costs" means fees, commission and any other expenditure wholly and exclusively incurred for the purpose of securing the acceptance of the bill.

(6) In this section "bank" means a bank carrying on a bona fide banking business in the United Kingdom and "discount house" means a person bona fide carrying on the business of a discount house in the United Kingdom.

79.—(1) Notwithstanding anything in section 74, but subject to the provisions of this section, where a person carrying on a trade, profession or vocation makes any contribution (whether in cash or in kind) to an approved local enterprise agency, any expenditure incurred by him in making the contribution may be deducted as an expense in computing the profits or gains of the trade, profession or vocation for the purposes of tax if it would not otherwise be so deductible.

(2) Where any such contribution is made by an investment company any expenditure allowable as a deduction under subsection (1) above shall for the purposes of section 75 be treated as expenses of management.

(3) Subsection (1) above does not apply in relation to a contribution made by any person if either he or any person connected with him receives or is entitled to receive a benefit of any kind whatsoever for or in connection with the making of that contribution, whether from the agency concerned or from any other person.

(4) In this section "approved local enterprise agency" means a body approved by the Secretary of State for the purposes of this section; but he shall not so approve a body unless he is satisfied that—

(a) its sole objective is the promotion or encouragement of industrial and commercial activity or enterprise in a particular area in the United Kingdom with particular reference to encouraging the formation and development of small businesses; or

(b) one of its principal objectives is that set out in paragraph (a) above and it maintains or is about to maintain a fund separate from its other funds which is or is to be applied solely in pursuance of that objective;

and where the Secretary of State approves a body by virtue of paragraph (b) above, the approval shall specify the fund concerned and, in relation to a body so approved, any reference in this section to a contribution is a reference to a contribution which is made wholly to or for the purposes of that fund.

(5) A body may be approved under subsection (4) above whether or not it is a body corporate or a body of trustees or any other association or organisation and whether or not it is described as a local enterprise agency.

(6) A body may not be approved under subsection (4) above unless it is precluded, by virtue of any enactment, contractual obligation, memorandum or otherwise, from making any direct or indirect payment or transfer to any of its members, or to any person charged with the control and direction of its affairs, of any of its income or profit by way of dividend, gift, division, bonus or otherwise howsoever by way of profit.

(7) For the purposes of subsection (6) above, the payment—

(a) of reasonable remuneration for goods, labour or power supplied or for services rendered, or

(b) of reasonable interest for money lent, or

(c) of reasonable rent for any premises,

does not constitute a payment or transfer which is required to be so precluded.

(8) Any approval given by the Secretary of State may be made conditional upon compliance with such requirements as to accounts, provision of information and other matters as he considers appropriate; and if it appears to the Secretary of State that—

(a) an approved local enterprise agency is not complying with any such requirement, or

(b) one or other of the conditions for his approval contained in subsection (4) above or the precondition for his approval in subsection (6) above has ceased to be fulfilled with respect to an approved local enterprise agency,

he shall by notice withdraw his approval from the body concerned with effect from such date as he may specify in the notice (which may be a date earlier than the date on which the notice is given).

(9) In any case where—

(a) a contribution has been made to an approved local enterprise agency in respect of which relief has been given under subsection (1) above, and

(b) any benefit received in any chargeable period by the contributor or any person connected with him is in any way attributable to that contribution,

the contributor shall in respect of that chargeable period be charged to tax under Case I or Case II of Schedule D or, if he is not chargeable to tax under either of those Cases for that period, under Case VI of Schedule D on an amount equal to the value of that benefit.

(10) Section 839 applies for the purposes of subsections (3) and (9) above.

(11) This section applies to contributions made on or after 1st April 1982 and before 1st April 1992.

80.—(1) This section applies in the case of a trade, profession or vocation carried on wholly outside the United Kingdom by an individual ("the taxpayer") who does not satisfy the Board as mentioned in section 65(4); and it is immaterial in the case of a trade or profession whether the taxpayer carries it on solely or in partnership.

(2) Expenses of the taxpayer—

(a) in travelling from any place in the United Kingdom to any place where the trade, profession or vocation is carried on;

(b) in travelling to any place in the United Kingdom from any place where the trade, profession or vocation is carried on; or

(c) on board and lodging for the taxpayer at any place where the trade, profession or vocation is carried on;

shall, subject to subsections (3) and (4) below, be treated for the purposes of section 74(a) as having been wholly and exclusively expended for the purposes of the trade, profession or vocation.

(3) Subsection (2) above does not apply unless the taxpayer's absence from the United Kingdom is occasioned wholly and exclusively for the purpose of performing the functions of the trade, profession or vocation

C

or of performing those functions and the functions of any other trade, profession or vocation (whether or not one in the case of which this section applies).

(4) Where subsection (2) above applies and more than one trade, profession or vocation in the case of which this section applies is carried on at the place in question, the expenses shall be apportioned on such basis as is reasonable between those trades, professions or vocations; and the expenses so apportioned to a particular trade, profession or vocation shall be treated for the purposes of section 74(a) as having been wholly and exclusively expended for the purposes of that trade, profession or vocation.

(5) Where the taxpayer is absent from the United Kingdom for a continuous period of 60 days or more wholly and exclusively for the purpose of performing the functions of one or more trades, professions or vocations in the case of which this section applies, expenses to which subsection (6) below applies shall be treated in accordance with subsection (7) or (8) below (as the case may be).

(6) This subsection applies to the expenses of any journey by the taxpayer's spouse, or any child of his, between any place in the United Kingdom and the place of performance of any of those functions outside the United Kingdom, if the journey—

(a) is made in order to accompany him at the beginning of the period of absence or to visit him during that period; or

(b) is a return journey following a journey falling within paragraph (a) above;

but this subsection does not apply to more than two outward and two return journeys by the same person in any year of assessment.

(7) The expenses shall be treated for the purposes of section 74(a) as having been wholly and exclusively expended for the purposes of the trade, profession or vocation concerned (if there is only one).

(8) The expenses shall be apportioned on such basis as is reasonable between the trades, professions or vocations concerned (if there is more than one) and the expenses so apportioned to a particular trade, profession or vocation shall be treated for the purposes of section 74(a) as having been wholly and exclusively expended for the purposes of that trade, profession or vocation.

(9) In subsection (6) above "child" includes a stepchild and an illegitimate child but does not include a person who is aged 18 or over at the beginning of the outward journey.

(10) Nothing in this section shall permit the same sum to be deducted for more than one trade, profession or vocation in respect of expenses in computing profits or gains.

Travel between trades etc.   **81.**—(1) Where a taxpayer (within the meaning of section 80) travels between a place where he carries on a trade, profession or vocation in the case of which section 80 applies and a place outside the United Kingdom where he carries on another trade, profession or vocation (whether or not one in the case of which that section applies) expenses of the taxpayer on such travel shall, subject to subsections (3) to (5) below, be treated for the purposes of section 74(a) as having been wholly and exclusively expended for the purposes of the trade, profession or vocation mentioned in subsection (2) below.

(2) The trade, profession or vocation is—

   (a) the one carried on at the place of the taxpayer's destination; or

   (b) if that trade, profession or vocation is not one in the case of which section 80 applies, the one carried on at the place of his departure.

(3) This section does not apply unless the journey was made—

   (a) after performing functions of the trade, profession or vocation carried on at the place of departure; and

   (b) for the purpose of performing functions of the trade, profession or vocation carried on at the place of destination.

(4) This section does not apply unless the taxpayer's absence from the United Kingdom is occasioned wholly and exclusively for the purpose of performing the functions of both the trades, professions or vocations concerned or of performing those functions and the functions of any other trade, profession or vocation.

(5) Where this section applies and more than one trade, profession or vocation in the case of which section 80 applies is carried on at the place of the taxpayer's destination or (in a case falling within subsection (2)(b) above) at the place of his departure, the expenses shall be apportioned on such basis as is reasonable between those trades, professions or vocations; and the expenses so apportioned to a particular trade, profession or vocation shall be treated for the purposes of section 74(a) as having been wholly and exclusively expended for the purposes of that trade, profession or vocation.

(6) Nothing in this section shall permit the same sum to be deducted for more than one trade, profession or vocation in respect of expenses in computing profits or gains.

82.—(1) In computing the profits or gains arising from a trade, profession or vocation, no sum shall be deducted in respect of any annual interest paid to a person not resident in the United Kingdom unless—

   (a) the person making the payment has deducted income tax from the payment in accordance with section 349(2) and accounts for the tax so deducted, or

   (b) the conditions set out in subsection (2) below are satisfied.

(2) The conditions referred to in subsection (1)(b) above are as follows—

   (a) that the trade, profession or vocation is carried on by a person residing in the United Kingdom, and

   (b) that the liability to pay the interest was incurred exclusively for the purposes of the trade, profession or vocation, and

   (c) that either—

PART IV

(i) the liability to pay the interest was incurred wholly or mainly for the purposes of activities of the trade, profession or vocation carried on outside the United Kingdom, or

(ii) the interest is payable in a currency other than sterling, and

(d) that, under the terms of the contract under which the interest is payable, the interest is to be paid, or may be required to be paid, outside the United Kingdom, and

(e) that the interest is in fact paid outside the United Kingdom.

(3) Where the trade, profession or vocation is carried on by a partnership, subsection (1)(b) above shall not apply to any interest which is payable to any of the partners, or is payable in respect of the share of any partner in the partnership capital.

(4) Subsection (1)(b) above shall not apply where—

(a) the trade, profession or vocation is carried on by a body of persons over whom the person entitled to the interest has control; or

(b) the person entitled to the interest is a body of persons over whom the person carrying on the trade, profession or vocation has control; or

(c) the person carrying on the trade, profession or vocation and the person entitled to the interest are both bodies of persons and some other person has control over both of them.

In this subsection, the references to a body of persons include references to a partnership, and "control" has the meaning given by section 840.

(5) If interest paid under deduction of tax in accordance with section 349(2) is deductible in computing the profits or gains of a trade, profession or vocation the amount so deductible shall be the gross amount.

(6) This section does not apply for the purposes of corporation tax.

Patent fees etc. and expenses.

83. Notwithstanding anything in section 74, in computing the profits or gains of a trade there may be deducted as expenses any fees paid or expenses incurred—

(a) in obtaining for the purposes of the trade the grant of a patent, an extension of the term of a patent, the registration of a design or trade mark, the extension of the period of copyright in a design or the renewal of registration of a trade mark, or

(b) in connection with a rejected or abandoned application for a patent made for the purposes of the trade.

1984 c. 19.

References in this section to a trade mark include references to a service mark within the meaning of the Trade Marks (Amendment) Act 1984.

Payments for technical education.

84.—(1) Notwithstanding anything in section 74, where a person carrying on a trade makes any payment to be used for the purposes of technical education related to that trade at any university or university college or at any such technical college or other similar institution as may for the time being be approved for the purposes of this section by the Secretary of State, the payment may be deducted as an expense in computing the profits or gains of the trade for the purposes of tax.

(2) For the purposes of this section, technical education shall be deemed to be related to a trade if, and only if, it is technical education of a kind specially requisite for persons employed in the class of trade to which that trade belongs.

(3) In relation to technical colleges or other institutions in Northern Ireland, this section shall have effect as if for the reference to the Secretary of State there were substituted a reference to the Department of Education for Northern Ireland.

85.—(1) Any sum expended in making a payment to the trustees of an approved profit sharing scheme by a company which is in relation to that scheme the grantor or a participating company—

> (a) shall be deducted in computing for the purposes of Schedule D the profits or gains of a trade carried on by that company; or
>
> (b) if that company is an investment company or a company in the case of which section 75 applies by virtue of section 76, shall be treated as expenses of management,

if, and only if, one of the conditions in subsection (2) below is fulfilled.

Payments to trustees of approved profit sharing schemes.

(2) The conditions referred to in subsection (1) above are—

> (a) that before the expiry of the relevant period the sum in question is applied by the trustees in the acquisition of shares for appropriation to individuals who are eligible to participate in the scheme by virtue of their being or having been employees or directors of the company making the payment; and
>
> (b) that the sum is necessary to meet the reasonable expenses of the trustees in administering the scheme.

(3) For the purposes of subsection (2)(a) above "the relevant period" means the period of nine months beginning on the day following the end of the period of account in which the sum in question is charged as an expense of the company incurring the expenditure or such longer period as the Board may allow by notice given to that company.

(4) For the purposes of this section, the trustees of an approved profit sharing scheme shall be taken to apply sums paid to them in the order in which the sums are received by them.

(5) In this section—

> "approved profit sharing scheme" means a profit sharing scheme approved under Schedule 9; and
>
> "the grantor" and "participating company" have the meaning given by paragraph 1(3) and (4) of that Schedule.

86.—(1) If a person ("the employer") carrying on a trade, profession, vocation or business for the purposes of which he employs a person ("the employee") makes available to a charity, on a basis which is expressed and intended to be of a temporary nature, the services of the employee

Employees seconded to charities and educational establishments.

then, notwithstanding anything in section 74 or 75, any expenditure incurred (or disbursed) by the employer which is attributable to the employment of that employee shall continue to be deductible in the manner and to the like extent as if, during the time that his services are so made available to the charity, they continued to be available for the purposes of the employer's trade, business, profession or vocation.

(2) In subsection (1) above—

"charity" has the same meaning as in section 506;

"deductible" means deductible as an expense in computing the profits or gains of the employer to be charged under Case I or II of Schedule D or, as the case may be, deductible as expenses of management for the purposes of section 75.

(3) With respect to expenditure attributable to the employment of a person on or after 26th November 1986 and before 1st April 1997, this section shall have effect as if the references to a charity included references to any of the following bodies, that is to say—

(a) in England and Wales, any local education authority and any educational institution maintained by such an authority;

(b) in Scotland, any education authority, any educational establishment maintained by such an authority, and any college of education or central institution within the meaning of the Education (Scotland) Act 1980;

1980 c. 44.

(c) in Northern Ireland, any education and library board, college of education or controlled school within the meaning of the Education and Libraries (Northern Ireland) Order 1986 and any institution of further education which is under the management of an education and library board by virtue of Article 28 of that Order; and

S.I. 1986/594
(N.I. 3).

(d) any other educational body which is for the time being approved for the purposes of this section by the Secretary of State or, in Northern Ireland, the Department of Education for Northern Ireland.

Taxable premiums etc.

87.—(1) This section applies where in relation to any land used in connection with a trade, profession or vocation—

(a) tax has become chargeable under section 34 or 35 on any amount (disregarding any reduction in that amount under section 37(2) and (3)); or

(b) tax would have become so chargeable on that amount but for the operation of section 37(2) and (3) or but for any exemption from tax;

and that amount is referred to below as "the amount chargeable".

(2) Subject to subsections (3) to (8) below, where—

(a) during any part of the relevant period the land in relation to which the amount chargeable arose is occupied by the person for the time being entitled to the lease as respects which it arose, and

(b) that occupation is for the purposes of a trade, profession or vocation carried on by him,

he shall be treated, in computing the profits or gains of the trade, profession or vocation chargeable to tax under Case I or II of Schedule D, as paying in respect of that land rent for the period (in addition to any actual rent), becoming due from day to day, of an amount which bears to the amount chargeable the same proportion as that part of the relevant period bears to the whole.

(3) As respects any period during which a part only of the land in relation to which the amount chargeable arose is occupied as mentioned in subsection (2) above, that subsection shall apply as if the whole were so occupied, but the amount chargeable shall be treated as reduced by so much thereof as, on a just apportionment, is attributable to the remainder of the land.

(4) Where a person, although not in occupation of the land or any part of the land, deals with his interest in the land or that part as property employed for the purposes of a trade, profession or vocation carried on by him, subsections (2) and (3) above shall apply as if the land or part were occupied by him for those purposes.

(5) Where section 37(2) and (3) has effect in relation to a lease granted out of the interest referred to in subsection (4) above, subsections (5) and (6) of that section shall apply for modifying the operation of subsections (2) and (3) above as they apply for modifying the operation of subsection (4) of that section.

(6) In computing profits or gains chargeable under Case I or II of Schedule D for any chargeable period, rent shall not by virtue of subsection (4) above be treated as paid by a person for any period in respect of land in so far as rent treated under section 37(4) as paid by him for that period in respect of the land has in any previous chargeable period been deducted, or falls in that chargeable period to be deducted under Part II.

(7) Where, in respect of expenditure on the acquisition of his interest in the land in relation to which the amount chargeable arose, a person has become entitled to an allowance under section 60 of the 1968 Act (mineral depletion) for any chargeable period, then—

(a) if the allowance is in respect of the whole of the expenditure, no deduction shall be allowed him under this section for that or any subsequent chargeable period; or

(b) if the allowance is in respect of part only of the expenditure ("the allowable part"), a deduction allowed him under this section for that or any subsequent chargeable period shall be the fraction—

$$\frac{A - B}{A}$$

of the amount which apart from this subsection would fall to be deducted, where—

A is the whole of the expenditure, and

B is the allowable part of the expenditure;

and the reference in this subsection to an allowance under section 60 of the 1968 Act includes a reference to an allowance under Part III of Schedule 13 to the Finance Act 1986 in respect of expenditure falling within paragraph 4(1)(b) of that Schedule.

(8) Where the amount chargeable arose under section 34(2) by reason of an obligation which included the carrying out of work in respect of which any capital allowance has fallen or will fall to be made, this section shall apply as if the obligation had not included the carrying out of that work and the amount chargeable had been calculated accordingly.

(9) In this section "the relevant period" means—

(a) where the amount chargeable arose under section 34, the period treated in computing that amount as the duration of the lease;

(b) where the amount chargeable arose under section 35, the period treated in computing that amount as the duration of the lease remaining at the date of the assignment.

88. Any sums paid by a person to the Export Credits Guarantee Department under an agreement entered into under arrangements made by the Secretary of State in pursuance of section 11 of the Export Guarantees and Overseas Investment Act 1978, or with a view to entering into such an agreement, shall be included—

(a) in the sums to be deducted in computing for the purposes of Case I or Case II of Schedule D the profits or gains of any trade, profession or vocation carried on by that person; or

(b) if that person is an investment company or a company in the case of which section 75 applies by virtue of section 76, in the sums to be deducted as expenses of management in computing the company's profits for the purposes of corporation tax;

whether or not they would fall to be so included apart from this section.

89. Where section 113 or 337(1) applies to treat a trade, profession or vocation as discontinued by reason of any event, then, in computing for tax purposes the profits or gains of the trade, profession or vocation in any period after the event, there may be deducted a sum equal to any amount proved during that period to be irrecoverable in respect of any debts credited in computing for tax purposes the profits or gains for any period before the event (being debts the benefit of which was assigned to the persons carrying on the trade, profession or vocation after the event) in so far as the total amount proved to be irrecoverable in respect of those debts exceeds any deduction allowed in respect of them under section 74(j) in a computation for any period before the event.

90.—(1) Where a payment is made by way of addition to a redundancy payment or to the corresponding amount of any other employer's payment and the additional payment would be—

(a) allowable as a deduction in computing for the purposes of Schedule D the profits or gains or losses of a trade, profession or vocation; or

(b) eligible for relief under section 75 or 76 as expenses of management of a business, but for the permanent discontinuance of the trade, profession, vocation PART IV or business, the additional payment shall, subject to subsection (2) below, be so allowable or so eligible notwithstanding that discontinuance and, if made after the discontinuance, shall be treated as made on the last day on which the trade, profession, vocation or business was carried on.

(2) Subsection (1) above applies to an additional payment only so far as it does not exceed three times the amount of the redundancy payment or of the corresponding amount of the other employer's payment.

(3) In this section references to the permanent discontinuance of a trade, profession, vocation or business include references to any occasion on which it is treated as permanently discontinued by virtue of section 113(1) or 337(1).

(4) In this section references to a redundancy payment or to the corresponding amount of an employer's payment shall be construed as in sections 579 and 580.

91.—(1) In computing the profits or gains or losses for any period of a Cemeteries. trade which consists of or includes the carrying on of a cemetery, there shall be allowed as a deduction—

    (a) any capital expenditure incurred by the person engaged in carrying on the trade in providing any land in the cemetery sold during that period for the purpose of interments, and

    (b) the appropriate fraction of the residue at the end of that period of the relevant capital expenditure.

(2) Subject to subsection (3) below, the relevant capital expenditure is capital expenditure incurred for the purposes of the trade in question by the person engaged in carrying it on, being—

    (a) expenditure on any building or structure other than a dwelling-house, being a building or structure in the cemetery likely to have little or no value when the cemetery is full; and

    (b) expenditure incurred in providing land taken up by any such building or structure, and any other land in the cemetery not suitable or adaptable for use for interments and likely to have little or no value when the cemetery is full.

(3) Relevant capital expenditure—

    (a) does not include expenditure incurred on buildings or structures which have been destroyed before the beginning of the first period to which subsection (1) above applies in the case of the trade in question; and

    (b) of other expenditure incurred before that time, includes only the fraction—

$$\frac{A}{A+B}$$

where—

    A is the number of grave-spaces which at that time were or could have been made available in the cemetery for sale, and

B is the number already sold.

(4) For the purposes of this section—

(a) the residue of any expenditure at the end of a period is the amount incurred before that time which remains after deducting—

(i) any amount allowed in respect of that expenditure under subsection (1)(b) above in computing the profits or gains or losses of the trade for any previous period, and

(ii) if, after the beginning of the first period to which subsection (1) above applies in the case of a trade and before the end of the period mentioned at the beginning of this subsection, any asset representing that expenditure is sold or destroyed, the net proceeds of sale or, as the case may be, any insurance money or other compensation of any description received by the person carrying on the trade in respect of the destruction and any money received by him for the remains of the asset; and

(b) the appropriate fraction of the residue of any expenditure at the end of any period is—

$$\frac{A}{A+B}$$

where—

A is the number of grave-spaces in the cemetery sold in the period, and

B is the number of grave-spaces which at the end of the period are or could be made available in the cemetery for sale.

(5) Where in any chargeable period there is a change in the persons engaged in carrying on a trade which consists of or includes the carrying on of a cemetery, any allowance to be made under this section to the persons carrying on the trade after the change shall, whether or not it is to be assumed for other purposes that the trade was discontinued and a new trade set up and commenced, be computed—

(a) as if they had at all times been engaged in carrying on the trade;

(b) as if everything done to or by any of their predecessors in carrying on the trade had been done to or by them; and

(c) without regard to the price paid on any sale on the occasion of any such change.

(6) No expenditure shall be taken into account under both paragraph (a) and paragraph (b) of subsection (1) above, whether for the same or different periods.

(7) This section shall apply in relation to a trade which consists of or includes the carrying on of a crematorium and, in connection therewith, the maintenance of memorial garden plots, as it applies in relation to a trade which consists of or includes the carrying on of a cemetery, but subject to the modifications that—

(a) references to the cemetery or land in the cemetery shall be taken as references to the land which is devoted wholly to memorial garden plots, and

(b) references to grave-spaces shall be taken as references to memorial garden plots, and

(c) references to the sale or use of land for interments shall be taken as references to its sale or use for memorial garden plots.

(8) In this section—

(a) references to the sale of land include references to the sale of a right of interment in land, and to the appropriation of part of a memorial garden in return for a dedication fee or similar payment;

(b) references to capital expenditure incurred in providing land shall be taken as references to the cost of purchase and to any capital expenditure incurred in levelling or draining it or otherwise rendering it suitable for the purposes of a cemetery or a memorial garden; and

(c) the reference in subsection (4)(a)(ii) to subsection (1) above includes a reference to section 141 of the 1970 Act and section 22 of the Finance Act 1952 (which made similar provision to that made by this section).

1952 c. 33.

(9) Section 84 of the 1968 Act (which relates to expenditure which is reimbursed to a person carrying on a trade) shall apply for the purposes of this section as it applies for the purposes of Part I of that Act.

Treatment of regional development and other grants and debts released etc.

92.—(1) A regional development grant which, apart from this subsection, would be taken into account as a receipt in computing the profits of a trade, profession or vocation which are chargeable under Case I or II of Schedule D, shall not be taken into account as a receipt in computing those profits.

Regional development grants.

(2) A regional development grant which is made to an investment company—

(a) shall not be taken into account as a receipt in computing its profits under Case VI of Schedule D; and

(b) shall not be deducted, by virtue of section 75(2), from the amount treated as expenses of management.

(3) In this section "regional development grant" means a payment by way of grant under Part II of the Industrial Development Act 1982.

1982 c. 52.

93.—(1) A payment to which this section applies which is made to a person carrying on a trade the profits of which are chargeable under Case I of Schedule D shall be taken into account as a receipt in computing those profits; and any such payment which is made to an investment company shall be taken into account as a receipt in computing its profits under Case VI of Schedule D.

Other grants under Industrial Development Act 1982 etc.

(2) This section applies to any payment which would not, apart from this section, be taken into account as mentioned in subsection (1) above, being a payment by way of a grant under—

1982 c. 52.
1972 c. 63.

    (a) section 7 or 8 of the Industrial Development Act 1982 or section 7 or 8 of the Industry Act 1972; or

1966 c. 36 (N.I.).
1971 c. 22 (N.I.).

    (b) section 1 of the Industries Development Act (Northern Ireland) 1966 or section 4 of the Industries Development Act (Northern Ireland) 1971; or

S.I. 1982/1083
(N.I. 15).

    (c) any of Articles 7, 9 and 30 of the Industrial Development (Northern Ireland) Order 1982;

other than a grant designated as made towards the cost of specified capital expenditure or as made by way of compensation for the loss of capital assets and other than a grant falling within subsection (3) below.

(3) A payment by way of grant which is made—

    (a) under Article 7 of the Order referred to in subsection (2)(c) above, and

    (b) in respect of a liability for corporation tax (including a liability which has already been met),

shall not be taken into account as mentioned in subsection (1) above, whether by virtue of this section or otherwise.

Debts deducted and subsequently released.

94. Where, in computing for tax purposes the profits or gains of a trade, profession or vocation, a deduction has been allowed for any debt incurred for the purposes of the trade, profession or vocation, then, if the whole or any part of the debt is thereafter released, the amount released shall be treated as a receipt of the trade, profession or vocation arising in the period in which the release is effected.

Taxation of dealer's receipts on purchase by company of own shares.

95.—(1) Where a company purchases its own shares from a dealer, the purchase price shall be taken into account in computing the profits of the dealer chargeable to tax under Case I or II of Schedule D; and accordingly—

    (a) tax shall not be chargeable under Schedule F in respect of any distribution represented by any part of the price, and

    (b) the dealer shall not be entitled in respect of the distribution to a tax credit under section 231, and

    (c) sections 208 and 234(1) shall not apply to the distribution.

(2) For the purposes of subsection (1) above a person is a dealer in relation to shares of a company if the price received on their sale by him otherwise than to the company would be taken into account in computing his profits chargeable to tax under Case I or II of Schedule D.

(3) Subject to subsection (4) below, in subsection (1) above—

    (a) the reference to the purchase of shares includes a reference to the redemption or repayment of shares and to the purchase of rights to acquire shares, and

(b) the reference to the purchase price includes a reference to any sum payable on redemption or repayment.

(4) Subsection (1) above shall not apply in relation to—

(a) the redemption of fixed-rate preference shares, or

(b) the redemption, on terms settled or substantially settled before 6th April 1982, of other preference shares issued before that date,

if in either case the shares were issued to and continuously held by the person from whom they are redeemed.

(5) In this section—

"fixed-rate preference shares" means shares which—

(a) were issued wholly for new consideration, and

(b) do not carry any right either to conversion into shares or securities of any other description or to the acquisition of any additional shares or securities, and

(c) do not carry any right to dividends other than dividends which—

(i) are of a fixed amount or at a fixed rate per cent. of the nominal value of the shares, and

(ii) together with any sum paid on redemption, represent no more than a reasonable commercial return on the consideration for which the shares were issued;

"new consideration" has the meaning given by section 254; and

"shares" includes stock.

Special provisions

96.—(1) Subject to the provisions of this section, a person who is or has been carrying on a trade of farming or market gardening in the United Kingdom may claim that subsection (2) or (3) below shall have effect in relation to his profits from that trade for any two consecutive years of assessment if his profits for either year do not exceed such part of his profits for the other year as is there specified.

Farming and market gardening: relief for fluctuating profits.

(2) If the claimant's profits for either year do not exceed seven-tenths of his profits for the other year or are nil, his profits for each year shall be adjusted so as to be equal to one-half of his profits for the two years taken together or, as the case may be, for the year for which there are profits.

(3) If the claimant's profits for either year exceed seven-tenths but are less than three-quarters of his profits for the other year, his profits for each year shall be adjusted by adding to the profits that are lower and deducting from those that are higher an amount equal to three times the difference between them less three-quarters of those that are higher.

(4) No claim shall be made under this section—

(a) in respect of any year of assessment before a year in respect of which a claim has already been made under this section; or

(b) in respect of a year of assessment in which the trade is (or by virtue of section 113(1) is treated as) set up and commenced or permanently discontinued.

(5) Any adjustment under this section shall have effect for all the purposes of the Income Tax Acts (including any further application of this section where the second of any two years of assessment is the first of a subsequent pair) except that—

(a) subsection (2) above shall not prevent a person obtaining relief under those Acts for a loss sustained by him in any year of assessment;

(b) any adjustment under this section shall be disregarded for the purposes of section 63(1)(b); and

(c) where, after a claim has been made under this section in respect of the profits for any two years of assessment, the profits for both or either of those years are adjusted for any other reason, this section shall have effect as if the claim had not been made but without prejudice to the making of a further claim in respect of those profits as so adjusted.

(6) This section applies to the profits of a trade carried on by a person in partnership as it applies to the profits of a sole trader except that—

(a) the profits to which the claim relates shall be those chargeable in accordance with section 111; and

(b) any claim in respect of those profits shall be made jointly by all the partners who are individuals;

and where during the years of assessment to which the claim relates there is a change in the persons engaged in carrying on the trade but a notice is given under section 113(2), the claim shall be made jointly by all the persons who are individuals and have been engaged in carrying on the trade at any time during those years.

Where a person who is required by this subsection to join in the making of a claim has died, this subsection shall have effect as if it required his personal representatives to join in making the claim.

(7) In this section references to profits from a trade for a year of assessment are references to the profits or gains from that trade which are chargeable to income tax for that year before—

(a) any deduction for losses sustained in any year of assessment;

(b) any deduction or addition for capital allowances or charges (not being allowances or charges given or made by deduction or addition in the computation of profits or gains);

1981 c. 35.

(c) any deduction for relief under Schedule 9 to the Finance Act 1981 (stock relief).

(8) Any claim under this section shall be made by notice given to the inspector not later than two years after the end of the second of the years of assessment to which the claim relates but any such further claim as is mentioned in subsection (5)(c) above shall not be out of time if made before the end of the year of assessment following that in which the adjustment is made.

(9) Where a person makes a claim under this section in respect of any year of assessment, any claim by him for relief for that year under any other provision of the Income Tax Acts—

    (a) shall not be out of time if made before the end of the period in which the claim under this section is required to be made; and

    (b) if already made, may be revoked or amended before the end of that period;

but no claim shall by virtue of this subsection be made, revoked or amended after the determination of the claim under this section.

(10) There shall be made all such alterations of assessments or repayments of tax (whether in respect of such profits as are mentioned in subsection (1) above or of other income of the person concerned) as may be required in consequence of any adjustment under this section.

(11) Nothing in this section shall be construed as applying to profits chargeable to corporation tax.

(12) This section applies where the first of the two years mentioned in subsection (1) above is the year 1987-88 or a subsequent year of assessment.

97. Schedule 5 shall have effect with respect to the treatment, in computing profits or gains for the purposes of Case I of Schedule D, of animals and other living creatures kept for the purposes of farming or any other trade.

98.—(1) In computing for tax purposes the profits or gains or losses of a trade carried on by a lessor of tied premises—

    (a) there shall be taken into account as a trading receipt any rent payable for the premises to him, and there shall be allowed as deduction any rent paid for the premises by him, but

    (b) no deduction shall be allowed in respect of the premises either by reference to his being entitled to a rent for the premises which is less than the rent which might have been obtained (or less than their annual value or the rent payable by him for them) or in respect of the annual value of the premises.

(2) For the purposes of this section, premises shall be deemed to be tied premises in relation to any lessor of the premises, and in relation to any trade carried on by him, if, but only if, in the course of that trade, he is concerned (whether as principal or agent) in the supply of goods sold or used on the premises and accordingly deals with the premises or his interest in the premises as property employed for the purposes of that trade; and in this section "the relevant trade", in relation to any tied premises and to any lessor thereof, means any trade carried on by him in relation to which they are tied premises.

(3) Where part only of premises in respect of which rent is paid by or payable to a lessor of the premises are tied premises in relation to him, the rent paid or payable for the tied premises shall for the purposes of this section be taken to be that part of the entire rent which, on a fair and just apportionment, is attributable to them.

(4) Subject to subsection (5) below, a lessor of tied premises who is chargeable to tax for any chargeable period in respect of the profits or gains of the relevant trade shall not be liable for that period (or for the part of it during which he carries on that trade) to any tax in respect of the premises under Schedule A.

(5) Where, for any chargeable period or part of a chargeable period, a lessor of tied premises becomes entitled to any rent under a lease comprising the tied premises and other premises, but is by virtue of subsection (4) above relieved of liability to tax in respect of the tied premises under Schedule A—

(a) his liability in respect of the rent shall be computed in the first instance as it would be apart from this section, but

(b) his total liability (so computed) in respect of the rent shall be reduced by the part which, on a fair and just apportionment, is attributable to the tied premises for the chargeable period or part thereof for which he is so relieved of liability in respect of them.

(6) If the lessor of tied premises outside the United Kingdom is chargeable to tax for any chargeable period in respect of the profits or gains of the relevant trade, he shall not be liable for that period (or for the part of it during which he carries on that trade) to tax under Case V of Schedule D in respect of any rent for the premises.

(7) Where the person carrying on a trade is, in the case of any premises, entitled in equity to the interest of any lessor of those premises, then, in relation to that person, subsections (1) to (3) above shall apply as if he were the lessor of the premises, and as if any rent payable to or paid by the lessor were payable to or paid by him; and, in relation to the lessor of the premises, subsections (4) and (5) above (or, in the case of premises outside the United Kingdom, subsection (6) above) shall apply as they would apply to the person carrying on the trade if the lessor's interest in the premises and in any other relevant land were vested in him.

(8) In this section "lease" includes an agreement for a lease if the term to be covered by the lease has begun, and any tenancy, but does not include a mortgage or heritable security, and "lessor" shall be construed accordingly, and includes the successors in title of a lessor.

Dealers in land.

99.—(1) In computing for tax purposes the profits or gains of a trade of dealing in land, there shall be disregarded—

(a) so much of the cost of woodlands in the United Kingdom purchased in the course of the trade as is attributable to trees or saleable underwood growing on the land; and

(b) where any amount has been disregarded under paragraph (a) above and, on a subsequent sale of the woodlands in the course of the trade, all or any of the trees or underwood to which the amount disregarded was attributable are still growing on the land, so much of the price for the land as is equal to the amount so disregarded in respect of those trees or underwood.

(2) In computing the profits or gains of a trade of dealing in land, any trading receipt falling within subsection (1), (4) or (5) of section 34 or section 35 or 36 shall be treated as reduced by the amount on which tax is chargeable by virtue of that section.

(3) Where, on a claim being made under subsection (2)(b) of section 36, the amount on which tax was chargeable by virtue of that section is treated as reduced, subsection (2) above shall be deemed to have applied to the amount as reduced, and any such adjustment of liability to tax shall be made (for all relevant chargeable periods) whether by means of an assessment or otherwise, as may be necessary, and may be so made at any time at which it could be made if it related only to tax for the chargeable period in which that claim is made.

(4) Subsection (1) above shall not apply where the purchase mentioned in paragraph (a) of that subsection was made under a contract entered into before 1st May 1963.

CHAPTER VI

DISCONTINUANCE, AND CHANGE OF BASIS OF COMPUTATION

Valuation of trading stock etc.

100.—(1) In computing for any tax purpose the profits or gains of a trade which has been discontinued, any trading stock belonging to the trade at the discontinuance shall be valued as follows—

Valuation of trading stock at discontinuance of trade.

    (a) if—

        (i) the stock is sold or transferred for valuable consideration to a person who carries on, or intends to carry on, a trade in the United Kingdom, and

        (ii) the cost of the stock may be deducted by the purchaser as an expense in computing for any tax purpose the profits or gains of that trade,

    the value of the stock shall be taken to be the amount realised on the sale or the value of the consideration given for the transfer; and

    (b) if the stock does not fall to be valued under paragraph (a) above, its value shall be taken to be the amount which it would have realised if it had been sold in the open market at the discontinuance of the trade.

(2) For the purposes of this section "trading stock", in relation to any trade—

    (a) means property of any description, whether real or personal, being either—

        (i) property such as is sold in the ordinary course of the trade, or would be so sold if it were mature or if its manufacture, preparation or construction were complete; or

        (ii) materials such as are used in the manufacture, preparation or construction of any such property as is referred to in sub-paragraph (i) above; and

(b) includes also any services, article or material which would, if the trade were a profession or vocation, be treated, for the purposes of section 101, as work in progress of the profession or vocation, and references to the sale or transfer of trading stock shall be construed accordingly.

Valuation of work in progress at discontinuance of profession or vocation.

101.—(1) Where, in computing for any tax purpose the profits or gains of a profession or vocation which has been discontinued, a valuation is taken of the work of the profession or vocation in progress at the discontinuance, that work shall be valued as follows—

(a) if—

(i) the work is transferred for money or any other valuable consideration to a person who carries on, or intends to carry on, a profession or vocation in the United Kingdom, and

(ii) the cost of the work may be deducted by that person as an expense in computing for any tax purpose the profits or gains of that profession or vocation,

the value of the work shall be taken to be the amount paid or other consideration given for the transfer; and

(b) if the work does not fall to be valued under paragraph (a) above, its value shall be taken to be the amount which would have been paid for a transfer of the work on the date of the discontinuance as between parties at arm's length.

(2) Where a profession or vocation is discontinued, and the person by whom it was carried on immediately before the discontinuance so elects by notice sent to the inspector at any time within 12 months after the discontinuance—

(a) the amount (if any) by which the value of the work in progress at the discontinuance (as ascertained under subsection (1) above) exceeds the actual cost of the work shall not be brought into account in computing the profits or gains of the period immediately before the discontinuance; but

(b) the amount by which any sums received for the transfer of the work exceed the actual cost of the work shall be included in the sums chargeable to tax by virtue of section 103 as if it were a sum to which that section applies received after the discontinuance.

(3) References in this section to work in progress at the discontinuance of a profession or vocation shall be construed as references to—

(a) any services performed in the ordinary course of the profession or vocation, the performance of which was wholly or partly completed at the time of the discontinuance and for which it would be reasonable to expect that a charge would have been made on their completion if the profession or vocation had not been discontinued; and

(b) any article produced, and any such material as is used, in the performance of any such services, and references in this section to the transfer of work in progress shall include references to the transfer of any benefits and rights which accrue, or might reasonably be expected to accrue, from the carrying out of the work.

PART IV

102.—(1) Any question arising under section 100(1)(a) or 101(1)(a) shall be determined as follows, for the purpose of computing for any tax purpose the profits or gains of both the trades or, as the case may be, the professions or vocations concerned—

Provisions supplementary to sections 100 and 101.

> (a) in a case where the same body of General Commissioners have jurisdiction with respect to both the trades, professions or vocations concerned, the question shall be determined by those Commissioners unless all parties concerned agree that it shall be determined by the Special Commissioners;

> (b) in any other case, the question shall be determined by the Special Commissioners; and

> (c) the General or Special Commissioners shall determine the question in like manner as an appeal.

(2) Where, by virtue of section 113 or 337(1), a trade, profession or vocation is treated as having been permanently discontinued for the purpose of computing tax, it shall also be so treated for the purposes of sections 100 and 101; but those sections shall not apply in a case where a trade, profession or vocation carried on by a single individual is discontinued by reason of his death.

Case VI charges on receipts

103.—(1) Where any trade, profession or vocation the profits or gains of which are chargeable to tax under Case I or II of Schedule D has been permanently discontinued, tax shall be charged under Case VI of that Schedule in respect of any sums to which this section applies which are received after the discontinuance.

Receipts after discontinuance: earnings basis charge and related charge affecting conventional basis.

(2) Subject to subsection (3) below, this section applies to the following sums arising from the carrying on of the trade, profession or vocation during any period before the discontinuance (not being sums otherwise chargeable to tax)—

> (a) where the profits or gains for that period were computed by reference to earnings, all such sums in so far as their value was not brought into account in computing the profits or gains for any period before the discontinuance, and

> (b) where those profits or gains were computed on a conventional basis (that is to say, were computed otherwise than by reference to earnings), any sums which, if those profits or gains had been computed by reference to earnings, would not have been brought into the computation for any period before the discontinuance because the date on which they became due, or the date on which the amount due in respect thereof was ascertained, fell after the discontinuance.

(3) This section does not apply to any of the following sums—

(a) sums received by a person beneficially entitled thereto who is not resident in the United Kingdom, or by a person acting on his behalf, which represent income arising directly or indirectly from a country or territory outside the United Kingdom, or

(b) a lump sum paid to the personal representatives of the author of a literary, dramatic, musical or artistic work as consideration for the assignment by them, wholly or partially, of the copyright in the work, or

(c) sums realised by the transfer of trading stock belonging to a trade at the discontinuance of the trade, or by the transfer of the work of a profession or vocation in progress at its discontinuance.

Paragraph (b) above shall have effect in relation to public lending right as it has effect in relation to copyright.

(4) Where—

(a) in computing for tax purposes the profits or gains of a trade, profession or vocation a deduction has been allowed for any debt incurred for the purposes of the trade, profession or vocation, and

(b) the whole or any part of that debt is thereafter released, and

(c) the trade, profession or vocation has been permanently discontinued at or after the end of the period for which the deduction was allowed and before the release was effected,

subsections (1) to (3) above shall apply as if the amount released were a sum received after the discontinuance.

(5) For the purposes of this section the value of any sum received in payment of a debt shall be treated as not brought into account in the computation of the profits or gains of a trade, profession or vocation to the extent that a deduction has been allowed in respect of that sum under section 74(j).

Conventional basis: general charge on receipts after discontinuance or change of basis.

104.—(1) Where any trade, profession or vocation the profits or gains of which are chargeable to tax under Case I or II of Schedule D has been permanently discontinued, and the profits or gains for any period before the discontinuance were computed on a conventional basis, tax shall be charged under Case VI of that Schedule in respect of any sums to which this subsection applies which are received on or after the discontinuance.

(2) Subject to subsection (3) below, subsection (1) above applies to all sums arising from the carrying on of the trade, profession or vocation during any period before the discontinuance, not being sums otherwise chargeable to tax, in so far as the amount or value of the sums was not brought into account in computing the profits or gains for any period before the discontinuance.

(3) In subsection (2) above the reference to sums otherwise chargeable to tax includes any sums which (disregarding this section) are chargeable to tax under section 103 or to which that section would have applied but for subsection (3)(a) and (b) of that section.

(4) Where, in the case of any trade, profession or vocation the profits or gains of which are chargeable to tax under Case I or II of Schedule D, there has been—

(a) a change from a conventional basis to the earnings basis, or

(b) a change of conventional basis which may result in receipts dropping out of computation,

tax shall be charged under Case VI of that Schedule in respect of sums to which this subsection applies which are received after the change and before the trade, profession or vocation is permanently discontinued.

(5) Subsection (4) above applies to all sums arising from the carrying on of the trade, profession or vocation during any period before the change, not being sums otherwise chargeable to tax, in so far as the amount or value of the sums was not brought into account in computing the profits or gains for any period.

(6) It is hereby declared that where work in progress at the discontinuance of a profession or vocation, or the responsibility for its completion, is transferred, the sums to which subsection (1) above applies include any sums received by way of consideration for the transfer, and any sums received by way of realisation by the transferee, on behalf of the transferor, of the work in progress transferred.

(7) Where in the case of any profession or vocation, the profits or gains of which are chargeable to tax under Case II of Schedule D—

(a) there has been a change from a conventional basis to the earnings basis, or a change of conventional basis, and

(b) the value of the work in progress at the time of the change was debited in the accounts and allowed as a deduction in computing profits for tax purposes for a period after the change,

then, in so far as no counterbalancing credit was brought into account in computing profits for tax purposes for any period ending before or with the date of the change, tax shall be charged under subsection (4) above in respect of that amount for the year of assessment in which the change occurred as if that amount were a sum to which that subsection applies, and the change of basis were a change of the kind described in that subsection.

105.—(1) In computing the charge to tax in respect of sums received by any person which are chargeable to tax by virtue of section 103 or 104(1) (including amounts treated as sums received by him by virtue of section 103(4)), there shall be deducted from the amount which, apart from this subsection, would be chargeable to tax—

Allowable deductions.

(a) any loss, expense or debit (not being a loss, expense or debit arising directly or indirectly from the discontinuance itself) which, if the trade, profession or vocation had not been discontinued, would have been deducted in computing for tax purposes the profits or gains of the person by whom it was carried on before the discontinuance, or would have been deducted from or set off against those profits or gains as so computed, and

(b) any capital allowance to which the person who carried on the trade, profession or vocation was entitled immediately before the discontinuance and to which effect has not been given by way of relief before the discontinuance.

(2) No amount shall be deducted under subsection (1) above if that amount has been allowed under any other provision of the Tax Acts.

(3) No amount shall be deducted more than once under subsection (1) above; and—

(a) any expense or debit shall be apportioned between a sum chargeable under section 103 and a sum chargeable under section 104(1) in such manner as may be just;

(b) as between sums chargeable, whether under section 103 or 104(1), for one chargeable period and sums so charged for a subsequent chargeable period, any deduction in respect of a loss or capital allowance shall be made against sums chargeable for the earlier chargeable period;

(c) subject to paragraph (b) above, as between sums chargeable for any chargeable period under section 103 and sums so chargeable under section 104(1), any deduction in respect of a loss or capital allowance shall be made against the last-mentioned sums rather than the first-mentioned;

but, in the case of a loss which is to be allowed after the discontinuance, not so as to authorise its deduction from any sum chargeable for a chargeable period preceding that in which the loss is incurred.

(4) In computing the charge to tax in respect of sums received by any person which are chargeable to tax by virtue of section 104(4), there shall be deducted any expense or debit which is not otherwise allowable and which, but for the change in basis, would have been deducted in computing for tax purposes the profits or gains of the trade, profession or vocation, but no amount shall be deducted more than once under this subsection.

Application of charges where rights to payments transferred.

106.—(1) Subject to subsection (2) below, in the case of a transfer for value of the right to receive any sum to which section 103, 104(1) or 104(4) applies, any tax chargeable by virtue of either of those sections shall be charged in respect of the amount or value of the consideration (or, in the case of a transfer otherwise than at arm's length, in respect of the value of the right transferred as between parties at arm's length), and references in this Chapter, except section 101(2), to sums received shall be construed accordingly.

(2) Where a trade, profession or vocation is treated as permanently discontinued by reason of a change in the persons carrying it on, and the right to receive any sum to which section 103 or 104(1) applies is or was transferred at the time of the change to the persons carrying on the trade, profession or vocation after the change, tax shall not be charged by virtue of either of those sections, but any sum received by those persons by virtue of the transfer shall be treated for all purposes as a receipt to be brought into the computation of the profits or gains of the trade, profession or vocation in the period in which it is received.

Reliefs

Treatment of receipts as earned income.

107. Where an individual is chargeable to tax by virtue of section 103 or 104, and the profits or gains of the trade, profession or vocation to which he was entitled before the discontinuance or, as the case may be, change of basis fell to be treated as earned income for the purposes of income tax, the sums in respect of which he is so chargeable shall also be treated as earned income for those purposes (but, in the case of sums chargeable by virtue of section 104, after any reduction in those sums under section 109).

108. Where any sum is—

(a) chargeable to tax by virtue of section 103 or 104, and

(b) received in any year of assessment beginning not later than six years after the discontinuance or, as the case may be, change of basis by the person by whom the trade, profession or vocation was carried on before the discontinuance or change, or by his personal representatives,

that person or (in either case) his personal representatives may, by notice sent to the inspector within two years after that year of assessment, elect that the tax so chargeable shall be charged as if the sum in question were received on the date on which the discontinuance took place or, as the case may be, on the last day of the period at the end of which the change of basis took place; and, in any such case, an assessment shall (notwithstanding anything in the Tax Acts) be made accordingly, and, in connection with that assessment, no further deduction or relief shall be made or given in respect of any loss or allowance deducted in pursuance of section 105.

109.—(1) If an individual born before 6th April 1917, or the personal representatives of such an individual, is chargeable to tax under section 104 and—

(a) the individual was engaged in carrying on a trade, profession or vocation on 18th March 1968, and

(b) the profits or gains of the trade, profession or vocation were not computed by reference to earnings in the period in which that 18th March fell, or in any subsequent period ending before or with the relevant date,

the net amount with which he is so chargeable to tax shall be reduced by multiplying that net amount by the fraction given below.

(2) Where section 104(4) applies in relation to a change of basis taking place on a date before 19th March 1968, then, in relation to tax chargeable by reference to that change of basis, that earlier date shall be substituted for the date in subsection (1)(a) above and subsection (1)(b) above shall be omitted.

(3) The fraction referred to in subsection (1) above is—

(a) where on 5th April 1968 the individual had not attained the age of 52—

$$\frac{19}{20}$$

(b) where on that date he had attained the age of 52, but had not attained the age of 53—

PART IV

$$\frac{18}{20}$$

and so on, reducing the fraction by—

$$\frac{1}{20}$$

for each year he had attained up to the age of 64;

   (c) where on that date he had attained the age of 65, or any greater age—

$$\frac{5}{20}$$

(4) In this section—

"the net amount" with which a person is chargeable to tax under section 104 means the amount with which he is so chargeable after making any deduction authorised by section 105 but before giving any relief under this section; and

"relevant date"—

      (a) in relation to tax under section 104(1), means the date of the permanent discontinuance, and

      (b) in relation to tax under section 104(4), means the date of the change of basis.

(5) Subsections (1) to (4) above shall apply as follows as respects the net amount of any sum chargeable under section 104 which is assessed by reference to a sum accruing to a partnership—

   (a) the part of that net amount which is apportioned to any partner (who is an individual), or the personal representative of such an individual, shall be a net amount with which that person is chargeable under that section, and

   (b) if the part of that net amount which is so apportioned is a greater proportion of that amount than is the individual's share (that is to say, the part to be included in his total income) of the total amount of the partnership profits assessed to income tax for the three years of assessment ending with the year in which the discontinuance or change of basis took place, the amount of the reduction to be given by way of relief shall not exceed the amount of relief which would have been so given if the apportionment had been made by reference to his share of that total amount.

(6) For the purposes of this section the trade, profession or vocation carried on before a permanent discontinuance shall not be treated as the same as any carried after the discontinuance.

Supplemental

Interpretation etc.

110.—(1) The following provisions have effect for the purposes of sections 103 to 109.

(2) For the purposes of those sections, any reference to the permanent discontinuance of a trade, profession or vocation includes a reference to the occurring of any event which, under section 113 or 337(1), is to be treated as equivalent to the permanent discontinuance of a trade, profession or vocation.

(3) The profits or gains of a trade, profession or vocation in any period shall be treated as computed by reference to earnings where all credits and liabilities accruing during that period as a consequence of its being carried on are brought into account in computing those profits or gains for tax purposes, and not otherwise, and "earnings basis" shall be construed accordingly.

(4) "Conventional basis" has the meaning given by section 103(2), so that profits or gains are computed on a conventional basis if computed otherwise than by reference to earnings.

(5) There is a change from a conventional basis to the earnings basis at the end of a period the profits or gains of which were computed on a conventional basis if the profits or gains of the next succeeding period are computed by reference to earnings; and, if the profits or gains of two successive periods are computed on different conventional bases, a change of conventional basis occurs at the end of the earlier period.

(6) In sections 103 and 104—

  (a) "trading stock" has the meaning given by section 100(2);

  (b) references to work in progress at the discontinuance of a profession or vocation, and to the transfer of work in progress, are to be construed in accordance with section 101(3); and

  (c) the reference to work in progress at the time of a change of basis is also to be construed in accordance with section 101(3), substituting therein for this purpose references to the change of basis for references to the discontinuance.

CHAPTER VII

PARTNERSHIPS AND SUCCESSIONS

General

111. Where a trade or profession is carried on by two or more persons jointly, income tax in respect thereof shall be computed and stated jointly, and in one sum, and shall be separate and distinct from any other tax chargeable on those persons or any of them, and a joint assessment shall be made in the partnership name.

Partnership assessments to income tax.

112.—(1) Where a trade or business is carried on by two or more persons in partnership, and the control and management of the trade or business is situated abroad, the trade or business shall be deemed to be carried on by persons resident outside the United Kingdom, and the partnership shall be deemed to reside outside the United Kingdom, notwithstanding the fact that some of the members of the partnership are resident in the United Kingdom and that some of its trading operations are conducted within the United Kingdom.

Partnerships controlled abroad.

(2) Where any part of the trade or business of a partnership firm whose management and control is situated abroad consists of trading operations within the United Kingdom, the firm shall, subject to subsection (3) below, be chargeable in respect of the profits of those trading operations within the United Kingdom to the same extent as, and no further than, a person resident abroad is chargeable in respect of trading operations by him within the United Kingdom, notwithstanding the fact that one or more members of the firm are resident in the United Kingdom.

(3) For the purpose of charging any such firm as is mentioned in subsection (2) above in respect of the profits of its trading operations within the United Kingdom, an assessment may be made on the firm in respect of those profits in the name of any partner resident in the United Kingdom.

(4) In any case where—

    (a) a person resident in the United Kingdom (in this subsection and subsection (5) below referred to as "the resident partner") is a member of a partnership which resides or is deemed to reside outside the United Kingdom; and

    (b) by virtue of any arrangements falling within section 788 any of the income or capital gains of the partnership is relieved from tax in the United Kingdom,

the arrangements referred to in paragraph (b) above shall not affect any liability to tax in respect of the resident partner's share of any income or capital gains of the partnership.

(5) If, in a case where subsection (4) above applies, the resident partner's share of the income of the partnership consists of or includes a share in a qualifying distribution made by a company resident in the United Kingdom, then, notwithstanding anything in the arrangements, the resident partner (and not the partnership as a whole) shall be regarded as entitled to that share of the tax credit in respect of the distribution which corresponds to his share of the distribution.

(6) Section 115(5) has effect as respects the application of this section where the partners in a partnership include a company.

113.—(1) Where there is a change in the persons engaged in carrying on any trade, profession or vocation chargeable under Case I or II of Schedule D, then, subject to the provisions of this section and of section 114(3)(b), the amount of the profits or gains of the trade, profession or vocation on which income tax is chargeable for any year of assessment and the persons on whom it is chargeable, shall be determined as if the trade, profession or vocation had been permanently discontinued, and a new one set up and commenced, at the date of the change.

(2) Subject to section 114(3)(b), where there is such a change as is mentioned in subsection (1) above, and a person engaged in carrying on the trade, profession or vocation immediately before the change continues to be so engaged immediately after it, the persons so engaged immediately before and the persons so engaged immediately after the change may, by notice signed by them and sent to the inspector at any time within two years after the date of the change, elect that subsection (1) above shall not apply to treat the trade, profession or vocation as discontinued or a new one as set up and commenced.

(3) Where there is in any year of assessment a change in the persons engaged in carrying on a trade, profession or vocation, and subsection (1) above does not apply by reason of a notice under subsection (2) above, then—

(a) income tax in respect of the trade, profession or vocation for that year shall be assessed and charged separately on those so engaged before the change and on those so engaged after the change, but the amount on which tax is chargeable shall be computed as if there had been no such change in that year, and shall be apportioned as may be just; and

(b) if, after the change but before the end of the second year of assessment following that in which the change occurred, there is a permanent discontinuance of the trade, profession or vocation (including a change treated as such), then, on that discontinuance, section 63 shall apply, as respects any period before the first-mentioned change, to the persons charged or chargeable for that period as it would apply if no such change had taken place and they had been charged to tax accordingly for the subsequent period up to the discontinuance.

(4) There shall be made any such assessment, reduction of an assessment or, on the making of a claim therefor, repayment of income tax as may in any case be necessary for giving effect to this section.

(5) Any question which arises as to the manner in which any sum is to be apportioned under subsection (3)(a) above shall be determined, for the purposes of the tax of all of the persons as respects whose liability to tax the apportionment is material—

(a) in a case where the same body of General Commissioners have jurisdiction with respect to all those persons, by those Commissioners, unless all those persons agree that it shall be determined by the Special Commissioners;

(b) in a case where different bodies of Commissioners have jurisdiction with respect to those persons, by such of those bodies as the Board may direct, unless all those persons agree that it shall be determined by the Special Commissioners; and

(c) in any other case, by the Special Commissioners;

and any such Commissioners shall determine the question in like manner as an appeal, except that all those persons shall be entitled to appear and be heard by the Commissioners who are to make the determination, or to make representations to them in writing.

(6) In the case of the death of a person who, if he had not died, would under the provisions of this section have become chargeable to tax for any year, the tax which would have been so chargeable shall be assessed and charged upon his executors or administrators, and shall be a debt due from and payable out of his estate; and where under those provisions an election may be made by any person, it may in the case of his death be made by his executors or administrators instead of by him.

(7) For the purposes of this section, a change in the personal representatives of any person, or in the trustees of any trust, shall not be treated as a change in the persons engaged in carrying on any trade, profession or vocation carried on by those personal representatives or trustees as such.

Partnerships involving companies

114.—(1) So long as a trade is carried on by persons in partnership, and any of those persons is a company, the profits and losses (including terminal losses) of the trade shall be computed for the purposes of corporation tax in like manner, and by reference to the like accounting periods, as if the partnership were a company, and without regard to any change in the persons carrying on the trade, except that—

  (a) references to distributions shall not apply; and

  (b) subject to section 116(5), no deduction or addition shall be made for charges on income, or for capital allowances and charges, nor in any accounting period for losses incurred in any other period nor for any expenditure to which section 401(1) applies; and

  (c) a change in the persons engaged in carrying on the trade shall be treated as the transfer of the trade to a different company if there continues to be a company so engaged after the change, but not a company that was so engaged before the change.

(2) A company's share in the profits or loss of any accounting period of the partnership, or in any matter excluded from the computation by subsection (1)(b) above, shall be determined according to the interests of the partners during that period, and corporation tax shall be chargeable as if that share derived from a trade carried on by the company alone in its corresponding accounting period or periods; and the company shall be assessed and charged to tax for its corresponding accounting period or periods accordingly.

In this subsection "corresponding accounting period or periods" means the accounting period or periods of the company comprising or together comprising the accounting period of the partnership, and any necessary apportionment shall be made between corresponding accounting periods if more than one.

(3) Where any of the persons engaged in carrying on the trade is an individual, income tax shall be chargeable in respect of his share of the profits, and he shall be entitled to relief for his share of any loss, as if all the partners had been individuals except that—

  (a) income tax shall be chargeable, and any relief from income tax shall be given, by reference to the computations made for corporation tax, but so that the amounts so computed for an accounting period of the capital allowances and charges falling to be made in taxing the trade shall (as regards the individual's share of them) be given or made for the year or years of assessment comprising that period and, where necessary, apportioned accordingly; and

  (b) section 113 shall not apply by reason of any change in the persons engaged in carrying on the trade unless an individual begins or ceases to be so engaged, and, where it does apply, an election under subsection (2) of that section shall be made only by the individuals so engaged, and only if an individual so engaged before the change continues to be so engaged after it; and

(c) sections 388 and 389 shall not apply except where section 394 applies to the partnership as a whole.

(4) Section 111 shall apply to income tax chargeable in accordance with this section, matters relevant only to corporation tax being omitted from the assessment.

115.—(1) Subsections (2) and (3) below have effect as respects income tax chargeable in accordance with section 114 for any year of assessment throughout all or any part of which one or more of the persons engaged in carrying on the trade is an individual.

(2) Notwithstanding any difference between the partners' interests during the basis period and their interests during the year of assessment, the amount of the individual's income from the partnership for the year of assessment, or the total of the amounts of the individuals' incomes from the partnership for that year, shall be deemed to be not less than the profits of the basis period, reduced, where any share was apportioned to a company under section 114(2), by the amount of that company's share.

(3) Where there are two or more individuals and, but for subsection (2) above, the total of the amounts of the individuals' incomes from the partnership for the year would fall short of the profits of the basis period reduced, where any share was apportioned to a company under section 114(2), by the amount of that company's share, that amount shall be apportioned—

(a) according to the individuals' interests during the year of assessment, disregarding any company's interest; and

(b) in so far as that does not determine, or fully determine, the apportionment, between the individuals in equal shares.

(4) Where a trade or business is carried on by two or more persons in partnership, and the control and management of the trade or business is situated abroad but those persons include a company resident in the United Kingdom, then as regards that company, this section and section 114 shall have effect as if the partnership were resident in the United Kingdom, and an assessment may be made on the company accordingly.

(5) Subject to subsection (4) above, where the partners in a partnership include a company, section 112 shall apply whether for corporation tax or for income tax; and this section and section 114 shall have effect accordingly.

(6) In this section and section 114—

"basis period", in relation to a year of assessment, means any accounting period or part of an accounting period which is, or forms part of, the period on the profits or gains of which income tax for the year of assessment in question falls to be computed under Schedule D in respect of the trade;

"capital allowances and charges" means any allowances or charges under any of the Capital Allowances Acts, not being allowances or charges which, for income tax, are given or made by deduction or addition in the computation of profits or gains;

and references in subsection (1) above to an individual's income from the partnership are references to that income before deduction of capital allowances or charges on income.

(7) For the purposes of this section and section 114 "profits" shall not be taken as including chargeable gains.

116.—(1) The provisions of subsection (2) below shall apply in relation to a company ("the partner company") which is a member of a partnership carrying on a trade if arrangements are in existence (whether as part of the terms of the partnership or otherwise) whereby—

(a) in respect of the whole or any part of the value of, or of any portion of, the partner company's share in the profits or loss of any accounting period of the partnership, another member of the partnership or any person connected with another member of the partnership receives any payment or acquires or enjoys, directly or indirectly, any other benefit in money's worth; or

(b) in respect of the whole or any part of the cost of, or of any portion of, the partner company's share in the loss of any accounting period of the partnership, the partner company or any person connected with that company receives any payment or acquires or enjoys, directly or indirectly, any other benefit in money's worth, other than a payment in respect of group relief to the partner company by a company which is a member of the same group as the partner company for the purposes of group relief.

(2) In any case where the provisions of this subsection apply in relation to the partner company—

(a) the company's share in the loss of the relevant accounting period of the partnership and its share in any charges on income, within the meaning of section 338, paid by the partnership in that accounting period shall not be available for set-off for the purposes of corporation tax except against its share in the profits of the trade carried on by the partnership; and

(b) except in accordance with paragraph (a) above, no trading losses shall be available for set-off for the purposes of corporation tax against the company's share in the profits of the relevant accounting period of the partnership; and

(c) except in accordance with paragraphs (a) and (b) above, no amount which, apart from this subsection, would be available for relief against profits shall be available for set-off for the purposes of corporation tax against so much of the company's total profits as consists of its share in the profits of the relevant accounting period of the partnership; and

(d) notwithstanding anything in section 239, no advance corporation tax may be set against the company's liability to corporation tax on its share in the profits of the relevant accounting period of the partnership.

(3) In subsection (2) above "relevant accounting period of the partnership" means any accounting period of the partnership in which any such arrangements as are specified in subsection (1) above are in existence or to which any such arrangements apply.

(4) If a company is a member of a partnership and tax in respect of any profits of the partnership is chargeable under Case VI of Schedule D, this section shall apply in relation to the company's share in the profits or loss of the partnership as if—

(a) the profits or loss to which the company's share is attributable were the profits of, or the loss incurred in, a trade carried on by the partnership; and

(b) any allowance which falls to be made under section 46(1) of the Finance Act 1971 (machinery and plant on lease) were an allowance made in taxing that trade.

1971 c. 68.

(5) For the purposes of this section, subsection (2) of section 114 shall have effect for determining a company's share in the profits or loss of any accounting period of a partnership as if, in subsection (1)(b) of that section, the words "or for capital allowances and charges" were omitted.

(6) In this section "arrangements" means arrangements of any kind whether in writing or not.

(7) Section 839 shall apply for the purposes of this section.

Limited partners

117.—(1) An amount which may be given or allowed to an individual under section 353, 380 or 381 below or section 71 of the 1968 Act—

Restriction on relief: individuals.

(a) in respect of a loss sustained by him in a trade, or of interest paid by him in connection with the carrying on of a trade, in a relevant year of assessment; or

(b) as an allowance falling to be made to him for a relevant year of assessment either in taxing a trade or by way of discharge or repayment of tax to which he is entitled by reason of his participation in a trade,

may be given or allowed otherwise than against income consisting of profits or gains arising from the trade only to the extent that the amount given or allowed or (as the case may be) the aggregate amount does not exceed the relevant sum.

(2) In this section—

"limited partner" means—

(i) a person who is carrying on a trade as a limited partner in a limited partnership registered under the Limited Partnerships Act 1907;

1907 c. 24.

(ii) a person who is carrying on a trade as a general partner in a partnership, who is not entitled to take part in the management of the trade and who is entitled to have his liabilities, or his liabilities beyond a certain limit, for debts or obligations incurred for the purposes of the trade discharged or reimbursed by some other person; or

(iii) a person who carries on a trade jointly with others and who, under the law of any territory outside the United Kingdom, is not entitled to take part in the management of the trade and is not liable beyond a certain limit for debts or obligations incurred for the purposes of the trade;

"relevant year of assessment" means a year of assessment at any time during which the individual carried on the trade as a limited partner;

"the aggregate amount" means the aggregate of any amounts given or allowed to him at any time under section 353, 380 or 381 below or section 71 of the 1968 Act—

(a) in respect of a loss sustained by him in the trade, or of interest paid by him in connection with carrying it on, in a relevant year of assessment; or

(b) as an allowance falling to be made to him for a relevant year of assessment either in taxing the trade or by way of discharge or repayment of tax to which he is entitled by reason of his participation in the trade;

"the relevant sum" means the amount of his contribution to the trade as at the appropriate time; and

"the appropriate time" is the end of the relevant year of assessment in which the loss is sustained or the interest paid or for which the allowance falls to be made (except that where he ceased to carry on the trade during that year of assessment it is the time when he so ceased).

(3) A person's contribution to a trade at any time is the aggregate of—

(a) the amount which he has contributed to it as capital and has not, directly or indirectly, drawn out or received back (other than anything which he is or may be entitled so to draw out or receive back at any time when he carries on the trade as a limited partner or which he is or may be entitled to require another person to reimburse to him), and

(b) the amount of any profits or gains of the trade to which he is entitled but which he has not received in money or money's worth.

(4) To the extent that an allowance is taken into account in computing profits or gains or losses in the year of the loss by virtue of section 383(1) it shall, for the purposes of this section, be treated as falling to be made in the year of the loss (and not the year of assessment for which the year of loss is the basis year).

Restriction on relief: companies.   **118.**—(1) An amount which may be given or allowed under section 338, 393(2) or 403(1) to (3) and (7) below or section 74 of the 1968 Act—

(a) in respect of a loss incurred by a company in a trade, or of charges paid by a company in connection with the carrying on of a trade, in a relevant accounting period; or

(b) as an allowance falling to be made to a company for a relevant accounting period either in taxing a trade or by way of discharge or repayment of tax to which it is entitled by reason of its participation in a trade,

may be given or allowed to that company ("the partner company") otherwise than against profits or gains arising from the trade, or to another company, only to the extent that the amount given or allowed or (as the case may be) the aggregate amount does not exceed the relevant sum.

(2) In this section—

"relevant accounting period" means an accounting period of the partner company at any time during which it carried on the trade as a limited partner (within the meaning of section 117(2));

"the aggregate amount" means the aggregate of any amounts given or allowed to the partner company or another company at any time under section 338, 393(2) or 403(1) to (3) and (7) below or section 74 of the 1968 Act—

(a) in respect of a loss incurred by the partner company in the trade, or of charges paid by it in connection with carrying it on, in any relevant accounting period; or

(b) as an allowance falling to be made to the partner company for any relevant accounting period either in taxing the trade or by way of discharge or repayment of tax to which it is entitled by reason of its participation in the trade;

"the relevant sum" means the amount of the partner company's contribution (within the meaning of section 117(3)) to the trade as at the appropriate time; and

"the appropriate time" is the end of the relevant accounting period in which the loss is incurred or the charges paid or for which the allowance falls to be made (except that where the partner company ceased to carry on the trade during that accounting period it is the time when it so ceased).

CHAPTER VIII

MISCELLANEOUS AND SUPPLEMENTAL

119.—(1) Where rent is payable in respect of any land or easement, and either—

(a) the land or easement is used, occupied or enjoyed in connection with any of the concerns specified in section 55(2); or

(b) the lease or other agreement under which the rent is payable provides for the recoupment of the rent by way of reduction of royalties or payments of a similar nature in the event of the land or easement being so used, occupied or enjoyed,

D

the rent shall, subject to section 122, be charged to tax under Schedule D, and, subject to subsection (2) below, shall be subject to deduction of income tax under section 348 or 349 as if it were a royalty or other sum paid in respect of the user of a patent.

(2) Where the rent is rendered in produce of the concern, it shall, instead of being treated as provided by subsection (1) above, be charged under Case III of Schedule D, and the value of the produce so rendered shall be taken to be the amount of the profits or income arising therefrom.

(3) For the purposes of this section—

"easement" includes any right, privilege or benefit in, over or derived from land; and

"rent" includes a rent service, rentcharge, fee farm rent, feuduty or other rent, toll, duty, royalty or annual or periodical payment in the nature of rent, whether payable in money or money's worth or otherwise.

Rent etc. payable in respect of electric line wayleaves.

120.—(1) Where rent is payable in respect of any easement enjoyed in the United Kingdom in connection with any electric, telegraphic or telephonic wire or cable (not being such an easement as is mentioned in section 119(1)), the rent shall be charged to tax under Schedule D, and, subject to subsections (2) to (5) below, shall be subject to deduction of income tax under section 348 or 349 as if it were a royalty or other sum paid in respect of the user of a patent.

(2) Any payment of rent to which subsection (1) above applies which does not exceed £2.50 per year may, if the payer so elects, be treated as not affected by so much of that subsection as provides that the rent shall be subject to deduction of income tax, and shall in that event be made without deduction of income tax accordingly.

(3) Any payment of rent to which subsection (1) above applies which is made without deduction of income tax, whether by virtue of subsection (2) above or otherwise, shall, unless income tax is assessed thereon under section 350, be chargeable to tax under Case III of Schedule D.

(4) Any payment of rent to which subsection (1) above applies which is made subject to deduction of income tax shall, if it is paid by a person carrying on a trade which consists of or includes the provision of a radio relay service and the wire or cable in question is used by that person for the purposes of that service—

(a) be deductible (notwithstanding anything in section 74(q)) in computing the amount of the profits or gains of the trade to be charged under Case I of Schedule D, and

(b) be deemed for the purposes of sections 348 and 349 not to be payable out of profits or gains brought into charge to income tax.

(5) In this section—

(a) "easement" and "rent" have the same meanings as in section 119;

(b) the reference to easements enjoyed in connection with any electric, telegraphic or telephonic wire or cable includes (without prejudice to the generality of that expression) references to easements enjoyed in connection with any pole or pylon supporting any such wire or cable, or with any apparatus (including any transformer) used in connection with any such wire or cable; and

(c) "radio relay service" means the retransmission by wire to their customers of broadcast programmes (which may or may not be television programmes) which the persons carrying on the service receive either by wire or by wireless from the British Broadcasting Corporation or from the persons outside the United Kingdom who broadcast the programmes in question.

121.—(1) Where for any year of assessment rights to work minerals in the United Kingdom are let, the lessor shall, subject to subsection (2) below, be entitled, on making a claim for the purpose, to be repaid so much of the income tax paid by him by deduction or otherwise in respect of the rent or royalties for that year as is equal to the amount of the tax on any sums proved to have been wholly, exclusively and necessarily disbursed by him as expenses of management or supervision of those minerals in that year.

Management expenses of owner of mineral rights.

(2) No repayment of tax shall be made under subsection (1) above if, or to such extent as, the expenses in question have been otherwise allowed as a deduction in computing income for the purposes of income tax.

(3) In computing for the purposes of corporation tax the income of a company for any accounting period from the letting of rights to work minerals in the United Kingdom, there may be deducted any sums disbursed by the company wholly, exclusively and necessarily as expenses of management or supervision of those minerals in that period.

122.—(1) Subject to the following provisions of this section, a person resident or ordinarily resident in the United Kingdom who in any year of assessment or accounting period is entitled to receive any mineral royalties under a mineral lease or agreement shall be treated—

Relief in respect of mineral royalties.

(a) for the purposes of income tax, or as the case may be for the purposes of corporation tax on profits exclusive of chargeable gains, as if the total of the mineral royalties receivable by him under that lease or agreement in that year or period and any management expenses available for set-off against those royalties in that year or period were each reduced by one-half; and

(b) for the purposes of the 1979 Act or as the case may be for the purposes of corporation tax on chargeable gains, as if there accrued to him in that year or period a chargeable gain equal to one-half of the total of the mineral royalties receivable by him under that lease or agreement in that year or period;

and this section shall have effect notwithstanding any provision of section 119(1) making the whole of certain kinds of mineral royalties chargeable to tax under Schedule D, but without prejudice to any provision of that section providing for any such royalties to be subject to deduction of income tax under section 348 or 349.

(2) For the purposes of subsection (1)(a) above, "management expenses available for set-off" against royalties means—

(a) where section 121 applies in respect of the royalties, any sum brought into account under subsection (1) of that section in determining the amount of the repayment of income tax in respect of those royalties or, as the case may be, deductible from those royalties under subsection (2) of that section in computing the income of a company for the purposes of corporation tax; and

(b) if the royalties are chargeable to tax under Schedule A, any sums deductible under Part II as payments made in respect of management of the property concerned;

and if neither paragraph (a) nor paragraph (b) above applies, the reference in subsection (1)(a) above to management expenses available for set-off shall be disregarded.

(3) The amount of the chargeable gain treated as accruing to any person by virtue of subsection (1)(b) above shall, notwithstanding anything in the enactments relating to the computation of chargeable gains, be the whole amount calculated in accordance with that subsection, and, accordingly, no reduction shall be made on account of expenditure incurred by that person or of any other matter whatsoever.

(4) Where subsection (1) above applies in relation to mineral royalties receivable under a mineral lease or agreement by a person not chargeable to corporation tax in respect of those royalties, then, in so far as the amount of income tax paid, by deduction or otherwise, by him in respect of those mineral royalties in any year of assessment exceeds the amount of income tax for which he is liable in respect of those royalties by virtue of subsection (1)(a) above—

(a) the amount of the excess shall in the first instance be set against the tax for which he is chargeable by virtue of subsection (1)(b) above; and

(b) on the making of a claim in that behalf, he shall be entitled to repayment of tax in respect of the balance of that excess.

(5) In this section references to mineral royalties refer only to royalties receivable on or after 6th April 1970, and the expression "mineral royalties" means so much of any rents, tolls, royalties and other periodical payments in the nature of rent payable under a mineral lease or agreement as relates to the winning and working of minerals; and the Board may by regulations—

(a) provide whether, and to what extent, payments made under a mineral lease or agreement and relating both to the winning and working of minerals and to other matters are to be treated as mineral royalties; and

(b) provide for treating the whole of such payments as mineral royalties in cases where the extent to which they relate to matters other than the winning and working of minerals is small.

(6) In this section—

"minerals" means all minerals and substances in or under land which are ordinarily worked for removal by underground or surface working but excluding water, peat, top-soil and vegetation; and

"mineral lease or agreement" means—

(a) a lease, profit à prendre, licence or other agreement conferring a right to win and work minerals in the United Kingdom;

(b) a contract for the sale, or a conveyance, of minerals in or under land in the United Kingdom; and

(c) a grant of a right under section 1 of the Mines (Working Facilities and Support) Act 1966, other than an ancillary right within the meaning of that Act.

1966 c. 4.

(7) In the application of this section to Northern Ireland—

(a) references to mineral royalties include references to periodical payments—

(i) of compensation under section 29 or 35 of the Mineral Development Act (Northern Ireland) 1969 ("the 1969 Act") or under section 4 of the Petroleum (Production) Act (Northern Ireland) 1964 ("the 1964 Act"); and

1969 c. 35 (N.I.).

1964 c. 28 (N.I.).

(ii) made as mentioned in section 37 of the 1969 Act or under section 55(4)(b) of that Act or under section 11 of the 1964 Act (payments in respect of minerals to persons entitled to a share of royalties under section 13(3) of the Irish Land Act 1903); and

1903 c. 37.

(b) in its application to any such payments as are mentioned in paragraph (a) above, references to the mineral lease or agreement under which mineral royalties are payable shall be construed as references to the enactment under which the payments are made.

(8) In any case where, before the commencement of this section, for the purposes of the 1979 Act or of corporation tax on chargeable gains, a person was treated as if there had accrued to him in any year of assessment or accounting period ending before 6th April 1988 a chargeable gain equal to the relevant fraction, determined in accordance with section 29(3)(b) of the Finance Act 1970, of the total of the mineral royalties receivable by him under that lease or agreement in that year or period, subsection (1)(b) above shall have effect in relation to any mineral royalties receivable by him under that lease or agreement in any later year or period with the substitution for the reference to one-half of a reference to the relevant fraction as so determined.

1970 c. 24.

123.—(1) In this section—

Foreign dividends.

(a) "foreign dividends" means any interest, dividends or other annual payments payable out of or in respect of the stocks, funds, shares or securities of any body of persons not resident in the United Kingdom (but not including any such payment to which section 348 or 349(1) applies) and references to dividends shall be construed accordingly;

(b) "relevant foreign dividends" means foreign dividends payable out of or in respect of stocks, funds, shares or securities which are not held in a recognised clearing system;

(c) "banker" includes a person acting as a banker; and

(d) references to coupons include, in relation to any dividends, warrants for or bills of exchange purporting to be drawn or made in payment of those dividends.

(2) Where relevant foreign dividends are entrusted to any person in the United Kingdom for payment to any persons in the United Kingdom, they shall be assessed and charged to income tax under Schedule D by the Board, and Parts III and IV of Schedule 3 shall apply in relation to the income tax to be so assessed and charged.

(3) Where—

(a) a banker or any other person in the United Kingdom, by means of coupons received from any other person or otherwise on his behalf, obtains payment of any foreign dividends elsewhere than in the United Kingdom, or

(b) any banker in the United Kingdom sells or otherwise realises coupons for foreign dividends, and pays over the proceeds to any person or carries them to his account, or

(c) any dealer in coupons in the United Kingdom purchases any such coupons otherwise than from a banker or another dealer in coupons,

tax under Schedule D shall extend, in the cases mentioned in paragraph (a) above, to the dividends, and, in the cases mentioned in paragraphs (b) and (c) above, to the proceeds of the sale or other realisation, and income tax shall be assessed and charged and paid under this subsection in accordance with Parts III and IV of Schedule 3.

(4) In the cases mentioned in subsections (2) and (3) above, no tax shall be chargeable if it is proved, on a claim in that behalf made to the Board, that the person owning the stocks, funds, shares or securities and entitled to the dividends or proceeds is not resident in the United Kingdom.

(5) Where stocks, funds, shares or securities are held under a trust, and the person who is the beneficiary in possession under the trust is the sole beneficiary in possession and can, by means either of the revocation of the trust or the exercise of any power under the trust, call upon the trustees at any time to transfer the stocks, funds, shares or securities to him absolutely free from the trust, that person shall, for the purposes of subsection (4) above, be deemed to be the person owning the stocks, funds, shares or securities.

(6) Where any income of any person is by virtue of any provision of the Tax Acts (and in particular, but without prejudice to the generality of the preceding words, Chapter III of Part XVII) to be deemed to be income of any other person, that income is not exempt from tax by virtue of subsection (4) above by reason of the first mentioned person not being resident in the United Kingdom.

Interest on quoted Eurobonds.　　　**124.**—(1) Section 349(2) shall not apply to interest paid on any quoted Eurobond where—

(a) the person by or through whom the payment is made is not in the United Kingdom; or

(b) the payment is made by or through a person who is in the United Kingdom but either of the conditions mentioned in subsection (2) below is satisfied.

(2) The conditions are—

(a) that it is proved, on a claim in that behalf made to the Board, that the person who is the beneficial owner of the quoted Eurobond and is entitled to the interest is not resident in the United Kingdom;

(b) that the quoted Eurobond is held in a recognised clearing system.

(3) In a case falling within subsection (1)(b) above the person by or through whom the payment is made shall deliver to the Board—

(a) on demand by the Board an account of the amount of any such payment; and

(b) not later than 12 months after making any such payment, and unless within that time he delivers an account with respect to the payment under paragraph (a) above, a written statement specifying his name and address and describing the payment.

(4) Where by virtue of any provision of the Tax Acts interest paid on any quoted Eurobond is deemed to be income of a person other than the person who is the beneficial owner of the quoted Eurobond, subsection (2)(a) above shall apply as if it referred to that other person.

(5) Subsections (3) to (6) of section 123 shall apply in relation to interest on quoted Eurobonds as they apply to foreign dividends but with the following modifications—

(a) subsection (4) shall apply as if it required a claim to have been made on or before the event by virtue of which tax would otherwise be chargeable; and

(b) paragraph 6(1) of Schedule 3 shall apply with the omission of paragraphs (a) and (b).

(6) In this section—

"quoted Eurobond" means a security which—

(a) is issued by a company;

(b) is quoted on a recognised stock exchange;

(c) is in bearer form; and

(d) carries a right to interest; and

"recognised clearing system" means any system for clearing quoted Eurobonds which is for the time being designated for the purposes of this section by order made by the Board, as a recognised clearing system.

(7) An order under subsection (6) above—

(a) may contain such transitional and other supplemental provisions as appear to the Board to be necessary or expedient; and

(b) may be varied or revoked by a subsequent order so made.

Annual payments for non-taxable consideration.

125.—(1) Any payment to which this subsection applies shall be made without deduction of income tax, shall not be allowed as a deduction in computing the income or total income of the person by whom it is made and shall not be a charge on income for the purposes of corporation tax.

(2) Subject to the following provisions of this section, subsection (1) above applies to any payment which—

(a) is an annuity or other annual payment charged with tax under Case III of Schedule D, not being interest; and

(b) is made under a liability incurred for consideration in money or money's worth all or any of which is not required to be brought into account in computing for the purposes of income tax or corporation tax the income of the person making the payment.

(3) Subsection (1) above does not apply to—

(a) any payment which in the hands of the recipient is income falling within section 683(1)(a) or (c) or (6);

(b) any payment made to an individual under a liability incurred in consideration of his surrendering, assigning or releasing an interest in settled property to or in favour of a person having a subsequent interest;

(c) any annuity granted in the ordinary course of a business of granting annuities; or

(d) any annuity charged on an interest in settled property and granted at any time before 30th March 1977 by an individual to a company whose business at that time consisted wholly or mainly in the acquisition of interests in settled property or which was at that time carrying on life assurance business in the United Kingdom.

(4) In the application of this section to Scotland the references in subsection (3) above to settled property shall be construed as references to property held in trust.

(5) Subsection (1) above applies to a payment made after 5th April 1988 irrespective of when the liability to make it was incurred.

Treasury securities issued at a discount.

126.—(1) Where a security to which this section applies is issued at a discount, tax shall not be charged in respect of the discount under Case III of Schedule D; but the discount shall not for that reason be regarded as annual profits or gains chargeable to tax under Case VI of Schedule D.

(2) This section applies to all securities issued by the Treasury after 6th March 1973 except Treasury bills.

Enterprise allowance.

127.—(1) This section applies to—

    (a) payments known as enterprise allowance and made by the
Manpower Services Commission in pursuance of arrangements
under section 2(2)(d) of the Employment and Training Act   1973 c. 50.
1973; and

    (b) corresponding payments made in Northern Ireland by the
Department of Economic Development.

(2) Any such payment which would (apart from this section) be charged to tax under Case I or II of Schedule D shall be charged to tax under Case VI of that Schedule.

(3) Nothing in subsection (2) above shall prevent such a payment—

    (a) being treated for the purposes of section 623(2)(c) or 833(4)(c) as immediately derived from the carrying on or exercise of a trade, profession or vocation; or

    (b) being treated for the purposes of paragraph 1 of Schedule 19 as trading income.

128. Any gain arising to any person in the course of dealing in   Commodity and
commodity or financial futures or in qualifying options, which apart from   financial futures
this section would constitute profits or gains chargeable to tax under   etc.: losses and
Schedule D otherwise than as the profits of a trade, shall not be   gains.
chargeable to tax under that Schedule.

In this section "commodity or financial futures" and "qualifying
options" have the same meaning as in section 72 of the Finance Act 1985,   1985 c. 54.
and the reference to a gain arising in the course of dealing in commodity
or financial futures includes any gain which is regarded as arising in the
course of such dealing by virtue of subsection (2A) of that section.

129.—(1) Subject to subsection (4) below, this section applies where a   Stock lending.
person ("A") has contracted to sell securities and, to enable him to fulfil
the contract, he enters into an arrangement under which—

    (a) another person ("B") is to transfer securities to A or his nominee; and

    (b) in return securities of the same kind and amount are to be transferred (whether or not by A or his nominee) to B or his nominee.

(2) Subject to subsection (4) below, this section also applies where, to enable B to make the transfer to A or his nominee, B enters into an arrangement under which—

    (a) another person ("C") is to transfer securities to B or his nominee; and

    (b) in return securities of the same kind and amount are to be transferred (whether or not by B or his nominee) to C or his nominee.

(3) Any transfer made in pursuance of an arrangement mentioned in subsection (1) or (2) above shall not be taken into account for the purposes of the Tax Acts in computing the profits or losses of any trade carried on by the transferor or transferee.

PART IV

(4) The Treasury may provide by regulations that this section or any provision of it or section 149B(9) of the 1979 Act does not apply unless such conditions as are specified in the regulations are fulfilled; and the conditions may relate to the capacity in which any person involved in any arrangement is acting, the Board's approval of any such person or of the arrangement, the nature of the securities or otherwise.

(5) In this section "securities" includes stocks and shares.

1986 c. 41.

(6) This section applies to transfers made after such date as is specified for this purpose by regulations made under section 61 of the Finance Act 1986 or, if no such regulations have been made before 6th April 1988, under this section.

Meaning of "investment company" for purposes of Part IV.

1985 c. 58.

130. In this Part of this Act "investment company", means any company whose business consists wholly or mainly in the making of investments and the principal part of whose income is derived therefrom, but includes any savings bank or other bank for savings except any which, for the purposes of the Trustee Savings Bank Act 1985, is a successor or a further successor to a trustee savings bank.

PART V

PROVISIONS RELATING TO THE SCHEDULE E CHARGE

CHAPTER I

SUPPLEMENTARY CHARGING PROVISIONS OF GENERAL APPLICATION

Miscellaneous provisions

131.—(1) Tax under Case I, II or III of Schedule E shall, except as provided to the contrary by any provision of the Tax Acts, be chargeable on the full amount of the emoluments falling under that Case, subject to such deductions only as may be authorised by the Tax Acts, and the expression "emoluments" shall include all salaries, fees, wages, perquisites and profits whatsoever.

Chargeable emoluments.

(2) Tax under Case III of Schedule E shall be chargeable whether or not tax is chargeable in repect of the same office or employment under Case I or II of that Schedule, but shall not be chargeable on any emoluments falling under Case I or II for the same or another chargeable period.

132.—(1) Where a person ordinarily performs the whole or part of the duties of his office or employment in the United Kingdom, then, for the purposes of Cases I and II of Schedule E, his emoluments for any period of absence from the office or employment shall be treated as emoluments for duties performed in the United Kingdom, except in so far as it is shown that, but for that absence, they would have been emoluments for duties performed outside the United Kingdom.

Place of performance, and meaning of emoluments received in the U.K.

(2) Where an office or employment is in substance one the duties of which fall in the chargeable period to be performed outside the United Kingdom, then, for the purposes of Cases I and II of Schedule E, there shall be treated as so performed any duties performed in the United Kingdom the performance of which is merely incidental to the performance of the other duties outside the United Kingdom.

(3) Subsection (2) above shall not be construed as affecting any question under section 193(1) or paragraph 3 of Schedule 12 as to where any duties are performed or whether a person is absent from the United Kingdom.

(4) For the purposes of Cases I and II of Schedule E, but subject to section 194(7) and paragraph 5 of Schedule 12, the following duties shall be treated as performed in the United Kingdom, namely—

    (a) the duties of any office or employment under the Crown which is of a public nature and the emoluments of which are payable out of the public revenue of the United Kingdom or of Northern Ireland; and

    (b) any duties which a person performs on a vessel engaged on a voyage not extending to a port outside the United Kingdom, or which a person resident in the United Kingdom performs on a vessel or aircraft engaged on a voyage or journey beginning or ending in the United Kingdom or on a part beginning or ending in the United Kingdom of any other voyage or journey.

(5) For the purposes of Case III of Schedule E, emoluments shall be treated as received in the United Kingdom if they are paid, used or enjoyed in, or in any manner or form transmitted or brought to, the United Kingdom, and subsections (6) to (9) of section 65 shall apply for the purposes of this subsection as they apply for the purposes of subsection (5) of that section.

Voluntary
pensions.

133.—(1) Where—

   (a) a person has ceased to hold any office or employment, and

   (b) a pension or annual payment is paid to him, or to his widow or child, or to any relative or dependant of his, by the person under whom he held the office or by whom he was employed, or by the successors of that person, and

   (c) that pension or annual payment is paid otherwise than by or on behalf of a person outside the United Kingdom,

then, notwithstanding that the pension or payment is paid voluntarily or is capable of being discontinued, it shall be deemed to be income for the purposes of assessment to tax, and shall be assessed and charged under Schedule E.

(2) For the avoidance of doubt, it is hereby declared that the expressions "annuity" and "pension" in Schedule E include respectively an annuity and a pension which is paid voluntarily or is capable of being discontinued.

Workers supplied
by agencies.

134.—(1) Subject to the provisions of this section, where—

   (a) an individual ("the worker") renders or is under an obligation to render personal services to another person ("the client") and is subject to, or to the right of, supervision, direction or control as to the manner in which he renders those services; and

   (b) the worker is supplied to the client by or through a third person ("the agency") and renders or is under an obligation to render those services under the terms of a contract between the worker and the agency ("the relevant contract"); and

   (c) remuneration receivable under or in consequence of that contract would not, apart from this section, be chargeable to income tax under Schedule E,

then, for all the purposes of the Income Tax Acts, the services which the worker renders or is under an obligation to render to the client under that contract shall be treated as if they were the duties of an office or employment held by the worker, and all remuneration receivable under or in consequence of that contract shall be treated as emoluments of that office or employment and shall be assessable to income tax under Schedule E accordingly.

(2) Subsection (1)(b) above includes cases in which the third person is an unincorporated body of which the worker is a member.

(3) Subsection (1) above shall apply whether or not the worker renders or is under an obligation to render the services in question as a partner in a firm or a member of an unincorporated body; and where, in any case in which that subsection applies, the worker is a partner in a firm or a member of such a body, remuneration receivable under or in consequence of the relevant contract shall be treated for all the purposes of the Income Tax Acts as income of the worker and not as income of the firm or body.

(4) For the purposes of this section, any remuneration which the client pays or provides by reason of the worker being a person who renders or is under an obligation to render the services in question shall be treated as receivable in consequence of the relevant contract.

(5) Subsection (1) above shall not apply—

(a) if the services in question are services as an actor, singer, musician or other entertainer or as a fashion, photographic or artist's model; or

(b) if the services in question are rendered wholly in the worker's own home or at other premises which are neither under the control or management of the client nor premises at which the worker is required, by reason of the nature of the services, to render them; or

(c) if in rendering the services the worker is or would be a sub-contractor within the meaning of section 560.

(6) Where an individual enters into arrangements with another person with a view to the rendering of personal services by the individual, being arrangements such that, if and when he renders any such services as a result of the arrangements, those services will be treated under subsection (1) above as if they were the duties of an office or employment held by him, then for all purposes of the Income Tax Acts any remuneration receivable under or in consequence of the arrangements shall be treated as emoluments of an office or employment held by the individual and shall be assessable to income tax under Schedule E accordingly.

(7) In this section "remuneration", in relation to an individual, does not include anything in respect of which he would not have been chargeable to tax under Schedule E if it had been receivable in connection with an office or employment held by him but, subject to that, includes every form of payment and all perquisites, benefits and profits whatsoever.

Shareholdings, loans etc.

135.—(1) Subject to section 185, where a person realises a gain by the exercise, or by the assignment or release, of a right to acquire shares in a body corporate obtained by that person as a director or employee of that or any other body corporate, he shall be chargeable to tax under Schedule E on an amount equal to the amount of his gain, as computed in accordance with this section.

Gains by directors and employees from share options.

(2) Without prejudice to section 185, where tax may by virtue of this section become chargeable in respect of any gain which may be realised by the exercise of a right which is not capable of being exercised more than seven years after it is obtained, tax shall not be chargeable under any other provision of the Tax Acts in respect of the receipt of the right.

(3) Subject to section 136(4)—

    (a) the gain realised by the exercise of any such right at any time shall be taken to be the difference between the amount that a person might reasonably expect to obtain from a sale in the open market at that time of the shares acquired and the amount or value of the consideration given whether for them or for the grant of the right; and

    (b) the gain realised by the assignment or release of any such right shall be taken to be the difference between the amount or value of the consideration for the assignment or release and the amount or value of the consideration given for the grant of the right;

(a just apportionment being made of any entire consideration given for the grant of the right to acquire those shares and other shares or otherwise for the grant of the right to acquire those shares and for something besides).

(4) For the purposes of subsection (3) above, neither the consideration given for the grant of the right nor any such entire consideration as is mentioned in that subsection shall be taken to include the performance of any duties in or in connection with the office or employment by reason of which the right was granted, and no part of the amount or value of the consideration given for the grant shall be deducted more than once under that subsection.

(5) Where such a right as is mentioned in subsection (1) above is obtained as mentioned therein and is capable of being exercised later than seven years after it is obtained, and the receipt of the right is chargeable to tax under any other provision of the Tax Acts, then—

    (a) the tax so charged shall be deducted from any tax which is chargeable under subsection (1) above by reference to the gain realised by the exercise, assignment or release of that right; and

    (b) for the purpose of any such charge to tax in relation to the receipt of the right, the value of the right shall be taken to be not less than the market value at the time the right is obtained—

        (i) of the shares which may be acquired by the exercise of the right, or

        (ii) of shares for which shares so acquired may be exchanged,

    reduced by the amount or value (or, if variable, the least amount or value) of the consideration for which the shares may be so acquired.

(6) Subject to subsection (7) below, a person shall, in the case of a right granted by reason of his office or employment, be chargeable to tax under this section in respect of a gain realised by another person—

    (a) if the right was granted to that other person, or

    (b) if the other person acquired the right otherwise than by or under an assignment made by way of a bargain at arm's length, or if the two are connected persons at the time when the gain is realised, but in a case within paragraph (b) above the gain realised shall be treated as reduced by the amount of any gain realised by a previous holder on an assignment of the right.

(7) A person shall not be chargeable to tax by virtue of subsection (6)(b) above in respect of any gain realised by another person if the first-mentioned person was divested of the right by operation of law on his bankruptcy or otherwise, but the other person shall be chargeable to tax in respect of the gain under Case VI of Schedule D.

(8) In any case where—

(a) a person has obtained any such right to acquire shares as is mentioned in subsection (1) above ("the first right"); and

(b) as to any of the shares to which the first right relates, he omits or undertakes to omit to exercise the right or grants or undertakes to grant to another a right to acquire the shares or any interest in them; and

(c) in consideration for or otherwise in connection with that omission, grant or undertaking, he receives any benefit in money or money's worth;

he shall be treated for the purposes of this section and section 136 as realising a gain by the assignment or release of the first right, so far as it relates to the shares in question, for a consideration equal to the amount or value of the benefit referred to in paragraph (c) above.

(9) Where subsection (8) above has had effect on any occasion, nothing in that subsection affects the application of this section in relation to a gain realised on a subsequent occasion, except that on that subsequent occasion so much of the consideration given for the grant of the first right as was deducted on the first occasion shall not be deducted again.

136.—(1) If a right to acquire shares in a body corporate is assigned or released in whole or in part for a consideration which consists of or comprises another right to acquire shares in that or any other body corporate, that other right shall not be treated as consideration for the assignment or release, but section 135 and this section shall apply in relation to it as they apply in relation to the right assigned or released and as if the consideration for its acquisition— Provisions supplementary to section 135.

(a) did not include the value of the right assigned or released, but

(b) did include the amount or value of the consideration given for the grant of the right assigned or released so far as that has not been offset by any valuable consideration for the assignment or release other than the consideration consisting of the other right.

(2) If—

(a) as a result of two or more transactions a person ceases to hold a right to acquire shares in a body corporate and he or a connected person comes to hold another right to acquire shares in that or any other body corporate (whether or not acquired from the person to whom the other right was assigned), and

(b) any of those transactions was effected under arrangements to which two or more persons holding rights in respect of which tax may be chargeable under this section were parties,

those transactions shall be treated for the purposes of subsection (1) above as a single transaction whereby the one right is assigned for a consideration which consists of or comprises the other right.

(3) Subsection (2) above applies in relation to two or more transactions whether they involve an assignment preceding, coinciding with or subsequent to an acquisition.

(4) In the case of a right to acquire shares granted before 3rd May 1966—

(a) the amount of the gain realised at any time by the exercise, or by the assignment or release, of the right shall not exceed the difference between the market value of those shares at that time and their market value on 3rd May 1966 (and no gain shall be treated as so realised unless the later value exceeds the earlier value); and

(b) subsection (2) of section 135 shall not affect tax chargeable under Case I of Schedule E in respect of the receipt of the right, but the amount, if any, on which tax is so chargeable shall be taken into account under subsection (3)(a) and (b) of that section in relation to the gain realised by the exercise or by the assignment or release, of the right as if that amount formed part (in addition to any other amount) of the consideration for the grant of the right.

(5) For the purposes of this section and section 135—

(a) references to the release of a right include references to agreeing to the restriction of the exercise of the right;

(b) "director" means—

(i) in relation to a body corporate the affairs of which are managed by a board of directors or similar body, a member of that board or similar body;

(ii) in relation to a body corporate the affairs of which are managed by a single director or similar person, that director or person;

(iii) in relation to a body corporate the affairs of which are managed by the members themselves, a member of the body corporate;

and includes any person who is to be or has been a director;

(c) "employee", in relation to a body corporate, includes any person taking part in the management of the affairs of the body corporate who is not a director, and includes a person who is to be or has been an employee; and

(d) in so far as the context permits, "shares" includes stock;

and this section and section 135 shall apply in relation to any securities issued by a body corporate as they apply to shares in that body corporate.

(6) Where in any year of assessment a body corporate grants a right in respect of which tax may become chargeable under section 135, or allots or transfers any shares in pursuance of such a right, or receives notice of the assignment of such a right or provides any benefit in money or money's worth—

(a) for the assignment or for the release in whole or in part of such a right; or

(b) for or in connection with an omission or undertaking to omit to exercise such a right; or

(c) for or in connection with the grant or undertaking to grant a right to acquire shares or an interest in shares to which such a right relates;

it shall deliver particulars thereof in writing to the inspector not later than 30 days after the end of that year.

137.—(1) In any case where—

(a) for any year of assessment a person is chargeable to tax under Schedule E, by virtue of section 135, on an amount equal to a gain realised by the exercise of a right to acquire shares which was obtained before 6th April 1984; and

(b) the shares acquired in the exercise of that right were acquired for a consideration which, subject to subsection (2) below, was not less than the market value (determined as for the purposes of the 1979 Act) of shares of the same class at the time the right was granted or, if the right was granted before 6th April 1982, 90 per cent. of that market value; and

(c) following an assessment for the year in which that right was exercised ("the relevant year") an amount of tax chargeable by virtue of section 135 in respect of the amount referred to in paragraph (a) above and exceeding £250 is payable to the collector pursuant to regulations under section 203; and

(d) the person concerned makes an election in accordance with subsection (3) below,

he shall be entitled to pay tax by instalments in accordance with subsection (4) below.

(2) Shares which are acquired for a consideration less than that required by paragraph (b) of subsection (1) above by reason only of a diminution in the market value of shares of that class (determined as for the purposes of the 1979 Act) which is attributable solely to the share capital of the company issuing the shares being varied after the right to acquire the shares was granted, shall for the purposes of that paragraph be regarded as having been acquired for a consideration not less than that required by that paragraph.

(3) An election under this section shall be made by notice to the inspector before the expiry of the period of 60 days beginning immediately after the end of the relevant year.

(4) Where an election has been made under this section the tax referred to in subsection (1)(c) above shall, subject to subsection (5) and (6) below, be paid in five equal instalments as follows—

    (a) the first shall be due and payable at the expiry of the period of 14 days beginning on the date on which application for the tax is made pursuant to regulations under section 203;

    (b) the fifth shall be due and payable on the last day of the fifth year following the end of the relevant year; and

    (c) the second, third and fourth instalments shall be due on such dates as will secure, so far as may be, that the interval between any two consecutive dates is the same.

(5) In any case where the date which, apart from this subsection, would be the due date for the fifth instalment of tax under subsection (4) above is earlier than the due date referred to in paragraph (a) of that subsection, all five instalments shall be due on the later date.

(6) Tax which, by virtue of an election under this section, is not yet due and payable in accordance with subsection (4) above may nevertheless be paid at any time and shall become due and payable forthwith if the person who made the election becomes bankrupt under the law of any part of the United Kingdom.

(7) Subject to any other provision of the Income Tax Acts requiring income of any description to be treated as the highest part of a person's income, for the purposes of paragraph (c) of subsection (1) above in determining what tax is chargeable on a person by virtue of section 135 in respect of the amount referred to in paragraph (a) of that subsection, that amount shall be treated as the highest part of his income for the relevant year.

Share acquisitions by directors and employees.

138.—(1) Subject to section 185 and the following provisions of this section, where a person has acquired or acquires shares or an interest in shares in a body corporate in pursuance of a right conferred on him or opportunity offered to him as a director or employee of that or any other body corporate, and not in pursuance of an offer to the public—

    (a) if the market value of the shares at the end of the period mentioned in subsection (9) below exceeds their market value at the time of the acquisition, he shall be chargeable to tax under Schedule E for the year of assessment in which that period ends on an amount equal, except as provided by subsection (8) below, to the excess (or, if his interest is less than the full beneficial ownership, such part of that amount as corresponds to his interest);

    (b) if he receives, by virtue of his ownership of or interest in the shares, any benefit not received by the majority of persons who—

        (i) hold shares forming part of the ordinary share capital of the same body corporate; and

        (ii) have acquired the shares otherwise than as mentioned above;

and the benefit is not otherwise chargeable to income tax, he shall be chargeable to tax under Schedule E for the year of assessment in which he receives the benefit on an amount equal to the value of the benefit;

and any amount chargeable under this subsection shall be treated as earned income, whether or not it would otherwise fall to be so treated.

(2) Subsection (1) above does not apply if the acquisition—

  (a) was made in pursuance of arrangements under which employees of a body corporate receive as part of their emoluments shares or interests in shares in that body or in a body controlling it to an extent determined in advance by reference to the profits of either body; and

  (b) where the arrangements were made or modified after 22nd March 1973, was of shares or an interest in shares which satisfy the conditions set out in subsection (4)(a) below and the arrangements satisfy the condition set out in subsection (4)(b) below.

(3) Subsection (1)(a) above does not apply if—

  (a) the acquisition was an acquisition of shares in a body and either of the following conditions was satisfied immediately after the acquisition, namely—

    (i) that the shares were not subject to such restrictions as are specified in subsection (6) below, and were not exchangeable for shares subject to such restrictions, and the majority of the available shares of the same class was acquired otherwise than as mentioned in subsection (1) above; or

    (ii) that the shares were not subject to such restrictions as are specified in paragraph (a) or (b) of subsection (6) below and were not exchangeable for shares subject to such restrictions, and the majority of the available shares of the same class was acquired by persons who were or had been employees or directors of, or of a body controlled by, that body and who were together able as holders of the shares to control that body; or

  (b) the acquisition was an acquisition after 5th April 1984 of an interest in shares which consists of units in an authorised unit trust and—

    (i) prior to the acquisition the unit trust was approved by the Board for the purposes of this section and, at the time of the acquisition, continues to be so approved, and

    (ii) the condition set out in subsection (7) below is fulfilled with respect to the body corporate (in that subsection referred to as "the relevant company") directorship of or employment by which gave rise to the right or opportunity by virtue of which the acquisition was made; or

  (c) the acquisition took place before 6th April 1981.

PART V   (4) The conditions referred to in subsection (2)(b) above are as follows—

  (a) that the shares—

      (i) are not subject to such restrictions as will or may result in the person acquiring the shares or an interest in the shares obtaining a benefit through an increase, subsequent to the acquisition, of the value or the value to him of the shares or interest; and

      (ii) cannot (whether by one transaction or a series of transactions) be exchanged for or converted into shares which are subject to such restrictions; and

      (iii) are either shares of a class quoted on a recognised stock exchange or are shares in a company which is not under the control of another company;

  (b) that the arrangements allow every full-time employee of the company concerned who—

      (i) has been a full-time employee of that company for a continuous period of not less than five years, and

      (ii) is chargeable to tax in respect of his employment under Case I of Schedule E, and

      (iii) is not less than 25 years old,

  to acquire shares or interests in shares of the same class on similar terms.

  (5) For the purposes of subsection (3)(a) above—

  (a) shares in a body are available shares if they are not held by or for the benefit of an associated company of that body; and

  (b) shares are exchangeable for other shares if (whether by one transaction or a series of transactions) they can be exchanged for or converted into the other shares.

  (6) The restrictions referred to in subsection (3)(a) above are—

  (a) restrictions not attaching to all shares of the same class; or

  (b) restrictions ceasing or liable to cease at some time after the acquisition; or

  (c) restrictions depending on the shares being or ceasing to be held by directors or employees of any body corporate (other than such restrictions imposed by a company's articles of association as require shares to be disposed of on ceasing to be so held).

  (7) The condition referred to in subsection (3)(b) above is fulfilled with respect to the relevant company if, for no continuous period of one month or more, throughout which any director or employee of the relevant company either—

  (a) has, by virtue of his office or employment, any such right or opportunity as is referred to in subsection (1) above to acquire units in the unit trust, or

  (b) retains any beneficial interest in any units in the unit trust which he acquired in pursuance of such a right or opportunity, do investments in the relevant company and in any other company in relation to which the relevant company is an associated company make up more than 10 per cent. by value of the investments subject to the trusts of the unit trust.

(8) The amount on which or on part of which the person making the acquisition is chargeable to tax under subsection (1)(a) above ("the chargeable amount") shall, in the following cases, be reduced as follows, that is to say—

(a) where, in accordance with the terms on which the acquisition of the shares was made, the consideration for the acquisition is subsequently increased, the chargeable amount shall be reduced by an amount equal to the increase; and

(b) where, in accordance with those terms, the shares are subsequently disposed of for a consideration which is less than their market value at the time of the disposal, the chargeable amount shall be reduced so as to be equal to the excess of that consideration over the market value of the shares at the time of the acquisition;

and similarly where the interest acquired is less than the full beneficial ownership, and such assessments, alterations of assessments or repayments of tax shall be made as may be necessary to give effect to the reduction.

(9) The period referred to in subsection (1)(a) above is a period ending at the earliest of the following times—

(a) the expiration of seven years from the acquisition of the shares or interest in the shares;

(b) the time when the person making the acquisition ceases to have any beneficial interest in the shares;

(c) in relation only to a person who acquires shares, the time when by reason of their ceasing to be subject to such restrictions as are specified in subsection (6) above either of the conditions in subsection (3)(a) above would be satisfied in relation to the shares if they had been acquired at that time;

and for the purposes of subsection (1)(a) and paragraph (b) above a person whose beneficial interest in shares is reduced shall be treated as ceasing to have an interest in such part of the shares as is proportionate to the reduction.

(10) Subsection (11) below applies where—

(a) a person has acquired shares or an interest in shares as mentioned in subsection (1) above (and the shares which he acquires or in which he acquires an interest are in sub-paragraphs (b) and (c) and subsection (11) below referred to as "the original shares"); and

(b) the circumstances of his acquisition of the original shares are such that the application of subsection (1)(a) above is not excluded; and

(c) after 18th March 1986 by virtue of his holding of the original shares or the interest in them he acquires (whether or not for consideration) additional shares or an interest in additional shares (and the shares which he so acquires or in which he so acquires an interest are in subsection (11) below referred to as "the additional shares").

(11) Where this subsection applies—

(a) the additional shares or, as the case may be, the interest in them shall be treated as having been acquired as mentioned in subsection (1) above and in circumstances falling within subsection (10)(b) above and, for the purposes of subsection (9)(a) above, as having been acquired at the same time as the original shares or the interest in them;

(b) for the purposes of subsections (1)(a) and (8) above, the additional shares and the original shares shall be treated as one holding of shares and the market value of the shares comprised in that holding at any time shall be determined accordingly (the market value of the original shares at the time of acquisition being attributed proportionately to all the shares in the holding); and

(c) for the purposes of those subsections, any consideration given for the acquisition of the additional shares or the interest in them shall be taken to be an increase falling within subsection (8)(a) above in the consideration for the original shares or the interest in them.

(12) Subsection (1)(b) above does not apply where the benefit is received by virtue of a person's ownership of or of an interest in shares which were acquired before 6th April 1972.

Provisions supplementary to section 138.

139.—(1) Where—

(a) a director or employee of a body corporate acquires shares in pursuance of an opportunity to acquire shares of that class offered to directors and employees of the body in their capacity as such ("the discount offer"); and

(b) the discount offer is made in conjunction with an offer to the public ("the main offer") under which shares of the same class may be acquired on the same terms, except that a discount in price is offered to directors and employees; and

(c) the director or employee is chargeable to tax under Schedule E on an amount equal to the discount in the price of the shares acquired by him; and

(d) at least 75 per cent. of the aggregate number of shares of the class in question which are acquired in pursuance of the discount offer and the main offer taken together are shares acquired in pursuance of the main offer, he shall be treated for the purposes of section 138(1) as acquiring the shares in pursuance of an offer to the public.

(2) Where a director or employee acquires an interest in shares, subsection (1) above shall apply as if the references in that subsection to the acquisition of shares were references to the acquisition of an interest in shares.

(3) For the purposes of section 138 and this section, where a person acquires any shares or an interest in shares in a body corporate in pursuance of a right conferred on him or opportunity offered to him as a person connected with a director or employee of that or any other body corporate, the shares or interest shall be deemed to be acquired by the director or employee, and section 32A(4) of the 1979 Act shall apply with the necessary modifications; and where that person receives a benefit as mentioned in section 138(1)(b) the benefit shall be deemed to be received by the director or employee.

(4) For the purposes of section 138, a person who disposes of shares or an interest in shares otherwise than by a bargain at arm's length with a person who is not connected with him shall be deemed not to cease to have a beneficial interest in the shares.

(5) Where in any year of assessment a person acquires shares or an interest in shares as mentioned in section 138(1) (disregarding subsections (1) and (2) above), the body from which the shares are or the interest is acquired shall deliver to the inspector within 30 days of the end of that year particulars in writing of the shares and the acquisition.

(6) The Board may by notice require the managers or trustees of any unit trust scheme which is an authorised unit trust approved by the Board for the purposes of section 138 to furnish to the Board within such time as they may direct (but not being less than 30 days) such information as the Board think necessary for the purposes of enabling them to determine—

(a) whether the condition in subsection (7) of that section is being or has at any time been fulfilled; and

(b) the liability to tax of any unit holder whose rights were acquired as mentioned in subsection (1) of that section.

(7) Subject to subsection (9) below, in determining for the purposes of section 138 (including any valuation made for those purposes) whether shares which, or interests in which, have been acquired or are or are to be acquired by any person are subject to any restrictions, there shall be regarded as a restriction attaching to the shares any contract, agreement, arrangement or condition by which his freedom to dispose of the shares or any interest in them or to exercise any right conferred by them is restricted or by which such a disposal or exercise may result in any disadvantages to him or a person connected with him, except where the restriction is imposed as a condition of a loan which is not a related loan as defined by subsection (8) below.

This subsection does not apply where the person acquired the shares before 19th October 1972.

(8) A loan made to any person is a related loan for the purposes of subsection (7) above if—

(a) it is made, arranged, guaranteed or in any way facilitated by—

      (i) the body corporate of which he is a director or employee, or

      (ii) an associated company of that body, or

      (iii) if that body or an associated company of it is a close company, any person having a material interest in the close company; or

    (b) it is made to a person connected with another person and would have been such a loan if it had been made to that other person;

but a loan made by the body corporate, associated company or person mentioned in paragraph (a) above is not a related loan if that body, company or person carries on a business of making personal loans and the loan is made in the ordinary course of that business.

(9) For the purposes of section 138(3)(a), shares acquired by any person shall not, by virtue of subsection (7) above, be regarded as subject to any restriction by reason only of any contract, agreement, arrangement or condition providing for the disposal of the shares, when that person ceases to hold the office or employment by virtue of which he acquired the shares, to a person nominated in accordance with the contract, agreement, arrangement or condition if he is required to dispose of them at a price not exceeding their market value.

(10) Any reference in subsection (7) above to a contract, agreement, arrangement or condition does not include a reference to so much of any contract, agreement, arrangement or condition as contains provisions similar in purpose and effect to any of the provisions of the Model Rules set out in the Model Code for Securities Transactions by Directors of Listed Companies issued by the Stock Exchange in November 1984.

(11) In section 138 and this section—

"associated company" has the meaning given by section 416;

"control" has the meaning given by section 840;

"director" includes a person who is to be a director;

"employee" includes a person who is to be an employee;

"full-time", in relation to an employee, means required to devote substantially the whole of his time to service as an employee;

"shares" includes stock and securities and references to an interest in any shares include references to the proceeds of sale of part of the shares; and

"units", in relation to an authorised unit trust, means an entitlement to a share in the investments subject to that trust.

(12) For the purposes of section 138 and this section, section 168(11) shall apply for determining whether a person has a material interest in a company, but with the omission of the words following "417(3)".

(13) If, on a person ceasing to have a beneficial interest in any shares, he acquires, after 18th March 1986, other shares or an interest in other shares and the circumstances are such that, for the purposes of sections 78

to 81 of the 1979 Act (reorganisations etc.) the shares in which he ceases to have a beneficial interest constitute original shares and the other shares constitute a new holding—

(a) section 78 of that Act (which equates the original shares with the new holding) shall apply for the purposes of this section and section 138;

(b) if any such consideration is given for the new holding as is mentioned in section 79(1) of that Act, it shall be treated for the purposes of this section and section 138 as an increase falling within section 138(8)(a) in the consideration for the shares; and

(c) if any such consideration is received for the disposal of the original shares as is mentioned in section 79(2) of the 1979 Act—

(i) the consideration shall be apportioned among the shares comprised in the new holding, and

(ii) the amount which, apart from this paragraph, would at any subsequent time be the market value of any of those shares shall be taken to be increased by the amount of the consideration apportioned to them;

and in paragraphs (a) to (c) above "the original shares" shall be construed in accordance with sections 78 to 81 of the 1979 Act.

(14) In any case where section 138(1) applies and the acquisition was an acquisition of units in an authorised unit trust—

(a) any reference in section 138(1)(a), (8) or (9) or subsection (4) above or section 32A(4) of the 1979 Act to shares shall be construed as references to units; and

(b) any reference in those provisions to an interest in shares shall be omitted.

140.—(1) For the purposes of section 135, 136, 138 or 139, a right to acquire shares is obtained by a person as a director or employee (within the meaning of the section in question) of a body corporate—

Further interpretation of sections 135 to 139.

(a) if it is granted to him by reason of his office or employment as such a director or employee who is chargeable to tax in respect of that office or employment under Case I of Schedule E; or

(b) if the right is assigned to him and was granted by reason of any such office or employment of his to some other person;

and paragraph (a) above shall apply to a right granted by reason of a person's office or employment after he has ceased to hold it if it would apply to a right so granted in the last chargeable period in which he did hold it.

(2) For those purposes any question whether a person is connected with another shall be determined in accordance with section 839.

(3) For those purposes—

"market value" has the same meaning as, for the purposes of the 1979 Act, it has by virtue of section 150 of that Act; and

"securities" has the meaning given by section 254(1).

Non-cash
vouchers.

Vouchers etc.

141.—(1) Subject to the following provisions of this section and section 157(3), where a non-cash voucher provided for an employee by reason of his employment is received by the employee, then, for the purposes of the Income Tax Acts—

> (a) he shall be treated as having received in the relevant year of assessment an emolument from his employment of an amount equal to the expense incurred by the person providing the voucher in or in connection with the provision of the voucher and the money, goods or services for which it is capable of being exchanged; and

> (b) any money, goods or services obtained by the employee or any other person in exchange for the voucher shall be disregarded;

and the expense incurred as mentioned in paragraph (a) above by the person providing the voucher is referred to below as "the chargeable expense".

(2) In subsection (1)(a) above "the relevant year of assessment" means—

> (a) in relation to a cheque voucher, the year of assessment in which the voucher is handed over in exchange for money, goods or services (a voucher which is posted being treated as handed over at the time of posting); and

> (b) in relation to any other non-cash voucher, the year of assessment in which the chargeable expense is incurred or, if later, the year of assessment in which the voucher is received by the employee.

(3) There shall be deductible under section 198, 201 or 332(3) from the amount taxable under subsection (1) above such amounts, if any, as would have been so deductible if the cost of the goods or services in question had been incurred by the employee out of his emoluments.

(4) The chargeable expense shall be treated as reduced by any part of that expense made good to the person incurring it by the employee.

(5) Where a non-cash voucher provided for an employee by reason of his employment is appropriated to him (whether by attaching it to a card held for him or in any other way), subsections (1) and (2) above shall have effect as if the employee had received the voucher at the time when it was so appropriated.

(6) Subsections (1) and (2) above shall not apply in relation to a transport voucher provided for an employee of a passenger transport undertaking under arrangements in operation on 25th March 1982 and intended to enable that employee or a relation of his to obtain passenger transport services provided by—

> (a) his employer;

> (b) a subsidiary of his employer;

> (c) a body corporate of which his employer is a subsidiary; or

> (d) another passenger transport undertaking.

(7) In this section—

"cheque voucher" means a cheque provided for an employee and intended for use by him wholly or mainly for payment for particular goods or services or for goods or services of one or more particular classes; and, in relation to a cheque voucher, references to a voucher being exchanged for goods or services shall be construed accordingly;

"passenger transport undertaking" means an undertaking whose business consists wholly or mainly in the carriage of passengers and includes a subsidiary of such an undertaking;

"subsidiary" means a wholly owned subsidiary within the meaning of section 736(5)(b) of the Companies Act 1985;

1985 c. 6.

"transport voucher" means any ticket, pass or other document or token intended to enable a person to obtain passenger transport services (whether or not in exchange for it) and, in relation to a transport voucher, references to a voucher being exchanged for services shall be construed as references to it being exchanged for, or otherwise being used to procure, services; and

"non-cash voucher" does not include a cash voucher within the meaning of section 143 but, subject to that, means any voucher, stamp or similar document or token capable of being exchanged (whether singly or together with other such vouchers, stamps, documents or tokens and whether immediately or only after a time) for money, goods or services (or for any combination of two or more of those things) and includes a transport voucher and a cheque voucher.

142.—(1) Subject to the provisions of this section and section 157(3), where a credit-token is provided for an employee by reason of his employment, then, for the purposes of the Income Tax Acts—

Credit-tokens.

(a) on each occasion on which the employee uses the credit-token to obtain money, goods or services he shall be treated as having received an emolument from his employment of an amount equal to the expense incurred by the person providing the credit-token in or in connection with the provision of the money, goods or services obtained; and

(b) any money, goods or services obtained by the employee by use of the credit-token shall be disregarded.

(2) There shall be deductible under section 198, 201 or 332(3) from the amount taxable under subsection (1) above such amounts, if any, as would have been so deductible if the cost of the goods or services in question had been incurred by the employee out of his emoluments.

(3) The expense incurred by the person providing the credit-token as mentioned in subsection (1)(a) above shall be treated as reduced by any part of that expense made good to that person by the employee.

(4) In this section "credit-token" means a card, token, document or other thing given to a person by another person who undertakes—

(a) that on the production of it (whether or not some other action is also required) he will supply money, goods and services (or any of them) on credit; or

(b) that where, on the production of it to a third party (whether or not some other action is also required) the third party supplies money, goods and services (or any of them), he will pay the third party for them (whether or not taking any discount or commission);

but does not include a non-cash voucher or a cash voucher.

(5) For the purposes of subsection (4) above, the use of an object to operate a machine provided by the person giving the object, or by a third party, shall be treated as production of the object to that person or, as the case may be, third party.

Cash vouchers taxable under P.A.Y.E.

143.—(1) Where a cash voucher provided for an employee by reason of his employment is received by the employee, then, subject to subsection (5) below, for the purposes of the Income Tax Acts (and in particular section 203)—

(a) he shall be treated as being paid by his employer, at the time when he receives the voucher, an emolument of his employment equal to the sum of money for which the voucher is capable of being exchanged as mentioned in subsection (3) below; and

(b) any money obtained by the employee or any other person in exchange for the voucher shall be disregarded.

(2) Where a cash voucher provided for an employee by reason of his employment is appropriated to him (whether by attaching it to a card held for him or in any other way), subsections (1) and (5) of this section shall have effect as if the employee had received the voucher at the time when it was so appropriated.

(3) In this section "cash voucher" (subject to subsection (4) below) means any voucher, stamp or similar document capable of being exchanged (whether singly or together with such other vouchers, stamps or documents, and whether immediately or only after a time) for a sum of money greater than, equal to or not substantially less than the expense incurred in providing the voucher by the person who provides it (whether or not it is also capable of being exchanged for goods or services), except that it does not include—

(a) any document intended to enable a person to obtain payment of the sum mentioned in the document, being a sum which if paid to him directly would not have been chargeable to income tax under Schedule E; or

(b) a savings certificate the accumulated interest payable in respect of which is exempt from tax (or would be so exempt if certain conditions were satisfied).

(4) Where—

(a) a voucher, stamp or similar document is capable of being exchanged (as mentioned above) for a sum of money substantially less than the expense incurred in providing the voucher by the person who provides it, and

(b) the difference or part of the difference represents the cost to that person of providing benefits in connection with sickness, personal injury or death,

then, in determining whether the voucher, stamp or document is a cash voucher within the meaning of this section, the expense incurred by him in providing it shall be treated as reduced by that difference or part.

(5) Subsection (1) above shall not apply to a cash voucher received by an employee if, at the time when the voucher is received, the scheme under which it was issued is a scheme approved by the Board for the purposes of this subsection; and the Board shall not approve a scheme for those purposes unless satisfied that it is practicable for income tax in respect of all payments made in exchange for vouchers issued under the scheme to be deducted in accordance with regulations under section 203.

144.—(1) If a person furnishes to the inspector a statement of the cases and circumstances in which non-cash vouchers or credit-tokens are provided for any employees (whether his own or those of anyone else) and the inspector is satisfied that no additional tax is payable under section 141 or 142 by reference to the vouchers or tokens mentioned in the statement, the inspector shall notify the person accordingly and nothing in those sections shall apply to the provision of those vouchers or tokens or their use.

Supplementary provisions.

(2) The inspector may, if in his opinion there is reason to do so, by notice served on the person to whom the notification under subsection (1) above was given, revoke the notification, either as from the date of its making or as from such later date as may be specified in the notice under this subsection; and all such income tax becomes chargeable, and all such returns are to be made by that person and by the employees in question, as would have been chargeable or would have had to be made in the first instance if the notification under subsection (1) above had never been given or, as the case may be, it had ceased to have effect on the specified date.

(3) For the purposes of sections 141 and 142 where a person incurs expense in or in connection with the provision by him of non-cash vouchers or credit-tokens for two or more employees as members of a group or class, the expense incurred in respect of any one of them shall be taken to be such part of that expense as is just and reasonable.

(4) For the purposes of sections 141, 142 and 143 and this section—

(a) a non-cash voucher, cash voucher or credit-token provided for an employee by his employer shall be deemed to be provided for him by reason of his employment; and

(b) any reference to a non-cash voucher, cash voucher or credit-token being provided for or received by an employee includes a reference to it being provided for or received by a relation of his.

(5) In sections 141, 142, 143 and this section—

"cash voucher" has the meaning given by section 143(3);

"credit-token" has the meaning given by section 142(4);

"employee" means the holder of any office or employment the emoluments in respect of which fall to be assessed under Schedule E; and related expressions shall be construed accordingly;

"non-cash voucher" has the meaning given by section 141(7); and

"relation", with respect to an employee, means his spouse, parent or child, the spouse of his child and any dependant of that employee.

Living accommodation

Living accommodation provided for employee.

145.—(1) Subject to the provisions of this section, where living accommodation is provided for a person in any period by reason of his employment, and is not otherwise made the subject of any charge to him by way of income tax, he is to be treated for the purposes of Schedule E as being in receipt of emoluments of an amount equal to the value to him of the accommodation for the period, less so much as is properly attributable to that provision of any sum made good by him to those at whose cost the accommodation is provided.

(2) The value of the accommodation to the employee in any period is the rent which would have been payable for the period if the premises had been let to him at an annual rent equal to their annual value as ascertained under section 837; but for a period in which those at whose cost the accommodation is provided pay rent at an annual rate greater than the annual value as so ascertained, the value of the accommodation to the employee is an amount equal to the rent payable by them for the period.

(3) From any amount to be treated as emoluments under subsection (1) above there are deductible under section 198 or 332(3) such amounts (if any) as would have been so deductible if the accommodation had been paid for by the employee out of his emoluments.

(4) Subject to subsection (5) below, subsection (1) above does not apply to accommodation provided for the employee in any of the following cases—

> (a) where it is necessary for the proper performance of the employee's duties that he should reside in the accommodation;

> (b) where the accommodation is provided for the better performance of the duties of his employment, and his is one of the kinds of employment in the case of which it is customary for employers to provide living accommodation for employees;

> (c) where there is a special threat to his security, special security arrangements are in force and he resides in the accommodation as part of those arrangements;

and in any such case there is no charge to tax under Schedule E (either by virtue of this section or under section 131 or otherwise) in respect of a liability for rates on the premises being discharged for or on behalf of the employee or the employee being reimbursed for the discharge of that liability.

(5) If the accommodation is provided by a company and the employee is a director of the company or of an associated company, then, except in a case where paragraph (c) of subsection (4) above applies, no exemption

is given by virtue of that subsection unless, for each employment of his which is employment as director of the company or an associated company, the following conditions are fulfilled, that is—

(a) he has no material interest in the company, and

(b) either his employment is as a full-time working director or the company is non-profit-making (meaning that neither does it carry on a trade nor do its functions consist wholly or mainly in the holding of investments or other property) or is established for charitable purposes only.

(6) If by reason of a person's employment accommodation is provided for others being members of his family or household, he is to be treated under subsections (1) to (3) above as if it were accommodation provided for him.

(7) For the purposes of this section, living accommodation provided for an employee, or for members of his family or household, by his employer is deemed to be provided by reason of his employment unless—

(a) the employer is an individual, and it can be shown that he makes the provision in the normal course of his domestic, family or personal relationships; or

(b) the accommodation is provided by a local authority for an employee of theirs, and it can be shown that the terms on which it is provided are no more favourable than those on which similar accommodation is provided by the authority for persons who are not their employees but are otherwise similarly circumstanced.

(8) For the purposes of this section—

(a) a company is associated with another if one has control of the other or both are under the control of the same person; and

(b) the expressions "employment", "family or household", "director", "full-time working director", "material interest" and (in relation to a body corporate) "control" shall be construed in accordance with subsections (2), (4) and (8) to (12) of section 168 as if this section were included in Chapter II of this Part.

146.—(1) This section applies where—

Additional charge in respect of certain living accommodation.

(a) living accommodation is provided for a person in any period, by reason of his employment;

(b) by virtue of section 145 he is treated for the purposes of Schedule E as being in receipt of emoluments of an amount calculated by reference to the value to him of that accommodation, or would be so treated if there were disregarded any sum made good by him to those at whose cost the accommodation is provided; and

(c) the cost of providing the accommodation exceeds £75,000.

(2) Where this section applies, the employee shall be treated for the purposes of Schedule E as being in receipt of emoluments (in addition to those which he is treated as receiving by virtue of section 145) of an amount equal to the additional value to him of the accommodation for

PART V
    the period, less so much of any rent paid by the employee, in respect of the accommodation, to the person providing it as exceeds the value to the employee of the accommodation for the period (as determined under section 145).

(3) The additional value of the accommodation to the employee in any period is the rent which would have been payable for that period if the premises had been let to him at an annual rent equal to the appropriate percentage of the amount by which the cost of providing the accommodation exceeds £75,000.

(4) For the purposes of this section, the cost of providing any living accommodation shall be taken to be the aggregate of—

    (a) the amount of any expenditure incurred in acquiring the estate or interest in the property held by a relevant person; and

    (b) the amount of any expenditure incurred by a relevant person before the year of assessment in question on improvements to the property.

(5) The aggregate amount mentioned in subsection (4) above shall be reduced by the amount of any payment made by the employee to a relevant person, so far as that amount represents a reimbursement of any such expenditure as is mentioned in paragraph (a) or (b) of that subsection or represents consideration for the grant to the employee of a tenancy of the property.

(6) Subject to subsection (8) below, where throughout the period of six years ending with the date when the employee first occupied the property, any estate or interest in the property was held by a relevant person (whether or not it was the same estate, interest or person throughout), the additional value shall be calculated as if in subsection (4) above—

    (a) the amount referred to in paragraph (a) were the market value of that property as at that date; and

    (b) the amount referred to in paragraph (b) did not include expenditure on improvements made before that date.

(7) In this section, "relevant person" means any of the following—

    (a) the person providing the accommodation;

    (b) where the person providing the accommodation is not the employee's employer, that employer;

    (c) any person, other than the employee, who is connected with a person falling within paragraph (a) or (b) above.

(8) Subsection (6) above does not apply where the employee first occupied the property before 31st March 1983.

(9) Any amount which is deductible, by virtue of section 145(3), from an amount to be treated as emoluments under that section may, to the extent to which it exceeds the amount of those emoluments, be deductible from the amount to be treated as emoluments under this section.

(10) For the purposes of this section, living accommodation shall be treated as provided for a person by reason of his employment if it is so treated for the purposes of section 145; and "employment" has the same meaning in this section as in that.

(11) In this section—

"the appropriate percentage" means the rate prescribed by the Treasury under section 160(5) as at the beginning of the year of assessment in question;

"property", in relation to any living accommodation, means the property consisting of that accommodation;

"market value", in relation to any property, means the price which that property might reasonably be expected to fetch on a sale in the open market with vacant possession, no reduction being made, in estimating the market value, on account of any option in respect of the property held by the employee, or a person connected with him, or by any of the persons mentioned in subsection (7) above; and

"tenancy" includes a sub-tenancy;

and section 839 shall apply for the purposes of this section.

147. Section 145 shall not apply in relation to the occupation of Chevening House or any other premises held on the trusts of the trust instrument set out in the Schedule to the Chevening Estate Act 1959 by a person nominated in accordance with those trusts.

Occupation of Chevening House.
1959 c. 49.

Payments on retirement, sick pay etc.

148.—(1) Subject to the provisions of this section and section 188, tax shall be charged under Schedule E in respect of any payment to which this section applies which is made to the holder or past holder of any office or employment, or to his executors or administrators, whether made by the person under whom he holds or held the office or employment or by any other person.

Payments on retirement or removal from office or employment.

(2) This section applies to any payment (not otherwise chargeable to tax) which is made, whether in pursuance of any legal obligation or not, either directly or indirectly in consideration or in consequence of, or otherwise in connection with, the termination of the holding of the office or employment or any change in its functions or emoluments, including any payment in commutation of annual or periodical payments (whether chargeable to tax or not) which would otherwise have been so made.

(3) For the purposes of this section and section 188, any payment made to the spouse or any relative or dependant of a person who holds or has held an office or employment, or made on behalf of or to the order of that person, shall be treated as made to that person, and any valuable consideration other than money shall be treated as a payment of money equal to the value of that consideration at the date when it is given.

(4) Any payment which is chargeable to tax by virtue of this section shall be treated as income received on the following date, that is to say—

(a) in the case of a payment in commutation of annual or other periodical payments, the date on which the commutation is effected; and

(b) in the case of any other payment, the date of the termination or change in respect of which the payment is made;

E

PART V

and shall be treated as emoluments of the holder or past holder of the office or employment assessable to tax under Schedule E; and any such payment shall be treated for all the purposes of the Income Tax Acts as earned income.

(5) In the case of the death of any person who, if he had not died, would have been chargeable to tax in respect of any such payment, the tax which would have been so chargeable shall be assessed and charged upon his executors or administrators and shall be a debt due from and payable out of his estate.

(6) This section shall not apply to any payment made in pursuance of an obligation incurred before 6th April 1960.

(7) Where any payment chargeable to tax under this section is made to any person in any year of assessment, it shall be the duty of the person by whom it is made to deliver particulars thereof in writing to the inspector not later than 30 days after the end of that year.

Sick pay.

149.—(1) Where a person holding an employment is absent from work for any period by reason of sickness or disability, any sums which—

(a) are paid to, or to the order or for the benefit of, that person (or a member of his family or household) in respect of any such absence from work; and

(b) are, by reason of his employment, paid as a result of any arrangements entered into by his employer,

shall be chargeable to income tax under Schedule E as emoluments of the employment for that period if, apart from this section, they would not be so chargeable for that or any other period.

(2) Where the funds for making payments under any arrangements are attributable partly to contributions made by the employer and partly to contributions made by the persons employed by him, subsection (1) above shall apply only to such part of the sums paid as a result of the arrangements as it is just and reasonable to regard as attributable to the employer's contributions.

(3) In this section "employment" means an office or employment the emoluments of which fall to be assessed under Schedule E and related expressions shall be construed accordingly; and the reference to a person's family or household is to his spouse, his sons and daughters and their spouses, his parents and his dependants.

Job release scheme allowances, maternity pay and statutory sick pay.

150. The following payments shall be charged to income tax under Schedule E by virtue of this section if they would not otherwise be, that is to say—

1977 c. 8.

(a) allowances paid under a scheme of the kind described in the Job Release Act 1977, being a scheme which provides for the payment of allowances for periods beginning earlier than one year before the date on which the recipient attains pensionable age, as defined in that Act;

(b) maternity pay (whether paid during the subsistence of a contract of employment or not) within the meaning of section 33 of the Employment Protection (Consolidation) Act 1978 or, in Northern Ireland, Article 15 of the Industrial Relations (No.2) (Northern Ireland) Order 1976;

PART V

1978 c. 44.
S.I. 1976/2147
(N.I. 28).

(c) payments of statutory sick pay within the meaning of section 1 of the Social Security and Housing Benefits Act 1982 or, in Northern Ireland, Article 3 of the Social Security (Northern Ireland) Order 1982; and

1982 c. 24.
S.I. 1982/1084
(N.I. 16).

(d) payments of statutory maternity pay under Part V of the Social Security Act 1986 or, in Northern Ireland, under Part VI of the Social Security (Northern Ireland) Order 1986.

1986 c. 50.
S.I. 1986/1888
(N.I. 18).

151.—(1) Subject to the following provisions of this section, payments to any person of income support under the Social Security Act 1986 in respect of any period shall be charged to income tax under Schedule E if during that period—

Income support etc.

(a) his right to income support is subject to the condition specified in section 20(3)(d)(i) of that Act (availability for employment); or

(b) he is one of a married or unmarried couple and section 23 of that Act (trade disputes) applies to him but not to the other person;

(2) In this section "married couple" and "unmarried couple" have the same meaning as in Part II of the Social Security Act 1986.

(3) Where the amount of income support paid to any person in respect of any week or part of a week exceeds the taxable maximum for that period as defined below, the excess shall not be taxable.

(4) Where payments of unemployment benefit and payments of income support are made to any person in respect of the same week or part of a week, the amount taxable in respect of that period in respect of those payments shall not exceed the taxable maximum for that period within the meaning of subsection (3) above.

(5) For the purposes of subsections (3) and (4) above, the taxable maximum in respect of a week shall be determined in accordance with subsections (6) to (8) below and the taxable maximum in respect of part of a week shall be equal to one-sixth of the taxable maximum in respect of a week multiplied by the number of days in the part.

(6) Where the income support is paid to one of a married or unmarried couple in a case not falling within subsection (1)(b) above, the taxable maximum in respect of a week shall be equal to the aggregate of—

(a) the weekly rate specified for the week in question in relation to unemployment benefit in paragraph 1 of Part I of Schedule 4 to the Social Security Act 1975; and

1975 c. 14.

(b) the increase for an adult dependant specified for that week in paragraph 1(a) of Part IV of that Schedule.

(7) Where the income support is paid to one of a married or unmarried couple in a case falling within subsection (1)(b) above, the taxable maximum in respect of a week shall—

(a) if the applicable amount (within the meaning of Part II of the Social Security Act 1986) consists only of an amount in respect of them, be equal to one half of that amount; and

(b) if the applicable amount includes other amounts, be equal to one half of the portion of it which is included in respect of them.

(8) Where the income support is paid to a person who is not one of a married or unmarried couple, the taxable maximum in respect of a week shall be equal to the weekly rate referred to in subsection (6)(a) above.

(9) In its application to Northern Ireland this section shall have effect as if—

(a) for the references to the Social Security Act 1986, to Part II of that Act and to sections 20(3)(d)(i) and 23 of that Act there were substituted respectively references to the Social Security (Northern Ireland) Order 1986, Part III of that Order and Articles 21(3)(d)(i) and 24 of that Order; and

(b) for the references to paragraph 1 of Part 1 of Schedule 4 to the Social Security Act 1975 and paragraph 1(a) of Part IV of that Schedule there were substituted respectively references to paragraph 1 of Part I of Schedule 4 to the Social Security (Northern Ireland) Act 1975 and paragraph 1(a) of Part IV of that Schedule.

152.—(1) A benefit officer may by notice notify a person who is taxable in respect of any unemployment benefit or income support of the amount on which he is taxable and any such notification shall state the date on which it is issued and shall inform the person to whom it is given that he may object to the notification by notice given within 60 days after the date of issue of the notification.

(2) Where—

(a) no objection is made to a notification of an amount under subsection (1) above within the period specified in that subsection (or such further period as may be allowed by virtue of subsection (5) below); or

(b) an objection is made but is withdrawn by the objector by notice,

that amount shall not be questioned in any appeal against any assessment in respect of income including that amount.

(3) Where—

(a) an objection is made to a notification of an amount under subsection (1) above within the period specified in that subsection (or such further period as may be allowed by virtue of subsection (5) below), and

(b) the benefit officer and the objector come to an agreement that the amount notified should be varied in a particular manner, and

(c) the officer confirms the agreement to vary in writing,

then, subject to subsection (4) below, that amount as so varied shall not be questioned in any appeal against any assessment in respect of income including that amount.

(4) Subsection (3) above shall not apply if, within 60 days from the date when the agreement was come to, the objector gives notice to the benefit officer that he wishes to repudiate or resile from the agreement.

(5) An objection to a notification may be made later than 60 days after the date of the issue of the notification if, on an application for the purpose—

(a) a benefit officer is satisfied that there was a reasonable excuse for not objecting within that time, and

(b) the objection was made thereafter without unreasonable delay, and

(c) the officer gives consent in writing;

and if the officer is not so satisfied he shall refer the application for determination—

(i) by the General Commissioners for the division in which the objector ordinarily resides or,

(ii) in a case where an appeal has been made against an assessment in respect of income including the amount in question, the General Commissioners or the Special Commissioners having jurisdiction in that appeal.

(6) Where a benefit officer has notified an amount to a person under subsection (1) above, he may by another notice notify the person of an alteration in the amount previously notified and, if he does so, the original notification shall be cancelled and this section shall apply to such a subsequent notification as it applies to the original notification.

(7) In this section "benefit officer" means the appropriate officer, in Great Britain, of the Department of Employment or of the Department of Health and Social Security, as the case may be, or, in Northern Ireland, of the Department of Health and Social Services.

CHAPTER II

SUPPLEMENTARY CHARGING PROVISIONS APPLICABLE TO DIRECTORS AND HIGHER-PAID EMPLOYEES AND OFFICE HOLDERS

Expenses

153.—(1) Subject to the provisions of this Chapter, where in any year a person is employed in director's or higher-paid employment and by reason of his employment there are paid to him in respect of expenses any sums which, apart from this section, are not chargeable to tax as his income, those sums are to be treated as emoluments of the employment and accordingly chargeable to income tax under Schedule E.

Payments in respect of expenses.

(2) Subsection (1) above is without prejudice to any claim for deductions under section 198, 201 or 332(3).

(3) The reference in subsection (1) above to sums paid in respect of expenses includes any sums put at the employee's disposal by reason of his employment and paid away by him.

Benefits in kind

General charging provision.

154.—(1) Subject to section 163, where in any year a person is employed in director's or higher-paid employment and—

(a) by reason of his employment there is provided for him, or for others being members of his family or household, any benefit to which this section applies; and

(b) the cost of providing the benefit is not (apart from this section) chargeable to tax as his income,

there is to be treated as emoluments of the employment, and accordingly chargeable to income tax under Schedule E, an amount equal to whatever is the cash equivalent of the benefit.

(2) The benefits to which this section applies are accommodation (other than living accommodation), entertainment, domestic or other services, and other benefits and facilities of whatsoever nature (whether or not similar to any of those mentioned above in this subsection), excluding however—

(a) any benefit consisting of the right to receive, or the prospect of receiving, any sums which would be chargeable to tax under section 149; and

(b) any benefit chargeable under section 157, 158, 160 or 162;

and subject to the exceptions provided for by section 155.

(3) For the purposes of this section and sections 155 and 156, the persons providing a benefit are those at whose cost the provision is made.

Exceptions from the general charge.

155.—(1) Where the benefit of a car is taxable under section 157, section 154 does not apply to any benefit in connection with the car other than a benefit in connection with the provision of a driver for the car.

(2) Section 154 does not apply where the benefit consists in provision for the employee, in premises occupied by the employer or others providing it, of accomodation, supplies or services used by the employee solely in performing the duties of his employment.

(3) Where living accommodation is provided by reason of a person's employment—

(a) alterations and additions to the premises concerned which are of a structural nature, and

1985 c. 70.

(b) repairs to the premises of a kind which, if the premises were let under a lease to which section 11 of the Landlord and Tenant Act 1985 (repairing obligations) applies, would be the obligation of the lessor under the covenants implied by subsection (1) of that section,

are not benefits to which section 154 applies.

(4) Section 154 does not apply to a benefit consisting in the provision by the employee's employer for the employee himself, or for the spouse, children or dependants of the employee, of any pension, annuity, lump sum, gratuity or other like benefit to be given on the employee's death or retirement.

(5) Section 154 does not apply to a benefit consisting in the provision by the employee's employer of meals in any canteen in which meals are provided for the staff generally.

(6) Section 154 does not apply where the benefit consists—

(a) in providing the employee with medical treatment outside the United Kingdom (including providing for him to be an in-patient) in a case where the need for the treatment arises while the employee is outside the United Kingdom for the purpose of performing the duties of his employment; or

(b) in providing insurance for the employee against the cost of such treatment in such a case;

and for the purpose of this subsection, medical treatment includes all forms of treatment for, and all procedures for diagnosing, any physical or mental ailment, infirmity or defect.

156.—(1) The cash equivalent of any benefit chargeable to tax under section 154 is an amount equal to the cost of the benefit, less so much (if any) of it as is made good by the employee to those providing the benefit.

Cash equivalents of benefits charged under section 154.

(2) Subject to the following subsections, the cost of a benefit is the amount of any expense incurred in or in connection with its provision, and (here and in those subsections) includes a proper proportion of any expense relating partly to the benefit and partly to other matters.

(3) Where the benefit consists in the transfer of an asset by any person, and since that person acquired or produced the asset it has been used or has depreciated, the cost of the benefit is deemed to be the market value of the asset at the time of transfer.

(4) Where the asset referred to in subsection (3) above is not a car and before the transfer a person (whether or not the transferee) has been chargeable to tax in respect of the asset in accordance with subsection (5) below, the amount which under subsection (3) above is deemed to be the cost of the benefit shall (if apart from this subsection it would be less) be deemed to be—

(a) the market value of the asset at the time when it was first applied (by those providing the benefit in question) for the provision of any benefit for a person, or for members of his family or household, by reason of his employment, less

(b) the aggregate of the amounts taken into account as the cost of the benefit in charging tax in accordance with subsection (5) below in the year or years up to and including that in which the transfer takes place.

(5) Where the benefit consists in an asset being placed at the employee's disposal, or at the disposal of others being members of his family or household, for his or their use (without any transfer of the property in the asset), or of its being used wholly or partly for his or their purposes, then the cost of the benefit in any year is deemed to be—

(a) the annual value of the use of the asset ascertained under subsection (6) below; plus

(b) the total of any expense incurred in or in connection with the provision of the benefit excluding—

(i) the expense of acquiring or producing it incurred by the person to whom the asset belongs; and

(ii) any rent or hire charge payable for the asset by those providing the benefit.

(6) Subject to subsection (7) below, the annual value of the use of the asset, for the purposes of subsection (5) above—

(a) in the case of land, is its annual value determined in accordance with section 837; and

(b) in any other case is 20 per cent. of its market value at the time when it was first applied (by those providing the benefit in question) in the provision of any benefit for a person, or for members of his family or household, by reason of his employment.

(7) Where there is payable, by those providing the benefit, any sum by way of rent or hire-charge for the asset, the annual amount of which is equal to, or greater than, the annual value of the use of the asset as ascertained under subsection (6) above, that amount shall be substituted for the annual value in subsection (5)(a) above.

(8) From the cash equivalent there are deductible in each case under section 198, 201 or 332(3) such amounts (if any) as would have been so deductible if the cost of the benefit had been incurred by the employee out of his emoluments.

(9) In the case of assets first applied before 6th April 1980 by those providing the benefit in question in the provision of any benefit for a person, or for members of his family or household, by reason of his employment—

(a) subsection (4) above shall not have effect; and

(b) in subsection (6)(b) above for the words "20 per cent." there shall be substituted the words "10 per cent.".

Cars available for private use.

157.—(1) Where in any year in the case of a person employed in director's or higher-paid employment, a car is made available (without any transfer of the property in it) either to himself or to others being members of his family or household, and—

(a) it is so made available by reason of his employment and it is in that year available for his or their private use; and

(b) the benefit of the car is not (apart from this section) chargeable to tax as the employee's income,

there is to be treated as emoluments of the employment, and accordingly chargeable to income tax under Schedule E, an amount equal to whatever is the cash equivalent of that benefit in that year.

(2) Subject to the provisions of this section, the cash equivalent of that benefit is to be ascertained—

(a) from Tables A and B in Part I of Schedule 6, in the case of cars with an original market value of up to £19,250; and

(b) from Table C in that Part in the case of cars with an original market value of more than that amount;

the equivalent in each case being shown in the second or third column of
the applicable Table by reference to the age of the car at the end of the
relevant year of assessment.

(3) Where in any year the benefit of a car is chargeable to tax under this
section as the employee's income he shall not be taxable—

(a) under Schedule E in respect of the discharge of any liability of his
in connection with the car;

(b) under section 141 or 142 in respect of any non-cash voucher or
credit-token to the extent that it is used by him—

(i) for obtaining money which is spent on goods or services
in connection with the car; or

(ii) for obtaining such goods or services;

(c) under section 153 in respect of any payment made to him in
respect of expenses incurred by him in connection with the car.

(4) The Treasury may by order taking effect from the beginning of any
year beginning after it is made—

(a) increase or further increase the money sum specified in
subsection (2)(a) above;

(b) with or without such an increase, substitute for any of the three
Tables a different Table of cash equivalents;

(c) increase or further increase the money sum specified in
paragraph 1(1) of Part II of Schedule 6.

(5) Part II of Schedule 6 has effect—

(a) with respect to the application of the Tables in Part I; and

(b) for the reduction of the cash equivalent under this section in
cases where the car has not been available for the whole of the
relevant year, or the use of it has been preponderantly business
use, or the employee makes any payment for the use of it.

158.—(1) Where in any year in the case of a person employed in
director's or higher-paid employment fuel is provided by reason of his
employment for a car which is made available as mentioned in section
157, an amount equal to whatever is the cash equivalent of that benefit in
that year shall be treated as emoluments of the employment and,
accordingly, shall be chargeable to income tax under Schedule E.

Car fuel.

(2) Subject to the provisions of this section, the cash equivalent of that
benefit shall be ascertained from Table A below where the car has an
internal combustion engine with one or more reciprocating pistons and
from Table B below in the case of other cars; and for the purposes of Table
A below a car's cylinder capacity is the capacity of its engine calculated as
for the purposes of the Vehicles (Excise) Act 1971 or the Vehicles (Excise)
Act (Northern Ireland) 1972.

1971 c. 10.
1972 c. 10 (N.I.).

TABLE A

Cylinder capacity of car in cubic centimetres	Cash equivalent
1,400 or less	£480
More than 1,400 but not more than 2,000	£600
More than 2,000	£900

TABLE B

Original market value of car	Cash equivalent
Less than £6,000	£480
£6,000 or more but less than £8,500	£600
£8,500 or more	£900

(3) Without prejudice to the generality of subsection (1) above, fuel is provided for a car if—

(a) any liability in respect of the provision of fuel for the car is discharged;

(b) a non-cash voucher or a credit-token is used to obtain fuel for the car or money which is spent on such fuel;

(c) any sum is paid in respect of expenses incurred in providing fuel for the car.

In this subsection "non-cash voucher" and "credit-token" have the meanings given by section 141(7) and 142(4) respectively.

(4) The Treasury may by order taking effect from the beginning of any year beginning after it is made substitute a different Table for either of the Tables in subsection (2) above.

(5) Where paragraph 2 or 3 of Part II of Schedule 6 applies to reduce the cash equivalent of the benefit of the car for which the fuel is provided, the same reduction shall be made to the cash equivalent of the benefit of the fuel ascertained under subsection (2) above.

(6) If in the relevant year—

(a) the employee is required to make good to the person providing the fuel the whole of the expense incurred by him in or in connection with the provision of fuel for his private use and he does so; or

(b) the fuel is made available only for business travel;

the cash equivalent is nil.

Pooled cars.

159.—(1) This section applies to any car in the case of which the inspector is satisfied (whether on a claim under this section or otherwise) that it has for any year been included in a car pool for the use of the employees of one or more employers.

(2) A car is to be treated as having been so included for a year if—

(a) in that year it was made available to, and actually used by, more than one of those employees and, in the case of each of them, it was made available to him by reason of his employment but it was not in that year ordinarily used by one of them to the exclusion of the others; and

(b) in the case of each of them any private use of the car made by him in that year was merely incidental to his other use of it in the year; and

(c) it was in that year not normally kept overnight on or in the vicinity of any residential premises where any of the employees was residing, except while being kept overnight on premises occupied by the person making the car available to them.

(3) Where this section applies to a car, then for the year in question the car is to be treated under sections 154 and 157 as not having been available for the private use of any of the employees.

(4) A claim under this section in respect of a car for any year may be made by any one of the employees mentioned in subsection (2)(a) above (referred to below as "the employees concerned") or by the employer on behalf of all of them.

(5) On an appeal against the decision of the inspector on a claim under this section all the employees concerned may take part in the proceedings, and the determination of the body of Commissioners or county court appealed to shall be binding on all those employees, whether or not they have taken part in the proceedings.

(6) Where an appeal against the decision of the inspector on a claim under this section has been determined, no appeal against the inspector's decision on any other such claim in respect of the same car and the same year shall be entertained.

160.—(1) Where in the case of a person employed in director's or higher-paid employment there is outstanding for the whole or part of a year a loan (whether to the employee himself or a relative of his) of which the benefit is obtained by reason of his employment and— Beneficial loan arrangements.

(a) no interest is paid on the loan for that year; or

(b) the amount of interest paid on it for the year is less than interest at the official rate,

there is to be treated as emoluments of the employment, and accordingly chargeable to income tax under Schedule E, an amount equal to whatever is the cash equivalent of the benefit of the loan for that year.

(2) Where in the case of a person employed in director's or higher-paid employment—

(a) there is in any year released or written off the whole or part of a loan (whether to the employee himself or a relative of his, and whether or not such a loan as is mentioned in subsection (1) above), and

(b) the benefit of that loan was obtained by reason of his employment,

PART V   then there is to be treated as emoluments of the employment, and accordingly chargeable to income tax under Schedule E, an amount equal to that which is released or written off.

(3) Where there was outstanding at any time when a person was in director's or higher-paid employment the whole or part of a loan to him (or to a relative of his) the benefit of which was obtained by reason of his employment, and that director's or higher-paid employment has terminated, whether on the employee ceasing to be employed or ceasing to be employed in director's or higher-paid employment, subsection (2) above applies as if it had not terminated.

(4) Part I of Schedule 7 has effect as to what is meant by the benefit of a loan obtained by reason of a person's employment; the cash equivalent of the benefit is to be ascertained in accordance with Part II of that Schedule; and Part III of that Schedule has effect for excluding from the operation of subsection (1) above loans on which interest is eligible for relief under subsection (1) of section 353 or which would be so eligible apart from subsection (2) of that section.

(5) In this section, sections 161 and 162 and Schedule 7—

(a) "loan" includes any form of credit;

(b) references to a loan include references to any other loan applied directly or indirectly towards the replacement of the first-mentioned loan;

(c) references to making a loan include arranging, guaranteeing or in any way facilitating a loan (related expressions being construed accordingly); and

(d) references to the official rate of interest are to the rate prescribed from time to time by the Treasury by order.

(6) For the purposes of this section and section 161, a person is a relative of another person if he or she is—

(a) the spouse of that other; or

(b) a parent or remoter forebear, child or remoter issue, or brother or sister of that other or of the spouse of that other; or

(c) the spouse of a person falling within paragraph (b) above.

(7) Subject to section 161, this section applies to loans whether made before or after this Act is passed.

Exceptions from section 160.   **161.**—(1) There is no charge to tax under section 160(1) if the cash equivalent does not exceed £200 or (for a year in which there are two or more loans outstanding) the total of all the cash equivalents does not exceed that amount.

(2) Where the amount of interest paid on a loan for the year in which it is made is not less than interest at the official rate applying for that year for the purposes of section 160 and the loan is made—

(a) for a fixed and unvariable period; and

(b) at a fixed and unvariable rate of interest,

subsection (1) of that section shall not apply to the loan in any subsequent year by reason only of an increase in the official rate since the year in which the loan was made.

(3) Where a loan was made at any time before 6th April 1978—

(a) for a fixed and unvariable period; and

(b) at a fixed and unvariable rate of interest,

section 160(1) shall not apply to the loan if it is shown that the rate of interest is not less than such rate as could have been expected to apply to a loan on the same terms (other than as to the rate of interest) made at that time between persons not connected with each other (within the meaning of section 839) dealing at arm's length.

(4) If the employee shows that he derived no benefit from a loan made to a relative of his, section 160(1) and (2) above shall not apply to that loan.

(5) Section 160(2) does not apply where the amount released or written off is chargeable to income tax as income of the employee apart from that section, except—

(a) where it is chargeable only by virtue of section 148; or

(b) to the extent that the amount exceeds the sums previously falling to be treated as the employee's income under section 677.

(6) On the employee's death—

(a) a loan within subsection (1) of section 160 ceases to be outstanding for the purposes of the operation of that subsection; and

(b) no charge arises under subsection (2) of that section by reference to any release or writing-off which takes effect on or after the death.

(7) Section 160(2) does not apply to benefits received in pursuance of arrangements made at any time with a view to protecting the holder of shares acquired before 6th April 1976 from a fall in their market value.

162.—(1) Where—

Employee shareholdings.

(a) a person employed or about to be employed in director's or higher-paid employment ("the employee"), or a person connected with him, acquires shares in a company (whether the employing company or not); and

(b) the shares are acquired at an under-value in pursuance of a right or opportunity available by reason of his employment,

section 160(1) and Schedule 7 apply as if the employee had the benefit of an interest-free loan obtained by reason of his employment ("the notional loan").

(2) The provisions of this section have effect subject to sections 185 and 186; and in this section—

(a) references to shares being acquired at an under-value are references to shares being acquired either without payment for them at the time or being acquired for an amount then paid which is less than the market value of fully paid up shares of that class (in either case with or without obligation to make payment or further payment at some later time); and

(b) any reference, in relation to any shares, to the under-value on acquisition is a reference to the market value of fully paid up shares of that class less any payment then made for the shares.

(3) The amount initially outstanding of the notional loan is so much of the under-value on acquisition as is not chargeable to tax as an emolument of the employee; and—

(a) the loan remains outstanding until terminated under subsection (4) below; and

(b) payments or further payments made for the shares after the initial acquisition go to reduce the amount outstanding of the notional loan.

(4) The notional loan terminates on the occurrence of any of the following events—

(a) the whole amount of it outstanding is made good by means of payments or further payments made for the shares; or

(b) the case being one in which the shares were not at the time of acquisition fully paid up, any outstanding or contingent obligation to pay for them is released, transferred or adjusted so as no longer to bind the employee or any person connected with him; or

(c) the shares are so disposed of by surrender or otherwise that neither he nor any such person any longer has a beneficial interest in the shares; or

(d) the employee dies.

(5) If the notional loan terminates as mentioned in subsection (4)(b) or (c) above, there is then for the year in which the event in question occurs the same charge to income tax on the employee, under section 160(2), as if an amount equal to the then outstanding amount of the notional loan had been released or written off from a loan within that section.

(6) Where after 6th April 1976 shares are acquired, whether or not at an under-value but otherwise as mentioned in subsection (1) above, and—

(a) the shares are subsequently disposed of by surrender or otherwise so that neither the employee nor any person connected with him any longer has a beneficial interest in them; and

(b) the disposal is for a consideration which exceeds the then market value of the shares,

then for the year in which the disposal is effected the amount of the excess is treated as emoluments of the employee's employment and accordingly chargeable to income tax under Schedule E.

(7) If at the time of the event giving rise to a charge in relation to any shares by virtue of subsection (5) or (6) above the employee has ceased to be in the director's or higher-paid employment by virtue of which he is the employee for the purposes of this section in relation to those shares, those subsections shall apply as if he had not so ceased.

(8) No charge arises under subsection (6) above by reference to any disposal effected after the death of the employee, whether by his personal representatives or otherwise.

(9) This section applies in relation to acquisition and disposal of an interest in shares less than full beneficial ownership (including an interest in the proceeds of sale of part of the shares but not including a share option) as it applies in relation to the acquisition and disposal of shares, subject to the following modifications—

(a) for references to the shares acquired there shall be substituted references to the interest in shares acquired;

(b) for the reference to the market value of the shares acquired there shall be substituted a reference to the proportion corresponding to the size of the interest of the market value of the shares in which the interest subsists;

(c) for the reference to shares of the same class as those acquired there shall be substituted a reference to shares of the same class as those in which the interest subsists; and

(d) for the reference to the market value of fully paid up shares of that class there shall be substituted a reference to the proportion of that value corresponding to the size of the interest.

(10) In this section—

(a) "shares" includes stock and also includes securities as defined in section 254(1);

(b) "acquisition" in relation to shares includes receipt by way of allotment or assignment or otherwise howsoever;

(c) any reference to payment for shares includes giving any consideration in money or money's worth or making any subscription, whether in pursuance of a legal liability or not;

(d) "market value" has the same meaning as, for the purposes of the 1979 Act, it has by virtue of section 150 of that Act;

and section 839 applies for the purposes of this section.

(11) This section, in respect of any shares or any interest in shares, operates only to include an amount in emoluments so far as any amount corresponding to it, and representing the same benefit, does not otherwise fall to be so included under the Tax Acts.

163.—(1) This section applies where, in the case of a person employed in director's or higher-paid employment, living accommodation is provided by reason of the employment and, accordingly, a charge to tax would arise in his case under section 145 but for the case being one of those specified in subsection (4) of that section.

(2) Where, by reason of expenditure incurred in one or more of the following, that is to say,—

(a) heating, lighting or cleaning the premises concerned;

(b) repairs to the premises, their maintenance or decoration;

(c) the provision in the premises of furniture or other appurtenances or effects which are normal for domestic occupation;

or by reason of such expenditure being reimbursed to the employee, an amount falls to be included in the emoluments of his employment, that amount shall not exceed the limit specified in subsection (3) below.

(3) That limit is—

(a) 10 per cent. of the net amount of the emoluments of the employment or, if the accommodation is provided for a period of less than a year, so much of that percentage of the net amount as is attributable to the period; less

(b) where the expenditure is incurred by a person other than the employee, so much as is properly attributable to the expenditure of any sum made good by the employee to that other.

(4) The net amount of the emoluments of a person's employment for the purposes of subsection (3) above is the amount of those emoluments (leaving out of account the expenditure in question) after—

(a) any capital allowance; and

(b) any deductions allowable under section 198, 199, 201, 332(3), 592(7), 594 or 619(1)(a);

and, for the purposes of this subsection, in the case of employment by a company there shall be taken into account, as emoluments of the employment, the emoluments of any employment by an associated company.

(5) For the purposes of subsection (4) above, a company is an associated company of another if one of them has control of the other or both are under the control of the same person.

Director's tax paid by employer.

164.—(1) Subject to the provisions of this Chapter, where in any year a person ("the recipient") is employed as a director of a company and—

(a) a payment of, or on account of, income assessable to income tax under Schedule E as emoluments of that employment is made to him in circumstances in which the person making the payment is required, by regulations made under section 203, to deduct an amount of income tax on making the payment; and

(b) the whole of that amount is not so deducted but is, or any part of it is, accounted for to the Board by someone other than the recipient;

the amount so accounted for to the Board, less so much (if any) as is made good by the recipient to that other person or so deducted, shall be treated as emoluments of the employment and accordingly chargeable to income tax under Schedule E.

(2) A person shall not be treated, for the purposes of subsection (1) above, as employed as a director of a company if he has no material interest in the company and either paragraph (a) or paragraph (b) of section 167(5) is satisfied.

(3) Where an amount treated as emoluments of a person's employment, by subsection (1) above, is accounted for to the Board at a time when the employment has come to an end, those emoluments shall be treated, for the purposes of the Income Tax Acts, as having arisen in the year in which the employment ended; but that subsection shall not apply in relation to any amount accounted for to the Board after the death of the director in question.

165.—(1) Nothing in section 331 shall be construed as conferring on any person other than the person holding the scholarship in question any exemption from the charge to tax under section 154.

Scholarships.

(2) For the purposes of this Chapter, any scholarship provided for a member of a person's family or household shall, without prejudice to any other provision of this Chapter, be taken to have been provided by reason of that person's employment if it is provided under arrangements entered into by, or by any person connected with, his employer (whether or not those arrangements require the employer or connected person to contribute directly or indirectly to the cost of providing the scholarship).

(3) Section 154 does not apply to a benefit consisting in a payment in respect of a scholarship—

(a) provided from a trust fund or under a scheme; and

(b) held by a person receiving full-time instruction at a university, college, school or other educational establishment; and

(c) which would not be regarded, for the purposes of this Chapter, as provided by reason of a person's employment were subsection (2) above and section 168(3) to be disregarded;

if, in the year in which the payment is made, not more than 25 per cent. of the total amount of the payments made from that fund, or under that scheme, in respect of scholarships held as mentioned in paragraph (b) above is attributable to relevant scholarships.

(4) This section does not have effect in relation to any payment if—

(a) it is made in respect of a scholarship awarded before 15th March 1983, and

(b) the first payment in respect of the scholarship was made before 6th April 1984; and

(c) in relation to payments made after 5th April 1989, the person holding the scholarship is receiving full-time instruction at the university, college, school or other educational establishment at which he was receiving such instruction on—

(i) 15th March 1983, in a case where the first payment in respect of the scholarship was made before that date; or

(ii) the date on which the first such payment was made, in any other case.

(5) For the purposes of subsection (4)(c) above, a payment made before 6th April 1989 in respect of any period beginning on or after that date shall be treated as made at the beginning of that period.

(6) In this section—

(a) "scholarship" includes an exhibition, bursary or other similar educational endowment;

(b) "relevant scholarship" means a scholarship which is provided by reason of a person's employment (whether or not that employment is director's or higher-paid employment); and for the purposes of this definition "employment" includes an office or employment whose emoluments do not fall to be assessed under Schedule E but would fall to be so assessed if the employee were resident, and ordinarily resident, and all the duties of the employment were performed wholly, in the United Kingdom;

and section 839 applies for the purposes of this section.

General supplementary provisions

Notice of nil liability under this Chapter.

166.—(1) If a person furnishes to the inspector a statement of the cases and circumstances in which payments of a particular character are made, or benefits or facilities of a particular kind are provided, for any employees (whether his own or those of anyone else), and the inspector is satisfied that no additional tax is payable under this Chapter by reference to the payments, benefits or facilities mentioned in the statement, the inspector shall notify the person accordingly; and then nothing in this Chapter applies to those payments, or to the provision of those benefits or facilities, or otherwise for imposing any additional charge to income tax.

(2) The inspector may, if in his opinion there is reason to do so, by notice served on the person to whom notification under subsection (1) above was given, revoke the notification, either as from the date of its making or from such later date as may be specified in the notice under this subsection; and then all such income tax becomes chargeable, and all such returns are to be made by that person and by the employees in question as would have been chargeable or would have had to be made in the first instance if the notification under subsection (1) had never been given or, as the case may be, it had ceased to have effect on the specified date.

(3) In relation to a notification given before 6th April 1988, the reference in subsection (2) above to income tax includes a reference to income tax chargeable under the corresponding enactments in force before that date, and accordingly, where the notification is revoked for any period before that date, that subsection has effect in relation to years of assessment before the year 1988-89.

1976 c. 40.

(4) The validity of any notification given under section 199 of the 1970 Act which was continued in force by paragraph 14 of Schedule 9 to the Finance Act 1976 shall not be affected by the repeal of that paragraph by this Act but shall continue in force as if made under subsection (1) above in relation to tax liability under sections 153 to 156; and subsection (2) above shall apply accordingly.

167.—(1) In this Chapter "director's or higher-paid employment" means—

(a) subject to subsection (5) below, employment as a director of a company; or

(b) employment with emoluments at the rate of £8,500 a year or more.

(2) For this purpose emoluments are to be calculated—

(a) on the basis that they include all such amounts as come or would but for section 157(3) come into charge under this Chapter or section 141, 142, 143 or, in the case of those in director's or higher-paid employment, 145; and

(b) without any deduction under section 198, 201 or 332(3).

(3) Where a person is employed in two or more employments by the same employer and either—

(a) the total of the emoluments of those employments (applying this section) is at the rate of £8,500 a year or more; or

(b) one or more of those employments is (apart from this subsection) director's or higher-paid,

all the employments are to be treated as director's or higher-paid.

(4) All employees of a partnership or body over which an individual or another partnership or body has control are to be treated for the purposes of this section (but not for any other purpose) as if the employment were an employment by the individual or by that other partnership or body as the case may be.

(5) A person's employment is not director's or higher-paid by reason only of its being employment as a director of a company (without prejudice to its being so under subsection (1)(b) or (3) above) if he has no material interest in the company and either—

(a) his employment is as a full-time working director; or

(b) the company is non-profit-making (meaning that neither does it carry on a trade nor do its functions consist wholly or mainly in the holding of investments or other property) or is established for charitable purposes only.

168.—(1) The following provisions of this section apply for the interpretation of expressions used in this Chapter.

(2) Subject to section 165(6)(b), "employment" means an office or employment the emoluments of which fall to be assessed under Schedule E; and related expressions shall be construed accordingly.

(3) For the purposes of this Chapter—

(a) all sums paid to an employee by his employer in respect of expenses, and

(b) all such provision as is mentioned in this Chapter which is made for an employee, or for members of his family or household, by his employer,

PART V

Meaning of "director's or higher-paid employment".

Other interpretative provisions.

PART V are deemed to be paid to or made for him or them by reason of his employment, except any such payment or provision made by the employer, being an individual, as can be shown to have been made in the normal course of his domestic, family or personal relationships.

(4) References to members of a person's family or household are to his spouse, his sons and daughters and their spouses, his parents and his servants, dependants and guests.

(5) As respects cars, the following definitions apply—

(a) "car" means any mechanically propelled road vehicle except—

(i) a vehicle of a construction primarily suited for the conveyance of goods or burden of any description,

(ii) a vehicle of a type not commonly used as a private vehicle and unsuitable to be so used,

1972 c. 20.

(iii) a motor cycle as defined in section 190(4) of the Road Traffic Act 1972, and

(iv) an invalid carriage as defined in section 190(5) of that Act;

(b) the age of a car at any time is the interval between the date of its first registration and that time;

(c) "business travel" means travelling which a person is necessarily obliged to do in the performance of the duties of his employment;

(d) the date of a car's first registration is the date on which it was first registered—

1971 c. 10.

(i) in Great Britain, under the Vehicles (Excise) Act 1971 or corresponding earlier legislation; or

(ii) elsewhere, under the corresponding legislation of any country or territory;

(e) the original market value of a car is the inclusive price which it might reasonably have been expected to fetch if sold in the United Kingdom singly in a retail sale in the open market immediately before the date of its first registration ("inclusive price" meaning the price inclusive of customs or excise duty, of any tax chargeable as if it were a duty of customs, and of value added tax and car tax); and

(f) "private use", in relation to a car made available to any person, or to others being members of his family or household, means any use otherwise than for his business travel.

(6) For the purposes of this Chapter—

(a) a car made available in any year to an employee, or to others being members of his family or household, by reason of his employment is deemed to be available in that year for his or their private use unless the terms on which the car is made available prohibit such use and no such use is made of the car in that year;

(b) a car made available to an employee, or to others being members of his family or household, by his employer is deemed to be made available to him or them by reason of his employment (unless the employer is an individual and it can be shown that the car was made so available in the normal course of his domestic, family or personal relationships).

(7) For the purposes of section 156, the market value of an asset at any time is the price which it might reasonably have been expected to fetch on a sale in the open market at that time.

(8) Subject to subsection (9) below, "director" means—

(a) in relation to a company whose affairs are managed by a board of directors or similar body, a member of that board or similar body;

(b) in relation to a company whose affairs are managed by a single director or similar person, that director or person; and

(c) in relation to a company whose affairs are managed by the members themselves, a member of the company,

and includes any person in accordance with whose directions or instructions the directors of the company (as defined above) are accustomed to act.

(9) A person is not under subsection (8) above to be deemed to be a person in accordance with whose directions or instructions the directors of the company are accustomed to act by reason only that the directors act on advice given by him in a professional capacity.

(10) "Full-time working director" means a director who is required to devote substantially the whole of his time to the service of the company in a managerial or technical capacity.

(11) A person shall be treated as having a material interest in a company—

(a) if he, either on his own or with any one or more of his associates, or if any associate of his with or without such other associates, is the beneficial owner of, or able, directly or through the medium of other companies or by any other indirect means, to control, more than 5 per cent. of the ordinary share capital of the company; or

(b) if, in the case of a close company, on an amount equal to the whole distributable income of the company falling to be apportioned under Part XI for the purpose of computing total income, more than 5 per cent. of that amount could be apportioned to him together with his associates (if any), or to any associate of his, or any such associates taken together.

In this subsection "associate" has the same meaning as in section 417(3), except that for this purpose "relative" in that subsection has the meaning given by section 160(6).

(12) "Control", in relation to a body corporate or partnership, has the meaning given to it by section 840; and the definition of "control" in that section applies (with the necessary modifications) in relation to an unincorporated association as it applies in relation to a body corporate.

PART V

(13) "Year" means year of assessment (except where the expression is used with reference to the age of a car).

CHAPTER III

PROFIT-RELATED PAY

Preliminary

Interpretation.

169.—(1) In this Chapter—

"employment" means an office or employment whose emoluments fall to be assessed under Schedule E, and related expressions have corresponding meanings;

"employment unit" means an undertaking, or that part of an undertaking, to which a profit-related pay scheme relates;

"pay" (except in the expression "profit-related pay") means emoluments paid under deduction of tax pursuant to section 203, reduced by any amounts included in them by virtue of Chapter II of Part V;

"profit period" means an accounting period by reference to which any profit-related pay is calcuated;

"profit-related pay" means emoluments from an employment which are paid in accordance with a profit-related pay scheme;

"profit-related pay scheme" means a scheme providing for the payment of emoluments calculated by reference to profits;

"profits", or "losses", in relation to a profit period, means the amount shown in the account prepared for that period in accordance with the relevant profit-related pay scheme as the profit, or as the case may be the loss, on ordinary activities after taxation;

"registered scheme" means a profit-related pay scheme registered under this Chapter;

"scheme employer" means the person on whose application a profit-related pay scheme is or may be registered under this Chapter.

(2) References in this Chapter to the employees to whom a profit-related pay scheme relates are references to the employees who will receive any payments of profit-related pay under the scheme.

Taxation of profit-related pay.

170. Any charge to income tax on profit-related pay paid in accordance with a registered scheme shall be made for the year of assessment in which it is paid (rather than the period for which it is paid).

The relief

Relief from tax.

171.—(1) One half of any profit-related pay to which this section applies shall be exempt from income tax.

(2) This section applies to any profit-related pay paid to an employee by reference to a profit period and in accordance with a registered scheme, but only so far as it does not exceed the lower of the two limits specified in the following provisions of this section.

(3) The first of the limits referred to in subsection (2) above is one fifth of the aggregate of—

(a) the pay (but not any profit-related pay) paid to the employee in the profit period in respect of his employment in the employment unit concerned (or, if the employee is eligible to receive profit-related pay by reference to part only of the period, so much of his pay, but not any profit-related pay, as is paid in that part); and

(b) the profit-related pay paid to him by reference to that period in respect of that employment.

(4) The second of the limits referred to in subsection (2) above is £3000 (or, if the profit period is less than 12 months, or the employee is eligible to receive profit-related pay by reference to part only of the profit period, a proportionately reduced amount).

172.—(1) Profit-related pay shall not be exempt from income tax by virtue of section 171 if— Exceptions from tax.

(a) it is paid to an employee in respect of his employment in an employment unit during a time when he also has another employment; and

(b) he receives in respect of that other employment during that time profit-related pay which is exempt from income tax by virtue of that section.

(2) Subject to subsection (3) below, profit-related pay in respect of which no secondary Class 1 contributions under Part I of the Social Security Act 1975 or Part I of the Social Security (Northern Ireland) Act 1975 are payable shall not be exempt from income tax by virtue of section 171. 1975 c. 14. 1975 c. 15.

(3) Subsection (2) above shall not apply to profit-related pay in respect of which no Class 1 contributions are payable only because the employee's earnings are below the lower earnings limit for such contributions.

Registration

173.—(1) Where the emoluments of all the employees to whom a profit-related pay scheme relates are paid by the same person, an application to register the scheme under this Chapter may be made to the Board by that person. Persons who may apply for registration.

(2) Where subsection (1) above does not apply to a profit-related pay scheme, no application to register it may be made unless all the persons who pay emoluments to employees to whom the scheme relates are bodies corporate which are members of the same group; and in that case an application may be made by the parent company of the group.

(3) In subsection (2) above—

"group" means a body corporate and its 51 per cent. subsidiaries, and

"parent company" means that body corporate; and

in applying for the purposes of this section the definition of "51 per cent. subsidiary" in section 838, any share capital of a registered industrial and provident society (within the meaning of section 486) shall be treated as ordinary share capital.

Excluded
employments.

174.—(1) No application may be made to register a scheme under this Chapter if any employment to which the scheme relates is—

(a) employment in an office under the Crown or otherwise in the service of the Crown; or

(b) employment by an excluded employer.

(2) For the purposes of this section "excluded employer" means—

(a) a person in an employment within subsection (1) above;

(b) a body under the control of the Crown, or of one or more persons acting on behalf of the Crown;

(c) a local authority;

(d) a body under the control of one or more local authorities, or of the Crown (or one or more persons acting on behalf of the Crown) and one or more local authorities.

(3) For the purposes of this section a person has control of a body only if one or more of the following conditions is satisfied—

(a) in the case of a body whose affairs are managed by its members, he has the power to appoint more than half of the members;

(b) in the case of a body having a share capital, he holds more than half of its issued share capital;

(c) in the case of a body whose members vote in general meeting, he has the power to exercise more than half of the votes exercisable in general meeting;

(d) the articles of association or other rules regulating the body give him the power to secure that the affairs of the body are conducted in accordance with his wishes.

(4) For the purposes of this section a person shall be taken to possess rights and powers possessed by—

(a) a person appointed by him to an office by virtue of which the rights or powers are exercisable; or

(b) a body which he controls;

including rights and powers which such an officer or body is taken to possess by virtue of this subsection.

(5) Subsections (3) and (4) above apply with the necessary modifications for the purpose of determining whether persons together have control of a body.

175.—(1) An application for the registration of a profit-related pay scheme under this Chapter—

(a) shall be in such form as the Board may prescribe;

(b) shall contain a declaration by the applicant that the scheme complies with the requirements of Schedule 8;

(c) shall contain an undertaking by the applicant that the emoluments paid to any employee to whom the scheme relates and to whom minimum wage legislation applies will satisfy that legislation without taking account of profit-related pay;

(d) shall specify the profit period or periods to which the scheme relates;

(e) shall be supported by such information as the Board may require.

(2) An application for the registration of a profit-related pay scheme under this Chapter shall be accompanied by a report by an independent accountant, in a form prescribed by the Board, to the effect that in his opinion—

(a) the scheme complies with the requirements of Schedule 8;

(b) the books and records maintained and proposed to be maintained by the applicant are adequate for the purpose of enabling the documents required by section 180(1) to be produced.

(3) An application for the registration of a profit-related pay scheme under this Chapter shall be made within the period of six months ending immediately before the beginning of the profit period, or the first of the profit periods, to which the scheme relates.

(4) In subsection (1) above "minimum wage legislation" means the provisions relating to remuneration in Part II of the Wages Act 1986, the Wages Councils (Northern Ireland) Order 1982, the Agricultural Wages Act 1948, the Agricultural Wages (Scotland) Act 1949 and the Agricultural Wages (Regulation) (Northern Ireland) Order 1977.

1986 c. 48.
S.I. 1982/1840 (N.I. 23).
1948 c. 47.
1949 c. 30.
S.I. 1977/2151 (N.I. 22).

176.—(1) If an application for registration of a profit-related pay scheme under this Chapter is made more than three months (but not more than six months) before the beginning of the profit period, or the first of the profit periods, to which the scheme relates, then subject to subsection (2) below, the Board shall register the scheme before the beginning of that period.

Registration.

(2) If the Board are not satisfied that an application made as mentioned in subsection (1) above complies with the requirements of this Chapter, they may within 30 days after the day on which they receive the application—

(a) refuse the application; or

(b) by notice to the applicant either require him to amend the application or require him to give them such further information as may be specified in the notice, and in either case to do so within such time, not exceeding 30 days after the day on which the notice is given, as may be so specified.

(3) If a notice under subsection (2) above is complied with and the Board are satisfied that the application complies with the requirements of this Chapter, the Board shall register the scheme before the beginning of the profit period.

(4) If a notice under subsection (2) above is complied with but the Board remain not satisfied that the application complies with the requirements of this Chapter, the Board shall refuse the application.

(5) If a notice under subsection (2) above is not complied with but the Board are before the beginning of the profit period satisfied that the application complies with the requirements of this Chapter, the Board may register the scheme before the beginning of the period; but if they do not do so, the application shall be regarded as having been refused.

(6) If an application for registration of a profit-related pay scheme under this Chapter is made within the period of three months before the beginning of the profit period, or the first of the profit periods, to which the scheme relates, then—

(a) if before the beginning of the profit period the Board are satisfied that the application complies with the requirements of this Chapter, they shall register the scheme before the beginning of the period; but

(b) in any other case, the application shall be regarded as having been refused.

(7) After registering a scheme under this Chapter, the Board shall by notice inform the applicant that they have done so.

(8) The Board shall give notice to the applicant if they refuse his application under subsection (2) or (4) above.

(9) For the purposes of this section an application does not comply with the requirements of this Chapter if the scheme to which it relates does not comply with the requirements of Schedule 8.

Change of scheme employer.

177.—(1) Where—

(a) a scheme employer ceases to fulfil the conditions which section 173 requires to be fulfilled by an applicant for registration of the scheme; and

(b) he is succeeded by a person who would be eligible to apply for registration to the scheme; and

(c) there is otherwise no other material change in the employment unit or in the circumstances relating to the scheme;

the scheme employer and his successor may make a joint written application to the Board under this section for the amendment of the registration of the scheme.

(2) If on receiving an application under this section the Board are satisfied—

(a) that the conditions in subsection (1)(a), (b) and (c) above are fulfilled; and

(b) that, apart from the change of scheme employer, there would be no grounds for cancelling the registration of the scheme, the Board shall amend the registration of the scheme by substituting the successor for the previous scheme employer.

(3) An application under this section shall be made before the end of the period of one month beginning with the date of the succession.

(4) Where the Board amend the registration of a scheme under this section, this Chapter shall (subject to any necessary modifications) have effect as if the successor had been the scheme employer throughout.

(5) The Board shall give notice to the applicants if they refuse an application under this section.

178.—(1) If after a scheme has been registered under this Chapter it Cancellation of appears to the Board— registration.

    (a) that the scheme has not been or will not be administered in accordance with this Chapter in relation to a profit period; or

    (b) that the circumstances relating to the scheme have during a profit period become such that (if it were not registered) an application to register it under this Chapter would be excluded by section 174; or

    (c) in the case of a scheme which employs (as the method of determining the distributable pool for a profit period) the method described as method B in paragraph 14 of Schedule 8, that losses were incurred in a profit period or in the preceding period of 12 months; or

    (d) that the undertaking given in compliance with section 175(1)(c) has not been complied with in relation to employment at any time during a profit period;

the Board may cancel the registration and, subject to subsection (5) below, the cancellation shall have effect from the beginning of that profit period.

(2) If after a scheme has been registered under this Chapter it appears to the Board—

    (a) that at the time of registration the scheme did not comply with the requirements of Schedule 8 or that the application did not comply with the requirements of this Chapter; or

    (b) in the case of a scheme which employs (as the method of determining the distributable pool for a profit period) the method described as method A in paragraph 13 of Schedule 8, that losses were incurred in the base year specified in the scheme;

the Board may cancel the registration with effect from the beginning of the profit period (or first profit period) to which the scheme related.

(3) If after a scheme has been registered under this Chapter the scheme employer fails to comply with the requirements of section 180 in relation to a profit period, the Board may cancel the registration with effect from the beginning of that profit period.

(4) If the scheme employer by notice requests the Board to cancel the registration of the scheme with effect from the beginning of a profit period specified in the notice, the Board shall comply with the request.

(5) Where—

    (a) the scheme employer has given to the Board in accordance with section 181(3) notice of a change in the employment unit, or in the circumstances relating to the scheme, which is a ground for cancellation of the registration of the scheme by virtue of subsection (1)(a) or (b) above, and

    (b) the Board are satisfied that the change is not brought about with a view to the registration of a new scheme, and

    (c) in the notice the scheme employer requests the Board to cancel the registration of the scheme with effect from the date of the change,

then, if the notice is given before the end of the period of one month beginning with that day, the Board shall comply with the request.

(6) The Board shall give notice to the scheme employer of the cancellation of a scheme's registration.

Administration

Recovery of tax from scheme employer.

179.—(1) This section applies where—

    (a) payments of profit-related pay are made to an employee in accordance with a registered scheme; and

    (b) in consequence of the relief given by this Chapter in respect of registered schemes, less income tax is deducted from the payments in accordance with section 203 than would have been deducted if the scheme had not been registered; and

    (c) the registration of the scheme is subsequently cancelled with effect from a time before that relevant for the purposes of the relief.

(2) Where this section applies, an amount equal to the shortfall in the deductions made in accordance with section 203 shall be payable by the scheme employer to the Board; and regulations under that section may include provision as to the collection and recovery of any such amount.

Annual returns etc.

180.—(1) After every profit period of a registered scheme, the scheme employer shall, within the period allowed by subsection (2) below, send to the Board—

    (a) a return in such form and containing such information as the Board may prescribe; and

    (b) a report by an independent accountant in such form and containing such information as the Board may prescribe and stating that in his opinion the terms of the scheme have been complied with in respect of the profit period.

(2) Subject to subsection (3) below, the period allowed for complying with subsection (1) above is—

(a) seven months from the end of the profit period if the employment unit to which the scheme relates is an undertaking or part of an undertaking of a public company; and

(b) ten months from the end of the profit period in any other case.

(3) If before the end of the period allowed by subsection (2) above the scheme employer gives the Board notice that an extension of three months has been allowed under section 242(3) of the Companies Act 1985, or under Article 250(3) of the Companies (Northern Ireland) Order 1986, in relation to a financial year of the employer which corresponds with the profit period in question, then the period allowed by subsection (2) above shall be correspondingly extended.

1985 c. 6.
S.I. 1986/1032
(N.I. 6).

(4) In subsection (2)(a) above, "public company" has the meaning given by section 1(3) of the Companies Act 1985 or Article 12(3) of the Companies (Northern Ireland) Order 1986.

181.—(1) The Board may by notice require any person to give them, within a period of 30 days or such longer period as may be specified in the notice, any information which is so specified and which—

Other information.

(a) that person has or can reasonably be required to obtain; and

(b) the Board consider they need to have in order to perform their functions under this Chapter.

(2) Without prejudice to the generality of subsection (1)(b) above, the Board may in particular require a person under subsection (1) to give them—

(a) information to enable them to determine whether the registration of a scheme should be cancelled;

(b) information to enable them to determine the liability to tax of any person who is or has been an employee to whom a registered scheme relates or who pays or has paid emoluments to such an employee;

(c) information about the administration of a profit-related pay scheme which is or has been a registered scheme;

(d) information about any change of person paying emoluments to employees to whom a registered scheme relates.

(3) The scheme employer of a registered scheme shall by notice inform the Board without delay if he becomes aware of anything that is or may be a ground for cancellation of the registration of the scheme.

182.—(1) An appeal to the Special Commissioners may be made by a scheme employer—

Appeals.

(a) against a refusal by the Board under section 176(2) or (4) of an application for registration of the scheme;

(b) against a refusal by the Board of an application under section 177;

(c) against the cancellation by the Board of the registration of the scheme.

PART V   (2) An appeal under this section shall be made by notice given to the Board within 30 days of the day on which the scheme employer was notified of the refusal or, as the case may be, the cancellation.

Supplementary

Partnerships.   **183.** For the purposes of this Chapter the members of a partnership which is a scheme employer shall be treated as a single continuing body of persons notwithstanding any change in their identity.

Independent accountants.

1985 c. 6.
S.I. 1986/1032
(N.I. 6).

184.—(1) For the purposes of this Chapter, "independent accountant", in relation to a profit-related pay scheme, means a person who—

(a) is within section 389(1)(a) or (b) of the Companies Act 1985 or Article 397(1)(a) or (b) of the Companies (Northern Ireland) Order 1986 (qualification for appointment as auditor); and

(b) is not excluded by subsections (2) to (5) below.

(2) A person is not an independent accountant in relation to a profit-related pay scheme if—

(a) he is the employer of employees to whom the scheme relates; or

(b) he is a partner or an employee of, or partner of an employee of, a person within subsection (3) below; or

(c) he is an employee of a person within paragraph (b) above.

(3) The persons within this subsection are—

(a) any person having employees to whom the scheme relates;

(b) any body corporate which is the subsidiary or holding company of a body corporate within paragraph (a) above or a subsidiary of such a body's holding company.

(4) For the purposes of this section—

(a) an auditor of a company is not to be regarded as an employee of it; and

(b) "holding company" and "subsidiary" are to be construed in accordance with section 736 of the Companies Act 1985 or Article 4 of the Companies (Northern Ireland) Order 1986.

(5) A body corporate cannot be an independent accountant in relation to a scheme.

(6) For the purposes of this Chapter, "independent accountant", in relation to a scheme, includes a Scottish firm all the partners of which are independent accountants in relation to the scheme.

CHAPTER IV

OTHER EXEMPTIONS AND RELIEFS

Share option and profit sharing schemes

Approved share option schemes.   **185.**—(1) The provisions of this section shall apply where, in accordance with the provisions of an approved share option scheme, an individual obtains a right to acquire shares in a body corporate by reason of his office or employment as a director or employee of that or any other body corporate and he obtains that right—

    (a) in the case of a savings-related share option scheme, on or after 15th November 1980; or

    (b) in the case of any other share option scheme, on or after 6th April 1984.

(2) Subject to subsections (4) and (6) below, tax shall not be chargeable under any provision of the Tax Acts in respect of the receipt of the right.

(3) Subject to subsections (4) and, except where paragraph 27(3) of Schedule 9 applies, (5) below, if he exercises the right in accordance with the provisions of the scheme at a time when it is approved—

    (a) tax shall not be chargeable under any provision of the Tax Acts in respect of the exercise nor under section 138(1)(a) in respect of an increase in the market value of the shares;

    (b) section 29A(1) of the 1979 Act (assets deemed to be acquired at market value) shall not apply in calculating the consideration for the acquisition of the shares by him or for any corresponding disposal of them to him.

(4) Subsections (2) and (3) above shall not apply in respect of a right, obtained by a person under a scheme which is a savings-related share option scheme, which is exercised within three years of its being obtained by virtue of a provision included in a scheme pursuant to paragraph 21 of Schedule 9.

(5) Subsection (3) above shall not apply in relation to the exercise by any person of a right in accordance with the provisions of a scheme which is not a savings-related share option scheme if—

    (a) the period beginning with his obtaining the right and ending with his exercising it is less than three, or greater than ten, years; or

    (b) the right is exercised within three years of the date on which he last exercised (in circumstances in which subsection (3) above applied) any right obtained under the scheme or under any other approved share option scheme which is not a savings-related share option scheme (any such right exercised on the same day being disregarded).

(6) Where, in the case of a right obtained by a person under a scheme which is not a savings-related share option scheme, the aggregate of—

    (a) the amount or value of any consideration given by him for obtaining the right, and

    (b) the price at which he may acquire the shares by exercising the right,

is less than the market value, at the time he obtains the right, of the same quantity of issued shares of the same class, he shall be chargeable to tax under Schedule E for the year of assessment in which he obtains the right on the amount of the difference; and the amount so chargeable shall be treated as earned income, whether or not it would otherwise fall to be so treated.

(7) For the purposes of section 32(1)(a) of the 1979 Act (computation of chargeable gains: allowable expenditure) the consideration given for shares acquired in the exercise of the right shall be taken to have included that part of any amount on which income tax is payable in accordance with subsection (6) above which is attributable to the shares disposed of.

This subsection applies whether or not the exercise is in accordance with the provisions of the scheme and whether or not the scheme is approved at the time of the exercise.

(8) Where a person is chargeable to tax under subsection (6) above on any amount (the "amount of the discount") and subsequently, in circumstances in which subsection (3) above does not apply—

(a) he is chargeable to tax under section 135, the amount of the gain on which he is chargeable to tax under that section shall be reduced by that part of the amount of the discount which is attributable to the shares in question; or

(b) he is treated by virtue of section 162 as having had the benefit of a notional interest-free loan, the amount of the notional loan initially outstanding shall be reduced by that part of the amount of the discount which is attributable to the shares in question.

(9) Where the provisions of a scheme which is not a savings-related share option scheme are approved in pursuance of an application made under paragraph 1 of Schedule 10 to the Finance Act 1984 before 1st January 1985 (and the approval has not been withdrawn), this section shall apply in relation to any right obtained before 1st July 1985 as if the scheme containing those provisions had been approved under that Schedule during the period beginning with the date on which that right was obtained and ending with the date on which those provisions were actually so approved.

1984 c. 43.

(10) In this section "savings-related share option scheme" has the meaning given by Schedule 9.

Approved profit sharing schemes.

186.—(1) The provisions of this section apply where, after 5th April 1979, the trustees of an approved profit sharing scheme appropriate shares—

(a) which have previously been acquired by the trustees, and

(b) as to which the conditions in Part II of Schedule 9 are fulfilled,

to an individual who participates in the scheme ("the participant").

(2) Notwithstanding that, by virtue of such an appropriation of shares as is mentioned in subsection (1) above, the beneficial interest in the shares passes to the participant to whom they are appropriated—

(a) the value of the shares at the time of the appropriation shall be treated as not being income of his chargeable to tax under Schedule E; and

(b) he shall not be chargeable to income tax under that Schedule by virtue of section 138(1)(a) in respect of an increase in the market value of the shares or by virtue of section 162 in any case where the shares are appropriated to him at an under-value within the meaning of that section.

(3) Subject to the provisions of this section and paragraph 4 of Schedule 10, if, in respect of or by reference to any of a participant's shares, the trustees become or the participant becomes entitled, before the release date, to receive any money or money's worth ("a capital receipt"), the participant shall be chargeable to income tax under Schedule E for the year of assessment in which the entitlement arises on the appropriate percentage (determined as at the time the trustees become or the participant becomes so entitled) of so much of the amount or value of the receipt as exceeds the appropriate allowance for that year, as determined under subsection (12) below.

(4) If the trustees dispose of any of a participant's shares at any time before the release date or, if it is earlier, the date of the participant's death, then, subject to subsections (6) and (7) below, the participant shall be chargeable to income tax under Schedule E for the year of assessment in which the disposal takes place on the appropriate percentage of the locked-in value of the shares at the time of the disposal.

(5) Subject to paragraphs 5 and 6(6) of Schedule 10, the locked-in value of a participant's shares at any time is—

    (a) if prior to that time he has become chargeable to income tax by virtue of subsection (3) above on a percentage of the amount or value of any capital receipt which is referable to those shares, the amount by which their initial market value exceeds the amount or value of that capital receipt or, if there has been more than one such receipt, the aggregate of them; and

    (b) in any other case, their initial market value.

(6) Subject to subsection (7) below, if, on a disposal of shares falling within subsection (4) above, the proceeds of the disposal are less than the locked-in value of the shares at the time of the disposal, subsection (4) above shall have effect as if that locked-in value were reduced to an amount equal to the proceeds of the disposal.

(7) If, at any time prior to the disposal of any of a participant's shares, a payment was made to the trustees to enable them to exercise rights arising under a rights issue, then, subject to subsection (8) below, subsections (4) and (6) above shall have effect as if the proceeds of the disposal were reduced by an amount equal to that proportion of that payment or, if there was more than one, of the aggregate of those payments which, immediately before the disposal, the market value of the shares disposed of bore to the market value of all the participant's shares held by the trustees at that time.

(8) For the purposes of subsection (7) above—

    (a) no account shall be taken of any payment to the trustees if or to the extent that it consists of the proceeds of a disposal of rights arising under a rights issue; and

    (b) in relation to a particular disposal the amount of the payment or, as the case may be, of the aggregate of the payments referred to in that subsection shall be taken to be reduced by an amount equal to the total of the reduction (if any) previously made under that subsection in relation to earlier disposals;

F

and any reference in subsection (7) or paragraph (a) above to the rights arising under a rights issue is a reference to rights conferred in respect of a participant's shares, being rights to be allotted, on payment, other shares or securities or rights of any description in the same company.

(9) If at any time the participant's beneficial interest in any of his shares is disposed of, the shares in question shall be treated for the purposes of the relevant provisions as having been disposed of at that time by the trustees for (subject to subsection (10) below) the like consideration as was obtained for the disposal of the beneficial interest; and for the purposes of this subsection there is no disposal of the participant's beneficial interest if and at the time when—

(a) in England and Wales or Northern Ireland, that interest becomes vested in any person on the insolvency of the participant or otherwise by operation of law, or

(b) in Scotland, that interest becomes vested in a judicial factor, in a trustee on the participant's sequestrated estate or in a trustee for the benefit of the participant's creditors.

(10) If—

(a) a disposal of shares falling within subsection (4) above is a transfer to which paragraph 2(2)(c) of Schedule 9 applies, or

(b) the Board is of opinion that any other disposal falling within that sub-paragraph is not at arm's length and accordingly direct that this subsection shall apply, or

(c) a disposal of shares falling within that sub-paragraph is one which is treated as taking place by virtue of subsection (9) above and takes place within the period of retention,

then for the purposes of the relevant provisions the proceeds of the disposal shall be taken to be equal to the market value of the shares at the time of the disposal.

(11) Where the trustees of an approved scheme acquire any shares as to which the requirements of Part II of Schedule 9 are fulfilled and, within the period of 18 months beginning with the date of their acquisition, those shares are appropriated in accordance with the scheme, section 686 shall not apply to income consisting of dividends on those shares received by the trustees; and, for the purpose of determining whether any shares are appropriated within that period, shares which were acquired at an earlier time shall be taken to be appropriated before shares of the same class which were acquired at a later time.

(12) For the purposes of subsection (3) above, "the appropriate allowance", in relation to any year of assessment, means a sum which, subject to a maximum of £100, is the product of multiplying £20 by 1 plus the number of years which fall within the period of five years immediately preceding the year in question and in which shares were appropriated to the participant under the scheme; and if in any year (and before the release date) the trustees become or the participant becomes entitled, in respect of or by reference to any of his shares, to more than one capital receipt, the receipts shall be set against the appropriate allowance for that year in the order in which they are received.

(13) Schedule 10 shall have effect with respect to profit sharing schemes.

187.—(1) In sections 185 and 186, this section and Schedules 9 and 10 "the relevant provisions" means those sections (including this section) and Schedules.

(2) For the purposes of the relevant provisions, except where the context otherwise requires—

"appropriate percentage" shall be construed in accordance with paragraph 3 of Schedule 10;

"approved", in relation to a scheme, means approved under Schedule 9;

"associated company" has the same meaning as in section 416, except that, for the purposes of paragraph 23 of Schedule 9, subsection (1) of that section shall have effect with the omission of the words "or at any time within one year previously";

"bonus date" has the meaning given by paragraph 17 of Schedule 9;

"capital receipt" means money or money's worth to which the trustees of or a participant in a profit sharing scheme become or becomes entitled as mentioned in section 186(3), but subject to paragraph 4 of Schedule 10;

"certified contractual savings scheme" has the meaning given by section 326;

"control" has the same meaning as in section 840;

"grantor", in relation to any scheme, means the company which has established the scheme;

"group scheme" and, in relation to such a scheme, "participating company" have the meanings given by paragraph 1(3) and (4) of Schedule 9;

"initial market value", in relation to shares in a profit sharing scheme, has the meaning given by paragraph 30(4) of Schedule 9;

"locked-in value", in relation to any shares, shall be construed in accordance with section 186(5);

"market value" has the same meaning as in Part VIII of the 1979 Act;

"new holding" has the meaning given by section 77(1)(b) of the 1979 Act;

"participant", in relation to a profit sharing scheme, means an individual to whom the trustees of the scheme have appropriated shares;

"participant's shares", in relation to a participant in a profit sharing scheme, means, subject to paragraph 5(4) of Schedule 10, shares which have been appropriated to the participant by the trustees;

"pensionable age" has the meaning given by Schedule 20 to the Social Security Act 1975;

"period of retention" has the meaning given by paragraph 2 of Schedule 10;

"release date", in relation to any of the shares of a participant in a profit sharing scheme, means the fifth anniversary of the date on which they were appropriated to him;

"relevant amount", in relation to a participant in a profit sharing scheme, means an amount which is not less than £1,250 and not more than £5,000 but which, subject to that, is 10 per cent. of his salary (determined under subsection (5) below) for the year of assessment in question or the preceding year of assessment, whichever is the greater;

"relevant requirements" has the meaning given by paragraph 1 of Schedule 9;

"savings-related share option scheme" has the meaning given by paragraph 1 of Schedule 9;

"scheme" means a savings-related share option scheme, a share option scheme which is not a savings-related share option scheme or a profit sharing scheme, as the context may require;

"shares" includes stock;

"the trustees", in relation to an approved profit sharing scheme or the shares of a participant in such a scheme, means the body of persons for the establishment of which the scheme must provide as mentioned in paragraph 30 of Schedule 9; and

"the trust instrument", in relation to an approved profit sharing scheme, means the instrument referred to in paragraph 30(1)(c) of Schedule 9.

(3) For the purposes of the application of the relevant provisions in relation to any share option scheme or profit sharing scheme, a person has a material interest in a company—

(a) if he, either on his own or with any one or more of his associates, or if any associate of his with or without any such other associates, is the beneficial owner of, or able, directly or through the medium of other companies or by any other indirect means, to control, more than 25 per cent., or in the case of a share option scheme which is not a savings-related share option scheme more than 10 per cent., of the ordinary share capital of the company; or

(b) if, on an amount equal to the whole distributable income of the company falling under Part XI to be apportioned for the purpose of computing total income, more than 25 per cent., or in the case of a share option scheme which is not a savings-related share option scheme more than 10 per cent., of that amount could be apportioned to him together with his associates (if any), or to any associate of his, or to any such associates taken together.

In this subsection "associate" has the meaning given by section 417(3) and (4).

(4) Subsection (3) above shall have effect subject to the provisions of Part VI of Schedule 9.

(5) For the purposes of subsection (2) above, a participant's salary for a year of assessment means such of the emoluments of the office or employment by virtue of which he is entitled to participate in a profit sharing scheme as are liable to be paid in that year under deduction of tax pursuant to section 203 after deducting therefrom amounts included by virtue of Chapter II of this Part.

(6) Section 839 shall apply for the purposes of the relevant provisions.

(7) For the purposes of the relevant provisions a company is a member of a consortium owning another company if it is one of a number of companies which between them beneficially own not less than three-quarters of the other company's ordinary share capital and each of which beneficially owns not less than one-twentieth of that capital.

(8) Where the disposal referred to in section 186(4) is made from a holding of shares which were appropriated to the participant at different times, then, in determining for the purposes of the relevant provisions—

(a) the initial market value and the locked-in value of each of those shares, and

(b) the percentage which is the appropriate percentage in relation to each of those shares,

the disposal shall be treated as being of shares which were appropriated earlier before those which were appropriated later.

(9) Any of the relevant provisions with respect to—

(a) the order in which any of a participant's shares are to be treated as disposed of for the purposes of those provisions, or

(b) the shares in relation to which an event is to be treated as occurring for any such purpose,

shall have effect in relation to a profit sharing scheme notwithstanding any direction given to the trustees with respect to shares of a particular description or to shares appropriated to the participant at a particular time.

(10) In the relevant provisions "workers' cooperative" means a registered industrial and provident society, within the meaning of section 486, which is a cooperative society and the rules of which include provisions which secure—

(a) that the only persons who may be members of it are those who are employed by, or by a subsidiary of, the society and those who are the trustees of its profit sharing scheme; and

(b) that, subject to any provision about qualifications for membership which is from time to time made by the members of the society by reference to age, length of service or other factors of any description, all such persons may be members of the society;

PART V

1965 c. 12.
1969 c. 24 (N.I.).

and in this subsection "cooperative society" has the same meaning as in section 1 of the Industrial and Provident Societies Act 1965 or, as the case may be, the Industrial and Provident Societies Act (Northern Ireland) 1969.

Retirement benefits etc.

Exemptions from
section 148.

188.—(1) Tax shall not be charged by virtue of section 148 in respect of the following payments, that is to say—

    (a) any payment made in connection with the termination of the holding of an office or employment by the death of the holder, or made on account of injury to or disability of the holder of an office or employment;

    (b) any sum chargeable to tax under section 313;

    (c) a benefit provided in pursuance of a retirement benefits scheme within the meaning of Chapter II of Part IX of the 1970 Act or Chapter I of Part XIV of this Act or of an agreement as described in section 220(2) of the 1970 Act, where under section 220 of that Act or section 595 of this Act the holder of the office or employment was chargeable to tax in respect of sums paid, or treated as paid, with a view to the provision of the benefit;

    (d) a benefit paid in pursuance of any such scheme or fund as was described in section 221(1) and (2) of the 1970 Act or as is described in section 596(1);

    (e) any terminal grant, gratuity or other lump sum paid under any Royal Warrant, Queen's Order, or Order in Council relating to members of Her Majesty's forces, and any payment made in commutation of annual or other periodical payments authorised by any such Warrant or Order;

    (f) a payment of benefit under any superannuation scheme administered by the government of an overseas territory within the Commonwealth, or of compensation for loss of career, interruption of service or disturbance made in connection with any change in the constitution of any such overseas territory to persons who, before the change, were employed in the public services of that territory;

1980 c. 63.

and references in paragraph (f) above to an overseas territory, to the government of such a territory, and to employment in the public service of such a territory shall be construed as if they occurred in the Overseas Development and Cooperation Act 1980, and sections 10(2) and 13(1) and (2) of that Act (which relate to the construction of such references) shall apply accordingly.

(2) Subsection (1)(d) above shall not apply to any compensation paid for loss of office or employment or for loss or diminution of emoluments unless the loss or diminution is due to ill-health; but this subsection shall not be taken to apply to any payment properly regarded as a benefit earned by past service.

(3) Tax shall not be charged by virtue of section 148 in respect of any payment in the case of which the following conditions are satisfied—

(a) that the payment is in respect of an office or employment in which the holder's service included foreign service; and

(b) that the foreign service comprised either—

(i) in any case, three-quarters of the whole period of service down to the relevant date, or

(ii) where the period of service down to the relevant date exceeded ten years, the whole of the last ten years, or

(iii) where the period of service down to the relevant date exceeded 20 years, one-half of that period, including any ten of the last 20 years.

(4) Tax shall not be charged by virtue of section 148 in respect of a payment of an amount not exceeding £25,000 ("the exempt sum") and, subject to subsection (5) below, in the case of a payment which exceeds that amount shall be charged only in respect of the excess.

(5) Where two or more payments in respect of which tax is chargeable by virtue of section 148, or would be so chargeable apart from subsection (4) above, are made to or in respect of the same person in respect of the same office or employment, or in respect of different offices or employments held under the same employer or under associated employers, subsection (4) above shall apply as if those payments were a single payment of an amount equal to that aggregate amount; and the amount of any one payment chargeable to tax shall be ascertained as follows, that is to say—

(a) where the payments are treated as income of different chargeable periods, the exempt sum shall be deducted from a payment treated as income of an earlier period before any payment treated as income of a later period; and

(b) subject to that, the exempt sum shall be deducted rateably from the payments according to their respective amounts.

(6) The person chargeable to tax by virtue of section 148 in respect of any payment may make a claim for such relief in respect of the payment as is applicable thereto under Schedule 11.

(7) For the purposes of this section and Schedule 11 offices or employments in respect of which payments to which section 148 applies are made shall be treated as held under associated employers if, on the date which is the relevant date in relation to any of those payments, one of those employers is under the control of the other or of a third person who controls or is under the control of the other on that or any other such date.

In this subsection "control" has the meaning given by section 840.

(8) In this section—

(a) "the relevant date" and "foreign service" have the same meaning as in Schedule 11; and

(b) references to an employer or to a person controlling or controlled by an employer include references to his successors.

189. A lump sum paid to a person on his retirement from an office or employment shall not be chargeable to income tax under Schedule E if—

Lump sum benefits on retirement.

(a) it is paid in pursuance of any such scheme or fund as was described in section 221(1) and (2) of the 1970 Act or as is described in section 596(1) and is neither a payment of compensation to which section 188(2) applies nor a payment chargeable to tax under section 600; or

(b) it is a benefit paid in pursuance of any such scheme or arrangement as was referred to in section 220 of the 1970 Act or a retirement benefits scheme within the meaning of section 611 of this Act and the person to whom it is paid was chargeable to tax under section 220 of the 1970 Act or section 595 of this Act in respect of sums paid, or treated as paid, with a view to the provision of the benefit; or

(c) it is paid under approved personal pension arrangements (within the meaning of Chapter IV of Part XIV).

Payments to Members of Parliament, Representatives to the European Parliament and others.

1984 c. 52.

1979 c. 50.

190. Grants and other payments made—

(a) in pursuance of a resolution of the House of Commons to a person ceasing to be a Member of that House on a dissolution of Parliament, or

(b) under section 13 of the Parliamentary Pensions etc. Act 1984 (grants to persons ceasing to hold certain Ministerial and other offices), or

(c) under section 3 of the European Parliament (Pay and Pensions) Act 1979 (resettlement grants to persons ceasing to be Representatives),

shall be exempt from income tax under Schedule E as emoluments, but without prejudice to their being taken into account, to the extent permitted by section 188(4), under section 148.

Job release scheme allowances not to be treated as income.

1977 c. 8.

191.—(1) A payment on account of an allowance to which this section applies shall not be treated as income for any purposes of the Income Tax Acts.

(2) This section applies to any allowance paid since the beginning of 1977 by the Secretary of State or the Department of Economic Development under any scheme of the kind described in the Job Release Act 1977, being a scheme which provides for the payment of allowances for periods beginning not earlier than one year before the date on which the recipient attains pensionable age as defined in that Act.

Foreign emoluments and earnings, pensions and certain travel facilities

Relief from tax for foreign emoluments.

192.—(1) In this Part "foreign emoluments" means the emoluments of a person not domiciled in the United Kingdom from an office or employment under or with any person, body of persons or partnership resident outside, and not resident in, the United Kingdom, but shall be taken not to include the emoluments of a person resident in the United Kingdom from an office or employment under or with a person, body of persons or partnership resident in the Republic of Ireland.

(2) Where the duties of an office or employment are performed wholly outside the United Kingdom and the emoluments from the office or employment are foreign emoluments, the emoluments shall be excepted from Case I of Schedule E.

(3) If it appears to the Board on a claim made by the holder of an office or employment that out of any foreign emoluments from the office or employment he has made payments in circumstances corresponding to those in which the payments would have reduced his liability to income tax, the Board may allow those payments as a deduction in computing the amount of the emoluments.

(4) Subject to subsection (2) above, there shall be allowed in charging tax on foreign emoluments from an office or employment under Case I or II of Schedule E for the year of assessment 1988-89 a deduction equal to one-quarter of the emoluments in any case where—

(a) the holder of the office or employment was in that year of assessment not resident in the United Kingdom or was not resident in the United Kingdom for at least two of the preceding ten years of assessment; and

(b) he—

(i) held an office or employment the emoluments of which were foreign emoluments chargeable under Case I or II of Schedule E at any time in the period beginning with 6th April 1983 and ending with 13th March 1984, or

(ii) in fulfilment of an obligation incurred before 14th March 1984, performed duties of such an office or employment in the United Kingdom before 1st August 1984,

and he held such an office or employment in the year 1984-85 and in each subsequent year of assessment.

(5) Paragraph 2(2) and (3) of Schedule 12 shall have effect with the necessary modifications in relation to the amount of emoluments to be excepted under subsection (2) above as they have effect in relation to the amount of emoluments in respect of which a deduction is allowed under section 193(1), and, subject to that, for the purposes of subsections (2) and (4) above the amount of any emoluments shall be taken to be the amount remaining after any capital allowance and after any deductions under subsection (3) above or section 193(4), 194(1), 195(7), 198, 199, 201, 332, 592 or 594.

193.—(1) Where in any year of assessment—

Foreign earnings and travel expenses.

(a) the duties of an office or employment are performed wholly or partly outside the United Kingdom; and

(b) any of those duties are performed in the course of a qualifying period (within the meaning of Schedule 12) which falls wholly or partly in that year and consists of at least 365 days;

then, in charging tax under Case I of Schedule E on the amount of the emoluments from that employment attributable to that period, or to so much of it as falls in that year of assessment, there shall be allowed a deduction equal to the whole of that amount.

Schedule 12 shall have effect for the purpose of supplementing this subsection.

(2) Subsections (3) and (4) below apply where a person ("the employee") who is resident and ordinarily resident in the United Kingdom holds an office or employment ("the overseas employment") the duties of which are performed wholly outside the United Kingdom and the emoluments from which are not foreign emoluments.

(3) For the purposes of section 198(1) there shall be treated as having been necessarily incurred in the performance of the duties of the overseas employment expenses of the employee in travelling from any place in the United Kingdom to take up the overseas employment and in travelling to any place in the United Kingdom on its termination; and if travel is partly for a purpose mentioned in this subsection and partly for another purpose this subsection applies only to such part of the expenses as is properly attributable to the former purpose.

(4) Where, for the purpose of enabling the employee to perform the duties of the overseas employment—

    (a) board and lodging outside the United Kingdom is provided for him and the cost of it is borne by or on behalf of his employer; or

    (b) he incurs expenses out of the emoluments of the employment on such board and lodging for himself and those expenses are reimbursed by or on behalf of his employer,

there shall be allowed, in charging tax under Case I of Schedule E on the emoluments from that employment, a deduction of an amount equal to so much of that cost, or, as the case may be, those expenses as falls to be included in those emoluments.

Where board and lodging is partly for the purpose mentioned in this subsection and partly for another purpose, this subsection applies only to such part of the cost or expenses as is properly attributable to the former purpose.

(5) Subsection (6) below applies where a person resident and ordinarily resident in the United Kingdom—

    (a) holds two or more offices or employments the duties of one or more of which are performed wholly or partly outside the United Kingdom; and

    (b) travels from one place having performed there duties of one office or employment to another place for the purpose of performing duties of another office or employment (the emoluments from which are not foreign emoluments);

and either or both of those places is outside the United Kingdom.

(6) For the purposes of section 198(1) expenses incurred by such a person on such travel shall be treated as having been necessarily incurred in the performance of the duties which he is to perform at his destination;

and if travel is partly for the purpose of performing those duties and partly for another purpose this subsection applies only to such part of the expenses as is properly attributable to the former purpose.

(7) References in the Income Tax Acts (including any provision of this Act, but without prejudice to any express reference to subsection (3) above) to section 198 and to deductions allowable under sections 198, 199, 201 or 332 shall be construed as including a reference to subsection (3) above and to deductions allowable under that subsection.

194.—(1) Where—

(a) travel facilities are provided for any journey to which this subsection applies and the cost of them is borne by or on behalf of the employer; or

(b) expenses are incurred out of the emoluments of any office or employment mentioned in subsection (2), (3) or (5) below on any such journey and those expenses are reimbursed by or on behalf of the employer,

there shall be allowed, in charging tax under Case I of Schedule E on the emoluments from that office or employment, a deduction of an amount equal to so much of that cost or, as the case may be, those expenses as falls to be included in those emoluments.

(2) Subsection (1) above applies where a person is absent from the United Kingdom for a continuous period of 60 days or more for the purpose of performing the duties of one or more offices or employments and applies to travel of the following descriptions between any place in the United Kingdom and the place of performance of any of those duties outside the United Kingdom, that is to say—

(a) any journey by his spouse or any child of his—

(i) accompanying him at the beginning of the period of absence; or

(ii) to visit him during that period;

(b) any return journey following a journey of a kind described in paragraph (a) above;

but that subsection does not extend to more than two outward and two return journeys by the same person in any year of assessment.

For the purposes of this subsection "child" includes a stepchild and an illegitimate child but does not include a person who is aged 18 or over at the beginning of the outward journey.

(3) Where a person holds an office or employment the duties of which are performed partly outside the United Kingdom, subsection (1) above applies, subject to subsection (4) below, to any journey by him—

(a) from any place in the United Kingdom to the place of performance of any of those duties outside the United Kingdom;

(b) from the place of performance of any of those duties outside the United Kingdom to any place in the United Kingdom.

PART V

(4) Subsection (1) does not apply by virtue of subsection (3) unless the duties concerned can only be performed outside the United Kingdom and the journey is made wholly and exclusively for the purpose—

    (a) where the journey falls within subsection (3)(a), of performing the duties concerned; or

    (b) where the journey falls within subsection (3)(b), of returning after performing the duties concerned.

(5) Where a person is absent from the United Kingdom for the purposes of performing the duties of one or more offices or employments, subsection (1) above applies, subject to subsection (6) below, to—

    (a) any journey by him from the place of performance of any of those duties outside the United Kingdom to any place in the United Kingdom;

    (b) any return journey following a journey of a kind described in paragraph (a) above.

(6) Subsection (1) does not apply by virtue of subsection (5) unless the duties concerned can only be performed outside the United Kingdom and the absence mentioned in subsection (5) was occasioned wholly and exclusively for the purpose of performing the duties concerned.

(7) For the purpose of applying this section in a case where the duties of the office or employment or (as the case may be) any of the offices or employments are performed on a vessel, in section 132(4)(b) the words from "or which" to the end shall be ignored.

(8) In such a case as is mentioned in subsection (7) above, subsection (4) above shall have effect as if "the duties concerned" in paragraphs (a) and (b) read "the duties concerned, or those duties and other duties of the office or employment".

(9) Where apart from this subsection a deduction in respect of any cost or expenses is allowable under a provision of this section or section 193 and a deduction in respect of the same cost or expenses is also allowable under another provision of this section or section 193 or of any other enactment, a deduction in respect of the cost or expenses may be made under either, but not both, of those provisions.

(10) References in the Income Tax Acts (including any provision of this Act, but without prejudice to any express reference to subsection (1) above) to section 198 and to deductions allowable under sections 198, 199, 201 or 332 shall be construed as including a reference to subsection (1) above and to deductions allowable under that subsection.

Travel expenses of employees not domiciled in the United Kingdom.

195.—(1) Subject to subsection (2) below, this section applies in the case of an office or employment in respect of which a person ("the employee") who is not domiciled in the United Kingdom is in receipt of emoluments for duties performed in the United Kingdom.

(2) This section does not apply unless subsection (3) below is satisfied in respect of a date on which the employee arrives in the United Kingdom to perform duties of the office or employment; and where subsection (3) is so satisfied, this section applies only for a period of five years beginning with that date.

(3) This subsection is satisfied in respect of a date if the employee—

(a) was not resident in the United Kingdom in either of the two years of assessment immediately preceding the year of assessment in which the date falls; or

(b) was not in the United Kingdom for any purpose at any time during the period of two years ending with the day immediately preceding the date.

(4) Where subsection (3) above is satisfied (by virtue of paragraph (a) of that subsection) in respect of more than one date in any year of assessment, only the first of those dates is relevant for the purposes of this section.

(5) Subsection (7) below applies to any journey by the employee—

(a) from his usual place of abode to any place in the United Kingdom in order to perform any duties of the office or employment there; or

(b) to his usual place of abode from any place in the United Kingdom after performing such duties there.

(6) Where the employee is in the United Kingdom for a continuous period of 60 days or more for the purpose of performing the duties of one or more offices or employments in the case of which this section applies, subsection (7) below applies to any journey by his spouse, or any child of his, between his usual place of abode and the place of performance of any of those duties in the United Kingdom, if the journey—

(a) is made to accompany him at the beginning of that period or to visit him during it; or

(b) is a return journey following a journey falling within paragraph (a) above;

but subsection (7) as it applies by virtue of this subsection does not extend to more than two journeys to the United Kingdom and two return journeys by the same person in any year of assessment.

(7) Subject to subsection (8) below, where—

(a) travel facilities are provided for any journey to which this subsection applies and the cost of them is borne by or on behalf of a person who is an employer in respect of any office or employment in the case of which this section applies; or

(b) expenses are incurred out of the emoluments of any office or employment in the case of which this section applies on such a journey and those expenses are reimbursed by or on behalf of the employer;

there shall be allowed, in charging tax under Case I or II of Schedule E on the emoluments from the office or employment concerned, a deduction of an amount equal to so much of that cost or, as the case may be, those expenses as falls to be included in those emoluments.

(8) If a journey is partly for a purpose mentioned in subsection (5) or (6) above and partly for another purpose, only so much of the cost or expenses referred to in subsection (7) as is properly attributable to the

PART V

former purpose shall be taken into account in calculating any deduction made under subsection (7) as it applies by virtue of subsection (5) or, as the case may be, (6).

(9) For the purposes of this section a person's usual place of abode is the country (outside the United Kingdom) in which he normally lives.

(10) In subsection (6) above "child" includes a step-child and an illegitimate child but does not include a person who is aged 18 or over at the beginning of the journey to the United Kingdom.

(11) References in the Income Tax Acts (including any provision of this Act, but without prejudice to any express reference to subsection (7) above) to section 198 and to deductions allowable under section 198, 199, 201 or 332 shall be construed as including a reference to subsection (7) above and to deductions allowable under it.

(12) Where apart from this subsection a deduction in respect of any cost or expenses is allowable under a provision of this section and a deduction in respect of the same cost or expenses is also allowable under another provision of this section or of any other enactment, a deduction in respect of the cost or expenses may be made under either, but not both, of those provisions.

1986 c. 41.

(13) Where by virtue of subsection (3) of section 38 of the Finance Act 1986 any provision of section 37 of that Act applied in the case of any employee at any time during the year 1984-85 or 1985-86 (and that section applied to him immediately before 6th April 1988), this section shall apply in his case for the years 1988-89 to 1990-91 as if the following were substituted for subsections (2) to (4)—

"(2) This section does not apply after 5th April 1991.".

Foreign pensions.

196. A deduction of one-tenth of its amount shall be allowed in charging any pension or annuity to tax under paragraph 4 of Schedule E.

Leave travel facilities for the armed forces.

197.—(1) No charge to tax under Schedule E shall arise in respect of travel facilities provided for members of the naval, military or air forces of the Crown going on, or returning from, leave.

(2) Subsection (1) above applies whether the charge would otherwise have arisen under section 131, 141 or 154 and applies not only to travel vouchers and warrants for particular journeys but also to allowances and other payments for and in respect of leave travel, whether or not a warrant was available.

Other expenses, subscriptions etc.

Relief for necessary expenses.

198.—(1) If the holder of an office or employment is necessarily obliged to incur and defray out of the emoluments of that office or employment the expenses of travelling in the performance of the duties of the office or employment, or of keeping and maintaining a horse to enable him to perform those duties, or otherwise to expend money wholly, exclusively and necessarily in the performance of those duties, there may be deducted from the emoluments to be assessed the expenses so necessarily incurred and defrayed.

(2) Subject to subsection (3) below, where the emoluments for any duties do not fall within Case I or II of Schedule E, then in relation to those or any other emoluments of the office or employment, subsection

(1) above and Chapter II of Part I of the 1968 Act and Chapter I of Part III of the Finance Act 1971 (capital allowances in respect of machinery and plant) shall apply as if the performance of those duties did not belong to that office or employment.

(3) There may be deducted from any emoluments chargeable under Case III of Schedule E the amount of—

(a) any expenses defrayed out of those emoluments, and

(b) any other expenses defrayed in the United Kingdom in the chargeable period or in an earlier chargeable period in which the holder of the office or employment has been resident in the United Kingdom,

being in either case expenses for which a deduction might have been made under subsection (1) above from emoluments of the office or employment if they had been chargeable under Case I of Schedule E for the chargeable period in which the expenses were incurred; but a deduction shall not be made twice, whether under this subsection or otherwise, in respect of the same expenses from emoluments of the office or employment.

(4) No deduction shall be made under this section in respect of expenditure incurred by a Member of the House of Commons in, or in connection with, the provision or use of residential or overnight accommodation to enable him to perform his duties as such a Member in or about the Palace of Westminster or his constituency.

199.—(1) Subject to the provisions of subsection (2) below, where the Treasury are satisfied with respect to any class of persons in receipt of any salary, fees or emoluments payable out of the public revenue that such persons are obliged to lay out and expend money wholly, exclusively and necessarily in the performance of the duties in respect of which such salary, fees or emoluments are payable, the Treasury may fix such sum as in the opinion of the Treasury represents a fair equivalent of the average annual amount laid out and so expended by persons of that class, and in charging income tax on that salary or those fees or emoluments there shall be deducted from the amount thereof the sums so fixed by the Treasury.

Expenses necessarily incurred and defrayed from official emoluments.

(2) If any such person would, but for the provisions of subsection (1) above, be entitled to deduct a larger amount than the sum so fixed, that amount may be deducted instead of the sum so fixed.

200. An allowance—

Expenses of Members of Parliament.

(a) which is paid to a Member of the House of Commons; and

(b) for which provision is made by resolution of that House, and

(c) which is expressed to be in respect of additional expenses necessarily incurred by the Member in staying overnight away from his only or main residence for the purpose of performing his parliamentary duties, either in the London area, as defined in such a resolution, or in his constituency,

shall not be regarded as income for any purpose of the Income Tax Acts.

201.—(1) Subject to the provisions of this section, the following may be deducted from the emoluments of any office or employment to be assessed to tax, if defrayed out of those emoluments, that is to say—

Fees and subscriptions to professional bodies, learned societies etc.

(a) any fee or contribution mentioned in subsection (2) below, and

(b) any annual subscription paid to a body of persons approved for the purposes of this section by the Board.

(2) The fees and contributions referred to in subsection (1)(a) above are—

(a) the fee payable in respect of the retention of a name in the Register of Architects;

(b) the fee payable in respect of the retention of a name in the dentists register or in a roll or record kept for a class of ancillary dental workers;

(c) the fee payable in respect of the retention of a name in either of the registers of ophthalmic opticians or in the register of dispensing opticians;

(d) the annual fee payable by a registered patent agent;

(e) the fee payable in respect of the retention of a name in the register of pharmaceutical chemists;

(f) the fee and contribution to the Compensation Fund or Guarantee Fund payable on the issue of a solicitor's practising certificate; and

(g) the annual fee payable by a registered veterinary surgeon or by a person registered in the Supplementary Veterinary Register.

(3) The Board may, on the application of the body, approve for the purposes of this section any body of persons not of a mainly local character whose activities are carried on otherwise than for profit and are solely or mainly directed to all or any of the following objects—

(a) the advancement or spreading of knowledge (whether generally or among persons belonging to the same or similar professions or occupying the same or similar positions);

(b) the maintenance or improvement of standards of conduct and competence among the members of any profession;

(c) the indemnification or protection of members of any profession against claims in respect of liabilities incurred by them in the exercise of their profession.

(4) If the activities of a body approved for the purposes of this section are to a significant extent directed to objects other than those mentioned in subsection (3) above, the Board may determine that such specified part only of any annual subscription paid to the body may be deducted under this section as corresponds to the extent to which its activities are directed to objects mentioned in that subsection; and in doing so the Board shall have regard to all relevant circumstances and, in particular, to the proportions of the body's expenditure attributable to the furtherance of objects so mentioned and other objects respectively.

(5) A fee, contribution or subscription shall not be deducted under this section from the emoluments of any office or employment unless—

(a) the fee is payable in respect of a registration (or retention of a name in a roll or record) or certificate which is a condition, or one of alternative conditions, of the performance of the duties of the office or employment or, as the case may be, the contribution is payable on the issue of such a certificate; or

(b) the subscription is paid to a body the activities of which, so far as they are directed to the objects mentioned in subsection (3) above, are relevant to the office or employment, that is to say, the performance of the duties of the office or employment is directly affected by the knowledge concerned or involves the exercise of the profession concerned.

(6) Any approval given and any determination made under this section may be withdrawn, and any such determination varied, so as to take account of any change of circumstances; and where a body is approved for the purposes of this section in pursuance of an application made before the end of any year of assessment, a deduction may be made under this section in respect of a subscription paid to the body in that year, whether the approval is given before or after the end of the year.

(7) Any body aggrieved by the failure of the Board to approve the body for the purposes of this section, or by their withdrawal of the approval, or by any determination made by them under this section or the variation of or refusal to withdraw or vary such a determination may, by notice given to the Board within 30 days from the date on which the body is notified of their decision, require the matter to be determined by the Special Commissioners, and the Special Commissioners shall thereupon hear and determine the matter in like manner as an appeal.

202.—(1) This section applies where an individual ("the employee") is entitled to receive payments from which income tax falls to be deducted by virtue of section 203 and regulations under that section, and the person liable to make the payments ("the employer") withholds sums from them.

Donations to charity: payroll deduction scheme.

(2) If the conditions mentioned in subsections (3) to (7) below are fulfilled the sums shall, in assessing tax under Schedule E, be allowed to be deducted as expenses incurred in the year of assessment in which they are withheld.

(3) The sums must be withheld in accordance with a scheme which is (or is of a kind) approved by the Board at the time they are withheld and which either contains provisions falling within subsection (4)(a) below, or contains provisions falling within subsection (4)(a) below and provisions falling within subsection (4)(b) below.

(4) The provisions are that—

(a) the employer is to pay sums withheld to a person ("the agent") who is approved by the Board at the time they are withheld, and the agent is to pay them to a charity or charities;

(b) the employer is to pay sums withheld directly to a charity which (or charities each of which) is at the time the sums are withheld approved by the Board as an agent for the purpose of paying sums to other charities.

(5) The sums must be withheld in accordance with a request by the employee that they be paid to a charity or charities in accordance with a scheme approved (or of a kind approved) by the Board.

(6) The sums must constitute gifts by the employee to the charity or charities concerned, must not be paid by the employee under a covenant, and must fulfil any conditions set out in the terms of the scheme concerned.

(7) The sums must not in any year of assessment exceed £120 in the case of any employee (however many offices or employments he holds or has held).

(8) The circumstances in which the Board may grant or withdraw approval of schemes (or kinds of schemes) or of agents shall be such as are prescribed by the Treasury by regulations; and the circumstances so prescribed (whether relating to the terms of schemes or the qualifications of agents or otherwise) shall be such as the Treasury think fit.

(9) The Treasury may by regulations make provision—

> (a) that a participating employer or agent shall comply with any notice which is served on him by the Board and which requires him within a prescribed period to make available for the Board's inspection documents of a prescribed kind or records of a prescribed kind;

> (b) that a participating employer or agent shall in prescribed circumstances furnish to the Board information of a prescribed kind;

> (c) for, and with respect to, appeals to the Special Commissioners against the Board's refusal to grant, or their withdrawal of, approval of any scheme (or any kind of scheme) or agent;

> (d) generally for giving effect to subsections (1) to (7) above.

In this subsection "prescribed" means prescribed by the regulations.

(10) For the purposes of subsection (9) above a person is a participating employer or agent if he is an employer or agent who participates, or has at any time participated, in a scheme under this section.

(11) In this section "charity" has the same meaning as in section 506.

CHAPTER V

ASSESSMENT, COLLECTION, RECOVERY AND APPEALS

Pay as you earn.

203.—(1) On the making of any payment of, or on account of, any income assessable to income tax under Schedule E, income tax shall, subject to and in accordance with regulations made by the Board under this section, be deducted or repaid by the person making the payment, notwithstanding that when the payment is made no assessment has been made in respect of the income and notwithstanding that the income is in whole or in part income for some year of assessment other than the year during which the payment is made.

(2) The Board shall make regulations with respect to the assessment, charge, collection and recovery of income tax in respect of all income assessable thereto under Schedule E, and those regulations may, in particular, include provision—

(a) for requiring any person making any payment of, or on account of, any such income, when he makes the payment, to make a deduction or repayment of income tax calculated by reference to tax tables prepared by the Board, and for rendering persons who are required to make any such deduction or repayment accountable to, or, as the case may be, entitled to repayment from, the Board;

(b) for the production to and inspection by persons authorised by the Board of wages sheets and other documents and records for the purpose of satisfying themselves that income tax has been and is being deducted, repaid and accounted for in accordance with the regulations;

(c) for the collection and recovery, whether by deduction from any such income paid in any later year or otherwise, of income tax in respect of any such income which has not been deducted or otherwise recovered during the year;

(d) for requiring the payment of interest on sums due to the Board—

(i) which are not paid by the due date; and

(ii) of which the amount is determined by the inspector (before or after the due date) in accordance with the regulations;

and for determining the date (being not less than 14 days after the end of the year of assessment in respect of which the sums are due) from which such interest is to be calculated;

(e) for the assessment and charge of income tax by the inspector in respect of income to which this section applies; and

(f) for appeals with respect to matters arising under the regulations which would otherwise not be the subject of an appeal;

and any such regulations shall have effect notwithstanding anything in the Income Tax Acts.

(3) The deductions of income tax required to be made by regulations under subsection (2)(a) above may be required to be made at the basic rate or other rates in such cases or classes of cases as may be provided for by the regulations.

(4) Any reference in this section to a payment of, or on account of, any income assessable under Schedule E includes a reference to anything which, in accordance with regulations under subsection (2) above, is to be treated as a payment of, or on account of, any such income.

(5) Regulations under this section shall not affect any right of appeal to the General or Special Commissioners which a person would have apart from the regulations.

(6) The tax tables referred to in subsection (2)(a) above shall be constructed with a view to securing that so far as possible—

(a) the total income tax payable in respect of any income assessable under Schedule E for any year of assessment is deducted from such income paid during that year; and

(b) the income tax deductible or repayable on the occasion of any payment of, or on account of, any such income is such that the total net income tax deducted since the beginning of the year of assessment bears to the total income tax payable for the year the same proportion that the part of the year which ends with the date of the payment bears to the whole year.

(7) In subsection (6) above references to the total income tax payable for the year shall be construed as references to the total income tax estimated to be payable for the year in respect of the income in question, subject to a provisional deduction for allowances and reliefs, and subject also, if necessary, to an adjustment for amounts overpaid or remaining unpaid on account of income tax in respect of income assessable under Schedule E for any previous year.

(8) For the purpose of estimating the total income tax payable as mentioned in subsection (6)(a) above, it may be assumed in relation to any payment of, or on account of, income assessable under Schedule E that the income paid in the part of the year of assessment which ends with the making of the payment will bear to the income for the whole of that year the same proportion as that part of the year bears to the whole year.

P.A.Y.E repayments.

204. Without prejudice to the generality of section 203, regulations under that section may provide that no repayment of income tax shall be made under that section to any person if at any time—

    (a) he has claimed unemployment benefit in respect of a period including that time; or

1986 c. 50.
S.I. 1986/1888 (N.I. 18).

    (b) he has claimed a payment of income support under the Social Security Act 1986 or the Social Security (Northern Ireland) Order 1986 in respect of a period including that time and his right to that income support is subject to the condition specified in section 20(3)(d)(i) of that Act or, in Northern Ireland, Article 21(3)(d)(i) of that Order (availability for employment); or

1975 c. 14.
1975 c. 15.

    (c) he is disqualified at the time from receiving unemployment benefit by virtue of section 19 of the Social Security Act 1975 or of section 19 of the Social Security (Northern Ireland) Act 1975 (loss of employment due to stoppage of work) or would be so disqualified if he otherwise satisfied the conditions for entitlement;

and such regulations may make different provision with respect to persons falling within paragraph (c) above from that made with respect to other persons.

Assessments unnecessary in certain circumstances.

205.—(1) Subject to the provisions of this section, no assessment under Schedule E need be made on a person in respect of income of his assessable to income tax under that Schedule for any year of assessment if the total net tax deducted in the year in question from that income is the same as it would have been if all the relevant circumstances had been known to all parties throughout the year, and deductions and repayments had throughout the year been made accordingly, and had been so made by reference to cumulative tax tables.

(2) In subsection (1) above—

(a) "cumulative tax tables" means tax tables prepared under section 203 which are so framed as to require the tax which is to be deducted or repaid on the occasion of each payment made in the year to be ascertained by reference to a total of emoluments paid in the year up to the time of making that payment; and

(b) references to the total net tax deducted shall be construed as references to the total income tax deducted during the year by virtue of regulations made under section 203, less any income tax repaid by virtue of any such regulations.

(3) Nothing in this section shall be construed as preventing an assessment being made on a person in respect of his income assessable under Schedule E, and, without prejudice to the generality of the preceding provisions of this subsection, an assessment shall be made in respect of the income of a person so assessable for any year of assessment if the person assessable requires an assessment to be made by notice given to the inspector within five years from the end of the year of assessment.

206. Where an assessment to income tax under Schedule E is made as respects income which—

Additional provision for certain assessments.

(a) has been taken into account in the making of deductions or repayments of tax under section 203, and

(b) was received not less than 12 months before the beginning of the year of assessment in which the assessment is made,

then, if the assessment is made after the expiration of the period of 12 months immediately following the year of assessment for which it is made, it shall be made in accordance with the practice generally prevailing at the expiration of that period.

207. Where a dispute arises under paragraph 1 of Schedule E or under section 192 whether a person is or has been ordinarily resident or domiciled in the United Kingdom, the question shall be referred to and determined by the Board; but any person who is aggrieved by their decision on the question may, by notice to that effect given to them within three months from the date on which notice is given to him, make an application to have the question heard and determined by the Special Commissioners, and where such an application is so made, the Special Commissioners shall hear and determine the question in like manner as an appeal.

Disputes as to domicile or ordinary residence.

PART VI

COMPANY DISTRIBUTIONS, TAX CREDITS ETC

CHAPTER I

TAXATION OF COMPANY DISTRIBUTIONS

U.K. company
distributions not
generally
chargeable to
corporation tax.

208. Except as otherwise provided by the Corporation Tax Acts, corporation tax shall not be chargeable on dividends and other distributions of a company resident in the United Kingdom, nor shall any such dividends or distributions be taken into account in computing income for corporation tax.

CHAPTER II

MATTERS WHICH ARE DISTRIBUTIONS FOR THE PURPOSES OF THE CORPORATION TAX ACTS

Meaning of
"distribution".

209.—(1) The following provisions of this Chapter, together with section 418, shall, subject to section 339(6) and to any other express exceptions, have effect with respect to the meaning of "distribution" and for determining the persons to whom certain distributions are to be treated as made, but references in the Corporation Tax Acts to distributions of a company shall not apply to distributions made in respect of share capital in a winding up.

(2) In the Corporation Tax Acts "distribution", in relation to any company, means—

(a) any dividend paid by the company, including a capital dividend;

(b) subject to subsections (5) and (6) below, any other distribution out of assets of the company (whether in cash or otherwise) in respect of shares in the company, except so much of the distribution, if any, as represents repayment of capital on the shares or is, when it is made, equal in amount or value to any new consideration received by the company for the distribution;

(c) subject to section 230, any redeemable share capital or any security issued by the company in respect of shares in or securities of the company otherwise than wholly for new consideration, or such part of any redeemable share capital or any security so issued as is not properly referable to new consideration;

(d) any interest or other distribution out of assets of the company in respect of securities of the company, where they are securities under which the consideration given by the company for the use of the principal thereby secured represents more than a reasonable commercial return for the use of that principal, except so much, if any, of any such distribution as represents that principal and so much as represents a reasonable commercial return for the use of that principal;

(e) any interest or other distribution out of assets of the company in respect of securities of the company (except so much, if any, of any such distribution as represents the principal thereby secured and except so much of any distribution as falls within paragraph (d) above), where the securities are—

    (i) securities issued as mentioned in paragraph (c) above, but excluding securities issued before 6th April 1965 in respect of shares and securities issued before 6th April 1972 in respect of securities; or

    (ii) securities convertible directly or indirectly into shares in the company or securities issued after 5th April 1972 and carrying any right to receive shares in or securities of the company, not being (in either case) securities quoted on a recognised stock exchange nor issued on terms which are reasonably comparable with the terms of issue of securities so quoted; or

    (iii) securities under which the consideration given by the company for the use of the principal secured is to any extent dependent on the results of the company's business or any part of it; or

    (iv) securities issued by the company ("the issuing company") and held by a company not resident in the United Kingdom where the issuing company is a 75 per cent. subsidiary of the other company or both are 75 per cent. subsidiaries of a third company which is not resident in the United Kingdom; or

    (v) securities issued by the company ("the issuing company") and held by a company not resident in the United Kingdom ("the non-resident company") where less than 90 per cent. of the share capital of the issuing company is directly owned by a company resident in the United Kingdom and both the issuing company and the non-resident company are 75 per cent. subsidiaries of a third company which is resident in the United Kingdom; or

    (vi) securities which are connected with shares in the company, and for this purpose securities are so connected if, in consequence of the nature of the rights attaching to the securities or shares and in particular of any terms or conditions attaching to the right to transfer the shares or securities, it is necessary or advantageous for a person who has, or disposes of or acquires, any of the securities also to have, or to dispose of or to acquire, a proportionate holding of the shares;

(f) any such amount as is required to be treated as a distribution by subsection (4) below or section 210.

(3) Without prejudice to section 254(11), no amount shall be regarded for the purposes of subsection (2)(d) and (e) above as representing the principal secured by a security issued after 5th April 1972 in so far as it exceeds any new consideration which has been received by the company for the issue of the security.

(4) Where on a transfer of assets or liabilities by a company to its members or to a company by its members, the amount or value of the benefit received by a member (taken according to its market value) exceeds the amount or value (so taken) of any new consideration given by him, the company shall, subject to subsections (5) and (6) below, be treated as making a distribution to him of an amount equal to the difference.

(5) Subsection (4) above shall not apply where the company and the member receiving the benefit are both resident in the United Kingdom and either the former is a subsidiary of the latter or both are subsidiaries of a third company also so resident; and any amount which would apart from this subsection be a distribution shall not constitute a distribution by virtue of subsection (2)(b) above.

(6) No transfer of assets (other than cash) or of liabilities between one company and another shall constitute, or be treated as giving rise to, a distribution by virtue of subsection (2)(b) or (4) above if they are companies—

(a) both of which are resident in the United Kingdom and neither of which is a 51 per cent. subsidiary of a company not so resident; and

(b) which, neither at the time of the transfer nor as a result of it, are under common control.

For the purposes of this subsection two companies are under common control if they are under the control of the same person or persons, and for this purpose "control" shall be construed in accordance with section 416.

(7) The question whether one body corporate is a subsidiary of another for the purpose of subsection (5) above shall be determined as a question whether it is a 51 per cent. subsidiary of that other, except that that other shall be treated as not being the owner—

(a) of any share capital which it owns directly in a body corporate, if a profit on a sale of the shares would be treated as a trading receipt of its trade; or

(b) of any share capital which it owns indirectly, and which is owned directly by a body corporate for which a profit on the sale of the shares would be a trading receipt; or

(c) of any share capital which it owns directly or indirectly in a body corporate not resident in the United Kingdom.

(8) For the purposes of subsection (2)(c) above—

(a) the value of any redeemable share capital shall be taken to be the amount of the share capital together with any premium payable on redemption, or in a winding up, or in any other circumstances; and

(b) the value of any security shall be taken to be the amount of the principal thereby secured (including any premium payable at maturity or in a winding up, or in any other circumstances);

and in determining the amount of the distribution constituted by the issue of any redeemable share capital or any security, the capital or security shall be taken at that value.

PART VI

210.—(1) Where a company—

Bonus issue following repayment of share capital.

    (a) repays any share capital or has done so at any time after 6th April 1965, and

    (b) at or after the time of that repayment issues any share capital as paid up otherwise than by the receipt of new consideration,

the amount so paid up shall, except as provided by any provision of the Corporation Tax Acts, be treated as a distribution made in respect of the shares on which it is paid up, except in so far as that amount exceeds the amount or aggregate amount of share capital so repaid less any amounts previously so paid up and treated by virtue of this subsection as distributions.

    (2) Subsection (1) above shall not apply where the repaid share capital consists of fully paid preference shares—

    (a) if those shares existed as issued and fully paid preference shares on 6th April 1965 and throughout the period from that date until the repayment those shares continued to be fully paid preference shares, or

    (b) if those shares were issued after 6th April 1965 as fully paid preference shares wholly for new consideration not derived from ordinary shares and throughout the period from their issue until the repayment those shares continued to be fully paid preference shares.

    (3) Except in relation to a company within paragraph D of section 704, subsection (1) above shall not apply if the issue of share capital mentioned in paragraph (b) of that subsection—

    (a) is of share capital other than redeemable share capital; and

    (b) takes place after 5th April 1973 and more than ten years after the repayment of share capital mentioned in paragraph (a) of that subsection.

    (4) In this section—

"ordinary shares" means shares other than preference shares;

"preference shares" means shares—

        (a) which do not carry any right to dividends other than dividends at a rate per cent. of the nominal value of the shares which is fixed, and

        (b) which carry rights in respect of dividends and capital which are comparable with those general for fixed-dividend shares quoted on the Stock Exchange; and

"new consideration not derived from ordinary shares" means new consideration other than consideration—

(a) consisting of the surrender, transfer or cancellation of ordinary shares of the company or any other company or consisting of the variation of rights in ordinary shares of the company or any other company, or

(b) derived from a repayment of share capital paid in respect of ordinary shares of the company or of any other company.

Matters to be treated or not to be treated as repayments of share capital.

211.—(1) Where—

(a) a company issues any share capital as paid up otherwise than by the receipt of new consideration, or has done so after 6th April 1965; and

(b) any amount so paid up does not fall to be treated as a qualifying distribution or, where the issue took place before 6th April 1973, did not fall to be treated as a distribution;

then, except as otherwise provided by any provision of the Corporation Tax Acts, for the purposes of sections 209 and 210, distributions afterwards made by the company in respect of shares representing that share capital shall not be treated as repayments of share capital, except to the extent to which those distributions, together with any relevant distributions previously so made, exceed the amounts so paid up (then or previously) on such shares after 6th April 1965 and not falling to be treated as qualifying distributions or, where the share capital was issued before 6th April 1973, as distributions.

(2) Except in relation to a company within paragraph D of section 704, subsection (1) above shall not prevent a distribution being treated as a repayment of share capital if it is made—

(a) more than ten years after the issue of share capital mentioned in paragraph (a) of that subsection; and

(b) in respect of share capital other than redeemable share capital.

(3) In subsection (1) above "relevant distribution" means so much of any distribution made in respect of shares representing the relevant share capital as apart from that subsection would be treated as a repayment of share capital, but by virtue of that subsection cannot be so treated.

(4) For the purposes of subsection (1) above all shares of the same class shall be treated as representing the same share capital, and where shares are issued in respect of other shares, or are directly or indirectly converted into or exchanged for other shares, all such shares shall be treated as representing the same share capital.

(5) Where share capital is issued at a premium representing new consideration, the amount of the premium is to be treated as forming part of that share capital for the purpose of determining under this Chapter whether any distribution made in respect of shares representing the share capital is to be treated as a repayment of share capital.

(6) Subsection (5) above shall not have effect in relation to any part of the premium after that part has been applied in paying up share capital.

(7) Subject to subsection (5) above, premiums paid on redemption of share capital are not to be treated as repayments of capital.

CHAPTER III

MATTERS WHICH ARE NOT DISTRIBUTIONS FOR THE PURPOSES OF THE CORPORATION TAX ACTS

Payments of interest

212.—(1) Any interest or other distribution—

Interest etc. paid in respect of certain securities.

(a) which is paid out of the assets of a company ("the borrower") to another company which is within the charge to corporation tax; and

(b) which is so paid in respect of securities of the borrower which fall within any of sub-paragraphs (i) to (iii) and (vi) of paragraph (e) of section 209(2); and

(c) which does not fall within paragraph (d) of section 209(2),

shall not be a distribution for the purposes of the Corporation Tax Acts unless the application of this subsection is excluded by subsection (2) or (3) below.

(2) Subsection (1) above does not apply in the case of any interest or other distribution which is paid in respect of a security of the borrower falling within section 209(2)(e)(iii) if—

(a) the principal secured does not exceed £100,000; and

(b) the borrower is under an obligation to repay the principal and interest before the expiry of the period of five years beginning on the date on which the principal was paid to the borrower; and

(c) that obligation either was entered into before 9th March 1982 or was entered into before 1st July 1982 pursuant to negotiations which were in progress on 9th March 1982; and

(d) where the period for repayment of either principal or interest is extended after 8th March 1982 (but paragraph (b) above still applies), the interest or other distribution is paid within the period which was applicable immediately before that date;

and for the purposes of paragraph (c) above negotiations shall not be regarded as having been in progress on 9th March 1982 unless, before that date, the borrower had applied to the lender for a loan and had supplied the lender with any documents required by him to support the application.

(3) Subsection (1) above does not apply in a case where the company to which the interest or other distribution is paid is entitled under any enactment, other than section 208, to an exemption from tax in respect of that interest or distribution.

Exempt
distributions.

Demergers

213.—(1) The provisions of this section and sections 214 to 218 have effect for facilitating certain transactions whereby trading activities carried on by a single company or group are divided so as to be carried on by two or more companies not belonging to the same group or by two or more independent groups.

(2) References in the Corporation Tax Acts to distributions of a company shall not apply to any distribution—

  (a) which falls within subsection (3) below, and

  (b) in respect of which the conditions specified in subsections (4) to (12) below are satisfied;

and any such distribution is referred to in this section as an "exempt distribution".

(3) The following distributions fall within this subsection—

  (a) a distribution consisting of the transfer to all or any of its members by a company ("the distributing company") of shares in one or more companies which are its 75 per cent. subsidiaries;

  (b) a distribution consisting of the transfer by a company ("the distributing company") to one or more other companies ("the transferee company or companies") of—

    (i) a trade or trades; or

    (ii) shares in one or more companies which are 75 per cent. subsidiaries of the distributing company,

    and the issue of shares by the transferee company or companies to all or any of the members of the distributing company;

and in this section and sections 214 to 217 references to a relevant company are to the distributing company, to each subsidiary whose shares are transferred as mentioned in paragraph (a) or (b) (ii) above and to each transferee company mentioned in paragraph (b) above.

(4) Each relevant company must be resident in the United Kingdom at the time of the distribution.

(5) The distributing company must at the time of the distribution be either a trading company or a member of a trading group and each subsidiary whose shares are transferred as mentioned in subsection (3)(a) or (b)(ii) above must at that time be either a trading company or the holding company of a trading group.

(6) In a case within subsection (3)(1)(a) above—

  (a) the shares must not be redeemable, must constitute the whole or substantially the whole of the distributing company's holding of the ordinary share capital of the subsidiary and must confer the whole or substantially the whole of the distributing company's voting rights in the subsidiary; and

  (b) subject to subsections (7) and (12)(b) below, the distributing company must after the distribution be either a trading company or the holding company of a trading group.

(7) Subsection (6)(b) above does not apply if the transfer relates to two or more 75 per cent. subsidiaries of the distributing company and that company is dissolved without there having been after the distribution any net assets of the company available for distribution in a winding up or otherwise.

(8) In a case within subsection (3)(b) above—

    (a) if a trade is transferred the distributing company must either not retain any interest or retain only a minor interest in that trade;

    (b) if shares in a subsidiary are transferred those shares must constitute the whole or substantially the whole of the distributing company's holding of the ordinary share capital of the subsidiary and must confer the whole or substantially the whole of the distributing company's voting rights in the subsidiary;

    (c) the only or main activity of the transferee company or each transferee company after the distribution must be the carrying on of the trade or the holding of the shares transferred to it;

    (d) the shares issued by the transferee company or each transferee company must not be redeemable, must constitute the whole or substantially the whole of its issued ordinary share capital and must confer the whole or substantially the whole of the voting rights in that company; and

    (e) subject to subsections (9) and (12)(b) below, the distributing company must after the distribution be either a trading company or the holding company of a trading group.

(9) Subsection (8)(e) above does not apply if there are two or more transferee companies each of which has a trade or shares in a separate 75 per cent. subsidiary of the distributing company transferred to it and the distributing company is dissolved without there having been after the distribution any net assets of the company available for distribution in a winding up or otherwise.

(10) The distribution must be made wholly or mainly for the purpose of benefiting some or all of the trading activities which before the distribution are carried on by a single company or group and after the distribution will be carried on by two or more companies or groups.

(11) The distribution must not form part of a scheme or arrangements the main purpose or one of the main purposes of which is—

    (a) the avoidance of tax (including stamp duty); or

    (b) without prejudice to paragraph (a) above, the making of a chargeable payment, as defined by section 214, or what would be such a payment if any of the companies mentioned in that section were an unquoted company; or

    (c) the acquisition by any person or persons other than members of the distributing company of control of that company, of any other relevant company or of any company which belongs to the same group as any such company; or

    (d) the cessation of a trade or its sale after the distribution.

In paragraph (c) above "group" means a company which has one or more 51 per cent. subsidiaries together with that or those subsidiaries.

(12) Where the distributing company is a 75 per cent. subsidiary of another company—

(a) the group (or, if more than one, the largest group) to which the distributing company belongs at the time of the distribution must be a trading group;

(b) subsections (6)(b) and (8)(e) above shall not apply; and

(c) the distribution must be followed by one or more other distributions falling within subsection (3)(a) or (b)(ii) above which satisfy the conditions of this section and result in members of the holding company of the group (or, if more than one, the largest group) to which the distributing company belonged at the time of the distribution becoming members of—

(i) the transferee company or each transferee company to which a trade was transferred by the distributing company; or

(ii) the subsidiary or each subsidiary whose shares were transferred by the distributing company; or

(iii) a company (other than that holding company) of which the company or companies mentioned in sub-paragraph (i) or (ii) above are 75 per cent. subsidiaries.

Chargeable payments connected with exempt distributions. **214.**—(1) If within five years after the making of an exempt distribution there is a chargeable payment—

(a) the amount or value of the payment shall be treated as income chargeable to tax under Case VI of Schedule D;

(b) unless the payment is a transfer of money's worth, sections 349(1) and 350 shall apply to the payment as if it were an annual sum payable otherwise than out of profits or gains charged to income tax;

(c) the payment shall be regarded as a distribution for the purposes of sections 337(2), 338(2)(a) and 427(4) and paragraph 3 of Schedule 19; and

(d) the payment shall not (if it otherwise would) be treated as a repayment of capital for the purposes of section 210 or 211.

(2) In this section "a chargeable payment" means any payment made otherwise than for bona fide commercial reasons or forming part of a scheme or arrangement the main purpose or one of the main purposes of which is the avoidance of tax (including stamp duty), being a payment which—

(a) a company concerned in an exempt distribution makes directly or indirectly to a member of that company or of any other company concerned in that distribution; and

(b) is made in connection with, or with any transaction affecting, the shares in that or any such company; and

(c) is not a distribution or exempt distribution or made to another company which belongs to the same group as the company making the payment.

(3) Where a company concerned in an exempt distribution is an unquoted company subsection (2)(a) above shall have effect as if any reference to the making of a payment by, or to a member of, a company concerned in the exempt distribution included a reference to the making of a payment by or to any other person in pursuance of a scheme or arrangements made with the unquoted company or, if the unquoted company is—

(a) under the control of five or fewer persons; and

(b) not under the control of (and only of) a company which is not itself under the control of five or fewer persons,

with any of the persons mentioned in paragraph (a) above.

(4) References in this section to a company concerned in an exempt distribution are to any relevant company and to any other company which was connected with any such company for the whole or any part of the period beginning with the exempt distribution and ending with the making of the payment which is in question under this section.

(5) For the purposes of subsection (4) above and this subsection a company shall be deemed to have been connected in the period referred to in that subsection with each company to which a company connected with it was connected in that period.

(6) References in this section to a payment include references to a transfer of money's worth including the assumption of a liability.

215.—(1) A distribution shall be treated as an exempt distribution in any case in which, before the distribution is made, the Board have, on the application of the distributing company, notified that company that the Board are satisfied that it will be such a distribution.

(2) A payment shall not be treated as a chargeable payment in any case in which, before the payment is made, the Board have, on the application of the person intending to make it, notified him that they are satisfied that it will be made for bona fide commercial reasons and will not form part of any scheme or arrangements the main purpose, or one of the main purposes, of which is the avoidance of tax (including stamp duty).

(3) A company which becomes or ceases to be connected with another company may make an application under subsection (2) above as respects any payments that may be made by it at any time after becoming or ceasing to be so connected (whether or not there is any present intention to make any payments); and where a notification is given by the Board on such an application no payment to which the notification relates shall be treated as a chargeable payment by reason only of the company being or having been connected with the other company.

(4) References in subsections (2) and (3) above to a payment shall be construed as in section 214.

(5) Any application under this section shall be in writing and shall contain particulars of the relevant transactions and the Board may, within 30 days of the receipt of the application or of any further

Advance clearance by Board of distributions and payments.

particulars previously required under this subsection, by notice require the applicant to furnish further particulars for the purposes of enabling the Board to make their decision; and if any such notice is not complied with within 30 days or such longer period as the Board may allow, the Board need not proceed further on the application.

(6) The Board shall notify their decision to the applicant within 30 days of receiving the application or, if they give a notice under subsection (5) above, within 30 days of the notice being complied with.

(7) If the Board notify the applicant that they are not satisfied as mentioned in subsection (1) or (2) above or do not notify their decision to the applicant within the time required by subsection (6) above, the applicant may within 30 days of the notification or of that time require the Board to transmit the application, together with any notice given and further particulars furnished under subsection (5) above, to the Special Commissioners; and in that event any notification by the Special Commissioners shall have effect for the purposes of this section as if it were a notification by the Board.

(8) If any particulars furnished under this section do not fully and accurately disclose all facts and circumstances material for the decision of the Board or the Special Commissioners, any resulting notification that the Board or Commissioners are satisfied as mentioned in subsection (1) or (2) above shall be void.

Returns.

216.—(1) Where a company makes an exempt distribution it shall within 30 days after the distribution make a return to the inspector giving particulars of the distribution and of the circumstances by reason of which it is exempt.

(2) Where within five years after the making of an exempt distribution a person makes a chargeable payment which consists of a transfer of money's worth, he shall within 30 days after the transfer make a return to the inspector giving particulars—

    (a) of the transaction effecting the transfer;

    (b) of the name and address of the recipient or each recipient and the value of what is transferred to him or each of them; and

    (c) if the transfer is accompanied by a chargeable payment consisting of a payment of money, of that payment.

(3) Subject to subsection (4) below, where within five years after the making of an exempt distribution a person makes a payment or a transfer of money's worth which would be a chargeable payment but for the fact that it is made for bona fide commercial reasons and does not form part of any such scheme or arrangements as are mentioned in section 214(2), that person shall within 30 days after making the payment or transfer make a return to the inspector giving particulars—

    (a) in the case of a transfer, of the transaction by which it is effected;

    (b) of the name and address of the recipient or each recipient and the amount of the payment made, or the value of what is transferred, to him or each of them; and

    (c) of the circumstances by reason of which the payment or transfer is not a chargeable payment.

(4) Subsection (3) above does not apply where the payment or transfer is one in relation to which a notification under section 215(3) has effect.

217.—(1) Where a distribution falling within section 213(3) has been made and the inspector has reason to believe that it may form part of any such scheme or arrangements as are mentioned in section 213(11), he may by notice require any relevant company or any person controlling any such company to furnish him within such time, not being less than 30 days, as may be specified in the notice with—

> (a) a declaration in writing stating whether or not, according to information which the company or that person has or can reasonably obtain, any such scheme or arrangements exist or have existed;

> (b) such other information as the inspector may reasonably require for the purposes of section 213(11) and the company or that person has or can reasonably obtain.

(2) If the inspector has reason to believe that a person has not delivered an account or made a return which he is required to deliver or make by virtue of section 214(1)(b) or 216(2) or (3) in respect of any payment or transfer, he may by notice require that person to furnish him within such time, not being less than 30 days, as may be specified in the notice with such information relating to the payment or transfer as he may reasonably require for the purposes of section 214.

(3) If the inspector has reason to believe that a payment or transfer has been made within five years after the making of an exempt distribution and that the payment or transfer is a chargeable payment by reason of the existence of any such scheme or arrangements as are mentioned in section 214(3), he may by notice require the person making the payment or transfer or, if that person is a company, any person controlling it to furnish him within such time, not being less than 30 days, as may be specified in the notice with—

> (a) a declaration in writing stating whether or not, according to information which that person has, or can reasonably obtain, any such scheme or arrangements exist or have existed;

> (b) such other information as the inspector may reasonably require for the purposes of section 214 and that person has or can reasonably obtain.

(4) Any recipient of a chargeable payment and any person on whose behalf such a payment is received shall, if so required by the inspector, state whether the payment received by him or on his behalf is received on behalf of any person other than himself and, if so, the name and address of that person.

218.—(1) In sections 213 to 217—

"chargeable payment" has the meaning given by section 214(2);

"control" shall be construed in accordance with section 416(2) to (6);

"distributing company" has the meaning given by section 213(3);

"exempt distribution" has the meaning given by section 213(2);

"group", except in section 213(11)(c), means a company which has one or more 75 per cent. subsidiaries together with that or those subsidiaries;

"holding company" means a company whose business (disregarding any trade carried on by it) consists wholly or mainly of the holding of shares or securities of one or more companies which are its 75 per cent. subsidiaries;

"member", where the reference is to a member of a company, does not, except in section 214(2)(a), include a person who is a member otherwise than by virtue of holding shares forming part of the company's ordinary share capital;

"relevant company" has the meaning given by section 213(3);

"shares" includes stock;

"trade", except in subsection (3) below, does not include dealing in shares, securities, land, trades or commodity futures and "trading activities" shall be construed accordingly;

"trading company" means a company whose business consists wholly or mainly of the carrying on of a trade or trades;

"trading group" means a group the business of whose members, taken together, consists wholly or mainly in the carrying on of a trade or trades; and

"unquoted company" means a company which does not satisfy the condition that its shares or some class thereof (disregarding debenture or loan stock, preferred shares or preferred stock) are listed in the Official List of the Stock Exchange and are dealt in on the Stock Exchange regularly or from time to time, so however that this definition does not apply to a company under the control of (and only of) one or more companies to which this definition does not apply.

(2) In determining for the purposes of section 213(3) to (9) whether a company whose shares are transferred by the distributing company is a 75 per cent. subsidiary of the distributing company there shall be disregarded any share capital of the first-mentioned company which is owned indirectly by the distributing company.

(3) In determining for the purposes of sections 213 to 217 whether one company is a 75 per cent. subsidiary of another, the other company shall be treated as not being the owner of—

(a) any share capital which it owns directly in a body corporate if a profit on a sale of the shares would be treated as a trading receipt of its trade; or

(b) any share capital which it owns indirectly and which is owned directly by a body corporate for which a profit on the sale of the shares would be a trading receipt.

(4) Section 839 applies for the purposes of sections 213 to 217.

Purchase of own shares

219.—(1) References in the Corporation Tax Acts to distributions of a company shall not include references to a payment made by a company on the redemption, repayment or purchase of its own shares if the company is an unquoted trading company or the unquoted holding company of a trading group and either—

    (a) the redemption, repayment or purchase is made wholly or mainly for the purpose of benefiting a trade carried on by the company or by any of its 75 per cent. subsidiaries, and does not form part of a scheme or arrangement the main purpose or one of the main purposes of which is—

        (i) to enable the owner of the shares to participate in the profits of the company without receiving a dividend, or

        (ii) the avoidance of tax; and

    the conditions specified in sections 220 to 224, so far as applicable, are satisfied in relation to the owner of the shares; or

    (b) the whole or substantially the whole of the payment (apart from any sum applied in paying capital gains tax charged on the redemption, repayment or purchase) is applied by the person to whom it is made in discharging a liability of his for inheritance tax charged on a death and is so applied within the period of two years after the death;

and in sections 220 to 224—

    "the purchase" means the redemption, repayment or purchase referred to in subsection (1)(a) above; and

    "the vendor" means the owner of the shares at the time it is made.

(2) Where, apart from this subsection, a payment falls within subsection (1)(b) above, subsection (1) above shall not apply to the extent that the liability in question could without undue hardship have been discharged otherwise than through the redemption, repayment or purchase of shares in the company or another unquoted company which is a trading company or the holding company of a trading group.

220.—(1) The vendor must be resident and ordinarily resident in the United Kingdom in the year of assessment in which the purchase is made and if the shares are held through a nominee the nominee must also be so resident and ordinarily resident.

(2) The residence and ordinary residence of trustees shall be determined for the purposes of this section as they are determined under section 52 of the 1979 Act for the purposes of that Act.

(3) The residence and ordinary residence of personal representatives shall be taken for the purposes of this section to be the same as the residence and ordinary residence of the deceased immediately before his death.

(4) The references in this section to a person's ordinary residence shall be disregarded in the case of a company.

(5) The shares must have been owned by the vendor throughout the period of five years ending with the date of the purchase.

(6) If at any time during that period the shares were transferred to the vendor by a person who was then his spouse living with him then, unless that person is alive at the date of the purchase but is no longer the vendor's spouse living with him, any period during which the shares were owned by that person shall be treated for the purposes of subsection (5) above as a period of ownership by the vendor.

(7) Where the vendor became entitled to the shares under the will or on the intestacy of a previous owner or is the personal representative of a previous owner—

(a) any period during which the shares were owned by the previous owner or his personal representatives shall be treated for the purposes of subsection (5) above as a period of ownership by the vendor, and

(b) that subsection shall have effect as if it referred to three years instead of five.

(8) In determining whether the condition in subsection (5) above is satisfied in a case where the vendor acquired shares of the same class at different times—

(a) shares acquired earlier shall be taken into account before shares acquired later, and

(b) any previous disposal by him of shares of that class shall be assumed to be a disposal of shares acquired later rather than of shares acquired earlier.

(9) If for the purposes of capital gains tax the time when shares were acquired would be determined under any provision of Chapter II of Part IV of the 1979 Act (reorganisation of share capital, conversion of securities, etc.) then, unless the shares were allotted for payment or were comprised in share capital to which section 249 applies, it shall be determined in the same way for the purposes of this section.

221.—(1) If immediately after the purchase the vendor owns shares in the company, then, subject to section 224, the vendor's interest as a shareholder must be substantially reduced.

(2) If immediately after the purchase any associate of the vendor owns shares in the company then, subject to section 224, the combined interests as shareholders of the vendor and his associates must be substantially reduced.

(3) The question whether the combined interests as shareholders of the vendor and his associates are substantially reduced shall be determined in the same way as is (under the following subsections) the question whether a vendor's interest as a shareholder is substantially reduced, except that the vendor shall be assumed to have the interests of his associates as well as his own.

(4) Subject to subsection (5) below, the vendor's interest as a shareholder shall be taken to be substantially reduced if and only if the total nominal value of the shares owned by him immediately after the purchase, expressed as a fraction of the issued share capital of the company at that time, does not exceed 75 per cent. of the corresponding fraction immediately before the purchase.

(5) The vendor's interest as a shareholder shall not be taken to be substantially reduced where—

(a) he would, if the company distributed all its profits available for distribution immediately after the purchase, be entitled to a share of those profits, and

(b) that share, expressed as a fraction of the total of those profits, exceeds 75 per cent. of the corresponding fraction immediately before the purchase.

(6) In determining for the purposes of subsection (5) above the division of profits among the persons entitled to them, a person entitled to periodic distributions calculated by reference to fixed rates or amounts shall be regarded as entitled to a distribution of the amount or maximum amount to which he would be entitled for a year.

(7) In subsection (5) above "profits available for distribution" has the same meaning as it has for the purposes of Part VIII of the Companies Act 1985, except that for the purposes of that subsection the amount of the profits available for distribution (whether immediately before or immediately after the purchase) shall be treated as increased— 1985 c. 6.

(a) in the case of every company, by £100, and

(b) in the case of a company from which any person is entitled to periodic distributions of the kind mentioned in subsection (6) above, by a further amount equal to that required to make the distribution to which he is entitled in accordance with that subsection;

and where the aggregate of the sums payable by the company on the purchase and on any contemporaneous redemption, repayment or purchase of other shares of the company exceeds the amount of the profits available for distribution immediately before the purchase, that amount shall be treated as further increased by an amount equal to the excess.

(8) References in this section to entitlement are, except in the case of trustees and personal representatives, references to beneficial entitlement.

222.—(1) Subject to section 224, where the company making the purchase is immediately before the purchase a member of a group and— Conditions applicable where purchasing company is member of group.

(a) immediately after the purchase the vendor owns shares in one or more other members of the group (whether or not he then owns shares in the company making the purchase), or

(b) immediately after the purchase the vendor owns shares in the company making the purchase and immediately before the purchase he owned shares in one or more other members of the group,

the vendor's interest as a shareholder in the group must be substantially reduced.

(2) In subsections (5) to (7) below "relevant company" means the company making the purchase and any other member of the group in which the vendor owns shares immediately before or immediately after the purchase, but subject to subsection (4) below.

(3) Subject to section 224, where the company making the purchase is immediately before the purchase a member of a group and at that time an associate of the vendor owns shares in any member of the group, the combined interests as shareholders in the group of the vendor and his associates must be substantially reduced.

(4) The question whether the combined interests as shareholders in the group of the vendor and his associates are substantially reduced shall be determined in the same way as is (under the following subsections) the question whether a vendor's interest as a shareholder in a group is substantially reduced, except that the vendor shall be assumed to have the interests of his associates as well as his own (and references in subsections (5) to (7) below to a relevant company shall be construed accordingly).

(5) The vendor's interest as a shareholder in the group shall be ascertained by—

(a) expressing the total nominal value of the shares owned by him in each relevant company as a fraction of the issued share capital of the company,

(b) adding together the fractions so obtained, and

(c) dividing the result by the number of relevant companies (including any in which he owns no shares).

(6) Subject to subsection (7) below, the vendor's interest as a shareholder in the group shall be taken to be substantially reduced if and only if it does not exceed 75 per cent. of the corresponding interest immediately before the purchase.

(7) The vendor's interest as a shareholder in the group shall not be taken to be substantially reduced if—

(a) he would, if every member of the group distributed all its profits available for distribution immediately after the purchase (including any profits received by it on a distribution by another member), be entitled to a share of the profits of one or more of them, and

(b) that share, or the aggregate of those shares, expressed as a fraction of the aggregate of the profits available for distribution of every member of the group which is—

(i) a relevant company, or

(ii) a 51 per cent. subsidiary of a relevant company,

exceeds 75 per cent. of the corresponding fraction immediately before the purchase.

(8) Subsections (6) and (7) of section 221 shall apply for the purposes of subsection (7) above as they apply for the purposes of subsection (5) of that section.

(9) Subject to the following subsections, in this section "group" means a company which has one or more 51 per cent. subsidiaries, but is not itself a 51 per cent. subsidiary of any other company, together with those subsidiaries.

(10) Where the whole or a significant part of the business carried on by an unquoted company ("the successor company") was previously carried on by—

(a) the company making the purchase, or

(b) a company which is (apart from this subsection) a member of a group to which the company making the purchase belongs,

the successor company and any company of which it is a 51 per cent. subsidiary shall be treated as being a member of the same group as the company making the purchase (whether or not, apart from this subsection, the company making the purchase is a member of a group).

(11) Subsection (10) above shall not apply if the successor company first carried on the business there referred to more than three years before the time of the purchase.

(12) For the purposes of this section a company which has ceased to be a 51 per cent. subsidiary of another company before the time of the purchase shall be treated as continuing to be such a subsidiary if at that time there exist arrangements under which it could again become such a subsidiary.

223.—(1) Subject to section 224, the vendor must not immediately after the purchase be connected with the company making the purchase or with any company which is a member of the same group as that company.

In this subsection "group" has the same meaning as it has for the purposes of section 222.

(2) Subject to section 224, the purchase must not be part of a scheme or arrangement which is designed or likely to result in the vendor or any associate of his having interests in any company such that, if he had those interests immediately after the purchase, any of the conditions in sections 221 and 222 and subsection (1) above could not be satisfied.

(3) A transaction occurring within one year after the purchase shall be deemed for the purposes of subsection (2) above to be part of a scheme or arrangement of which the purchase is also part.

Other conditions.

224. Where—

(a) any of the conditions in sections 221 to 223 which are applicable are not satisfied in relation to the vendor, but

(b) he proposed or agreed to the purchase in order that the condition in section 221(2) or 222(3) could be satisfied in respect of the redemption, repayment or purchase of shares owned by a person of whom he is an associate,

then, to the extent that that result is produced by virtue of the purchase, section 219(1)(a) shall have effect as if the conditions in sections 221 to 223 were satisfied in relation to the vendor.

Relaxation of conditions in certain cases.

225.—(1) A payment made by a company on the redemption, repayment or purchase of its own shares shall be deemed—

(a) to be one to which section 219 applies if, before it is made, the Board have on the application of the company notified the company that they are satisfied that the section will apply; and

Advance clearance of payments by Board.

PART VI

(b) to be one to which section 219 does not apply if, before it is made, the Board have on the application of the company notified the company that they are satisfied that the section will not apply.

(2) An application under this section shall be in writing and shall contain particulars of the relevant transactions; and the Board may, within 30 days of the receipt of the application or of any further particulars previously required under this subsection, by notice require the applicant to furnish further particulars for the purpose of enabling the Board to make their decision.

(3) If a notice under subsection (2) above is not complied with within 30 days or such longer period as the Board may allow, the Board need not proceed further on the application.

(4) The Board shall notify their decision to the applicant within 30 days of receiving the application or, if they give a notice under subsection (2) above, within 30 days of the notice being complied with.

(5) If particulars furnished under this section do not fully and accurately disclose all facts and circumstances material for the decision of the Board, any resulting notification by the Board shall be void.

Returns and information.

226.—(1) A company which treats a payment made by it as one to which section 219 applies shall within 60 days after making the payment make a return to the inspector giving particulars of the payment and of the circumstances by reason of which that section is regarded as applying to it.

(2) Where a company treats a payment made by it as one to which section 219(1)(a) applies, any person connected with the company who knows of any such scheme or arrangement affecting the payment as is mentioned in section 223(2) shall, within 60 days after he first knows of both the payment and the scheme or arrangement, give a notice to the inspector containing particulars of the scheme or arrangement.

(3) Where the inspector has reason to believe that a payment treated by the company making it as one to which section 219(1)(a) applies may form part of a scheme or arrangement of the kind referred to therein or in section 223(2), he may by notice require the company or any person who is connected with the company to furnish him within such time, not being less than 60 days, as may be specified in the notice with—

(a) a declaration in writing stating whether or not, according to information which the company or that person has or can reasonably obtain, any such scheme or arrangement exists or has existed, and

(b) such other information as the inspector may reasonably require for the purposes of the provision in question and the company or that person has or can reasonably obtain.

(4) The recipient of a payment treated by the company making it as one to which section 219 applies, and any person on whose behalf such a payment is received, shall if so required by the inspector state whether the payment received by him or on his behalf is received on behalf of any person other than himself and, if so, the name and address of that person.

227.—(1) Any question whether a person is an associate of another in relation to a company shall be determined for the purposes of sections 219 to 226 and 228 in accordance with the following provisions of this section.

(2) A husband and wife living together are associates of one another, a person under the age of 18 is an associate of his parents, and his parents are his associates.

(3) A person connected with a company is an associate of the company and of any company controlled by it, and the company and any company controlled by it are his associates.

(4) Where a person connected with one company has control of another company, the second company is an associate of the first.

(5) Where shares in a company are held by trustees (other than bare trustees) then in relation to that company, but subject to subsection (8) below, the trustees are associates of—

(a) any person who directly or indirectly provided property to the trustees or has made a reciprocal arrangement for another to do so,

(b) any person who is, by virtue of subsection (2) above, an associate of a person within paragraph (a) above, and

(c) any person who is or may become beneficially entitled to a significant interest in the shares;

and any such person is an associate of the trustees,

(6) Where shares in a company are comprised in the estate of a deceased person, then in relation to that company the deceased's personal representatives are associates of any person who is or may become beneficially entitled to a significant interest in the shares, and any such person is an associate of the personal representatives.

(7) Where one person is accustomed to act on the directions of another in relation to the affairs of a company, then in relation to that company the two persons are associates of one another.

(8) Subsection (5) above shall not apply to shares held on trusts which—

(a) relate exclusively to an exempt approved scheme as defined in Chapter I of Part XIV, or

(b) are exclusively for the benefit of the employees, or the employees and directors, of the company referred to in that subsection or of companies in a group to which that company belongs, or their dependants (and are not wholly or mainly for the benefit of directors or their relatives);

and for the purposes of this subsection "group" means a company which has one or more 51 per cent. subsidiaries, together with those subsidiaries.

(9) For the purposes of subsections (5) and (6) above a person's interest is significant if its value exceeds 5 per cent. of the value of all the property held on the trusts or, as the case may be, comprised in the estate concerned, excluding any property in which he is not and cannot become beneficially entitled to an interest.

228.—(1) Any question whether a person is connected with a company shall be determined for the purposes of sections 219 to 227 in accordance with the following provisions of this section.

(2) A person is connected with a company if he directly or indirectly possesses or is entitled to acquire more than 30 per cent. of—

(a) the issued ordinary share capital of the company, or

(b) the loan capital and issued share capital of the company, or

(c) the voting power in the company.

(3) Where a person—

(a) acquired or became entitled to acquire loan capital of a company in the ordinary course of a business carried on by him, being a business which includes the lending of money, and

(b) takes no part in the management or conduct of the company,

his interest in that loan capital shall be disregarded for the purposes of subsection (2) above.

(4) A person is connected with a company if he directly or indirectly possesses or is entitled to acquire such rights as would, in the event of the winding up of the company or in any other circumstances, entitle him to receive more than 30 per cent. of the assets of the company which would then be available for distribution to equity holders of the company; and for the purposes of this subsection—

(a) the persons who are equity holders of the company, and

(b) the percentage of the assets of the company to which a person would be entitled,

shall be determined in accordance with paragraphs 1 and 3 of Schedule 18, taking references in paragraph 3 to the first company as references to an equity holder and references to a winding up as including references to any other circumstances in which assets of the company are available for distribution to its equity holders.

(5) A person is connected with a company if he has control of it.

(6) References in this section to the loan capital of a company are references to any debt incurred by the company—

(a) for any money borrowed or capital assets acquired by the company, or

(b) for any right to receive income created in favour of the company, or

(c) for consideration the value of which to the company was (at the time when the debt was incurred) substantially less than the amount of the debt (including any premium thereon).

(7) For the purposes of this section a person shall be treated as entitled to acquire anything which he is entitled to acquire at a future date or will at a future date be entitled to acquire.

(8) For the purposes of this section a person shall be assumed to have the rights or powers of his associates as well as his own.

229.—(1) In sections 219 to 228— PART VI
Other
interpretative
provisions.

"control" has the meaning given by section 840;

"holding company" means a company whose business (disregarding any trade carried on by it) consists wholly or mainly of the holding of shares or securities of one or more companies which are its 75 per cent. subsidiaries;

"personal representatives" means persons responsible for administering the estate of a deceased person;

"quoted company" means a company whose shares (or any class of whose shares) are listed in the official list of a stock exchange;

"shares" includes stock;

"trade" does not include dealing in shares, securities, land or futures and "trading activities" shall be construed accordingly;

"trading company" means a company whose business consists wholly or mainly of the carrying on of a trade or trades;

"trading group" means a group the business of whose members, taken together, consists wholly or mainly of the carrying on of a trade or trades, and for this purpose "group" means a company which has one or more 75 per cent. subsidiaries together with those subsidiaries; and

"unquoted company" means a company which is neither a quoted company nor a 51 per cent. subsidiary of a quoted company.

(2) References in sections 219 to 228 to the owner of shares are references to the beneficial owner except where the shares are held on trusts (other than bare trusts) or are comprised in the estate of a deceased person, and in such a case are references to the trustees or, as the case may be, to the deceased's personal representatives.

(3) References in sections 219 to 228 to a payment made by a company include references to anything else that is, or would but for section 219 be, a distribution.

Stock dividends

230. Any share capital to which section 249 applies and which is issued by a company either as mentioned in subsection (4), (5) or (6) of that section or to a close company as mentioned in paragraph 12(1) of Schedule 19 (read in either case with subsection (3) of that section)— Stock dividends: distributions.

(a) shall, notwithstanding section 209(2)(c), not constitute a distribution within the meaning of section 209(2); and

(b) for purposes of sections 210 and 211 shall not be treated as issued "as paid up otherwise than by the receipt of new consideration".

CHAPTER IV

TAX CREDITS

Tax credits for certain recipients of qualifying distributions.

231.—(1) Subject to sections 95(1)(b) and 247, where a company resident in the United Kingdom makes a qualifying distribution and the person receiving the distribution is another such company or a person resident in the United Kingdom, not being a company, the recipient of the distribution shall be entitled to a tax credit equal to such proportion of the amount or value of the distribution as corresponds to the rate of advance corporation tax in force for the financial year in which the distribution is made.

(2) Subject to section 241(5), a company resident in the United Kingdom which is entitled to a tax credit in respect of a distribution may claim to have the amount of the credit paid to it if—

(a) the company is wholly exempt from corporation tax or is only not exempt in respect of trading income; or

(b) the distribution is one in relation to which express exemption is given (otherwise than by section 208), whether specifically or by virtue of a more general exemption from tax, under any provision of the Tax Acts.

(3) A person, not being a company resident in the United Kingdom, who is entitled to a tax credit in respect of a distribution may claim to have the credit set against the income tax chargeable on his income under section 3 or on his total income for the year of assessment in which the distribution is made and where the credit exceeds that income tax, to have the excess paid to him.

(4) Where a distribution mentioned in subsection (1) above is, or falls to be treated as, or under any provision of the Tax Acts is deemed to be, the income of a person other than the recipient, that person shall be treated for the purposes of this section as receiving the distribution (and accordingly the question whether he is entitled to a tax credit in respect of it shall be determined by reference to where he, and not the actual recipient, is resident); and where any such distribution is income of a United Kingdom trust the trustees shall be entitled to a tax credit in respect of it if no other person falls to be treated for the purposes of this section as receiving the distribution.

(5) In subsection (4) above "United Kingdom trust" means a trust administered under the law of any part of the United Kingdom, not being a trust the general administration of which is ordinarily carried on outside the United Kingdom and the trustees, or a majority of the trustees, of which are resident or ordinarily resident outside the United Kingdom.

Tax credits for non-U.K. residents.

232.—(1) An individual who, having made a claim in that behalf, is entitled to relief under Chapter I of Part VII by virtue of section 278(2) in respect of any year of assessment shall be entitled to a tax credit in respect of any qualifying distribution received by him in that year to the same extent as if he were resident in the United Kingdom.

(2) Where a qualifying distribution is income of a fund to which section 615(2)(b) or (c) applies the persons entitled to receive the income shall be entitled to a tax credit in respect of the distribution to the same extent as a recipient mentioned in section 231(1).

(3) Where a qualifying distribution is income of, or of the government of, any sovereign power or of any international organisation, that power, government or organisation shall be entitled to a tax credit in respect of the distribution to the same extent as a recipient mentioned in section 231(1).

In this subsection "international organisation" means an organisation of which two or more sovereign powers, or the governments of two or more sovereign powers, are members; and if in any proceedings a question arises whether a person is within this subsection, a certificate issued by or under the authority of the Secretary of State stating any fact relevant to that question shall be conclusive evidence of that fact.

233.—(1) Where in any year of assessment the income of any person, not being a company resident in the United Kingdom, includes a distribution in respect of which that person is not entitled to a tax credit—

> (a) no assessment shall be made on that person in respect of income tax at the basic rate on the amount or value of the distribution;
>
> (b) that person's liability under any assessment made in respect of income tax at a higher rate on the amount or value of the distribution or on any part of the distribution shall be reduced by a sum equal to income tax at the basic rate on so much of the distribution as is assessed at that higher rate;
>
> (c) the amount or value of the distribution shall be treated for the purposes of sections 348 and 349(1) as not brought into charge to income tax.

(2) Where a person has paid tax ("the tax paid") in respect of excess liability on, or on any part of, a non-qualifying distribution, then if, apart from this subsection, he would be liable to pay an amount of tax in respect of excess liability on, or on any part of, a repayment of the share capital or of the principal of the security which constituted that non-qualifying distribution, he shall be so liable only to the extent (if any) to which that amount exceeds the amount of the tax paid.

In this subsection—

> "excess liability" means the excess of liability to income tax over what it would be if all income tax were charged at the basic rate to the exclusion of any higher rate;
>
> "non-qualifying distribution" means a distribution which is not a qualifying distribution.

234.—(1) Without prejudice to subsections (3) and (4) below but subject to section 95(1)(c), a company which makes a qualifying distribution shall, if the recipient so requests in writing, furnish to him a statement in writing showing the amount or value of the distribution and (whether or not the recipient is a person entitled to a tax credit in respect of the distribution) the amount of the tax credit to which a recipient who is such a person is entitled in respect of that distribution.

(2) The duty imposed by subsection (1) above shall be enforceable at the suit or instance of the person requesting the information.

(3) Every warrant or cheque or other order drawn or made, or purporting to be drawn or made, in payment of any dividend or interest distributed by any company, being a company within the meaning of the Companies Act 1985 or the Companies (Northern Ireland) Order 1986, or a company created by letters patent or by or in pursuance of an Act, shall have annexed to itself or be accompanied by a statement in writing showing—

    (a) in the case of interest which is not a qualifying distribution—

        (i) the gross amount which, after deduction of the income tax appropriate thereto, corresponds to the net amount actually paid;

        (ii) the rate and the amount of income tax appropriate to such gross amount, and

        (iii) the net amount actually paid;

    (b) in the case of a dividend or interest which is a qualifying distribution, each of the following amounts—

        (i) the amount of the dividend or interest paid, and

        (ii) (whether or not the recipient is a person entitled to a tax credit in respect of that distribution) the amount of the tax credit to which a recipient who is such a person is entitled in respect of that distribution.

(4) If a company fails to comply with the provisions of subsection (3) above, the company shall in respect of each offence incur a penalty of £10 except that the aggregate amount of any penalties imposed under this subsection on any company in respect of offences connected with any one distribution of dividends or interest shall not exceed £100.

(5) Where a company makes a distribution which is not a qualifying distribution it shall make a return to the inspector—

    (a) within 14 days from the end of the accounting period in which the distribution is made; or

    (b) if the distribution is made on a date not falling in an accounting period, within 14 days from that date.

(6) A return under subsection (5) above shall contain—

    (a) particulars of the transaction giving rise to the distribution; and

    (b) the name and address of the person, or each of the persons, receiving the distribution, and the amount or value of the distribution received by him or by each of them.

(7) Where it is not in the circumstances apparent whether a transaction gives rise to a distribution in respect of which a return is required to be made under subsection (5) above, the company shall—

    (a) within the time within which such a return would be required to be made if the transaction did give rise to such a distribution, make a return to the inspector containing particulars of the transaction in question; and

(b) if required by a notice served on the company by the inspector, furnish him within the time specified in the notice with such further information in relation to the transaction as he may reasonably require.

(8) If it appears to the inspector that particulars of any transaction ought to have been and have not been included in a return under subsection (5) or (7) above, he may by a notice served on the company require the company to furnish him within the time specified in the notice with such information relating thereto as he may reasonably require.

(9) Any power which the inspector may exercise under paragraph 17 of Schedule 19 for the purposes of that Schedule may be exercised by him for the purposes of subsections (5) to (8) above.

235.—(1) Where a person entitled to a tax credit in respect of a distribution to which this section applies is, by reason of any exemption from tax, entitled to recover tax and his holding (together with any associated holding) of any one class of the shares, securities or rights by virtue of which he is entitled to the distribution amounts to not less than 10 per cent. thereof, subsection (3) below shall apply to the income represented by any part of the distribution which is not a part— Distributions of exempt funds etc.

(a) to which profits arising after the date of acquisition are attributable in accordance with section 236; or

(b) in relation to which the date of acquisition is earlier than 6th April 1965.

(2) For the purposes of this section and section 236, the date of acquisition, in relation to any part of a distribution or profits attributable to it, is the date on which the shares, securities or rights by virtue of which a person is entitled to that part were acquired by him.

(3) Where this subsection applies to any income—

(a) the exemption from tax shall not extend to that income; and

(b) it shall be treated for the purposes of sections 348 and 349(1) as not brought into charge to income tax; and

(c) no amount of interest shall be deducted from or set off against it under section 353.

(4) Where, by virtue of this section, an exemption from tax does not apply to any income represented by a distribution or part of a distribution, the person entitled to the income shall be liable to tax or, as the case may be, additional tax, on it at a rate equal to the additional rate in force at the time the distribution is made and shall be assessable to income tax or corporation tax accordingly.

(5) This section applies to any qualifying distribution except any amount which is treated as such in accordance with section 209(3) or sections 210 and 211.

236.—(1) Section 235 shall be construed in accordance with the following provisions of this section. Provisions supplementary to section 235.

(2) Two or more holdings are associated if they were acquired by persons acting in concert or under arrangements made by any person.

(3) There shall be attributed—

    (a) to the distributions made by a company at any time (whether before or after the passing of this Act) in respect of any class of shares, securities or rights such of its relevant profits arising after the date of acquisition and before that time as remain after allowing for earlier distributions made in respect of that or any other class of shares, securities or rights, and for distributions made at or to be made after that time in respect of other classes of shares, securities or rights; and

    (b) to any part of a distribution made at any time to which a person is entitled by virtue of any part of his holding of any class of shares, securities or rights, such proportion of the profits attributable under paragraph (a) above to the distributions made at that time in respect of that class as corresponds to that part of his holding.

(4) For the purposes of subsection (3) above profits arising in part of an accounting period shall be taken to be a proportionate part of the profits arising in the whole of the accounting period except where a different method of arriving at the profits arising in that part can be shown to be fair and reasonable.

(5) For the purposes of this section the relevant profits of a company are, subject to subsection (6) below, its profits computed on a commercial basis after allowing for any provision properly made for corporation tax; and the computation shall be made without regard to any capital gains or losses or to any such amount as is mentioned in section 235(5), and—

    (a) shall include franked investment income received from any company not related to the first-mentioned company; and

    (b) shall exclude group income and franked investment income received from a company related to the first-mentioned company.

(6) There shall be treated as included in the relevant profits of a company the appropriate portion of the relevant profits of any company related to it.

(7) For the purposes of this section a company ("the owned company") is related to another company ("the owning company") if—

    (a) the owning company owns not less than 10 per cent. of any one class of shares in the owned company; or

    (b) any company related to the owning company owns not less than 10 per cent. of any one class of shares in the owned company;

and the appropriate proportion of the relevant profits of a related company is that proportion of those profits which the owning company would receive by virtue of the shares, securities or rights owned by it, if all the relevant profits of the owned company were distributed and, so far as received directly or indirectly by a company related to the owning company, were distributed by that related company, no account being taken of any profits arising at a time when the owned company was not related to the owning company.

237.—(1) This section has effect where any person ("the recipient") receives an amount treated as a distribution by virtue of section 209(3) or 210 or 211(1); and in this section—

PART VI

Disallowance of reliefs in respect of bonus issues.

(a) any such distribution is referred to as a bonus issue; and

(b) "relevant tax credit" in relation to a bonus issue means the tax credit to which the recipient becomes entitled in respect of the bonus issue.

(2) Subject to subsection (6) below, if the recipient is entitled by reason of—

(a) any exemption from tax, or

(b) the setting-off of losses against profits or income,

to recover tax in respect of any distribution received by him, no account shall be taken for the purposes of any such exemption or set-off of any bonus issue or relevant tax credit received by him.

(3) Subject to subsection (6) below, where, by virtue of this section, no account is to be taken for the purposes of any exemption from tax of any bonus issue and the relevant tax credit, the person entitled to that issue and that credit shall be liable to tax or, as the case may be, additional tax, on them at a rate equal to the additional rate in force at the time the bonus issue is made and shall be assessable to income tax or corporation tax accordingly.

(4) Subject to subsection (6) below, a bonus issue and the relevant tax credit shall be treated for the purposes of sections 241 and 244 as not being franked investment income.

(5) Subject to subsection (6) below—

(a) the relevant tax credit relating to a bonus issue shall not be available to set against any income tax which the recipient is entitled to deduct under section 348 or with which he is chargeable by virtue of section 349(1), and

(b) no interest may be deducted or set off under section 353 from or against so much of a person's income as consists of bonus issues and relevant tax credits.

(6) Nothing in subsections (2) to (5) above shall affect the proportion (if any) of any bonus issue made in respect of any shares or securities which, if it were declared as a dividend, would represent a normal return to the recipient on the consideration provided by him for the relevant shares or securities, that is to say, those in respect of which the bonus issue was made and, if those securities are derived from shares or securities previously acquired by the recipient, the shares or securities which were previously acquired; nor shall anything in those subsections affect the like proportion of the relevant tax credit relating to that bonus issue.

(7) For the purposes of subsection (6) above—

(a) if the consideration provided by the recipient for any of the relevant shares or securities was in excess of their market value at the time he acquired them, or if no consideration was provided by him for any of the relevant shares or securities, the recipient shall be taken to have provided for those shares or securities consideration equal to their market value at the time he acquired them; and

(b) in determining whether an amount received by way of dividend exceeds a normal return, regard shall be had to the length of time previous to the receipt of that amount since the recipient first acquired any of the relevant shares or securities and to any dividends and other distributions made in respect of them during that time.

CHAPTER V

ADVANCE CORPORATION TAX AND FRANKED INVESTMENT INCOME

Interpretation of terms and collection of ACT.

238.—(1) In this Chapter—

"franked investment income" means income of a company resident in the United Kingdom which consists of a distribution in respect of which the company is entitled to a tax credit (and which accordingly represents income equal to the aggregate of the amount or value of the distribution and the amount of that credit), but subject to section 247(2);

"franked payment" means the sum of the amount or value of a qualifying distribution and such proportion of that amount or value as corresponds to the rate of advance corporation tax in force for the financial year in which the distribution is made, but subject to section 247(2);

"surplus advance corporation tax" has the meaning given by section 239(3);

"surplus of franked investment income" means any such excess as is mentioned in subsection (3) of section 241 (calculated without regard to franked investment income which by virtue of subsection (5) of that section cannot be used to frank distributions);

"tax credit" means a tax credit under section 231;

and references to any accounting or other period in which a franked payment is made are references to the period in which the distribution in question is made.

(2) References in this Chapter to distributions or payments received by a company apply to any received by another person on behalf of or in trust for the company but not to any received by the company on behalf of or in trust for another person.

(3) References in this Chapter to using franked investment income to frank distributions of a company shall be construed in accordance with section 241(5).

(4) References in this Chapter to an amount of profits on which corporation tax falls finally to be borne are references to the amount of those profits after making all deductions and giving all reliefs that for the

purposes of corporation tax are made or given from or against those profits, including deductions and reliefs which under any provision are treated as reducing them for those purposes.

(5) Schedule 13 shall have effect for the purpose of regulating the time and manner in which advance corporation tax is to be accounted for and paid.

239.—(1) Subject to section 497 and subsection (2) below, advance corporation tax paid by a company (and not repaid) in respect of any distribution made by it in an accounting period shall be set against its liability to corporation tax on any profits charged to corporation tax for that accounting period and shall accordingly discharge a corresponding amount of that liability.

Set-off of ACT against liability to corporation tax.

(2) The amount of advance corporation tax to be set against a company's liability for any accounting period under subsection (1) above shall not exceed the amount of advance corporation tax that would have been payable (apart from section 241) in respect of a distribution made at the end of that period of an amount which, together with the advance corporation tax so payable in respect of it, is equal to the company's profits charged to corporation tax for that period.

(3) Where in the case of any accounting period of a company there is an amount of surplus advance corporation tax, the company may, within two years after the end of that period, claim to have the whole or any part of that amount treated for the purposes of this section (but not of any further application of this subsection) as if it were advance corporation tax paid in respect of distributions made by the company in any of its accounting periods beginning in the six years preceding that period (but so that the amount which is the subject of the claim is set, so far as possible, against the company's liability for a more recent accounting period before a more remote one) and corporation tax shall, so far as may be required, be repaid accordingly.

In this subsection "surplus advance corporation tax", in relation to any accounting period of a company, means advance corporation tax which cannot be set against the company's liability to corporation tax for that period because the company has no profits charged to corporation tax for that period or because of subsection (2) above or section 797(4).

(4) Where in the case of any accounting period of a company there is an amount of surplus advance corporation tax which has not been dealt with under subsection (3) above, that amount shall be treated for the purposes of this section (including any further application of this subsection) as if it were advance corporation tax paid in respect of distributions made by the company in the next accounting period.

(5) Effect shall be given to subsections (1) and (4) above as if on a claim in that behalf by the company and, for that purpose, a return made by the company under section 11 of the Management Act containing particulars of advance corporation tax or surplus advance corporation tax which falls to be dealt with under those subsections shall be treated as a claim.

(6) For the purposes of this section the profits of a company charged to corporation tax for any period shall be taken to be the amount of its profits for that period on which corporation tax falls finally to be borne.

(7) This section has effect subject to subsections (5) to (7) of section 430 and the following provisions of this Chapter.

Set-off of company's surplus ACT against subsidiary's liability to corporation tax.

240.—(1) Where a company ("the surrendering company") has paid an amount of advance corporation tax in respect of a dividend or dividends paid by it in an accounting period and the advance corporation tax has not been repaid, it may, on making a claim, surrender the benefit of the whole or any part of that amount—

(a) to any company which was a subsidiary of the surrendering company throughout that accounting period, or

(b) in such proportions as the surrendering company may determine, to any two or more companies which were subsidiaries of the surrendering company throughout that period.

(2) Subject to subsections (4) and (5) below, where the benefit of any amount of advance corporation tax ("the surrendered amount") is surrendered under this section to a subsidiary, then—

(a) if the advance corporation tax mentioned in subsection (1) above was paid in respect of one dividend only or of dividends all of which were paid on the same date, the subsidiary shall be treated for the purposes of section 239 as having paid an amount of advance corporation tax equal to the surrendered amount in respect of a distribution made by it on the date on which the dividend or dividends were paid;

(b) if the advance corporation tax mentioned in subsection (1) above was paid in respect of dividends paid on different dates, the subsidiary shall be treated for the purposes of section 239 as having paid an amount of advance corporation tax equal to the appropriate part of the surrendered amount in respect of a distribution made by it on each of those dates.

(3) For the purposes of paragraph (b) of subsection (2) above "the appropriate part of the surrendered amount", in relation to any distribution treated as made on the same date as that on which a dividend was paid, means such part of that amount as bears to the whole of it the same proportion as the amount of that dividend bears to the total amount of the dividends mentioned in that paragraph.

(4) No advance corporation tax which a subsidiary is treated as having paid by virtue of subsection (2) above shall be set against the subsidiary's liability to corporation tax under subsection (3) of section 239; but in determining for the purposes of subsections (3) and (4) of that section what (if any) amount of surplus advance corporation tax there is in any accounting period of a subsidiary, an amount so treated as having been paid shall be set against its liability to corporation tax before any advance corporation tax paid in respect of any distribution made by the subsidiary.

(5) No advance corporation tax which a subsidiary is treated as having paid by virtue of subsection (2) above shall be set against the subsidiary's liability to corporation tax for any accounting period in which, or in any part of which, it was not a subsidiary of the surrendering company.

(6) Any claim under this section shall be made within six years after the end of the accounting period to which it relates and shall require the consent, notified to the inspector in such form as the Board may require, of the subsidiary or subsidiaries concerned.

(7) No amount of advance corporation tax which has been dealt with under section 239(3) shall be available for the purposes of a claim under this section; and no amount of advance corporation tax the benefit of which has been surrendered under this section shall be treated for the purposes of that section as advance corporation tax paid by the surrendering company.

(8) A payment made by a subsidiary to a surrendering company in pursuance of an agreement between them as respects the surrender of the benefit of an amount of advance corporation tax, being a payment not exceeding that amount—

    (a) shall not be taken into account in computing profits or losses of either company for corporation tax purposes; and

    (b) shall not for any of the purposes of the Corporation Tax Acts be regarded as a distribution or a charge on income.

(9) References in this section to dividends shall be construed as including references to distributions made on the redemption, repayment or purchase by a company of its own shares, and references to the payment of dividends shall be construed accordingly.

(10) References in this section to a company apply only to bodies corporate resident in the United Kingdom; and, subject to subsection (11) below, for the purposes of this section the question whether one body corporate is the subsidiary of another shall be determined as a question whether it is a 51 per cent. subsidiary of that other, except that that other shall be treated as not being the owner—

    (a) of any share capital which it owns directly in a body corporate if a profit on the sale of the shares would be treated as a trading receipt of its trade; or

    (b) of any share capital which it owns indirectly, and which is owned directly by a body corporate for which a profit on the sale of the shares would be a trading receipt; or

    (c) of any share capital which it owns directly or indirectly in a body corporate not resident in the United Kingdom.

(11) Notwithstanding that, apart from this subsection, one company ("the subsidiary company") would at any time, by virtue of subsection (10) above, be a subsidiary of another company ("the parent company") for the purposes of this section, the subsidiary company shall not be treated at that time as a subsidiary for those purposes—

    (a) if arrangements are in existence by virtue of which any person has or could obtain, or any persons together have or could obtain, control of the subsidiary company but not of the parent company; and

(b) unless the following conditions are also fulfilled, namely—

(i) that the parent company is beneficially entitled to more than 50 per cent. of any profits available for distribution to equity holders of the subsidiary company; and

(ii) that the parent company would be beneficially entitled to more than 50 per cent. of any assets of the subsidiary company available for distribution to its equity holders on a winding up.

In this subsection "control" has the meaning given by section 840 and "arrangements" means arrangements of any kind, whether in writing or not.

(12) Where by virtue of any enactment a Minister of the Crown or Northern Ireland department has power to give directions to a statutory body as to the disposal of assets belonging to, or to a subsidiary of, that body, the existence of that power shall not be regarded as constituting (or as having at any time constituted) an arrangement within the meaning of subsection (11) above.

(13) Schedule 18 shall have effect for the purposes of subsection (11)(b) above, subject to the following modifications—

(a) for any reference to section 413(7) to (10) there shall be substituted a reference to subsection (11)(b) above; and

(b) paragraph 7(1) shall be omitted and for any reference to the relevant accounting period there shall be substituted a reference to the accounting period current at the time in question.

Calculation of ACT where company receives franked investment income.

241.—(1) Where in any accounting period a company receives franked investment income the company shall not be liable to pay advance corporation tax in respect of qualifying distributions made by it in that period unless the amount of the franked payments made by it in that period exceeds the amount of that income.

(2) If in an accounting period there is such an excess, advance corporation tax shall be payable on an amount which, when the advance corporation tax payable thereon is added to it, is equal to the excess.

(3) If the amount of franked investment income received by a company in an accounting period exceeds the amount of the franked payments made by it in that period the excess shall be carried forward to the next accounting period and treated for the purposes of this section (including any further application of this subsection) as franked investment income received by the company in that period.

(4) Without prejudice to section 238(5), Schedule 13 shall apply for the purpose of regulating the manner in which effect is to be given to subsections (1) to (3) above.

(5) No franked investment income shall be used to frank distributions of a company (that is to say, used in accordance with this section and Schedule 13 so as to relieve the company from, or obtain repayment of, advance corporation tax for which the company would otherwise be liable) if the amount of the tax credit comprised in it has been paid under subsection (2) of section 231; and no payment shall be made under that subsection in respect of the tax credit comprised in franked investment income which has been so used.

242.—(1) Where a company has a surplus of franked investment income for any accounting period—

PART VI

Set-off of losses etc. against surplus of franked investment income.

> (a) the company may, on making a claim for the purpose, require that the amount of the surplus shall for all or any of the purposes mentioned in subsection (2) below be treated as if it were a like amount of profits chargeable to corporation tax; and
>
> (b) subject to subsection (4) below, the provisions mentioned in subsection (2) below shall apply in accordance with this section to reduce the amount of the surplus for purposes of section 241(3); and
>
> (c) the company shall be entitled to have paid to it the amount of the tax credit comprised in the amount of franked investment income by which the surplus is so reduced.

(2) The purposes for which a claim may be made under subsection (1) above are those of—

> (a) the setting of trading losses against total profits under section 393(2);
>
> (b) the deduction of charges on income under section 338 or paragraph 5 of Schedule 4;
>
> (c) the deduction of expenses of management under section 75 or 76;
>
> (d) the setting of certain capital allowances against total profits under section 74(3) of the 1968 Act;
>
> (e) the setting of losses against income under section 573(2).

(3) Where a company makes a claim under this section for any accounting period, the reduction falling to be made in profits of that accounting period shall be made, as far as may be, in profits chargeable to corporation tax rather than in the amount treated as profits so chargeable under this section.

(4) Where a claim under this section relates to section 393(2) or 573(2) of this Act or to section 74(3) of the 1968 Act and an accounting period of the company falls partly before and partly within the time mentioned in that subsection, then—

> (a) the restriction imposed by section 393(3) or 573(3) of this Act or by section 74(4) of the 1968 Act on the amount of the relief shall be applied only to any relief to be given apart from this section, and shall be applied without regard to any amount treated as profits of the accounting period under this section; but
>
> (b) relief under this section shall be given only against a part of the amount so treated proportionate to the part of the accounting period falling within that time.

(5) Where—

> (a) on a claim made under this section for any accounting period relief is given in respect of the whole or part of any loss incurred in a trade, or of any amount which could be treated as a loss under section 393(9); and

Part VI

(b) in a later accounting period the franked payments made by the company exceed its franked investment income;

then (unless the company has ceased to carry on the trade or to be within the charge to corporation tax in respect of it) the company shall, for the purposes of section 393(1), be treated as having, in the accounting period ending immediately before the beginning of the later accounting period mentioned in paragraph (b) above, incurred a loss equal to whichever is the lesser of—

(i) the excess referred to in paragraph (b) above; and

(ii) the amount in respect of which relief was given as mentioned in paragraph (a) above or so much of that amount as remains after deduction of any part of it dealt with under this subsection in relation to an earlier accounting period.

(6) Subject to subsection (7) below, subsection (5) above shall apply, with the necessary adaptations—

(a) in relation to relief given in respect of management expenses; and

(b) in relation to relief given in respect of capital allowances; and

(c) in relation to relief given in respect of losses under section 573(2);

as it applies in relation to relief given in respect of a loss (the reference to the company ceasing to be within the charge to corporation tax in respect of the trade being construed as a reference to its ceasing to be within that charge at all, and as respects the relief mentioned in paragraph (c) above, the reference to the purposes of section 393(1) being construed as a reference to the purposes of corporation tax on chargeable gains).

(7) Any amount which may be dealt with under subsection (5) above as a loss shall be so dealt with rather than under subsection (6) above, except in so far as the company concerned otherwise elects.

(8) The time limits for claims under this section shall be as follows—

(a) if and so far as the purpose for which the claim is made is the setting of trading losses against total profits under section 393(2), two years from the end of the accounting period in which the trading loss is incurred;

(b) if and so far as the purpose for which the claim is made is the deduction of charges on income under section 338 or paragraph 5 of Schedule 4 or of expenses of management under section 75 or 76, six years from the end of the accounting period in which the charges were paid or the expenses of management were incurred;

(c) if and so far as the purpose for which the claim is made is the setting of capital allowances against total profits under section 74(3) of the 1968 Act, two years from the end of the accounting period for which the capital allowances fall to be made;

(d) if and so far as the purpose for which the claim is made is the setting of a loss against income under section 573(2), two years from the end of the accounting period in which the loss was incurred.

(9) For the purposes of a claim under this section for any accounting period, the surplus of franked investment income for that accounting period shall be calculated without regard to the part, if any, carried forward from an earlier accounting period; and for the purposes of subsection (5) above franked investment income which by virtue of section 241(5) cannot be used to frank distributions of a company shall be left out of account.

243.—(1) Where a company has a surplus of franked investment income for any accounting period, the company, instead of or in addition to making a claim under section 242, may on making a claim for the purpose require that the surplus shall be taken into account for relief under section 393(1) or 394, up to the amount of franked investment income for the accounting period which, if chargeable to corporation tax, would have been so taken into account by virtue of section 393(8); and (subject to the restriction to that amount of franked investment income) the following subsections shall have effect where the company makes a claim under this section for any accounting period.

(2) The amount to which the claim relates shall for the purposes of the claim be treated as trading income of the accounting period.

(3) The reduction falling to be made in trading income of an accounting period shall be made as far as possible in trading income chargeable to corporation tax rather than in the amount treated as trading income so chargeable under this section.

(4) If the claim relates to section 393(1), section 242(5) shall apply in relation to it.

(5) If the claim relates to section 394 and an accounting period of the company falls partly outside the three years mentioned in subsection (1) of that section, then—

(a) the restriction imposed by subsection (2) of that section on the amount of the reduction that may be made in the trading income of that period shall be applied only to any relief to be given apart from this section, and shall be applied without regard to any amount treated as trading income of the accounting period by virtue of this section, but

(b) relief under this section shall be given only against a part of the amount so treated proportionate to the part of the accounting period falling within the three years in question.

(6) The time limits for claims under this section shall be as follows—

(a) if and so far as the purpose for which the claim is made is the allowance of relief under section 393(1), six years from the end of the accounting period for which the claim is made,

(b) if and so far as the purpose for which the claim is made is the allowance of relief under section 394, six years from the time when the company ceases to carry on the trade.

(7) For the purposes of a claim under this section for any accounting period the surplus of franked investment income for that period shall be calculated without regard to the part, if any, carried forward from an earlier accounting period.

244.—(1) Without prejudice to section 242(9) or 243(7), the surplus of franked investment income for an accounting period for which a claim is made under either of those sections shall be calculated without regard to any part of that surplus which, when the claim is made, has been used to frank distributions made by the company in a later accounting period.

(2) Where in consequence of a claim under either section 242 or section 243 for any accounting period a company is entitled to payment of a sum in respect of tax credit—

(a) an amount equal to that sum shall be deducted from any advance corporation tax which apart from this subsection would fall, under section 239, to be set against the company's liability to corporation tax for the next accounting period or the benefit of which could be surrendered under section 240; and

(b) if that amount exceeds that advance corporation tax or there is no such advance corporation tax, that excess or that amount (as the case may be) shall be carried forward and similarly deducted in relation to the following accounting period and so on.

Calculation etc. of
ACT on change of
ownership of
company.

245.—(1) This section applies if—

(a) within any period of three years there is both a change in the ownership of a company and (either earlier or later in that period, or at the same time) a major change in the nature or conduct of a trade or business carried by the company; or

(b) at any time after the scale of the activities in a trade or business carried on by a company has become small or negligible, and before any considerable revival of the trade or business, there is a change in the ownership of the company.

(2) Sections 239 and 241 and Schedule 13 shall apply to an accounting period in which the change of ownership occurs as if the part ending with the change of ownership, and the part after, were two separate accounting periods; and for that purpose the profits of the company charged to corporation tax for the accounting period (as defined in section 239(6)) shall be apportioned between those parts.

(3) No advance corporation tax paid by the company in respect of distributions made in an accounting period beginning before the change of ownership shall be treated under section 239(4) as paid by it in respect of distributions made in an accounting period ending after the change of ownership; and this subsection shall apply to an accounting period in which the change of ownership occurs as if the part ending with the change of ownership, and the part after, were two separate accounting periods.

(4) In subsection (1) above "a major change in the nature or conduct of a trade or business" includes—

(a) a major change in the type of property dealt in, or services or facilities provided, in the trade or business; or

(b) a major change in customers, outlets or markets of the trade or business; or

(c) a change whereby the company ceases to be a trading company and becomes an investment company or vice versa; or

(d) where the company is an investment company, a major change in the nature of the investments held by the company;

and this section applies even if the change is the result of a gradual process which began outside the period of three years mentioned in subsection (1)(a) above.

(5) In this section—

"trading company" means a company whose business consists wholly or mainly of the carrying on of a trade or trades;

"investment company" means a company (other than a holding company) whose business consists wholly or mainly in the making of investments and the principal part of whose income is derived therefrom;

"holding company" means a company whose business consists wholly or mainly in the holding of shares or securities of companies which are its 90 per cent. subsidiaries and which are trading companies.

(6) Subsection (3) above applies to advance corporation tax which a company is treated as having paid by virtue of section 240 as it applies to advance corporation tax which it has actually paid.

(7) Sections 768(8) and (9) and 769 shall apply also for the purposes of this section and as if in subsection (3) of section 769 the reference to the benefit of the losses were a reference to the benefit of advance corporation tax.

246.—(1) If, at the beginning of any financial year, the basic rate percentage for the appropriate year of assessment has not been determined (whether under the Provisional Collection of Taxes Act 1968 or otherwise), then, subject to subsection (2) below, advance corporation tax in respect of distributions made in that financial year shall be payable under Schedule 13 and may be assessed under that Schedule according to the rate of advance corporation tax fixed for the previous financial year.

Charge of ACT at previous rate until new rate fixed, and changes of rate.

1968 c. 2

(2) Subsection (1) above does not apply with respect to any distribution made in a financial year after—

(a) the date on which is determined the basic rate percentage for the appropriate year of assessment; or

(b) 5th August in that year,

whichever is the earlier.

(3) If a rate of advance corporation tax for any financial year is not fixed, under section 14(3) or any other enactment, or if advance corporation tax for any financial year is charged otherwise than as it has been paid or assessed, the necessary adjustment shall be made by discharge or repayment of tax or by a further assessment.

(4) In subsections (1) and (2) above "the basic rate percentage for the appropriate year of assessment", in relation to a financial year, means the percentage at which income tax at the basic rate is charged for the year of assessment which begins on 6th April in that financial year.

(5) Where different rates of advance corporation tax are in force in different parts of an accounting period, the maximum set-off permitted for that accounting period under section 239(2) shall be determined by apportioning the profits of the company charged to corporation tax for that period (as defined in section 239(6)) between the different parts of the period, calculating the maximum for each part as if it were a separate accounting period and aggregating the result.

(6) Where the rate of advance corporation tax for any financial year differs from the rate last fixed—

(a) any advance corporation tax payable in respect of a distribution made in that financial year on or before 5th April shall be calculated according to the rate last fixed and—

(i) the definition of "franked payment" in section 238(1), and

(ii) section 231(1) and Schedule 13;

shall have effect in relation to the distribution as if the rate for that year were the same as the rate last fixed;

(b) if a distribution is made on or before 5th April in an accounting period which extends beyond 5th April in that year and another distribution is made, or franked investment income is received, in that period after that date, then—

(i) the company's liability for advance corporation tax,

(ii) the amount of any such tax, and

(iii) the amount of any surplus of franked investment income,

for that accounting period, shall be determined under section 241 and Schedule 13 as if the part of the accounting period ending with, and the part of it beginning after, that date were separate accounting periods.

CHAPTER VI

MISCELLANEOUS AND SUPPLEMENTAL

Group income

Dividends etc. paid by one member of a group to another.

247.—(1) Where a company ("the receiving company") receives dividends from another company ("the paying company"), both being bodies corporate resident in the United Kingdom, and the paying company is—

(a) a 51 per cent. subsidiary of the other or of a company so resident of which the other is a 51 per cent. subsidiary; or

(b) a trading or holding company owned by a consortium the members of which include the receiving company,

then, subject to the following provisions of this section, the receiving company and the paying company may jointly elect that this subsection shall apply to the dividends received from the paying company by the receiving company ("the election dividends").

(2) So long as an election under subsection (1) above is in force the election dividends shall be excluded from sections 14(1) and 231 and are accordingly not included in references to franked payments made by the paying company or the franked investment income of the receiving company but are in the Corporation Tax Acts referred to as "group income" of the receiving company.

(3) Where an election under subsection (1) above is in force the paying company may by notice to the collector state that it does not wish the election to have effect in relation to any amount of dividends specified in the notice and the Corporation Tax Acts shall then have effect in relation to that amount as if there had been no such election.

(4) Where a company ("the recipient company") receives from another company ("the payer company"), both being bodies corporate resident in the United Kingdom, any payments which are for corporation tax charges on income of the payer company and either—

    (a) the conditions in subsection (1)(a) or (b) above would be satisfied in relation to the companies if the payments were dividends, or

    (b) the recipient company is a 51 per cent. subsidiary of the payer company,

then, subject to the following provisions of this section, the recipient company and the payer company may jointly elect that this subsection shall apply to any such payments received from the payer company by the recipient company, and so long as the election is in force those payments may be made without deduction of income tax and neither section 349 nor section 350 shall apply thereto.

(5) Subsections (1) to (4) above shall not apply to dividends or other payments received by a company on any investments, if a profit on the sale of those investments would be treated as a trading receipt of that company, and shall not apply to a dividend in any case where, if those subsections do not apply to it, the receiving company will, or would but for section 235 or 237, be entitled by virtue of any exemption to claim payment of the tax credit to which it is entitled in respect of the dividend.

(6) Where—

    (a) the paying company purports by virtue of an election under subsection (1) above to pay any dividends without paying advance corporation tax, or

    (b) the payer company purports by virtue of an election under subsection (4) above to make any payment without deduction of income tax,

and advance corporation tax ought to have been paid or income tax ought to have been deducted, as the case may be, the inspector may make such assessments, adjustments or set-offs as may be required for securing that the resulting liabilities to tax (including interest on unpaid tax) of the paying or payer company and the receiving or recipient company are, so far as possible, the same as they would have been if the advance corporation tax had been duly paid or the income tax had been duly deducted.

(7) Where tax assessed under subsection (6) above on the paying or payer company is not paid by that company before the expiry of the period of three months from the date on which that tax is payable, that tax shall, without prejudice to the right to recover it from that company, be recoverable from the receiving or recipient company.

(8) In determining for the purposes of this section whether one body corporate is a 51 per cent. subsidiary of another, that other shall be treated as not being the owner—

    (a) of any share capital which it owns directly or indirectly in a body corporate not resident in the United Kingdom, or

    (b) of any share capital which it owns indirectly, and which is owned directly by a body corporate for which a profit on the sale of the shares would be a trading receipt.

(9) For the purposes of this section—

    (a) "trading or holding company" means a trading company or a company the business of which consists wholly or mainly in the holding of shares or securities of trading companies which are its 90 per cent. subsidiaries;

    (b) "trading company" means a company whose business consists wholly or mainly of the carrying on of a trade or trades; and

    (c) a company is owned by a consortium if three-quarters or more of the ordinary share capital of the company is beneficially owned between them by companies resident in the United Kingdom of which none beneficially owns less than one-twentieth of that capital, and those companies are called the members of the consortium.

(10) References in this section to dividends or payments received by a company apply to any received by another person on behalf of or in trust for the company, but not to any received by the company on behalf of or in trust for another person, and references to "group income" shall be construed accordingly.

248.—(1) The Board may make regulations with respect to the procedure to be adopted for giving effect to section 247 and as to the information and evidence to be furnished by a company in connection with that section and, subject to the provisions of such regulations, an election under that section ("the election") shall be made by notice to the inspector which shall set out the facts necessary to show that the companies are entitled to make the election.

(2) The election shall not have effect in relation to dividends or other payments paid less than three months after the giving of the notice and before the inspector is satisfied that the election is validly made, and has so notified the companies concerned; but shall be of no effect if within those three months the inspector notifies the companies concerned that the validity of the election is not established to his satisfaction.

(3) The companies concerned shall have the like right of appeal against any decision that the validity of the election is not established as the company paying the dividends or other payments would have if it were an assessment made on that company, and Part V of the Management Act shall apply accordingly.

Provisions supplementary to section 247.

(4) The election shall cease to be in force if at any time the companies cease to be entitled to make the election, and on that happening each company shall forthwith notify the inspector.

(5) Either of the companies making the election may at any time give the inspector notice revoking the election; and any such notice shall have effect from the time it is given.

(6) The Board shall not make any regulations under subsection (1) above unless a draft of them has been laid before and approved by a resolution of the House of Commons.

Stock dividends

249.—(1) Subject to subsections (7) to (9) below, this section applies to any of the following share capital, that is to say—

> (a) any share capital issued by a company resident in the United Kingdom in consequence of the exercise by any person of an option conferred on him to receive in respect of shares in the company (whether the last-mentioned shares were issued before or after the coming into force of this section) either a dividend in cash or additional share capital; and

> (b) any bonus share capital issued by a company so resident in respect of any shares in the company of a relevant class (whether the last-mentioned shares were issued before or after the coming into force of this section).

(2) For the purposes of subsection (1)(b) above a class of shares is a relevant class if—

> (a) shares of that class carry the right to receive bonus share capital in the company of the same or a different class; and

> (b) that right is conferred by the terms on which shares of that class were originally issued or by those terms as subsequently extended or otherwise varied.

(3) Where a company issues any share capital in a case in which two or more persons are entitled thereto, the following provisions of this section and paragraph 12(1) to (3) of Schedule 19 shall have effect as if the company had issued to each of those persons separately a part of that share capital proportionate to his interest therein on the due date of issue.

(4) Subject to the following provisions of this section, where a company issues any share capital in a case in which an individual is beneficially entitled to that share capital, that individual shall be treated as having received on the due date of issue income of an amount which, if reduced by an amount equal to income tax on that income at the basic rate for the year of assessment in which that date fell, would be equal to the appropriate amount in cash, and—

> (a) no assessment shall be made on the individual in respect of income tax at the basic rate on that income but he shall be treated as having paid tax at the basic rate on it or, if his total income is reduced by any deductions, on so much of it as is part of his total income as so reduced;

(b) no repayment shall be made of income tax treated by virtue of paragraph (a) above as having been paid; and

(c) that income shall be treated for the purposes of sections 348 and 349(1) as not brought into charge to income tax.

(5) Where a company issues any share capital to the personal representatives of a deceased person as such during the administration period, the amount of income which, if the case had been one in which an individual was beneficially entitled to that share capital, that individual would have been treated under subsection (4) above as having received shall be deemed for the purposes of Part XVI to be part of the aggregate income of the estate of the deceased.

This subsection shall be construed as if it were contained in Part XVI.

(6) Where a company issues any share capital to trustees in respect of any shares in the company held by them (or by them and one or more other persons) in a case in which a dividend in cash paid to the trustees in respect of those shares would have been to any extent income to which section 686 applies, then—

(a) there shall be ascertained the amount of income which, if the case had been one in which an individual was beneficially entitled to that share capital, that individual would have been treated under subsection (4) above as having received; and

(b) income of that amount shall be treated as having arisen to the trustees on the due date of issue and as if it had been chargeable to income tax at the basic rate; and

(c) paragraphs (a) to (c) of subsection (4) above shall, with the substitution of "income" for "total income" and with all other necessary modifications, apply to that income as they apply to income which an individual is treated as having received under that subsection.

(7) This section does not apply to—

(a) any share capital of which the due date of issue is earlier than 6th April 1975; or

(b) any share capital issued by a company in respect of shares in the company which confer on the holder a right to convert or exchange them into or for shares in the company of a class which is not a relevant class for the purposes of subsection (1)(b) above where the due date of issue of the share capital so issued precedes the earlier of the following dates, namely—

(i) the day next after the earliest date after 5th August 1975 on which conversion or exchange of the shares could be effected by an exercise of that right; and

(ii) 6th April 1976 or, in the case of share capital issued by an investment trust, 6th April 1977.

(8) Where, in a case within subsection (4) above, the share capital in question is issued in respect of shares in the company issued before 6th April 1975 which confer on the holder a right to convert or exchange them into or for shares of a different class, this section shall not apply to so much (if any) of any bonus share capital issued by the company after 5th

April 1976 in connection with an exercise of that right as would have been issued if that right had been exercised so as to effect the conversion or exchange of the shares on the earliest possible date after 5th April 1975; and subsections (5) and (6) above shall, where applicable, have effect accordingly.

(9) Where any bonus share capital falling within subsection (1)(b) above is after 5th April 1975 converted into or exchanged for shares in the company in question of a different class, then—

    (a) this section shall not apply to any shares in the company issued, in connection with the conversion or exchange, in consideration of the cancellation, extinguishment or acquisition by the company of that bonus share capital; but

    (b) section 230(a) and (b) shall apply to any shares in the company issued, in connection with the conversion or exchange, in consideration of the cancellation, extinguishment or acquisition by the company of so much of that bonus share capital as caused an individual to be treated under subsection (4) above as having received an amount of income on the due date of issue (or would have done so if the case had been one in which an individual was beneficially entitled to that share capital).

250.—(1) A company shall for each of its accounting periods make, in accordance with this section, returns to the inspector of all share capital to which section 249 applies ("relevant share capital") and which was issued by it in that period.   Returns.

(2) A return shall be made for—

    (a) each complete quarter falling within the accounting period, that is to say, each of the periods of three months ending with 31st March, 30th June, 30th September or 31st December which falls within that period;

    (b) each part of the accounting period which is not a complete quarter and ends on the first (or only), or begins immediately after the last (or only), of those dates which falls within the accounting period;

    (c) if none of those dates falls within the accounting period, the whole accounting period.

(3) A return for any period for which a return is required to be made under this section (a "return period") shall be made within 30 days from the end of that period.

(4) No return need be made under this section by a company for any period in which it has issued no relevant share capital.

(5) The return made by a company for any return period shall state—

    (a) the date on which any relevant share capital issued by it in the period was issued and, if different, the date on which the company was first required to issue it;

    (b) particulars of the terms on which any such share capital so issued by it was issued; and

H

(c) what is, in relation to any such share capital so issued, the appropriate amount in cash.

(6) If it appears to the inspector that a company ought to have, but has not, made a return for any return period, he may (notwithstanding subsection (4) above) by notice require the company to make a return for that period within such time (not being less than 30 days) as may be specified in the notice; and a return required to be made under this subsection shall, if such be the case, state that no relevant share capital was issued in the period in question.

(7) As regards any share capital included in a return made under this section by a company, the inspector may by notice require the company to furnish him within such time (not being less than 30 days) as may be specified in the notice with such further information relating thereto as he may reasonably require for the purposes of sections 230 and 249, this section and section 251 and paragraph 12 of Schedule 19.

Interpretation of
sections 249 and
250.

251.—(1) For the purposes of sections 249 and 250 —

(a) "bonus share capital", in relation to a company, means share capital issued by the company otherwise than wholly for new consideration or such part of any share capital so issued as is not properly referable to new consideration;

(b) "due date of issue", in relation to any share capital issued by a company, means the earliest date on which the company was required to issue that share capital;

(c) an option to receive either a dividend in cash or additional share capital is conferred on a person not only where he is required to choose one or the other, but also where he is offered the one subject to a right, however expressed, to choose the other instead, and a person's abandonment of, or failure to exercise, such a right is to be treated as an exercise of the option;

and in section 254 the definition of "security" (in subsection (1)) and subsections (5) and (11) shall not apply.

(2) In sections 249 and 250 "the appropriate amount in cash", in relation to any share capital to which section 249 applies—

(a) in a case where that share capital was issued —

(i) in consequence of the exercise of an option such as is mentioned in section 249(1)(a); or

(ii) in a quantity which is determined by or determines the amount of a dividend in cash payable in respect of share capital in the company of a different class,

and where the relevant cash dividend is not substantially greater nor substantially less than the market value of that share capital on the relevant date, means the amount of the relevant cash dividend or, in a case in which section 249(3) applies, a due proportion of that amount;

(b) in a case where paragraph (a) above does not apply, means the market value of that share capital on the relevant date or, in a case in which section 249(3) applies, a due proportion of that market value.

(3) In subsection (2) above—

> "the relevant cash dividend", in a case falling within subsection (2)(a)(i) above, means the cash dividend mentioned in section 249(1)(a) or, in a case falling within subsection (2)(a)(ii) above, means the cash dividend there mentioned (subject to subsection (4) below);

> "the relevant date", in the case of share capital listed in the Stock Exchange Daily Official List, means the date of first dealing and, in the case of share capital not so listed, means the due date of issue; and

> "market value", in relation to any share capital in a company, means, subject to the provisions applied by subsections (5) and (6) below, the price which that share capital might reasonably be expected to fetch on a sale in the open market.

(4) Where, in a case falling within subsection (2)(a)(ii) above, the company on the occasion on which it issues the share capital in question also issues a dividend in cash ("the accompanying cash dividend") in respect of the shares in the company in respect of which that share capital is issued, "the relevant cash dividend" means the cash dividend mentioned in subsection (2)(a)(ii) above reduced by the amount of the accompanying cash dividend.

(5) Section 150(3) of the 1979 Act (market value of shares or securities listed in the Stock Exchange Daily Official List) shall apply for the purposes of subsection (3) above as it applies for the purposes of that Act.

(6) In the case of shares or securities which are not quoted on a recognised stock exchange at the time when their market value for the purposes of subsection (2) above falls to be determined, subsection (3) of section 152 of the 1979 Act shall apply with respect to the determination of their market value for those purposes as it applies with respect to a determination falling within subsection (1) of that section.

Supplemental

252.—(1) If an inspector discovers that—

Rectification of excessive set-off etc. of ACT or tax credit.

(a) any set-off of advance corporation tax under section 239, or

(b) any set-off or payment of tax credit,

ought not to have been made, or is or has become excessive, the inspector may make any such assessments as may in his judgment be required for recovering any tax that ought to have been paid or any payment of tax credit that ought not to have been made and generally for securing that the resulting liabilities to tax (including interest on unpaid tax) of the persons concerned are what they would have been if only such set-offs or payments had been made as ought to have been made.

(2) In any case where—

(a) interest has been paid under section 826 on a payment of tax credit; and

(b) interest ought not to have been paid on that payment, either at all or to any extent, an assessment under this section may be made for recovering any interest that ought not to have been paid.

(3) Where—

    (a) an assessment is made under this section to recover tax credit paid to a company in respect of franked investment income received by the company in an accounting period; and

    (b) more than one payment of tax credit has been made in respect of that period,

any sum recovered shall as far as possible be treated as relating to a payment of tax credit made later rather than to a payment made earlier.

(4) Subsections (2) and (3) above shall have effect in relation to payments of tax credit claimed in respect of accounting periods ending after such day as may be appointed for the purpose of those subsections by order made by the Treasury, not being earlier than 31st March 1992.

(5) The Management Act shall apply to any assessment under this section for recovering a payment of tax credit or interest on such a payment as if it were an assessment to income tax for the year of assessment, or in the case of a company, corporation tax for the accounting period, in respect of which the payment was claimed, and as if that payment represented a loss of tax to the Crown; and any sum charged by any such assessment shall, subject to any appeal against the assessment, be due within 14 days after the issue of the notice of assessment.

Power to modify or replace section 234(5) to (9) and Schedule 13.

253.—(1) The Board may by regulations—

    (a) modify, supplement or replace any of the provisions of subsections (5) to (9) of section 234 for the purpose of requiring companies resident in the United Kingdom to make returns and give information to the inspector in respect of distributions made by them, whether before or after the passing of this Act, which are not qualifying distributions;

    (b) modify, supplement or replace any of the provisions of Schedule 13 for the purpose of regulating the time and manner in which advance corporation tax is to be accounted for and paid or the manner in which effect is to be given to section 241(1) to (3);

and references in this Act and in any other enactment to section 234(5) to (9) and to Schedule 13 shall be construed as including references to any such regulations.

(2) Without prejudice to the generality of subsection (1) above, regulations under that subsection may, in relation to advance corporation tax, modify any provision of Parts II to VI of the Management Act or apply any such provision with or without modifications.

(3) Regulations under this section may—

    (a) make different provision for different descriptions of companies and for different circumstances and may authorise the Board, where in their opinion there are special circumstances justifying it, to make special arrangements as respects advance corporation tax or the repayment of income tax borne by a company or the payment to a company of amounts in respect of any tax credit to which it is entitled;

(b) include such transitional and other supplemental provisions as appear to the Board to be expedient or necessary.

(4) The Board shall not make any regulations under this section unless a draft of them has been laid before and approved by a resolution of the House of Commons.

254.—(1) In this Part, except where the context otherwise requires—

"new consideration" means, subject to subsections (5) and (6) below, consideration not provided directly or indirectly out of the assets of the company, and in particular does not include amounts retained by the company by way of capitalising a distribution;

"security" includes securities not creating or evidencing a charge on assets, and interest paid by a company on money advanced without the issue of a security for the advance, or other consideration given by a company for the use of money so advanced, shall be treated as if paid or given in respect of a security issued for the advance by the company;

"share" includes stock, and any other interest of a member in a company;

and in this section "a 90 per cent. group" means a company and all of its 90 per cent. subsidiaries.

(2) In this Part, the expressions "in respect of shares in the company" and "in respect of securities of the company", in relation to a company which is a member of a 90 per cent. group, mean respectively in respect of shares in that company or any other company in the group and in respect of securities of that company or any other company in the group.

(3) Without prejudice to section 209(2)(b) as extended by subsection (2) above, in relation to a company which is a member of a 90 per cent. group, "distribution" includes anything distributed out of assets of the company (whether in cash or otherwise) in respect of shares in or securities of another company in the group.

(4) Nothing in subsections (2) and (3) above shall require a company to be treated as making a distribution to any other company which is in the same group and is resident in the United Kingdom.

(5) Where share capital has been issued at a premium representing new consideration, any part of that premium afterwards applied in paying up share capital shall be treated as new consideration also for that share capital, except in so far as the premium has been taken into account under section 211(5) so as to enable a distribution to be treated as a repayment of share capital.

(6) Subject to subsection (7) below, no consideration derived from the value of any share capital or security of a company, or from voting or other rights in a company, shall be regarded for the purposes of this Part as new consideration received by the company unless the consideration consists of—

PART VI

(a) money or value received from the company as a qualifying distribution;

(b) money received from the company as a payment which for those purposes constitutes a repayment of that share capital or of the principal secured by the security; or

(c) the giving up of the right to the share capital or security on its cancellation, extinguishment or acquisition by the company.

(7) No amount shall be regarded as new consideration by virtue of subsection (6)(b) or (c) above in so far as it exceeds any new consideration received by the company for the issue of the share capital or security in question or, in the case of share capital which constituted a qualifying distribution on issue, the nominal value of that share capital.

(8) Where two or more companies enter into arrangements to make distributions to each other's members, all parties concerned (however many) may for the purposes of this Part be treated as if anything done by any one of those companies had been done by any of the others.

(9) A distribution shall be treated under this Part as made, or consideration as provided, out of assets of a company if the cost falls on the company.

(10) References in this Part to issuing share capital as paid up apply also to the paying up of any issued share capital.

(11) Where securities are issued at a price less than the amount repayable on them, and are not quoted on a recognised stock exchange, the principal secured shall not be taken for the purposes of this Part to exceed the issue price, unless the securities are issued on terms reasonably comparable with the terms of issue of securities so quoted.

(12) For the purposes of this Part a thing is to be regarded as done in respect of a share if it is done to a person as being the holder of the share, or as having at a particular time been the holder, or is done in pursuance of a right granted or offer made in respect of a share; and anything done in respect of shares by reference to share holdings at a particular time is to be regarded as done to the then holders of the shares or the personal representatives of any share holder then dead.

This subsection shall apply in relation to securities as it applies in relation to shares.

"Gross rate" and "gross amount" of distributions to include ACT.

255.—(1) Where any right or obligation created before 6th April 1973 is expressed by reference to a dividend at a gross rate or of a gross amount, that right or obligation shall continue to have effect, in relation to a dividend payable on or after that date, as if the reference were to a dividend of an amount which, when there is added to it such proportion thereof as corresponds to the rate of advance corporation tax in force on that date, that is to say, 6th April 1973, is equal to a dividend at that gross rate or of that gross amount.

(2) Subsection (1) above shall apply with the necessary modifications to a dividend partly at a gross rate or of a gross amount and shall apply to any distribution other than a dividend as it applies to a dividend.

PART VII

GENERAL PROVISIONS RELATING TO TAXATION OF INCOME OF INDIVIDUALS

CHAPTER I

PERSONAL RELIEFS

The reliefs

256. An individual who makes a claim in that behalf or, in the case of relief under section 266, who satisfies the conditions of that section, shall be entitled to such relief as is specified in sections 257 to 274, subject however to the provisions of sections 275 to 278 and 287 and 288.

General.

257.—(1) Subject to the provisions of this section and section 261, the claimant shall be entitled—

Personal relief.

    (a) if he proves—

        (i) that for the year of assessment he has his wife living with him, or

        (ii) that his wife is wholly maintained by him during the year of assessment, and that he is not entitled in computing the amount of his income for that year for income tax purposes to make any deduction in respect of the sums paid for the maintenance of his wife,

    to a deduction of £3,795 from his total income;

    (b) in any other case, to a deduction of £2,425 from his total income.

(2) Subject to the provisions of this section, subsection (1) above shall have effect—

    (a) in relation to a claim by a person who proves that he or his wife was at any time within the year of assessment of the age of 65 or upwards, as if the sum specified in paragraph (a) were £4,675; and

    (b) in relation to a claim by a person who proves that he was at any time within the year of assessment of the age of 65 or upwards, as if the sum specified in paragraph (b) were £2,960;

and for the purposes of this subsection a person who would have been of the age of 65 or upwards within the year of assessment if he had not died in the course of it shall be treated as having been of that age within that year.

(3) Subject to the provisions of this section, subsection (1) above shall have effect—

    (a) in relation to a claim by a person who proves that he or his wife was at any time within the year of assessment of the age of 80 or upwards, as if the sum specified in paragraph (a) were £4,845; and

(b) in relation to a claim by a person who proves that he was at any time within the year of assessment of the age of 80 or upwards, as if the sum specified in paragraph (b) were £3,070;

and for the purposes of this subsection, a person who would have been of the age of 80 or upwards within the year of assessment if he had not died in the course of it shall be treated as having been of that age within that year.

(4) For any year of assessment for which a person is entitled to increased personal relief by virtue of subsection (3) above, he shall not be entitled to increased relief under subsection (2) above.

(5) Where the claimant's total income for the year of assessment exceeds £9,800, subsections (2) and (3) above shall not apply except in a case where the deduction to be allowed under subsection (1) above will be increased by virtue of this subsection; and in such a case subsection (2) or (3), as the case may be, shall apply as if the sums mentioned in it were reduced by two-thirds of the excess of that total income over £9,800.

(6) If the total income of the claimant includes any earned income of his wife, the deduction to be allowed under this section shall be increased by the amount of that earned income or by £2,425, whichever is the less.

(7) For the purposes of subsection (6) above—

(a) any earned income of the claimant's wife arising in respect of any pension, superannuation or other allowance, deferred pay or compensation for loss of office, given in respect of his past services in any office or employment, shall be deemed not to be earned income of his wife; and

(b) no payment of benefit under the Social Security Acts 1975 or the Social Security (Northern Ireland) Acts 1975 except—

1975 c. 60.
S.I. 1975/1503.
(N.I. 15).

(i) a Category A retirement pension (exclusive of any increase under section 10 of the Social Security Pensions Act 1975 or Article 12 of the Social Security Pensions (Northern Ireland) Order 1975);

(ii) unemployment benefit, and

(iii) invalid care allowance,

shall be treated as earned income.

(8) Subsection (1) above shall have effect in relation to any claim by a man who becomes married in the year of assessment for which the claim is made and has not previously in that year been entitled to relief under paragraph (a) of that subsection, as if the sum specified in that paragraph were reduced, for each month of that year ending before the date of the marriage, by one-twelfth of the amount by which it exceeds the sum specified in paragraph (b) of that subsection.

In this subsection "month" means a month beginning with the 6th day of a month of the calendar year.

(9) If the retail prices index for the month of December preceding a year of assessment is higher than it was for the previous December, then, unless Parliament otherwise determines, this section shall apply for that year as if for each amount specified in subsections (1) to (6) above as they applied for the previous year (whether by virtue of this subsection or

otherwise) there were substituted an amount arrived at by increasing the amount for the previous year by the same percentage as the percentage increase in the retail prices index, and if—

    (a) in the case of an amount specified in subsection (5) above, the result is not a multiple of £100, rounding it up to the nearest amount which is such a multiple;

    (b) in the case of any other amount, the increase is not a multiple of £10, rounding the increase up to the nearest amount which is such a multiple.

(10) Subsection (9) above shall not require any change to be made in the amounts deductible or repayable under section 203 between the beginning of a year of assessment and 5th May in that year.

(11) The Treasury shall in each year of assessment make an order specifying the amounts which by virtue of subsection (9) above will be treated as specified for the following year of assessment in subsections (1) to (6) above.

258.—(1) If the claimant proves that he is a widower and that for the year of assessment a person, being a relative of his or of his deceased wife, is resident with him in the capacity of a housekeeper, or that he has no relative of his own or of his deceased wife who is able and willing to act in such capacity and that he has employed some other person to reside with him for the purpose, he shall be entitled to a deduction of £100 from his total income in respect of that relative or person.

Widower's or widow's housekeeper.

(2) No relief shall be allowed under this section—

    (a) unless the claimant proves that no other individual is entitled to relief in respect of the relative under the provisions of this Chapter, or, if any other individual is so entitled, that the other individual has relinquished his claim thereto; or

    (b) where the relative is a married woman living with her husband, and the husband has claimed and been allowed the higher relief under section 257(1), or the relative is a man who has claimed and been allowed that higher relief; or

    (c) to a person entitled to relief under section 259.

(3) Not more than one deduction shall be allowed under this section to any claimant for any year.

(4) This section shall apply to a claimant being a widow as it applies to a claimant being a widower, with the substitution of "her deceased husband" for "his deceased wife".

259.—(1) This section applies—

Additional relief in respect of children.

    (a) to any individual who is not entitled for the year of assessment to the higher (married persons) relief under section 257(1); and

    (b) to any married man who is entitled for the year of assessment to that higher relief but whose wife was throughout that year totally incapacitated by physical or mental infirmity.

(2) Subject to subsections (3) and (4) below and to section 260, if the claimant, being a person to whom this section applies, proves in the case of a year of assessment that a qualifying child is resident with him for the whole or part of the year, he shall be entitled to a deduction from his total income of an amount equal to the difference between the higher (married persons) relief and the lower (single persons) relief under subsection (1) of section 257 as it applies to persons not falling within subsection (2) or (3) of that section.

(3) A claimant is entitled to only one deduction under subsection (2) above for any year of assessment irrespective of the number of qualifying children resident with him in that year.

(4) A person to whom this section applies by virtue of subsection (1)(a) above shall not be entitled to relief under this section for a year of assessment during any part of which that person is married and living with his or her spouse unless the child in connection with whom the relief is claimed is resident with that person during a part of the year in which that person is not married and living with his or her spouse.

(5) For the purposes of this section a qualifying child means, in relation to any claimant and any year of assessment, a child who—

(a) is born in, or is under the age of 16 years at the commencement of, the year or, being over that age at the commencement of that year, is receiving full-time instruction at any university, college, school or other educational establishment; and

(b) is a child of the claimant or, not being such a child, is born in, or is under the age of 18 years at the commencement of, the year and maintained for the whole or part of that year by the claimant at his own expense.

(6) In subsection (5)(a) above the reference to a child receiving full-time instruction at an educational establishment includes a reference to a child undergoing training by any person ("the employer") for any trade, profession or vocation in such circumstances that the child is required to devote the whole of his time to the training for a period of not less than two years.

For the purposes of a claim in connection with a child undergoing training, the inspector may require the employer to furnish particulars with respect to the training of the child in such form as may be prescribed by the Board.

(7) If any question arises under this section whether a child is receiving full-time instruction at an educational establishment, the Board may consult the Secretary of State or the Department of Education for Northern Ireland.

(8) In subsection (5)(b) above the reference to a child of the claimant includes a reference to a stepchild of his, an illegitimate child of his if he has married the other parent after the child's birth and an adopted child of his if the child was under the age of 18 years when he was adopted.

1969 c. 46.
1969 c. 28 (N.I.).

(9) Notwithstanding anything in section 9 of the Family Law Reform Act 1969 or section 5 of the Age of Majority Act (Northern Ireland) 1969 or any rule of law in Scotland, for the purposes of subsection (5) above a child whose birthday falls on 6th April shall be taken to be over the age of

16 at the commencement of the year which begins with his 16th birthday and over the age of 18 at the commencement of the year which begins with his 18th birthday.

260.—(1) Where for any year of assessment two or more individuals are entitled to relief under section 259 in connection with the same child—

> Apportionment of relief under section 259.

    (a) the amount referred to in subsection (2) of that section shall be apportioned between them; and

    (b) the deduction to which each of them is entitled under that section shall, subject to subsection (2) below, be equal to so much of that amount as is apportioned to him.

(2) Where for any year of assessment amounts are apportioned to an individual under this section in respect of two or more children, the deduction to which he is entitled for that year under section 259 shall be equal to the sum of those amounts or the amount referred to in subsection (2) of that section, whichever is the less.

(3) Any amount required to be apportioned under this section shall be apportioned between the individuals concerned in such proportions as may be agreed between them or, in default of agreement, in proportion to the length of the periods for which the child in question is resident with them respectively in the year of assessment; and where the proportions are not so agreed, the apportionment shall be made by such body of General Commissioners, being the General Commissioners for a division in which one of the individuals resides, as the Board may direct, or, if none of the individuals resides in Great Britain, by the Special Commissioners.

(4) Where a claim is made under section 259 and it appears that, if the claim is allowed, an apportionment will be necessary under this section, the Board may if they think fit direct that the claim itself shall be dealt with by any specified body of Commissioners which could under this section be directed to make the apportionment and that the same Commissioners shall also make any apportionment which proves to be necessary; and where a direction is given under this subsection no other body of Commissioners shall have jurisdiction to determine the claim.

(5) The Commissioners making any apportionment under this section shall hear and determine the case in like manner as an appeal, but any individual who is, or but for the provisions of this section would be, entitled to relief in connection with the child shall be entitled to appear and be heard by the Commissioners or to make representations to them in writing.

(6) For the purposes of this section an individual shall not be regarded as entitled to relief under section 259 for any year of assessment in connection with the same child as another individual if there is another child in connection with whom he, and he alone, is entitled to relief under that section for that year.

261. A man who becomes married during a year of assessment may by notice to the inspector elect that his marriage be disregarded for the purposes of any claim for that year under section 258 or 259, and, in that case, the marriage shall also be disregarded for the purposes of any claim for that year under section 257.

> Claims under sections 258 and 259 for year of marriage.

262. Where a man dies in a year of assessment for which he is entitled to the higher (married persons) relief under section 257(1), or would be so entitled but for an election under section 261 or 287, his widow shall be entitled—

(a) for that year of assessment, and

(b) unless she marries again before the beginning of it, for the next following year of assessment,

to a deduction from her total income of an amount equal to that referred to in section 259(2).

Dependent
relatives.

263.—(1) If the claimant proves that he maintains at his own expense—

(a) any relative of his or of his wife who is incapacitated by old age or infirmity from maintaining himself; or

(b) his or his wife's mother who, whether or not incapacitated, is either widowed, or living apart from her husband, or a single woman in consequence of dissolution or annulment of marriage,

being (whether falling within paragraph (a) or (b) above) a person whose total income does not in a year exceed by more than £100 a sum equal to the basic retirement pension for that year, he shall be entitled in respect of each such person whom he so maintains to a deduction from his total income of £100 reduced, if the total income of the person so maintained exceeds the basic retirement pension, by the amount of the excess.

(2) Where the claimant under subsection (1) above is a woman—

(a) the references in that subsection to the claimant's wife shall be construed as references to the claimant's husband; and

(b) unless she is a married woman living with her husband, for each reference in that subsection to £100 there shall be substituted a reference to £145.

(3) For the purposes of this section "the basic retirement pension" for any year means the aggregate of the payments to which a person would be entitled in that year on account of a Category A retirement pension under the Social Security Acts 1975 or the Social Security (Northern Ireland) Acts 1975 if the weekly rate of his pension consisted (and consisted only) of the full amount of the basic component.

(4) Subject to subsection (7) below, where two or more persons jointly maintain any such person as is mentioned in subsection (1) above, the deduction of £100 or less mentioned in that subsection in respect of the person so maintained shall be apportioned between them in proportion to the amount or value of their respective contributions towards the maintenance of that person.

The apportionment under this subsection may be effected as the persons entitled to claim the relief agree, and, subject to any such agreement, subsections (5) and (6) below shall apply to the apportionment.

(5) Any apportionment under subsection (4) above shall be made by such body of General Commissioners, being the General Commissioners for a division in which one of the individuals resides, as the Board may direct, or, if none of the individuals resides in Great Britain, by the Special Commissioners.

(6) Where a claim is made under subsection (1) above and it appears that, if the claim is allowed, an apportionment will be necessary under subsection (4) above, the Board may if they think fit direct that the claim itself shall be dealt with by any specified body of Commissioners which could under this section be directed to make the apportionment and that the same Commissioners shall also make any apportionment which proves to be necessary; and where a direction is given under this subsection no other body of Commissioners shall have jurisdiction to determine the claim.

(7) Where, without subsection (2)(b) above, the claimant's relief would fall to be reduced by any proportion under subsection (4) above, any increase in the claimant's relief attributable to subsection (2)(b) above shall be reduced by the same proportion; and accordingly subsection (4) above shall be read without reference to the modifications made by subsection (2)(b).

264. If the claimant, by reason of old age or infirmity, is compelled to depend upon the services of a son or daughter resident with and maintained by him, he shall be entitled to a deduction of £55 from his total income.

Claimant depending on services of a son or daughter.

265.—(1) Subject to subsection (3) below, if the claimant proves—

Relief for blind persons.

    (a) that he is a married man who for the year of assessment has his wife living with him, and that one of them was, and the other was not, a registered blind person for the whole or part of the year; or

    (b) that, not being such a married man, he was a registered blind person for the whole or part of the year,

he shall be entitled to a deduction of £540 from his total income.

(2) Subject to subsection (3) below, if the claimant proves—

    (a) that he is a married man who for the year of assessment has his wife living with him, and

    (b) that he was a registered blind person for the whole or part of the year and his wife was also a registered blind person for the whole or part of the year,

he shall be entitled to a deduction of £1,080 from his total income.

(3) Unless a claimant who is entitled to relief for the year of assessment under section 264 in respect of the services of a son or daughter relinquishes his claim to that relief, he shall not be allowed relief under this section for that year.

(4) In this section "registered blind person" means a person registered as a blind person in a register compiled under section 29 of the National Assistance Act 1948 or, in the case of a person ordinarily resident in Scotland or in Northern Ireland, a person who is a blind person within the meaning of section 64(1) of that Act.

Life assurance premiums.

266.—(1) Subject to the provisions of this section, sections 274 and 619(6) and Schedules 14 and 15, an individual who pays any such premium as is specified in subsection (2) below or makes a payment falling within subsection (7) below shall (without making any claim) be entitled to relief under this section.

(2) The premiums referred to in subsection (1) above are any premiums paid by an individual under a policy of insurance or contract for a deferred annuity, where—

(a) the payments are made to —

(i) any insurance company legally established in the United Kingdom or any branch in the United Kingdom of an insurance company lawfully carrying on in the United Kingdom life assurance business (as defined in section 431); or

1982 c. 50.

(ii) underwriters being members of Lloyd's who comply with the requirements set forth in section 83 of the Insurance Companies Act 1982; or

(iii) a registered friendly society; or

(iv) in the case of a deferred annuity, the National Debt Commissioners; and

(b) the insurance or, as the case may be, the deferred annuity is on the life of the individual or on the life of his spouse; and

(c) the insurance or contract was made by him or his spouse.

(3) Subject to subsections (7), (10) and (11) below, no relief under this section shall be given—

(a) except in respect of premiums payable under policies for securing a capital sum on death, whether in conjunction with any other benefit or not;

(b) in respect of premiums payable under any policy issued in respect of an insurance made after 19th March 1968 unless the policy is a qualifying policy;

(c) in respect of premiums payable under any policy issued in respect of an insurance made after 13th March 1984, except where the relief relates to part only of any such payment as falls within subsection (6) below;

(d) in respect of premiums payable during the period of deferment in respect of a policy of deferred assurance.

(4) Subject to subsections (6) to (8) below, relief under this section in respect of any premiums paid by an individual in a year of assessment shall be given by making good to the person to whom they are paid any deficiency arising from the deductions authorised under subsection (5)

below; and this section and Schedule 14 shall have effect in relation to any
premium or part of a premium which is paid otherwise than in the year of
assessment in which it becomes due and payable as if it were paid in that
year.

(5) Subject to the provisions of Schedule 14—

(a) an individual resident in the United Kingdom who is entitled to
relief under this section in respect of any premium may deduct
from any payment in respect of the premium and retain an
amount equal to 15 per cent. of the payment; and

(b) the person to whom the payment is made shall accept the
amount paid after the deduction in discharge of the individual's
liability to the same extent as if the deduction had not been
made and may recover the deficiency from the Board.

(6) Where—

(a) a person is entitled to relief under this section in respect of part
only of a payment made to a registered friendly society; and

(b) the insurance or contract was made by the society in the course
of tax exempt life or endowment business (as defined in section
466(2)),

subsection (4) above shall not apply with respect to that relief but there
shall be deducted from his total income an amount equal to one-half of
that part of the payment.

(7) Where a person makes a payment to a trade union as defined in
section 28(1) of the Trade Union and Labour Relations Act 1974, and   1974 c. 52.
part of that payment is attributable to the provision of superannuation,
life insurance or funeral benefits, he shall be entitled to relief under this
section in respect of that part of the payment, but—

(a) subsection (4) above shall not apply; and

(b) there shall be deducted from his total income an amount equal
to one-half of that part of the payment.

This subsection shall also apply in relation to any payment made to an
organisation of persons in police service but only where the annual
amount of the part of the payment attributable to the provision of the
benefits in question is £20 or more.

(8) Where the individual is not resident in the United Kingdom but is
entitled to relief by virtue of section 278(2), subsection (4) above shall not
apply but (subject to section 278(3)) the like relief shall be given to him
under paragraph 6 of Schedule 14.

(9) Subsections (5) and (8) above shall apply in relation to an
individual who is not resident in the United Kingdom but is a member of
the armed forces of the Crown or the wife (but not the husband) of such
a member as if the individual were so resident.

(10) Subsection (3)(b) above shall not apply—

(a) to any policy of life insurance having as its sole object the
provision on an individual's death or disabililty of a sum
substantially the same as any amount then outstanding under a
mortgage of his residence, or of any premises occupied by him

PART VII

for the purposes of a business, being a mortgage the principal amount secured by which is repayable by instalments payable annually or at shorter regular intervals; or

(b) to any policy of life insurance issued in connection with an approved scheme as defined in Chapter I of Part XIV.

1924 c. 27.

In the application of this subsection to Scotland, for any reference to a mortgage there shall be substituted a reference to a heritable security within the meaning of the Conveyancing (Scotland) Act 1924 (but including a security constituted by ex facie absolute disposition or assignation).

(11) Subsection (3)(a) and (d) above shall not affect premiums payable—

(a) under policies or contracts made in connection with any superannuation or bona fide pension scheme for the benefit of the employees of any employer, or of persons engaged in any particular trade, profession, vocation or business, or for the benefit of the wife or widow of any such employee or person or of his children or other dependants, or

(b) under policies taken out by teachers in the schools known in the year 1918 as secondary schools, pending the establishment of a superannuation or pension scheme for those teachers.

(12) Schedule 14 shall have effect for the purpose of modifying, for certain cases, and supplementing the provisions of this section.

Qualifying policies.

267. Schedule 15, Part I of which contains the basic rules for determining whether or not a policy is a qualifying policy, Part II of which makes provision for the certification etc. of policies as qualifying policies and Part III of which modifies Parts I and II in their application to certain policies issued by non-resident companies, shall have effect for the purpose of determining whether or not a policy is a qualifying policy; and, accordingly, any reference in this Act to a qualifying policy shall be construed in accordance with that Schedule.

Early conversion or surrender of life policies.

268.—(1) Where a policy of life insurance to which this section applies has been issued and, within four years from the making of the insurance in respect of which it was issued, any of the following events happens, that is to say—

(a) the surrender of the whole or part of the rights conferred by the policy;

(b) the falling due (otherwise than on death) of a sum payable in pursuance of a right conferred by the policy to participate in profits; and

(c) the conversion of the policy into a paid-up or partly paid-up policy;

the body by whom the policy was issued shall pay to the Board, out of the sums payable by reason of the surrender or, as the case may be, out of the sum falling due or out of the fund available to pay the sums which will be due on death or on the maturity of the policy, a sum determined in accordance with the following provisions of this section, unless the body is wound up and the event is a surrender or conversion effected in connection with the winding-up.

(2) The sum payable under subsection (1) above shall, subject to the following provisions of this section, be equal to the lower of the following, that is to say—

    (a) the appropriate percentage of the premiums payable under the policy up to the happening of the event; and

    (b) the surrender value of the policy at the time of the happening of the event less the complementary percentage of the premiums mentioned in paragraph (a) above.

(3) If the event is one of those mentioned below, the sum payable to the Board shall not exceed the following limit, that is to say—

    (a) if it is the surrender of part of the rights conferred by the policy, the value of the rights surrendered at the time of the surrender;

    (b) if it is the conversion of the policy into a partly paid-up policy, the surrender value at the time of the conversion, of so much of the policy as is paid up; and

    (c) if it is the falling due of a sum, that sum.

(4) If the event was preceded by the happening of such an event as is mentioned in subsection (1) above, subsection (2) above shall apply—

    (a) as if the lower of the amounts mentioned therein were reduced by the sum paid under this section in respect of the earlier event; and

    (b) if the earlier event was such an event as is mentioned in paragraph (a) or (c) of subsection (3) above, as if the surrender value of the policy were increased by the amount which, under that paragraph, limited or might have limited the sum payable under this section in respect of the earlier event.

(5) For the purposes of this section the appropriate percentage, in relation to any event, is the percentage equal to the following fraction of the percentage found by doubling that mentioned in section 266(5)(a) as in force for the year of assessment in which the event happened, that is to say—

    (a) if the event happens in the first two of the four years mentioned in subsection (1) above, three-sixths;

    (b) if it happens in the third of those years, two-sixths; and

    (c) if it happens in the last of those years, one-sixth;

and the complementary percentage, in relation to any event, is 100 per cent. less the appropriate percentage.

(6) Where the annual amount of the premiums payable under a policy of life insurance is at any time increased (whether under the policy or by any contract made after its issue) so as to exceed by more than 25 per cent.—

(a) if the insurance was made on or before 26th March 1974, the annual amount as at that date, or

(b) in the case of any other insurance, the first annual amount so payable,

the additional rights attributable to the excess shall be treated for the purposes of this section as conferred by a new policy issued in respect of an insurance made at that time, and the excess shall be treated as premiums payable under the new policy.

(7) This section applies to any policy of life insurance which is a qualifying policy unless—

(a) it is a policy in respect of the premiums on which relief under section 266 is not available by virtue of subsection (3)(c) of that section; or

(b) it is a policy of life insurance issued in connection with an approved scheme, as defined in Chapter I of Part XIV;

and in relation to a policy of life insurance issued in respect of an insurance made before 27th March 1974 applies only in accordance with subsection (6) above.

Surrender etc. of policies after four years.

269.—(1) Where a policy of life insurance to which this section applies has been issued and, in the fifth or any later year from the making of the insurance in respect of which it was issued, either of the following events happens, that is to say—

(a) the surrender of the whole or part of the rights conferred by the policy; and

(b) the falling due (otherwise than on death or maturity) of a sum payable in pursuance of a right conferred by the policy to participate in profits;

then, if either of those events has happened before, the body by whom the policy was issued shall pay to the Board, out of the sums payable by reason of the surrender, or, as the case may be, out of the sum falling due, a sum determined in accordance with the following provisions of this section.

(2) The sum payable under subsection (1) above shall, subject to the following provisions of this section, be equal to the applicable percentage of the lower of the following—

(a) the total of the premiums which are payable in that year under the policy; and

(b) the sums payable by reason of the surrender or, as the case may be, the sum falling due;

and the percentage to be applied for this purpose shall be a percentage equal to that mentioned in section 266(5)(a) as in force for the year of assessment in which the event happens.

(3) Where, after a sum has become payable under subsection (1) above, and within the same year from the making of the insurance, another such event happens as is mentioned therein, the sums payable

under that subsection in respect of both or all of the events shall not exceed the applicable percentage of the total mentioned in subsection (2)(a) above.

(4) Where, on the happening of an event in the fifth or any later year from the making of the insurance, any sum is payable under subsection (1) of section 268 as applied by subsection (6) of that section as well as under subsection (1) above, subsection (2) above shall apply as if the sums or sum mentioned in paragraph (b) thereof were reduced by the sum payable under that section.

(5) This section applies to any policy of life insurance which is a qualifying policy unless—

    (a) it is a policy in respect of the premiums on which relief under section 266 is not available by virtue of subsection (3)(c) of that section; or

    (b) it is a policy issued in the course of an industrial insurance business; or

    (c) it was issued in respect of an insurance made before 27th March 1974.

270.—(1) Where on the happening of an event in relation to a policy of life insurance a sum is payable under section 268 or 269, relief under section 266 in respect of the relevant premiums paid under the policy shall be reduced by the sum so payable or, as the case may be, by so much of the sum as does not exceed the amount of that relief.(or as does not exceed so much of that amount as remains after any previous reduction under this section).

(2) For the purposes of this section the relevant premiums are—

    (a) in relation to a sum payable under section 268, the premiums payable under the policy up to the happening of the event by reason of which the sum is payable; and

    (b) in relation to a sum payable under section 269, the premiums payable in the year (from the making of the insurance) in which the event happens by reason of which the sum is payable.

(3) Where the relevant premiums are payable in more than one year of assessment the reduction in relief under this section shall, so far as possible, reduce relief for an earlier year of assessment before reducing relief for a later one.

(4) Any sum paid under section 268 or 269 by reason of any event shall be treated—

    (a) as between the parties, as received by the person by whom the premiums under the policy were paid; and

    (b) for the purposes of section 266, as a sum paid by that person in satisfaction of his liability resulting from the reduction of relief under this section;

and where that sum exceeds that liability he shall be entitled, on a claim made by him not later than six years after the end of the year of assessment in which the event happens, to repayment of the excess.

271.—(1) Where—

(a) under section 547 a gain arising in connection with a policy or contract would be treated as forming part of an individual's total income; and

(b) the policy was issued in respect of an insurance made after 26th March 1974 or the contract was made after that date; and

(c) any sum is at any time after the making of the insurance or contract lent to or at the direction of that individual by or by arrangement with the body issuing the policy or, as the case may be, the body with which the contract was made;

then, subject to subsection (2) below, the same results shall follow under sections 268 to 270 as if at the time the sum was lent there had been a surrender of part of the rights conferred by the policy or contract and the sum had been paid as consideration for the surrender (and if the policy is a qualifying policy, whether or not the premiums under it are eligible for relief under section 266, those results shall follow under section 269, whether or not a gain would be treated as arising on the surrender).

(2) Subsection (1) above does not apply—

(a) in relation to a policy if—

(i) it is a qualifying policy; and

(ii) either interest at a commercial rate is payable on the sum lent or the sum is lent to a full-time employee of the body issuing the policy for the purpose of assisting him in the purchase or improvement of a dwelling used or to be used as his only or main residence; or

(b) in relation to a contract if and to the extent that interest on the sum lent is eligible for relief under section 353 by virtue of section 365.

272.—(1) Any body by whom a policy to which section 268 or 269 applies has been issued shall, within 30 days of the end of each period of 12 months ending with 31st March in every year, make a return to the collector of the sums which, in that period, have become payable by it under either of those sections.

(2) Any sum which is to be included in a return made under subsection (1) above shall be due at the time by which the return is to be made and shall be paid without being demanded.

(3) Where any sum which was or ought to have been included in such a return is not paid by the end of the period for which the return was to be made, it may be recovered by an assessment as if it were income tax for the year of assessment in which that period ends; and where it appears to the inspector that a sum which ought to have been so included had not been included or that a return is not correct he may make such an assessment to the best of his judgment.

(4) All the provisions of the Income Tax Acts relating to the assessment and collection of tax, interest on unpaid tax, appeals and penalties shall, with the necessary modifications, apply in relation to sums due under this section; and for the purposes of those provisions so far as

they relate to interest on unpaid tax, a sum assessed in pursuance of this section shall be treated as having been payable when it would have been payable had it been included in a return under subsection (1) above.

(5) Where, on an appeal against an assessment made in pursuance of this section, it is determined that a greater sum has been assessed than was payable, the excess, if paid, shall be repaid.

(6) Where a body has paid a sum which is payable under section 268 or 269 it shall give within 30 days to the person by whom the sum is, under section 270(4), treated as received a statement specifying that sum and showing how it has been arrived at.

(7) The Board or an inspector may, by notice served on the body by whom a policy to which section 268 or 269 applies has been issued, require the body, within such time, not being less than 30 days, as may be specified in the notice—

(a) to furnish such particulars; or

(b) to make available for inspection by an officer authorised by the Board such books and other documents in the possession or under the control of the body;

as the Board or officer may reasonably require for the purposes of those sections or this section.

273. Subject to sections 274, 617(3) and 619(6), if the claimant is, under any Act of Parliament or under the terms or conditions of his employment, liable to the payment of any sum, or to the deduction from his salary or stipend of any sum, for the purpose of securing a deferred annuity to his widow or provision for his children after his death, he shall be entitled to a deduction from the amount of income tax with which he is chargeable equal to income tax at the basic rate on the amount of the sum paid by him or deducted from his salary or stipend.

Payments securing widows' and children's annuities.

274.—(1) The aggregate of the premiums or other sums in respect of which relief is given to any person under section 266 shall not exceed £1,500 in any year of assessment or one-sixth of that person's total income, whichever is the greater.

Limits on relief under sections 266 and 273.

(2) The aggregate of the relief given under sections 266 and 273 in respect of premiums or sums payable for securing any benefits other than capital sums on death shall not exceed the amount of the income tax calculated at the appropriate rate on £100.

(3) In subsection (2) above "the appropriate rate"—

(a) in relation to premiums to which section 266 applies, means 15 per cent.;

(b) in relation to other payments, means the basic rate of income tax.

(4) War insurance premiums shall not be taken into account in calculating the limits of one-sixth of total income or of £100 mentioned in this section.

In this subsection "war insurance premiums" means any additional premium or other sum paid in order to extend an existing life insurance policy to risks arising from war or war service abroad, and any part of any

PART VII

premium or other sum paid in respect of a life insurance policy covering those risks, or either of them, which appears to the inspector to be attributable to those risks, or either of them.

Supplemental

Meaning of "relative".

275. In this Chapter "relative" includes any person of whom the person claiming a relief had the custody and whom he maintained at his own expense while that person was under the age of 16 years.

Effect on relief of charges on income.

276.—(1) Where any of the claimant's income is income the income tax on which (at the basic rate) he is entitled to charge against any other person, or to deduct, retain or satisfy out of any payment, he shall not be entitled to relief under this Chapter in respect of that income, except to the extent, if any, that the relief would exceed tax at the basic rate on that income.

(2) Notwithstanding subsection (1) above, relief under section 273 may be given to the extent that the deduction from tax provided for by that section can be made from so much of the income tax with which the claimant is chargeable as exceeds what would be the amount of that tax if all income tax were chargeable at the basic rate to the exclusion of any other rate.

Partners.

277.—(1) Subject to subsection (2) below, the following persons having joint interests, that is to say—

(a) coparceners, joint tenants, or tenants in common of the profits of any property, and

(b) joint tenants, or tenants of land or tenements in partnership, being in the actual and joint occupation thereof in partnership, who are entitled to the profits thereof in shares, and

(c) partners carrying on a trade, profession or vocation together who are entitled to the profits thereof in shares,

may claim any relief under this Chapter according to their respective shares and interests, and any such claims which are proved may be dealt with in the same manner as in the case of several interests.

(2) The income of a partner from a partnership carrying on any trade, profession or vocation shall be deemed to be the share to which he is entitled during the year to which the claim relates in the partnership profits, such profits being estimated according to the provisions of the Income Tax Acts.

Non-residents.

278.—(1) Subject to the provisions of this section, no relief under this Chapter shall be given in the case of any individual who is not resident in the United Kingdom.

(2) Subject to subsection (3) below, subsection (1) above shall not apply in the case of any individual who satisfies the Board that he or she—

(a) is a Commonwealth citizen or a citizen of the Republic of Ireland; or

(b) is a person who is or who has been employed in the service of the Crown, or who is employed in the service of any missionary society or in the service of any territory under Her Majesty's protection; or

(c) is resident in the Isle of Man or the Channel Islands; or

(d) has previously resided within the United Kingdom, and is resident abroad for the sake of his or her health, or the health of a member of his or her family resident with him or her; or

(e) is a widow whose late husband was in the service of the Crown.

(3) No relief under this Chapter shall be given so as to reduce the amount of the income tax payable by the individual below the amount which results from applying the fraction—

$$\frac{A}{B}$$

to the amount which would have been payable by him by way of income tax if the tax were chargeable on his total income from all sources (including income which is not subject to income tax charged in the United Kingdom) where—

A is the amount of his income subject to income tax charged in the United Kingdom; and

B is the amount of his total income.

(4) Subsection (3) above shall have effect as if the amount of any relief to which an individual is entitled under section 266(4) were an amount by which his liability to income tax is reduced.

(5) For the purposes of subsection (3) above as it applies to an individual whose income includes income eligible for double taxation relief—

(a) in computing the amount of the income tax payable by the individual, the tax chargeable in respect of the income eligible for double taxation relief shall be disregarded;

(b) in computing the amount of his income subject to income tax charged in the United Kingdom, the income eligible for double taxation relief shall be disregarded; and

(c) in computing his total income from all sources, including income which is not subject to income tax charged in the United Kingdom, income eligible for double taxation relief shall be included, and the income tax which would be chargeable on that total income shall be computed without regard to the double taxation relief available in respect of the income eligible for double taxation relief;

and, accordingly, where this subsection applies, the amount of the tax chargeable in respect of the income eligible for double taxation relief shall not be affected by subsections (2) and (3) above.

PART VII

(6) Subsection (5) shall not operate so as to make the tax payable by an individual for a year of assessment higher than it would have been if the double taxation relief had not been available.

(7) In subsection (5) above "income eligible for double taxation relief" means any dividends, interest, royalties or other profits which are chargeable to income tax but in respect of which relief (other than credit) is available under an Order in Council under section 788 so as to limit the rate of income tax so chargeable (but not so as to confer an exemption and make it income which is not subject to income tax charged in the United Kingdom).

(8) Any claim which an individual is entitled to make by virtue of subsection (2) above shall be made to the Board.

CHAPTER II

TAXATION OF INCOME OF SPOUSES

General rules

Aggregation of wife's income with husband's.

279.—(1) Subject to the provisions of this Chapter, a woman's income chargeable to income tax shall, so far as it is income for—

(a) a year of assessment; or

(b) any part of a year of assessment, being a part beginning with 6th April,

during which she is a married woman living with her husband, be deemed for income tax purposes to be his income and not to be her income.

(2) The question whether there is any income of hers chargeable to income tax for any year of assessment and, if so, what is to be taken to be the amount thereof for income tax purposes shall not be affected by the provisions of subsection (1) above.

(3) Any tax falling to be assessed in respect of any income which, under subsection (1) above, is to be deemed to be the income of a woman's husband shall, instead of being assessed on her, or on her trustee, guardian, curator, receiver or committee, or on her executors or administrators, be assessable on him or, in the appropriate cases, on his trustee, guardian, curator, receiver or committee, or on his executors or administrators.

(4) Nothing in subsection (3) above shall affect the operation of section 111.

(5) Any deduction from a man's total income made under section 257(6) and (7) shall be treated as reducing the earned income of his wife.

(6) References in this section to a woman's income include references to any sum which, apart from the provisions of this section, would fall to be included in computing her total income, and this subsection has effect in relation to any such sum notwithstanding that some enactment (including, except so far as the contrary is expressly provided, an enactment passed after the passing of this Act) requires that that sum should not be treated as income of any person other than her.

(7) For the purposes of sections 380 and 381 of this Act and section 71 of the 1968 Act (set off of capital allowances against general income), subsection (1)(b) above shall have effect as if the words "being a part beginning with 6th April" were omitted.

280.—(1) Where during any part of a year of assessment a husband and wife are living together but his income for that year does not or, if there were any, would not include any of hers, then if either of them—

> (a) would, if he or she had sufficient income for that year, be entitled to have any amount deducted from or set off against it under a provision to which this subsection applies, and

> (b) makes a claim in that behalf,

that amount or, as the case may be, so much of it as cannot be deducted from or set off against his or her own income for that year shall instead be deducted from and set off against the income for that year of the other spouse.

(2) Subsection (1) above applies—

> (a) in the case of the husband, to any provision of Chapter I of this Part and sections 289 and 353;

> (b) in the case of the wife, to—

>> (i) any provision of that Chapter except sections 257(1)(b), (2)(b) and (3)(b), 258, 259 and 262;

>> (ii) section 289 but only in respect of amounts subscribed by her for shares issued in the part of the year of assessment mentioned in subsection (1) above; and

>> (iii) section 353 so far as applicable to interest paid in the part of the year mentioned in subsection (1) above.

Transfer of reliefs.

281.—(1) Where in any year of assessment tax has been deducted under section 203 from the earned income of a wife and, apart from this section, a repayment of tax for that year would fall to be made to her husband in consequence of an assessment under Schedule E, so much of the repayment as is attributable to the tax so deducted shall be made to her and not to him.

(2) The amount of a repayment attributable to tax deducted as mentioned in subsection (1) above is the excess (if any) of the total net tax so deducted in the year of assessment over the tax chargeable on the wife's relevant earned income included in her husband's total income for that year after allowing—

> (a) any relief for that year under section 266 in respect of any payment made by her of the kind mentioned in paragraph 5 of Schedule 14; and

> (b) any relief for that year to which her husband is entitled under any other provision of the Income Tax Acts to the extent to which it cannot be allowed because his income, exclusive of her earned income, is insufficient;

Tax repayments to wives.

but that amount shall not exceed the aggregate of the amounts repayable for that year in respect of the total net tax deducted in that year under section 203 from the income of the wife and the income of her husband.

(3) Where in consequence of an assessment under Schedule E any amount is repayable under this section to the wife of the person on whom the assessment is made the inspector shall notify both of them of his determination of that amount and, subject to subsection (4) below, an appeal shall lie against the determination as if it were a decision on a claim.

(4) Any appeal under subsection (3) above shall be to the General Commissioners for the division in which the spouses reside or, if they reside in different divisions, for the division in which one of them resides, as the Board may direct, or, if neither of them resides in Great Britain, to the Special Commissioners; and on any such appeal by one of the spouses the other shall have the same rights as an appellant, including any right to require the statement of a case for the opinion of the court.

(5) The Board may make regulations—

(a) modifying subsection (2) above in relation to such cases as may be specified in the regulations;

(b) modifying section 824 in relation to cases in which a repayment falls to be made under this section.

(6) This section does not apply to any repayment for a year of assessment—

(a) for which the husband is chargeable to income tax at a rate or rates higher than the basic rate; or

(b) for which any earned income of the wife has been assessed otherwise than under Schedule E.

(7) For the purposes of this section earned income of a wife has the same meaning as for the purposes of subsection (6) of section 257 and relevant earned income of a wife means so much of her earned income as exceeds the relief available in respect of it under that subsection.

(8) References in this section to the total net tax deducted in any year under section 203 are references to the total income tax deducted during that year by virtue of regulations made under that section less any income tax repaid by virtue of any such regulations.

Construction of references to married women living with their husbands.

282.—(1) A married woman shall be treated for income tax purposes as living with her husband unless—

(a) they are separated under an order of a court of competent jurisdiction, or by deed of separation, or

(b) they are in fact separated in such circumstances that the separation is likely to be permanent.

(2) Where a married woman is living with her husband and either—

(a) one of them is, and the other is not, resident in the United Kingdom for a year of assessment, or

(b) both of them are resident in the United Kingdom for a year of assessment, but one of them is, and the other is not, absent from the United Kingdom throughout that year,

the same consequences shall follow for income tax purposes as would have followed if, throughout that year of assessment, they had been in fact separated in such circumstances that the separation was likely to be permanent.

(3) Where subsection (2) above applies and the net aggregate amount of income tax falling to be borne by the husband and the wife for the year is greater than it would have been but for that subsection, the Board shall cause such relief to be given (by the reduction of such assessments on the husband or the wife or the repayment of such tax paid, by deduction or otherwise, by the husband or the wife, as the Board may direct) as will reduce that net aggregate amount by the amount of the excess.

Separate assessments

283.—(1) If, within six months before the 6th July in any year of assessment for which his income would include any of hers, a husband or a wife makes an application for the purpose in such manner and form as the Board may prescribe, income tax for that year shall be assessed, charged and recovered on the income of the husband and on the income of the wife as if they were not married, and all the provisions of the Income Tax Acts with respect to the assessment, charge and recovery of income tax shall, save as otherwise provided by those Acts, apply as if they were not married.

Option for separate assessment.

(2) Notwithstanding an application under subsection (1) above the income of the husband and the wife shall be treated as one in estimating total income; and the amount of tax payable by each of them shall be ascertained by first dividing between them, in proportion to the amounts of their respective incomes, the amount that would be payable by them if no reliefs were given under Chapter I or III of this Part and then applying section 284 to give effect to those reliefs.

(3) Subject to subsection (4) below, an application duly made by a husband or wife under subsection (1) above shall have effect, not only as respects the year of assessment for which it is made, but also for any subsequent year of assessment.

(4) A person who has made any such application for any year of assessment may give, for any subsequent year of assessment, a notice to withdraw that application, and where such a notice is given, the application shall not have effect with respect to the year for which the notice is given or any subsequent year.

(5) A notice of withdrawal under subsection (4) above shall be in such form, and be given in such manner, as may be prescribed by the Board, and shall not be valid unless it is given within the period allowed by law for making, for the year for which the notice is given, applications similar to that to which the notice relates.

284.—(1) Where, by virtue of an application under section 283(1), income tax for any year of assessment is to be assessable and chargeable on the incomes of a husband and wife as if they were not married, the total relief given to the husband and the wife by way of personal reliefs shall be

Effect of separate assessment on personal reliefs.

PART VII   the same as if the application had not had effect with respect to the year and, subject to subsections (2) and (3) below, the reduction of tax flowing from the personal reliefs shall be allocated to the husband and the wife—

(a) so far as it flows from relief under section 273 or Chapter III of this Part, to the husband or the wife according as he or she made the payment giving rise to the relief;

(b) so far as it flows from relief in respect of a dependent relative under section 263 or relief in respect of a son or daughter under section 264, to the husband or the wife according as he or she maintains the relative or son or daughter; and

(c) as to the balance, in proportion to the amounts of tax which would have been payable by them respectively if no personal reliefs had been allowable.

(2) Subject to subsection (3) below, the amount of reduction of tax allocated to the wife by virtue of subsection (1) above shall not be less than the reduction resulting from section 279(5) in the tax chargeable in respect of her earned income, and the amount of reduction of tax allocated to the husband shall be correspondingly reduced.

(3) Where the amount of reduction of tax allocated to the husband under subsection (1) above exceeds the tax chargeable on the income of the husband for the year of assessment, the balance shall be applied to reduce the tax chargeable on the income of the wife for that year; and where the amount of reduction of tax allocated to the wife under that subsection exceeds the tax chargeable on her income for the year of assessment, the balance shall be applied to reduce the tax chargeable on the income of the husband for that year.

(4) Returns of the total incomes of the husband and the wife may be made for the purposes of this section either by the husband or by the wife, but, if the Board are not satisfied with any such return, they may obtain a return from the wife or the husband, as the case may be.

(5) In this section "personal reliefs" means the reliefs provided for by Chapters I and III of this Part.

Collection from wife of tax assessed on husband but attributable to her income.

285.—(1) Where—

(a) an assessment to income tax ("the original assessment") is made on a man, or on a man's trustee, guardian, curator, receiver or committee, or on a man's executors or administrators; and

(b) the Board are of opinion that, if an application for separate assessment under section 283(1) had been in force with respect to the year for which the assessment is made, an assessment ("the potential assessment") in respect of, or of part of, the same income would have fallen to be made on, or on the trustee, guardian, curator, receiver or committee of, or on the executors or administrators of, a woman who is that man's wife, or was his wife in that year of assessment; and

(c) the whole or part of the amount payable under the original assessment has remained unpaid at the expiration of 28 days from the time when it became due;

the Board may serve on her, or, if she is dead, on her executors or administrators, or, if the potential assessment could in the event referred to in paragraph (b) above have been made on her trustee, guardian, curator, receiver or committee, on her or on her trustee, guardian, curator, receiver or committee, a notice—

> (i) giving particulars of the original assessment, and of the amount remaining unpaid thereunder, and

> (ii) giving particulars, to the best of their judgment, of the potential assessment,

and requiring the person on whom the notice is served to pay the amount which would have been payable under the potential assessment if it conformed with those particulars, or the amount remaining unpaid under the original assessment, whichever is the less.

(2) The same consequences as respects—

(a) the imposition of a liability to pay, and the recovery of, the tax, with or without interest; and

(b) priority for the tax in bankruptcy, or in the administration of the estate of a deceased person; and

(c) appeals to the General or Special Commissioners, and the stating of cases for the opinion of the High Court; and

(d) the ultimate incidence of the liability imposed,

shall follow on the service of a notice under subsection (1) above on a woman, or on her trustee, guardian, curator, receiver or committee, or on her executors or administrators, as would have followed on the making on her, or on her trustee, guardian, curator, receiver or committee, or on her executors or administrators, as the case may be, of the potential assessment, being an assessment which—

> (i) was made on the day of the service of the notice, and

> (ii) charged the same amount of income tax as is required to be paid by the notice, and

> (iii) fell to be made, and was made, by the authority who made the original assessment, and

> (iv) was made by that authority to the best of their judgment,

and the provisions of the Income Tax Acts relating to the matters specified in paragraphs (a) to (d) above shall, with the necessary adaptations, have effect accordingly.

(3) Where an appeal against the original assessment has been heard in whole or in part by the Special Commissioners, any appeal from the notice under subsection (1) above shall be an appeal to the Special Commissioners, and where an appeal against the original assessment has been heard in whole or in part by the General Commissioners for any division, any appeal from the notice shall be an appeal to the General Commissioners for that division.

(4) Where a notice is given under subsection (1) above—

    (a) income tax up to the amount required to be paid by the notice shall cease to be recoverable under the original assessment, and

    (b) where the tax charged by the original assessment carried interest under section 86 of the Management Act, such adjustment shall be made of the amount payable under that section in relation to that assessment, and such repayment shall be made of any amounts previously paid under that section in relation thereto, as are necessary to secure that the total sum, if any, paid or payable under that section in relation to that assessment is the same as it would have been if the amount which ceases to be recoverable had never been charged.

(5) Where the amount payable under a notice given under subsection (1) above is reduced as the result of an appeal, or of the stating of a case for the opinion of the High Court—

    (a) the Board shall, if in the light of that result they are satisfied that the original assessment was excessive, cause such relief to be given by way of repayment or otherwise as appears to them to be just, but

    (b) subject to any relief so given, a sum equal to the reduction in the amount payable under the notice shall again become recoverable under the original assessment.

(6) The Board and the inspector shall have the like powers of obtaining information with a view to the giving of, and otherwise in connection with, a notice under subsection (1) above as they would have had with a view to the making of, and otherwise in connection with, the potential assessment if the necessary conditions had been fulfilled for the making of such an assessment.

Right of husband to disclaim liability for tax on deceased wife's income.

286.—(1) Where a woman dies who at any time before her death was a married woman living with her husband, he or, if he is dead, his executors or administrators, may, not later than two months from the date of the grant of probate or letters of administration in respect of her estate or, with the consent of her executors or administrators, at any later date, serve on her executors or administrators and on the inspector a notice declaring that, to the extent permitted by this section, he disclaims or they disclaim responsibility for unpaid income tax in respect of all income of hers for any year of assessment or part of a year of assessment during which he was her husband and she was living with him.

(2) A notice under subsection (1) above shall not be deemed to be validly served on the inspector unless it specifies the names and addresses of the woman's executors or administrators.

(3) Where a notice under subsection (1) above has been duly served on a woman's executors or administrators and on the inspector—

    (a) it shall be the duty of the Board to exercise such powers as they may then or thereafter be entitled to exercise under section 285 in connection with any assessment made on or before the date when the service of the notice is completed, being an assessment in respect of any of the income to which the notice relates; and

(b) the assessments (if any) which may be made after that date shall in all respects, and in particular as respects the persons assessable and the tax payable, be the assessments which would have fallen to be made if—

(i) an application for separate assessment under section 283(1) had been in force in respect of the year of assessment in question; and

(ii) all assessments previously made had been made accordingly.

(4) In the application of this section to Scotland, the reference to the date of the grant of probate or letters of administration shall be construed as a reference to the date of confirmation.

Separate taxation

287.—(1) Where a man and his wife living with him jointly so elect or have elected for any year of assessment, the wife's earnings and their other income shall be chargeable to income tax as provided in the following provisions of this section.

(2) References in this section to the wife's earnings are references to any earned income of hers other than—

(a) income arising in respect of any pension, superannuation or other allowance, deferred pay or compensation for loss of office given in respect of the husband's past services in any office or employment; or

(b) any payment of benefit under the Social Security Acts except a Category A retirement pension (exclusive of any increase under section 10 of the Social Security Pensions Act 1975 or Article 12 of the Social Security Pensions (Northern Ireland) Order 1975), unemployment benefit or invalid care allowance.

In this subsection "the Social Security Acts" means the Social Security Acts 1975 and the Social Security (Northern Ireland) Acts 1975.

(3) In charging the income of the husband and wife in accordance with section 279—

(a) the wife's earnings shall be charged to income tax as if she were a single woman with no other income; and

(b) the husband's other income shall be charged to income tax as if the wife's earnings were nil.

(4) Subject to subsections (5) and (6) below, the reliefs to be given under Chapter I of this Part shall be determined as if the husband and the wife were not married and—

(a) the wife's earnings were her only income; and

(b) the husband's income included all income of the wife, other than her earnings;

PART VII

Separate taxation of wife's earnings.

1975 c. 60.
S.I. 1975/1503
(N.I. 15).

and accordingly the reliefs to be given under that Chapter in respect of the income chargeable under either paragraph (a) or paragraph (b) of subsection (3) above shall not reduce the tax or the income chargeable under the other of those paragraphs.

(5) No relief shall be given to either the husband or the wife under section 257(2) or (3) or 259.

(6) References in Chapter I of this Part to the claimant shall be construed as including the wife.

(7) Notwithstanding anything to the contrary in the Income Tax Acts, where any amount is under any provision of those Acts to be deducted from or set off against income in respect of any payments, loss or capital allowance, then—

> (a) if under that provision it is (or is in the first instance) to reduce the wife's earned income, or is to be deducted or set off in respect of payments made by her or, in the case of relief under Chapter III of this Part, in respect of a payment made by her as a subscription for shares, it shall be treated as reducing her earnings and as not reducing any other income; and

> (b) in any other case, it shall be treated as not reducing the wife's earnings.

(8) Subsection (7) above shall not affect the giving of any relief under section 388 for a year of assessment for which no election under this section was in force.

(9) Income tax charged on the wife's earnings under subsection (3)(a) above shall, whether or not an application under section 283 is in force, be assessed and recovered as if she were a single woman, and any repayment of tax assessed in pursuance of this subsection shall be made to her.

(10) Where subsection (4) of section 284 applies for the purposes of subsections (1) to (3) of that section, it shall apply also for the purposes of this section; but, subject to that, nothing in this section shall be taken to affect the provisions of the Management Act as to returns.

Elections under
section 287.

288.—(1) An election under section 287 ("an election") must be made in such form and manner as the Board may prescribe and must be made not earlier than six months before the beginning of the year of assessment for which it is made nor later than 12 months after the end of that year or such later time as the Board may in any particular case allow.

(2) An election for any year of assessment shall, unless revoked, have effect for any subsequent year of assessment.

(3) An election in force for any year may be revoked by notice in such form and manner as the Board may prescribe and any such notice must be given jointly by the husband and the wife not later than 12 months after the end of that year or such later time as the Board may in any particular case allow.

(4) An election or revocation of an election under this section that could have been made jointly with a person who has died may, within the time permitted by this section, be made jointly with his personal representatives.

CHAPTER III

RELIEF FOR INVESTMENT IN CORPORATE TRADES: THE BUSINESS EXPANSION SCHEME

289.—(1) This Chapter has effect for affording relief from income tax where an individual who qualifies for the relief subscribes for eligible shares in a qualifying company, and either— *The relief.*

(a) those shares are issued to him after 5th April 1983 for the purpose of raising money for a qualifying trade which is being carried on by the company or which it intends to carry on; or

(b) those shares are issued to him after 18th March 1986 for the purpose of raising money—

(i) for research and development which is being carried on by the company or by any subsidiary of the company on the date on which the shares are issued, or begins so to be carried on immediately thereafter, and from which it is intended that a qualifying trade (to be so carried on) will be derived; or

(ii) both for any such research and development and the resulting trade; or

(c) those shares are issued to him after 5th April 1985 and before 19th March 1986 for the purpose of raising money—

(i) for research and development which is being carried on at the time when the shares are issued, or begins immediately thereafter, and from which the company intends to derive a qualifying trade which will be carried on by it; or

(ii) both for any such research and development and the resulting trade; or

(d) those shares are issued to him after the passing of the Finance Act 1986 (25th July 1986) for the purpose of raising money for oil exploration which— *1986 c. 41.*

(i) is being carried on by the company, or by any subsidiary of the company, on the date on which the shares are issued; or

(ii) begins so to be carried on immediately thereafter;

and from which it is intended that a qualifying trade (to be so carried on) will be derived.

(2) Subsection (1)(d) above shall not apply unless—

(a) throughout the period of three years beginning with the date on which the shares were issued the company, or any subsidiary of the company, holds an exploration licence which was granted to it, or to another such subsidiary;

(b) the exploration is carried out solely within the area to which the licence applies; and

I

PART VII

(c) on the date on which the shares are issued, neither the company nor any subsidiary of the company holds an appraisal licence or a development licence relating to that area or any part of that area.

(3) Where, at any time after the issue of the shares but before the end of the period mentioned in subsection (2)(a) above, the company, or any subsidiary of the company, comes to hold an appraisal licence or development licence which relates to the area, or any part of the area, to which the exploration licence relates, the exploration licence and that other licence shall be treated for the purposes of subsection (2)(a) above as a single exploration licence.

(4) In this Chapter "eligible shares" means new ordinary shares which, throughout the period of five years beginning with the date on which they are issued, carry no present or future preferential right to dividends or to a company's assets on its winding up and no present or future preferential right to be redeemed.

(5) Subject to subsection (6) below, the relief in respect of the amount subscribed by an individual for any eligible shares shall be given as a deduction of that amount from his total income for the year of assessment in which the shares are issued, and references in this Chapter to the amount of the relief are references to the amount of that deduction.

(6) If—

(a) the shares are issued before 6th October in a year of assessment; and

(b) the claimant so requests in his claim for relief;

the relief shall be given partly by way of deduction from the claimant's total income for the year of assessment in which the shares are issued and partly by way of deduction from his total income for the preceding year of assessment.

(7) A deduction from the claimant's total income for the year of assessment preceding that in which the shares are issued shall be of such amount as may be specified in the claim; but

(a) that amount shall not exceed one half of the total relief in respect of the shares; and

(b) the aggregate of that amount and the amounts of any other deductions made by virtue of subsection (6) above from the claimant's total income for the year of assessment preceding that in which the shares are issued shall not exceed £5,000.

(8) The relief shall be given on a claim and shall not be allowed—

(a) in a case falling within subsection (1)(a)—

(i) unless and until the company has carried on the trade for four months; and

(ii) if the company is not carrying on that trade at the time when the shares are issued, unless the company begins to carry it on within two years after that time;

(b) in a case falling within subsection (1)(b) or (c) unless and until the company or (as the case may be) the subsidiary has carried on the research and development for four months;

(c) in a case falling within subsection (1)(d) unless and until the company has carried on the exploration for four months.

(9) A claim for relief may be allowed—

(a) under subsection (1)(a), (c) or (d) at any time after the trade, the research and development or the exploration (as the case may be) has been carried on by the company for four months;

(b) under subsection (1)(b) at any time after the research and development has been carried on for four months;

if the conditions for the relief are then satisfied.

(10) In the case of a claim allowed before the end of the relevant period, the relief shall be withdrawn if by reason of any subsequent event it appears that the claimant was not entitled to the relief allowed.

(11) An individual is not entitled to relief in respect of any shares unless the shares are subscribed for and issued for bona fide commercial purposes and not as part of a scheme or arrangement the main purpose, or one of the main purposes of which, is the avoidance of tax.

(12) In this Chapter "the relevant period", in relation to relief in respect of any eligible shares issued by a company, means—

(a) as respects sections 291, 299, 300, 302 and 303, the period beginning with the incorporation of the company (or, if the company was incorporated more than two years before the date on which the shares were issued, beginning two years before that date) and ending five years after the issue of the shares; and

(b) as respects sections 293, 294, 297, 308 and 309, the period beginning with the date on which the shares were issued and ending either—

(i) three years after that date; or

(ii) in a case falling within subsection (1)(a), where the company was not at that date carrying on a qualifying trade, three years after the date on which it subsequently began to carry on such a trade.

(13) Where by reason of its being wound up, or dissolved without winding up, the company carries on the qualifying trade for a period shorter than four months, subsection (8)(a) above shall have effect as if it referred to that shorter period but only if it is shown that the winding up or dissolution was for bona fide commercial reasons and not as part of a scheme or arrangement the main purpose or one of the main purposes of which was the avoidance of tax.

(14) The relief shall be treated for the purposes of section 835(5) as a deduction to be made under Chapter I of this Part after all other deductions under that Chapter and shall be disregarded for the purposes of calculating relief under section 550(2), paragraph 3 of Schedule 2 and paragraphs 4 and 16 of Schedule 11 where an election has effect under paragraph 12 of that Schedule.

(15) Where effect is given to a claim for relief by repayment of tax, section 824 shall have effect in relation to the repayment as if the time from which the 12 months mentioned in subsections (1)(b) and (3)(a) of that section are to be calculated were the end of the year of assessment in which the shares are issued or, if the period mentioned in subsection (8)(a) above ends in a later year, the end of that later year.

Minimum and maximum subscriptions.

290.—(1) Subject to section 311(3), the relief shall not be given in respect of any amount subscribed by an individual for eligible shares issued to him by any company in any year of assessment unless the amount or total amount subscribed by him for the eligible shares issued to him by the company in that year is £500 or more.

(2) No more than £40,000 may be deducted by way of relief under section 289 from the total income of an individual for a year of assessment.

Individuals qualifying for relief.

291.—(1) Subject to section 292, an individual qualifies for the relief if he—

(a) subscribes for the eligible shares on his own behalf,

(b) is resident and ordinarily resident in the United Kingdom at the time when they are issued, and

(c) is not at any time in the relevant period connected with the company;

and, in relation to shares issued after 5th April 1986, an individual who is at any time performing duties which are treated by virtue of section 132(4)(a) as performed in the United Kingdom shall be treated for the purposes of this section as resident and ordinarily resident in the United Kingdom at that time.

(2) An individual is connected with the company if he, or an associate of his, is—

(a) an employee of the company or of a partner of the company;

(b) a partner of the company; or

(c) subject to subsection (3) below, a director of the company or of another company which is a partner of that company.

(3) An individual is not connected with a company by reason only that he, or an associate of his, is a director unless he or his associate (or a partnership of which he or his associate is a member) receives a payment from the company during the period of five years beginning with the date on which the shares are issued or is entitled to receive such a payment in respect of that period or any part of it; but for that purpose there shall be disregarded—

(a) any payment or reimbursement of travelling or other expenses wholly, exclusively and necessarily incurred by him or his associate in the performance of his duties as a director of the company;

(b) any interest which represents no more than a reasonable commercial return on money lent to the company;

(c) any dividend or other distribution which does not exceed a normal return on the investment;

(d) any payment for the supply of goods which does not exceed their market value; and

(e) any reasonable and necessary remuneration which —

(i) is paid for services rendered to the company in the course of a trade or profession (not being secretarial or managerial services or services of a kind provided by the company itself); and

(ii) is taken into account in computing the profits or gains of the trade or profession under Case I or II of Schedule D or would be so taken into account if it fell in a period on the basis of which those profits or gains are assessed under that Schedule.

(4) An individual is connected with the company if he directly or indirectly possesses or is entitled to acquire more than 30 per cent. of—

(a) the issued ordinary share capital of the company; or

(b) the loan capital and issued share capital of the company; or

(c) the voting power in the company.

(5) For the purposes of subsection (4)(b) above the loan capital of a company shall be treated as including any debt incurred by the company—

(a) for any money borrowed or capital assets acquired by the company; or

(b) for any right to receive income created in favour of the company; or

(c) for consideration the value of which to the company was (at the time when the debt was incurred) substantially less than the amount of the debt (including any premium thereon).

(6) An individual is connected with the company if he directly or indirectly possesses or is entitled to acquire such rights as would, in the event of the winding up of the company or in any other circumstances, entitle him to receive more than 30 per cent. of the assets of the company which would then be available for distribution to equity holders of the company, and for the purposes of this subsection—

(a) the persons who are equity holders of the company, and

(b) the percentage of the assets of the company to which the individual would be entitled,

shall be determined in accordance with paragraphs 1 and 3 of Schedule 18, taking references in paragraph 3 to the first company as references to an equity holder and references to a winding up as including references to any other circumstances in which assets of the company are available for distribution to its equity holders.

(7) An individual is connected with a company if he has control of it within the meaning of section 840.

PART VII

(8) For the purposes of this section an individual shall be treated as entitled to acquire anything which he is entitled to acquire at a future date or will at a future date be entitled to acquire, and there shall be attributed to any person any rights or powers of any other person who is an associate of his.

(9) In determining for the purposes of this section whether an individual is connected with a company, no debt incurred by the company by overdrawing an account with a person carrying on a business of banking shall be treated as loan capital of the company if the debt arose in the ordinary course of that business.

(10) Where an individual subscribes for shares in a company with which he is not connected (either within the meaning of this section or by virtue of section 309(6)(b)) he shall nevertheless be treated as connected with it if he subscribes for the shares as part of any arrangement which provides for another person to subscribe for shares in another company with which that or any other individual who is a party to the arrangement is connected (within the meaning of this section or by virtue of section 309(6)(b)).

Parallel trades.

292.—(1) An individual is not entitled to relief in respect of any shares in a company which are issued after 18th March 1986 where, at the date mentioned in subsection (2) below—

(a) he is one of a group of persons—

(i) who control the company; or

(ii) to whom belongs an interest amounting in the aggregate to more than a half share in the trade carried on by the company;

(b) he is also an individual, or one of a group of persons—

(i) controlling another company; or

(ii) to whom belongs an interest amounting in the aggregate to more than a half share in another trade; and

(c) the trade carried on by the company, or a substantial part of it—

(i) is concerned with the same or similar types of property or parts thereof or provides the same or similar services or facilities; and

(ii) serves substantially the same or similar outlets or markets;

as the other trade or (as the case may be) the trade carried on by the other company.

(2) The date mentioned in subsection (1) above is—

(a) the date on which the shares are issued; or

(b) if later, the date on which the company begins to carry on the trade.

(3) For the purposes of subsection (1) above—

    (a) the persons to whom a trade belongs, and (where a trade belongs to two or more persons) their respective shares in that trade, shall be determined in accordance with section 344(1)(a) and (b), (2) and (3); and

    (b) any interest, rights or powers of a person who is an associate of another person shall be treated as those of that other person.

(4) For the purposes of this section—

    (a) references to a company's trade include references to the trade of any of its subsidiaries; and

    (b) "trade" in the expressions "another trade", "other trade" and "trade carried on by the other company" includes any business, profession or vocation.

293.—(1) Subject to section 294, a company is a qualifying company if it is incorporated in the United Kingdom and complies with the requirements of this section.

Qualifying companies.

(2) The company must, throughout the relevant period, be an unquoted company which is resident in the United Kingdom and not resident elsewhere, and be—

    (a) a company which exists wholly, or substantially wholly, for the purpose of carrying on wholly or mainly in the United Kingdom one or more qualifying trades; or

    (b) a company whose business consists wholly of—

        (i) the holding of shares or securities of, or the making of loans to, one or more qualifying subsidiaries of the company; or

        (ii) both the holding of such shares or securities, or the making of such loans, and the carrying on wholly or mainly in the United Kingdom of one or more qualifying trades.

(3) In this section "qualifying subsidiary", in relation to a company, means a subsidiary of that company of a kind which may be held by virtue of sections 308 and 309.

(4) Where a company has one or more qualifying subsidiaries, it shall not be a qualifying company in relation to shares issued after 18th March 1986 if the qualifying trade or trades carried on by the company and its subsidiaries, taken as a whole, are not carried out wholly or mainly in the United Kingdom.

(5) Without prejudice to the generality of subsection (2) above, but subject to subsection (6) below, a company ceases to comply with that subsection if before the end of the relevant period a resolution is passed, or an order is made, for the winding up of the company (or, in the case of a winding up otherwise than under the Insolvency Act 1986 or the Companies (Northern Ireland) Order 1986, any other act is done for the like purpose) or the company is dissolved without winding up.

1986 c. 45.
S.I. 1986/1032
(N.I. 6).

(6) A company shall not be regarded as ceasing to comply with subsection (2) above if it does so by reason of being wound up or dissolved without winding up and—

    (a) it is shown that the winding up or dissolution is for bona fide commercial reasons and not part of a scheme or arrangement the main purpose or one of the main purposes of which is the avoidance of tax; and

    (b) the company's net assets, if any, are distributed to its members or dealt with as bona vacantia before the end of the relevant period or, in the case of a winding up, the end (if later) of three years from the commencement of the winding up.

(7) The company's share capital must not, at any time in the relevant period, include any issued shares that are not fully paid up.

(8) Subject to sections 308 and 309, the company must not at any time in the relevant period—

    (a) control (or together with any person connected with it control) another company or be under the control of another company (or another company and any other person connected with that other company); or

    (b) be a 51 per cent. subsidiary of another company or itself have a 51 per cent. subsidiary;

and no arrangements must be in existence at any time in that period by virtue of which the company could fall within paragraph (a) or (b) above.

(9) A company is not a qualifying company in relation to shares issued before 19th March 1986 if—

    (a) an individual has acquired a controlling interest in the company's trade after 5th April 1983; and

    (b) at any time in the period mentioned in subsection (10) below he has, or has had, a controlling interest in another trade; and

    (c) the trade carried on by the company or a substantial part of it—

        (i) is concerned with the same or similar types of property or parts thereof or provides the same or similar services or facilities as the other trade, or

        (ii) serves substantially the same or similar outlets or markets as the other trade.

Section 298(1) and (2) shall apply for the purposes of this subsection.

(10) The period referred to in subsection (9) above is the period beginning two years before and ending three years after—

    (a) the date on which the shares were issued; or

    (b) if later, the date on which the company began to carry on the trade.

(11) In subsections (9) and (10) above references to a company's trade include references to the trade of any of its subsidiaries.

294.—(1) Subject to section 296, a company is not a qualifying company in relation to shares issued after 18th March 1986 if at any time during the relevant period—

    (a) the value of the interests in land held by the company at that time; or

    (b) where lower, the value of the interests in land which were held by the company immediately after the issue of the shares (adjusted in accordance with section 295);

is greater than half the value of the company's assets as a whole.

(2) For the purposes of this section, the value of the interests in land held by a company on any date shall be arrived at by first aggregating the market value on that date of each of those interests and then deducting—

    (a) the amount of any debts of the company which are secured on any of those interests (including any debt secured by a floating charge on property which comprises any of those interests);

    (b) the amount of any unsecured debts of the company which do not fall due for payment before the expiry of the period of 12 months beginning with that date; and

    (c) the amount paid up in respect of those shares of the company (if any) which carry a present or future preferential right to the company's assets on its winding up.

(3) For the purposes of this section, the value of a company's assets as a whole shall be arrived at by first aggregating the market value of each of those assets and then deducting the amount of the debts and liabilities of the company.

(4) For the purposes of subsection (3) above, the amount paid up in respect of those shares of a company (if any) which carry a present or future preferential right to the company's assets on its winding up shall be treated as a debt of the company, but otherwise a company's share capital, share premium account and reserves shall not be treated for those purposes as debts or liabilities of the company.

(5) In this section "interest in land" means any estate or interest in land, any right in or over land or affecting the use or disposition of land, and any right to obtain such an estate, interest or right from another which is conditional on that other's ability to grant the estate, interest or right in question, except that it does not include—

    (a) the interest of a creditor (other than a creditor in respect of a rentcharge) whose debt is secured by way of a mortgage, an agreement for a mortgage or a charge of any kind over land; or

    (b) in Scotland, the interest of a creditor in a charge or security of any kind over land.

(6) In arriving at the value of any interest in land for the purposes of this section—

    (a) it shall be assumed that there is no source of mineral deposits in the land of a kind which it would be practicable to exploit by extracting them from underground otherwise than by means of opencast mining or quarrying; and

    (b) any borehole on the land shall be disregarded if it was made in the course of oil exploration.

(7) Where a company is a member of a partnership which holds any interest in land—

(a) that interest shall, for the purposes of this section and sections 295 and 296, be treated as an interest in land held by the company; but

(b) its value at any time shall, for those purposes, be taken to be such fraction of its value (apart from this subsection) as is equal to the fraction of the assets of the partnership to which the company would be entitled if the partnership were dissolved at that time.

(8) Where a qualifying company has one or more subsidiaries, the company and its subsidiaries ("the group") shall be treated as a single company for the purposes of this section and sections 295 and 296; but any debt owed by, or liability of, one member of the group to another shall be disregarded for those purposes.

(9) The Treasury may by order amend subsection (1) above by substituting a different fraction for the fraction for the time being specified there.

Valuation of interests in land for purposes of section 294(1)(b).

295.—(1) For the purposes of section 294(1)(b), the value of the interests in land held by a company immediately after the issue of the shares in question ("the original interests") shall be adjusted by—

(a) adding—

(i) the cost of any interests in land subsequently acquired by the company ("the later interests"); and

(ii) any expenditure (whenever payable) incurred by the company wholly and exclusively in enhancing the value of any of the original or later interests;

(b) deducting any consideration received by the company on the disposal of any of the original or later interests or on the grant by the company of any interest in land out of any of those interests;

(c) deducting any consideration otherwise derived by the company from its ownership of any of the original or later interests.

(2) Any sum which is received by a company by way of rent, or which is attributable to the use of any premises by the company, shall be disregarded for the purposes of subsection (1)(c) above.

(3) For the purposes of this section—

(a) the cost of an interest in land acquired by a company shall be taken to be the amount or value of the consideration given by the company, or on its behalf, wholly and exclusively for the acquisition of the interest;

(b) consideration shall be brought into account without any discount for the postponement of the right to receive any part of it; and

(c) the grant of an interest in land out of any of the original interests shall be treated as a disposal of the original interest in question.

(4) Where—

    (a) the interest of a company as lessee under a lease ("the lease") falls to be valued at any time for the purposes of section 294 or the cost of acquiring that interest falls to be calculated for the purposes of this section; and

    (b) the aggregate amount of the rent payable by the lessee under the lease before the end of the relevant period exceeds that which would be so payable under a lease of the premises at a full market rent (but otherwise on the same terms and conditions as the lease);

the value of the company's interest at that time shall be calculated on the assumption that the aggregate amount payable as mentioned in paragraph (b) above is a nominal amount and, where the interest was acquired after the issue of the shares in question, it shall be assumed that the company paid the appropriate premium when acquiring the interest.

(5) In determining, for the purposes of this section, the consideration for the disposal or acquisition of an interest in land, no account shall be taken in the first instance of any contingent liability assumed by the company or by any other person.

(6) If it is subsequently shown to the satisfaction of the Board that a contingent liability which was not taken into account in determining the consideration for a disposal or acquisition has become enforceable and is being or had been enforced, such adjustment, whether by way of a further assessment or the discharge or repayment of tax or otherwise, shall be made as is required in consequence.

(7) Where the relief obtainable under subsection (6) above requires a discharge or repayment of tax, it shall be given on a claim to the Board and such a claim may be made at any time.

296.—(1) Where a company raises any amount through the issue of eligible shares, section 294—

Section 294 disapplied where amounts raised total £50,000 or less.

    (a) shall not have effect to deny relief in relation to those shares if the aggregate of that amount and of all other amounts (if any) so raised within the period of 12 months ending with the date of that issue does not exceed £50,000; and

    (b) where that aggregate exceeds £50,000, shall have effect to deny relief only in relation to the excess.

(2) Where—

    (a) at any time within the relevant period, the company in question or any of its subsidiaries carries on any trade or part of a trade in partnership, or as a party to a joint venture, with one or more other persons; and

    (b) that other person, or at least one of those other persons, is a company;

each reference to £50,000 in subsection (1)(a) and (b) above shall have effect as if it were a reference to—

$$\frac{£50,000}{1 + A}$$

Part VII

where A is the total number of companies (apart from the company in question or any of its subsidiaries) which are members of any such partnership or parties to any such joint venture during the relevant period.

(3) Where section 294, as read with this section, requires a restriction to be placed on the relief given on claims in respect of shares issued to two or more individuals, the available relief shall be divided between them in proportion to the amounts which have been respectively subscribed by them for the shares to which their claims relate and which would, apart from the restrictions, be eligible for the relief.

(4) A claimant who is dissatisfied with the manner in which the available relief is divided under this section between him and any other claimant or claimants may apply to the appropriate Commissioners who shall, after giving the other claimant or claimants an opportunity to appear and be heard or to make representations in writing, determine the question for all the claimants in the same way as an appeal.

(5) In this section "the appropriate Commissioners" means—

(a) in a case where the same body of General Commissioners has jurisdiction with respect to all the claimants, those Commissioners, unless all the claimants agree that the question should be determined by the Special Commissioners;

(b) in a case where different bodies of General Commissioners have jurisdiction with respect to the claimants, such of those bodies as the Board may direct, unless all the claimants agree that the question should be determined by the Special Commissioners;

(c) in any other case, the Special Commissioners.

(6) In calculating the aggregate mentioned in subsection (1)(a) above in respect of any period of 12 months which begins on or before 18th March 1986, any amount raised by the issue of eligible shares on or before that date shall be disregarded.

Qualifying trades.

297.—(1) Subject to section 298(6) and (7) below, a trade is a qualifying trade if it complies with the requirements of this section.

(2) Subject to subsection (9) below, the trade must not at any time in the relevant period consist of one or more of the following activities if that activity amounts, or those activities when taken together amount, to a substantial part of the trade—

(a) dealing in commodities, shares, securities, land or futures;

(b) dealing in goods otherwise than in the course of an ordinary trade of wholesale or retail distribution;

(c) banking, insurance, money-lending, debt-factoring, hire-purchase financing or other financial activities;

(d) oil extraction activities;

(e) leasing (including letting ships on charter or other assets on hire) or receiving royalties or licence fees;

(f) providing legal or accountancy services;

(g) providing services or facilities for any trade carried on by another person which consists to any substantial extent of activities within any of paragraphs (a) to (f) above and in which a controlling interest is held by a person who also has a controlling interest in the trade carried on by the company;

(h) property development;

(j) farming.

(3) For the purposes of subsection (2)(b) above—

(a) a trade of wholesale distribution is one in which the goods are offered for sale and sold to persons for resale by them, or for processing and resale by them, to members of the general public for their use or consumption;

(b) a trade of retail distribution is one in which the goods are offered for sale and sold to members of the general public for their use or consumption;

(c) a trade is not an ordinary trade of wholesale or retail distribution if—

(i) it consists to a substantial extent of dealing in goods of a kind which are collected or held as an investment or of that activity and any other activity of a kind falling within subsection (2) above, taken together; and

(ii) a substantial proportion of those goods are held by the company for a period which is significantly longer than the period for which a vendor would reasonably be expected to hold them while endeavouring to dispose of them at their market value; and

(d) in determining whether a trade is an ordinary trade of wholesale or retail distribution regard shall be had to the extent to which it has the following features, that is to say—

(i) the goods are bought by the trader in quantities larger than those in which he sells them;

(ii) the goods are bought and sold by the trader in different markets;

(iii) the trader employs staff and incurs expenses in the trade in addition to the cost of the goods and, in the case of a trade carried on by a company, in addition to any remuneration paid to any person connected with it;

(iv) there are purchases or sales from or to persons who are connected with the trader;

(v) purchases are matched with forward sales or vice versa;

(vi) the goods are held by the trader for longer than is normal for goods of the kind in question;

(vii) the trade is carried on otherwise than at a place or places commonly used for wholesale or retail trade;

(viii) the trader does not take physical possession of the goods;

those features in sub-paragraphs (i) to (iii) being regarded as indications that the trade is such an ordinary trade and those in sub-paragraphs (iv) to (viii) being regarded as indications of the contrary.

(4) A trade shall not be treated as failing to comply with this section by reason only of its consisting to a substantial extent of receiving royalties or licence fees if—

(a) the company carrying on the trade is engaged throughout the relevant period in—

(i) the production of films; or

(ii) the production of films and the distribution of films produced by it in the relevant period; and

(b) all royalties and licence fees received by it in that period are in respect of films produced by it in that period or sound recordings in relation to such films or other products arising from such films.

(5) A trade shall not be treated as failing to comply with this section by reason only that at any time after 19th March 1985 it consists to a substantial extent of receiving royalties or licence fees if—

(a) the company carrying on the trade is engaged in research and development throughout the relevant period; and

(b) all royalties and licence fees received by it in that period are attributable to research and development which it has carried out.

(6) A trade shall not be treated as failing to comply with this section by reason only of its consisting of letting ships, other than oil rigs or pleasure craft, on charter if—

(a) every ship let on charter by the company carrying on the trade is beneficially owned by the company;

(b) every ship beneficially owned by the company is registered in the United Kingdom; and

(c) throughout the relevant period the company is solely responsible for arranging the marketing of the services of its ships; and

(d) the conditions mentioned in subsection (7) below are satisfied in relation to every letting on charter by the company;

but where any of the requirements mentioned in paragraphs (a) to (d) above are not satisfied in relation to any lettings of such ships, the trade shall not thereby be treated as failing to comply with this section if those lettings and any other activity of a kind falling within subsection (2) above do not, when taken together, amount to a substantial part of the trade.

(7) The conditions are that—

(a) the letting is for a period not exceeding 12 months and no provision is made at any time (whether in the lease or otherwise) for extending it beyond that period otherwise than at the option of the lessee;

(b) during the period of the letting there is no provision in force (whether made in the lease or otherwise) for the grant of a new letting to end, otherwise than at the option of the lessee, more than 12 months after that provision is made;

(c) the letting is by way of a bargain made at arm's length between the company and a person who is not connected with it;

(d) under the terms of the charter the company is responsible as principal—

(i) for taking, throughout the period of the charter, management decisions in relation to the ship, other than those of a kind generally regarded by persons engaged in trade of the kind in question as matters of husbandry; and

(ii) for defraying all expenses in connection with the ship throughout that period, or substantially all such expenses, other than those directly incidental to a particular voyage or to the employment of the ship during that period; and

(e) no arrangements exist by virtue of which a person other than the company may be appointed to be responsible for the matters mentioned in paragraph (d) above on behalf of the company;

but this subsection shall have effect, in relation to any letting between the company in question and its subsidiary, or between it and another company of which it is a subsidiary or between it and a company which is a subsidiary of the same company of which it is a subsidiary, as if paragraph (c) were omitted.

(8) The trade must, during the relevant period, be conducted on a commercial basis and with a view to the realisation of profits.

(9) A trade which consists to any substantial extent of oil extraction activities shall, if it would be a qualifying trade were it not for subsection (2)(d) above, be treated as a qualifying trade for the purposes of section 289(1)(d).

298.—(1) For the purposes of sections 293(9) and 297 a person has a controlling interest in a trade— *Provisions supplementary to sections 293 and 297.*

(a) in the case of a trade carried on by a company, if—

(i) he controls the company;

(ii) the company is a close company and he or an associate of his is a director of the company and the beneficial owner of, or able directly or through the medium of other companies or by any other indirect means to control, more than 30 per cent. of the ordinary share capital of the company; or

(iii) not less than half of the trade could in accordance with section 344(2) be regarded as belonging to him;

(b) in any other case, if he is entitled to not less than half of the assets used for, or the income arising from, the trade.

(2) For the purposes of subsection (1) above, there shall be attributed to any person any rights or powers of any other person who is an associate of his.

(3) References in this section and section 297 to a trade shall be construed without regard to so much of the definition of "trade" in section 832(1) as relates to adventures or concerns in the nature of trade; but the foregoing provisions do not affect the construction of references in section 297(2)(g) or subsection (1) above to a trade carried on by a person other than the company and those references shall be construed as including a reference to any business, profession or vocation.

(4) The Treasury may by order amend section 297 and this section, except in relation to shares issued before 19th March 1986, in such manner as they consider expedient.

(5) In section 297—

"film" means an original master negative of a film, an original master film disc or an original master film tape;

1971 c. 61.

"oil rig" means any ship which is an offshore installation for the purposes of the Mineral Workings (Offshore Installations) Act 1971;

"pleasure craft" means any ship of a kind primarily used for sport or recreation;

"property development" means the development of land, by a company which has, or at any time has had, an interest in the land (within the meaning of section 294(5)), with the sole or main object of realising a gain from disposing of the land when developed; and

"sound recording" means, in relation to a film, its sound track, original master audio disc or, as the case may be, original master audio tape.

(6) Section 297 shall have effect in relation to shares issued before 19th March 1986 subject to the following modifications—

(a) in subsection (2) the words "or those activities when taken together amount" shall be omitted;

(b) subsection (2)(h) shall not apply unless the shares were issued after 19th March 1985;

(c) subsection (2)(j) shall not apply unless the shares were issued after 13th March 1984;

(d) in subsection (3) the words in paragraph (a) "to members of the general public for their use or consumption" and paragraph (c) shall be omitted; and

(e) subsections (6) and (7) shall be omitted;

and in relation to shares issued after 18th March 1986 section 297(2) shall have effect with the omission of paragraphs (h) and (j).

(7) Section 297(2) shall have effect so far as it relates to oil extraction only in relation to shares issued after 25th July 1986.

(8) Section 297(4) shall have effect in relation to shares issued before 17th March 1987 with the omission of paragraph (a)(ii), together with the word "or" immediately before it, (but not the word "and" at the end of it) and the words in paragraph (b) "in that period" in the second place where they appear.

299.—(1) Where an individual disposes of any eligible shares before the end of the relevant period, then—

Disposal of shares.

> (a) if the disposal is otherwise than by way of a bargain made at arm's length, he shall not be entitled to any relief in respect of those shares; and
>
> (b) in any other case, the amount of relief to which he is entitled in respect of those shares shall be reduced by the amount or value of the consideration which he receives for them.

(2) Where after 18th March 1986 an option, the exercise of which would bind the grantor to purchase any shares, is granted to an individual during the relevant period, the individual shall not be entitled to any relief in respect of the shares to which the option relates.

(3) Where an individual holds ordinary shares of any class in a company and the relief has been given (and not withdrawn) in respect of some shares of that class but not others, any disposal by him of ordinary shares of that class in the company, and any option of the kind mentioned in subsection (2) above, shall be treated for the purposes of this section as relating—

> (a) first, to those (if any) in respect of which relief has been given (and not withdrawn) under Chapter II of Part IV of the Finance Act 1981 rather than to others; and

1981 c. 35.

> (b) then, to those in respect of which relief has been given (and not withdrawn) under this Chapter (or Schedule 5 to the Finance Act 1983).

1983 c. 28.

(4) Where the relief has been given (and not withdrawn) to an individual in respect of shares of any class in a company which have been issued to him at different times, any disposal by him of shares of that class shall, subject to subsection (3) above, be treated for the purposes of this section as relating to those issued earlier rather than to those issued later.

(5) Where shares in respect of which the relief was given have by virtue of any such allotment as is mentioned in section 77(2)(a) of the 1979 Act (not being an allotment for payment) fallen to be treated under section 78 of that Act as the same asset as a new holding—

> (a) a disposal of the whole or part of the new holding shall be treated for the purposes of this section as a disposal of the whole or a corresponding part of those shares; and
>
> (b) the new holding shall be treated for the purposes of subsection (3) above as shares in respect of which the relief has been given.

(6) For the purposes of this section—

(a) shares in a company shall not be treated as being of the same class unless they would be so treated if dealt with on the Stock Exchange; and

(b) references to a disposal of shares include references to the grant of an option (after 18th March 1986) the exercise of which would bind the grantor to sell the shares.

Value received from company.

300.—(1) Subject to section 299, where an individual who subscribes for eligible shares in a company—

(a) has, before the issue of the shares but within the relevant period, received any value from the company; or

(b) after their issue but before the end of the relevant period, receives any such value;

1983 c. 28.

the amount of the relief to which he is entitled in respect of the shares shall be reduced by the value received; but the value received shall be disregarded to the extent to which relief under Schedule 5 to the Finance Act 1983 or under this Chapter has been reduced on its account.

(2) For the purposes of this section an individual receives value from the company if the company—

(a) repays, redeems or repurchases any of its share capital or securities which belong to the individual or makes any payment to him for giving up his right to any of the company's share capital or any security on its cancellation or extinguishment;

(b) repays any debt owed to the individual other than a debt which was incurred by the company—

(i) on or after the date on which he subscribed for the shares in respect of which the relief is claimed; and

(ii) otherwise than in consideration of the extinguishment of a debt incurred before that date;

(c) makes to the individual any payment for giving up his right to any debt (other than a debt in respect of a payment of the kind mentioned in section 291(3)(a) or (e) or an ordinary trade debt) on its extinguishment;

(d) releases or waives any liability of the individual to the company or discharges, or undertakes to discharge, any liability of his to a third person;

(e) makes a loan or advance to the individual which has not been repaid in full before the issue of the shares in respect of which relief is claimed;

(f) provides a benefit or facility for the individual;

(g) transfers an asset to the individual for no consideration or for consideration less than its market value or acquires an asset from him for consideration exceeding its market value; or

(h) makes to him any other payment except a payment of the kind mentioned in section 291(3)(a), (b), (c), (d) or (e) or a payment in discharge of an ordinary trade debt.

(3) For the purposes of this section an individual also receives value from the company if he receives in respect of ordinary shares held by him any payment or asset in a winding up or in connection with a dissolution of the company, being a winding up or dissolution falling within section 293(6).

(4) The value received by an individual is—

(a) in a case within paragraph (a), (b) or (c) of subsection (2) above, the amount receivable by the individual or, if greater, the market value of the shares, securities or debt in question;

(b) in a case within paragraph (d) of that subsection, the amount of the liability;

(c) in a case within paragraph (e) of that subsection, the amount of the loan or advance reduced by the amount of any repayment made before the issue of the shares in respect of which relief is claimed;

(d) in a case within paragraph (f) of that subsection, the cost to the company of providing the benefit or facility less any consideration given for it by the individual;

(e) in a case within paragraph (g) of that subsection, the difference between the market value of the asset and the consideration (if any) given for it;

(f) in a case within paragraph (h) of that subsection, the amount of the payment; and

(g) in a case within subsection (3) above, the amount of the payment or, as the case may be, the market value of the asset.

(5) For the purposes of this section an individual also receives value from the company if any person who would, for the purposes of section 291, be treated as connected with the company—

(a) purchases any of its share capital or securities which belong to the individual; or

(b) makes any payment to him for giving up any right in relation to any of the company's share capital or securities;

and the value received by the individual is the amount receivable by the individual or, if greater, the market value of the shares or securities in question.

301.—(1) Where by virtue of section 300 any relief is withheld or withdrawn in the case of an individual to whom ordinary shares in a company have been issued at different times before 19th March 1986 the relief shall be withheld or withdrawn in respect of shares issued earlier rather than in respect of shares issued later.

Provisions supplementary to section 300.

(2) Where relief to which an individual is entitled in respect of eligible shares issued after 18th March 1986 is reduced by virtue of section 300, effect shall be given to the reduction by apportioning it, as between any such eligible shares held by him, in such a way as appears to the inspector, or on an appeal to the Commissioners concerned, to be just and reasonable.

(3) For the purposes of section 300(2)(d) a company shall be treated as having released or waived a liability if the liability is not discharged within 12 months of the time when it ought to have been discharged.

(4) For the purposes of section 300(2)(e) there shall be treated as if it were a loan made by the company to the individual—

(a) the amount of any debt (other than an ordinary trade debt) incurred by the individual to the company; and

(b) the amount of any debt due from the individual to a third person which has been assigned to the company.

(5) In this section and section 300, "an ordinary trade debt" means any debt for goods or services supplied in the ordinary course of a trade or business where the credit given does not exceed six months and is not longer than that normally given to the customers of the person carrying on the trade or business.

(6) In this section and section 300—

(a) any reference to a payment or transfer to an individual includes a reference to a payment or transfer made to him indirectly or to his order or for his benefit; and

(b) any reference to an individual includes a reference to an associate of his and any reference to the company includes a reference to any person connected with the company.

(7) Section 300 shall apply in relation to shares issued before 19th March 1986 with the omission—

(a) in subsection (2)(e) of the words "which has not been repaid in full before the issue of the shares in respect of which relief is claimed"; and

(b) in subsection (4)(c) of the words "reduced by the amount of any repayment made before the issue of the shares in respect of which relief is claimed".

Replacement capital.

302.—(1) An individual is not entitled to relief in respect of any shares in a company where—

(a) at any time in the relevant period, the company or any of its subsidiaries—

(i) begins to carry on as its trade or as part of its trade a trade which was previously carried on at any time in that period otherwise than by the company or any of its subsidiaries; or

(ii) acquires the whole, or greater part, of the assets used for the purposes of a trade previously so carried on; and

(b) subsection (2) below applies in relation to that individual.

(2) This subsection applies in relation to an individual where—

(a) any person or group of persons to whom an interest amounting in the aggregate to more than a half share in the trade (as previously carried on) belonged, at any time in the relevant period, is or are a person or group of persons to whom such an interest in the trade carried on by the company belongs or has, at any such time, belonged; or

(b) any person or group of persons who control or, at any such time, have controlled the company is or are a person or group of persons who, at any such time, controlled another company which previously carried on the trade;

and the individual is that person or one of those persons.

(3) An individual is not entitled to relief in respect of any shares in a company where—

(a) the company comes to acquire all of the issued share capital of another company, at any time in the relevant period; and

(b) any person or group of persons who control or have, at any such time, controlled the company is or are a person or group of persons who, at any such time, controlled that other company;

and that individual is that person or one of those persons.

(4) For the purposes of subsection (2) above—

(a) the persons to whom a trade belongs and, where a trade belongs to two or more persons, their respective shares in that trade shall be determined in accordance with section 344(1)(a) and (b), (2) and (3); and

(b) any interest, rights or powers of a person who is an associate of another person shall be treated as those of that other person.

(5) In this section—

"subsidiary" means a subsidiary of a kind which a qualifying company may have by virtue of sections 308 and 309; and

"trade" includes any business, profession or vocation, and references to a trade previously carried on include references to part of such a trade.

303.—(1) The relief to which an individual is entitled in respect of any shares in a company shall be reduced in accordance with subsection (2) below if at any time in the relevant period the company repays, redeems or repurchases any of its share capital which belongs to any member other than—

(a) that individual; or

(b) another individual whose relief is thereby withdrawn or reduced by virtue of section 299 or reduced by virtue of section 300(2)(a);

or makes any payment to any such member for giving up his right to any of the company's share capital on its cancellation or extinguishment.

(2) Where subsection (1) above applies, the amount of relief to which an individual is entitled shall be reduced by the amount receivable by the member or, if greater, the nominal value of the share capital in question; and where, apart from this subsection, two or more individuals would be

entitled to relief the reduction shall be made in proportion to the amounts of relief to which they would, apart from this subsection, have been entitled.

(3) Where at any time in the relevant period a member of a company receives or is entitled to receive any value from the company within the meaning of this subsection, then, for the purposes of section 291(4) in its application to any subsequent time—

(a) the amount of the company's issued ordinary share capital; and

(b) the amount of the part of that capital which consists of the shares which (within the meaning of section 291) the individual directly or indirectly possesses or is entitled to acquire, and the amount of the part consisting of the remainder,

shall each be treated as reduced in accordance with subsection (4) below.

(4) The amount of each of the parts mentioned in subsection (3)(b) above shall be treated as equal to such proportion of that amount as the amount subscribed for that part less the relevant value bears to the amount subscribed; and the amount of the issued share capital shall be treated as equal to the sum of the amounts treated under this subsection as the amount of those parts respectively.

(5) In subsection (4) above "the relevant value", in relation to each of the parts there mentioned, means the value received by the member or members entitled to the shares of which that part consists.

(6) For the purposes of subsection (3) above a member of a company receives or is entitled to receive value from the company in any case in which an individual would receive value from the company by virtue of section 300(2)(d), (e), (f), (g) or (h) (but treating as excepted from paragraph (h) all payments made for full consideration) and the value received shall be determined as for the purposes of that section.

(7) For the purposes of subsection (6) above a person shall be treated as entitled to receive anything which he is entitled to receive at a future date or will at a future date be entitled to receive.

(8) Subsection (1) above does not apply in relation to the redemption of any share capital for which the redemption date was fixed before 15th March 1983.

(9) Where—

(a) a company issues share capital ("the original shares") of nominal value equal to the authorised minimum (within the meaning of the Companies Act 1985) for the purposes of complying with the requirements of section 117 of that Act (public company not to do business unless requirements as to share capital complied with); and

1985 c. 6.

(b) after the registrar of companies has issued the company with a certificate under section 117, it issues eligible shares;

subsection (1) above shall not apply in relation to any redemption of any of the original shares within 12 months of the date on which those shares were issued.

In relation to companies incorporated under the law of Northern Ireland references in this subsection to the Companies Act 1985 and to section 117 of that Act shall have effect as references to the Companies (Northern Ireland) Order 1986 and to Article 127 of that Order.

(10) Where relief to which an individual is entitled in respect of eligible shares issued after 18th March 1986 is reduced by virtue of this section, effect shall be given to the reduction by apportioning it as between any such eligible shares held by him in such a way as appears to the inspector, or on appeal to the Commissioners concerned, to be just and reasonable.

(11) In relation to shares issued before 19th March 1986, subsection (1)(b) above shall have effect with the omission of the words "withdrawn or reduced by virtue of section 299 or".

304.—(1) In the case of any amount subscribed by a married woman for eligible shares issued to her at a time— *Husband and wife.*

    (a) when she is living with her husband; and

    (b) which falls in a year of assessment for which his income includes (or, if there were any, would include) any of hers,

the deduction under section 289(5) shall, subject to Chapter II of this Part and subsections (2) to (5) below, be made from his total income, and references in this Chapter to the relief to which an individual is entitled in respect of any shares shall be construed accordingly.

(2) The limits in section 290 shall apply jointly to a husband and wife as respects amounts subscribed for shares at a time—

    (a) when they are married and living together; and

    (b) which falls in a year of assessment for which his income includes (or, if there were any, would include) any of hers;

but if the husband dies or they are divorced or cease to live together before the end of any such year those limits shall apply to the wife as respects amounts subscribed by her for shares issued in the remainder of the year as if it were a separate year of assessment.

(3) Where an application under section 283(1) or an election under section 287(1) is in force for a year of assessment in which shares are issued for which amounts have been subscribed both by the husband and the wife, then, if section 290(2) requires a restriction to be placed on the relief given on a claim or claims in respect of those amounts, the available relief shall be divided between the husband and wife in proportion to the amounts which have been respectively subscribed by them for the shares to which the claim or claims relate and which would, apart from the restriction, be eligible for the relief.

(4) Subsections (2) and (3) above shall apply in relation to the limit of £5,000 imposed by section 289(7) as it applies in relation to the limit of £40,000 imposed by section 290(2); and for this purpose the reference in subsection (3) above to a division in proportion to the amounts subscribed by the husband and wife shall be construed as a reference to a division in proportion to the aggregate amounts of the relevant deductions sought by each of them in their claims under section 289(6).

(5) Subsection (1) of section 299 shall not apply to a disposal made by a married woman to her husband at a time when she is living with him or to a disposal made at such a time by him to her; but where shares issued to one of them have been transferred to the other by a transaction inter vivos—

(a) that subsection shall apply on the disposal of the shares by the transferee to a third person; and

(b) if at any time the husband and wife are divorced or cease to live together and any of those shares have not been disposed of by the transferee before that time, any assessment for withdrawing relief in respect of those shares shall be made on the transferee.

(6) Where a husband and wife are divorced or cease to live together, then, if any relief given in respect of shares for which either of them has subscribed and which were issued while they were married and living together falls to be withdrawn by virtue of a subsequent disposal of those shares by the person who subscribed for them, any assessment for withdrawing that relief shall be made on the person making the disposal and shall be made by reference to the reduction of tax flowing from the amount of the relief regardless of any allocation of that relief under section 280 or of any allocation of the reduction under section 284.

Reorganisation of share capital.

305.—(1) Where shares in respect of which relief has been given and not withdrawn have by virtue of any such allotment, otherwise than for payment, as is mentioned in section 77(2)(a) of the 1979 Act fallen to be treated under section 78 of that Act as the same asset as a new holding—

(a) a disposal of the whole or part of the new holding shall be treated for the purposes of this Part as a disposal of the whole or a corresponding part of those shares; and

(b) the new holding shall be treated for the purposes of section 299(3) as shares in respect of which relief has been given and not withdrawn.

(2) Where—

(a) there is, by virtue of any such allotment for payment as is mentioned in section 77(2)(a) of the 1979 Act, a reorganisation affecting ordinary shares in respect of which relief has been given; and

(b) immediately before the reorganisation the relief had not been withdrawn; and

(c) the amount of relief (or, where the relief has been reduced, the amount remaining) and the market value of the shares immediately before the reorganisation, exceeds their market value immediately after the reorganisation;

the relief shall be reduced by an amount equal to whichever is the smaller of those excesses.

(3) Subsection (2) above shall also apply where—

(a) an individual who has received, or become entitled to receive, in respect of any ordinary shares in a company, a provisional allotment of shares in or debentures of the company disposes of his rights; and

(b) subsection (2) above would have applied (apart from this subsection) had those rights not been disposed of but an allotment of shares or debentures made to him.

(4) This section has effect in relation to reorganisations occurring after 18th March 1986.

306.—(1) A claim for relief in respect of eligible shares issued by a company in any year of assessment shall be made— Claims.

(a) not earlier than the end of the period of four months mentioned in section 289(8)(a), (b) or (c), as the case may be; and

(b) not later than two years after the end of that year of assessment or, if that period of four months ended after the end of that year, not later than two years after the end of that period.

(2) A claim for relief in respect of eligible shares in a company shall not be allowed unless it is accompanied by a certificate issued by the company in such form as the Board may direct and certifying that the conditions for the relief, so far as applying to the company and the trade, are satisfied in relation to those shares.

(3) Before issuing a certificate for the purposes of subsection (2) above a company shall furnish the inspector with a statement to the effect that it satisfies the conditions for the relief, so far as they apply in relation to the company and the trade, and has done so at all times since the beginning of the relevant period.

(4) No such certificate shall be issued without the authority of the inspector or where the company, or a person connected with the company, has given notice to the inspector under section 310(2).

(5) Any statement under subsection (3) above shall contain such information as the Board may reasonably require, shall be in such form as the Board may direct and shall contain a declaration that it is correct to the best of the company's knowledge and belief.

(6) Where a company has issued a certificate for the purposes of subsection (2) above, or furnished a statement under subsection (3) above and—

(a) the certificate or statement is made fraudulently or negligently; or

(b) the certificate was issued in contravention of subsection (4) above;

the company shall be liable to a penalty not exceeding £250 or, in the case of fraud, £500.

(7) For the purposes of regulations made under section 203 no regard shall be had to the relief unless a claim for it has been duly made and admitted.

(8) No application shall be made under section 55(3) or (4) of the Management Act (application for postponement of payment of tax pending appeal) on the ground that the applicant is entitled to the relief unless a claim for the relief has been duly made by him.

(9) For the purposes of section 86 of the Management Act (interest on overdue tax), tax charged by an assessment—

(a) shall be regarded as due and payable notwithstanding that relief from the tax (whether by discharge or repayment) is subsequently given on a claim for the relief; but

(b) shall, unless paid earlier or due and payable later, be regarded as paid on the date of the making of the claim on which the relief is given;

and section 91 of that Act (effect on interest of reliefs) shall not apply in consequence of any discharge or repayment for giving effect to the relief.

(10) For the purposes of the provisions of the Management Act relating to appeals against decisions on claims, the refusal of the inspector to authorise the issue of a certificate under subsection (2) above shall be taken to be a decision refusing a claim made by the company.

This subsection shall not apply in relation to shares issued before 19th March 1986.

Withdrawal of relief.

307.—(1) Where any relief has been given which is subsequently found not to have been due, it shall be withdrawn by the making of an assessment to tax under Case VI of Schedule D for the year of assessment for which the relief was given; but where by virtue of section 289(6) relief has been given for each of two consecutive years of assessment, any withdrawal of relief shall be made for the first of those years before being made for the second.

(2) Subject to subsections (3) to (7) below, any assessment for withdrawing relief which is made by reason of an event occurring after the date of the claim may be made within six years after the end of the year of assessment in which that event occurs.

(3) No assessment for withdrawing relief in respect of shares issued to any person shall be made by reason of any event occurring after his death.

(4) Where a person has, by a disposal or disposals to which section 299(1)(b) applies, disposed of all the ordinary shares issued to him by a company, no assessment for withdrawing relief in respect of any of those shares shall be made by reason of any subsequent event unless it occurs at a time when he is connected with the company within the meaning of section 291.

(5) Subsection (2) above is without prejudice to section 36 of the Management Act (fraud and wilful default) and section 37 of that Act (neglect).

(6) In its application to an assessment made by virtue of this section, section 86 of the Management Act (interest on overdue tax) shall have effect as if the reckonable date were—

(a) in the case of relief withdrawn by virtue of section 289(11)—

(i) so far as effect has been given to the relief in accordance with regulations under section 203, 5th April in the year of assessment in which effect was so given;

(ii) so far as effect has not been so given, the date on which the relief was granted.

(b) in the case of relief withdrawn by virtue of section 291, 293, 297, 302, 303(1) or 305 in consequence of any event after the grant of the relief, the date of that event;

(c) in the case of relief withdrawn by virtue of section 299(1) in consequence of a disposal after the grant of the relief, the date of the disposal;

(d) in the case of relief withdrawn by virtue of section 300 in consequence of a receipt of value after the grant of the relief, the date of the receipt.

(7) For the purposes of subsection (6) above the date on which the relief is granted is the date on which a repayment of tax for giving effect to the relief was made or, if there was no such repayment, the date on which the inspector issued a notice to the claimant showing the amount of tax payable after giving effect to the relief.

(8) Where a company has ceased to be a qualifying company in consequence of the operation of section 294, subsection (6) above shall apply as if the relief was withdrawn in consequence of an event which occurred at the time when the company so ceased to be a qualifying company.

(9) Subsections (1) to (7) above apply in relation to relief under Chapter II of Part IV of the Finance Act 1981 as they apply in relation to relief under this Chapter (or Schedule 5 to the Finance Act 1983) but—

(a) with the substitution for references to sections 299 (in both places), 291, 289(11), 293, 297, 302, 303(1), 305 and 300 of this Act of references respectively to sections 57, 54, 59(1), 53(7), 54, 55, 56, 59(2) and 58 of the Finance Act 1981; and

(b) with the omission of subsection (6)(a)(i).

308.—(1) A qualifying company may, in the relevant period, have one or more subsidiaries if—

(a) the conditions mentioned in subsection (2) below are satisfied in respect of the subsidiary or, as the case may be, each subsidiary and, except as provided by subsection (3) below, continue to be so satisfied until the end of the relevant period; and

(b) the subsidiary or, as the case may be, each subsidiary exists wholly, or substantially wholly, for the purpose of carrying on one or more qualifying trades or is a property managing, or dormant, subsidiary.

(2) The conditions referred to are—

(a) that the qualifying company, or another of its subsidiaries, possesses not less than 90 per cent. of the issued share capital of, and not less than 90 per cent. of the voting power in, the subsidiary;

(b) that the qualifying company, or another of its subsidiaries, would in the event of a winding up of the subsidiary or in any other circumstances be beneficially entitled to receive not less than 90 per cent. of the assets of the subsidiary which would then be available for distribution to the equity holders of the subsidiary;

(c) that the qualifying company or another of its subsidiaries is beneficially entitled to not less than 90 per cent. of any profits of the subsidiary which are available for distribution to the equity holders of the subsidiary;

(d) that no person other than the qualifying company or another of its subsidiaries has control of the subsidiary within the meaning of section 840; and

(e) that no arrangements are in existence by virtue of which the conditions in paragraphs (a) to (d) above could cease to be satisfied.

(3) The conditions shall not be regarded as ceasing to be satisfied by reason only of the subsidiary or the qualifying company being wound up, or dissolved without winding up, if—

(a) it is shown that the winding up or dissolution is for bona fide commercial reasons and not part of a scheme or arrangement the main purpose or one of the main purposes of which is the avoidance of tax; and

(b) the net assets, if any, of the subsidiary or, as the case may be, the qualifying company are distributed to its members or dealt with as bona vacantia before the end of the relevant period, or in the case of a winding up, the end (if later) of three years from the commencement of the winding up.

(4) The conditions shall not be regarded as ceasing to be satisfied by reason only of the disposal by the qualifying company or (as the case may be) by another subsidiary, within the relevant period, of all its interest in the subsidiary if it is shown that the disposal is for bona fide commercial reasons and not part of a scheme or arrangement the main purpose or one of the main purposes of which is the avoidance of tax.

(5) For the purposes of this section—

(a) a subsidiary of a qualifying company is a property managing subsidiary if it exists wholly, or substantially wholly, for the purpose of holding and managing property used by the qualifying company, or by any of its subsidiaries, for the purposes of—

(i) research and development from which it is intended that a qualifying trade to be carried on by the company or any of its subsidiaries will be derived; or

(ii) one or more qualifying trades so carried on;

(b) a subsidiary is a dormant subsidiary if it has no profits for the purposes of corporation tax and no part of its business consists in the making of investments; and

(c) the persons who are equity holders of a subsidiary and the percentage of the assets of a subsidiary to which an equity holder would be entitled shall be determined in accordance with paragraphs 1 and 3 of Schedule 18, taking references in paragraph 3 to the first company as references to an equity holder and references to a winding up as including references to any other circumstances in which assets of the subsidiary are available for distribution to its equity holders.

(6) In relation to shares issued before 19th March 1986 this section shall have effect subject to the following modifications—

(a) the following paragraph shall be substituted for subsection (1)(b)—

"(b) the subsidiary or each subsidiary was incorporated in the United Kingdom and is a company falling within section 293(2)(a).";

(b) the following subsection shall be substituted for subsection (2)—

"(2) The conditions referred to in subsection (1)(a) above are—

(a) that the qualifying company possesses all the issued share capital of, and all the voting power in, the subsidiary; and

(b) that no other person has control of the subsidiary within the meaning of section 840; and

(c) that no arrangements are in existence by virtue of which the conditions in paragraphs (a) and (b) above could cease to be satisfied."; and

(c) subsections (4) and (5) shall be omitted.

309.—(1) Where a qualifying company has one or more subsidiaries in the relevant period, this Chapter shall have effect subject to subsections (2) to (8) below.

(2) The shares issued by the qualifying company may, instead of or as well as being issued for the purpose mentioned in subsection (1)(a) of section 289, be issued for the purpose of raising money for a qualifying trade which is being carried on by a subsidiary or which a subsidiary intends to carry on; and, where shares are so issued, subsections (8), (9), (12)(b)(ii) and (13) of that section shall have effect as if references to the company were or, as the case may be, included references to the subsidiary.

(3) In relation to a qualifying trade carried on by a subsidiary the reference in section 297(2)(g) to another person shall not include a reference to the company of which it is a subsidiary.

(4) In section 303(1) references to the company (except the first) shall include references to a company which during the relevant period is a subsidiary of the company whether it becomes a subsidiary before or after the redemption, repayment, repurchase or payment referred to in that subsection.

(5) In subsections (2), (4) and (6) of section 291, references to the company (except, in each subsection, the first such reference) include references to a company which is during the relevant period a subsidiary of that company—

(a) whether it becomes a subsidiary before, during or after the year of assessment in respect of which the individual concerned claims relief; or

(b) whether or not it is such a subsidiary while he is such an employee, partner or director as is mentioned in subsection (2) or while he has or is entitled to acquire such capital or voting power or rights as are mentioned in subsections (4) and (6).

(6) Without prejudice to the provisions of section 291 (as it has effect in accordance with subsection (5) above), an individual shall be treated as connected with a company if—

(a) he has at any time in the relevant period had control (within the meaning of section 840) of another company which has since that time and before the end of the relevant period become a subsidiary of the company; or

(b) he directly or indirectly possesses or is entitled to acquire any loan capital of a subsidiary of that company.

(7) Section 291(5) and (8) shall apply for the purposes of this section.

(8) In sections 300(1) and 303(3) references to the receipt of value from the company shall include references to the receipt of value from any company which during the relevant period is a subsidiary of that company, whether it becomes a subsidiary before or after the individual concerned receives any value from it, and other references to the company in sections 300 and 301 and in section 303(6) shall be construed accordingly.

Information.   **310.**—(1) Where an event occurs by reason of which any relief given to an individual falls to be withdrawn by virtue of sections 291, 299, 300 or 304(2) to (6), the individual shall within 60 days of his coming to know of the event give a notice to the inspector containing particulars of the event.

(2) Where an event occurs by reason of which any relief in respect of any shares in a company falls to be withdrawn by virtue of section 289(11), 293, 297, 300, 302 or 303—

(a) the company; and

(b) any person connected with the company who has knowledge of that matter;

shall within 60 days of the event or, in the case of a person within paragraph (b) above, of his coming to know of it, give a notice to the inspector containing particulars of the event or payment.

(3) Where—

(a) a company has issued a certificate under section 306(2) in respect of any eligible shares in the company; and

(b) it appears to the company, or to any person connected with the company who has knowledge of the matter, that section 294 may have effect to deny relief in respect of those shares;

the company or (as the case may be) that person or (where it so appears to each of them) both the company and that person shall give notice to the inspector setting out the particulars of the case.

(4) If the inspector has reason to believe that a person has not given a notice which he is required to give under subsection (1) or (2) above in respect of any event, or under subsection (3) above in respect of any particular case, the inspector may by notice require that person to furnish him within such time (not being less than 60 days) as may be specified in the notice with such information relating to the event or case as the inspector may reasonably require for the purposes of this Chapter.

(5) Where relief is claimed in respect of shares in a company and the inspector has reason to believe that it may not be due by reason of any such arrangement or scheme as is mentioned in section 289(11), 291(10), 293(8) or 308(2)(e), he may by notice require any person concerned to furnish him within such time (not being less than 60 days) as may be specified in the notice with—

(a) a declaration in writing stating whether or not, according to the information which that person has or can reasonably obtain, any such arrangement or scheme exists or has existed;

(b) such other information as the inspector may reasonably require for the purposes of the provision in question and as that person has or can reasonably obtain.

(6) References in subsection (5) above to the person concerned are references, in relation to sections 289(11), 291(10) and 308(2)(e), to the claimant and, in relation to sections 289(11), 293(8) and 308(2)(e), to the company and any person controlling the company.

(7) Where relief has been given in respect of shares in a company—

(a) any person who receives from the company any payment or asset which may constitute value received (by him or another) for the purposes of sections 300, 301 and 303(3); and

(b) any person on whose behalf such a payment or asset is received,

shall, if so required by the inspector, state whether the payment or asset received by him or on his behalf is received on behalf of any person other than himself and, if so, the name and address of that person.

(8) Where relief has been claimed in respect of shares in a company, any person who holds or has held shares in the company and any person on whose behalf any such shares are or were held shall, if so required by the inspector, state whether the shares which are or were held by him or on his behalf are or were held on behalf of any person other than himself and, if so, the name and address of that person.

(9) No obligation as to secrecy imposed by statute or otherwise shall preclude the inspector from disclosing to a company that relief has been given or claimed in respect of a particular number or proportion of its shares.

(10) This section shall have effect in relation to relief under Chapter II of Part IV of the Finance Act 1981 as it has effect in relation to relief under this Chapter but with the substitution—

    (a) in subsection (1) for "291, 299, 300 or 304(2) to (6)" of "54, 57, 58 and 60(6) of the Finance Act 1981";

    (b) for subsection (3) of the following subsection—

        "(3) Where the company is notified by the inspector that relief has been given in respect of any shares issued by the company on a specified date, then, if any shares in the company (whether or not shares in respect of which relief has been given) are transferred at any time in the period of five years beginning with that date, the company shall within 60 days of—

        (a) coming to know of the transfer; or

        (b) receiving the notification from the inspector,

        whichever is the later, give a notice to the inspector containing particulars of the transfer.";

    (c) in subsection (5) for references to sections 289(11), 291(10), 293(8) and 308(2)(e) of references to sections 54(9), 55(8) and 59(1) of the 1981 Act;

    (d) in subsection (6) for "289(11), 293(10) and 308(2)(e)" and "289(11), 293(8) and 308(2)(e)" of "54(9) and 59(1) of the Finance Act 1981" and "55(8) and 59(1) of that Act", respectively;

    (e) in subsection (7) for "300, 301 or 303(3)" of "58 or 59(4) of the Finance Act 1981".

(11) In any case where this section has effect in accordance with subsection (10) above and the qualifying company has one or more subsidiaries—

    (a) subsection (3) above shall, where the inspector has notified the subsidiary that relief has been given in respect of shares in the company of which it is a subsidiary, apply to the subsidiary as respects any transfer of its shares as it applies to the company as respects any transfer of shares in the company; and

    (b) subsections (5) and (6) above shall have effect in relation to any such arrangements as are mentioned in paragraph (c) of subsection (2) of section 308 (as that subsection has effect by virtue of subsection (6) of that section) as they have effect in relation to any such arrangement as is mentioned in section 289(11).

Nominees, bare trustees and approved investment funds.

311.—(1) Shares subscribed for, issued to, held by or disposed of for an individual by a nominee shall be treated for the purposes of this Chapter as subscribed for, issued to, held by or disposed of by that individual.

(2) Where eligible shares issued after 18th March 1986 are held on a bare trust for two or more beneficiaries, this Chapter shall have effect (with the necessary modifications) as if—

    (a) each beneficiary had subscribed as an individual for all of those shares; and

    (b) the amount subscribed by each beneficiary was equal to the total amount subscribed on the issue of those shares divided by the number of beneficiaries.

(3) Section 290(1) shall not apply where the amount is subscribed as nominee for an individual by the person or persons having the management of an investment fund approved for the purposes of this section by the Board ("the managers of an approved fund").

(4) Where an individual claims relief in respect of eligible shares in a company which have been issued to the managers of an approved fund as nominee for that individual, section 306(2) shall apply as if it required—

    (a) the certificate referred to in that section to be issued by the company to the managers;

    (b) the claim for relief to be accompanied by a certificate issued by the managers, in such form as the Board may authorise, certifying that the managers hold certificates issued to them by the companies concerned, for the purposes of sections 306(2), in respect of the holdings of eligible shares shown on the managers' certificate.

(5) The managers of an approved fund may be required by a notice given to them by an inspector or other officer of the Board to deliver to the officer, within the time limited by the notice, a return of the holdings of eligible shares shown on certificates issued by them in accordance with subsection (4) above in the year of assessment to which the return relates.

(6) Section 306(6) shall not apply in relation to any certificate issued by the managers of an approved fund for the purposes of subsection (4) above.

312.—(1) In this Chapter—

    "associate" has the meaning given in subsections (3) and (4) of section 417 except that in those subsections "relative" shall not include a brother or sister;

    "appraisal licence" means an appraisal licence incorporating the model clauses set out in Schedule 4 to the 1984 Regulations or a Northern Ireland licence granted for the five year renewal term and includes in either case any modified appraisal licence;

    "control", except in sections 291(7), 308(2) and 309(6)(a), shall be construed in accordance with section 416(2) to (6);

    "debenture" has the meaning given by section 744 of the Companies Act 1985;

    "development licence" means a development licence incorporating the model clauses set out in Schedule 5 to the 1984 Regulations or a Northern Ireland licence granted for the 30 year renewal term and includes in either case any modified development licence;

    "director" shall be construed in accordance with section 417(5);

Interpretation of Chapter III.

1985 c. 6.

K

"exploration licence" means an exploration licence incorporating the model clauses set out in Schedule 3 to the 1984 Regulations or a Northern Ireland licence granted for the initial term and includes in either case any modified exploration licence;

"fixed-rate preference share capital" means share capital consisting of shares which—

(a) are issued for consideration which is or includes new consideration; and

(b) do not carry any right either to conversion into shares or securities of any other description or to the acquisition of any additional shares or securities; and

(c) do not carry any right to dividends other than dividends which—

(i) are of a fixed amount or at a fixed rate per cent. of the nominal value of the shares, and

(ii) represent no more than a reasonable commercial return on the new consideration received by the company in respect of the issue of the shares; and

(d) on repayment do not carry any rights to an amount exceeding that new consideration except in so far as those rights are reasonably comparable with those general for fixed dividend shares listed in the Official List of the Stock Exchange;

"modified appraisal licence", "modified development licence" and "modified exploration licence" mean, respectively, any appraisal licence, development licence or exploration licence in which any of the relevant model clauses have been modified or excluded by the Secretary of State or in Northern Ireland the Department of Economic Development;

"new consideration" has the same meaning as in Part VI;

1964 c. 28 (N.I.).

S.R.& O.(N.I.) 1965 No.47.

"Northern Ireland licence" means a licence granted under the Petroleum (Production) Act (Northern Ireland) 1964 and incorporating the model clauses set out in Schedule 2 to the Petroleum Production (Licences) Regulations (Northern Ireland) 1965, and in relation to such a licence the references above to "the initial term", "the 30 year renewal term" and "the five year renewal term" shall be construed in accordance with Clause 2 of Schedule 2 to those Regulations;

"oil" and "oil extraction activities" have the same meanings as they have in Chapter V of Part XII;

"oil exploration" means searching for oil;

"ordinary shares" means shares forming part of a company's ordinary share capital;

"the relevant period" has the meaning given in section 289(12);

"research and development" means any activity which is intended to result in a patentable invention (within the meaning of the Patents Act 1977) or in a computer program;

PART VII

1977 c. 37.

"the relief" and "relief", except where the reference is to relief under Chapter II of Part IV of the Finance Act 1981, means relief under section 289 (and includes relief under Schedule 5 to the Finance Act 1983), and references to the amount of the relief shall be construed in accordance with section 289(5); and

1981 c. 35.

1983 c. 28.

"unquoted company" means a company none of whose shares, stocks or debentures are listed in the Official List of the Stock Exchange or dealt in on the Unlisted Securities Market;

and "the 1984 Regulations" means the Petroleum (Production) (Landward Areas) Regulations 1984.

S.I. 1984/1832.

(2) Section 839 applies for the purposes of this Chapter other than section 291.

(3) References in this Chapter to a disposal of shares include references to a disposal of an interest or right in or over the shares and an individual shall be treated for the purposes of this Chapter as disposing of any shares which he is treated by virtue of section 86(1) of the 1979 Act as exchanging for other shares.

(4) References in this Chapter to the reduction of any amount include references to its reduction to nil.

(5) For the purposes of this Chapter—

(a) in relation to shares issued after 18th March 1986, the market value at any time of any asset shall be taken to be the price which it might reasonably be expected to fetch on a sale at that time in the open market free from any interest or right which exists by way of security in or over it;

(b) in relation to shares issued before 19th March 1986, "market value" shall be construed in accordance with section 150 of the 1979 Act.

(6) References in this Chapter to relief given to an individual in respect of eligible shares, and to the withdrawal of such relief, include respectively references to relief given to him in respect of those shares at any time after he has disposed of them and references to the withdrawal of such relief at any such time.

(7) In relation to any case falling within section 289(1)(d), any reference in that section to any licence being held by, or granted to, any person shall be read as including a reference to such a licence being held by, or (as the case may be) granted to, that person together with one or more other persons.

(8) The Treasury may by order amend any of the definitions set out in subsection (1) above which relate to licences under the Petroleum (Production) Act 1934 or the Petroleum (Production) Act (Northern Ireland) 1964.

1934 c. 36.

1964 c. 28 (N.I.).

CHAPTER IV

SPECIAL PROVISIONS

Taxation of
consideration for
certain restrictive
undertakings.

313.—(1) Where—

(a) an individual who holds, has held, or is about to hold, an office or employment gives in connection with his holding that office or employment an undertaking (whether absolute or qualified, and whether legally valid or not) the tenor or effect of which is to restrict him as to his conduct or activities; and

(b) in respect of the giving of that undertaking by him, or of the total or partial fulfilment of that undertaking by him, any sum is paid either to him or to any other person; and

(c) apart from this section, the sum paid would neither fall to be treated as income of any person for the purposes of income tax for any year of assessment nor fall to be taken into account as a receipt in computing, for the purposes of income tax for any year of assessment, the amount of any income of, or loss incurred by, any person;

that sum shall be treated for the purpose of computing that individual's total income as received by him after deduction of income tax from a corresponding gross amount ("the gross amount").

(2) In any case where subsection (1) above applies—

(a) no assessment shall be made on the individual in respect of income tax at the basic rate on the gross amount but he shall be treated as having paid income tax at the basic rate on that amount or, if his total income is reduced by any deductions, on so much of that amount as is part of his total income as so reduced;

(b) no repayment shall be made of income tax treated by virtue of paragraph (a) above as having been paid; and

(c) the gross amount shall be treated for the purposes of sections 348 and 349 as not brought into charge to income tax.

(3) Where the individual has died before the payment of the sum referred to in subsection (1) above, so much of subsections (1) and (2) above as relates to the results which are to follow from the matters specified in paragraphs (a) to (c) of subsection (1) above shall have effect as if that sum had been paid immediately before the death.

(4) Where valuable consideration otherwise than in the form of money is given in respect of the giving of, or of the total or partial fulfilment of, any undertaking, subsections (1) to (3) above shall apply as if a sum had instead been paid equal to the value of that consideration.

(5) Where any sum is paid or valuable consideration given to any person in any year of assessment in respect of the giving of, or the total or partial fulfilment of, an undertaking satisfying the conditions specified in subsection (1)(a) above (not being a sum from which income tax is duly deducted under any provision of the Income Tax Acts), it shall be the duty of the person paying over the sum or giving the consideration to deliver particulars thereof in writing to the inspector not later than one month

after the end of that year, identifying the recipient of the payment or consideration, the undertaking in connection with which it was made or given and the individual who gave that undertaking.

(6) In this section—

(a) "office or employment" means any office or employment whatsoever such that the emoluments thereof, if any, are or would be chargeable to income tax under Case I or II of Schedule E; and

(b) references to the giving of valuable consideration do not include references to the mere assumption of an obligation to make over or provide valuable property, rights or advantages, but do include references to the doing of anything in or towards the discharge of such an obligation.

314.—(1) Where the duties of any employment which are performed by a person in the United Kingdom or a designated area consist wholly or mainly—

Divers and diving supervisors.

(a) of taking part, as a diver, in diving operations concerned with the exploration or exploitation of the seabed, its subsoil and their natural resources; or

(b) of acting, in relation to any such diving operations, as a diving supervisor,

the Income Tax Acts shall have effect as if the performance by that person of those duties constituted the carrying on by him of a trade within Case I of Schedule D; and accordingly Schedule E shall not apply to the emoluments from the employment so far as attributable to his performance of those duties.

(2) In this section "designated area" means any area designated under section 1(7) of the Continental Shelf Act 1964.

1964 c. 29.

315.—(1) Income from wounds and disability pensions to which this subsection applies shall be exempt from income tax and shall not be reckoned in computing income for any purposes of the Income Tax Acts.

Wounds and disability pensions.

(2) Subsection (1) above applies to—

(a) wounds pensions granted to members of the naval, military or air forces of the Crown;

(b) retired pay of disabled officers granted on account of medical unfitness attributable to or aggravated by naval, military or air-force service;

(c) disablement or disability pensions granted to members, other than commissioned officers, of the naval, military or air forces of the Crown on account of medical unfitness attributable to or aggravated by naval, military or air-force service;

(d) disablement pensions granted to persons who have been employed in the nursing services of any of the naval, military or air forces of the Crown on account of medical unfitness attributable to or aggravated by naval, military or air-force service; and

PART VII
1914 c. 30.
1914 c. 18 (5 & 6
Geo. 5 c. 18).
1915 c. 24.

(e) injury and disablement pensions payable under any scheme made under the Injuries in War (Compensation) Act 1914, the Injuries in War Compensation Act 1914 (Session 2) and the Injuries in War (Compensation) Act 1915 or under any War Risks Compensation Scheme for the Mercantile Marine.

(3) Where the amount of any retired pay or pensions to which subsection (1) above applies is not solely attributable to disablement or disability, the relief conferred by that subsection shall extend only to such part as is certified by the Secretary of State for Social Services, after consultation with the appropriate government department, to be attributable to disablement or disability.

Allowances,
bounties and
gratuities.

1939 c. 62.

316.—(1) Where, under the scheme relating to men in the Armed Forces of the Crown announced on behalf of His Majesty's Government in the United Kingdom on 15th April 1946 or under any other scheme certified by the Treasury to make analogous provision for classes of persons to whom the first-mentioned scheme does not apply, a person who has served in the armed forces of the Crown at any time during the continuance in force of the Emergency Powers (Defence) Act 1939 voluntarily undertakes to serve therein for a further period, any sum payable to him in pursuance of the scheme out of moneys provided by Parliament by way of gratuity at the end of his further period of service shall not be regarded as income for any income tax purposes.

(2) Where, under the scheme relating to members of the Women's Royal Naval Service, the Auxiliary Territorial Service and the Women's Auxiliary Air Force announced on behalf of His Majesty's Government in the United Kingdom on 20th November 1946, or under any other scheme certified by the Treasury to make analogous provision for classes of persons to whom the first-mentioned scheme does not apply, a woman who has served in or with the armed forces of the Crown at any time during the continuance in force of the Emergency Powers (Defence) Act 1939 voluntarily undertakes to serve in or with those forces for a further period, any sum payable to her in pursuance of the scheme out of moneys provided by Parliament by way of gratuity at the end of her further period of service shall not be regarded as income for any income tax purposes.

(3) Any allowance payable out of the public revenue to or in respect of any class of persons, being members of the armed forces of the Crown, as respects which the Treasury certifies either—

(a) that it is payable to the persons in question in lieu of food or drink normally supplied in kind to members of the armed forces, or

(b) that it is payable in respect of the persons in question as a contribution to the expenses of a mess,

shall not be regarded as income for any income tax purposes.

(4) The sums known as training expenses allowances payable out of the public revenue to members of the reserve and auxiliary forces of the Crown, and the sums payable by way of bounty out of the public revenue to such members in consideration of their undertaking prescribed training and attaining a prescribed standard of efficiency, shall not be treated as income for any income tax purpose.

(5) Any sum which, in pursuance of the scheme as to service emoluments contained in the Command Paper laid before Parliament in August 1950, becomes payable out of moneys provided by Parliament by way of bounty to a person who, having served in the armed forces of the Crown, voluntarily undertakes to serve for a further period shall not be regarded as income for any income tax purpose.

317.—The following shall be disregarded for all the purposes of the Income Tax Acts—

    (a) annuities and additional pensions paid to holders of the Victoria Cross;

    (b) annuities and additional pensions paid to holders of the George Cross;

    (c) annuities paid to holders of the Albert Medal or of the Edward Medal;

    (d) additional pensions paid to holders of the Military Cross;

    (e) additional pensions paid to holders of the Distinguished Flying Cross;

    (f) additional pensions paid to holders of the Distinguished Conduct Medal;

    (g) additional pensions paid to holders of the Conspicuous Gallantry Medal;

    (h) additional pensions paid to holders of the Distinguished Service Medal;

    (i) additional pensions paid to holders of the Military Medal;

    (j) additional pensions paid to holders of the Distinguished Flying Medal;

where paid by virtue of holding the award.

318.—(1) Payments of pensions or allowances to which this section applies shall not be treated as income for any purposes of the Income Tax Acts.

(2) This section applies to—

    (a) any pension or allowance payable by or on behalf of the Department of Health and Social Security under so much of any Order in Council, Royal Warrant, order or scheme as relates to death due to—

        (i) service in the armed forces of the Crown or war-time service in the merchant navy, or

        (ii) war injuries;

    (b) any pension or allowance at similar rates and subject to similar conditions which is payable by the Ministry of Defence in respect of death due to peacetime service in the armed forces of the Crown before 3rd September 1939; and

PART VII

(c) any pension or allowance which is payable under the law of a country other than the United Kingdom and is of a character substantially similar to a pension or allowance falling within paragraph (a) or (b) above.

(3) Where a pension or allowance falling within subsection (2) above is withheld or abated by reason of the receipt of another pension or allowance not falling within that subsection, there shall be treated as falling within that subsection so much of the other pension or allowance as is equal to the pension or allowance that is withheld or, as the case may be, to the amount of the abatement.

Crown servants: foreign service allowance.

319.—Where any allowance to any person in the service of the Crown is certified by the Treasury to represent compensation for the extra cost of having to live outside the United Kingdom in order to perform his duties, that allowance shall not be regarded as income for any income tax purpose.

Commonwealth Agents-General and official agents etc.
1964 c. 81.

320.—(1) An Agent-General who is resident in the United Kingdom shall be entitled to the same immunity from income tax as that to which the head of a mission so resident is entitled under the Diplomatic Privileges Act 1964.

(2) Any person having or exercising any employment to which this subsection applies (not being a person employed in any trade, business or other undertaking carried on for the purposes of profit) shall be entitled to the same immunity from income tax as that to which a member of the staff of a mission is entitled under the Diplomatic Privileges Act 1964.

(3) The employments to which subsection (2) above applies are the employment in the United Kingdom as—

(a) a member of the personal staff of any Agent-General; or

(b) an official agent for, or for any state or province of, any of the countries for the time being mentioned in Schedule 3 to the British Nationality Act 1981 or the Republic of Ireland; or

1981 c. 81.

(c) an official agent for any self-governing colony,

of a person certified by the High Commissioner of the country in question or, as the case may be, by the Agent-General for the state, province or self-governing colony in question to be ordinarily resident outside the United Kingdom and to be resident in the United Kingdom solely for the purpose of the performance of his duties as such member or official agent.

(4) In this section—

"Agent-General" means the Agent-General for any state or province of a country within subsection (3)(b) above or for any self-governing colony;

"High Commissioner" includes the head of the mission of a country within subsection (3)(b) above by whatever name called;

"mission" has the same meaning as in the Diplomatic Privileges Act 1964, and references to the head of a mission and a member of the staff of a mission shall be construed in accordance with that Act;

"self-governing colony" means any colony certified by a Secretary of State to be a self-governing colony.

321.—(1) Income arising from any office or employment to which this section applies shall be exempt from income tax, and no account shall be taken of any such income in estimating the amount of income for any income tax purposes.

(2) The offices and employments to which this section applies are the following, that is to say—

    (a) the office of a consul in the United Kingdom in the service of any foreign state; and

    (b) the employment of an official agent in the United Kingdom for any foreign state, not being an employment exercised by a Commonwealth citizen or a citizen of the Republic of Ireland or exercised in connection with any trade, business or other undertaking carried on for the purposes of profit.

(3) In this section—

"consul" means a person recognised by Her Majesty as being a consul-general, consul, vice-consul or consular agent; and

"official agent" means a person, not being a consul, who is employed on the staff of any consulate, official department or agency of a foreign state, not being a department or agency which carries on any trade, business or other undertaking for the purposes of profit.

322.—(1) Where a consular officer or employee in the United Kingdom of any foreign state to which this section applies—

    (a) is not a British citizen, a British Dependent Territories citizen or a British Overseas citizen, and

    (b) is not engaged in any trade, profession, vocation or employment in the United Kingdom, otherwise than as such a consular officer or employee, and

    (c) either is a permanent employee of that state or was not ordinarily resident in the United Kingdom immediately before he became a consular officer or employee in the United Kingdom of that state;

then any income of his falling within Case IV or V of Schedule D shall be exempt from income tax, and he shall be treated as not resident in the United Kingdom for the purposes of sections 48 and 123(4).

(2) Without prejudice to section 321, the income arising from a person's employment in the United Kingdom as a consular employee of any foreign state to which this section applies shall be exempt from income tax, except in the case of a person who is not a national of that state but is a British citizen, a British Dependent Territories citizen or a British Overseas citizen.

(3) For the purposes of this section "consular employee" includes any person employed, for the purposes of the official business of a consular officer, at any consulate or consular establishment or at any other premises used for those purposes.

(4) This section shall apply to any foreign state to which Her Majesty by Order in Council directs that it shall apply for the purpose of giving effect to any consular convention or other arrangement with that state making similar provision in the case of Her Majesty's consular officers or employees in that state.

(5) An Order in Council under subsection (4) above—

(a) may limit the operation of this section in relation to any state in such manner as appears to Her Majesty to be necessary or expedient having regard to the arrangement with that state;

(b) may be made so as to have effect from a date earlier than the making of the Order or the passing of this Act (but not earlier than the coming into force of the arrangement with regard to which it is made); and

(c) may contain such transitional provisions as appear to Her Majesty to be necessary or expedient;

and any statutory instrument under this section shall be subject to annulment in pursuance of a resolution of the House of Commons.

Visiting forces.

323.—(1) The emoluments paid by the government of any designated country to any member of a visiting force of that country who is not a British citizen, a British Dependent Territories citizen or a British Overseas citizen shall be exempt from income tax.

(2) A period during which a member of a visiting force to whom subsection (1) above applies is in the United Kingdom by reason solely of his being a member of that force shall not be treated for the purposes of income tax either as a period of residence in the United Kingdom or as creating a change of his residence or domicile.

(3) Subsection (2) above shall not affect the operation of section 278 in relation to any person for any year of assessment.

(4) In subsections (1) and (2) above references to a visiting force shall apply to a civilian component of such a force as they apply to the force itself; and those subsections shall be construed as one with the Visiting Forces Act 1952, but so that, for the purposes of this section, references to a designated country shall be substituted in that Act for references to a country to which a provision of that Act applies.

1952 c. 67.

(5) For the purpose of conferring on persons attached to any designated allied headquarters the like benefits as are conferred by subsections (1) and (2) above on members of a visiting force or civilian component, any members of the armed forces of a designated country shall, while attached to any such headquarters, be deemed to constitute a visiting force of that country, and there shall be a corresponding extension of the class of persons who may be treated as members of a civilian component of such a visiting force.

(6) In the case of persons of any category for the time being agreed between Her Majesty's government in the United Kingdom and the other members of the North Atlantic Council—

(a) employment by a designated allied headquarters shall be treated for the purposes of subsection (2) above as if it were service as a member of a visiting force of a designated country; and

(b) the emoluments paid by a designated allied headquarters to persons employed by such a headquarters shall be exempt from income tax.

(7) The exemption conferred by subsection (6)(b) above shall cease to apply to British citizens, British Dependent Territories citizens and British Overseas citizens if it becomes unnecessary that it should so apply for the purpose of giving effect to any agreement between parties to the North Atlantic Treaty.

(8) For the purposes of this section—

"allied headquarters" means any international military headquarters established under the North Atlantic Treaty, and

"designated" means designated for the purpose in question by or under any Order in Council made for giving effect to any international agreement.

324.—(1) The Treasury may by order designate for the purposes of this section—

Designated international organisations.

(a) any international organisation—

(i) if one of its members is the United Kingdom or any of the Communities; and

(ii) if the agreement under which that member became a member provides for exemption from tax, in relation to the organisation, of the kind for which provision is made by this section; or

(b) any of the Communities or the European Investment Bank.

(2) Where an organisation has been so designated, a person not resident in the United Kingdom shall not be liable to income tax in respect of income from any security issued by the organisation if he would not be liable but for the fact that—

(a) the security or income is issued, made payable or paid in the United Kingdom or in sterling; or

(b) the organisation maintains an office or other place of business in the United Kingdom.

325.—Where the total income of an individual for the year of assessment includes, or would but for this section include, any sums paid or credited in respect of interest on deposits with the National Savings Bank, other than investment deposits, those sums shall be disregarded for all purposes of the Income Tax Acts, other than the furnishing of information, if or in so far as they do not exceed £70; and for this purpose the question whether or how far those sums exceed £70 shall, where by virtue of section 279 a woman's income is deemed to be her husband's, be determined separately as regards the part of his income which is his by virtue of that section and the part which is his apart from that section.

Interest on deposits with National Savings Bank.

326.—(1) Any terminal bonus, or interest or other sum, payable under a certified contractual savings scheme—

Interest etc. under contractual savings schemes.

PART VII
1968 c. 13.

(a) in respect of money raised under section 12 of the National Loans Act 1968, or

(b) in respect of shares in a building society,

shall be disregarded for all purposes of the Income Tax Acts.

(2) In this section "certified contractual savings scheme" means, except in relation to a building society, a scheme—

1958 c. 6 (7 & 8
Eliz. 2).
1969 c. 32.

(a) governed by regulations made under section 12 of the National Debt Act 1958 or section 52 of the Finance Act 1969; and

(b) providing for periodical contributions by individuals for a specified period, and the repayment in accordance with the regulations of contributions together with any additional sum by way of bonus or interest, and

(c) certified by the Treasury as qualifying for exemption under this section.

(3) In this section "certified contractual savings scheme" means, in relation to a building society, a scheme—

(a) providing for periodical contributions by individuals for a specified period, being contributions by way of investment in shares in the building society, and

(b) certified by the Treasury as corresponding to a scheme certified under subsection (2) above, and as qualifying for exemption under this section.

Disabled person's
vehicle
maintenance
grant.
1977 c. 49.
1978 c. 29.
S.I. 1972/1265
(N.I. 14).

327.—A grant made under paragraph 2 of Schedule 2 to the National Health Service Act 1977 or section 46(3) of the National Health Service (Scotland) Act 1978 (cost of maintenance etc. of vehicles belonging to disabled persons) or under Article 30 of the Health and Personal Social Services (Northern Ireland) Order 1972 to any person owning a vehicle shall not be treated as income for any purpose of the Income Tax Acts.

Funds in court.
1982 c. 53.

328.—(1) If any common investment fund established under section 42 of the Administration of Justice Act 1982 is for the time being designated for the purposes of this subsection by an agreement between the Board and the investment manager of the fund—

(a) subject to subsection (2) below, the investment manager shall be entitled to exemption from income tax in respect of so much of the income derived from that fund or any investment thereof as is paid by him by way of dividend on the shares into which the fund is divided; and

(b) dividends on those shares shall be paid without deduction of income tax and shall be chargeable under Case III of Schedule D.

A claim for exemption under paragraph (a) shall be made to the Board.

(2) Where the income or part of the income derived in a year of assessment from the fund or its investments consists of interest on securities, the income or part (as the case may be) shall for the purposes

of subsection (1)(a) above be calculated by treating it as the amount it would be apart from section 714(5), but reduced by an amount (if any) equal to the excess of A over B.

(3) In subsection (2) above—

> A is the total amount of allowances to which, by virtue of section 714(4), the investment manager of the fund is entitled in the year of assessment in respect of all securities comprised in the fund; and

> B is the total amount of annual profits or gains which, by virtue of section 714(2), he is treated as receiving in the year of assessment in respect of those securities.

(4) In subsections (2) and (3) above "interest" and "securities" have the same meanings as in sections 710 and 711.

(5) Where at any time by virtue of subsection (1) above the income of any person from any source becomes chargeable to income tax as provided by that subsection, not having previously been chargeable by direct assessment on that person, section 66(3) shall apply as if the source of that income were a new source of income acquired by that person at that time.

(6) The Accountant General and any other person authorised to invest in a fund designated for the purposes of subsection (1) above shall as respects each year of assessment furnish to the Board, at such time and in such manner as they may direct, particulars of any sums paid without deduction of tax by virtue of that subsection and of the persons to whom they were paid, except that particulars shall not be required of any case where the total of such sums paid to any person in that year did not exceed £15.

(7) An agreement designating a fund for the purposes of subsection (1) above may provide for incidental and consequential matters, including arrangements for giving effect to subsection (1)(a) above by provisional repayments of tax deducted at source, and may be determined by the Board or the investment manager of the fund by one year's notice expiring at the end of any year of assessment.

(8) The reference to the Accountant General is a reference to the Accountant General of the Supreme Court of England and Wales and in relation to money in the Supreme Court of Judicature of Northern Ireland, or money in a county court in Northern Ireland, and in relation to investments representing such money, includes a reference to the Accountant General of the Supreme Court of Judicature of Northern Ireland or any other person by whom such funds are held.

329.—(1) The following interest shall not be regarded as income for any income tax purpose—

> (a) any interest on damages in respect of personal injuries to a plaintiff or any other person, or in respect of a person's death, which is included in any sum for which judgment is given by virtue of a provision to which this paragraph applies; and

PART VII

(b) any interest on damages or solatium in respect of personal injuries sustained by a pursuer or by any other person, decree for payment of which is included in any interlocutor by virtue of 1958 c. 61.   section 1 of the Interest on Damages (Scotland) Act 1958.

(2) The provisions to which subsection (1)(a) above applies are—

1934 c. 41.

(a) section 3 of the Law Reform (Miscellaneous Provisions) Act 1934;

1937 c. 9 (N.I.).

(b) section 17 of the Law Reform (Miscellaneous Provisions) Act (Northern Ireland) 1937;

1981 c. 54.

(c) section 35A of the Supreme Court Act 1981;

1984 c. 28.

(d) section 69 of the County Courts Act 1984;

1978 c. 23 (N.I.).

(e) section 33A of the Judicature (Northern Ireland) Act 1978; and

S.I. 1980/397 (N.I. 13).

(f) Article 45A of the County Courts (Northern Ireland) Order 1980.

(3) A payment in satisfaction of a cause of action, including a payment into court, shall not be regarded as income for any income tax purpose to the extent to which it is in respect of interest which would fall within subsection (1) above if included in a sum for which a judgment is given or if decree for payment of it were included in an interlocutor.

(4) In this section "personal injuries" includes any disease and any impairment of a person's physical or mental condition.

Compensation for National-Socialist persecution.

330.—Annuities and pensions payable under any special provision for victims of National-Socialist persecution which is made by the law of the Federal Republic of Germany or any part of it or of Austria shall not be regarded as income for any income tax purpose.

Scholarship income.

331.—(1) Income arising from a scholarship held by a person receiving full-time instruction at a university, college, school or other educational establishment shall be exempt from income tax, and no account shall be taken of any such income in computing the amount of income for income tax purposes.

(2) In this section "scholarship" includes an exhibition, bursary or any other similar educational endowment.

Expenditure and houses of ministers of religion.

332.—(1) Subsection (2) below applies where an interest in any premises belongs to a charity or any ecclesiastical corporation and (in right of that interest)—

(a) the persons from time to time holding any full-time office as clergyman or minister of any religious denomination, or

(b) any particular person holding such an office,

have or has a residence in those premises from which to perform the duties of the office.

(2) In the case of such a clergyman or minister, for the purposes of income tax with which he may be chargeable under Schedule E, there shall be disregarded—

(a) the making good to him, in consequence of his being the holder of his office, of statutory amounts payable in connection with the premises or statutory deductions falling to be made in connection therewith, except in so far as an amount or deduction is properly attributable to a part of the premises in respect of which he receives rent;

(b) the payment on his behalf, except as aforesaid, of such a statutory amount; and

(c) unless he is in director's or higher-paid employment (as defined in section 167), the value to him of any expenses incurred in connection with the provision in the premises of living accommodation for him, being expenses incurred in consequence of his being the holder of his office.

(3) In assessing the income tax chargeable (whether under Schedule E or any other Schedule) upon a clergyman or minister of any religious denomination, the following deductions may be made from any profits, fees or emoluments of his profession or vocation—

(a) any sums of money paid or expenses incurred by him wholly, exclusively and necessarily in the performance of his duty as a clergyman or minister;

(b) such part of the rent (not exceeding one-quarter) as the inspector by whom the assessment is made may allow, paid by him in respect of a dwelling-house any part of which is used mainly and substantially for the purposes of his duty as such clergyman or minister; and

(c) in respect of expenses borne by him in the maintenance, repairs, insurance or management of any premises in which, in right of such an interest as is mentioned in subsection (1) above, he has such a residence as is mentioned in that subsection, such part of the expenses as, together with any deduction allowable in respect of such expenses under paragraph (a) above, is equal to one-quarter of the amount of the expenses.

On an appeal to the General Commissioners or Special Commissioners, the Commissioners shall have jurisdiction to review the inspector's decision under paragraph (b) above.

(4) In this section "statutory amount" and "statutory deduction" mean an amount paid and a deduction made in pursuance of any provision contained in or having the force of an Act.

333.—(1) The Treasury may make regulations providing that an individual who invests under a plan shall be entitled to relief from income tax in respect of the investments.

Personal equity plans.

(2) The regulations shall set out the conditions subject to which plans are to operate and the extent to which investors are to be entitled to relief from tax.

(3) In particular, the regulations may—

(a) specify the description of individuals who may invest and the kind of investments they may make;

(b) specify maximum investment limits and minimum periods for which investments are to be held;

(c) provide that investments are to be held by persons ("plan managers") on behalf of investors;

(d) specify how relief from tax is to be claimed by, and granted to, investors or plan managers on their behalf;

(e) provide that plans and plan managers must be such as are approved by the Board;

(f) specify the circumstances in which approval may be granted and withdrawn.

(4) The regulations may include provision—

(a) that in prescribed circumstances—

(i) an investor under a plan shall cease to be, and be treated as not having been, entitled to relief from tax in respect of the investments; and

(ii) he or the plan manager concerned (depending on the terms of the regulations) shall account to the Board for tax from which relief has already been given on the basis that the investor was so entitled;

(b) that an investor under a plan or the plan manager concerned (depending on the terms of the regulations) shall account to the Board for tax from which relief has been given in circumstances such that the investor was not entitled to it;

(c) adapting, or modifying the effect of, any enactment relating to income tax in order to—

(i) secure that investors under plans are entitled to relief from tax in respect of investments;

(ii) secure that investors under plans cease to be, and are treated as not having been, so entitled;

(iii) secure that investors under plans or plan managers account for tax as mentioned in paragraph (a) or (b) above;

(d) that a person who is, or has at any time been, either an investor under a plan or a plan manager—

(i) shall comply with any notice which is served on him by the Board and which requires him within a prescribed period to make available for the Board's inspection documents (of a prescribed kind) relating to a plan or to investments which are or have been held under it;

(ii) shall, within a prescribed period of being required to do so by the Board, furnish to the Board information (of a prescribed kind) about a plan or about investments which are or have been held under it;

(e) generally for the purpose of bringing plans into existence, and generally for the purpose of the administration of plans and the administration of income tax and corporation tax in relation to them.

(5) In this section "prescribed" means prescribed by the regulations.

CHAPTER V

RESIDENCE OF INDIVIDUALS

334.—Every Commonwealth citizen or citizen of the Republic of Ireland—

(a) shall, if his ordinary residence has been in the United Kingdom, be assessed and charged to income tax notwithstanding that at the time the assessment or charge is made he may have left the United Kingdom, if he has so left the United Kingdom for the purpose only of occasional residence abroad, and

(b) shall be charged as a person actually residing in the United Kingdom upon the whole amount of his profits or gains, whether they arise from property in the United Kingdom or elsewhere, or from any allowance, annuity or stipend, or from any trade, profession, employment or vocation in the United Kingdom or elsewhere.

335.—(1) Where—

(a) a person works full-time in one or more of the following, that is to say, a trade, profession, vocation, office or employment; and

(b) no part of the trade, profession or vocation is carried on in the United Kingdom and all the duties of the office or employment are performed outside the United Kingdom;

the question whether he is resident in the United Kingdom shall be decided without regard to any place of abode maintained in the United Kingdom for his use.

(2) Where an office or employment is in substance one of which the duties fall in the year of assessment to be performed outside the United Kingdom there shall be treated for the purposes of this section as so performed any duties performed in the United Kingdom the performance of which is merely incidental to the performance of the other duties outside the United Kingdom.

336.—(1) A person shall not be charged to income tax under Schedule D as a person residing in the United Kingdom, in respect of profits or gains received in respect of possessions or securities out of the United Kingdom, if—

(a) he is in the United Kingdom for some temporary purpose only and not with any view or intent of establishing his residence there, and

(b) he has not actually resided in the United Kingdom at one time or several times for a period equal in the whole to six months in any year of assessment, but if any such person resides in the United Kingdom for such a period he shall be so chargeable for that year.

(2) For the purposes of Cases I, II and III of Schedule E, a person who is in the United Kingdom for some temporary purpose only and not with the intention of establishing his residence there shall not be treated as resident in the United Kingdom if he has not in the aggregate spent at least six months in the United Kingdom in the year of assessment, but shall be treated as resident there if he has.

PART VIII

TAXATION OF INCOME AND CHARGEABLE GAINS OF COMPANIES

Taxation of income

337.—(1) Where a company begins or ceases to carry on a trade, or to be within the charge to corporation tax in respect of a trade, the company's income shall be computed as if that were the commencement or, as the case may be, discontinuance of the trade, whether or not the trade is in fact commenced or discontinued.

(2) Subject to subsection (3) below and to any other provision of the Corporation Tax Acts which expressly authorises such a deduction, no deduction shall be made in computing income from any source—

    (a) in respect of dividends or other distributions; nor

    (b) in respect of any yearly interest, annuity or other annual payment or in respect of any such other payments as are mentioned in section 348(2), but not including sums which are, or but for any exemption would be, chargeable under Schedule A.

(3) In computing income from a trade, subsection (2)(b) above shall not prevent the deduction of yearly interest payable in the United Kingdom on an advance from a bank carrying on a bona fide banking business in the United Kingdom.

Companies beginning or ceasing to carry on a trade.

338.—(1) Subject to sections 339, 494 and 787, in computing the corporation tax chargeable for any accounting period of a company any charges on income paid by the company in the accounting period, so far as paid out of the company's profits brought into charge to corporation tax, shall be allowed as deductions against the total profits for the period as reduced by any other relief from tax, other than group relief.

Allowance of charges on income and capital.

(2) Subject to the following subsections, to section 339 and to any other express exceptions, "charges on income" means for the purposes of corporation tax—

    (a) payments of any description mentioned in subsection (3) below, not being dividends or other distributions of the company; and

    (b) payments which are qualifying donations (within the meaning of section 339);

but no payment which is deductible in computing profits or any description of profits for purposes of corporation tax shall be treated as a charge on income.

(3) Subject to subsections (4) to (6) below, the payments referred to in subsection (2)(a) above are—

    (a) any yearly interest (whether charged to revenue or capital), annuity or other annual payment and any such other payments as are mentioned in section 348(2) but not including sums which are or, but for any exemption would be, chargeable under Schedule A; and

(b) any other interest (whether charged to revenue or capital) payable in the United Kingdom on an advance from a bank carrying on a bona fide banking business in the United Kingdom, or from a person who in the opinion of the Board is bona fide carrying on business as a member of the Stock Exchange or bona fide carrying on the business of a discount house in the United Kingdom;

and for the purposes of this section any interest payable by a company as mentioned in paragraph (b) above shall be treated as paid on its being debited to the company's account in the books of the person to whom it is payable.

(4) No such payment as is mentioned in subsection (3)(a) above made by a company to a person not resident in the United Kingdom shall be treated as a charge on income unless the company is so resident and either—

(a) the company deducts income tax from the payment in accordance with section 349, and accounts under Schedule 16 for the tax so deducted, or

(b) it is a payment of interest on a quoted Eurobond falling within section 124; or

(c) the payment is a payment of interest falling within section 340; or

(d) the payment is one payable out of income brought into charge to tax under Case IV or V of Schedule D.

(5) No such payment made by a company as is mentioned in subsection (3) above shall be treated as a charge on income if—

(a) the payment, not being interest, is charged to capital or the payment is not ultimately borne by the company; or

(b) the payment is not made under a liability incurred for a valuable and sufficient consideration (and, in the case of a company not resident in the United Kingdom, incurred wholly and exclusively for the purposes of a trade carried on by it in the United Kingdom through a branch or agency), and is not a covenanted donation to charity (within the meaning of section 339).

(6) No such payment of interest as is mentioned in subsection (3) above made by a company shall be treated as a charge on income unless—

(a) the company exists wholly or mainly for the purpose of carrying on a trade; or

(b) the payment of interest is wholly and exclusively laid out or expended for the purposes of a trade carried on by the company; or

(c) the company is an investment company, within the meaning of section 130 and including an authorised unit trust; or

(d) the payment of interest would, on the assumptions made below, be eligible for relief under section 353 by virtue of section 354 if it were made by an individual.

For the purposes of paragraph (d) above, it shall be assumed that if the land concerned is occupied by the company the conditions of section 355(1) are satisfied if the land either—

  (i) is not used as a residence; or

  (ii) is used as an individual's main or only residence;

but the limit imposed by section 357 shall apply only in a case falling within paragraph (ii) above and shall then apply without regard to any loan made in connection with any other land.

(7) Any payment to which section 125(1) applies shall not be a charge on income for the purposes of corporation tax.

339.—(1) A qualifying donation is a payment made by a company to a charity, other than—

  (a) a covenanted payment to charity, as defined in section 660(3); and

  (b) a payment which is deductible in computing profits or any description of profits for purposes of corporation tax.

Charges on income: donations to charity.

(2) A qualifying donation shall not constitute a charge on the income of the company unless a claim is made by the company and the company is resident in the United Kingdom and is not a close company.

(3) A payment made by a company is not a qualifying donation unless, on the making of it, the company deducts out of it a sum representing the amount of income tax on it.

(4) Where, with a view to securing relief under section 338 a company makes a payment subject to such a deduction as is mentioned in subsection (3) above, then, whether or not it proves to be a qualifying donation, the payment—

  (a) shall be treated as a relevant payment for the purposes of Schedule 16; and

  (b) shall in the hands of the recipient (whether a charity or not) be treated for the purposes of this Act as if it were an annual payment.

(5) In any accounting period of a company, the maximum amount allowable under section 338 by virtue of subsection (2)(b) of that section in respect of qualifying donations made by the company shall be a sum equal to 3 per cent. of the dividends paid on the company's ordinary share capital in that accounting period.

(6) A covenanted donation to charity shall not be regarded for the purposes of the definition of "charges on income" in section 338, or for any of the other purposes of the Corporation Tax Acts, as being, by reason of any provision of this Act, a distribution.

(7) Notwithstanding anything in any other provision of the Tax Acts, a covenanted donation to charity made by a company shall not be a charge on income for the purposes of section 338 unless the company—

  (a) deducts out of it a sum representing the amount of income tax on it; and

(b) accounts for that tax in accordance with Schedule 16;

and any such payment from which a deduction is made as mentioned in paragraph (a) above shall be treated as a relevant payment for the purposes of Schedule 16, whether or not it would otherwise fall to be so treated.

(8) In this section "covenanted donation to charity" means a payment under a disposition or covenant made by the company in favour of a charity whereby the like annual payments (of which the donation is one) become payable for a period which may exceed three years and is not capable of earlier termination under any power exercisable without the consent of the persons for the time being entitled to the payments.

(9) For the purposes of this section "charity" includes the Trustees of the National Heritage Memorial Fund and the Historic Buildings and Monuments Commission for England and, additionally, in subsections (1) to (5) above includes the Trustees of the British Museum, the Trustees of the British Museum (Natural History) and any Association of a description specified in section 508, but, subject to that, in this section "charity" has the same meaning as in section 506.

Charges on income: interest payable to non-residents.

340.—(1) A payment of interest by a company is one to which section 338(4)(c) applies if the company is carrying on a trade and—

(a) under the terms of the contract under which the interest is payable, the interest is to be paid, or may be required to be paid, outside the United Kingdom; and

(b) the interest is in fact paid outside the United Kingdom; and

(c) either—

(i) the liability to pay the interest was incurred wholly or mainly for the purposes of activities of the company's trade carried on outside the United Kingdom; or

(ii) the interest is payable in a currency other than sterling and, subject to subsection (2) below, the liability to pay the interest was incurred wholly or mainly for the purposes of activities of that trade, wherever carried on.

(2) Subsection (1)(c)(ii) above does not apply where—

(a) the trade is carried on by a body of persons over whom the person entitled to the interest has control; or

(b) the person entitled to the interest is a body of persons over whom the person carrying on the trade has control; or

(c) the person carrying on the trade and the person entitled to the interest are both bodies of persons, and some other person has control over both of them.

In this subsection references to a body of persons include references to a partnership and "control" has the meaning given by section 840.

(3) For the purposes of subsection (1) above the company paying the interest shall be treated as carrying on any trade carried on by a 75 per cent. subsidiary of it (both being bodies corporate) if the subsidiary (as well as the company making the payment) is resident in the United Kingdom.

(4) In determining for the purposes of this section whether one company is a 75 per cent. subsidiary of another that other company shall be treated as not being the owner—

(a) of any share capital which it owns directly in a body corporate if a profit on a sale of the shares would be treated as a trading receipt of its trade; or

(b) of any share capital which it owns indirectly, and which is owned directly by a body corporate for which a profit on the sale of the shares would be a trading receipt; or

(c) of any share capital which it owns directly or indirectly in a body corporate not resident in the United Kingdom.

341.—(1) This section applies where—

(a) the relationship between two companies is as mentioned in subsection (2) below;

(b) one of the companies makes to the other a payment which, for the purposes of corporation tax, is a charge on income of the company making it; and

(c) in the hands of the company receiving it, the payment is chargeable to tax under Case III of Schedule D.

(2) The relationship between two companies which is referred to in subsection (1)(a) above is—

(a) that one company controls the other; or

(b) that another person controls both companies; or

(c) that one company is a 51 per cent. subsidiary of the other; or

(d) that both companies are 51 per cent. subsidiaries of another company;

and section 840 applies for the purposes of this section.

(3) In a case where this section applies, the payment referred to in subsection (1)(b) above shall be treated for the purposes of corporation tax as received by the company to which it is paid on the same day as that on which it is for those purposes treated as paid by the company paying it.

(4) Subject to subsection (5) below, where the payment referred to in subsection (1)(b) above is a "relevant payment" for the purposes of Schedule 16, it shall be treated for the purposes of that Schedule as received on the same day as that on which, by virtue of subsection (3) above, it is treated as received for the purposes of corporation tax; and the reference in paragraph 5(1) of that Schedule to the accounting period in which the payment is received shall be construed accordingly.

(5) Subsection (4) above does not apply if the day on which the payment would be treated as received apart from that subsection falls within the same accounting period (of the receiving company) as the day on which it would be treated as received under that subsection.

Tax on company in liquidation.

342.—(1) In this section references to a company's final year are references to the financial year in which the affairs of the company are completely wound up, and references to a company's penultimate year are references to the last financial year preceding its final year.

(2) Subject to subsection (3) below—

(a) corporation tax shall be charged on the profits of the company arising in the winding-up in its final year at the rate of corporation tax fixed or proposed for the penultimate year; but

(b) where the corporation tax charged on the company's income included in those profits falls to be calculated or reduced in accordance with section 13, it shall be so calculated or reduced in accordance with such rate or fraction fixed or proposed for the penultimate year as is applicable under that section.

(3) If, before the affairs of the company are completely wound up, any of the rates or fractions mentioned in subsection (2) above has been fixed or proposed for the final year, that subsection shall have effect in relation to that rate or fraction as if for the references to the penultimate year there were substituted references to the final year.

(4) An assessment on the company's profits for an accounting period which falls after the commencement of the winding-up shall not be invalid because made before the end of the accounting period.

(5) In making an assessment after the commencement of the winding-up of the company but before the date when its affairs are completely wound up, the inspector may, with the concurrence of the liquidator, act on an assumption as to when that date will fall, so far as it governs section 12(7).

(6) The assumption of the wrong date shall not alter the company's final and penultimate year, and, if the right date is later, an accounting period shall end on the date assumed, and a new accounting period shall begin and section 12(7) shall thereafter apply as if that new accounting period began with the commencement of the winding-up.

(7) References in this section to a rate or fraction fixed or proposed are references to a rate or fraction fixed by an Act passed before the completion of the winding-up or, if not so fixed, proposed by a Budget resolution (and without regard to any subsequent Act); except that if a rate or fraction so fixed is proposed to be altered by a Budget resolution any such reference to it is a reference to it as proposed to be so altered.

In this subsection "Budget resolution" means a resolution of the House of Commons for fixing any such rate or fraction as is mentioned in this section.

(8) Where the winding-up commenced before the company's final year, paragraphs (a) and (b) of subsection (2) (but not subsection (3)) above shall apply in relation to the company's profits arising at any time in its penultimate year.

(9) Any assessment made by virtue of section 8(4) shall be subject to any such adjustment by discharge or repayment of tax or by a further assessment as may be required to give effect to this section.

343.—(1) Where, on a company ("the predecessor") ceasing to carry on a trade, another company ("the successor") begins to carry it on, and—

Company reconstructions without a change of ownership.

    (a) on or at any time within two years after that event the trade or an interest amounting to not less than a three-fourths share in it belongs to the same persons as the trade or such an interest belonged to at some time within a year before that event; and

    (b) the trade is not, within the period taken for the comparison under paragraph (a) above, carried on otherwise than by a company which is within the charge to tax in respect of it;

then the Corporation Tax Acts shall have effect subject to subsections (2) to (6) below.

In paragraphs (a) and (b) above references to the trade shall apply also to any other trade of which the activities comprise the activities of the first mentioned trade.

(2) The trade shall not be treated as permanently discontinued nor a new trade as set up and commenced for the purpose of the allowances and charges provided for by the Capital Allowances Acts; but—

    (a) there shall be made to or on the successor in accordance with those Acts all such allowances and charges as would, if the predecessor had continued to carry on the trade, have fallen to be made to or on it; and

    (b) the amount of any such allowance or charge shall be computed as if—

        (i) the successor had been carrying on the trade since the predecessor began to do so, and

        (ii) everything done to or by the predecessor had been done to or by the successor (but so that no sale or transfer which on the transfer of the trade is made to the successor by the predecessor of any assets in use for the purpose of the trade shall be treated as giving rise to any such allowance or charge).

The preceding provisions of this subsection shall not apply if the successor is a dual resident investing company (within the meaning of section 404) which begins to carry on the trade after 31st March 1987.

(3) The predecessor shall not be entitled to relief under section 394, except as provided by subsection (6) below; and, subject to subsection (4) below and to any claim made by the predecessor under section 393(2), the successor shall be entitled to relief under section 393(1), as for a loss sustained by the successor in carrying on the trade, for any amount for which the predecessor would have been entitled to claim relief if it had continued to carry on the trade.

(4) Where the amount of relevant liabilities exceeds the value of relevant assets, the successor shall be entitled to relief by virtue of subsection (3) above only if, and only to the extent that, the amount of that excess is less than the amount mentioned in that subsection.

This subsection does not apply where the predecessor ceased to carry on the trade or part of a trade before 19th March 1986 nor, in a case where subsection (7) below applies, in relation to any earlier event, within the meaning of that subsection, which occurred before that date (but without prejudice to its application in relation to any later event which occurred on or after that date).

(5) Any securities, within the meaning of section 731, which at the time when the predecessor ceases to carry on the trade form part of the trading stock belonging to the trade shall be treated for the purposes of that section as having been sold at that time in the open market by the predecessor and as having been purchased at that time in the open market by the successor.

(6) On the successor ceasing to carry on the trade—

(a) if the successor does so within four years of succeeding to it, any relief which might be given to the successor under section 394 on its ceasing to carry on the trade may, so far as it cannot be given to the successor, be given to the predecessor as if the predecessor had incurred the loss (including any amount treated as a loss under subsection (4) of that section); and

(b) if the successor ceases to carry on the trade within one year of succeeding to it, relief may be given to the predecessor under that section in respect of any loss incurred by it (or amount treated as such a loss under subsection (4) of that section);

but for the purposes of that section, as it applies by virtue of this subsection to the giving of relief to the predecessor, the predecessor shall be treated as ceasing to carry on the trade when the successor does so.

(7) Where the successor ceases to carry on the trade within the period taken for the comparison under subsection (1)(a) above and on its doing so a third company begins to carry on the trade, then no relief shall be given to the predecessor by virtue of subsection (6) above by reference to that event, but, subject to that, subsections (2) to (6) above shall apply both in relation to that event (together with the new predecessor and successor) and to the earlier event (together with the original predecessor and successor), but so that—

(a) in relation to the earlier event "successor" shall include the successor at either event; and

(b) in relation to the later event "predecessor" shall include the predecessor at either event;

and if the conditions of this subsection are thereafter again satisfied, it shall apply again in like manner.

(8) Where, on a company ceasing to carry on a trade, another company begins to carry on the activities of the trade as part of its trade, then that part of the trade carried on by the successor shall be treated for the purposes of this section as a separate trade, if the effect of so treating it is that subsection (1) or (7) above has effect on that event in relation to

that separate trade; and where, on a company ceasing to carry on part of a trade, another company begins to carry on the activities of that part as its trade or part of its trade, the predecessor shall for purposes of this section be treated as having carried on that part of its trade as a separate trade if the effect of so treating it is that subsection (1) or (7) above has effect on that event in relation to that separate trade.

(9) Where under subsection (8) above any activities of a company's trade fall, on the company ceasing or beginning to carry them on, to be treated as a separate trade, such apportionments of receipts, expenses, assets or liabilities shall be made as may be just.

(10) Where, by virtue of subsection (9) above, any item falls to be apportioned and, at the time of the apportionment, it appears that it is material as respects the liability to tax (for whatever period) of two or more companies, any question which arises as to the manner in which the item is to be apportioned shall be determined, for the purposes of the tax of all those companies—

    (a) in a case where the same body of General Commissioners have jurisdiction with respect to all those companies, by those Commissioners, unless all the companies agree that it shall be determined by the Special Commissioners;

    (b) in a case where different bodies of Commissioners have jurisdiction with respect to those companies, by such of those bodies as the Board may direct, unless all the companies agree that it shall be determined by the Special Commissioners; and

    (c) in any other case, by the Special Commissioners,

and any such Commissioners shall determine the question in like manner as if it were an appeal except that all those companies shall be entitled to appear and be heard by the Commissioners who are to make the determination or to make representations to them in writing.

(11) Any relief obtainable under this section by way of discharge or repayment of tax shall be given on the making of a claim.

(12) In the application of this section to any case in relation to which subsection (4) above does not apply—

    (a) subsection (9) above shall have effect with the substitution for the words following "separate trade" of the words "any necessary apportionment shall be made of receipts or expenses"; and

    (b) subsection (10) above shall have effect with the substitution for "item" of "sum".

344.—(1) For the purposes of section 343—

    (a) a trade carried on by two or more persons shall be treated as belonging to them in the shares in which they are entitled to the profits of the trade;

    (b) a trade or interest in a trade belonging to any person as trustee (otherwise than for charitable or public purposes) shall be treated as belonging to the persons for the time being entitled to the income under the trust; and

Company reconstructions: supplemental.

    (c) a trade or interest in a trade belonging to a company shall, where the result of so doing is that subsection (1) or (7) of section 343 has effect in relation to an event, be treated in any of the ways permitted by subsection (2) below.

(2) For the purposes of section 343, a trade or interest in a trade which belongs to a company engaged in carrying it on may be regarded—

    (a) as belonging to the persons owning the ordinary share capital of the company and as belonging to them in proportion to the amount of their holdings of that capital, or

    (b) in the case of a company which is a subsidiary company, as belonging to a company which is its parent company, or as belonging to the persons owning the ordinary share capital of that parent company, and as belonging to them in proportion to the amount of their holdings of that capital,

and any ordinary share capital owned by a company may, if any person or body of persons has the power to secure by means of the holding of shares or the possession of voting power in or in relation to any company, or by virtue of any power conferred by the articles of association or other document regulating any company, that the affairs of the company owning the share capital are conducted in accordance with his or their wishes, be regarded as owned by the person or body of persons having that power.

(3) For the purposes of subsection (2) above—

    (a) references to ownership shall be construed as references to beneficial ownership;

    (b) a company shall be deemed to be a subsidiary of another company if and so long as not less than three-quarters of its ordinary share capital is owned by that other company, whether directly or through another company or other companies, or partly directly and partly through another company or other companies;

    (c) the amount of ordinary share capital of one company owned by a second company through another company or other companies, or partly directly and partly through another company or other companies, shall be determined in accordance with section 838(5) to (10); and

    (d) where any company is a subsidiary of another company, that other company shall be considered as its parent company unless both are subsidiaries of a third company.

(4) In determining, for the purposes of section 343, whether or to what extent a trade belongs at different times to the same persons, persons who are relatives of one another and the persons from time to time entitled to the income under any trust shall respectively be treated as a single person, and for this purpose "relative" means husband, wife, ancestor, lineal descendant, brother or sister.

(5) For the purposes of section 343(4), relevant assets are—

   (a) assets which were vested in the predecessor immediately before it ceased to carry on the trade, which were not transferred to the successor and which, in a case where the predecessor was the predecessor on a previous application of section 343, were not by virtue of subsection (9) of that section apportioned to a trade carried on by the company which was the successor on that application; and

   (b) consideration given to the predecessor by the successor in respect of the change of company carrying on the trade;

and for the purposes of paragraph (b) above the assumption by the successor of any liabilities of the predecessor shall not be treated as the giving of consideration to the predecessor by the successor.

(6) For the purposes of section 343(4), relevant liabilities are liabilities which were outstanding and vested in the predecessor immediately before it ceased to carry on the trade, which were not transferred to the successor and which, in a case where the predecessor was the predecessor on a previous application of section 343, were not by virtue of subsection (9) of that section apportioned to a trade carried on by the company which was the successor on that application; but a liability representing the predecessor's share capital, share premium account, reserves or relevant loan stock is not a relevant liability.

(7) For the purposes of section 343(4)—

   (a) the value of assets (other than money) shall be taken to be the price which they might reasonably be expected to have fetched on a sale in the open market immediately before the predecessor ceased to carry on the trade; and

   (b) the amount of liabilities shall be taken to be their amount at that time.

(8) Where the predecessor transferred a liability to the successor but the creditor concerned agreed to accept settlement of part of the liability as settlement of the whole, the liability shall be treated for the purposes of subsection (6) above as not having been transferred to the successor except as to that part.

(9) A liability representing the predecessor's share capital, share premium account, reserves or relevant loan stock shall, for the purposes of subsection (6) above, be treated as not doing so if, in the period of one year ending with the day on which the predecessor ceased to carry on the trade, the liability arose on a conversion of a liability not representing its share capital, share premium account, reserves or relevant loan stock.

(10) Where a liability of the predecessor representing its relevant loan stock is not a relevant liability for the purposes of section 343(4) but is secured on an asset of the predecessor not transferred to the successor, the value of the asset shall, for the purposes of section 343(4), be reduced by an amount equal to the amount of the liability.

(11) In this section "relevant loan stock" means any loan stock or similar security (whether secured or unsecured) except any in the case of which subsection (12) below applies.

(12) This subsection applies where, at the time the liability giving rise to the loan stock or other security was incurred, the person who was the creditor was carrying on a trade of lending money.

Chargeable gains

Computation of chargeable gains.

345.—(1) Subject to the provisions of this section and sections 400 and 435, the amount to be included in respect of chargeable gains in a company's total profits for any accounting period shall be the total amount of chargeable gains accruing to the company in the accounting period after deducting any allowable losses accruing to the company in the period and, so far as they have not been allowed as a deduction from chargeable gains accruing in any previous accounting period, any allowable losses previously accruing to the company while it has been within the charge to corporation tax.

(2) Except as otherwise provided by the Corporation Tax Acts, the total amount of the chargeable gains to be included in respect of chargeable gains in a company's total profits for any accounting period shall for purposes of corporation tax be computed in accordance with the principles applying for capital gains tax, all questions—

(a) as to the amounts which are or are not to be taken into account as chargeable gains or as allowable losses, or in computing gains or losses, or charged to tax as a person's gain; or

(b) as to the time when any such amount is to be treated as accruing,

being determined in accordance with the provisions relating to capital gains tax as if accounting periods were years of assessment.

(3) Subject to subsection (4) below, where the enactments relating to capital gains tax contain any reference to income tax or to the Income Tax Acts the reference shall, in relation to a company, be construed as a reference to corporation tax or to the Corporation Tax Acts; but—

(a) this subsection shall not affect the references to income tax in section 33(2) of the 1979 Act (exclusion of expenditure by reference to hypothetical income tax); and

(b) in so far as those enactments operate by reference to matters of any specified description, account shall for corporation tax be taken of matters of that description which are confined to companies, but not of any which are confined to individuals.

(4) The 1979 Act as extended by this section shall not be affected in its operation by the fact that capital gains tax and corporation tax are distinct taxes but, so far as is consistent with the Corporation Tax Acts, shall apply in relation to capital gains tax and corporation tax on chargeable gains as if they were one tax, so that, in particular, a matter which in a case involving two individuals is relevant for both of them in relation to capital gains tax shall in a like case involving an individual and a company be relevant for him in relation to that tax and for it in relation to corporation tax.

1986 c. 45.
S.I. 1986/1032
(N.I. 6)

(5) Where assets of a company are vested in a liquidator under section 145 of the Insolvency Act 1986 or Article 498 of the Companies (Northern Ireland) Order 1986 or otherwise, this section and the enactments applied by this section shall apply as if the assets were vested in, and the acts of

the liquidator in relation to the assets were the acts of, the company (acquisitions from or disposals to him by the company being disregarded accordingly).

346.—(1) This section applies where a person who is connected with a company resident in the United Kingdom receives or becomes entitled to receive in respect of shares in the company any capital distribution from the company, other than a capital distribution representing a reduction of capital, and—

  (a) the capital so distributed derives from the disposal of assets in respect of which a chargeable gain accrued to the company; or

  (b) the distribution constitutes such a disposal of assets;

and that person is referred to below as "the shareholder".

(2) If the corporation tax assessed on the company for the accounting period in which the chargeable gain accrues included any amount in respect of chargeable gains, and any of the tax assessed on the company for that period is not paid within six months from the date determined under subsection (3) below, the shareholder may by an assessment made within two years from that date be assessed and charged (in the name of the company) to an amount of that corporation tax—

  (a) not exceeding the amount or value of the capital distribution which the shareholder has received or become entitled to receive; and

  (b) not exceeding a proportion equal to the shareholder's share of the capital distribution made by the company of corporation tax on the amount of that gain at the rate in force when the gain accrued.

(3) The date referred to in subsection (2) above is whichever is the later of—

  (a) the date when the tax becomes due and payable by the company; and

  (b) the date when the assessment was made on the company.

(4) Where the shareholder pays any amount of tax under this section, he shall be entitled to recover from the company a sum equal to that amount together with any interest paid by him under section 87A of the Management Act on that amount.

(5) The provisions of this section are without prejudice to any liability of the shareholder in respect of a chargeable gain accruing to him by reference to the capital distribution as constituting a disposal of an interest in shares in the company.

(6) With respect to chargeable gains accruing in accounting periods ending on or before the day, not being earlier than 31st March 1992, appointed by order by the Treasury for the purposes of this section, this section shall have effect—

  (a) with the substitution for the words in subsection (3) after "above" of the words "is the date when the tax becomes payable by the company"; and

(b) with the omission of the words in subsection (4) from "together" to the end of the subsection.

(7) In this section "capital distribution" has the same meaning as in section 72(5)(b) of the 1979 Act and "connected with" shall be construed in accordance with section 839.

Tax on one
member of group
recoverable from
another member.

347.—(1) If at any time a chargeable gain accrues to a company which at that time is a member of a group of companies and any of the corporation tax assessed on the company for the accounting period in which the chargeable gain accrues is not paid within six months from the date determined under subsection (2) below by the company, then, if the tax so assessed included any amount in respect of chargeable gains—

(a) a company which was at the time when the gain accrued the principal company of the group; and

(b) any other company which in any part of the period of two years ending with that time was a member of that group of companies and owned the asset disposed of or any part of it, or where that asset is an interest or right in or over another asset, owned either asset or any part of either asset;

may at any time within two years from the date determined under subsection (2) below be assessed and charged (in the name of the company to whom the chargeable gain accrued) to an amount of that corporation tax not exceeding corporation tax on the amount of that gain at the rate in force when the gain accrued.

(2) The date referred to in subsection (1) above is whichever is the later of—

(a) the date when the tax becomes due and payable by the company; and

(b) the date when the assessment is made on the company.

(3) A company paying any amount of tax under subsection (1) above shall be entitled to recover a sum of that amount—

(a) from the company to which the chargeable gain accrued, or

(b) if that company is not the company which was the principal company of the group at the time when the chargeable gain accrued, from that principal company,

and a company paying any amount under paragraph (b) above shall be entitled to recover a sum of that amount from the company to which the chargeable gain accrued, and so far as it is not so recovered, to recover from any company which is for the time being a member of the group and which has while a member of the group owned the asset disposed of or any part of it (or where that asset is an interest or right in or over another asset, owned either asset or any part of it) such proportion of the amount unrecovered as is just having regard to the value of the asset at the time when the asset, or an interest or right in or over it, was disposed of by that company.

(4) Any reference in subsection (3) above to an amount of tax includes a reference to any interest paid under section 87A of the Management Act on that amount.

(5) Section 272 of the 1970 Act shall apply for the interpretation of this section as it applies for the interpretation of sections 273 to 281 of that Act.

(6) In relation to any chargeable gains accruing in accounting periods ending on or before the day, not being earlier than 31st March 1992, appointed by order by the Treasury for the purposes of this section, this section shall have effect—

    (a) with the substitution for the words in subsection (2) after "above" of the words "is the date when the tax becomes payable by the company"; and

    (b) with the omission of subsection (4).

L

PART IX

ANNUAL PAYMENTS AND INTEREST

Annual payments

Payments out of profits or gains brought into charge to income tax: deduction of tax.

348.—(1) Subject to any provision to the contrary in the Income Tax Acts, where any annuity or other annual payment charged with tax under Case III of Schedule D, not being interest, is payable wholly out of profits or gains brought into charge to income tax—

> (a) the whole of the profits or gains shall be assessed and charged with income tax on the person liable to the annuity or other annual payment, without distinguishing the annuity or other annual payment; and
>
> (b) the person liable to make the payment, whether out of the profits or gains charged with income tax or out of any annual payment liable to deduction, or from which a deduction has been made, shall be entitled on making the payment to deduct and retain out of it a sum representing the amount of income tax thereon; and
>
> (c) the person to whom the payment is made shall allow the deduction on receipt of the residue of the payment, and the person making the deduction shall be acquitted and discharged of so much money as is represented by the deduction, as if that sum had been actually paid; and
>
> (d) the deduction shall be treated as income tax paid by the person to whom the payment is made.

(2) Subject to any provision to the contrary in the Income Tax Acts, where—

> (a) any royalty or other sum paid in respect of the user of a patent; or
>
> (b) any rent, royalty or other payment which, by section 119 or 120, is declared to be subject to deduction of income tax under this section or section 349 as if it were a royalty or other sum paid in respect of the user of a patent;

is paid wholly out of profits or gains brought into charge to income tax, the person making the payment shall be entitled on making the payment to deduct and retain out of it a sum representing the amount of the income tax thereon.

(3) This section does not apply to a small maintenance payment within the meaning of section 351 or to any payment to which section 687 applies.

Payments not out of profits or gains brought into charge to income tax, and annual interest.

349.—(1) Where—

> (a) any annuity or other annual payment charged with tax under Case III of Schedule D, not being interest; or
>
> (b) any royalty or other sum paid in respect of the user of a patent; or

(c) any rent, royalty or other payment which, by section 119 or 120, is declared to be subject to deduction of income tax under this section or section 348 as if it were a royalty or other sum paid in respect of the user of a patent,

is not payable or not wholly payable out of profits or gains brought into charge to income tax, the person by or through whom any payment thereof is made shall, on making the payment, deduct out of it a sum representing the amount of income tax thereon.

This subsection does not apply to any payment to which section 687 applies.

(2) Subject to subsection (3) below and to any other provision to the contrary in the Income Tax Acts, where any yearly interest of money chargeable to tax under Case III of Schedule D is paid—

(a) otherwise than in a fiduciary or representative capacity, by a company or local authority; or

(b) by or on behalf of a partnership of which a company is a member; or

(c) by any person to another person whose usual place of abode is outside the United Kingdom;

the person by or through whom the payment is made shall, on making the payment, deduct out of it a sum representing the amount of income tax thereon for the year in which the payment is made.

(3) Subsection (2) above does not apply—

(a) to interest payable in the United Kingdom on an advance from a bank carrying on a bona fide banking business in the United Kingdom; or

(b) to interest paid by such a bank in the ordinary course of that business; or

(c) to any payment to which section 124 applies; or

(d) to any payment to which section 369 or 479(1) applies;

and subsection (1) above does not apply to any small maintenance payment within the meaning of section 351.

350.—(1) Where any payment within section 349 is made by or through any person, that person shall forthwith deliver to the inspector an account of the payment, and shall be assessable and chargeable with income tax at the basic rate on the payment, or on so much thereof as is not made out of profits or gains brought into charge to income tax.

Charge to tax where payments made under section 349.

(2) In section 349(1) any reference to a payment or sum as being not payable, or not wholly payable, out of profits or gains brought into charge to income tax shall be construed as a reference to it as being payable wholly or in part out of a source other than profits or gains brought into charge; and any such reference elsewhere in the Tax Acts shall be construed accordingly.

(3) All the provisions of the Income Tax Acts relating to persons who are to be chargeable with income tax, to income tax assessments, and to the collection and recovery of income tax, shall, so far as they are applicable, apply to the charge, assessment, collection and recovery of income tax under this section.

(4) Section 349 and this section have effect subject to the provisions of Schedule 16 which has effect for the purpose of regulating the time and manner in which companies resident in the United Kingdom—

(a) are to account for and pay income tax in respect of payments from which tax is deductible under section 349, and

(b) are to be repaid income tax in respect of payments received by them;

and for that purpose the Board may by regulations modify, supplement or replace any of the provisions of Schedule 16; and references in this Act and in any other enactment to any of those provisions shall be construed as including references to any such regulations.

(5) Without prejudice to the generality of subsection (4) above, regulations under that subsection may, in relation to income tax for which a company is liable to account, modify any provision of Parts II to VI of the Management Act or apply any such provision with or without modifications.

(6) Regulations under this section may—

(a) make different provision for different descriptions of companies and for different circumstances and may authorise the Board, where in their opinion there are special circumstances justifying it, to make special arrangements as respects income tax for which a company is liable to account or the repayment of income tax borne by a company;

(b) include such transitional and other supplemental provisions as appear to the Board to be expedient or necessary.

(7) The Board shall not make any regulations under this section unless a draft of them has been laid before and approved by a resolution of the House of Commons.

Small maintenance payments.

351.—(1) In this section "small maintenance payments" means payments under an order made by a court in the United Kingdom—

(a) by one of the parties to a marriage (including a marriage which has been dissolved or annulled) to or for the benefit of the other party to that marriage for that other party's maintenance,

(b) to any person under 21 years of age for his own benefit, maintenance or education, or

(c) to any person for the benefit, maintenance or education of a person under 21 years of age,

in respect of which the two conditions mentioned in subsection (2) below are satisfied; and "small maintenance order" means an order providing for the making of small maintenance payments.

(2) The first of the conditions referred to in subsection (1) above is—

(a) in the case of payments falling within paragraph (a) of that subsection, that the order for the time being requires them to be made—

  (i) weekly at a rate not exceeding £48 per week, or

  (ii) monthly at a rate not exceeding £208 per month;

(b) in the case of payments falling within paragraph (b) (but not within paragraph (a)) of that subsection, that the order for the time being requires them to be made—

  (i) weekly at a rate not exceeding £48 per week, or

  (ii) monthly at a rate not exceeding £208 per month;

(c) in the case of payments falling within paragraph (c) (but not within paragraph (a) or (b)) of that subsection, that the order for the time being requires them to be made—

  (i) weekly at a rate not exceeding £25 per week, or

  (ii) monthly at a rate not exceeding £108 per month;

and the second of those conditions is that the payments would fall within section 348 or 349(1), apart from subsection (3) of each of those sections and subsection (3) below.

(3) Small maintenance payments shall be made without deduction of income tax.

(4) Any sums paid in or towards the discharge of a small maintenance payment shall be chargeable under Case III of Schedule D, but the tax shall (notwithstanding anything in sections 64 to 67) be computed in all cases on the payments falling due in the year of assessment, so far as paid in that or any other year.

(5) A person making a claim in that behalf shall be entitled, in computing his total income for any year of assessment for any of the purposes of the Income Tax Acts, to deduct sums paid by him in or towards the discharge of any small maintenance payments which fall due in that year; and, for the purposes of section 276, any amount which can be deducted under this subsection in computing the total income of a person shall be treated as if it were income the tax on which that person is entitled to charge against another person.

(6) The Treasury may from time to time by order increase any, or all, of the amounts for the time being specified in subsection (2) above.

(7) An order under subsection (6) above which increases the amount for the time being specified in sub-paragraph (i) of paragraph (a), (b) or (c) of subsection (2) above shall increase the amount for the time being specified in sub-paragraph (ii) of that paragraph so that it is 52 twelfths of the amount specified in sub-paragraph (i) by virtue of the order or, if that does not give a convenient round sum, such other amount as appears to the Treasury to be the nearest convenient round sum; and an order under that subsection may contain provision whereby it—

(a) does not in general affect payments falling due in the year of assessment in which it comes into force under small maintenance orders made before its coming into force, but

(b) in the case of a small maintenance order which was made before that time but is varied or revived after that time, does apply in relation to payments falling due under that order at any time after the variation or revival.

(8) Where a court—

(a) makes or revives a small maintenance order, or

(b) varies or revives an order so that it becomes, or ceases to be, a small maintenance order, or

(c) changes the persons who are entitled to small maintenance payments,

the court shall furnish to the Board, in such form as the Board may prescribe, particulars of the order or variation, as the case may be, the names of the persons affected by the order, and, so far as is known to the court, the addresses of those persons.

In this subsection—

(i) "the persons affected", in relation to a small maintenance order, means the person liable to make the payments under the order and any person for the time being entitled to the payments, and

(ii) references to the variation of an order include references to the making of an order changing the persons entitled to the payments under it.

Certificates of deduction of tax.

352.—(1) A person making any payment which is subject to deduction of income tax by virtue of section 339, 348, 349 or 687 shall, if the recipient so requests in writing, furnish him with a statement in writing showing the gross amount of the payment, the amount of tax deducted, and the actual amount paid.

(2) The duty imposed by subsection (1) above shall be enforceable at the suit or instance of the person requesting the statement.

Relief for payments of interest (excluding MIRAS)

General provision.

353.—(1) Where a person pays in any year of assessment—

(a) annual interest chargeable to tax under Case III of Schedule D; or

(b) interest payable in the United Kingdom or the Republic of Ireland on an advance from a bank carrying on a bona fide banking business in the United Kingdom or the Republic of Ireland or from a person bona fide carrying on a business as a member of the Stock Exchange or bona fide carrying on the business of a discount house in the United Kingdom or the Republic of Ireland;

and the interest is stated in sections 354 to 365 to be eligible for relief under this section, then, if he makes a claim to the relief and subject to the following provisions of this section, sections 354 to 368 and section

237(5)(b), the amount of the interest shall be deducted from or set off against his income for that year of assessment, and income tax shall be discharged or repaid accordingly.

(2) This section does not apply to a payment of relevant loan interest to which section 369 applies.

(3) Relief under this section shall not be given in respect of—

    (a) interest on a debt incurred by overdrawing an account or by debiting the account of any person as the holder of a credit card or under similar arrangements; or

    (b) where interest is paid at a rate in excess of a reasonable commercial rate, so much of the interest as represents the excess.

354.—(1) Subject to sections 355 to 358 and subsections (2) to (6) below, interest is eligible for relief under section 353 if it is paid by a person for the time being owning an estate or interest in land, or the property in a caravan or house-boat, in the United Kingdom or the Republic of Ireland on a loan to defray money applied—

    (a) in purchasing that estate, interest or property, or another estate, interest or property absorbed into, or given up to obtain, that estate, interest or property; or

    (b) in improving or developing the land, or buildings on the land; or

    (c) in paying off another loan, if interest on that other loan would have been eligible for relief under section 353 had the loan not been paid off (on the assumption, if the loan was free of interest, that it carried interest) or would have been so eligible apart from section 353(2).

(2) In this section and section 355—

    (a) references to money applied in improving or developing land or buildings include references to payments in respect of maintenance or repairs incurred by reason of dilapidation attributable to a period before the estate or interest was acquired, but otherwise do not include references to payments in respect of maintenance or repairs, or any of the other payments mentioned in section 25(1); and

    (b) references to money applied in improving or developing land include references to expenditure incurred or defrayed directly or indirectly in respect of street works, other than works of maintenance or repair, for any highway or road, or in Scotland any right of way, adjoining or serving the land.

(3) Interest is eligible for relief under section 353 in the case of a caravan only if the caravan—

    (a) is a large caravan, or

    (b) taken with the land on which it stands, is for the time being a rateable hereditament for the purposes of a relevant enactment and the owner or the wife or husband of the owner has as occupier of the caravan duly paid rates under the relevant enactment for the period in which the interest was paid.

In this subsection—

"relevant enactment" means the General Rate Act 1967, any corresponding enactment in force in Scotland or the Republic of Ireland or the Rates (Northern Ireland) Order 1977; and

"hereditament", in relation to Scotland, means lands and heritages.

(4) References in this section and in section 355 to an estate or interest do not include references—

    (a) to a rentcharge or, in Scotland, a superiority or the interest of a creditor in a contract of ground annual; or

    (b) to the interest of a chargee or mortgagee or, in Scotland, the interest of a creditor in a charge or security of any kind over land.

(5) Where this section applies to a loan by reason of the land, caravan or house-boat concerned being used as a person's only or main residence, and the borrower raises another loan to defray money to be applied as mentioned in subsection (1) above with a view to the use of other land or another caravan or house-boat as that person's only or main residence and the disposal of the first-mentioned land, caravan or house-boat, then in relation to interest payable within 12 months from the making of the other loan, this section—

    (a) shall continue to apply to the first-mentioned loan, whether or not the first-mentioned land, caravan or house-boat continues to be so used; and

    (b) shall apply to the other loan to the same extent (if any) as if no interest were payable on the first-mentioned loan.

(6) If it appears to the Board reasonable to do so, having regard to all the circumstances of a particular case, they may direct that in relation to that case subsection (5) above shall have effect as if for the reference to 12 months there were substituted a reference to such longer period as meets the circumstances of that case.

(7) Where interest is payable by the tenant occupier of any property to the landlord in pursuance of arrangements whereby money advanced at interest by the landlord is applied by the tenant in purchasing the landlord's estate or interest, or in the case of a caravan or house-boat the property in the caravan or house-boat, but that estate or interest or property is not to pass to the tenant until some time after the interest begins to be payable, this section and section 355(5) shall have effect in relation to the tenant as if he were the owner of the landlord's estate, interest or property.

355.—(1) Subject to the following provisions of this section and sections 356 to 358, section 354 shall not apply unless the land, caravan or house-boat in question—

    (a) is at the time the interest is paid used as the only or main residence of the person by whom it is paid ("the borrower") or of a dependent relative or former or separated spouse of his, or, if the interest is paid less than 12 months after the date on which the loan is made, is so used within 12 months after that date; or

(b) is, in any period of 52 weeks comprising the time at which the interest is payable and falling wholly or partly within the year of assessment, let at a commercial rent for more than 26 weeks and, when not so let, either available for letting at such a rent or used as mentioned in paragraph (a) above or prevented from being so available or used by any works of construction or repair;

and shall in a case within paragraph (a) above apply only within the limit imposed by section 357.

(2) If it appears to the Board reasonable to do so, having regard to all the circumstances of a particular case, they may direct that in relation to that case subsection (1) above shall have effect as if for the references to 12 months there were substituted references to such longer period as meets the circumstances of that case.

(3) The land, caravan or house-boat does not fall within subsection (1)(a) above by reason of its being used as the only or main residence of a dependent relative of the borrower unless it is provided rent-free and without any other consideration.

(4) Relief under section 353 for interest eligible for it by virtue of section 354 in a case where it is eligible only because the land, caravan or house-boat referred to in it falls under subsection (1)(b) above shall be given only against income from the letting of that or any other land, caravan or house-boat, but may, if and to the extent that such income for the year of assessment is insufficient, be given against such income for the following year, and so on, provided the first-mentioned land, caravan or house-boat continues to fall under that subsection.

(5) Subsection (1)(a) of section 354 shall not apply—

(a) where the seller and purchaser are husband and wife and either sells to the other, or

(b) where the purchaser, or the wife or husband of the purchaser, has since 15th April 1969 disposed of an estate or interest in the land, or the property in the caravan or house-boat, in question, and it appears that the main purpose of the disposal and purchase was to obtain relief in respect of interest on the loan, or

(c) where the purchasers are the trustees of a settlement, and the seller is the settlor, or the wife or husband of the settlor, and it appears that the main purpose of the purchase is to obtain relief in respect of interest on the loan, or

(d) where the purchaser is directly or indirectly purchasing from a person who is connected with him, and the price substantially exceeds the value of what is acquired;

and subsection (1)(b) of that section shall not apply where the person spending the money is connected with the person who directly or indirectly receives the money, and the money substantially exceeds the value of the work done.

For the purposes of this subsection—

(i) references to a husband and wife are references to a husband and his wife living with him; and

(ii) one person is connected with another if he is so connected within the terms of section 839.

Job-related accommodation.

356.—(1) Section 355(1) shall not prevent relief being given under section 353 in a case where the land, caravan or house-boat in question—

(a) is, at the time the interest is paid, used by the borrower as a residence or, if it is paid less than 12 months after the date on which the loan is made, is so used by him within 12 months after that date; or

(b) is intended at that time to be used in due course as his only or main residence;

and at that time he resides in living accommodation which is for him job-related.

(2) A borrower for whom there are two or more properties falling within subsection (1) above may not by virtue of this section claim relief for any period under section 353 in respect of more than one of them.

(3) Subject to subsections (4) and (5) below, living accommodation is job-related for a person if—

(a) it is provided for him by reason of his employment, or for his spouse by reason of her employment, in any of the following cases—

(i) where it is necessary for the proper performance of the duties of the employment that the employee should reside in that accommodation;

(ii) where the accommodation is provided for the better performance of the duties of the employment, and it is one of the kinds of employment in the case of which it is customary for employers to provide living accommodation for employees;

(iii) where, there being a special threat to the employee's security, special security arrangements are in force and the employee resides in the accommodation as part of those arrangements; or

(b) under a contract entered into at arm's length and requiring him or his spouse to carry on a particular trade, profession or vocation, he or his spouse is bound—

(i) to carry on that trade, profession or vocation on premises or other land provided by another person (whether under a tenancy or otherwise); and

(ii) to live either on those premises or on other premises provided by that other person.

(4) If the living accommodation is provided by a company and the employee is a director of that or an associated company, subsection (3)(a)(i) or (ii) above shall not apply unless—

(a) the company of which the employee is a director is one in which he or she has no material interest; and

(b) either—

(i) the employment is as a full-time working director, or

(ii) the company is non-profit making, that is to say, it does not carry on a trade nor do its functions consist wholly or mainly in the holding of investments or other property, or

(iii) the company is established for charitable purposes only.

(5) Subsection (3)(b) above does not apply if the living accommodation concerned is in whole or in part provided by—

(a) a company in which the borrower or his spouse has a material interest; or

(b) any person or persons together with whom the borrower or his spouse carries on a trade or business in partnership.

(6) For the purposes of this section—

(a) a company is an associated company of another if one of them has control of the other or both are under the control of the same person; and

(b) "employment", "director", "full-time working director", "material interest" and "control", in relation to a body corporate, have the same meanings as they have for the purposes of Chapter II of Part V.

357.—(1) Interest on a loan ("the limited loan") which (apart from this subsection) is eligible for relief under section 353 by virtue of section 355(1)(a) or 356(1) shall be so eligible for relief only to the extent that the amount on which it is payable does not exceed the following limit, that is to say, the qualifying maximum for the year of assessment reduced by the amount on which interest is payable by the borrower under any earlier loans so eligible for relief, so that—

> Limit on amount of loan eligible for relief by virtue of section 354.

(a) if the amount on which interest is payable under the limited loan exceeds the limit, so much only of that interest is eligible for relief as bears to the whole of that interest the same proportion as that part of that amount which does not exceed the limit bears to the whole of that amount; and

(b) if the amount on which interest is payable under any earlier loans is equal to or exceeds the qualifying maximum for the year of assessment, none of the interest on the limited loan is eligible for relief.

(2) Where a loan on which interest is payable by the borrower was made jointly to the borrower and another person, not being the borrower's husband or wife, then, if—

(a) the land, caravan or house-boat concerned is used as the main or only residence of that other person, or of a dependent relative or former or separated spouse of his, and

(i) that other person owns an estate or interest in the land or the property in the caravan or house-boat, and

(ii) that other person pays part of the interest payable on the loan; or

(b) that other person falls within sub-paragraphs (i) and (ii) of paragraph (a) above and is by virtue of section 356 entitled to claim relief under section 353 in respect of that part of the interest,

the amount on which interest is payable under the loan shall be treated for the purposes of this section as being such part only of that amount as bears to the whole thereof the same proportion as the amount of interest paid by the borrower bears to the whole of the interest paid on the loan.

(3) For the purposes of this section—

(a) any interest payable on a loan made to the borrower's husband or wife shall be treated as payable on a loan made to the borrower; and

(b) where interest is payable on more than one loan made or treated as made to the borrower and the loans were made simultaneously it shall be treated as payable on one loan.

(4) Where section 354 continues to apply to a loan by virtue of section 354(5)(a), this section shall also continue to have effect in relation to the loan as if section 354 applied to it by virtue of section 355(1)(a).

(5) References in this section to the borrower's husband or wife do not include references to a separated husband or wife.

(6) In determining whether the amount on which interest is payable under a loan exceeds the limit in subsection (1) above, no account shall be taken of so much (if any) of that amount as consists of interest which has been added to capital and does not exceed £1000.

Relief where borrower deceased.

358.—(1) Where any interest paid by persons as the personal representatives of a deceased person or as the trustees of a settlement made by his will would, on the assumptions required by this section, be eligible for relief under section 353 by virtue of section 354 above and, in a case where subsection (3) below applies, one of the conditions in subsection (4) below is satisfied, that interest shall be so eligible notwithstanding sections 354 to 357.

(2) For the purposes of subsection (1) above it shall be assumed that the deceased would have survived and been the borrower.

(3) If, at his death,—

(a) the land, caravan or house-boat concerned was used as his only or main residence, or

(b) it was used by him as a residence or was intended to be used in due course as his only or main residence and, in either case, he resided in job-related living accommodation;

that shall be assumed for the purposes of subsection (1) above to have continued to be the case.

(4) The conditions referred to in subsection (1) above are—

(a) that, at the time the interest is paid, the land, caravan or house-boat concerned is used as the only or main residence of the deceased's widow or widower or of any dependent relative of the deceased;

(b) that, at that time, it is used by the deceased's widow or widower as a residence or is intended to be used in due course as his or her only or main residence and, in either case, he or she resides in job-related living accommodation.

(5) In this section "personal representatives" has the meaning given by section 701; and subsections (3) to (6) of section 356 apply in relation to this section as they apply in relation to that.

359.—(1) Where an individual is a member of a partnership which, under section 44 of the 1968 Act, is entitled to a capital allowance or liable to a balancing charge for any year of assessment in respect of machinery or plant belonging to the individual, any interest paid by him in the basis period (as defined in section 72 of that Act) for that year on a loan to defray money applied as capital expenditure on the provision of that machinery or plant is eligible for relief under section 353, except interest falling due and payable more than three years after the end of the year of assessment in which the debt was incurred.

Loan to buy machinery or plant.

(2) Where the machinery or plant is in use partly for the purposes of the trade, profession or vocation carried on by the partnership and partly for other purposes, such part only of the interest is eligible for relief under section 353 as is just and reasonable to attribute to the purposes of the trade, profession or vocation, having regard to all the relevant circumstances and, in particular, to the extent of the use for those other purposes.

(3) Where the holder of an office or employment—

(a) is under Chapter II of Part I of the 1968 Act or Chapter I of Part III of the Finance Act 1971 entitled to a capital allowance or liable to a balancing charge, (or would be so entitled or liable but for some contribution made by the employer), for any year of assessment in respect of machinery or plant belonging to him and in use for the purposes of the office or employment; and

1971 c. 68.

(b) pays interest in that year on a loan to defray money applied as capital expenditure on the provision of that machinery or plant;

the interest so paid is eligible for relief under section 353 unless it is interest falling due and payable more than three years after the end of the year of assessment in which the debt was incurred.

(4) Where the machinery or plant is in use partly for the purposes of the office or employment and partly for other purposes, such part only of the interest is eligible for relief under section 353 as it is just and reasonable to attribute to the purposes of the office or employment, having regard to all the relevant circumstances and, in particular, to the extent of the use for those other purposes.

360.—(1) Subject to the following provisions of this section and sections 361 to 364, interest is eligible for relief under section 353 if it is interest on a loan to an individual to defray money applied—

Loan to buy interest in close company.

(a) in acquiring any part of the ordinary share capital of a close company satisfying any of the conditions of section 424(4); or

(b) in lending money to such a close company which is used wholly and exclusively for the purposes of the business of the company or of any associated company of it which is a close company satisfying any of those conditions; or

(c) in paying off another loan interest on which would have been eligible for relief under section 353 had the loan not been paid off (on the assumption, if the loan was free of interest, that it carried interest);

and either the conditions stated in subsection (2) below or those stated in subsection (3) below are satisfied.

(2) The conditions first referred to in subsection (1) above are—

(a) that, when the interest is paid, the company continues to satisfy any of the conditions of section 424(4) and the individual has a material interest in the company; and

(b) that he shows that in the period from the application of the proceeds of the loan to the payment of the interest he has not recovered any capital from the company, apart from any amount taken into account under section 363(1); and

(c) that, if the company exists wholly or mainly for the purpose of holding investments or other property, no property held by the company is used as a residence by the individual;

but the condition in paragraph (c) above shall not apply in a case where the individual has worked for the greater part of his time in the actual management or conduct of the business of the company, or of an associated company of the company.

(3) The conditions secondly referred to in subsection (1) above are—

(a) that, when the interest is paid, the company continues to satisfy any of the conditions of section 424(4) and the individual holds any part of the ordinary share capital of the company; and

(b) that in the period from the application of the proceeds of the loan to the payment of the interest the individual has worked for the greater part of his time in the actual management or conduct of the company or of an associated company of the company; and

(c) that he shows in the period from the application of the proceeds of the loan to the payment of the interest he has not recovered any capital from the company, apart from any amount taken into account under section 363(1).

(4) In this section expressions to which a meaning is assigned by Part XI have that meaning, but—

(a) in relation to any loan made after 5th April 1987, paragraph 39 of Schedule 9 shall have effect for determining whether the interest on the loan is eligible for relief under section 353 by virtue of this section; and

(b) in relation to any loan made before 14th November 1986, section 417 shall have effect subject to the following modifications—

(i) in subsection (3)(c) for the words following "deceased person" there shall be substituted the words "subject to subsection (3A) below, any other person interested therein"; and

(ii) after subsection (3) there shall be added—

"(3A) Subsection (3)(c) above shall not apply so as to make an individual an associate as being entitled or eligible to benefit under a trust—

(a) if the trust relates exclusively to an exempt approved scheme as defined in section 592; or

(b) if the trust is exclusively for the benefit of the employees, or the employees and directors, of the company or their dependants (and not wholly or mainly for the benefit of directors or their relatives), and the individual in question is not (and could not as a result of the operation of the trust become), either on his own or with his relatives, the beneficial owner of more than 5 per cent. of the ordinary share capital of the company;

and in applying paragraph (b) above any charitable trusts which may arise on the failure or determination of other trusts shall be disregarded."

361.—(1) Subject to the following provisions of this section and sections 363 and 364, interest is eligible for relief under section 353 if it is interest on a loan to an individual to defray money applied—

(a) in acquiring a share or shares in a body which is a co-operative as defined by section 363(5); or

(b) in lending money to any such body which is used wholly and exclusively for the purposes of the business of that body or of a subsidiary of that body; or

(c) in paying off another loan interest on which would have been eligible for relief under section 353 had the loan not been paid off (on the assumption, if it was free of interest, that it carried interest);

and the conditions in subsection (2) below are satisfied.

(2) The conditions referred to in subsection (1) above are—

(a) that the loan was made after 10th March 1981;

(b) that, when the interest is paid, the body continues to be a co-operative; and

(c) that in the period from the application of the proceeds of the loan to the payment of the interest the individual has worked for the greater part of his time as an employee of the body or of a subsidiary of the body; and

(d) that he shows that in that period he has not recovered any capital from the body apart from any taken into account under section 363(1).

Loan to buy interest in co-operative or employee-controlled company.

(3) Subject to sections 362 to 365, interest is eligible for relief under section 353 if it is interest on a loan to an individual to defray money applied—

(a) in acquiring any part of the ordinary share capital of an employee-controlled company; or

(b) in paying off another loan, interest on which would have been eligible for relief under section 353 had the loan not been paid off (on the assumption, if it was free of interest, that it carried interest);

and the conditions stated in subsection (4) below are satisfied.

(4) The conditions referred to in subsection (3) above are that—

(a) the company is, throughout the period beginning with the date on which the shares are acquired and ending with the date on which the interest is paid—

(i) an unquoted company resident in the United Kingdom and not resident elsewhere; and

(ii) a trading company or the holding company of a trading group;

(b) the shares are acquired before, or not later than 12 months after, the date on which the company first becomes an employee-controlled company;

(c) during the year of assessment in which the interest is paid the company either—

(i) first becomes an employee-controlled company; or

(ii) is such a company throughout a period of at least nine months;

(d) the individual or his spouse is a full-time employee of the company throughout the period beginning with the date on which the proceeds of the loan are applied and ending with the date on which the interest is paid or, if at that date he has ceased to be such an employee, ending with whichever is the later of—

(i) the date on which he ceased to be such an employee;

(ii) the date 12 months before the payment of the interest; and

(e) the individual shows that in the period from the application of the proceeds of the loan to the payment of the interest he has not recovered any capital from the company, apart from any amount taken into account under section 363(1).

(5) For the purposes of this section a company is employee-controlled at any time when more than 50 per cent.—

(a) of the issued ordinary share capital of the company, and

(b) of the voting power in the company,

is beneficially owned by persons who, or whose spouses, are full-time employees of the company.

(6) Where an individual owns beneficially, or he and his spouse together own beneficially, more than 10 per cent. of the issued ordinary share capital of, or voting power in, a company, the excess shall be treated for the purposes of subsection (5) above as being owned by an individual who is neither a full-time employee of the company nor the spouse of such an employee.

(7) Where an individual and his spouse are both full-time employees of the company, subsection (6) above shall apply in relation to them with the omission of the words "or he and his spouse together own beneficially".

(8) In this section—

"full-time employee", in relation to a company, means a person who works for the greater part of his time as an employee or director of the company or of a 51 per cent. subsidiary of the company;

"holding company" means a company whose business (disregarding any trade carried on by it) consists wholly or mainly of the holding of shares or securities of one or more companies which are its 75 per cent. subsidiaries;

"trading company" means a company whose business consists wholly or mainly of the carrying on of a trade or trades;

"trading group" means a group the business of whose members taken together consists wholly or mainly of the carrying on of a trade or trades, and for this purpose "group" means a company which has one or more 75 per cent. subsidiaries together with those subsidiaries; and

"unquoted company" means a company none of whose shares are listed in the Official List of the Stock Exchange.

362.—(1) Subject to sections 363 to 365, interest is eligible for relief under section 353 if it is interest on a loan to an individual to defray money applied—

Loan to buy into partnership.

(a) in purchasing a share in a partnership; or

(b) in contributing money to a partnership by way of capital or premium, or in advancing money to a partnership, where the money contributed or advanced is used wholly for the purposes of the trade, profession or vocation carried on by the partnership; or

(c) in paying off another loan interest on which would have been eligible for relief under that section had the loan not been paid off (on the assumption, if the loan was free of interest, that it carried interest);

and the conditions stated in subsection (2) below are satisfied.

(2) The conditions referred to in subsection (1) above are—

(a) that, throughout the period from the application of the proceeds of the loan until the interest was paid, the individual has been a member of the partnership otherwise than as a limited partner; and

(b) that he shows that in that period he has not recovered any capital from the partnership, apart from any amount taken into account under section 363(1).

Provisions supplementary to sections 360 to 362.

363.—(1) If at any time after the application of the proceeds of the loan the individual has recovered any amount of capital from the close company, co-operative, employee-controlled company or partnership without using that amount in repayment of the loan, he shall be treated for the purposes of sections 353, 360, 361 and 362 as if he had at that time repaid that amount out of the loan, so that out of the interest otherwise eligible for relief (or, where section 367(4) applies, out of the proportion so eligible) and payable for any period after that time there shall be deducted an amount equal to interest on the amount of capital so recovered.

(2) The individual shall be treated as having recovered an amount of capital from the close company, co-operative, employee-controlled company or partnership if—

(a) he receives consideration of that amount or value for the sale, exchange or assignment of any part of the ordinary share capital of the company or of his share or shares in the co-operative or of his interest in the partnership, or of any consideration of that amount or value by way of repayment of any part of that ordinary share capital or of his share or shares in the co-operative; or

(b) the close company, co-operative, employee-controlled company or partnership repays that amount of a loan or advance from him or the partnership returns that amount of capital to him; or

(c) he receives consideration of that amount or value for assigning any debt due to him from the close company, co-operative, employee-controlled company or partnership;

and where a sale or assignment is not a bargain made at arm's length, the sale or assignment shall be deemed to be for a consideration of an amount equal to the market value of what is disposed of.

(3) In the application of this section to Scotland for the word "assignment" wherever it occurs there shall be substituted the word "assignation".

(4) Section 360, or, as the case may be, 361(2) or (4) or 362(2) and subsections (1) to (3) above, shall apply to a loan within section 360(1)(c), 361(1)(c) or (3)(b) or 362(1)(c) as if it, and any loan it replaces, were one loan, and so that—

(a) references to the application of the proceeds of the loan were references to the application of the proceeds of the original loan; and

(b) any restriction under subsection (1) above which applies to any loan which has been replaced shall apply to the loan which replaces it.

(5) In this section and sections 361 and 362—

"co-operative" means a common ownership enterprise or a co-operative enterprise as defined in section 2 of the Industrial Common Ownership Act 1976; and

"subsidiary" has the same meaning as for the purposes of section 2 of that Act.

364.—(1) Interest is eligible for relief under section 353 if it is interest on a loan to the personal representatives of a deceased person, the proceeds of which are applied—

(a) in paying, before the grant of representation or confirmation, capital transfer tax or inheritance tax payable on the delivery of the personal representatives' account and attributable to the value of personal property to which the deceased was beneficially entitled immediately before his death and which vests in the personal representatives or would vest in them if the property were situated in the United Kingdom; or

(b) in paying off another loan interest on which would have been eligible for that relief by virtue of this section if the loan had not been paid off (on the assumption, if the loan was free of interest, that it carried interest);

and the interest is paid in respect of a period ending within one year from the making of the loan within paragraph (a) above.

(2) If or to the extent that any relief in respect of interest eligible for it under subsection (1) above cannot be given against income of the year in which the interest is paid because of an insufficiency of income in that year, it may instead be given against income of the preceding year of assessment, and so on; and if or to the extent that it cannot be so given it may instead be given against income of the year following that in which the interest is paid, and so on.

(3) Sufficient evidence of the amount of capital transfer tax or inheritance tax paid as mentioned in subsection (1)(a) above and of any statements relevant to its computation may be given by the production of a document purporting to be a certificate from the Board.

(4) For the purposes of subsections (1) to (3) above—

(a) references to capital transfer tax or inheritance tax include any interest payable on that tax; and

(b) references to interest in respect of a period ending within a given time apply whether or not interest continues to run after that time.

365.—(1) Subject to the following provisions of this section, interest is eligible for relief under section 353 if it is interest on a loan in respect of which the following conditions are satisfied—

(a) that the loan was made as part of a scheme under which not less than nine-tenths of the proceeds of the loan were applied to the purchase by the person to whom it was made of an annuity ending with his life or with the life of the survivor of two or more persons ("the annuitants") who include the person to whom the loan was made;

(b) that at the time the loan was made the person to whom it was made or each of the annuitants had attained the age of 65 years;

(c) that the loan was secured on land in the United Kingdom or the Republic of Ireland and the person to whom it was made or one of the annuitants owns an estate or interest in that land; and

(d) that, if the loan was made after 26th March 1974, the person to whom it was made or each of the annuitants uses the land on which it was secured as his only or main residence at the time the interest is paid.

(2) Interest is not eligible for relief by virtue of this section unless it is payable by the person to whom the loan was made or by one of the annuitants.

(3) If the loan was made after 26th March 1974 interest on it is eligible for relief by virtue of this section only to the extent that the amount on which it is payable does not exceed the qualifying maximum for the year of assessment; and if the interest is payable by two or more persons the interest payable by each of them is so eligible only to the extent that the amount on which it is payable does not exceed such amount as bears to the qualifying maximum for the year of assessment the same proportion as the interest payable by him bears to the interest payable by both or all of them.

Information.

366.—(1) A person who claims relief under section 353 in respect of any payment of interest shall furnish to the inspector a statement in writing by the person to whom the payment is made, showing—

(a) the date when the debt was incurred;

(b) the amount of the debt when incurred;

(c) the interest paid in the year of assessment for which the claim is made (or, in the case of relief by virtue of section 355(4) or 364(2), the year of assessment for which the claim would be made but for an insufficiency of income); and

(d) the name and address of the debtor.

(2) Where any such interest as is mentioned in section 353 is paid, the person to whom it is paid shall, if the person who pays it so requests in writing, furnish him with such statement as regards that interest as is mentioned in subsection (1) above; and the duty imposed by this subsection shall be enforceable at the suit or instance of the person making the request.

(3) Subsections (1) and (2) above do not apply to interest paid to a building society, or to a local authority.

Provisions supplementary to sections 354 to 366.

1960 c. 62.

367.—(1) In sections 354 to 366 as they apply throughout the United Kingdom and in relation to the Republic of Ireland—

"caravan" has the meaning given by section 29(1) of the Caravan Sites and Control of Development Act 1960;

"dependent relative" means, in relation to any person, a relative of his, or of his spouse, who is incapacitated by old age or infirmity from maintaining himself, or the mother of that person, or of his spouse, if the mother is widowed or living apart from her husband, or, in consequence of dissolution or annulment of marriage, a single woman;

"house-boat" means a boat or similar structure designed or adapted for use as a place of permanent habitation;

"large caravan" means one which has either or both of the following dimensions—

> (a) an overall length (excluding any draw bar) exceeding 22 feet;

> (b) an overall width exceeding seven feet six inches;

where "overall length" and "overall width" have the meanings given in Regulation 3 of the Motor Vehicles (Construction and Use) Regulations 1966;   S.I. 1966/1288.

"separated" means separated under an order of a court of competent jurisdiction or by deed of separation or in such circumstances that the separation is likely to be permanent; and

"street works" means any works for the sewering, levelling, paving, metalling, flagging, channelling and making good of a road, and includes the provision of proper means for lighting a road.

(2) Sections 354(1) and 360 to 364 do not apply to a loan unless it is made—

(a) in connection with the application of money, and

(b) on the occasion of, or within what is in the circumstances a reasonable time from, the application of the money;

and those sections do not apply to a loan the proceeds of which are applied for some other purpose before being applied as mentioned in those sections.

(3) For the purposes of sections 354 to 364, the giving of credit for any money due from the purchaser under any sale shall be treated as the making of a loan to defray money applied by him in making the purchase.

(4) Where part only of a debt fulfils the conditions required under sections 354 to 364 for interest on the debt to be eligible for relief under section 353, such proportion of the interest shall be treated as eligible for relief under that section as is equal to the portion of the debt fulfilling those conditions at the time of the application of the money in question.

(5) In sections 357(1) and 365(3) references to the qualifying maximum for the year of assessment are references to such sum as Parliament may determine for the purpose for that year.

368.—(1) Interest in respect of which relief is given under section 353 shall not be allowable as a deduction for any other purpose of the Income Tax Acts.   Exclusion of double relief etc.

(2) Relief shall not be given under section 353 against income chargeable to corporation tax, and shall not be given against any other income of a company, except where both of the following conditions are satisfied, that is to say—

    (a) that the company is not resident in the United Kingdom; and

    (b) that the interest cannot be taken into account in computing corporation tax chargeable on the company.

(3) Where interest on any debt or liability is taken into account in the computation of profits or gains or losses for the purposes of Case I or II of Schedule D no relief shall be given under section 353—

    (a) in respect of the payment of that interest; or

    (b) in respect of interest on the same debt or liability which is paid in any year of assessment for which that computation is relevant.

(4) Where relief is given under section 353 in respect of the interest paid in any year of assessment on any debt or liability—

    (a) that interest shall not be taken into account in the computation of profits or gains or losses for the purposes of Case I or II of Schedule D for any year of assessment; and

    (b) interest on that debt or liability shall not be taken into account in that computation for any year of assessment for which the interest so paid could have been taken into account but for the relief.

(5) For the purposes of subsections (3) and (4) above, all interest capable of being taken into account in such a computation as is mentioned in those subsections which is payable by any person on money advanced to him on current account, whether advanced on one or more accounts or by the same or separate banks or other persons, shall be treated as interest payable on the same debt.

(6) References in subsections (3) and (4) above to relief given or an amount taken into account are references to relief given or an amount taken into account on a claim or in an assessment which has been finally determined.

Mortgage interest relief at source

Mortgage interest payable under deduction of tax.

369.—(1) If a person who is a qualifying borrower makes a payment of relevant loan interest to which this section applies, he shall be entitled, on making the payment, to deduct and retain out of it a sum equal to income tax thereon at the basic rate for the year of assessment in which the payment becomes due.

(2) Where a sum is deducted under subsection (1) above from a payment of relevant loan interest—

    (a) the person to whom the payment is made shall allow the deduction on receipt of the residue;

    (b) the borrower shall be acquitted and discharged of so much money as is represented by the deduction as if the sum had been actually paid; and

    (c) the sum deducted shall be treated as income tax paid by the person to whom the payment is made.

(3) Where payments of relevant loan interest to which this section applies become due in any year, the borrower shall be charged with tax at the basic rate for that year on an amount of income equal, subject to subsection (4) below, to the deduction which, in computing his total income, falls to be made on account of those payments.

(4) In any case where—

    (a) payments of relevant loan interest to which this section applies become due in any year; and

    (b) the total income of the borrower for that year is such that he cannot benefit from any or, as the case may be, the full amount of the relevant personal reliefs to which he is entitled;

so much of that full amount as cannot be deducted from his total income shall be deducted from the amount of income on which he is chargeable to tax by virtue of subsection (3) above.

(5) In subsection (4) above "relevant personal relief" means any relief to which the borrower concerned is entitled under Chapter I of Part VII other than—

    (a) relief under section 266 which is given either by deduction by virtue of subsection (5) of that section or in accordance with paragraph 6 of Schedule 14; and

    (b) relief under section 273;

and for the purposes of subsection (4) above the full amount of those reliefs means the amount of them determined without regard to section 276.

(6) Any person by whom a payment of relevant loan interest to which this section applies is received shall be entitled to recover from the Board, in accordance with regulations, an amount which by virtue of subsection (2)(c) above is treated as income tax paid by him; and any amount so recovered shall be treated for the purposes of the Tax Acts in like manner as the payment of relevant loan interest to which it relates.

370.—(1) Subject to this section and sections 371 to 376, in this Part "relevant loan interest" means interest which is paid and payable in the United Kingdom to a qualifying lender and to which subsection (2) or (3) below applies.

Relevant loan interest.

(2) Subject to subsection (4) below, this subsection applies to interest if, disregarding section 353(2)—

    (a) it is interest falling within section 354(1) or 365; and

    (b) apart from section 74(o) and, where applicable, section 357 or 365(3), the whole of the interest either would be eligible for relief under section 353 or would be taken into account in a computation of profits or gains or losses for the purposes of Case I, II or VI of Schedule D for any year of assessment; and

    (c) except in the case of interest falling within section 365, at the time the interest is paid, the condition in either section 355(1) or 356(1) is fulfilled with respect to the land, caravan or house-boat to which the loan concerned relates.

(3) This subsection applies to interest which is payable on a loan—

(a) in respect of which there was in force on 31st March 1983—

> (i) an option notice given under section 24(2) of the Housing Subsidies Act 1967 (option mortgages) other than one falling within section 27(3)(b) of the Finance Act 1982; or

> (ii) an option notice given under Article 142(2) of the Housing (Northern Ireland) Order 1981 (option mortgages in Northern Ireland) other than one falling within section 27(4)(b) of the Finance Act 1982; and

(b) which relates to a dwelling in respect of which, at the time the interest is paid, the condition in section 355(1) is fulfilled.

(4) Subsection (2) above does not apply to interest payable on a loan the only security for which is a contract of insurance on human life or a contract to pay an annuity on human life.

(5) In determining whether subsection (2) above applies to any interest, sections 354(1) and 365 shall each have effect as if the words "or the Republic of Ireland" were omitted.

(6) In determining whether subsection (2)(c) above applies to any interest, section 355(1) shall have effect as if—

(a) in paragraph (a) after the word "used", where it first occurs, there were inserted the words "wholly or to a substantial extent"; and

(b) paragraph (b) and the word "or" immediately preceding it were omitted.

(7) In determining for the purposes of subsection (3)(b) above whether the condition in section 355(1) is for the time being fulfilled with respect to any dwelling—

(a) subsection (1) of that section shall have effect as if for the words from "section 354" to "used" (where it first occurs) there were substituted the words "interest shall not be relevant loan interest for the purposes of section 369 unless the dwelling to which the loan relates is at the time the interest is paid used wholly or partly" and paragraph (b) and the word "or" immediately preceding it were omitted; and

(b) subsection (3) of that section shall have effect as if for "land, caravan or house-boat" there were substituted "dwelling".

371.—(1) Where at a time when interest on a loan ("the first loan") is relevant loan interest, the borrower raises another loan to defray money to be applied as mentioned in section 354(1) with a view—

(a) to the use of other land or another caravan or house-boat wholly or partly as that person's only or main residence, and

(b) to the disposal of the land, caravan, house-boat or dwelling to which the first loan relates,

then, in relation to interest payable within 12 months from the making of the other loan, the condition in section 355(1) shall be treated as continuing to be fulfilled.

(2) If in a case falling within subsection (1) above the interest on the first loan is interest to which section 370(2) applies and a direction is given under section 354(6) extending the period within which section 354 applies to that loan, subsection (1) above shall have effect in relation to that case as if for the reference to 12 months there were substituted a reference to such longer period as is specified in the direction.

(3) If in a case falling within subsection (1) above the interest on the first loan is interest to which section 370(3) applies and, having regard to the circumstances of that case, it appears to the Board reasonable to do so, they may direct that, in relation to that case, subsection (1) above shall have effect as if for the reference to 12 months there were substituted a reference to such longer period as meets the circumstances of the case.

372.—(1) Notwithstanding anything in section 370(2), interest on a home improvement loan (other than interest to which section 370(3) applies) is not relevant loan interest unless—

    (a) the qualifying lender to whom the interest is payable is a building society or a local authority or the Northern Ireland Housing Executive; or

    (b) the qualifying lender to whom the interest is payable has given notice to the Board in accordance with regulations that he is prepared to have those home improvement loans in respect of which he is the lender and which were made after such date as he may specify in the notice brought within the tax deduction scheme.

Home improvement loans.

(2) A qualifying lender may not specify a date in a notice under subsection (1) above which is earlier than the earliest date on which paragraph 2 of Schedule 7 to the Finance Act 1982 applied, or, if that paragraph did not apply, section 370 applies to interest on any loan (whether or not a home improvement loan) made by him.

1982 c. 39.

(3) In this section "home improvement loan" means a loan made to defray money applied wholly in improving or developing land or buildings on land or in paying off another loan which was itself to defray money so applied.

(4) Section 354(2) shall apply for the purposes of this section as it applies for the purposes of sections 354 and 355.

373.—(1) The provisions of this section have effect in relation to a loan where, by virtue of section 357(1) or section 365(3), only part of the interest on the loan would (apart from section 353(2)) be eligible for relief under section 353; and in this section any such loan is referred to as a "limited loan".

Loans in excess of the qualifying maximum, and joint borrowers.

(2) None of the interest on a limited loan is relevant loan interest unless—

    (a) the loan is made on or after 6th April 1987; or

    (b) the qualifying lender to whom the interest is payable has given notice to the Board in accordance with regulations that he is prepared to have limited loans of a description which includes that limited loan brought within the tax deduction scheme.

(3) If in a case where subsection (2) above applies section 357(1) requires an earlier loan to be taken into account for the purpose of determining that part of the limited loan interest on which would (apart from section 353(2)) be eligible for relief under section 353, none of the interest on the limited loan is relevant loan interest unless that earlier loan was made by the same qualifying lender as the limited loan.

(4) The reference in subsection (1) above to a loan only part of the interest on which would (apart from section 353(2)) be eligible for relief under section 353 includes a reference to each of two or more loans if, by virtue of subsection (3)(b) of section 357, the interest on the loans falls to be treated for the purposes of that section as payable on one loan; but, notwithstanding that each of those loans is accordingly a limited loan for the purposes of this section, none of the interest on any of them is relevant loan interest unless each of the loans was made by the same qualifying lender.

(5) Where the condition in paragraph (a) or (b) of subsection (2) above is fulfilled and, if subsection (3) or (4) above also applies, the condition in that subsection is also fulfilled only so much of the interest as (apart from section 353(2)) would be eligible for relief under section 353 is relevant loan interest.

(6) Where a loan on which interest is payable by the borrower was made jointly to the borrower and another person who is not the borrower's husband or wife, the interest on the loan is not relevant loan interest unless—

> (a) each of the persons to whom the loan was made is a qualifying borrower; and

> (b) in relation to each of them considered separately, the whole of that interest is relevant loan interest, in accordance with sections 370 to 372 and this section.

(7) In subsection (6) above references to the borrower's husband or wife do not include references to a separated husband or wife, and for this purpose "separated" has the meaning given by section 367(1).

Conditions for application of section 369.

374.—(1) Section 369 does not apply to any relevant loan interest unless—

> (a) in the case of a loan of a description specified by regulations for the purposes of this paragraph, the borrower or, in the case of joint borrowers, each of them has given notice to the lender in the prescribed form certifying—

>> (i) that he is a qualifying borrower; and

>> (ii) that the interest is relevant loan interest; and

>> (iii) such other matters as may be prescribed; or

> (b) the Board have given notice to the lender and the borrower that the interest may be paid under deduction of tax; or

> (c) it is interest to which section 370(3) applies; or

> (d) the loan to which the interest relates is of a description specified by regulations for the purposes of this paragraph and was made—

>> (i) if sub-paragraph (2) of paragraph 2 of Schedule 7 to the Finance Act 1982 applied to interest on the loan which

became due on or after a date earlier than 6th April 1983, being a date specified by the Board in pursuance of sub-paragraph (5) of that paragraph, before that earlier date; or

(ii) if the qualifying lender is a building society or a local authority, before 1st April 1983; or

(iii) if sub-paragraphs (i) and (ii) above do not apply and the interest falls within section 370(2), before 6th April 1983.

(2) Where notice has been given as mentioned in paragraph (a) or (b) of subsection (1) above, section 369 applies to any relevant loan interest to which the notice relates and which becomes due on or after the relevant date, as defined by subsection (3) below; and in a case falling within paragraph (c) or (d) of subsection (1) above, section 369 applies to the relevant loan interest referred to in that paragraph.

(3) In subsection (2) above "the relevant date" means—

(a) in the case of a notice under subsection (1)(a) above, the date the notice is given, and

(b) in the case of a notice under subsection (1)(b) above, a date specified in the notice as being the relevant date (which may be earlier than the date so specified as the date from which the interest may be paid under deduction of tax).

375.—(1) If at any time—

(a) the interest on a loan ceases to be relevant loan interest; or

(b) a person making payments of relevant loan interest ceases to be a qualifying borrower;

the borrower shall give notice of the fact to the lender.

(2) Without prejudice to subsection (3) below, in relation to a payment of interest—

(a) which is due after the time referred to in subsection (1) above and before the date on which notice is given under that subsection, and

(b) from which a deduction was made as mentioned in section 369(1),

section 369 shall have effect as if the payment were a payment of relevant loan interest made by a qualifying borrower.

(3) Nothing in subsection (2) above entitles the borrower to any relief from tax or other benefit and, accordingly, where the amount of any such relief or other benefit which is allowed by virtue of that subsection exceeds that which ought to have been allowed, he shall be liable to make good the excess and an inspector may make such assessments as may in his judgment be required for recovering the excess.

(4) The Management Act shall apply to an assessment under subsection (3) above as if it were an assessment to tax for the year of assessment in which the relief was given and as if—

Interest ceasing to be relevant loan interest etc.

    (a) the assessment were among those specified in sections 55(1) (recovery of tax not postponed) and 86(2) (interest on overdue tax) of that Act; and

    (b) the sum charged by the assessment were tax specified in paragraph 3 of the Table in section 86(4) of that Act (reckonable date).

(5) If, as a result of receiving a notice under subsection (1) above or otherwise, a qualifying lender has reason to believe that any interest is no longer relevant loan interest or that a borrower is no longer a qualifying borrower, the lender shall furnish the Board with such information as is in his possession with respect to those matters.

(6) Where it appears to the Board that any of the provisions of sections 370 to 373 is not or may not be fulfilled with respect to any interest, or that a qualifying borrower has or may have ceased to be a qualifying borrower, they shall give notice of that fact to the lender and the borrower specifying the description of relevant loan interest concerned or, as the case may be, that the borrower has or may have ceased to be a qualifying borrower.

(7) Section 369 shall not apply to any payment of relevant loan interest of a description to which a notice under subsection (6) above relates and which becomes due or is made after such date as may be specified in the notice and before such date as may be specified in a further notice given by the Board to the lender and the borrower.

(8) In any case where—

    (a) section 369 applies to any relevant loan interest by virtue of a notice under section 374(1)(b), and

    (b) the relevant date specified in the notice is earlier than the date from which the interest begins to be paid under deduction of tax, and

    (c) a payment of that interest was made on or after the relevant date but not under deduction of tax,

regulations may provide for a sum to be paid by the Board of an amount equal to that which the borrower would have been able to deduct from that payment by virtue of section 369 if it had been made after the relevant date.

(9) No obligation as to secrecy imposed by statute or otherwise on persons employed in relation to Inland Revenue shall prevent information relating to any loan in respect of which an option notice has been given as mentioned in section 370(3)(a) from being disclosed to the Secretary of State or the Department of the Environment for Northern Ireland, or to an officer of either of them authorised to receive such information, in connection with the exercise by the Secretary of State or that Department of any of his or its functions in relation to any such loan.

(10) Subsection (9) above extends only to disclosure by or under the authority of the Inland Revenue; and information which is disclosed to any person by virtue of that subsection shall not be further disclosed to any other person unless—

(a) it could have been disclosed to that other person in accordance with that subsection; or

(b) the disclosure is made for the purposes of any civil or criminal proceedings concerned with the loan to which the disclosure relates.

376.—(1) Subject to subsection (2) below, an individual is a qualifying borrower with respect to the interest on any loan.

(2) In relation to interest paid at a time when the borrower or the borrower's husband or wife holds an office or employment in respect of the emoluments of which he or she would but for some special exemption or immunity from tax be chargeable to tax under Case I, II or III of Schedule E, the borrower is not a qualifying borrower.

(3) In subsection (2) above references to the borrower's husband or wife do not include references to a separated husband or wife, and for this purpose "separated" has the meaning given by section 367(1).

(4) The following bodies are qualifying lenders:—

(a) a building society;

(b) a local authority;

(c) the Bank of England;

(d) the Post Office;

(e) a company which is authorised under section 3 or 4 of the Insurance Companies Act 1982 to carry on in the United Kingdom any of the classes of business specified in Schedule 1 to that Act;   1982 c. 50.

(f) any company to which property and rights belonging to a trustee savings bank were transferred by section 3 of the Trustee Savings Bank Act 1985;   1985 c. 50.

(g) a registered friendly society or branch, within the meaning of the Friendly Societies Act 1974 or the Friendly Societies Act (Northern Ireland) 1970;   1974 c. 46.   1970 c. 31 (N.I.).

(h) a development corporation within the meaning of the New Towns Act 1981 or the New Towns (Scotland) Act 1968;   1981 c.64.   1968 c. 16.

(j) the Commission for the New Towns;

(k) the Housing Corporation;

(l) the Northern Ireland Housing Executive;

(m) the Scottish Special Housing Association;

(n) the Development Board for Rural Wales;

(o) the Church of England Pensions Board;

(p) any of the following which is prescribed under subsection (5) below, namely, an institution authorised under the Banking Act 1987, a company which is authorised as mentioned in paragraph (e) above to carry on in the United Kingdom any of the classes   1987 c. 22.

PART IX
1982 c. 50.

of business specified in Schedule 2 to the Insurance Companies Act 1982, and a 90 per cent. subsidiary of any such institution or company or of a company within paragraph (e) above and any other body whose activities and objects appear to the Treasury to qualify it for inclusion in this paragraph.

(5) The Treasury may by order prescribe for the purposes of subsection (4) above generally or in relation to any specified description of loan any of the bodies referred to in paragraph (p) of subsection (4) above; and a body which is prescribed by such an order shall become a qualifying lender generally or, as the case may be, in relation to such description of loan as is specified in the order with effect from such date as may be so specified.

(6) Without prejudice to subsection (4) above, in relation to interest to which section 370(3) applies, the person who, as a qualifying lender for the purposes of Part II of the Housing Subsidies Act 1967 or Part VIII of the Housing (Northern Ireland) Order 1981, was the lender in relation to the loan referred to in section 370(3) shall also be a qualifying lender.

1967 c. 29.
S.I. 1981/156
(N.I.3).

Variation of terms
of repayment of
certain loans.

377.—(1) If relevant loan interest payable by a qualifying borrower—

(a) is payable under a loan agreement requiring combined payments, and

(b) is payable to a qualifying lender who, in accordance with subsection (5) below, is specified for the purposes of this section, and

(c) is interest on a loan made before 1st April 1983, or if it is interest in respect of which the Board notified an earlier date to the lender under paragraph 2(5) of Schedule 7 to the Finance Act 1982, before that earlier date,

1982 c. 39.

then, subject to subsection (2) below, the terms of repayment are by virtue of this section varied in accordance with subsection (3) below.

(2) Subsection (1) above does not apply to any combined payments unless—

(a) the qualifying lender concerned has, in accordance with regulations, given notice to the qualifying borrower that this section is to apply to combined payments which the borrower is required to make under the loan agreement; and

(b) the qualifying borrower has not, in accordance with regulations, given notice to the qualifying lender that he wishes to continue with combined payments which, allowing for any sums he is entitled to deduct by virtue of section 369, do not exceed the combined payments which he would have been required to make but for the provisions of that section.

(3) Where subsection (1) applies, the amount of any combined payment payable by the qualifying borrower concerned which includes a payment of relevant loan interest shall be determined by the lender so as to secure, so far as practicable—

(a) that the principal and interest are repaid over the period which is for the time being agreed between the lender and the borrower; and

(b) that, unless there is a change in that period or in the basic rate of income tax or in the rate of interest charged by the lender, the amount of each net payment due from the borrower to the lender will be of the same amount;

and for the purposes of paragraph (b) above "net payment" means a payment which, so far as it is a payment of interest, consists of interest from which the sum provided for by section 369(1) has been deducted.

(4) Where the qualifying borrower gives a notice under subsection (2)(b) above, the amount of any combined payment payable by him which includes a payment of relevant loan interest and the period over which the principal and interest on the loan are to be repaid shall be determined by the lender so as to secure, so far as practicable, that, unless there is a change in the basic rate of income tax or in the rate of interest charged by the lender—

(a) the amount of each net payment as defined in subsection (3) above which is due from the borrower to the lender will be of the same amount; and

(b) the amount of each such payment does not exceed what, apart from section 369, would have been the amount of the combined payment payable by the borrower on the effective date of the notice under subsection (2)(a) above, less tax at the basic rate for the year of assessment in which that effective date falls on so much of that combined payment as would have consisted of interest.

(5) Nothing in this section or in the loan agreement shall prevent the borrower from making, at such time or times as he chooses, additional repayments of capital of any amount so as to secure that the principal and interest on the loan are repaid within a period which is not shorter than that referred to in subsection (3)(a) above.

(6) For the purposes of subsection (4)(b) above the effective date of a notice under subsection (2)(a) above is the date which, in accordance with regulations, is the due date for the first combined payment which, in consequence of that notice and the notice under subsection (2)(b) above, is a net payment for the purposes of subsection (3)(b) above.

(7) The repeal by this Act of section 28 of the Finance Act 1982 shall not affect the variation of any agreement in pursuance of that section before 26th July 1984 and accordingly, where the borrower gave a notice under subsection (2)(b) of that section, the maximum amount of any combined payment payable under the agreement as so varied which includes a payment of relevant loan interest shall continue to be the amount which would, apart from section 369, have been the first combined payment payable by the borrower after the date referred to in subsection (1)(c) above less tax at the basic rate for the year 1983-84 on so much of that combined payment as would have consisted of interest (subject to any change in the basic rate of income tax or in the rate of interest charged by the lender); and subsection (5) above shall apply in relation to any agreement as so varied.

1982 c. 39.

(8) A building society is by virtue of this subsection specified for the purposes of this section; and the Treasury may by order specify any other qualifying lender or class of qualifying lender for the purposes of this section.

(9) The giving of a notice under subsection (2)(a) or (b) above does not affect the right of the qualifying lender and the qualifying borrower to vary, by agreement, the terms on which interest or capital or both is to be repaid.

(10) In this section—

"loan agreement" means an agreement governing the terms of payment of interest and repayment of capital of a loan the interest on which is relevant loan interest; and

"combined payment" means one of a number of regular payments which are attributable in part to repayment of capital and in part to payment of interest.

Supplementary regulations.

378.—(1) The Treasury may by regulations make provision for the application of sections 369 to 377 in relation to—

(a) a housing association which is for the time being approved for the purposes of section 488 and which borrows or has borrowed from a qualifying lender on the security of a freehold or leasehold estate of that association on land in the United Kingdom; and

(b) a self-build society which is for the time being approved for the purposes of section 489 and which borrows or has borrowed from a qualifying lender on the security of a freehold or leasehold estate of that society on land in the United Kingdom.

(2) Regulations under subsection (1) above—

(a) may contain such modifications of the provisions of sections 369 to 377, and

(b) may make the application of any of those provisions subject to such special conditions,

as appear to the Treasury to be appropriate.

(3) The Board may by regulations make provision—

(a) for the purposes of any provision of sections 369 to 377 which relates to any matter or thing to be specified by or done in accordance with regulations;

(b) for the application of those sections in relation to loan interest paid by personal representatives and trustees;

(c) with respect to the furnishing of information by borrowers or lenders, including, in the case of lenders, the inspection of books, documents and other records on behalf of the Board;

(d) for, and with respect to, appeals to the General Commissioners or the Special Commissioners against the refusal of the Board to issue a notice under section 374(1)(b) or the issue of a notice under section 375(6) or (7); and

(e) generally for giving effect to sections 369 to 377.

(4) In this section—

(a) references to a self-build society are references to a self-build society within the meaning of Part I of the Housing Associations Act 1985 or, in Northern Ireland, Part VII of the Housing (Northern Ireland) Order 1981; and

1985 c. 69.
S.I. 1981/156
(N.I.3).

(b) in its application to Scotland —

(i) "a freehold or leasehold estate" means any interest in land, and

(ii) any reference to a loan on the security of such an estate is a reference to a loan upon a heritable security within the meaning of section 9(8)(a) of the Conveyancing and Feudal Reform (Scotland) Act 1970.

1970 c. 35.

379. In sections 369 to 378—

Interpretation of sections 369 to 378.

"prescribed", except in section 376(4) and (5), means prescribed by the Board;

"qualifying borrower" has the meaning given by section 376(1) to (3);

"qualifying lender" has the meaning given by section 376(4) to (6);

"regulations", except in sections 378(1) and (2), means regulations made by the Board under section 378;

"relevant loan interest" has the meaning given by section 370(1).

M

PART X

LOSS RELIEF AND GROUP RELIEF

CHAPTER I

LOSS RELIEF: INCOME TAX

Trade etc. losses

Set-off against general income.

380.—(1) Where any person sustains a loss in any trade, profession, vocation or employment carried on by him either solely or in partnership, he may, by notice given within two years after the year of assessment, make a claim for relief from income tax on an amount of his income equal to the amount of the loss.

(2) Subject to section 492(2), relief may be given under subsection (1) above in respect of a person's loss sustained in the last preceding year of assessment in any trade, profession, vocation or employment still carried on by him in the year for which the claim is made, in so far as relief in respect of that loss has not already been given under that subsection or otherwise; and where relief is claimed by virtue of this subsection it shall be given in priority to any relief under that subsection in respect of a loss sustained in the year for which the relief is claimed.

(3) Where there is in any year of assessment a change on which a trade, profession or vocation is treated under section 113(1) as permanently discontinued, and a person engaged in carrying it on immediately before the change continues to be so engaged immediately afterwards, it shall, notwithstanding the discontinuance, be treated as the same trade, profession or vocation for the purposes of subsection (2) above, except as respects the computation of profits or gains and losses.

(4) This section applies in relation to losses sustained in the occupation of woodlands in respect of which a person has elected under section 54 to be charged to income tax under Schedule D as it applies in relation to losses sustained in a trade.

Further relief for individuals for losses in early years of trade.

381.—(1) Where an individual carrying on a trade sustains a loss in the trade in—

(a) the year of assessment in which it is first carried on by him; or

(b) any of the next three years of assessment;

he may, by notice given within two years after the year of assessment in which the loss is sustained, make a claim for relief under this section.

(2) Subject to section 492 and this section, relief shall be given under subsection (1) above from income tax on an amount of the claimant's income equal to the amount of the loss, being income for the three years of assessment last preceding that in which the loss is sustained, taking income for an earlier year before income for a later year.

(3) Relief shall not be given for the same loss or the same portion of a loss both under subsection (1) above and under any other provision of the Income Tax Acts.

(4) Relief shall not be given under subsection (1) above in respect of a loss sustained in any period unless it is shown that the trade was carried on throughout that period on a commercial basis and in such a way that profits in the trade (or, where the carrying on of the trade forms part of a larger undertaking, in the undertaking as a whole) could reasonably be expected to be realised in that period or within a reasonable time thereafter.

(5) Relief shall not be given under subsection (1) above in respect of a loss sustained by an individual in a trade if—

(a) at the time when it is first carried on by him he is married to and living with another individual who has previously carried on the trade; and

(b) the loss is sustained in a year of assessment later than the third year of assessment after that in which the trade was first carried on by the other individual.

(6) For the purposes of this section an individual carries on a trade whether he does so solely or in partnership; and (except as respects the computation of profits or gains and losses) an individual continues to carry on the same trade notwithstanding a change in the persons engaged in carrying it on if he is engaged in carrying it on immediately before and immediately after the change.

(7) This section applies, with the necessary modifications, in relation to a profession or vocation as it applies in relation to a trade.

382.—(1) A claim for relief under section 380 or 381 may require that the relief be given only by reference to the income of the person sustaining the loss, without extending to the income of that person's wife or husband.

Provisions supplementary to sections 380 and 381.

(2) Subject to any requirement under subsection (1) above, relief under section 380 or 381 shall be given in respect of a loss sustained by any person by treating the loss as reducing first his income of the corresponding class, then his other income, then the income of the corresponding class of that person's wife or husband, then the other income of the wife or husband.

For the purposes of this subsection "income of the corresponding class" means earned or unearned income according as income arising during the same period as the loss to the person sustaining it from profits or gains of the same trade, profession, vocation or employment would have been that person's earned or unearned income.

(3) Where relief under section 380 or 381 has been given to a person for any year of assessment, he shall not be entitled, in computing the amount of the assessment for any subsequent year, to a deduction of any portion of the amount in respect of which such relief has been obtained.

(4) For the purposes of sections 380 and 381, the amount of a loss sustained in a trade, (including the occupation of woodlands in a case where section 380(4) applies), profession or vocation shall be computed in like manner as the profits or gains arising or accruing from the trade, profession or vocation are computed under the provisions of the Income Tax Acts applicable to Case I or II of Schedule D.

Part X
Extension of right
of set-off to
capital allowances.

383.—(1) Subject to the provisions of this section, any claim made under section 380 or 381 for relief in respect of a loss sustained by the claimant in any trade in any year of assessment ("the year of loss") may require the amount of that loss to be determined as if an amount equal to the capital allowances for the year of assessment for which the year of loss is the basis year were to be deducted in computing the profits or gains or losses of the trade in the year of loss; and a claim may be so made notwithstanding that apart from those allowances the claimant has not sustained a loss in the trade in the year of loss.

(2) Capital allowances for any year of assessment shall be taken into account by virtue of this section only if and so far as they are not required to offset balancing charges for the year; and, for the purposes of this subsection, the capital allowances for a year of assessment shall be treated as required to offset balancing charges for the year up to the amount on which the balancing charges fall to be made after deducting from that amount the amount (if any) of capital allowances for earlier years which is carried forward to that year and would, without the balancing charges, be non-effective in that year.

(3) In the case of a claim under section 380, where the capital allowances taken into account by virtue of this section are those for the year of assessment for which the claim is made or for the preceding year (the year of loss being the basis year for that year itself, or the claim being made by way of carry-forward of the loss by virtue of section 380(2)) relief shall not be given by reference to those allowances in respect of an amount greater than the amount non-effective in the year for which the claim is made, or, in the case of allowances for the preceding year, the amount non-effective in both years.

(4) In the case of a claim under section 381, where the capital allowances taken into account by virtue of this section are those for the year of loss, relief shall not be given by reference to those allowances in respect of an amount greater than the amount non-effective in that year.

(5) For the purposes of this section—

    (a) where the end of the basis period for a year of assessment (as defined in section 72 of the 1968 Act) falls in, or coincides with the end of, any year of assessment, that year is the basis year for the first-mentioned year of assessment, but so that, if a year of assessment would under the foregoing provision be the basis year both for that year itself and for another year of assessment, it shall be the basis year for the year itself and not for the other year;

    (b) any reference to the capital allowances or balancing charges for a year of assessment shall be construed as a reference to those falling to be made in taxing the trade for that year (but not including, in the case of allowances, any part of the allowances for an earlier year carried forward under section 70(4) of the 1968 Act);

    (c) any reference to an amount of capital allowances non-effective in a year shall be construed as referring to the amount to which, by reason of an insufficiency of profits or gains, effect cannot be given in taxing the trade for the year; and

(d) effect shall be deemed to be given in taxing the trade to allowances carried forward from an earlier year before it is given to allowances arising in a later year.

(6) Where, on a claim made by virtue of this section, relief is not given under section 380 or 381 for the full amount of the loss determined as mentioned in subsection (1) above, the relief shall be referred as far as may be to the loss sustained by the claimant in the trade rather than to the capital allowances in respect of the trade.

(7) Subject to subsection (8) below, where for any year of assessment relief is given under section 380 or 381 by reference to any capital allowances, then, for all the purposes of the Income Tax Acts, effect shall be deemed to have been given to those allowances up to the amount in respect of which relief is so given, as if (in accordance with section 70(2) of the 1968 Act) a deduction in respect thereof had been allowed in taxing the trade for that year, or—

(a) where relief is given under section 380, in the case of allowances for the following year, in taxing the trade for that following year;

(b) where relief is given under section 381, in the case of allowances for any later year, in taxing the trade for that later year;

and any relief previously given for a subsequent year on the basis that effect had not been given to the allowances as aforesaid shall be adjusted where necessary by an assessment.

(8) Where in any year of assessment a trade is permanently discontinued, or is treated for the purposes of section 113 as permanently discontinued, and, immediately before the discontinuance, the trade was being carried on in partnership, then, notwithstanding subsection (7) above, for the purposes of any claim for relief made by virtue of section 385(5)(c) or 388 and relating to that discontinuance, effect shall not be deemed to have been given either—

(a) to any part of the capital allowances falling to be made in taxing the trade for that year by reason of relief given under section 380 or 381 by reference to those allowances; or

(b) to any part of the capital allowances falling to be made in taxing the trade for the preceding year by reason of relief so given by reference to them, in so far as that relief must be referred to the part of the allowances apportionable to the part of the year within 12 months of the discontinuance on an apportionment made by reference to the comparative lengths of the two parts of the year;

but where the same partner claims relief both under section 380 or 381 and under section 385(5) or 388 in respect of the same allowances, the total amount for which relief is to be given to him by reference thereto shall not exceed the greater of the amounts for which, apart from any deficiency of income, relief might have been given under either section separately, and the total amount for which relief is to be given to all the partners under those sections in respect of any allowances shall not in any event exceed the amount of the allowances to which effect has not been given apart from those sections.

(9) Where a person claiming relief under section 380 or 381 has, since the end, where the claim is under section 380, of the year for which the claim is made, or, where the claim is under section 381, of the year of loss, carried on the trade in question in partnership, effect shall not be given to this section in relation to that claim except with the written consent of, or of the personal representatives of, every other person who has been engaged in carrying on the trade between the end of that year and the making of the claim.

(10) Where the claim is for a loss sustained before an event treated as the permanent discontinuance of the trade, subsection (9) above shall not require the consent of any person as having been so engaged since that discontinuance, or as the personal representative of such a person.

(11) Relief from tax may be given by virtue of this section by reference to capital allowances for a year of assessment before the passing of any Act granting income tax for that year, as if income tax had been granted for the year without alteration; but if relief given to a person by virtue of this section for any year of assessment is affected by a subsequent alteration of the law, or by any discontinuance of the trade or other event occurring after the end of the year, any necessary adjustment may be made, and so much of any repayment of tax as exceeded the amount repayable in the events that happened may, if not otherwise made good, be assessed under Case VI of Schedule D and recovered from that person accordingly.

(12) This section applies (with any necessary adaptations)—

(a) in the case of a claim under section 380, in relation to a profession, vocation or employment and in relation to the occupation of woodlands the profits or gains of which are assessable under Schedule D by virtue of an election under section 54; and

(b) in relation to a claim under section 381, in relation to a profession or vocation,

as it applies in relation to a trade.

Restrictions on right of set-off.

384.—(1) Subject to subsection (2) below, a loss (including any amount in respect of capital allowances which, by virtue of section 383, is to be treated as a loss) shall not be available for relief under section 380 unless it is shown that, for the year of assessment in which the loss is claimed to have been sustained, the trade was being carried on on a commercial basis and with a view to the realisation of profits in the trade or, where the carrying on of the trade formed part of a larger undertaking, in the undertaking as a whole.

(2) Subsection (1) above shall not apply—

(a) to a loss made, or an allowance in respect of expenditure incurred, by any person in the exercise of functions conferred by or under any enactment (including an enactment contained in a local or private Act); or

(b) to an allowance in respect of expenditure incurred before 6th April 1960.

(3) Where during a year of assessment there is a change in the manner in which a trade is being carried on, it shall be treated for the purposes of this section as having been carried on throughout the year in the way in which it was being carried on by the end of the year.

(4) Subject to subsection (5) below, where a trade is (or falls to be treated as being) carried on for a part only of a year of assessment by reason of its being (or falling to be treated as being) set up and commenced, or discontinued, or both, in that year, subsections (1) to (3) above shall have effect in relation to the trade as regards that part of that year as if any reference to the manner of carrying on the trade for or by the end of that year were a reference to the manner of carrying it on for or by the end of that part of that year.

(5) Where in any year of assessment there is a change in the persons engaged in carrying on a trade, then, for the purposes of the application of subsections (1) to (4) above in the case of any person who, being engaged in carrying on the trade immediately before the change, continues to be so engaged immediately after it, the trade carried on by that person immediately before the change shall be treated as continuing to be carried on by him notwithstanding the change, whether or not it falls to be treated for any other purpose as having been discontinued on the change.

(6) There shall be disregarded for the purposes of section 383 any allowances made to an individual under Chapter I of Part III of the Finance Act 1971 in respect of expenditure incurred on the provision of machinery or plant for leasing in the course of a trade unless—   1971 c. 68.

(a) the trade is carried on by him (alone or in partnership) for a continuous period of at least six months in, or beginning or ending in, the year of the loss (as defined in section 383); and

(b) he devotes substantially the whole of his time to carrying it on (alone or in partnership) throughout that year or if it is set up or permanently discontinued (or both) in that year, for a continuous period of at least six months beginning or ending in that year.

(7) Subsection (6) above shall apply also to expenditure incurred by an individual on the provision for the purposes of a trade carried on by him (alone or in partnership) of an asset which is not to be leased if payments in the nature of royalties or licence fees are to accrue from rights granted by him in connection with that asset.

(8) Where relief has been given in a case to which subsection (6) above applies it shall be withdrawn by the making of an assessment under Case VI of Schedule D.

(9) For the purposes of subsection (1) above, the fact that a trade was being carried on at any time so as to afford a reasonable expectation of profit shall be conclusive evidence that it was then being carried on with a view to the realisation of profits.

(10) Subsections (1) to (5) and (9) above—

(a) apply to professions and vocations as they apply to trades, with references to a commercial basis construed accordingly; and

(b) have effect without prejudice to section 397;

Carry-forward
against subsequent
profits.

and subsection (6) above is without prejudice to section 41 of the Finance Act 1976.

385.—(1) Where a person has, in any trade, profession or vocation carried on by him either alone or in partnership, sustained a loss (to be computed in the same way as profits or gains under the provisions of the Income Tax Acts applicable to Cases I and II of Schedule D) in respect of which relief has not been wholly given either under section 380 or under any other provision of those Acts, he may make a claim requiring that any portion of the loss for which relief has not been so given shall be carried forward and, as far as may be, deducted from or set off against the amount of profits or gains on which he is assessed to income tax under Schedule D in respect of that trade, profession or vocation for subsequent years of assessment.

(2) In the application of this section to a loss sustained by a partner in a partnership, "the amount of profits or gains on which he is assessed" shall, in respect of any year, be taken to mean such portion of the amount on which the partnership is assessed to income tax under Schedule D in respect of the trade, profession or vocation as he would be required to include in a return of his total income for that year.

(3) Any relief under this section shall be given as far as possible from the first subsequent assessment, and so far as it cannot be so given, then from the next assessment, and so on.

(4) Where in any year of assessment relief cannot be given, or cannot be wholly given, in respect of a loss carried forward under this section because the amount of the profits or gains of the trade assessed under Case I of Schedule D for that year is insufficient, any interest or dividends being interest or dividends—

(a) on investments arising in that year, and

(b) which would fall to be taken into account as trading receipts in computing the profits or gains of the trade for the purposes of assessment under that Case but for the fact that they have been subjected to tax under other provisions of the Income Tax Acts,

shall be treated for the purposes of the application of this section as if they were profits or gains on which the person carrying on the trade was assessed under that Case in respect of that trade for that year of assessment, and relief shall be given accordingly by repayment or otherwise.

(5) Where there is in any year of assessment a change on which a trade, profession or vocation is treated under section 113 as permanently discontinued, and a person engaged in carrying it on immediately before the change continues to be so engaged immediately thereafter, then—

(a) the trade, profession or vocation carried on by him immediately before and that carried on immediately after the change shall, notwithstanding the discontinuance, be treated as the same for the purposes of this section, except as respects the computation of profits or gains and losses; and

(b) in respect of a loss sustained by him in the trade, profession or vocation in the part of that year before the change, relief shall be given under this section from the assessment relating to the part of the year after the change as if it were an assessment for a subsequent year; and

(c) for the purposes of this section, there shall be treated as a loss so sustained in the part of the year before the change his share of the non-effective amount (if any) of any capital allowances falling to be made in taxing the trade, profession or vocation for that part of that year.

For the purposes of paragraph (c) above—

(i) the persons engaged in carrying on the trade, profession or vocation immediately before the change shall be treated as entitled to capital allowances in the shares in which they are then entitled to the profits of the trade, profession or vocation, and

(ii) "the non-effective amount" means, in relation to any such allowances, the amount to which, because of an insufficiency of profits or gains, effect cannot be given in taxing the trade, profession or vocation.

(6) Where a loss is sustained by a person in the occupation of woodlands, and that person, if he had made a profit, would by reason of his election under section 54 have been chargeable for the following year to income tax under Schedule D computed on the amount of that profit, this section shall apply so as to give relief in respect of that loss in the same manner, and to the same extent, as if it were a loss sustained in a trade.

(7) In so far as relief in respect of any loss has been given to any person under this section, that person shall not be entitled to claim relief in respect of that loss under any other provision of the Income Tax Acts.

(8) So far as a claim under this section concerns the amount of the loss for any year of assessment it must be made within six years after the year of assessment in question, but the question whether any and if so how much relief on that amount should be given under this section against tax for any year of assessment may be the subject of a separate claim made not later than six years after that year of assessment.

386.—(1) Where—

Carry-forward where business transferred to a company.

(a) a business carried on by any individual, or any individuals in partnership, has been transferred to a company in consideration solely or mainly of the allotment of shares in the company to that individual or those individuals; and

(b) in the case of any individual to whom, or to whose nominee or nominees, shares have been so allotted, his total income for any year of assessment throughout which he is the beneficial owner of the shares, and throughout which the company carries on the business, includes any income derived by him from the company, whether by way of dividends on those shares or otherwise;

PART X

then, subject to subsection (2) below, section 385 (except subsection (5)) shall apply as if the income so derived were profits or gains on which that individual was assessed under Schedule D in respect of that business for that year.

(2) Where under section 385 as applied by subsection (1) above a loss falls to be deducted from or set off against any income for any year of assessment, the deduction or set-off shall be made in the first place against that part, if any, of the income in respect of which the individual has been, or is liable to be, assessed to tax for that year.

(3) This section, in its application to the year of assessment in which a business is transferred, shall have effect as if, for the reference in subsection (1)(b) to the year of assessment throughout which the individual is the beneficial owner of the shares and the business is carried on by the company, there were substituted a reference to the period from the date of the transfer to the following 5th April.

(4) Where a change to which subsection (5) of section 385 applies has occurred before a transfer to which this section applies, paragraph (a), but not paragraph (c), of that subsection shall for the purposes of this section apply in relation to the earlier change as it applies for the purposes of that section.

Carry-forward as losses of amounts taxed under section 350.

387.—(1) Subject to the provisions of this section, where under section 350 a person has been assessed to income tax in respect of a payment made wholly and exclusively for the purposes of a trade, profession or vocation, the amount on which tax has been paid under that assessment shall be treated for the purposes of sections 385 and 386 as though it were a loss sustained in that trade, profession or vocation, and relief in respect of the loss shall be allowed accordingly.

(2) Relief shall not be allowed by virtue of this section in respect of any payment, or part of a payment, which is not ultimately borne by the person assessed, or which is charged to capital.

(3) This section shall not apply—

(a) to any payment falling within section 349(2);

(b) to any payment falling within section 349 by virtue of section 43(1);

(c) to any such payment of rent as is referred to in section 120(4);

(d) to any capital sum paid in respect of any patent rights assessed under section 349(1) by virtue of section 524;

(e) to any payment of, or on account of, copyright royalties to which section 536 applies; or

(f) to any payment to which section 349(1) applies by virtue of section 737.

Carry-back of terminal losses.

388.—(1) Where a trade, profession or vocation is permanently discontinued in the year 1988-89 or any later year, and any person then carrying it on, either alone or in partnership, has sustained therein a loss to which this section applies ("a terminal loss"), that person may, subject to the provisions of this section and of section 389, make a claim requiring that the amount of the terminal loss shall, as far as may be, be deducted from or set off against the amount of profits or gains on which he has been charged to income tax under Schedule D in respect of the trade, profession or vocation for the three years of assessment last preceding that in which the discontinuance occurs; and there shall be made all such reductions of assessments or repayments of tax as may be necessary to give effect to the claim.

(2) Relief shall not be given in respect of the same matter both under this section and under some other provision of the Income Tax Acts.

(3) Any relief under this section shall be given as far as possible from the assessment for a later rather than an earlier year.

(4) Where—

   (a) a claim under this section is made in respect of a terminal loss sustained in a trade, and

   (b) relief cannot be given, or cannot be wholly given, against the profits or gains of the trade charged to income tax under Schedule D for any year because the amount of those profits or gains is insufficient,

any relevant interest or dividends arising in that year shall be treated for the purposes of the application of this section as if they were profits or gains on which the person carrying on the trade was assessed under Case I of Schedule D in respect of that trade for that year of assessment, and relief shall be given accordingly by repayment or otherwise.

For the purposes of this subsection "any relevant interest or dividends" means interest or dividends which would fall to be taken into account as trading receipts in computing the profits or gains of the trade for the purpose of assessment under Case I of Schedule D but for the fact that they have been subjected to tax under other provisions of the Income Tax Acts.

(5) The profits or gains on which a person or partnership has been charged to income tax for any year of assessment shall be treated for the purposes of any relief under this section from the assessment for that year as reduced by the amount of those profits or gains applied in making any payment from which income tax was deducted, but was not accounted for because the payment was made out of profits or gains brought into charge to income tax; and the like reduction shall be made in the amount of the terminal loss for which relief may be given under this section from the assessments for earlier years unless the payment was one which, if not made out of profits or gains brought into charge to income tax—

   (a) could have been assessed to income tax under section 350, and

   (b) if so assessed, could have been treated as a loss by virtue of section 387.

(6) The question whether a person has sustained any and, if so, what terminal loss in a trade, profession or vocation shall be determined for the purposes of this section by taking the amounts (if any) of the following, in so far as they have not otherwise been taken into account so as to reduce or relieve any charge to tax—

   (a) the loss sustained by him in the trade, profession or vocation in the year of assessment in which it is permanently discontinued;

   (b) the relevant capital allowances for that year of assessment;

   (c) the loss sustained by him in the trade, profession or vocation in the part of the preceding year of assessment beginning 12 months before the discontinuance; and

   (d) the same fraction of the relevant capital allowances for that preceding year of assessment as the part thereof beginning 12 months before the discontinuance is of a year.

(7) In subsection (6) above "the relevant capital allowances" means, in relation to any year of assessment, any capital allowances falling to be made in taxing the trade, profession or vocation for that year, excluding amounts carried forward from an earlier year; and for the purposes of paragraphs (a) and (c) of that subsection the amount of a loss shall, subject to the provisions of this section, be computed in the same way as profits or gains under the provisions of the Income Tax Acts applicable to Cases I and II of Schedule D.

Supplementary provisions relating to carry-back of terminal losses.

389.—(1) Sections 387, 458 and 474 shall apply to the computation of losses, or of profit or loss, for any purpose of this section or section 388 as they apply to any such computation for the corresponding purposes of section 385.

1986 c. 41.

(2) Where on the permanent discontinuance of a trade which consists of or includes the working of a mine, oil well or other source of mineral deposits within the meaning of Schedule 13 to the Finance Act 1986, a claim for relief is made both under section 388 above and section 15(1) of the 1968 Act (carry-back of balancing allowances), the balancing allowance in respect of which the claim is made under section 15(1) shall be left out of account for the purposes of section 388(6), but relief under section 388 shall be given in priority to relief under section 15(1).

(3) Where a person claiming relief under section 388 on a discontinuance has, since the beginning of the third year of assessment preceding that in which the discontinuance occurs, carried on the trade, profession or vocation in partnership—

   (a) in section 388(1) "the amount of profits or gains on which he has been charged to income tax" shall be taken to mean, in respect of any year or part of a year for which the partnership was assessed in respect of the trade, profession or vocation, such portion of the amount of the profits or gains on which the partnership has been, or is treated by virtue of section 388(5) as having been, charged to income tax in respect of it for that year or part of a year as would be required to be included in a return of his total income for that year;

   (b) any reduction in the amount of his terminal loss which falls to be made under section 388(5) by reason of profits or gains having been applied by the partnership in any such year or part of a year in making any payment shall be limited to the same proportion of the profits or gains brought into charge which were so applied; and

   (c) if he was carrying on the trade, profession or vocation immediately before the discontinuance, the amounts to be included in his terminal loss by virtue of section 388(6)(b) or (d) shall be such part only of the amounts therein mentioned (in so far as they have not otherwise been taken into account so as to reduce or relieve any charge to tax) as would fall to his share on a division made according to the shares in which the partners were then entitled to the profits of the trade, profession or vocation.

(4) For all purposes of this section and section 388 a trade, profession or vocation shall be treated as discontinued, and a new one as set up and commenced, when it is so treated for the purposes of section 113; but—

(a) a person who continues to be engaged in carrying it on immediately after such a discontinuance shall not be entitled to relief in respect of any terminal loss on that discontinuance; and

(b) on any discontinuance, a person not continuing to be so engaged may be given relief in respect of a terminal loss against profits or gains on which he was charged in respect of the same trade, profession or vocation for a period before a previous discontinuance, if he has been continuously engaged in carrying it on between the two discontinuances, and, in his case, if the previous discontinuance occurred within 12 months before the other—

(i) it shall be disregarded for the purposes of paragraphs (a) and (c) of section 388(6), except that those paragraphs shall be taken to include any amount on which relief could have been allowed to him as for a loss sustained before the previous discontinuance by virtue of section 385(5)(c), so far as it is referable to a period within those 12 months; and

(ii) paragraph (d) of section 388(6) shall be taken to include the whole amount of the allowances in question instead of the fraction there mentioned.

(5) Where a trade, profession or vocation is being carried on by any persons in partnership immediately before it is permanently discontinued, relief under section 388 given to one of them on the discontinuance shall not, in relation to a claim made by another of them by virtue of paragraph (c) of section 385(5), be taken to affect the non-effective amount of any allowances within the meaning of that paragraph.

(6) Subject to subsection (7) below, a claim for relief under section 388 may require that, in so far as they have not been otherwise taken into account so as to reduce or relieve any charge to tax, capital allowances in respect of the trade under Part I of the 1968 Act or Chapter I of Part III of the Finance Act 1971, being allowances which—   1971 c. 68.

(a) fall to be made to the claimant by way of discharge or repayment of tax, and

(b) fall to be so made for the year of assessment in which the discontinuance occurs or the preceding year of assessment,

shall be added to the terminal loss sustained by him (or, if he has not sustained a terminal loss computed in accordance with the provisions of this section and section 388, shall be treated as a terminal loss so sustained), and the allowances to be taken into account for this purpose may include allowances arising before a previous discontinuance.

(7) For the purposes of subsection (6) above—

(a) there shall be taken into account such fraction only of the allowances for the preceding year of assessment referred to in that subsection as the part of that year beginning 12 months before the discontinuance giving rise to the claim is of a year; and

(b) the allowances for any year shall not be treated as including any amounts carried forward from an earlier year.

(8) Where a person occupying woodlands has elected to be charged to income tax in respect thereof under Schedule D, this section and section 388 shall apply to a terminal loss sustained by him in the occupation of the woodlands as they apply to a terminal loss sustained in a trade.

Treatment of interest as a loss for purposes of carry-forward and carry-back.

390. Where—

(a) a payment of interest eligible for relief under section 353 is money wholly and exclusively laid out or expended for the purposes of a trade, profession or vocation the profits of which are chargeable to tax under Case I or II of Schedule D, and

(b) full effect cannot be given to such relief in respect of the payment by reason of a want or deficiency of income of the year of assessment in which the payment is made,

the amount unallowed may be carried forward to succeeding years of assessment as if it were a loss carried forward under section 385, or may be treated for the purposes of sections 388 and 389 as a loss sustained at the date of payment.

Losses from trade etc. carried on abroad.

391.—(1) Subject to the following provisions of this section, sections 380 to 386 and 388 and 389, so far as applicable, shall apply in relation to a loss incurred by any person in the carrying on of a trade, profession or vocation chargeable in accordance with section 65(3) as they apply to a loss incurred in a trade, profession or vocation chargeable to tax under Case I or II of Schedule D.

(2) Relief shall not be given by virtue of subsection (1) above except on income falling within section 65(2) or (3), 192(2), (3) or (4) or 196.

Case VI losses

Case VI losses.

392.—(1) Where in any year of assessment a person sustains a loss in any transaction, whether he was engaged therein solely or in partnership, being a transaction of such a nature that, if any profits had arisen therefrom, he would have been liable to be assessed to income tax in respect thereof under Case VI of Schedule D, he may make a claim requiring—

(a) that the amount of the loss sustained by him shall, as far as may be, be deducted from or set off against the amount of any profits or gains arising from any transaction in respect of which he is assessed for that year under that Case, and

(b) that any portion of the loss for which relief is not so given shall, as far as may be, be carried forward and deducted from or set off against the amount of any profits or gains arising from any transaction in respect of which he is assessed to income tax under that Case for any subsequent year of assessment.

(2) In the application of this section to a loss sustained by a partner in a partnership, "the amount of any profits or gains arising from any transaction in respect of which he is assessed" shall be taken to mean in respect of any year such portion of the amount on which the partnership is assessed under Case VI of Schedule D in respect of any transaction as falls to be taken into account in computing his total income for that year.

(3) Any relief under this section by way of the carrying forward of the loss shall be given as far as possible from the first subsequent assessment in respect of any profits or gains arising from any transaction in respect of which he is assessed under Case VI of Schedule D for any year, and, so far as it cannot be so given, then from the next such assessment, and so on.

(4) This section does not apply to any loss sustained in a transaction falling within section 34, 35 or 36.

(5) So far as a claim under this section concerns the amount of the loss for any year of assessment, it must be made within six years after the year of assessment in question; but the question whether any and if so how much relief on that amount should be given under this section against tax for any year of assessment may be the subject of a separate claim made not later than six years after that year of assessment.

CHAPTER II

LOSS RELIEF: CORPORATION TAX

Trade etc. losses

393.—(1) Where in any accounting period a company carrying on a trade incurs a loss in the trade, the company may make a claim requiring that the loss be set off for the purposes of corporation tax against any trading income from the trade in succeeding accounting periods; and (so long as the company continues to carry on the trade) its trading income from the trade in any succeeding accounting period shall then be treated as reduced by the amount of the loss, or by so much of that amount as cannot, on that claim or on a claim (if made) under subsection (2) below, be relieved against income or profits of an earlier accounting period.

Losses other than terminal losses.

(2) Subject to section 492(2), where in any accounting period ending after 5th April 1988 a company carrying on a trade incurs a loss in the trade, then (subject to subsection (5) below) the company may make a claim requiring that the loss be set off for the purposes of corporation tax against profits (of whatever description) of that accounting period and, if the company was then carrying on the trade and the claim so requires, of preceding accounting periods ending within the time specified in subsection (3) below; and, subject to that subsection and to any relief for an earlier loss, the profits of any of those periods shall then be treated as reduced by the amount of the loss, or by so much of that amount as cannot be relieved under this subsection against profits of a later accounting period.

(3) The time referred to in subsection (2) above is a time equal in length to the accounting period in which the loss is incurred; but the amount of the reduction which may be made under that subsection in the profits of an accounting period falling partly before that time shall not exceed a part of those profits proportionate to the part of the period falling within that time.

(4) Where a company incurs a loss in a trade in an accounting period for which one or more first-year allowances fall to be made to it under Chapter I of Part III of the Finance Act 1971 in respect of expenditure on the provision for the purposes of the trade of machinery or plant, subsections (2) and (3) above shall have effect in relation to so much of the loss as does not exceed the allowance or allowances which are so made as if the time specified in subsection (3) above were a period of three years ending immediately before the accounting period in which the loss is incurred.

(5) Subsection (2) above shall not apply to trades falling within Case V of Schedule D; and, except in so far as it represents an excess in respect of expenditure incurred before the year 1960-61 of capital allowances over balancing charges, a loss incurred in a trade in any accounting period shall not be relieved under that subsection unless the trade is one carried on in the exercise of functions conferred by or under any enactment (including an enactment contained in a local or private Act), or it is shown that for that accounting period the trade was being carried on on a commercial basis and with a view to the realisation of gain in the trade or in any larger undertaking of which the trade formed part.

This subsection has effect without prejudice to section 397.

(6) For the purposes of subsection (5) above, the fact that a trade was being carried on at any time so as to afford a reasonable expectation of gain shall be conclusive evidence that it was then being carried on with a view to the realisation of gain; and where in an accounting period there is a change in the manner in which a trade is being carried on, it shall for those purposes be treated as having throughout the accounting period been carried on in the way in which it was being carried on by the end of that period.

(7) The amount of a loss incurred in a trade in an accounting period shall be computed for the purposes of this section in the same way as trading income from the trade in that period would have been computed.

(8) For the purposes of this section "trading income" means, in relation to any trade, the income which falls or would fall to be included in respect of the trade in the total profits of the company; but where—

(a) in an accounting period a company incurs a loss in a trade in respect of which it is within the charge to corporation tax under Case I or V of Schedule D, and

(b) in any later accounting period to which the loss or any part of it is carried forward under subsection (1) above relief in respect thereof cannot be given, or cannot wholly be given, because the amount of the trading income of the trade is insufficient, any interest or dividends on investments which would fall to be taken into account as trading receipts in computing that trading income but for the fact that they have been subjected to tax under other provisions shall be treated for the purposes of subsection (1) above as if they were trading income of the trade.

(9) Where in an accounting period the charges on income paid by a company—

(a) exceed the amount of the profits against which they are deductible, and

(b) include payments made wholly and exclusively for the purposes of a trade carried on by the company,

then, up to the amount of that excess or of those payments, whichever is the less, the charges on income so paid shall in computing a loss for the purposes of subsection (1) above be deductible as if they were trading expenses of the trade.

(10) In this section references to a company carrying on a trade refer to the company carrying it on so as to be within the charge to corporation tax in respect of it.

(11) A claim under subsection (1) above must be made within six years after the end of the accounting period in which the loss is incurred, and must be so made notwithstanding that relief cannot be given in respect of the loss until after the end of that period of six years; and a claim under subsection (2) above must be made within two years from the end of the accounting period in which the loss is incurred.

394.—(1) Where a company ceasing to carry on a trade after 5th April 1988 has in any accounting period falling wholly or partly within the previous 12 months incurred a loss in the trade, the company may make a claim requiring that the loss be set off for the purposes of corporation tax against trading income from the trade in accounting periods falling wholly or partly within the three years preceding those 12 months (or within any less period throughout which the company has carried on the trade); and, subject to subsections (2) to (6) below and to any relief for earlier losses, the trading income of any of those periods shall be then treated as reduced by the amount of the loss, or by so much of that amount as cannot be relieved under this subsection against income of a later accounting period. *Terminal losses.*

(2) Relief under subsection (1) above shall not be given in respect of any loss in so far as the loss has been or can be otherwise taken into account so as to reduce or relieve any charge to tax.

(3) Where a loss is incurred in an accounting period falling partly outside the 12 months mentioned in subsection (1) above, relief shall be given under that subsection in respect of a part only of that loss proportionate to the part of the period falling within those 12 months; and the amount of the reduction which may be made under that subsection in the trading income of an accounting period falling partly outside the three years there mentioned shall not exceed a part of that income proportionate to the part of the period falling within those three years.

(4) A claim for relief under this section may require that capital allowances in respect of the trade, being allowances which fall to be made to the company by way of discharge or repayment of tax, and to be so made for an accounting period falling wholly or partly within the 12 months ending when the company ceases to carry on the trade, shall (so far as they cannot be otherwise taken into account so as to reduce or relieve any charge to corporation tax) be added to the loss incurred by the company in that accounting period or, if the company has not incurred a loss in the period, shall be treated as a loss so incurred.

For the purposes of this subsection the allowances for any period shall not be treated as including amounts carried forward from an earlier period.

(5) Subsections (7) to (10) of section 393 shall apply for the purposes of this section as they apply for the purposes of subsection (1) of that section; and relief shall not be given under this section in respect of a loss incurred in a trade so as to interfere with any relief under section 338 in respect of payments made wholly and exclusively for the purposes of that trade.

(6) A claim under this section must be made within six years from the time when the company ceases to carry on the trade.

Leasing contracts and company reconstructions.

395.—(1) Subject to the provisions of this section, if—

    (a) under a contract entered into on or after 6th March 1973 a company ("the first company") incurs capital expenditure on the provision of machinery or plant which the first company lets to another person by another contract (a "leasing contract"); and

    (b) apart from this subsection, the first company would be entitled to claim relief under subsection (1) or (2) of section 393 in respect of losses incurred on the leasing contract; and

1971 c. 68.

    (c) in the accounting period for which a first-year allowance, within the meaning of Chapter I of Part III of the Finance Act 1971, in respect of the expenditure referred to in paragraph (a) above is made to the first company, arrangements are in existence by virtue of which, at some time during or after the expiry of that accounting period, a successor company will be able to carry on any part of the first company's trade which consists of or includes the performance of all or any of the obligations which, apart from the arrangements, would be the first company's obligations under the leasing contract,

then, in the accounting period specified in paragraph (c) above and in any subsequent accounting period, the first company shall not be entitled to claim relief as mentioned in paragraph (b) above except in computing its profits (if any) arising under the leasing contract.

(2) For the purposes of this section a company is a successor of the first company if the circumstances are such that—

    (a) section 343 applies in relation to the first company and the other company as the predecessor and the successor within the meaning of that section; or

(b) the two companies are connected with each other within the terms of section 839.

(3) For the purposes of this section losses incurred on a leasing contract and profits arising under such a contract shall be computed as if the performance of the leasing contract were a trade begun to be carried on by the first company, separately from any other trade which it may carry on, at the commencement of the letting under the leasing contract.

(4) In determining whether the first company would be entitled to claim relief as mentioned in subsection (1)(b) above, any losses incurred on the leasing contract shall be treated as incurred in a trade carried on by that company separately from any other trade which it may carry on.

(5) In this section "arrangements" means arrangements of any kind whether in writing or not.

Case VI losses

396.—(1) Subject to subsection (2) below, where in any accounting period a company incurs a loss in a transaction in respect of which the company is within the charge to corporation tax under Case VI of Schedule D, the company may make a claim requiring that the loss be set off against the amount of any income arising from transactions in respect of which the company is assessed to corporation tax under that Case for the same or any subsequent accounting period; and the company's income in any accounting period from such transactions shall then be treated as reduced by the amount of the loss, or by so much of that amount as cannot be relieved under this section against income of an earlier accounting period.

Case VI losses.

(2) This section shall not apply to a loss incurred in a transaction falling within section 34, 35 or 36.

(3) A claim under this section must be made within six years after the end of the accounting period in which the loss is incurred and must be so made notwithstanding that relief cannot be given in respect of the loss until after the end of that period of six years.

CHAPTER III

LOSS RELIEF: MISCELLANEOUS PROVISIONS

397.—(1) Any loss incurred in a trade of farming or market gardening shall be excluded from section 380 if in each of the prior five years a loss was incurred in carrying on that trade; and where a loss is so excluded any related capital allowance shall also be excluded from that section.

Restriction of relief in case of farming and market gardening.

(2) Any loss incurred in any accounting period by a company in carrying on a trade of farming or market gardening shall be excluded from section 393(2) if a loss, computed without regard to capital allowances, was incurred in carrying on that trade in that accounting period, and in each of the chargeable periods wholly or partly comprised in the prior five years.

(3) Subsections (1) and (2) above shall not restrict relief for any loss or for any capital allowance, if it is shown by the claimant—

(a) that the whole of the farming or market gardening activities in the year next following the prior five years are of such a nature, and carried on in such a way, as would have justified a reasonable expectation of the realisation of profits in the future if they had been undertaken by a competent farmer or market gardener, but

(b) that, if that farmer or market gardener had undertaken those activities at the beginning of the prior period of loss, he could not reasonably have expected the activities to become profitable until after the end of the year next following the prior period of loss.

(4) Subsections (1) and (2) above shall not restrict relief where the carrying on of the trade forms part of, and is ancillary to, a larger trading undertaking.

(5) In this section—

"basis year", in relation to any capital allowance, shall be construed in accordance with section 383(5)(a);

"chargeable period", in relation to a company, means any accounting period, or any basis period ending before its first accounting period, "basis period" having the meaning given by section 72 of the 1968 Act;

"prior five years"—

    (a) in relation to a loss incurred in a year of assessment, means the last five years of assessment before that year, and

    (b) in relation to a loss incurred in a company's accounting period, means the last five years before the beginning of the accounting period;

"prior period of loss" means the prior five years, except that, if losses were incurred in the trade in successive years of assessment or chargeable periods amounting in all to a period longer than five years (and ending when the prior five years end), it means that longer period, and in applying this definition to a chargeable period of a company "losses" means losses computed without regard to capital allowances; and

"farming" and "market gardening" shall be construed in accordance with the definitions of those terms in section 832, but as if those definitions were not restricted to activities in the United Kingdom.

(6) For the purposes of this section, a capital allowance is related to a loss incurred in a trade if it falls to be made in taxing that trade and its basis year is the year of assessment in which the loss was incurred.

(7) In ascertaining for the purposes of this section whether a loss was incurred in any part of the prior five years or earlier, the rules applicable to Case I of Schedule D shall be applied; and in this section "loss computed without regard to capital allowances" means, in relation to a chargeable period of a company, a loss so ascertained, but so that, notwithstanding section 73(2) of the 1968 Act, no account shall be taken of any allowance or charge under any of the Capital Allowances Acts.

(8) Subsections (1) and (2) above shall not restrict relief for any loss or capital allowance if the trade was set up and commenced within the prior five years, and, for the purposes of this subsection, a trade shall be treated as discontinued, and a new trade set up, in any event which under any of the provisions of the Tax Acts is to be treated as equivalent to the permanent discontinuance or setting up of a trade.

(9) For the purposes of subsection (8) above a trade shall not be treated as discontinued if, under section 343(2), it is not to be treated as discontinued for the purpose of capital allowances and charges.

(10) Where at any time there has been a change in the persons engaged in carrying on a trade, this section shall, notwithstanding subsection (8) above, apply to any person who was engaged in carrying on the trade immediately before and immediately after the change as if the trade were the same before and after without any discontinuance, and as if—

(a) a husband and his wife were the same person, and

(b) a husband or his wife were the same person as any company of which either the husband or the wife has control, or of which the two of them have control;

and accordingly relief from income tax or from corporation tax may be restricted under this section by reference to losses some of which are incurred in years of assessment and some, computed without regard to capital allowances, are incurred in a company's chargeable periods.

In this subsection "control" has the same meaning as in Part XI.

398. Where a person sustains a loss on the exercise or disposal of a right to receive any amount, being a right to which section 56(2) applies, in a case where— Transactions in deposits with and without certificates or in debts.

(a) if a profit had arisen from that exercise or disposal, that profit would have been chargeable to tax by virtue of section 56(2), and

(b) he is chargeable to tax under Schedule C or D in respect of interest payable on that amount,

then the amount of that interest shall be included in the amounts against which he may claim to set off the amount of his loss under section 392 or, as the case may be, 396.

399.—(1) If, apart from section 72(1) of the Finance Act 1985 or section 128 above, gains arising to any person in the course of dealing in commodity or financial futures or in qualifying options would constitute, for the purposes of the Tax Acts, profits or gains chargeable to tax under Schedule D otherwise than as the profits of a trade, then any loss arising in the course of that dealing shall not be allowable against profits or gains which are chargeable to tax under Schedule D. Dealings in commodity futures etc: withdrawal of loss relief.
1985 c. 54.

(2) Relief shall not be given to any person under section 380, 381 or 393(2) in respect of a loss sustained in a trade of dealing in commodity futures if—

(a) the loss was sustained in a trade carried on in partnership and that person or one or more of the other partners was a company; and

(b) a scheme has been effected or arrangements have been made (whether by the partnership agreement or otherwise) such that the sole or main benefit that might be expected to accrue to that person from his interest in the partnership was the obtaining of a reduction in tax liability by means of any such relief.

(3) Where relief has been given in a case to which subsection (2) above applies it shall be withdrawn by the making of an assessment under Case VI of Schedule D.

(4) Subsection (2) above does not apply where the scheme was effected or the arrangements were made wholly before 6th April 1976.

(5) In this section "commodity futures", "financial futures" and "qualifying options" have the same meanings as in section 72 of the Finance Act 1985, and the reference in subsection (1) to a loss arising in the course of dealing in commodity or financial futures includes any loss which is regarded as arising in the course of such dealing by virtue of subsection (2A) of that section.

1985 c. 54.

Write-off of government investment.

400.—(1) Where any amount of government investment in a body corporate is written-off on or after 6th April 1988, an amount equal to the amount written-off shall be set off against the body's tax losses as at the end of the accounting period ending last before the write-off date and, to the extent to which that amount exceeds those losses, against the body's tax losses as at the end of the next accounting period and so on.

(2) For the purposes of subsection (1) above a body's tax losses as at the end of an accounting period are—

(a) any losses which under section 393(1) are or, if a claim had been made under that subsection, would be available for relief against its trading income for the next accounting period;

(b) in the case of an investment company, any expenses of management or charges on income which under section 75(3) are available for carry forward to the next accounting period;

(c) any allowances which under section 74(2) of the 1968 Act are available for carry forward to the next accounting period;

(d) any amount paid by way of charges on income so far as it exceeds the company's profit for the period and is not taken into account under 75(3) or 393(9); and

(e) any allowable losses available under 345 so far as not allowed in that or a previous accounting period.

(3) The set off to be made under subsection (1) above for any accounting period shall be made first against the amounts in paragraphs (a) to (d) of subsection (2) above and, so far as it cannot be so made, against the amount in paragraph (e) of that subsection.

(4) For the purposes of subsection (1) above there shall be excluded from a body's tax losses as at the end of the accounting period ending last before the write-off date any amounts in respect of which a claim has been made before the write-off date under section 393(2) or 402 of this Act or section 74(3) of the 1968 Act but the body's tax losses as at the end of any subsequent accounting period shall be determined as if no such claim had been made on or after that date.

(5) Any amount that could be set off under subsection (1) above against a body's tax losses as at the end of an accounting period (or could be so set off if that body then had any such losses) may be set off against the tax losses of any other body corporate which at the end of that period is a member of the same group as the first-mentioned body, or partly against the tax losses of one member of that group and partly against those of the other or any of the others, as may be just and reasonable.

(6) Expenditure shall not be treated for the purposes of section 84 of the 1968 Act or section 42 of the 1979 Act as met by the Crown by reason only of the writing-off of any government investment in the body in question and a sum shall not by reason only of any such writing-off be treated as not having been deductible in computing the profits or gains of that body for the purposes of Case I or II of Schedule D.

(7) For the purposes of this section an amount of government investment in a body corporate is written-off—

    (a) if its liability to repay any money lent to it out of public funds by a Minister of the Crown is extinguished;

    (b) if any of its shares for which a Minister of the Crown has subscribed out of public funds are cancelled; or

    (c) if its commencing capital debt is reduced otherwise than by being paid off or its public dividend capital is reduced otherwise than by being repaid (including, in either case, a reduction to nil);

and the amount written-off and the write-off date are the amount in respect of which the liability is extinguished and the date on which it is extinguished, the amount subscribed for the shares that are cancelled and the date of cancellation or the amount of reduction in the commencing capital debt or public dividend capital and the date of the reduction, as the case may be.

(8) In subsection (7) above "commencing capital debt" means any debt to a Minister of the Crown assumed as such under an enactment and "public dividend capital" means any amount paid by a Minister of the Crown under an enactment in which that amount is so described or under an enactment corresponding to an enactment in which a payment made on similar terms to another body is so described.

(9) This section shall not have effect in relation to any amount written-off if and to the extent to which it is replaced by money lent, or a payment made, out of public funds or by shares subscribed for, whether for money or money's worth, by a Minister of the Crown.

(10) In this section—

"body corporate" means any body corporate which is a company for the purposes of corporation tax;

"group" means a company having one or more 51 per cent. subsidiaries and that or those subsidiaries; and

"Minister of the Crown" includes a Northern Ireland department.

401.—(1) Where a person incurs expenditure for the purposes of a trade, profession or vocation before the time when he begins to carry it on and the expenditure—

    (a) is incurred not more than three years before that time; and

Relief for pre-trading expenditure.

(b) is not allowable as a deduction in computing his profits or gains from the trade, profession or vocation for the purposes of Case I or II of Schedule D but would have been so allowable if incurred after that time,

the expenditure shall be treated for the purposes of corporation tax as incurred on the day on which the trade, profession or vocation is first carried on by him and for the purposes of relief under Chapter I of this Part as if it were the amount of a loss sustained by him in the trade, profession or vocation in the year of assessment in which it is set up and commenced.

(2) A claim for relief under the Income Tax Acts in respect of an amount treated as a loss by virtue of subsection (1) above shall be made separately from any claim for relief under those Acts in respect of any other loss.

CHAPTER IV

GROUP RELIEF

Surrender of relief between members of groups and consortia.

402.—(1) Subject to and in accordance with this Chapter and section 492(8), relief for trading losses and other amounts eligible for relief from corporation tax may, in the cases set out in subsections (2) and (3) below, be surrendered by a company ("the surrendering company") and, on the making of a claim by another company ("the claimant company") may be allowed to the claimant company by way of a relief from corporation tax called "group relief".

(2) Group relief shall be available in a case where the surrendering company and the claimant company are both members of the same group.

A claim made by virtue of this subsection is referred to as a "group claim".

(3) Group relief shall also be available in the case of a surrendering company and a claimant company either where one of them is a member of a consortium and the other is—

(a) a trading company which is owned by the consortium and which is not a 75 per cent. subsidiary of any company; or

(b) a trading company—

(i) which is a 90 per cent. subsidiary of a holding company which is owned by the consortium; and

(ii) which is not a 75 per cent. subsidiary of a company other than the holding company; or

(c) a holding company which is owned by the consortium and which is not a 75 per cent. subsidiary of any company;

or, in accordance with section 406, where one of them is a member of a group of companies and the other is owned by a consortium and another company is a member of both the group and the consortium.

A claim made by virtue of this subsection is referred to as "a consortium claim".

(4) A consortium claim shall not be made if the share in the consortium of the member in the relevant accounting period of the surrendering company (or, where that company is a trading company falling within subsection (3)(b) above, its holding company) is nil or if a profit on a sale of the share capital of the other company or its holding company which the member owns would be treated as a trading receipt of that member.

(5) Subject to the provisions of this Chapter, two or more claimant companies may make claims relating to the same surrendering company, and to the same accounting period of that surrendering company.

(6) A payment for group relief—

(a) shall not be taken into account in computing profits or losses of either company for corporation tax purposes, and

(b) shall not for any of the purposes of the Corporation Tax Acts be regarded as a distribution or a charge on income;

and in this subsection "a payment for group relief" means a payment made by the claimant company to the surrendering company in pursuance of an agreement between them as respects an amount surrendered by way of group relief, being a payment not exceeding that amount.

403.—(1) Subject to the provisions of this Chapter, if in any accounting period the surrendering company has incurred a loss, computed as for the purposes of section 393(2), in carrying on a trade, the amount of the loss may be set off for the purposes of corporation tax against the total profits of the claimant company for its corresponding accounting period.

Losses etc. which may be surrendered by way of group relief.

(2) Subsection (1) above shall not apply to so much of a loss as is excluded from subsection (2) of section 393 by subsection (5) of that section or by section 397.

(3) Subject to the provisions of this Chapter, if for any accounting period any capital allowances fall to be made to the surrendering company which—

(a) are to be given by discharge or repayment of tax, and

(b) are to be available primarily against a specified class of income,

so much of the amount of those allowances (exclusive of any carried forward from an earlier period) as exceeds its income of the relevant class arising in that accounting period (before deduction of any losses of any other period or of any capital allowances) may be set off for purposes of corporation tax against the total profits of the claimant company for its corresponding accounting period.

(4) Subject to the provisions of this Chapter, if for any accounting period the surrendering company (being an investment company) may under subsection (1) of section 75 deduct as expenses of management any amount disbursed for that accounting period, so much of that amount (exclusive of any amount deductible only by virtue of subsection (3) of that section) as exceeds the company's profits of that accounting period

PART X   may be set off for purposes of corporation tax against the total profits of the claimant company (whether an investment company or not) for its corresponding accounting period.

(5) The surrendering company's profits of the period shall be determined for the purposes of subsection (4) above without any deduction under section 75 and without regard to any deduction falling to be made in respect of losses or allowances of any other period.

(6) References in subsections (4) and (5) above to section 75 do not include references to that section as applied by section 76 to companies carrying on life assurance business.

(7) Subject to the provisions of this Chapter and section 494(4), if in any accounting period the surrendering company has paid any amount by way of charges on income, so much of that amount as exceeds its profits of the period may be set off for the purposes of corporation tax against the total profits of the claimant company for its corresponding accounting period.

(8) The surrendering company's profits of the period shall be determined for the purposes of subsection (7) above without regard to any deduction falling to be made in respect of losses or allowances of any other period, or to expenses of management deductible only by virtue of section 75(3).

(9) In applying any of the preceding subsections in the case of a consortium claim—

(a) where the claimant company is a member of a consortium, only a fraction of the loss referred to in subsection (1) above, or of the excess referred to in subsection (3), (4) or (7) above, as the case may be, may be set off under the subsection in question;

(b) where the surrendering company is a member of a consortium that loss or excess shall not be set off under the subsection in question against more than a fraction of the total profits of the claimant company;

and that fraction shall be equal to that member's share in the consortium in the accounting period referred to in section 402(4), subject to any further reduction under section 408(2) and subject also to sections 405(4) and 406(2) and (6).

(10) Where a company owned by a consortium—

(a) has in any relevant accounting period incurred such a loss as is referred to in subsection (1) above, and

(b) has profits (of whatever description) of that accounting period against which that loss could be set off under section 393(2),

the amount of that loss which is available to any member of the consortium on a consortium claim shall be determined on the assumption that the company owned by the consortium has made a claim under section 393(2) requiring the loss to be so set off.

(11) Where the company referred to in subsection (10) above is a group/consortium company, the amount of the loss shall be determined under that subsection before any reduction is made under section 405(1) to (3).

404.—(1) Notwithstanding any other provision of this Chapter, no loss or other amount shall be available for set off by way of group relief in accordance with section 403 if, in the material accounting period of the company which would otherwise be the surrendering company, that company is for the purposes of this section a dual resident investing company.

(2) In this section "the material accounting period" means, according to the kind of group relief which would be appropriate, the accounting period—

(a) in which the loss is incurred; or

(b) for which the capital allowances fall to be made; or

(c) for which the expenses of management are disbursed; or

(d) for which the amount is paid by way of charges on income;

but subsection (1) above does not have effect unless the material accounting period begins on or after 1st April 1987.

(3) In Schedule 17—

(a) Part I has effect where an accounting period of a company in which it is a dual resident investing company begins before and ends on or after 1st April 1987 and references in subsections (1) and (2) above to the material accounting period shall be construed accordingly; and

(b) Part II has effect with respect to the time at which certain interest and other payments are to be treated as paid.

(4) A company is for the purposes of this section a dual resident company in any accounting period in which—

(a) it is resident in the United Kingdom; and

(b) it is also within a charge to tax under the laws of a territory outside the United Kingdom—

(i) because it derives its status as a company from those laws; or

(ii) because its place of management is in that territory; or

(iii) because under those laws it is for any other reason regarded as resident in that territory for the purposes of that charge.

(5) In any accounting period throughout which it is not a trading company, a dual resident company is for the purposes of this section an investing company.

(6) In any accounting period of a dual resident company in which it is a trading company, the company is nevertheless for the purposes of this section an investing company if—

(a) in that period it carries on a trade of such a description that its main function or one of its main functions consists of all or any of the following, namely—

(i) acquiring and holding, directly or indirectly, shares, securities or investments of any other description, including interests in companies (resident outside, as well as in, the United Kingdom) with which the dual resident company is connected, within the terms of section 839;

(ii) making payments which, by virtue of any enactment, are charges on income for the purposes of corporation tax;

(iii) making payments (of interest or other sums) which are similar to those referred to in sub-paragraph (ii) above but which are deductible in computing the profits of the company for the purposes of corporation tax;

(iv) obtaining funds (by borrowing or in any other manner whatsoever) for the purpose of, or otherwise in connection with, any of the activities referred to in sub-paragraphs (i) to (iii) above; or

(b) it does not fall within paragraph (a) above, but in that accounting period it carries on all or any of the activities referred to in sub-paragraphs (i) to (iv) of that paragraph and does so—

(i) to an extent which does not appear to be justified by any trade which it does carry on; or

(ii) for a purpose which does not appear to be appropriate to any such trade; or

(c) in that period—

(i) the amount paid by the company by way of charges on income exceeds its profits of the period, determined as mentioned in section 403(8); and

(ii) those charges include an amount which falls to be treated as a charge on income by virtue of section 78(2) or paragraph 5(2) of Schedule 4; and

(iii) the paying of those charges by the company is its main activity or one of its main activities.

Claims relating to losses etc. of members of both group and consortium.

405.—(1) For the purposes of a consortium claim in respect of the loss or other amount of any relevant accounting period of a group/consortium company, that loss or other amount shall be treated as reduced (or, as the case may be, extinguished) by first deducting therefrom the potential relief attributable to group claims.

(2) Subject to subsection (3) below, in relation to the loss or other amount of a relevant accounting period of a group/consortium company, the potential relief attributable to group claims is the aggregate amount of group relief that would be claimed if every company which, as a member of the same group of companies as the group/consortium company, could make a group claim in respect of that loss or other amount made such a claim for an amount which, when set against the claimant company's total profits for its corresponding accounting period, would equal those profits.

(3) Where for any accounting period another member of the group of companies of which the group/consortium company is a member has a loss or other amount available for relief and one or more group claims is or are in fact made in respect of that loss or other amount, account shall be taken of the relief so claimed before determining (in relation to the loss or other amount of the group/consortium company) the potential relief attributable to group claims under subsection (2) above.

(4) In any case where—

(a) a consortium claim is made by a group/consortium company in respect of a loss or other amount of an accounting period of a member of the consortium, and

(b) the corresponding accounting period of the group/consortium company is a relevant accounting period,

the total profits of the corresponding accounting period of the group/consortium company against a fraction of which that loss or other amount may be set off (in accordance with section 403(9)(b)) shall be treated as reduced (or as the case may be extinguished) by deducting therefrom the potential relief available to the group/consortium company by way of group claims.

(5) Subject to subsection (6) below, in relation to a relevant accounting period of a group/consortium company, the potential relief available to the company by way of group claims is the maximum amount of group relief that could be claimed by the company for that accounting period on group claims relating to the losses or other amounts available for relief of other members of the group of companies of which the group/consortium company is a member.

(6) Where another member of the group of companies of which the group/consortium company is a member in fact makes one or more group claims in respect of losses or other amounts of other members of the group, account shall be taken of the relief already claimed by that company in determining the potential relief available to the group/consortium company by way of group claims under subsection (5) above.

406.—(1) In this section—

(a) "link company" means a company which is a member of a consortium and is also a member of a group of companies; and

(b) "consortium company", in relation to a link company, means a company owned by the consortium of which the link company is a member; and

(c) "group member", in relation to a link company, means a company which is a member of the group of which the link company is also a member but is not itself a member of the consortium of which the link company is a member.

(2) Subject to subsections (3) and (4) below, where the link company could (disregarding any deficiency of profits) make a consortium claim in respect of the loss or other amount eligible for relief of a relevant accounting period of a consortium company, a group member may make any consortium claim which could be made by the link company; and the

PART X

fraction which is appropriate under section 403(9) where a group member is the claimant company shall be the same as that which would be appropriate if the link company were the claimant company.

(3) A group member may not, by virtue of subsection (2) above, make a consortium claim in respect of the loss or other amount of any accounting period of a consortium company unless the claimant company was a member of the group concerned throughout the whole of the accounting period or, as the case may be, each accounting period of the link company which, if that company were making the claim, would be a corresponding accounting period in relation to that accounting period of the consortium company.

(4) The maximum amount of relief which, in the aggregate, may be claimed by group members and the link company by consortium claims relating to the loss or other amount of a relevant accounting period of a consortium company shall not exceed the relief which could have been claimed by the link company (disregarding any deficiency of profits) if subsections (2) and (3) above had not been enacted.

(5) Subject to subsections (6) to (8) below, where a group member has for a relevant accounting period a loss or other amount available for relief, a consortium company may make any claim in respect of that loss or other amount which it could make if the group member were a member of the consortium at all times when the link company was such a member, but not at any other time.

(6) The fraction which is appropriate under section 403(9) in relation to a consortium claim made by virtue of subsection (5) above shall be the same as that which would be appropriate if the link company were the surrendering company, except that the accounting period in respect of which the member's share in the consortium is to be ascertained shall be that of the group member which is in fact the surrendering company.

(7) A consortium company may not, by virtue of subsection (5) above, make a consortium claim in respect of the loss or other amount of any accounting period of a group member unless the group member was a member of the group in question throughout the whole of that accounting period.

(8) For any accounting period of a consortium company ("the claimant company's accounting period") the maximum amount of relief which, in the aggregate, may be claimed by that company by consortium claims relating to the losses or other amounts of accounting periods of the link company and group members shall not exceed that fraction of the total profits of the claimant company's accounting period which would be brought into account under section 403(9)(b) on a consortium claim in respect of which—

(a) the link company was the surrendering company; and

(b) the link company's accounting period was the same as the claimant company's accounting period.

Relationship between group relief and other relief.

407.—(1) Group relief for an accounting period shall be allowed as a deduction against the claimant company's total profits for the period—

(a) before reduction by any relief derived from a subsequent accounting period, but

(b) as reduced by any other relief from tax (including relief in respect of charges on income under section 338(1)) determined on the assumption that the company makes all relevant claims under section 393(2) of this Act and section 74(3) of the 1968 Act (set-off of capital allowances against total profits).

(2) For the purposes of this section "relief derived from a subsequent accounting period" means—

(a) relief under section 393(2) or 394 in respect of a loss incurred in an accounting period after the accounting period the profits of which are being computed; and

(b) relief under section 74(3) of the 1968 Act in respect of capital allowances falling to be made for an accounting period after the accounting period the profits of which are being computed.

(3) The reductions to be made in total profits of an accounting period against which any relief derived from a subsequent accounting period is to be set off shall include any group relief for that first-mentioned accounting period.

408.—(1) For the purposes of group relief an accounting period of the claimant company which falls wholly or partly within an accounting period of the surrendering company corresponds to that accounting period. Corresponding accounting periods.

(2) If an accounting period of the surrendering company and a corresponding accounting period of the claimant company do not coincide—

(a) the amount which may be set off against the total profits of the claimant company for the corresponding accounting period shall be reduced by applying the fraction—

$$\frac{A}{B}$$

(if that fraction is less than unity); and

(b) the total profits of the claimant company for the corresponding accounting period shall be reduced by applying the fraction—

$$\frac{A}{C}$$

(if that fraction is less than unity);

where—

A is the length of the period common to the two accounting periods;

B is the length of the accounting period of the surrendering company;

C is the length of the corresponding accounting period of the claimant company.

409.—(1) Subject to the following provisions of this section, group relief shall be given if, and only if, the surrendering company and the claimant company are members of the same group, or fulfil the conditions for relief for a consortium, throughout the whole of the surrendering company's accounting period to which the claim relates, and throughout the whole of the corresponding accounting period of the claimant company.

(2) Where on any occasion two companies become or cease to be members of the same group, then, for the purposes specified in subsection (3) below, it shall be assumed as respects each company that—

(a) on that occasion (unless a true accounting period of the company begins or ends then) an accounting period of the company ends and a new one begins, the new accounting period to end with the end of the true accounting period (unless before then there is a further break under this subsection); and

(b) the losses or other amounts of the true accounting period are apportioned to the component accounting periods; and

(c) the amount of total profits for the true accounting period of the company against which group relief may be allowed in accordance with section 407(1) is also apportioned to the component accounting periods;

and an apportionment under this subsection shall be on a time basis according to the respective lengths of the component accounting periods except that, if it appears that that method would work unreasonably or unjustly, such other method shall be used as appears just and reasonable.

(3) Where the one company is the surrendering company and the other company is the claimant company—

(a) references in section 403 to accounting periods, to profits, and to losses, allowances, expenses of management or charges on income of the surrendering company shall be construed in accordance with subsection (2) above;

(b) references in subsection (1) above and section 408 to accounting periods shall be so construed (so that if the two companies are members of the same group in the surrendering company's accounting period, they must under that section also be members of the same group in any corresponding accounting period of the claimant company);

(c) references in section 408 to profits, and amounts to be set off against the profits, shall be so construed (so that an amount apportioned under subsection (2) above to a component accounting period may fall to be reduced under subsection (2) of that section).

(4) Subsections (2) and (3) above shall apply with the necessary modifications where a company begins or ceases to fulfil the conditions for relief for a consortium, either as a surrendering company or as a claimant company, as it applies where two companies become or cease to be members of the same group except that, in a case where—

(a) the surrendering company is owned by a consortium and two or more members of the consortium claim relief in respect of losses or other amounts of the surrendering company, or

(b) the claimant company is owned by a consortium and claims relief in respect of losses or other amounts of two or more members of the consortium,

the basis of apportionment which is adopted under subsection (2) above in relation to the losses or other amounts or, as the case may be, the total profits of the true accounting period of the company owned by the consortium shall be the same on each of the claims.

(5) In subsection (6) below—

"the primary claim" means a consortium claim made in respect of the loss or other amount of a relevant accounting period of a company owned by a consortium;

"the principal surrendering company" means that company; and

"the principal accounting period" means that accounting period.

(6) In any case where—

(a) the company making the primary claim or, if that claim is made by virtue of section 406(2), the company which is the link company for the purposes of that subsection was not a member of the consortium throughout the whole of the principal accounting period; and

(b) on or after the date on which the primary claim is made, a consortium claim is made which—

(i) is in respect of the loss or other amount of an accounting period of a surrendering company (being a company owned by the consortium referred to in paragraph (a) above, other than the principal surrendering company); and

(ii) is made by the company making the primary claim or, in a case where it or the primary claim is made by virtue of section 406(2), is made by any member of the group in question other than the company making the primary claim;

and the accounting period to which the claim relates falls, in whole or in part, within the principal accounting period; and

(c) at any time during the principal accounting period the surrendering company is a member of the same group of companies as the principal surrendering company;

no relief shall be allowed on the primary claim, or, as the case may be, any relief which was so allowed shall be withdrawn.

(7) In any case where—

(a) a company ("the principal claimant company") owned by a consortium makes a consortium claim ("the principal claim") in respect of the loss or other amount of an accounting period of a member of the consortium or, if the principal claim is made by

N

virtue of section 406(5), of a company which, in relation to that member of the consortium, is a group member, within the meaning of that section; and

(b) the member of the consortium concerned (whether as the surrendering company or the link company, within the meaning of section 406) was not a member of the consortium throughout the whole of that accounting period; and

(c) on or after the date on which the principal claim is made, a consortium claim is made—

(i) by a company, other than the principal claimant company, which is owned by the consortium and which is a member of the same group of companies as the principal claimant company; and

(ii) which relates to the loss or other amount of an accounting period of the consortium member referred to in paragraph (b) above or of a company which in relation to that consortium member is a group member, within the meaning of section 406;

and that accounting period falls, in whole or in part, in the accounting period referred to in paragraph (a) above;

no relief shall be allowed on the principal claim or, as the case may be, any relief which was so allowed shall be withdrawn.

(8) Where any relief which has been allowed is withdrawn by virtue of subsection (6) or (7) above, all such adjustments shall be made, whether by way of assessment or otherwise, as may be necessary in consequence of that withdrawal.

Arrangements for transfer of company to another group or consortium.

410.—(1) If, apart from this section, two companies ("the first company" and "the second company") would be treated as members of the same group of companies and—

(a) in an accounting period one of the two companies has trading losses or other amounts eligible for relief from corporation tax which it would, apart from this section, be entitled to surrender by way of group relief; and

(b) arrangements are in existence by virtue of which, at some time during or after the expiry of that accounting period—

(i) the first company or any successor of it could cease to be a member of the same group of companies as the second company and could become a member of the same group of companies as a third company; or

(ii) any person has or could obtain, or any persons together have or could obtain, control of the first company but not of the second; or

(iii) a third company could begin to carry on the whole or any part of a trade which, at any time in that accounting period, is carried on by the first company and could do so either as a successor of the first company or as a successor of another company which is not a third company but which, at some time during or after the expiry of that accounting period, has begun to carry on the whole or any part of that trade;

then, for the purposes of this Chapter, the first company shall be treated as not being a member of the same group of companies as the second company.

(2) If a trading company is owned by a consortium or is a 90 per cent. subsidiary of a holding company which is owned by a consortium and—

(a) in any accounting period the trading company or a member of the consortium has trading losses or other amounts eligible for relief from corporation tax which it would, apart from this section, be entitled to surrender by way of group relief; and

(b) arrangements are in existence by virtue of which—

(i) the trading company or any successor of it could, at some time during or after the expiry of that accounting period, become a 75 per cent. subsidiary of a third company; or

(ii) any person who owns, or any persons who together own, less than 50 per cent. of the ordinary share capital of the trading company has or together have, or could at some time during or after the expiry of that accounting period obtain, control of the trading company; or

(iii) any person, other than a holding company of which the trading company is a 90 per cent. subsidiary, either alone or together with connected persons, holds or could obtain, or controls or could control the exercise of not less than 75 per cent. of the votes which may be cast on a poll taken at a general meeting of that trading company in that accounting period or in any subsequent accounting period; or

(iv) a third company could begin to carry on, at some time during or after the expiry of that accounting period, the whole or any part of a trade which, at any time in that accounting period, is carried on by the trading company and could do so either as a successor of the trading company or as a successor of another company which is not a third company but which, at some time during or after the expiry of that accounting period, has begun to carry on the whole or any part of that trade;

then, for the purposes of this Chapter, the trading company shall be treated as though it did not (as the surrendering company or the claimant company) fall within section 402(3).

(3) In any case where a trading company is a 90 per cent. subsidiary of a holding company which is owned by a consortium, any reference in subsection (2) above to the trading company, other than a reference in paragraph (b)(iv), shall be construed as including a reference to the holding company.

(4) In this section "third company" means a company which, apart from any provision made by or under any such arrangements as are specified in paragraph (b) of either subsection (1) or subsection (2) above,

PART X   is not a member of the same group of companies as the first company or, as the case may be, the trading company or the holding company to which subsection (2) above applies.

(5) In subsections (1) and (2) above—

"arrangements" means arrangements of any kind whether in writing or not;

"connected persons" shall be construed in accordance with section 839; and

"control" has the meaning assigned by section 840.

(6) For the purposes of subsections (1) and (2) above a company is the successor of another if it carries on a trade which, in whole or in part, the other company has ceased to carry on and the circumstances are such that—

(a) section 343 applies in relation to the two companies as the predecessor and the successor within the meaning of that section; or

(b) the two companies are connected with each other within the meaning of section 839.

(7) Where by virtue of any enactment a Minister of the Crown or Northern Ireland department has power to give directions to a statutory body as to the disposal of assets belonging to, or to a subsidiary of, that body, the existence of that power shall not be regarded as constituting or as having at any time constituted an arrangement within the meaning of this section.

Exclusion of double allowances.

411.—(1) Relief shall not be given more than once in respect of the same amount, whether by giving group relief and by giving some other relief (in any accounting period) to the surrendering company, or by giving group relief more than once.

(2) In accordance with subsection (1) above, two or more claimant companies cannot, in respect of any one loss or other amount for which group relief may be given, and whatever their accounting periods corresponding to that of the surrendering company, obtain in all more relief than could be obtained by a single claimant company whose corresponding accounting period coincided with the accounting period of the surrendering company.

(3) Subject to subsections (4) and (5) below, if claims for group relief relating to the same accounting period of the same surrendering company are made by two or more claimant companies which themselves are members of a group of companies, and—

(a) all the claims so made are admissible only by virtue of subsection (2) and (3) of section 409, and

(b) there is a part of the surrendering company's accounting period during which none of those claimant companies is a member of the same group as the surrendering company, those claimant companies shall not obtain in all more relief than could be obtained by a single claimant company which was not a member of the same group as the surrendering company during that part of the surrendering company's accounting period (but was a member during the remainder of that accounting period).

(4) If companies which are members of different groups make claims falling within subsection (3) above, that subsection shall apply separately in relation to the companies in each group.

(5) For the purposes of subsection (3) above, there shall be left out of account a claim made by a company if—

(a) the claimant company joins or leaves a group of companies at the same time as the surrendering company; and

(b) both before and after that time either the claimant company is a 75 per cent. subsidiary of the surrendering company or the surrendering company is a 75 per cent. subsidiary of the claimant company or both companies are 75 per cent. subsidiaries of another company.

(6) Subject to subsection (7) below, if claims as respects two or more surrendering companies which themselves are members of a group of companies are made by a claimant company for group relief to be set off against its total profits for any one accounting period, and—

(a) all the claims so made are admissible only by virtue of subsections (2) and (3) of section 409, and

(b) there is a part of the claimant company's accounting period during which none of the surrendering companies by reference to which the claims are made is a member of the same group as the claimant company,

the claimant company shall not obtain in all more relief to be set off against its profits for the accounting period than it could obtain on a claim as respects a single surrendering company (with unlimited losses and other amounts eligible for relief) which was not a member of the same group as the claimant company during that part of the claimant company's accounting period (but was a member during the remainder of that accounting period).

(7) If claims falling within subsection (6) above are made as respects surrendering companies which are members of different groups, that subsection shall apply separately in relation to claims as respects the surrendering companies in each group.

(8) For the purposes of subsection (6) above there shall be left out of account a claim made as respects a surrendering company if—

(a) the surrendering company joins or leaves the group of companies concerned at the same time as the claimant company; and

(b) both before and after that time either the surrendering company is a 75 per cent. subsidiary of the claimant company or the claimant company is a 75 per cent. subsidiary of the surrendering company or both companies are 75 per cent. subsidiaries of another company.

(9) References in subsections (3) to (6) above to claims for group relief do not include references to consortium claims.

(10) Without prejudice to the provisions of section 87(3) of the 1968 Act, any reference in Part I of that Act to an allowance made includes a reference to an allowance which would be made but for the granting of group relief, or but for that and but for an insufficiency of profits or other income against which to make it.

Claims and adjustments.   **412.**—(1) A claim for group relief—

(a) need not be for the full amount available,

(b) shall require the consent of the surrendering company notified to the inspector in such form as the Board may require,

(c) must be made within two years from the end of the surrendering company's accounting period to which the claim relates.

(2) A consortium claim shall require the consent of each member of the consortium, notified to the inspector in such form as the Board may require, in addition to the consent of the surrendering company.

(3) If the inspector discovers that any group relief which has been given is or has become excessive he may make an assessment to corporation tax under Case VI of Schedule D in the amount which ought in his opinion to be charged.

(4) Subsection (3) above is without prejudice to the making of an assessment under section 29(3)(c) of the Management Act and to the making of all such adjustments by way of discharge or repayment of tax or otherwise as may be required where a claimant company has obtained too much relief, or a surrendering company has forgone relief in respect of a corresponding amount.

Interpretation of Chapter IV.   **413.**—(1) The following provisions of this section have effect for the interpretation of this Chapter.

(2) In this Chapter—

"claimant company" has the meaning given by section 402(1);

"consortium claim" means a claim for group relief made by virtue of section 402(3);

"group claim" means a claim for group relief made by virtue of section 402(2);

"group/consortium company" means a company which is both a member of a group of companies and a company owned by a consortium;

"group relief" has the meaning given by section 402(1);

"relevant accounting period" means an accounting period beginning after 31st July 1985; and

"surrendering company" has the meaning given by section 402(1).

(3) For the purposes of this Chapter—

(a) two companies shall be deemed to be members of a group of companies if one is the 75 per cent. subsidiary of the other or both are 75 per cent. subsidiaries of a third company;

(b) "holding company" means a company the business of which consists wholly or mainly in the holding of shares or securities of companies which are its 90 per cent. subsidiaries and which are trading companies; and

(c) "trading company" means a company the business of which consists wholly or mainly in the carrying on of a trade or trades.

(4) In applying for the purposes of this Chapter the definition of "75 per cent. subsidiary" in section 838, any share capital of a registered industrial and provident society shall be treated as ordinary share capital.

(5) References in this Chapter to a company apply only to bodies corporate resident in the United Kingdom; and in determining for the purposes of this Chapter whether one company is a 75 per cent. subsidiary of another, the other company shall be treated as not being the owner—

(a) of any share capital which it owns directly in a body corporate if a profit on a sale of the shares would be treated as a trading receipt of its trade; or

(b) of any share capital which it owns indirectly, and which is owned directly by a body corporate for which a profit on a sale of the shares would be a trading receipt; or

(c) of any share capital which it owns directly or indirectly in a body corporate not resident in the United Kingdom.

(6) References to a company being owned by a consortium shall be construed in accordance with paragraph (a) below except for the purposes of the definition of "group/consortium company" in subsection (2) above and of sections 403(10), 406(1)(b) and 409(5), (6) and (7), and for those purposes shall be construed in accordance with paragraph (b) below—

(a) a company is owned by a consortium if three-quarters or more of the ordinary share capital of the company is beneficially owned between them by companies of which none beneficially owns less than one-twentieth of that capital;

(b) a company is owned by a consortium if—

(i) it is either such a trading company as is referred to in paragraph (a) or (b) of subsection (3) of section 402 or such a holding company as is referred to in paragraph (c) of that subsection, and

(ii) three-quarters or more of the ordinary share capital of the company or, in the case of a company within section 402(3)(b), of its holding company is beneficially owned between them by companies of which none beneficially owns less than one-twentieth of that capital;

and the companies which so own three-quarters or more of that ordinary share capital are in this Chapter called the members of the consortium.

(7) Notwithstanding that at any time a company ("the subsidiary company") is a 75 per cent. subsidiary or a 90 per cent. subsidiary of another company ("the parent company") it shall not be treated at that time as such a subsidiary for the purposes of this Chapter unless, additionally at that time—

(a) the parent company is beneficially entitled to not less than 75 per cent. or, as the case may be, 90 per cent. of any profits available for distribution to equity holders of the subsidiary company; and

(b) the parent company would be beneficially entitled to not less than 75 per cent. or, as the case may be, 90 per cent. of any assets of the subsidiary company available for distribution to its equity holders on a winding-up.

(8) Subject to subsection (9) below, for the purposes of this Chapter, a member's share in a consortium, in relation to an accounting period of the surrendering company, shall be whichever is the lowest in that period of the following percentages, namely—

(a) the percentage of the ordinary share capital of the surrendering or claimant company which is beneficially owned by that member;

(b) the percentage to which that member is beneficially entitled of any profits available for distribution to equity holders of the surrendering or claimant company; and

(c) the percentage to which that member would be beneficially entitled of any assets of the surrendering or claimant company available for distribution to its equity holders on a winding-up;

and if any of those percentages have fluctuated in that accounting period, the average percentage over the period shall be taken for the purposes of this subsection.

(9) In any case where the surrendering or claimant company is a subsidiary of a holding company which is owned by a consortium, for references in subsection (8) above to the surrendering or claimant company there shall be substituted references to the holding company.

(10) Schedule 18 shall have effect for supplementing this section.

PART XI

CLOSE COMPANIES

CHAPTER I

INTERPRETATIVE PROVISIONS

414.—(1) For the purposes of the Tax Acts, a "close company" is one   Close companies.
which is under the control of five or fewer participators, or of
participators who are directors, except that the expression does not
apply—

(a) to a company not resident in the United Kingdom;

(b) to a registered industrial and provident society within the
meaning of section 486(12) or to a building society;

(c) to a company controlled by or on behalf of the Crown, and not
otherwise a close company; or

(d) to a company falling within section 415 or subsection (5) below.

(2) Subject to section 415 and subsection (5) below, a company
resident in the United Kingdom (but not falling within subsection (1)(b)
above) is also a close company if—

(a) on the assumption that it is so, or

(b) on the assumption that it and any other such company or
companies are so,

more than half of any amount falling to be apportioned under section 423
in the case of the company (including any sum which has been
apportioned to it, or could on either of those assumptions be apportioned
to it, under that section) could be apportioned among five or fewer
participators, or among participators who are directors.

(3) In ascertaining under subsection (2) above whether any amount
could be apportioned among five or fewer participators or among
participators who are directors, account shall, in cases where an original
apportionment and any sub-apportionment are involved, be taken only
of persons among whom that amount could finally be apportioned as the
result of the whole process of original apportionment and sub-
apportionment and those persons shall be treated as participators or
directors if they are participators or directors of any company in the case
of which either an original apportionment or any sub-apportionment
could be made.

(4) For the purposes of this section—

(a) a company is to be treated as controlled by or on behalf of the
Crown if, but only if, it is under the control of the Crown or of
persons acting on behalf of the Crown, independently of any
other person, and

(b) where a company is so controlled, it shall not be treated as being
otherwise a close company unless it can be treated as a close
company as being under the control of persons acting
independently of the Crown.

(5) A company is not to be treated as a close company—

   (a) if—

> (i) it is controlled by a company which is not a close company, or by two or more companies none of which is a close company; and

> (ii) it cannot be treated as a close company except by taking as one of the five or fewer participators requisite for its being so treated a company which is not a close company;

   (b) if it cannot be treated as a close company except by virtue of paragraph (c) of section 416(2) and it would not be a close company if the reference in that paragraph to participators did not include loan creditors who are companies other than close companies.

(6) References in subsection (5) above to a close company shall be treated as applying to any company which, if resident in the United Kingdom, would be a close company.

(7) If shares in any company ("the first company") are held on trust for an exempt approved scheme as defined in section 592, then, unless the scheme is established wholly or mainly for the benefit of persons who are, or are dependants of, directors or employees or past directors or employees of—

   (a) the first company; or

   (b) an associated company of the first company; or

   (c) a company which is under the control of any director or associate of a director of the first company or of two or more persons each of whom is such a director or associate; or

   (d) a close company;

the persons holding the shares shall, for the purposes of subsection (5) above, be deemed to be the beneficial owners of the shares and, in that capacity, to be a company which is not a close company.

Certain quoted
companies not to
be close
companies.

415.—(1) Subject to the following provisions of this section, a company is not to be treated as being at any time a close company if—

   (a) shares in the company carrying not less than 35 per cent. of the voting power in the company (and not being shares entitled to a fixed rate of dividend, whether with or without a further right to participate in profits) have been allotted unconditionally to, or acquired unconditionally by, and are at that time beneficially held by, the public, and

   (b) any such shares have within the preceding 12 months been the subject of dealings on a recognised stock exchange, and the shares have within those 12 months been quoted in the official list of a recognised stock exchange.

(2) Subsection (1) above shall not apply to a company at any time when the total percentage of the voting power in the company possessed by all of the company's principal members exceeds 85 per cent.

(3) For the purposes of subsection (1) above shares in a company shall be deemed to be beneficially held by the public if, and only if, they—

    (a) fall within subsection (4) below, and

    (b) are not within the exceptions in subsection (5) below,

and a corresponding construction shall be given to the reference to shares which have been allotted unconditionally to, or acquired unconditionally by, the public.

(4) Shares shall fall within this subsection (as being beneficially held by the public)—

    (a) if beneficially held by a company resident in the United Kingdom which is not a close company, or by a company not so resident which would not be a close company if it were so resident, or

    (b) if held on trust for an exempt approved scheme as defined in section 592, or

    (c) if they are not comprised in a principal member's holding.

(5) Shares shall not be deemed to be held by the public if they are held—

    (a) by any director or associate of a director of the company, or

    (b) by any company which is under the control of any such director or associate, or of two or more persons each of whom is such a director or associate, or

    (c) by any associated company of the company, or

    (d) as part of any fund the capital or income of which is applicable or applied wholly or mainly for the benefit of, or of the dependants of, the employees or directors, or past employees or directors, of the company, or of any company within paragraph (b) or (c) above.

References in this subsection to shares held by any person include references to any shares the rights or powers attached to which could, for the purposes of section 416, be attributed to that person under subsection (5) of that section.

(6) For the purposes of this section—

    (a) a person is a principal member of a company if he possesses a percentage of the voting power in the company of more than 5 per cent. and, where there are more than five such persons, if he is one of the five persons who possess the greatest percentages or if, because two or more persons possess equal percentages of the voting power in the company, there are no such five persons, he is one of the six or more persons (so as to include those two or more who possess equal percentages) who possess the greatest percentages, and

    (b) a principal member's holding consists of the shares which carry the voting power possessed by him.

(7) In arriving at the voting power which a person possesses, there shall be attributed to him any voting power which, for the purposes of section 416, would be attributed to him under subsection (5) or (6) of that section.

(8) In this section "shares" include stock.

416.—(1) For the purposes of this Part, except paragraphs 2 and 9(1)(a), (2)(a) and (3)(a) of Schedule 19, a company is to be treated as another's "associated company" at a given time if, at that time or at any other time within one year previously, one of the two has control of the other, or both are under the control of the same person or persons.

(2) For the purposes of this Part, a person shall be taken to have control of a company if he exercises, or is able to exercise or is entitled to acquire, direct or indirect control over the company's affairs, and in particular, but without prejudice to the generality of the preceding words, if he possesses or is entitled to acquire—

    (a) the greater part of the share capital or issued share capital of the company or of the voting power in the company; or

    (b) such part of the issued share capital of the company as would, if the whole of the income of the company were in fact distributed among the participators (without regard to any rights which he or any other person has as a loan creditor), entitle him to receive the greater part of the amount so distributed; or

    (c) such rights as would, in the event of the winding-up of the company or in any other circumstances, entitle him to receive the greater part of the assets of the company which would then be available for distribution among the participators.

(3) Where two or more persons together satisfy any of the conditions of subsection (2) above, they shall be taken to have control of the company.

(4) For the purposes of subsection (2) above a person shall be treated as entitled to acquire anything which he is entitled to acquire at a future date, or will at a future date be entitled to acquire.

(5) For the purposes of subsections (2) and (3) above, there shall be attributed to any person any rights or powers of a nominee for him, that is to say, any rights or powers which another person possesses on his behalf or may be required to exercise on his direction or behalf.

(6) For the purposes of subsections (2) and (3) above, there may also be attributed to any person all the rights and powers of any company of which he has, or he and associates of his have, control or any two or more such companies, or of any associate of his or of any two or more associates of his, including those attributed to a company or associate under subsection (5) above, but not those attributed to an associate under this subsection; and such attributions shall be made under this subsection as will result in the company being treated as under the control of five or fewer participators if it can be so treated.

417.—(1) For the purposes of this Part, a "participator" is, in relation to any company, a person having a share or interest in the capital or income of the company, and, without prejudice to the generality of the preceding words, includes—

(a) any person who possesses, or is entitled to acquire, share capital or voting rights in the company;

(b) any loan creditor of the company;

(c) any person who possesses, or is entitled to acquire, a right to receive or participate in distributions of the company (construing "distributions" without regard to section 418) or any amounts payable by the company (in cash or in kind) to loan creditors by way of premium on redemption; and

(d) any person who is entitled to secure that income or assets (whether present or future) of the company will be applied directly or indirectly for his benefit.

In this subsection references to being entitled to do anything apply where a person is presently entitled to do it at a future date, or will at a future date be entitled to do it.

(2) The provisions of subsection (1) above are without prejudice to any particular provision of this Part requiring a participator in one company to be treated as being also a participator in another company.

(3) For the purposes of this Part "associate" means, in relation to a participator—

(a) any relative or partner of the participator;

(b) the trustee or trustees of any settlement in relation to which the participator is, or any relative of his (living or dead) is or was, a settlor ("settlement" and "settlor" having here the same meaning as in section 681(4)); and

(c) where the participator is interested in any shares or obligations of the company which are subject to any trust, or are part of the estate of a deceased person—

(i) the trustee or trustees of the settlement concerned or, as the case may be, the personal representatives of the deceased; and

(ii) if the participator is a company, any other company interested in those shares or obligations;

and has a corresponding meaning in relation to a person other than a participator.

(4) In subsection (3) above "relative" means husband or wife, parent or remoter forebear, child or remoter issue, or brother or sister.

(5) For the purposes of this Part "director" includes any person occupying the position of director by whatever name called, any person in accordance with whose directions or instructions the directors are accustomed to act, and any person who—

(a) is a manager of the company or otherwise concerned in the management of the company's trade or business, and

(b) is, either on his own or with one or more associates, the beneficial owner of, or able, directly or through the medium of other companies or by any other indirect means, to control 20 per cent. or over of the ordinary share capital of the company.

(6) In subsection (5)(b) above the expression "either on his own or with one or more associates" requires a person to be treated as owning or, as the case may be, controlling what any associate owns or controls, even if he does not own or control share capital on his own.

(7) Subject to subsection (9) below, for the purposes of this Part "loan creditor", in relation to a company, means a creditor in respect of any debt incurred by the company—

(a) for any money borrowed or capital assets acquired by the company; or

(b) for any right to receive income created in favour of the company; or

(c) for consideration the value of which to the company was (at the time when the debt was incurred) substantially less than the amount of the debt (including any premium thereon);

or in respect of any redeemable loan capital issued by the company.

(8) Subject to subsection (9) below, a person who is not the creditor in respect of any debt or loan capital to which subsection (7) above applies but nevertheless has a beneficial interest therein shall, to the extent of that interest, be treated for the purposes of this Part as a loan creditor in respect of that debt or loan capital.

(9) A person carrying on a business of banking shall not be deemed to be a loan creditor in respect of any loan capital or debt issued or incurred by the company for money lent by him to the company in the ordinary course of that business.

Additional matters to be treated as distributions

"Distribution" to include certain expenses of close companies.

418.—(1) Subject to such exceptions as are mentioned in section 209(1), in the Corporation Tax Acts "distribution", in relation to a close company, includes, unless otherwise stated, any such amount as is required to be treated as a distribution by subsection (2) below.

(2) Subject to subsection (3) below, where a close company incurs expense in or in connection with the provision for any participator of living or other accommodation, of entertainment, of domestic or other services, or of other benefits or facilities of whatever nature, the company shall be treated as making a distribution to him of an amount equal to so much of that expense as is not made good to the company by the participator.

(3) Subsection (2) above shall not apply to expense incurred in or in connection with the provision—

(a) for a person employed in director's or higher-paid employment (within the meaning of section 167) of such benefits as are mentioned in any of sections 154 to 165; or

(b) of living accommodation for any person if the accommodation is (within the meaning of section 145) provided by reason of his employment; or

(c) for the spouse, children or dependants of a person employed by the company of any pension, annuity, lump sum, gratuity or other like benefit to be given on that person's death or retirement.

(4) The amount of the expense to be taken into account under subsection (2) above as a distribution shall be the same as would under Chapter II of Part V be the cash equivalent of the resultant benefit to the participator.

(5) Subsection (2) above shall not apply if the company and the participator are both resident in the United Kingdom and—

(a) one is a subsidiary of the other or both are subsidiaries of a third company also so resident, and

(b) the benefit to the participator arises on or in connection with a transfer of assets or liabilities by the company to him, or to the company by him.

(6) The question whether one body corporate is a subsidiary of another for the purposes of subsection (5) above shall be determined as a question whether it is a 51 per cent. subsidiary of that other, except that that other shall be treated as not being the owner—

(a) of any share capital which it owns directly in a body corporate if a profit on a sale of the shares would be treated as a trading receipt of its trade; or

(b) of any share capital which it owns indirectly, and which is owned directly by a body corporate for which a profit on a sale of the shares would be a trading receipt; or

(c) of any share capital which it owns directly or indirectly in a body corporate not resident in the United Kingdom.

(7) Where each of two or more close companies makes a payment to a person who is not a participator in that company, but is a participator in another of those companies, and the companies are acting in concert or under arrangements made by any person, then each of those companies and any participator in it shall be treated as if the payment made to him had been made by that company.

This subsection shall apply, with any necessary adaptations, in relation to the giving of any consideration, and to the provision of any facilities, as it applies in relation to the making of a payment.

(8) For the purposes of this section any reference to a participator includes an associate of a participator, and any participator in a company which controls another company shall be treated as being also a participator in that other company.

CHAPTER II

CHARGES TO TAX IN CONNECTION WITH LOANS

419.—(1) Subject to the following provisions of this section and section 420, where a close company, otherwise than in the ordinary course of a business carried on by it which includes the lending of money, makes any

Loans to participators etc.

Part XI   loan or advances any money to an individual who is a participator in the company or an associate of a participator, there shall be assessed on and recoverable from the company, as if it were an amount of corporation tax chargeable on the company for the accounting period in which the loan or advance is made, an amount equal to such proportion of the amount of the loan or advance as corresponds to the rate of advance corporation tax in force for the financial year in which the loan or advance is made.

In relation to a loan or advance made in an accounting period ending after the day, not being earlier than 31st March 1992, appointed by order by the Treasury for the purpose of this provision, this subsection shall have effect with the substitution for "assessed on and recoverable" of "due".

(2) For the purposes of this section the cases in which a close company is to be regarded as making a loan to any person include a case where—

(a) that person incurs a debt to the close company; or

(b) a debt due from that person to a third party is assigned to the close company;

and then the close company shall be regarded as making a loan of an amount equal to the debt.

(3) Tax shall be assessable by virtue of this section whether or not the whole or any part of the loan or advance in question has been repaid at the time of the assessment; and tax assessed by virtue of this section shall, subject to any appeal against the assessment, be due within 14 days after the issue of the notice of assessment.

The preceding provisions of this subsection shall not apply in relation to a loan or advance made in an accounting period ending after the day, not being earlier than 31st March 1992, appointed by order by the Treasury for the purpose of this provision, but in relation to any such loan or advance tax due by virtue of this section shall be due and payable within 14 days after the end of the accounting period in which the loan or advance was made.

(4) Where a close company has made a loan or advance which gave rise to a charge to tax on the company under subsection (1) above and the loan or advance or any part of it is repaid to the company, relief shall be given from that tax, or a proportionate part of it, by discharge or repayment.

Relief under this subsection shall be given on a claim, which must be made within six years from the end of the financial year in which the repayment is made.

(5) Where, under arrangements made by any person otherwise than in the ordinary course of a business carried on by him—

(a) a close company makes a loan or advance which, apart from this subsection, does not give rise to any charge on the company under subsection (1) above, and

(b) some person other than the close company makes a payment or transfers property to, or releases or satisfies (in whole or in part) a liability of, an individual who is a participator in the company or an associate of a participator, then, unless in respect of the matter referred to in paragraph (b) above there falls to be included in the total income of the participator or associate an amount not less than the loan or advance, this section shall apply as if the loan or advance had been made to him.

(6) In subsections (1) and (5)(b) above the references to an individual shall apply also to a company receiving the loan or advance in a fiduciary or representative capacity, and to a company not resident in the United Kingdom.

(7) For the purposes of this section any participator in a company which controls another company shall be treated as being also a participator in that other company.

420.—(1) Section 419(2)(a) shall not apply to a debt incurred for the supply by the close company of goods or services in the ordinary course of its trade or business unless the credit given exceeds six months or is longer than that normally given to the company's customers.

Exceptions from section 419.

(2) Section 419(1) shall not apply to a loan made to a director or employee of a close company, or of an associated company of the close company, if—

(a) neither the amount of the loan, nor that amount when taken together with any other outstanding loans which—

(i) were made by the close company or any of its associated companies to the borrower or the wife or husband of the borrower; and

(ii) if made before 31st March 1971, were made for the purpose of purchasing a dwelling which was or was to be the borrower's only or main residence;

exceeds £15,000 and the outstanding loans falling within sub-paragraph (ii) above do not together exceed £10,000; and

(b) the borrower works full-time for the close company or any of its associated companies; and

(c) the borrower does not have a material interest in the close company or in any associated company of the close company;

but if the borrower acquires such a material interest at a time when the whole or part of any such loan made after 30th March 1971 remains outstanding the close company shall be regarded as making to him at that time a loan of an amount equal to the sum outstanding.

Section 168(11) shall apply for the purpose of determining whether a person has, for the purpose of this subsection, a material interest in a company, but with the omission of the words following "417(3)".

421.—(1) Subject to the following provisions of this section, where a company is assessed or liable to be assessed under section 419 in respect of a loan or advance and releases or writes off the whole or part of the debt in respect of it, then—

Taxation of borrower when loan under section 419 released etc.

(a) for the purpose of computing the total income of the person to whom the loan or advance was made, a sum equal to the amount so released or written off shall be treated as income received by him after deduction of income tax from a corresponding gross amount;

(b) no repayment of income tax shall be made in respect of that income and no assessment shall be made on him in respect of income tax at the basic rate on that income;

(c) the income included by virtue of paragraph (a) above in his total income shall, notwithstanding that paragraph, be treated for the purposes of sections 348 and 349(1) as not brought into charge to income tax;

(d) for the purpose of determining whether any or what amount of tax is, by virtue of paragraph (a) above, to be taken into account as having been deducted from a gross amount in the case of an individual whose total income is reduced by any deductions so much only of that gross amount shall be taken into account as is part of his total income as so reduced.

(2) If the loan or advance referred to in subsection (1) above was made to a person who has since died, or to trustees of a trust which has come to an end, this section, instead of applying to the person to whom it was made, shall apply to the person from whom the debt is due at the time of release or writing off (and if it is due from him as personal representative, within the meaning of Part XVI, the amount treated as received by him shall accordingly be included for the purposes of that Part in the aggregate income of the estate) and subsection (1) above shall apply accordingly with the necessary modifications.

(3) This section shall not have effect in relation to a loan or advance made to a person if any sum falls in respect of the loan or advance to be included in his income by virtue of section 677, except so far as the amount released or written off exceeds the sums previously falling to be so included (without the addition for income tax provided for by subsection (6) of that section).

(4) This section shall be construed as one with section 419.

Extension of section 419 to loans by companies controlled by close companies.

422.—(1) Subject to subsection (4) below, where a company which is controlled by a close company makes a loan which, apart from this section, does not give rise to a charge under subsection (1) of section 419, that section and section 420 shall apply as if the loan had been made by the close company.

(2) Subject to subsection (4) below, where a company which is not controlled by a close company makes a loan which, apart from this section, does not give rise to a charge under subsection (1) of section 419 and a close company subsequently acquires control of it, that section and section 420 shall apply as if the loan had been made by the close company immediately after the time when it acquired control.

(3) Where two or more close companies together control the company that makes or has made the loan, subsections (1) and (2) above shall have effect—

(a) as if each of them controlled that company; and

(b) as if the loan had been made by each of those close companies,

but the loan shall be apportioned between those close companies in such proportion as may be appropriate having regard to the nature and amount of their respective interests in the company that makes or has made the loan.

(4) Subsections (1) and (2) above do not apply if it is shown that no person has made any arrangements (otherwise than in the ordinary course of a business carried on by him) as a result of which there is a connection—

(a) between the making of the loan and the acquisition of control; or

(b) between the making of the loan and the provision by the close company of funds for the company making the loan;

and the close company shall be regarded as providing funds for the company making the loan if it directly or indirectly makes any payment or transfers any property to, or releases or satisfies (in whole or in part) a liability of, the company making the loan.

(5) Where, by virtue of this section, sections 419 and 420 have effect as if a loan made by one company had been made by another, any question under those sections or section 421 whether—

(a) the company making the loan did so otherwise than in the ordinary course of a business carried on by it which includes the lending of money;

(b) the loan or any part of it has been repaid to the company;

(c) the company has released or written off the whole or part of the debt in respect of the loan,

shall be determined by reference to the company that makes the loan.

(6) This section shall be construed as one with section 419 and section 420 and in this section—

(a) "loan" includes advance; and

(b) references to a company making a loan include references to cases in which the company is, or if it were a close company would be, regarded as making a loan by virtue of section 419(2).

CHAPTER III

APPORTIONMENT OF UNDISTRIBUTED INCOME ETC.

423.—(1) Subject to section 424, there shall, for the purposes of this Chapter, be apportioned by the inspector among the participators in a close company—

Apportionment of certain income, deductions and interest.

(a) the income of the company for any accounting period; and

(b) as if it were the income of the company for an accounting period, any amount—

(i) which was deducted in respect of annual payments made by the company in arriving at its distributable income for that period, and

(ii) which in the case of an individual would not have been deductible or would (apart from section 683(3)) have been treated as his income in computing his total income; and

(c) as if it were the income of the company for an accounting period, any interest paid by the company in that period.

(2) Any amount apportionable under any paragraph of subsection (1) above shall be in addition to the amount (if any) which may be apportioned under any other provision of that subsection.

(3) Any amount apportioned to a close company under this section, or by one or more sub-apportionments under this subsection, shall be further apportioned among the participators in that company.

(4) If any amount of interest apportionable by virtue of paragraph (c) of subsection (1) above is interest paid to a participator in the close company or is (apart from that paragraph) treated for the purposes of income tax as the income of such a participator, the amount so apportionable to that participator shall be reduced by the first-mentioned amount (and without requiring the reduction to be reflected in the amount apportioned to any other person).

(5) In determining for the purposes of this Chapter the person to whom any amount is to be apportionable by virtue of subsection (1)(c) above, any interest which any person possesses as a loan creditor shall be disregarded (but without prejudice to the making of an apportionment to him in any other capacity).

(6) Subject to paragraph 10 of Schedule 19, this section shall, notwithstanding the winding up of a company, or the passing of any resolution or the making of any order or anything else done for the purpose of winding up a company, continue to apply as if the company were not being wound up.

(7) Schedule 19, which makes provision for determining the relevant income and distributions of a company for an accounting period and whether there is any such excess as is mentioned in section 424(1), shall have effect for the purpose of supplementing this Chapter.

Exclusions from section 423.

424.—(1) Subject to the following provisions of this Chapter, an apportionment shall not be made under subsection (1)(a) of section 423 of any relevant income of a company unless—

(a) its relevant income for the accounting period exceeds its distributions for that period; and

(b) if the company is a trading company or a member of a trading group by virtue of paragraph 7(2)(a) of Schedule 19, that excess is more than £1,000;

and the amount apportioned shall be the amount of that excess.

(2) Subject to paragraphs 10(5) and 11(2) of Schedule 19, there may be apportioned under section 423(1)(a), if the inspector sees reason for it, the whole of the relevant income for an accounting period of a close company which is not a trading company whether or not there is any such excess as is mentioned in subsection (1) above.

(3) Subsection (1)(b) of section 423 does not apply to annual payments which consist of interest or are made wholly and exclusively for the purposes of the company's trade.

(4) Subsection (1)(c) of section 423 does not apply to a company—

    (a) if it is a trading company, or

    (b) if it is a member of a trading group, or

    (c) if more than 75 per cent. of its income is of one or more of the following descriptions, that is—

        (i) estate or trading income;

        (ii) interest, and dividends or other distributions, received from a 51 per cent. subsidiary of it (both companies being bodies corporate) if the subsidiary is itself within paragraph (a) or (b) above or this paragraph;

and for the purposes of paragraph (c) above no account shall be taken of any deduction from the company's profits for charges on income, expenses of management or other amounts which can be deducted from or set off against or treated as reducing profits of more than one description.

(5) In determining for the purposes of subsection (4)(c)(ii) above whether one body corporate is a 51 per cent. subsidiary of another, that other shall be treated as not being the owner—

    (a) of any share capital which it owns directly or indirectly in a body corporate not resident in the United Kingdom, or

    (b) of any share capital which it owns indirectly and which is owned directly by a body corporate for which a profit on the sale of the shares would be a trading receipt.

(6) Subsection (1)(c) of section 423 shall not apply to interest which—

    (a) would be eligible for relief under section 353 if paid by an individual; or

    (b) is money wholly and exclusively laid out or expended for the purposes of a trade carried on by the company.

425.—(1) Subject to the provisions of this section, any apportionment under section 423, including any sub-apportionment of an amount directly or indirectly apportioned to a company, shall be made according to the respective interests in the company in question of the participators.

Manner of apportionment.

(2) In determining for the purposes of this section the respective interests of the participators, the inspector may, if it seems proper to him to do so, attribute to each participator an interest corresponding to his interest in the assets of the company available for distribution among the participators in the event of a winding up or in any other circumstances.

(3) Where income of a company which is not a trading company is apportioned under section 423, the inspector may, if it seems proper to him to do so, treat a loan creditor as having an interest for the purposes of this section to the extent to which the income to be apportioned, or assets representing it, has or have been expended or applied, or is or are

available to be expended or applied, in redemption, repayment or discharge of the loan capital or debt (including any premium thereon) in respect of which he is a loan creditor.

Charge to income tax where apportionment is to an individual.

426.—(1) Where a sum has been apportioned under section 423 to an individual (whether by an original apportionment or a sub-apportionment), income tax shall be assessed and charged in respect of that sum in accordance with the following provisions of this section and sections 427 and 428.

(2) Where a sum has been so apportioned to an individual—

(a) it shall be treated for the purpose of computing his total income as income received by him at the end of the accounting period to which the apportionment relates and, subject to section 833(3), shall be deemed to be the highest part of his total income;

(b) no assessment shall be made on the individual in respect of income tax at the basic rate on that sum (nor, in the case mentioned in section 427(1), in respect of income tax at any other rate) but he shall be treated as having paid income tax at the basic rate on that sum or, if his total income is reduced by any deductions, on so much of that sum as is part of his total income as so reduced;

(c) no repayment shall be made of the income tax treated by virtue of paragraph (b) above as having been paid; and

(d) the sum so apportioned shall be treated for the purposes of sections 348 and 349(1) as not brought into charge to income tax.

(3) Where a sum is so apportioned to the personal representatives of a deceased person it shall be treated, in ascertaining the aggregate income of the estate for the purposes of Part XVI, as having been received as mentioned in paragraph (a) of subsection (2) above, and paragraphs (b) to (d) of that subsection shall apply accordingly with the necessary modifications.

Reduction of charge under section 426 in certain cases.

427.—(1) No individual shall be assessed to income tax by virtue of any apportionment unless the sum or, where there is a sub-apportionment, the aggregate sum on which he is so assessable amounts at least to—

(a) £1,000; or

(b) 5 per cent. of the amount apportioned;

whichever is the less.

(2) Where an apportionment is made by virtue of section 424(2), an individual shall not be charged to tax on a sum treated in consequence of the apportionment or any sub-apportionment as being his income except in so far as it exceeds the amount which, apart from the apportionment, falls in respect of distributions made by the company for the accounting period to be included in his total income.

(3) Where as a result of a company or companies making covenanted payments to charity a sum or sums are apportioned by virtue of section 423(1)(b) and form part of the total income of an individual for any year of assessment, then, except in so far as any such sum is referable to a

payment which, if made by the individual, would be treated by virtue of section 683(1) as the income of the individual for the purposes of excess liability, his total income for that year and the total amount assessable for that year in respect of that sum or those sums shall be reduced by the amount of that sum or those sums.

In this subsection "covenanted payments to charity" has the same meaning as in section 683.

(4) Where the income of a company for any accounting period has been apportioned under section 423 of this Act or 296 of the 1970 Act and the distributions of the company for a later accounting period for which it is a close company—

    (a) consist of or include a distribution of all or any of the apportioned income; and

    (b) exceed the company's relevant income for that later period,

then, if any individual who was charged to tax under section 426 or section 297 of the 1970 Act in respect of any of the apportioned income is entitled to any of that income on that subsequent distribution, there shall be deemed not to form part of his income for the purposes of excess liability an amount of the income subsequently distributed (or of the excess mentioned in paragraph (b) above if it is less) equal to such fraction as corresponds to—

        (i) the fraction of the apportioned income in respect of which he was charged to tax; or

        (ii) the fraction to which he is entitled of the subsequent distribution of that income,

whichever is the smaller.

(5) In this section "excess liability" means the excess of liability to income tax over what it would be if all income tax were chargeable at the basic rate to the exclusion of any higher rate.

428.—(1) For the purposes of sections 426 and 427—

    (a) the sum apportioned to any person;

    (b) the amount mentioned in section 427(1)(b); and

    (c) the amount to be excluded from a person's income in accordance with section 427(4),

Increase of apportioned sum etc. by reference to ACT.

shall respectively be taken to consist of the aggregate of that sum or amount and such proportion of it as corresponds to the appropriate rate of advance corporation tax; but paragraphs (a) and (b) above shall not apply in the case of any apportionment so far as made by virtue of section 423(1)(b) or (c).

(2) For the purposes of paragraphs (a) and (b) of subsection (1) above, the appropriate rate of advance corporation tax is the rate applicable to a distribution made at the end of the accounting period to which the apportionment relates, and for the purposes of paragraph (c) of that subsection the appropriate rate of advance corporation tax is the rate applicable to the distribution mentioned in section 427(4)(a).

429.—(1) Any income tax chargeable under section 426 in respect of a sum apportioned to a participator shall be assessed on the participator and, subject to the provisions of this section, all the provisions of the Income Tax Acts relating to assessment and the collection and recovery of tax shall with any necessary modifications apply to tax chargeable under that section.

(2) If the whole or any part of the tax assessed on the participator is not paid within 30 days from the date on which the assessment became final and conclusive or by 1st December in the year next following the year of assessment, whichever is the later, a notice of liability to tax under this section may be served on the company and the tax or the part remaining unpaid, as the case may be, shall be payable by the company upon service of the notice.

(3) Where a notice of liability is served under subsection (2) above, any interest due on the tax assessed on the participator and not paid by him, and any interest accruing due on that tax after the date of service, shall be payable by the company.

(4) Where a notice of liability is served on the company and the relevant tax and any interest payable by the company under subsection (3) above is not paid by the company before the expiry of three months from the date of service, that tax and interest may, without prejudice to the right of recovery from the company, be recovered from the participator.

(5) Where, in consequence of a sub-apportionment, subsections (1) to (4) above apply in relation to a participator in a company other than the company in relation to which the original apportionment was made, references in those subsections to the company shall be taken as references to the company in relation to which the original apportionment was made.

430.—(1) This section has effect where the income of a company is apportioned under section 423(1)(a); and in this section "the apportioned amount" means the aggregate of the amount of that income which is so apportioned (subject to subsection (2) below) and such proportion of the amount as corresponds to the rate of advance corporation tax applicable to a distribution made at the end of the accounting period to which the apportionment relates ("the relevant period").

(2) Where a company issues to a close company any share capital to which section 249 applies, the amount of the company's income apportioned under section 423(1)(a) shall, for the purposes of the definition of "apportioned amount" in subsection (1) above, be treated as reduced by an amount equal to the appropriate amount in cash (within the meaning of section 251(2)).

(3) If in the relevant period the company has a surplus of franked investment income, the surplus (so far as not already reduced in consequence of a claim under section 242 or 243 or of being used to frank distributions made by the company in a subsequent accounting period) shall be treated for all purposes as reduced by a sum equal to the apportioned amount or, if that is greater, as extinguished.

(4) If in the relevant period the company has no such surplus (so far as not already reduced as mentioned in subsection (3) above) or the apportioned amount exceeds that surplus (so far as not already so

reduced), subsections (5) to (7) below shall have effect in relation to a sum equal to the advance corporation tax comprised in a franked payment made at the end of the relevant period of an amount equal to the apportioned amount or to that excess, as the case may be.

(5) If, apart from this section, surplus advance corporation tax of a later accounting period could by virtue of subsection (3) of section 239 be set against the company's liability to corporation tax for the relevant period, that advance corporation tax shall not be so set except to such extent, if any, as would be possible if the sum mentioned in subsection (4) above had been advance corporation tax available to be so set against that liability for the relevant period and had, so far as permitted by that section, already been set against that liability.

(6) If the sum mentioned in subsection (4) above exceeds the amount that could, if it were advance corporation tax available for the purpose, be set as mentioned in subsection (5) above against the company's liability for the relevant period—

   (a) there shall be deducted from the excess an amount equal to the advance corporation tax, if any, that could by virtue of subsection (3) of section 239 be set against the company's liability to corporation tax for earlier accounting periods after taking into account advance corporation tax so set in consequence of a claim already made under that subsection; and

   (b) if no such claim has already been made, advance corporation tax shall not by virtue of any such claim be set against the company's liability to corporation tax for any such earlier accounting periods except to such extent, if any, as would be possible if an amount equal to any deduction under paragraph (a) above had been advance corporation tax available to be so set and had, so far as permitted by section 239, already been set against that liability.

(7) Any excess of the sum mentioned in subsection (4) above remaining after the deduction mentioned in subsection (6)(a) above—

   (a) shall be assessed on and recoverable from the company as if it were advance corporation tax payable by the company in respect of a distribution made by it at the end of the relevant period; and

   (b) shall carry interest as if it were advance corporation tax so payable; and

   (c) shall be treated as surplus advance corporation tax of the relevant period falling to be dealt with in accordance with section 239(4).

(8) Tax assessed by virtue of subsection (7)(a) above shall, subject to any appeal against the assessment, be due within 14 days after the issue of the notice of assessment.

(9) Subsection (7)(c) above shall not be construed as authorising any sum to be carried forward to a later accounting period in any case in which section 245 would prevent the carry-forward of advance corporation tax.

(10) Section 238 shall apply for the interpretation of this section as it applies for the interpretation of Chapter V of Part VI.

PART XII

SPECIAL CLASSES OF COMPANIES AND BUSINESSES

CHAPTER I

INSURANCE COMPANIES, UNDERWRITERS AND CAPITAL REDEMPTION BUSINESS

Insurance companies: general

431.—(1) This section has effect for the interpretation of this Chapter.

(2) Unless the context otherwise requires—

"annuity business" means the business of granting annuities on human life;

"general annuity business" means any annuity business which is not pension business, and "pension business" shall be construed in accordance with subsections (3) and (4) below;

"annuity fund" means, where an annuity fund is not kept separately from the life assurance fund of an insurance company, such part of the life assurance fund as represents the liability of the company under its annuity contracts, as stated in its periodical returns;

"insurance company" means a company to which Part II of the Insurance Companies Act 1982 applies;

"life assurance business" includes annuity business;

"offshore income gain" has the same meaning as in Chapter V of Part XVII;

"overseas life insurance company" means an insurance company having its head office outside the United Kingdom but carrying on life assurance business through a branch or agency in the United Kingdom; and

"periodical return", in relation to an insurance company, means a return deposited with the Secretary of State under Part II of the Insurance Companies Act 1982.

(3) Subject to section 439, any division to be made between general annuity business, pension business and other life assurance business shall be made on the principle of—

(a) referring to pension business any premiums falling within subsection (4) below, together with the incomings, outgoings and liabilities referable to those premiums and the policies and contracts under which they are or have been paid;

(b) allocating to general annuity business all other annuity business;

and references to "pension fund" and "general annuity fund" shall be construed accordingly, whether or not any such funds are kept separate from the insurance company's life assurance fund.

Margin notes:

Interpretative provisions relating to insurance companies.

1982 c. 50.

(4) The premiums to be referred to pension business are those payable under contracts falling within one or other of the following descriptions, that is to say—

(a) any contract with an individual who is, or would but for an insufficiency of profits or gains be, chargeable to income tax in respect of relevant earnings (as defined in section 623(1) and (2)) from a trade, profession, vocation, office or employment carried on or held by him (being a contract approved by the Board under section 620), or any substituted contract within the meaning of section 622(3);

(b) any contract (including a contract of insurance) entered into for the purposes of, and made with the persons having the management of, an exempt approved scheme as defined in Chapter I of Part XIV, being a contract so framed that the liabilities undertaken by the insurance company under the contract correspond with liabilities against which the contract is intended to secure the scheme;

(c) any contract made under approved personal pension arrangements within the meaning of Chapter IV of Part XIV;

(d) any annuity contract entered into for the purposes of—

   (i) a scheme which is approved or is being considered for approval under Chapter I of Part XIV;

   (ii) a statutory scheme as defined by section 612(1); or

   (iii) a fund to which section 608 applies,

being a contract which is approved by the Board and made with the persons having the management of the scheme or fund (or those persons and a member of or contributor to the scheme or fund) and by means of which relevant benefits as defined by section 612(1) (but no other benefits) are secured;

(e) any annuity contract approved by the Board which is entered into in substitution for a contract within paragraph (d) above;

(f) any contract with the trustees or other persons having the management of a scheme approved under section 620 or, subject to subsection (5) below, of a superannuation fund which was approved under section 208 of the 1970 Act, being a contract which—

   (i) was entered into for the purposes only of that scheme or fund or, in the case of a fund part only of which was approved under section 208, for the purposes only of that part of that fund, and

   (ii) (in the case of a contract entered into or varied after 1st August 1956) is so framed that the liabilities undertaken by the insurance company under the contract correspond with liabilities against which the contract is intended to secure the scheme or fund (or the relevant part of the fund).

(5) Subsection (4)(c) above shall not apply to premiums payable under a contract where the fund in question was approved under section 208 of the 1970 Act unless—

(a) immediately before 6th April 1980 premiums paid under the contract with the trustees or other persons having the management of the fund fell within section 323(4) of that Act (premiums referable to pension business); and

(b) the terms on which benefits are payable from the fund have not been altered since that time; and

(c) section 608 applies to the fund.

(6) In subsections (3) to (5) above "premium" includes any consideration for an annuity.

432.—(1) Where an insurance company carries on life assurance business in conjunction with insurance business of any other class, the life assurance business shall, for the purposes of the Corporation Tax Acts, be treated as a separate business from any other class of business carried on by the company.

Separation of different classes of business.

(2) Where an insurance company carries on both ordinary life assurance business and industrial life assurance business, the business of each such class shall, for the purposes of the Corporation Tax Acts, be treated as though it were a separate business, and section 76 shall apply separately to each such class of business.

433. Where the profits of an insurance company in respect of its life assurance business are, for the purposes of this Act, computed in accordance with the provisions of this Act applicable to Case I of Schedule D, such part of those profits as belongs or is allocated to, or is reserved for, or expended on behalf of, policy holders or annuitants shall be excluded in making the computation, but if any profits so excluded as being reserved for policy holders or annuitants cease at any time to be so reserved and are not allocated to or expended on behalf of policy holders or annuitants, those profits shall be treated as profits of the company for the accounting period in which they ceased to be so reserved.

Profits reserved for policy holders and annuitants.

434.—(1) Section 208 shall not prevent franked investment income of a company resident in the United Kingdom which carries on life assurance business from being taken into account as part of the profits in computing trading income in accordance with the provisions applicable to Case I of Schedule D.

Franked investment income etc.

(2) In ascertaining for the purposes of section 393 or 394 whether and to what extent a company has incurred a loss on its life assurance business, any profits derived from the investments of its life assurance fund (including franked investment income of a company so resident) shall be treated as part of the profits of that business.

(3) Any such part of the franked investment income from investments held in connection with a company's life assurance business as is specified in subsection (4) below ("the specified part") shall not be used under Chapter V of Part VI to frank distributions made by the company.

(4) Subject to subsection (5) below, the specified part shall be, in the case of any unrelieved income, the same fraction of it as the fraction which, on a computation of the profits of the company in respect of its life assurance business in accordance with the provisions applicable to Case I of Schedule D (whether or not the company is in fact charged to tax under that Case for the relevant accounting period or periods), would be

connoted by the words in section 433 "such part of those profits as belongs or is allocated to, or is reserved for, or expended on behalf of, policy holders or annuitants".

(5) If the income exceeds the profits as computed in accordance with the provisions applicable to Case I of Schedule D other than section 433, the specified part shall be that fraction of the income so far as not exceeding the profits, together with the amount of the excess.

(6) For the purposes of section 239 the profits charged to corporation tax for any accounting period (as defined in subsection (6) of that section) shall be reduced by deducting therefrom such fraction thereof as is equal to the fraction of the profits of the company in respect of its life assurance business which under section 433 is excluded from the computation of those profits or would be so excluded if the profits were computed in accordance with the provisions applicable to Case I of Schedule D.

(7) For the purposes of subsection (4) above "unrelieved income" means income which has not been excluded from charge to tax by virtue of any provision and against which no relief has been allowed by deduction or set-off.

(8) Where subsection (3) or (6) above would deny to a company any relief to which it would have been entitled if it had been charged to tax in respect of its life assurance business under Case I of Schedule D, corresponding relief shall be afforded to the company by repayment of, or set-off against, corporation tax or by payment of tax credit comprised in franked investment income from investments held in connection with that business.

Taxation of gains reserved for policy holders and annuitants.

435.—(1) This section has effect in relation to any accounting period of an insurance company carrying on life assurance business and for the purposes of this section—

(a) the life assurance gains are such part of the amount to be included, in accordance with section 345, in the company's total profits as is attributable to gains from investments held in connection with the company's life assurance business;

(b) the policy holders' share of the life assurance gains or of the relevant reliefs is such fraction thereof as is equal to the fraction of the profits of the company in respect of its life assurance business which, under section 433, is excluded from the computation of those profits or would be so excluded if the profits were computed in accordance with the provisions applicable to Case I of Schedule D; and

(c) the relevant reliefs are such of the sums to be deducted from or set off against the company's profits as are deducted from or set off against the life assurance gains.

(2) Corporation tax charged on so much of the policy holders' share of the life assurance gains as remains after setting against it the amounts referred to in subsection (3)(c) below shall be calculated on the basis of a rate of corporation tax of 30 per cent.

(3) For the purposes of this section there shall be ascertained the policy holders' share and the remainder ("the residual part") of the life assurance gains and of the relevant reliefs; and—

(a) the residual part of the relevant reliefs shall be set against the residual part of those gains; and

(b) if the residual part of the relevant reliefs exceeds the residual part of those gains, the excess (or so much of it as does not, together with the policy holders' share of the relevant reliefs, exceed the policy holders' share of those gains) shall be added to the policy holders' share of the relevant reliefs; and

(c) the policy holders' share of the relevant reliefs, with any addition made under paragraph (b) above, shall be set against the policy holders' share of the life assurance gains.

436.—(1) Subject to the provisions of this section, profits arising to an insurance company from general annuity business or pension business shall be treated as income within Schedule D, and be chargeable under Case VI of that Schedule, and for that purpose—

Annuity business and pension business: separate charge on profits.

(a) the business of each such class shall be treated separately, and

(b) subject to paragraph (a) above, and to subsection (3) below, the profits therefrom shall be computed in accordance with the provisions of this Act applicable to Case I of Schedule D.

(2) Subsection (1) above shall not apply to an insurance company charged to corporation tax in accordance with the provisions applicable to Case I of Schedule D in respect of the profits of its ordinary life assurance business.

(3) In making the computation referred to in subsection (1) above—

(a) section 433 shall apply with the necessary modifications and in particular with the omission of all references to policy holders (other than holders of policies referable to pension business);

(b) no deduction shall be allowed in respect of any expenses of management deductible under section 76;

(c) there may be set off against the profits any loss, to be computed on the same basis as the profits, which has arisen from pension business or general annuity business in any previous accounting period or year of assessment;

(d) where the computation in question is of profits arising to an insurance company from pension business—

(i) group income shall not be taken into account as part of those profits, and

(ii) annuities shall be deductible notwithstanding section 337(2);

and the company shall not be entitled to treat as paid out of profits or gains brought into charge to income tax any part of the annuities paid by the company which is referable to pension business; and

(e) distributions which are not qualifying distributions shall not be taken into account where the computation in question is of the profits arising to an insurance company or overseas life insurance company from general annuity business or pension business.

(4) Section 396 shall not be taken to apply to a loss incurred by a company on its general annuity business or pension business.

(5) Nothing in section 128 or 399(1) shall affect the operation of this section.

437.—(1) In the case of a company carrying on general annuity business, the annuities paid by the company, so far as referable to that business and so far as they do not exceed the taxed income of the part of the annuity fund so referable, shall be treated as charges on income.

(2) In computing under section 436 the profits arising to an insurance company from general annuity business—

(a) taxed income, group income and income attributable to offshore income gains shall not be taken into account as part of those profits; and

(b) of the annuities paid by the company and referable to general annuity business—

(i) those which under subsection (1) above are treated as charges on income shall not be deductible, and

(ii) those which are not so treated shall (notwithstanding section 337(2)) be deductible.

(3) In subsections (1) and (2) above "taxed income" means income charged to corporation tax otherwise than under section 436, and franked investment income.

(4) Subject to subsection (5) below, franked investment income which is taken into account under subsection (2) above to enable annuities referable to general annuity business to be treated as charges on income shall not be used under Chapter V of Part VI to frank distributions made by the company.

(5) For the purposes of subsection (4) above there shall be deducted from the amount of the franked investment income of the company arising in any accounting period and taken into account under subsection (1) above—

(a) the amount of any profit arising in that accounting period to the company from general annuity business and computed under section 436; and

(b) the amount of any group income arising in that accounting period to the company and referable to its general annuity business.

(6) A company which is not resident in the United Kingdom but carries on through a branch or agency there any general annuity business shall not be entitled to treat any part of the annuities paid by it which are referable to that business as paid out of profits or gains brought into charge to income tax.

438.—(1) Exemption from corporation tax shall be allowed in respect of income from, and chargeable gains in respect of, investments and deposits of so much of an insurance company's life assurance fund and separate annuity fund, if any, as is referable to pension business.

PART XII
Pension business: exemption from tax.

(2) The exemption from tax conferred by subsection (1) above shall not exclude any sums from being taken into account as receipts in computing profits or losses for any purpose of the Corporation Tax Acts.

(3) Subject to subsection (6) below, the exclusion by section 208 from the charge to corporation tax of franked investment income shall not prevent such income being taken into account as part of the profits in computing under section 436 income from pension business.

(4) If in the case of any company the income referred to in subsection (1) above includes a distribution in respect of which the company is entitled to a tax credit, the company may, subject to subsections (5) and (6) below, claim to have the amount of that credit paid to it.

(5) If the company is resident in the United Kingdom (so that the distribution and the tax credit in question constitute franked investment income of that company), no franked investment income comprising any tax credit which is paid under subsection (4) above shall, subject to subsection (6) below, be used under Chapter V of Part VI to frank the company's distributions.

(6) If for any accounting period there is, apart from this subsection, a profit arising to an insurance company from pension business and computed under section 436, and the company so elects as respects all or any part of its franked investment income arising in that period, being an amount of franked investment income not exceeding the amount of that profit, subsections (3) to (5) above shall not apply to the franked investment income to which the election relates.

(7) An election under subsection (6) above shall be made by notice given to the inspector not later than two years after the end of the accounting period to which the election relates or within such longer period as the Board may by notice allow.

(8) Nothing in sections 431(4)(c) or 643(2) of this Act or section 149B(1)(h) of the 1979 Act shall be construed as affording relief in respect of any sums to be brought into account under this section.

439.—(1) This section applies where for any accounting period —

Restricted government securities.

(a) any division falls to be made between the pension business and any other kind of long-term business of an insurance company, and

(b) any of the income or gains or losses of the company for that period relate to restricted government securities;

and where this section applies section 431(3) shall have effect subject to the provisions of this section.

(2) All income, gains or losses of the company which relate to restricted government securities shall be referred to its pension business.

o

(3) Where the division of the other income, gains or losses of the company is made by reference to the liabilities at any time in the accounting period which are referable to pension business or to two or more kinds of business including pension business, those liabilities shall be treated as reduced by the appropriate amount.

(4) In subsection (3) above "the appropriate amount" means—

(a) in a case in which the total liabilities of the company at the time in question which are referable to long-term business are less than the market value at that time of the investments and deposits held by the company relating to all such business, such proportion of the market value of the restricted government securities held by the company at that time as those liabilities bear to the market value of those investments and deposits, and

(b) in any other case, the market value of the restricted government securities at that time.

(5) In this section—

1982 c. 50.
"long-term business" has the same meaning as in section 1(1) of the Insurance Companies Act 1982;

"restricted government securities" means, subject to the following provisions of this section, government securities issued on the condition that, except in such circumstances as may be specified in the conditions of issue, they are to be held by insurance companies against and applied solely towards meeting pension business liabilities.

(6) Subject to subsection (7) below, the following Treasury Stock, namely—

(a) 2 per cent. Index-linked Treasury Stock 1996;

(b) 2 per cent. Index-linked Treasury Stock 2006;

(c) $2\frac{1}{2}$ per cent. Index-linked Treasury Stock 2011;

are not restricted government securities for the purposes of this section.

(7) If any of the index-linked stock referred to in subsection (6) above was on 27th March 1982 held by an insurance company against and applied solely towards meeting the liabilities of the company's pension business, then—

(a) if and so long as the stock continues to be so held by that company, it shall continue to be treated as restricted government securities for the purposes of this section; and

(b) if the stock ceases to be restricted government securities otherwise than by virtue of being actually disposed of or redeemed, on the day on which it so ceases the stock shall be deemed for the purposes of corporation tax, including (subject to subsection (8) below) corporation tax on chargeable gains, to have been disposed of and immediately re-acquired at its market value on that date.

(8) For the purposes of sections 67 and 68 of the 1979 Act (gilt-edged securities)—

(a) in ascertaining the date on which securities were acquired, no account shall be taken of any deemed disposal and re-acquisition resulting from subsection (7)(b) above; and

(b) so long as any index-linked stock continues, by virtue of subsection (7)(a) above, to be treated as restricted government securities for the purposes of this section, it shall be regarded as being stock of a different kind from the index-linked stock referred to in subsection (6) above which is not so treated.

440.—(1) The provisions of this section apply to any insurance company which carries on or has carried on long term business, and shall have effect for all purposes of the Corporation Tax Acts.

Identification or exchange of long term assets.

(2) Subject to subsection (4) below, a profit or loss shall not be taken to arise in respect of any asset of the company by reason only that at any time after the base date the asset was or is exchanged for other assets of the company so as to become or cease to be part of the long term assets.

(3) Subject to subsection (5) below, if an asset of the company which has at any time after 29th April 1975 been exchanged as mentioned in subsection (2) above is—

(a) within the period of one year beginning with the date of that exchange ("the relevant exchange") exchanged again for other assets of the company so as to cease to be or, as the case may be, become part of the long term assets; or

(b) within the period of six months beginning with the date of the relevant exchange disposed of by the company,

then any income arising in respect of the asset after the relevant exchange, and any profit, gain or loss accruing to the company on a disposal of the asset made after the relevant exchange, shall be treated as if the relevant exchange had not taken place.

(4) If an insurance company to which this section applies by notice given to the inspector so elects, then, where in the relevant period any relevant asset of the company was or is exchanged as mentioned in subsection (2) above—

(a) that subsection shall not apply in relation to that asset as regards that exchange; and

(b) the company shall be treated as if the asset had been disposed of at market value by the company at the time of the exchange.

In this and the following subsection—

"the relevant period", in relation to a notice under this subsection, means the period of six years from the end of the accounting period of the company in which the notice is given;

"relevant asset", in relation to an insurance company, means an asset of the company such that, if it were sold, the proceeds would be taken into account in any computation of profits of the company in accordance with the provisions of this Act applicable to Case I of Schedule D.

(5) Where an insurance company has given a notice under subsection (4) above, subsection (3) above shall, as regards relevant assets disposed of by the company in the relevant period, have effect as if paragraph (b) and the reference to any profit, gain or loss accruing to the company on a disposal made after the relevant exchange were omitted.

(6) If at any time after the base date an insurance company to which this section applies disposed or disposes of an asset which—

(a) was or is part of the long term assets at the time of the disposal, but without having been continuously part of those assets since its acquisition by the company; or

(b) was or is not part of the long term assets at the time of the disposal, but without having been continuously not part of those assets since its acquisition by the company,

the asset shall be treated, in a case falling within paragraph (a) above, as if it had been continuously part of the long term assets from the time of its acquisition by the company to the time of the disposal, or, in a case falling within paragraph (b) above, as if it had been continuously not part of the long term assets from the time of its acquisition by the company to the time of its disposal; and if the disposal is one as respects which subsection (3) above applies, this subsection shall apply as if the relevant exchange (within the meaning of that subsection) had not taken place.

(7) Without prejudice to subsection (6) above, if—

(a) an insurance company to which this section applies disposes of an asset which, since its acquisition by the company, has on one or more occasions (whether after the base date or not) been exchanged for other assets of the company; and

(b) as regards that occasion or one or more of those occasions the company was assessed to income tax or corporation tax in an amount computed by reference to the value of the asset at the time of the exchange,

then, in computing for any purpose of the Corporation Tax Acts the profit, gain or loss (if any) arising on the disposal, the asset shall be deemed to have been acquired by the company on the occasion or latest of the occasions mentioned in paragraph (b) above at a cost equal to the value by reference to which the company was so assessed as regards that occasion.

(8) There shall be made such assessments, reductions of assessments or, on a claim in that behalf, repayments of tax as may in any case be required in order to give effect to subsection (3) or (4) above.

(9) In this section, unless the context otherwise requires, "asset" includes part of an asset and any reference to a disposal of part of an asset includes a reference to a part disposal of an asset within the meaning of section 19(2)(b) of the 1979 Act; and where part of an asset is exchanged or disposed of as mentioned in any of subsections (2) to (7) above, that subsection shall have effect as if that part of the asset and the part not exchanged or disposed of were separate assets.

(10) For the purposes of this section—

"the base date", in relation to an insurance company, means the last day of the financial year of the company which ended next after 7th December 1973;

"financial year" has the meaning given by section 96 of the Insurance Companies Act 1982;

"long term assets", in relation to an insurance company, means assets representing the fund or funds maintained by the company in respect of its long term business; and

"long term business" has the meaning given by section 1(1) of the Insurance Companies Act 1982.

441.—(1) Corporation tax under Cases IV and V on income arising from investments of the foreign life assurance fund of an insurance company shall be computed as in the case mentioned in section 65(4), that is to say, by reference to the amount of income received in the United Kingdom; and this subsection shall apply notwithstanding that that section relates only to income tax.

(2) Where any of the following securities, namely—

(a) securities issued by the Treasury with the condition that the interest thereon shall not be liable to income tax so long as it is shown, in manner directed by the Treasury, that the securities are in the beneficial ownership of persons who are not ordinarily resident in the United Kingdom; or

(b) securities issued by the Treasury with the condition that—

(i) so long as the securities are in the beneficial ownership of persons who are not ordinarily resident in the United Kingdom, the interest thereon shall be exempt from income tax, and

(ii) so long as the securities are in the beneficial ownership of persons who are neither domiciled nor ordinarily resident in the United Kingdom, neither the capital thereof nor the interest thereon shall be liable to any taxation present or future; or

(c) securities to which section 581 applies;

for the time being form part of the investments of the foreign life assurance fund of an insurance company, the income arising from those securities, if applied for the purposes of that fund or reinvested so as to form part of that fund, shall not be liable to tax.

(3) Where any income arising abroad from the investments of the foreign life assurance fund of an insurance company has been remitted to the United Kingdom and invested, as part of the investments of that fund, in any such securities as are mentioned in subsection (2) above, that income shall not be liable to tax and any tax paid thereon shall, if necessary, be repaid to the company on the making of a claim.

(4) Any securities issued by the Treasury in pursuance of the power conferred by section 60(1) of the Finance Act 1940 with a modified form of the condition specified in subsection (2)(b) above shall, save in so far as

the terms of the issue otherwise provide, be deemed for the purposes of subsections (2) and (3) above to be such securities as are mentioned in subsection (2) above.

(5) Where income arising from the investments of the foreign life assurance fund of an insurance company has been relieved from tax in pursuance of the provisions of this section, a corresponding reduction shall be made—

(a) in the relief granted under section 76 in respect of expenses of management; and

(b) in any amount on which the company is chargeable to tax by virtue of section 436.

(6) In this section "foreign life assurance fund"—

(a) means any fund representing the amount of the liability of an insurance company in respect of its life assurance business with policy holders and annuitants residing outside the United Kingdom whose proposals were made to, or whose annuity contracts were granted by, the company at or through a branch or agency outside the United Kingdom; and

(b) where such a fund is not kept separately from the life assurance fund, means such part of the life assurance fund as represents the liability of the company under such policies and contracts, such liability being estimated in the same manner as it is estimated for the purpose of the company's periodical return.

(7) Where this section has effect in relation to income arising from investments of any part of an insurance company's life assurance fund, it shall have the like effect in relation to chargeable gains accruing from the disposal of any such investments, and losses so accruing shall not be allowable losses.

(8) For the purposes of this section, an offshore income gain accruing to an insurance company carrying on life assurance business shall, if it accrues in respect of investments held in connection with that business, be treated as if it were income from investments held in connection with that business.

(9) Where any payment is made by the Export Credits Guarantee Department—

1978 c. 18.

(a) under any agreement entered into under arrangements made by the Secretary of State in pursuance of section 11 of the Export Guarantees and Overseas Investment Act 1978, and

(b) in respect of any income —

(i) which cannot be transferred to the United Kingdom, and

(ii) which arises from investments of the foreign life assurance fund of an insurance company,

then, to the extent of the payment, this section shall apply in relation to the income as if it had been received in the United Kingdom (and accordingly cannot be received again in the United Kingdom).

PART XII
Overseas business
of U.K.
companies.

442.—(1) Subsections (2) and (3) below apply where a company resident in the United Kingdom carries on insurance business outside the United Kingdom through a branch or agency and—

    (a) that business, or part of it, together with the whole assets of the company used for the purposes of that business or part (or together with the whole of those assets other than cash), is transferred to a company not resident in the United Kingdom;

    (b) the business or part is so transferred wholly or partly in exchange for shares, or for shares and loan stock, issued by the transferee company to the transferor company; and

    (c) the shares so issued, either alone or taken together with any other shares in the transferee company already held by the transferor company, amount in all to not less than one quarter of the ordinary share capital of the transferee company.

(2) In making any computation in accordance with the provisions of this Act applicable to Case I of Schedule D of the profits or losses of the transferor company for the accounting period in which the transfer occurs, there shall be disregarded any profit or loss in respect of any asset transferred which, apart from this subsection, would fall to be taken into account in making that computation.

(3) Where by virtue of subsection (2) above any profit or loss is disregarded in making any computation otherwise than for the purposes of section 76(2) the profit or loss shall be treated for the purposes of the 1979 Act as a chargeable gain or allowable loss accruing to the transferor company on the transfer.

(4) Where at any time a company resident in the United Kingdom—

    (a) which carries on insurance business wholly outside the United Kingdom, and

    (b) the whole or part of whose ordinary share capital is beneficially owned by one or more companies resident in the United Kingdom,

ceases to be resident in the United Kingdom, the profits or losses of the company in respect of that business for the accounting period ending at that time shall be computed for tax purposes without regard to the whole, or, as the case may be, a corresponding part of any profit or loss in respect of any asset which, apart from this subsection, would fall to be calculated in accordance with section 100(1)(b) and taken into account in making that computation.

443. Where any investments or other assets are or have been, in accordance with a policy issued in the course of life assurance business carried on by an insurance company, transferred to the policy holder on or after 6th April 1967, the policy holder's acquisition of the assets, and the disposal of them to him, shall be deemed to be for a consideration equal to the market value of the assets for the purposes of computing income in accordance with Case I or VI of Schedule D.

Life policies
carrying rights not
in money.

444.—(1) This section applies in relation to policies of life assurance issued before 5th August 1965 by a company carrying on life assurance business, being policies which—

Life policies issued
before 5th August
1965.

(a) provide for benefits consisting to any extent of investments of a specified description or of a sum of money to be determined by reference to the value of such investments, but

(b) do not provide for the deduction from those benefits of any amount by reference to tax chargeable in respect of chargeable gains.

(2) Where—

(a) the investments of the company's life assurance fund, so far as referable to those policies, consist wholly or mainly of investments of the description so specified, and

(b) on the company becoming liable under any of those policies for any such benefits (including benefits to be provided on the surrender of a policy), a chargeable gain accrues to the company from the disposal, in meeting or for the purpose of meeting that liability, of investments of that description forming part of its life assurance fund, or would so accrue if the liability were met by or from the proceeds of such a disposal,

then the company shall be entitled as against the person receiving the benefits to retain out of those benefits a part not exceeding in amount or value corporation tax, at the rate specified in subsection (3) below, in respect of the chargeable gain referred to in paragraph (b) above, computed without regard to any amount retained under this subsection.

(3) The amount to be retained under subsection (2) above shall, subject to subsection (4) below, be computed by reference to the rate of corporation tax for the time being in force or, if no rate of corporation tax has yet been fixed for the financial year, the rate last in force.

(4) In so far as the chargeable gain represents or would represent a gain belonging or allocated to, or reserved for, policy holders, the amount to be retained shall be computed by reference to a rate of tax not exceeding 37.5 per cent.

Provisions applying only to overseas life insurance companies

Charge to tax on investment income.

445.—(1) Any income of an overseas life insurance company from the investments of its life assurance fund (excluding the pension fund and general annuity fund, if any), wherever received, shall, to the extent provided in this section, be deemed to be profits comprised in Schedule D and shall be charged to corporation tax under Case III of Schedule D.

(2) In subsection (1) above "income" shall not include—

(a) distributions which are not qualifying distributions or income attributable to offshore income gains; or

(b) annual profits or gains chargeable to tax by virtue of section 714(2) or 716(3).

(3) Qualifying distributions received from companies resident in the United Kingdom shall be brought into account under this section notwithstanding their exclusion from the charge to corporation tax.

(4) A portion only of the income from the investments of the life assurance fund (excluding the pension fund and general annuity fund, if any) shall be charged in accordance with subsection (1) above, and for any accounting period that portion shall be determined by the formula—

$$\frac{A \times B}{C}$$

where—

A is the total income from those investments for that period;

B is the average of the liabilities for that period to policy holders resident in the United Kingdom and to policy holders resident abroad whose proposals were made to the company at or through its branch or agency in the United Kingdom; and

C is the average of the liabilities for that period to all the company's policy holders;

but any reference in this subsection to liabilities does not include liabilities in respect of general annuity and pension business.

(5) For the purposes of subsection (4) above the average of any liabilities for an accounting period shall be taken as one half of the aggregate of the liabilities at the beginning and end of the valuation period which coincides with that accounting period or in which that accounting period falls.

(6) For the purposes of this section the liabilities of an insurance company attributable to any business at any time shall be ascertained by reference to the net liabilities of the company as valued by an actuary for the purposes of the relevant periodical return.

(7) Section 73 shall not apply to tax in respect of income to which subsection (1) above applies.

(8) In the case of an overseas life insurance company—

(a) in computing for the purposes of this section the income from the investments of the life assurance fund of the company, any interest, dividends and other payments whatsoever to which section 48 or 123(4) extends shall be included notwithstanding the exemption from tax conferred by those sections respectively; and

(b) where in computing that income any interest on any securities issued by the Treasury is excluded by virtue of a condition of the issue of those securities regulating the treatment of the interest on them for tax purposes, the relief under section 76 shall be reduced so as to bear to the amount of relief which would be granted but for the provisions of this paragraph the same proportion as the amount of that income, excluding that interest, bears to the amount of that income including that interest.

446.—(1) Nothing in the Corporation Tax Acts shall prevent the qualifying distributions of companies resident in the United Kingdom from being taken into account as part of the profits in computing, under section 436, the profits arising from pension business and general annuity business to an overseas life insurance company.

Annuity business.

PART XII

(2) Any charge to tax under section 436 for any accounting period on profits arising to an overseas life insurance company from general annuity business shall extend only to a portion of the profits arising from that business and that portion shall be determined by the formula—

$$\frac{A \times B}{C}$$

where—

A is the total amount of those profits;

B is the average of the liabilities attributable to that business for the relevant accounting period in respect of contracts with persons resident in the United Kingdom or contracts with persons resident abroad whose proposals were made to the company at or through its branch or agency in the United Kingdom; and

C is the average of the liabilities attributable to that business for that accounting period in respect of all contracts.

(3) For the purposes of subsection (2) above, the average of any liabilities for an accounting period shall be taken as one half of the aggregate of the liabilities at the beginning and end of the valuation period which coincides with that accounting period or in which that accounting period falls.

(4) For the purposes of this section the liabilities of an insurance company attributable to general annuity business at any time shall be ascertained by reference to the net liabilities of the company as valued by an actuary for the purposes of the relevant periodical return.

Set-off of income tax and tax credits against corporation tax.

447.—(1) For the purposes of subsection (3) of section 11 as it applies to life insurance companies, the amount of the income tax referred to in that subsection which shall be available for set-off under that subsection in an accounting period shall be limited in accordance with subsections (2) to (4) below.

(2) If the company is chargeable to corporation tax for an accounting period in accordance with section 445 in respect of the income from the investments of its life assurance fund, the amount of income tax available for set-off against any corporation tax assessed for that period on that income shall not exceed an amount equal to income tax at the basic rate on the portion of income from investments which is chargeable to corporation tax by virtue of subsection (4) of that section.

(3) If the company is chargeable to corporation tax for an accounting period in accordance with section 446 on a proportion of the total amount of the profits arising from its general annuity business, the amount of income tax available for set-off against any corporation tax assessed for

that period on those profits shall not exceed an amount equal to income tax at the basic rate on the like proportion of the income from investments included in computing those profits.

(4) Where an overseas life insurance company receives a distribution in respect of which it is entitled to a tax credit the company may claim to have that credit set off against any corporation tax assessed on the company under section 445 or 446 for the accounting period in which the distribution is received, but the restriction in subsections (2) and (3) above on the amount of income tax that may be set off against corporation tax so assessed shall apply to the aggregate of that income tax and of the tax credit that can be so set off by virtue of this subsection.

448.—(1) Where an overseas life insurance company receives a qualifying distribution made by a company resident in the United Kingdom and relief in respect of the distribution is not available or is not claimed under arrangements specified in an Order in Council made under section 788, the overseas life insurance company shall be deemed for the purposes of sections 76(3) and (4), 434(8), 436, 438 and 445 to 447 to be entitled to such a tax credit in respect of the distribution as it would be entitled to under section 231 if it were resident in the United Kingdom; and accordingly the distribution shall be treated for the purposes of those provisions as representing income equal to the aggregate of the amount or value of the distribution and the amount of that credit.

(2) Where under subsection (1) above an overseas life insurance company is deemed to be entitled to a tax credit in respect of a distribution, it may claim to have the income represented by the distribution set, subject to subsection (3) below, against its profits chargeable to tax under section 436 or against its income chargeable to tax in accordance with section 445 or partly against the one and partly against the other; but to the extent that any income is so set the tax credit included in it shall not be payable and shall not be set against corporation tax under section 447(4).

(3) The amounts that an overseas life insurance company may by virtue of subsection (2) above set against profits or income of any description shall not exceed the amount of the profits or income of that description and shall be further limited as follows—

(a) the amount set against profits arising from general annuity business shall not exceed a portion of the company's income from investments referable to that business, and that portion shall be determined by the same formula as determines under section 446 the portion of those profits which is chargeable to tax; and

(b) the amount set against profits from pension business shall not exceed such of its income referable to that business as is represented by distributions in respect of which the company is deemed to be entitled to a tax credit by virtue of this section, and shall not reduce any other income.

(4) Where by virtue of a set-off under this section income or profits of any description are reduced by any amount, that amount shall be left out of account in determining the amount of income tax which is available for set-off against corporation tax under section 11(3).

(5) A claim under this section in respect of a distribution shall not prevent the making of a subsequent claim for relief in respect of that distribution under arrangements specified in an Order in Council made under section 788; but where such a subsequent claim is made the claim under this section shall be deemed never to have been made, and no adjustment (whether by additional assessments or otherwise) to which the subsequent claim gives rise shall be out of time if it is made within 12 months after the making of the subsequent claim.

Double taxation agreements.

449.—(1) This section applies to an overseas life insurance company if, by virtue of arrangements specified in an Order in Council made under section 788, no charge to corporation tax under Case III of Schedule D arises under section 445 in respect of any income of the company from the investments of its life assurance fund (excluding the pension fund and general annuity fund, if any).

(2) For the purposes of section 242 so much of any relevant distributions as is received in any year of assessment by an overseas life insurance company to which this section applies in respect of the portion of the investments of its life assurance fund (excluding the pension fund and general annuity fund, if any) attributable to the business of its branch or agency in the United Kingdom shall be deemed to be franked investment income of that company, and accordingly the company may make a claim under subsection (1) of section 242 for any of the purposes specified in subsection (2) of that section.

(3) In subsection (2) above "relevant distributions" means distributions in respect of which the company receiving them is entitled to a tax credit.

Underwriters

Assessment, set-off of losses and reinsurance.

450.—(1) Income tax, for any year of assessment, on the profits or gains arising from a member's underwriting business or from assets forming part of a premiums trust fund shall be computed on the profits or gains of that year of assessment; but for this purpose and all other purposes of the Income Tax Acts—

(a) the profits or gains arising in any year of assessment from a member's underwriting business shall be taken to be those arising in the corresponding underwriting year; and

(b) the profits or gains arising from assets forming part of a premiums trust fund shall be taken to be those allocated under the rules or practice of Lloyd's to the corresponding underwriting year.

(2) Income tax on the profits or gains arising to a member from assets forming part of a premiums trust fund may be assessed on the underwriting agent through whom his business is carried on.

(3) Relief under section 380 in respect of a loss sustained by a member in his underwriting business in any year of assessment shall not be given under subsection (2) of that section but may, if the member so claims and he was a member in the preceding year of assessment, be given against his income for that preceding year, so far as it cannot be given against the income for the year in which the loss was sustained and can be given after any relief for a loss sustained in that preceding year.

(4) In any case where a member has taken out an insurance against losses in his underwriting business—

    (a) any premium paid by him on that insurance shall be deducted as an expense in computing the profits or gains arising from that business; and

    (b) any insurance money paid to him under that insurance shall be taken into account as a trading receipt in computing those profits or gains for the year of assessment for which the premium was allowed as a deduction.

(5) Where, in accordance with the rules or practice of Lloyd's, and in consideration of the payment of a premium, one member agrees with another to meet liabilities arising from the latter's business for an underwriting year so that the accounts of the business for that year may be closed—

    (a) in computing for the purposes of income tax the profits or gains of his business, the amount of the premium shall be deductible as an expense of the member by whom it is payable only to the extent that it is shown not to exceed a fair and reasonable assessment of the value of the liabilities in respect of which it is payable; and

    (b) any part of a premium which, by virtue of paragraph (a) above, is not deductible as an expense of the member by whom it is payable, shall be disregarded in computing for the purposes of income tax the profits or gains of the business of the member to whom it is payable;

and the assessment referred to above shall be taken to be fair and reasonable only if it is arrived at with a view to producing the result that a profit does not accrue to the member to whom the premium is payable but that he does not suffer a loss.

This subsection has effect in relation to premiums payable in connection with the closing of the accounts of a member's business for an underwriting year ending in the year of assessment 1985-86 or any later year of assessment.

(6) The cost of acquisition and the consideration for the disposal of assets forming part of a premiums trust fund shall be left out of account in computing the profits or gains or losses of a member's underwriting business for the purposes of Schedule D (and accordingly shall not be excluded for the purposes of capital gains tax under section 31 or 33 of the 1979 Act).

451.—(1) The Board may by regulations provide—   Regulations.

    (a) for the assessment and collection of tax charged in accordance with section 450;

    (b) for modifying the provisions of section 450 in relation to syndicates continuing for more than two years after the end of an underwriting year;

    (c) for giving credit for foreign tax.

(2) The Treasury may by regulations modify any of the provisions specified in paragraphs (a) to (c) below in their application to companies permitted by the Council of Lloyd's to act as underwriting agents at Lloyd's—

(a) section 11 of the Management Act (return of profits);

(b) section 87A of that Act (interest on overdue corporation tax); and

(c) section 10(1) of this Act.

(3) Regulations under subsection (2) above shall not have effect with respect to accounting periods ending on or before such day, not being earlier than 31st March 1992, as the Treasury may by order appoint for the purposes of that subsection.

1973 c. 51.

(4) Regulations made under paragraph 17(1)(b) of Schedule 16 to the Finance Act 1973 which are in force immediately before the coming into operation of this Act shall continue in force notwithstanding the repeal of that paragraph by this Act, and shall be deemed to have been made under this section.

Special reserve funds.

452.—(1) If in the case of Lloyd's—

(a) arrangements are made for the setting up in relation to each underwriting member of such a special reserve fund as is referred to in the following provisions of this section and sections 453 to 456; and

(b) the arrangements comply with the requirements of this section and sections 453 to 455, are approved by the Board and are certified by the Secretary of State to be in the public interest;

then, subject to section 456(4), the provisions of this section and sections 453 to 456 relating to taxation shall have effect in relation to any underwriting member.

(2) The arrangements must provide for the setting up, in relation to the underwriter, of a special reserve fund vested in trustees who have control over it and power to invest the capital thereof and to vary the investments.

(3) Where part of the business of the underwriter is carried on through an underwriting agent and part is not so carried on, or where different parts of his business are carried on through different underwriting agents, the arrangements may provide for separate special reserve funds being constituted in relation to the different parts of his business.

(4) The arrangements must provide—

(a) for the income arising from the investments of the underwriter's special reserve fund or funds being held on trust for the underwriter, his personal representatives or assigns; and

(b) that, on the underwriter ceasing to carry on his business, the capital of his special reserve fund or funds, so far as not required for giving effect to the requirements of section 453, shall be paid over to the underwriter or his personal representatives or assigns.

(5) The arrangements must be such as to secure that if, for an underwriting year corresponding to a year of assessment during the whole or any part of which the underwriter continues to carry on his business (subject to section 456(4)), the underwriter makes a profit from his business, he has the right to make, into his special reserve fund or funds, payments ("permissible payments") the gross amount of which is not in the aggregate greater than £7,000 or 50 per cent. of the profit, whichever is the less, or such less sum as may be specified in the arrangements.

(6) The amount of any permissible payment shall be notified to the inspector not later than 12 months after the date at which the accounts of the business for that underwriting year are deemed by the Board to be closed for the purposes of the arrangements, and no permissible payment shall be made more than 30 days after the date on which the inspector has notified his agreement in writing or, if later, 30 days after the expiration of those 12 months.

(7) Where the underwriter carries on his business during part only of the year of assessment referred to in subsection (5) above, the maximum gross amount of the permissible payments shall be reduced by the application thereto of the proportion which the part of that year of assessment for which he is entitled to profits from the business bears to a full year.

(8) In subsection (5) above "profit" means a profit computed in the manner in which the profits or gains of the business of the underwriting year in question would fall to be computed under Case I of Schedule D if—

(a) income arising from the investments forming part of the premiums trust fund of the underwriter, his special reserve fund or funds and any other fund required or authorised by the rules of Lloyd's or required by the underwriting agent through whom the business or any part thereof is carried on, to be kept in connection with the business fell to be taken into account; and

(b) all shares of the profits of the business and all charges related to those profits or to the income mentioned in paragraph (a) above, being shares and charges payable to persons other than the underwriter and not otherwise taken into account, fell to be deducted.

In paragraph (a) above "income" includes annual profits or gains chargeable to tax by virtue of section 714(2) or 716(3).

453.—(1) The arrangements must be such as to secure that, if it is certified that the underwriter has sustained a loss in his business for an underwriting year subsequent to that which corresponds to the first year of assessment to which section 452(5) applies, there shall be made into his premiums trust fund, out of the capital of his special reserve fund or funds, payments the gross amount of which is equal in the aggregate to the certified amount of the loss. *Payments into premiums trust fund on account of losses.*

(2) If the capital of the underwriter's special reserve fund or funds, reduced by so much thereof as represents sums paid into it or them as a consequence of a profit for a year later than the year of the loss, is less than the net amount of the payments required to be made by subsection (1) above, those payments shall be reduced so that the net amount thereof is equal to the capital of the fund or funds as so reduced.

(3) In this section—

(a) "loss" means a loss computed in the manner in which the profits or gains of the business of the underwriting year in question would fall to be computed under section 452(8); and

(b) where, under any arrangement between the underwriter and another person which provides for the sharing of losses, any amount is paid to the underwriter by that person as that person's share of a loss for that year, the loss (as so computed) shall be reduced by that amount.

(4) In this section "certified" means certified by a certificate of the inspector, but—

(a) no certificate shall be given by the inspector until 30 days have elapsed from the date on which he has given notice to the underwriter or his personal representatives stating his intention to give a certificate and stating the amount which he proposes to specify as the amount of the loss;

(b) the underwriter or his personal representatives may, on giving notice to the inspector within that 30 day period, appeal to the Special Commissioners;

(c) where notice is so given by the underwriter or his personal representatives, the inspector shall not without the consent of the underwriter or his personal representatives give any certificate until after the hearing of the appeal; and

(d) on the hearing of the appeal, the Special Commissioners may direct the inspector not to give a certificate or to give it with such an amount specified as the amount of the loss as may be specified in the direction.

(5) The arrangements may authorise the making of payments pursuant to subsection (1) above on a provisional basis before the amount of the loss has been finally ascertained and certified by the inspector.

(6) The amount so withdrawn shall not exceed such proportion of the estimated loss as may be specified in the arrangements.

(7) When the amount of the loss has been certified by the inspector such adjustments shall be made by repayment to the underwriter's special reserve fund or funds, or by further withdrawal of sums for payment into the underwriter's premiums trust fund, as will secure that the net amount withdrawn from the underwriter's special reserve fund or funds in respect of the loss is that required pursuant to subsection (1) above; and no tax consequences shall ensue on the withdrawal of sums in respect of a loss until the amount of the loss has been so certified and any such adjustments have been made.

Income tax consequences on payments into and out of special reserve fund.

454.—(1) Where such a payment as is mentioned in section 452(5) is made into a special reserve fund of an underwriter by reason of the making by him of a profit for an underwriting year—

(a) subject to subsection (2) below, the payment shall be deemed to be an annual payment chargeable to income tax by way of deduction and payable and paid in the year of assessment corresponding to that underwriting year; and

(b) the sum actually paid shall be deemed for the purposes of sections 452 to 456 and for all income tax purposes to be a net amount corresponding to a gross amount from which income tax has been duly deducted.

(2) Subsection (1)(a) above—

(a) shall not reduce any income other than income derived from the underwriter's underwriting business or from any deposit made or assets held on trust in connection with that business; and

(b) subject to paragraph (a) above, shall reduce income other than investment income before reducing investment income.

(3) Where such a payment as is mentioned in section 453(1) is made out of a special reserve fund of an underwriter into a premiums trust fund of his by reason that he has sustained a loss for an underwriting year then, subject to section 453(7)—

(a) the payment shall be deemed for all income tax purposes—

(i) to be an annual payment chargeable to income tax by way of deduction and paid out of profits or gains brought into charge to income tax; and

(ii) to have been payable and paid to the underwriter; and

(iii) to have been payable and paid to him on the last day of the year of assessment corresponding to that underwriting year or, if he ceased to carry on his business before that day, on the last day on which he carried on his business; and

(b) the sum actually paid shall be deemed for the purposes of sections 452 to 456 and for all income tax purposes to be a net amount corresponding to a gross amount from which income tax has been duly deducted for the year of assessment in which the payment is so deemed to have been payable and paid.

(4) Where such a payment as is mentioned in section 453(1) is made out of a special reserve fund of an underwriter by reason that he has sustained a loss, relief in respect of the loss shall, so far as possible, be given by treating the loss as reducing the income represented by the payment.

(5) Where the underwriter ceases to carry on his business before his death and under so much of the arrangements as gives effect to section 452(4)(b) a sum is paid to him or his personal representatives or assigns—

(a) the payment shall be deemed for all income tax purposes—

(i) to be an annual payment chargeable to income tax by way of deduction and paid out of profits or gains brought into charge to income tax; and

(ii) to have been payable and paid to the underwriter; and

(iii) to have been payable and paid to him on the last day on which he carried on his business; and

(b) the sum actually paid shall be deemed for the purposes of sections 452 to 456 and for all income tax purposes to be a net amount corresponding to a gross amount from which income tax has been duly deducted.

PART XII

Income tax consequences on death of underwriter.

(6) Neither the arrangements, nor any disposition, trust, covenant, agreement or arrangement entered into for the purposes of the arrangements, shall be treated as included in the expression "settlement" for the purposes of Chapter III or IV of Part XV.

455.—(1) In this section "the lower limit" means the limit which would be imposed by section 452(5) if the words "£5,000 or 35 per cent. of that profit, whichever is the less" stood in that subsection in place of the words "£7,000 or 50 per cent. of that profit, whichever is the less".

(2) Where an underwriter dies while carrying on his business and, after giving effect to the requirements of section 453, his special reserve fund or funds include an amount which represents an excess in the payments made into the fund or funds for any underwriting year over the lower limit—

(a) he shall be deemed for all income tax purposes to have received in the year of assessment corresponding to that underwriting year a payment of that amount—

(i) which was an annual payment chargeable to income tax by way of deduction and paid out of profits or gains brought into charge to income tax, and

(ii) which was payable in the year of assessment in which it is deemed to have been paid, and

(b) the payment (to that actual amount) shall be deemed for the purposes of sections 452 to 456 and for all income tax purposes to be a net amount corresponding to a gross amount from which tax has been duly deducted.

(3) Where, to give effect to the requirements of section 453 as to the meeting of a loss, any withdrawal was made at any time from the capital of the underwriter's special reserve fund or funds, the amount withdrawn shall be regarded for the purposes of subsection (2) above—

(a) as having been met out of payments made into the fund or funds for underwriting years before that in which the loss was incurred, and as having been met before any withdrawal to meet a loss for a later underwriting year; and

(b) as having been met out of so much of the payments made for any underwriting year as was not in excess of the lower limit, rather than out of such part of the payments made for any underwriting year as was in excess of the lower limit; and

(c) subject to that, as having been met out of payments in excess of the lower limit for a later year rather than out of payments in excess of the lower limit for an earlier year;

and, where payments have been made into the underwriter's special reserve fund or funds for any underwriting year in excess of the lower limit, his fund or funds shall be deemed at all subsequent times to include an amount representing that excess except to the extent that any withdrawal is, under the provisions of this subsection, to be regarded as having been met out of that amount.

(4) Any tax chargeable by virtue of this section shall be assessed and charged upon the underwriter's personal representatives and tax so charged shall be a debt due from and payable out of his estate; and, notwithstanding section 34(1) of the Management Act (which requires assessments to be made not later than six years after the end of the year to which they relate), assessments in respect of tax so chargeable may be made at any time not later than three years after the end of the year of assessment in which the underwriter died.

(5) References in this section to payments made into a special reserve fund or funds for any underwriting year are references to payments made, as described in section 452(5), by reference to the profits made for that underwriting year.

456.—(1) So much of an underwriter's income as is attributable to payments from his special reserve fund or to such an excess as is mentioned in section 455 shall (so far as remaining after allowing for any relief by which it is reduced) be treated as unearned income if, but only if, his income from his underwriting business falls to be so treated.

(2) Where, as a result of a change in the circumstances in which an underwriting business is carried on, an underwriter's income from the business falls to be treated as unearned income, the change shall be disregarded for the purposes of subsection (1) above except to the extent that the special reserve fund represents payments made into it after the change; and for this purpose any amount withdrawn after the change to give effect to the requirements of section 453 shall, so far as possible and notwithstanding section 455(3), be regarded as having been met by payments into the fund made after the change.

(3) The arrangements may from time to time be varied with the consent of the Board and the Secretary of State.

(4) If, after giving notice of their intention so to do to the Council of Lloyd's, the Board or the Secretary of State cancel the approval or certificate which they have or he has given with respect to the arrangements, section 452(5) to (9) shall not apply, in the case of any underwriter, to any year of assessment after the year of assessment in which the approval or certificate is cancelled.

457.—(1) In sections 450 to 456—

"arrangements" means any such arrangements as are referred to in section 452(1);

"business", in relation to an underwriter, means his underwriting business as a member of Lloyd's, whether carried on personally or through an underwriting agent, and does not include any other business carried on by him, and in particular, where he is himself an underwriting agent, does not include his business as such an agent;

"member" means an underwriting member of Lloyd's;

"net amount" and "gross amount", in relation to any payment, mean respectively the sum actually paid and the sum which, after deduction of income tax, is equal to the sum actually paid;

"premiums trust fund" means such a trust fund as is referred to in section 83 of the Insurance Companies Act 1982;

"underwriting year" means the calendar year.

(2) For the purpose of construing any reference in sections 450 to 456 to the year of assessment which corresponds to an underwriting year or to the underwriting year which corresponds to a year of assessment, an underwriting year and a year of assessment shall be deemed to correspond to each other if the underwriting year ends in the year of assessment.

Capital redemption business

Capital
redemption
business.

458.—(1) Where any person carries on capital redemption business in conjunction with business of any other class, the capital redemption business shall, for the purposes of the Corporation Tax Acts (including the provisions about corporation tax on chargeable gains) and the Income Tax Acts, be treated as a separate business from any other class of business carried on by that person.

(2) In ascertaining whether and to what extent any person has incurred a loss on his capital redemption business for the purposes of section 380 or sections 393 and 394—

(a) any profits derived from investments held in connection with the capital redemption business (including franked investment income of a company resident in the United Kingdom) shall be treated as part of the profits of that business, and

(b) in determining whether any, and if so what, relief can be given under section 385(4) in the case of capital redemption business, the loss which may be carried forward under subsection (1) of that section shall be similarly computed.

(3) In this section "capital redemption business" means the business (not being life assurance business or industrial assurance business) of effecting and carrying out contracts of insurance, whether effected by the issue of policies, bonds or endowment certificates or otherwise, whereby, in return for one or more premiums paid to the insurer, a sum or a series of sums is to become payable to the insured in the future.

(4) This section shall not apply to any capital redemption business in so far as it consists of carrying out contracts of insurance effected before 1st January 1938.

CHAPTER II

FRIENDLY SOCIETIES, TRADE UNIONS AND EMPLOYERS' ASSOCIATIONS

Unregistered friendly societies

Exemption from
tax.

459. An unregistered friendly society whose income does not exceed £160 a year shall, on making a claim, be entitled to exemption from income tax and corporation tax (whether on income or chargeable gains).

Registered friendly societies

460.—(1) Subject to subsection (2) below, a registered friendly society shall, on making a claim, be entitled to exemption from income tax and corporation tax (whether on income or chargeable gains) on its profits arising from life or endowment business.

(2) Subsection (1) above—

(a) shall not, subject to section 462, exempt a friendly society registered after 31st December 1957 which at any time in the period of three months ending 3rd May 1966 entered into any transaction in return for a single premium, being a transaction forming part of its life or endowment business;

(b) shall not apply to profits arising from pension business;

(c) shall not apply to profits arising from life or endowment business consisting—

(i) where the profits relate to contracts made after 31st August 1987, of the assurance of gross sums under contracts under which the total premiums payable in any period of 12 months exceed £100 or of the granting of annuities of annual amounts exceeding £156;

(ii) where the profits relate to contracts made after 13th March 1984 but before 1st September 1987, of the assurance of gross sums exceeding £750 or of the granting of annuities of annual amounts exceeding £156;

(iii) where the profits relate to contracts made before 14th March 1984, of the assurance of gross sums exceeding £500 or of the granting of annuities of annual amounts exceeding £104; and

(d) as respects other life or endowment business ("tax exempt life or endowment business"), has effect subject to the following provisions of this Chapter.

(3) In determining for the purposes of subsection (2)(c)(i) above the total premiums payable in any period of 12 months—

(a) where those premiums are payable more frequently than annually, there shall be disregarded an amount equal to 10 per cent. of those premiums; and

(b) so much of any premium as is charged on the ground that an exceptional risk of death is involved shall be disregarded;

and in applying the limit of £156 in subsection (2)(c)(i) above, any bonus or addition declared upon an annuity shall be disregarded.

(4) In applying the limits referred to in subsection (2)(c)(ii) and (iii) above, any bonus or addition which either is declared upon an assurance of a gross sum or annuity or accrues upon such an assurance by reference to an increase in the value of any investments shall be disregarded.

(5) A registered friendly society is within this subsection if its rules make no provision for it to carry on life or endowment business consisting of the assurance of gross sums exceeding £2,000 or of the granting of annuities of annual amounts exceeding £416.

(6) In the case of a registered friendly society within subsection (5) above—

(a) subsection (2)(c)(iii) above shall have effect with the substitution of references to £2,000 and £416 respectively for the references to £500 and £104; and

(b) references in this Chapter to tax exempt life or endowment business shall be construed accordingly.

(7) Where at any time a registered friendly society within subsection (5) above amends its rules so as to cease to be within that subsection, any part of its life or endowment business consisting of business which—

(a) relates to contracts made before that time; and

(b) immediately before that time was tax exempt life or endowment business,

shall thereafter continue to be tax exempt life or endowment business for the purposes of this Chapter.

(8) Where at any time a registered friendly society not within subsection (5) above amends its rules so as to bring itself within that subsection, any part of its life or endowment business consisting of business which—

(a) related to contracts made before that time; and

(b) immediately before that time was not tax exempt life or endowment business,

shall thereafter continue not to be tax exempt life or endowment business for the purposes of this Chapter.

(9) Where at any time a registered friendly society not within subsection (5) above acquires by way of transfer of engagements or amalgamation from another registered friendly society any life or endowment business consisting of business which—

(a) relates to contracts made before that time; and

(b) immediately before that time was tax exempt life or endowment business,

that business shall thereafter continue to be tax exempt life or endowment business for the purposes of this Chapter.

(10) Where at any time a registered friendly society within subsection (5) above acquires by way of transfer of engagements or amalgamation from another registered friendly society any life or endowment business consisting of business which—

(a) relates to contracts made before that time; and

(b) immediately before that time was not tax exempt life or endowment business,

that business shall thereafter continue not to be tax exempt life or endowment business for the purposes of this Chapter.

(11) Where at any time a registered friendly society ceases by virtue of section 84 of the Friendly Societies Act 1974 or by virtue of section 72 of the Friendly Societies Act (Northern Ireland) 1970 (conversion into company) to be registered under that Act, any part of its life or endowment business consisting of business which—

(a) relates to contracts made before that time; and

(b) immediately before that time was tax exempt life or endowment business,

shall thereafter continue to be tax exempt life or endowment business for the purposes of this Chapter.

(12) For the purposes of the Corporation Tax Acts any part of a company's business which continues to be tax exempt life or endowment business by virtue of subsection (11) above shall be treated as a separate business from any other business carried on by the company.

461.—(1) Subject to the following provisions of this section, a registered friendly society other than a society to which subsection (2) below applies shall, on making a claim, be entitled to exemption from income tax and corporation tax (whether on income or chargeable gains) on its profits other than those arising from life or endowment business.

(2) This subsection applies to any society registered after 31st May 1973 unless—

(a) its business is limited to the provision, in accordance with the rules of the society, of benefits for or in respect of employees of a particular employer or such other group of persons as is for the time being approved for the purposes of this section by the registrar; or

(b) it was registered before 27th March 1974 and its rules limit the aggregate amount which may be paid by a member by way of contributions and deposits to not more than £1 per month or such greater amount as the registrar may authorise for the purposes of this section;

and also applies to any society registered before 1st June 1973 with respect to which a direction under subsection (8) below is in force.

(3) If a society to which subsection (2) above applies, after 26th March 1974 or such later date as may be specified in a direction under this section, makes a payment to a member in respect of his interest in the society and the payment is made otherwise than in the course of life or endowment business and exceeds the aggregate of any sums paid by him to the society by way of contributions or deposits, after deducting from that aggregate the amount of—

(a) any previous payment so made to him by the society after that date, and

(b) any earlier repayment of such sums paid by him,

the excess shall be treated for the purposes of corporation tax and income tax as a qualifying distribution.

PART XII

1974 c. 46.

1970 c. 31 (N.I.).

Taxation in respect of other business.

(4) Where a registered friendly society—

    (a) at any time ceases by virtue of section 84 of the Friendly Societies Act 1974 or by virtue of section 72 of the Friendly Societies Act (Northern Ireland) 1970 (conversion into company) to be registered under that Act; and

    (b) immediately before that time was exempt from income tax or corporation tax on profits arising from any business carried on by it other than life or endowment business,

the company into which the society is converted shall be so exempt on its profits arising from any part of that business which relates to contracts made before that time so long as there is no increase in the scale of benefits which it undertakes to provide in the course of carrying on that part of its business.

(5) For the purposes of the Corporation Tax Acts any part of a company's business in respect of the profits from which the company is exempt by virtue of subsection (4) above shall be treated as a separate business from any other business carried on by the company.

(6) If—

    (a) a friendly society registered before 1st June 1973 begins after 26th March 1974 to carry on business other than life or endowment business or, in the opinion of the registrar, begins to carry on business other than life or endowment business on an enlarged scale or of a new character; and

    (b) it appears to the registrar, having regard to the restrictions imposed by this section on friendly societies registered later, that for the protection of the revenue it is expedient to do so;

he may serve a notice on the society referring to the provisions of this subsection and stating that he is considering the question whether, for the protection of the revenue, it is expedient to give a direction that subsection (2) above shall apply to the society as from the date of the notice.

(7) The registrar shall consider any representations or undertakings made or offered to him by the society within the period of one month from service of the notice, and if the society so requests shall afford it an opportunity of being heard by him not later than three weeks after the end of that period.

(8) If, after consideration of any such representations or undertakings, the registrar remains of the opinion that it is expedient to do so, he shall direct that subsection (2) above shall apply to the society as from the date of the notice, but subject to any further direction given by him cancelling that direction.

(9) A friendly society may, within one month from the giving of a direction under subsection (8) above, appeal against it to the court to which or person to whom it might appeal under section 92 of the Friendly Societies Act 1974 or section 81 of the Friendly Societies Act (Northern Ireland) 1970 against cancellation of its registration.

(10) For the purposes of this section a registered friendly society formed on the amalgamation of two or more friendly societies shall be treated as registered before 1st June 1973 if at the time of the amalgamation subsection (2) above did not apply to any of the societies amalgamated, but otherwise shall be treated as registered at that time.

462.—(1) Subject to subsections (2) to (4) below, section 460(1) shall not apply to so much of the profits arising from tax exempt life or endowment business as is attributable to a policy which, by virtue of paragraph 6(2) of Schedule 15—

(a) is not a qualifying policy; and

(b) would not be a qualifying policy if all policies with other friendly societies were left out of account.

(2) Section 460(2)(a) and subsection (1) above shall not withdraw exemption under section 460(1) for profits arising from any part of a life or endowment business relating to contracts made not later than 3rd May 1966.

(3) If, with respect to a policy issued in respect of an insurance made on or after 1st June 1984 and before 19th March 1985 for the assurance of a gross sum, there is or has been an infringement of any of the conditions in paragraph 3(2) to (11) of Schedule 15, section 460(1) shall not apply to so much as is attributable to that policy of the profits of the registered friendly society or branch concerned which arise from tax exempt life or endowment business.

(4) Nothing in subsection (3) above shall be taken to affect the status of a policy as a qualifying policy.

463. Subject to section 460(1), the Corporation Tax Acts shall apply to the life or endowment business carried on by registered friendly societies in the same way as they apply to mutual life assurance business carried on by insurance companies, so however that the Treasury may by regulations provide that those Acts as so applied shall have effect subject to such modifications and exceptions as may be prescribed by the regulations, and those regulations may in particular require any part of any business to be treated as a separate business.

464.—(1) Subject to subsections (2) and (3) below, a member of a registered friendly society or branch shall not be entitled to have at any time outstanding contracts with any one or more such societies or branches (taking together all such societies or branches throughout the United Kingdom) for the assurance of—

(a) more than £750 by way of gross sum under tax exempt life or endowment business;

(b) more than £156 by way of annuity under tax exempt life or endowment business.

In any case where the member's outstanding contracts were all made before 14th March 1984 this subsection shall have effect with the substitution for "£750" and "£156" of "£2,000" and "£416" respectively.

(2) Subsection (1)(a) above shall not apply as respects sums assured under contracts made after 31st August 1987.

(3) With respect to contracts for the assurance of gross sums under tax exempt life or endowment business, a member of a registered friendly society or branch shall not be entitled to have outstanding with any one or more such societies or branches (taking together all such societies or branches throughout the United Kingdom) contracts under which the total premiums payable in any period of 12 months exceed £100 unless all those contracts were entered into before 1st September 1987.

(4) In applying the limit in subsection (3) above, the premiums under any contract for an annuity which was made before 1st June 1984 by a new society shall be brought into account as if the contract were for the assurance of a gross sum.

(5) In applying the limits in this section there shall be disregarded—

(a) any bonus or addition which either is declared upon assurance of a gross sum or annuity or accrues upon such an assurance by reference to an increase in the value of any investments;

(b) any approved annuities as defined in section 620(9) or any policy of insurance or annuity contract by means of which the benefits to be provided under an occupational pension scheme as defined 1973 c. 38.   in section 51(3)(a) of the Social Security Act 1973 are secured;

(c) any increase in a benefit under a friendly society contract, as 1969 c. 19.   defined in section 6 of the Decimal Currency Act 1969, resulting from the adoption of a scheme prescribed or approved in pursuance of subsection (3) of that section; and

(d) so far as concerns the total premiums payable in any period of 12 months—

(i) 10 per cent. of the premiums payable under any contract under which the premiums are payable more frequently than annually; and

(ii) £10 of the premiums payable under any contract made before 1st September 1987 by a society which is not a new society; and

(iii) so much of any premium as is charged on the ground that an exceptional risk of death is involved.

(6) In applying the limits in this section in any case where a member has outstanding with one or more society or branch one or more contracts made after 13th March 1984 and one or more contracts made on or before that date, any contract for an annuity which was made before 1st June 1984 by a new society shall be regarded not only as a contract for the annual amount concerned but also as a contract for the assurance of a gross sum equal to 75 per cent. of the total premiums which would be payable under the contract if it were to run for its full term or, as the case may be, if the member concerned were to die at the age of 75 years.

(7) A registered friendly society or branch may require a member to make and sign a statutory declaration that the total amount assured under outstanding contracts entered into by that member with any one or more registered friendly societies or branches (taking together all such societies or branches throughout the United Kingdom) does not exceed the limits applicable by virtue of this section and that the total premiums under those contracts do not exceed those limits.

465.—(1) In this section "old society" means a friendly society which is not a new society.

(2) This section applies if, on or after 19th March 1985, an old society—

> (a) begins to carry on tax exempt life or endowment business; or

> (b) in the opinion of the Board begins to carry on such business on an enlarged scale or of a new character.

(3) If it appears to the Board, having regard to the restrictions placed on qualifying policies issued by new societies by paragraphs 3(1)(b) and (c) and 4(3)(b) of Schedule 15, that for the protection of the revenue it is expedient to do so, the Board may give a direction to the old society under subsection (4) below.

(4) A direction under this subsection is that (and has the effect that) the old society to which it is given is to be treated for the purposes of this Act as a new society with respect to business carried on after the date of the direction.

(5) An old society to which a direction is given may, within 30 days of the date on which it is given, appeal against the direction to the Special Commissioners on the ground that—

> (a) it has not begun to carry on business as mentioned in subsection (2) above; or

> (b) that the direction is not necessary for the protection of the revenue.

466.—(1) In this Chapter "life or endowment business" means any business within any of paragraphs (1), (2), (4) and (5) of Schedule 1 to the Friendly Societies Act 1974 or paragraphs 1, 2, 4 and 5 of Schedule 1 to the Friendly Societies Act (Northern Ireland) 1970, any pension business and any other life assurance business, but—

> (a) shall not include the issue of a policy affording provision for sickness or other infirmity (whether bodily or mental) unless—

>> (i) it also affords assurance for a gross sum independent of sickness or other infirmity; and

>> (ii) not less than 60 per cent. of the amount of the premiums is attributable to the provision afforded during sickness or other infirmity; and

>> (iii) there is no bonus or addition which may be declared or accrue upon the assurance of the gross sum;

> (b) shall not include the assurance of any annuity the consideration for which consists of sums obtainable on the maturity, or on the surrender, of any other policy of assurance issued by the friendly society, being a policy of assurance forming part of the tax exempt life or endowment business of the friendly society.

(2) In this Chapter—

> "life assurance business" means the issue of, or the undertaking of liability under, policies of assurance upon human life, or the

granting of annuities upon human life, not being industrial assurance business;

"new society" means a friendly society which was registered after 3rd May 1966 or which was registered in the period of three months ending on that date but which at no time earlier than that date carried on any life or endowment business;

"pension business" shall be construed in accordance with section 431;

"policy", in relation to life or endowment business, includes an instrument evidencing a contract to pay an annuity upon human life;

"registrar" means the Chief Registrar of Friendly Societies or, in the application of this Chapter to Scotland, the assistant registrar for Scotland or, in the application of this Chapter to Northern Ireland, the Registrar of Friendly Societies for Northern Ireland;

"tax exempt life or endowment business" has, subject to subsections (7) to (11) of section 460, the meaning given by subsection (2)(d) of that section, that is to say, it means (subject to those subsections) life or endowment business other than business profits arising from which are excluded from subsection (1) of that section by subsection (2)(b) or (c) of that section (read, where appropriate, with subsection (6) of that section);

and references in sections 460 to 465 and this subsection to a friendly society include references to any branch of that friendly society.

(3) It is hereby declared that for the purposes of this Chapter (except where provision to the contrary is made) a registered friendly society formed on the amalgamation of two or more friendly societies is to be treated as different from the amalgamated societies.

(4) A registered friendly society formed on the amalgamation of two or more friendly societies shall, for the purposes of this Chapter, be treated as registered not later than 3rd May 1966 if at the time of the amalgamation—

(a) all the friendly societies amalgamated were registered friendly societies eligible for the exemption conferred by section 460(1); and

(b) at least one of them was not a new society;

or, if the amalgamation took place before 19th March 1985, the society was treated as registered not later than 3rd May 1966 by virtue of the proviso to section 337(4) of the 1970 Act.

Trade unions and employers' associations

Exemption for trade unions and employers' associations.

467.—(1) A trade union which is precluded by Act of Parliament or by its rules from assuring to any person a sum exceeding £3,000 by way of gross sum or £625 by way of annuity shall on making a claim be entitled—

(a) to exemption from income tax and corporation tax in respect of its income which is not trading income and which is applicable and applied for the purpose of provident benefits;

(b) to exemption from tax in respect of chargeable gains which are applicable and applied for the purpose of provident benefits.

(2) In this section "provident benefits" includes any payment, expressly authorised by the rules of the trade union, which is made to a member during sickness or incapacity from personal injury or while out of work, or to an aged member by way of superannuation, or to a member who has met with an accident, or has lost his tools by fire or theft, and includes a payment in discharge or aid of funeral expenses on the death of a member or the wife of a member or as provision for the children of a deceased member.

(3) In determining for the purposes of this section whether a trade union is by Act of Parliament or its rules precluded from assuring to any person a sum exceeding £625 by way of annuity, there shall be disregarded any approved annuities (as defined in section 620(9)).

(4) In this section "trade union" means—

(a) any trade union the name of which is entered in the list of trade unions maintained by the Registrar of Friendly Societies under section 8 of the Trade Union and Labour Relations Act 1974;   1974 c. 52.

(b) any employers' association the name of which is entered in the list of employers' associations maintained by the Registrar of Friendly Societies under section 8 of the Trade Union and Labour Relations Act 1974 and which on 30th September 1971 was a registered trade union for the purposes of section 338 of the 1970 Act; and

(c) the Police Federation for England and Wales, the Police Federation for Scotland, the Police Federation for Northern Ireland and any other organisation of persons in police service which has similar functions.

CHAPTER III

UNIT TRUST SCHEMES, DEALERS IN SECURITIES ETC.

Unit trust schemes

468.—(1) In respect of income arising to the trustees of an authorised unit trust, and for the purposes of the provisions relating to relief for capital expenditure, the Tax Acts shall have effect as if—   Authorised unit trusts.

(a) the trustees were a company resident in the United Kingdom; and

(b) the rights of the unit holders were shares in the company.

(2) The Tax Acts shall also have effect as if the aggregate amount shown in the accounts of the trust as income available for payment to unit holders or for investment were dividends on the shares referred to in

PART XII

subsection (1) above paid to them in proportion to their rights, the date of payment, in the case of income not paid to unit holders, being taken to be—

(a) the date or latest date provided by the terms of the authorised unit trust for any distribution in respect of the distribution period in question;

(b) if no date is so provided, the last day of the distribution period.

This subsection shall not apply to any authorised unit trust which is also an approved personal pension scheme (within the meaning of Chapter IV of Part XIV).

(3) References in the Corporation Tax Acts to a body corporate shall be construed in accordance with subsections (1) and (2) above, and section 234(3) and (4) shall apply with any necessary modifications.

(4) Section 75 shall apply in relation to an authorised unit trust whether or not it is an investment company within the meaning of section 130; and sums periodically appropriated for managers' remuneration shall be treated for the purposes of section 75 as sums disbursed as expenses of management.

(5) Subsection (1) above shall not apply in relation to an authorised unit trust under the terms of which the funds of the trust cannot be invested in such a way that income can arise to the trustees which will be chargeable to tax in the hands of the trustees otherwise than—

(a) under Schedule C as profits arising from United Kingdom public revenue dividends, or

(b) under Case III of Schedule D;

and in this subsection "United Kingdom public revenue dividends" means public revenue dividends payable in the United Kingdom (whether they are also payable outside the United Kingdom or not) out of the public revenue of the United Kingdom.

(6) In this section—

"authorised unit trust" means, as respects an accounting period, a unit trust scheme in the case of which an order under section 78 of the Financial Services Act 1986 is in force during the whole or part of that accounting period;

1986 c. 60.

"distribution period" means a period beginning on or after 1st April 1987 over which income from the investments subject to the trusts is aggregated for the purposes of ascertaining the amount available for distribution to unit holders;

"unit holder" means a person entitled to a share of the investments subject to the trusts of a unit trust scheme; and

"unit trust scheme" has the same meaning as in section 469.

Other unit trusts.

469.—(1) This section applies to—

(a) any unit trust scheme that is not an authorised unit trust; and

(b) any authorised unit trust to which, by virtue of subsection (5) of section 468, that section does not apply, except where the trustees of the scheme are not resident in the United Kingdom.

(2) Income arising to the trustees of the scheme shall be regarded for the purposes of the Tax Acts as income of the trustees (and not as income of the unit holders); and the trustees (and not the unit holders) shall be regarded as the persons to or on whom allowances or charges are to be made under the provisions of those Acts relating to relief for capital expenditure.

(3) For the purposes of the Tax Acts the unit holders shall be treated as receiving annual payments (made by the trustees under deduction of tax) in proportion to their rights.

This subsection shall not apply to any authorised unit trust which is also an approved personal pension scheme (within the meaning of Chapter IV of Part XIV).

(4) The total amount of those annual payments in respect of any distribution period shall be the amount which, after deducting income tax at the basic rate in force for the year of assessment in which the payments are treated as made, is equal to the aggregate amount shown in the accounts of the scheme as income available for payment to unit holders or for investment.

(5) The date on which the annual payments are treated as made shall be the date or latest date provided by the terms of the scheme for any distribution in respect of the distribution period in question, except that, if—

    (a) the date so provided is more than 12 months after the end of the period; or

    (b) no date is so provided,

the date on which the payments are treated as made shall be the last day of the period.

(6) In this section "distribution period" has the same meaning as in section 468, but—

    (a) if the scheme does not make provision for distribution periods, then for the purposes of this section its distribution periods shall be taken to be successive periods of 12 months the first of which began with the day on which the scheme took effect; and

    (b) if the scheme makes provision for distribution periods of more than 12 months, then for the purposes of this section each of those periods shall be taken to be divided into two (or more) distribution periods, the second succeeding the first after 12 months (and so on for any further periods).

(7) In this section "unit trust scheme" has the same meaning as in the Financial Services Act 1986, except that the Treasury may by regulations provide that any scheme of a description specified in the regulations shall be treated as not being a unit trust scheme for the purposes of this section.

1986 c. 60.

(8) Regulations under this section may contain such supplementary and transitional provisions as appear to the Treasury to be necessary or expedient.

(9) Sections 686 and 687 shall not apply to a scheme to which this section applies.

(10) Section 720(5) shall not apply in relation to profits or gains treated as received by the trustees of a scheme to which this section applies if or to the extent that those profits or gains represent accruals of interest (within the meaning of Chapter II of Part XVII) which are treated as income in the accounts of the scheme.

(11) This section shall have effect in relation to distribution periods beginning on or after 6th April 1987.

Transitional
provisions relating
to unit trusts.
1987 c. 16.

470.—(1) Any transitional provisions contained in an order made under section 40(5) of the Finance Act 1987 appointing a day for the coming into force of subsections (1) and (2) of that section and made in connection therewith shall after the coming into force of this section have effect for the purposes of this Act as they had effect for the purposes of that section, with such modifications if any as may be necessary.

(2) If such an order as is mentioned in subsection (1) above has not been made before the coming into force of this Act, section 468 shall have effect with the substitution for the definition of "authorised unit trust" contained in subsection (6) of the following definition—

1958 c. 45.
1940 c. 9 (N.I.).

"authorised unit trust" means, as respects any accounting period, a unit trust scheme in the case of which an order under section 17 of the Prevention of Frauds (Investments) Act 1958 or under section 16 of the Prevention of Frauds (Investments) Act (Northern Ireland) 1940 is in force during the whole or some part of that accounting period;

and sections 468 and 832 shall have effect with the omission of the definition of "unit trust scheme".

(3) If such an order as is mentioned in subsection (1) above has not been made before the coming into force of this Act, subsection (2) above shall cease to have effect on such day as the Board may by order appoint; and an order under this subsection may contain such transitional provisions as appear to the Board to be necessary or expedient.

Dealers in securities, banks and insurance businesses

Exchange of
securities in
connection with
conversion
operations,
nationalisation
etc.

471.—(1) If—

(a) any securities to which a person who is carrying on a trade which consists wholly or partly in dealing in securities is beneficially entitled are exchanged for other securities; and

(b) the exchange is one to which this section applies,

then, whether or not any additional consideration is given for the exchange but subject to subsection (2) below, that person shall be treated for tax purposes (except as regards any tax payable in respect of dividends or interest), both at the time of the exchange and thereafter, as if the exchange had not taken place, and in that case the produce of any subsequent realisation of any of the securities received by him under the exchange (together with any additional consideration, or the appropriate part of any additional consideration, received by him under the exchange) shall be treated as the produce of the realisation of the corresponding securities surrendered by or transferred from him under the exchange, or of a corresponding part thereof, as the case may be.

(2) Subsection (1) above shall not apply to any person who gives notice to the inspector not later than two years after the end of the chargeable period in which the exchange takes place that he desires not to be treated as mentioned in that subsection.

(3) The exchanges to which this section applies are—

(a) any exchange effected under any arrangement carried out under section 2 of the National Loans Act 1939 or section 14 of the National Loans Act 1968 if the Treasury direct, in pursuance of that arrangement, that this section shall apply to exchanges thereunder;

1939 c. 117.
1968 c. 13.

(b) any exchange of securities effected by section 1 of the Bank of England Act 1946; and

1946 c. 27.

(c) any exchange of securities effected in pursuance of any enactment passed after 5th April 1946 which provides for the compulsory acquisition of any securities and the issue of other securities in lieu thereof, if the Treasury direct that this section shall apply to exchanges of securities effected in pursuance of that enactment.

(4) In this section "securities" includes shares, stock, bonds, debentures and debenture stock.

472.—(1) Where—

Distribution of securities issued in connection with nationalisation etc.

(a) in pursuance of any enactment passed after 5th April 1946 any securities are issued to any body corporate as, or as part of, the consideration for the compulsory acquisition of any property under that enactment; and

(b) that body corporate is wound up or the capital thereof is reduced or any bonds, debentures or debenture stock thereof are redeemed, and, in or in connection with the winding up, reduction of capital or redemption, all or any of the securities so issued are distributed to holders of securities of the body corporate ("the distributed securities"); and

(c) the Treasury direct that this section shall apply in relation to the distribution,

any person ("the dealer") who is carrying on a trade which consists wholly or partly in dealing in securities and is beneficially entitled to any securities ("the relevant securities") to the holders of which the distribution is made shall, in relation to that distribution, be treated for tax purposes in the manner specified in subsections (2) and (3) below, unless he gives notice to the inspector not later than two years after the end of the chargeable period in which the distribution takes place that he desires not to be so treated in relation to that distribution.

(2) If the result of the winding up, reduction of capital or redemption of bonds, debentures or debenture stock is that the relevant securities to which the dealer is beneficially entitled are wholly extinguished without his receiving anything in respect thereof except the distributed securities,

P

he shall be treated for tax purposes (except as regards any tax payable in respect of dividends or interest), both then and thereafter, as if neither the extinction nor the distribution had taken place but as if the produce of any subsequent realisation of any of the distributed securities were the produce of the realisation of the relevant securities or a corresponding part thereof, as the case may be.

(3) In any other case—

(a) the dealer shall be treated as having acquired the distributed securities at a cost equal to such proportion of the cost to him of the relevant securities as may be specified in the direction of the Treasury referred to in subsection (1) above and the question whether he has made any, and if so what, profit or suffered any, and if so what, loss on any subsequent realisation of the distributed securities shall be determined accordingly; and

(b) in considering whether he has, either as the result of the winding up, reduction of capital or redemption of bonds, debentures or debenture stock and the distribution of the securities, or on any subsequent realisation of any of the relevant securities, made any, and if so what, profit or suffered any, and if so what, loss in connection with the relevant securities, the distributed securities shall be left out of account and the cost to him of the relevant securities shall be deemed to be reduced by the amount of the cost at which, under paragraph (a) above, he is taken to have acquired the distributed securities.

(4) In this section "securities" includes shares, stock, bonds, debentures and debenture stock.

Conversion etc. of securities held as circulating capital.

473.—(1) Subsections (3) and (4) below shall have effect where a transaction to which this section applies occurs in relation to any securities ("the original holding")—

(a) to which a person carrying on a banking business, an insurance business or a business consisting wholly or partly in dealing in securities is beneficially entitled; and

(b) which are such that a profit on their sale would form part of the trading profits of that business.

(2) This section applies to any transaction which, if the securities were not such as are mentioned in subsection (1)(b) above—

(a) would result in the original holding being equated with a new holding by virtue of sections 77 to 86 of the 1979 Act (capital gains tax roll-over relief in cases of conversion etc.); or

(b) would be treated by virtue of section 84 of that Act (compensation stock) as an exchange for a new holding which does not involve a disposal of the the original holding;

but does not apply to any transaction in relation to which section 471 applies or would apply if the person concerned had not given a notice under that section.

(3) Subject to subsection (4) below, in making any computation in accordance with the provisions of this Act applicable to Case I of Schedule D of the profits or losses of the business —

(a) the transaction shall be treated as not involving any disposal of the original holding, and

(b) the new holding shall be treated as the same asset as the original holding.

(4) Where under the transaction the person concerned receives or becomes entitled to receive any consideration in addition to the new holding, subsection (3) above shall have effect as if references to the original holding were references to the proportion of it which the market value of the new holding at the time of the transaction bears to the aggregate of that value and the market value at that time (or, if it is cash, the amount) of the consideration.

(5) Subsections (3) and (4) above shall have effect with the necessary modifications in relation to any computation made for the purposes of section 76(2) in a case where securities held by the company concerned are equated with a new holding by virtue of any of sections 77 to 86 of the 1979 Act or are treated as not disposed of by virtue of section 84 of that Act.

(6) In this section "securities" includes shares, any security within the meaning of section 82 of the 1979 Act and any rights, interests or options which by virtue of section 86(7), 93 or 139 of that Act are treated as shares for the purposes of sections 77 to 86 of that Act.

(7) In determining for the purposes of subsection (2)(a) above whether a transaction would result in the original holding being equated with a new holding by virtue of section 85 or 86 of the 1979 Act the reference in section 87(1) of that Act to capital gains tax shall be construed as a reference to income tax.

474.—(1) Where a banking business, an insurance business or a business consisting wholly or partly in dealing in securities is carried on in the United Kingdom by a person not resident there, then— Treatment of tax-free income.

(a) in computing for any of the purposes of the Tax Acts the profits arising from, or loss sustained in, the business, and

(b) in the case of an insurance business, also in computing the profits or loss from pension business and general annuity business under section 436,

all interest, dividends and other payments whatsoever to which section 48 or 123(4) extends shall be included notwithstanding the exemption from tax conferred by those sections respectively.

In this subsection "securities" includes stocks and shares.

(2) Where a banking business, an insurance business or a business consisting wholly or partly in dealing in securities—

(a) is carried on in the United Kingdom by a person not ordinarily resident there, and

(b) in making any such computation as is referred to in subsection (1) above with respect to that business, any interest on any securities issued by the Treasury is excluded by virtue of a condition of the issue thereof regulating the treatment of the interest on those securities for tax purposes, then any expenses attributable to the acquisition or holding of, or to any transaction in, the securities (but not including in those expenses any interest on borrowed money), and any profits or losses so attributable, shall also be excluded in making that computation.

Tax-free Treasury securities: exclusion of interest on borrowed money.

475.—(1) This section has effect where paragraphs (a) and (b) of section 474(2) apply to a business for any accounting period or year of assessment.

(2) Up to the amount determined under this section ("the amount ineligible for relief"), interest on money borrowed for the purposes of the business—

(a) shall be excluded in any computation under the Tax Acts of the profits (or losses) arising from the business or, where subsection (6) below applies, arising from any annuity business forming part of the life assurance business, and

(b) shall be excluded from the definition of "charges on income" in section 338.

(3) Subject to subsection (4) below, in determining the amount ineligible for relief, account shall be taken of all money borrowed for the purposes of the business which is outstanding in the accounting or basis period, up to the total cost of the tax-free Treasury securities held for the purpose of the business in that period.

(4) Where the person carrying on the business is a company, account shall not be taken of any borrowed money carrying interest which, apart from subsection (2) above, does not fall to be included in the computations under paragraph (a) of that subsection, and is not to be treated as a charge on income for the purposes of the Corporation Tax Acts.

(5) Subject to subsection (6) below, the amount ineligible for relief shall be equal to a year's interest on the amount of money borrowed which is to be taken into account under subsection (3) above at a rate equal to the average rate of interest in the accounting or basis period on money borrowed for the purposes of the business, except that in the case of a period of less than 12 months interest shall be taken for that shorter period instead of for a year.

(6) Where relief for expenses of management is to be granted to an insurance company for any accounting period, and that relief falls to be reduced under section 445(8)(b) (by applying the fraction which is investment income of the life assurance fund other than income from tax-free Treasury securities divided by that total investment income)—

(a) the amount ineligible for relief shall be a fraction of the amount of interest in the accounting period on money borrowed for the purposes of the business; and

(b) that fraction shall be the fraction which is income from tax-free Treasury securities divided by total investment income of the life assurance fund (that is to say, one minus the fraction to be applied under section 445(8)(b)).

(7) In this section "tax-free Treasury securities" means securities issued by the Treasury with a condition regulating the treatment of the interest thereon for income tax or corporation tax purposes such that interest on the securities is excluded in computing the income or profits.

(8) For the purposes of this section the cost of a holding of tax-free Treasury securities which has fluctuated in the accounting or basis period shall be the average cost of acquisition of the initial holding, and of any subsequent acquisitions in the accounting or basis period, applied to the average amount of the holding in the accounting or basis period, and this subsection shall be applied separately to securities of different classes.

(9) In this section "accounting or basis period" means the company's accounting period or the period by reference to which the profits or gains arising in the year of assessment are to be computed.

CHAPTER IV

BUILDING SOCIETIES, BANKS, SAVINGS BANKS, INDUSTRIAL AND PROVIDENT SOCIETIES AND OTHERS

476.—(1) The Board may by regulations make provision with respect to any year of assessment requiring building societies, on such sums as may be determined in accordance with the regulations (including sums paid or credited before the beginning of the year but not previously brought into account under this subsection), to account for and pay an amount representing income tax calculated in part at the basic rate and in part at the reduced rate determined for the year of assessment concerned under section 483(1)(a); and in this section and section 477 such sums are referred to as "aggregate rate sums".

Building societies: regulations for payment of tax.

(2) Regulations under subsection (1) may contain such incidental and consequential provisions as appear to the Board to be appropriate, including provisions requiring the making of returns.

(3) For any year of assessment to which regulations under subsection (1) above apply, dividends or interest payable in respect of shares in, or deposits with or loans to, a building society shall be dealt with for the purposes of corporation tax as follows—

    (a) in computing for any accounting period ending in the year of assessment the income of the society from the trade carried on by it, there shall be allowed as a deduction the actual amount paid or credited in the accounting period of any such dividends or interest, together with any amount accounted for and paid by the society in respect thereof as representing income tax;

    (b) in computing the income of a company which is paid or credited in the year of assessment with any such dividends or interest which are aggregate rate sums, the company shall—

        (i) be treated as having received an amount which, after deduction of income tax, is equal to the amount paid or credited, and

        (ii) be entitled to a set-off or repayment of income tax accordingly;

(c) no part of any such dividends or interest paid or credited in the year of assessment shall be treated as a distribution of the society or as franked investment income of any company resident in the United Kingdom.

(4) Nothing in section 326 shall be taken as affecting subsection (3)(a) above and that paragraph shall apply to any terminal bonus paid by the society under a certified contractual savings scheme as if it were a dividend on a share in the society.

(5) Except in so far as regulations under subsection (1) above otherwise provide, for any year of assessment to which such regulations apply—

(a) notwithstanding anything in sections 348 to 350, income tax shall not be deducted from any dividends or interest payable in that year in respect of shares in or deposits with or loans to a building society;

(b) subject to subsections (3)(b), (6) and (7) of this section, no repayment of income tax and no assessment to income tax shall be made in respect of any such dividends or interest to or on the person receiving or entitled to the dividends or interest;

(c) any amounts paid or credited in respect of any such dividends or interest shall in computing the total income of an individual entitled thereto be treated as income for that year received by him after deduction of income tax from a corresponding gross amount;

(d) subject to section 7(1), the amounts so paid or credited (and no more) shall, in applying sections 348 and 349(1) to other payments, be treated as profits or gains which have been brought into charge to income tax.

(6) Subsection (5)(b) above shall not prevent an assessment in respect of income tax at a rate other than the basic rate.

(7) Subsection (5)(b) above shall not apply to sums which are payable to exempt pension funds and which are aggregate rate sums; but the amounts paid or credited in respect of such sums shall be treated as paid or credited after deduction of income tax from a corresponding gross amount.

In this subsection "exempt pension fund" means any fund or scheme in the case of which provision is made by section 592(2), 613(4), 614(1), (2) or (3), 620(6) or 643(2) for exempting the whole or part of its income from income tax.

(8) For the purpose of determining whether any or what amount of tax is, by virtue of subsection (5)(c) above, to be taken into account as having been deducted from a gross amount in the case of an individual whose total income is reduced by any deductions, so much only of that gross amount shall be taken into account as is part of his total income as so reduced.

(9) Notwithstanding anything in sections 348 to 350, for any year of assessment to which regulations under subsection (1) above apply income tax shall not be deducted upon payment to the society of any interest on advances, being interest payable in that year.

(10) Subsection (9) above shall not apply to any payment of relevant loan interest to which section 369 applies.

(11) In this section "dividend" has the meaning given by regulations under subsection (1) above, but any sum which is paid by a building society by way of dividend and which is not an aggregate rate sum shall be treated for the purposes of Schedule D as paid by way of interest.

477.—(1) Where a building society investment which is a source of income of any person ("the lender") is not a relevant building society investment but at any time becomes such an investment, section 67 shall apply as if the investment were a source of income which the lender ceased to possess immediately before that time.

Investments becoming or ceasing to be relevant building society investments.

(2) Where a building society investment which is a source of income of any person ceases at any time to be a relevant building society investment, section 66(3) shall apply as if the investment were a new source of income acquired by him immediately after that time.

(3) In this section "building society investment" does not include a quoted Eurobond (as defined in section 124(1)) but, subject to that, means any share in, deposit with or loan to a building society; and for the purposes of this section a building society investment is relevant if dividends or interest payable in respect of it are aggregate rate sums.

478.—(1) This section shall apply, in place of the provisions of section 10, with respect to any accounting period ending before 6th April 1990 of a building society to which section 344 of the 1970 Act applied immediately before the coming into force of this Act.

Building societies: time for payment of tax.

(2) Where this section applies to a building society, then —

(a) corporation tax assessed on the society for any accounting period shall be paid within 30 days from the date of the issue of the notice of assessment, except that if the society's basis period for the year 1965-66 did not extend into the year 1966, the tax shall not be payable before the like time after the last day of the accounting period as 1st January 1966 is after the last day of that basis period; but

(b) if corporation tax has not become payable by the society for an accounting period by the like time from the beginning of that period as there is between the beginning of the society's basis period for the year 1965-66 and 1st January 1966, the society shall at that time from the beginning of the accounting period make a provisional payment of tax computed on the amount on which the society is chargeable to corporation tax for the accounting period last ended with such adjustments, if any, as may be required for periods of different length or as may be agreed between the society and the inspector.

(3) References in section (2) above to a society's basis period for the year 1965-66 are references to the period by reference to which the society was assessed to income tax for that year under arrangements entered into under section 445 of the Income Tax Act 1952.

1952 c. 10.

(4) Where, by virtue of subsection (2)(a) above, corporation tax assessed on a building society in respect of a 1989 accounting period would, apart from this subsection, be payable by a date which is earlier than the end of the period of two months from the end of that accounting period, the tax shall be payable within that period of two months.

(5) If, apart from this subsection, the date on which, under subsection (2)(b) above, a building society would be required to make a provisional payment of corporation tax for a 1989 accounting period would fall before the end of the period of two months from the end of that accounting period, that date shall be postponed until the end of that period of two months.

(6) With respect to a 1989 accounting period of a building society to which subsection (4) above applies, in section 825(8)(b) of this Act and paragraph 5(c) in the second column of the Table in section 86(4) of the Management Act (the reckonable date for interest on overdue tax), the reference to the time limit imposed by section (2)(a) above shall be construed as a reference to the limit imposed by subsection (4) above.

(7) In subsections (4) to (6) above a "1989 accounting period" means an accounting period ending in the year 1989-90.

Interest paid on deposits with banks etc.

479.—(1) Any deposit-taker making a payment of interest in respect of a relevant deposit shall be liable to account for and pay an amount representing income tax on that payment, calculated by applying the composite rate (determined in accordance with section 483) to the grossed-up amount of the payment, that is to say, to the amount which after deduction of tax at the composite rate would be equal to the amount actually paid.

(2) Where in relation to any payment of interest a deposit-taker is liable to account for and pay an amount under subsection (1) above—

(a) subject to subsection (3) below, no assessment to income tax shall be made on, and no repayment of income tax shall be made to, the person receiving or entitled to the payment in respect of it;

(b) the payment shall, in computing the total income of the person entitled to it, be treated as income for that year received by him after deduction of income tax at the basic rate from a corresponding gross amount; and

(c) the payment (and no more) shall, in applying sections 348 and 349 to other payments, be treated as profits or gains which have been brought into charge to income tax.

(3) Subsection (2)(a) above shall not prevent an assessment in respect of income tax at a rate other than the basic rate.

(4) For the purpose of determining whether any or what amount of tax is, by virtue of subsection (2)(b) above, to be taken into account as having been deducted from a gross amount in the case of an individual whose total income is reduced by any deductions, so much only of that gross amount shall be taken into account as is part of his total income as so reduced.

(5) Any payment of interest in respect of which an amount is payable under subsection (1) above shall be a relevant payment for the purposes of Schedule 16 whether or not the deposit-taker making the payment is resident in the United Kingdom.

(6) Schedule 16 shall apply in relation to any payment which is a relevant payment by virtue of subsection (5) above—

(a) with the substitution for any reference to a company of a reference to a deposit-taker;

(b) as if any amount payable under subsection (1) above were payable as income tax;

(c) as if paragraph 5 applied only in relation to payments received by the deposit-taker and falling to be taken into account in computing his income chargeable to corporation tax; and

(d) as if in paragraph 7 the reference to section 7(2) included a reference to sections 11(3) and 349(1).

(7) In relation to any deposit-taker who is not a company, Schedule 16 shall have effect as if—

(a) paragraph 5 were omitted; and

(b) references to accounting periods were references to periods for which the deposit-taker makes up his accounts.

480.—(1) Where a deposit which is a source of income of any person ("the lender") is not a composite rate deposit but at any time becomes such a deposit, section 67 shall apply as if the deposit were a source of income which the lender ceased to possess immediately before it became a composite rate deposit.

Deposits becoming or ceasing to be composite rate deposits.

(2) Section 67 shall apply in relation to a deposit which became a composite rate deposit on 6th April 1985 with the omission from subsection (1)(b) of the words from "and shall" to "this provision".

(3) Where a deposit which is a source of income of any person ceases to be a composite rate deposit, section 66(3) shall apply as if the deposit were a new source of income acquired by him immediately after it ceased to be a composite rate deposit.

(4) For the purposes of this section a deposit is at any time a composite rate deposit if, were the person holding it to make a payment of interest in respect of it at that time, he would be liable to account for and pay an amount on that payment under section 479(1).

481.—(1) In this section "the relevant provisions" means sections 479 and 480, this section and section 482.

"Deposit-taker", "deposit" and "relevant deposit".

(2) In the relevant provisions "deposit-taker" means any of the following—

(a) the Bank of England;

(b) any institution authorised under the Banking Act 1987 or municipal bank within the meaning of that Act;

1987 c. 22.

(c) the Post Office;

(d) any company to which property and rights belonging to a trustee savings bank were transferred by section 3 of the Trustee Savings Bank Act 1985;

(e) any bank formed under the Savings Bank (Scotland) Act 1819; and

(f) any person or class of person who receives deposits in the course of his business or activities and which is for the time being prescribed by order made by the Treasury for the purposes of this paragraph.

(3) In the relevant provisions "deposit" means a sum of money paid on terms under which it will be repaid with or without interest and either on demand or at a time or in circumstances agreed by or on behalf of the person making the payment and the person to whom it is made.

(4) For the purposes of the relevant provisions a deposit is a relevant deposit if, but only if—

(a) the person who is beneficially entitled to any interest in respect of the deposit is an individual or, where two or more persons are so entitled, all of them are individuals; or

(b) in Scotland, the person who is so entitled is a partnership all the partners of which are individuals; or

(c) the person entitled to any such interest receives it as a personal representative in his capacity as such;

and the deposit is not prevented from being a relevant deposit by subsection (5) below.

(5) A deposit is not a relevant deposit if—

(a) a qualifying certificate of deposit has been issued in respect of it or it is a qualifying time deposit;

(b) it is a debt on a debenture ("debenture" having the meaning given in section 744 of the Companies Act 1985) issued by the deposit-taker;

(c) it is a loan made by a deposit-taker in the ordinary course of his business or activities;

(d) it is a debt on a security which is listed on a recognised stock exchange;

(e) it is a general client account deposit;

(f) it forms part of a premiums trust fund (within the meaning of section 457) of an underwriting member of Lloyd's;

(g) it is made by a Stock Exchange money broker (recognised by the Bank of England) in the course of his business as such a broker;

(h) in the case of a deposit-taker resident in the United Kingdom for the purposes of income tax or corporation tax, it is held at a branch of his situated outside the United Kingdom;

(j) in the case of a deposit-taker who is not so resident, it is held otherwise than at a branch of his situated in the United Kingdom; or

(k) the appropriate person has declared in writing to the deposit-taker liable to pay interest in respect of the deposit that—

(i) at the time when the declaration is made, the person who is beneficially entitled to the interest is not, or, as the case may be, all the persons who are so entitled are not, ordinarily resident in the United Kingdom;

(ii) in a case falling within subsection (4)(c) above the deceased was, immediately before his death, not ordinarily resident in the United Kingdom.

(6) The Treasury may by order make amendments in this section and sections 479(2) to (7), 480 and 482 providing for deposits of a kind specified in the order to be or, as the case may be, not to be relevant deposits in relation to all deposit-takers or such deposit-takers or classes of deposit-takers as may be so specified.

482.—(1) For the purposes of sections 479, 480 and 481 and this section, any amount which is credited as interest in respect of a relevant deposit shall be treated as a payment of interest.

Supplementary provisions.

(2) A declaration under section 481(5)(k) shall—

(a) if made under sub-paragraph (i), contain an undertaking by the person making it that if the person, or any of the persons in respect of whom it is made, becomes ordinarily resident in the United Kingdom he will notify the deposit-taker accordingly; and

(b) in any case, be in such form as may be prescribed or authorised, and contain such information as may reasonably be required, by the Board.

(3) A deposit-taker shall, on being so required by notice given to him by an inspector, make all declarations which have been made to him under section 481(5) available for inspection by the inspector or by a named officer of the Board.

(4) Where a notice has been given to a deposit-taker under subsection (3) above, the declarations shall be made available within such time as may be specified in the notice, and the person to whom they are to be made available may take copies of or extracts from them.

(5) A deposit-taker shall treat every deposit made with him as a relevant deposit unless satisfied that it is not a relevant deposit, but where he has satisfied himself that a deposit is not a relevant deposit he shall be entitled to continue to so treat it until such time as he is in possession of information which can reasonably be taken to indicate that the deposit is or may be a relevant deposit.

(6) In section 481(5)—

"appropriate person", in relation to a deposit, means any person who is beneficially entitled to any interest in respect of the deposit or entitled to receive any such interest as a personal representative in his capacity as such or to whom any such interest is payable;

"general client account deposit" means a deposit, held by the deposit-taker in a client account (other than one which is identified by the deposit-taker as one in which sums are held only for one or more particular clients of the person whose account it is) in respect of which that person is required by provision made under any enactment to make payments representing interest to some or all of the clients for whom, or on whose account, he received the sums deposited in the account;

"qualifying certificate of deposit" means a certificate of deposit, as defined in section 56(5), which is issued by a deposit-taker and under which—

(a) the amount payable by the deposit-taker, exclusive of interest, is not less than £50,000 (or, for a deposit denominated in foreign currency, not less than the equivalent of £50,000 at the time when the deposit is made); and

(b) the obligation of the deposit-taker to pay that amount arises after a period of not less than seven days beginning with the date on which the deposit is made; and

"qualifying time deposit" means a deposit which is made by way of loan for an amount which is not less than £50,000 (or, for a deposit denominated in foreign currency, not less than the equivalent of £50,000 at the time when the deposit is made) and on terms which—

(a) prevent repayment of the deposit before the expiry of the period of seven days beginning with the date on which the deposit is made, but which require repayment at the end of a specified period;

(b) do not make provision for the transfer of the right to repayment; and

(c) prevent partial withdrawals of, or additions to, the deposit.

In relation to deposits made before 20th May 1986 this subsection shall have effect with the substitution for "seven" of "28" (in both places).

(7) For the purposes of section 481(5)(h) and (j) a deposit is held at a branch of a deposit-taker if it is recorded in his books as a liability of that branch.

(8) A certificate of deposit, as defined in section 56(5), which was issued before 13th March 1984 on terms which provide for interest to be payable on the deposit at any time after 5th April 1985 (whether or not interest is payable on it before that date) shall, if it is not a qualifying certificate of deposit, be treated for the purposes of section 481(5) as if it were a qualifying certificate of deposit.

(9) Any deposit which was made before 6th July 1984 but which is not
a qualifying time deposit shall, where it is made on terms which—

    (a) do not make provision for the transfer of the right to repayment;

    (b) prevent partial withdrawals of, or additions to, the deposit; and

    (c) require—

        (i) the deposit-taker to repay the sum at the end of a specified period which ends after 5th April 1985; or

        (ii) in a case where interest is payable only at the time of repayment of the deposit, the deposit-taker to repay the sum on demand or on notice;

be treated for the purposes of section 481(5) as if it were a qualifying time deposit.

(10) An order under section 481(2)(f) may prescribe a person or class of person in relation to all relevant deposits or only in relation to relevant deposits of a kind specified in the order.

(11) The Board may by regulations make provision—

    (a) requiring any declaration under section 481(5)(k)(i) which does not give the address of the person making it, to be supported by a certificate given by the deposit-taker concerned—

        (i) in such form as may be prescribed or authorised by the Board; and

        (ii) containing such information as may reasonably be required by the Board; and

    (b) generally for giving effect to sections 479 to 481 and this section.

(12) Regulations under subsection (11) above or an order under section 481(6) may contain such incidental and consequential provision as appears to the Board or the Treasury, as the case may be, to be appropriate.

483.—(1) In every year of assessment the Treasury shall by order determine a rate which shall, for the following year of assessment, be—   Determination of reduced rate for building societies and composite rate for banks etc.

    (a) the reduced rate for the purposes of section 476; and

    (b) the composite rate for the purposes of section 479.

(2) The order made under subsection (1) above in each year of assessment shall—

    (a) be made before 31st December in that year; and

    (b) be based only on information relating to periods before the end of the year of assessment in which the order is made.

(3) Whenever they exercise their powers under this section the Treasury shall aim at securing that (assuming for the purposes of this subsection that the amounts payable by building societies under section 476 and by deposit-takers under section 479 are income tax) the total income tax becoming payable to, and not being repayable by, the Crown

PART XII

is (when regard is had to the operation of those sections) as nearly as may be the same in the aggregate as it would have been if those sections had not been enacted.

1984 c. 43.

(4) If the order made under section 26 of the Finance Act 1984 in the year 1987-88 is made in pursuance of subsection (4) of that section, that order shall, notwithstanding that that subsection is not re-enacted by this Act, apply for the purposes of sections 476 and 479 for the year 1988-89.

(5) For the purposes of enabling the Treasury to comply with the requirements of subsection (3) above, the Board may by notice require any deposit-taker (within the meaning of section 481) or building society to furnish to the Board such information about its depositors as the Board may reasonably require for those purposes.

In this subsection "depositors", in relation to a building society, includes shareholders.

Savings banks: exemption from tax.

484.—(1) Any savings bank other than a savings bank which is the successor or further successor to an existing trustee savings bank shall on making a claim be entitled to exemption from income tax and corporation tax in respect of the income of its funds to the extent that such income is applied in the payment or credit of interest to any depositor; but, subject to section 325, any such interest shall be chargeable under Case III of Schedule D.

(2) Any gain or loss accruing to a savings bank which is the successor to an existing trustee savings bank on a disposal of an exempt investment held by that existing bank on 21st November 1979, may, if that existing bank has so elected, be computed by reference to the cost of the investment instead of by reference to its market value on the latter date and, in the case of a loss, without any restriction under section 270(4) of the 1970 Act.

1980 c. 48.

(3) In subsection (2) above the reference to an election is a reference to an election under paragraph 2(3) of Schedule 11 to the Finance Act 1980 (under which the election must have been by notice in writing given to the Board within two years after 21st November 1979, and has effect in relation to all exempt investments held by the bank on that date).

(4) Where a savings bank which is the successor to an existing trustee savings bank holds investments which include both exempt investments held by the existing bank on 21st November 1979 and other investments of the same class, any investments of that class which are disposed of by the successor shall be treated for the purposes of subsection (2) above as consisting of the other investments rather than of the exempt investments held on that date.

(5) In this section references to exempt investments held by an existing trustee savings bank on 21st November 1979 are to investments on the disposal of which immediately before that date no chargeable gain or allowable loss would have accrued to the bank by virtue of section 67 of the 1979 Act (gilt-edged securities held for more than a year).

1985 c. 58.

(6) In this section "successor" and "existing", in relation to a trustee savings bank, have the meanings given by section 1 of the Trustee Savings Bank Act 1985, and "further successor" has the meaning given by paragraph 9 of Schedule 2 to that Act.

485.—(1) Where the business of a trustee savings bank has been transferred to another trustee savings bank after 21st November 1979 and before the day which was the vesting day for the purposes of the Trustee Savings Bank Act 1985—

PART XII
Savings banks: supplemental.
1985 c. 58.

    (a) any exempt investment which was held on that date by the first bank and was transferred with the business shall be treated for the purposes of section 484 in its application to any savings bank which is the successor to the second bank as if it had been held on that date by the second bank but without prejudice to any election made in respect of the investment by the first bank under sub-paragraph (3) of paragraph 2 of Schedule 11 to the Finance Act 1980; and

1980 c. 48.

    (b) the cost of the investment shall be taken for the purposes of that sub-paragraph as equal to the cost of the investment to the first bank.

(2) Where the business of a trustee savings bank was transferred to another trustee savings bank before 21st November 1979 the cost of any exempt investment held by the second bank on that date which—

    (a) was transferred to it with the business; and

    (b) was an exempt investment on the date of the transfer,

shall be taken for the purposes of section 484(2) in its application to any savings bank which is the successor to the second bank as equal to the cost of the investment to the first bank.

(3) In this section references to exempt investments held by a trustee savings bank on 21st November 1979 or the date of the transfer are to investments on the disposal of which immediately before that date no chargeable gain or allowable loss would have accrued to the bank by virtue of section 67 of the 1979 Act (gilt-edged securities held for more than a year) or, in the case of a transfer which took place before that section came into force, section 41 of the Finance Act 1969 (which was re-enacted by section 67 of the 1979 Act).

1969 c. 32.

486.—(1) Notwithstanding anything in the Tax Acts, share interest or loan interest paid by a registered industrial and provident society shall not be treated as a distribution; and, subject to subsection (7) below and section 487(3), any share or loan interest paid in an accounting period of the society—

Industrial and provident societies and co-operative associations.

    (a) shall be deductible in computing, for the purposes of corporation tax, the income of the society for that period from the trade carried on by the society, or

    (b) if the society is not carrying on a trade, shall be treated for those purposes as a charge on the income of the society.

(2) Notwithstanding anything in sections 348 to 350, any share interest or loan interest paid by a registered industrial and provident society, except any to which subsection (3) below applies, shall be paid without deduction of income tax.

(3) This subsection applies to any share interest or loan interest payable to a person whose usual place of abode is not within the United Kingdom, and in any such case section 349(2) shall apply to the payment as it applies to a payment of yearly interest, and income tax shall be deducted accordingly.

(4) Any share interest or loan interest paid by a registered industrial and provident society shall be chargeable under Case III of Schedule D.

(5) Where at any time, by virtue of this section, the income of a person from any source, not having previously been chargeable by direct assessment on that person, becomes so chargeable, section 66(3) shall apply as if the source of that income were a new source of income acquired by that person at that time.

(6) Every registered industrial and provident society shall, within three months after the end of any accounting period of the society, deliver to the inspector a return showing—

   (a) the name and place of residence of every person to whom the society has by virtue of this section paid without deduction of income tax sums amounting to more than £15 in that period; and

   (b) the amount so paid in that period to each of those persons.

(7) If for any accounting period a return under subsection (6) above is not duly made by a registered industrial and provident society, share and loan interest paid by the society in that period shall not be deductible in computing its income, or be treated as a charge on income.

(8) If in the course of, or as part of, a union or amalgamation of two or more registered industrial and provident societies, or a transfer of engagements from one registered industrial and provident society to another, there is a disposal of an asset by one society to another, both shall be treated for the purposes of corporation tax in respect of chargeable gains as if the asset were acquired from the society making the disposal for a consideration of such amount as would secure that neither a gain nor a loss would accrue to that society on the disposal.

(9) Subsections (1) and (8) above shall have effect as if references to a registered industrial and provident society included any co-operative association established and resident in the United Kingdom, and having as its object or primary object to assist its members in the carrying on of agricultural or horticultural businesses on land occupied by them in the United Kingdom or in the carrying on of businesses consisting in the catching or taking of fish or shellfish.

(10) It is hereby declared that, in computing, for the purposes of any provision of the Tax Acts relating to profits or gains chargeable under Case I of Schedule D ("the tax computation"), any profits or gains of—

   (a) any registered industrial and provident society which does not sell to persons not members thereof; or

   (b) any registered industrial and provident society the number of the shares in which is not limited by its rules or practice;

there are to be deducted as expenses any sums which—

> (i) represent a discount, rebate, dividend or bonus granted by the company to members or other persons in respect of amounts paid or payable by or to them on account of their transactions with the company, being transactions which are taken into account in the tax computation; and

> (ii) are calculated by reference to those amounts or to the magnitude of those transactions and not by reference to the amount of any share or interest in the capital of the company.

(11) No dividends or bonus deductible in computing income as mentioned in subsection (10) above shall be regarded as a distribution.

(12) In this section—

"co-operative association" means a body of persons having a written constitution from which the Minister is satisfied, having regard to the provision made as to the manner in which the income of the body is to be applied for the benefit of its members and all other relevant provisions, that the body is in substance a co-operative association;

"the Minister" means—

> the Minister of Agriculture, Fisheries and Food, as regards England and Wales;

> the Secretary of State, as regards Scotland; and

> the Department of Agriculture for Northern Ireland, as regards Northern Ireland;

"registered industrial and provident society" means a society registered or deemed to be registered under the Industrial and Provident Societies Act 1965 or under the Industrial and Provident Societies Act (Northern Ireland) 1969;   1965 c. 12.
1969 c. 24 (N.I.).

"share interest" means any interest, dividend, bonus or other sum payable to a shareholder of the society by reference to the amount of his holding in the share capital of the society;

"loan interest" means any interest payable by the society in respect of any mortgage, loan, loan stock or deposit;

and references to the payment of share interest or loan interest include references to the crediting of such interest.

487.—(1) Subject to subsection (2) below, in computing for the purposes of corporation tax the income of a credit union for any accounting period—   Credit unions.

(a) neither the activity of the credit union in making loans to its members nor in placing on deposit or otherwise investing from time to time its surplus funds shall be regarded as the carrying on of a trade or part of a trade; and

(b) interest received by the credit union on loans made by it to its members shall not be chargeable to tax under Case III of Schedule D or otherwise.

(2) Paragraph (b) of subsection (1) above shall not apply to an accounting period of a credit union for which the credit union is obliged to make a return under section 486(6) and has not done so within three months after the end of that accounting period or such longer period as the inspector shall allow.

(3) No share interest, loan interest or annuity or other annual payment paid or payable by a credit union in any accounting period shall be deductible in computing for the purposes of corporation tax the income of the credit union for that period from any trade carried on by it or be treated for those purposes as a charge on income.

(4) A credit union shall not be regarded as an investment company for the purposes of section 75 above or section 306 of the 1970 Act (capital allowances).

(5) In this section—

1965 c. 12.
S.I. 1985/1205
(N.I. 12.).

"credit union" means a society registered as a credit union under the Industrial and Provident Societies Act 1965 or the Credit Unions (Northern Ireland) Order 1985;

"share interest" and "loan interest" have the same meaning as in section 486;

"surplus funds", in relation to a credit union, means funds not immediately required for its purposes;

and references to the payment of share interest or loan interest include references to the crediting of such interest.

Co-operative
housing
associations.

488.—(1) Where a housing association makes a claim in that behalf for any year or part of a year of assessment during which the association was approved for the purposes of this section—

(a) rent to which the association was entitled from its members for the year or part shall be disregarded for tax purposes; and

(b) any yearly interest payable by the association for the year or part shall be treated for tax purposes as payable not by the association but severally by the members of the association who during the year or part were tenants of property of the association, in the proportion which the rents payable by those members for the year or part bear to the aggregate of the rents to which the association was entitled for the year or part from the properties to which the interest relates; and

(c) each member of the association shall be treated for the purposes of section 354 as if he were the owner of the association's estate or interest in the property of which he is the tenant.

(2) Where the property, or any of the properties, to which any such interest as is mentioned in paragraph (b) of subsection (1) above relates is for any period not subject to a tenancy—

(a) that paragraph shall not apply in relation to so much of the interest as is attributable to the property not subject to a tenancy; and

(b) for the purposes of that paragraph as it applies in relation to a tenant of any other property to which the interest relates, the association shall be deemed to have received, in respect of the property not subject to a tenancy, rent at the rate payable therefor when it was last let by the association.

(3) In computing the income of the association no payments shall be deductible under section 25(3) to (7) in so far as attributable to a period as respects which a claim under subsection (1) above has effect.

(4) Where a claim under subsection (1) above has effect, any adjustment of the liability to tax of a member or of the association which is required in consequence of the claim may be made by an assessment or by repayment or otherwise, as the case may require.

(5) Where a housing association makes a claim in that behalf for an accounting period or part of an accounting period during which it was approved for the purposes of this section, the housing association shall be exempt from corporation tax on chargeable gains accruing to it in the accounting period or part on the disposal by way of sale of any property which has been or is being occupied by a tenant of the housing association.

(6) References in this section to the approval of an association shall be construed as references to approval—

(a) by the Secretary of State in the case of a housing association in Great Britain;

(b) by the Head of the Department of the Environment for Northern Ireland in the case of a housing association in Northern Ireland;

and an association shall not be approved unless the approving authority is satisfied—

(i) that the association is, or is deemed to be, duly registered under the Industrial and Provident Societies Act 1965 or the Industrial and Provident Societies Act (Northern Ireland) 1969, and is a housing association within the meaning of the Housing Associations Act 1985 or Article 114 of the Housing (Northern Ireland) Order 1981;

1965 c. 12.
1969 c.24 (N.I.).

1985 c. 68.
S.I. 1981/156 (N.I. 3).

(ii) that the rules of the association restrict membership to persons who are tenants or prospective tenants of the association, and preclude the granting or assignment (or, in Scotland, the granting or assignation) of tenancies to persons other than members; and

(iii) that the association satisfies such other requirements as may be prescribed by the approving authority, and will comply with such conditions as may for the time being be so prescribed.

(7) An approval given for the purposes of this section shall have effect as from such date (whether before or after the giving of the approval) as may be specified by the approving authority and shall cease to have effect if revoked.

(8) The Secretary of State as respects Great Britain, or the Head of the Department of the Environment for Northern Ireland as respects Northern Ireland, may make regulations for the purpose of carrying out the provisions of this section; and, from the coming into operation of regulations under this subsection prescribing requirements or conditions for the purposes of subsection (6)(iii) above, "prescribed" in subsection (6)(iii) above shall mean prescribed by or under such regulations.

The power to make regulations under this subsection shall be exercisable by the Secretary of State by statutory instrument and by the Head of the Department of the Environment for Northern Ireland by

statutory rule for the purposes of the Statutory Rules (Northern Ireland) Order 1979.

(9) A claim under this section shall be made to the inspector, and shall be made not later than two years after the end of the year of assessment or accounting period to which, or to a part of which, it relates.

Section 42 of the Management Act shall not apply to a claim under this section.

(10) Subject to subsection (11) below, no claim under this section shall have effect unless it is proved that during the year or accounting period, or part thereof, to which the claim relates—

    (a) no property belonging to the association making the claim was let otherwise than to a member of the association;

    (b) no property let by the association, and no part of such property, was occupied, whether solely or as joint occupier, by a person not being a member of the association;

    (c) the association making the claim satisfies the conditions specified in subsection (6)(i) and (ii) above and has complied with the conditions prescribed under subsection (6)(iii) for the time being in force; and

    (d) any covenants required to be included in grants of tenancies by those conditions have been observed.

For the purposes of paragraph (b) above occupation by any other person in accordance with the will, or the provisions applicable on the intestacy, of a deceased member, shall be treated during the first six months after the death as if it were occupation by a member.

(11) Where the Board are satisfied that the requirements of subsection (10) above are substantially complied with they may direct that the claim shall have effect; but if subsequently information comes to the knowledge of the Board which satisfies them that the direction was not justified they may revoke the direction and thereupon the liability of all persons concerned to tax for all relevant years or accounting periods shall be adjusted by the making of assessments or otherwise.

(12) A claim under this section shall be in such form and contain such particulars as may be prescribed by the Board, and, without prejudice to the generality of this provision, the required particulars may include an authority granted by all members of the association for any relevant information contained in any return made by a member under the

provisions of the Income Tax Acts to be used by the Board in such manner as the Board may think fit for determining whether the claim ought to be allowed.

489.—(1) Where a self-build society makes a claim in that behalf for any year or part of a year of assessment during which the society was approved for the purposes of this section, rent to which the society was entitled from its members for the year or part shall be disregarded for tax purposes.

Self-build societies.

(2) Where a claim under subsection (1) above has effect, any adjustment of the society's liability to tax which is required in consequence of the claim may be made by an assessment or by repayment or otherwise, as the case may require.

(3) Where a self-build society makes a claim in that behalf for an accounting period or part during which it was approved for the purposes of this section, the society shall be exempt from corporation tax on chargeable gains accruing to it in the accounting period or part thereof on the disposal of any land to a member of the society.

(4) References in this section to the approval of a self-build society are references to its approval by the Secretary of State, and the Secretary of State shall not approve a self-build society for the purposes of this section unless he is satisfied—

  (a) that the society is, or is deemed to be, duly registered under the Industrial and Provident Societies Act 1965; and

1965 c. 12.

  (b) that the society satisfies such other requirements as may be prescribed by or under regulations under subsection (6) below and will comply with such conditions as may for the time being be so prescribed.

(5) An approval given for the purposes of this section shall have effect as from such date (whether before or after the giving of the approval) as may be specified by the Secretary of State and shall cease to have effect if revoked by him.

(6) The Secretary of State may by statutory instrument make regulations for the purpose of carrying out the provisions of this section; and a statutory instrument containing any such regulations shall be subject to annulment in pursuance of a resolution of the House of Commons.

(7) Section 42 of the Management Act shall not apply to a claim under this section, but such a claim shall be made to the inspector and shall be made not later than two years after the end of the year of assessment or accounting period to which, or to a part of which, it relates.

(8) Subject to subsection (9) below, no claim under this section shall have effect unless it is proved that during the year or accounting period, or part thereof, to which the claim relates—

  (a) no land owned by the society was occupied, in whole or in part and whether solely or as joint occupier, by a person who was not, at the time of his occupation, a member of the society; and

(b) the society making the claim satisfies the condition specified in paragraph (a) of subsection (4) above and has complied with the conditions prescribed under paragraph (b) of that subsection and for the time being in force;

and for the purposes of paragraph (a) above, occupation by any other person in accordance with the will, or the provisions applicable on the intestacy, of a deceased member, shall be treated during the first six months after the death as if it were occupation by a member.

(9) Notwithstanding the provisions of subsection (8) above, where, on a claim under this section, the Board are satisfied that the requirements of paragraphs (a) and (b) of that subsection are substantially complied with, they may direct that the claim shall have effect; but if, subsequently, information comes to the knowledge of the Board which satisfies them that the direction was not justified, they may revoke the direction and thereupon the liability of the society to tax for all relevant years or accounting periods shall be adjusted by the making of assessments or otherwise.

(10) A claim under this section shall be in such form and contain such particulars as may be prescribed by the Board.

(11) In this section—

1985 c. 68.

S.I. 1981/156 (N.I. 3).

"self-build society" has the same meaning as in the Housing Associations Act 1985 or, in Northern Ireland, Part VII of the Housing (Northern Ireland) Order 1981; and

"rent" includes any sums to which a self-build society is entitled in respect of the occupation of any of its land under a licence or otherwise.

(12) In the application of this section to Northern Ireland—

(a) any reference in subsections (4) and (5) above to the Secretary of State shall be construed as a reference to the Department of the Environment for Northern Ireland;

1965 c. 12.

1969 c. 24 (N.I.).

(b) the reference in subsection (4)(a) to the Industrial and Provident Societies Act 1965 shall be construed as a reference to the Industrial and Provident Societies Act (Northern Ireland) 1969; and

(c) for subsection (6) there shall be substituted the following subsection—

S.I. 1979/1573 (N.I. 12).

1954 c. 33 (N.I.).

"(6) The Department of the Environment for Northern Ireland may by statutory rule for the purposes of the Statutory Rules (Northern Ireland) Order 1979 make regulations for the purpose of carrying out the provisions of this section; and a statutory rule containing any such regulations shall be subject to negative resolution within the meaning of section 41(6) of the Interpretation Act (Northern Ireland) 1954".

Companies carrying on a mutual business or not carrying on a business.

490.—(1) Subject to subsection (2) below, where a company carries on any business of mutual trading or mutual insurance or other mutual business the provisions of the Tax Acts relating to distributions shall apply to distributions made by the company notwithstanding that they are made to persons participating in the mutual activities of that business and derive from those activities, but shall so apply only to the extent to which the distributions are made out of profits of the company which are brought into charge to corporation tax or out of franked investment income (including group income).

(2) In the case of a company carrying on any mutual life assurance business, the provisions of the Tax Acts relating to distributions shall not apply to distributions made to persons participating in the mutual activities of that business and derived from those activities; but if the business includes annuity business, the annuities payable in the course of that business shall not be treated as charges on the income of the company to any greater extent than if the business were not mutual but were being carried on by the company with a view to the realisation of profits for the company.

(3) Subject to subsections (1) and (2) above, the fact that a distribution made by a company carrying on any such business is derived from the mutual activities of that business and the recipient is a person participating in those activities shall not affect the character which the payment or other receipt has for purposes of corporation tax or income tax in the hands of the recipient.

(4) Where a company does not carry on, and never has carried on, a trade or a business of holding investments, and is not established for purposes which include the carrying on of a trade or of such a business, the provisions of the Tax Acts relating to distributions shall apply to distributions made by the company only to the extent to which the distributions are made out of profits of the company which are brought into charge to corporation tax or out of franked investment income.

491.—(1) Where any person receives any money or money's worth—

(a) forming part of the assets of a body corporate, other than assets representing capital; or

(b) forming part of the consideration for the transfer of the assets of a body corporate, other than assets representing capital, as part of a scheme of amalgamation or reconstruction which involves the winding up of the body corporate; or

(c) consisting of the consideration for a transfer or surrender of a right to receive anything falling under paragraph (a) or (b) above, being a receipt not giving rise to any charge to tax on the recipient apart from this section,

Distribution of assets of body corporate carrying on mutual business.

and the body corporate has at any time carried on a trade which consists of or includes the conducting of any mutual business (whether confined to members of the body corporate or not), and is being or has been wound up or dissolved, the provisions of this section shall apply to the receipt.

(2) If a transfer or surrender of a right under subsection (1)(c) above is not at arm's length, the person making the transfer or surrender shall, for the purposes of this section, be deemed then to have received consideration equal to the value of the right.

(3) If in respect of a payment of any amount made to the body corporate for the purposes of its mutual business any deduction has been allowed for the purposes of tax in computing the profits or gains or losses of a trade, then—

(a) if at the time of the receipt the recipient is the person, or one of the persons, carrying on that trade, the amount or value of the receipt shall be treated for the purposes of tax as a trading receipt of that trade; and

(b) if at the time of the receipt the recipient is not the person, or one of the persons, carrying on that trade, but was the person, or one of the persons, carrying on that trade when any payment was made to the body corporate for the purposes of its mutual business in respect of which a deduction was allowed for the purposes of tax in computing the profits or gains or losses of the trade, the recipient shall, subject to subsection (6) below, be charged under Case VI of Schedule D for the chargeable period in which the receipt falls on an amount equal to the amount or value of the receipt.

(4) Subsection (3)(a) above applies notwithstanding that, as a result of a change in the persons carrying on the trade, the profits or gains are under section 113 or 337(1) determined as if it had been permanently discontinued and a new trade set up and commenced.

(5) Where an individual is chargeable to tax by virtue of subsection (3)(b) above and the profits or gains of the trade there mentioned fell to be treated as earned income for the purposes of the Income Tax Acts, the sums in respect of which he is so chargeable shall also be treated for those purposes as earned income.

(6) If the trade mentioned in subsection (3)(b) above was permanently discontinued before the time of the receipt, then in computing the charge to tax under subsection (3)(b) above there shall be deducted from the amount or value of the receipt—

(a) any loss, expense or debit (not being a loss, expense or debit arising directly or indirectly from the discontinuance itself) which, if the trade had not been discontinued, would have been deducted in computing for tax purposes the profits or gains or losses of the person by whom it was carried on before the discontinuance, or would have been deducted from or set off against those profits as so computed, and

(b) any capital allowance to which the person who carried on the trade was entitled immediately before the discontinuance and to which effect has not been given by way of relief before discontinuance.

(7) Relief shall not be given under subsection (6) above or under section 105(1) in respect of any loss, expense, debit or allowance if and so far as it has been so given by reference to another charge to tax under this section or under section 103.

(8) For the purposes of subsection (1) above assets representing capital consist of—

(a) assets representing any loan or other capital subscribed, including income derived from any investment of any part of that capital, but not including profits from the employment of that capital for the purposes of the mutual business of the body corporate;

(b) assets representing any profits or gains charged to tax as being profits or gains of any part of the trade carried on by the body corporate which does not consist of the conducting of any mutual business;

(c) (so far as not comprised in paragraphs (a) and (b) above) assets representing taxed income from any investments.

(9) In this section "mutual business" includes any business of mutual insurance or mutual trading.

(10) Subsections (3) to (7) above shall apply with any necessary modifications—

(a) to a profession or vocation; and

(b) to the occupation of woodlands the profits or gains of which are assessable under Schedule D;

as they apply to a trade.

(11) It is hereby declared that the description of trades in subsection (1) above does not include any trade all the profits or gains of which are chargeable to tax and, in particular, does not include such a trade carried on by any registered industrial and provident society.

CHAPTER V

PETROLEUM EXTRACTION ACTIVITIES

492.—(1) Where a person carries on as part of a trade—

Treatment of oil extraction activities etc. for tax purposes.

(a) any oil extraction activities; or

(b) any of the following activities, namely, the acquisition, enjoyment or exploitation of oil rights; or

(c) activities of both those descriptions,

those activities shall be treated for all purposes of income tax, and for the purposes of the charge of corporation tax on income, as a separate trade, distinct from all other activities carried on by him as part of the trade.

(2) Relief in respect of a loss incurred by a person shall not be given under section 380 or 381 against income arising from oil extraction activities or from oil rights ("ring fence income") except to the extent that the loss arises from such activities or rights.

(3) Relief in respect of a loss incurred by a person shall not be given under section 393(2) against his ring fence profits except to the extent that the loss arises from oil extraction activities or from oil rights.

(4) In any case where—

(a) in any chargeable period a person incurs a loss in activities ("separate activities") which, for that or any subsequent chargeable period, are treated by virtue of subsection (1) above as a separate trade for the purposes specified in that subsection; and

(b) in any subsequent chargeable period any of his trading income is derived from activities ("related activities") which are not part of the separate activities but which, apart from subsection (1) above, would together with those activities constitute a single trade,

then, notwithstanding anything in that subsection, the amount of the loss may be set off, in accordance with section 385 or 393(1), against so much of his trading income in any subsequent chargeable period as is derived from the related activities.

(5) Subject to subsection (7) below, a capital allowance which is to be given to any person by discharge or repayment of tax shall not to any extent be given effect under section 71 of the 1968 Act by deduction from or set off against his ring fence income.

(6) Subject to subsection (7) below, a capital allowance which is to be given to any person by discharge or repayment of tax shall not to any extent be given effect under section 74 of the 1968 Act by deduction from or set off against his ring fence profits.

(7) Subsection (5) or (6) above shall not apply to a capital allowance which falls to be made to a company for any accounting period in respect of an asset used in the relevant accounting period by a company associated with it and so used in carrying on oil extraction activities.

For the purposes of this subsection, the relevant accounting period is that in which the allowance in question first falls to be made to the company (whether or not it can to any extent be given effect in that period under section 74(1) of the 1968 Act).

(8) On a claim for group relief made by a claimant company in relation to a surrendering company, group relief shall not be allowed against the claimant company's ring fence profits except to the extent that the claim relates to losses incurred by the surrendering company that arose from oil extraction activities or from oil rights.

Valuation of oil disposed of or appropriated in certain circumstances.
1975 c. 22

493.—(1) Where a person disposes of any oil in circumstances such that the market value of that oil in a particular month falls to be taken into account under section 2 of the Oil Taxation Act 1975 ("the 1975 Act"), otherwise than by virtue of paragraph 6 of Schedule 3 to that Act, in computing for the purposes of petroleum revenue tax the assessable profit or allowable loss accruing to him in any chargeable period from an oil field (or as would so fall but for section 10 of that Act), then—

(a) for all purposes of income tax, and

(b) for the purposes of the charge of corporation tax on income,

the disposal of the oil and its acquisition by the person to whom it was disposed of shall be treated as having been for a consideration equal to the market value of the oil as so taken into account under section 2 of that Act (or as would have been so taken into account under that section but for section 10 of that Act).

(2) Where a person makes a relevant appropriation of any oil without disposing of it and does so in circumstances such that the market value of that oil in a particular month falls to be taken into account under section 2 of the 1975 Act in computing for the purposes of petroleum revenue tax the assessable profit or allowable loss accruing to him in any chargeable

period from an oil field (or would so fall but for section 10 of that Act), then for all the purposes of income tax and for the purposes of the charge of corporation tax on income, he shall be treated—

(a) as having, at the time of the appropriation—

(i) sold the oil in the course of the separate trade consisting of activities falling within section 492(1)(a) or (b); and

(ii) bought it in the course of the separate trade consisting of activities not so falling; and

(b) as having so sold and bought it at a price equal to its market value as so taken into account under section 2 of the 1975 Act (or as would have been so taken into account under that section but for section 10 of that Act).

In this subsection "relevant appropriation" has the meaning given by section 12(1) of the 1975 Act.

(3) Where—

(a) a person disposes otherwise than in a sale at arm's length (as defined in paragraph 1 of Schedule 3 to the 1975 Act) of oil acquired by him in the course of oil extraction activities carried on by him or by virtue of oil rights held by him, and

(b) subsection (1) above does not apply in relation to the disposal,

then, for all purposes of income tax and for the purposes of the charge of corporation tax on income, the disposal of the oil and its acquisition by the person to whom it was disposed of shall be treated as having been for a consideration equal to the market value of the oil in the calendar month in which the disposal was made.

(4) If a person appropriates oil acquired by him in the course of oil extraction activities carried on by him or by virtue of oil rights held by him and the appropriation is to refining or to any use except for production purposes of an oil field, within the meaning of Part I of the 1975 Act, then, unless subsection (2) above applies, for all purposes of income tax and for the purposes of the charge of corporation tax on income—

(a) he shall be treated as having, at the time of the appropriation, sold and bought the oil as mentioned in subsection (2)(a)(i) and (ii) above; and

(b) that sale and purchase shall be deemed to have been at a price equal to the market value of the oil in the calendar month in which it was appropriated.

(5) For the purposes of subsections (3) and (4) above—

(a) "calendar month" means a month of the calendar year; and

(b) paragraph 2 of Schedule 3 to the 1975 Act shall apply as it applies for the purposes of Part I of that Act, but with the following modifications, that is to say—

(i) for sub-paragraph (2)(f) there shall be substituted—

"(f) the contract is for the sale of the whole quantity of oil of which the market value falls to be ascertained for the purposes of section 493(3) or (4) of the Income and Corporation Taxes Act 1988 and of no other oil; and for the avoidance of doubt it is hereby declared that the terms as to payment which are to be implied in the contract shall be those which are customarily contained in contracts for sale at arm's length of oil of the kind in question."; and

(ii) sub-paragraphs (3) and (4) shall be omitted.

Charges on income.

494.—(1) Section 338 shall have effect subject to the following provisions of this section.

(2) Interest paid by a company shall not be allowable under section 338 as a deduction against the company's ring fence profits except—

(a) to the extent that it was payable in respect of money borrowed by the company which is shown to have been used to meet expenditure incurred by the company in carrying on oil extraction activities or in acquiring oil rights otherwise than from a connected person or to have been appropriated to meeting expenditure to be so incurred by the company; and

(b) in the case of interest paid by the company to a company associated with it, to the extent that (subject always to paragraph (a) above) the rate at which it was payable did not exceed what, having regard to all the terms on which the money was borrowed and the standing of the borrower, was a reasonable commercial rate.

Section 839 shall apply for the purposes of this subsection.

(3) Where a company pays to a company associated with it a charge on income not consisting of a payment of interest, the charge shall not be allowable to any extent under section 338 against the first-mentioned company's ring fence profits.

(4) In any case where—

(a) such of the charges on income which are paid by a company and allowable under section 338 as, by virtue of subsections (2) and (3) above, are not allowable against the company's ring fence profits exceed the remaining part of its profits (the company's "non-oil profits"), and

(b) the amount of that excess is greater than the amount (if any) by which the total of the charges on income which are allowable to the company under that section exceeds the total of the company's profits,

then, for the purpose of enabling the company to surrender the excess referred to in paragraph (a) above by way of group relief, section 403(7) shall have effect as if in that subsection—

(i) the reference to the amount paid by the surrendering company by way of charges on income were a reference to so much of that amount as is allowable only against the company's non-oil profits; and

(ii) the reference to the surrendering company's profits were a reference to its non-oil profits alone.

495.—(1) Subsection (2) below applies in any case where—

Regional development grants.

(a) a person has incurred expenditure (by way of purchase, rent or otherwise) on the acquisition of an asset in a transaction to which paragraph 2 of Schedule 4 to the 1975 Act applies (transactions between connected persons and otherwise than at arm's length), and

(b) the expenditure incurred by the other person referred to in that paragraph in acquiring, bringing into existence or enhancing the value of the asset as mentioned in that paragraph has been or is to be met by a regional development grant and, in whole or in part, falls to be taken into account under Chapter I of Part I, or under Part II, of the 1968 Act (industrial buildings and structures and scientific research) or Chapter I of Part III of the Finance Act 1971 (machinery or plant).

1971 c. 68.

(2) Where this subsection applies, for the purposes of the charge of income tax or corporation tax on the income arising from those activities of the person referred to in paragraph (a) of subsection (1) above which are treated by virtue of section 492(1) as a separate trade for those purposes, the expenditure referred to in that paragraph shall be treated as reduced by the amount of the regional development grant referred to in paragraph (b) of that subsection.

(3) Subsections (4) to (6) below apply where—

(a) expenditure incurred by any person in relation to an asset in any relevant period ("the initial period") has been or is to be met by a regional development grant; and

(b) notwithstanding the provisions of section 137 of the Finance Act 1982 and subsections (1) and (2) above, in determining that person's liability to income tax or corporation tax for the initial period the whole or some part of that expenditure falls to be taken into account under Chapter I of Part I, or under Part II, of the 1968 Act or Chapter I of Part III of the Finance Act 1971; and

1982 c. 39.

(c) in a relevant period subsequent to the initial period either expenditure on the asset becomes allowable under section 3 or 4 of the 1975 Act or the proportion of any such expenditure which is allowable is different as compared with the initial period;

and in subsections (4) to (6) below the subsequent relevant period referred to in paragraph (c) above is referred to as "the adjustment period".

(4) Where this subsection applies—

(a) there shall be redetermined for the purposes of subsections (5) and (6) below the amount of the expenditure referred to in subsection (3)(a) above which would have been taken into account as mentioned in subsection (3)(b) if the circumstances referred to in subsection (3)(c) had existed in the initial period; and

PART XII

(b) according to whether the amount as so redetermined is greater or less than the amount actually taken into account as mentioned in subsection (3)(b), the difference is in subsections (5) and (6) below referred to as the increase or the reduction in the allowance.

(5) If there is an increase in the allowance, then, for the purposes of the provisions referred to in subsection (3)(b) above, an amount of capital expenditure equal to the increase shall be deemed to have been incurred by the person concerned in the adjustment period on an extension of or addition to the asset referred to in subsection (3)(a) above.

(6) If there is a reduction in the allowance, then, for the purpose of determining the liability to income tax or corporation tax of the person concerned, he shall be treated as having received in the adjustment period, as income of the trade in connection with which the expenditure referred to in subsection (3)(a) above was incurred, a sum equal to the amount of the reduction in the allowance.

(7) In this section—

1982 c. 52.
1972 c. 63.

"regional development grant" means a grant made under the provisions of Part II of the Industrial Development Act 1982 or Part I of the Industry Act 1972 or such grant made under an enactment of the Parliament of Northern Ireland or Measure of the Northern Ireland Assembly as has been or may be declared by the Treasury under section 84 or 95 of the 1968 Act to correspond to a grant made under those provisions; and

"relevant period" means an accounting period of a company or a year of assessment.

Tariff receipts.

496.—(1) Any sum which—

(a) constitutes a tariff receipt of a person who is a participator in an oil field, and

(b) constitutes consideration in the nature of income rather than capital, and

(c) would not, apart from this subsection, be treated for the purposes of this Chapter as a receipt of the separate trade referred to in section 492(1),

shall be so treated for those purposes.

(2) To the extent that they would not otherwise be so treated, the activities of a participator in an oil field or a person connected with him in making available an asset in a way which gives rise to tariff receipts of the participator shall be treated for the purposes of this Chapter as oil extraction activities.

(3) In determining for the purposes of subsection (1) above whether any sum constitutes a tariff receipt of a person who is a participator, no account shall be taken of any sum which—

(a) is in fact received or receivable by a person connected with the participator, and

(b) constitutes a tariff receipt of the participator,

but in relation to the person by whom such a sum is actually received, subsection (1) above shall have effect as if he were a participator and as if the condition in paragraph (a) of that subsection were fulfilled.

(4) References in this section to a person connected with a participator include references to a person with whom the person is associated within the meaning of paragraph 11 of Schedule 2 to the Oil Taxation Act 1983.

497.—(1) Section 239 shall have effect subject to the following provisions of this section; and in those provisions any reference to a company's ring fence income shall be construed, except in relation to relief under section 380 of this Act and section 71 of the 1968 Act, as a reference to the company's ring fence profits.

(2) Where advance corporation tax is paid by a company ("the distributing company") in respect of any distribution made by it to a company associated with it and resident in the United Kingdom or, where subsection (3) below applies, in respect of any distribution consisting of a dividend on a redeemable preference share—

(a) that advance corporation tax shall not be set against the distributing company's liability to corporation tax on any ring fence income of the distributing company; and

(b) if the benefit of any amount of that advance corporation tax is surrendered under section 240 to a subsidiary of the distributing company, the corresponding amount of advance corporation tax which under that section the subsidiary is treated for the purposes of section 239 as having paid shall not be set against the subsidiary's liability to corporation tax on any ring fence income of the subsidiary.

(3) Subject to subsection (4) below, this subsection applies in relation to the payment of a dividend on redeemable preference shares if the dividend is paid on or after 17th March 1987 and—

(a) at the time the shares are issued, or

(b) at the time the dividend is paid,

the company paying the dividend is under the control of a company resident in the United Kingdom, and in this subsection "control" shall be construed in accordance with section 416.

(4) Subsection (3) above does not apply if or to the extent that it is shown that the proceeds of the issue of the redeemable preference shares—

(a) were used to meet expenditure incurred by the company issuing them in carrying on oil extraction activities or in acquiring oil rights otherwise than from a connected person; or

(b) were appropriated to meeting expenditure to be so incurred by that company;

and section 839 applies for the purposes of this subsection.

(5) Where in the case of any accounting period of a company there is an amount of advance corporation tax which because of subsection (2) above is not available to be set against the company's liability to corporation tax for that period on ring fence income of the company,

section 239(2) shall as regards that period have effect as if the reference to the company's profits charged to corporation tax for that period were a reference to the company's profits so charged exclusive of any ring fence income.

(6) For the purposes of subsections (2) to (4) above, shares in a company are redeemable preference shares either if they are so described in the terms of their issue or if, however they are described, they fulfil the condition in paragraph (a) below and either or both of the conditions in paragraphs (b) and (c) below—

    (a) that, as against other shares in the company, they carry a preferential entitlement to a dividend or to any assets in a winding up or both;

    (b) that, by virtue of the terms of their issue, the exercise of a right by any person or the existence of any arrangements, they are liable to be redeemed, cancelled or repaid, in whole or in part;

    (c) that, by virtue of any material arrangements, the holder has a right to require another person to acquire the shares or is obliged in any circumstances to dispose of them or another person has a right or is in any circumstances obliged to acquire them.

(7) For the purposes of paragraph (a) of subsection (6) above, shares are to be treated as carrying a preferential entitlement to a dividend as against other shares if, by virtue of any arrangements, there are circumstances in which a minimum dividend will be payable on those shares but not on others; and for the purposes of paragraph (c) of that subsection arrangements relating to shares are material arrangements if the company which issued the shares or a company associated with that company is a party to the arrangements.

Limited right to carry back surrendered ACT.

498.—(1) In any case where,—

    (a) on a date not earlier than 17th March 1987, a company which is the surrendering company for the purposes of section 240 paid a dividend; and

    (b) at no time in the accounting period of the surrendering company in which that dividend was paid was the surrendering company under the control of a company resident in the United Kingdom (construing "control" in accordance with section 416); and

    (c) under section 240(1) the benefit of the advance corporation tax paid in respect of that dividend was surrendered to a subsidiary of the surrendering company; and

    (d) that advance corporation tax is not such that the restriction in paragraph (a) or paragraph (b) of section 497(2) applies with respect to it; and

    (e) in one or more of the accounting periods of the subsidiary beginning in the six years preceding the accounting period in which falls the date referred to in paragraph (a) above, the subsidiary has a liability to corporation tax in respect of profits which consist of or include ring fence profits, sections 239 and 240 shall have effect subject to subsections (3) to (7) below.

(2) Where the conditions in subsection (1) above are fulfilled, the subsidiary to which the benefit of the advance corporation tax is surrendered is in the following provisions of this section referred to as a "qualifying subsidiary"; and in those provisions—

(a) "the surrendering company" has the same meaning as in section 240;

(b) "surrendered advance corporation tax" means advance corporation tax which, by virtue of section 240(2), a qualifying subsidiary is treated as having paid in respect of a distribution made on a particular date; and

(c) "the principal accounting period" means the accounting period of the qualifying subsidiary in which that date falls.

(3) So much of section 240(4) as would prevent surrendered advance corporation tax being set against a qualifying subsidiary's liability to corporation tax under section 239(3) shall not apply, but section 239(3) shall instead have effect subject to the following provisions of this section.

(4) Surrendered advance corporation tax may not under section 239(3) be set against a qualifying subsidiary's liability to corporation tax for an accounting period earlier than the principal accounting period unless throughout—

(a) that period,

(b) the principal accounting period, and

(c) any intervening accounting period,

the qualifying subsidiary was carrying on activities which, under and for the purposes specified in section 492, constitute a separate trade.

(5) Subject to subsection (6) below, for each accounting period of the surrendering company in which is paid a dividend the advance corporation tax on which gives rise, under section 240, to surrendered advance corporation tax, the total amount of that surrendered advance corporation tax in respect of which claims may be made under section 239(3) (whether by one qualifying subsidiary of the surrendering company or by two or more taken together) shall not exceed whichever of the following limits is appropriate to the accounting period of the surrendering company—

(a) for periods ending on or after 17th March 1987 and before 1st April 1989, £10 million;

(b) for periods ending on or after 1st April 1989 and before 1st April 1991, £15 million;

(c) for later periods, £20 million.

(6) In any case where an accounting period of the surrendering company is less than 12 months, the amount which is appropriate to it under subsection (5)(a) to (c) above shall be proportionately reduced.

Q

(7) The amount of surrendered advance corporation tax of the principal accounting period which, on a claim under section 239(3), may be treated as if it were advance corporation tax paid in respect of distributions made by the qualifying subsidiary concerned in any earlier accounting period shall not exceed the amount of advance corporation tax that would have been payable in respect of a distribution made at the end of that earlier period of an amount which, together with the advance corporation tax so payable in respect of it, would equal the qualifying subsidiary's ring fence profits of that period.

(8) In determining the amount (if any) of advance corporation tax which may be repayable—

(a) under section 17(3) of the 1975 Act, or

1981 c. 35.
        (b) under section 127(5) of the Finance Act 1981,

any advance corporation tax in respect of a distribution actually made on or after 17th March 1987 shall be left out of account.

Surrender of ACT where oil extraction company etc. owned by a consortium.

499.—(1) In any case where—

(a) a company (in this section referred to as "the consortium company") is owned by a consortium consisting of two members only, each of which owns 50 per cent. of the issued share capital of the company; and

(b) the consortium company carries on a trade consisting of or including activities falling within section 492(1)(a) to (c); and

(c) all of the issued share capital of the consortium company is of the same class and carries the same rights as to voting, dividends and distribution of assets on a winding up,

section 240 shall have effect, subject to the following provisions of this section, as if the company were a subsidiary of each member of the consortium.

(2) This section has effect with respect to advance corporation tax paid by either member of the consortium in respect of a dividend paid by it on or after 17th March 1987; and, in relation to a surrender under section 240 of the benefit of the advance corporation tax paid in respect of such a dividend—

(a) "surrendered advance corporation tax" means advance corporation tax which, by virtue of section 240(2), the consortium company is treated as having paid; and

(b) "the notional distribution date" means the date of the distribution in respect of which the surrendered advance corporation tax is treated as paid.

(3) No surrender under section 240 of the benefit of advance corporation tax may be made by virtue of this section—

(a) unless the conditions in paragraphs (a) to (c) of subsection (1) above are fulfilled throughout that accounting period of the consortium company in which falls the notional distribution date; or

(b) if arrangements are in existence by virtue of which any person could cause one or more of those conditions to cease to be fulfilled at some time during that or any later accounting period.

(4) In the application of section 239 in relation to surrendered advance corporation tax resulting from a surrender by either one of the consortium members under section 240, the reference in section 239(2) to the consortium company's profits charged to corporation tax shall be construed as a reference to one half of so much of those profits as consists of ring fence profits.

(5) So much of any surplus advance corporation tax as consists of or includes surrendered advance corporation tax shall not be treated under section 239(4) as if it were advance corporation tax paid in respect of distributions made by the consortium company in a later accounting period unless the conditions in paragraphs (a) to (c) of subsection (1) above are fulfilled throughout that later period.

(6) In any case where—

(a) as a result of a surrender by one of the consortium members, the consortium company is treated as paying an amount of surrendered advance corporation tax which exceeds the limit applicable under section 239(2) (as modified by subsection (4) above), and

(b) that excess falls to be treated under section 239(4) as advance corporation tax paid by the consortium company in respect of distributions made in a later accounting period,

then, for the purposes of the application of section 239(2) (as modified by subsection (4) above) in relation to that later accounting period, the excess of the surrendered advance corporation tax shall be treated as resulting from a surrender by that one of the consortium members referred to in paragraph (a) above.

(7) Where section 240 has effect as mentioned in subsection (2) above, subsection (11) of that section shall have effect with the omission of paragraph (b) (and the word "and" immediately preceding it).

(8) Notwithstanding the provisions of subsection (1) above the consortium company shall not be regarded as a subsidiary for the purposes of section 498.

500.—(1) Where a participator in an oil field has paid any petroleum revenue tax with which he was chargeable for a chargeable period, then, in computing for corporation tax the amount of his income arising in the relevant accounting period from oil extraction activities or oil rights, there shall be deducted an amount equal to that petroleum revenue tax.

Deduction of PRT in computing income for corporation tax purposes.

(2) There shall be made all such adjustments of assessments to corporation tax as are required in order to give effect to subsection (1) above.

(3) For the purposes of subsection (1) above, the relevant accounting period, in relation to any petroleum revenue tax paid by a company, is—

(a) the accounting period of the company in or at the end of which the chargeable period for which that tax was charged ends; or

(b) if that chargeable period ends after the accounting period of the company in or at the end of which the trade giving rise to the income referred to above is permanently discontinued, that accounting period.

(4) If some or all of the petroleum revenue tax in respect of which a deduction has been made under subsection (1) above is subsequently repaid, that deduction shall be reduced or extinguished accordingly; and any additional assessment to corporation tax required in order to give effect to this subsection may be made at any time not later than six years after the end of the accounting period in which the first-mentioned tax was repaid.

(5) In this section "chargeable period" has the same meaning as in Part I of the 1975 Act.

Interest on repayment of PRT.

501. Where any amount of petroleum revenue tax paid by a participator in an oil field is, under any provision of Part I of the 1975 Act, repaid to him with interest, the amount of the interest paid to him shall be disregarded in computing the amount of his income for the purposes of corporation tax.

Interpretation of Chapter V.
1975 c. 22.

1934 c. 36.
1964 c. 28 (N.I.).

502.—(1) In this Chapter—

"the 1975 Act" means the Oil Taxation Act 1975;

"oil" means any substance won or capable of being won under the authority of a licence granted under either the Petroleum (Production) Act 1934 or the Petroleum (Production) Act (Northern Ireland) 1964, other than methane gas won in the course of operations for making and keeping mines safe;

"oil extraction activities" means any activities of a person—

(a) in searching for oil in the United Kingdom or a designated area or causing such searching to be carried out for him; or

(b) in extracting or causing to be extracted for him oil at any place in the United Kingdom or a designated area under rights authorising the extraction and held by him or, if the person in question is a company, by the company or a company associated with it; or

(c) in transporting or causing to be transported for him as far as dry land in the United Kingdom oil extracted at any such place not on dry land under rights authorising the extraction and so held; or

(d) in effecting or causing to be effected for him the initial treatment or initial storage of oil won from any oil field under rights authorising its extraction and so held;

"oil field" has the same meaning as in Part I of the 1975 Act;

"oil rights" means rights to oil to be extracted at any place in the United Kingdom or a designated area, or to interests in or to the benefit of such oil;

"participator" has the same meaning as in Part I of the 1975 Act; and "ring fence income" means income arising from oil extraction activities or oil rights; and

"ring fence profits" has the same meaning as in section 79(5) of the Finance Act 1984 or, in any case where that subsection does not apply, means ring fence income.

(2) For the purposes of subsection (1) above—

(a) "designated area" means an area designated by Order in Council under section 1(7) of the Continental Shelf Act 1964;

(b) "initial treatment" has the same meaning as in Part I of the 1975 Act; and

(c) the definition of "initial storage" in section 12(1) of the 1975 Act shall apply but, in its application for those purposes in relation to the person mentioned in subsection (1)(d) above and to oil won from any one oil field shall have effect as if the reference to the maximum daily production rate of oil for the field as there mentioned were a reference to that person's share of that maximum daily production rate, that is to say, a share thereof proportionate to his share of the oil won from that field.

(3) For the purposes of this Chapter two companies are associated with one another if—

(a) one is a 51 per cent. subsidiary of the other;

(b) each is a 51 per cent. subsidiary of a third company; or

(c) one is owned by a consortium of which the other is a member.

Section 413(6) shall apply for the purposes of paragraph (c) above.

(4) Without prejudice to subsection (3) above, for the purposes of this Chapter, two companies are also associated with one another if one has control of the other or both are under the control of the same person or persons; and in this subsection "control" shall be construed in accordance with section 416.

CHAPTER VI

MISCELLANEOUS BUSINESSES AND BODIES

503.—(1) Subject to the following provisions of this section, for the purposes of sections 5(2), 380 to 390, 393, 394, 401, 623(2)(c), 644(2)(c) and 833(4)(c) and of Chapter I of Part III of the Finance Act 1971—

(a) the commercial letting of furnished holiday accommodation in the United Kingdom in respect of which the profits or gains are chargeable under Case VI of Schedule D shall be treated as a trade; and

(b) all such lettings made by a particular person or partnership or body of persons shall be treated as one trade.

(2) In their application by virtue of subsection (1) above sections 390(1) and 401(1) shall have effect as if for the references in those sections to Case I of Schedule D there were substituted references to Case VI of that Schedule.

(3) No relief shall be given to an individual under section 381 as it has effect by virtue of subsection (1) above, in respect of a loss sustained in any year of assessment, if any of the accommodation in respect of which the trade is carried on in that year was first let by him as furnished accommodation more than three years before the beginning of that year of assessment.

(4) Relief shall not be given for the same loss or the same portion of a loss both under any provision of Chapters I and II of Part X except sections 391, 392, 395 and 396, as those Chapters apply by virtue of this section, and under any other provision of the Tax Acts.

(5) In computing the profits or gains arising from the commercial letting of furnished holiday accommodation which are chargeable to tax under Case VI of Schedule D, such expenditure may be deducted as would be deductible if the letting were a trade and those profits or gains were accordingly to be computed in accordance with the rules applicable to Case I of that Schedule.

(6) Where there is a letting of accommodation only part of which is holiday accommodation such apportionments shall be made for the purposes of this section as appear to the inspector, or on appeal the Commissioners, to be just and reasonable.

(7) Where a person has been charged to income tax or corporation tax otherwise than in accordance with the provisions of this section, such assessment, reduction or discharge of an assessment or, where a claim for repayment is made, such repayment, shall be made as may be necessary to give effect to those provisions.

Supplementary provisions.

504.—(1) This section has effect for the purposes of section 503.

(2) A letting—

(a) is a commercial letting if it is let on a commercial basis and with a view to the realisation of profits; and

(b) is of furnished accommodation if the tenant is entitled to the use of furniture.

(3) Accommodation shall not be treated as holiday accommodation for the purposes of this section unless—

(a) it is available for commercial letting to the public generally as holiday accommodation for periods which amount, in the aggregate, to not less than 140 days;

(b) the periods for which it is so let amount in the aggregate to at least 70 days; and

(c) for a period comprising at least seven months (which need not be continuous but includes any months in which it is let as mentioned in paragraph (b) above) it is not normally in the same occupation for a continuous period exceeding 31 days.

(4) Any question whether accommodation let by any person other than a company is, at any time in a year of assessment, holiday accommodation shall be determined—

(a) if the accommodation was not let by him as furnished accommodation in the preceding year of assessment but is so let in the following year of assessment, by reference to the 12 months beginning with the date on which he first so let it in the year of assessment;

(b) if the accommodation was let by him as furnished accommodation in the preceding year of assessment but is not so let in the following year of assessment, by reference to the 12 months ending with the date on which he ceased so to let it in the year of assessment; and

(c) in any other case, by reference to the year of assessment.

(5) Any question whether accommodation let by a company is at any time in an accounting period holiday accommodation shall be determined—

(a) if the accommodation was not let by it as furnished accommodation in the period of 12 months immediately preceding the accounting period but is so let in the period of 12 months immediately following the accounting period, by reference to the 12 months beginning with the date in the accounting period on which it first so let it;

(b) if the accommodation was let by it as furnished accommodation in the period of 12 months immediately preceding the accounting period but is not so let by it in the period of 12 months immediately following the accounting period, by reference to the 12 months ending with the date in the accounting period on which it ceased so to let it;

(c) in any other case, by reference to the period of 12 months ending with the last day of the accounting period.

(6) Where, in any year of assessment or accounting period, a person lets furnished accommodation which is treated as holiday accommodation for the purposes of this section in that year or period ("the qualifying accommodation"), he may make a claim under this subsection, within two years after that year or period, for averaging treatment to apply for that year or period to that and any other accommodation specified in the claim which was let by him as furnished accommodation during that year or period and would fall to be treated as holiday accommodation in that year or period if subsection (3)(b) above were satisfied in relation to it.

(7) Where a claim is made under subsection (6) above in respect of any year of assessment or accounting period, any such other accommodation shall be treated as being holiday accommodation in that year or period if the number of days for which the qualifying accommodation and any other such accommodation was let by the claimant as mentioned in subsection (3)(a) above during the year or period amounts on average to at least 70.

(8) Qualifying accommodation may not be specified in more than one claim in respect of any one year of assessment or accounting period.

(9) For the purposes of this section a person lets accommodation if he permits another person to occupy it, whether or not in pursuance of a lease; and "letting" and "tenant" shall be construed accordingly.

505.—(1) Subject to subsections (2) and (3) below, the following exemptions shall be granted on a claim in that behalf to the Board—

(a) exemption from tax under Schedules A and D in respect of the rents and profits of any lands, tenements, hereditaments or heritages belonging to a hospital, public school or almshouse, or vested in trustees for charitable purposes, so far as the same are applied to charitable purposes only;

(b) exemption from tax under Schedule B in respect of any lands occupied by a charity;

(c) exemption—

(i) from tax under Schedule C in respect of any interest, annuities, dividends or shares of annuities,

(ii) from tax under Schedule D in respect of any yearly interest or other annual payment, and

(iii) from tax under Schedule F in respect of any distribution,

where the income in question forms part of the income of a charity, or is, according to rules or regulations established by Act of Parliament, charter, decree, deed of trust or will, applicable to charitable purposes only, and so far as it is applied to charitable purposes only;

(d) exemption from tax under Schedule C in respect of any interest, annuities, dividends or shares of annuities which are in the names of trustees and are applicable solely towards the repairs of any cathedral, college, church or chapel, or of any building used solely for the purposes of divine worship, so far as the same are applied to those purposes;

(e) exemption from tax under Schedule D in respect of the profits of any trade carried on by a charity, if the profits are applied solely to the purposes of the charity and either—

(i) the trade is exercised in the course of the actual carrying out of a primary purpose of the charity; or

(ii) the work in connection with the trade is mainly carried out by beneficiaries of the charity.

(2) Any payment which—

(a) is received by a charity from another charity; and

(b) is not made for full consideration in money or money's worth; and

(c) is not chargeable to tax apart from this subsection; and

(d) is not, apart from this subsection, of a description which (on a claim) would be eligible for relief from tax by virtue of any provision of subsection (1) above;

shall be chargeable to tax under Case III of Schedule D but shall be eligible for relief from tax under subsection (1)(c) above as if it were an annual payment.

(3) If in any chargeable period of a charity—

   (a) its relevant income and gains are not less than £10,000; and

   (b) its relevant income and gains exceed the amount of its qualifying expenditure; and

   (c) the charity incurs, or is treated as incurring, non-qualifying expenditure;

relief shall not be available under either subsection (1) above or section 145 of the 1979 Act for so much of the excess as does not exceed the non-qualifying expenditure incurred in that period.

(4) In relation to a chargeable period of less than 12 months, subsection (3) above shall have effect as if the amount specified in paragraph (a) of that subsection were proportionately reduced.

(5) In subsection (3) above "relevant income and gains" means—

   (a) income which apart from subsection (1) above would not be exempt from tax together with any income which is taxable notwithstanding that subsection; and

   (b) gains which apart from section 145 of the 1979 Act would be chargeable gains together with any gains which are chargeable gains notwithstanding that section.

(6) Where by virtue of subsection (3) above there is an amount of a charity's relevant income and gains for which relief under subsection (1) above and section 145 of the 1979 Act is not available, the charity may, by notice to the Board, specify which items of its relevant income and gains are, in whole or in part, to be attributed to that amount, and, for this purpose, all covenanted payments to charity (within the meaning of section 660(3)) shall be treated as a single item; and if within 30 days of being required to do so by the Board, a charity does not give notice under this subsection, the items of its relevant income and gains which are to be attributed to the amount in question shall be such as the Board may determine.

(7) Where it appears to the Board that two or more charities acting in concert are engaged in transactions of which the main purpose or one of the main purposes is the avoidance of tax (whether by the charities or by any other person), the Board may by notice given to the charities provide that, for such chargeable periods as may be specified in the notice, subsection (3) above shall have effect in relation to them with the omission of paragraph (a).

(8) An appeal may be brought against a notice under subsection (7) above as if it were notice of the decision of the Board on a claim made by the charities concerned.

506.—(1) In this section, section 505 and Schedule 20—

   "charity" means any body of persons or trust established for charitable purposes only;

   "qualifying expenditure", in relation to a chargeable period of a charity, means, subject to subsection (3) below, expenditure incurred in that period for charitable purposes only; and

Qualifying expenditure and non-qualifying expenditure.

"non-qualifying expenditure" means expenditure which is not qualifying expenditure.

(2) For the purposes of section 505 and subsection (1) above, where expenditure which is not actually incurred in a particular chargeable period properly falls to be charged against the income of that chargeable period as being referable to commitments (whether or not of a contractual nature) which the charity has entered into before or during that period, it shall be treated as incurred in that period.

(3) A payment made (or to be made) to a body situated outside the United Kingdom shall not be qualifying expenditure by virtue of this section unless the charity concerned has taken such steps as may be reasonable in the circumstances to ensure that the payment will be applied for charitable purposes.

(4) If in any chargeable period a charity—

(a) invests any of its funds in an investment which is not a qualifying investment, as defined in Part I of Schedule 20; or

(b) makes a loan (not being an investment) which is not a qualifying loan, as defined in Part II of that Schedule;

then, subject to subsection (5) below, the amount so invested or lent in that period shall be treated for the purposes of this section as being an amount of expenditure incurred by the charity, and, accordingly, as being non-qualifying expenditure.

(5) If, in any chargeable period, a charity which has in that period made an investment or loan falling within subsection (4) above—

(a) realises the whole or part of that investment; or

(b) is repaid the whole or part of that loan;

any further investment or lending in that period of the sum realised or repaid shall, to the extent that it does not exceed the sum originally invested or lent, be left out of account in determining the amount which, by virtue of subsection (4) above, is treated as non-qualifying expenditure incurred in that period.

(6) If the aggregate of the qualifying and non-qualifying expenditure incurred by a charity in any chargeable period exceeds the relevant income and gains of that period, Part III of Schedule 20 shall have effect to treat, in certain cases, some or all of that excess as non-qualifying expenditure incurred in earlier periods.

507.—(1) There shall on a claim in that behalf to the Board be allowed in the case of—

(a) the Trustees of the National Heritage Memorial Fund;

(b) the Historic Buildings and Monuments Commission for England;

such exemption from tax as falls to be allowed under section 505 in the case of a charity the whole income of which is applied to charitable purposes.

(2) The Trustees of the British Museum and the Trustees of the British Museum (Natural History) shall each be entitled, on a claim in that behalf to the Board, to the following exemptions—

(a) exemption from tax under Schedules A and D in respect of any land, or interest in or right over land, vested in them; and

(b) the like exemptions in respect of any dividends of stock vested in them, or in any other person for their use, and in respect of distributions charged under Schedule F, as are granted to charities under section 505.

508.—(1) Where—

(a) an Association which has as its object the undertaking of scientific research which may lead to or facilitate an extension of any class or classes of trade is approved for the purposes of this section by the Secretary of State; and

(b) the memorandum of association or other similar instrument regulating the functions of the Association precludes the direct or indirect payment or transfer to any of its members of any of its income or property by way of dividend, gift, division, bonus or otherwise howsoever by way of profit;

there shall, on a claim in that behalf to the Board, be allowed in the case of the Association such exemption from tax as falls to be allowed under section 505 in the case of a charity the whole income of which is applied to charitable purposes.

(2) The condition specified in paragraph (b) of subsection (1) above shall not be deemed not to be complied with in the case of any Association by reason only that the memorandum or other similar instrument regulating its functions does not prevent the payment to its members of reasonable remuneration for goods, labour or power supplied, or for services rendered, of reasonable interest for money lent, or of reasonable rent for any premises.

(3) In this section "scientific research" means any activities in the fields of natural or applied science for the extension of knowledge.

509.—(1) Where a body established by or under any enactment and having as its object, or one of its objects, the marketing of an agricultural product or the stabilising of the price of an agricultural product is required, by or under any scheme or arrangements approved by or made with a Minister of the Crown or government department, to pay the whole or part of any surplus derived from its trading operations or other trade receipts into a reserve fund satisfying the conditions specified in subsection (2) below, then, in computing for the purposes of tax the profits or gains or losses of the body's trade—

(a) there shall be allowed as deductions any sums so required to be paid by the body into the reserve fund out of the profits or gains of the trade, and

(b) there shall be taken into account as trading receipts any sums withdrawn by the body from the fund, except so far as they are so required to be paid to a Minister or government department, or are distributed to producers of the product in question or refunded to persons paying any levy or duty.

(2) The conditions to be satisfied by the reserve fund are as follows—

(a) that no sum may be withdrawn from the fund without the authority or consent of a Minister of the Crown or government department; and

(b) that where money has been paid to the body by a Minister of the Crown or government department in connection with arrangements for maintaining guaranteed prices, or in connection with the body's trading operations, and is repayable to that Minister or department, sums afterwards standing to the credit of the fund are required as mentioned in subsection (1) above to be applied in whole or in part in repaying the money; and

(c) that the fund is reviewed by a Minister of the Crown at intervals fixed by or under the scheme or arrangements in question, and any amount by which it appears to the Minister to exceed the reasonable requirements of the body is withdrawn therefrom.

(3) In this section references to a Minister of the Crown or government department include references to a Head of a Department or a Department in Northern Ireland, and references to producers of a product include references to producers of one type or quality of a product from another.

Agricultural societies.

510.—(1) Profits or gains arising to an agricultural society from any exhibition or show held for the purposes of the society shall be exempt from tax if applied solely to the purposes of the society.

(2) In this section "agricultural society" means any society or institution established for the purpose of promoting the interests of agriculture, horticulture, livestock breeding or forestry.

The Electricity Council and Boards, the Northern Ireland Electricity Service and the Gas Council.

511.—(1) For the purposes of the Corporation Tax Acts, the Electricity Council shall be treated as carrying on a trade, and those Acts shall have effect as if the trade carried on by the Central Electricity Authority at any time before 1st January 1958 had been the trade of the Electricity Council.

(2) For the purposes of the Corporation Tax Acts—

(a) any trade carried on by a Board shall be treated as if it were part of the trade carried on by the Electricity Council;

(b) subject to paragraph (c) below, any property, rights or liabilities of a Board shall be treated as property, rights or liabilities of the Electricity Council, and anything done by or to a Board shall be deemed to have been done by or to the Electricity Council;

(c) any rights, liabilities or things done —

(i) of, by or to the Electricity Council against, to or by a Board, or

(ii) of, by or to a Board against, to or by the Electricity Council or any other Board,

shall be left out of account;

and corporation tax shall be charged accordingly.

(3) For the purposes of the operation of the Corporation Tax Acts in accordance with subsections (1) and (2) above, the Electricity Council shall be deemed to have been in existence as from 1st April 1948, and anything done by, to or in relation to the Central Electricity Authority shall be treated as if it had been done by, to or in relation to the Electricity Council.

(4) The Corporation Tax Acts shall have effect as if the trade carried on at any time before 1st April 1973 by any predecessor of the Northern Ireland Electricity Service had been carried on by the Service; and for that purpose the Service shall be deemed to have been in existence as from the time when the predecessor began to carry on its trade and anything done by, to or in relation to the predecessor shall be treated as if it had been done by, to or in relation to the Service.

(5) In subsection (4) above references to a predecessor of the Northern Ireland Electricity Service are references to any body whose functions were transferred to the Service on the 1st April 1973, and references to the trade of a predecessor are references to its activities in the discharge of the functions that were so transferred.

(6) In subsections (1) and (2) above "Board" means—

(a) any Area Board established by or under the provisions of the Electricity Act 1947; and

1947 c. 54.

(b) in relation to any time on or after 1st January 1958, the Central Electricity Generating Board.

(7) The Corporation Tax Acts shall apply in relation to the trade of the Gas Council as if before the beginning of April 1962 it had consisted of the trades of the Area Boards (within the meaning of the Gas Act 1948), and (without prejudice to the generality of the foregoing) allowances and balancing charges shall be made to or on the Gas Council accordingly by reference to the capital expenditure of Area Boards and to the allowances made to Area Boards in respect of that expenditure.

1948 c. 67.

512.—(1) The United Kingdom Atomic Energy Authority and the National Radiological Protection Board shall be entitled to exemption from income tax and corporation tax—

Atomic Energy Authority and National Radiological Protection Board.

(a) under Schedules A, B and C;

(b) under Schedule D in respect of any yearly interest or other annual payment received by the Authority or Board;

(c) under Schedule F in respect of distributions received by the Authority or Board.

(2) Income arising from investments or deposits held for the purposes of any pension scheme provided and maintained by the Authority shall be treated for the purposes of this section as if that income and the source thereof belonged to the Authority.

Part XII
British Airways
Board and
National Freight
Corporation.
1980 c. 60.
1980 c. 34.

513.—(1) Subject to subsection (2) below, the successor company in which the property, rights, liabilities and obligations of the British Airways Board are vested by the Civil Aviation Act 1980 shall be treated for all purposes of corporation tax as if it were the same person as the British Airways Board; and the successor company to which the undertaking of the National Freight Corporation is transferred by the Transport Act 1980 shall be treated for those purposes as if it were the same person as the National Freight Corporation.

(2) The transfer by the Civil Aviation Act 1980 from the British Airways Board to the successor company of liability for any loan made to the Board shall not affect any direction in respect of the loan which has been given by the Treasury under section 581.

(3) A successor company shall not by virtue of subsection (1) above be regarded as a body falling within section 272(5) of the 1970 Act.

514. Where any property is held upon trust in accordance with directions which are valid and effective under section 9 of the Superannuation and other Trust Funds (Validation) Act 1927 (which provides for the validation of trust funds for the reduction of the national debt), any income arising from that property or from any accumulation of any such income, and any profits of any description otherwise accruing to the property and liable to be accumulated under the trust, shall be exempt from income tax.

515.—(1) An overseas signatory to the Operating Agreement made pursuant to the Convention on the International Maritime Satellite Organisation which came into force on 16th July 1979 shall be exempt from income tax and corporation tax in respect of any payment received by that signatory from the Organisation in accordance with that Agreement.

(2) In this section "an overseas signatory" means a signatory other than one designated for the purposes of the Agreement by the United Kingdom in accordance with the Convention.

516.—(1) Tax shall not be chargeable on dividends (within the meaning of Schedule C) paid out of the public revenue of the United Kingdom where they are income of any bank or issue department of a bank to which this subsection for the time being applies.

(2) Subsection (1) above shall not prevent any such dividends being taken into account in computing profits or gains or losses of a business carried on in the United Kingdom.

(3) A bank or issue department of a bank to which this subsection for the time being applies shall be exempt from tax in respect of chargeable gains accruing to it.

(4) Her Majesty may by Order in Council direct that subsection (1) or (3), or both, shall apply to any bank, or to its issue department, if it appears to Her Majesty that the bank is not resident in the United

Kingdom and is entrusted by the government of a territory outside the United Kingdom with the custody of the principal foreign exchange reserves of that territory.

(5) No recommendation shall be made to Her Majesty in Council to make an order under this section unless a draft of the order has been laid before the House of Commons and has been approved by resolution of that House.

517. There shall be exempt from tax any profits or income arising or accruing to the issue department of the Reserve Bank of India constituted under an Act of the Indian legislature called the Reserve Bank of India Act 1934, or to the issue department of the State Bank of Pakistan constituted under certain orders made under section 9 of the Indian Independence Act 1947.

518.—(1) This section has effect where the trade of any body corporate other than a limited liability company is transferred to a harbour authority by or under a certified harbour reorganisation scheme which provides also for the dissolution of the transferor.

(2) For the purposes of the Corporation Tax Acts, the trade shall not be treated as permanently discontinued, nor shall a new trade be treated as set up and commenced.

(3) The transferee shall be entitled to relief from corporation tax under section 393(1), as for a loss sustained by it in carrying on the transferred trade or any trade of which it comes to form part, for any amount which, if the transferor had continued to carry it on, would have been available to the transferor for carry-forward against chargeable profits of succeeding accounting periods, but subject to any claim made by the transferor under section 393(2).

(4) There shall be made to or on the transferee in accordance with the provisions of the Capital Allowances Acts all such allowances and charges as would, if the transferor had continued to carry on the trade, have fallen to be made to or on it under those Acts and the amount of any such allowance or charge shall be computed as if the transferee had been carrying on the trade since the transferor had begun to do so and as if everything done to or by the transferor had been done to or by the transferee.

(5) No sale or transfer which on the transfer of the trade is made by the transferor to the transferee of any assets in use for the purposes of the trade shall be treated as giving rise to any such allowance or charge as is mentioned in subsection (4) above.

(6) The transferor shall not be entitled to relief under section 394 in respect of the trade.

(7) The transferee shall be entitled to relief from corporation tax in respect of chargeable gains for any amount for which the transferor would have been entitled to claim relief in respect of allowable losses if it had continued to carry on the trade.

(8) Where part only of such trade is transferred to a harbour authority by or under a certified harbour organisation scheme, and the transferor continues to carry on the remainder of the trade, or any such trade is, by or under a certified harbour reorganisation scheme which provides also

for the dissolution of the transferor, transferred in parts to two or more harbour authorities, this section shall apply as if the transferred part, or each of the transferred parts, had at all times been a separate trade.

(9) Where a part of any trade is to be treated by virtue of subsection (8) above as having been a separate trade over any period there shall be made any necessary adjustments of accounting periods, and such apportionments as may be just of receipts, expenses, allowances or charges.

Subsection (10) of section 343 shall apply to any apportionment under this subsection as it applies to an apportionment under subsection (9) of that section.

(10) In this section—

1964 c. 40.

"harbour authority" has the same meaning as in the Harbours Act 1964;

"harbour reorganisation scheme" means any statutory provision providing for the management by a harbour authority of any harbour or group of harbours in the United Kingdom, and "certified", in relation to any harbour reorganisation scheme, means certified by a Minister of the Crown or government department as so providing with a view to securing, in the public interest, the efficient and economical development of the harbour or harbours in question;

"limited liability company" means a company having a limit on the liability of its members;

"statutory provision" means any enactment, or any scheme, order or other instrument having effect under an enactment, and includes an enactment confirming a provisional order; and

"transferor", in relation to a trade, means the body from whom the trade is transferred, whether or not the transfer is effected by that body.

Local authorities.

519.—(1) A local authority in the United Kingdom—

(a) shall be exempt from all charge to income tax in respect of its income;

(b) shall be exempt from corporation tax;

and so far as the exemption from income tax conferred by this subsection calls for repayment of tax, effect shall be given thereto by means of a claim.

(2) Subsection (1) above shall apply to a local authority association as it applies to a local authority.

(3) In this Act "local authority association" means any incorporated or unincorporated association—

(a) of which all the constituent members are local authorities, groups of local authorities or local authority associations, and

(b) which has for its object or primary object the protection and furtherance of the interests in general of local authorities or any description of local authorities;

and for this purpose, if a member of an association is a representative of or appointed by any authority, group of authorities or association, that authority, group or association (and not he) shall be treated as a constituent member of the association.

(4) In this Act "local authority" means—

(a) any authority having power to make or determine a rate;

(b) any authority having power to issue a precept, requisition or other demand for the payment of money to be raised out of a rate;

and in this subsection "rate" means a rate the proceeds of which are applicable for public local purposes and which is leviable by reference to the value of land or other property.

PART XIII

MISCELLANEOUS SPECIAL PROVISIONS

CHAPTER I

INTELLECTUAL PROPERTY

Patents and know-how

Allowances for expenditure on purchase of patent rights: post-31st March 1986 expenditure.

520.—(1) Subject to subsection (3) below, where a person incurs capital expenditure after 31st March 1986 on the purchase of patent rights, allowances and charges shall, in accordance with subsections (4) and (6) below, be made to and on him in respect of that expenditure.

(2) No allowance shall be made to a person under subsection (1) above in respect of any expenditure unless—

(a) the allowance falls in accordance with section 528(1) to be made to him in taxing his trade; or

(b) any income receivable by him in respect of the rights would be liable to tax.

(3) For the purposes of this section and section 521 any expenditure incurred for the purposes of a trade by a person about to carry it on shall be treated as if it had been incurred by that person on the first day on which he does carry it on, unless, before that first day, he has sold all the rights on the purchase of which the expenditure was incurred.

(4) For any chargeable period for which a person within subsection (1) above has qualifying expenditure which exceeds any disposal value to be brought into account by him in accordance with section 521(2) there shall be made to him—

(a) except where paragraph (b) or (c) below applies, a writing-down allowance of an amount equal, subject to subsection (5) below, to—

(i) 25 per cent. of the excess; or

(ii) a proportionately reduced percentage of the excess if the period is part only of a year, or if, in a case where the period is a year of assessment and the allowance falls to be made in taxing a trade, the trade has been carried on for part only of that year;

(b) if an allowance falls to be made to that person in taxing his trade and the period is the chargeable period related to the permanent discontinuance of the trade, a balancing allowance equal to the whole of the excess; and

(c) if paragraph (b) above does not apply but the period is the chargeable period in which the last of the relevant patent rights comes to an end without any of those rights being revived, a balancing allowance equal to the whole of the excess.

(5) For the purposes of subsection (4)(c) above the "relevant patent rights" at any time are those—

(a) on the purchase of which the person concerned has incurred capital expenditure which has been taken into account in determining his qualifying expenditure for any chargeable period; and

(b) which he has not wholly disposed of.

(6) For any chargeable period for which a person's qualifying expenditure is less than the disposal value which he is to bring into account, there shall be made on him a balancing charge and the amount on which the charge is made shall be an amount equal to the difference.

521.—(1) For the purposes of section 520(4) to (6), a person's qualifying expenditure for a chargeable period is the aggregate of the following amounts—

(a) any capital expenditure incurred by him on the purchase of patent rights, being expenditure incurred during the chargeable period or its basis period or at any previous time, other than expenditure which, or any part of which, has formed part of his qualifying expenditure for any previous chargeable period; and

(b) if, for the chargeable period immediately preceding the chargeable period in question, there was an excess of qualifying expenditure over disposal value, the balance of that excess after deducting any writing-down allowance under section 520(4)(a) made by reference to that excess.

(2) If, in any chargeable period or its basis period, a person sells the whole or any part of any patent rights on the purchase of which he has incurred capital expenditure, then, for the purposes of section 520(4) to (6) and subsection (1) above, he is required to bring into account for that chargeable period disposal value equal, subject to subsections (3) and (4) below, to the net proceeds to him of that sale.

(3) The disposal value to be brought into account by any person in respect of any patent rights as a result of one or more sales falling within subsection (2) above shall not (or, as the case may be, shall not in the aggregate) exceed the capital expenditure incurred by him on the purchase of those rights.

(4) Where the person mentioned in subsection (3) above has acquired the patent rights as a result of a transaction which was, or a series of transactions each of which was, between persons who are connected with each other within the terms of section 839, that subsection shall have effect as if it referred to the capital expenditure on the purchase of the rights incurred by whichever party to that transaction or to any of those transactions incurred the greatest such expenditure.

(5) Where a person incurs capital expenditure on the purchase of patent rights and either—

(a) he and the seller are connected with each other within the terms of section 839, or

(b) it appears with respect to the sale, or with respect to transactions of which the sale is one, that the sole or main benefit which, but for this subsection, might have been expected to accrue to the parties was the obtaining of an allowance under section 520(4),

PART XIII

there shall be disregarded for the purposes of section 520(4) and (6) and subsection (1) above so much (if any) of that expenditure as exceeds the disposal value to be brought into account by virtue of subsections (2) to (4) above by reason of the sale.

Allowances for expenditure on purchase of patent rights: pre-1st April 1986 expenditure.

522.—(1) Subject to subsection (2) below, where a person incurred capital expenditure before 1st April 1986 on the purchase of patent rights, there shall, subject to and in accordance with the following provisions of this Chapter, be made to him writing-down allowances in respect of that expenditure during the writing-down period.

(2) No writing-down allowance shall be made to a person under subsection (1) above in respect of any expenditure unless—

(a) the allowance falls in accordance with section 528(1) to be made to him in taxing his trade; or

(b) any income receivable by him in respect of the rights would be liable to tax.

(3) Subject to subsections (4) to (6) below, the writing-down period referred to in subsection (1) above is 17 years beginning with the chargeable period related to the expenditure.

(4) Where the rights are purchased for a specified period, subsection (3) above shall have effect with the substitution for the reference to 17 years of a reference to 17 years or the number of years comprised within that period, whichever is the less.

(5) Where the rights purchased begin one complete year or more after the commencement of the patent and subsection (4) above does not apply, subsection (3) above shall have effect with the substitution for the reference to 17 years of a reference to 17 years less the number of complete years which, when the rights began, have elapsed since the commencement of the patent or, if 17 complete years have so elapsed, of a reference to one year.

(6) Any expenditure incurred for the purposes of a trade by a person about to carry it on shall be treated for the purposes of subsections (3) to (5) above as if it had been incurred by that person on the first day on which he does carry it on, unless, before that first day, he has sold all the rights on the purchase of which the expenditure was incurred.

(7) Subsections (2) and (3) of section 75 of the 1968 Act (effect of providing for writing-down allowances during a writing-down period of a specified length) shall apply to this section as they apply to the provisions specified in subsection (1) of that section.

Lapses of patent rights, sales etc.

523.—(1) Where a person incurred capital expenditure before 1st April 1986 on the purchase of patent rights and, before the end of the writing-down period under section 522, any of the following events occurs, that is to say—

(a) the rights come to an end without being subsequently revived; or

(b) he sells all those rights or so much of them as he still owns; or

(c) he sells part of those rights and the net proceeds of the sale (so far as they consist of capital sums) are not less than the amount of the capital expenditure remaining unallowed, no writing-down allowance shall be made to that person for the chargeable period related to the event or for any subsequent chargeable period.

(2) Where a person incurred capital expenditure before 1st April 1986 on the purchase of patent rights and, before the end of the writing-down period under section 522, either of the following events occurs, that is to say—

(a) the rights come to an end without being subsequently revived, or

(b) he sells all those rights, or so much of them as he still owns, and the net proceeds of the sale (so far as they consist of capital sums) are less than the amount of the capital expenditure remaining unallowed,

there shall, subject to and in accordance with the following provisions of this Chapter, be made to him for the chargeable period related to the event an allowance ("a balancing allowance") equal, if the event is the rights coming to an end, to the amount of the capital expenditure remaining unallowed and, if the event is a sale, to the amount of the capital expenditure remaining unallowed less the net proceeds of the sale.

(3) Where—

(a) a person who incurred capital expenditure before 1st April 1986 on the purchase of patent rights sells all or any part of those rights, and

(b) the net proceeds of the sale (so far as they consist of capital sums) exceed the amount of the capital expenditure remaining unallowed, if any,

there shall, subject to and in accordance with the following provisions of this Chapter, be made on him for the chargeable period related to the sale a charge ("a balancing charge") on an amount equal to the excess or, where the amount of the capital expenditure remaining unallowed is nil, to those net proceeds.

(4) Where a person who incurred capital expenditure before 1st April 1986 on the purchase of patent rights sells a part of those rights and subsection (3) above does not apply, the amount of any writing-down allowance made in respect of that expenditure for the chargeable period related to the sale or any subsequent chargeable period shall be the amount arrived at by—

(a) subtracting the net proceeds of the sale (so far as they consist of capital sums) from the amount of the expenditure remaining unallowed at the time of the sale, and

(b) dividing the result by the number of complete years of the writing-down period which remained at the beginning of the chargeable period related to the sale,

and so on for any subsequent sales.

(5) References in this section to the amount of any capital expenditure remaining unallowed shall, in relation to any event, be construed as references to the amount of that expenditure less any writing-down allowances made in respect thereof for chargeable periods before that

related to the event, and less also the net proceeds of any previous sale by the person who incurred the expenditure of any part of the rights acquired by the expenditure, so far as those proceeds consist of capital sums.

(6) Notwithstanding anything in subsections (1) to (5) above—

(a) no balancing allowance shall be made in respect of any expenditure incurred before 1st April 1986 unless a writing-down allowance has been, or, but for the happening of the event giving rise to the balancing allowance, could have been, made in respect of that expenditure, and

(b) the total amount on which a balancing charge is made in respect of any expenditure incurred before 1st April 1986 shall not exceed the total writing-down allowances actually made in respect of that expenditure, less, if a balancing charge has previously been made in respect of that expenditure, the amount on which that charge was made.

Taxation of receipts from sale of patent rights.

524.—(1) Subject to subsection (2) below, where a person resident in the United Kingdom sells all or any part of any patent rights and the net proceeds of the sale consist wholly or partly of a capital sum, he shall, subject to the provisions of this Chapter, be charged to tax under Case VI of Schedule D, for the chargeable period in which the sum is received by him and successive chargeable periods, being charged in each period on the same fraction of the sum as the period is of six years (or such less fraction as has not already been charged).

(2) If the person by notice served on the inspector not later than two years after the end of the chargeable period in which the sum was received, elects that the whole of the sum shall be charged to tax for that chargeable period, it shall be charged to tax accordingly.

(3) Subject to subsection (4) below, where a person not resident in the United Kingdom sells all or any part of any patent rights and the net proceeds of the sale consist wholly or partly of a capital sum, and the patent is a United Kingdom patent, then, subject to the provisions of this Chapter—

(a) he shall be chargeable to tax in respect of that sum under Case VI of Schedule D; and

(b) section 349(1) shall apply to that sum as if it was an annual sum payable otherwise than out of profits or gains charged to income tax; and

(c) all other provisions of the Tax Acts shall, save as therein otherwise provided, have effect accordingly.

(4) If, not later than two years after the end of the year of assessment in which the sum is paid, the person to whom it is paid, by notice to the Board, elects that the sum shall be treated for the purpose of income tax for that year and each of the five succeeding years as if one-sixth thereof, and no more, were included in his income chargeable to tax for all those years respectively, it shall be so treated, and all such repayments and assessments of tax for each of those years shall be made as are necessary to give effect to the election, but—

(a) the election shall not affect the amount of tax which is to be deducted and assessed under section 349(1) and 350; and

(b) where any sum is deducted under section 349(1), any adjustments necessary to give effect to the election shall be made by way of repayment of tax; and

(c) those adjustments shall be made year by year and as if one-sixth of the sum deducted had been deducted in respect of tax for each year, and no repayment of, or of any part of, that portion of the tax deducted which is to be treated as deducted in respect of tax for any year shall be made unless and until it is ascertained that the tax ultimately falling to be paid for that year is less than the amount of tax paid for that year.

(5) In subsections (3) and (4) above, "tax" shall mean income tax or, in subsection (3) in a case where the seller of the patent rights, being a company, would be within the charge to corporation tax in respect of any proceeds of the sale not consisting of a capital sum, corporation tax.

(6) Where subsection (3) applies to charge a company to corporation tax in respect of a sum paid to it, subsection (4) shall not apply, but the company may, by notice given to the Board not later than two years after the end of the accounting period in which the sum is paid, elect that the sum shall be treated as arising rateably in the accounting periods ending not later than six years from the beginning of that in which the sum is paid (being accounting periods during which the company remains within the charge to corporation tax in respect of any proceeds of the sale not consisting of a capital sum), and there shall be made all such repayments of tax and assessments to tax as are necessary to give effect to any such election.

(7) Subject to subsections (8) and (9) below, where the person selling all or any part of any patent rights ("the seller") acquired the rights sold, or the rights out of which they were granted, by purchase and the price paid by him consisted wholly or partly of a capital sum, the preceding provisions of this section shall apply as if any capital sum received by him when he sells the rights were reduced by the amount of that sum.

(8) Where between the purchase and the sale the seller has sold part of the rights acquired by him and the net proceeds of that sale consist wholly or partly of a capital sum, the amount of the reduction falling to be made under subsection (7) above in respect of the subsequent sale shall be itself reduced by the amount of that sum.

(9) Nothing in subsections (7) and (8) above shall affect the amount of income tax which is to be deducted and assessed under section 349(1) and (3) by virtue of subsection (3) above, and, where any sum is deducted under section 349(1), any adjustment necessary to give effect to the provisions of this subsection shall be made by way of repayment of tax.

(10) A claim for relief under this section shall be made to the Board.

525.—(1) Where a person on whom, by reason of the receipt of a capital sum, a charge falls or would otherwise fall to be made under section 524 dies or, being a body corporate, commences to be wound up—

Capital sums: death, winding up or partnership change.

(a) no sums shall be charged under that section on that person for any chargeable period subsequent to that in which the death takes place or the winding up commences; and

(b) the amount falling to be charged for the chargeable period in which the death occurs or the winding up commences shall, subject to subsection (2) below, be increased by the total amounts which, but for the death or winding up, would have fallen to be charged for subsequent chargeable periods.

(2) In the case of a death the personal representatives may, by notice served on the inspector not later than 30 days after notice has been served on them of the charge falling to be made by virtue of subsection (1) above, require that the income tax payable out of the estate of the deceased by reason of the increase provided for by that subsection shall be reduced so as not to exceed the total amount of income tax which would have been payable by him or out of his estate by reason of the operation of section 524 in relation to that sum, if, instead of the amount falling to be charged for the year in which the death occurs being increased by the whole amount of the sums charged for subsequent years, the several amounts falling to be charged for the years beginning with that in which the capital sum was received and ending with that in which the death occurred had each been increased by that whole amount divided by the number of those years.

(3) Where, under section 79 of the 1968 Act (succession to trades) as applied by section 532, a charge under section 524 falls to be made on two or more persons jointly as being the persons for the time being carrying on a trade, and that trade is discontinued, subsection (1) above shall have effect in relation to the discontinuance as it has effect where a body corporate commences to be wound up.

(4) Where subsection (3) above applies—

(a) the additional sum which, under subsection (1) above, falls to be charged for the chargeable period in which the discontinuance occurs shall be apportioned among the members of the partnership immediately before the discontinuance, according to their respective interests in the partnership profits before the discontinuance, and each partner (or, if he is dead, his personal representatives) shall be charged separately for his proportion; and

(b) each partner (or, if he is dead, his personal representatives) shall have the same right to require a reduction of the total income tax payable by him or out of his estate by reason of the increase as would have been exercisable by the personal representatives under subsection (2) above in the case of a death, and that subsection shall have effect accordingly, but as if references to the amount of income tax which would have been payable by the deceased or out of his estate in the event therein mentioned were a reference to the amount of income tax which would in that event have fallen to be paid or borne by the partner in question or out of his estate.

(5) In this section any references to income tax paid or borne or payable or falling to be paid or borne by a person include, in cases where the income of a wife is deemed to be income of the husband, references to the income tax paid or borne, or payable or falling to be paid or borne, by his wife or her husband, as the case may be.

526.—(1) Where—

(a) a person, otherwise than for the purposes of a trade carried on by him, pays any fees or incurs any expenses in connection with the grant or maintenance of a patent, or the obtaining of an extension of a term of a patent, or a rejected or abandoned application for a patent, and

(b) those fees or expenses would, if they had been paid or incurred for the purposes of a trade, have been allowable as a deduction in estimating the profits or gains of that trade,

there shall be made to him, for the chargeable period in which those expenses were paid or incurred, an allowance equal to the amount thereof.

(2) Where a patent is granted in respect of any invention, an allowance equal to so much of the net amount of any expenses incurred by an individual who, whether alone or in conjunction with any other person, actually devised the invention as is properly ascribable to the devising thereof (not being expenses in respect of which, or of assets representing which, an allowance falls to be made under any other provision of the Income Tax Acts) shall be made to that individual for the year of assessment in which the expenses were incurred.

527.—(1) Where a royalty or other sum to which section 348 or 349(1) applies is paid in respect of the user of a patent, and that user extended over a period of six complete years or more, the person receiving the payment may on the making of a claim require that the income tax or corporation tax payable by him by reason of the receipt of that sum shall be reduced so as not to exceed the total amount of income tax or corporation tax which would have been payable by him if that royalty or sum had been paid in six equal instalments at yearly intervals, the last of which was paid on the date on which the payment was in fact made.

(2) Subsection (1) above shall apply in relation to a royalty or other sum where the period of the user is two complete years or more but less than six complete years as it applies to the royalties and sums mentioned in that subsection, but with the substitution for the reference to six equal instalments of a reference to so many equal instalments as there are complete years comprised in that period.

(3) In this section any reference to the income tax payable by a person includes, in cases where the income of a wife is deemed to be the income of the husband, references to the income tax payable by his wife or her husband, as the case may be.

(4) Nothing in this section shall apply to any sum to which section 349(1) applies by virtue of section 524(3)(b).

528.—(1) An allowance or charge under section 520, 522 or 523 shall be made to or on a person in taxing his trade if—

(a) he is carrying on a trade the profits or gains of which are, or, if there were any, would be, chargeable to tax under Case I of Schedule D for the chargeable period for which the allowance or charge is made, and

(b) at any time in that chargeable period or its basis period the patent rights in question, or other rights out of which they were granted, were or were to be used for the purposes of that trade.

PART XIII

(2) Where an allowance falls to be made to a person for any year of assessment under section 520, 522, 523 or 526 as those provisions apply for the purposes of income tax, and the allowance is not to be made in taxing a trade—

(a) the amount of the allowance shall be deducted from or set off against his income from patents for that year of assessment, and

(b) if the amount to be allowed is greater than the amount of his income from patents for that year of assessment, the balance shall be deducted from or set off against his income from patents for the next year of assessment, and so on for subsequent years of assessment, and tax shall be discharged or repaid accordingly.

Relief shall be given under this subsection on the making of a claim.

(3) Where an allowance falls to be made to a company for any accounting period under section 520, 522, 523 or 526 as those provisions apply for the purposes of corporation tax, and is not to be made in taxing a trade—

(a) the allowance shall, as far as may be, be given effect by deducting the amount of the allowance from the company's income from patents of the accounting period;

(b) where the allowance cannot be given full effect under paragraph (a) above in that period by reason of a want or deficiency of income from patents, then (so long as the company remains within the charge to corporation tax) the amount unallowed shall be carried forward to the succeeding accounting period, and shall be treated for the purposes of that paragraph, and of any further application of this paragraph, as the amount of a corresponding allowance for that period.

(4) Effect shall be given to any balancing charge under section 520 or 523 which is not to be made in taxing a trade—

(a) if a charge to income tax, by making the charge under Case VI of Schedule D;

(b) if a charge to corporation tax, by treating the amount on which the charge is to be made as income from patents.

Patent income to be earned income in certain cases.

529.—(1) Subject to subsection (2) below, any income from patent rights arising to an individual where the patent was granted for an invention actually devised by him, whether alone or jointly with any other person, shall be treated for all purposes as earned income.

(2) Where any part of the rights in question or of any rights out of which they were granted has at any time belonged to any other person, so much only of that income shall be treated as earned income as is not properly attributable to the rights which have belonged to that other person.

Disposal of know-how.

530.—(1) Subject to section 531, where after 31st March 1986 a person—

(a) acquires know-how for use in a trade carried on by him, or

(b) acquires know-how, and thereafter sets up and commences a trade in which it is used,

allowances and charges shall, in accordance with subsections (2) and (3) below, be made to and on him in respect of his expenditure on the acquisition, so far as not otherwise deducted for the purposes of corporation tax or income tax.

(2) For any chargeable period for which a person within subsection (1) above has qualifying expenditure which exceeds any disposal value to be brought into account by him in accordance with subsection (5) below, there shall be made to him—

(a) unless the period is the chargeable period related to the permanent discontinuance of the trade, a writing-down allowance of an amount equal to—

(i) 25 per cent. of the excess, or

(ii) a proportionately reduced percentage of the excess if the period is part only of a year, or if the period is a year of assessment but the trade had been carried on for part only of the year; and

(b) if the period is the chargeable period related to the permanent discontinuance of the trade, a balancing allowance equal to the whole of the excess.

(3) For any chargeable period for which a person's qualifying expenditure is less than the disposal value which he is to bring into account, there shall be made on him a balancing charge and the amount on which the charge is made shall be an amount equal to the difference.

(4) For the purposes of subsections (2) and (3) above a person's qualifying expenditure for a chargeable period is the aggregate of the following amounts—

(a) any capital expenditure incurred by him on the acquisition of know-how, being expenditure incurred during the chargeable period or its basis period or at any previous time, other than expenditure which, or any part of which, has formed part of his qualifying expenditure for any previous chargeable period; and

(b) if, for the chargeable period immediately preceding the chargeable period in question, there was an excess of qualifying expenditure over disposal value, the balance of that excess after deducting any writing-down allowance under subsection (2)(a) above made by reference to that excess.

(5) If, in any chargeable period or its basis period, a person sells any know-how on the acquisition of which for use in a trade carried on by him he has incurred expenditure falling within subsection (1) above, then, for the purposes of subsections (2) to (4) above, he is required to bring into account for that chargeable period disposal value equal to the net proceeds to him of that sale.

(6) Subject to section 531, where after 19th March 1968 and before 1st April 1986 a person—

(a) acquired know-how for use in a trade carried on by him, or

(b) acquired know-how, and thereafter sets up and commences a trade in which it is used,

writing-down allowances in respect of his expenditure on the acquisition, so far as not otherwise deducted for the purposes of corporation tax or income tax, shall be made in taxing the trade during a writing-down period of six years beginning with the chargeable period related to the expenditure; and if during that period he ceases to carry on the trade, an allowance equal to the amount of that expenditure then unallowed shall be made in taxing the trade for the chargeable period related to the discontinuance.

(7) For the purposes of subsections (1) and (6) above, a person incurring expenditure on know-how before the setting up and commencement of the trade in which it is used shall be treated as incurring it on that setting up and commencement.

(8) Subsection (2) of section 75 of the 1968 Act (effect of providing writing-down allowances during writing-down period of a specified length) shall apply to subsection (6) above as it applies to the provisions specified in subsection (1) of that section.

Provisions supplementary to section 530.

531.—(1) Subject to subsection (7) below, where, after 19th March 1968, a person disposes of know-how which has been used in a trade carried on by him, and continues to carry on the trade after the disposal, the amount or value of any consideration received by him for the disposal shall—

(a) if it is received in respect of the disposal of know-how after 31st March 1986, so far as it is not brought into account as disposal value under section 530(5), nor is chargeable to tax as a revenue or income receipt;

(b) in any other case, so far as it is not chargeable to tax as a revenue or income receipt,

be treated for all purposes as a trading receipt.

(2) Subject to subsection (3) below, where, after 19th March 1968, a person disposes of a trade or part of a trade and, together with that trade or part, of know-how used in it, any consideration received by him for the know-how shall be dealt with in relation both to him and to the person acquiring the know-how, if that person provided the consideration, and for the purposes of corporation tax, income tax and capital gains tax, as a payment for goodwill.

(3) Subsection (2) above shall not apply—

(a) to either of the persons concerned if they so elect by notice given jointly to the inspector within two years of the disposal, or

(b) to the person acquiring the know-how if the trade in question was, before the acquisition, carried on wholly outside the United Kingdom;

and where know-how is disposed of with a trade or part of a trade, but that subsection is excluded in relation to the person acquiring it, section 530(1) and (6) shall apply as if that person had acquired it for use in a trade previously carried on by him.

(4) Subject to subsections (5) and (7) below, any consideration received by a person for the disposal of know-how shall—

(a) if it is received in respect of the disposal of know-how after 31st March 1986 and is not brought into account as disposal value under section 530(5), or

(b) if it is neither chargeable to tax under subsection (1) above or otherwise as a revenue or income receipt, nor dealt with in relation to him as a payment for goodwill as mentioned in subsection (2) above, (whether the disposal took place before or after 31st March 1986),

be treated as a profit or gain chargeable to tax under Case VI of Schedule D.

(5) Where the person concerned has incurred expenditure wholly and exclusively in the acquisition or disposal of the know-how, the amount which would apart from this subsection be treated as a profit or gain chargeable to tax under Case VI of Schedule D shall be reduced by the amount of that expenditure; but a deduction shall not be twice made in respect of the same expenditure, whether under this subsection or otherwise.

(6) Where subsection (4) above has effect in the case of an individual who devised the know-how in question, whether alone or jointly with any other person, the amount in respect of which he is chargeable to tax by virtue of that subsection shall be treated for all purposes as earned income.

(7) Subsections (1) and (3) to (6) above and section 530(1) and (6) shall not apply on any sale of know-how where the buyer is a body of persons over whom the seller has control, or the seller is a body of persons over whom the buyer has control, or both the seller and the buyer are bodies of persons and some other person has control over both of them; and subsection (2) above shall apply in any such case with the omission of the words "Subject to subsection (3) below".

In this subsection references to a body of persons include references to a partnership.

(8) Where in connection with any disposal of know-how a person gives an undertaking (whether absolute or qualified, and whether legally valid or not) the tenor or effect of which is to restrict his or another's activities in any way, any consideration received in respect of the giving of the undertaking or its total or partial fulfilment shall be treated for the purposes of this section as consideration received for the disposal of the know-how.

532.—(1) Subject to subsection (2) below, the Tax Acts shall have effect as if sections 520 to 531, this section and section 533 were contained in Part I of the 1968 Act, and any reference in the Tax Acts to any capital allowance to be given "by way of discharge or repayment of tax and to be available or available primarily against a specified class of income" shall include a reference to any capital allowance given in accordance with subsection (2) or (3) of section 528.

Application of the 1968 Act.

(2) Schedule 7 to the 1968 Act (special provisions as to controlled sales) shall not (by virtue of subsection (1) above) apply with respect to expenditure incurred after 31st March 1986 on the purchase of patent rights.

(3) Subject to subsection (2) above, in Part I of the 1968 Act, as applied by virtue of subsection (1) above to patent rights, the sum referred to in paragraph 4(1)(a) of Schedule 7 to that Act (special provisions as to controlled sales) is the amount of any capital expenditure on the acquisition of the patent rights remaining unallowed, computed in accordance with the provisions of section 523.

(4) The reference in section 82(1) of the 1968 Act (certain payments not to be treated as capital expenditure) to any expenditure or sum in the case of which a deduction of income tax falls or may fall to be made under sections 348 to 350 does not include a sum in the case of which such a deduction falls or may fall to be so made by virtue of section 524(3)(b).

(5) In Part I of the 1968 Act as so applied to know-how—

(a) references in that Part to property and its purchase or sale include references to know-how and its acquisition or disposal;

(b) section 78, together with Schedule 7 to that Act (special provisions as to controlled sales), shall be omitted.

Interpretation of sections 520 to 532.

533.—(1) In sections 520 to 532—

"income from patents" means—

(a) any royalty or other sum paid in respect of the user of a patent; and

(b) any amount on which tax is payable for any chargeable period by virtue of section 520(6), 523(3), 524 or 525;

"the commencement of the patent" means, in relation to a patent, the date as from which the patent rights become effective;

"patent rights" means the right to do or authorise the doing of anything which would, but for that right, be an infringement of a patent;

"United Kingdom patent" means a patent granted under the laws of the United Kingdom.

(2) Subject to subsection (3) below, in sections 520 to 532 any reference to the sale of part of patent rights includes a reference to the grant of a licence in respect of the patent in question, and any reference to the purchase of patent rights includes a reference to the acquisition of a licence in respect of a patent.

(3) If a licence granted by a person entitled to any patent rights is a licence to exercise those rights to the exclusion of the grantor and all other persons for the whole of the remainder of the term for which the right subsists, the grantor shall be treated for the purposes of sections 520 to 532 as thereby selling the whole of the rights.

(4) Where, under sections 46 to 49 of the Patents Act 1949 or any corresponding provisions of the law of any country outside the United Kingdom, an invention which is the subject of a patent is made, used, or

exercised or vended by or for the service of the Crown or the government of the country concerned, sections 520 to 532 shall have effect as if the making, user, exercise or vending of the invention had taken place in pursuance of a licence, and any sums paid in respect thereof shall be treated accordingly.

(5) Expenditure incurred in obtaining a right to acquire in the future patent rights as respects any invention in respect of which the patent has not yet been granted shall be deemed for all the purposes of sections 520 to 532 to be expenditure on the purchase of patent rights, and if the patent rights are subsequently acquired the expenditure shall be deemed for those purposes to have been expenditure on the purchase of those rights.

(6) Any sum received from a person which by virtue of subsection (5) above is deemed to be expenditure incurred by him on the purchase of patent rights shall be deemed to be proceeds of a sale of patent rights.

(7) In sections 530 and 531 "know-how" means any industrial information and techniques likely to assist in the manufacture or processing of goods or materials, or in the working of a mine, oil-well or other source of mineral deposits (including the searching for, discovery or testing of deposits or the winning of access thereto), or in the carrying out of any agricultural, forestry or fishing operations.

Copyright and public lending right

534.—(1) Where—

(a) an author of a literary, dramatic, musical or artistic work assigns the copyright in the work wholly or partially, or grants any interest in the copyright by licence; and

(b) the consideration for the assignment or grant consists wholly or partially of a payment to which this section applies, being a payment the whole amount of which would, but for this section, be included in computing the amount of his profits or gains for a single year of assessment; and

(c) the author was engaged on the making of the work for a period of more than 12 months;

he may, on making a claim, require that effect shall be given to the following provisions of this section in connection with that payment.

(2) If the period for which he was engaged on the making of the work does not exceed 24 months, then, for all income tax purposes, one-half only of the amount of the payment shall be treated as having become receivable on the date on which it actually became receivable, and the remaining half shall be treated as having become receivable 12 months before that date.

(3) If the period for which he was engaged on the making of the work exceeds 24 months, then, for all income tax purposes, one-third only of the amount of the payment shall be treated as having become receivable on the date on which it actually became receivable, and one-third shall be treated as having become receivable 12 months, and one-third 24 months, before that date.

PART XIII

(4) This section applies to—

    (a) a lump sum payment, including an advance on account of royalties which is not returnable, and

    (b) any payment of or on account of royalties or sums payable periodically,

except that it shall not by virtue of paragraph (b) above apply to payments in respect of the copyright in any work which only become receivable more than two years after its first publication.

(5) A claim under this section with respect to any payment to which it applies by virtue only of subsection (4)(b) above shall have effect as a claim with respect to all such payments in respect of the copyright in the same work which are receivable by the claimant, whether before or after the claim; and such a claim may be made at any time not later than 5th April next following the expiration of eight years after the work's first publication.

(6) A claim cannot be made under this section in respect of a payment if a prior claim has been made under section 535 as respects that payment.

(7) In this section—

    (a) "author" includes a joint author; and

    (b) any reference to the first publication of a work is a reference to the first occasion on which the work or a reproduction of it is published, performed or exhibited.

Relief where copyright sold after ten years or more.

535.—(1) Where not less than ten years after the first publication of the work the author of a literary, dramatic, musical or artistic work assigns the copyright in the work wholly or partially, or grants any interest in the copyright by licence, and—

    (a) the consideration for the assignment or grant consists wholly or partially of a lump sum payment the whole amount of which would, but for this section, be included in computing the amount of his profits or gains for a single year of assessment, and

    (b) the copyright or interest is not assigned or granted for a period of less than two years,

he may by making a claim require that effect shall be given to the following provisions of this section in connection with that payment.

(2) Except where the copyright or interest is assigned or granted for a period of less than six years, the amount of the payment shall for income tax purposes be treated as becoming receivable in six equal instalments at yearly intervals the first of which becomes receivable on the date when the payment actually became receivable.

(3) Where the copyright or interest is assigned or granted for a period of less than six years, the amount of the payment shall for income tax purposes be treated as becoming receivable in a number of equal instalments at yearly intervals the first of which becomes receivable on the date when the payment actually became receivable, the number being the number of whole years in that period.

(4) Subject to subsection (5) below, if the author dies, any instalment which under this section would, but for the death, be treated as becoming receivable after the death shall for income tax purposes be treated as becoming receivable on the date when the last instalment before the death is to be treated as becoming receivable.

(5) If the personal representatives so elect—

(a) the total amount of income tax which would have been payable by the deceased or out of his estate in respect of the payment if the copyright or interest had been assigned or granted for a period beginning with the date when the first instalment is treated as becoming receivable and ending with the day before the death shall be computed, and

(b) the income tax payable out of the estate by reason of the provisions of subsection (4) above shall be reduced so as not to exceed the amount at (a) above.

The references in this subsection to the income tax payable by a person include, in cases where the income of a wife is deemed to be the income of the husband, references to the income tax payable by his wife or her husband, as the case may be.

(6) If—

(a) the payment would, apart from this section, have been taken into account in assessing the profits or gains of a profession or vocation, and

(b) the profession or vocation is permanently discontinued (otherwise than on death) after the date on which the payment actually became receivable,

any instalment which under this section would, but for the discontinuance, be treated as receivable on a date after the discontinuance shall for income tax purposes be treated as becoming receivable when the last instalment before the discontinuance is to be treated as becoming receivable, unless the author elects to be treated (for all purposes) as if the copyright or interest had been assigned or granted for a period beginning with the date when the first instalment is treated as becoming receivable and ending with the day before the discontinuance.

(7) Notice of any election under subsection (5) or (6) above shall be served on the inspector within two years of the death, or as the case may be of the discontinuance.

(8) In any case where—

(a) but for this section, the payment would be included in computing any profits or gains chargeable to tax under Case VI of Schedule D, and

(b) any amount would be deductible from that payment in computing those profits or gains (whether under the general provisions relating to Case VI or under section 105(1)),

the amount which, under this section, is to be treated as receivable in instalments shall be the amount of the payment after that deduction, and effect shall not be given to that deduction in any other way.

R

(9) A claim cannot be made under this section in respect of a payment if a prior claim has been made under section 534 as respects that payment.

(10) Where it is necessary, in order to give effect to a claim or election under this section, or as a result of the claim or election, to make any adjustment by way of an assessment on any person, the assessment shall not be out of time if it is made within one year of the final determination of the claim or, as the case may be, within one year from the giving of notice of the election.

(11) In this section—

"author" includes a joint author;

"lump sum payment" includes an advance on account of royalties which is not returnable;

and any reference to the first publication of a work is a reference to the first occasion on which the work or a reproduction of it is published, performed or exhibited.

Taxation of royalties where owner abroad.

536.—(1) Subject to the provisions of this section, where the usual place of abode of the owner of a copyright is not within the United Kingdom, section 349(1) shall apply to any payment of or on account of any royalties or sums paid periodically for or in respect of that copyright as it applies to annual payments not payable out of profits or gains brought into charge to income tax.

(2) In subsection (1) above—

"copyright" does not include a copyright in any dramatic work being a cinematograph production, or in any artistic work being a photograph intended to be used for the purposes of the exhibition of pictures or other optical effects by means of a cinematograph or other similar apparatus; and

"owner of a copyright" includes a person who, notwithstanding that he has assigned a copyright to some other person, is entitled to receive periodical payments in respect of that copyright;

and the reference to royalties or sums paid periodically for or in respect of a copyright does not include royalties or sums paid in respect of copies of works which are shown on a claim to have been exported from the United Kingdom for distribution outside the United Kingdom.

(3) Subject to subsection (4) below, where any payment to which subsection (1) above applies is made through an agent resident in the United Kingdom and that agent is entitled as against the owner of the copyright to deduct any sum by way of commission in respect of services rendered, the amount of the payment shall for the purposes of section 349(1) be taken to be diminished by the sum which the agent is so entitled to deduct.

(4) Where the person by or through whom the payment is made does not know that any such commission is payable or does not know the amount of any such commission, any income tax deducted by or assessed and charged on him shall be computed in the first instance on, and the account to be delivered of the payment shall be an account of, the total amount of the payment without regard being had to any diminution thereof, and in that case, on proof of the facts on a claim, there shall be

made to the agent on behalf of the owner of the copyright such repayment of income tax as is proper in respect of the sum deducted by way of commission.

(5) The time of the making of a payment to which subsection (1) above applies shall, for all tax purposes, be taken to be the time when it is made by the person by whom it is first made and not the time when it is made by or through any other person.

(6) Any agreement for the making of any payment to which subsection (1) above applies in full and without deduction of income tax shall be void.

537. Sections 534, 535 and 536 shall have effect in relation to public lending right as they have effect in relation to copyright.

Public lending right.

Artists' receipts

538.—(1) Where the artist obtains any sum for the sale of a painting, sculpture or other work of art, or by way of commission or fee for the creation of the work of art, and—

Relief for painters, sculptors and other artists.

    (a) he was engaged on the making of the work of art for a period of more than 12 months, or

    (b) he was engaged for a period of more than 12 months in making a number of works of art for an exhibition, and the work is one of them,

he may, by making a claim, require that effect shall be given to the following provisions of this section as respects that sum.

(2) If the period for which he was engaged on the making of the work does not exceed 24 months, then, for all income tax purposes, one-half only of the amount of the payment shall be treated as having become receivable on the date on which it actually became receivable, and the remaining half shall be treated as having become receivable 12 months before that date.

(3) If the period for which he was engaged on the making of the work exceeds 24 months, then, for all income tax purposes, one-third only of the amount of the payment shall be treated as having become receivable on the date on which it actually became receivable, and one-third shall be treated as having become receivable 12 months, and one-third 24 months, before that date.

CHAPTER II

LIFE POLICIES, LIFE ANNUITIES AND CAPITAL REDEMPTION POLICIES

539.—(1) This Chapter shall have effect for the purposes of imposing, in the manner and to the extent therein provided, charges to tax, including tax under section 426, in respect of gains to be treated in accordance with this Chapter as arising in connection with policies of life insurance, contracts for life annuities and capital redemption policies.

Introductory.

(2) Nothing in this Chapter shall apply—

(a) to any policy of life insurance having as its sole object the provision on an individual's death or disability of a sum substantially the same as any amount then outstanding under a mortgage of his residence, or of any premises occupied by him for the purposes of a business, being a mortgage the principal amount secured by which is repayable by instalments payable annually or at shorter regular intervals; or

(b) to any policy of life insurance issued in connection with an approved scheme, as defined in Chapter I of Part XIV; or

(c) to a policy of insurance which constitutes, or is evidence of, a contract for the time being approved under section 621.

1924 c. 27.

In the application of this subsection to Scotland, for the reference to a mortgage there shall be substituted a reference to a heritable security within the meaning of the Conveyancing (Scotland) Act 1924 (but including a security constituted by ex facie absolute disposition or assignation).

(3) In this Chapter—

"assignment", in relation to Scotland, means an assignation;

"capital redemption policy" means any insurance effected in the course of a capital redemption business as defined in section 458(3); and

"life annuity" means any annuity to which sections 656 and 657 apply and any annuity the contract for which is made on or after 1st June 1984 by a friendly society or branch thereof in the course of life or endowment business as defined in section 466.

(4) For the purposes of this Chapter the falling due of a sum payable in pursuance of a right conferred by a policy or contract to participate in profits shall be treated as the surrender of rights conferred by the policy or contract.

(5) This Chapter shall have effect only as respects policies of life insurance issued in respect of insurances made after 19th March 1968, contracts for life annuities entered into after that date, and capital redemption policies effected after that date.

(6) A policy of life insurance issued in respect of an insurance made on or before 19th March 1968 shall be treated for the purposes of subsection (5) above and the following provisions of this Chapter as issued in respect of one made after that date if it is varied after that date so as to increase the benefits secured or to extend the term of the insurance.

1968 c. 44.

(7) A variation effected before the end of the year 1968 shall be disregarded for the purposes of subsection (6) above if its only effect was to bring into conformity with paragraph 2 of Schedule 9 to the Finance Act 1968 (which is re-enacted, as amended, by paragraph 2 of Schedule 15 to this Act) a policy previously conforming therewith except as respects the amount guaranteed on death, and no increase was made in the premiums payable under the policy.

(8) Subsections (1) to (7) above do not apply in relation to section 554.

Life policies: chargeable events.

540.—(1) Subject to the provisions of this section, in this Chapter "chargeable event" means, in relation to a policy of life insurance—

(a) if it is not a qualifying policy, any of the following—

> (i) any death giving rise to benefits under the policy;

> (ii) the maturity of the policy;

> (iii) the surrender in whole of the rights conferred by the policy;

> (iv) the assignment for money or money's worth of those rights; and

> (v) an excess of the reckonable aggregate value mentioned in subsection (2) of section 546 over the allowable aggregate amount mentioned in subsection (3) of that section, being an excess occurring at the end of any year (as defined in subsection (4) of that section) except, if it ends with another chargeable event, the final year; and

(b) if it is a qualifying policy (whether or not the premiums thereunder are eligible for relief under section 266), any of the above events, but—

> (i) in the case of death or maturity, only if the policy is converted into a paid-up policy before the expiry of ten years from the making of the insurance, or, if sooner, of three-quarters of the term for which the policy is to run if not ended by death or disability;

> (ii) in the case of a surrender or assignment or such an excess as is mentioned in paragraph (a)(v) above, only if it is effected or occurs within that time, or the policy has been converted into a paid-up policy within that time.

(2) The maturity of a policy is not a chargeable event in relation thereto if—

(a) a new policy is issued in consequence of the exercise of an option conferred by the maturing policy, and

(b) the whole of the sums becoming payable under the maturing policy are retained by the company with whom the insurance was made and applied in the payment of one or more premiums under the new policy,

unless the circumstances are such that the person making the insurance in respect of which the new policy is issued was an infant when the former policy was issued, and the former policy was one securing a capital sum payable either on a specified date falling not later than one month after his attaining 25 or on the anniversary of the policy immediately following his attainment of that age.

(3) Except as provided by section 544, no event is a chargeable event in relation to a policy issued in respect of an insurance made before 26th June 1982 if the rights conferred by the policy have at any time before that date and before the event been assigned for money or money's worth and are not at the time of the event held by the original beneficial owner.

(4) No account shall be taken for the purposes of this section of any assignment effected by way of security for a debt, or on the discharge of a debt secured by the rights or share concerned, or of any assignment between spouses living together.

(5) Where subsection (1)(b) applies to a policy which has been varied so as to increase the premiums payable thereunder, it shall so apply as if the references in subsection (1)(b)(i) to the making of the insurance and the term of the policy were references respectively to the taking effect of the variation and the term of the policy as from the variation.

(6) This section has effect subject to paragraph 20 of Schedule 15.

Life policies: computation of gain.

541.—(1) On the happening of a chargeable event in relation to any policy of life insurance, there shall be treated as a gain arising in connection with the policy—

(a) if the event is a death, the excess (if any) of the surrender value of the policy immediately before the death, plus the amount or value of any relevant capital payments, over the sum of the following—

(i) the total amount previously paid under the policy by way of premiums; and

(ii) the total amount treated as a gain by virtue of paragraph (d) below on the previous happening of chargeable events;

(b) if the event is the maturity of the policy, or the surrender in whole of the rights thereby conferred, the excess (if any) of the amount or value of the sum payable or other benefits arising by reason of the event, plus the amount or value of any relevant capital payments, over the sum of the following—

(i) the total amount previously paid under the policy by way of premiums; and

(ii) the total amount treated as a gain by virtue of paragraph (d) below on the previous happening of chargeable events;

(c) if the event is an assignment, the excess (if any) of the amount or value of the consideration, plus the amount or value of any relevant capital payments or of any previously assigned share in the rights conferred by the policy, over the sum of the following—

(i) the total amount previously paid under the policy by way of premiums; and

(ii) the total amount treated as a gain by virtue of paragraph (d) below on the previous happening of chargeable events;

(d) if the event is the occurrence of such an excess as is mentioned in section 540(1)(a)(v), the amount of the excess.

(2) Where, in a case falling within subsection (1)(b) above, a right to periodical payments arises by reason of the event, there shall be treated as payable by reason thereof an amount equal to the capital value of those payments at the time the right arises.

(3) Where, in a case falling within subsection (1)(c) above, the assignment is between persons who are connected with each other within the meaning of section 839, the assignment shall be deemed to have been made for a consideration equal to the market value of the rights or share assigned.

(4) Where there is an assignment, otherwise than for money or money's worth, of all the rights conferred by the policy, the calculations required to be made by section 546 shall be made, in the first instance, without regard to any surrender or assignment of part of or a share in those rights which takes place after the assignment, and any gain treated as arising under subsection (1)(d) above on the calculation so made shall be treated as arising to the assignor.

(5) In this section—

(a) "relevant capital payments" means, in relation to any policy, any sum or other benefit of a capital nature, other than one attributable to a person's disability, paid or conferred under the policy before the happening of the chargeable event; and

(b) references in this subsection and (in relation to premiums) in subsection (1) above to "the policy" include references to any related policy, that is to say, to any policy in relation to which the policy is a new policy within the meaning of paragraph 17 of Schedule 15, and any policy in relation to which that policy is such a policy, and so on;

and the provisions of this section are subject to paragraph 20 of Schedule 15.

(6) There shall be disregarded for the purposes of this section any amount which was treated under section 72(9) of the Finance Act 1984 as an additional premium.

542.—(1) Subject to subsections (2) and (3) below, in this Chapter "chargeable event" means, in relation to any contract for a life annuity— Life annuity contracts: chargeable events.

(a) the surrender in whole of the rights conferred by the contract, or

(b) the assignment for money or money's worth of those rights, or

(c) an excess of the reckonable aggregate value mentioned in subsection (2) of section 546 over the allowable aggregate amount mentioned in subsection (3) of that section, being an excess occurring at the end of any year (as defined in subsection (4) of that section) except, if it ends with another chargeable event, the final year.

(2) Where the terms of a contract provide for the payment of a capital sum as an alternative, in whole or in part, to payments by way of annuity, the taking of the capital sum shall be treated for the purposes of this section and section 543 as a surrender in whole or in part of the rights conferred by the contract, and where the terms of the contract provide for

the payment of a capital sum on death and the contract was made on or after 10th December 1974, the death shall be treated for those purposes as a surrender in whole of the rights conferred by the contract.

(3) Except as provided by section 544, an event referred to in subsection (1) above is not a chargeable event in relation to any contract made before 26th June 1982 if the rights conferred by the contract have at any time before that date and before the event been assigned for money or money's worth and are not at the time of the event held by the original beneficial owner.

(4) Subsection (4) of section 540 shall, with any necessary modifications, apply for the purposes of this section as it applies for the purposes of that section.

Life annuity contracts: computation of gain.

543.—(1) On the happening of a chargeable event in relation to any contract for a life annuity, there shall be treated as a gain arising in connection with the contract—

(a) if the event is the surrender in whole of the rights conferred by the contract, the excess (if any) of the amount payable by reason of the event plus the amount or value of any relevant capital payments over the sum of the following—

(i) the total amount previously paid under the contract, whether by way of premiums or as lump sum consideration, reduced, if before the happening of the event one or more payments have been made on account of the annuity, by the capital element in that payment or payments, as determined in accordance with section 656; and

(ii) the total amount treated as a gain by virtue of paragraph (c) below on the previous happening of chargeable events;

(b) if the event is an assignment, the excess (if any) of the amount or value of the consideration, plus the amount or value of any relevant capital payments or of any previously assigned share in the rights conferred by the contract, over the sum of the following—

(i) the amount specified in paragraph (a)(i) above; and

(ii) any amount treated as a gain by virtue of paragraph (c) below on the previous happenings of chargeable events;

(c) if the event is the occurrence of such an excess as is mentioned in section 542(1), the amount of the excess.

(2) Subsection (3) of section 541 shall apply for the purposes of subsection (1) above as it applies for the purposes of subsection (1)(c) of that section, and subsection (4) of that section shall apply for the purposes of this section with the substitution of references to the contract for references to the policy.

(3) In this section "relevant capital payments" means, in relation to any contract, any sum or other benefit of a capital nature paid or conferred under the contract before the happening of the chargeable event.

544.—(1) In this section "assigned policy" means a policy of life assurance—

(a) which was issued in respect of an insurance made before 26th June 1982; and

(b) the rights conferred by which have been assigned for money or money's worth before that date; and

(c) in relation to which an event occurring on or after that date would not, apart from this section, be a chargeable event.

(2) In this section "assigned contract" means a contract for a life annuity—

(a) which was made before 26th June 1982; and

(b) the rights conferred by which have been assigned for money or money's worth before that date; and

(c) in relation to which an event occurring on or after that date would not, apart from this section, be a chargeable event.

(3) In any case where after 23rd August 1982—

(a) the rights conferred by an assigned policy or, as the case may be, an assigned contract are again assigned for money or money's worth; or

(b) a payment is made by way of premium or as lump sum consideration under the policy or contract; or

(c) subject to subsections (5) and (7) below, a sum is lent by or by arrangement with the body issuing the policy or, as the case may be, the body with which the contract was made;

section 540(3) shall cease to apply to the policy or section 542(3) shall cease to apply to the contract, as the case may be.

(4) No account shall be taken for the purposes of subsection (3)(a) above of any assignment effected by way of security for a debt, or on the discharge of a debt secured by the rights concerned, or of an assignment between spouses living together.

(5) Subsection (3)(c) above does not apply unless—

(a) the policy was issued in respect of an insurance made after 26th March 1974 or, as the case may be, the contract was entered into after that date; and

(b) the sum concerned is lent to or at the direction of the individual who, in accordance with subsection (6) below, is at the time of the loan the chargeable individual.

(6) The individual who is at any time the chargeable individual for the purposes of subsection (5)(b) above shall be determined as follows—

(a) if at the time the rights conferred by the policy or contract are vested in an individual as beneficial owner or are held on trusts created by an individual (including such trusts as are referred to in section 547(1)(a)), that individual is the chargeable individual; and

(b) if at that time those rights are held as security for a debt owed by an individual, that individual is the chargeable individual.

(7) Subsection (3)(c) above does not apply in relation to a policy if—

(a) it is a qualifying policy; and

(b) either interest at a commercial rate is payable on the sum lent or the sum is lent to a full-time employee of the body issuing the policy for the purpose of assisting him in the purchase or improvement of a dwelling-house to be used as his only or main residence.

(8) Where section 540(3) or 542(3) ceases to apply to an assigned policy or assigned contract by virtue of paragraph (c) of subsection (3) above, the lending of the sum concerned shall be regarded for the purposes of the Income Tax Acts (other than that paragraph) as taking place immediately after the time at which section 540(3) or, as the case may be, 542(3) ceases so to apply.

Capital redemption policies.

545.—(1) Subject to subsection (2) below, in this Chapter "chargeable event" means, in relation to a capital redemption policy, any of the following—

(a) the maturity of the policy, except where the sums payable on maturity are annual payments chargeable to tax under Schedule D;

(b) the surrender in whole of the rights conferred by the policy;

(c) the assignment for money or money's worth of those rights; and

(d) an excess of the reckonable aggregate value mentioned in subsection (2) of section 546 over the allowable aggregate amount mentioned in subsection (3) of that section, being an excess occurring at the end of any year (as defined in subsection (4) of that section), except, if it ends with another chargeable event, the final year.

(2) Subsection (4) of section 540 shall apply for the purposes of this section as it applies for purposes of that section.

(3) The provisions of section 541, except subsection (3), shall, so far as appropriate and subject to subsection (4) below, apply to capital redemption policies as they apply to policies of life assurance.

(4) Where a chargeable event happens in relation to a capital redemption policy which has previously been assigned for money or money's worth, section 541 shall have effect in relation thereto as if, for the references to the total amount previously paid under the policy by way of premiums, there were substituted references to the amount or value of the consideration given for the last such assignment, plus the total amount of the premiums paid under the policy since that assignment.

Calculation of certain amounts for purposes of sections 540, 542 and 545.

546.—(1) For the purposes of sections 540, 542 and 545, there shall be calculated as at the end of each year—

(a) the value, as at the time of surrender or assignment, of any part of or share in the rights conferred by the policy or contract which has been assigned or surrendered during the period ending with the end of that year and beginning with the commencement of the first year which falls wholly after 13th March 1975; and

(b) the appropriate portion of any payment made up to the end of that period by way of premium or as a lump sum consideration;

and the appropriate portion of any payment shall be one-twentieth for the year in which it is made, increased by a further one-twentieth for each of the subsequent years, up to a maximum of nineteen, but excluding therefrom any such one-twentieth for any year before that first year.

(2) The reckonable aggregate value referred to in those sections shall be—

(a) the sum of the values calculated under subsection (1) above; less

(b) the sum of the values so calculated for a previous year and brought into account on the previous happening of a chargeable event.

(3) The allowable aggregate amount referred to in those sections shall be—

(a) the aggregate of the appropriate portions calculated under subsection (1) above;

less

(b) the aggregate of the appropriate portions so calculated for a previous year and brought into account on the previous happening of a chargeable event.

(4) In this section "year" means the 12 months beginning with the making of the insurance or contract and any subsequent period of 12 months; except that—

(a) death, the maturity of the policy or the surrender of the rights conferred by the policy or contract shall be treated as ending the final year; and

(b) if the final year would by virtue of paragraph (a) above begin and end in the same year of assessment, the final year and the year preceding it shall together be one year.

(5) There shall be disregarded for the purposes of this section any amount which was treated under section 72(9) of the Finance Act 1984 as an additional premium.

1984 c. 43.

547.—(1) Where under section 541, 543 or 545 a gain is to be treated as arising in connection with any policy or contract—

Method of charging gain to tax.

(a) if, immediately before the happening of the chargeable event in question, the rights conferred by the policy or contract were vested in an individual as beneficial owner, or were held on trusts created by an individual (including trusts arising under section 11 of the Married Women's Property Act 1882, section 2 of the Married Women's Policies of Assurance (Scotland) Act 1880 or section 4 of the Law Reform (Husband and Wife) Act (Northern Ireland) 1964 or as security for a debt owed by an

1882 c. 75.
1880 c. 56.
1964 c. 23 (N.I.).

individual, the amount of the gain shall be deemed to form part of that individual's total income for the year in which the event happened;

(b) if, immediately before the happening of that event, those rights were in the beneficial ownership of a close company, or were held on trusts created, or as security for a debt owed, by a close company, then, for the purposes of Chapter III of Part XI—

(i) the amount of the gain shall be deemed to form part of the company's income for the accounting period in which the event happened, and

(ii) the company's distributable income (but not its estate or trading income) for that period shall be treated as increased by the amount of the gain;

(c) if, immediately before the happening of that event, those rights were vested in personal representatives, within the meaning of Part XVI, the amount of the gain shall be deemed for the purposes of that Part to be part of the aggregate income of the estate of the deceased.

(2) Nothing in subsection (1) above shall apply to any amount which is chargeable to tax apart from that subsection.

(3) Where, immediately before the happening of a chargeable event, the rights conferred by any policy or contract were vested beneficially in two or more persons, or were held on trusts created, or as security for a debt owed, by two or more persons, subsection (1)(a) and (b) above shall have effect in relation to each of those persons as if he had been the sole owner, settlor or debtor, but with references to the amount of the gain construed as references to the part of it proportionate to his share in the rights at the time of the event or, as the case may require, when the trusts were created.

(4) References in subsections (1) and (3) above to the rights conferred by a policy or contract are, in the case of an assignment of a share only in any rights, references to that share.

(5) Subject to subsections (6) and (7) below and section 550, where by virtue of subsection (1) above, a sum is included in an individual's total income—

(a) no assessment shall be made on him in respect of income tax at the basic rate on that sum but he shall be treated as having paid income tax at the basic rate on that sum or, if his total income is reduced by any deductions, on so much of that sum as is part of his total income as so reduced;

(b) no repayment shall be made of the income tax treated by virtue of paragraph (a) above as having been paid; and

(c) the sum so included shall be treated for the purposes of sections 348 and 349(1) as not brought into charge to income tax.

(6) Where under section 543 a gain is to be treated as arising in connection with a contract for a life annuity made after 26th March 1974—

(a) this section shall have effect, in relation to the gain, as if subsection (5) were omitted; and

(b) the gain shall be chargeable to tax under Case VI of Schedule D; but

(c) any relief under section 550 shall be computed as if this subsection had not been enacted.

(7) Where under section 541 or 543 a gain is to be treated as arising in connection with a policy issued by a friendly society in the course of tax exempt life or endowment business, this section shall have effect in relation to the gain as if subsection (5) were omitted, but any relief under section 550 shall be computed as if this subsection had not been enacted.

548.—(1) Where—

(a) under section 547 a gain arising in connection with a policy or contract would be treated as forming part of an individual's total income; and

(b) the policy was issued in respect of an insurance made after 26th March 1974 or the contract was made after that date; and

(c) any sum is at any time after the making of the insurance or contract lent to or at the direction of that individual by or by arrangement with the body issuing the policy or, as the case may be, the body with which the contract was made;

then, subject to subsection (3) below, the same results shall follow under this Chapter as if at the time the sum was lent there had been a surrender of part of the rights conferred by the policy or contract and the sum had been paid as consideration for the surrender.

(2) If the whole or any part of the sum is repaid the repayment shall be treated, for the purpose of computing any gain arising on the happening, at the end of the final year, of a chargeable event, as a payment of a premium or lump sum consideration.

(3) Subsections (1) and (2) above do not apply in relation—

(a) to a policy if—

(i) it is a qualifying policy; and

(ii) either interest at a commercial rate is payable on the sum lent or the sum is lent to a full-time employee of the body issuing the policy for the purpose of assisting him in the purchase or improvement of a dwelling used or to be used as his only or main residence;

(b) to a contract if and to the extent that interest on the sum lent is eligible for relief under section 353 by virtue of section 365.

(4) In this section "final year" has the same meaning as in section 546.

549.—(1) Subject to subsection (2) below, where such an excess as is mentioned in section 541(1)(a) or (b) or 543(1)(a)—

(a) would be treated as a gain arising in connection with a policy or contract, and

(b) would form part of an individual's total income for the year of assessment in which the final year ends,

a corresponding deficiency occurring at the end of the final year shall be allowable as a deduction from his total income for that year of assessment, so far as it does not exceed the total amount treated as a gain by virtue of section 541(1)(d) or 543(1)(c) on the previous happenings of chargeable events.

(2) Except where the deficiency mentioned in subsection (1) above occurs in connection with a contract for a life annuity made after 26th March 1974, the deduction allowable under that subsection shall be made only for the purposes of ascertaining the individual's excess liability, that is to say, the excess (if any) of his liability to income tax over what it would be if all income tax were chargeable at the basic rate to the exclusion of any higher rate.

(3) In this section "final year" has the same meaning as in section 546.

Relief where gain charged at a higher rate.

550.—(1) The following provisions of this section shall have effect for the purposes of giving relief, on a claim in that behalf being made by him to the Board, in respect of any increase in an individual's liability to tax which is attributable to one or more amounts being included in his total income for a year of assessment by virtue of section 547(1)(a).

(2) Where one amount only is so included, there shall be computed—

(a) the tax which would be chargeable in respect of the amount if relief under this section were not available and it constituted the highest part of the claimant's total income for the year, and

(b) the tax (if any) which would be chargeable in respect of the amount if calculated, in accordance with subsection (3) below, by reference to its appropriate fraction;

and the relief shall consist of a reduction or repayment of tax equal to the difference between the two amounts of tax so computed, or, if tax would not be chargeable on a calculation by reference to the appropriate fraction, of a reduction or repayment of the tax equal to the tax computed under paragraph (a) above.

(3) In subsection (2) above "appropriate fraction" means, in relation to any amount, such a sum as bears thereto the same proportion as that borne by one to the number of complete years for which the policy or contract has run before the happening of the chargeable event; and the computation required by paragraph (b) of that subsection shall be made by applying to the amount in question such rate or rates of income tax, other than the basic rate, as would apply if it were reduced to that fraction and, as so reduced, still constituted the highest part of the claimant's total income for the year.

(4) For the purposes of subsection (3) above the number of years for which a policy of life insurance has run before the happening of a chargeable event shall be calculated, where appropriate, from the issue of the earliest related policy, meaning, any policy in relation to which the policy is a new policy within the meaning of paragraph 17 of Schedule 15, any policy in relation to which that policy is such a policy, and so on.

(5) Where a chargeable event on the happening of which an amount is included in an individual's total income by virtue of section 547(1)(a) follows the happening of another chargeable event in relation to the same policy or contract, and each of those events is such an excess as is mentioned in section 540(1)(a)(v), 542(1) or 545(1)(d), subsections (3) and (4) above shall have effect in relation to that amount as if the number of complete years referred to in subsection (3) were the number of complete years elapsing between that other event (or, if more than one, the last of them) and the first-mentioned event.

(6) Where by virtue of section 547(1)(a) two or more amounts are included in an individual's total income for any year of assessment, subsections (2) and (3) above shall apply as if they together constituted a single amount, but with the appropriate fraction of the whole determined by adding together the appropriate fractions of the individual amounts.

(7) A provision of this section requiring tax to be calculated as if an amount constituted the highest part of a claimant's total income shall apply notwithstanding any other provision of the Income Tax Acts directing any other amount to be treated as the highest part thereof, but, for the purposes of this section, a claimant's total income shall be deemed not to include any amount in respect of which he is chargeable to tax under section 34, 35, 36 or 148.

551.—(1) Where—

(a) an amount is included in an individual's income by virtue of section 547(1)(a), and

(b) the rights or share in question were held immediately before the happening of the chargeable event on trust,

Right of individual to recover tax from trustees.

the individual shall be entitled to recover from the trustees, to the extent of any sums, or to the value of any benefits, received by them by reason of the event, an amount equal to that (if any) by which the tax with which he is chargeable for the year of assessment in question, reduced by the amount of any relief available under section 550 in respect of the amount so included, exceeds the tax with which he would have been chargeable for the year if that amount had not been so included.

(2) Where, for the purposes of relief under section 550, two or more amounts are to be treated as one, the reduction required by subsection (1) above on account of the relief available in respect of any of them shall consist of a proportionate part of the relief available in respect of their aggregate.

(3) An individual may require the Board to certify any amount recoverable by him by virtue of this section, and the certificate shall be conclusive evidence of the amount.

552.—(1) Subject to subsections (2) to (5) below, where a chargeable event within the meaning of this Chapter has happened in relation to any policy or contract, the body by or with whom the policy or contract was issued, entered into or effected shall, within three months of the event or, if it is a death or an assignment, within three months of their receiving written notification thereof, deliver to the inspector a certificate specifying—

Information: duty of insurers.

(a) the name and address of the policy holder;

(b) the nature of the event, and the date on which it happened;

(c) as may be required for computing the gain to be treated as arising by virtue of this Chapter—

    (i) the surrender value of the policy, or the sum payable, or other benefits to be conferred, by the body in question by reason of the event;

    (ii) the amount or value of any relevant capital payments;

    (iii) the amounts previously paid under the policy or contract by way of premiums, or otherwise by way of consideration for an annuity; and

    (iv) the capital element in any payment previously made on account of an annuity;

(d) the number of years relevant for computing the appropriate fraction of the gain for the purposes of section 550(3).

(2) Subsection (1) above shall not apply where—

(a) the body in question are satisfied that no gain is to be treated as arising by reason of the event, or

(b) the amount of the surrender value or sum, or the value of the other benefits, referred to in paragraph (c)(i) of that subsection, together with the amount or value of any payments within paragraph (c)(ii) of that subsection, does not exceed £500,

but the inspector may by notice require a like certificate in any such case, and it shall be the duty of the body to deliver the certificate within 30 days of receipt of the notice.

(3) Where the chargeable event is an assignment of all the rights conferred by the policy or contract the certificate shall also specify any such excess as is mentioned in section 540(1)(a)(v), 542(1) or 545(1)(d) which has occurred since the relevant date, the date on which it occurred and the value of the part of or share in the rights which have been surrendered or assigned since the relevant date.

(4) Where the chargeable event is the occurrence of such an excess as is mentioned in section 540(1)(a)(v), 542(1) or 545(1)(d), subsections (1) and (2) above shall apply with the omission of paragraph (b) of subsection (2) and the certificate shall also specify the value of the part of or share in the rights surrendered or assigned in any year since the relevant date and the amounts paid by way of premiums in any year since the relevant date.

(5) In subsections (3) and (4) above—

"year" has the same meaning as in section 546(4); and

"the relevant date", in relation to any certificate, means the date of the chargeable event in respect of which the last certificate under this section was delivered or, if none was delivered, the commencement of the policy or contract.

553.—(1) If, in the case of a substitution of policies falling within paragraph 25(1) or (3) of Schedule 15, the new policy is a qualifying policy, section 540 shall have effect with the following modifications—

PART XIII
Non-resident
policies and off-
shore capital
redemption
policies.

> (a) the surrender of the rights conferred by the old policy shall not be a chargeable event (within the meaning of that section); and

> (b) the new policy shall be treated as having been issued in respect of an insurance made on the day referred to in paragraph 26 of that Schedule.

(2) If at any time neither the conditions in sub-paragraph (3) nor those in sub-paragraph (4) of paragraph 24 of Schedule 15 are fulfilled with respect to a new non-resident policy which has previously become a qualifying policy, then, from that time onwards, this Chapter shall apply in relation to the policy as if it were not a qualifying policy.

(3) Subject to subsection (5) below, on the happening of a chargeable event in relation to a new non-resident policy or a new offshore capital redemption policy, the amount which, apart from this subsection, would by virtue of section 541 be treated as a gain arising in connection with the policy shall be reduced by multiplying it by the fraction—

$$\frac{A}{B}$$

where—

> A is the number of days on which the policy holder was resident in the United Kingdom in the period for which the policy has run before the happening of the chargeable event; and

> B is the number of days in that period.

(4) The calculation of the number of days in the period referred to in subsection (3) above shall be made in like manner as is provided in section 550(4), substituting a reference to the number of days for the reference to the number of years.

(5) If, on the happening of the chargeable event referred to in subsection (3) above or at any time during the period referred to in that subsection, the policy is or was held by a trustee resident outside the United Kingdom or by two or more trustees any of whom is or was so resident, no reduction shall be made under that subsection unless—

> (a) the policy was issued in respect of an insurance made on or before 19th March 1985; and

> (b) on that date the policy was held by a trustee who was so resident or, as the case may be, by two or more trustees any of whom was so resident.

(6) Subject to subsection (7) below, where, under section 541, a gain (reduced in accordance with subsection (3) above) is to be treated as arising in connection with a new non-resident policy or a new offshore capital redemption policy—

> (a) section 547 shall have effect, in relation to the gain, as if subsection (5) were omitted; and

> (b) the gain shall be chargeable to tax under Case VI of Schedule D;

but any relief under section 550 shall be computed as if this subsection had not been enacted.

(7) Paragraphs (a) and (b) of subsection (6) above do not apply to a gain arising in connection with a new non-resident policy if the conditions in either sub-paragraph (3) or sub-paragraph (4) of paragraph 24 of Schedule 15 are fulfilled at all times between the date on which the policy was issued and the date on which the gain is treated as arising.

(8) Where a claim is made under section 550 in respect of the amount of a gain treated as arising in connection with a new non-resident policy or a new offshore capital redemption policy (with or without other amounts), the "appropriate fraction" which, in accordance with subsection (2) of that section, is to be applied to that amount shall be modified by deducting from the number of complete years referred to in subsection (3) of that section any complete years during which the policy holder was not resident in the United Kingdom.

(9) Subsection (5) of section 550 shall not apply in relation to a new non-resident policy or a new offshore capital redemption policy.

(10) In this section—

"chargeable event" has, subject to subsection (1) above, the meaning given by section 540 or, as the case may be, 545;

"new non-resident policy" has the meaning given by paragraph 24 of Schedule 15; and

"new offshore capital redemption policy" means a capital redemption policy, as defined in section 539(3), which—

(a) is issued in respect of an insurance made after 22nd February 1984; and

(b) is so issued by a company resident outside the United Kingdom.

Borrowings on life policies to be treated as income in certain cases.

554.—(1) Where—

(a) under any contract or arrangements made on or after 7th April 1949, provision is made for the making to any person, at intervals until the happening of an event or contingency dependent on human life, of payments by way of loan; and

(b) under the contract or arrangements, the loans are secured upon a policy of life assurance which assures moneys payable on the happening of such an event or contingency and need not be repaid until the policy moneys become payable; and

(c) the amount of the moneys payable on the happening of the event or contingency is made by the policy to increase by reference to the length of a period ending on the happening of that event or contingency;

the payments made by way of loan shall be treated for tax purposes as annual payments falling within Case III of Schedule D, or, if they are made to a person residing in the United Kingdom and the contract or arrangements were made outside the United Kingdom, as income from a possession out of the United Kingdom and, for income tax, as falling within section 65(1).

PART XIII

(2) The amount of the moneys payable under a policy of life assurance shall not be deemed for the purposes of this section to be made to increase by reference to the length of a period ending on the happening of an event or contingency dependent on human life by reason only that those moneys are to increase from time to time if profits are made by the person liable under the policy.

(3) This section shall not apply to any payments by way of loan if the Board are satisfied as respects those payments that it is not one of the objects of the contract or arrangements under which the payments are made that the recipient of them should enjoy the advantages which would, apart from any question of liability to tax, be enjoyed by a person in receipt of payments of the same amounts paid at the same times by way of annuity.

CHAPTER III

ENTERTAINERS AND SPORTSMEN

Payment of tax.

555.—(1) Where a person who is an entertainer or sportsman of a prescribed description performs an activity of a prescribed description in the United Kingdom ("a relevant activity"), this Chapter shall apply if he is not resident in the United Kingdom in the year of assessment in which the relevant activity is performed.

(2) Where a payment is made (to whatever person) and it has a connection of a prescribed kind with the relevant activity, the person by whom it is made shall on making it deduct out of it a sum representing income tax and shall account to the Board for the sum.

(3) Where a transfer is made (to whatever person) and it has a connection of a prescribed kind with the relevant activity, the person by whom it is made shall account to the Board for a sum representing income tax.

(4) The sums mentioned in subsections (2) and (3) above shall be such as are calculated in accordance with prescribed rules but shall in no case exceed the relevant proportion of the payment concerned or of the value of what is transferred, as the case may be; and "relevant proportion" here means a proportion equal to the basic rate of income tax for the year of assessment in which the payment or, as the case may be, the transfer is made.

(5) In this Chapter—

   (a) references to a payment include references to a payment by way of loan of money; and

   (b) references to a transfer do not include references to a transfer of money but, subject to that, include references to a temporary transfer (as by way of loan) and to a transfer of a right (whether or not a right to receive money).

(6) This section shall not apply to payments or transfers of such a kind as may be prescribed.

(7) Regulations may—

(a) make provision enabling the Board to serve notices requiring persons who make payments or transfers to which subsection (2) or (3) above applies to furnish to the Board particulars of a prescribed kind in respect of payments or transfers;

(b) make provision requiring persons who make payments or transfers to which subsection (2) or (3) above applies to make, at prescribed times and for prescribed periods, returns to the Board containing prescribed information about payments or transfers and the income tax for which those persons are accountable in respect of them;

(c) make provision for the collection and recovery of such income tax, provision for assessments and claims to be made in respect of it, and provision for the payment of interest on it;

(d) adapt, or modify the effect of, any enactment relating to income tax for the purpose of making any such provision as is mentioned in paragraphs (a) to (c) above.

(8) Where in accordance with subsections (2) to (7) above a person pays a sum to the Board, they shall treat it as having been paid on account of a liability of another person to income tax or corporation tax; and the liability and the other person shall be such as are found in accordance with prescribed rules.

(9) Where the sum exceeds the liability concerned, the Board shall pay such of the sum as is appropriate to the other person mentioned in subsection (8) above.

(10) Where no liability is found as mentioned in subsection (8) above, the Board shall pay the sum to the person to whom the payment or transfer to which subsection (2) or (3) above applies, and which gave rise to the payment of the sum concerned to the Board, was made.

(11) In construing references to a sum in subsections (8) to (10) above, anything representing interest shall be ignored.

Activity treated as trade etc. and attribution of income.

556.—(1) Where a payment is made (to whatever person) and it has a connection of the prescribed kind with the relevant activity, the activity shall be treated for the purposes of the Tax Acts as performed in the course of a trade, profession or vocation exercised by the entertainer or sportsman within the United Kingdom, to the extent that (apart from this subsection) it would not be so treated.

This subsection shall not apply where the relevant activity is performed in the course of an office or employment.

(2) Where a payment is made to a person who fulfils a prescribed description but is not the entertainer or sportsman and the payment has a connection of the prescribed kind with the relevant activity—

(a) the entertainer or sportsman shall be treated for the purposes of the Tax Acts as the person to whom the payment is made; and

(b) the payment shall be treated for those purposes as made to him in the course of a trade, profession or vocation exercised by him within the United Kingdom (whether or not he would be treated as exercising such a trade, profession or vocation apart from this paragraph).

(3) Regulations may provide—

    (a) for the deduction, in computing any profits or gains of the entertainer or sportsman arising from the payment, of expenses incurred by other persons in relation to the payment;

    (b) that any liability to tax (whether of the entertainer or sportsman or of another person) which would, apart from subsection (2) above, arise in relation to the payment shall not arise or shall arise only to a prescribed extent.

(4) References in this section to a payment include references to a transfer.

(5) This section shall not apply unless the payment or transfer is one to which section 555(2) or (3) applies, and subsections (2) and (3) above shall not apply in such circumstances as may be prescribed.

557.—(1) Where income tax is chargeable under Case I or II of Schedule D on the profits or gains arising from payment (made to whatever person) and the payments have a connection of the prescribed kind with relevant activities of the entertainer or sportsman, such tax shall be charged— *Charge on profits or gains.*

    (a) as if those payments were received in the course of one trade, profession or vocation exercised by the entertainer or sportsman within the United Kingdom separately from any other trade, profession or vocation exercised by him; and

    (b) for each year of assessment, on the full amount of the profits or gains arising in the year from those payments.

(2) Regulations may—

    (a) provide for the apportionment of profits or gains between different trades, professions or vocations of the entertainer or sportsman;

    (b) provide for the apportionment between different years of assessment of the profits or gains arising from relevant activities of the entertainer or sportsman;

    (c) provide for losses sustained in any trade, profession or vocation of the entertainer or sportsman to be deducted from or set off against the profits or gains of another trade, profession or vocation of the entertainer or sportsman;

    (d) provide that prescribed provisions of the Tax Acts about losses, or about expenditure, shall not apply (or shall apply with prescribed modifications) in prescribed circumstances relating to the entertainer or sportsman.

(3) References in subsection (2)(a) and (c) above to a trade, profession or vocation of the entertainer or sportsman include references to that first mentioned in subsection (1)(a) above as well as to any other exercised by him.

(4) References in this section to a payment include references to a transfer.

PART XIII

(5) This section shall not apply in the case of a payment or transfer unless it is one to which section 555(2) or (3) applies.

Supplementary provisions.

558.—(1) A payment to which subsection (2) of section 555 applies shall be treated for the purposes of the Tax Acts as not diminished by the sum mentioned in that subsection.

(2) Regulations may provide that for the purposes of the Tax Acts the value of what is transferred by a transfer to which section 555(3) applies shall be calculated in accordance with prescribed rules.

(3) In particular, rules may include provision for the calculation of an amount representing the actual worth of what is transferred, for that amount to be treated as a net amount corresponding to a gross amount from which income tax at the basic rate has been deducted, and for the gross amount to be taken to be the value of what is transferred.

(4) No obligation as to secrecy imposed by statute or otherwise shall preclude the Board or an authorised officer of the Board from disclosing to any person who appears to the Board to have an interest in the matter information which may be relevant to determining whether section 555(2) or (3) applies to a payment or transfer.

(5) Regulations may make provision generally for giving effect to this Chapter, and may make different provision for different cases or descriptions of case.

(6) In this Chapter—

"regulations" means regulations made by the Treasury; and

"prescribed" means prescribed by regulations.

CHAPTER IV

SUB-CONTRACTORS IN THE CONSTRUCTION INDUSTRY

Deductions on account of tax etc. from payments to certain sub-contractors.

559.—(1) Subject to subsection (2) below, where a contract relating to construction operations is not a contract of employment but—

(a) one party to the contract is a sub-contractor; and

(b) another party to the contract ("the contractor") either is a sub-contractor under another such contract relating to all or any of the construction operations or is a person to whom section 560(2) applies,

this section shall apply to any payments which are made under the contract and are so made by the contractor to—

(i) the sub-contractor;

(ii) a person nominated by the sub-contractor or the contractor; or

(iii) a person nominated by a person who is a sub-contractor under another such contract relating to all or any of the construction operations.

(2) Subsection (1) above shall not apply to any payment made under the contract in question if the person to whom it is made or, if it is made to a nominee, each of the following persons, that is to say, the nominee,

the person who nominated him and the person for whose labour (or, where that person is a company, for whose employees' or officers' labour) the payment is made, is excepted from this section in relation to those payments by virtue of section 561.

(3) Subsection (2) above does not apply to so much of any payment made under the contract in question to a person falling within subsection (4) of section 561 as exceeds, or in aggregate with other payments specified in regulations made under subsection (5) of that section exceeds, the limit prescribed by those regulations.

(4) On making a payment to which this section applies the contractor shall deduct from it a sum equal to 27 per cent. of so much of the payment as is not shown to represent the direct cost to any other person of materials used or to be used in carrying out the construction operations to which the contract under which the payment is to be made relates; and the sum so deducted shall be paid to the Board and shall be treated for the purposes of income tax or, as the case may be, corporation tax—

    (a) as not diminishing the payment; but

    (b) subject to subsection (5) below, as being income tax or, as the case may be, corporation tax paid in respect of the profits or gains of the trade, profession or vocation of the person for whose (or for whose employees' or officers') labour the contractor makes the payment.

(5) Where a sum deducted and paid to the Board under subsection (4) above is more than sufficient to discharge the liability to income tax of the person referred to in paragraph (b) of that subsection in respect of the profits or gains mentioned in that paragraph, so much of the excess as is required to discharge any liability of that person for Class 4 contributions shall be treated as being, for the purposes of the Social Security Act, Class 4 contributions paid in respect of the profits or gains so mentioned.

(6) References in section 1(1) of the Preferential Payments (Bankruptcies and Arrangements) Act (Northern Ireland) 1964 to sums due on account of tax deductions for any period shall be construed as including references to any amounts due from any person in respect of deductions required to be made by him under this section. 1964 c. 32 (N.I.).

(7) For the purposes of this Chapter a payment (including a payment by way of loan) that has the effect of discharging an obligation under a contract relating to construction operations shall be taken to be made under the contract; and if—

    (a) the obligation is to make a payment to a person within subsection (1)(i) to (iii) above, but

    (b) the payment discharging that obligation is made to a person not within those paragraphs,

the payment shall for those purposes be taken to be made to the first-mentioned person.

(8) In this section—

    "Class 4 contributions" means Class 4 contributions within the meaning of the Social Security Act 1975 or, as the case may be, the Social Security (Northern Ireland) Act 1975; and 1975 c. 14.
1975 c. 15.

PART XIII

Persons who are sub-contractors or contractors for purposes of Chapter IV.

"the Social Security Act" means whichever of those Acts is the one under which the contribution in question is payable.

560.—(1) For the purposes of this Chapter a party to a contract relating to construction operations is a sub-contractor if, under the contract—

(a) he is under a duty to the contractor to carry out the operations, or to furnish his own labour (that is to say, in the case of a company, the labour of employees or officers of the company) or the labour of others in the carrying out of the operations or to arrange for the labour of others to be furnished in the carrying out of the operations; or

(b) he is answerable to the contractor for the carrying out of the operations by others, whether under a contract or under other arrangements made or to be made by him.

(2) This subsection applies to the following persons, that is to say—

(a) any person carrying on a business which includes construction operations;

(b) any local authority;

(c) any development corporation or new town commission;

(d) the Commission for the New Towns;

(e) the Housing Corporation, a housing association, a housing trust, the Scottish Special Housing Association, and the Northern Ireland Housing Executive;

(f) a person carrying on a business at any time if—

(i) his average annual expenditure on construction operations in the period of three years ending with the end of the last period of account before that time exceeds £250,000, or

(ii) where he was not carrying on the business at the beginning of that period of three years, one-third of his total expenditure on construction operations for the part of that period during which he has been carrying on the business exceeds £250,000;

and in paragraph (f) "period of account" means a period for which an account is made up in relation to the business in question.

(3) Where section 559(1)(b) begins to apply to any person in any period of account by virtue of his falling within subsection (2)(f) above, it shall continue to apply to him until he satisfies the Board that his expenditure on construction operations has been less than £250,000 in each of three successive years beginning in or after that period of account.

(4) Where the whole or part of a trade is transferred by a company ("the transferor") to another company ("the transferee") and section 343 has effect in relation to the transfer, then in determining for the purposes of this section the amount of expenditure incurred by the transferee—

(a) the whole or, as the case may be, a proportionate part of any expenditure incurred by the transferor at a time before the transfer shall be treated as if it had been incurred at that time by the transferee; and

(b) where only a part of the trade is transferred the expenditure shall be apportioned in such manner as appears to the Board, or on appeal to the Commissioners, to be just and reasonable.

(5) In this section—

"development corporation" has the same meaning as in the New Towns Act 1981 or the New Towns (Scotland) Act 1968;

1981 c. 64.
1968 c. 16.

"housing association" has the same meaning as in the Housing Associations Act 1985 or the Housing (Northern Ireland) Order 1981;

1985 c. 69.
S.I. 1981/156
(N.I. 3).

"housing trust" has the same meaning as in the Housing Associations Act 1985; and

"new town commission" has the same meaning as in the New Towns Act (Northern Ireland) 1965.

1965 c. 13 (N.I.).

561.—(1) Subject to the provisions of regulations under subsection (5) below or section 566(2), a person is excepted from section 559 in relation to payments made under a contract if a certificate under this section has been issued to that person and is in force when the payment is made, but—

Exceptions from section 559.

(a) where the certificate has been issued to a person who becomes a partner in a firm, that person is not excepted in relation to payments made under contracts under which the firm or, where a person has nominated the firm to receive payments, the person who has nominated the firm is a sub-contractor; and

(b) where a certificate has been issued to a person as a partner in a firm, that person is excepted in relation only to payments made under contracts under which the firm or, where a person has nominated the firm to receive payments, the person who has nominated the firm, is a sub-contractor.

(2) If the Board are satisfied, on the application of an individual or a company, that—

(a) where the application is for the issue of a certificate to an individual (otherwise than as a partner in a firm), he satisfies the conditions set out in section 562;

(b) where the application is for the issue of a certificate to a person as a partner in a firm, that person satisfies the conditions set out in section 563 if he is an individual or, if a company, the conditions set out in section 565 and, in either case, the firm itself satisfies the conditions set out in section 564;

(c) where the application is for the issue of a certificate to a company, the company satisfies the conditions set out in section 565 and, if the Board have given a direction under subsection (4) below, each of the persons to whom any of the conditions set out in section 562 applies in accordance with the direction satisfies the conditions which so apply to him, the Board shall issue to that individual or company a certificate excepting that individual or company (or, in a case falling within paragraph (b) above, that individual or company as a partner in the firm specified in the certificate) from section 559.

(3) References in subsection (2) above to an individual, a company or a firm satisfying conditions set out in section 562, 563, 564 or 565 include, in relation to a condition which may, by virtue of a provision of that section, be treated as being satisfied, references to that individual, company or firm being treated as satisfying that condition.

(4) This subsection applies to the holder of a certificate in force under this section if it was issued to him on the basis—

(a) that the condition in subsection (3) of section 562 was inapplicable to him by reason of paragraph (b) of that subsection; or

(b) that he satisfied that condition by virtue of subsection (7) of that section.

(5) The Board may make regulations securing that a person to whom subsection (4) above applies shall not be excepted from subsection (1) above in relation to a payment to the extent that the amount of the payment, or the aggregate amount of the payment and such other payments as may be prescribed by the regulations, exceeds a limit so prescribed.

(6) Where it appears to the Board, on an application made under subsection (2) above by a company, that the company—

(a) was incorporated on a date within the period of three years ending with the date of the application; or

(b) has not carried on business continuously throughout that period; or

(c) has carried on business continuously throughout that period but the business has not at all times in that period consisted of or included the carrying out of construction operations; or

(d) does not at the date of the application hold a certificate which is then in force under this section;

the Board may direct that the conditions set out in section 562 or such of them as are specified in the direction shall apply to the directors of the company and, if the company is a close company, to the persons who are the beneficial owners of shares in the company or to such of those directors or persons as are so specified as if each of them were an applicant for a certificate under this section (not being a certificate to the holder of which section 561(4) would apply).

In this subsection "director" has the same meaning as in Chapter II of Part V.

(7) Where it appears to the Board that there has been a change in the control of a company holding or applying for a certificate, the Board may make any such direction as is referred to in subsection (6) above.

(8) The Board may at any time cancel a certificate which has been issued to a person and is in force under this section if it appears to them that—

    (a) it was issued on information which was false;

    (b) if an application for the issue of a certificate under this section to that person were made at that time, the Board would refuse to issue a certificate;

    (c) that person has permitted the certificate to be misused; or

    (d) in the case of a certificate issued to a company, there has been a change in the control of the company and information with respect to that change has not been furnished in accordance with regulations under section 566(2);

and may by notice require that person to deliver the certificate to the Board within the time specified in the notice.

Section 840 shall apply for the purposes of paragraph (d) above.

(9) A person aggrieved by the refusal of an application for a certificate under this section or the cancellation of such a certificate may, by notice given to the Board within 30 days after the refusal or, as the case may be, cancellation, appeal to the General Commissioners or, if he so elects in the notice, to the Special Commissioners; and the jurisdiction of the Commissioners on such an appeal shall include jurisdiction to review any relevant decision taken by the Board in the exercise of their functions under this section.

(10) If any person, for the purpose of obtaining a certificate under this section—

    (a) makes any statement, or furnishes any document, which he knows to be false in a material particular; or

    (b) recklessly makes any statement, or furnishes any document, which is false in a material particular,

he shall be liable on summary conviction to a fine not exceeding £5,000.

(11) A person to whom a certificate is issued under this section or a voucher is given as required by regulations under section 566(2)(j) shall take all reasonable steps to ensure its safety; and any person who, without lawful authority or lawful excuse—

    (a) disposes of any such certificate or voucher or any form supplied by the Board in connection with regulations made by virtue of section 566(2)(e); or

    (b) possesses such a certificate, voucher or form or any document purporting to be such a certificate, voucher or form,

shall be liable on summary conviction to a fine not exceeding £5,000.

(12) Notwithstanding any enactment prescribing the period within which summary proceedings may be commenced, proceedings for an offence under subsection (10) or (11) above may be commenced at any time within three years from the commission of the offence.

Part XIII

1975 c. 45.

(13) Without prejudice to section 843(3), this section shall come into force on 6th April 1988 to the exclusion of the provisions of section 70 of the Finance (No.2) Act 1975 which are re-enacted in this section, but any offence committed before that date shall not be punishable under this section and neither this subsection nor any other provision of this Act shall prevent any such offence from being punishable as if this Act had not been passed.

Conditions to be satisfied by individuals.

562.—(1) In the case of an application for the issue of a certificate under section 561 to an individual (otherwise than as a partner in a firm) the following conditions are required to be satisfied by that individual.

(2) The applicant must be carrying on a business in the United Kingdom which satisfies the following conditions, that is to say—

(a) the business consists of or includes the carrying out of construction operations or the furnishing or arranging for the furnishing of labour in carrying out construction operations;

(b) the business is, to a substantial extent, carried on by means of an account with a bank;

(c) the business is carried on with proper records and in particular with records which are proper having regard to the obligations referred to in subsections (8) to (12) below; and

(d) the business is carried on from proper premises and with proper equipment, stock and other facilities.

(3) Unless the applicant—

(a) is the holder of a certificate in force under section 561 (other than a holder to whom section 561(4) applies), or

(b) supplies the Board with a guarantee by such person, for such amount and in such form as may be prescribed in regulations made by the Board,

he must throughout the period of three years ending with the date of his application for a certificate under section 561, have been employed in the United Kingdom as the holder of an office or employment or as a person carrying on a trade, profession or vocation.

(4) The applicant must not be receiving full-time education or full-time training.

(5) An applicant shall be treated as satisfying the condition in subsection (3) above if—

(a) he satisfies the Board that he has been employed as mentioned in that subsection throughout a period of three years beginning not more than six years before the date of his application and ending on a date before that date;

(b) he satisfies the Board either—

(i) that he has not been so employed throughout the whole of the period between those dates, or

(ii) that he has not been so employed during any part of that period other than a part for which he specifies he has been so employed; and

(c) where the applicant states that he has been outside the United Kingdom for the whole or part of the period mentioned in paragraph (b) above, he satisfies the Board of that fact by such evidence as may be prescribed in regulations made by the Board.

(6) The Board may for the purposes of subsections (3) and (5) above treat a person as having been employed as mentioned in subsection (3) above throughout a period of three years if during a period of three years he has been so employed except for a period or periods not exceeding six months or six months in aggregate.

(7) If the applicant satisfies the Board that he has during any period within six years before the date of his application attended a school or other establishment for the purpose of receiving full-time education or full-time training, this section shall have effect as if that period were one during which he was employed as mentioned in subsection (3) above.

(8) The applicant must, subject to subsection (10) below, have complied with all obligations imposed on him by or under the Tax Acts or the Management Act in respect of periods ending within the qualifying period and with all requests to supply to an inspector accounts of, or other information about, any business of his in respect of periods so ending.

(9) An applicant who at any time in the qualifying period had control of a company shall be taken not to satisfy the condition in subsection (8) above unless the company has satisfied that condition in relation to periods ending at a time within that period when he had control of it; and for this purpose "control" has the meaning given by section 840.

(10) An applicant or company that has failed to comply with such an obligation or request as is referred to in subsection (8) above shall nevertheless be treated as satisfying that condition as regards that obligation or request if the Board are of the opinion that the failure is minor and technical and does not give reason to doubt that the conditions mentioned in subsection (13) below will be satisfied.

(11) An applicant who must satisfy the Board under subsection (5) above that he has been outside the United Kingdom for the whole or part of the period mentioned in subsection (5)(b) above must also satisfy them by such evidence as may be prescribed in regulations made by the Board that he has complied with any obligations imposed under the tax laws of any country in which he was living during that period which are comparable to the obligations mentioned in subsection (8) above.

(12) The applicant must, if any contribution has at any time during the qualifying period become due from him under Part I of the Social Security Act 1975 or Part I of the Social Security (Northern Ireland) Act 1975, have paid the contribution when it became due. 1975 c. 14. 1975 c. 15.

(13) There must be reason to expect that the applicant will, in respect of periods ending after the end of the qualifying period, comply with such obligations as are referred to in subsections (8) to (12) above and with such requests as are referred to in subsection (8) above.

(14) In this section "the qualifying period" means—

(a) in relation to a person who is within subsection (5) above, the period starting at the beginning of the last period of three years before his application throughout which he has been employed as mentioned in subsection (3) above (or is by virtue of subsection (6) above treated as having been so employed) and ending on the date of his application; and

(b) in the case of any other person, the period of three years ending with the date of his application.

563.—(1) In the case of an application for the issue of a certificate under section 561 to an individual who is a partner in a firm, the following conditions are required to be satisfied by that individual.

(2) The partner, unless he is the holder of a certificate in force under section 561 (other than a holder to whom section 561(4) applies), must throughout the period of three years ending with the date of his application for a certificate under section 561 have been employed in the United Kingdom as the holder of an office or employment or as a person carrying on a trade, profession or vocation.

(3) A partner who has not fulfilled the condition in subsection (2) above shall nevertheless be treated as satisfying that condition if—

(a) he satisfies the Board that he has been employed as mentioned in that subsection throughout a period of three years beginning not more than six years before the date of his application and ending on a date before that date;

(b) he satisfies the Board either—

(i) that he has not been so employed throughout the whole of the period between those dates, or

(ii) that he has not been so employed during any part of that period other than a part for which he specifies he has been so employed; and

(c) where the partner states that he has been outside the United Kingdom for the whole or part of the period mentioned in paragraph (b) above, he satisfies the Board of that fact by such evidence as may be prescribed in regulations made by the Board.

(4) The Board may for the purposes of this paragraph treat a person as having been employed as mentioned in subsection (2) above throughout a period of three years if during a period of three years he has been so employed except for a period or periods not exceeding six months or six months in aggregate.

(5) The partner must, subject to subsection (6) below, have complied with all obligations imposed on him by or under the Income Tax Acts or the Management Act in respect of periods ending within the qualifying period and with all requests to supply to an inspector accounts of, or other information about, any business of his in respect of periods so ending.

(6) A partner who has failed to comply with such an obligation or request as is referred to in subsection (5) above shall nevertheless be treated as satisfying that condition as regards that obligation or request if the Board are of the opinion that the failure is minor and technical and does not give reason to doubt that the conditions mentioned in subsection (9) below will be satisfied.

(7) A partner who must satisfy the Board under subsection (3) above that he has been outside the United Kingdom for the whole or part of the period mentioned in subsection (3)(b) above must also satisfy them by such evidence as may be prescribed in regulations made by the Board that he has complied with any obligations imposed under the tax laws of any country in which he was living during that period which are comparable to the obligations mentioned in subsection (5) above.

(8) The partner must, if any contribution has at any time during the qualifying period become due from him under Part I of the Social Security Act 1975 or Part I of the Social Security (Northern Ireland) Act 1975, have paid the contribution when it became due.

1975 c. 14.
1975 c. 15.

(9) There must be reason to expect that the partner will, in respect of periods ending after the end of the qualifying period, comply with such obligations as are referred to in subsections (5) to (8) above and with such requests as are referred to in subsection (5) above.

(10) In this section "the qualifying period" means—

(a) in relation to a person who is within subsection (3) above, the period starting at the beginning of the last period of three years before his application throughout which he has been employed as mentioned in subsection (2) above (or is by virtue of subsection (4) above treated as having been so employed) and ending on the date of his application, and

(b) in the case of any other person, the period of three years ending with the date of his application.

564.—(1) In the case of an application for the issue of a certificate under section 561 to an individual or a company as a partner in a firm the following conditions are required to be satisfied by the firm.

Conditions to be satisfied by firms.

(2) The firm's business must be carried on in the United Kingdom and must satisfy the conditions mentioned in section 562(2)(a) to (d).

(3) Subject to subsection (4) below, any income tax or corporation tax which became due from any partner in the firm in respect of the firm's business at any time in the period of three years ending with the date of the application for a certificate under section 561 must have been paid when the tax was demanded.

(4) Where the obligation referred to in subsection (3) above has not been complied with in the case of any firm, the firm shall nevertheless be treated as satisfying that condition as regards that tax if the Board are of the opinion that the failure is minor and technical and does not give reason to doubt that the conditions mentioned in subsection (5) below will be satisfied.

(5) There must be reason to expect that income tax or corporation tax becoming due in respect of the firm's business in respect of periods ending after the end of the period referred to in subsection (3) above will be paid when it is demanded.

565.—(1) In the case of an application for the issue of a certificate under section 561 to a company (whether as a partner in a firm or otherwise), the following conditions are required to be satisfied by the company.

Conditions to be satisfied by companies.

(2) The company must be carrying on (whether or not in partnership) a business in the United Kingdom and that business must satisfy the conditions mentioned in section 562(2)(a) to (d).

(3) The company must, subject to subsection (4) below, have complied with all obligations imposed on it by or under the Tax Acts or the Management Act in respect of periods ending within the qualifying period and with all requests to supply to an inspector accounts of, or other information about, the business of the company in respect of periods so ending.

(4) A company which has failed to comply with such an obligation or request as is referred to in subsection (3) above shall nevertheless be treated as satisfying this condition as regards that obligation or request if the Board are of the opinion that the failure is minor and technical and does not give reason to doubt that the conditions mentioned in subsection (8) below will be satisfied.

(5) The company must, if any contribution has at any time during the qualifying period become due from the company under Part I of the Social Security Act 1975 or Part I of the Social Security (Northern Ireland) Act 1975 have paid the contribution when it became due.

1975 c. 14.
1975 c. 15.

(6) The company must have complied with any obligations imposed on it by the following provisions of the Companies Act 1985, in so far as those obligations fell to be complied with within the qualifying period, that is to say—

1985 c. 6.

(a) sections 227 and 241 (contents, laying and delivery of annual accounts);

(b) section 287 (registered office and notification of changes therein);

(c) section 288(2) (return of directors and secretary and notification of changes therein);

(d) sections 363, 364 and 365 (annual returns);

(e) section 691 (registration of constitutional documents and list of directors and secretary of oversea company);

(f) section 692 (notification of changes in constitution or directors or secretary of oversea company);

(g) section 693 (oversea company to state its name and country of incorporation);

(h) section 699 (obligations of companies incorporated in Channel Islands or Isle of Man);

(j) Chapter II of Part XXIII (accounts of oversea company).

(7) The company must have complied with any obligations imposed on it by the following provisions of the Companies (Northern Ireland) Order 1986, in so far as those obligations fell to be complied with within the qualifying period, that is to say—

S.I. 1986/1032
(N.I. 6).

(a) Articles 235, 247 and 249 (annual accounts, documents included in annual accounts and laying and delivery of accounts);

(b) Article 295 (registered office and notification of changes therein);

(c) Article 296(2) (return of directors and secretary and notification of changes therein);

(d) Articles 371, 372 and 373 (annual returns);

(e) Article 641 (registration of constitutional documents and list of directors and secretary of oversea company);

(f) Article 642 (notification of changes in constitution or directors or secretary of oversea company);

(g) Article 643 (oversea company to state its name and country of incorporation);

(h) Article 649 (accounts of oversea company).

(8) There must be reason to expect that the company will, in respect of periods ending after the end of the qualifying period, comply with all such obligations as are referred to in subsections (2) to (7) above and with such requests as are referred to in subsection (3) above.

(9) In this section "qualifying period" means the period of three years ending with the date of the company's application for a certificate under section 561.

566.—(1) The Board shall make regulations with respect to the collection and recovery, whether by assessment or otherwise, of sums required to be deducted from any payments under section 559 and for the giving of receipts by persons receiving the payments to persons making them; and those regulations may include any matters with respect to which regulations may be made under section 203.

General powers to make regulations under Chapter IV.

(2) The Board may make regulations—

(a) prescribing the period for which certificates under section 561 are to be issued and the form of such certificates;

(b) providing for the renewal of such certificates;

(c) providing for the issue, renewal or cancellation of such certificates or the giving of directions under section 561(6) by inspectors on behalf of the Board;

(d) requiring the furnishing of information with respect to changes in the control of a company holding or applying for such a certificate;

(e) requiring the production of such certificates to such persons and in such circumstances as may be specified in the regulations and providing for the completion and return to the Board of forms certifying such production;

(f) requiring the surrender to the Board of such certificates in such circumstances as may be specified in the regulations;

(g) requiring persons who make payments under contracts relating to construction operations to keep such records and to make to the Board such returns relating to payments so made by them as may be specified in the regulations, and requiring persons who hold such certificates to keep such records relating to payments so made to them as may be so specified;

(h) with respect to the production, copying and removal of, and the making of extracts from, any records kept by virtue of any such requirement as is referred to in paragraph (g) above and with respect to rights of access to or copies of any such records which are removed;

(j) requiring vouchers for payments made under contracts relating to construction operations to persons who hold such certificates to be obtained by the person making, and given by the person receiving, the payment, prescribing the form of the vouchers, and requiring their production or surrender to the Board in such circumstances as may be specified in the regulations; and

(k) excluding payments from the operation of section 561 where, in such circumstances as may be specified in the regulations, the requirements of regulations relating to the production of certificates or the obtaining, production or surrender of vouchers have not been complied with;

and any such regulations may make different provision for different circumstances.

Section 840 shall apply for the purposes of paragraph (d) above.

Meaning of "construction operations".

567.—(1) In this Chapter "construction operations" means operations of any description specified in subsection (2) below, not being operations of any description specified in subsection (3) below; and references to construction operations shall be taken—

(a) except where the context otherwise requires, as including references to the work of individuals participating in the carrying out of such operations; and

(b) except in the case of offshore installations, as not including references to operations carried out or to be carried out otherwise than in the United Kingdom.

(2) The following operations are, subject to subsection (3) below, construction operations for the purposes of this Chapter—

(a) construction, alteration, repair, extension, demolition or dismantling of buildings or structures (whether permanent or not), including offshore installations;

(b) construction, alteration, repair, extension or demolition of any works forming, or to form, part of the land, including (without prejudice to the foregoing) walls, roadworks, power-lines, telecommunication apparatus, aircraft runways, docks and harbours, railways, inland waterways, pipe-lines, reservoirs, water-mains, wells, sewers, industrial plant and installations for purposes of land drainage, coast protection or defence;

(c) installation in any building or structure of systems of heating, lighting, air-conditioning, ventilation, power supply, drainage, sanitation, water supply or fire protection;

(d) internal cleaning of buildings and structures, so far as carried out in the course of their construction, alteration, repair, extension or restoration;

(e) operations which form an integral part of, or are preparatory to, or are for rendering complete, such operations as are previously described in this subsection, including site clearance, earth-moving, excavation, tunnelling and boring, laying of foundations, erection of scaffolding, site restoration, landscaping and the provision of roadways and other access works;

(f) painting or decorating the internal or external surfaces of any building or structure.

(3) The following operations are not construction operations for the purposes of this Chapter—

(a) drilling for, or extraction of, oil or natural gas;

(b) extraction (whether by underground or surface working) of minerals; tunnelling or boring, or construction of underground works, for this purpose;

(c) manufacture of building or engineering components or equipment, materials, plant or machinery, or delivery of any of these things to site;

(d) manufacture of components for systems of heating, lighting, air-conditioning, ventilation, power supply, drainage, sanitation, water supply or fire protection, or delivery of any of these things to site;

(e) the professional work of architects or surveyors, or of consultants in building, engineering, interior or exterior decoration or in the laying-out of landscape;

(f) the making, installation and repair of artistic works, being sculptures, murals and other works which are wholly artistic in nature;

(g) signwriting and erecting, installing and repairing signboards and advertisements;

(h) the installation of seating, blinds and shutters;

(j) the installation of security systems, including burglar alarms, closed circuit television and public address systems.

(4) In this section "offshore installations" means installations which are maintained, or are intended to be established, for underwater exploitation or exploration to which the Mineral Workings (Offshore Installations) Act 1971 applies.

1971 c. 61.

(5) The Treasury may by order—

(a) include in subsection (2) above any description of operations as to which they are satisfied that it is a normal activity of the construction industry and that its inclusion in that subsection is necessary for achieving the object of section 559;

(b) include in subsection (3) above any description of operations as to which they are satisfied that it cannot properly be considered a normal activity of the construction industry and ought to be excluded from subsection (2) above.

(6) An order under subsection (5) above shall not have effect unless a draft of the instrument containing it has been laid before and approved by a resolution of the House of Commons.

CHAPTER V

SCHEMES FOR RATIONALIZING INDUSTRY

Deductions from profits of contributions paid under certified schemes.

568.—(1) Notwithstanding anything contained in section 74 but subject to the following provisions of this Chapter, where a person pays, wholly and exclusively for the purposes of a trade in respect of which he is chargeable under Case I of Schedule D, a contribution in furtherance of a scheme which is for the time being certified by the Secretary of State under this section, the contribution shall, in so far as it is paid in furtherance of the primary object of the scheme, be allowed to be deducted as an expense in computing the profits or gains of that trade.

(2) The Secretary of State shall certify a scheme under this section if he is satisfied—

   (a) that the primary object of the scheme is the elimination of redundant works or machinery or plant from use in an industry in the United Kingdom; and

   (b) that the scheme is in the national interest and in the interests of that industry as a whole; and

   (c) that such number of persons engaged in that industry as are substantially representative of the industry are liable to pay contributions in furtherance of the primary object of the scheme by agreement between them and the body of persons carrying out the scheme.

References in this subsection to an industry in the United Kingdom shall include references to the business carried on by owners of ships or of a particular class of ships, wherever that business is carried on, and, in relation to that business, references in this subsection to works or machinery or plant shall include references to ships.

(3) The Secretary of State shall cancel any certificate granted under this section if he ceases to be satisfied as to any of the matters referred to in subsection (2) above.

(4) The Secretary of State may at any time require the body of persons carrying out a scheme certified under this section to produce any books or documents of whatever nature relating to the scheme and, if the requirement is not complied with, he may cancel the certificate.

(5) In this section and in section 569 "contribution", in relation to a scheme, does not include a sum paid by a person by way of loan or subscription of share capital, or in consideration of the transfer of assets to him, or by way of a penalty for contravening or failing to comply with the scheme.

Repayment of contributions.

569.—(1) In the event of the repayment, whether directly or by way of distribution of assets on a winding up or otherwise, of a contribution or any part of a contribution which has been allowed to be deducted under section 568, the deduction of the contribution, or so much of it as has been repaid, shall be deemed to be an unauthorised deduction in respect of which an assessment shall be made, and, notwithstanding the provisions of the Tax Acts requiring assessments to be made within six years after the end of the chargeable period to which they relate, any such assessment and any consequential assessment may be made at any time within three years after the end of the chargeable period in which the repayment was made.

(2) For the purposes of this section, a sum received by any person by way of repayment of contributions shall be deemed to be by way of repayment of the last contribution paid by him, and, if the sum exceeds the amount of that contribution, by way of repayment of the penultimate contribution so paid, and so on.

570.—(1) Subject to the provisions of this section, where, under any scheme which is for the time being certified or has at any time been certified by the Secretary of State under section 568, any payment (not being a payment made by way of repayment of contributions) is made to a person carrying on a trade to which the scheme relates, that payment shall be treated for the purposes of the Tax Acts as a trading receipt of the trade, and shall accordingly be taken into account in computing the profits or gains of the trade for those purposes.

(2) Where on a claim it is shown in accordance with the provisions of Part II of Schedule 21 that the payments which have been made under such a scheme in respect of a trade (not being payments made by way of repayment of contributions) have been made wholly or partly in respect of damage in respect of which no relief may be given under the Tax Acts, then, subject to and in accordance with the provisions of that Schedule—

(a) relief shall be given in respect of those payments by reducing the amounts which are to be treated as trading receipts of the trade under subsection (1) above; but

(b) where such relief is given, section 568 shall, in relation to contributions subsequently paid under the scheme in respect of the trade, have effect subject to the modifications specified in Part III of that Schedule.

(3) The provisions of this section and Schedule 21 shall apply in relation to any payment made to a person who has ceased to carry on a trade to which any such scheme as is mentioned in subsection (1) above relates as they apply in relation to payments made to a person carrying on such a trade, subject to the modification that so much of that payment as falls to be treated as a trading receipt by virtue of those provisions shall be deemed for the purposes of those provisions to have been made to him on the last day on which he was engaged in carrying on the trade.

(4) In determining for the purposes of this section and of Schedule 21—

(a) whether any trade has ceased to be carried on; or

(b) whether any contribution is paid in respect of a trade in respect of which a payment has been made; or

(c) whether any payment is made in respect of a trade in respect of which a contribution has been paid, no regard shall be had to any event which, by virtue of any of the provisions of section 113 or section 337(1), is to be treated as effecting a discontinuance of a trade.

Cancellation of certificates.

571.—(1) Where any certificate granted with respect to a scheme under section 568 is cancelled by the Secretary of State, and any deductible contributions paid in furtherance of the scheme have not been repaid at the expiration of one year from the cancellation, the body of persons carrying out the scheme shall, for the chargeable period in which that year expires, be charged to tax under Case VI of Schedule D upon the aggregate amount of the deductible contributions which have not been repaid at that time.

(2) The charge to tax under subsection (1) above shall not be made if the total amount of any contributions, other than deductible contributions, which have been paid under the scheme and have not been repaid before that time is greater than the available resources of the scheme, and shall not in any case be made upon an amount greater than the excess, if any, of those resources over that total amount.

(3) In subsection (2) above "the available resources", in relation to any scheme, means a sum representing the total funds held for the purposes of the scheme at the expiration of one year from the cancellation of the certificate plus a sum representing any funds held for the purposes of the scheme which, during that year, have been applied otherwise than in accordance with the provisions of the scheme as in force when the certificate was granted.

(4) Where the body of persons carrying out a scheme are charged to tax by virtue of subsection (1) above, and, after the expiration of one year from the cancellation of the certificate, any deductible contribution paid in furtherance of the scheme is repaid, the amount upon which the charge is made shall on the making of a claim be reduced by the amount repaid, and all such repayments of tax shall be made as are necessary to give effect to the provisions of this subsection.

(5) In this section "contribution" includes a part of a contribution, and "deductible contribution" means a contribution allowed to be deducted under section 568, any reduction under Part III of Schedule 21 being left out of account.

(6) For the purposes of this section, a sum received by any person by way of repayment of contributions shall be deemed to be by way of repayment of the last contribution paid by him, and, if the sum exceeds the amount of that contribution, by way of repayment of the penultimate contribution so paid, and so on.

Application to statutory redundancy schemes.

572.—(1) Sections 569 to 571 and Schedule 21 shall, subject to the adaptations specified in subsection (2) below, apply in relation to a statutory redundancy scheme as they apply in relation to a scheme certified under section 568.

(2) The adaptations referred to above are as follows, that is to say—

(a) for any reference to a contribution allowed to be deducted under section 568 there shall be substituted a reference to a contribution allowed to be deducted under any provision of the Tax Acts other than that section;

(b) any provision that section 568 shall, in relation to contributions, have effect subject to modifications, shall be construed as a provision that so much of any provision of the Tax Acts other than that section as authorises the deduction of contributions shall, in relation to the contributions in question, have effect subject to the modifications in question;

(c) for any reference to the cancellation of a certificate with respect to a scheme there shall be substituted a reference to the scheme ceasing to have effect; and

(d) for any reference to the provisions of the scheme as in force when the certificate was granted there shall be substituted a reference to the provisions of the scheme as in force when the contributions were first paid thereunder.

(3) In this section "statutory redundancy scheme" means a scheme for the elimination or reduction of redundant works, machinery or plant, or for other similar purposes, to which effect is given by or under any Act, whether passed before or after this Act.

CHAPTER VI

OTHER PROVISIONS

Relief for losses on unquoted shares in trading companies

573.—(1) Subsection (2) below has effect where a company which has subscribed for shares in a qualifying trading company incurs an allowable loss (for the purpose of corporation tax on chargeable gains) on the disposal of the shares in any accounting period and the company disposing of the shares—

(a) is an investment company on the date of the disposal and either—

(i) has been an investment company for a continuous period of six years ending on that date; or

(ii) has been an investment company for a shorter continuous period ending on that date and has not before the beginning of that period been a trading company or an excluded company; and

(b) was not associated with, or a member of the same group as, the qualifying trading company at any time in the period beginning with the date when it subscribed for the shares and ending with the date of the disposal.

(2) The company disposing of the shares may, within two years after the end of the accounting period in which the loss was incurred, make a claim requiring that the loss be set off for the purposes of corporation tax against income—

(a) of that accounting period; and

(b) if the company was then an investment company and the claim so requires, of preceding accounting periods ending within the time specified in subsection (3) below;

and, subject to any relief for an earlier loss, the income of any of those periods shall then be treated as reduced by the amount of the loss or by so much of it as cannot be relieved under this subsection against income of a later accounting period.

(3) The time referred to in subsection (2) above is the period of 12 months ending immediately before the accounting period in which the loss is incurred; but the amount of the reduction which may be made under that subsection in the income of an accounting period falling partly before that time shall not exceed a part of that income proportionate to the part of the accounting period falling within that time.

(4) Relief under subsection (2) above shall be given before any deduction for charges on income, expenses of management or other amounts which can be deducted from or set against or treated as reducing profits of any description; and where relief is given under that subsection in respect of the amount of a loss no deduction shall be made in respect of that amount for the purposes of corporation tax on chargeable gains.

(5) For the purposes of subsection (1)(b) above companies are associated with each other if one controls the other or both are under the control of the same person or persons; and section 416(2) to (6) shall apply for the purposes of this subsection.

(6) For the purposes of this section a company subscribes for shares in another company if they are issued to it by that other company in consideration of money or money's worth.

Relief for individuals.

574.—(1) Where an individual who has subscribed for shares in a qualifying trading company incurs an allowable loss (for capital gains tax purposes) on the disposal of the shares in any year of assessment, he may, by notice given within two years after that year, make a claim for relief from income tax on an amount of his income equal to the amount of the loss; and where such relief is given in respect of the amount of a loss no deduction shall be made in respect of that amount under the 1979 Act.

(2) The following provisions shall have effect as respects relief under this section—

    (a) relief may, by notice given within two years after a year of assessment, be claimed for that year in respect of a loss incurred in the preceding year of assessment so far as relief under this section in respect of that loss has not already been given in that year, and relief claimed by virtue of this paragraph shall be given in priority to any relief in respect of a loss incurred in the year for which the relief is claimed;

    (b) a claim for relief may require it to be given only by reference to the income of the individual without extending to the income of his spouse;

    (c) subject to paragraph (b) above, relief shall be given by treating the loss as reducing first the earned income of the individual, then his other income, then the earned income of his spouse and then his spouse's other income;

    (d) the relief shall be given in priority to relief under section 380 or 381.

(3) For the purposes of this section—

   (a) an individual subscribes for shares if they are issued to him by the company in consideration of money or money's worth; and

   (b) an individual shall be treated as having subscribed for shares if his spouse did so and transferred them to him by a transaction inter vivos.

575.—(1) Sections 573 and 574 do not apply unless the disposal is—

   (a) by way of a bargain made at arm's length for full consideration; or

   (b) by way of a distribution in the course of dissolving or winding up the company; or

   (c) a deemed disposal under section 22(2) of the 1979 Act (claim that value of asset has become negligible).

Exclusion of relief under section 573 or 574 in certain cases.

(2) Where a person disposes of shares ("the new shares") which by virtue of section 78 of the 1979 Act (reorganisation etc. treated as not involving disposal) are identified with other shares ("the old shares") previously held by him, relief shall not be given under section 573 or 574 on the disposal of the new shares unless—

   (a) relief under section 573 or 574 could (or if this section had been in force could) have been given on a disposal of the old shares if he had incurred an allowable loss in disposing of them as mentioned in subsection (1)(a) above on the occasion of the disposal that would have occurred but for section 78 of the 1979 Act; or

   (b) he gave new consideration for the new shares;

but in a case within paragraph (b) above the amount of relief under section 573 or 574 on the disposal of the new shares shall not exceed the amount or value of the new consideration taken into account as a deduction in computing the loss incurred on their disposal.

(3) Where the shares are the subject of an exchange or arrangement of the kind mentioned in section 85 or 86 of the 1979 Act (company reconstructions etc.) which by reason of section 87 of that Act involves a disposal of the shares, section 573 or 574 shall not apply to any allowable loss incurred on the disposal.

576.—(1) Where a person holds shares in a company which constitute a holding and comprise—

   (a) shares for which he has subscribed ("qualifying shares"); and

   (b) shares which he has acquired otherwise than by subscription,

Provisions supplementary to sections 573 to 575.

any question whether a disposal by him of shares forming part of the holding is of qualifying shares shall be determined by treating that and any previous disposal by him out of the holding as relating to shares acquired later rather than earlier; and if a disposal by him is of qualifying shares forming part of a holding and he makes a claim under section 573 or 574 in respect of a loss incurred on their disposal, the amount of relief under that section on the disposal shall not exceed the sums that would be allowed as deductions in computing the loss if the shares had not been part of the holding.

(2) Where a claim is made under section 573 or 574 in respect of a loss accruing on the disposal of shares, section 26 of the 1979 Act (value-shifting) shall have effect in relation to the disposal as if for the references in subsections (1)(b) and (4) to a tax-free benefit there were substituted references to any benefit whether tax-free or not.

(3) There shall be made all such adjustments of corporation tax on chargeable gains or capital gains tax, whether by way of assessment or by way of discharge or repayment of tax, as may be required in consequence of relief being given under section 573 or 574 in respect of an allowable loss or in consequence of the whole or part of such a loss in respect of which a claim is made not being relieved under that section.

(4) For the purposes of sections 573 to 575 and this section a qualifying trading company is a company none of whose shares have at any time in the relevant period been quoted on a recognised stock exchange and which—

(a) either—

(i) is a trading company on the date of the disposal; or

(ii) has ceased to be a trading company at a time which is not more than three years before that date and has not since that time been an excluded company or an investment company; and

(b) either—

(i) has been a trading company for a continuous period of six years ending on that date or at that time; or

(ii) has been a trading company for a shorter continuous period ending on that date or at that time and has not before the beginning of that period been an excluded company or an investment company; and

(c) has been resident in the United Kingdom throughout the period from its incorporation until that date.

(5) In sections 573 to 575 and this section—

"excluded company" means a company—

(a) which has a trade which consists wholly or mainly of dealing in shares, securities, land, trades or commodity futures or is not carried on on a commercial basis and in such a way that profits in the trade can reasonably be expected to be realised; or

(b) which is the holding company of a group other than a trading group; or

(c) which is a building society or a registered industrial and provident society as defined in section 486(12);

"group" means a company which has one or more 51 per cent. subsidiaries together with that or those subsidiaries;

"holding" means a holding within the meaning of section 65 of the 1979 Act;

"holding company" means a company whose business consists wholly or mainly in the holding of shares or securities of one or more companies which are its 51 per cent. subsidiaries;

"investment company" has the meaning given by section 130 except that it does not include the holding company of a trading group;

"new consideration" means consideration in money or money's worth other than consideration of the kind excluded by the first proviso to section 79(1) of the 1979 Act;

"relevant period" means the period ending with the date on which the shares in question are disposed of and beginning with the incorporation of the company, or, if later, one year before the date on which the shares were subscribed for;

"shares" includes stock but except in the definition of "excluded company" does not include shares or stock not forming part of a company's ordinary share capital;

"spouse" refers to one of two spouses who are living together (construed in accordance with section 155(2) of the 1979 Act);

"trading company" means a company other than an excluded company which is—

> (a) a trading company within the meaning of paragraph 7 of Schedule 19; or

> (b) the holding company of a trading group;

"trading group" means a group the business of whose members, taken together, consists wholly or mainly in the carrying on of a trade or trades, but for the purposes of this definition any trade carried on by a subsidiary which is an excluded company or not resident in the United Kingdom shall be treated as not consituting a trade.

Miscellaneous

577.—(1) Subject to the provisions of this section—

Business entertaining expenses.

> (a) no deduction shall be made in computing profits or gains chargeable to tax under Schedule A or Schedule D for any expenses incurred in providing business entertainment, and such expenses shall not be included in computing any expenses of management in respect of which relief may be given under the Tax Acts;

> (b) no deduction for expenses so incurred shall be made from emoluments chargeable to tax under Schedule E; and

> (c) for the purposes of Chapter II of Part I of the 1968 Act and Chapter I of Part III of the Finance Act 1971, the use of any asset for providing business entertainment shall be treated as use otherwise than for the purposes of trade.

1971 c. 68.

(2) Subsection (1) above shall not apply to expenses incurred in, or the use of an asset for, the provision by a person carrying on a trade in the United Kingdom ("a United Kingdom trader"), or by a member of his staff, of entertainment for an overseas customer of that person, being entertainment of a kind and on a scale which is reasonable having regard to all the circumstances.

(3) The expenses to which paragraph (a) of subsection (1) above applies include, in the case of any person, any sums paid by him to, or on behalf of, or placed by him at the disposal of a member of his staff exclusively for the purpose of defraying expenses incurred or to be incurred by him in providing business entertainment, but where—

(a) any such sum falls to be included in his emoluments chargeable to tax under Schedule E; and

(b) the deduction or inclusion of that sum as mentioned in that paragraph falls to be disallowed in whole or in part by virtue of this section;

paragraph (b) of that subsection shall not preclude the deduction of any expenses defrayed out of that sum.

(4) Where by virtue of subsection (2) above a person claims to deduct or include any expenses as mentioned in paragraph (a) or (b) of subsection (1) above or claims any allowance under the provisions mentioned in paragraph (c) of that subsection he shall, if the inspector so requires, furnish particulars of the entertainment in question and of the person for whom it was provided.

(5) For the purposes of this section "business entertainment" means entertainment (including hospitality of any kind) provided by a person, or by a member of his staff, in connection with a trade carried on by that person, but does not include anything provided by him for bona fide members of his staff unless its provision for them is incidental to its provision also for others.

(6) For the purposes of this section "overseas customer" means, in relation to any United Kingdom trader—

(a) any person who is not ordinarily resident nor carrying on a trade in the United Kingdom and avails himself, or may be expected to avail himself, in the course of a trade carried on by him outside the United Kingdom, of any goods, services or facilities which it is the trade of the United Kingdom trader to provide; and

(b) any person who is not ordinarily resident in the United Kingdom and is acting, in relation to such goods, services or facilities, on behalf of an overseas customer within paragraph (a) above or on behalf of any government or public authority of a country outside the United Kingdom.

(7) In this section—

(a) any reference to expenses incurred in, or to the use of an asset for, providing entertainment includes a reference to expenses incurred in, or to the use of an asset for, providing anything incidental thereto;

(b) references to a trade include references to any business, profession or vocation; and

(c) references to the members of a person's staff are references to persons employed by that person, directors of a company or persons engaged in the management of a company being for this purpose deemed to be persons employed by it.

(8) This section shall apply in relation to the provision of a gift as it applies in relation to the provision of entertainment, except that it shall not by virtue of this subsection apply in relation to the provision for any person of a gift consisting of an article incorporating a conspicuous advertisement for the donor, being an article—

(a) which is not food, drink, tobacco or a token or voucher exchangeable for goods; and

(b) the cost of which to the donor, taken together with the cost to him of any other such articles given by him to that person in the same year, does not exceed £10.

(9) Subsection (8) above shall not preclude the deduction, in computing profits or gains under Case I or II of Schedule D, of expenditure incurred in making a gift to a body of persons or trust established for charitable purposes only; and for the purposes of this subsection the Historic Buildings and Monuments Commission for England and the Trustees of the National Heritage Memorial Fund shall each be treated as such a body of persons.

(10) Nothing in this section shall be taken as precluding the deduction of expenses incurred in, or any claim for capital allowances in respect of the use of an asset for, the provision by any person of anything which it is his trade to provide, and which is provided by him in the ordinary course of that trade for payment or, with the object of advertising to the public generally, gratuitously.

578.—(1) Where, under any enactment relating to the giving of financial assistance for the provision, maintenance or improvement of housing accommodation or other residential accommodation, a payment is made to a person by way of grant or other contribution towards expenses incurred, or to be incurred, by that or any other person, the payment shall not be treated as a receipt in computing income for any tax purpose.

Housing grants.

(2) Subsection (1) above shall not apply to a payment in so far as it is made in respect of an expense giving rise to a deduction in computing income for any tax purpose.

579.—(1) Any redundancy payment, and the corresponding amount of any other employer's payment, shall be exempt from income tax under Schedule E.

Statutory redundancy payments.

(2) Where a redundancy payment or other employer's payment is made in respect of employment wholly in a trade, profession or vocation carried on by the employer, and within the charge to tax, the amount of the redundancy payment or the corresponding amount of the other employer's payment shall (if not otherwise so allowable) be allowable as a deduction in computing for the purposes of Schedule D the profits or gains or losses of the trade, profession or vocation, but—

(a) if it is so allowed by virtue of this section the amount of the rebate recoverable shall (if it is not otherwise to be so treated) be treated as a receipt to be brought into account in computing those profits or gains; and

(b) if the employer's payment was made after the discontinuance of the trade, profession or vocation the net amount so deductible shall be treated as if it were a payment made on the last day on which the trade, profession or vocation was carried on.

(3) Where a redundancy payment or other employer's payment is made in respect of employment wholly in a business carried on by the employer and expenses of management of the business are eligible for relief under section 75 or 76—

(a) the amount by which the redundancy payment, or the corresponding amount of the other employer's payment, exceeds the recoverable rebate shall (if not otherwise so allowable) be allowable as expenses of management eligible for relief under that section, and

(b) if the employer's payment was made after the discontinuance of the business the net amount so allowable shall be treated as if it were expenses of management incurred on the last day on which the business was carried on.

(4) Where a redundancy payment or other employer's payment is made in respect of employment wholly in maintaining or managing property the expenses of maintaining or managing which were eligible for relief under the provisions of section 25(1) or 28—

(a) the amount by which the redundancy payment or the corresponding amount of the other employer's payment exceeds the recoverable rebate shall (if not otherwise allowable under those provisions) be treated for the purposes of those provisions as a payment made by the employer in respect of the maintenance or management of the property, or of such part of it as he may elect; and

(b) if the employer's payment was made after the latest time when it could be taken into account for the purposes of relief under those provisions as a payment in respect of the maintenance or management of the property or any part of it, it shall be treated as having been made at that time.

(5) Relief shall not be given under subsections (2), (3) and (4) above, or otherwise, more than once in respect of any employer's payment, and if the employee was being employed in such a way that different parts of his remuneration fell for tax purposes to be treated in different ways—

(a) the amount by which the redundancy payment or the corresponding amount of the other employer's payment exceeds the recoverable rebate shall be apportioned to the different capacities in which the employee was employed; and

(b) subsections (2), (3) and (4) above shall apply separately to the employment in those capacities, and by reference to the apportioned part of that amount, instead of by reference to the full amount of the employer's payment, and the full amount of the rebate.

(6) Where the Minister pays a sum under section 106 of the Employment Protection (Consolidation) Act 1978 or section 42 of the Contracts of Employment and Redundancy Payments Act (Northern Ireland) 1965 in respect of an employer's payment this section shall apply as if—

(a) that sum had been paid on account of that redundancy or other employer's payment, and

(b) so far as the employer has reimbursed the Minister, it had been so paid by the employer.

580.—(1) In section 579—

(a) "redundancy payment", "employer's payment" and "rebate" have the same meaning as in the Employment Protection (Consolidation) Act 1978 ("the 1978 Act") or Part III of the Contracts of Employment and Redundancy Payments Act (Northern Ireland) 1965 ("the 1965 Act");

(b) references to the corresponding amount of an employer's payment (other than a redundancy payment) are references to the amount of that employer's payment so far as not in excess of the amount of the relevant redundancy payment (and so that, where in consequence of section 104(2) of the 1978 Act or section 40(2) of the 1965 Act there is no relevant redundancy payment, the corresponding amount of an employer's payment is nil);

(c) "the Minister" in relation to the 1978 Act means the Secretary of State and in relation to the 1965 Act means the Department of Health and Social Services.

(2) For the purposes of subsection (1) above "relevant redundancy payment" shall be construed in accordance with paragraph 8 of Schedule 6 to the 1978 Act or paragraph 8 of Schedule 6 to the 1965 Act.

(3) In section 579(1) the reference to tax under Schedule E does not include a reference to tax under section 148 and accordingly payments exempted by section 579(1) may be taken into account under section 148.

581.—(1) If the Treasury direct that this section shall apply to any securities issued by a local authority and expressed in a currency other than sterling, interest on those securities—

(a) shall be paid without deduction of income tax, and

(b) so long as the beneficial owner is not resident in the United Kingdom, shall be exempt from income tax (but not corporation tax).

(2) Where for repayment of the principal amount due under the securities there is an option between sterling and one or more currencies other than sterling, that subsection shall be applicable to the securities if the option is exercisable only by the holder of the securities, and shall not be applicable to the securities in any other case.

(3) Where any income of any person is by virtue of any provision of the Income Tax Acts to be deemed to be income of any other person, that income shall not be exempt from tax by virtue of this section by reason of the first-mentioned person not being resident in the United Kingdom.

(4) This section shall have effect in relation to any securities issued by or loan made to a statutory corporation as it has effect in relation to any securities issued by a local authority, the references to the beneficial owner or holder of the securities being for this purpose read, in the case of such a loan, as references to the person for the time being entitled to repayment or eventual repayment of the loan.

(5) In subsection (4) above "statutory corporation" means —

(a) a corporation incorporated by an Act; or

(b) any other corporation, being a corporation to which functions in respect of the carrying on of an undertaking are entrusted by an Act or by an order made under or confirmed by an Act;

1985 c. 6.
S.I. 1986/1032
(N.I. 6).

but, save as is provided by paragraph (b) above, does not include any company within the meaning of the Companies Act 1985 or the Companies (Northern Ireland) Order 1986.

1947 c. 14.

(6) In relation to securities issued before 6th April 1982 subsections (1) and (2) above shall have effect with the substitution for references to sterling of references to a currency of a country which at the time of the issue was specified in Schedule 1 to the Exchange Control Act 1947.

Funding bonds issued in respect of interest on certain debts.

582.—(1) Where any funding bonds are issued to a creditor in respect of any liability to pay interest on any debt to which this section applies—

(a) the issue of the bonds shall be treated for all the purposes of the Tax Acts as if it were the payment of an amount of that interest equal to the value of the bonds at the time of their issue, and

(b) the redemption of the bonds shall not be treated for those purposes as the payment of any amount of that interest.

(2) Where an issue of bonds is treated by virtue of subsection (1) above as if it were the payment of an amount of interest, and any person by or through whom the bonds are issued would be required by virtue of any provision of the Tax Acts to deduct income tax from that amount of interest if it had been actually paid by or through him, the following provisions shall have effect—

(a) subject to paragraph (b) below, any such person—

(i) shall retain bonds the value of which at the time of their issue is equal to income tax on that amount of interest at the basic rate for the year of assessment in which the bonds are issued, and

(ii) shall be acquitted in respect of any such retention in the same way as if he had deducted such tax from the interest, and

(iii) shall be chargeable with that tax accordingly, but may tender the bonds retained in satisfaction thereof;

(b) where the Board are satisfied that it is impracticable to retain bonds on account of income tax under paragraph (a) above—

(i) they may relieve any such person from the obligation to retain bonds and account for income tax under that paragraph, on his furnishing to them a statement of the names and addresses of the persons to whom the bonds have been issued and the amount of the bonds issued to each such person; and

(ii) tax in respect of the amount of interest treated by virtue of this section as having been paid by the issue of the bonds shall be charged under Case VI of Schedule D for the chargeable period in which the bonds are issued on the persons receiving or entitled to the bonds.

(3) This section applies to any debt incurred, whether in respect of any money borrowed or otherwise, by any government, public authority or public institution whatsoever, or by any body corporate whatsoever.

(4) For the purposes of this section "funding bonds" includes any bonds, stocks, shares, securities or certificates of indebtedness.

583. A person not resident in the United Kingdom shall not be liable to income tax in respect of income from any security issued by the Inter-American Development Bank if he would not be liable but for the fact that—

Inter-American Development Bank.

(a) the security or income is issued, made payable or paid in the United Kingdom or in sterling; or

(b) the Bank maintains an office or other place of business in the United Kingdom.

584.—(1) Where a person is chargeable to tax by reference to the amount of any income arising in a territory outside the United Kingdom ("overseas income"), then for the purposes of tax this section shall apply to the overseas income in so far as—

Relief for unremittable overseas income

(a) he is prevented from transferring the amount of the overseas income to the United Kingdom, either by the laws of that territory or any executive action of its government or by the impossibility of obtaining foreign currency in that territory; and

(b) he has not realised the overseas income outside that territory for a consideration in sterling or a consideration in some other currency which he is not prevented from transferring to the United Kingdom.

Overseas income to which this section applies is referred to below as unremittable.

(2) Subject to subsection (3) below, where a person so chargeable gives notice of his desire to be assessed in accordance with this subsection, then, in the first instance, account shall not be taken of the overseas income to the extent to which he shows to the satisfaction of the Board that the following conditions are satisfied with respect to it, that is to say—

(a) that it is unremittable; and

(b) that subsection (1)(a) above would continue to apply notwithstanding any reasonable endeavours on his part, and tax shall be assessed and charged on all persons concerned and for all periods accordingly; but, on the Board ceasing, as respects any part of the income, to be satisfied that those conditions are satisfied, such assessments, reductions of assessments and repayments of tax shall be made as may be necessary to take account of it, and of any tax payable in respect of it under the law of the territory where it arises, according to their value at the date when, in the opinion of the Board, those conditions cease to be satisfied with respect to it, and may be so made at any time not later than six years after that date.

(3) Where the tax chargeable is corporation tax, subsection (2) above shall have effect as if—

    (a) for the word "assessed" in the second place where it occurs, there were substituted "assessable";

    (b) for the words from "on the Board ceasing" to "take account" there were substituted "on the said conditions ceasing to be satisfied as respects any part of the income, it shall be treated as income arising on the date when those conditions cease to be satisfied with respect to it and account shall be taken"; and

    (c) for the words from "the date" onwards there were substituted "that date".

(4) Where a company becomes chargeable to corporation tax in respect of income from any source by virtue of subsections (2) and (3) above after it has ceased to possess that source of income, the income shall be chargeable under Case VI of Schedule D.

(5) Where under an agreement entered into under arrangements made by the Secretary of State in pursuance of section 11 of the Export Guarantees and Overseas Investment Act 1978 any payment is made by the Export Credit Guarantee Department in respect of any income which cannot be transferred to the United Kingdom, then, to the extent of the payment, the income shall be treated as income with respect to which the conditions mentioned in subsection (2) above are not satisfied (and accordingly cannot cease to be satisfied).

(6) Any notice under subsection (2) above shall be delivered to the inspector before an assessment made by reference to that income otherwise than in accordance with that subsection has become final and conclusive; and there shall be made all such assessments, reductions of assessments or repayments of tax as may be required by reason of any such notice.

(7) In the case of the death of a person who, if he had not died, would, under subsection (2) above, have become chargeable to any income tax, the tax which would have been so chargeable shall be assessed and charged upon his executors or administrators, and shall be a debt due from and payable out of his estate.

(8) Subject to subsections (2) and (3) above, the amount of any unremittable overseas income shall be determined by reference to the generally recognised market value in the United Kingdom (if any), or, in the absence of any such value, according to the official rate of exchange of the territory where the income arises.

(9) Any appeal against an assessment which involves a question as to the operation of this section shall be made to the Special Commissioners and not to the General Commissioners.

(10) This section shall have effect as respects any accounting period in which the conditions in subsection (2) above cease to be satisfied in relation to any income, being an accounting period ending on or before such day, not being earlier than 31st March 1992, as the Treasury may by order appoint for the purposes of this section, with the omission of subsections (3) and (4).

585.—(1) A person charged or chargeable for any year of assessment in respect of income from any source with tax which (apart from this section) falls to be computed under Case IV or V of Schedule D, or under Case III of Schedule E, on the amount of income received in the United Kingdom in the basis year for that year of assessment, may by making a claim require that the following provisions of this section shall apply, on showing that the following conditions are satisfied, that is to say—

  (a) that of the income so received all or part arose before the basis year but he was unable to transfer it to the United Kingdom before that year; and

  (b) subject to subsection (2) below, that that inability was due to the laws of the territory where the income arose, or to executive action of its government, or to the impossibility of obtaining foreign currency in that territory; and

  (c) that the inability was not due to any want of reasonable endeavours on his part.

(2) For the purposes of this section, where in any year of assessment a person is granted a pension or increase of pension retrospectively, the amount paid in respect of any previous year of assessment by virtue of the grant shall be treated as income arising in that previous year, whenever it is paid, and he shall be treated as having possessed the source of income from the time as from which the grant has effect; and subsection (1)(b) above shall not apply in relation to any amount so paid, except as respects the period after it becomes payable.

(3) Where a person claims that the provisions of this section shall apply for any year of assessment as respects the income from any source, then for the purposes of income tax—

  (a) there shall be deducted from the income received in the United Kingdom in the basis year for that year the amount as respects which the conditions in paragraphs (a), (b) and (c) of subsection (1) above are satisfied, so far as applicable; but

  (b) the part (if any) of that amount arising in each previous year of assessment shall be treated as if it were income received in the United Kingdom in the basis year for that previous year.

(4) Nothing in this section shall alter the year which is to be taken as the basis year for computing tax chargeable for any year of assessment under Case IV or V of Schedule D, and where under subsection (3)(b) above income is treated as received in the United Kingdom in a year which is the basis year for two years of assessment, it shall not by reason thereof be taken into account except in the year in which it arose.

(5) Where—

(a) a person makes a claim under this section for any year of assessment as respects income from any source chargeable under Case IV or V of Schedule D, and

(b) that year is the basis year for computing the tax with which he is chargeable on the income from that source both for that and for the succeeding year of assessment,

tax shall not be chargeable for either of those years of assessment on the amount referred to in paragraph (a) of subsection (3) above (without however being charged a second time by virtue of paragraph (b) of that subsection).

(6) No claim under this section shall be made in respect of any income more than six years after the end of the year of assessment in which the income is received in the United Kingdom.

(7) There shall be made all such adjustments, whether by way of repayment of tax, assessment or otherwise, as may be necessary to give effect to this section, and notwithstanding anything in the Income Tax Acts, any adjustment to give effect to a claim under this section may be made at any time.

(8) A person's executors or administrators may make any claim under this section which he might have made, if he had not died, and after a person's death—

(a) any tax paid by him and repayable by virtue of a claim under this section (whoever made the claim) shall be repaid to his executors or administrators; and

(b) any additional tax chargeable by virtue of such a claim shall be assessed and charged upon his executors or administrators and shall be a debt due from and payable out of his estate.

(9) In this section "basis year" means—

(a) in relation to tax chargeable for any year of assessment under Case IV or V of Schedule D in respect of income from any source, the year by reference to which the amount of the income chargeable finally falls to be computed; and

(b) in relation to tax chargeable for any year of assessment under Case III of Schedule E, that year of assessment;

and any reference in this section to a source of income includes a part of a source.

Disallowance of deductions for war risk premiums.

586.—(1) In computing the amount of the profits or gains of any person for any tax purpose, no sum shall be deducted in respect of any payment made by him to which this section applies.

(2) No payment to which this section applies shall be included in computing the expenses of management in respect of which relief may be given under section 75 or 76.

(3) Subject to subsections (4) and (5) below, this section applies to any payment made by any person under any contract or arrangement under which that person is, in the event of war damage, entitled or eligible, either

absolutely or conditionally, to or for any form of indemnification, PART XIII
whether total or partial, and whether by way of a money payment or not,
in respect of that war damage.

(4) Where the payment is made in respect of the right or eligibility
mentioned in subsection (3) above and also in respect of other matters,
the deduction or inclusion of so much of the payment as is properly
attributable to the other matters shall not be disallowed by virtue only of
subsection (1) or (2) above.

(5) This section shall not apply to any payment made under any
contract of marine insurance, or any contract of insurance of an aircraft,
or any contract of insurance of goods in transit.

(6) In this section "war damage" means loss or damage arising from
action taken by an enemy of Her Majesty, or action taken in combating
such an enemy or in repelling an imagined attack by such an enemy, or
action taken in anticipation of or in consequence of an attack by such an
enemy.

587.—(1) In computing the amount of the profits or gains, or total Disallowance of
income, of any person for any tax purpose, no sum shall be deducted in certain payments
respect of any payment made by him to which this section applies. in respect of war
injuries to
(2) No payment to which this section applies shall be included in employees.
computing—

(a) the expenses of management in respect of which relief may be
given under section 75 or 76; or

(b) the expenses of management or supervision in respect of which
relief may be given under section 121.

(3) Subject to subsections (4) and (5) below, this section applies—

(a) to any payments by way of benefit made by any person to, or to
the personal representatives or dependants of, any employees of
his on account of their incapacity, retirement or death owing to
war injuries, whether sustained in the United Kingdom or
elsewhere; and

(b) to any payments made by any person by way of premium or
contribution under any policy, agreement, scheme or
arrangement providing for the payment of benefits to, or to the
personal representatives or dependants of, any employees of his
on account of their incapacity, retirement or death owing to
such war injuries.

(4) This section shall not apply to any payment (whether by way of
benefit or by way of premium or contribution) which is payable under any
policy, agreement, scheme or arrangement made before 3rd September
1939, except to the extent that the amount of the payment is increased by
any variation of the terms of that policy, agreement, scheme or
arrangement made on or after that date.

(5) This section shall not apply to any payment by way of benefit if, in
the opinion of the Board, that payment was made under an established
practice which was such that the same or a greater payment would have
been made if the incapacity, retirement or death had not been due to war
injuries.

(6) Where a person makes a payment by way of benefit to which this section applies and, in the opinion of the Board, there is an established practice under which a smaller payment would have been made if the incapacity, retirement or death had not been due to war injuries, the deduction or inclusion of an amount equal to that smaller payment shall not be disallowed by virtue only of subsection (1) or (2) above.

(7) Where a person makes a payment to which this section applies by way of premium or contribution, and the policy, agreement, scheme or arrangement provides for the payment of any benefit in the event of incapacity, retirement or death not due to war injuries, the deduction or inclusion of so much of the payment of premium or contribution as, in the opinion of the Board, is properly attributable to benefit payable in the event of incapacity, retirement or death not due to war injuries shall not be disallowed by virtue only of subsection (1) or (2) above.

(8) In this section "war injuries" means physical injuries—

    (a) caused by—

        (i) the discharge of any missile (including liquids and gas);

        (ii) the use of any weapon, explosive or other noxious thing; or

        (iii) the doing of any other injurious act,

    either by the enemy or in combating the enemy or in repelling an imagined attack by the enemy; or

    (b) caused by the impact on any person or property of any enemy aircraft, or any aircraft belonging to, or held by any person on behalf of, or for the benefit of, Her Majesty or any allied power, or any part of, or anything dropped from, any such aircraft.

Training courses for employees.
    588.—(1) Where, on or after 6th April 1987, a person (in this section referred to as the "employer") incurs expenditure in paying or reimbursing relevant expenses incurred in connection with a qualifying course of training which—

    (a) is undertaken by a person (in this section referred to as the "employee") who is the holder or past holder of any office or employment under the employer; and

    (b) is undertaken with a view to retraining the employee,

the employee shall not thereby be regarded as receiving any emolument which forms part of his income for any purpose of Schedule E.

(2) Section 589 shall have effect to determine for the purposes of this section—

    (a) what is a qualifying course of training;

    (b) whether such a course is undertaken by an employee with a view to retraining; and

    (c) what are relevant expenses in relation to such a course.

(3) Subject to subsection (4) below, where—

(a) an employer incurs expenditure in paying or reimbursing relevant expenses as mentioned in subsection (1) above; and

(b) that subsection has effect in relation to the income of the employee for the purposes of Schedule E;

then, if and so far as that expenditure would not, apart from this subsection, be so deductible, it shall be deductible in computing for the purposes of Schedule D the profits or gains of the trade, profession or vocation of the employer for the purposes of which the employee is or was employed.

(4) If the employer carries on a business, the expenses of management of which are eligible for relief under section 75, subsection (3) above shall have effect as if for the words from "in computing" onwards there were substituted "as expenses of management for the purposes of section 75".

(5) In any case where—

(a) an employee's liability to tax for any year of assessment is determined (by assessment or otherwise) on the assumption that subsection (1) above applies in his case and, subsequently, there is a failure to comply with any provision of section 589(3) and (4); or

(b) an employer's liability to tax for any year is determined (by assessment or otherwise) on the assumption that, by virtue only of subsection (3) above (or subsections (3) and (4) above), he is entitled to a deduction on account of any expenditure and, subsequently, there is such a failure as is referred to in paragraph (a) above;

an assessment under section 29(3) of the Management Act of an amount due in consequence of the failure referred to above may be made at any time not later than six years after the end of the chargeable period in which the failure occurred.

(6) Where an event occurs by reason of which there is a failure to comply with any provision of section 589(3) and (4), the employer of the employee concerned shall within 60 days of coming to know of the event give a notice to the inspector containing particulars of the event.

(7) If the inspector has reason to believe that an employer has not given a notice which he is required to give under subsection (6) above in respect of any event, the inspector may by notice require the employer to furnish him within such time (not less that 60 days) as may be specified in the notice with such information relating to the event as the inspector may reasonably require for the purposes of this section.

589.—(1) Subject to subsection (2) below, a course is a qualifying course of training if—

Qualifying courses of training etc.

(a) it provides a course of training designed to impart or improve skills or knowledge relevant to, and intended to be used in the course of, gainful employment (including self-employment) of any description; and

(b) the course is entirely devoted to the teaching or practical application of the skills or knowledge (or to both such teaching and practical application); and

PART XIII

(c) the duration of the course does not exceed one year; and

(d) all teaching and practical application forming part of the course takes place within the United Kingdom.

(2) A course shall not be regarded as a qualifying course of training in relation to a particular employee unless—

(a) he attends the course on a full-time or substantially full-time basis; and

(b) he is employed by the employer full-time throughout the period of two years ending at the time when he begins to undertake the course or, if it is earlier, at the time he ceases to be employed by him; and

(c) the opportunity to undertake the course, on similar terms as to payment or reimbursement of relevant expenses, is available either generally to holders or past holders of offices or employment under the employer or to a particular class or classes of such holders or past holders.

(3) An employee shall not be regarded as undertaking a course with a view to retraining unless—

(a) he begins to undertake the course of training while he is employed by the employer or within the period of one year after he ceases to be so employed; and

(b) he ceases to be employed by the employer not later than the end of the period of two years beginning at the end of the qualifying course of training.

(4) An employee shall not be regarded as having undertaken a course with a view to retraining if, any time within the period of two years beginning at the time when he ceased to be employed as mentioned in subsection (3)(b) above, he is again employed by the employer.

(5) Where an employee undertakes a qualifying course of training, the relevant expenses consist of—

(a) fees for attendance at the course;

(b) fees for any examination which is taken during or at the conclusion of the course;

(c) the cost of any books which are essential for a person attending the course, and

(d) travelling expenses falling within subsection (6) below.

(6) The travelling expenses referred to in subsection (5)(d) above are those which would be deductible under section 198—

(a) on the assumption that attendance at the course is one of the duties of the employee's office or employment; and

(b) if the employee has in fact ceased to be employed by the employer, on the assumption that he continues to be employed by him.

(7) Any reference in this section to an employee being employed by an employer is a reference to the employee holding office or employment under the employer.

PART XIV

PENSION SCHEMES, SOCIAL SECURITY BENEFITS, LIFE
ANNUITIES ETC.

CHAPTER I

RETIREMENT BENEFIT SCHEMES

Approval of schemes

Conditions for
approval of
retirement benefit
schemes.

590.—(1) Subject to section 591, the Board shall not approve any retirement benefits scheme for the purposes of this Chapter unless the scheme satisfies all of the conditions set out in subsection (2) below.

(2) The conditions are—

(a) that the scheme is bona fide established for the sole purpose of providing relevant benefits in respect of service as an employee, being benefits payable to, or to the widow, children or dependants or personal representatives of, the employee;

(b) that the scheme is recognised by the employer and employees to whom it relates, and that every employee who is, or has a right to be, a member of the scheme has been given written particulars of all essential features of the scheme which concern him;

(c) that there is a person resident in the United Kingdom who will be responsible for the discharge of all duties imposed on the administrator of the scheme under this Chapter;

(d) that the employer is a contributor to the scheme;

(e) that the scheme is established in connection with some trade or undertaking carried on in the United Kingdom by a person resident in the United Kingdom;

(f) that in no circumstances, whether during the subsistence of the scheme or later, can any amount be paid by way of repayment of an employee's contributions under the scheme.

(3) Subject to subsection (1) above, the Board shall approve a retirement benefits scheme for the purposes of this Chapter if the scheme satisfies all the conditions of this subsection, that is to say—

(a) that any benefit for an employee is a pension on retirement at a specified age not earlier than 60 or, if the employee is a woman, 55, and not later than 70, which does not exceed one-sixtieth of the employee's final remuneration for each year of service up to a maximum of 40;

(b) that any benefit for any widow of an employee is a pension payable on his death after retirement such that the amount payable to the widow by way of pension does not exceed two-thirds of any pension or pensions payable to the employee;

(c) that no other benefits are payable under the scheme;

(d) that no pension is capable in whole or in part of surrender, commutation or assignment, except in so far as the scheme allows an employee on retirement to obtain, by commutation of his pension, a lump sum or sums not exceeding in all three-eightieths of his final remuneration (disregarding any excess of that remuneration over the permitted maximum) for each year of service up to a maximum of 40.

In paragraph (d) above "the permitted maximum" means £100,000 or such other sum as may for the time being be specified in an order made by the Treasury.

(4) The conditions set out in subsections (2) and (3) above are in this Chapter referred to as "the prescribed conditions".

(5) If in the opinion of the Board the facts concerning any scheme or its administration cease to warrant the continuance of their approval of the scheme, they may at any time by notice to the administrator withdraw their approval on such grounds, and from such date (which shall not be earlier than the date when those facts first ceased to warrant the continuance of their approval or 17th March 1987, whichever is the later), as may be specified in the notice.

(6) Where an alteration has been made in a retirement benefits scheme, no approval given as regards the scheme before the alteration shall apply after the date of the alteration unless the alteration has been approved by the Board.

(7) For the purpose of determining whether a retirement benefits scheme, so far as it relates to a particular class or description of employees, satisfies or continues to satisfy the prescribed conditions—

(a) that scheme shall be considered in conjunction with any other retirement benefits scheme or schemes relating to employees of that class or description, and

(b) if those conditions are satisfied in the case of both or all of those schemes taken together, they shall be taken to be satisfied in the case of each of them, but otherwise those conditions shall be taken to be satisfied in the case of none of them.

591.—(1) The Board may, if they think fit having regard to the facts of a particular case, and subject to such conditions, if any, as they think proper to attach to the approval, approve a retirement benefits scheme for the purposes of this Chapter notwithstanding that it does not satisfy one or more of the prescribed conditions; but this subsection has effect subject to subsection (5) below.

(2) The Board may in particular approve by virtue of this section a scheme—

(a) which exceeds the limits imposed by the prescribed conditions as respects benefits for less than 40 years; or

(b) which provides pensions for the widows of employees on death in service, or for the children or dependants of employees; or

(c) which provides on death in service a lump sum of up to four times the employee's final remuneration (exclusive of any refunds of contributions); or

(d) which allows benefits to be payable on retirement within ten years of the specified age, or on earlier incapacity; or

(e) which provides for the return in certain contingencies of employees' contributions; or

(f) which relates to a trade or undertaking carried on only partly in the United Kingdom and by a person not resident in the United Kingdom; or

(g) which provides in certain contingencies for securing relevant benefits (but no other benefits) by means of an annuity contract approved by the Board and made with an insurance company of the employee's choice; or

(h) to which the employer is not a contributor and which provides benefits additional to those provided by a scheme to which he is a contributor.

(3) In subsection (2)(g) above "insurance company" means a company to which Part II of the Insurance Companies Act 1982 applies.

(4) In applying this section to a scheme which was in existence on 6th April 1980, the Board shall exercise their discretion, in such cases as appear to them to be appropriate, so as to preserve—

(a) benefits earned or rights arising out of service before 6th April 1980; and

(b) any rights to death-in-service benefits conferred by rules of the scheme in force on 26th February 1970.

(5) The Board shall not approve a scheme by virtue of this section if to do so would be inconsistent with regulations made for the purposes of this section.

(6) Regulations made for the purposes of this section may restrict the Board's discretion to approve a scheme by reference to the benefits provided by the scheme, the investments held for the purposes of the scheme, the manner in which the scheme is administered or any other circumstances whatever.

Tax reliefs

Exempt approved schemes.

592.—(1) This section has effect as respects—

(a) any approved scheme which is shown to the satisfaction of the Board to be established under irrevocable trusts; or

(b) any other approved scheme as respects which the Board, having regard to any special circumstances, direct that this section shall apply;

and any scheme which is for the time being within paragraph (a) or (b) above is in this Chapter referred to as an "exempt approved scheme".

(2) Exemption from income tax shall, on a claim being made in that behalf, be allowed in respect of income derived from investments or deposits if, or to such extent as the Board are satisfied that, it is income from investments or deposits held for the purposes of the scheme.

(3) Exemption from income tax shall, on a claim being made in that behalf, be allowed in respect of underwriting commissions if, or to such extent as the Board are satisfied that, the underwriting commissions are applied for the purposes of the schemes and would, but for this subsection, be chargeable to tax under Case VI of Schedule D.

(4) Any sum paid by an employer by way of contribution under the scheme shall, for the purposes of Case I or II of Schedule D and of sections 75 and 76, be allowed to be deducted as an expense, or expense of management, incurred in the chargeable period in which the sum is paid.

(5) The amount of an employer's contributions which may be deducted under subsection (4) above shall not exceed the amount contributed by him under the scheme in respect of employees in a trade or undertaking in respect of the profits of which the employer is assessable to tax (that is to say, to United Kingdom income tax or corporation tax).

(6) A sum not paid by way of ordinary annual contribution shall for the purposes of subsection (4) above be treated, as the Board may direct, either as an expense incurred in the chargeable period in which the sum is paid, or as an expense to be spread over such period of years as the Board think proper.

(7) Any contribution paid under the scheme by an employee shall, in assessing tax under Schedule E, be allowed to be deducted as an expense incurred in the year of assessment in which the contribution is paid.

(8) The amount allowed to be deducted by virtue of subsection (7) above in respect of contributions paid by an employee in a year of assessment (whether under a single scheme or under two or more schemes) shall not exceed 15 per cent., or such higher percentage as the Board may in a particular case prescribe, of his remuneration for that year.

(9) Relief shall not be given under section 266 or 273 in respect of any payment in respect of which an allowance can be made under subsection (7) above.

(10) Subsection (2) of section 468 and subsection (3) of section 469 shall not apply to any authorised unit trust which is also an exempt approved scheme if the employer is not a contributor to the exempt approved scheme and that scheme provides benefits additional to those provided by another exempt approved scheme to which he is a contributor.

(11) Nothing in this section shall be construed as affording relief in respect of any sums to be brought into account under section 438.

(12) This section has effect only as respects income arising or contributions paid at a time when the scheme is an exempt approved scheme.

593.—(1) Relief under section 592(7) shall be given in accordance with subsections (2) and (3) below in such cases and subject to such conditions as the Board may prescribe by regulations under section 612(3) in respect of schemes—

    (a) to which employees, but not their employers, are contributors; and

Relief by way of deductions from contributions.

(b) which provide benefits additional to benefits provided by schemes to which their employers are contributors.

(2) An employee who is entitled to relief under section 592(7) in respect of a contribution may deduct from the contribution when he pays it, and may retain, an amount equal to income tax at the basic rate on the contribution.

(3) The administrator of the scheme—

(a) shall accept the amount paid after the deduction in discharge of the employee's liability to the same extent as if the deduction had not been made; and

(b) may recover an amount equal to the deduction from the Board.

(4) Regulations under subsection (3) of section 612 may, without prejudice to the generality of that subsection—

(a) provide for the manner in which claims for the recovery of a sum under subsection (3)(b) above may be made;

(b) provide for the giving of such information, in such form, as may be prescribed by or under the regulations;

(c) provide for the inspection by persons authorised by the Board of books, documents and other records.

Exempt statutory schemes.

594.—(1) Any contribution paid by any officer or employee under a statutory scheme established under a public general Act shall, in assessing tax under Schedule E, be allowed to be deducted as an expense incurred in the year of assessment in which the contribution is paid; and relief shall not be given under section 266 or 273 in respect of any contribution allowable as a deduction under this section.

(2) The amount allowed to be deducted by virtue of subsection (1) above in respect of contributions paid by a person in a year of assessment (whether under a single scheme or under two or more schemes) shall not exceed 15 per cent., or such higher percentage as the Board may in a particular case prescribe, of his remuneration for that year.

Charge to tax in certain cases

Charge to tax in respect of certain sums paid by employer etc.

595.—(1) Subject to the provisions of this Chapter, where, pursuant to a retirement benefits scheme, the employer in any year of assessment pays a sum with a view to the provision of any relevant benefits for any employee of that employer, then (whether or not the accrual of the benefits is dependent on any contingency)—

(a) the sum paid, if not otherwise chargeable to income tax as income of the employee, shall be deemed for all purposes of the Income Tax Acts to be income of that employee for that year of assessment and assessable to tax under Schedule E; and

(b) where the payment is made under such an insurance or contract as is mentioned in section 266, relief, if not otherwise allowable, shall be given to that employee under that section in respect of the payment to the extent, if any, to which such relief would have been allowable to him if the payment had been made by him and the insurance or contract under which the payment is made had been made with him.

(2) Subject to the provisions of this Chapter, where—

(a) the circumstances in which any relevant benefits under a retirement benefits scheme are to accrue are not such as will render the benefits assessable to income tax under Schedule E as emoluments of the employee in respect of whom the benefits are paid, and

(b) the provision of those benefits is not, or is not fully, secured by the payment of sums by the employer with a view to the provision of those benefits,

then (whether or not the accrual of the benefits is dependent on any contingency) an amount equal to the cost, estimated in accordance with subsection (3) below, of securing the provision by a third person of the benefits or, as the case may be, of the benefits so far as not already secured by the payment of such sums as are mentioned in subsection (1) above, shall be deemed for all purposes of the Income Tax Acts to be income of the employee for the year or years of assessment specified in subsection (3) below and assessable to income tax under Schedule E.

(3) The cost referred to in subsection (2) above shall be estimated either—

(a) as an annual sum payable in each year of assessment in which the scheme in question is in force or the employee is serving, up to and including the year of assessment in which the benefits accrue or there ceases to be any possibility of the accrual thereof, or

(b) as a single sum payable in the year of assessment in which falls the date when the employee acquired the right to the relevant benefits, or the date when he acquired the right to any increase in the relevant benefits;

as may be more appropriate in the circumstances of the case.

(4) Where the employer pays any sum as mentioned in subsection (1) above in relation to more than one employee, the sum so paid shall, for the purpose of that subsection, be apportioned among those employees by reference to the separate sums which would have had to be paid to secure the separate benefits to be provided for them respectively, and the part of the sum apportioned to each of them shall be deemed for that purpose to have been paid separately in relation to that one of them.

(5) Any reference in this section to the provision for an employee of relevant benefits includes a reference to the provision of benefits payable to that employee's wife or widow, children, dependants or personal representatives.

596.—(1) Neither subsection (1) nor subsection (2) of section 595 shall apply where the retirement benefits scheme in question is—

(a) an approved scheme, or

(b) a statutory scheme, or

(c) a scheme set up by a government outside the United Kingdom for the benefit, or primarily for the benefit of, its employees.

(2) Neither subsection (1) nor subsection (2) of section 595 shall apply for any year of assessment—

(a) where the employee performs the duties of his employment in such circumstances that no tax is chargeable under Case I or II of Schedule E in respect of the emoluments of his employment (or would be so chargeable were there such emoluments), or

(b) where the emoluments from the employment are foreign emoluments within the meaning of section 192 and the Board are satisfied, on a claim made by the employee, that the retirement benefits scheme in question corresponds to such a scheme as is mentioned in paragraph (a), (b) or (c) of subsection (1) above.

(3) Where, in respect of the provision for an employee of any relevant benefits—

(a) a sum has been deemed to be income of his by virtue either of subsection (1) or subsection (2) of section 595, and

(b) subsequently, the employee proves to the satisfaction of the Board that—

(i) no payment in respect of, or in substitution for, the benefits has been made, and

(ii) some event has occurred by reason of which no such payment will be made,

and makes application for relief under this subsection within six years from the time when that event occurred,

the Board shall give relief in respect of tax on that sum by repayment or otherwise as may be appropriate; and if the employee satisfies the Board as mentioned above in relation to some particular part, but not the whole, of the benefits, the Board may give such relief as may seem to them just and reasonable.

Charge to tax: pensions.

597.—(1) Subject to subsection (2) below, all pensions paid under any scheme which is approved or is being considered for approval under this Chapter shall be charged to tax under Schedule E, and section 203 shall apply accordingly.

(2) As respects any scheme which is approved or is being considered for approval under this Chapter, the Board may direct that, until such date as the Board may specify, pensions under the scheme shall be charged to tax as annual payments under Case III of Schedule D, and tax shall be deductible under sections 348 and 349 accordingly.

Charge to tax: repayment of employee's contributions.

598.—(1) Subject to the provisions of this section, tax shall be charged under this section on any repayment to an employee during his lifetime of any contributions (including interest on contributions, if any) if the payment is made under—

(a) a scheme which is or has at any time been an exempt approved scheme, or

(b) a statutory scheme established under a public general Act.

(2) Where any payment is chargeable to tax under this section, the administrator of the scheme shall be charged to income tax under Case VI of Schedule D and, subject to subsection (3) below, the rate of tax shall be 10 per cent.

(3) The Treasury may by order from time to time increase or decrease the rate of tax under subsection (2) above.

(4) The tax shall be charged on the amount paid or, if the rules permit the administrator to deduct the tax before payment, on the amount before deduction of tax, and the amount so charged to tax shall not be treated as income for any other purpose of the Tax Acts.

(5) Subsection (1)(a) above shall not apply in relation to a contribution made after the scheme ceases to be an exempt approved scheme (unless it again becomes an exempt approved scheme).

(6) This section shall not apply where the employee's employment was carried on outside the United Kingdom.

(7) In relation to a statutory scheme, "employee" in this section includes any officer.

599.—(1) Where a scheme to which this section applies contains a rule allowing, in special circumstances, a payment in commutation of an employee's entire pension, and any pension is commuted, whether wholly or not, under the rule, tax shall be charged on the amount by which the sum receivable exceeds—

Charge to tax: commutation of entire pension in special circumstances.

(a) the largest sum which would have been receivable in commutation of any part of the pension if the scheme had secured that the aggregate value of the relevant benefits payable to an employee on or after retirement, excluding any pension which was not commutable, could not exceed three-eightieths of his final remuneration (disregarding any excess of that remuneration over the permitted maximum) for each year of service up to a maximim of 40; or

(b) the largest sum which would have been receivable in commutation of any part of the pension under any rule of the scheme authorising the commutation of part (but not the whole) of the pension, or which would have been so receivable but for those special circumstances;

whichever gives the lesser amount chargeable to tax.

(2) This section applies to—

(a) a scheme which is or has at any time been an approved scheme, or

(b) a statutory scheme established under a public general Act.

(3) Where any amount is chargeable to tax under this section the administrator of the scheme shall be charged to income tax under Case VI of Schedule D on that amount, and section 598(2), (3) and (4) shall apply as they apply to tax chargeable under that section.

T

(4) This section shall not apply where the employee's employment was carried on outside the United Kingdom.

(5) In relation to a statutory scheme, "employee" in this section includes any officer.

(6) In applying paragraph (a) or (b) of subsection (1) above—

(a) the same considerations shall be taken into account, including the provisions of any other relevant scheme, as would have been taken into account by the Board in applying section 590; and

(b) where the scheme has ceased to be an approved scheme, account shall only be taken of the rules in force when the scheme was last an approved scheme.

(7) Where the pension has been secured by means of an annuity contract with an insurance company and the sum receivable is payable under that contract by the insurance company, the references to the administrator of the scheme in subsection (3) above and in section 598(2) and (4) as applied by that subsection are to be read as references to the insurance company.

(8) In subsection (7) above "insurance company" means—

1982 c. 50.

(a) a person authorised under section 3 or 4 of the Insurance Companies Act 1982 to carry on long term business and acting through a branch or agency in the United Kingdom; or

1974 c. 46.
1970 c. 30 (N.I.).

(b) a society registered as a friendly society under the Friendly Societies Act 1974 or the Friendly Societies Act (Northern Ireland) 1970.

(9) In relation to payments made under schemes approved or established before 17th March 1987 to employees who became members before that date, subsection (1)(a) above shall have effect with the omission of the words "(disregarding any excess of that remuneration over the permitted maximum)".

Charge to tax:
unauthorised
payments to or for
employees.

600.—(1) This section applies to any payment to or for the benefit of an employee, otherwise than in course of payment of a pension, being a payment made out of funds which are or have been held for the purposes of a scheme which is or has at any time been approved for the purposes of—

(a) this Chapter;

1970 c. 24.

(b) Chapter II of Part II of the Finance Act 1970; or

(c) section 208 or Chapter II of Part IX of the 1970 Act.

(2) If the payment—

(a) is not expressly authorised by the rules of the scheme, or

(b) is made at a time when the scheme is not approved for the purposes of any of the enactments mentioned in subsection (1) above, and would not have been expressly authorised by the rules of the scheme when it was last so approved, the employee (whether or not he is the recipient of the payment) shall be chargeable to tax on the amount of the payment under Schedule E for the year of assessment in which the payment is made.

(3) Any payment chargeable to tax under this section shall not be chargeable to tax under section 598 or 599 or under the Regulations mentioned in paragraph 8 of Schedule 3 to the Finance Act 1971.

1971 c. 68.

(4) References in this section to any payment include references to any transfer of assets or other transfer of money's worth.

601.—(1) Subsection (2) below applies where a payment is made to an employer out of funds which are or have been held for the purposes of a scheme which is or has at any time been an exempt approved scheme and whether or not the payment is made in pursuance of Schedule 22.

Charge to tax: payments to employers.

(2) An amount equal to 40 per cent. of the payment shall be recoverable by the Board from the employer.

(3) Subsection (2) above does not apply to any payment—

(a) to the extent that, if this section had not been enacted, the employer would have been exempt, or entitled to claim exemption, from income tax or corporation tax in respect of the payment; or

(b) made before the scheme became an exempt approved scheme; or

(c) of any prescribed description; or

(d) made in pursuance of the winding-up of the scheme where the winding-up commenced on or before 18th March 1986; or

(e) made in pursuance of an application which —

(i) was made to the Board on or before that date and was not withdrawn before the making of the payment, and

(ii) sought the Board's assurance that the payment would not lead to a withdrawal of approval under section 19(3) of the Finance Act 1970;

1970 c.24.

(4) Subsection (2) above does not apply where the employer is a charity (within the meaning of section 506).

(5) Where any payment is made or becomes due to an employer out of funds which are or have been held for the purposes of a scheme which is or has at any time been an exempt approved scheme then—

(a) if the scheme relates to a trade, profession or vocation carried on by the employer, the payment shall be treated for the purposes of the Tax Acts as a receipt of that trade, profession or vocation receivable when the payment falls due or on the last day on which the trade, profession or vocation is carried on by the employer, whichever is the earlier;

(b) if the scheme does not relate to such a trade, profession or vocation, the employer shall be charged to tax on the amount of the payment under Case VI of Schedule D.

This subsection shall not apply to a payment which fell due before the scheme became an exempt approved scheme or to a payment to which subsection (2) above applies or would apply but for subsection (3)(a) or (4) above.

(6) In this section—

    (a) references to any payment include references to any transfer of assets or other transfer of money's worth; and

    (b) "prescribed" means prescribed by regulations made by the Treasury.

Regulations relating to pension fund surpluses.

602.—(1) In relation to an amount recoverable as mentioned in section 601(2), the Treasury may by regulations make any of the provisions mentioned in subsection (2) below; and for this purpose the amount shall be treated as if it were—

    (a) an amount of income tax chargeable on the employer under Case VI of Schedule D for the year of assessment in which the payment is made; or

    (b) where the employer is a company, an amount of corporation tax chargeable on the company for the accounting period in which the payment is made.

(2) The provisions are—

    (a) provision requiring the administrator of the scheme or the employer (or both) to furnish to the Board, in respect of the amount recoverable and of the payment concerned, information of a prescribed kind;

    (b) provision enabling the Board to serve a notice or notices requiring the administrator or employer (or both) to furnish to the Board, in respect of the amount and payment, particulars of a prescribed kind;

    (c) provision requiring the administrator to deduct out of the payment the amount recoverable and to account to the Board for it;

    (d) provision as to circumstances in which the employer may be assessed in respect of the amount recoverable;

    (e) provision that, in a case where the employer has been assessed in respect of an amount recoverable but has not paid it (or part of it) within a prescribed period, the administrator may be assessed and charged (in the employer's name) in respect of the amount (or part unpaid);

    (f) provision that, in a case where the amount recoverable (or part of it) has been recovered from the administrator by virtue of an assessment in the employer's name, the administrator is entitled to recover from the employer a sum equal to the amount (or part);

(g) provision enabling the employer or administrator (as the case may be) to appeal against an assessment made on him in respect of the amount recoverable;

(h) provision as to when any sum in respect of the amount recoverable is payable to the Board by the administrator or employer and provision requiring interest to be paid on any sum so payable;

(j) provision that an amount paid to the Board by the adminstrator shall be treated as paid on account of the employer's liability under section 601(2).

(3) For the purpose of giving effect to any provision mentioned in subsection (2)(c) to (j) above, regulations under this section may include provision applying (with or without modifications) provisions of the enactments relating to income tax and corporation tax.

(4) Subject to any provision of regulations under this section—

(a) a payment to which section 601(2) applies shall not be treated as a profit or gain brought into charge to income tax or corporation tax and shall not be treated as part of the employer's income for any purpose of this Act; and

(b) the amount recoverable shall not be subject to any exemption or reduction (by way of relief, set-off or otherwise) or be available for set-off against other tax.

(5) If the employer is a company and a payment to which section 601(1) and (2) applies is made at a time not otherwise within an accounting period of the company, an accounting period of the company shall for the purposes of subsection (1)(b) above be treated as beginning immediately before the payment is made.

603. Schedule 22 (which provides for the reduction of certain pension fund surpluses) shall have effect.

Reduction of surpluses.

Supplementary provisions

604.—(1) An application for the approval for the purposes of this Chapter of any retirement benefits scheme shall be made in writing by the administrator of the scheme to the Board before the end of the first year of assessment for which approval is required, and shall be accompanied by—

Application for approval of a scheme.

(a) two copies of the instrument or other document constituting the scheme; and

(b) two copies of the rules of the scheme and, except where the application is being sought on the setting up of the scheme, two copies of the accounts of the scheme for the last year for which such accounts have been made up; and

(c) such other information and particulars (including copies of any actuarial report or advice given to the administrator or employer in connection with the setting up of the scheme) as the Board may consider relevant.

(2) The form in which an application for approval is to be made, or in which any information is to be given, in pursuance of this section may be prescribed by the Board.

Information.

605.—(1) In the case of every approved scheme, the administrator of the scheme, and every employer who pays contributions under the scheme, shall, within 30 days from the date of a notice from the inspector requiring them so to do —

    (a) furnish to the inspector a return containing such particulars of contributions paid under the scheme as the notice may require;

    (b) prepare and deliver to the inspector a return containing particulars of all payments under the scheme, being —

        (i) payments by way of return of contributions (including interest on contributions, if any);

        (ii) payments by way of commutation of, or in lieu of, pensions, or other lump sum payments;

        (iii) other payments made to an employer;

    (c) furnish to the inspector a copy of the accounts of the scheme up to the last date previous to the notice to which such accounts have been made up together with such other information and particulars (including copies of any actuarial report or advice given to the administrator or employer in connection with the conduct of the scheme during the period to which the accounts relate) as the inspector considers relevant.

(2) Where benefits provided for an employee under an approved scheme or a statutory scheme have been secured by means of an annuity contract with an insurance company (within the meaning given by section 599(8)), the insurance company shall, within 30 days from the date of a notice from the inspector requiring it to do so, prepare and deliver to the inspector a return containing particulars of—

    (a) any payments under the contract by way of commutation of, or in lieu of, a pension, or any other lump sum payments under the contract; and

    (b) any payments made under the contract to the employer.

(3) It shall be the duty of every employer—

    (a) if there subsists in relation to any of his employees a retirement benefits scheme to which he contributes and which is neither an approved scheme nor a statutory scheme, to deliver particulars of that scheme to the Board within three months beginning with the date on which the scheme first comes into operation in relation to any of his employees, and

    (b) when required to do so by notice given by the Board, to furnish within the time limited by the notice such particulars as the Board may require with regard to—

        (i) any retirement benefits scheme relating to the employer which is neither an approved scheme nor a statutory scheme; and

(ii) the employees of his to whom any such scheme relates.

(4) It shall be the duty of the administrator of a retirement benefits scheme which is neither an approved scheme nor a statutory scheme, when required to do so by notice given by the Board, to furnish within the time limited by the notice such particulars as the Board may require with regard to the scheme.

606.—(1) If the administrator of a retirement benefits scheme defaults or cannot be traced or dies, the employer shall be responsible in his place for the discharge of all duties imposed on the administrator under this Chapter and shall be liable for any tax due from him in his capacity as administrator. Responsibilities of administrator of scheme, and employer.

This subsection does not apply if the employer is not a contributor to the scheme.

(2) No liability incurred under this Chapter by the administrator of a scheme, or by an employer, shall be affected by the termination of the scheme or by it ceasing to be an approved scheme, or to be an exempt approved scheme.

(3) References in this section to the employer include, where the employer is resident outside the United Kingdom, references to any branch or agent of the employer in the United Kingdom, and in this subsection "branch or agent" has the meaning given by section 118(1) of the Management Act.

(4) This section does not apply for the purposes of sections 602 and 603 and Schedule 22.

607.—(1) The Board may, if they think fit, and subject to such conditions as they think proper to attach to the approval, approve a pilots' benefit fund for the purposes of this Chapter as if it were a retirement benefits scheme and notwithstanding that it does not satisfy one or more of the conditions set out in section 590(2) and (3). Pilots' benefit fund.

(2) If a fund is approved by virtue of this section—

(a) sections 592, 597 to 600 and 604 to 606 shall have effect in relation to the fund with the modifications specified in subsection (3) below;

(b) pensions paid out of the fund and any sums chargeable to tax in connection with the fund under section 600 shall be treated for the purposes of the Income Tax Acts as earned income; and

(c) Chapter III of this Part shall have effect as if a member of the fund were the holder of a pensionable office or employment and his earnings as a pilot (estimated in accordance with the provisions of Case II of Schedule D) were remuneration from such an office or employment.

(3) The modifications referred to in subsection (2)(a) above are as follows—

(a) in section 592, for the references in subsection (7) to an employee and Schedule E there shall be substituted respectively references to a member of the fund and Schedule D, and subsections (4) to (6), and in subsection (7) the words from "incurred" onwards, shall be omitted;

(b) in sections 597 to 606 (except sections 601 to 603)—

    (i) for references to an employee there shall be substituted references to a member or former member of the fund;

    (ii) in section 599(1)(a) for the reference to a year of service there shall be substituted a reference to a year as a pilot licensed by a pilotage authority or authorised by a competent harbour authority;

    (iii) section 606(1) and (3) and so much of any other provision as applies to an employer shall be omitted; and

    (iv) in section 600, for references to Schedule E there shall be substituted references to Case VI of Schedule D.

(4) In this section "pilots' benefit fund" means a fund established under section 15(1)(i) of the Pilotage Act 1983 or any scheme supplementing or replacing any such fund.

1983 c. 21.

Superannuation funds approved before 6th April 1980.

608.—(1) This section applies to any fund which immediately before 6th April 1980 was an approved superannuation fund for the purposes of section 208 of the 1970 Act if—

1970 c. 24.

(a) it has not been approved under this Chapter (or under Chapter II of Part II of the Finance Act 1970); and

(b) no sum has been paid to it by way of contribution since 5th April 1980.

(2) Subject to subsection (3) below, exemption from income tax shall, on a claim being made in that behalf, be allowed to a fund to which this section applies in respect of—

(a) income derived from investments or deposits of the fund;

(b) any underwriting commissions which apart from this subsection would be chargeable to tax under Case VI of Schedule D; and

(c) any profits or gains which (apart from this subsection) would be chargeable to tax under Case VI of Schedule D by virtue of section 56(1)(a) and (2);

if, or to such extent as the Board are satisfied that, the income, commissions, profits or gains are applied for the purposes of the fund.

(3) No claim under subsection (2) above shall be allowed unless the Board are satisfied that the terms on which benefits are payable from the fund have not been altered since 5th April 1980.

(4) An annuity paid out of a fund to which this section applies shall be charged to tax under Schedule E and section 203 shall apply accordingly.

Schemes approved before 23rd July 1987.

609. Schedule 23 to this Act, which makes provision with respect to retirement benefit schemes approved before 23rd July 1987, shall have effect.

610.—(1) This section applies to any amendment of a retirement benefits scheme proposed in connection with an application for the Board's approval for the purposes of this Chapter which is needed in order to ensure that approval is so given, or designed to enhance the benefits under the scheme up to the limits suitable in a scheme for which approval is sought.

(2) A provision, however expressed, designed to preclude any amendment of a scheme which would have prejudiced its approval under section 208 or 222 of the 1970 Act shall not prevent any amendment to which this section applies.

(3) In the case of a scheme which contains no powers of amendment, the administrator of the scheme may, with the consent of all the members of the scheme, and of the employer (or of each of the employers), make any amendment to which this section applies.

PART XIV
Amendments of schemes.

611.—(1) In this Chapter "retirement benefits scheme" means, subject to the provisions of this section, a scheme for the provision of benefits consisting of or including relevant benefits, but does not include any national scheme providing such benefits.

Definition of "retirement benefits scheme".

(2) References in this Chapter to a scheme include references to a deed, agreement, series of agreements, or other arrangements providing for relevant benefits notwithstanding that it relates or they relate only to—

(a) a small number of employees, or to a single employee, or

(b) the payment of a pension starting immediately on the making of the arrangements.

(3) The Board may, if they think fit, treat a retirement benefits scheme relating to employees of two or more different classes or descriptions as being for the purposes of this Chapter two or more separate retirement benefits schemes relating respectively to such one or more of those classes or descriptions of those employees as the Board think fit.

(4) For the purposes of this section, and of any other provision of this Chapter—

(a) employees may be regarded as belonging to different classes or descriptions if they are employed by different employers; and

(b) a particular class or description of employee may consist of a single employee, or any number of employees, however small.

(5) Without prejudice to subsections (3) and (4) above, the Board may continue to treat as two different schemes, for the purposes of this Chapter, any retirement benefits scheme which, in pursuance of paragraph 5 of Schedule 3 to the Finance Act 1971 (schemes in existence before 5th April 1973), they treated, immediately before the coming into force of this Chapter, as two separate schemes for the purposes of Chapter II of Part II of the Finance Act 1970.

1971 c. 68.

1970 c. 24.

612.—(1) In this Chapter, except where the context otherwise requires—

"administrator", in relation to a retirement benefits scheme, means the person or persons having the management of the scheme;

Other interpretative provisions, and regulations for purposes of this Chapter.

"approved scheme" means a retirement benefits scheme for the time being approved by the Board for the purposes of this Chapter;

"director" in relation to a company includes—

(a) in the case of a company the affairs of which are managed by a board of directors or similar body, a member of that board or body,

(b) in the case of a company the affairs of which are managed by a single director or similar person, that director or person,

(c) in the case of a company the affairs of which are managed by the members themselves, a member of that company;

and includes a person who is to be or has been a director;

"employee"—

(a) in relation to a company, includes any officer of the company, any director of the company and any other person taking part in the management of the affairs of the company, and

(b) in relation to any employer, includes a person who is to be or has been an employee;

and "employer" and other cognate expressions shall be construed accordingly;

"exempt approved scheme" has the meaning given by section 592(1);

"final remuneration" means the average annual remuneration of the last three years' service;

"pension" includes annuity;

"the permitted maximum" has the meaning given by section 590(3);

"relevant benefits" means any pension, lump sum, gratuity or other like benefit given or to be given on retirement or on death, or in anticipation of retirement, or, in connection with past service, after retirement or death, or to be given on or in anticipation of or in connection with any change in the nature of the service of the employee in question, except that it does not include any benefit which is to be afforded solely by reason of the disablement by accident of a person occurring during his service or of his death by accident so occurring and for no other reason;

"remuneration" does not include—

(a) anything in respect of which tax is chargeable under Schedule E and which arises from the acquisition or disposal of shares or an interest in shares or from a right to acquire shares; or

(b) anything in respect of which tax is chargeable by virtue of section 148;

"service" means service as an employee of the employer in question and other expressions, including "retirement", shall be construed accordingly; and

"statutory scheme" means a retirement benefits scheme established by or under any enactment—

> (a) the particulars of which are set out in any enactment, or in any regulations made under any enactment, or

> (b) which has been approved as an appropriate scheme by a Minister or government department (including the head of a Northern Ireland department or a Northern Ireland department).

(2) Any reference in this Chapter to the provision of relevant benefits, or of a pension, for employees of an employer includes a reference to the provision of relevant benefits or a pension by means of a contract between the administrator or the employer or the employee and a third person; and any reference to pensions or contributions paid, or payments made, under a scheme includes a reference to pensions or contributions paid, or payments made, under such a contract entered into for the purposes of the scheme.

(3) The Board may make regulations generally for the purpose of carrying the preceding provisions of this Chapter into effect.

CHAPTER II

OTHER PENSION FUNDS AND SOCIAL SECURITY BENEFITS AND CONTRIBUTIONS

613.—(1) The salary of a Member of the House of Commons shall, for all the purposes of the Income Tax Acts, be treated as reduced by the amounts deducted in pursuance of section 1 of the House of Commons Members' Fund Act 1939; but a Member shall not by reason of any such deduction be entitled to relief under any other provision of the Income Tax Acts.

Parliamentary pension funds. 1939 c. 49.

(2) In subsection (1) above the reference to salary shall be construed as mentioned in subsection (3) of section 1 of the House of Commons Members' Fund Act 1939, the reference to amounts deducted includes a reference to amounts required to be set aside under that subsection, and "deduction" shall be construed accordingly.

(3) Periodical payments granted out of the House of Commons Members' Fund (including periodical payments granted out of sums appropriated from that Fund or out of the income from those sums) shall be charged to income tax under Schedule E.

(4) The respective trustees of—

> (a) the House of Commons Members' Fund established under section 1 of that Act of 1939;

> (b) the Parliamentary Contributory Pension Fund;

> (c) the Members' Contributory Pension (Northern Ireland) Fund constituted under section 3(2) of the Ministerial Salaries and Members' Pensions Act (Northern Ireland) 1965; and

1965 c. 18 (N.I.).

(d) the Assembly Contributory Pension Fund constituted under the Assembly Pensions (Northern Ireland) Order 1976;

shall be entitled to exemption from income tax in respect of all income derived from those Funds or any investment of those Funds.

A claim under this subsection shall be made to the Board.

Exemptions and reliefs in respect of income from investments etc. of certain pension schemes.
1975 c.14.
1975 c. 15.

1935 c. 2.
1973 c. 21.

614.—(1) All income receivable from any source whatsoever for the purposes of any supplementary scheme under section 158 of the Social Security Act 1975 or section 149 of the Social Security (Northern Ireland) Act 1975, or under the enactments replaced by those sections, by the body charged with the administration of the scheme shall be exempt from income tax.

(2) Any interest or dividends received by the person in whom is vested any of the Family Pension Funds mentioned in section 273 of the Government of India Act 1935, and having effect as a scheme made under section 2 of the Overseas Pensions Act 1973, on sums forming part of that fund shall be exempt from income tax.

(3) Income derived from investments or deposits of any fund referred to in paragraph (b), (c), (d) or (f) of subsection (2) of section 615 shall not be charged to income tax, and any income tax deducted from any such income shall be repaid by the Board to the persons entitled to receive the income.

1966 c. 21.

(4) In respect of income derived from investments or deposits of the Overseas Service Pensions Fund established pursuant to section 7(1) of the Overseas Aid Act 1966, the Board shall give by way of repayment such relief from income tax as is necessary to secure that the income is exempt to the like extent (if any) as if it were income of a person not domiciled, ordinarily resident or resident in the United Kingdom.

(5) In respect of dividends and other income derived from investments, deposits or other property of a superannuation fund to which section 615(3) applies the Board shall give by way of repayment such relief from income tax as is necessary to secure that the income is exempt to the like extent (if any) as if it were income of a person not domiciled, ordinarily resident or resident in the United Kingdom.

(6) A claim under this section shall be made to the Board.

Exemption from tax in respect of certain pensions.

615.—(1) A pension to which this subsection applies shall not be liable to charge to income tax if it is the income of a person who satisfies the Board that he is not resident in the United Kingdom.

A claim under this subsection shall be made to the Board.

(2) Subsection (1) above applies to any of the following pensions—

1955 c. 22.

(a) a pension paid under the authority of the Pensions (India, Pakistan and Burma) Act 1955 (which has effect, by virtue of subsection (3) of section 2 of the Overseas Pensions Act 1973, as a scheme made under that section);

(b) a pension paid out of any fund established in the United Kingdom by the government of any country which is, or forms part of, a country to which this paragraph applies, an associated state, a colony, a protectorate, a protected state or a United

Kingdom trust territory, or by a government constituted for two or more such countries, if the fund was established for the sole purpose of providing pensions, whether contributory or not, payable in respect of service under that government;

(c) a pension paid out of the fund formed under the Overseas Superannuation Scheme (formerly known as the Colonial Superannuation Scheme);

(d) a pension paid under section 1 of the Overseas Pensions Act 1973, whether or not paid out of a fund established under a scheme made under that section;

1973 c. 21.

(e) so much of any pension paid to or in respect of any person—

(i) under an order made under section 2 of the Overseas Service Act 1958 and having effect as if it were a scheme under section 2 of the Overseas Pensions Act 1973 or under a pension scheme originally provided and maintained under such an order and having such effect, or

1958 c. 14.

(ii) under section 4(2) of the Overseas Service Act 1958, which has effect as if it were a scheme under section 2 of the Overseas Pensions Act 1973,

as may be certified by the Secretary of State to be attributable to the employment of that person in the public services of an overseas territory;

(f) a pension paid out of the fund established under the name "the Central African Pension Fund" by section 24 of the Federation of Rhodesia and Nyasaland (Dissolution) Order in Council 1963;

S.I. 1963/2085.

(g) a pension paid out of the Overseas Service Pensions Fund established under section 7(1) of the Overseas Aid Act 1966.

1966 c. 21.

(3) Where an annuity is paid from a superannuation fund to which this subsection applies to a person who is not resident in the United Kingdom, income tax shall not be deducted from any payment of the annuity or accounted for under section 349(1) by the trustees or other persons having the control of the fund.

(4) Subsection (1) above shall not apply to so much of any pension falling within paragraph (a) or (d) of subsection (2) above as is paid by virtue of the application to the pension of the Pensions (Increase) Acts.

(5) Paragraph (b) of subsection (2) above applies to any country mentioned in Schedule 3 to the British Nationality Act 1981 except Australia, Canada, New Zealand, India, Sri Lanka and Cyprus.

1981 c. 61.

(6) Subsection (3) above applies to any superannuation fund which—

(a) is bona fide established under irrevocable trusts in connection with some trade or undertaking carried on wholly or partly outside the United Kingdom;

(b) has for its sole purpose the provision of superannuation benefits in respect of persons' employment in the trade or undertaking wholly outside the United Kingdom; and

(c) is recognised by the employer and employed persons in the trade or undertaking;

and for the purposes of this subsection duties performed in the United Kingdom the performance of which is merely incidental to the performance of other duties outside the United Kingdom shall be treated as performed outside the United Kingdom.

(7) In this section—

"pension" includes a gratuity or any sum payable on or in respect of death or, in the case of a pension falling within subsection (2)(g) above, ill-health, and a return of contributions with or without interest thereon or any other addition thereto;

"overseas territory" means any territory or country outside the United Kingdom;

1971 c. 56.

"the Pensions (Increase) Acts" means the Pensions (Increase) Act 1971 and any Act passed after that Act for purposes corresponding to the purposes of that Act;

"United Kingdom trust territory" means a territory administered by the government of the United Kingdom under the trusteeship system of the United Nations.

(8) In this section—

(a) references to a government constituted for two or more countries include references to any authority established for the purpose of providing or administering services which are common to, or relate to matters of common interest to, two or more countries;

1980 c. 63.

(b) any reference to employment in the public services of an overseas territory shall be construed as if it occurred in the Overseas Development and Cooperation Act 1980 and section 10(2) of that Act shall apply accordingly; and

1973 c. 21.

(c) any reference to an enactment or order having effect as if it were a scheme constituted under section 2 of the Overseas Pensions Act 1973 includes a reference to a scheme made under that section and certified by the Secretary of State for the purpose of the 1970 Act or this Act to correspond to that enactment or order.

Other overseas pensions.

616.—(1) If and so long as provision is made by double taxation relief arrangements for a pension of a description specified in subsection (2) below to be exempt from tax in the United Kingdom and, by reason of Her Majesty's Government in the United Kingdom having assumed responsibility for the pension, payments in respect of it are made under section 1 of the Overseas Pensions Act 1973, then, to the extent that those payments are made to, or to the widow or widower of, an existing pensioner, the provision made under the arrangements shall apply in relation to the pension, exclusive of any statutory increases in it, as if it continued to be paid by the government which had responsibility for it before that responsibility was assumed by Her Majesty's Government in the United Kingdom.

(2) The pensions referred to in subsection (1) above are pensions paid by—

(a) the Government of Malawi for services rendered to that Government or to the Government of the Federation of Rhodesia and Nyasaland in the discharge of governmental functions;

(b) the Government of Trinidad and Tobago in respect of services rendered to that Government in the discharge of governmental functions;

(c) the Government of the Republic of Zambia for services rendered to that Government or to the Government of Northern Rhodesia or to the Government of the Federation of Rhodesia and Nyasaland in the discharge of governmental functions.

(3) If—

(a) immediately before 6th April 1973 a person resident in the United Kingdom was entitled to receive a pension as or as the widow or widower of an existing pensioner, and

(b) by reason of Her Majesty's Government in the United Kingdom having assumed responsibility for the pension, payments in respect of it are made under section 1 of the Overseas Pensions Act 1973,

1973 c. 21.

then, if and so long as the pension is received by that person or, where that person is an existing pensioner, by his or her widow or widower, the provisions of this Act shall apply in relation to it, exclusive of any statutory increases in it, as if it continued to be paid by the government or other body or fund which had responsibility for it before that responsibility was assumed by Her Majesty's Government in the United Kingdom.

(4) In this section—

"double taxation relief arrangements" means arrangements specified in an Order in Council making any such provisions as are referred to in section 788;

"existing pensioner", in relation to a pension, means a person by virtue of whose service the pension is payable and who retired from that service before 6th April 1973; and

"statutory increases", in relation to a pension, means so much (if any) of the pension as is paid by virtue of the application to it of any provision of the Pensions (Increase) Act 1971;

1971 c. 56.

and in this subsection "pension" has the same meaning as in section 1 of the Overseas Pensions Act 1973.

617.—(1) Payments of benefit under Chapters I to III of Part II of the Social Security Act 1975, Part II of the Social Security Pensions Act 1975, Chapters I to III of Part II of the Social Security (Northern Ireland) Act 1975 or Part III of the Social Security Pensions (Northern Ireland) Order 1975, except—

Social security benefits and contributions.
1975 c. 14.
1975 c. 60.
1975 c. 15.
S.I. 1975/1503 (N.I. 15).

(a) sickness benefit, invalidity benefit, attendance allowance, mobility allowance, severe disablement allowance, maternity allowance, widow's payments, child's special allowance and guardian's allowance; and

(b) so much of any benefit as is attributable to an increase in respect of a child,

shall be charged to income tax under Schedule E.

(2) The following payments shall not be treated as income for any purpose of the Income Tax Acts—

(a) payments of income support, family credit or housing benefit under the Social Security Act 1986 or the Social Security (Northern Ireland) Order 1986 other than payments of income support which are taxable by virtue of section 151;

(b) payments of child benefit; and

(c) payments excepted by subsection (1) above from the charge to tax imposed by that subsection.

(3) Subject to subsection (4) and (5) below, no relief or deduction shall be given or allowed in respect of any contribution paid by any person under—

(a) Part I of the Social Security Act 1975, or

(b) Part I of the Social Security (Northern Ireland) Act 1975.

(4) Subsection (3) above shall not apply to any secondary Class I contributions within the meaning of the Social Security Act 1975 or the Social Security (Northern Ireland) Act 1975 which is allowable as a deduction in computing profits or gains, in computing expenses of management under section 75 or under that section as applied by section 76 or in computing expenses of management or supervision under section 121.

(5) An individual making a claim in that behalf shall be entitled, in computing his total income for any year of assessment, to deduct one-half of any amount (as finally settled) which is determined under subsection (2) of section 9 of the Social Security Act 1975 or of the Social Security (Northern Ireland) Act 1975 and which he is liable to pay in respect of that year by way of Class 4 contributions under either of those sections.

(6) Until such day as may be appointed by the Secretary of State by order made by statutory instrument, subsection (1)(a) above shall have effect with the omission of the words "widow's payments".

CHAPTER III

RETIREMENT ANNUITIES

618.—(1) Nothing in this Chapter shall apply in relation to—

(a) a contract made or trust scheme established on or after 4th January 1988; or

(b) a person by whom contributions are first paid on or after that date under a trust scheme established before that date.

(2) Subject to subsection (4) below, the terms of a contract made, or the rules of a trust scheme established, on or after 17th March 1987 and before 4th January 1988 and approved by the Board under section 620 shall have effect (notwithstanding anything in them to the contrary) as if

they did not allow the payment to the individual by whom the contract is made, or an individual paying contributions under the scheme, of a lump sum exceeding £150,000 or such other sum as may for the time being be specified in an order under section 635(4).

(3) Subject to subsection (5) below, the rules of a trust scheme established before 17th March 1987 and approved by the Board under section 620 shall have effect (notwithstanding anything in them to the contrary) as if they did not allow the payment to any person first paying contributions under the scheme on or after 17th March 1987 of a lump sum such as is mentioned in subsection (2) above.

(4) Subsection (2) above shall not apply—

(a) to a contract if, before the end of January 1988, the persons by and to whom premiums are payable under it jointly give notice to the Board that subsection (2) is not to apply; or

(b) to a scheme if, before the end of January 1988, the trustees or other persons having the management of the scheme give notice to the Board that subsection (2) is not to apply;

and where notice is given to the Board under this subsection, the contract or scheme shall, with effect from the date with effect from which it was approved, cease to be approved.

(5) Subsection (3) above shall not apply in the case of any person paying contributions under a scheme if, before the end of January 1988, he and the trustees or other persons having the management of the scheme jointly give notice to the Board that subsection (3) is not to apply; and where notice is given to the Board, the scheme shall cease to be approved in relation to the contributor with effect from the date on which he first paid a contribution under it or (if later) the date with effect from which it was approved.

619.—(1) Where in any year of assessment an individual is (or would but for an insufficiency of profits or gains be) chargeable to income tax in respect of relevant earnings from any trade, profession, vocation, office or employment carried on or held by him, and pays a qualifying premium, then— Exemption from tax in respect of qualifying premiums.

(a) relief from income tax shall be given under this section in respect of that qualifying premium, but only on a claim made for the purpose, and where relief is to be so given, the amount of that premium shall, subject to the provisions of this section, be deducted from or set off against his relevant earnings for the year of assessment in which the premium is paid; and

(b) any annuity payable to the same or another individual shall be treated as earned income of the annuitant to the extent to which it is payable in return for any amount on which relief is so given.

Paragraph (b) above applies only in relation to the annuitant to whom the annuity is made payable by the terms of the annuity contract under which it is paid.

(2) Subject to the provisions of this section and section 626, the amount which may be deducted or set off in any year of assessment (whether in respect of one or more qualifying premiums, and whether or

not including premiums in respect of a contract approved under section 621) shall not be more than $17\frac{1}{2}$ per cent. of the individual's net relevant earnings for that year.

(3) Subject to the provisions of this section, the amount which may be deducted or set off in any year of assessment in respect of qualifying premiums paid under a contract approved under section 621 (whether in respect of one or more such premiums) shall not be more than 5 per cent. of the individual's net relevant earnings for that year.

(4) An individual who pays a qualifying premium in a year of assessment (whether or not a year for which he has relevant earnings) may before the end of that year elect that the premium shall be treated as paid—

(a) in the last preceding year of assessment; or

(b) if he had no net relevant earnings in the year referred to in paragraph (a) above, in the last preceding year of assessment but one;

and where an election is made under this subsection in respect of a premium the other provisions of this Chapter shall have effect as if the premium had been paid in the year specified in the election and not in the year in which it was actually paid.

(5) Where relief under this section for any year of assessment is claimed and allowed (whether or not relief then falls to be given for that year), and afterwards there is made any assessment, alteration of an assessment, or other adjustment of the claimant's liability to tax, there shall be made also such adjustments, if any, as are consequential thereon in the relief allowed or given under this section for that or any subsequent year of assessment.

(6) Where relief under this section is claimed and allowed for any year of assessment in respect of any payment, relief shall not be given in respect of it under any other provision of the Income Tax Acts for the same or a later year of assessment nor (in the case of a payment under an annuity contract) in respect of any other premium or consideration for an annuity under the same contract; and references in the Income Tax Acts to relief in respect of life assurance premiums shall not be taken to include relief under this section.

(7) If any person, for the purpose of obtaining for himself or any other person any relief from or repayment of tax under this section, knowingly makes any false statement or false representation, he shall be liable to a penalty not exceeding £500.

Qualifying premiums.

620.—(1) In this Chapter "qualifying premium" means, subject to subsection (5) below, a premium or other consideration paid by an individual—

(a) under an annuity contract for the time being approved by the Board under this section as having for its main object the provision for the individual of a life annuity in old age, or

(b) under a contract for the time being approved under section 621.

(2) Subject to subsection (3) and (4) below, the Board shall not approve a contract under this section unless it appears to them to satisfy the conditions that it is made by the individual with a person lawfully carrying on in the United Kingdom the business of granting annuities on human life, and that it does not—

    (a) provide for the payment by that person during the life of the individual of any sum except sums payable by way of annuity to the individual; or

    (b) provide for the annuity payable to the individual to commence before he attains the age of 60 or after he attains the age of 75; or

    (c) provide for the payment by that person of any other sums except sums payable by way of annuity to the individual's widow or widower and any sums which, in the event of no annuity becoming payable either to the individual or to a widow or widower, are payable by way of return of premiums, by way of reasonable interest on premiums or by way of bonuses out of profits; or

    (d) provide for the annuity, if any, payable to a widow or widower of the individual to be of a greater annual amount than that paid or payable to the individual; or

    (e) provide for the payment of any annuity otherwise than for the life of the annuitant;

and that it does include provision securing that no annuity payable under it shall be capable in whole or in part of surrender, commutation or assignment.

(3) A contract shall not be treated as not satisfying the requirements of subsection (2) above by reason only that it—

    (a) gives the individual the right to receive, by way of commutation of part of the annuity payable to him, a lump sum not exceeding three times the annual amount of the remaining part of the annuity, taking, where the annual amount is or may be different in different years, the initial annual amount, and

    (b) makes any such right depend on the exercise by the individual of an election at or before the time when the annuity first becomes payable to him.

(4) The Board may, if they think fit, and subject to any conditions they think proper to impose, approve, under this section, a contract otherwise satisfying the preceding conditions, notwithstanding that the contract provides for one or more of the following matters—

    (a) for the payment after the individual's death of an annuity to a dependant not the widow or widower of the individual;

    (b) for the payment to the individual of an annuity commencing before he attains the age of 60, if the annuity is payable on his becoming incapable through infirmity of body or mind of carrying on his own occupation or any occupation of a similar nature for which he is trained or fitted;

      (c) if the individual's occupation is one in which persons customarily retire before attaining the age of 60, for the annuity to commence before he attains that age;

      (d) for the annuity payable to any person to continue for a term certain (not exceeding ten years), notwithstanding his death within that term, or for the annuity payable to any person to terminate, or be suspended, on marriage (or re-marriage) or in other circumstances;

      (e) in the case of an annuity which is to continue for a term certain, for the annuity to be assignable by will, and in the event of any person dying entitled to it, for it to be assignable by his personal representatives in the distribution of the estate so as to give effect to a testamentary disposition, or to the rights of those entitled on intestacy, or to an appropriation of it to a legacy or to a share or interest in the estate.

(5) Subject to section 621(5), section 619 and subsections (1) to (4) above shall apply in relation to a contribution under a trust scheme approved by the Board as they apply in relation to a premium under an annuity contract so approved, with the modification that, for the condition as to the person with whom the contract is made, there shall be substituted a condition that the scheme—

      (a) is established under the law of any part of, and administered in, the United Kingdom; and

      (b) is established for the benefit of individuals engaged in or connected with a particular occupation (or one or other of a group of occupations), and for the purpose of providing retirement annuities for them, with or without subsidiary benefits for their families or dependants; and

      (c) is so established under irrevocable trusts by a body of persons comprising or representing a substantial proportion of the individuals so engaged in the United Kingdom, or of those so engaged in England, Wales, Scotland or Northern Ireland;

and with the necessary adaptations of other references to the contract or the person with whom it is made.

(6) Exemption from income tax shall be allowed in respect of income derived from investments or deposits of any fund maintained for the purpose mentioned in subsection (5)(b) above under a scheme for the time being approved under that subsection.

(7) The Board may at any time, by notice given to the persons by and to whom premiums are payable under any contract for the time being approved under this section, or to the trustees or other persons having the management of any scheme so approved, withdraw that approval on such grounds and from such date as may be specified in the notice.

1867 c. 144.   (8) Nothing in sections 4 and 6 of the Policies of Assurance Act 1867 (obligations of assurance companies in respect of notices of assignment of policies of life assurance) shall be taken to apply to any contract approved under this section.

(9) For the purposes of any provision applying this subsection "approved annuities" means—

(a) annuities under contracts approved by the Board under this section, being annuities payable wholly in return for premiums or other consideration paid by a person who (when the premiums or other consideration are or is payable) is, or would but for an insufficiency of profits or gains be, chargeable to tax in respect of relevant earnings from a trade, profession, vocation, office or employment carried on or held by him; and

(b) annuities or lump sums under approved personal pension arrangements within the meaning of Chapter IV of this Part.

621.—(1) The Board may approve under this section—

    (a) a contract the main object of which is the provision of an annuity for the wife or husband of the individual, or for any one or more dependants of the individual,

    (b) a contract the sole object of which is the provision of a lump sum on the death of the individual before he attains the age of 75.

(2) The Board shall not approve the contract unless it appears to them that it is made by the individual with a person lawfully carrying on in the United Kingdom the business of granting annuities on human life.

(3) The Board shall not approve a contract under subsection (1)(a) above unless it appears to them to satisfy all the following conditions, that is to say—

    (a) that any annuity payable to the wife or husband or dependant of the individual commences on the death of the individual,

    (b) that any annuity payable to the individual commences at a time after the individual attains the age of 60, and, unless the individual's annuity is one to commence on the death of a person to whom an annuity would be payable under the contract if that person survived the individual, cannot commence after the time when the individual attains the age of 75;

    (c) that the contract does not provide for the payment by the person contracting with the individual of any sum, other than any annuity payable to the individual's wife or husband or dependant, or to the individual, except, in the event of no annuity becoming payable under the contract, any sums payable by way of return of premiums, by way of reasonable interest on premiums or by way of bonuses out of profits;

    (d) that the contract does not provide for the payment of any annuity otherwise than for the life of the annuitant;

    (e) that the contract does include provision securing that no annuity payable under it shall be capable in whole or in part of surrender, commutation or assignment.

(4) The Board may, if they think fit, and subject to any conditions that they think proper to impose, approve a contract under subsection (1)(a) above notwithstanding that, in one or more respects, they are not satisfied that the contract complies with the provisions of paragraphs (a) to (e) of subsection (3) above.

(5) The main purpose of a trust scheme, or part of a trust scheme, within section 620(5) may be to provide annuities for the wives, husbands and dependants of the individuals, or lump sums payable on death and in that case—

(a) approval of the trust scheme shall be subject to subsections (1) to (4) above with any necessary modifications, and not subject to section 620(2) to (4);

(b) the provisions of this Chapter shall apply to the scheme or part of the scheme when duly approved as they apply to a contract approved under this section; and

(c) section 620(6) shall apply to any duly approved trust scheme, or part of a trust scheme.

(6) Except as otherwise provided in this Chapter (and in particular except in section 620), any reference in the Tax Acts to a contract or scheme approved under that section shall include a reference to a contract or scheme approved under this section.

Substituted retirement annuity contracts.

622.—(1) The Board may, if they think fit, and subject to any conditions they think proper to impose, approve an annuity contract under section 620 notwithstanding that the contract provides that the individual by whom it is made—

(a) may agree with the person with whom it is made that a sum representing the value of the individual's accrued rights under it should be applied as the premium or other consideration either under another annuity contract made between them and approved by the Board under section 620, or under personal pension arrangements made between them and approved by the Board under Chapter IV of this Part; or

(b) may require the person with whom it is made to pay such a sum to such other person as the individual may specify, to be applied by that other person as the premium or other consideration either under an annuity contract made beween the individual and him and approved by the Board under section 620, or under personal pension arrangements made between the individual and him and approved by the Board under Chapter IV of this Part.

(2) References in subsection (1) above to the individual by whom the contract is made include references to any widow, widower or dependant having accrued rights under the contract.

(3) Where in pursuance of any such provision as is mentioned in subsection (1) above of an annuity contract approved under section 620, or of a corresponding provision of a contract approved under section 621(1)(a), a sum representing the value of accrued rights under one contract ("the original contract") is paid by way of premium or other consideration under another contract ("the substituted contract"), any annuity payable under the substituted contract shall be treated as earned income of the annuitant to the same extent that an annuity payable under the original contract would have been so treated.

623.—(1) For the purposes of this Chapter, a married woman's relevant earnings shall not be treated as her husband's relevant earnings, notwithstanding that her income chargeable to tax is treated as his income.

(2) Subject to subsection (1) above, "relevant earnings", in relation to any individual, means, for the purposes of this Chapter, any income of his chargeable to tax for the year of assessment in question, being either—

(a) income arising in respect of remuneration from an office or employment held by him other than a pensionable office or employment; or

(b) income from any property which is attached to or forms part of the emoluments of any such office or employment held by him; or

(c) income which is chargeable under Schedule B or Schedule D and is immediately derived by him from the carrying on or exercise by him of his trade, profession or vocation either as an individual or, in the case of a partnership, as a partner personally acting therein; or

(d) income treated as earned income by virtue of section 529;

but does not include any remuneration as director of a company whose income consists wholly or mainly of investment income (construed in accordance with paragraph 7 of Schedule 19), being a company of which he is a controlling director.

(3) For the purposes of this Chapter, an office or employment is a pensionable office or employment if, and only if, service in it is service to which a sponsored superannuation scheme relates (not being a scheme under which the benefits provided in respect of that service are limited to a lump sum payable on the termination of the service through death or disability before the age of 75 or some lower age); but references to a pensionable office or employment apply whether or not the duties are performed wholly or partly in the United Kingdom or the holder is chargeable to tax in respect of it.

(4) Service in an office or employment shall not for the purposes of subsection (3) above be treated as service to which a sponsored superannuation scheme relates by reason only of the fact that the holder of the office or employment might (though he does not) participate in the scheme by exercising or refraining from exercising an option open to him by virtue of that service.

(5) For the purposes of relief under section 619, an individual's relevant earnings are those earnings before giving effect to any capital allowances, other than deductions allowable in computing profits or gains, but after taking into account the amounts on which charges fall to be made under any of the Capital Allowances Acts; and references to income in the following provisions of this section (other than references to total income) shall be construed similarly.

(6) Subject to the following provisions of this section "net relevant earnings" means, in relation to an individual, the amount of his relevant earnings for the year of assessment in question, less the amount of any deductions falling to be made from the relevant earnings in computing for the purposes of income tax his total income for that year, being—

(a) deductions which but for section 74(m), (p) or (q) could be made in computing his profits or gains; or

(b) deductions in respect of relief under Schedule 9 of the Finance Act 1981 (stock relief); or

(c) deductions in respect of losses or capital allowances arising from activities profits or gains of which would be included in computing relevant earnings of the individual or of the individual's wife or husband.

(7) Where in any year of assessment for which an individual claims and is allowed relief under section 619—

(a) there falls to be made in computing the total income of the individual or that of his wife or her husband a deduction in respect of any such loss or allowance of the individual as is mentioned in subsection (6)(c) above; and

(b) the deduction or part of it falls to be so made from income other than relevant earnings,

the amount of the deduction made from that other income shall be treated as reducing the individual's net relevant earnings for subsequent years of assessment (being deducted as far as may be from those of the immediately following year, whether or not he claims or is entitled to claim relief under this section for that year, and so far as it cannot be so deducted, then from those of the next year, and so on).

(8) An individual's net relevant earnings for any year of assessment are to be computed without regard to any relief which falls to be given for that year under section 619 either to that individual or to that individual's wife or husband.

(9) An individual's relevant earnings, in the case of partnership profits, shall be taken to be his share of the partnership income, estimated in accordance with the Income Tax Acts, but the amount to be included in respect of those earnings in arriving at his net relevant earnings shall be his share of that income after making therefrom all such deductions (if any) in respect of payments made by the partnership or of relief given to the partnership under Schedule 9 of the Finance Act 1981 (stock relief) or in respect of capital allowances falling to be made to the partnership as would be made in computing the tax payable in respect of that income.

Sponsored superannuation schemes and controlling directors.

624.—(1) In section 623 "a sponsored superannuation scheme" means a scheme or arrangement—

(a) relating to service in particular offices or employments, and

(b) having for its object or one of its objects to make provision in respect of persons serving in those offices or employments against future retirement or partial retirement, against future termination of service through death or disability, or against similar matters,

being a scheme or arrangement under which any part of the cost of the provision so made is or has been borne otherwise than by those persons by reason of their service (whether it is the cost or part of the cost of the benefits provided, or of paying premiums or other sums in order to provide those benefits, or of administering or instituting the scheme or arrangement).

(2) For the purposes of subsection (1) above a person shall be treated as bearing by reason of his service the cost of any payment made or agreed to be made in respect of his service, if that payment or the agreement to make it is treated under the Income Tax Acts as increasing his income, or would be so treated if he were chargeable to tax under Case I of Schedule E in respect of his emoluments from that service.

(3) In section 623 "controlling director" means a director of a company, the directors of which have a controlling interest in the company, who is the beneficial owner of, or able either directly or through the medium of other companies or by any other indirect means to control, more than 5 per cent. of the ordinary share capital of the company; and for the purposes of this definition—

"company" means one within the Companies Act 1985 or the Companies (Northern Ireland) Order 1986; and

1985 c. 6.
S.I. 1986/1032
(N.I. 6).

"director" means—

(a) in relation to a body corporate the affairs of which are managed by a board of directors or similar body, a member of that board or similar body;

(b) in relation to a body corporate the affairs of which are managed by a single director or similar person, that director or person;

(c) in relation to a body corporate the affairs of which are managed by the members themselves, a member of the body corporate;

and includes any person who is to be or has been a director.

625.—(1) Where—

Carry-forward of unused relief under section 619.

(a) in any year of assessment an individual is (or would but for an insufficiency of profits or gains be) chargeable to income tax in respect of relevant earnings from any trade, profession, vocation, office or employment carried on or held by him, but

(b) there is unused relief for that year, that is to say, an amount which could have been deducted from or set off against the individual's relevant earnings for that year under subsection (1) of section 619 if—

(i) he had paid a qualifying premium in that year; or

(ii) the qualifying premium or premiums paid by him in that year had been greater;

then, subject to section 655(1)(b), relief may be given under that section, up to the amount of the unused relief, in respect of so much of any qualifying premium or premiums paid by the individual in any of the next six years of assessment as exceeds the maximum applying for that year under subsection (2) of that section.

(2) Relief by virtue of this section shall be given for an earlier year rather than a later year, the unused relief taken into account in giving relief for any year being deducted from that available for giving relief in subsequent years and unused relief derived from an earlier year being exhausted before unused relief derived from a later year.

(3) Where a relevant assessment to tax in respect of a year of assessment becomes final and conclusive more than six years after the end of that year and there is an amount of unused relief for that year which results from the making of the assessment—

(a) that amount shall not be available for giving relief by virtue of this section for any of the six years following that year, but

(b) the individual may, within the period of six months beginning with the date on which the assessment becomes final and conclusive, elect that relief shall be given under section 619, up to that amount, in respect of so much of any qualifying premium or premiums paid by him within that period as exceeds the maximum applying under subsection (2) of that section for the year of assessment in which they were paid;

and to the extent to which relief in respect of any premium or premiums is given by virtue of this subsection it shall not be given by virtue of subsection (1) above.

(4) In this section "a relevant assessment to tax" means an assessment on the individual's relevant earnings or on the profits or gains of a partnership from which the individual derives relevant earnings.

Modification of section 619 in relation to persons over 50.

626. In the case of an individual whose age at the beginning of a year of assessment is within a range specified in the first column of the Table set out below, section 619(2) shall have effect for that year with the substitution for the reference to $17\frac{1}{2}$ per cent. of a reference to the relevant percentage specified in the second column of the Table.

TABLE

Age range	Percentage
51 to 55	20
56 to 60	$22\frac{1}{2}$
61 or more	$27\frac{1}{2}$

Lloyd's underwriters.

627.—(1) Where for any year of assessment an individual—

(a) is chargeable to income tax in respect of relevant earnings derived from Lloyd's underwriting activities; and

(b) there is an amount of unused relief attributable to those earnings,

the individual may, subject to subsection (2) below, elect that there shall be treated as paid in that year any qualifying premium paid by him in the next year of assessment but two.

(2) An election under this section shall not have effect in relation to so much of any qualifying premium as exceeds the amount of unused relief referred to in subsection (1)(b) above.

(3) Any election under this section shall be made before the end of the year of assessment in which the premium is paid.

(4) Where an election is made under this section the provisions of this Chapter, other than section 619(4), shall have effect as if the premium or, as the case may be, the part of the premium in question had been paid in the year specified in the election and not in the year in which it was actually paid.

(5) In this section—

"unused relief" has the same meaning as in section 625; and

"relevant earnings derived from Lloyd's underwriting activities" means relevant earnings as an underwriting member of Lloyd's or by way of commission calculated by reference to the profits of Lloyd's underwriting business.

628.—(1) Where a person ("the former partner") has ceased to be a member of a partnership on retirement, because of age or ill-health or on death and, under—

Partnership retirement annuities.

(a) the partnership agreement; or

(b) an agreement replacing the partnership agreement or supplementing it or supplementing an agreement replacing it; or

(c) an agreement made with an individual who acquires the whole or part of the business carried on by the partnership;

annual payments are made for the benefit of the former partner or his widow or a dependant of his and are for the purposes of income tax income of the person for whose benefit they are made, the payments shall be treated as earned income of that person, except to the extent that they exceed the limit specified in subsection (2) below.

(2) The limit mentioned in subsection (1) above is 50 per cent. of the average of the amounts which, in the best three of the relevant years of assessment, were the former partner's shares of the relevant profits or gains; and for this purpose—

(a) the former partner's share in any year of the relevant profits or gains is, subject to subsection (3) below, so much of the relevant profits or gains as fell to be included in a return of his income for that year; and

(b) the relevant profits or gains are the profits or gains of any trade, profession or vocation on which the partnership or any other partnership of which the former partner was a member was assessed to income tax; and

(c) the relevant years of assessment are the last seven years of assessment in which he was required to devote substantially the whole of his time to acting as a partner in the partnership or those partnerships; and

(d) the best three of the relevant years of assessment are those three of them in which the amounts of his shares of the relevant profits were highest;

but where, in any of the relevant years, the circumstances were such that any of the profits or gains of a partnership were not assessable to income tax, paragraphs (a), (b) and (d) above shall apply as they would apply had those profits or gains been so assessable.

(3) If the retail prices index for the month of December in the last of the seven years referred to in paragraph (c) of subsection (2) above is higher than it was for the month of December in any of the other years referred to in that paragraph, the amount which, for that other year, was the former partner's share of the relevant profits or gains shall be treated for the purposes of that subsection as increased by the same percentage as the percentage increase in that index.

(4) If the retail prices index for the month of December preceding a year of assessment after that in which the former partner ceased to be a member of the partnership is higher than it was for the month of December in the year of assessment in which he ceased to be such a member, the amount which under subsection (2) above is the limit for the first-mentioned year of assessment shall be treated as increased by the same percentage as the percentage increase in that index.

(5) Where the former partner ceased to be a member of the partnership before the year 1974-75, subsection (4) above shall have effect as if he had ceased to be a member in that year.

Annuity premiums of Ministers and other officers.

629.—(1) For the purposes of this Chapter so much of any salary which—

(a) is payable to the holder of a qualifying office who is also a Member of the House of Commons, and

(b) is payable for a period in respect of which the holder is not a participant in relation to that office in arrangements contained in the Parliamentary pension scheme but is a participant in relation to his membership of the House of Commons in any such arrangements, or for any part of such a period,

as is equal to the difference between a Member's pensionable salary and the salary which (in accordance with any such resolution as is mentioned in subsection (3)(a) below) is payable to him as a Member holding that qualifying office shall be treated as remuneration from the office of Member and not from the qualifying office.

(2) In this section—

"Member's pensionable salary" means a Member's ordinary salary under any resolution of the House of Commons which, being framed otherwise than as an expression of opinion, is for the time being in force relating to the remuneration of Members or, if the resolution provides for a Member's ordinary salary thereunder to be treated for pension purposes as being at a higher rate, a notional yearly salary at that higher rate;

1987 c. 45.

"qualifying office" means an office mentioned in section 2(2)(b), (c) or (d) of the Parliamentary and other Pensions Act 1987;

"the Parliamentary pension scheme" has the same meaning as in that Act;

and without prejudice to the power conferred by virtue of paragraph 13 of Schedule 1 to that Act, regulations under section 2 of that Act may make provision specifying the circumstances in which a person is to be regarded for the purposes of this section as being or not being a participant in relation to his Membership of the House of Commons, or in relation to any office, in arrangements contained in the Parliamentary pension scheme.

(3) In subsection (2) above "a Member's ordinary salary", in relation to any resolution of the House of Commons, means—

(a) if the resolution provides for salary to be paid to Members at different rates according to whether or not they are holders of particular offices, or are in receipt of salaries or pensions as the holders or former holders of particular offices, a Member's yearly salary at the higher or highest rate; and

(b) in any other case, a Member's yearly salary at the rate specified in or determined under the resolution.

CHAPTER IV

PERSONAL PENSION SCHEMES

Preliminary

630. In this Chapter—

Interpretation.

"approved"—

(a) in relation to a scheme, means approved by the Board under this Chapter; and

(b) in relation to arrangements, means made in accordance with a scheme which is for the time being, and was when the arrangements were made, an approved scheme;

but does not refer to cases in which approval has been withdrawn;

"authorised insurance company" means either—

(a) a person authorised under section 3 or 4 of the Insurance Companies Act 1982 to carry on long term business and acting through a branch or office in the United Kingdom; or

1982 c. 50.

(b) a society registered as a friendly society under the Friendly Societies Act 1974 or the Friendly Societies Act (Northern Ireland) 1970;

1974 c. 46.
1970 c. 31 (N.I.).

"member", in relation to a personal pension scheme, means an individual who makes arrangements in accordance with the scheme;

"personal pension arrangements" means arrangements made by an individual in accordance with a personal pension scheme;

"personal pension scheme" means a scheme whose sole purpose is the provision of annuities or lump sums under arrangements made by individuals in accordance with the scheme;

"scheme administrator" means the person referred to in section 638(1).

Approval of schemes.

631.—(1) An application to the Board for their approval of a personal pension scheme shall be in such form, shall contain such information, and shall be accompanied by such documents, in such form, as the Board may prescribe.

(2) The Board may at their discretion grant or refuse an application for approval of a personal pension scheme, but their discretion shall be subject to the restrictions set out in sections 632 to 638.

(3) The Board shall give notice to the applicant of the grant or refusal of an application; and in the case of a refusal the notice shall state the grounds for the refusal.

(4) If an amendment is made to an approved scheme without being approved by the Board, their approval of the scheme shall cease to have effect.

Restrictions on approval

Establishment of schemes.

632.—(1) The Board shall not approve a personal pension scheme established by any person other than—

1986 c. 60.

(a) a person who is authorised under Chapter III of Part I of the Financial Services Act 1986 to carry on investment business and who carries on business of a kind mentioned in subsection (2) below;

1986 c. 53.

(b) a building society within the meaning of the Building Societies Act 1986;

1987 c. 22.

(c) an institution authorised under the Banking Act 1987;

1979 c. 37.

(d) a recognised bank or licensed institution within the meaning of the Banking Act 1979.

(2) The kinds of business referred to in subsection (1)(a) above are—

(a) issuing insurance policies or annuity contracts;

(b) managing unit trust schemes authorised under section 78(1) of the Financial Services Act 1986.

(3) Subsection (1) above shall not apply in relation to a scheme approved by the Board by virtue of section 620(5) if it was established before 4th January 1988.

(4) The Treasury may by order amend this section as it has effect for the time being.

Scope of benefits.

633.—(1) The Board shall not approve a personal pension scheme which makes provision for any benefit other than—

(a) the payment of an annuity satisfying the conditions in section 634;

(b) the payment to a member of a lump sum satisfying the conditions in section 635;

(c) the payment after the death of a member of an annuity satisfying the conditions in section 636;

(d) the payment on the death of a member of a lump sum satisfying either the conditions in section 637(1) or those in section 637(2).

(2) Subsection (1) above shall not prevent the approval of a scheme which makes provision for insurance against a risk relating to the non-payment of contributions.

634.—(1) The annuity must be payable by an authorised insurance company which may be chosen by the member.

Annuity to member.

(2) Subject to subsection (3) below, the annuity must not commence before the member attains the age of 50 or after he attains the age of 75.

(3) The annuity may commence before the member attains the age of 50 if—

(a) it is payable on his becoming incapable through infirmity of body or mind of carrying on his own occupation or any occupation of a similar nature for which he is trained or fitted; or

(b) the Board are satisfied that his occupation is one in which persons customarily retire before that age.

(4) Subject to subsection (5) below, the annuity must be payable to the member for his life.

(5) The annuity may continue for a term certain not exceeding ten years, notwithstanding the member's death within that term; and for this purpose an annuity shall be regarded as payable for a term certain notwithstanding that it may terminate, after the death of the member and before expiry of that term, on the happening of any of the following—

(a) the marriage of the annuitant;

(b) his attaining the age of 18;

(c) the later of his attaining that age and ceasing to be in full-time education.

(6) The annuity must not be capable of assignment or surrender, except that an annuity for a term certain may be assigned by will or by the annuitant's personal representatives in the distribution of his estate so as to give effect to a testamentary disposition, or to the rights of those entitled on an intestacy, or to an appropriation of it to a legacy or to a share or interest in the estate.

635.—(1) The lump sum must be payable only if the member so elects on or before the date on which an annuity satisfying the conditions in section 634 is first payable to him under the arrangements made in accordance with the scheme.

Lump sum to member.

(2) The lump sum must be payable when that annuity is first payable.

(3) The lump sum must not exceed one quarter of the total value, at the time when the lump sum is paid, of the benefits for the member provided for by the arrangements made by him in accordance with the scheme.

(4) The lump sum must not exceed £150,000 or such other sum as may for the time being be specified in an order made by the Treasury.

(5) The right to payment of the lump sum must not be capable of assignment or surrender.

Annuity after death of member.

636.—(1) The annuity must be payable by an authorised insurance company which may be chosen by the member or by the annuitant.

(2) The annuity must be payable to the surviving spouse of the member, or to a person who was at the member's death a dependant of his.

(3) The aggregate annual amount (or, if that amount varies, the aggregate of the initial annual amounts) of all annuities to which this section applies and which are payable under the same personal pension arrangements shall not exceed—

(a) where before his death the member was in receipt of an annuity under the arrangements, the annual amount (or, if it varied, the highest annual amount) of that annuity; or

(b) where paragraph (a) does not apply, the highest annual amount of the annuity that would have been payable under the arrangements to the member (ignoring any entitlement of his to commute part of it for a lump sum) if it had vested on the day before his death.

(4) Subject to subsections (5) to (9) below, the annuity must be payable for the life of the annuitant.

(5) Where the annuity is payable to the surviving spouse of the member and at the time of the member's death the surviving spouse is under the age of 60, the annuity may be deferred to a time not later than—

(a) the time when the surviving spouse attains that age; or

(b) where the member's annuity is payable to the surviving spouse for a term certain as mentioned in section 634(5) and the surviving spouse attains the age of 60 before the time when the member's annuity terminates, that time.

(6) The annuity may cease to be payable on the marriage of the annuitant.

(7) Where the annuity is payable to the surviving spouse of the member, it may cease before the death of the surviving spouse if—

(a) the member was survived by one or more dependants under the age of 18 and at the time of the member's death the surviving spouse was under the age of 45; and

(b) at some time before the surviving spouse attains that age no such dependant remains under the age of 18.

(8) Where the annuity is payable to a person who is under the age of 18 when it is first payable, it must cease to be payable either—

(a) on his attaining that age; or

(b) on the later of his attaining that age and ceasing to be in full-time education, unless he was a dependant of the member otherwise than by reason only that he was under the age of 18.

(9) The annuity may continue for a term certain not exceeding ten years, notwithstanding the original annuitant's death within that term; and for this purpose an annuity shall be regarded as payable for a term certain notwithstanding that it may terminate, after the death of the original annuitant and before the expiry of that term, on the happening of any of the following—

(a) the marriage of the annuitant to whom it is payable;

(b) his attaining the age of 18;

(c) the later of his attaining that age and ceasing to be in full-time education.

(10) The annuity must not be capable of assignment or surrender, except that an annuity for a term certain may be assigned by will or by the annuitant's personal representatives in the distribution of his estate so as to give effect to a testamentary disposition, or to the rights of those entitled on an intestacy, or to an appropriation of it to a legacy or to a share or interest in the estate.

637.—(1) The lump sum—

(a) must be payable by an authorised insurance company; and

(b) must be payable on the death of the member before he attains the age of 75.

(2) The lump sum—

(a) must be payable only if no annuity satisfying the conditions in either section 634 or section 636 has become payable; and

(b) subject to subsection (3) below, must represent no more than the return of contributions together with reasonable interest on contributions or bonuses out of profits.

(3) To the extent that contributions are invested in units under a unit trust scheme, the lump sum referred to in subsection (2) above may represent the sale or redemption price of the units.

638.—(1) The Board shall not approve a personal pension scheme unless they are satisfied that there is a person resident in the United Kingdom who will be responsible for the management of the scheme.

(2) The Board shall not approve a personal pension scheme unless it makes such provision for the making, acceptance and application of transfer payments as satisfies any requirements imposed by or under regulations made by the Board.

(3) The Board shall not approve a personal pension scheme unless it makes provision, in relation to arrangements made in accordance with the scheme, for ensuring that—

(a) the aggregate amount of the contributions that may be made in a year of assessment by the member and an employer of his under the arrangements, together with the aggregate amounts

U

of such contributions under other approved personal pension arrangements made by that member, does not exceed the permitted maximum for that year; and

(b) any excess is repaid to the member to the extent of his contributions and otherwise to his employer.

(4) In subsection (3) above "the permitted maximum" for a year of assessment means an amount equal to the aggregate of—

(a) the relevant percentage of the member's net relevant earnings for the year; and

(b) so much of any relief given under section 639(1) for that year as is given by virtue of section 642;

and references in subsection (3) to contributions by the member do not include references to contributions treated by virtue of section 649(3) as paid by him.

(5) In subsection (4) above "the relevant percentage" means 17.5 per cent. or, in a case where section 640(2) applies, the relevant percentage there specified.

(6) The Board shall not approve a personal pension scheme which permits the acceptance of contributions other than—

(a) contributions by members;

(b) contributions by employers of members; .

1986 c.50.

S.I. 1986/1888
(N.I. 18).

(c) minimum contributions paid by the Secretary of State under Part I of the Social Security Act 1986 or by the Department of Health and Social Services for Northern Ireland under Part II of the Social Security (Northern Ireland) Order 1986.

(7) The Board shall not approve a personal pension scheme which permits the acceptance of minimum contributions paid as mentioned in subsection (6)(c) above in respect of an individual's service—

(a) as director of the company, if his emoluments as such are within section 644(5); or

(b) in an office or employment to which section 645 applies.

Tax reliefs

Member's
contributions.

639.—(1) A contribution paid by an individual under approved personal pension arrangements made by him shall, subject to the provisions of this Chapter, be deducted from or set off against any relevant earnings of his for the year of assessment in which the payment is made.

Except where subsections (2) to (4) below apply, relief under this subsection in respect of a contribution shall be given only on a claim made for the purpose.

(2) In such cases and subject to such conditions as the Board may prescribe in regulations, relief under subsection (1) above shall be given in accordance with subsections (3) and (4) below.

(3) An individual who is entitled to such relief in respect of a contribution may deduct from the contribution when he pays it, and may retain, an amount equal to income tax at the basic rate on the contribution.

(4) The scheme administrator—

    (a) shall accept the amount paid after the deduction in discharge of the individual's liability to the same extent as if the deduction had not been made; and

    (b) may recover an amount equal to the deduction from the Board.

(5) Regulations under this section may make provision for carrying subsections (3) and (4) above into effect and, without prejudice to the generality of that, may provide—

    (a) for the manner in which claims for the recovery of a sum under subsection (4)(b) may be made;

    (b) for the giving of such information, in such form, as may be prescribed by or under the regulations;

    (c) for the inspection by persons authorised by the Board of books, documents and other records.

(6) Where relief under this section for any year of assessment is claimed and allowed (whether or not it then falls to be given for that year), and afterwards an assessment, alteration of an assessment, or other adjustment of the claimant's liability to tax is made, there shall also be made such consequential adjustments in the relief allowed or given under this section for that or any subsequent year as are appropriate.

(7) Where relief under this section is claimed and allowed for any year of assessment in respect of a contribution, relief shall not be given in respect of it under any other provision of the Income Tax Acts for the same or any subsequent year, nor (in the case of a contribution under an annuity contract) in respect of any other premium or consideration for an annuity under the same contract.

(8) References in the Income Tax Acts to relief in respect of life assurance premiums shall not be taken to include relief under this section.

640.—(1) The maximum amount that may be deducted or set off in any year of assessment by virtue of section 639(1) shall be 17.5 per cent. of the individual's net relevant earnings for that year.

Maximum amount of deductions.

(2) In the case of an individual whose age at the beginning of the year of assessment is within a range specified in the first column of the following table, subsection (1) above shall have effect with the substitution for 17.5 per cent. of the relevant percentage specified in the second column.

51 to 55	20 per cent.
56 to 60	22.5 per cent.
61 or more	27.5 per cent.

(3) Without prejudice to subsection (1) above, the maximum amount that may be deducted or set off in any year of assessment in respect of contributions paid by an individual to secure benefits satisfying the conditions in section 637(1) shall be 5 per cent. of the individual's net relevant earnings for that year.

(4) Where personal pension arrangements are made by an employee whose employer makes contributions under the arrangements, the maximum amount that may be deducted or set off in any year of assessment shall be reduced by the amount of the employer's contributions in the year.

(5) Any minimum contributions treated by virtue of section 649(3) as paid by the individual in respect of whom they are paid shall be disregarded for the purposes of this section.

Carry-back of contributions.

641.—(1) An individual who pays a contribution under approved personal pension arrangements in a year of assessment (whether or not a year for which he has relevant earnings) may elect that the contribution, or part of it, shall be treated as paid—

 (a) in the year of assessment preceding that year; or

 (b) if he had no net relevant earnings in that preceding year of assessment, in the year of assessment before that.

(2) Where for any year of assessment an individual—

 (a) has relevant earnings as an underwriting member of Lloyd's or by way of commission calculated by reference to the profits of Lloyd's underwriting business; and

 (b) there is an amount of unused relief attributable to those earnings,

the individual may elect that there shall be treated as paid in that year so much of any contributions paid by him under approved personal pension arrangements in the next year of assessment but two as does not exceed the amount of the unused relief.

(3) Subject to section 655(2), references in subsection (2) above to an amount of unused relief attributable to the earnings mentioned in subsection (2)(a) are to an amount which could have been deducted from or set off against those earnings under section 639(1) if—

 (a) the individual had paid contributions under approved personal pension arrangements in the year of assessment for which he has the earnings; or

 (b) any such contributions paid by him in that year had been greater.

(4) An election under this section must be made not later than three months after the end of the year of assessment in which the contributions treated as paid in another year are actually paid.

(5) Where an election is made under this section in respect of a contribution or part of a contribution, the other provisions of this Chapter shall have effect as if the contribution or part had been paid in the year specified in the election and not in the year in which it was actually paid.

642.—(1) Where—

(a) for any year of assessment an individual has relevant earnings from any trade, profession, vocation, office or employment carried on or held by him, and

(b) there is an amount of unused relief for that year,

relief may be given under section 639(1), up to the amount of the unused relief, in respect of so much of any contributions paid by him under approved personal pension arrangements in any of the next six years of assessment as exceeds the maximum applying for that year under section 640.

(2) In this section, references to an amount of unused relief for any year are to an amount which could have been deducted from or set off against the individual's relevant earnings for that year under section 639(1) if—

(a) the individual had paid contributions under approved personal pension arrangements in that year; or

(b) any such contributions paid by him in that year had been greater.

(3) Relief by virtue of this section shall be given for an earlier year rather than a later year, the unused relief taken into account in giving relief for any year being deducted from that available for giving relief in subsequent years and unused relief derived from an earlier year being exhausted before unused relief derived from a later year.

(4) Where a relevant assessment to tax in respect of a year of assessment becomes final and conclusive more than six years after the end of that year and there is an amount of unused relief for that year which results from the making of the assessment—

(a) that amount shall not be available for giving relief by virtue of this section for any of the six years following that year; but

(b) the individual may, within the period of six months beginning with the date on which the assessment becomes final and conclusive, elect that relief shall be given under section 639(1), up to that amount, in respect of so much of any contributions paid by him under approved personal pension arrangements within that period as exceeds the maximum applying under section 640 for the year of assessment in which they are paid;

and to the extent to which relief in respect of any contributions is given by virtue of this subsection it shall not be given by virtue of subsection (1) above.

(5) In this section "a relevant assessment to tax" means an assessment on the individual's relevant earnings or on the profits or gains of a partnership from which the individual derives relevant earnings.

643.—(1) Where contributions are paid by an employer under approved personal pension arrangements made by his employee, those contributions shall not be regarded as emoluments of the employment chargeable to tax under Schedule E.

(2) Income derived by a person from investments or deposits held by him for the purposes of an approved personal pension scheme shall be exempt from income tax.

(3) An annuity payable under approved personal pension arrangements shall be treated as earned income of the annuitant.

(4) Subsection (3) above applies only in relation to the annuitant to whom the annuity is made payable by the terms of the arrangements.

Meaning of "relevant earnings".

644.—(1) In this Chapter, "relevant earnings", in relation to an individual, means any income of his which is chargeable to tax for the year of assessment in question and is within subsection (2) below.

(2) Subject to subsections (3) to (5) below, income is within this subsection if it is—

    (a) emoluments chargeable under Schedule E from an office or employment held by the individual;

    (b) income from any property which is attached to or forms part of the emoluments of an office or employment held by him;

    (c) income which is chargeable under Schedule D and is immediately derived by him from the carrying on or exercise by him of his trade, profession or vocation (either as an individual or as a partner acting personally in a partnership);

    (d) income treated as earned income by virtue of section 529.

(3) Where section 645 applies to an office or employment held by the individual, neither emoluments from the office or employment nor income from any property which is attached to it or forms part of its emoluments are within subsection (2) above.

(4) The following are not income within subsection (2) above—

    (a) anything in respect of which tax is chargeable under Schedule E and which arises from the acquisition or disposal of shares or an interest in shares or from a right to acquire shares;

    (b) anything in respect of which tax is chargeable by virtue of section 148.

(5) Emoluments of an individual as director of a company are not income within subsection (2) above if—

    (a) the income of the company consists wholly or mainly of investment income; and

    (b) the individual, either alone or together with any other persons who are or have been at any time directors of the company, controls the company;

and section 840 shall apply for the purposes of this subsection.

(6) For the purposes of subsection (5) above—

    "director" includes any person occupying the position of director by whatever name called; and

    "investment income" shall be construed in accordance with paragraph 7 of Schedule 19.

(7) For the purposes of this Chapter, a married woman's relevant earnings shall not be treated as her husband's relevant earnings, notwithstanding that her income chargeable to tax is treated as his income.

645.—(1) This section applies to an office or employment held by an individual if— Earnings from pensionable employment.

(a) service in it is service to which a relevant superannuation scheme relates; and

(b) the individual is a participant in the scheme; and

(c) neither subsection (4) nor subsection (5) below applies to his participation in the scheme.

(2) This section applies whether or not the duties of the office or employment are performed wholly or partly in the United Kingdom or the individual is chargeable to tax in respect of it.

(3) In subsection (1) above "a relevant superannuation scheme" means a scheme or arrangement—

(a) the object or one of the objects of which is the provision, in respect of persons serving in particular offices or employments, of relevant benefits within the meaning of section 612; and

(b) which is established by a person other than the individual.

(4) This subsection applies to an individual's participation in a scheme if the scheme provides no benefits in relation to him other than—

(a) an annuity payable to his surviving spouse or a dependant of his;

(b) a lump sum payable on his death in service.

(5) This subsection applies to an individual's participation in a scheme if any sums paid pursuant to the scheme with a view to the provision of relevant benefits for him are treated as his income for the purposes of the Income Tax Acts.

646.—(1) Subject to subsections (3) to (7) below, in this Chapter "net relevant earnings", in relation to an individual, means the amount of his relevant earnings for the year of assessment in question, less the amount of any deductions within subsection (2) below which fall to be made from the relevant earnings in computing for the purposes of income tax his total income for that year. Meaning of "net relevant earnings".

(2) Deductions are within this subsection if they are—

(a) deductions which but for section 74(m), (p) or (q) could be made in computing the profits or gains of the individual;

(b) deductions made by virtue of section 198, 201 or 332(3);

(c) deductions in respect of relief under Schedule 9 to the Finance Act 1981 (stock relief); 1981 c. 35.

(d) deductions in respect of losses or capital allowances, being losses or capital allowances arising from activities profits or gains of which would be included in computing relevant earnings of the individual or the individual's wife or husband.

(3) For the purposes of this section, an individual's relevant earnings shall be taken to be those earnings before giving effect to any capital allowances, other than deductions allowable in computing profits or gains, but after taking into account the amounts on which charges fall to be made under the 1968 Act (including the enactments which under this Act or the 1970 Act are to be treated as contained in Part I of the 1968 Act); and in subsections (4) and (5) below, references to income (other than references to total income) shall be construed similarly.

(4) In the case of an individual's partnership profits, the amount to be included in arriving at his net relevant earnings shall be his share of the partnership income (estimated in accordance with the Income Tax Acts) after making from it any such deductions in respect of—

(a) payments made by the partnership;

(b) relief given to the partnership under Schedule 9 to the Finance Act 1981; or

(c) capital allowances falling to be made to the partnership,

as would be made in computing the tax payable in respect of that income.

(5) Where, in a year of assessment for which an amount is deducted or set off under section 639(1) against the net relevant earnings of an individual—

(a) a deduction in respect of such a loss or allowance of the individual as is mentioned in subsection (2)(d) above falls to be made in computing the total income of the individual or the individual's wife or husband; and

(b) the deduction or part of it falls to be so made from income other than relevant earnings;

the amount of the deduction made from that other income shall be treated as reducing the individual's net relevant earnings for subsequent years of assessment in accordance with subsection (6) below.

(6) The deduction shall be made so far as possible from the individual's net relevant earnings for the first of the subsequent years of assessment (whether or not he is entitled to relief under section 639(1) for that year), and then, so far as it cannot be so made, from those of the next year, and so on.

(7) An individual's net relevant earnings for any year of assessment shall be computed without regard to any deduction or set off under section 639(1) which falls to be made for that year in respect of the individual or the individual's wife of husband.

Charge to tax

Unauthorised payments.

647.—(1) This section applies to any payment within subsection (2) below which is made—

(a) out of funds which are or have been held for the purposes of a personal pension scheme which is or has at any time been approved; and

(b) to or for the benefit of an individual who has made personal pension arrangements in accordance with the scheme.

(2) A payment is within this subsection if—

(a) it is not expressly authorised by the rules of the scheme; or

(b) it is made at a time when the scheme or the arrangements are not approved and it would not have been expressly authorised by the rules of the scheme or by the arrangements when the scheme, or as the case may be the arrangements, were last so approved.

(3) The individual referred to in subsection (1)(b) above, whether or not he is the recipient of the payment, shall be chargeable to tax under Schedule E on the amount of the payment for the year of assessment in which the payment is made.

(4) This section applies to a transfer of assets or other transfer of money's worth as it applies to a payment, and in relation to such a transfer the reference in subsection (3) above to the amount of the payment shall be read as a reference to the value of the transfer.

648. Where contributions are paid by an employer under personal pension arrangements made by his employee then, if those arrangements are not approved arrangements and the contributions are not otherwise chargeable to income tax as income of the employee, the contributions shall be regarded for all the purposes of the Income Tax Acts as emoluments of the employment chargeable to tax under Schedule E.

Contributions under unapproved arrangements.

Miscellaneous

649.—(1) Where under Part I of the Social Security Act 1986 the Secretary of State pays minimum contributions for the purposes of approved personal pension arrangements, the amount of the employee's share of those contributions shall, instead of being the amount provided for in that Part, be the grossed-up equivalent of the amount so provided for.

Minimum contributions under Social Security Act 1986.
1986 c. 50.

(2) For the purposes of this section—

"the employee's share" of minimum contributions is so much of the contributions as is attributable to the percentage mentioned in paragraph (a) of the definition of "rebate percentage" in section 3(3) of the Social Security Act 1986;

"the grossed-up equivalent" of an amount is such sum as, after deduction of income tax at the basic rate in force for the year of assessment for which the contributions are paid, is equal to that amount.

(3) The employee's share of minimum contributions paid for a year of assessment by the Secretary of State for the purposes of approved personal pension arrangements shall be treated for the purposes of income tax—

(a) as the income for that year of the individual in respect of whom it is paid; and

(b) as contributions paid in that year by that individual under those arrangements.

(4) The Board may make regulations—

(a) providing for the recovery by the Secretary of State from the Board, in such circumstances as may be prescribed by the regulations, of any increase attributable to this section in the sums paid by the Secretary of State out of the National Insurance Fund;

(b) requiring the Secretary of State to give the Board such information as may be so prescribed about minimum contributions paid by the Secretary of State;

(c) prescribing circumstances in which this section or any provision of it shall not apply;

(d) making such provision as appears to the Board to be necessary or expedient for the purposes of supplementing the provisions of this section.

(5) Any payment received by the Secretary of State by virtue of this section shall be paid into the National Insurance Fund.

(6) In relation to Northern Ireland, this section shall have effect as if—

(a) references to the Secretary of State were references to the Department of Health and Social Services for Northern Ireland;

1986 c. 50.
S.I. 1986/1888
(N.I. 18).

(b) references to Part I and section 3(3) of the Social Security Act 1986 were references to Part II and Article 5(3) of the Social Security (Northern Ireland) Order 1986; and

(c) references to the National Insurance Fund were references to the Northern Ireland National Insurance Fund.

Withdrawal of approval.

650.—(1) If in the opinion of the Board the facts concerning an approved personal pension scheme or its administration or arrangements made in accordance with it do not warrant the continuance of their approval of the scheme, they may at any time by notice given to the scheme administrator withdraw their approval of the scheme.

(2) If in the opinion of the Board the facts concerning any approved personal pension arrangements do not warrant the continuance of their approval in relation to the arrangements, they may at any time by notice given to the individual who made them and to the scheme administrator withdraw their approval in relation to the arrangements.

(3) Without prejudice to the generality of subsection (2) above, the Board may withdraw their approval in relation to any personal pension arrangements if they are of the opinion that securing the provision of benefits under the arrangements was not the sole purpose of the individual in making them.

(4) A notice under subsection (1) or (2) above shall state the grounds on which, and the date from which, approval is withdrawn.

(5) The Board may not withdraw their approval from a date earlier than the date when the facts were first such that they did not warrant the continuance of their approval (so, however, that in a case within subsection (3) above their approval may be withdrawn from the day the arrangements in question were made).

PART XIV

651.—(1) Where the Board—

Appeals.

    (a) refuse an application by notice under section 631; or

    (b) withdraw an approval by notice under section 650;

the person to whom the notice is given may appeal to the Special Commissioners against the refusal or, as the case may be, the withdrawal.

(2) An appeal under this section shall be made by notice stating the grounds for the appeal and given to the Board before the end of the period of 30 days beginning with the day on which the notice of refusal or withdrawal was given to the appellant.

(3) On an appeal under this section against the withdrawal of an approval, the Special Commissioners may, instead of allowing or dismissing the appeal, order that the withdrawal shall have effect from a date other than that determined by the Board.

(4) The bringing of an appeal under this section shall not affect the validity of the decision appealed against pending the determination of the proceedings.

652.—(1) An inspector may give a notice to a scheme administrator requiring him to provide the inspector with—

Information about payments.

    (a) such particulars as the notice may require relating to contributions paid under approved personal pension arrangements made in accordance with the scheme;

    (b) such particulars as the notice may require relating to payments by way of return of contributions;

    (c) copies of such accounts as the notice may require.

(2) A person to whom a notice is given under this section shall comply with the notice within the period of 30 days beginning with the day on which it is given.

653. A person who knowingly makes a false statement or false representation on making an application under section 631 or for the purpose of obtaining for himself or any other person any relief from or repayment of tax under this Chapter shall be liable to a penalty not exceeding £500.

Information: penalties.

654.—(1) This section applies to any salary—

Remuneration of Ministers and other officers.

    (a) payable to the holder of a qualifying office who is also a Member of the House of Commons; and

(b) payable for a period in respect of which the holder is not a participant in relation to that office in arrangements contained in the Parliamentary pension scheme but is a participant in relation to his membership of the House of Commons in any such arrangements, or for any part of such a period.

(2) So much of any salary to which this section applies as is equal to the difference between a Member's pensionable salary and the salary which (in accordance with any such resolution as is mentioned in subsection (4)(a) below) is payable to him as a Member holding that qualifying office, shall be treated for the purposes of this Chapter as remuneration from the office of Member and not from the qualifying office.

(3) In this section—

"Member's pensionable salary" means a Member's ordinary salary under any resolution of the House of Commons which, being framed otherwise than as an expression of opinion, is for the time being in force relating to the remuneration of Members or, if the resolution provides for a Member's ordinary salary thereunder to be treated for pension purposes as being at a higher rate, a notional yearly salary at that higher rate;

1987 c. 45.

"qualifying office" means an office mentioned in paragraph (b), (c) or (d) of subsection (2) of section 2 of the Parliamentary and other Pensions Act 1987;

"the Parliamentary pension scheme" has the same meaning as in that Act;

and, without prejudice to the power conferred by virtue of paragraph 13 of Schedule 1 to that Act, regulations under section 2 of that Act may make provision specifying the circumstances in which a person is to be regarded for the purposes of this section as being or not being a participant in relation to his membership of the House of Commons, or in relation to any office, in arrangements contained in the Parliamentary pension scheme.

(4) In subsection (3) above "a Member's ordinary salary", in relation to any resolution of the House of Commons, means—

(a) if the resolution provides for salary to be paid to Members at different rates according to whether or not they are holders of particular offices or are in receipt of salaries or pensions as the holders or former holders of particular offices, a Member's yearly salary at the higher or highest rate; and

(b) in any other case, a Member's yearly salary at the rate specified in or determined under the resolution.

Transitional provisions.

655.—(1) Where approved personal pension arrangements are made by an individual who pays qualifying premiums within the meaning of section 620(1)—

(a) the amount that may be deducted or set off by virtue of section 639(1) in any year of assessment shall be reduced by the amount of any qualifying premiums which are paid in the year by the individual and in respect of which relief is given for the year under section 619(1)(a); and

(b) the relief which, by virtue of section 625, may be given under section 619 by reference to the individual's unused relief for any year shall be reduced by the amount of any contributions paid by him in that year under the approved personal pension arrangements.

(2) Where an individual elects under section 641 that a contribution or part of a contribution shall be treated as paid in the year of assessment 1984-85, 1985-86 or 1986-87, the payment shall be treated as the payment of a qualifying premium for the purposes of Chapter III of this Part; and in such a case references in section 641 to an amount of unused relief shall be construed in accordance with section 625.

(3) The references in section 642 to unused relief for any year are, for years of assessment before 1987-88, references to unused relief within the meaning of section 625.

(4) The Board shall not grant any application under section 631 so as to approve a scheme with effect from a date earlier than 4th January 1988.

(5) The Board may by regulations make provision for applications for approval of personal pension schemes to be granted provisionally in cases where the applications are made before 1st August 1989, notwithstanding that the Board have not satisfied themselves that the schemes comply with the requirements of sections 632 to 638; and such regulations may, in particular, provide—

(a) for the contents and form of certificates or other documents which the Board may require the applicant to give them before they grant an application provisionally;

(b) for the making of such amendments of the rules of the scheme after the provisional grant of an application as are necessary to enable the scheme to comply with the requirements of sections 632 to 638, and for those amendments to have effect as from the date of approval of the scheme;

(c) for the withdrawal of approval of the scheme as from that date if it does not comply with the requirements of sections 632 to 638 and such amendments as are mentioned in paragraph (b) above are not made;

and may make such supplementary provision as appears to the Board to be necessary or expedient.

CHAPTER V

PURCHASED LIFE ANNUITIES

656.—(1) Subject to section 657, a purchased life annuity shall, for the purposes of the provisions of the Tax Acts relating to tax on annuities and other annual payments, be treated as containing a capital element and, to the extent of the capital element, as not being an annual payment or in the nature of an annual payment; but the capital element in such an annuity shall be taken into account in computing profits or gains or losses for other purposes of the Tax Acts in any circumstances in which a lump sum payment would be taken into account.

Purchased life annuities other than retirement annuities.

(2) Where, in the case of any purchased life annuity to which this section applies, the amount of any annuity payment (but not the term of the annuity) depends on any contingency other than the duration of a human life or lives—

(a) the capital element shall be determined by reference—

(i) to the amount or value of the payments made or other consideration given for the grant of the annuity ("the purchase price"); and

(ii) to the expected term of the annuity, as at the date when the first annuity payment began to accrue, expressed in years (and any odd fraction of a year), and determined by reference to the prescribed tables of mortality;

and in head (ii) above "term" means the period from the date when the first annuity payment begins to accrue to the date when the last payment becomes payable;

(b) the capital element in any annuity payment made in respect of a period of 12 months shall be a fraction—

$$\frac{1}{E}$$

of the purchase price, where E is the expected term referred to in paragraph (a)(ii) above;

(c) the capital element in any annuity payment made in respect of a period of less than, or more than, 12 months shall be the amount at (b) above reduced or, as the case may be, increased, in the same proportion as the length of that period bears to a period of 12 months;

(d) subsection (3) below shall not apply but paragraphs (a) and (b) of subsection (4) below shall apply as they apply to that subsection.

(3) Subject to subsection (2) above, in the case of any purchased life annuity to which this section applies—

(a) the capital element shall be determined by reference to the amount or value of the payments made or other consideration given for the grant of the annuity; and

(b) the proportion which the capital element in any annuity payment bears to the total amount of that payment shall be constant for all payments on account of the annuity; and

(c) where neither the term of the annuity nor the amount of any annuity payment depends on any contingency other than the duration of a human life or lives, that proportion shall be the same proportion which the total amount or value of the consideration for the grant of the annuity bears to the actuarial value of the annuity payments as determined in accordance with subsection (4) below; and

(d) where either the term of the annuity or the amount of any annuity payment (but not both) depends on any contingency other than the duration of a human life or lives, that proportion shall be such as may be just, having regard to paragraph (c) above and to the contingencies affecting the annuity; and

(e) where both the term of the annuity and the amount of any annuity payment depend on any contingency other than the duration of a human life or lives, that proportion shall be such as may be just, having regard to subsection (2) above and to the contingencies affecting the annuity.

(4) For the purposes of subsection (3) above—

(a) any entire consideration given for the grant of an annuity and for some other matter shall be apportioned as appears just (but so that a right to a return of premiums or other consideration for an annuity shall not be treated for this purpose as a distinct matter from the annuity);

(b) where it appears that the amount or value of the consideration purporting to be given for the grant of an annuity has affected, or has been affected by, the consideration given for some other matter, the aggregate amount or value of those considerations shall be treated as one entire consideration given for both and shall be apportioned under paragraph (a) above accordingly; and

(c) the actuarial value of any annuity payments shall be taken to be their value as at the date when the first of those payments begins to accrue, that value being determined by reference to the prescribed tables of mortality and without discounting any payment for the time to elapse between that date and the date it is to be made.

(5) Where a person making a payment on account of any life annuity has been notified in the prescribed manner of any decision as to its being or not being a purchased life annuity to which this section applies or as to the amount of the capital element (if any), and has not been notified of any alteration of that decision, the notice shall be conclusive as to those matters for the purpose of determining the amount of income tax which he is entitled or required to deduct from the payment, or for which he is chargeable in respect of it.

(6) Where a person making a payment on account of a purchased life annuity to which this section applies has not been notified in the prescribed manner of the amount of the capital element, the amount of income tax which he is entitled or required to deduct from the payment, or for which he is chargeable in respect of it, shall be the same as if the annuity were not a purchased life annuity to which this section applies.

657.—(1) For the purposes of section 656—

"life annuity" means an annuity payable for a term ending with (or at a time ascertainable only by reference to) the end of a human life, whether or not there is provision for the annuity to end

Purchased life annuities to which section 656 applies.

during the life on the expiration of a fixed term or on the happening of any event or otherwise, or to continue after the end of the life in particular circumstances; and

"purchased life annuity" means a life annuity granted for consideration in money or money's worth in the ordinary course of a business of granting annuities on human life.

(2) Section 656 does not apply—

(a) to any annuity which would, apart from that section, be treated for the purposes of the provisions of the Tax Acts relating to tax on annuities and other annual payments as consisting to any extent in the payment or repayment of a capital sum;

(b) to any annuity where the whole or part of the consideration for the grant of the annuity consisted of sums satisfying the conditions for relief under section 266, 273 or 619 or to any annuity payable under a substituted contract within the meaning of section 622(3);

(c) to any annuity purchased in pursuance of any direction in a will, or to provide for an annuity payable by virtue of a will or settlement out of income of property disposed of by the will or settlement (whether with or without resort to capital);

(d) to any annuity purchased under or for the purposes of any sponsored superannuation scheme (as defined in section 624) or any scheme approved under section 620 or in pursuance of any obligation imposed, or offer or invitation made, under or in connection with any such scheme or to any other annuity purchased by any person in recognition of another's services (or past services) in any office or employment; or

(e) to any annuity payable under approved personal pension arrangements within the meaning of Chapter IV of this Part.

Supplementary.

658.—(1) Any question whether an annuity is a purchased life annuity to which section 656 applies, or what is the capital element in such an annuity, shall be determined by the inspector; but a person aggrieved by the inspector's decision on any such question may appeal within the prescribed time to the Special Commissioners.

(2) Save as otherwise provided in this Chapter, the procedure to be adopted in giving effect to this Chapter shall be such as may be prescribed.

(3) The Board may make regulations for prescribing anything which is to be prescribed under this Chapter, and the regulations may apply for the purposes of this Chapter or of the regulations any provision of the Income Tax Acts, with or without modifications.

(4) Regulations under subsection (3) above may in particular make provision as to the time limit for making any claim for relief from or repayment of tax under this Chapter and as to all or any of the following matters, that is to say—

(a) as to the information to be furnished in connection with the determination of any question whether an annuity is a purchased life annuity to which section 656 applies or what is the capital element in an annuity, and as to the persons who may be required to furnish any such information;

(b) as to the manner of giving effect to the decision on any such question, and (notwithstanding anything in section 348) as to the making of assessments for the purpose on the person entitled to the annuity; and

(c) as to the extent to which the decision on any such question is to be binding, and the circumstances in which it may be reviewed.

(5) If any person, for the purpose of obtaining for himself or for any other person any relief from or repayment of tax under this Chapter, knowingly makes any false statement or false representation, he shall be liable to a penalty not exceeding £500.

CHAPTER VI

MISCELLANEOUS

659. For the purposes of sections 592(2), 608(2)(a), 613(4), 614(3) and (4), 620(6) and 643(2) of this Act and section 149B(1)(g) and (h) and (2) of the 1979 Act, a contract entered into in the course of dealing in financial futures or traded options shall be regarded as an investment; and in this section "traded option" means an option which is for the time being quoted on a recognised stock exchange or on the London International Financial Futures Exchange.

Financial futures and traded options.

PART XV

SETTLEMENTS

CHAPTER I

DISPOSITIONS FOR SHORT PERIODS

Dispositions for period which cannot exceed six years.

660.—(1) Subject to subsection (2) below, any income which by virtue or in consequence of any disposition made, directly or indirectly, by any person (other than a disposition made for valuable and sufficient consideration), is payable to or applicable for the benefit of any other person for a period which cannot exceed six years shall be deemed for all the purposes of the Income Tax Acts to be the income of the person, if living, by whom the disposition was made, and not to be the income of any other person.

(2) Subsection (1) above shall not apply in relation to income which is payable as a covenanted payment to charity.

(3) In this Chapter, unless the context otherwise requires—

"disposition" includes any trust, covenant, agreement or arrangement, and

"a covenanted payment to charity" means a payment made under a covenant made otherwise than for consideration in money or money's worth in favour of a body of persons or trust established for charitable purposes only whereby the like annual payments (of which the payment in question is one) become payable for a period which may exceed three years and is not capable of earlier termination under any power exercisable without the consent of the persons for the time being entitled to the payments.

(4) For the purposes of subsection (3) above the Trustees of the National Heritage Memorial Fund and the Historic Buildings and Monuments Commission for England shall each be treated as a body of persons established for charitable purposes only.

Adjustments between disponor and trustees.

661.—(1) Where, by virtue of this Chapter, any income tax becomes chargeable on and is paid by the person by whom a disposition was made, that person shall be entitled—

(a) to recover from any trustee or other person to whom the income is payable by virtue or in consequence of the disposition the amount of the tax so paid; and

(b) for that purpose to require an inspector to furnish to him a certificate specifying the amount of the income in respect of which he has so paid tax and the amount of the tax so paid;

and any certificate so furnished shall be conclusive evidence of the facts appearing thereby.

(2) Where any person obtains in respect of any allowance or relief a repayment of income tax in excess of the amount of the repayment to which he would but for the provisions of this Chapter have been entitled, an amount equal to the excess shall be paid by him to the trustee or other

person to whom the income is payable by virtue or in consequence of the disposition, or, where there are two or more such persons, shall be apportioned among those persons as the case may require.

If any question arises as to the amount of any payment or as to any apportionment to be made under this subsection, that question shall be decided by the General Commissioners whose decision thereon shall be final.

(3) Subject to section 833(3), any income which is deemed by virtue of this Chapter to be the income of any person shall be deemed to be the highest part of his income.

662.—(1) In the case of any disposition where there is more than one person who made the disposition, this Chapter shall, subject to the provisions of this section, have effect in relation to each person who made the disposition as if he were the only person who had made it.

(2) In the case of any such disposition, references in this Chapter to income payable or applicable by virtue or in consequence of the disposition include, in relation to any person making the disposition, only—

(a) income from property which that person has provided directly or indirectly for the purposes of the disposition ("the settled property"); and

(b) income from property representing the settled property; and

(c) income from so much of any property which represents both the settled property and other property as, on a just apportionment, represents the settled property; and

(d) income provided directly or indirectly by that person.

(3) In this section references to property which represents other property include references to property which represents accumulated income from that other property.

CHAPTER II

SETTLEMENTS ON CHILDREN

663.—(1) Where, by virtue or in consequence of any settlement to which this Chapter applies and during the life of the settlor, any income is paid to or for the benefit of a child of the settlor in any year of assessment, the income shall, if at the time of the payment the child was unmarried and below the age of 18, be treated for all the purposes of the Income Tax Acts as the income of the settlor for that year and not as the income of any other person.

(2) Where an offshore income gain (within the meaning of Chapter V of Part XVII) accrues in respect of a disposal of assets made by a person holding them as trustee for a person who would be absolutely entitled as against the trustee but for being an infant, the income which by virtue of section 761(1) is treated as arising by reference to that gain shall for the purposes of this Chapter be deemed to be paid to the infant; and in this subsection, in relation to Scotland, "infant" means pupil or minor.

(3) This Chapter applies to every settlement, wheresoever it was made or entered into, and whether it was made or entered into before or after the passing of this Act, except a settlement made or entered into before 22nd April 1936 which immediately before that date was irrevocable.

Paragraph 10 of Schedule 30 shall have effect as respects certain earlier settlements on children.

(4) Income paid to or for the benefit of a child of a settlor shall not be treated as provided in subsection (1) above for any year of assessment in which the aggregate amount of the income paid to or for the benefit of that child, which, but for this subsection, would be so treated by virtue of subsection (1) above, does not exceed £5.

(5) This Chapter shall not apply in relation to any income arising under a settlement in any year of assessment for which the settlor is not chargeable to income tax as a resident in the United Kingdom, and references in this Chapter to income shall be construed accordingly.

Accumulation settlements.

664.—(1) Subject to the provisions of this section, for the purposes of this Chapter—

(a) income which, by virtue or in consequence of a settlement to which this Chapter applies, is so dealt with that it, or assets representing it, will or may become payable or applicable to or for the benefit of a child of the settlor in the future (whether on fulfilment of a condition, or the happening of a contingency, or as the result of the exercise of a power or discretion conferred on any person, or otherwise) shall be deemed to be paid to or for the benefit of that child; and

(b) any income so dealt with which is not required by the settlement to be allocated, at the time when it is so dealt with, to any particular child or children of the settlor shall be deemed to be paid in equal shares to or for the benefit of each of the children to or for the benefit of whom or any of whom the income or assets representing it will or may become payable or applicable.

(2) Where any income is dealt with as mentioned in subsection (1) above by virtue or in consequence of a settlement to which this Chapter applies, being a settlement which, at the time when the income is so dealt with, is an irrevocable settlement—

(a) subsection (1) above shall not apply to that income unless and except to the extent that that income consists of, or represents directly or indirectly, sums paid by the settlor which are allowable as deductions in computing his total income; and

(b) subject to subsection (3) below, any sum whatsoever paid thereafter by virtue or in consequence of the settlement, or any enactment relating thereto, to or for the benefit of a child of the settlor, being a child who at the time of the payment is unmarried and below the age of 18, shall be deemed for the purposes of section 663 to be paid as income.

(3) Subsection (2)(b) above shall not apply if and to the extent that the sum paid as mentioned in that paragraph together with any other sums previously so paid (whether to that child or to any other child who, at the time of the payment, was unmarried and below the age of 18) exceeds the aggregate amount of the income which, by virtue or in consequence of the

settlement, has been paid to or for the benefit of a child of the settlor, or dealt with as mentioned in subsection (1) above, since the date when the settlement took effect or the date when it became irrevocable, whichever is the later.

665.—(1) For the purposes of this Chapter, a settlement shall not be deemed to be irrevocable if its terms provide—

Meaning of "irrevocable".

(a) for the payment to the settlor or, during the life of the settlor, to the wife or husband of the settlor for his or her benefit, or for the application for the benefit of the settlor or, during the life of the settlor, of the wife or husband of the settlor, of any income or assets in any circumstances whatsoever during the life of the settlor's child; or

(b) for the determination of the settlement by the act or on the default of any person; or

(c) for the payment of any penalty by the settlor in the event of his failing to comply with the provisions of the settlement.

In this section "the settlor's child", in relation to any settlement, means any child of the settlor to or for the benefit of whom any income, or assets representing it, is or are or may be payable or applicable by virtue or in consequence of the settlement.

(2) For the purposes of this Chapter, a settlement shall not be deemed to be revocable by reason only—

(a) that it contains a provision under which any income or assets will or may become payable to or applicable for the benefit of the settlor, or the wife or husband of the settlor, on the bankruptcy of the settlor's child or in the event of an assignment of or charge on that income or those assets being executed by the settlor's child; or

(b) that it provides for the determination of the settlement by the act or on the default of any person in such a manner that the determination will not, during the lifetime of the settlor's child, benefit the settlor or the wife or husband of the settlor; or

(c) in the case of a settlement to which section 33 of the Trustee Act 1925 applies, that it directs income to be held for the benefit of the settlor's child on protective trusts, unless the trust period is a period less than the life of the child or the settlement specifies some event on the happening of which the child would, if the income were payable during the trust period to him absolutely during that period, be deprived of the right to receive all or part of the income.

1925 c. 19.

666.—(1) Where interest is paid by the trustees of a settlement to which this Chapter applies there shall be deemed for the purposes of this Chapter to be paid to or for the benefit of a child of the settlor who at the time of the payment is unmarried and below the age of 18 (in addition to any other amount deemed to be so paid) an amount equal to a fraction—

Interest paid by trustees.

$$\frac{B}{A}$$

of the interest, where—

> A is the whole of the income arising under the settlement in the year of assessment, less any expenses of the trustees of the settlement paid in that year which, in the absence of any express provision of the settlement, would be properly chargeable to income, and

> B is such part of A as is paid to or for the benefit of any child of the settlor who is unmarried and below the age of 18.

(2) This section shall not apply to interest in respect of which relief from tax is allowable under any provision of the Income Tax Acts or to interest payable to the settlor or the wife or husband of the settlor (if living with the settlor).

(3) Nothing in this section shall be construed as affecting the liability to tax of the person receiving or entitled to the interest.

(4) For the purpose of this section "income arising under the settlement" has the meaning given by section 681, which for that purpose shall be deemed to apply in relation to settlements to which this Chapter applies as it applies in relation to settlements to which Chapter III of this Part applies.

(5) In this section the reference to the trustees' expenses excludes sums mentioned in section 682(1)(a).

Adjustments between disponor and trustees.

667.—(1) Where, by virtue of this Chapter, any income tax becomes chargeable on and is paid by the person by whom a settlement was made or entered into, that person shall be entitled—

> (a) to recover from any trustee or other person to whom the income is payable by virtue or in consequence of the settlement the amount of the tax so paid; and

> (b) for that purpose to require an inspector to furnish to him a certificate specifying the amount of income in respect of which he has so paid tax and the amount of the tax so paid,

and any certificate so furnished shall be conclusive evidence of the facts appearing thereby.

(2) Where any person obtains in respect of any allowance or relief a repayment of income tax in excess of the amount of the repayment to which he would but for the provisions of this Chapter have been entitled, an amount equal to the excess shall be paid by him to the trustee or other person to whom the income is payable by virtue or in consequence of the settlement, or, where there are two or more such persons, shall be apportioned among those persons as the case may require.

If any question arises as to the amount of any payment or as to any apportionment to be made under this subsection, that question shall be decided by the General Commissioners whose decision thereon shall be final.

(3) Subject to section 833(3), any income which is deemed by virtue of this Chapter to be the income of any person shall be deemed to be the highest part of his income.

668.—(1) In the case of any settlement where there is more than one settlor, this Chapter shall, subject to the provisions of this section, have effect in relation to each settlor as if he were the only settlor.

(2) In the case of any such settlement, only the following can, for the purposes of this Chapter, be taken into account, in relation to any settlor, as income paid by virtue or in consequence of the settlement to or for the benefit of a child of the settlor, that is to say—

    (a) income originating from that settlor; and

    (b) in a case in which section 664(2)(b) applies, any sums which are under that paragraph to be deemed to be paid as income.

(3) In applying section 664(2)(b) to any settlor—

    (a) the references to sums paid by virtue or in consequence of the settlement or any enactment relating thereto include only sums paid out of property originating from that settlor or income originating from that settlor; and

    (b) the reference to income which by virtue or in consequence of the settlement has been paid to or for the benefit of a child of the settlor or dealt with as mentioned in section 664(1) includes only income originating from that settlor.

(4) References in this section to property originating from a settlor are references to—

    (a) property which that settlor has provided directly or indirectly for the purposes of the settlement; and

    (b) property representing that property; and

    (c) so much of any property which represents both property provided as mentioned in paragraph (a) above and other property as, on a just apportionment, represents the property so provided.

(5) References in this section to income originating from a settlor are references to—

    (a) income from property originating from that settlor; and

    (b) income provided directly or indirectly by that settlor.

(6) In subsections (4) and (5) above—

    (a) references to property or income which a settlor has provided directly or indirectly include references to property or income which has been provided directly or indirectly by another person in pursuance of reciprocal arrangements with that settlor but do not include references to property or income which that settlor has provided directly or indirectly in pursuance of reciprocal arrangements with another person; and

PART XV

(b) references to property which represents other property include references to property which represents accumulated income from that other property.

Power to obtain information under Chapter II.

669. An inspector may by notice require any party to a settlement to furnish him within such time as he may direct (not being less than 28 days) with such particulars as he thinks necessary for the purposes of this Chapter.

Interpretation of Chapter II.

670. In this Chapter—

"child" includes a stepchild and an illegitimate child;

"settlement" includes any disposition, trust, covenant, agreement, arrangement or transfer of assets;

"settlor", in relation to a settlement, includes any person by whom the settlement was made or entered into directly or indirectly, and in particular (but without prejudice to the generality of the preceding words of this definition) includes any person who has provided or undertaken to provide funds directly or indirectly for the purpose of the settlement, or has made with any other person a reciprocal arrangement for that other person to make or enter into the settlement;

"income", except in the phrase (occurring in section 663(1)) "be treated for all the purposes of the Income Tax Acts as the income of the settlor for that year and not as the income of any other person", includes any income chargeable to income tax by deduction or otherwise and any income which would have been so chargeable if it had been received in the United Kingdom by a person resident and ordinarily resident in the United Kingdom.

CHAPTER III

REVOCABLE SETTLEMENTS ETC.

Revocable settlements allowing release of obligation.

671.—(1) If and so long as the terms of any settlement (wherever made) are such that—

(a) any person has or may have power, whether immediately or in the future, and whether with or without the consent of any other person, to revoke or otherwise determine the settlement or any provision thereof and, in the event of the exercise of the power, the settlor or the wife or husband of the settlor will or may cease to be liable to make any annual payments payable by virtue or in consequence of any provision of the settlement; or

(b) the settlor or the wife or husband of the settlor may, whether immediately or in the future, cease, on the payment of a penalty, to be liable to make any annual payments payable by virtue or in consequence of any provision of the settlement,

any sums payable by the settlor or the wife or husband of the settlor by virtue or in consequence of that provision of the settlement in any year of assessment shall be treated for all the purposes of the Income Tax Acts as the income of the settlor for that year and not as the income of any other person.

(2) Where any such power as is referred to in subsection (1)(a) above cannot be exercised—

(a) in the case of a covenanted payment to charity (as defined by section 660(3)), within the period of three years, or

(b) in any other case, within the period of six years,

from the time when the first of the annual payments so referred to becomes payable, and the like annual payments are payable in each year throughout that period, subsection (1)(a) above shall not apply so long as that power cannot be exercised.

(3) In subsections (1) and (2) above—

(a) the references to a power to revoke or otherwise determine a settlement or any provision thereof shall be deemed to include references to any power to diminish the amount of any payments which are or may be payable under the settlement or any provision thereof and to any power to diminish the amount of any annual payments which the settlor or the wife or husband of the settlor is or may be liable to make by virtue or in consequence of any provision of the settlement;

(b) the references to the settlor or the wife or husband of the settlor ceasing to be liable to make any annual payments payable by virtue or in consequence of any provision of the settlement shall be deemed to include references to a diminution of the amount of any such annual payments which the settlor or the wife or husband of the settlor is or may be liable to make;

but the sums to be treated under subsections (1) and (2) above as the income of the settlor for any year of assessment and not as the income of any other person shall, where those subsections would not apply but for paragraph (b) above, be such part only of the sums payable as mentioned in that paragraph by the settlor or the wife or husband of the settlor in that year as corresponds to the diminution mentioned in that paragraph.

672.—(1) If and so long as the terms of any settlement (wherever made) are such that—

(a) any person has or may have power, whether immediately or in the future, and whether with or without the consent of any other person, to revoke or otherwise determine the settlement or any provision thereof; and

(b) in the event of the exercise of the power, the settlor or the wife or husband of the settlor will or may become beneficially entitled to the whole or any part of the property then comprised in the settlement or of the income arising from the whole or any part of the property so comprised,

any income arising under the settlement from the property comprised in the settlement in any year of assessment or from a corresponding part of that property, or a corresponding part of any such income, as the case may be, shall, subject to subsection (2) below, be treated for all the purposes of the Income Tax Acts as the income of the settlor for that year and not as the income of any other person.

(2) Where any such power cannot be exercised within six years from the time when any particular property first becomes comprised in the settlement, subsection (1) above shall not apply to income arising under the settlement from that property, or from property representing that property, so long as the power cannot be exercised.

(3) In subsection (1) above the references to a power to revoke or otherwise determine a settlement or any provision thereof shall be deemed to include references to—

(a) any power to diminish the property comprised in the settlement; and

(b) any power to diminish the amount of any payments which are or may be payable under the settlement or any provision thereof to any person other than the settlor and the wife or husband of the settlor.

Settlements where settlor retains an interest.

673.—(1) If and so long as the settlor has an interest in any income arising under or property comprised in a settlement (wherever made), any income so arising during the life of the settlor in any year of assessment shall, to the extent to which it is not distributed, be treated for all the purposes of the Income Tax Acts as the income of the settlor for that year and not as the income of any other person except that—

(a) if and so long as that interest is an interest neither in the whole of the income arising under the settlement nor in the whole of the property comprised in the settlement, the amount of income to be treated as the income of the settlor by virtue of this subsection shall be such part of the income which, but for this paragraph, would be so treated as is proportionate to the extent of that interest; and

(b) where it is shown that any amount of the income which is not distributed in any year of assessment consists of income which falls to be treated as the income of the settlor for that year by virtue of section 671 or 672, that amount shall be deducted from the amount of income which, but for this paragraph, would be treated as his for that year by virtue of this subsection.

(2) Subject to subsection (3) below, the settlor shall, for the purpose of subsection (1) above, be deemed to have an interest in income arising under or property comprised in a settlement if any income or property which may at any time arise under or be comprised in that settlement is, or will or may become, payable to or applicable for the benefit of the settlor or the wife or husband of the settlor in any circumstances whatsoever.

(3) The settlor shall not be deemed to have an interest in any income arising under or property comprised in a settlement—

(a) if and so long as that income or property cannot become payable or applicable as mentioned in subsection (2) above except in the event of—

(i) the bankruptcy of some person who is or may become beneficially entitled to that income or property; or

(ii) any assignment of or charge on that income or property being made or given by some such person; or

(iii) in the case of a marriage settlement, the death of both the parties to the marriage and of all or any of the children of the marriage; or

(iv) the death under the age of 25 or some lower age of some person who would be beneficially entitled to that income or property on attaining that age; or

(b) if and so long as some person is alive and under the age of 25 during whose life that income or property cannot become payable or applicable as mentioned in subsection (2) above except in the event of that person becoming bankrupt or assigning or charging his interest in that income or property.

674.—(1) This section applies to any settlement (wherever made) if and so long as the terms of the settlement are such that any person has or may have power, exercisable at his discretion, whether immediately or in the future, and whether with or without the consent of any person— Settlements: discretionary power for benefit of settlor etc.

(a) to pay or apply to or for the benefit of the settlor or the wife or husband of the settlor the whole or any part of the income or property which may at any time arise under or be comprised in the settlement; or

(b) to secure the payment or application to or for the benefit of the settlor or the wife or husband of the settlor of the whole or any part of that income or property.

(2) Subject to subsections (3) and (4) below, any income arising in any year of assessment under a settlement to which this section applies or, as the case may be, any income so arising from the property comprised in any such settlement or from a corresponding part of that property, or a corresponding part of any such income, shall (so far as it is not so treated apart from this section) be treated for all the purposes of the Income Tax Acts as the income of the settlor for that year and not as the income of any other person.

(3) Where the power mentioned in subsection (1) of this section cannot be exercised within six years from the time when any income or class of income first arises under the settlement or from the time when any particular property first becomes comprised in the settlement, then, so long as the power cannot be exercised, subsection (2) above shall not apply to any income arising under the settlement or, as the case may be, any income of that class or income from that property or property representing that property.

(4) Where, under section 673(3), the settlor is not deemed to have an interest in any income arising under or property comprised in the settlement, subsection (2) above shall not apply to that income or, as the case may be, to income arising from that property.

675.—(1) Tax chargeable by virtue of section 671, 672, 673 or 674 shall be charged under Case VI of Schedule D. Provisions supplementary to sections 671 to 674.

(2) In computing the liability to income tax of a settlor chargeable by virtue of any of those sections the same deductions and reliefs shall be allowed as would have been allowed if the income treated as his by virtue of that section had been received by him.

PART XV

(3) Where, by virtue of any of those sections, any income tax becomes chargeable on and is paid by a settlor, he shall be entitled—

(a) to recover from any trustee, or other person to whom income arises under the settlement, the amount of the tax so paid; and

(b) for that purpose to require an inspector to furnish to him a certificate specifying the amount of income in respect of which he has so paid tax and the amount of tax so paid.

Any certificate so furnished shall be conclusive evidence of the facts stated therein.

(4) Where any person obtains, in respect of any allowance or relief, a repayment of income tax in excess of the amount of the repayment to which he would, but for section 671, 672, 673 or 674, have been entitled, an amount equal to the excess shall be paid by him to the trustee or other person to whom income arises under the settlement, or, where there are two or more such persons, shall be apportioned among those persons as the case may require.

If any question arises as to the amount of any payment or as to any apportionment to be made under this subsection, that question shall be decided by the General Commissioners whose decision thereon shall be final.

(5) Subject to section 833(3), any income which is treated by virtue of section 671, 672, 673 or 674 as income of a settlor shall be deemed for the purpose of this section to be the highest part of his income.

Disallowance of deduction from total income of certain sums paid by settlor.

676.—(1) Where, by virtue or in consequence of any settlement to which this section applies, the settlor pays directly or indirectly in any year of assessment to the trustees of the settlement any sums which would, but for this subsection, be allowable as deductions in computing his total income for that year, those sums shall not be so allowable to the extent to which the aggregate amount thereof falls within the amount of income arising under the settlement in that year which has not been distributed, less—

(a) so much of any income arising under the settlement in that year which has not been distributed as is shown to consist of income which has been treated as the income of the settlor by virtue of section 671, 672 or 674, and

(b) the amount of income so arising in that year which is treated as the income of the settlor by virtue of section 673.

(2) For the purposes of subsection (1) above, any sum paid in any year of assessment by the settlor to any body corporate connected with the settlement in that year shall be treated as if it had been paid to the trustees of the settlement in that year by virtue or in consequence of the settlement.

(3) No relief shall be given under any of the provisions of the Income Tax Acts on account of tax paid in respect of so much of any income arising under a settlement in any year of assessment as is equal to the aggregate amount of any sums paid by the settlor in that year which are not allowable as deductions by virtue of this section.

(4) This section shall apply to any settlement (wherever made) made after 26th April 1938, and where income arising under any settlement (wherever made) made on or before that date is treated as the income of the settlor by virtue of section 671 or 672 but ceases to be so treated by reason of any variation of the terms of the settlement made after that date, or would have been so treated but for such a variation, this section shall apply to that settlement as from the date when the variation takes effect.

(5) In this section, references to sums paid by a settlor include references to sums paid by the wife or husband of the settlor.

677.—(1) Any capital sum paid directly or indirectly in any year of assessment by the trustees of a settlement to which this section applies to the settlor shall—

(a) to the extent to which the amount of that sum falls within the amount of income available up to the end of that year, be treated for all the purposes of the Income Tax Acts as the income of the settlor for that year;

(b) to the extent to which the amount of that sum is not by virtue of this subsection treated as his income for that year and falls within the amount of the income available up to the end of the next following year, be treated for those purposes as the income of the settlor for the next following year;

and so on for each subsequent year up to a maximum of ten subsequent years, taking the reference in paragraph (b) to the year mentioned in paragraph (a) as a reference to that and any other year before the subsequent year in question.

(2) For the purposes of subsection (1) above, the amount of income available up to the end of any year shall, in relation to any capital sum paid as mentioned in that subsection, be taken to be the aggregate amount of income arising under the settlement in that year and any previous year which has not been distributed, less—

(a) the amount of that income taken into account under that subsection in relation to that sum in any previous year or years; and

(b) the amount of any other capital sums paid to the settlor in any year before that sum was paid; and

(c) so much of any income arising under the settlement in that year and any previous year which has not been distributed as is shown to consist of income which has been treated as income of the settlor by virtue of section 671, 672, 674 or 683; and

(d) any income arising under the settlement in that year and any previous year which has been treated as the income of the settlor by virtue of section 673; and

(e) any sums paid by virtue or in consequence of the settlement, to the extent that they are not allowable, by virtue of section 676, as deductions in computing the settlor's income for that year or any previous year; and

(f) any sums paid by virtue or in consequence of the settlement in that year or any previous year which have been treated as the income of the settlor by virtue of section 664(2)(b); and

(g) any sums included in the income arising under the settlement as amounts which have been or could have been apportioned to a beneficiary as mentioned in section 681(1)(b); and

(h) an amount equal to the sum of tax at the basic rate and tax at the additional rate on—

(i) the aggregate amount of income arising under the settlement in that year and any previous year which has not been distributed, less

(ii) the aggregate amount of the income and sums referred to in paragraphs (c), (d), (e), (f) and (g) above.

(3) Where any amount is included in a person's income by virtue of section 421 in respect of any loan or advance, there shall be a corresponding reduction in the amount (if any) afterwards falling to be so included in respect of it by virtue of this section.

(4) Where the capital sum paid to the settlor is a sum paid by way of loan, then—

(a) if the whole of it is repaid, no part of that sum shall by virtue of subsection (1) above be treated as the settlor's income for any year of assessment after that in which the repayment occurs; and

(b) if one or more capital sums have previously been paid to him by way of loan and wholly repaid, the amount of that capital sum shall be treated as equal to its excess, if any, over so much of the sum or sums previously paid as has already fallen to be treated as his income by virtue of that subsection.

(5) Where the capital sum paid to the settlor is a sum paid by way of complete repayment of a loan, then, if an amount not less than that sum is thereafter lent by the settlor to the trustees of the settlement, no part of that sum shall by virtue of subsection (1) above be treated as his income for any year of assessment after that in which the further loan is made.

(6) Where the whole or any part of any sum is treated by virtue of this section as income of the settlor for any year, it shall be treated as income of such an amount as, after deduction of both tax at the basic rate and tax at the additional rate for that year, would be equal to that sum or that part of that sum.

(7) Tax chargeable by virtue of this section shall be charged under Case VI of Schedule D; and there shall be set off against the tax charged on any amount treated by virtue of this section as income of the settlor for any year an amount equal to—

(a) the sum of tax at the basic rate and tax at the additional rate for that year on the amount so treated as his income; or

(b) so much of that sum as is equal to the tax charged,

whichever is the less.

(8) In computing the liability to income tax of a settlor chargeable by virtue of this section, the same deductions and reliefs shall be allowed as would have been allowed if the amount treated as his income by virtue of this section had been received by him as income.

(9) This section applies to any settlement wherever made, and whether made before or after the passing of this Act, and in this section—

> (a) "capital sum" means, subject to subsection (10) below—
>
>> (i) any sum paid by way of loan or repayment of a loan; and
>>
>> (ii) any other sum paid otherwise than as income, being a sum which is not paid for full consideration in money or money's worth,
>
> but does not include any sum which could not have become payable to the settlor except in one of the events specified in section 673(3); and
>
> (b) references to sums paid to the settlor include references to sums paid to the wife or husband of the settlor or to the settlor (or the husband or wife of the settlor) jointly with another person.

(10) For the purposes of this section there shall be treated as a capital sum paid to the settlor by the trustees of the settlement any sum which—

> (a) is paid by them to a third party at the settlor's direction or by virtue of the assignment by him of his right to receive it where the direction or assignment was given or made on or after 6th April 1981; or
>
> (b) is otherwise paid or applied by them for the benefit of the settlor,

and which would not apart from this subsection be treated as a capital sum paid to him.

678.—(1) Where—

> (a) a capital sum is paid after 5th April 1981 to the settlor in a year of assessment by any body corporate connected with the settlement in that year; and
>
> (b) an associated payment has been or is made directly or indirectly to that body by the trustees of the settlement,

the capital sum shall, in accordance with subsection (2) below, be treated for the purposes of section 677 as having been paid to the settlor by the trustees of the settlement.

(2) A capital sum to which subsection (1) above applies shall—

> (a) to the extent to which the amount of that sum falls within the total of the associated payment or payments made up to the end of the year of assessment in which it is paid, be treated as having been paid to the settlor in that year;
>
> (b) to the extent to which the amount of that sum is not treated as paid to the settlor in that year and falls within the total of the associated payment or payments made up to the end of the next following year (less what was taken into account under this

subsection in relation to that sum in the previous year), be treated as having been paid to the settlor in the next following year,

and so on for each subsequent year, taking the references in paragraph (b) to the year mentioned in paragraph (a) as references to that and any other year before the subsequent year in question.

(3) In this section "associated payment", in relation to any capital sum paid to the settlor by a body corporate, means—

(a) any capital sum paid to that body by the trustees of the settlement; and

(b) any other sum paid or asset transferred to that body by those trustees which is not paid or transferred for full consideration in money or money's worth,

being a sum paid or asset transferred in the five years ending or beginning with the date on which the capital sum is paid to the settlor.

(4) For the purposes of this section any capital sum paid by a body corporate, and any associated payment made to a body corporate, at a time when it is, within the meaning of section 416, associated with another body corporate may be treated as paid by or made to that other body corporate.

(5) In this section "capital sum" has the same meaning as in section 677; and any question whether a capital sum has been paid to the settlor by a body corporate or to a body corporate by the trustees shall be determined in the same way as any question under that section whether a capital sum has been paid to the settlor by the trustees.

(6) Subsection (1) above does not apply to any sum paid to the settlor by way of loan or repayment of a loan if—

(a) the whole of the loan is repaid within 12 months of the date on which it was made; and

(b) the period for which amounts are outstanding in respect of loans made to the settlor by that or any other body corporate connected with the settlement, or by him to that or any other such body, in any period of five years does not exceed 12 months.

(7) Where a capital sum is paid to the settlor in a year of assessment by a body corporate connected with the settlement in that year it shall be assumed until the contrary is shown that an associated payment of an amount not less than that of the capital sum has been made to that body by the trustees of the settlement.

Application of Chapter III to settlements by two or more settlors.

679.—(1) In the case of any settlement where there is more than one settlor, this Chapter shall, subject to the provisions of this section, have effect in relation to each settlor as if he were the only settlor.

(2) In this Chapter—

(a) references to the property comprised in a settlement include, in relation to any settlor, only property originating from that settlor, and

(b) references to income arising under the settlement include, in relation to any settlor, only income originating from that settlor.

(3) In considering for the purposes of this Chapter, in relation to any settlor, whether any, and if so, how much, of the income arising under the settlement has been distributed, any sums paid partly out of income originating from that settlor and partly out of other income must (so far as not apportioned by the terms of the settlement) be apportioned evenly over all that income.

(4) References in sections 671(1) and 676 to sums payable by virtue or in consequence of any provision of the settlement or sums paid by virtue or in consequence of the settlement include, in relation to any settlor, only sums payable or paid by that settlor.

(5) References in this section to property originating from a settlor are references to—

(a) property which that settlor has provided directly or indirectly for the purposes of the settlement; and

(b) property representing that property; and

(c) so much of any property which represents both property so provided and other property as, on a just apportionment, represents the property so provided.

(6) References in this section to income originating from a settlor are references to—

(a) income from property originating from that settlor; and

(b) so much of any such income of a body corporate as is mentioned in section 681(1)(b) as corresponds to property originating from the settlor which is comprised in the settlement; and

(c) income provided directly or indirectly by that settlor.

(7) In subsections (5) and (6) above—

(a) references to property or income which a settlor has provided directly or indirectly include references to property or income which has been provided directly or indirectly by another person in pursuance of reciprocal arrangements with that settlor, but do not include references to property or income which that settlor has provided directly or indirectly in pursuance of reciprocal arrangements with another person; and

(b) references to property which represents other property include references to property which represents accumulated income from that other property.

680. An inspector may by notice require any person, being a party to a settlement, to furnish him within such time as he may direct (not being less than 28 days) with such particulars as he thinks necessary for the purposes of any of the provisions of this Chapter.

Power to obtain information for purposes of Chapter III.

681.—(1) In this Chapter, "income arising under a settlement" includes—

Interpretation of Chapter III.

v

(a) any income chargeable to income tax by deduction or otherwise, and any income which would have been so chargeable if it had been received in the United Kingdom by a person domiciled, resident and ordinarily resident in the United Kingdom; and

(b) where the amount of the income of any body corporate has been apportioned under section 423 for any year or period, or could have been so apportioned if the body corporate were incorporated and resident in any part of the United Kingdom, so much of the income of the body corporate for that year or period as is equal to the amount which has been or could have been so apportioned to the trustees of or a beneficiary under the settlement,

but, where the settlor is not domiciled, or not resident, or not ordinarily resident, in the United Kingdom in any year of assessment, does not include income arising under the settlement in that year in respect of which the settlor, if he were actually entitled thereto, would not be chargeable to income tax by deduction or otherwise by reason of his not being so domiciled, resident or ordinarily resident.

(2) Where the income of a body corporate has been, or could have been, apportioned under section 423 any amount of that income which by virtue of subsection (1)(b) above is to be included in the income arising under a settlement shall be increased by such proportion thereof as corresponds to the rate of advance corporation tax applicable to a distribution made at the end of the accounting period to which the apportionment relates.

(3) In subsections (1) and (2) above references to income that could have been apportioned to a person if a body corporate were incorporated and resident in any part of the United Kingdom include references to income that could have been apportioned to that person indirectly through any other body corporate if that other body had also been so incorporated and resident.

(4) In this Chapter—

"settlement" includes any disposition, trust, covenant, agreement or arrangement, and

"settlor", in relation to a settlement, means any person by whom the settlement was made;

and a person shall be deemed for the purposes of this Chapter to have made a settlement if he has made or entered into the settlement directly or indirectly, and, in particular, but without prejudice to the generality of the preceding words, if he has provided or undertaken to provide funds directly or indirectly for the purpose of the settlement, or has made with any other person a reciprocal arrangement for that other person to make or enter into the settlement.

(5) For the purposes of this Chapter, a body corporate shall be deemed to be connected with a settlement in any year of assessment if at any time in that year—

(a) it is a close company (or only not a close company because it is not resident in the United Kingdom) and the participators then include the trustees of the settlement; or

(b) it is controlled (within the meaning of section 840) by a company falling within paragraph (a) above.

(6) The provisions of this Chapter shall be in addition to and not in derogation of any other provisions of this Act.

682.—(1) For the purposes of this Chapter, income arising under a settlement in any year of assessment shall be deemed not to have been distributed if and to the extent that it exceeds the aggregate amount of—

(a) the sums, excluding all payments of interest, paid in that year by the trustees of the settlement to any persons (not being a body corporate connected with the settlement and not being the trustees of another settlement made by the settlor or the trustees of the settlement) in such manner that they fall to be treated in that year, otherwise than by virtue of section 677, as the income of those persons for the purposes of income tax, or would fall to be so treated if those persons were domiciled, resident and ordinarily resident in the United Kingdom and the sums had been paid to them there, and

(b) subject to subsections (2) to (5) below, any expenses of the trustees of the settlement paid in that year which, in the absence of any express provision of the settlement, would be properly chargeable to income, in so far as such expenses are not included in the sums mentioned in paragraph (a) above, and

(c) in a case where the trustees of the settlement are trustees for charitable purposes, the amount by which any income arising under the settlement in that year in respect of which exemption from tax may be granted under section 505 exceeds the aggregate amount of any such sums or expenses as are mentioned in paragraphs (a) and (b) above paid in that year which are properly chargeable to that income.

(2) Subsection (1)(b) above shall apply to any interest paid by the trustees of the settlement subject to subsections (3) to (6) below.

(3) If no sums within subsection (1)(a) were paid to any person other than the settlor, or the wife or husband of the settlor, the whole of any interest paid by the trustees of the settlement shall be excluded from subsection (1)(b) above.

(4) If any sum was so paid, there shall be excluded from subsection (1)(b) above a fraction—

$$\frac{A - B}{A}$$

of any interest paid by the trustees of the settlement where—

A is the whole of the income arising under the settlement in the year of assessment, less the sums referred to in subsection (1)(b) above apart from subsections (2), (3) and (5) of this section; and

B is so much of the sums within subsection (1)(a) above as is paid to persons other than the settlor, or the wife or husband of the settlor.

(5) Subsections (2) to (4) above shall not apply to interest in respect of which relief from tax is allowable under any provision of the Income Tax Acts or to interest payable to the settlor or the wife or husband of the settlor if living with the settlor.

(6) Nothing in subsections (2) to (5) above shall be construed as affecting the liability to tax of the person receiving or entitled to the interest.

CHAPTER IV

LIABILITY TO HIGHER RATE AND ADDITIONAL RATE TAX

Liability of settlors

683.—(1) Where, during the life of the settlor, income arising under a settlement made after 6th April 1965 is, under the settlement and in the events that occur, payable to or applicable for the benefit of any person other than the settlor, then, unless, under the settlement and in those events, the income either—

(a) consists of annual payments made under a partnership agreement to or for the benefit of a former member, or the widow or dependants of a deceased former member, of the partnership, being payments made under a liability incurred for full consideration; or

(b) is excluded by subsection (3), (6) or (9) below; or

(c) is income arising under a settlement made by one party to a marriage by way of provision for the other after the dissolution or annulment of the marriage, or while they are separated under an order of a court or under a separation agreement or in such circumstances that the separation is likely to be permanent, being income payable to or applicable for the benefit of that other party; or

(d) is income from property of which the settlor has divested himself absolutely by the settlement; or

(e) is income which, by virtue of some provision of the Income Tax Acts not contained in this Chapter, is to be treated for the purposes of those Acts as income of the settlor;

the income shall, for the purposes of excess liability, be treated as the income of the settlor and not as the income of any other person.

(2) In subsection (1) above "excess liability" means the excess of liability to income tax over what it would be if all income tax were charged at the basic rate to the exclusion of any higher rate.

(3) Subject to subsection (4) below, subsection (1) above shall not apply to so much of an individual's income as consists of covenanted payments to charity.

(4) If at least £1,000 of an individual's income for any year of assessment consists of covenanted payments to charity which, in the hands of the charities receiving them, consitute income for which, by virtue of subsection (3) of section 505, relief is not available under

subsection (1) of that section, so much of the individual's income as consists of those payments shall not be excluded from the operation of subsection (1) above by virtue of subsection (3) above.

(5) If, for any chargeable period of a charity—

(a) the income of the charity includes two or more covenanted payments to charity; and

(b) only a part of the aggregate of those payments constitutes income for which, by virtue of subsection (3) of section 505 relief is not available under subsection (1) of that section,

each of the payments which make up the aggregate shall be treated for the purposes of subsection (4) above as apportioned rateably between the part of the aggregate referred to in paragraph (b) above and the remainder.

(6) Subsection (1) above shall not apply to income consisting of annual payments made by an individual, in connection with the acquisition by him of the whole or part of a business—

(a) to or for the benefit of the individual from whom it is acquired or, if he is dead, to or for the benefit of his widow or dependants, or

(b) if the acquisition was from a partnership, to or for the benefit of a former member, or the widow or dependants of a deceased former member, of that or any preceding partnership, or to or for the benefit of an individual from whom the business or part was acquired by that or any preceding partnership or, if he is dead, to or for the benefit of the widow or dependants of such an individual;

being payments made under a liability incurred for full consideration.

(7) Payments made in respect of any individual under a liability incurred in connection with an acquisition from a partnership shall only be excluded from the operation of subsection (1) above by virtue of subsection (6)(b) above if, and to the extent that, they are made in substitution for, or matched by reductions in, other payments which would themselves be excluded from its operation.

(8) Where the right of a former member of a partnership to payments falling due not more than ten years after he ceased to be a member of that partnership has devolved on his death, subsections (1)(a) and (6) above shall apply to the payments as they would apply if he had not died.

(9) Where for any year of assessment there is made to or for the benefit of a former member, or the widow or a dependant of a deceased former member, of a partnership an annual payment which—

(a) is excluded from the operation of subsection (1) above by virtue of paragraph (a) of that subsection or by virtue of subsection (6) above; and

(b) falls short of the limit applying for that year under section 628;

any additional annual payment made to or for the benefit of that person shall, notwithstanding that it is not made under a liability incurred for full consideration, be excluded from the operation of subsection (1) above to the extent to which it makes good that shortfall.

(10) For the purposes of this section—

(a) "former member", in relation to a partnership, means an individual who has ceased to be a member of that partnership on retirement or death;

(b) a partnership becomes a "preceding partnership" of another if it transfers its business or part of its business to another and one or more individuals are members of both, and any preceding partnership of the transferor by reference to any part of the business transferred shall also become a preceding partnership of the transferee;

(c) "covenanted payments to charity" has the meaning given by section 660(3).

684.—(1) Where, during the life of the settlor, income arising under a settlement made before 7th April 1965, but after 9th April 1946, is, under the settlement and in the events that occur, payable to or applicable for the benefit of any person other than the settlor, then, unless under the settlement and in those events, the income either—

(a) is payable to an individual for his own use; or

(b) is applicable for the benefit of an individual named in that behalf in the settlement or of two or more individuals so named; or

(c) is applicable for the benefit of a child or children of an individual named in that behalf in the settlement; or

(d) is income from property of which the settlor has divested himself absolutely by the settlement; or

(e) is income which, by virtue of some provision of the Income Tax Acts not contained in this Chapter, is to be treated for the purposes of those Acts as income of the settlor;

the income shall, for the purposes of excess liability, be treated as the income of the settlor and not as the income of any other person.

(2) In subsection (1) above "excess liability" means the excess of liability to income tax over what it would be if all income tax were charged at the basic rate to the exclusion of any higher rate.

(3) The exceptions provided for by paragraphs (a), (b) and (c) of subsection (1) above shall not apply where the named individual or individuals or, in the case of paragraph (c), either the named individual or the child or any of the children in question, is in the service of the settlor or accustomed to act as the solicitor or agent of the settlor.

685.—(1) For the purposes of sections 683 and 684, the settlor shall not be deemed to have divested himself absolutely of any property if that property or any derived property is, or will or may become, in any circumstances whatsoever, payable to or applicable for the benefit of the settlor or, in the case of a settlement made after 6th April 1965, the wife or husband of the settlor.

(2) For those purposes, the settlor shall not be deemed not to have divested himself absolutely of any property by reason only that the property or any derived property may become payable to or applicable for the benefit of the settlor, or, in the case of a settlement made after 6th April 1965, the wife or husband of the settlor, in the event of—

(a) the bankruptcy of some person who is or may become beneficially entitled to the property or any of the derived property; or

(b) an assignment of or charge on the property or any of the derived property being made or given by some such person; or

(c) in the case of a marriage settlement, the death of both parties to the marriage and of all or any of the children of the marriage; or

(d) the death under the age of 25 or some lower age of some person who would be beneficially entitled to the property or the derived property on attaining that age.

(3) In subsections (1) and (2) above "derived property", in relation to any property, means income from that property or any other property directly or indirectly representing proceeds of, or of income from, that property or any income therefrom.

(4) In sections 683 and 684 and this section "income arising under a settlement", "settlement" and "settlor" have the meanings assigned to them for the purposes of Chapter III of this Part by section 681.

(5) Section 679 shall have effect in relation to sections 683 and 684 and this section as it has effect in relation to Chapter III of this Part.

Liability of trustees

686.—(1) So far as income arising to trustees is income to which this section applies it shall, in addition to being chargeable to income tax at the basic rate, be chargeable at the additional rate.

Liability to additional rate tax of certain income of discretionary trusts.

(2) This section applies to income arising to trustees in any year of assessment so far as it—

(a) is income which is to be accumulated or which is payable at the discretion of the trustees or any other person (whether or not the trustees have power to accumulate it); and

(b) is neither (before being distributed) the income of any person other than the trustees nor treated for any of the purposes of the Income Tax Acts as the income of a settlor; and

(c) is not income arising under a trust established for charitable purposes only or income from investments, deposits or other property held for the purposes of a fund or scheme established for the sole purpose of providing relevant benefits within the meaning of section 612; and

(d) exceeds the income applied in defraying the expenses of the trustees in that year which are properly chargeable to income (or would be so chargeable but for any express provisions of the trust).

(3) This section also applies to sums apportioned to the trustees under section 423 and treated, under 426(2) as applied by subsection (4) below, as income received by the trustees.

(4) Sections 426(1) and (2), 427 and 428 shall, with the omission in section 426(2)(a) of the words following "the apportionment relates", the substitution of "income" for "total income" and all other necessary modifications, apply to a sum apportioned to trustees as they apply to sums apportioned to an individual; and section 429 shall apply accordingly.

(5) For the purposes of this section sums paid or credited to trustees in any year of assessment in respect of dividends or interest payable in respect of shares in or deposits with or loans to a building society being sums in respect of which the society is required to account for and pay an amount in accordance with regulations under section 476(1) shall be treated as income for that year received by the trustees after deduction of income tax from a corresponding gross amount.

In this subsection expressions used in section 476 have the same meanings as in that section.

(6) In this section "trustees" does not include personal representatives; but where personal representatives, on or before the completion of the administration of the estate, pay to trustees any sum representing income which, if personal representatives were trustees within the meaning of this section, would be income to which this section applies, that sum shall be deemed to be paid to the trustees as income and to have borne income tax at the basic rate.

This subsection shall be construed as if it were contained in Part XVI.

Payments under discretionary trusts.

687.—(1) Where, in any year of assessment, trustees make a payment to any person in the exercise of a discretion exercisable by them or any person other than the trustees, then, if the sum paid is for all the purposes of the Income Tax Acts income of the person to whom it is paid (but would not be his income apart from the payment), the following provisions of this section shall apply with respect to the payment in lieu of section 348 or 349(1).

(2) The payment shall be treated as a net amount corresponding to a gross amount from which tax has been deducted at a rate equal to the sum of the basic rate and the additional rate in force for the year in which the payment is made; and the sum treated as so deducted shall be treated—

(a) as income tax paid by the person to whom the payment is made; and

(b) so far as not set off under the following provisions of this section, as income tax assessable on the trustees.

(3) The following amounts, so far as not previously allowed, shall be set against the amount assessable (apart from this subsection) on the trustees in pursuance of subsection (2)(b) above—

(a) the amount of any tax on income arising to the trustees and charged at the additional as well as at the basic rate in pursuance of section 686;

(b) the amount of tax at the additional rate on any sum treated, under section 426(2) as applied by section 686(4) or under section 249(6), as income of the trustees;

(c) the amount of tax at the basic rate on any amount taken for the purposes of sections 426 to 428 as applied by section 686(4) to be the amount to be excluded from the income of the trustees in accordance with section 427(4);

(d) an amount of tax in respect of income found on a claim made by the trustees to have been available to them for distribution at the end of the year 1972-73, which shall be taken to be two-thirds of the net amount of that income;

(e) the amount of any tax on income arising to the trustees by virtue of section 761(1) and charged at a rate equal to the sum of the basic rate and the additional rate by virtue of section 764; and

(f) the amount of any tax on annual profits or gains treated as received by trustees by virtue of section 714(2) or 716(3) of this Act or paragraph 2(2) or (3) of Schedule 22 to the Finance Act 1985 and charged at a rate equal to the sum of the basic rate and the additional rate by virtue of section 720(5) of this Act or paragraph 8(1) of Schedule 23 to that Act;

1985 c. 54.

(g) the amount of any tax on income which arose to the trustees by virtue of section 38(2) of the Finance Act 1974 (development gains) and charged at a rate equal to the basic rate and the additional rate in pursuance of section 43(1) of that Act;

1974 c. 30.

but tax on any income represented by amounts paid or credited as mentioned in section 686(5) shall be taken into account under paragraph (a) above only on production of a certificate from the building society concerned specifying those amounts and stating that an amount representing income tax on that income calculated at the basic rate has been or will be accounted for.

(4) In this section "trustees" does not include personal representatives within the meaning of section 701(4).

688. Where under a scheme set up to comply with section 153(4)(b) of the Companies Act 1985 or Article 163(4)(b) of the Companies (Northern Ireland) Order 1986 (financial assistance for company employees and salaried directors acquiring shares) trustees receive interest from such employees or directors then, if and so far as the scheme requires an equivalent amount to be paid by way of interest by the trustees to the company, the trustees shall be exempt from tax under Case III of Schedule D on that interest received by them.

Schemes for employees and directors to acquire shares. 1985 c. 6. S.I. 1986/1032 (N.I. 6).

689.—(1) The provisions of this section shall have effect in relation to the excess amount of the income tax due from any person ("the beneficiary") to whom, or for whose benefit, any income or any capital may in the discretion of some other person be paid or applied under a trust.

Recovery from trustees of discretionary trusts of higher rate tax due from beneficiaries.

(2) In this section "the excess amount" means so much of the income tax payable in respect of the beneficiary's income as exceeds what would be the amount thereof if all income tax were chargeable at the basic rate to the exclusion of any higher rate.

(3) If the whole or part of the excess amount of the income tax charged in respect of the income of the beneficiary is not paid before the expiry of six months from the date when it became due and payable, the Board may at any time thereafter, so long as the excess amount or any part thereof remains unpaid, cause to be served on the trustees of the trust a notice that the excess amount or any part thereof remains unpaid.

(4) Where such a notice is served in accordance with the provisions of this section on the trustees of the trust, it shall be the duty of the trustees, as soon as may be, and if necessary from time to time, to pay to the Board in or towards satisfaction of the excess amount or any part thereof from time to time remaining unpaid any income or capital which, by virtue of any exercise of the discretion under the trust, the beneficiary may become entitled to receive or to have applied for his benefit.

(5) Any payments made out of income by trustees on account of tax in respect of which a notice under this section has been served shall be deemed for all the purposes of the Income Tax Acts to represent income paid to the beneficiary.

(6) Any sum which the trustees are liable to pay by virtue of this section shall be recoverable from them as a debt due to the Crown.

(7) Where there are two or more trustees under the trust, a notice under this section shall be deemed to have been validly served upon the trustees if served upon any one of them, but nothing in this section shall render a trustee personally liable for anything done by him in good faith and in ignorance of the fact that such a notice has been served.

CHAPTER V

MAINTENANCE FUNDS FOR HISTORIC BUILDINGS

Schedule 4
directions.
1984 c. 51.

690. In this Chapter "a Schedule 4 direction" means a direction under paragraph 1 of Schedule 4 to the Inheritance Tax Act 1984 (maintenance funds for historic buildings); and any reference in this Chapter to paragraph 1 or Schedule 4 is a reference to that paragraph or that Schedule, as the case may be.

Certain income
not to be income
of settlor etc.

691.—(1) This section applies to any settlement in relation to which a Schedule 4 direction has effect.

(2) The trustees of the settlement may elect that this subsection shall have effect in relation to any year of assessment, and if they do so—

    (a) any income arising in that year from the property comprised in the settlement which, apart from this subsection, would be treated by virtue of this Part as income of the settlor shall not be so treated; and

    (b) no sum applied in that year out of the property for the purposes mentioned in paragraph 3(1)(a)(i) of Schedule 4 (maintenance etc. of qualifying property) shall be treated for any purposes of the Income Tax Acts as the income of any person—

(i) by virtue of any interest of that person in, or his occupation of, the qualifying property in question; or

(ii) by virtue of section 677.

(3) Where income arising from the property comprised in the settlement in a year of assessment for which no election is made under subsection (2) above is treated by virtue of this Part as income of the settlor, paragraph (b) of that subsection shall have effect in relation to any sums in excess of that income which are applied in that year as mentioned in that paragraph.

(4) Any election under subsection (2) above shall be by notice to the Board in such form as the Board may require and shall be made within two years of the end of the year of assessment to which it relates.

(5) Where—

(a) for part of a year of assessment a Schedule 4 direction has effect and circumstances obtain by virtue of which income arising from property comprised in the settlement is treated as income of a settlor under this Part; and

(b) for the remainder of that year either no such direction has effect, or no such circumstances obtain, or both,

subsections (1) to (4) above shall apply as if each of those parts were a separate year of assessment and separate elections may be made accordingly.

692.—(1) This section applies to income arising from settled property in respect of which a Schedule 4 direction has effect if the income—

Reimbursement of settlor.

(a) is treated by virtue of this Part as income of the settlor, and

(b) is applied in reimbursing the settlor for expenditure incurred by him for a purpose within paragraph 3(1)(a)(i) of Schedule 4,

and if that expenditure is (or would apart from the reimbursement be) deductible in computing the profits of a trade carried on by the settlor.

(2) Income to which this section applies shall not be treated as reducing the expenditure deductible in computing the profits referred to in subsection (1) above, and shall not be regarded as income of the settlor otherwise than by virtue of this Part.

693. Where settled property in respect of which a Schedule 4 direction has effect constitutes part only of the property comprised in a settlement, it and the other property shall be treated as comprised in separate settlements for the purposes of sections 27 and 380 to 387 and this Part.

Severance of settled property for certain purposes.

694.—(1) If in the case of a settlement in respect of which a Schedule 4 direction has effect—

Trustees chargeable to income tax at 30 per cent. in certain cases.

(a) any of the property comprised in the settlement (whether capital or income) is applied otherwise than as mentioned in paragraph 3(1)(a)(i) or (ii) of Schedule 4; or

(b) any of that property on ceasing to be comprised in the settlement devolves otherwise than on any such body or charity as is mentioned in paragraph 3(1)(a)(ii) of that Schedule; or

(c) the direction ceases to have effect;

then, unless subsection (6) below applies, income tax shall be charged under this section in respect of the settlement.

(2) Subject to subsection (3) below, tax chargeable under this section shall be charged at the rate of 30 per cent. on the whole of the income which has arisen in the relevant period from the property comprised in the settlement and has not been applied (or accumulated and then applied) as mentioned in paragraph 3(1)(a)(i) or (ii) of Schedule 4.

In this subsection "the relevant period" means, if tax has become chargeable under this section in respect of the settlement on a previous occasion, the period since the last occasion and, in any other case, the period since the settlement took effect.

(3) Tax shall not be chargeable under this section in respect of income which by virtue of Chapters I to IV of this Part is treated as income of the settlor; but where income arising in any year of assessment is exempted by this subsection any sums applied in that year as mentioned in paragraph 3(1)(a)(i) or (ii) of Schedule 4 shall be treated as paid primarily out of that income and only as to the excess, if any, out of income not so exempted.

(4) Tax charged under this section shall be in addition to any tax chargeable apart from this section and—

(a) the persons assessable and chargeable with tax under this section shall be the trustees of the settlement; and

(b) all the provisions of the Income Tax Acts relating to assessments and to the collection and recovery of income tax shall, so far as applicable, apply to the charge, assessment, collection and recovery of tax under this section.

(5) Tax shall also be chargeable in accordance with subsections (1) to (4) above if—

(a) any of the property comprised in a settlement to which subsection (1) above applies, on ceasing at any time to be comprised in the settlement, devolves on any such body or charity as is referred to in paragraph (b) of that subsection, and

(b) at or before that time an interest under the settlement is or has been acquired for a consideration in money or money's worth by that or another such body or charity;

but for the purposes of this subsection any acquisition from another such body or charity shall be disregarded.

(6) Tax shall not be chargeable under this section in respect of a settlement on an occasion when the whole of the property comprised in it is transferred tax-free into another settlement; but on the first occasion on which tax becomes chargeable under this section in respect of a settlement ("the current settlement") comprising property which was previously comprised in another settlement or settlements and has become comprised in the current settlement as a result of, or of a series of, tax-free transfers, the relevant period for the purposes of subsection (2) above shall, as respects that property, be treated as having begun—

(a) on the last occasion on which tax became chargeable under this section in respect of the other settlement or any of the other settlements; or

(b) if there has been no such occasion, when the other settlement or the first of the other settlements took effect.

(7) For the purposes of subsection (6) above, property is transferred tax-free from one settlement into another if either—

(a) it ceases to be comprised in the first-mentioned settlement and becomes comprised in the other settlement in circumstances such that by virtue of paragraph 9(1) of Schedule 4 there is (or, but for paragraph 9(4), there would be) no charge to capital transfer tax or inheritance tax in respect of the property; or

(b) both immediately before and immediately after the transfer it is property in respect of which a Schedule 4 direction has effect.

PART XVI

ESTATES OF DECEASED PERSONS IN COURSE OF ADMINISTRATION

Limited interests in residue.

695.—(1) The following provisions of this section shall have effect in relation to a person who, during the period commencing on the death of a deceased person and ending on the completion of the administration of his estate ("the administration period") or during a part of that period, has a limited interest in the residue of the estate or in a part thereof.

(2) When any sum has been paid during the administration period in respect of that limited interest, the amount of that sum shall, subject to subsection (3) below, be deemed for all tax purposes to have been paid to that person as income for the year of assessment in which that sum was paid or, in the case of a sum paid in respect of an interest that has ceased, for the last year of assessment in which it was subsisting.

(3) On the completion of the administration of the estate—

(a) the aggregate amount of all sums paid before, or payable on, the completion of the administration in respect of that limited interest shall be deemed to have accrued due to that person from day to day during the administration period or the part of that period during which he had that interest, as the case may be, and to have been paid to him as it accrued due; and

(b) the amount deemed to have been paid to that person by virtue of paragraph (a) above in any year of assessment shall be deemed for all tax purposes to have been paid to him as income for that year; and

(c) where the amount which is deemed to have been paid to that person as income for any year by virtue of this subsection is less or greater than the amount deemed to have been paid to him as income for that year by virtue of subsection (2) above, such adjustments shall be made as are provided in section 700.

(4) Any amount which is deemed to have been paid to that person as income for any year by virtue of this section shall—

(a) in the case of a United Kingdom estate, be deemed to be income of such an amount as would after deduction of income tax for that year be equal to the amount deemed to have been so paid, and to be income which has borne income tax at the basic rate; and

(b) in the case of a foreign estate, be deemed to be income of the amount deemed to have been so paid, and shall be chargeable to income tax under Case IV of Schedule D as if it were income arising from securities in a place out of the United Kingdom.

(5) Where—

(a) a person has been charged to income tax for any year by virtue of this section in respect of an amount deemed to have been paid to him as income in respect of an interest in a foreign estate ("the deemed income"), and

(b) any part of the aggregate income of that estate for that year has borne United Kingdom income tax by deduction or otherwise ("the aggregate income"),

the tax so charged on him shall, on proof of the facts on a claim, be reduced by an amount bearing the same proportion thereto as the amount of the deemed income which has borne United Kingdom income tax, less the tax so borne, bears to the amount of the aggregate income, less the tax so borne.

(6) Where relief has been given under subsection (5) above, such part of the amount in respect of which he has been charged to income tax as corresponds to the proportion mentioned in that subsection shall, for the purpose of computing his total income, be deemed to represent income of such an amount as would after deduction of income tax be equal to that part of the amount charged.

696.—(1) The following provisions of this section shall have effect in relation to a person who, during the administration period or during a part of that period, has an absolute interest in the residue of the estate of a deceased person or in a part thereof.

(2) There shall be ascertained in accordance with section 697 the amount of the residuary income of the estate for each whole year of assessment, and for each broken part of a year of assessment, during which—

(a) the administration period was current, and

(b) that person had that interest;

and the amount so ascertained in respect of any year or part of a year or, in the case of a person having an absolute interest in a part of a residue, a proportionate part of that amount, is in this Part referred to as the "residuary income" of that person for that year of assessment.

(3) When any sum or sums has or have been paid during the administration period in respect of that absolute interest, the amount of that sum or the aggregate amount of those sums shall, subject to subsection (5) below, be deemed for all tax purposes to have been paid to that person as income to the extent to which, and for the year or years of assessment for which, he would have been treated for those purposes as having received income if he had had a right to receive in each year of assessment—

(a) in the case of a United Kingdom estate, his residuary income for that year less income tax at the basic rate for that year; and

(b) in the case of a foreign estate, his residuary income for that year;

and that sum or the aggregate of those sums had been available for application primarily in or towards satisfaction of those rights as they accrued and had been so applied.

(4) In the case of a United Kingdom estate, any amount which is deemed to have been paid to that person as income for any year by virtue of subsection (3) above shall be deemed to be income of such an amount as would, after deduction of income tax for that year, be equal to the amount deemed to have been so paid, and to be income that has borne income tax at the basic rate.

(5) On the completion of the administration of the estate—

    (a) the amount of the residuary income of that person for any year of assessment shall be deemed for all tax purposes to have been paid to him as income for that year, and in the case of a United Kingdom estate shall be deemed to have borne income tax at the basic rate; and

    (b) where the amount which is deemed to have been paid to that person as income for any year by virtue of this subsection is less or greater than the amount deemed to have been paid to him as income for that year by virtue of subsection (3) above, such adjustments shall be made as are provided in section 700.

(6) In the case of a foreign estate, any amount which is deemed to have been paid to that person as income for any year by virtue of this section shall be deemed to be income of that amount and shall be chargeable to income tax under Case IV of Schedule D as if it were income arising from securities in a place out of the United Kingdom.

(7) Where—

    (a) a person has been charged to income tax for any year by virtue of this section in respect of an amount deemed to have been paid to him as income in respect of an interest in a foreign estate ("the deemed income"), and

    (b) any part of the aggregate income of that estate for that year has borne United Kingdom income tax by deduction or otherwise ("the aggregate income"),

the tax so charged on him shall, on proof of the facts on a claim, be reduced by an amount bearing the same proportion thereto as the amount of the deemed income which has borne United Kingdom income tax bears to the amount of the aggregate income.

(8) For the purposes of any charge to corporation tax under this section, the residuary income of a company shall be computed in the first instance by reference to years of assessment, and the residuary income for any such year shall be apportioned between the accounting periods (if more than one) comprising that year.

Supplementary provisions as to absolute interests in residue.

697.—(1) The amount of the residuary income of an estate for any year of assessment shall be ascertained by deducting from the aggregate income of the estate for that year—

    (a) the amount of any annual interest, annuity or other annual payment for that year which is a charge on residue and the amount of any payment made in that year in respect of any such expenses incurred by the personal representatives as such in the management of the assets of the estate as, in the absence of any express provision in a will, would be properly chargeable to income, but excluding any such interest, annuity or payment allowed or allowable in computing the aggregate income of the estate; and

(b) the amount of any of the aggregate income of the estate for that year to which a person has on or after assent become entitled by virtue of a specific disposition either for a vested interest during the administration period or for a vested or contingent interest on the completion of the administration.

(2) In the event of its appearing, on the completion of the administration of an estate in the residue of which, or in a part of the residue of which, a person had an absolute interest at the completion of the administration, that the aggregate of the benefits received in respect of that interest does not amount to as much as the aggregate for all years of the residuary income of the person having that interest, his residuary income for each year shall be reduced for the purpose of section 696 by an amount bearing the same proportion thereto as the deficiency bears to the aggregate for all years of his residuary income.

(3) In subsection (2) above "benefits received" in respect of an absolute interest means the following amounts in respect of all sums paid before, or payable on, the completion of the administration in respect of that interest, that is to say—

(a) as regards a sum paid before the completion of the administration, in the case of a United Kingdom estate such an amount as would, after deduction of income tax for the year of assessment in which that sum was paid, be equal to that sum, or in the case of a foreign estate the amount of that sum; and

(b) as regards a sum payable on the completion of the administration, in the case of a United Kingdom estate such an amount as would, after deduction of income tax for the year of assessment in which the administration is completed, be equal to that sum, or in the case of a foreign estate the amount of that sum.

(4) In the application of subsection (2) above to a residue or a part of a residue in which a person other than the person having an absolute interest at the completion of the administration had an absolute interest at any time during the administration period, the aggregates mentioned in that subsection shall be computed in relation to those interests taken together, and the residuary income of that other person also shall be subject to reduction under that subsection.

698.—(1) Where the personal representatives of a deceased person have as such a right in relation to the estate of another deceased person such that, if that right were vested in them for their own benefit, they would have an absolute or limited interest in the residue of that estate or in a part of that residue, they shall be deemed to have that interest notwithstanding that that right is not vested in them for their own benefit, and any amount deemed to be paid to them as income by virtue of this Part shall be treated as part of the aggregate income of the estate of the person whose personal representatives they are.

Special provisions as to certain interests in residue.

(2) Where different persons have successively during the administration period absolute interests in the residue of the estate of a deceased person or in a part of such residue, sums paid during that period in respect of the residue or of that part, as the case may be, shall be treated for the purposes of this Part as having been paid in respect of the interest of the person who first had an absolute interest in that residue or that part up to the amount of—

 (a) in the case of a United Kingdom estate, the aggregate for all years of that person's residuary income less income tax at the basic rate; or

 (b) in the case of a foreign estate, the aggregate for all years of that person's residuary income;

and, as to any balance up to a corresponding amount, in respect of the interest of the person who next had an absolute interest in that residue or part, and so on.

(3) Where, upon the exercise of a discretion, any of the income of the residue of the estate of a deceased person for any period (being the administration period or a part of the administration period) would, if the residue had been ascertained at the commencement of that period, be properly payable to any person, or to another in his right, for his benefit, whether directly by the personal representatives or indirectly through a trustee or other person—

 (a) the amount of any sum paid pursuant to an exercise of the discretion in favour of that person shall be deemed for all tax purposes to have been paid to that person as income for the year of assessment in which it was paid; and

 (b) section 695(4) to (6) shall have effect in relation to an amount which is deemed to have been paid as income by virtue of paragraph (a) above.

Relief from higher rate tax for inheritance tax on accrued income.

699.—(1) Where any income, having accrued before the death of any person, is taken into account both—

 (a) in determining the value of his estate for the purposes of any inheritance tax chargeable on his death; and

 (b) in ascertaining for the purposes of this Part the residuary income of his estate for any year of assessment;

then, in ascertaining the excess liability of any person having an absolute interest in the residue of that or any other estate or part thereof, that residuary income shall be treated as reduced by an amount calculated in accordance with the following provisions of this section.

(2) In subsection (1) above "excess liability" means the excess of liability to income tax over what it would be if all income tax were chargeable at the basic rate to the exclusion of any higher rate.

(3) The amount of the reduction shall be an amount which, after deduction of income tax for the year of assessment in question, would be equal to the amount of inheritance tax attributable to so much of the income taken into account as mentioned in subsection (1) above as exceeds any liabilities so taken into account.

(4) The amount of any income accruing before the death of any person and taken into account in estimating the value of an estate shall (whether or not the income was valued separately or its amount known at the date of the death) be taken to be the actual amount so accruing less income tax at the basic rate for the year of assessment in which the death occurred.

(5) The amounts agreed between the persons liable for inheritance tax and the Board, or determined in the proceedings between them, as being respectively the value of an estate and the amount of any inheritance tax payable shall be conclusive for the purposes of this section; and evidence of those amounts and of any facts relevant to their computation may be given by the production of a document purporting to be a certificate from the Board.

(6) In this section—

(a) references to liabilities taken into account in ascertaining the amount of the residuary income of an estate include references to liabilities allowed or allowable in computing its aggregate income; and

(b) references to inheritance tax include references to capital transfer tax.

700.—(1) Where on the completion of the administration of an estate any amount is deemed by virtue of this Part to have been paid to any person as income for any year of assessment and—

(a) that amount is greater than the amount that has previously been deemed to have been paid to him as income for that year by virtue of this Part; or

(b) no amount has previously been so deemed to have been paid to him as income for that year;

an assessment may be made upon him for that year and tax charged accordingly or, on a claim being made for the purpose, any relief or additional relief to which he may be entitled shall be allowed accordingly.

(2) Where on the completion of the administration of an estate any amount is deemed by virtue of this Part to have been paid to any person as income for any year of assessment, and that amount is less than the amount that has previously been so deemed to have been paid to him, then—

(a) if an assessment has already been made upon him for that year, such adjustments shall be made in that assessment as may be necessary for the purpose of giving effect to the provisions of this Part which take effect on the completion of the administration, and any tax overpaid shall be repaid; and

(b) if—

(i) any relief has been allowed to him by reference to the amount which has been previously deemed by virtue of this Part to have been paid to him as income for that year, and

(ii) the amount of that relief exceeds the amount of relief which could have been given by reference to the amount which, on the completion of the administration, is deemed to have been paid to him as income for that year,

the relief so given in excess may, if not otherwise made good, be charged under Case VI of Schedule D and recovered from that person accordingly.

(3) Notwithstanding anything in the Tax Acts, the time within which an assessment may be made for the purposes of this Part, or an assessment may be adjusted for those purposes, or a claim for relief may be made by virtue of this Part, shall not expire before the end of the third year following the year of assessment in which the administration of the estate in question was completed.

(4) An inspector may by notice require any person being or having been a personal representative of a deceased person, or having or having had an absolute or limited interest in the residue of the estate of a deceased person or in a part of such residue, to furnish him within such time as he may direct (not being less than 28 days) with such particulars as he thinks necessary for the purposes of this Part.

Interpretation.

701.—(1) The following provisions of this section shall have effect for the purpose of the interpretation of sections 695 to 700.

(2) A person shall be deemed to have an absolute interest in the residue of the estate of a deceased person, or in a part of such residue, if and so long as the capital of the residue or of that part would, if the residue had been ascertained, be properly payable to him, or to another in his right, for his benefit, or is properly so payable, whether directly by the personal representatives or indirectly through a trustee or other person.

(3) A person shall be deemed to have a limited interest in the residue of the estate of a deceased person, or in a part of such residue, during any period, being a period during which he has not an absolute interest in the residue or in that part, where the income of the residue or of that part for that period would, if the residue had been ascertained at the commencement of that period, be properly payable to him, or to another in his right, for his benefit, whether directly by the personal representatives or indirectly through a trustee or other person.

(4) "Personal representatives" means, in relation to the estate of a deceased person, his personal representatives as defined in relation to England and Wales by section 55 of the Administration of Estates Act 1925, and persons having in relation to the deceased under the law of another country any functions corresponding to the functions for administration purposes under the law of England and Wales of personal representatives as so defined; and references to "personal representatives as such" shall be construed as references to personal representatives in their capacity as having such functions.

1925 c. 23.

(5) "Specific disposition" means a specific devise or bequest made by a testator, and includes the disposition of personal chattels made by section 46 of the Administration of Estates Act 1925 and any disposition having, whether by virtue of any enactment or otherwise, under the law of another country an effect similar to that of a specific devise or bequest under the law of England and Wales.

Real estate included (either by a specific or general description) in a residuary gift made by the will of a testator shall be deemed to be a part of the residue of his estate and not to be the subject of a specific disposition.

(6) Subject to subsection (7) below, "charges on residue" means, in relation to the estate of a deceased person, the following liabilities, properly payable thereout and interest payable in respect of those liabilities, that is to say—

(a) funeral, testamentary and administration expenses and debts, and

(b) general legacies, demonstrative legacies, annuities and any sum payable out of residue to which a person is entitled under the law of intestacy of any part of the United Kingdom or any other country, and

(c) any other liabilities of his personal representatives as such.

(7) Where, as between persons interested under a specific disposition or in a general or demonstrative legacy or in an annuity and persons interested in the residue of the estate, any such liabilities as are mentioned in subsection (6) above fall exclusively or primarily upon the property that is the subject of the specific disposition or upon the legacy or annuity, only such part (if any) of those liabilities as falls ultimately upon the residue shall be treated as charges on residue.

(8) References to the aggregate income of the estate of a deceased person for any year of assessment shall be construed as references to the aggregate income from all sources for that year of the personal representatives of the deceased as such, treated as consisting of—

(a) any such income which is chargeable to United Kingdom income tax by deduction or otherwise, such income being computed at the amount on which that tax falls to be borne for that year; and

(b) any such income which would have been so chargeable if it had arisen in the United Kingdom to a person resident and ordinarily resident there, such income being computed at the full amount thereof actually arising during that year, less such deductions as would have been allowable if it had been charged to United Kingdom income tax;

but excluding any income from property devolving on the personal representatives otherwise than as assets for payment of the debts of the deceased.

This subsection has effect subject to sections 249(5), 421(2), 426(3) and 547(1)(c).

(9) "United Kingdom estate" means, as regards any year of assessment, an estate the income of which comprises only income which either—

(a) has borne United Kingdom income tax by deduction, or

(b) in respect of which the personal representatives are directly assessable to United Kingdom income tax,

not being an estate any part of the income of which is income in respect of which the personal representatives are entitled to claim exemption from United Kingdom income tax by reference to the fact that they are not resident, or not ordinarily resident, in the United Kingdom.

(10) "Foreign estate" means, as regards any year of assessment, an estate which is not a United Kingdom estate.

(11) In a case in which different parts of the estate of a deceased person are the subjects respectively of different residuary dispositions, this Part shall have effect in relation to each of those parts with the substitution—

PART XVI

(a) for references to the estate of references to that part of the estate; and

(b) for references to the personal representatives of the deceased as such of references to his personal representatives in their capacity as having the functions referred to in subsection (4) above in relation to that part of the estate.

(12) In this Part—

(a) references to sums paid include references to assets that are transferred or that are appropriated by a personal representative to himself, and to debts that are set off or released;

(b) references to sums payable include references to assets as to which an obligation to transfer or a right of a personal representative to appropriate to himself is subsisting on the completion of the administration and to debts as to which an obligation to release or set off, or a right of a personal representative so to do in his own favour, is then subsisting; and

(c) references to amount shall be construed, in relation to such assets as are referred to in paragraph (a) or (b) above, as references to their value at the date on which they were transferred or appropriated, or at the completion of the administration, as the case may require, and, in relation to such debts as are so referred to, as references to the amount thereof.

(13) In this Part references to the administration period shall be construed in accordance with section 695(1).

(14) In relation to so much of any residuary income for any year of assessment which has borne income tax at a rate equal to the sum of the basic rate and the additional rate for that year, section 696(3) shall have effect with the substitution for paragraph (a) of the following paragraph—

"(a) in the case of a United Kingdom estate—

(i) in the first instance, as regards so much of his residuary income for that year as has borne income tax at the basic rate for that year, that much of that income less income tax at that rate; and

(ii) subject to sub-paragraph (i), as regards so much of his residuary income for that year as has borne income tax at a rate equal to the sum of the basic rate and the additional rate for that year, that much of that income less income tax at the sum of those rates; and";

and the references in sections 696(4) and (5)(a) and 698(2)(a) to income tax at the basic rate shall have effect as references to income tax at a rate equal to that sum.

Application to Scotland.

702. For the purpose of the application of this Part to Scotland—

(a) any reference to the completion of the administration of an estate shall be construed as a reference to the date at which, after discharge of, or provision for, liabilities falling to be met out of the deceased's estate (including, without prejudice to the generality of the foregoing, debts, legacies immediately payable, prior rights of surviving spouse on intestacy and legal rights of surviving spouse or children), the free balance held in trust for behoof of the residuary legatees has been ascertained;

(b) for paragraph (b) of section 697(1) the following paragraph shall be substituted—

> "(b) the amount of any of the aggregate income of the estate for that year to which a person has become entitled by virtue of a specific disposition";

(c) "real estate" means heritable estate, and

(d) "charge on residue" shall include, in addition to the liabilities specified in section 701(6), any sums required to meet claims in respect of prior rights by surviving spouse or in respect of legal rights by surviving spouse or children.

PART XVII

TAX AVOIDANCE

CHAPTER I

CANCELLATION OF TAX ADVANTAGES FROM CERTAIN TRANSACTIONS IN SECURITIES

Cancellation of
tax advantage.

703.—(1) Where—

(a) in any such circumstances as are mentioned in section 704, and

(b) in consequence of a transaction in securities or of the combined effect of two or more such transactions,

a person is in a position to obtain, or has obtained, a tax advantage, then unless he shows that the transaction or transactions were carried out either for bona fide commercial reasons or in the ordinary course of making or managing investments, and that none of them had as their main object, or one of their main objects, to enable tax advantages to be obtained, this section shall apply to him in respect of that transaction or those transactions.

(2) For the purposes of this Chapter a tax advantage obtained or obtainable by a person shall be deemed to be obtained or obtainable by him in consequence of a transaction in securities or of the combined effect of two or more such transactions, if it is obtained or obtainable in consequence of the combined effect of the transaction or transactions and the liquidation of a company.

(3) Where this section applies to a person in respect of any transaction or transactions, the tax advantage obtained or obtainable by him in consequence thereof shall be counteracted by such of the following adjustments, that is to say an assessment, the nullifying of a right to repayment or the requiring of the return of a repayment already made (the amount to be returned being chargeable under Case VI of Schedule D and recoverable accordingly), or the computation or recomputation of profits or gains, or liability to tax, on such basis as the Board may specify by notice served on him as being requisite for counteracting the tax advantage so obtained or obtainable.

(4) Where, by virtue of an assessment under subsection (3) above to counteract a tax advantage obtained in circumstances falling within paragraph D or paragraph E of section 704 and consisting of the avoidance of a charge to income tax, income tax has been paid by any person on an amount specified in the assessment and it appears to the Board that, as a result of that payment, it is just and reasonable in the circumstances that an amount should be treated as having been paid by way of advance corporation tax, the Board shall serve a notice under subsection (5) below on every company which appears to them to be concerned in the transaction or transactions in consequence of which the tax advantage was obtained.

(5) A notice under this subsection—

(a) shall provide that, for the purposes of section 239 (but not for the purposes of entitling any person to a tax credit under section 231), such company or each of such companies as may be specified in the notice is to be treated as having paid, on such date as may be so specified, such amount of advance corporation tax as may be so specified in relation to that company;

(b) shall specify the amount which is equal to income tax at the basic rate on the amount on which income tax has been paid as mentioned in subsection (4) above; and

(c) may contain such supplementary or incidental directions as appear to the Board to be appropriate;

but the total amount of advance corporation tax which, by virtue of paragraph (a) above, a notice under this subsection may treat as having been paid shall not exceed the amount specified in accordance with paragraph (b) above.

(6) If, in a case falling within subsection (4) above, it does not appear to the Board that any amount should be treated as having been paid by way of advance corporation tax, the Board shall serve on every company which appears to them to be concerned in the transaction or transactions in consequence of which the tax advantage was obtained in a notice informing the company of the Board's decision that no amount is to be treated as having been paid by way of advance corporation tax.

(7) In the case of a man and his wife living with him (whether or not she is separately assessed to tax), this Chapter shall, subject to subsection (8) below, be treated as applying to him in respect of any transaction or transactions as it would apply if any property, rights or liabilities of the wife were his property, rights or liabilities in relation to which she had acted only as nominee for him, and shall be treated as applying to the wife in respect of any transaction or transactions as it would apply if any property, rights or liabilities of the man were her property, rights or liabilities in relation to which he had acted only as nominee for her.

(8) No adjustment made under subsection (3) above by reference to any transaction or transactions to counteract any tax advantage shall by virtue of subsection (7) above be so made that a person bears more tax than if the transaction or transactions had not had as a consequence that any relief or increased relief from, or repayment or increased repayment of, income tax, or any deduction in computing profits or gains, was obtained or obtainable, or that the way in which receipts accrued was such that the recipient did not pay or bear tax on them.

(9) The Board shall not give a notice under subsection (3) above until they have notified the person in question that they have reason to believe that this section may apply to him in respect of a transaction or transactions specified in the notification; and if within 30 days of the issue of the notification that person, being of opinion that this section does not so apply to him, makes a statutory declaration to that effect stating the facts and circumstances upon which his opinion is based, and sends it to the Board, then subject to subsection (10) below, this section shall not apply to him in respect of the transaction or transactions.

(10) If, when a statutory declaration has been sent to the Board under subsection (9) above, they see reason to take further action in the matter—

(a) the Board shall send to the tribunal a certificate to that effect, together with the statutory declaration, and may also send therewith a counter-statement with reference to the matter;

(b) the tribunal shall take into consideration the declaration and the certificate, and the counter-statement, if any, and shall determine whether there is or is not a prima facie case for proceeding in the matter, and if they determine that there is no such case this section shall not apply to the person in question in respect of the transaction or transactions;

but any such determination shall not affect the operation of this section in respect of transactions which include that transaction or some or all of those transactions and also include another transaction or other transactions.

(11) Any notice or notification under subsection (3) or subsection (9) above, or under section 708, concerning the application of this section to a person who has died may be given or issued to his personal representatives, and the provisions of this Chapter relating to the making of a statutory declaration, to rights of appeal and to the giving of information shall be construed accordingly.

(12) This section applies whether the tax advantage in question relates to a chargeable period ending before or after the commencement of this Act, but nothing in this section shall authorise the making of an assessment later than six years after the chargeable period to which the tax advantage relates; and no other provision contained in the Tax Acts shall be construed as limiting the powers conferred by this section.

The prescribed circumstances.

704. The circumstances mentioned in section 703(1) are—

A. That in connection with the distribution of profits of a company, or in connection with the sale or purchase of securities being a sale or purchase followed by the purchase or sale of the same or other securities, the person in question receives an abnormal amount by way of dividend, and the amount so received is taken into account for any of the following purposes—

(a) any exemption from tax, or

(b) the setting-off of losses against profits or income, or

(c) the giving of group relief, or

(d) the application of franked investment income in calculating a company's liability to pay advance corporation tax, or

(e) the application of a surplus of franked investment income under section 242 or 243, or

(f) the computation of profits or gains out of which are made payments falling within section 348 or 349(1), or

(g) the deduction from or set-off against income of interest under section 353.

OR

B.—(1) That in connection with the distribution of profits of a company, or in connection with the sale or purchase of securities being sale or purchase followed by the purchase or sale of the same or other securities, the person in question becomes entitled—

(a) in respect of securities held or sold by him, or

(b) in respect of securities formerly held by him (whether sold by him or not),

to a deduction in computing profits or gains by reason of a fall in the value of the securities resulting from the payment of a dividend thereon or from any other dealing with any assets of a company.

(2) Where a company in the circumstances mentioned in sub-paragraph (1) above becomes entitled to a deduction as there mentioned, section 703 shall apply in relation to any tax advantage obtained or obtainable in consequence of that deduction by another company by way of group relief as if obtained or obtainable by the other company in circumstances falling within sub-paragraph (1) above.

OR

C.—(1) That the person in question receives, in consequence of a transaction whereby any other person—

(a) subsequently receives, or has received, an abnormal amount by way of dividend; or

(b) subsequently becomes entitled, or has become entitled, to a deduction as mentioned in paragraph B(1) above,

a consideration which either—

(i) is, or represents the value of, assets which are (or apart from anything done by the company in question would have been) available for distribution by way of dividend, or

(ii) is received in respect of future receipts of the company, or

(iii) is, or represents the value of, trading stock of the company,

and the person in question so receives the consideration that he does not pay or bear tax on it as income.

(2) The assets mentioned in sub-paragraph (1) above do not include assets which (while of a description which under the law of the country in which the company is incorporated is available for distribution by way of dividend) are shown to represent a return of sums paid by subscribers on the issue of securities.

OR

D.—(1) That in connection with the distribution of profits of a company to which this paragraph applies, the person in question so receives as is mentioned in paragraph C(1) above such a consideration as is therein mentioned.

(2) The companies to which this paragraph applies are—

(a) any company under the control of not more than five persons, and

(b) any other company which does not satisfy the condition that its shares or stocks or some class thereof (disregarding debenture stock, preferred shares or preferred stock), are authorised to be dealt in on the Stock Exchange, and are so dealt in (regularly or from time to time),

so, however, that this paragraph does not apply to a company under the control of one or more companies to which this paragraph does not apply.

(3) Subsections (2) to (6) of section 416 shall apply for the purposes of this paragraph.

OR

E.—(1) That in connection with the transfer directly or indirectly of assets of a company to which paragraph D above applies to another such company, or in connection with any transaction in securities in which two or more companies to which paragraph D above applies are concerned, the person in question receives non-taxable consideration which is or represents the value of assets available for distribution by such a company, and which consists of any share capital or any security (as defined by section 254(1)) issued by such a company.

(2) So far as sub-paragraph (1) above relates to share capital other than redeemable share capital, it shall not apply unless and except to the extent that the share capital is repaid (in a winding-up or otherwise), and, where section 703 applies to a person by virtue of sub-paragraph (1) above on the repayment of any share capital, any assessment to tax under subsection (3) of that section shall be an assessment to tax for the year in which the share capital is repaid.

(3) In this paragraph—

"assets available for distribution" means assets which are, or apart from anything done by the company in question would have been, available for distribution by way of dividend, or trading stock of the company;

"non-taxable", in relation to a person receiving consideration, means that the recipient does not pay or bear tax on it as income (apart from the provisions of this Chapter);

"share" includes stock and any other interest of a member in a company;

and the references in sub-paragraph (2) above to the repayment of share capital include references to any distribution made in respect of any shares in a winding-up or dissolution of the company.

Appeals against Board's notices under section 703.

705.—(1) Any person to whom notice has been given under section 703(3) may within 30 days by notice to the Board appeal to the Special Commissioners on the grounds that section 703 does not apply to him in respect of the transaction or transactions in question, or that the adjustments directed to be made are inappropriate.

(2) If he or the Board are dissatisfied with the determination of the Special Commissioners he or they may, on giving notice to the clerk to the Special Commissioners within 30 days after the determination, require the appeal to be re-heard by the tribunal, and the Special Commissioners shall transmit to the tribunal any document in their possession which was delivered to them for the purposes of the appeal.

(3) Where notice is given under subsection (2) above, the tribunal shall re-hear and determine the appeal and shall have and exercise the same powers and authorities in relation to the appeal as the Special Commissioners might have and exercise, and the determination of the tribunal thereon shall be final and conclusive.

(4) Section 56 of the Management Act (statement of case for opinion of High Court etc.) shall apply with the necessary modifications in the case of any such rehearing and determination as it applies in the case of appeals to the General or Special Commissioners.

(5) On an appeal under subsections (1) to (3) above the Special Commissioners or the tribunal shall have power to cancel or vary a notice under subsection (3) of section 703 or to vary or quash an assessment made in accordance with such a notice, but the bringing of an appeal or the statement of a case shall not affect the validity of a notice given or of any other thing done in pursuance of that subsection pending the determination of the proceedings.

(6) A company on which a notice has been served under section 703(5) or (6) may within 30 days by notice to the Board appeal to the Special Commissioners on the ground that it is just and reasonable in the circumstances that the company should be treated, for the purposes specified in section 703(6), as having paid an amount of advance corporation tax or, as the case may require, a greater amount of advance corporation tax than is specified in the notice.

(7) Notwithstanding that a company on which a notice has been served as mentioned in subsection (6) above has made no appeal under that subsection, the company—

(a) shall be entitled, to the same extent as the appellant, to receive notice of, and to appear and be heard in, any proceedings arising from the notice referred to in subsection (6) above, whether the proceedings are before the Special Commissioners, by way of further appeal or otherwise;

(b) if it does appear, shall be treated as a party to the proceedings and as having the same rights in respect of those proceedings and any decision made therein as the appellant; and

(c) whether or not it so appears, shall be bound by any order made in any such proceedings;

and no agreement under section 54 of the Management Act (settling of appeals by agreement) shall have effect except with the consent of each company which, by virtue of this subsection, would have been entitled to appear and be heard on the appeal if it had been proceeded with.

(8) On an appeal under subsection (6) above, the Special Commissioners—

(a) may cancel or vary any notice served under section 703(5), or

(b) if no such notice was served, may by order make any provision which could have been made by the Board in such a notice.

The tribunal.

706. For the purposes of this Chapter the tribunal shall consist of—

(a) a chairman, appointed by the Lord Chancellor, and

(b) two or more persons appointed by the Lord Chancellor as having special knowledge of and experience in financial or commercial matters.

Procedure for clearance in advance.

707.—(1) The following provisions shall have effect where in pursuance of this section a person furnishes to the Board particulars of a transaction or transactions effected or to be effected by him, that is to say—

(a) if the Board are of opinion that the particulars, or any further information furnished in pursuance of this paragraph, are not sufficient for the purposes of this section, they shall within 30 days of the receipt thereof notify to that person what further information they require for those purposes, and unless that further information is furnished to the Board within 30 days from the notification, or such further time as the Board may allow, they shall not be required to proceed further under this section;

(b) subject to paragraph (a) above, the Board shall within 30 days of the receipt of the particulars, or, where that paragraph has effect, of all further information required, notify that person whether or not they are satisfied that the transaction or transactions as described in the particulars were or will be such that no notice under section 703(3) ought to be given in respect of it or them;

and, subject to the following provisions of this section, if the Board notify him that they are so satisfied, section 703 shall not apply to him in respect of that transaction or those transactions.

(2) If the particulars, and any further information given under this section with respect to any transaction or transactions, are not such as to make full and accurate disclosure of all facts and considerations relating thereto which are material to be known to the Board, any notification given by the Board under this section shall be void.

(3) In no event shall the giving of a notification under this section with respect to any transaction or transactions prevent section 703 applying to a person in respect of transactions which include that transaction or all or some of those transactions and also include another transaction or other transactions.

Power to obtain information.

708. Where it appears to the Board that by reason of any transaction or transactions a person may be a person to whom section 703 applies, the Board may by notice served on him require him, within such time not less than 28 days as may be specified in the notice, to furnish information in his possession with respect to the transaction or any of the transactions, being information as to matters, specified in the notice, which are relevant to the question whether a notice under section 703(3) should be given in respect of him.

709.—(1) In this Chapter "tax advantage" means a relief or increased relief from, or repayment or increased repayment of, tax, or the avoidance or reduction of a charge to tax or an assessment to tax or the avoidance of a possible assessment thereto, whether the avoidance or reduction is effected by receipts accruing in such a way that the recipient does not pay or bear tax on them, or by a deduction in computing profits or gains.

(2) In this Chapter—

"company" includes any body corporate;

"securities"—

(a) includes shares and stock, and

(b) in relation to a company not limited by shares (whether or not it has a share capital) includes also a reference to the interest of a member of the company as such, whatever the form of that interest;

"trading stock" has the same meaning as in section 100(1);

"transaction in securities" includes transactions, of whatever description, relating to securities, and in particular—

(i) the purchase, sale or exchange of securities;

(ii) the issuing or securing the issue of, or applying or subscribing for, new securities;

(iii) the altering, or securing the alteration of, the rights attached to securities;

and references to dividends include references to other qualifying distributions and to interest.

(3) In section 704—

(a) references to profits include references to income, reserves or other assets;

(b) references to distribution include references to transfer or realisation (including application in discharge of liabilities); and

(c) references to the receipt of consideration include references to the receipt of any money or money's worth.

(4) For the purposes of section 704 an amount received by way of dividend shall be treated as abnormal if the Board, the Special Commissioners or the tribunal, as the case may be, are satisfied—

(a) in the case of a dividend at a fixed rate, that it substantially exceeds the amount which the recipient would have received if the dividend had accrued from day to day and he had been entitled only to so much of the dividend as accrued while he held the securities, so however that an amount shall not be treated as abnormal by virtue only of this paragraph if during the six months beginning with the purchase of the securities the recipient does not sell or otherwise dispose of, or acquire an option to sell, any of those securities or any securities similar to those securities; or

(b) in any case, that it substantially exceeds a normal return on the consideration provided by the recipient for the relevant securities, that is to say, the securities in respect of which the dividend was received and, if those securities are derived from securities previously acquired by the recipient, the securities which were previously acquired.

(5) For the purposes of subsection (4)(a) above securities shall be deemed to be similar if they entitle their holders to the same rights against the same persons as to capital and interest and the same remedies for the enforcement of those rights, notwithstanding any difference in the total nominal amounts of the respective securities or in the form in which they are held or the manner in which they can be transferred, and for those purposes rights guaranteed by the Treasury shall be treated as rights against the Treasury.

(6) For the purposes of subsection (4)(b) above—

(a) if the consideration provided by the recipient for any of the relevant securities was in excess of their market value at the time he acquired them, or if no consideration was provided by him for any of the relevant securities, the recipient shall be taken to have provided for those securities consideration equal to their market value at the time he acquired them; and

(b) in determining whether an amount received by way of dividend exceeds a normal return, regard shall be had to the length of time previous to the receipt of that amount that the recipient first acquired any of the relevant securities and to any dividends and other distributions made in respect of them during that time.

CHAPTER II

TRANSFERS OF SECURITIES

Transfers with or without accrued interest: introductory

Meaning of "securities", "transfer" etc. for purposes of sections 711 to 728.

710.—(1) This section has effect for the interpretation of sections 711 to 728.

(2) "Securities" does not include shares in a company but, subject to subsection (3) below, includes any loan stock or similar security—

(a) whether of the government of the United Kingdom, any other government, any public or local authority in the United Kingdom or elsewhere, or any company or other body; and

(b) whether or not secured, whether or not carrying a right to interest of a fixed amount or at a fixed rate per cent. of the nominal value of the securities, and whether or not in bearer form.

(3) "Securities" does not include—

(a) securities on which the whole of the return is a distribution by virtue of section 209(2)(e)(iv) and (v);

(b) national savings certificates (including Ulster Savings Certificates);

(c) war savings certificates;

(d) certificates of deposit (within the meaning of section 56(5));

(e) any security which fulfils the following conditions, namely, it is redeemable, the amount payable on its redemption exceeds its issue price, and no return other than the amount of that excess is payable on it.

(4) Securities are to be taken to be of the same kind if they are treated as being of the same kind by the practice of a recognised stock exchange or would be so treated if dealt with on such a stock exchange.

(5) "Transfer", in relation to securities, means transfer by way of sale, exchange, gift or otherwise.

(6) Where an agreement for the transfer of securities is made, they are transferred, and the person to whom they are agreed to be transferred becomes entitled to them, when the agreement is made and not on a later transfer made pursuant to the agreement; and "entitled", "transfer" and cognate expressions shall be construed accordingly.

(7) A person holds securities—

(a) at a particular time if he is entitled to them at the time;

(b) on a day if he is entitled to them throughout the day or he becomes and does not cease to be entitled to them on the day.

(8) A person acquires securities when he becomes entitled to them.

(9) Where—

(a) one individual holds securities at a particular time, and

(b) any interest on them would, if it became payable at that time, be treated for the purposes of the Tax Acts as part of another individual's income,

then, for the purposes of section 715(1)(b) and section 715(2)(b) so far as relating to section 715(1)(b), each of them shall be treated as holding at that time the securities which the other holds as well as those which he actually holds.

(10) Where in Scotland two or more persons carry on a trade or business in partnership, any partnership dealings shall be treated as dealings by the partners and not by the firm as such and the partners as being entitled to securities held by the firm.

(11) The nominal value of securities is—

(a) where the interest on them is expressed to be payable by reference to a given value, that value; and

(b) in any other case, the price of the securities when they were issued.

(12) Where apart from this subsection the nominal value of securities would be a value ("the foreign value") expressed in a currency other than sterling, then, for the purposes of section 715, their nominal value on a particular day is the sterling equivalent on that day of the foreign value.

W

For the purposes of this subsection the sterling equivalent of a value on a particular day is the sterling equivalent calculated by reference to the London closing rate of exchange for that day.

(13) Where there is a conversion of securities then,—

(a) the person who was entitled to them immediately before the conversion shall be treated as transferring them on the day of the conversion (if there is no actual transfer); and

(b) the interest period in which the conversion is made shall be treated as ending on the day on which it would have ended had the conversion not been made.

In this subsection "conversion" means a conversion within the meaning of section 82 of the 1979 Act.

(14) In relation to an underwriting member of Lloyd's, "business" and "premiums trust fund" have the meanings given by section 457.

Meaning of "interest", "transfers with or without accrued interest" etc.

711.—(1) This section has effect for the interpretation of sections 710 and 712 to 728.

(2) An interest payment day, in relation to securities, is a day on which interest on them is payable; and, in a case where a particular payment of interest may be made on one of a number of days, the interest is for the purposes of this subsection payable on the first of those days.

(3) Subject to subsection (4) below, the following are interest periods in relation to securities—

(a) the period beginning with the day following that on which they are issued and ending with the first interest payment day to fall;

(b) the period beginning with the day following one interest payment day and ending with the next to fall.

(4) A period which would (apart from this subsection) be an interest period exceeding 12 months ("a long period") is not an interest period, but the following shall apply to it—

(a) the period of 12 months beginning with the day on which it begins is an interest period;

(b) each successive period (if any) of 12 months falling within it is an interest period;

(c) any period of it which remains after applying paragraphs (a) and (b) above is an interest period.

(5) Securities are transferred with accrued interest if they are transferred with the right to receive interest payable on—

(a) the settlement day, if that is an interest payment day; or

(b) the next (or first) interest payment day to fall after the settlement day, in any other case;

and they are transferred without accrued interest if they are transferred without that right.

(6) Where section 710(13), 715(3), 720(4), 721(1) or 722(1) or (2) applies, the transfer shall be treated as made with accrued interest if the person treated as making the transfer was entitled to receive in respect of the securities interest payable on—

    (a) the settlement day, if that is an interest payment day; or

    (b) the next (or first) interest payment day to fall after that day, in any other case;

and they shall be treated as transferred without accrued interest if he was not so entitled.

(7) The interest applicable to securities for an interest period is, subject to subsection (8) below, the interest payable on them on the interest payment day with which the period ends.

(8) In the case of a period which is an interest period by virtue only of subsection (4) above or section 725(9)—

    (a) the interest applicable to securities for the period is the interest payable on them on the interest payment day with which the long or straddling period concerned ends; and

    (b) section 713(6) shall have effect as if the references to the period were to the long or straddling period concerned.

(9) "Interest" includes dividends and any other return (however described) except a return consisting of an amount by which the amount payable on a security's redemption exceeds its issue price.

712.—(1) This section has effect to determine, for the purposes of sections 711 and 713 to 728, the settlement day in relation to a transfer of securities.

Meaning of "settlement day" for purposes of sections 711 to 728.

(2) Where the securities are transferred in accordance with the rules of a recognised market, the settlement day is the day on which the transferee agrees to settle or, if he may settle on one of a number of days, the day on which he settles; and, where they are transferred otherwise, subsections (3) to (5) below apply.

(3) Where the consideration for the transfer is money alone, and the transferee agrees to pay the whole of it on or before the next (or first) interest payment day to fall after an agreement for transfer is made, the settlement day is the day on which he agrees to make the payment or, if payment may be made on one of a number of days, or on a number of different days, the latest of them to fall.

(4) Where there is no consideration for the transfer, or the transfer is a transfer by virtue of sections 710(13), 715(3), 717(8), 720(4), 721 and 722, the settlement day is the day on which the securities are transferred.

(5) In any other case, the settlement day is such day as an inspector decides; and the jurisdiction of the General Commissioners or the Special Commissioners on any appeal shall include jurisdiction to review such a decision of the inspector.

Transfers with or without accrued interest: charge to tax and reliefs

713.—(1) Subject to sections 714 to 728, this section applies whether the

Deemed sums and reliefs.

PART XVII   securities in question are transferred before, on or after 6th April 1988; and in this section references to a period are references to the interest period in which the settlement day falls.

(2) If securities are transferred with accrued interest—

(a) the transferor shall be treated as entitled to a sum on them in the period of an amount equal to the accrued amount; and

(b) the transferee shall be treated as entitled to relief on them in the period of the same amount.

(3) If securities are transferred without accrued interest—

(a) the transferor shall be treated as entitled to relief on them in the period of an amount equal to the rebate amount; and

(b) the transferee shall be treated as entitled to a sum on them in the period of the same amount.

(4) In subsection (2) above "the accrued amount" means—

(a) if the securities are transferred under an arrangement by virtue of which the transferee accounts to the transferor separately for the consideration for the securities and for gross interest accruing to the settlement day, an amount equal to the amount (if any) of gross interest so accounted for; and

(b) in any other case, an amount equal to the accrued proportion of the interest applicable to the securities for the period.

(5) In subsection (3) above "the rebate amount" means—

(a) if the securities are transferred under an arrangement by virtue of which the transferor accounts to the transferee for gross interest accruing from the settlement day to the next interest payment day, an amount equal to the amount (if any) of gross interest so accounted for; and

(b) in any other case, an amount equal to the rebate proportion of the interest applicable to the securities for the period.

(6) In this section—

(a) the accrued proportion is—

$$\frac{A}{B}$$

(b) the rebate proportion is—

$$\frac{B-A}{B}$$

where—

A is the number of days in the period up to (and including) the settlement day, and

B is the number of days in the period.

(7) For the purposes of subsection (2) above, in a case where the interest on the securities is payable in a currency other than sterling the accrued amount is to be determined as follows—

    (a) if subsection (4)(a) above applies and the sterling equivalent of the amount of gross interest there mentioned is shown in an agreement for transfer, the accrued amount is the sterling equivalent so shown;

    (b) if subsection (4)(a) applies but paragraph (a) above does not, or if subsection (4)(b) above applies, the accrued amount is the sterling equivalent on the settlement day of the amount found by virtue of subsection (4)(a) or (b) (as the case may be).

(8) For the purposes of subsection (3) above, in a case where the interest on the securities is payable in a currency other than sterling the rebate amount is to be determined as follows—

    (a) if subsection (5)(a) above applies and the sterling equivalent of the amount of gross interest there mentioned is shown in an agreement for transfer, the rebate amount is the sterling equivalent so shown;

    (b) if subsection (5)(a) applies but paragraph (a) above does not, or if subsection (5)(b) above applies, the rebate amount is the sterling equivalent on the settlement day of the amount found by virtue of subsection (5)(a) or (b) (as the case may be).

(9) For the purposes of subsections (7) and (8) above the sterling equivalent of an amount on a particular day is the sterling equivalent calculated by reference to the London closing rate of exchange for that day.

714.—(1) Subsection (2) below applies if a person is treated as entitled under section 713 to a sum on securities of a particular kind in an interest period, and either—

Treatment of deemed sums and reliefs.

    (a) he is not treated as entitled under that section to relief on securities of that kind in the period; or

    (b) the sum (or total sum) to which he is treated as entitled exceeds the amount (or total amount) of relief to which he is treated as entitled under that section on securities of that kind in the period.

(2) The person shall be treated as receiving on the day the period ends annual profits or gains whose amount is (depending on whether subsection (1)(a) or (1)(b) above applies) equal to the sum (or total sum) to which he is treated as entitled or equal to the amount of the excess; and the profits or gains shall be chargeable to tax under Case VI of Schedule D for the chargeable period in which they are treated as received.

(3) Subsection (4) below applies if a person is treated as entitled under section 713 to relief on securities of a particular kind in an interest period, and either—

    (a) he is not treated as entitled under that section to a sum on securities of that kind in the period; or

(b) the amount (or total amount) of relief to which he is treated as entitled exceeds the sum (or total sum) to which he is treated as entitled under that section on securities of that kind in the period.

(4) The person shall be entitled to an allowance whose amount is (depending on whether subsection (3)(a) or (3)(b) above applies) equal to the amount (or total amount) of relief to which he is treated as entitled or equal to the amount of the excess; and subsection (5) below shall apply.

(5) Any amount to which the person is entitled by way of interest which—

(a) falls due on the securities at the end of the interest period, and

(b) is taken into account in computing tax charged for the chargeable period in which the interest period ends,

shall for the purposes of the Tax Acts be treated as reduced by the amount of the allowance; but if the period is one which does not end with an interest payment day, he shall be treated as becoming, in the next interest period, entitled under section 713 to relief on the securities of an amount equal to the amount of the allowance.

(6) Where, but for this subsection, a company would by virtue of subsection (2) above be treated as receiving profits or gains on a day which does not fall within an accounting period of the company, the profits or gains shall instead be treated as received by the company on the latest day of the interest period which does so fall.

Exceptions from sections 713 and 714.

715.—(1) Section 713(2)(a) or (3)(a) (as the case may be) does not apply—

(a) if the transferor carries on a trade and the transfer falls to be taken into account for the purposes of the Tax Acts in computing the profits or losses of that trade;

(b) if the transferor is an individual and on no day in the year of assessment in which the interest period ends or the previous year of assessment the nominal value of securities held by him exceeded £5,000;

(c) if the securities transferred form part of the estate of a deceased person, the transferor is that person's personal representative and on no day in the year of assessment in which the interest period ends or the previous year of assessment the nominal value of securities held by him as the deceased's personal representative exceeded £5,000;

(d) where—

(i) if the transferor became entitled to any interest on the securities transferred and applied it for charitable purposes only, exemption could be granted under section 505(1)(c) in respect of the interest;

(ii) if the transferor became entitled to any interest on the securities transferred and applied it for the purposes mentioned in paragraph (d) of section 505(1), exemption could be granted under that paragraph in respect of the interest;

(e) if the securities transferred are held on a disabled person's trusts, the transferor is trustee of the settlement and on no day in the year of assessment in which the interest period ends or the previous year of assessment the nominal value of securities held by him as trustee of the settlement exceeded £5,000;

(f) if the transferor does not fulfil the residence requirement for the chargeable period in which the transfer is made and is not a non-resident United Kingdom trader in that period;

(g) if the transferor is not ordinarily resident in the United Kingdom during the chargeable period in which the transfer occurs and, if he became entitled in the period to any interest on the securities transferred, it would not be liable to income tax by virtue of section 47;

(h) if the securities transferred are FOTRA securities, the transferor is not domiciled in the United Kingdom at any time in the chargeable period in which the transfer occurs, and he is either not ordinarily resident in the United Kingdom during that period or a non-resident United Kingdom trader in that period;

(j) if the transferor is an individual who, if he became entitled in the year of assessment in which the transfer occurs to any interest on the securities transferred, would be liable, in respect of the interest, to tax chargeable under Case IV or V of Schedule D and computed on the amount of sums received in the United Kingdom; or

(k) where, if the transferor became entitled to any interest on the securities transferred, exemption could be allowed under section 592(2) in respect of the interest.

(2) Section 713(2)(b) or (3)(b) (as the case may be) does not apply if—

(a) the transferee carries on a trade, and if at the time he acquired the securities he were to transfer them that transfer would fall to be taken into account for the purposes of the Tax Acts in computing the profits or losses of that trade; or

(b) any provision of subsection (1) above except paragraph (a) would apply if "transferor" read "transferee".

(3) If securities held on charitable trusts cease to be subject to charitable trusts the trustees shall be treated for the purposes of sections 710 to 728 as transferring the securities (in their capacity as charitable trustees) to themselves (in another capacity) at the time when the securities cease to be so subject.

(4) For the purposes of this section a person fulfils the residence requirement for a chargeable period if he is resident in the United Kingdom during any part of the period or is ordinarily resident in the United Kingdom during the period.

(5) For the purposes of this section a person is a non-resident United Kingdom trader in a chargeable period if during any part of it he is (though neither resident during any part of it nor ordinarily resident during it) carrying on a trade in the United Kingdom through a branch or agency and the securities transferred—

(a) were situated in the United Kingdom and used or held for the purposes of the branch or agency at or before the time of the transfer (where the person concerned is a transferor); or

(b) were so situated at the time of the transfer and were acquired for use by or for the purposes of the branch or agency (where the person concerned is a transferee);

but the provisions of this subsection relating to the situation of the securities in the United Kingdom do not apply where the person concerned is a company.

(6) In any case where securities are transferred without accrued interest to a person ("the seller") and a contract is made for the sale by the seller of securities of that kind ("the seller's contract") and the seller's contract or any contract under which the securities are transferred to the seller is one in the case of which section 737 has effect and in relation to which the seller is the dividend manufacturer, then—

(a) where the nominal value of the securities subject to the seller's contract is greater than or equal to that of the securities transferred, the seller shall not be treated as entitled to any sum to which, but for this subsection, he would be treated as entitled under section 713(3)(b) on the securities transferred;

(b) where the nominal value of the securities subject to the seller's contract is less than that of the securities transferred, any sum (or the aggregate of any sums) to which he is treated as entitled under section 713(3)(b) on the securities transferred shall be reduced by the amount of any part of the sum (or aggregate) attributable to securities ("relevant securities") of a nominal value equal to that of the securities subject to the seller's contract;

and for the purposes of sections 710 to 728 the securities which the seller contracts to sell shall not be treated as transferred by him (though treated as transferred to the person to whom he contracts to sell).

(7) In determining for the purposes of subsection (6)(b) above which of the securities transferred are relevant securities, those transferred to the seller earlier must be chosen before those transferred to him later.

(8) For the purposes of this section—

"disabled person's trusts" means trusts falling within paragraph 5(1) of Schedule 1 to the 1979 Act;

"branch or agency" has the meaning given by section 12(3) of the 1979 Act;

"FOTRA securities" means securities issued with the condition mentioned in section 22(1) of the Finance (No.2) Act 1931 (securities free of tax for residents abroad) as modified by virtue of section 60(1) of the Finance Act 1940;

and the place where securities are situated shall be determined in accordance with section 18(4) of the 1979 Act.

716.—(1) This section applies where securities are transferred (whether before or after 6th April 1988) with the right to receive interest ("unrealised interest") payable on them on an interest payment day falling before the settlement day.

(2) Where the settlement day falls within an interest period, section 714 shall (subject to subsection (5) below) apply as if the transferor were entitled under section 713 to a sum on them in the period of an amount equal to the unrealised interest (in addition to any other sum to which he may be treated as so entitled).

(3) Where the settlement day falls after the end of the last interest period in relation to the securities, the transferor shall be treated as receiving on the settlement day annual profits or gains of an amount equal to the unrealised interest; and the profits or gains shall be chargeable to tax under Case VI of Schedule D for the chargeable period in which they are treated as received.

(4) Where the transferee receives the unrealised interest, and but for this subsection it would be taken into account in computing tax charged for the chargeable period in which the interest is received, it shall for the purposes of the Tax Acts be left out of account.

(5) Section 715 shall apply for the purposes of this section as if—

    (a) in subsection (1)—

         (i) the reference to section 713(2)(a) or (3)(a) were a reference to subsection (2) or (3) above; and

         (ii) references to the year of assessment in which the interest period ends were references to the year in which the settlement day falls; and

    (b) in subsection (2) the reference to section 713(2)(b) or (3)(b) were a reference to subsection (4) above.

Paragraph (b) above does not apply where the securities in question were transferred before 19th March 1986.

(6) Where the unrealised interest is payable in a currency other than sterling its amount is for the purposes of this section the sterling equivalent on the settlement day of the amount it would be apart from this subsection; and for this purpose the sterling equivalent is to be calculated by reference to the London closing rate of exchange for the day.

717.—(1) This section applies to securities other than securities falling within subsection (2) or (4) below.

(2) Securities fall within this subsection if their terms of issue provide that throughout the period from issue to redemption (whenever redemption might occur) they are to carry interest at a rate which falls into one, and one only, of the following categories—

    (a) a fixed rate which is the same throughout the period;

    (b) a rate which bears to a standard published base rate the same fixed relationship throughout the period;

(c) a rate which bears to a published index of prices the same fixed relationship throughout the period.

(3) In subsection (2)(c) above "published index of prices" means the retail prices index or any similar general index of prices which is published by, or by an agent of, the government of any territory outside the United Kingdom.

(4) Securities fall within this subsection if they are deep discount securities and the rate of interest for each (or their only) interest period is equal to or less than the yield to maturity.

(5) In subsection (4) above "deep discount securities" and "yield to maturity" have the same meanings as in Schedule 4; and for the purposes of that subsection the rate of interest for an interest period is, in relation to securities, the rate of return (expressed as a percentage) attributable to the interest applicable to them for the interest period.

(6) Subsections (7) to (11) below apply if securities to which this section applies are transferred at any time between the time they are issued and the time they are redeemed.

(7) If the securities are transferred without accrued interest they shall be treated for the purposes of sections 710 to 728 as transferred with accrued interest.

(8) The person entitled to the securities immediately before they are redeemed shall be treated for the purposes of those sections as transferring them with accrued interest on the day they are redeemed.

(9) Where there is a transfer as mentioned in subsection (6) above or by virtue of subsection (8) above, section 713 shall have effect with the omission of subsection (2)(b) and with the substitution for subsections (3) to (6) of the following subsection—

"(3) In subsection (2) above "the accrued amount" means such amount (if any) as an inspector decides is just and reasonable; and the jurisdiction of the General Commissioners or the Special Commissioners on any appeal shall include jurisdiction to review such a decision of the inspector.".

(10) Subsection (11) below applies where there is a transfer by virtue of subsection (8) above and the settlement day in relation to the transfer falls after the end of a period which would (by virtue of section 711(3) and (4) and apart from this subsection) be the only or last interest period in relation to the securities.

(11) For the purposes of sections 710 to 728 the period beginning with the day following that interest period and ending with the settlement day shall be treated as an interest period in relation to the securities; and section 711(4) shall not apply to it.

Interest in default.   **718.**—(1) This section applies where, because of any failure to fulfil the obligation to pay interest on securities, the value (on a day mentioned in section 711(7) or (8)(a), as the case may be) of the right to receive the interest payable on them on that day is less than the interest so payable.

(2) Section 711(7) or (8)(a), as the case may be, shall be construed as if the reference to that interest were to an amount equal to that value.

719.—(1) Where securities are transferred as mentioned in section 716(1) and, because of any failure to fulfil the obligation to pay interest on them, the value (on the day of the transfer) of the right to receive the unrealised interest is less than the amount of the unrealised interest, section 716 shall have effect as modified by subsections (2) to (4) below.

(2) In subsections (2) and (3) for "the unrealised interest" there shall be substituted "amount A".

(3) For subsection (4) there shall be substituted—

"(4) Where the transferee receives an amount by way of the unrealised interest (amount B) and that amount falls to be taken into account in computing tax charged for the chargeable period in which it is received, it shall for the purposes of the Tax Acts be treated as reduced by an amount (amount C) equal to—

(a) nil, if the amounts have been previously received by the transferee by way of the unrealised interest and their aggregate is equal to or greater than the value (on the day of the transfer to the transferee) of the right to receive the unrealised interest;

(b) amount B, if that value is equal to or greater than amount B (aggregated with other amounts previously so received, if any);

(c) that value, if no amount has been previously so received and that value is less than amount B; or

(d) so much of that value as exceeds the aggregate of amounts previously so received, in any other case.".

(4) The following shall be substituted for subsection (6)—

"(6) In this section "amount A" means, in a case where the transferor acquired the securities on or after 28th February 1986 with the right to received unrealised interest—

(a) an amount equal to amount D less amount E; or

(b) if amount D is equal to or less than amount E, nil.

(7) In this section "amount A" means, in a case not falling within subsection (6) above, an amount equal to amount D.

(8) In this section "amount D" means an amount equal to the value (on the day of the transfer by the transferor) of the right to receive the unrealised interest.

(9) In this section "amount E" means, in a case where the transferor (as transferee) has received in respect of the securities an amount or amounts falling within subsection (4) above—

(a) an amount equal to amount F less the total received; or

(b) if amount F is equal to or less than the total received, nil.

(10) In this section "amount E" means, in any other case, an amount equal to amount F.

(11) In this section "amount F" means an amount equal to the value (on the day of the transfer to the transferor) of the right to receive the unrealised interest.

(12) In determining for the purposes of this section which securities of a particular kind a person has transferred, he is to be taken to have transferred securities of that kind which he acquired later before securities of that kind which he acquired earlier.

(13) Where the unrealised interest is payable in a currency other than sterling—

    (a) any amount received by way of the interest is for the purposes of this section the sterling equivalent on the day it is received of the amount it would be apart from this subsection; and

    (b) the value (on the day of a transfer) of the right to receive the interest is for the purposes of this section the sterling equivalent (on that day) of the value it would be apart from this subsection;

and for this purpose the sterling equivalent is to be calculated by reference to the London closing rate of exchange for the day concerned."

Transfers with or without accrued interest: supplemental

Nominees, trustees etc.

720.—(1) Where securities are transferred by or to a person as nominee for another person, or as trustee for another person absolutely entitled as against the trustee, or for any person who would be so entitled but for being an infant or other person under disability, or for two or more persons who are or would be jointly so entitled, sections 713, 715 and 716 shall apply as if references to the transferor or the transferee (as the case may be) were to the person or persons for whom the nominee or trustee disposes or acquires.

(2) It is hereby declared that for the purposes of subsection (1) above—

    (a) securities are transferred by a person as trustee for another person absolutely entitled as against the trustee if that other person has immediately before the transfer the exclusive right to direct how the securities shall be dealt with, subject only to satisfying any outstanding charge, lien or other right of the trustee to resort to the securities for payment of duty, taxes, costs or other outgoings; and

    (b) securities are transferred to a person as trustee for another person so entitled if that other person has that right immediately after the transfer.

(3) An underwriting member of Lloyd's shall be treated for the purposes of sections 710 to 728 as absolutely entitled as against the trustees to the securities forming part of his premiums trust fund, his special reserve fund (if any) and any other trust fund required or authorised by the rules of Lloyd's or required by the underwriting agent through whom his business or any part of it is carried on, to be kept in connection with the business.

(4) Where a person who is entitled to securities becomes trustee of them, he shall be treated for the purposes of sections 710 to 728 as transferring them (in a capacity other than trustee) to himself (in his capacity as trustee), or to himself and any other trustees, at the time he becomes trustee.

(5) Annual profits or gains which by virtue of 714(2) or 716(3) are treated as received in a year of assessment by trustees shall be chargeable to income tax at a rate equal to the sum of the basic rate and the additional rate for that year.

This subsection does not apply where the profits or gains are treated as received by the investment manager of a common investment fund for the time being designated as mentioned in section 328(1).

(6) In any case where—

    (a) a trustee of a settlement is treated as receiving annual profits or gains under section 714(2), or

    (b) a trustee of a settlement who is resident or domiciled outside the United Kingdom throughout any chargeable period in which an interest period (or part of it) falls would, at the end of the interest period, have been treated under section 714(2) as receiving annual profits or gains or annual profits or gains of a greater amount if he had been resident or domiciled in the United Kingdom during a part of each such chargeable period,

Chapters II to IV of Part XV shall have effect as if the amount which the trustee is or would be treated as receiving were income (within Chapter II) or income arising under the settlement (within Chapter III or IV).

(7) In any case where income of a trustee of a settlement who is resident or domiciled outside the United Kingdom throughout any chargeable period in which an interest period (or part of it) falls consists of interest which—

    (a) falls due at the end of the interest period; and

    (b) would have been treated under section 714(5) as reduced by an allowance or an allowance of a greater amount if he had been resident or domiciled in the United Kingdom during a part of each such chargeable period;

then, for the purposes of Chapters II to IV of Part XV, the interest shall be treated as being reduced by the amount of the allowance or by the additional amount (as the case may be).

(8) In subsections (6) and (7) above—

    (a) "settlement" means settlement within the meaning of Chapter II, III or IV of Part XV (as the case may be); and

    (b) references to a trustee of a settlement are, where there is no trustee of the settlement, to any person entitled to securities comprised in the settlement.

721.—(1) Where an individual who is entitled to securities dies, he shall be treated for the purposes of sections 710 to 728 as transferring the securities to his personal representatives immediately before his death.

Death.

(2) Where the securities are transferred with accrued interest by the personal representatives to a legatee in the interest period in which the individual died—

    (a) section 713 shall not apply to the transfer, and

    (b) the transfer of the securities which the individual is treated as making by virtue of subsection (1) above shall be treated as made to the legatee (and not to the personal representatives).

(3) In subsection (2) above "legatee" includes any person taking (whether beneficially or as trustee) under a testamentary disposition or on an intestacy or partial intestacy, including any person taking by virtue of an appropriation by the personal representatives in or towards satisfaction of a legacy or other interest or share in the deceased's property.

(4) In the case of an individual who dies in an interest period, section 714(2) shall have effect as if the reference to the day the period ends were to the day he dies.

(5) Subsections (1) to (4) above do not apply where the individual concerned is an underwriting member of Lloyd's and the securities concerned form part of a premiums trust fund, a special reserve fund or any other trust fund required or authorised by the rules of Lloyd's or required by the underwriting agent through whom the individual's business or any part of it is carried on, to be kept in connection with the business.

(6) In a case where subsection (5) above applies the deceased's personal representatives shall be treated for the purposes of sections 710 to 728 as the transferor or transferee in relation to transfers of securities as to which the deceased was the transferor or transferee (as the case may be) in the interest period in which he died.

Trading stock.

722.—(1) Where securities acquired by a person otherwise than as trading stock of a trade carried on by him are appropriated by him for the purposes of the trade as trading stock (whether on the commencement of the trade or otherwise), he shall be treated for the purposes of sections 710 to 728 as transferring them otherwise than in the course of the trade and re-acquiring them in the course of the trade on the day the appropriation is made.

(2) Where securities forming part of the trading stock of a person's trade are appropriated by him for any other purpose, or are retained by him on his ceasing to carry on the trade, he shall be treated for the purposes of sections 710 to 728 as transferring them in the course of the trade and re-acquiring them otherwise than in the course of the trade on the day the appropriation is made or (as the case may be) he ceases to carry on the trade.

Foreign securities: delayed remittances.

723.—(1) This section applies where in an interest period a person is treated as entitled to a sum or sums under section 713(2)(a) in respect of a transfer or transfers of securities of a particular kind which are situated outside the United Kingdom.

(2) Subject to subsection (3) below, the amount of any annual profits or gains which the person is treated under section 714 as receiving on the day the period ends in respect of securities of that kind shall be reduced—

(a) if the amount of the sum or aggregate of the sums exceeds the amount of the profits or gains, to nil; or

(b) in any other case, by the amount of the sum or aggregate.

(3) No reduction shall be made unless the person makes a claim and shows that the conditions in subsection (5) below are, so far as applicable, satisfied in the chargeable period in which the profits or gains are treated as received.

(4) The claimant (or his personal representatives) shall be charged to tax under Case VI of Schedule D on the amount of the reduction for the chargeable period in which the conditions in subsection (5) below cease to be satisfied.

(5) The conditions are—

(a) that the claimant was unable to remit the proceeds of the transfer or transfers to the United Kingdom;

(b) that the inability was due to the laws of the territory in which the securities are situated, or to the executive action of its government, or to the impossibility of obtaining foreign currency in that territory; and

(c) that the inability was not due to any want of reasonable endeavours on the part of the claimant.

(6) No claim under this section shall be made in respect of a transfer more than six years after the end of the interest period in which the transfer occurred.

(7) The personal representatives of a deceased person may make any claim which he might have made under this section if he had not died.

(8) For the purposes of this section the place where securities are situated shall be determined in accordance with section 18(4) of the 1979 Act.

724.—(1) The references in section 715(1)(a) and (2)(a) to computing the profits or losses of a trade shall not be taken as applying to a computation of income for the purposes of section 76(2).

(2) Where an insurance company carrying on life assurance business is treated as receiving annual profits or gains under section 714(2) or 716(3) in respect of securities held as investments in connection with that business, the profits or gains shall be treated for the purposes of section 434(3) to (5) as if they were income from investments held in connection with that business.

(3) Section 713(2)(a) or (3)(a) (as the case may be) shall not apply if the transferor is an insurance company and—

(a) the transfer falls to be taken into account in computing its profits or losses for the purposes of section 436; or

(b) if the company became entitled to any interest on the securities transferred, it would by virtue of section 441(1) be liable, in respect of the interest, to tax computed by reference to the amount of income received in the United Kingdom; or

(c) if the company became entitled to any interest on the securities transferred and applied the interest for the purposes of its foreign life assurance fund, it would by virtue of section 441(2) not be liable to tax in respect of the interest.

(4) Section 713(2)(b) or (3)(b) (as the case may be) shall not apply if subsection (3) above would apply if in that subsection "transferor" read "transferee".

(5) Where an overseas life insurance company (within the meaning of section 431) is entitled to an allowance under section 714(4), section 714(5) and (6) shall not apply but subsections (6) and (7) below shall apply.

(6) If the company is treated under section 714(2) as receiving annual profits or gains in an accounting period, the profits or gains shall be treated as reduced by any amount ("the deductible amount") equal to the allowance or aggregate of the allowances, as the case may be, to which the company is entitled under section 714(4) in relation to an interest period or periods ending in the accounting period.

(7) Where the deductible amount exceeds the amount of those annual profits or gains, the company may claim to have the excess treated as reducing any annual profits or gains the company is treated as receiving under section 714(2) in the company's next accounting period or, if there is still an excess, the one after (and so on for future accounting periods).

(8) Subsections (5) to (7) above do not apply to an overseas life insurance company if, by virtue of arrangements specified in an Order in Council under section 788, no charge to corporation tax under Case III of Schedule D arises under section 445 in respect of any income of the company.

Lloyd's underwriters.

725.—(1) The securities forming part of a premiums trust fund at the beginning of 1st January of any year shall be treated for the purposes of sections 710 to 728 as transferred on that day to the trustees of the fund, and in relation to such a transfer, the settlement day is the day preceding that of the transfer (notwithstanding section 712).

(2) The securities shall be treated as transferred with accrued interest if the trustees are entitled to receive in respect of them interest payable on—

(a) the day of the transfer, if that is an interest payment day, or

(b) the next (or first) interest payment day to fall after that day, in any other case;

and they shall be treated as transferred without accrued interest if they are not so entitled.

(3) Subsections (1) and (2) above do not apply as regards securities if the day preceding 1st January concerned is an interest payment day in relation to them.

(4) The securities forming part of a premiums trust fund at the end of 31st December of any year shall be treated for the purposes of sections 710 to 728 as transferred on that day by the trustees of the fund, and in relation to such a transfer, the settlement day is the day of the transfer (notwithstanding section 712).

(5) The securities shall be treated as transferred with accrued interest if the trustees are entitled to receive in respect of them interest payable on the next (or first) interest payment day to fall after the day of the transfer, and they shall be treated as transferred without accrued interest if they are not so entitled.

(6) Subsections (4) and (5) above do not apply as regards securities if 31st December concerned is an interest payment day in relation to them.

(7) Where securities are transferred by or to the trustees of a premiums trust fund, subsections (8) and (9) below shall have effect in relation to the trustees, though not in relation to the transferee or transferor (unless in turn constituting trustees of such a fund).

(8) In subsection (9) below "straddling period" means a period which would (by virtue of section 711(3) and (4) and apart from subsection (9)) be in relation to the securities an interest period beginning on or before and ending after 31st December of any year.

(9) For the purposes of sections 710 to 728 a straddling period is not an interest period, but—

    (a) the period beginning with the day on which the straddling period begins and ending with 31st December concerned is an interest period; and

    (b) the period beginning with the day following 31st December concerned and ending with the day with which the straddling period ends is an interest period.

726.—(1) Subsections (2) to (5) below apply where securities are transferred and the interest which falls due on them either before the settlement day or at the end of the interest period in which the settlement day falls is subject to the provisions of regulations under section 476(1) but would not on being paid (to whatever person) be a gross payment within the meaning of those regulations ("a gross payment").   Building societies.

(2) Section 713(4) shall be construed as if the following were substituted for paragraphs (a) and (b)—

    "(a) if the securities are transferred under an arrangement by virtue of which the transferee accounts to the transferor separately for the consideration for the securities and for an amount equal to the grossed up equivalent of the interest (if any) accruing to the settlement day, an amount equal to that amount; and

    (b) in any other case, an amount equal to the accrued proportion of the grossed up equivalent of the interest applicable to the securities for the period.".

(3) Section 713(5) shall be construed as if the following were substituted for paragraphs (a) and (b)—

    "(a) if the securities are transferred under an arrangement by virtue of which the transferor accounts to the transferee for an amount equal to the grossed up equivalent of the interest (if any) accruing from the settlement day to the next interest payment day, an amount equal to that amount; and

(b) in any other case, an amount equal to the rebate proportion of the grossed up equivalent of the interest applicable to the securities for the period.".

(4) Section 716 shall be construed as if in subsections (2) and (3) "the unrealised interest" read "the grossed up equivalent of the unrealised interest".

(5) In calculating the grossed up equivalent of interest for the purposes of sections 713(4)(b) and (5)(b) and 716(2) and (3) of this Act (as substituted or amended as mentioned in this section) and section 33A(5)(c) of the 1979 Act, the interest shall be treated as if it would, on being paid, not be a gross payment.

(6) For the purposes of the provisions mentioned in subsection (5) above, the grossed up equivalent of interest is to be calculated by adding to the interest a sum found by applying the formula—

$$\frac{S}{I + S} = R$$

where—

S is the sum to be found;

I is the interest; and

R is the basic rate of income tax (expressed as a fraction) for the year of assessment in which the interest is payable.

(7) Where a sum is both interest mentioned in section 714(5), 720(7) or 742(6) and dividends or interest in the case of which section 476(3)(b) or (5)(c) applies—

(a) in calculating the deduction of income tax as mentioned in section 476(3)(b) or (5)(c) any reduction mentioned in section 714(5), 720(7) or 742(6) shall be disregarded; and

(b) the amount which is treated as reduced as mentioned in section 714(5), 720(7) or 742(6) shall be the amount the person concerned is treated as receiving by virtue of section 476(3)(b) or (5)(c) (rather than the interest which falls due).

Stock lending.

727.—(1) The effect of section 129(3) shall be disregarded in construing section 715(1)(a) and (2)(a).

(2) Where securities are transferred in circumstances such that by virtue of section 149B(9) of the 1979 Act (capital gains tax exemption) any disposal and acquisition are disregarded for the purposes of capital gains tax, sections 713(2) and (3) and 716 shall not apply.

Information.

728.—(1) In order to obtain for the purposes of sections 710 to 727 particulars relating to securities, an inspector may by notice require a return under subsection (2) or (3) below.

(2) A member of the Stock Exchange, other than a market maker, may be required to make a return giving, in relation to any transactions effected by him in the course of his business in the period specified in the notice, such particulars as may be so specified.

In relation to transactions before 27th October 1986 this subsection shall have effect with the substitution of "jobber" for "market maker".

(3) A person (other than a member of the Stock Exchange), who acts as an agent or broker in the United Kingdom in transactions in securities, may be required to make a return giving, in relation to any such transactions effected by him in the period specified in the notice, such particulars as may be so specified.

(4) No person shall be required under subsection (2) or (3) above to include in a return particulars of any transaction effected more than three years before the service of the notice requiring him to make the return.

(5) In order to obtain for the purposes of sections 710 to 727 particulars relating to securities, the Board or an inspector may by notice require any person in whose name any securities are registered to state whether or not he is the beneficial owner of those securities and, if he is not the beneficial owner of them or any of them, to furnish the name and address of the person or persons on whose behalf the securities are registered in his name.

(6) In this section "market maker", in relation to securities, means a person who—

(a) holds himself out at all normal times in compliance with the rules of the Stock Exchange as willing to buy and sell securities of the kind concerned at a price specified by him; and

(b) is recognised as doing so by the Council of the Stock Exchange.

(7) The Board may by regulations provide that—

(a) subsections (2), (3) and (6)(a) above shall have effect as if references to the Stock Exchange were to any recognised investment exchange (within the meaning of the Financial Services Act 1986) or to any of those exchanges specified in the regulations; and

1986 c. 60.

(b) subsection (6)(b) shall have effect as if the reference to the Council of the Stock Exchange were to the investment exchange concerned.

(8) Regulations under subsection (7) above shall apply in relation to transactions effected on or after such day as may be specified in the regulations.

Other transfers of securities

729.—(1) Where the owner of any securities ("the owner") agrees to sell or transfer those securities and by the same or any collateral agreement—

Sale and repurchase of securities.

(a) agrees to buy back or re-acquire the securities, or

(b) acquires an option, which he subsequently exercises, to buy back or re-acquire the securities,

then, if the result of the transaction is that any interest becoming payable in respect of the securities is receivable otherwise than by the owner, the following provisions shall have effect—

(i) the interest so payable shall, whether it would or would not have been chargeable to tax apart from the provisions of this section, be deemed for all the purposes of the Tax Acts to be the income of the owner and not to be the income of any other person; and

(ii) if the securities are of such a character that the interest payable in respect thereof may be paid without deduction of tax, the owner shall be chargeable to tax under Case VI of Schedule D in respect of the interest which is so deemed to be his income, but shall be entitled to credit for any tax which that income is shown to have borne.

(2) In relation to corporation tax—

(a) subject to the provisions of the Tax Acts about distributions, interest deemed under subsection (1)(i) above to be the income of the owner shall be chargeable under Case VI of Schedule D, and

(b) subsection (1)(ii) above shall not apply.

(3) The references in subsection (1) above to buying back or re-acquiring the securities shall be deemed to include references to buying or acquiring similar securities, so, however, that where similar securities are bought or acquired, the owner shall be under no greater liability to tax than he would have been under if the original securities had been bought back or re-acquired.

(4) Where any person carrying on a trade which consists wholly or partly in dealing in securities agrees to buy or acquire any securities, and by the same or any collateral agreement—

(a) agrees to sell back or re-transfer the securities, or

(b) acquires an option, which he subsequently exercises, to sell back or re-transfer the securities,

then, if the result of the transaction is that any interest becoming payable in respect of the securities is receivable by him, no account shall be taken of the transaction in computing for any of the purposes of the Tax Acts the profits arising from or loss sustained in the trade.

(5) Subsection (4) above shall have effect, subject to any necessary modifications, as if references to selling back or re-transferring the securities included references to selling or transferring similar securities.

(6) This section shall not apply to any income to which section 786(4) applies.

(7) Subsections (1) and (2) above shall not apply where—

(a) the securities are Eurobonds or foreign government stock; and

(b) the owner of the securities carries on a trade which consists wholly or partly in dealing in securities and the person who agrees to buy or acquire the securities carries on such a trade.

(8) Subsection (4) above shall not apply where—

(a) the securities are Eurobonds or foreign government stock; and

(b) the person from whom the person there mentioned agrees to buy or acquire the securities carries on a trade which consists wholly or partly in dealing in securities.

(9) In subsections (7) and (8) above—

"Eurobond" has the same meaning as in section 732(5); and

"foreign government stock" means stock which is issued by a government other than that of the United Kingdom and is denominated in a currency other than sterling.

(10) For the purposes of this section—

(a) "interest" includes a dividend;

(b) "securities" includes stocks and shares, except securities which are securities for the purposes of sections 710 to 728; and

(c) securities shall be deemed to be similar if they entitle their holders to the same rights against the same persons as to capital and interest and the same remedies for the enforcement of those rights, notwithstanding any difference in the total nominal amounts of the respective securities or in the form in which they are held or the manner in which they can be transferred.

(11) The Board may by notice require any person to furnish them within such time as they may direct (not being less than 28 days), in respect of all securities of which he was the owner at any time during the period specified in the notice, such particulars as they consider necessary for the purposes of this section and for the purpose of discovering whether tax has been borne in respect of the interest on all those securities.

(12) In any case where the owner agrees to sell or transfer before such day as the Board may by order appoint for the purposes of this section or the person referred to in subsection (4) above agreed to buy or acquire before that day—

(a) subsections (1) and (2) above shall not apply if the owner's agreement to sell or transfer constitutes a transfer to which section 713(2)(a) applies; and

(b) subsection (10)(b) above shall have effect with the omission of the words "except securities which are securities for the purposes of sections 710 to 728".

730.—(1) Where in any chargeable period the owner of any securities ("the owner") sells or transfers the right to receive any interest payable (whether before or after the sale or transfer) in respect of the securities without selling or transferring the securities, then, for all the purposes of the Tax Acts, that interest, whether it would or would not be chargeable to tax apart from the provisions of this section— *Transfers of income arising from securities.*

(a) shall be deemed to be the income of the owner or, in a case where the owner is not the beneficial owner of the securities and some other person ("a beneficiary") is beneficially entitled to the income arising from the securities, the income of the beneficiary, and

(b) shall be deemed to be the income of the owner or beneficiary for that chargeable period, and

(c) shall not be deemed to be the income of any other person.

(2) For the purposes of subsection (1) above, in the case of a sale or other realisation the proceeds of which are chargeable to tax under Schedule C or under section 123(3) the interest so deemed to be the income of the owner or beneficiary shall be deemed to be equal in amount to the amount of those proceeds.

(3) Nothing in subsection (1) above shall affect any provision of this Act authorising or requiring the deduction of income tax—

    (a) from any interest which, under that subsection, is deemed to be the income of the owner or beneficiary, or

    (b) from the proceeds of any subsequent sale or other realisation of the right to receive that interest;

but the proceeds of any such subsequent sale or other realisation shall not, for any of the purposes of the Tax Acts, be deemed to be the income of the seller or the person on whose behalf the right is otherwise realised.

(4) Where—

    (a) the securities are of such a character that the interest payable in respect thereof may be paid without deduction of income tax, and

    (b) the owner or beneficiary does not show that the proceeds of any sale or other realisation of the right to receive the interest which is deemed to be his income by virtue of this section have been charged to tax under Schedule C or under section 123(3),

then the owner or beneficiary shall be chargeable to tax under Case VI of Schedule D in respect of that interest, but shall be entitled to credit for any tax which that interest is shown to have borne.

(5) For the purposes of subsection (4) above, in any case where, if the interest had been chargeable under Case IV or Case V of Schedule D, the computation of tax would have been made by reference to the amount received in the United Kingdom, the tax under Case VI shall be computed on the full amount of the sums which have been or will be received in the United Kingdom in the year of assessment or any subsequent year in which the owner remains the owner of the securities.

(6) In relation to corporation tax, subsections (4) and (5) above shall not apply but, subject to the provisions of the Tax Acts about distributions, the owner or beneficary shall, in respect of any interest which is deemed to be his income by virtue of this section, be chargeable to corporation tax under Case VI of Schedule D unless he shows that the proceeds of any sale or other realisation of the right to receive that interest have been charged to tax under Schedule C or under section 123(3).

(7) In this section—

"interest" includes dividends, annuities and shares of annuities, and

"securities" includes stocks and shares.

(8) The Board may by notice require any person to furnish them within such time as they may direct (not being less than 28 days), in respect of all securities of which he was the owner at any time during the period specified in the notice, with such particulars as they consider necessary for the purposes of this section and for the purpose of discovering whether—

(a) tax has been borne in respect of the interest on all those securities; or

(b) the proceeds of any sale or other realisation of the right to receive the interest on the securities have been charged to tax under Schedule C or section 123(3).

Purchase and sale of securities

731.—(1) In this section "the relevant provisions" means sections 732, 733, 734 and this section.

(2) Subject to subsections (3) to (10) below, the relevant provisions relate to cases of a purchase by a person ("the first buyer") of any securities and their subsequent sale by him, the result of the transaction being that interest becoming payable in respect of the securities ("the interest") is receivable by the first buyer.

(3) The relevant provisions do not relate to cases where—

(a) the time elapsing between the purchase by the first buyer and his taking steps to dispose of the securities exceeded six months, or

(b) that time exceeded one month and it is shown to the satisfaction of the Board that the purchase and sale were each effected at the current market price, and that the sale was not effected in pursuance of an agreement or arrangement made before or at the time of the purchase.

The jurisdiction of the General Commissioners or Special Commissioners on any appeal shall include jurisdiction to review any relevant decision taken by the Board in the exercise of their functions under this subsection.

(4) The reference in subsection (3) above to the first buyer taking steps to dispose of the securities shall be construed—

(a) if he sold them in the exercise of an option he had acquired, as a reference to his acquisition of the option,

(b) in any other case, as a reference to his selling them.

(5) For the purposes of the relevant provisions, a sale of securities similar to, and of the like nominal amount as, securities previously bought ("the original securities") shall be equivalent to a sale of the original securities, and subsection (4) above shall apply accordingly; and where the first buyer bought parcels of similar securities at different times a subsequent sale of any of the securities shall, so far as may be, be related to the last to be bought of the parcels, and then to the last but one, and so on.

(6) A person shall be under no greater liability to tax by virtue of subsection (5) above than he would have been under if instead of selling the similar securities he had sold the original securities.

PART XVII

(7) Where at the time when a trade is, or is deemed to be, set up and commenced any securities form part of the trading stock belonging to the trade, those securities shall be treated for the purposes of this section—

(a) as having been sold at that time in the open market by the person to whom they belonged immediately before that time, and

(b) as having been purchased at that time in the open market by the person thereafter engaged in carrying on the trade.

(8) Subject to subsection (7) above, where there is a change in the persons engaged in carrying on a trade which is not a change on which the trade is deemed to be discontinued, the provisions of this section shall apply in relation to the person so engaged after the change as if anything done to or by his predecessor had been done to or by him.

(9) For the purposes of the relevant provisions—

"interest" includes a qualifying distribution and any dividend which is not a qualifying distribution, and in applying references to interest in relation to a qualifying distribution—

(a) "gross interest" means the qualifying distribution together with the tax credit to which the recipient of the distribution is entitled in respect of it; and

(b) "net interest" means the qualifying distribution exclusive of any such tax credit;

"person" includes any body of persons, and references to a person entitled to any exemption from tax include, in a case of an exemption expressed to apply to income of a trust or fund, references to the persons entitled to make claims for the granting of that exemption;

"securities" includes stocks and shares, except securities which are securities for the purposes of sections 710 to 728.

(10) For the purposes of the relevant provisions, securities shall be deemed to be similar if they entitle their holders to the same rights against the same persons as to capital and interest and the same remedies for the enforcement of those rights, notwithstanding any difference in the total nominal amounts of the respective securities or in the form in which they are held or the manner in which they can be transferred; and for the purposes of this subsection, rights guaranteed by the Treasury shall be treated as rights against the Treasury.

Dealers in securities.

732.—(1) Subject to the provisions of this section, if the first buyer is engaged in carrying on a trade which consists of or comprises dealings in securities, then, in computing for any of the purposes of the Tax Acts the profits arising from or loss sustained in the trade, the price paid by him for the securities shall be reduced by the appropriate amount in respect of the interest, as determined in accordance with section 735.

(2) Subsection (1) above shall not apply if the subsequent sale is carried out by the first buyer after 26th October 1986 in the ordinary course of his business as a market maker in securities of the kind concerned.

(3) Subsection (1) above shall not apply if the purchase of the securities by the first buyer and their resale, or as the case may be the subsequent sale of similar securities, constitute a transaction which is to be left out

of account in computing profits or losses by virtue of section 729(4), or a transaction which would fall to be so left out of account apart from section 729(8).

(4) Subsection (1) above shall not apply if the securities are overseas securities bought by the first buyer on a stock exchange outside the United Kingdom in the ordinary course of his trade as a dealer in securities and the following conditions are satisfied, namely—

    (a) the interest is brought into account in computing for the purposes of the Tax Acts the profits arising from or loss sustained in the trade, and

    (b) where credit against tax would fall to be allowed in respect of the interest under section 788 or 790, the first buyer elects that credit shall not be so allowed.

In this subsection "overseas securities" means securities of the government of, or of a body of persons resident in, any country or territory outside the United Kingdom and the Republic of Ireland.

(5) Subsection (1) above shall not apply if the securities are Eurobonds bought by the first buyer in the ordinary course of his trade as a dealer in Eurobonds; and in this subsection "Eurobond" means a security—

    (a) which is neither preference stock nor preference share capital; and

    (b) which is issued in bearer form; and

    (c) which carries a right to interest either at a fixed rate or at a rate bearing a fixed relationship to a standard published base rate; and

    (d) which does not carry a right to any other form of benefit, whether in the nature of interest, participation in profits or otherwise; and

    (e) the interest on which is payable without any deduction in respect of income tax or of any tax of a similar character imposed by the laws of a territory outside the United Kingdom;

but, notwithstanding anything in paragraph (d) above, a security is not prevented from being a Eurobond by reason only that it carries a right to convert into a security of another description or to subscribe for further securities (whether of the same description or not).

(6) For the purposes of subsection (2) above a person is a market maker in securities of a particular kind if he—

    (a) holds himself out at all normal times in compliance with the rules of the Stock Exchange as willing to buy and sell securities of that kind at a price specified by him; and

    (b) is recognised as doing so by the Council of the Stock Exchange.

733.—(1) If the first buyer is entitled under any enactment to an exemption from tax which, apart from this subsection, would extend to the interest, then the exemption shall not extend to an amount equal to the appropriate amount in respect of the interest, as determined in accordance with section 735.

(2) If the first buyer is so entitled and any annual payment is payable by him out of the interest, the annual payment shall be deemed as to the whole thereof to be paid out of profits or gains not brought into charge to income tax, and section 349(1) shall apply accordingly.

Persons other than dealers in securities.

734.—(1) If the first buyer carries on a trade not falling within section 732, then in ascertaining whether any or what repayment of income tax is to be made to him under section 380 or 381 by reference to any loss sustained in the trade and the amount of his income for the year of assessment his income for which includes the interest, there shall be left out of account—

(a) the appropriate amount in respect of the interest, as determined in accordance with section 735, and

(b) any tax paid on that amount.

(2) Where the first buyer is a company which does not carry on a trade falling within section 732—

(a) the appropriate amount in respect of the interest, as determined in accordance with section 735(2), and

(b) any tax paid in respect of or deducted from that amount,

shall be disregarded except that, for the purposes of corporation tax on chargeable gains, the appropriate proportion of the net interest receivable by the first buyer as mentioned in section 735(2) shall be treated as if it were a capital distribution within the meaning of section 72(5)(b) of the 1979 Act received in respect of the holding of the securities concerned.

(3) In applying references in this section to interest in relation to a qualifying distribution, references to any tax paid on or in respect of an amount shall be construed as references to so much of any related tax credit as is attributable to that amount; and for this purpose "related tax credit", in relation to an amount, means the tax credit to which the recipient of the distribution of which that amount is a proportion is entitled.

Meaning of "appropriate amount in respect of" interest.

735.—(1) For the purposes of section 732 the appropriate amount in respect of the interest is the appropriate proportion of the net interest receivable by the first buyer.

(2) For the purposes of sections 733 and 734 the appropriate amount in respect of the interest is the gross amount corresponding with the appropriate proportion of the net interest receivable by the first buyer.

(3) For the purposes of this section the appropriate proportion is the proportion which—

(a) the period beginning with the date on which the securities were first listed in The Stock Exchange Daily Official List at a price excluding the value of the interest payment last payable before the interest receivable by the first buyer, and ending with the day before the day on which the first buyer bought the securities,

bears to—

(b) the period beginning with that date and ending with the day before the first date after the purchase by the first buyer on which the securities are quoted in that List at a price excluding the value of the interest receivable by the first buyer.

(4) Where the interest receivable by the first buyer was the first interest payment payable in respect of the securities, paragraphs (a) and (b) of subsection (3) above shall have effect with the substitution, for references to the date on which the securities were first quoted as mentioned in paragraph (a), of the beginning of the period for which the interest was payable; except that where the capital amount of the securities was not fully paid at the beginning of that period and one or more instalments of capital were paid during that period—

(a) the interest shall be treated as divided into parts, calculated by reference to the amount of the interest attributable to the capital paid at or before the beginning of that period and the amount thereof attributable to each such instalment, and

(b) treating each of those parts as interest payable for that period or, where the part was calculated by reference to any such instalment, as interest payable for the part of that period beginning with the payment of the instalment, there shall be calculated, in accordance with the preceding provisions of this section, the amount constituting the appropriate proportion of each part, and

(c) the appropriate proportion of the interest for the purposes of this section shall be the proportion thereof constituted by the sum of those amounts.

(5) In relation to securities not listed in the Stock Exchange Daily Official List, subsection (3) above shall have effect with the substitution for the periods therein mentioned of such periods as in the opinion of the Commissioners having jurisdiction in the matter, correspond therewith in the case of the securities in question.

Miscellaneous provisions relating to securities

736.—(1) Subection (2) below applies where a company has, as a dealing company, a holding in another company resident in the United Kingdom (being a body corporate), and—

Company dealing in securities: distribution materially reducing value of holding.

(a) the holding amounts to, or is an ingredient in a holding amounting to, 10 per cent. of all holdings of the same class in that company, and

(b) a distribution is, or two or more distributions are, made in respect of the holding, and

(c) the value (at any accounting date or immediately before realisation or appropriation) of any security comprised in the holding is materially reduced below the value of the security at the time when it was acquired, and the whole or any part of this reduction is attributable to any distribution falling within paragraph (b) above;

and in relation to any security comprised in the holding, the company having the holding is in subsection (2) below referred to as "the dealing company" and so much of any reduction in the value of the security as is attributable to any distribution falling within paragraph (b) above is in that subsection referred to as "the relevant reduction".

(2) Where this subsection applies, an amount equal to the relevant reduction in the value of a security comprised in the holding—

> (a) shall, if and so long as the security is not realised or appropriated as mentioned below, be added to the value of the security for the purposes of any valuation;

> (b) shall be treated, on any realisation of the security in the course of trade, as a trading receipt of the dealing company or, in the event of a partial realisation, shall be so treated to an appropriate extent, and

> (c) shall be treated as a trading receipt of the dealing company if the security is appropriated in such circumstances that a profit on the sale of the security would no longer form part of the dealing company's trading profits.

(3) References in this section to a holding in a company refer to a holding of securities by virtue of which the holder may receive distributions made by the company, but so that—

> (a) a company's holdings of different classes in another company shall be treated as separate holdings, and

> (b) holdings of securities which differ in the entitlements or obligations they confer or impose shall be regarded as holdings of different classes.

(4) For the purposes of subsection (2) above—

> (a) all a company's holdings of the same class in another company are to be treated as ingredients constituting a single holding, and

> (b) a company's holding of a particular class shall be treated as an ingredient in a holding amounting to 10 per cent. of all holdings of that class if the aggregate of that holding and other holdings of that class held by connected persons amounts to 10 per cent. of all holdings of that class;

and section 839 shall have effect in relation to paragraph (b) above as if, in subsection (7) of that section, after the words "or exercise control of" in each place where they occur there were inserted the words "or to acquire a holding in".

(5) Where this section applies in relation to a distribution which consists of or includes interest to which section 732 applies, any reduction under that section in the price paid for the securities in respect of which the distribution is made shall be adjusted in such manner as seems appropriate to the Board to take account of subsection (2) above.

(6) For the purposes of this section "security" includes a share or other right and a company is a "dealing company" in relation to a holding if a profit on a sale of the holding would be taken into account in computing the company's trading profits.

737.—(1) Subject to the provisions of this section, where—

(a) under a contract for the sale of securities one of the parties to the contract ("the dividend manufacturer") is required to pay to the other the amount of a periodical payment of interest on the securities, and

(b) the dividend manufacturer does not satisfy the following condition, that is to say, that he is entitled to that payment of interest either as the registered holder of the securities or from a person from whom the dividend manufacturer purchased them,

section 350(1) and Schedule 16 shall apply as if the payment by the dividend manufacturer were an annual payment made, after due deduction of tax, wholly out of a source other than profits or gains brought into charge to income tax.

(2) Subsection (1) of this section shall not apply where otherwise than by virtue of section 476(5)(a) the interest in question is payable without deduction of tax or where, under the rules of the stock exchange governing the transaction, the payment required to be made in respect of the interest is of the amount of the interest before deduction of tax.

(3) If for any chargeable period the liability to tax of a market maker is determined on the footing that any excess of his payments in respect of interest on securities over his receipts in respect thereof, being payments made or receipts accrued in pursuance of a contract for the sale or purchase of the securities, is to be treated for all the purposes of the Tax Acts as an annual payment made by him, then as respects that chargeable period subsection (1) above shall not apply to him if he sold or purchased the securities in the ordinary course of his business as a market maker in securities of the kind concerned.

(4) Where the dividend manufacturer is resident in the United Kingdom and purchased the securities (otherwise than through a broker) from a person not so resident, then paragraph (b) of subsection (1) above shall have effect as if after the word "say" there were inserted the word "either" and as if for the words from "either as" to the end of the paragraph there were inserted the words "as the registered holder of the securities or that he shows that he acquired the securities, directly or indirectly, from a person who was so entitled to the payment".

(5) Where the dividend manufacturer in relation to such a contract as is mentioned in paragraph (a) of subsection (1) above is not resident in the United Kingdom, and the sale is effected through a broker, that subsection shall not apply; but unless the broker shows either—

(a) that the dividend manufacturer was entitled to the payment of interest as the registered holder of the securities, or

(b) that the dividend manufacturer acquired the securities, directly or indirectly, from a person who was so entitled to the payment,

section 350(1) shall apply as if the payment through the broker of the amount of the payment of interest were an annual payment by the broker made, after due deduction of tax, wholly out of such a source as is mentioned in subsection (1) above.

(6) In this section—

"broker", in relation to securities, means a member of the Stock Exchange who carries on business in the United Kingdom and is not, at the time the contract is made, a market maker in securities of the kind concerned;

"market maker", in relation to securities of a particular kind, means a person who—

(a) holds himself out at all normal times in compliance with the rules of the Stock Exchange as willing to buy and sell securities of that kind at a price specified by him; and

(b) is recognised as doing so by the Council of the Stock Exchange;

"securities" includes shares and stock;

and references to a periodical payment of interest include references to a qualifying distribution and any dividend which is not a qualifying distribution.

(7) In the application of this section in a case where the references in subsection (1) above to a periodical payment of interest are construed as references to a qualifying distribution, subsection (2) above shall be omitted.

(8) Where it appears to the Board that by reason of any transaction or transactions a person may by virtue of this section have incurred any liability to tax, the Board may by notice served on him require him, within such time not less than 28 days as may be specified in the notice, to furnish information in his possession with respect to the transaction or any of the transactions, being information as to matters, specified in the notice, which are relevant to the question whether he has incurred any such liability.

Supplemental

Power to amend sections 732, 735 and 737.

738.—(1) The Board may by regulations provide for all or any of the following—

(a) that section 732(2) shall not apply unless the subsequent sale is carried out in compliance with further conditions specified in the regulations;

(b) that section 732(6) shall have effect as if the reference to the Stock Exchange in paragraph (a) were to any recognised investment exchange or to any of those exchanges specified in the regulations, and as if the reference to the Council of the Stock Exchange in paragraph (b) were to the investment exchange concerned;

(c) that for section 735(3) and (5) (which refer to the Stock Exchange Daily Official List) there shall be substituted such provisions as the Board think fit to take account of recognised investment exchanges.

Regulations under this subsection shall apply where the subsequent sale is carried out by the first buyer on or after such day as is specified in the regulations.

(2) The Board may by regulations provide that section 737(6) shall have effect—

    (a) as if references to the Stock Exchange in the definition of "broker" and in paragraph (a) of the definition of "market maker" were to any recognised investment exchange or to any of those exchanges specified in the regulations; and

    (b) as if the reference to the Council of the Stock Exchange in paragraph (b) of the definition of "market maker" were to the investment exchange concerned.

(3) The Board may by regulations substitute for subsection (3) of section 737 a provision that subsection (1) of that section shall not apply to such persons and in such circumstances as are specified in the substituted provision, and make such incidental and consequential provisions (which may include the amendment of other provisions of section 737) as appear to the Board to be appropriate.

(4) Regulations under subsections (2) and (3) above shall apply where the contract for the sale of securities is made on or after such day as is specified in the regulations.

(5) In this section "recognised investment exchange" means a recognised investment exchange within the meaning of the Financial Services Act 1986.

1986 c. 60.

CHAPTER III

TRANSFER OF ASSETS ABROAD

739.—(1) Subject to section 747(4)(b), the following provisions of this section shall have effect for the purpose of preventing the avoiding by individuals ordinarily resident in the United Kingdom of liability to income tax by means of transfers of assets by virtue or in consequence of which, either alone or in conjunction with associated operations, income becomes payable to persons resident or domiciled outside the United Kingdom.

Prevention of avoidance of income tax.

(2) Where by virtue or in consequence of any such transfer, either alone or in conjunction with associated operations, such an individual has, within the meaning of this section, power to enjoy, whether forthwith or in the future, any income of a person resident or domiciled outside the United Kingdom which, if it were income of that individual received by him in the United Kingdom, would be chargeable to income tax by deduction or otherwise, that income shall, whether it would or would not have been chargeable to income tax apart from the provisions of this section, be deemed to be income of that individual for all purposes of the Income Tax Acts.

(3) Where, whether before or after any such transfer, such an individual receives or is entitled to receive any capital sum the payment of which is in any way connected with the transfer or any associated operation, any income which, by virtue or in consequence of the transfer, either alone or in conjunction with associated operations, has become the income of a person resident or domiciled outside the United Kingdom shall, whether it would or would not have been chargeable to income tax apart from the provisions of this section, be deemed to be income of that individual for all purposes of the Income Tax Acts.

(4) In subsection (3) above "capital sum" means, subject to subsection (5) below—

(a) any sum paid or payable by way of loan or repayment of a loan, and

(b) any other sum paid or payable otherwise than as income, being a sum which is not paid or payable for full consideration in money or money's worth.

(5) For the purposes of subsection (3) above, there shall be treated as a capital sum which an individual receives or is entitled to receive any sum which a third person receives or is entitled to receive at the individual's direction or by virtue of the assignment by him of his right to receive it.

(6) Income shall not by virtue of subsection (3) above be deemed to be that of an individual for any year of assessment by reason only of his having received a sum by way of loan if that sum has been wholly repaid before the beginning of that year.

Liability of non-transferors.

740.—(1) This section has effect where—

(a) by virtue or in consequence of a transfer of assets, either alone or in conjunction with associated operations, income becomes payable to a person resident or domiciled outside the United Kingdom; and

(b) an individual ordinarily resident in the United Kingdom who is not liable to tax under section 739 by reference to the transfer receives a benefit provided out of assets which are available for the purpose by virtue or in consequence of the transfer or of any associated operations.

(2) Subject to the provisions of this section, the amount or value of any such benefit as is mentioned in subsection (1) above, if not otherwise chargeable to income tax in the hands of the recipient, shall—

(a) to the extent to which it falls within the amount of relevant income of years of assessment up to and including the year of assessment in which the benefit is received, be treated for all the purposes of the Income Tax Acts as the income of the individual for that year;

(b) to the extent to which it is not by virtue of this subsection treated as his income for that year and falls within the amount of relevant income of the next following year of assessment, be treated for those purposes as his income for the next following year,

and so on for subsequent years, taking the reference in paragraph (b) to the year mentioned in paragraph (a) as a reference to that and any other year before the subsequent year in question.

(3) Subject to subsection (7) below and section 744(1), the relevant income of a year of assessment, in relation to an individual, is any income which arises in that year to a person resident or domiciled outside the United Kingdom and which by virtue or in consequence of the transfer or associated operations referred to in subsection (1) above can directly or indirectly be used for providing a benefit for the individual or for enabling a benefit to be provided for him.

(4) Income tax chargeable by virtue of this section shall be charged under Case VI of Schedule D.

(5) An individual who is domiciled outside the United Kingdom shall not, in respect of any benefit not received in the United Kingdom, be chargeable to tax under this section by reference to relevant income which is such that if he had received it he would not, by reason of his being so domiciled, have been chargeable to income tax in respect of it; and subsections (6) to (9) of section 65 shall apply for the purposes of this subsection as they would apply for the purposes of subsection (5) of that section if the benefit were income arising from possessions outside the United Kingdom.

(6) Where—

(a) the whole or part of the benefit received by an individual in a year of assessment is a capital payment within the meaning of section 80 or 81(2) of the Finance Act 1981 (chargeable gains: non-resident and migrant settlements) (because not falling within the amount of relevant income referred to in paragraph (a) of subsection (2) above); and

1981 c.35.

(b) chargeable gains are by reason of that payment treated under either of those sections as accruing to him in that or a subsequent year,

paragraph (b) of that subsection shall apply in relation to any year of assessment ("a year of charge") after one in which chargeable gains have been so treated as accruing to him as if a part of the amount or value of the benefit corresponding to the amount of those gains had been treated under that subsection as his income for a year of assessment before the year of charge.

(7) This section applies irrespective of when the transfer or associated operations referred to in subsection (1) above took place, but applies only to relevant income arising on or after 10th March 1981.

741. Sections 739 and 740 shall not apply if the individual shows in writing or otherwise to the satisfaction of the Board either—

(a) that the purpose of avoiding liability to taxation was not the purpose or one of the purposes for which the transfer or associated operations or any of them were effected; or

(b) that the transfer and any associated operations were bona fide commercial transactions and were not designed for the purpose of avoiding liability to taxation.

The jurisdiction of the Special Commissioners on any appeal shall include jurisdiction to review any relevant decision taken by the Board in exercise of their functions under this section.

742.—(1) For the purposes of sections 739 to 741 "an associated operation" means, in relation to any transfer, an operation of any kind effected by any person in relation to any of the assets transferred or any assets representing, whether directly or indirectly, any of the assets transferred, or to the income arising from any such assets, or to any assets representing, whether directly or indirectly, the accumulations of income arising from any such assets.

X

(2) An individual shall, for the purposes of section 739, be deemed to have power to enjoy income of a person resident or domiciled outside the United Kingdom if—

> (a) the income is in fact so dealt with by any person as to be calculated, at some point of time, and whether in the form of income or not, to enure for the benefit of the individual; or

> (b) the receipt or accrual of the income operates to increase the value to the individual of any assets held by him or for his benefit; or

> (c) the individual receives or is entitled to receive, at any time, any benefit provided or to be provided out of that income or out of moneys which are or will be available for the purpose by reason of the effect or successive effects of the associated operations on that income and on any assets which directly or indirectly represent that income; or

> (d) the individual may, in the event of the exercise or successive exercise of one or more powers, by whomsoever exercisable and whether with or without the consent of any other person, become entitled to the beneficial enjoyment of the income; or

> (e) the individual is able in any manner whatsoever, and whether directly or indirectly, to control the application of the income.

(3) In determining whether an individual has power to enjoy income within the meaning of subsection (2) above—

> (a) regard shall be had to the substantial result and effect of the transfer and any associated operations, and

> (b) all benefits which may at any time accrue to the individual (whether or not he has rights at law or in equity in or to those benefits) as a result of the transfer and any associated operations shall be taken into account irrespective of the nature or form of the benefits.

(4) Subsection (5) below applies where a person resident or domiciled outside the United Kingdom throughout any chargeable period in which an interest period (or part of it) falls would, at the end of the interest period, have been treated under section 714(2) as receiving annual profits or gains or annual profits or gains of a greater amount if he had been resident or domiciled in the United Kingdom during a part of each such chargeable period.

(5) Sections 739 to 741 shall have effect as if the amount which the person would be treated as receiving or the additional amount (as the case may be) were income becoming payable to him; and, accordingly, any reference in those sections to income of (or payable or arising to) such a person shall be read as including a reference to such an amount.

(6) Where income of a person resident or domiciled outside the United Kingdom throughout any chargeable period in which an interest period (or part of it) falls consists of interest—

> (a) which falls due at the end of the interest period, and

(b) which would have been treated under section 714(5) as reduced by an allowance or an allowance of a greater amount if he had been resident or domiciled in the United Kingdom during a part of each such chargeable period,

then for the purposes of sections 739 to 741, the interest shall be treated as being reduced by the amount of the allowance or by the additional amount (as the case may be).

(7) In subsections (4) to (6) above "interest period" has the meaning given by section 711.

(8) For the purposes of sections 739 to 741, any body corporate incorporated outside the United Kingdom shall be treated as if it were resident outside the United Kingdom whether it is so resident or not.

(9) For the purposes of sections 739 to 741—

(a) a reference to an individual shall be deemed to include the wife or husband of the individual;

(b) "assets" includes property or rights of any kind and "transfer", in relation to rights, includes the creation of those rights;

(c) "benefit" includes a payment of any kind;

(d) references to income of a person resident or domiciled outside the United Kingdom shall, where the amount of the income of a company for any year or period has been apportioned under section 423, include references to so much of the income of the company for that year or period as is equal to the amount so apportioned to that person, and that amount shall be treated as increased by such proportion of itself as corresponds to the rate of advance corporation tax applicable to a distribution made at the end of the accounting period to which the apportionment relates;

(e) references to assets representing any assets, income or accumulations of income include references to shares in or obligations of any company to which, or obligations of any other person to whom, those assets, that income or those accumulations are or have been transferred.

(10) Any amount which by virtue of subsection (9)(d) above is treated as the income of any person for the purposes of sections 739 to 741 shall also be treated for those purposes as payable to that person.

743.—(1) Income tax at the basic rate shall not be charged by virtue of section 739 in respect of income which has borne tax at the basic rate by deduction or otherwise but, subject to that, income tax so chargeable shall be charged under Case VI of Schedule D.

Supplemental provisions.

(2) In computing the liability to income tax of an individual chargeable by virtue of section 739, the same deductions and reliefs shall be allowed as would have been allowed if the income deemed to be his by virtue of that section had actually been received by him.

(3) An individual who is domiciled outside the United Kingdom shall not be chargeable to tax in respect of any income deemed to be his by virtue of that section if he would not, by reason of his being so domiciled, have been chargeable to tax in respect of it if it had in fact been his income.

(4) Where an individual has been charged to income tax on any income deemed to be his by virtue of section 739 and that income is subsequently received by him, it shall be deemed not to form part of his income again for the purposes of the Income Tax Acts.

(5) In any case where an individual has for the purposes of that section power to enjoy income of a person abroad by reason of his receiving any such benefit as is referred to in section 742(2)(c), then notwithstanding anything in subsection (1) above, the individual shall be chargeable to income tax by virtue of section 739 for the year of assessment in which the benefit is received on the whole of the amount or value of that benefit except in so far as it is shown that the benefit derives directly or indirectly from income on which he has already been charged to tax for that or a previous year of assessment.

No duplication of charge.

744.—(1) No amount of income shall be taken into account more than once in charging tax under the provisions of sections 739 and 740; and where there is a choice as to the persons in relation to whom any amount of income can be so taken into account—

(a) it shall be so taken into account in relation to such of them, and if more than one in such proportions respectively, as appears to the Board to be just and reasonable; and

(b) the jurisdiction of the Special Commissioners on any appeal against an assessment charging tax under those provisions shall include jurisdiction to review any relevant decision taken by the Board under this subsection.

(2) In subsection (1) above references to an amount of income taken into account in charging tax are—

(a) in the case of tax which under section 739 is charged on income, to the amount of that income;

(b) in the case of tax charged under that section by virtue of section 743(5), to an amount of the income out of which the benefit is provided equal to the amount or value of the benefit charged;

(c) in the case of tax charged under section 740, to the amount of relevant income taken into account under subsection (2) of that section in charging the benefit.

Power to obtain information.

745.—(1) The Board may by notice require any person to furnish them within such time as they may direct (not being less than 28 days) with such particulars as they think necessary for the purposes of this Chapter.

(2) The particulars which a person must furnish under this section, if he is required by such a notice so to do, include particulars—

(a) as to transactions with respect to which he is or was acting on behalf of others;

(b) as to transactions which in the opinion of the Board it is proper that they should investigate for the purposes of this Chapter notwithstanding that, in the opinion of the person to whom the notice is given, no liability to tax arises under this Chapter; and

   (c) as to whether the person to whom the notice is given has taken or is taking any, and if so what, part in any, and if so what, transactions of a description specified in the notice.

(3) Notwithstanding anything in subsection (2) above, a solicitor shall not be deemed for the purposes of paragraph (c) of that subsection to have taken part in a transaction by reason only that he has given professional advice to a client in connection with that transaction, and shall not, in relation to anything done by him on behalf of his client, be compellable under this section, except with the consent of his client, to do more than state that he is or was acting on behalf of a client, and give the name and address of the client and also—

   (a) in the case of anything done by the solicitor in connection with the transfer of any asset by or to an individual ordinarily resident in the United Kingdom to or by any such body corporate as is mentioned in subsection (4) below, or in connection with any associated operation in relation to any such transfer, the names and addresses of the transferor and the transferee or of the persons concerned in the associated operations, as the case may be;

   (b) in the case of anything done by the solicitor in connection with the formation or management of any such body corporate as is mentioned in subsection (4) below, the name and address of the body corporate;

   (c) in the case of anything done by the solicitor in connection with the creation, or with the execution of the trusts, of any settlement by virtue or in consequence of which income becomes payable to a person resident or domiciled outside the United Kingdom, the names and addresses of the settlor and of that person.

(4) The bodies corporate mentioned in subsection (3) above are bodies corporate resident or incorporated outside the United Kingdom which are, or if resident in the United Kingdom would be, close companies, but not trading companies (as defined in paragraph 7 of Schedule 19).

(5) Nothing in this section shall impose on any bank the obligation to furnish any particulars of any ordinary banking transactions between the bank and a customer carried out in the ordinary course of banking business, unless the bank has acted or is acting on behalf of the customer in connection with the formation or management of any such body corporate as is mentioned in subsection (4) above or in connection with the creation, or with the execution of the trusts, of any such settlement as is mentioned in subsection (3)(c) above.

(6) In this section "settlement" and "settlor" have the meanings given by section 681(4).

746. In relation to amounts which by virtue of any provision of section 34, 35 or 36 would, in the case of a person resident in the Republic of Ireland and not resident in the United Kingdom, be included in his income if he were not resident in the Republic of Ireland, sections 739, 742(1) to (3), 743 and 745 shall apply—

   (a) as if his income included those amounts; and

(b) as if references to an individual included references to any person (and so that in accordance with section 9 those sections then apply for corporation tax as well as for income tax);

but section 741 shall not apply in any such case.

CHAPTER IV

CONTROLLED FOREIGN COMPANIES

Imputation of chargeable profits and creditable tax of controlled foreign companies.

747.—(1) If the Board have reason to believe that in any accounting period a company—

(a) is resident outside the United Kingdom, and

(b) is controlled by persons resident in the United Kingdom, and

(c) is subject to a lower level of taxation in the territory in which it is resident,

and the Board so direct, the provisions of this Chapter shall apply in relation to that accounting period.

(2) A company which falls within paragraphs (a) to (c) of subsection (1) above is in this Chapter referred to as a "controlled foreign company".

(3) Where, by virtue of a direction under subsection (1) above, the provisions of this Chapter apply in relation to an accounting period of a controlled foreign company, the chargeable profits of that company for that period and its creditable tax (if any) for that period shall each be apportioned in accordance with section 752 among the persons (whether resident in the United Kingdom or not) who had an interest in that company at any time during that accounting period.

(4) Where, on such an apportionment of a controlled foreign company's chargeable profits for an accounting period as is referred to in subsection (3) above, an amount of those profits is apportioned to a company resident in the United Kingdom then, subject to subsection (5) below—

(a) a sum equal to corporation tax at the appropriate rate on that apportioned amount of profits, less the portion of the controlled foreign company's creditable tax for that period (if any) which is apportioned to the resident company, shall be assessed on and recoverable from the resident company as if it were an amount of corporation tax chargeable on that company; and

(b) if, apart from this paragraph, section 739 would deem any sum forming part of the company's chargeable profits for that accounting period to be the income of an individual for the purposes of the Income Tax Acts, that section shall not apply to such portion of that sum as corresponds to the portion of those chargeable profits which is apportioned to companies which are resident in the United Kingdom and which, by virtue of paragraph (a) above, have a liability to tax in respect thereof;

and for the purposes of paragraph (a) above "the appropriate rate" means the rate of corporation tax applicable to profits of that accounting period of the resident company in which ends the accounting period of the controlled foreign company to which the direction under subsection (1) above relates or, if there is more than one such rate, the average rate over the whole of that accounting period of the resident company.

(5) Tax shall not, by virtue of subsection (4) above, be assessed and recoverable from a company resident in the United Kingdom unless, on the apportionment in question, the aggregate of—

(a) the amount of the controlled foreign company's chargeable profits for the accounting period in question which is apportioned to the resident company, and

(b) any amounts of those chargeable profits which are apportioned to persons who are connected or associated with the resident company,

is at least 10 per cent. of the total of those chargeable profits.

(6) In relation to a company resident outside the United Kingdom—

(a) any reference in this Chapter to its chargeable profits for an accounting period is a reference to the amount which, on the assumptions in Schedule 24, would be the amount of the total profits of the company for that period on which, after allowing for any deductions available against those profits, corporation tax would be chargeable; and

(b) any reference in this Chapter to profits does not include a reference to chargeable gains but otherwise (except as provided by paragraph (a) above) has the same meaning as it has for the purposes of corporation tax.

748.—(1) No direction may be given under section 747(1) with respect to an accounting period of a controlled foreign company if— Limitations on direction-making power.

(a) in respect of that period the company pursues, within the meaning of Part 1 of Schedule 25, an acceptable distribution policy; or

(b) throughout that period the company is, within the meaning of Part II of that Schedule, engaged in exempt activities; or

(c) the public quotation condition set out in Part III of that Schedule is fulfilled with respect to that period; or

(d) the chargeable profits of the accounting period do not exceed £20,000 or, if the accounting period is less than 12 months, a proportionately reduced amount.

(2) Without prejudice to any right of appeal, nothing in subsection (1) above prevents the Board from giving a direction with respect to an accounting period after the end of that period but before it is known whether the company has paid such a dividend as establishes that it is pursuing an acceptable distribution policy in respect of the profits arising in that period.

(3) Notwithstanding that none of paragraphs (a) to (d) of subsection (1) above applies to an accounting period of a controlled foreign company, no direction may be given under section 747(1) with respect to that accounting period if it appears to the Board that—

(a) in so far as any of the transactions the results of which are reflected in the profits arising in that accounting period, or any two or more of those transactions taken together, achieved a reduction in United Kingdom tax, either the reduction so achieved was minimal or it was not the main purpose or one of the main purposes of that transaction or, as the case may be, of those transactions taken together to achieve that reduction, and

(b) it was not the main reason or, as the case may be, one of the main reasons for the company's existence in that accounting period to achieve a reduction in United Kingdom tax by a diversion of profits from the United Kingdom,

and Part IV of Schedule 25 shall have effect with respect to the preceding provisions of this subsection.

Residence and interest.

749.—(1) Subject to subsections (2) and (4) below, in any accounting period in which a company is resident outside the United Kingdom, it shall be regarded for the purposes of this Chapter as resident in that territory in which, throughout that period, it is liable to tax by reason of domicile, residence or place of management.

(2) If, in the case of any company, there are in any accounting period two or more territories falling within subsection (1) above, the company shall in that accounting period be regarded for the purposes of this Chapter as resident in only one of them, namely—

(a) if, throughout the accounting period, the company's place of effective management is situated in one of those territories only, in that territory; and

(b) if, throughout the accounting period, the company's place of effective management is situated in two or more of those territories, in that one of them in which, at the end of the accounting period, the greater amount of the company's assets is situated; and

(c) if neither paragraph (a) nor paragraph (b) above applies, in that one of the territories falling within subsection (1) above in which, at the end of the accounting period, the greater amount of the company's assets is situated; and

(d) if paragraph (a) above does not apply and neither paragraph (b) nor paragraph (c) above produces one, and only one, of those territories, in that one of them which may be specified in a direction under section 747(1) relating to that accounting period.

(3) If, in the case of any company, there is in any accounting period no territory falling within subsection (1) above, then, for the purposes of this Chapter, it shall be conclusively presumed that the company is in that accounting period resident in a territory in which it is subject to a lower level of taxation.

(4) In any case where it becomes necessary for the purposes of subsection (2) above to determine in which of two or more territories the greater amount of a company's assets is situated at the end of an accounting period, account shall be taken only of those assets which,

immediately before the end of that period, are situated in those territories and the amount of them shall be determined by reference to their market value at that time.

(5) For the purposes of this Chapter, the following persons have an interest in a controlled foreign company—

(a) any person who possesses, or is entitled to acquire, share capital or voting rights in the company,

(b) any person who possesses, or is entitled to acquire, a right to receive or participate in distributions of the company or any amounts payable by the company (in cash or in kind) to loan creditors by way of premium on redemption,

(c) any person who is entitled to secure that income or assets (whether present or future) of the company will be applied directly or indirectly for his benefit, and

(d) any other person who, either alone or together with other persons, has control of the company,

and for the purposes of paragraph (b) above the definition of "distribution" in Part VI shall be construed without any limitation to companies resident in the United Kingdom.

(6) References in subsection (5) above to being entitled to do anything apply where a person is presently entitled to do it at a future date, or will at a future date be entitled to do it; but a person whose entitlement to secure that any income or assets of the company will be applied as mentioned in paragraph (c) of that subsection is contingent upon a default of the company or any other person under any agreement shall not be treated as falling within that paragraph unless the default has occurred.

(7) Without prejudice to subsection (5) above, the Board may, if they think it appropriate, treat a loan creditor of a controlled foreign company as having an interest in the company for the purposes of this Chapter.

750.—(1) Without prejudice to subsection (3) of section 749, a company which, by virtue of subsection (1) or subsection (2) of that section, is to be regarded as resident in a particular territory outside the United Kingdom shall be considered to be subject to a lower level of taxation in that territory if the amount of tax ("the local tax") which is paid under the law of that territory in respect of the profits of the company which arise in any accounting period is less than one-half of the corresponding United Kingdom tax on those profits.

Territories with a lower level of taxation.

(2) For the purposes of this Chapter, the amount of the corresponding United Kingdom tax on the profits arising in an accounting period of a company resident outside the United Kingdom is the amount of corporation tax which, on the assumptions set out in Schedule 24 and subject to subsection (3) below, would be chargeable in respect of the chargeable profits of the company for that accounting period.

(3) In determining the amount of corporation tax which, in accordance with subsection (2) above, would be chargeable in respect of the chargeable profits of an accounting period of a company resident outside the United Kingdom—

PART XVII

(a) it shall be assumed for the purposes of Schedule 24—

(i) that a direction has been given under section 747(1) in respect of that period; and

(ii) that the Board have made any declaration which they could have made under sub-paragraph (3) of paragraph 11 of that Schedule and of which they gave notice as mentioned in that sub-paragraph; and

(b) there shall be disregarded so much of any relief from corporation tax in respect of income as would be attributable to the local tax and would fall to be given by virtue of any provision of Part XVIII other than section 810; and

(c) there shall be deducted from what would otherwise be the amount of that corporation tax—

(i) any amount which (on the assumptions set out in Schedule 24) would fall to be set off against corporation tax by virtue of section 7(2); and

(ii) any amount of income tax or corporation tax actually charged in respect of any of those chargeable profits.

(4) The references in subsection (3)(c) above to an amount falling to be set off or an amount actually charged do not include so much of any such amount as has been or falls to be repaid to the company whether on the making of a claim or otherwise.

Accounting periods and creditable tax.

751.—(1) For the purposes of this Chapter, an accounting period of a company resident outside the United Kingdom shall begin—

(a) whenever the company comes under the control of the persons resident in the United Kingdom;

(b) whenever the company, not being the subject of an earlier direction under section 747(1), commences to carry on business; and

(c) whenever an accounting period of the company ends without the company then ceasing either to carry on business or to have any source of income whatsoever.

(2) For the purposes of this Chapter, an accounting period of a company resident outside the United Kingdom shall end if and at the time when—

(a) the company ceases to be under the control of persons resident in the United Kingdom; or

(b) the company becomes, or ceases to be, liable to tax in a territory; or

(c) the company ceases to have any source of income whatsoever;

and for the purposes of paragraph (b) above "liable to tax" means liable to tax by reason of domicile, residence or place of management.

(3) Without prejudice to subsections (1) and (2) above, subsections (3), (5) and (7) of section 12 shall apply for the purposes of this Chapter as they apply for the purposes of corporation tax, but with the omission of so much of those provisons as relates to a company coming or ceasing to be within the charge to corporation tax.

(4) Where it appears to the Board that the beginning or end of any accounting period of a company resident outside the United Kingdom is uncertain, a direction under section 747(1) may specify as an accounting period of the company such period, not exceeding 12 months, as appears to the Board to be appropriate, and that period shall be treated for the purposes of this Chapter as an accounting period of the company unless the direction is subsequently amended under subsection (5) below.

(5) If, on further facts coming to the knowledge of the Board after the making of a direction (including facts emerging on an appeal against notice of the making of the direction), it appears to the Board that any accounting period specified in the direction is not the true accounting period, the Board shall amend the direction so as to specify the true period.

(6) In this Chapter, in relation to an accounting period of a controlled foreign company in respect of which a direction is given under section 747(1), the creditable tax means the aggregate of—

(a) the amount of any relief from corporation tax in respect of income which (on the assumptions set out in Schedule 24 and assuming the company to be liable for corporation tax on the chargeable profits of that accounting period) would fall to be given to the company by virtue of any provision of Part XVIII in respect of foreign tax attributable to any income which is brought into account in determining those chargeable profits; and

(b) any amount which (on those assumptions) would fall to be set off against corporation tax on those chargeable profits by virtue of section 7(2); and

(c) the amount of any income tax or corporation tax actually charged in respect of the chargeable profits of that accounting period, less any of that tax which has been or falls to be repaid to the company, whether on the making of a claim or otherwise.

752.—(1) Where a direction has been given under section 747(1) in respect of an accounting period of a controlled foreign company, then, subject to subsections (2) and (3) below, the apportionment of the company's chargeable profits and creditable tax (if any) for that period shall be made among, and according to the respective interests of, the persons who at any time during that period had interests in the company.

(2) In determining for the purposes of this Chapter the respective interests of persons who (in accordance with section 749) have interests in a controlled foreign company, the Board may, if it seems to them just and reasonable to do so, attribute to each of those persons an interest corresponding to his interest in the assets of the company available for distribution among those persons in the event of a winding up or in any other circumstances.

(3) Where the controlled foreign company is not a trading company, the Board may, if it seems to them just and reasonable to do so, treat a loan creditor as having for the purposes of this section an interest in the company to the extent to which the income of the company has been, or is available to be, expended in redemption, repayment or discharge of the loan capital or debt (including any premium thereon) in respect of which he is a loan creditor.

(4) Subject to subsections (5) and (7) below, as between persons each of whom has an unvarying holding of shares of the same class throughout a particular accounting period of a controlled foreign company, the amount of the company's chargeable profits and creditable tax which is apportioned to each of them by virtue of his holding of those shares shall be in direct proportion to the numbers of shares comprised in their holdings; and similar principles shall apply in relation to an apportionment among other persons each of whom holds an interest of the same description in the controlled foreign company.

(5) Where the same interest in a controlled foreign company is held directly by one person and indirectly by another or others (as in a case where one company has a shareholding in the controlled foreign company and the first company is controlled by a third company or by two or more persons together) then, subject to subsection (6) below, the Board, in apportioning the company's chargeable profits and creditable tax—

(a) may treat that interest as held solely by a person who holds that interest indirectly or, as the case may be, by two or more persons (the "holders") who, taken together, hold that interest indirectly, and

(b) in particular, if that person or one or more of those holders is resident in the United Kingdom, may treat the interest as held solely by that one or, as the case may be, those holders.

(6) In any case where the same interest is held directly by one person and indirectly by another and the circumstances are as set out in any of paragraphs (a) to (c) below, the Board shall treat the interest as held solely by the company which is described in the paragraph concerned as "the assessable company"—

(a) where the interest is held directly by a company resident in the United Kingdom, that company is the assessable company; and

(b) where the interest is held directly by a person resident outside the United Kingdom and indirectly by only one company resident in the United Kingdom, that company is the assessable company; and

(c) where the interest is held directly by a person resident outside the United Kingdom and indirectly by two or more companies resident in the United Kingdom, the assessable company is that one of the companies which so holds the interest by virtue of holding directly an interest in a foreign holding company;

and for the purposes of paragraph (c) above a foreign holding company is a company resident outside the United Kingdom which holds directly or indirectly the interest in the controlled foreign company.

(7) Without prejudice to subsection (5) above, in any case where an interest in a controlled foreign company is held in a fiduciary or representative capacity in such circumstances that there is or are an identifiable beneficiary or beneficiaries, the Board may treat the interest as held by that beneficiary or, as the case may be, as apportioned among those beneficiaries; and any such apportionment shall be made on such basis as seems to the Board to be just and reasonable.

(8) Subject to the preceding provisions of this section, the apportionment of the chargeable profits and creditable tax of a controlled foreign company for any accounting period shall be made on such basis as seems to the Board to be just and reasonable.

753.—(1) Where the Board have given a direction under section 747(1) with respect to an accounting period of a controlled foreign company, notice of the making of the direction shall be given to every company resident in the United Kingdom which appears to the Board to have had an interest in the controlled foreign company at any time during that period.

(2) A notice under subsection (1) above shall—

(a) specify the date on which the direction was made and the controlled foreign company to which it relates;

(b) specify the accounting period to which the direction relates and the amount of the chargeable profits and creditable tax computed for that period;

(c) specify the reliefs (if any) which it has been assumed that the company has claimed by virtue of paragraph 4(1) of Schedule 24;

(d) specify, in a case where paragraph (d) of subsection (2) of section 749 applies, the territory which, by virtue of that paragraph, was specified in the direction and, in any other case, specify the territory (if any) in which, by virtue of that section, the Board consider that the company is to be regarded as resident for the purposes of this Chapter;

(e) inform the recipient of the notice of the right of appeal conferred on him by subsection (4) below and of the right to give notice under paragraph 4(2) of Schedule 24; and

(f) specify any declaration with respect to the accounting period concerned which was made prior to or at the same time as the notice by virtue of paragraph 11(3) of Schedule 24 or paragraph 3(2) of Schedule 25;

and, in the case of a notice given after the direction concerned has been amended by virtue of section 751(5), the notice shall specify the date of the amendment and (so far as paragraphs (b) and (c) above are concerned) shall relate to the position resulting from the amendment.

(3) Where, by virtue of section 751(5), the Board have amended a direction so as to specify a revised accounting period, notice of the making of the amendment shall be given to every company which was previously given notice of the making of the direction; and a notice under this subsection—

(a) shall identify the direction which is amended and state the effect of the amendment, including the extent to which the matters specified in the notice of the making of the direction are superseded; and

(b) shall contain the provisions required, by virtue of paragraphs (b) to (f) of subsection (2) above, to be included in a notice under subsection (1) above.

(4) Any company to which notice is given under subsection (1) or subsection (3) above may, by giving notice of appeal to the Board within 60 days of the date of the notice given to the company, appeal to the Special Commissioners against that notice on all or any of the following grounds—

(a) that the direction should not have been given or, where the direction has been amended, that the amendment should not have been made;

(b) that the amount of chargeable profits or creditable tax specified in the notice is incorrect;

(c) that the company did not have an interest in the controlled foreign company concerned at any time during the accounting period in question;

(d) that, if the notice specifies a declaration made by virtue of sub-paragraph (3) of paragraph 11 of Schedule 24, the condition for the making of that declaration in sub-paragraph (5) of that paragraph was not fulfilled; and

(e) that, if the notice specifies a declaration made by virtue of paragraph 3(2) of Schedule 25, the condition for the making of that declaration was not fulfilled;

and the notice of appeal shall specify the grounds of appeal, but on the hearing of the appeal the Special Commissioners may allow the appellant to put forward any ground not specified in the notice and take it into consideration if satisfied that the omission was not wilful or unreasonable.

(5) If, after the time at which notice is given under subsection (1) above with respect to an accounting period of a controlled foreign company, the Board make a declaration by virtue of—

(a) paragraph 11(3) of Schedule 24; or

(b) paragraph 3(2) of Schedule 25,

then, unless the effect of the declaration is such that a notice (which, among other matters, will specify the declaration) will be required to be given under subsection (3) above, the Board shall give notice specifying the declaration to every company which was previously given notice of the making of the direction; and subsection (4) above shall apply in relation to a notice under this subsection as it applies in relation to a notice under subsection (3) above but with the omission of paragraphs (a) to (c).

(6) If it appears to the inspector that the amount of the chargeable profits or creditable tax specified in a notice under subsection (1) or subsection (3) above is incorrect, he shall give notice of the revised

amount to every company to which notice was given under subsection (1) or subsection (3) above and, except where the revised amount results from—

(a) an appeal under this section, or

(b) a notice given to the Board under paragraph 4(2) of Schedule 24 or by virtue of paragraph 12 of that Schedule,

any company to which notice is given under this subsection may, by giving notice of appeal to the Board within 60 days of the date of the notice given to the company, appeal to the Special Commissioners against the revised amount specified in the notice.

(7) The jurisdiction of the Special Commissioners on an appeal under this section shall include jurisdiction to review any decision of the Board or the inspector which is relevant to a ground of the appeal.

(8) The Board may make regulations—

(a) as respects the conduct of appeals under this section;

(b) entitling any person who has received, or is connected or associated with a person who has received, a notice under subsection (1) above with respect to a particular accounting period of a controlled foreign company to appear on an appeal brought by another person who has received such a notice; and

(c) with respect to the joinder of appeals brought by different persons with respect to the same direction or the same amount of chargeable profits or creditable tax.

754.—(1) Subject to the following provisions of this section, the provisions of section 747(4)(a) relating to assessment and recovery of a sum as if it were an amount of corporation tax shall be taken as applying, subject to the provisions of the Taxes Acts, and to any necessary modifications, all enactments applying generally to corporation tax, including those relating to the assessing, collecting and receiving of corporation tax, those conferring or regulating a right of appeal and those concerning administration, penalties, interest on unpaid tax and priority of tax in cases of insolvency under the law of any part of the United Kingdom.

Assessment, recovery and postponement of tax.

(2) For the purposes of the Taxes Acts, any sum assessable and recoverable under section 747(4)(a) shall be regarded as corporation tax which falls to be assessed for the accounting period in which ends that one of the controlled foreign company's accounting periods the chargeable profits of which give rise to that sum; and a notice of assessment relating to such a sum shall (in addition to any other matter required to be contained in such a notice) specify separately—

(a) the total amount of those chargeable profits and of any creditable tax which has been apportioned to persons falling within each of paragraphs (a) to (d) of subsection (5), or within subsection (7), of section 749, and

(b) where there is more than one class of shares in the controlled foreign company, the total amount apportioned to persons holding shares of each class, but such a notice shall not identify any particular person (other than the person assessed) as having an interest of any description in the controlled foreign company.

(3) On an appeal against an assessment to tax under section 747(4)(a), the jurisdiction of the Special Commissioners shall include jurisdiction to review any relevant decision taken by the Board under section 752 in connection with the apportionment of chargeable profits or creditable tax.

(4) No appeal may be brought against an assessment to tax under section 747(4)(a) on a ground on which an appeal has or could have been brought under section 753(4) or (6).

(5) Schedule 26 shall have effect with respect to the reliefs which may be claimed by a company resident in the United Kingdom which has a liability for tax in respect of an amount of chargeable profits; and no reliefs other than those provided for by that Schedule shall be allowed against any such liability.

(6) In any case where—

(a) the whole or any part of the tax assessed on a company ("the assessable company") by virtue of section 752(6) is not paid before the date on which it is due and payable in accordance with this Act or, as the case may be, the Management Act; and

(b) the Board serve a notice of liability to tax under this subsection on another company ("the responsible company") which is resident in the United Kingdom and holds or has held (whether directly or indirectly) the same interest in the controlled foreign company as is or was held by the assessable company,

the tax assessed on the assessable company or, as the case may be, so much of it as remains unpaid shall be payable by the responsible company upon service of the notice.

(7) Where a notice of liability is served under subsection (6) above—

(a) any interest due on the tax assessed on the assessable company and not paid; and

(b) any interest accruing due on that tax after the date of service,

shall be payable by the responsible company.

(8) In any case where—

(a) a notice of liability is served on the responsible company under subsection (6) above, and

(b) the relevant tax and any interest payable by the responsible company under subsection (7) above is not paid by that company before the expiry of the period of three months beginning on the date of service of the notice,

that tax and interest may, without prejudice to the right of recovery from the responsible company, be recovered from the assessable company.

(9) In this section "the Taxes Acts" has the same meaning as in the Management Act.

PART XVII

Information relating to controlled foreign companies.

755.—(1) Where it appears to the Board that a company resident outside the United Kingdom (in this section referred to as a "foreign subsidiary") may be a controlled foreign company, the Board may, by notice given to any company which appears to them to be a controlling company of the foreign subsidiary, require that company to give to the Board, within such time (not being less than 30 days) as may be specified in the notice, such particulars (which may include details of documents) as may be so specified with respect to any matter concerning the foreign subsidiary, being particulars required by the Board for the purposes of this Chapter as being relevant to the affairs of the controlling company, the foreign subsidiary or any connected or associated company.

(2) In this section "controlling company", in relation to a foreign subsidiary or any other company, means a company which is resident in the United Kingdom and has, alone or together with other persons so resident, control of the foreign subsidiary or, as the case may be, that other company.

(3) The Board may by notice given to a company which appears to them to be a controlling company in relation to a foreign subsidiary require that company to make available for inspection any relevant books, accounts, or other documents or records whatsoever of the company itself or, subject to subsection (6) below, of any other company, including the foreign subsidiary, in relation to which it appears to the Board to be a controlling company.

(4) In subsection (3) above "relevant" means relevant to—

(a) the computation of any profits of the foreign subsidiary; or

(b) the question whether a direction should be given under section 747(1) with respect to the foreign subsidiary or a connected or associated company or whether any such direction should be amended; or

(c) any question as to the amount of the chargeable profits or creditable tax for any accounting period of the foreign subsidiary or a connected or associated company; or

(d) any question as to the sum which, in accordance with section 747(4)(a), should be assessed on and recoverable from any person.

(5) In subsections (1) and (4) above "connected or associated company" means a controlled foreign company with which the foreign subsidiary or the controlling company is connected or associated.

(6) In any case where—

(a) under subsection (3) above a company is by notice required to make available for inspection any books, accounts, documents or records of a company other than itself, and

(b) it appears to the Board, on the application of the company, that the circumstances are such that the requirement ought not to have effect,

the Board shall direct that the company need not comply with the requirement.

(7) If, on an application under subsection (6) above, the Board refuse to give a direction under that subsection, the company concerned may, by notice given to the Board within 30 days after the refusal, appeal to the Special Commissioners who, if satisfied that the requirement in question ought in the circumstances not to have effect, may determine accordingly.

Interpretation and construction of Chapter IV.

756.—(1) In this Chapter "trading company" means a company whose business consists wholly or mainly of the carrying on of a trade or trades.

(2) For the purposes of this Chapter—

    (a) section 839 applies; and

    (b) subsection (10) of section 783 applies as it applies for the purposes of that section.

(3) The following provisions of Part XI apply for the purposes of this Chapter as they apply for the purposes of that Part—

    (a) section 416; and

    (b) section 417(7) to (9);

but, in the application of subsection (6) of section 416 for the purposes of this Chapter, for the words "five or fewer participators" there shall be substituted the words "persons resident in the United Kingdom".

CHAPTER V

OFFSHORE FUNDS

Material interests in non-qualifying offshore funds

Disposal of material interests in non-qualifying offshore funds.

757.—(1) This Chapter applies to a disposal by any person of an asset if—

    (a) at the time of the disposal, the asset constitutes a material interest in an offshore fund which is or has at any material time been a non-qualifying offshore fund; or

    (b) at the time of the disposal, the asset constitutes an interest in a company resident in the United Kingdom or in a unit trust scheme, the trustees of which are at that time resident in the United Kingdom and at a material time after 31st December 1984 the company or unit trust scheme was a non-qualifying offshore fund and the asset constituted a material interest in that fund;

and for the purpose of determining whether the asset disposed of falls within paragraph (b) above, section 78 of the 1979 Act (equation of original shares and new holding) shall have effect as it has effect for the purposes of that Act.

(2) Subject to the following provisions of this section and section 758, there is a disposal of an asset for the purposes of this Chapter if there would be such a disposal for the purposes of the 1979 Act.

(3) Notwithstanding anything in paragraph (b) of subsection (1) of section 49 of the 1979 Act (general provisions applicable on death: no deemed disposal by the deceased) where a person dies and the assets of

which he was competent to dispose include an asset which is or has at any time been a material interest in a non-qualifying offshore fund, then, for the purposes of this Chapter, other than section 758—

(a) immediately before the acquisition referred to in paragraph (a) of that subsection, that interest shall be deemed to be disposed of by the deceased for such a consideration as is mentioned in that subsection; but

(b) nothing in this subsection affects the determination, in accordance with subsection (1) above, of the question whether that deemed disposal is one to which this Chapter applies.

(4) Subject to subsection (3) above, section 49 of the 1979 Act applies for the purposes of this Chapter as it applies for the purposes of that Act, and the reference in that subsection to the assets of which a deceased person was competent to dispose shall be construed in accordance with subsection (10) of that section.

(5) Notwithstanding anything in section 85 of the 1979 Act (exchange of securities for those in another company) in any case where—

(a) the company which is company B for the purposes of subsection (1) of that section is or was at a material time a non-qualifying offshore fund and the company which is company A for those purposes is not such a fund, or

(b) under section 86 of that Act (reconstruction or amalgamation involving issue of securities) persons are to be treated, in consequence of an arrangement, as exchanging shares, debentures or other interests in or of an entity which is or was at a material time a non-qualifying offshore fund for assets which do not constitute interests in such a fund;

then, subsection (3) of section 85 of that Act (which applies provisions of that Act treating transactions as not being disposals and equating original shares with a new holding in certain cases) shall not apply for the purposes of this Chapter.

(6) In any case where, apart from subsection (5) above, section 85(3) of the 1979 Act would apply, the exchange concerned of shares, debentures or other interests in or of a non-qualifying offshore fund shall for the purposes of this Chapter constitute a disposal of interests in the offshore fund for a consideration equal to their market value at the time of the exchange.

(7) For the purposes of this section—

(a) a material time, in relation to the disposal of an asset, is the earliest date on which any relevant consideration was given for the acquisition of the asset or, if that date is earlier than 1st January 1984, any time on or after 1st January 1984; and

(b) "relevant consideration" means consideration which, assuming the application to the disposal of Chapter II of Part II of the 1979 Act, would fall to be taken into account in determining the amount of the gain or loss accruing on the disposal, whether that consideration was given by or on behalf of the person making the disposal or by or on behalf of a predecessor in title of his whose acquisition cost represents, directly or indirectly, the whole or any part of the acquisition cost of the person making the disposal.

Offshore funds operating equalisation arrangements.

758.—(1) For the purposes of this Chapter, an offshore fund operates equalisation arrangements if, and at a time when, arrangements are in existence which have the result that where—

(a) a person acquires by way of initial purchase a material interest in the fund at some time during a period relevant to the arrangements; and

(b) the fund makes a distribution for a period which begins before the date of his acquisition of that interest;

the amount of that distribution which is paid to him (assuming him still to retain that interest) will include a payment of capital which is debited to an account maintained under the arrangements ("the equalisation account") and which is determined by reference to the income which had accrued to the fund at the date of his acquisition.

(2) For the purposes of this section, a person acquires an interest in an offshore fund by way of initial purchase if—

(a) his acquisition is by way of subscription for or allotment of new shares, units or other interests issued or created by the fund; or

(b) his acquisition is by way of direct purchase from the persons concerned with the management of the fund and their sale to him is made in their capacity as managers of the fund.

(3) Without prejudice to section 757(1), this Chapter applies, subject to the following provisions of this section, to a disposal by any person of an asset if—

(a) at the time of the disposal, the asset constitutes a material interest in an offshore fund which at that time is operating equalisation arrangements; and

(b) the fund is not and has not at any material time (within the meaning of section 757(7)) been a non-qualifying offshore fund; and

(c) the proceeds of the disposal do not fall to be taken into account as a trading receipt.

(4) This Chapter does not, by virtue of subsection (3) above, apply to a disposal if—

(a) it takes place during such a period as is mentioned in subsection (1)(a) above; and

(b) throughout so much of that period as precedes the disposal, the income of the offshore fund concerned has been of such a nature as is referred to in paragraph 3(1) of Schedule 27.

(5) An event which, apart from section 78 of the 1979 Act (reorganisations etc.), would constitute a disposal of an asset shall constitute such a disposal for the purpose of determining whether, by virtue of subsection (3) above, there is a disposal to which this Chapter applies.

(6) The reference in subsection (5) above to section 78 of the 1979 Act includes a reference to that section as applied by section 85 of that Act (exchange of securities) but not as applied by section 82 of that Act (conversion of securities).

759.—(1) In this Chapter references to a material interest in an offshore fund are references to such an interest in any of the following, namely—

Material interests in offshore funds.

(a) a company which is resident outside the United Kingdom;

(b) a unit trust scheme the trustees of which are not resident in the United Kingdom; and

(c) any arrangements which do not fall within paragraph (a) or (b) above, which take effect by virtue of the law of a territory outside the United Kingdom and which, under that law, create rights in the nature of co-ownership (without restricting that expression to its meaning in the law of any part of the United Kingdom);

and any reference in this Chapter to an offshore fund is a reference to any such company, unit trust scheme or arrangements in which any person has an interest which is a material interest.

(2) Subject to the following provisions of this section, a person's interest in a company, unit trust scheme or arrangements is a material interest if, at the time when he acquired the interest, it could reasonably be expected that, at some time during the period of seven years beginning at the time of his acquisition, he would be able to realise the value of the interest (whether by transfer, surrender or in any other manner).

(3) For the purposes of subsection (2) above, a person is at any time able to realise the value of an interest if at that time he can realise an amount which is reasonably approximate to that portion which the interest represents (directly or indirectly) of the market value at that time of the assets of the company or, as the case may be, of the assets subject to the scheme or arrangements.

(4) For the purposes of subsections (2) and (3) above—

(a) a person is able to realise a particular amount if he is able to obtain that amount either in money or in the form of assets to the value of that amount; and

(b) if at any time an interest in an offshore fund has a market value which is substantially greater than the portion which the interest represents, as mentioned in subsection (3) above, of the market value at that time of the assets concerned, the ability to realise such a market value of the interest shall not be regarded as an ability to realise such an amount as is referred to in that subsection.

(5) An interest in a company, scheme or arrangements is not a material interest if—

(a) it is an interest in respect of any loan capital or debt issued or incurred for money which, in the ordinary course of a business of banking, is lent by a person carrying on that business; or

(b) it is a right arising under a policy of insurance.

(6) Shares in a company falling within subsection (1)(a) above (an "overseas company") do not constitute a material interest if—

(a) the shares are held by a company and the holding of them is necessary or desirable for the maintenance and development of a trade carried on by the company or a company associated with it; and

(b) the shares confer at least 10 per cent. of the total voting rights in the overseas company and a right, in the event of a winding-up, to at least 10 per cent. of the assets of that company remaining after the discharge of all liabilities having priority over the shares; and

(c) not more than ten persons hold shares in the overseas company and all the shares in that company confer both voting rights and a right to participate in the assets on a winding-up; and

(d) at the time of its acquisition of the shares, the company had such a reasonable expectation as is referred to in subsection (2) above by reason only of the existence of—

(i) an arrangement under which, at some time within the period of seven years beginning at the time of acquisition, that company may require the other participators to purchase its shares; or

(ii) provisions of either an agreement between the participators or the constitution of the overseas company under which the company will be wound up within a period which is, or is reasonably expected to be, shorter than the period referred to in subsection (2) above; or

(iii) both such an arrangement and such provisions;

and in this paragraph "participators" means the persons holding shares falling within paragraph (c) above.

(7) For the purposes of subsection (6)(a) above, a company is associated with another company if one of them has control of the other within the meaning of section 416 or both of them are under the control, within the meaning of that section, of the same person or persons.

(8) An interest in a company falling within subsection (1)(a) above is not a material interest at any time when the following conditions are satisfied, namely—

(a) that the holder of the interest has the right to have the company wound up; and

(b) that, in the event of a winding up, the holder is, by virtue of the interest and any other interest which he then holds in the same capacity, entitled to more than 50 per cent. of the assets remaining after the discharge of all liabilities having priority over the interest or interests concerned.

(9) The market value of any asset for the purposes of this Chapter shall be determined in like manner as it would be determined for the purposes of the 1979 Act except that, in the case of an interest in an offshore fund for which there are separate published buying and selling prices, section 150(4) of that Act (meaning of "market value" in relation to rights of unit

holders in a unit trust scheme) shall apply with any necessary modifications for determining the market value of the interest for the purposes of this Chapter.

760.—(1) For the purposes of this Chapter, an offshore fund is a non-qualifying fund except during an account period of the fund in respect of which the fund is certified by the Board as a distributing fund.

(2) An offshore fund shall not be certified as a distributing fund in respect of any account period unless, with respect to that period, the fund pursues a full distribution policy, within the meaning of Part I of Schedule 27.

(3) Subject to Part II of that Schedule, an offshore fund shall not be certified as a distributing fund in respect of any account period if, at any time in that period—

(a) more than 5 per cent. by value of the assets of the fund consists of interests in other offshore funds; or

(b) subject to subsections (4) and (5) below, more than 10 per cent. by value of the assets of the fund consists of interests in a single company; or

(c) the assets of the fund include more than 10 per cent. of the issued share capital of any company or of any class of that share capital; or

(d) subject to subsection (6) below, there is more than one class of material interest in the offshore fund and they do not all receive proper distribution benefits, within the meaning of subsection (7) below.

(4) For the purposes of subsection (3)(b) above, in any account period the value, expressed as a percentage of the value of all the assets of an offshore fund, of that portion of the assets of the fund which consists of an interest in a single company shall be determined as at the most recent occasion (whether in that account period or an earlier one) on which the fund acquired an interest in that company for consideration in money or money's worth; but for this purpose there shall be disregarded any occasion—

(a) on which the interest acquired constituted the "new holding" for the purposes of section 78 of the 1979 Act (equation of original shares and new holding), including that section as applied by any later provision of Chapter II of Part IV of that Act (reorganisation of share capital etc.); and

(b) on which no consideration fell to be given for the interest acquired, other than the interest which constituted the "original shares" for the purposes of that section.

(5) Except for the purpose of determining the total value of the assets of an offshore fund, an interest in a company shall be disregarded for the purposes of subsection (3)(b) above if—

(a) the company carries on (in the United Kingdom or elsewhere) a banking business providing current or deposit account facilities in any currency for members of the public and bodies corporate; and

(b) the interest consists of a current or deposit account provided in the normal course of the company's banking business.

(6) There shall be disregarded for the purposes of subsection (3)(d) above any interests in an offshore fund—

(a) which are held solely by persons employed or engaged in or about the management of the assets of the fund; and

(b) which carry no right or expectation to participate, directly or indirectly, in any of the profits of the fund; and

(c) which, on a winding up or on redemption, carry no right to receive anything other than the return of the price paid for the interests.

(7) If in any account period of an offshore fund there is more than one class of material interests in the fund, the classes of interest do not, for the purposes of subsection (3)(d) above, all receive proper distribution benefits unless, were each class of interests and the assets which that class represents interests in and assets of a separate offshore fund, each of those separate funds would, with respect to that period, pursue a full distribution policy, within the meaning of Part I of Schedule 27.

(8) For the purposes of this Chapter, an account period of an offshore fund shall begin—

(a) whenever the fund begins to carry on its activities; and

(b) whenever an account period of the fund ends without the fund then ceasing to carry on its activities.

(9) For the purposes of this Chapter, an account period of an offshore fund shall end on the first occurrence of any of the following—

(a) the expiration of 12 months from the beginning of the period;

(b) an accounting date of the fund or, if there is a period for which the fund does not make up accounts, the end of that period; and

(c) the fund ceasing to carry on its activities.

(10) For the purposes of this Chapter—

(a) an account period of an offshore fund which is a company falling within section 759(1)(a) shall end if, and at the time when, the company ceases to be resident outside the United Kingdom; and

(b) an account period of an offshore fund which is a unit trust scheme falling within section 759(1)(b) shall end if, and at the time when, the trustees of the scheme become resident in the United Kingdom.

(11) The provisions of Part III of Schedule 27 shall have effect with respect to the procedure for and in connection with the certification of an offshore fund as a distributing fund, and the supplementary provisions in Part IV of that Schedule shall have effect.

Charge to tax of offshore income gains

761.—(1) If a disposal to which this Chapter applies gives rise in accordance with section 758 and Schedule 28 to an offshore income gain, then, subject to the provisions of this section, the amount of that gain shall be treated for all the purposes of the Tax Acts as—

> Charge to income tax or corporation tax of offshore income gain.

    (a) income arising at the time of the disposal to the person making the disposal, and

    (b) constituting profits or gains chargeable to tax under Case VI of Schedule D for the chargeable period in which the disposal is made.

(2) Subject to subsection (3) below, sections 2 and 12 of the 1979 Act (persons chargeable to tax in respect of chargeable gains) and section 11(2)(b) shall have effect in relation to income tax or corporation tax in respect of offshore income gains as they have effect in relation to capital gains tax or corporation tax in respect of chargeable gains.

(3) In the application of section 12 of the 1979 Act in accordance with subsection (2) above, paragraphs (a) and (b) of subsection (1) of that section (which define the assets on the disposal of which chargeable gains are taxable) shall have effect with the omission of the words "situated in the United Kingdom and".

(4) In a case where section 12 of the 1979 Act has effect as modified by subsection (3) above, section 11 shall have effect as if, in subsection (2)(b), the words "situated in the United Kingdom" were omitted.

(5) In the case of individuals resident or ordinarily resident but not domiciled in the United Kingdom, section 14 of the 1979 Act (which provides for taxation on a remittance basis) shall have effect in relation to income tax chargeable by virtue of subsection (1) above on an offshore income gain as it has effect in relation to capital gains tax in respect of gains accruing to such individuals from the disposal of assets situated outside the United Kingdom.

(6) A charity shall be exempt from tax in respect of an offshore income gain if the gain is applicable and applied for charitable purposes; but if property held on charitable trusts ceases to be subject to charitable trusts and that property represents directly or indirectly an offshore income gain, the trustees shall be treated as if they had disposed of and immediately reacquired that property for a consideration equal to its market value, any gain (calculated in accordance with Schedule 28) accruing being treated as an offshore income gain not accruing to a charity.

In this subsection "charity" has the same meaning as in section 506 and "market value" has the same meaning as in the 1979 Act.

(7) In any case where—

    (a) a disposal to which this Chapter applies is a disposal of settled property, within the meaning of the 1979 Act, and

    (b) for the purposes of the 1979 Act, the general administration of the trusts is ordinarily carried on outside the United Kingdom and the trustees or a majority of them for the time being are not resident or not ordinarily resident in the United Kingdom, subsection (1) above shall not apply in relation to any offshore income gain to which the disposal gives rise.

Offshore income
gains accruing to
persons resident
or domiciled
abroad.

762.—(1) Section 15 of the 1979 Act (chargeable gains accruing to certain non-resident companies) shall have effect in relation to offshore income gains subject to the following modifications—

(a) for any reference to a chargeable gain there shall be substituted a reference to an offshore income gain;

(b) for the reference in subsection (7) to capital gains tax there shall be substituted a reference to income tax or corporation tax; and

(c) paragraphs (b) and (c) of subsection (5) and subsection (8) shall be omitted.

1981 c. 35.

(2) Subject to subsections (3) and (4) below, sections 80 to 84 of the Finance Act 1981 (gains of non-resident settlements) shall have effect in relation to offshore income gains subject to the following modifications—

(a) for any reference to chargeable gains, other than the reference in section 80(5), there shall be substituted a reference to offshore income gains;

(b) in section 80(2) for the words "tax under section 4(1) of the Capital Gains Tax Act 1979" there shall be substituted the words "income tax by virtue of section 761 of the Taxes Act";

(c) in section 80(6) the reference to tax shall be construed as a reference to income tax or corporation tax; and

(d) sections 80(8) and 83(6) shall be omitted.

(3) In section 80(5) of the Finance Act 1981, both as it applies apart from subsection (2) above and as applied by subsection (2) above, the reference to chargeable gains shall be construed as including a reference to offshore income gains.

(4) If, in any year of assessment—

(a) under subsection (3) of section 80 of the Finance Act 1981, as it applies apart from subsection (2) above, a chargeable gain falls to be attributed to a beneficiary, and

(b) under that subsection, as applied by subsection (2) above, an offshore income gain also falls to be attributed to him,

subsection (4) of that section (gains attributed in proportion to capital payments received) shall have effect as if it required offshore income gains to be attributed before chargeable gains.

(5) Subject to subsection (6) below, for the purpose of determining whether an individual ordinarily resident in the United Kingdom has a liability for income tax in respect of an offshore income gain which arises on a disposal to which this Chapter applies where the disposal is made by a person resident or domiciled outside the United Kingdom—

(a) sections 739 and 740 shall apply as if the offshore income gain arising to the person resident or domiciled outside the United Kingdom constituted income becoming payable to him, and

(b) any reference in those sections to income of (or payable or arising to) such a person accordingly includes a reference to the offshore income gain arising to him by reason of the disposal to which this Chapter applies.

(6) To the extent that an offshore income gain is treated, by virtue of subsection (1) or subsection (2) above, as having accrued to any person resident or ordinarily resident in the United Kingdom, that gain shall not be deemed to be the income of any individual for the purposes of section 739 or 740 or any provision of Part XV.

763.—(1) The provisions of this section apply where a disposal to which this Chapter applies gives rise to an offshore income gain; and, if that disposal also constitutes the disposal of the interest concerned for the purposes of the 1979 Act, then that disposal is in the following provisions of this section referred to as "the 1979 Act disposal".

Deduction of offshore income gain in determining capital gain.

(2) So far as relates to an offshore income gain which arises on a material disposal (within the meaning of Part I of Schedule 28), subsections (3) and (4) below shall have effect in relation to the 1979 Act disposal in substitution for section 31(1) of that Act (deduction of consideration chargeable to tax on income).

(3) Subject to the following provisions of this section, in the computation under Chapter II of Part II of the 1979 Act of any gain accruing on the 1979 Act disposal, a sum equal to the offshore income gain shall be deducted from the sum which would otherwise constitute the amount or value of the consideration for the disposal.

(4) Where the 1979 Act disposal is of such a nature that, by virtue of section 35 of that Act (part disposals) an apportionment falls to be made of certain expenditure, no deduction shall be made by virtue of subsection (3) above in determining, for the purposes of the fraction in subsection (2) of that section, the amount or value of the consideration for the disposal.

(5) If the 1979 Act disposal forms part of a transfer to which section 123 of that Act applies (roll-over relief on transfer of business in exchange wholly or partly for shares) then, for the purposes of subsection (4) of that section (determination of the amount of the deduction from the gain on the old assets) "B" in the fraction in that subsection (the value of the whole of the consideration received by the transferor in exchange for the business) shall be taken to be what it would be if the value of the consideration other than shares so received by the transferor were reduced by a sum equal to the offshore income gain.

(6) Where the disposal to which this Chapter applies constitutes such a disposal by virtue of section 757(6) or 758(5), the 1979 Act shall have effect as if an amount equal to the offshore income gain to which the disposal gives rise were given (by the person making the exchange concerned) as consideration for the new holding, within the meaning of section 79 of that Act (consideration given or received for new holding on a reorganisation).

(7) In any case where—

(a) a disposal to which this Chapter applies by virtue of subsection (3) of section 758 is made otherwise than to the offshore fund concerned or the persons referred to in subsection (2)(b) of that section; and

   (b) subsequently, a distribution which is referable to the asset disposed of is paid either to the person who made the disposal or to a person connected with him; and

   (c) the disposal gives rise (in accordance with Part II of Schedule 28) to an offshore income gain;

then, for the purposes of the Tax Acts, the amount of the first distribution falling within paragraph (b) above shall be taken to be reduced or, as the case may be, extinguished by deducting therefrom an amount equal to the offshore income gain referred to in paragraph (c) above and, if that amount exceeds the amount of that first distribution, the balance shall be set against the second and, where necessary, any later distribution falling within paragraph (b) above, until the balance is exhausted.

   (8) Section 839 shall apply for the purposes of subsection (7)(b) above.

Offshore income gains of trustees.   **764.** Income arising in a year of assessment by virtue of section 761(1) to trustees shall be chargeable to income tax at a rate equal to the sum of the basic rate and the additional rate for that year.

CHAPTER VI

MISCELLANEOUS

Migration etc. of company

Migration etc. of companies.   **765.**—(1) Subject to the provisions of this section, all transactions of the following classes shall be unlawful unless carried out with the consent of the Treasury, that is to say—

   (a) for a body corporate resident in the United Kingdom to cease to be so resident; or

   (b) for the trade or business or any part of the trade or business of a body corporate so resident to be transferred from that body corporate to a person not so resident; or

   (c) for a body corporate so resident to cause or permit a body corporate not so resident over which it has control to create or issue any shares or debentures; or

   (d) except for the purpose of enabling a person to be qualified to act as a director, for a body corporate so resident to transfer to any person, or cause or permit to be transferred to any person, any shares or debentures of a body corporate not so resident over which it has control, being shares or debentures which it owns or in which it has an interest.

   (2) Nothing in subsection (1)(c) above shall apply to the giving to the bankers of the body corporate not resident in the United Kingdom of any security for the payment of any sum due or to become due from it to them by reason of any transaction entered into with it by them in the ordinary course of their business as bankers.

   (3) Nothing in subsection (1)(c) above shall apply to the giving by the body corporate not resident in the United Kingdom to an insurance company of any security for the payment of any sum due or to become due from that body corporate to that company by reason of any

transaction entered into with that body corporate by that company in the ordinary course of that company's business by way of investment of its funds.

(4) Any consent granted by the Treasury under this section—

    (a) may be given either specially (that is to say, so as to apply only to specified transactions of or relating to a specified body corporate) or generally (that is to say, so as not only so to apply); and

    (b) may, if given generally, be revoked by the Treasury; and

    (c) may in any case be absolute or conditional; and

    (d) shall be published in such a way as to give any person entitled to the benefit of it an adequate opportunity of getting to know of it, unless in the opinion of the Treasury publication is not necessary for that purpose.

766.—(1) Any person who, whether within or outside the United Kingdom, does or is a party to the doing of any act which to his knowledge amounts to or results in, or forms part of a series of acts which together amount to or result in, or will amount to or result in, something which is unlawful under section 765(1) shall be guilty of an offence under this section.

Offences under section 765.

(2) In any proceedings in respect of such an offence against a director of the body corporate in question (that is to say, the body corporate which is or was resident in the United Kingdom) or against any person who was purporting to act in that capacity—

    (a) it shall be presumed that he was a party to every act of that body corporate unless he proves that it was done without his consent or connivance; and

    (b) it shall, unless the contrary is proved, be presumed that any act which in fact amounted to or resulted in, or formed part of a series of acts which together amounted to or resulted in or would amount to or result in, something which is unlawful under section 765(1) was to his knowledge such an act.

(3) Any person who is guilty of an offence under this section shall be liable on conviction on indictment—

    (a) to imprisonment for not more than two years or to a fine, or to both; or

    (b) where the person in question is a body corporate which is or was resident in the United Kingdom, to a fine not exceeding an amount equal to three times the corporation tax, capital gains tax and income tax paid or payable which is attributable to the income, profits or gains (including chargeable gains) arising in the 36 months immediately preceding the commission of the offence, or £10,000, whichever is the greater;

and proceedings in respect of such an offence alleged to have been committed by a person may be taken before the appropriate court in the United Kingdom having jurisdiction in the place where that person is for the time being.

(4) No proceedings for an offence under this section shall be instituted, in England or Wales, except by or with the consent of the Attorney General, or in Northern Ireland, except by or with the consent of the Attorney General for Northern Ireland.

Interpretation and commencement of sections 765 and 766.

767.—(1) A body corporate shall be deemed for the purposes of sections 765 and 766 to be resident or not to be resident in the United Kingdom according as the central management and control of its trade or business is or is not exercised in the United Kingdom.

(2) If it is shown that it has been established as between the Crown and a body corporate for any income tax or corporation tax purpose that the body corporate was resident or ordinarily resident in the United Kingdom for any year of assesment or other period, it shall be presumed, except so far as the contrary is proved, that that body corporate was resident in the United Kingdom for the purposes of sections 765 and 766 at the beginning of that year of assesment or other period and that it continued to be so resident at all times thereafter.

(3) Where the functions of a body corporate consist wholly or mainly in the holding of investments or other property, the holding of the investments or property shall be deemed for the purposes of this section and sections 765 and 766 to be a business carried on by the body corporate.

(4) Notwithstanding anything in the preceding provisions of this section or in sections 765 and 766, in no event shall a mere transfer of assets by a body corporate not resulting in a substantial change in the character or extent of the trade or business of that body corporate be treated for the purposes of sections 765 and 766 as a transfer of part of its trade or business.

(5) In this section and in sections 765 and 766—

"share", "debenture" and "director" have, in relation to any body corporate, the meanings respectively assigned to them by Part XXVI of the Companies Act 1985 in relation to a company;

1985 c. 6.

"control" (except in the expression "central management and control") has, in relation to a body corporate, the meaning given by section 840;

"transfer", in relation to shares or debentures, includes a transfer of any beneficial interest therein;

"insurance company" means a body corporate lawfully carrying on business as an insurer, whether in the United Kingdom or elsewhere; and

"funds" in relation to an insurance company means the funds held by it in connection with that business;

and a body corporate shall not be deemed for the purposes of this section and sections 765 and 766 to cease to be resident in the United Kingdom by reason only that it ceases to exist.

(6) This section and sections 765 and 766 shall come into force on 6th April 1988 to the exclusion of section 482 of the 1970 Act (which is re-enacted by those sections); but any offence committed before 6th April

1988 shall not be punishable under section 766 and neither this subsection nor any other provision of this Act shall prevent any such offence from being punishable as if this Act had not been passed.

Change in ownership of company

768.—(1) If—

    (a) within any period of three years there is both a change in the ownership of a company and (either earlier or later in that period, or at the same time) a major change in the nature or conduct of a trade carried on by the company, or

    (b) at any time after the scale of the activities in a trade carried on by a company has become small or negligible, and before any considerable revival of the trade, there is a change in the ownership of the company,

no relief shall be given under section 393 by setting a loss incurred by the company in an accounting period beginning before the change of ownership against any income or other profits of an accounting period ending after the change of ownership.

(2) In applying this section to the accounting period in which the change of ownership occurs, the part ending with the change of ownership, and the part after, shall be treated as two separate accounting periods, and the profits or losses of the accounting period shall be apportioned to the two parts.

(3) The apportionment under subsection (2) above shall be on a time basis according to the respective lengths of those parts except that if it appears that that method would work unreasonably or unjustly such other method shall be used as appears just and reasonable.

(4) In subsection (1) above "major change in the nature or conduct of a trade" includes—

    (a) a major change in the type of property dealt in, or services or facilities provided, in the trade; or

    (b) a major change in customers, outlets or markets of the trade;

and this section applies even if the change is the result of a gradual process which began outside the period of three years mentioned in subsection (1)(a) above.

(5) In relation to any relief available under section 343 to a successor company, subsection (1) above shall apply as if any loss sustained by a predecessor company had been sustained by a successor company and as if the references to a trade included references to the trade as carried on by a predecessor company.

(6) Where relief in respect of a company's losses has been restricted under this section then, notwithstanding section 87(3) of the 1968 Act, in applying the provisions of that Act about balancing charges to the company by reference to any event after the change of ownership of the company, any allowance or deduction falling to be made in taxing the company's trade for any chargeable period before the change of ownership shall be disregarded unless the profits or gains of that

chargeable period or of any subsequent chargeable period before the change of ownership were sufficient to give effect to the allowance or deduction.

(7) In applying subsection (6) above it shall be assumed that any profits or gains are applied in giving effect to any such allowance or deduction in preference to being set off against any loss which is not attributable to such an allowance or deduction.

(8) Where the operation of this section depends on circumstances or events at a time after the change of ownership (but not more than three years after), an assessment to give effect to the provisions of this section shall not be out of time if made within six years from that time, or the latest of those times.

(9) Any person in whose name any shares, stock or securities of a company are registered shall, if required by notice by an inspector given for the purposes of this section, state whether or not he is the beneficial owner of those shares or securities and, if not the beneficial owner of those shares or securities of any of them, shall furnish the name and address of the person or persons on whose behalf those shares, stock or securities are registered in his name.

Rules for ascertaining change in ownership of company.

769.—(1) For the purposes of section 768 there is a change in the ownership of a company—

   (a) if a single person acquires more than half the ordinary share capital of the company; or

   (b) if two or more persons each acquire a holding of 5 per cent. or more of the ordinary share capital of the company, and those holdings together amount to more than half the ordinary share capital of the company; or

   (c) if two or more persons each acquire a holding of the ordinary share capital of the company, and the holdings together amount to more than half the ordinary share capital of the company, but disregarding a holding of less that 5 per cent. unless it is an addition to an existing holding and the two holdings together amount to 5 per cent. or more of the ordinary share capital of the company.

(2) In applying subsection (1) above—

   (a) the circumstances at any two points of time with not more than three years between may be compared, and a holder at the later time may be regarded as having acquired whatever he did not hold at the earlier time, irrespective of what he has acquired or disposed of in between;

   (b) to allow for any issue of shares or other reorganisation of capital, the comparison may be made in terms of percentage holdings of the total ordinary share capital at the respective times, so that a person whose percentage holding is greater at the later time may be regarded as having acquired a percentage holding equal to the increase;

   (c) to decide for the purposes of subsection (1)(b) or (c) above if any person has acquired a holding of at least 5 per cent., or a holding which makes at least 5 per cent. when added to an existing holding, acquisitions by, and holdings of, two or more persons who are connected persons within the meaning of section 839 shall be aggregated as if they were acquisitions by, and holdings of, one and the same person;

(d) any acquisition of shares under the will or on the intestacy of a deceased person and, if it is shown that the gift is unsolicited and made without regard to the provisions of section 768, any gift of shares, shall be left out of account.

(3) Where, because persons, whether company members or not, possess extraordinary rights or powers under the articles of association or under any other document regulating the company, ownership of the ordinary share capital may not be an appropriate test of whether there has been a major change in the persons for whose benefit the losses may ultimately enure, then, in considering whether there has been a change in the ownership of the company for the purposes of section 768, holdings of all kinds of share capital, including preference shares, or of any particular category of share capital, or voting power or any other special kind of power, may be taken into account instead of ordinary share capital.

(4) Where section 768 has operated to restrict relief by reference to a change of ownership taking place at any time, no transaction or circumstances before that time shall be taken into account in determining whether there is any subsequent change of ownership.

(5) A change in the ownership of a company shall be disregarded for the purposes of section 768 if—

(a) immediately before the change the company is the 75 per cent. subsidiary of another company, and

(b) (although there is a change in the direct ownership of the company) that other company continues after the change to own the first-mentioned company as a 75 per cent. subsidiary.

(6) If there is a change in the ownership of a company which has a 75 per cent. subsidiary (whether owned directly or indirectly) then, unless under subsection (5) above that change in ownership is to be disregarded, section 768 shall apply as if there had also been a change in the ownership of that 75 per cent. subsidiary.

(7) For the purposes of this section—

(a) references to ownership shall be construed as references to beneficial ownership, and references to acquisition shall be construed accordingly;

(b) a company shall be deemed to be a 75 per cent. subsidiary of another company if and so long as not less than three-quarters of its ordinary share capital is owned by that other company, whether directly or through another company or other companies, or partly directly and partly through another company or other companies;

(c) the amount of ordinary share capital of one company owned by a second company through another company or other companies or partly directly and partly through another company or other companies, shall be determined in accordance with subsections (5) to (10) of section 838; and

Y

(d) "shares" includes stock.

(8) If any acquisition of ordinary share capital or other property or rights taken into account in determining that there has been a change of ownership of a company was made in pursuance of a contract of sale or option or other contract, or the acquisition was made by a person holding such a contract, then the time when the change in the ownership of the company took place shall be determined as if the acquisition had been made when the contract was made with the holder or when the benefit of it was assigned to him so that, in the case of a person exercising an option to purchase shares, he shall be regarded as having purchased the shares when he acquired the option.

Transactions between associated persons

Sales etc. at an undervalue or overvalue.

770.—(1) Subject to the provisions of this section and section 771, where any property is sold and—

(a) the buyer is a body of persons over whom the seller has control or the seller is a body of persons over whom the buyer has control or both the buyer and the seller are bodies of persons over whom the same person or persons has or have control; and

(b) the property is sold at a price ("the actual price") which is either—

(i) less than the price which it might have been expected to fetch if the parties to the transaction had been independent persons dealing at arm's length ("the arm's length price"), or

(ii) greater than the arm's length price,

then, in computing for tax purposes the income, profits or losses of the seller where the actual price was less than the arm's length price, and of the buyer where the actual price was greater than the arm's length price, the like consequences shall ensue as would have ensued if the property had been sold for the arm's length price.

(2) Subsection (1) above shall not apply—

(a) in any case where—

(i) the actual price is less than the arm's length price, and

(ii) the buyer is resident in the United Kingdom and is carrying on a trade there, and

(iii) the price of the property falls to be taken into account as a deduction in computing the profits or gains or losses of that trade for tax purposes; or

(b) in any case where—

(i) the actual price is greater than the arm's length price, and

(ii) the seller is resident in the United Kingdom and is carrying on a trade there, and

(iii) the price of the property falls to be taken into account as a trading receipt in computing the profits or gains or losses of that trade for tax purposes; or

(c) in relation to any transaction in relation to which section 493(1) or (3) applies; or

(d) in relation to any other sale, unless the Board so direct.

(3) Where a direction is given under subsection (2)(d) above all such adjustments shall be made, whether by assessment, repayment of tax or otherwise, as are necessary to give effect to the direction.

771.—(1) For the purposes of this section a company is a petroleum company if—

Transactions by petroleum companies.

(a) its activities include any relevant activities; or

(b) it is associated with a company whose activities include any relevant activities and its own activities include the ownership, operation or management of ships or pipelines (as defined in section 65 of the Pipelines Act 1962) used for transporting or conveying petroleum or petroleum products.

1962 c. 58.

(2) "Relevant activities" means any of the following—

(a) the acquisition or disposal of petroleum or of rights to acquire or dispose of petroleum;

(b) the importation into or exportation from the United Kingdom of petroleum products or the acquisition or disposal of rights to such importation or exportation;

(c) the acquisition otherwise than for importation into the United Kingdom of petroleum products outside the United Kingdom or the disposal outside the United Kingdom of petroleum products not exported from the United Kingdom by the company making the disposal;

(d) the refining or processing of crude petroleum; and

(e) the extraction of petroleum, either under rights authorising it or under contractual or other arrangements with persons by whom such rights are exercisable.

(3) Section 770(2) shall have effect with the omission of paragraphs (a) and (b) in any case where—

(a) either party to the transaction is a petroleum company or both are petroleum companies; and

(b) the activities of either or both are or include activities—

(i) the profits from which are or would be chargeable to overseas tax for which credit could be given under section 790 or in pursuance of arrangements having effect by virtue of section 788; or

(ii) which are exploration or exploitation activities within the meaning of section 830; and

(c) the transaction is part of such activities or is connected with them.

(4) Where both the buyer and the seller are resident in the United Kingdom and the Board, in pursuance of this section, direct that section 770(1) is to apply to the computation of the income, profits or losses of the one, the direction may extend the application of that subsection to the computation of the income, profits or losses of the other, and where it does so adjustments shall be made under section 770(3) accordingly.

(5) Where any property is sold and either the buyer or the seller is a petroleum company or both are petroleum companies, then if—

   (a) the sale is part of a transaction or series of transactions (whether or not between the same persons) and its terms are affected by those of the remainder of the transaction or transactions; or

   (b) what is sold is petroleum extracted under rights exercisable by a company other than the buyer, and not less than 20 per cent. of that company's ordinary share capital was at the time of the sale owned directly or indirectly by one or more of the following, that is to say, the buyer and any companies associated with the buyer;

section 770 shall apply in relation to the sale as if in subsection (1) of that section paragraph (a) were omitted.

(6) Where a petroleum company was a party to a sale of property, then, in determining for the purposes of section 770 what price the property might have been expected to fetch had the parties to the transaction been independent persons dealing at arm's length and what consequences would have ensued in computing the income, profits or losses of the seller or the buyer for tax purposes if the property had been sold for that price, it shall be assumed—

   (a) that the terms of the transaction would have been such as might have been expected to secure both to the buyer and to the seller a reasonable profit from transactions of the same kind carried out on similar terms over a reasonable period; and

   (b) that the seller would not have been compelled by law or by executive action of any government to demand a price fixed by law or such action or a price not less than one so fixed; and

   (c) that, if the transaction was part of a transaction or series of transactions (whether or not between the same persons), its terms would not have been affected by those of the remainder of the transaction or transactions; and

   (d) in a case where the whole of the property sold is not delivered by the seller within 12 months after the date of the sale—

      (i) that such part of the property as is delivered within that time would have fetched a price equal to that which it might have been expected to fetch if sold under a contract for the sale of that part and of no other property, being a contract made at the date of the sale; and

      (ii) that such part of the property not so delivered as is delivered in any calendar month would have fetched a price equal to that which it might have been expected to fetch if sold under a contract for the sale of that part and of no other property, being a contract made at the material time in that month;

and no regard shall be had to the terms of similar transactions which were capable of being varied.

In this subsection "calendar month" means a month of the calendar year and "material time", in relation to a calendar month, means noon on the middle day of the month which, in the case of a month containing an even number of days, shall be taken to be the last day of the first half of the month.

(7) In this section—

"petroleum" includes any mineral oil or relative hydrocarbon and, except in the expression "crude petroleum", includes natural gas;

"petroleum products" means products derived from petroleum and wholly or substantially of a hydrocarbon nature.

(8) For the purposes of this section—

(a) two companies are associated with one another if one is under the control of the other or both are under the control of the same person or persons, and "control" has the meaning given by section 840;

(b) any question whether ordinary share capital is owned by a company directly or indirectly shall be determined as for the purposes of section 838;

(c) rights are exercisable by a company if they are exercisable by that company alone or jointly with another company or companies.

772.—(1) The Board may, by notice given to any body corporate, require it to give to the Board, within such time (not being less than 30 days) as may be specified in the notice, such particulars (which may include details of relevant documents) as may be so specified of any related transaction which appears to the Board— Information for purposes of section 770, and appeals.

(a) to be, or to be connected with, a transaction with respect to which the Board might give a direction under section 770; or

(b) to be relevant for determining whether such a direction could or should be given in any case; or

(c) to be relevant for determining for the purposes of that section what price any property sold would have fetched had the sale been one between independent persons dealing at arm's length.

(2) For the purposes of a notice under subsection (1) above, a transaction is a related transaction if, but only if, it is one to which the body corporate to which the notice is given, or a body corporate associated with that body, was a party; and for the purposes of this subsection two bodies corporate are associated with one another if one is under the control of the other or both are under the control of the same person or persons.

(3) Where, in the case of a transaction with respect to which it appears to the Board that a direction under section 770 might be given—

    (a) one of the parties is a body corporate resident outside the United Kingdom and a 51 per cent. subsidiary of a body corporate ("the parent body") resident in the United Kingdom; and

    (b) the other party is, or is a 51 per cent. subsidiary of, the parent body,

the Board may, by notice given to the parent body, require it to make available for inspection any books, accounts or other documents or records whatsoever of the parent body or, subject to subsection (4) below, of any body of persons over which it has control which relate to that transaction, to any other transaction (of whatever nature) in the same assets, or to transactions (of whatever nature) in assets similar to those to which the first-mentioned transaction related.

(4) If, in a case in which under subsection (3) above the parent body is by notice required to make available for inspection any books, accounts, documents or records of a body of persons resident outside the United Kingdom over which the parent body has control, it appears to the Board, on the application of the parent body, that the circumstances are such that the requirement ought not to have effect, the Board shall direct that the parent body need not comply with the requirement.

(5) If, on an application under subsection (4) above, the Board refuse to give a direction under that subsection, the parent body may, by notice given to the Board within 30 days after the refusal, appeal to the Special Commissioners who, if satisfied that the requirement in question ought in the circumstances not to have effect, may determine accordingly.

(6) Where it appears to the Board that a body of persons may be a party to a transaction or transactions with respect to which a direction under section 770 might be given, then, for the purpose of assisting the Board to determine whether such a direction should be given, an inspector specifically authorised in that behalf by the Board may, at any reasonable time, on production if so required of his authority—

    (a) enter any premises used in connection with the relevant trade carried on by that body of persons (that is to say, the trade in the course of which the transaction or transactions were effected),

    (b) inspect there any books, accounts or other documents or records whatsoever relating to that trade which he considers it necessary for him to inspect for that purpose, and

    (c) require any such books, accounts or other documents or records to be produced to him there for inspection.

(7) An inspector's authority for entering any premises under subsection (6) above shall state the name of the inspector and the name of the body of persons carrying on the trade in connection with which the premises are used.

(8) If and so far as the question in dispute on an appeal to the General Commissioners or, in Northern Ireland, to a county court against an assessment to tax arises from a direction of the Board under section 770 the question shall be referred to and determined by the Special Commissioners.

773.—(1) Nothing in sections 770 and 771 shall be construed as affecting the operation of any of the provisions of the 1968 Act or of Chapter I of Part III of the Finance Act 1971.

(2) In sections 770 and 772—

"body of persons" includes a partnership, and

"control" has the meaning given by section 840;

and, for the purposes of this section, a sale shall be deemed to take place at the time of completion or when possession is given, whichever is the earlier.

(3) In determining for the purposes of sections 770 and 771 whether any person (alone or with others) has control over a body of persons—

> (a) there shall be attributed to him any rights or powers of a nominee for him, that is to say, any rights or powers which another possesses on his behalf or may be required to exercise on his direction or behalf;

> (b) there may also be attributed to him any rights or powers of a person with whom he is connected (within the meaning of section 839 but omitting subsections (5) to (7) and the exception in subsection (4)), including any rights or powers of a nominee for such a person, that is to say, any rights or powers which another possesses on behalf of such a person or may be required to exercise on his direction or behalf.

(4) Sections 770, 771, except subsection (5)(b), and 772 and this section shall, with the necessary adaptations, have effect in relation to lettings and hirings of property, grants and transfers of rights, interests or licences and the giving of business facilities of whatever kind as they have effect in relation to sales, and the references in those sections to sales, sellers, buyers and prices shall be deemed to be extended accordingly.

774.—(1) Subject to the provisions of this section, where—

> (a) a dealing company becomes entitled to a deduction, in computing the profits or gains of the company for tax purposes for any period, in respect of the depreciation in the value of any right subsisting against an associated company, being a non-dealing company; or

> (b) a dealing company makes any payment to such an associated company, being a payment in respect of which the dealing company is entitled to a deduction in computing its profits or gains for tax purposes for any period;

and the depreciation or payment is not brought into account in computing the profits or gains of the non-dealing company, that company shall be deemed to have received on the last day of the period income of an amount equal to the amount of the deduction and shall be chargeable in respect thereof under Case VI of Schedule D.

(2) Where the non-dealing company is carrying on a trade, the income referred to in subsection (1) above shall, if the company so elects, not be so chargeable but shall be deemed to have been a receipt of the trade, or, if the company is carrying on more than one trade, to have been a receipt of such one of the trades as the company may choose.

(3) Where the non-dealing company is carrying on, or was formed to carry on a trade, then if—

    (a) either—

        (i) the right subsisting against it was a right to the repayment of moneys lent for meeting expenditure which has proved (in whole or in part) abortive, or

        (ii) the payment to the company was made for meeting such expenditure, and

    (b) that expenditure is such that the company is not entitled in respect of it to any allowance or deduction in computing losses or gains,

subsection (1) above shall not apply in so far as the expenditure proved abortive.

(4) For the purposes of this section—

    (a) "company" includes any body corporate;

    (b) "dealing company" means a company dealing in securities, land or buildings and includes any company whose profits on the sale of securities, land or buildings are part of its trading profits;

    (c) "non-dealing company" means any company which is not a dealing company;

    (d) two or more companies shall be treated as associated companies if one has control of the other or others, or any person has control of both or all of them;

    (e) references to a company ("the first company") having control of another company ("the second company") shall be construed as references to the first company having control of the second company either by itself or in conjunction with any person having control over the first company, and "control" has the meaning given by section 840;

    (f) "securities" includes shares and stock.

(5) Where it appears to the Board that by reason of any transaction or transactions a person may by virtue of this section have incurred any liability to tax, the Board may by notice served on him require him, within such time not less than 28 days as may be specified in the notice, to furnish information in his possession with respect to the transaction or any of the transactions, being information as to matters, specified in the notice, which are relevant to the question whether he has incurred any such liability to tax.

Other provisions

Sale by individual of income derived from his personal activities.

775.—(1) Subject to subsection (7) below, this section has effect where—

    (a) transactions or arrangements are effected or made to exploit the earning capacity of an individual in any occupation by putting some other person in a position to enjoy all or any part of the profits or gains or other income, or of the receipts, derived from the individual's activities in that occupation, or anything derived directly or indirectly from any such income or receipts; and

(b) as part of, or in connection with, or in consequence of, the transactions or arrangements any capital amount is obtained by the individual for himself or for any other person; and

(c) the main object or one of the main objects of the transactions was the avoidance or reduction of liability to income tax.

(2) Any such capital amount shall for all the purposes of the Income Tax Acts be treated as being earned income of the individual which arises when the capital amount is receivable, and which is chargeable to tax under Case VI of Schedule D.

(3) In this section—

(a) references to any occupation are references to any activities of any of the kinds pursued in any profession or vocation, irrespective of whether the individual is engaged in a profession or vocation, or is employed by or holds office under some other person; and

(b) references in subsection (1) above to income or receipts include references to payments for any description of copyright or licence or franchise or other right deriving its value from the activities, including past activities, of the individual.

(4) This section shall not apply to a capital amount obtained from the disposal—

(a) of assets (including any goodwill) of a profession or vocation, or of a share in a partnership which is carrying on a profession or vocation, or

(b) of shares in a company,

in so far as the value of what is disposed of, at the time of disposal, is attributable to the value of the profession or vocation as a going concern, or as the case may be to the value of the company's business, as a going concern.

(5) If the value of the profession, vocation or business as a going concern is derived to a material extent from prospective income or receipts derived directly or indirectly from the individual's activities in the occupation, and for which, when all capital amounts are disregarded, the individual will not have received full consideration, whether as a partner in a partnership or as an employee or otherwise, subsection (4) above shall not exempt the part of the capital amount so derived.

(6) In subsections (4) and (5) above references to the company's business include references to the business of any other company in which it holds shares directly or indirectly.

(7) Where on any occasion an individual obtains a capital amount consisting of any property or right which derives substantially the whole of its value from the activities of the individual, or (as in the case where the individual acquires a stock option and subsequently exercises the stock option) there are two or more occasions on which an individual obtains a capital amount consisting of any such property or right, then—

(a) tax under this section shall not be charged on any such occasion, but

(b) without prejudice to the generality of the provisions of this section or section 777, tax under this section shall be charged on the occasion when the capital amount, or any such capital amount, is sold or otherwise realised, and shall be so charged by reference to the proceeds of sale or the realised value.

(8) For the purposes of subsection (1)(b) above the cases where an individual obtains any capital amount for some other person include cases where the individual has put some other person in a position to receive the capital amount by providing that other person with something of value derived, directly or indirectly, from the individual's activities in the occupation.

(9) This section shall apply to all persons, whether resident in the United Kingdom or not, if the occupation of the individual is carried on wholly or partly in the United Kingdom.

Transactions in land: taxation of capital gains.

776.—(1) This section is enacted to prevent the avoidance of tax by persons concerned with land or the development of land.

(2) This section applies wherever—

(a) land, or any property deriving its value from land, is acquired with the sole or main object of realising a gain from disposing of the land; or

(b) land is held as trading stock; or

(c) land is developed with the sole or main object of realising a gain from disposing of the land when developed;

and any gain of a capital nature is obtained from the disposal of the land—

(i) by the person acquiring, holding or developing the land, or by any connected person, or

(ii) where any arrangement or scheme is effected as respects the land which enables a gain to be realised by any indirect method, or by any series of transactions, by any person who is a party to, or concerned in, the arrangement or scheme;

and this subsection applies whether any such person obtains the gain for himself or for any other person.

(3) Where this section applies, the whole of any such gain shall for all the purposes of the Tax Acts be treated—

(a) as being income which arises when the gain is realised, and which constitutes profits or gains chargeable to tax under Case VI of Schedule D for the chargeable period in which the gain is realised; and

(b) subject to the following provisions of this section, as being income of the person by whom the gain is realised.

(4) For the purposes of this section—

(a) land is disposed of if, by any one or more transactions, or by any arrangement or scheme, whether concerning the land or property deriving its value from the land, the property in the land, or control over the land, is effectually disposed of; and

(b) references in subsection (2) above to the acquisition or development of property with the sole or main object of realising the gain from disposing of the land shall be construed accordingly.

(5) For those purposes—

(a) where, whether by a premature sale or otherwise, a person directly or indirectly transmits the opportunity of making a gain to another person, that other person's gain is obtained for him by the first-mentioned person; and

(b) any number of transactions may be regarded as constituting a single arrangement or scheme if a common purpose can be discerned in them, or if there is other sufficient evidence of a common purpose.

(6) For the purposes of this section, such method of computing a gain shall be adopted as is just and reasonable in the circumstances, taking into account the value of what is obtained for disposing of the land, and allowing only such expenses as are attributable to the land disposed of; and in applying this subsection—

(a) where a freehold is acquired and the reversion is retained on disposal, account may be taken of the way in which the profits or gains under Case I of Schedule D of a person dealing in land are computed in such a case; or

(b) account may be taken of the adjustments to be made in computing such profits or gains under subsections (2) and (3) of section 99.

In the application of this subsection to Scotland, "freehold" means the estate or interest of the proprietor of the *dominium utile* or, in the case of property other than feudal property, of the owner, and "reversion" means the interest of the landlord in property subject to a lease.

(7) Subsection (2)(c) above shall not apply to so much of any gain as is fairly attributable to the period, if any, before the intention to develop the land was formed, and which would not fall under paragraph (a) or (b) of that subsection; and in applying this subsection account shall be taken of the treatment under Case I of Schedule D of a person who appropriates land as trading stock.

(8) If all or any part of the gain accruing to any person is derived from value, or an opportunity of realising a gain, provided directly or indirectly by some other person, whether or not put at the disposal of the first-mentioned person, subsection (3)(b) above shall apply to the gain, or that part of it, with the substitution of that other person for the person by whom the gain was realised.

(9) This section shall not apply to a gain accruing to an individual which by virtue of sections 101 to 105 of the 1979 Act (private residences) is exempt from capital gains tax, or which would be so exempt but for the provisions of section 103(3) of that Act (residences acquired partly with a view to making a gain).

(10) Where—

(a) there is a disposal of shares in—

(i) a company which holds land as trading stock; or

(ii) a company which owns directly or indirectly 90 per cent. or more of the ordinary share capital of another company which holds land as trading stock; and

(b) all the land so held is disposed of—

(i) in the normal course of its trade by the company which held it, and

(ii) so as to procure that all opportunity of profit in respect of the land arises to that company,

then this section shall not by virtue of subsection (2)(i) above apply to any gain to the holder of shares as being a gain on property deriving value from that land (but without prejudice to any liability under subsection (2)(ii) above).

(11) Where a person who considers that paragraph (a) or (c) of subsection (2) above may apply as respects a gain of a capital nature which that person has obtained from the disposal of land, or which he would obtain from a proposed disposal of land, supplies to the inspector to whom he makes his return of income written particulars showing how the gain has arisen or would arise—

(a) the inspector shall, within 30 days from his receipt of the particulars, notify that person whether or not he is satisfied that, in the circumstances as described in the particulars, the gain will not, or would not, be chargeable to tax on that person under this section; and

(b) if the inspector notifies that person that he is so satisfied, the gain shall not be chargeable on that person under this section.

(12) If the particulars given under this section with respect to the gain are not such as to make full and accurate disclosure of all facts and considerations relating thereto which are material to be known to the inspector, any notification given by the inspector under subsection (11) above shall be void.

(13) In this section—

(a) references to the land include references to all or any part of the land, and "land" includes buildings, and any estate or interest in land or buildings;

(b) references to property deriving its value from land include—

(i) any shareholding in a company, or any partnership interest, or any interest in settled property, deriving its value directly or indirectly from land, and

(ii) any option, consent or embargo affecting the disposition of land;

and for the purposes of this section any question whether a person is connected with another shall be determined in accordance with section 839.

(14) This section shall apply to all persons, whether resident in the United Kingdom or not, if all or any part of the land in question is situated in the United Kingdom.

777.—(1) This section has effect to supplement sections 775 and 776, and those sections and this section are together referred to as the relevant provisions.

(2) In applying the relevant provisions account shall be taken of any method, however indirect, by which—

(a) any property or right is transferred or transmitted; or

(b) the value of any property or right is enhanced or diminished;

and accordingly the occasion of the transfer or transmission of any property or right, however indirect, and the occasion when the value of any property or right is enhanced, may be an occasion when, under sections 775 and 776, tax becomes chargeable.

(3) Subsection (2) above applies in particular—

(a) to sales, contracts and other transactions made otherwise than for full consideration or for more than full consideration; and

(b) to any method by which any property or right, or the control of any property or right, is transferred or transmitted by assigning share capital or other rights in a company or any partnership or interest in settled property; and

(c) to the creation of any option or consent or embargo affecting the disposition of any property or right, and to the consideration given for the option, or for the giving of the consent or the release of the embargo; and

(d) to the disposal of any property or right on the winding up, dissolution or termination of any company, partnership or trust.

(4) In ascertaining for the purposes of the relevant provisions the intentions of any person, the objects and powers of any company, partners or trustees, as set out in any memorandum, articles of association or other document, shall not be conclusive.

(5) In order to ascertain whether and to what extent the value of any property or right is derived from any other property or right, value may be traced through any number of companies, partnerships and trusts, and the property held by any company, partnership or trust shall be attributed to the shareholders, partners or beneficiaries at each stage in such manner as is appropriate in the circumstances.

(6) In applying the relevant provisions—

    (a) any expenditure or receipt or consideration or other amount may be apportioned by such method as is just and reasonable in the circumstances;

    (b) all such valuations shall be made as are appropriate to give effect to sections 775 and 776.

(7) For the purposes of the relevant provisions (and in particular for the purpose of the reference in section 775 to an individual putting some other person in a position to enjoy income or receipts) partners, or the trustees of settled property, or personal representatives, may be regarded as persons distinct from the individuals or other persons who are for the time being partners or trustees or personal representatives.

(8) Where a person is assessed to tax under the relevant provisions in respect of consideration receivable by another person—

    (a) he shall be entitled to recover from that other person any part of that tax which he has paid; and

    (b) if any part of that tax remains unpaid at the expiration of six months from the date when it became due and payable, it shall be recoverable from that other person as though he were the person assessed, but without prejudice to the right to recover it from the person actually assessed;

and for the purposes of paragraph (a) above the Board or an inspector shall on request furnish a certificate specifying the amount of income in respect of which tax has been paid, and the amount of tax so paid; and the certificate shall be conclusive evidence of any facts stated in it.

For the purposes of this subsection any income which a person is treated as having by virtue of sections 775 and 776 shall, subject to section 833(3), be treated as the highest part of his income.

(9) If it appears to the Board that any person entitled to any consideration or other amount taxable under sections 775 and 776 is not resident in the United Kingdom, the Board may direct that section 349(1) shall apply to any payment forming part of that amount as if it were an annual payment charged with tax under Case III of Schedule D, but without prejudice to the final determination of the liability of that person, including any liability under subsection (8)(b) above.

(10) Sections 775 and 776 have effect subject to Part XV and to any other provision of the Tax Acts deeming income to belong to a particular person.

(11) Where under section 776(2)(c) any person is charged to tax on the realisation of a gain, and the computation of the gain proceeded on the footing that the land or some other property was appropriated at any time as trading stock, that land or other property shall be treated on that footing also for the purposes of section 122 of the 1979 Act (property becoming or ceasing to be stock in trade).

(12) Where under section 775(1)(b) or 776(8) the person charged to tax is a person other than the person for whom the capital amount was obtained or the person by whom the gain was realised, and the tax has been paid, then, for the purposes of sections 31 and 33 of the 1979 Act

(profits taxable as income excluded from tax on capital gains), the person for whom the capital amount was obtained or the person by whom the gain was realised shall be regarded as having been charged to that tax.

(13) For the purposes of the relevant provisions—

"capital amount" means any amount, in money or money's worth, which, apart from the sections 775 and 776, does not fall to be included in any computation of income for purposes of the Tax Acts, and other expressions including the word "capital" shall be construed accordingly;

"company" includes any body corporate; and

"share" includes stock;

and any amount in money or money's worth shall not be regarded as having become receivable by some person until that person can effectively enjoy or dispose of it.

778.—(1) The Board or an inspector may by notice require any person to furnish them within such time as the Board or the inspector may direct (not being less than 30 days) with such particulars as the Board or the inspector think necessary for the purposes of sections 775 and 776.

Power to obtain information.

(2) The particulars which a person must furnish under this section, if he is required by a notice from the Board or the inspector so to do, include particulars—

(a) as to transactions or arrangements with respect to which he is or was acting on behalf of others;

(b) as to transactions or arrangements which in the opinion of the Board or the inspector should properly be investigated for the purposes of sections 775 and 776 notwithstanding that, in the opinion of the person to whom the notice is given, no liability to tax arises under those sections; and

(c) as to whether the person to whom the notice is given has taken or is taking any, and if so what, part in any, and if so what, transactions or arrangements of a description specified in the notice.

(3) Notwithstanding anything in subsection (2) above, a solicitor—

(a) shall not be deemed for the purposes of paragraph (c) of that subsection to have taken part in any transaction or arrangement by reason only that he has given professional advice to a client in connection with the transaction or arrangement, and

(b) shall not, in relation to anything done by him on behalf of a client, be compellable under this section, except with the consent of his client, to do more than state that he is or was acting on behalf of a client, and give the name and address of his client.

779.—(1) If land or any estate or interest in land is transferred from one person to another and—

Sale and lease-back: limitation on tax reliefs.

(a) as a result of a lease of the land or any part of the land granted at that time or subsequently by the transferee to the transferor, or

(b) as a result of any other transaction or series of transactions affecting the land or any estate or interest in the land,

the transferor, or any person who is associated with the transferor, becomes liable at the time of the transfer or subsequently to pay any rent under a lease of the land or any part of the land, this section shall apply to all rent due under the lease from the transferor, or from any person who is associated with the transferor.

(2) If—

   (a) land or any estate or interest in land is transferred from one person to another, and

   (b) as a result of any transaction or series of transactions affecting the land or any estate or interest in the land, the transferor, or any person who is associated with the transferor, becomes liable at the time of the transfer or subsequently to make any payment (other than rent under a lease) for which any relevant tax relief is available, being a payment by way of rentcharge on the land or any part of the land or a payment in any other way connected with the land,

then this section shall apply to all such payments under the rentcharge or other transaction due from the transferor, or from any person who is associated with the transferor.

(3) The references in subsections (1) and (2) above to the transfer of an estate or interest in land include references to—

   (a) the granting of a lease or any other transaction involving the creation of a new estate or interest in the land;

   (b) the transfer of the lessee's interest under a lease by surrender or forfeiture of the lease; and

   (c) any transaction or series of transactions affecting land or an estate or interest in land, such that some person is the owner, or one of the owners, before and after the carrying out of the transaction or transactions, but another person becomes or ceases to become one of the owners;

and in relation to any such transaction or series of transactions any person who is an owner before the carrying out of the transaction or transactions, and is not the sole owner thereafter, shall be regarded for the purposes of this section as a transferor.

(4) A deduction by way of any relevant tax relief, being a deduction in respect of rent or of any other payment to which this section applies, shall not exceed the commercial rent for the period for which the rent or other payment is made of the land in respect of which that payment is made.

(5) If—

   (a) under subsection (4) above part of a payment which would otherwise be allowable as a deduction by way of any relevant tax relief is not so allowable, and

   (b) one or more subsequent payments are made by the transferor, or a person who is associated with the transferor, under the lease or other transaction, that part of the first-mentioned payment may be carried forward and treated for the purposes of any such deduction by way of tax relief as if it were made at the time when the next of those subsequent payments was made, and so made for the period for which that subsequent payment was made.

(6) For the purposes of subsection (4) above—

(a) if more than one payment is made for the same period the payments shall be taken together;

(b) if payments are made for periods which overlap, the payments shall be apportioned, and the apportioned payments which belong to the common part of the overlapping periods shall be taken together;

(c) the preceding references to payments include references to parts of payments which under subsection (5) above are treated as if made at a time subsequent to that at which they were made, and to the extent that a part of a payment so carried forward under that subsection is not so allowable as a deduction by way of tax relief, it may again be carried forward under that subsection;

(d) so much of any payment as is in respect of services or the use of assets or rates usually borne by the tenant shall be excluded, and in determining the amount to be so excluded provisions in any lease or agreement fixing the payments or parts of payments which are in respect of services or the use of assets may be overridden.

(7) A payment made for a period all of which falls more than one year after the payment is made shall be treated for the purposes of this section as made for that period of one year beginning with the date on which the payment was made, and a payment for a period part of which falls after the end of that year shall be treated for those purposes as if a corresponding part of the payment was made for that year (and no part for any later period).

(8) For the purpose of making a comparison under subsection (4) above between a payment consisting of rent under a lease ("the actual lease"), or such payments taken together, and the commercial rent of the land, "commercial rent" shall mean the rent which might be expected to be paid under a lease of the land negotiated in the open market at the time when the actual lease was created, being a lease which is of the same duration as the actual lease, which is, as respects liability for maintenance and repairs, subject to the terms and conditions of the actual lease and which provides for rent payable at uniform intervals and—

(a) at a uniform rate, or

(b) if the rent payable under the actual lease is rent at a progressive rate (and such that the amount of rent payable for any year is never less than the amount payable for any previous year), a rent which progresses by gradations proportionate to those provided by the actual lease.

(9) For the purpose of making a comparison under subsection (4) above between a payment which does not consist of rent under a lease (or such a payment taken together with other payments) and the commercial rent of the land, "commercial rent" shall mean the rent which might be

expected to be paid under a tenant's repairing lease negotiated in the open market at the time when the transaction was effected under which the payment or payments became due, being—

(a) where the period over which payments are to be made under that transaction is not less than 200 years, or the obligation to make such payments is perpetual, a lease for 200 years; and

(b) where that period is less than 200 years, a lease which is of the same duration as that period.

(10) In this section references to rent under a lease include references to rent which the person entitled to the lease is under subsection (4), (5) or (6) of section 37 or under section 87 treated, for any purpose, as paying in respect of land comprised in the lease, and such rent shall be treated for the purposes of this section as having been paid from day to day as it has become due.

(11) For the purposes of this section the following persons shall be deemed to be associated with one another, that is—

(a) the transferor in any such transaction as is described in subsection (1) or (2) above, and the transferor in another such transaction, if those two persons are acting in concert, or if the two transactions are in any way reciprocal, and any person who is an associate of either of those associated transferors;

(b) any two or more bodies corporate participating in, or incorporated for the purposes of, a scheme for the reconstruction of any body or bodies corporate or for the amalgamation of any two or more bodies corporate;

(c) any persons who are associates as defined in section 783(10).

(12) In this section—

"asset" means any description of property or rights other than land or an interest in land;

"lease" includes an underlease, sublease or any tenancy or licence, and any agreement for a lease, underlease, sublease or tenancy or licence and, in the case of land outside the United Kingdom, any interest corresponding to a lease as so defined; and in relation to such land, expressions in this section relating to interests in land and their disposition shall be construed accordingly;

"rent" includes any payment made under a lease; and

"tenant's repairing lease" means a lease where the lessee is under an obligation to maintain and repair the whole, or substantially the whole, of the premises comprised in the lease.

(13) For the purposes of this section the following are deductions by way of relevant tax relief, that is to say—

(a) a deduction in computing profits or gains chargeable under Schedule A allowable by virtue of sections 25, 26 and 28 to 31 and Schedule 1;

(b) a deduction in computing profits or gains or losses of a trade, profession or vocation for the purposes of tax;

(c) a deduction in computing profits or gains chargeable under Case VI of Schedule D, or in computing any loss for which relief is allowable under section 392 or 396;

(d) allowance of a payment under section 75 or 76;

(e) a deduction from emoluments to be assessed under Schedule E made in pursuance of section 198(1) or allowable in computing losses in an employment for tax purposes;

(f) a deduction allowable for tax purposes in computing profits or gains or losses arising from woodlands.

(14) This section shall not apply if the transfer described in subsection (1) or (2) above was on or before 14th April 1964.

780.—(1) If, in any case where a person ("the lessee") who is a lessee of land under a lease having not more than 50 years to run ("the original lease") is entitled in respect of the rent under the lease to a deduction by way of tax relief which is a relevant tax relief for the purposes of section 779—

Sale and lease-back: taxation of consideration received.

(a) the lessee assigns the original lease to another person, or surrenders it to his landlord, for a consideration which apart from this section would not be taxable otherwise than as capital in the hands of the lessee, and

(b) there is granted or assigned to the lessee another lease ("the new lease") of or including the whole or any part of the land which was the subject of the original lease for a term not exceeding 15 years;

then, subject to the following provisions of this section, the provisions of this Act providing for deductions or allowances by way of tax relief in respect of payments of rent shall apply in relation to the rent under the new lease, and for the purposes of the Tax Acts a proportion of the consideration received by the lessee shall be treated not as a capital receipt but in accordance with subsection (3) below.

(2) For the purposes of this section—

(a) if the aggregate of the rent payable under the new lease in respect of any rental period ending on a date falling before the 15th anniversary of the date on which the term of the new lease begins is greater than the aggregate of the rent payable under the new lease in respect of the period of equal duration beginning on the day following that date, then unless the term of the new lease would be treated as ending on an earlier date by virtue of paragraph (b) below, that term shall be treated as ending on that date;

(b) if under the terms of the new lease —

(i) the lessor or the lessee has power to determine the new lease at a time before the expiry of the term for which it was granted, or

(ii) the lessee has power to vary his obligations under the new lease so as to reduce the rent which he would otherwise have to pay or in any other manner beneficial to him,

then, unless the term of the new lease would be treated as ending on an earlier date by virtue of paragraph (a) above, that term shall be treated as ending on the earliest date with effect from which, in exercise of that power, the lessor or the lessee could determine the new lease or, as the case may be, the lessee could so vary his obligations;

and in any case where a rentcharge payable by the lessee is secured on the whole or any part of the property which is the subject of the new lease, the rent payable under the new lease shall be treated for the purposes of paragraphs (a) and (b) above as equal to the aggregate of the rentcharge and the rent payable under the terms of that lease.

(3) Subject to the following provisions of this section, the proportion of the consideration received by the lessee as mentioned in subsection (1) above, or of any instalment of that consideration, which for the purposes of the Tax Acts is to be treated not as a capital receipt but in accordance with this subsection shall be determined by the formula—

$$\frac{16 - N}{15}$$

where N is the term of the new lease expressed in years or, if that term is less than a year, where N is 1; and that proportion shall be treated for the purposes of the Tax Acts—

(a) as a receipt of a trade, profession or vocation, if the rent payable by the lessee under the new lease is allowable as a deduction in computing profits or gains or losses of a trade, profession or vocation for the purposes of tax and if the consideration is received by the lessee in the course of that trade, profession or vocation; and

(b) in any other case, as a profit or gain chargeable under Case VI of Schedule D.

(4) In any case where the property which is the subject of the new lease does not include the whole of the property which was the subject of the original lease, the consideration received by the lessee shall be treated for the purposes of subsection (3) above as reduced to that portion of the consideration which is reasonably attributable to such part of the property which was the subject of the original lease as consists of, or is included in, the property which is the subject of the new lease.

(5) Schedule 2 shall have effect for the purposes of giving relief, on a claim being made in that behalf, from any increase in an individual's liability to income tax which is attributable to any amount being treated, by virtue of subsection (3) above, as an income receipt for a single year of assessment rather than as a series of such receipts during the term of the new lease; and in the application of that Schedule by virtue of this subsection for the definitions of "chargeable sum" and "relevant period" there shall be substituted the following definitions—

"chargeable sum" means the amount in respect of which, by virtue of subsection (3) above, the claimant is chargeable to income tax for the year of assessment;

"relevant period", in relation to any chargeable sum, means the term of the new lease.

(6) Where by agreement with his landlord, the lessee varies the terms of the original lease in such a manner that, in return for such a consideration as is specified in subsection (1)(a) above, the lessee undertakes to pay, during a period ending not later than 15 years after the date on which the consideration, or if the consideration is paid in instalments, the last such instalment, is paid to the lessee, a rent greater than that payable under the original lease, he shall be treated for the purposes of this section—

(a) as having surrendered the original lease for that consideration, and

(b) as having been granted a new lease for a term not exceeding 15 years but otherwise on the terms of the original lease as so varied.

(7) References in this section to the lessee (other than in subsection (1)(a) above) include references to a person who is a partner or associate of the lessee or an associate of a partner of the lessee; and for the purposes of this section the expression "associate" shall be construed in accordance with 783(10).

(8) Subject to subsection (7) above, expressions used in this section have the meanings assigned to them by section 24, and in subsection (2)(a) above "rental period" means a period in respect of which a payment of rent falls to be made, and for the purposes of that subsection, in a case where the rental period is a quarter or a month, each such period shall be treated as of equal duration.

(9) The preceding provisions of this section shall not apply if the lessee had, before 22nd June 1971, a right enforceable at law or in equity to the grant of the new lease, but in any case where, apart from this subsection, those provisions would apply, no part of the rent paid under the new lease shall be treated as a payment of capital, and the provisions of this Act providing for deductions or allowances by way of tax relief in respect of payments of rent shall apply accordingly.

781.—(1) Subject to section 782, where—   Assets leased to traders and

(a) a deduction by way of tax relief which is one of the kinds listed in   others. subsection (4) below is allowable in respect of a payment made under a lease of an asset of any description, and

(b) before, at or after the time when the payment is made, either—

(i) the person who made the payment has obtained or obtains a capital sum in respect of the lessee's interest in the lease, or

(ii) the lessor's interest in the lease, or any other interest in the asset, has belonged to an associate of the person who made the payment, and that associate has obtained a capital sum in respect of that interest, the person obtaining that sum shall be charged under Case VI of Schedule D for the chargeable period in which the sum is obtained with tax on an amount equal to the amount of the payment in respect of which tax relief is so allowed.

(2) A person shall not be assessed to tax under subsection (1) above on any amount to the extent to which it exceeds the capital sum by reference to which he is so assessed.

(3) Subsection (1) above shall not apply to payments under a lease created on or before 14th April 1964.

(4) The kinds of deductions by way of tax relief to which subsection (1) above applies are as follows—

  (a) a deduction in computing profits or gains or losses of a trade, profession or vocation for the purposes of tax;

  (b) a deduction in computing profits or gains chargeable under Case VI of Schedule D, or in computing any loss for which relief is allowable under section 392 or 396;

  (c) allowance of a payment under section 75 or 76;

  (d) a deduction from emoluments to be assessed under Schedule E made in pursuance of section 198(1) or allowable in computing losses in an employment for tax purposes;

  (e) a deduction allowable for tax purposes in computing profits or gains or losses arising from woodlands.

(5) Where—

  (a) the deduction by way of tax relief mentioned in subsection (1)(a) above is a deduction in computing, for income tax purposes, profits or gains or losses of a trade, profession or vocation, or arising from woodlands, and

  (b) any part of the payments made under the lease by the person obtaining the capital sum is a payment in respect of which a deduction is not allowed for the reason that the whole or any part of the period in which the payment would fall to be allowed is not a period on the profits or gains of which income tax falls to be computed in respect of the trade, profession or vocation,

for the reference in subsection (2) above to the amount of the capital sum there shall be substituted a reference to that amount after deducting the amount of the payment in respect of which a deduction is not allowed for that reason.

(6) So far as in respect of a capital sum any part of a payment allowed as a deduction by way of tax relief of a kind to which this section applies is taken into account in making an assessment under subsection (1) above, that part of the payment shall be left out of account in determining whether any and if so what amount should be assessed by reference to any other capital sum; and the order in which this subsection is applied shall be the order in which the capital sums are obtained.

(7) There shall be made all such adjustments of tax, whether by way of making assessments or by repayment of tax, as are required after the making of any such payment as is described in subsection (1) above to give effect to the charge under that subsection in respect of a sum obtained before the making of the payment.

(8) Notwithstanding anything in the Tax Acts limiting the time within which an assessment may be made or a claim for relief may be admitted any such adjustment may be made, by making an assessment or otherwise, at any time not more than six years from the end of the chargeable period in which the payment was made.

(9) This section shall not apply if the capital sum obtained in respect of the lessee's interest in a lease constituting a hire-purchase agreement for machinery or plant is a sum which is required to be brought into account as the whole or part of the disposal value of the machinery or plant under section 45(2) of the Finance Act 1971.

1971 c. 68.

782.—(1) This section shall apply, and section 781 shall not apply, to payments—

Leased assets: special cases.

    (a) which are allowable by way of deductions in computing the profits or gains or losses of a trade, and

    (b) which are made under a lease of an asset which at any time before the creation of the lease was used for the purposes—

        (i) of that trade; or

        (ii) of another trade carried on by the person who at that time or later was carrying on the first-mentioned trade;

        and when so used was owned by the person carrying on the trade in which it was being used.

(2) Subject to the following provisions of this section, the deduction allowable in computing the profits or gains or losses of the trade for the purposes of tax as respects any such payment shall not exceed the commercial rent of the asset for the period for which the payment was made.

(3) If under subsection (2) above part of a payment which would otherwise be allowable as a deduction is not so allowable, and one or more subsequent payments are made by the same person under the same lease, that part of the first-mentioned payment may be carried forward and treated for the purposes of computing the profits or gains or losses of the trade for the purposes of tax as if it were made at the time when the next of those subsequent payments was made, and so made for the period for which that subsequent payment was made.

(4) For the purposes of subsection (2) above—

    (a) if more than one payment is made for the same period the payments shall be taken together;

    (b) if the payments are made for periods which overlap, the payments shall be apportioned, and the apportioned payments which belong to the common part of the overlapping periods shall be taken together;

(c) the preceding references to payments include references to parts of payments which under subsection (3) above are treated as if made at a time subsequent to that at which they were made;

and to the extent that a part of a payment carried forward under subsection (3) above is not allowable as a deduction it may again be carried forward under that subsection.

(5) A payment made for a period all of which falls more than one year after the payment is made shall be treated for the purposes of this section as made for that period of one year beginning with the date on which the payment is made, and a payment for a period part of which falls after the end of that year shall be treated for those purposes as if a corresponding part of the payment was made for that year (and no part for any later period).

(6) For the purpose of making a comparison under subsection (2) above between a payment, or payments taken together, and the commercial rent of the asset, "commercial rent" shall mean the rent which might at the relevant time be expected to be paid under a lease of the asset for the remainder of the anticipated normal working life of the asset, being a rent payable at uniform intervals and at a uniform rate which would afford a reasonable return for its market value at the relevant time, having regard to the terms and conditions of the lease; and in this subsection—

"anticipated normal working life" means, in the case of any asset, the period which might be expected, when the asset is first put into use, to be going to elapse before it is finally put out of use as being unfit for further use, it being assumed that the asset is going to be used in the normal manner and to the normal extent, and is going to be so used throughout that period; and

"the relevant time" means the time when the lease was created under which the payment was made with which the commercial rent is to be compared.

(7) If the asset is used at the same time partly for the purposes of the trade and partly for other purposes the commercial rent as defined in subsection (6) above shall be determined by reference to what would be paid for such a partial use of the asset.

(8) This section shall not apply in relation to payments made under a lease created on or before 14th April 1964.

(9) In this section references to the person carrying on a trade are references to the person carrying on the trade for the time being, and where at any time a person succeeds to a trade which until that time was carried on by another person, and by virtue of section 113 or 337(1) the trade is to be treated as discontinued, the trade shall, nonetheless, be treated as the same trade for the purposes of this section.

(10) In this section references to a trade include references to a profession or vocation.

Leased assets: supplemental.

783.—(1) References in section 781 to a sum obtained in respect of the lessee's interest in a lease of an asset, or in respect of any other interest in an asset include—

(a) in the case of a lessee's interest, references to sums representing the consideration in money or money's worth obtained on a surrender of the rights to the lessor, or on an assignment of the lease, or on creating a sublease or any other interest out of the lease; and

(b) references to any insurance moneys payable in respect of the asset, so far as payable to the owner of the interest in the asset.

(2) Such references also include references to sums representing money or money's worth obtained by the person entitled to the interest by a transaction or series of transactions disposing of the asset, or of an interest in the asset, and in particular transactions which comprise arrangements under which the rights of the lessee under a lease of the asset are merged in any way with the rights of the lessor, or with any other rights as respects the asset, so far as the money or money's worth so obtained is attributable to the rights of the lessee under the lease.

(3) References in section 781 to sums obtained in respect of any interest in an asset include references to money or money's worth so obtained in any transaction (including a transaction of the kind described in subsection (1) or (2) above) by way of consideration received by a person who is an associate of the person entitled to the interest in the asset.

(4) If an interest in the asset is disposed of by any person to a person who is his associate, the person disposing of the interest shall (unless in fact he obtains a greater sum) be treated for the purposes of section 781 as having obtained in respect of the interest—

(a) the value of the interest in the open market; or

(b) the value of the interest to the person to whom it is, in effect, transferred;

whichever is the greater.

(5) For the purposes of subsections (3) and (4) above a disposition may be direct or indirect and may be effected by any such transaction as is described in subsection (2) above.

(6) For the purposes of sections 781 and 784 and this section any sum obtained by any persons carrying on a trade, profession or vocation in partnership in respect of an interest in an asset which is and continues to be used for the purposes of the trade, profession or vocation shall be regarded as apportionable between them in the shares in which they are then entitled to the profits of the trade, profession or vocation.

(7) Subject to subsection (6) above, for those purposes a sum obtained by persons jointly entitled to an interest in an asset shall be apportionable according to their respective interests in the rights.

(8) For those purposes, any payment in respect of which a deduction is allowable by way of tax relief which is made by persons carrying on a trade, profession or vocation in partnership shall be apportioned in such manner as may be just.

(9) Where under this section any sum or payment falls to be apportioned and, at the time of the apportionment, it appears that it is material as respects the liability to tax (for whatever period) of two or

PART XVII

more persons, any question which arises as to the manner in which the sum or payment is to be apportioned shall be determined, for the purposes of tax of all those persons—

(a) in a case where the same body of General Commissioners have jurisdiction with respect to all those persons, by those Commissioners unless all those persons agree that it shall be determined by the Special Commissioners;

(b) in a case where different bodies of Commissioners have jurisdiction with respect to those persons, by such of those bodies as the Board may direct unless all those persons agree that it shall be determined by the Special Commissioners; and

(c) in any other case, by the Special Commissioners;

and any such Commissioners shall determine the question in like manner as if it were an appeal, except that all those persons shall be entitled to appear and be heard by the Commissioners who are to make the determination or to make representations to them in writing.

(10) For the purposes of this section and in construing the expressions "associate" and "associated" in section 781 and this section, the following persons shall be deemed to be associated with each other, that is to say—

(a) any individual and that individual's husband or wife, and any relative, or husband or wife of a relative, of that individual or that individual's husband or wife ("relative" meaning, for this purpose, brother, sister, ancestor or lineal descendant);

(b) any person in his capacity of trustee of a settlement and any individual who in relation to the settlement is a settlor, and any person associated with that individual ("settlement" and "settlor" having, for this purpose, the meanings given by section 670(2));

(c) any person and a body of persons of which that person, or persons associated with him, or that person and persons associated with him, has or have control;

(d) any two or more bodies of persons associated with the same person by virtue of paragraph (c) above;

(e) in relation to a disposal by joint owners, the joint owners and any person associated with any of them.

(11) In subsection (10) above "body of persons" includes a partnership and "control" has the meaning given by section 840.

Leased assets subject to hire-purchase agreements.

784.—(1) In the application of section 781 to a lease which constitutes a hire-purchase agreement, for the reference in subsection (2) of that section to the amount of the capital sum there shall, where that capital sum was obtained in respect of the lessee's interest in the lease constituting the hire-purchase agreement, be substituted references to the amount of the capital sum (adjusted, if necessary, under subsection (5) of that section) after deducting any capital expenditure which was incurred by the person obtaining the capital sum in providing the lessee's interest.

(2) In subsection (1) above "capital expenditure which was incurred by the person obtaining the capital sum in providing the lessee's interest" means—

(a) so much of any payment made under the lease by the person obtaining the capital sum (or, where the capital sum was obtained by the personal representatives of a deceased person, so made by that deceased person) as is not a payment in respect of which a deduction is allowable by way of tax relief which is one of the kinds listed in subsection (4) of section 781, plus

(b) where the lessee's interest was assigned to the person obtaining the capital sum, any capital payment made by that person as consideration for the assignment.

(3) If the amount to be deducted in pursuance of subsection (1) above exceeds the amount of the capital sum from which it is to be deducted, no charge shall arise under section 781(1) in respect of the capital sum.

(4) If the capital sum represents the consideration for part only of the lessee's interest in the lease which constitutes a hire-purchase agreement, the amount to be deducted under subsection (1) above shall be such proportion of the capital expenditure which is still unallowed as is reasonable having regard to the degree to which the capital expenditure has contributed to the value of what is disposed of in return for the capital sum.

(5) If more than one capital sum is, or is to be regarded as, obtained by the same person in respect of the lessee's interest in the lease which constitutes a hire-purchase agreement, then, so far as in respect of one of those capital sums any deduction is made in respect of capital expenditure in pursuance of subsection (1) above that capital expenditure shall be left out of account in applying subsections (1) and (3) above to any other such capital sum; and the order in which this subsection is applied shall be the order in which the capital sums are obtained.

(6) In this section—

"hire-purchase agreement" means an agreement, other than a conditional sale agreement, under which—

(a) goods are bailed or, in Scotland, hired in return for periodical payments by the person to whom they are bailed or hired, and

(b) the property in the goods will pass to that person if the terms of the agreement are complied with and one or more of the following occurs—

(i) the exercise of an option to purchase by that person;

(ii) the doing of any other specified act by any party to the agreement;

(iii) the happening of any other specified event; and

"conditional sale agreement" means an agreement for the sale of goods under which the purchase price or part of it is payable by instalments, and the property in the goods is to remain in the seller (notwithstanding that the buyer is to be in possession of the goods) until such conditions as to the payment of instalments or otherwise as may be specified in the agreement are fulfilled.

Meaning of "asset", "capital sum" and "lease" for purposes of sections 781 to 784.

785. In sections 781 to 784—

"asset" means any description of property or rights other than land or an interest in land;

"capital sum" means any sum of money, or any money's worth, except so far as it or any part of it is to be treated for the purposes of tax as a receipt to be taken into account in computing the profits or gains or losses of a trade, profession or vocation, or profits or gains or losses arising from woodlands, or is, apart from section 781, chargeable under Case VI of Schedule D; and

"lease", in relation to an asset, means any kind of agreement or arrangement under which payments are made for the use of, or otherwise in respect of, an asset, and includes, in particular, any agreement or arrangement all or any of the payments under which represent instalments of, or payments towards, a purchase price.

Transactions associated with loans or credit.

786.—(1) This section applies as respects any transaction effected with reference to the lending of money or the giving of credit, or the varying of the terms on which money is lent or credit is given, or which is effected with a view to enabling or facilitating any such arrangement concerning the lending of money or the giving of credit.

(2) Subsection (1) above has effect whether the transaction is effected between the lender or creditor and the borrower or debtor, or between either of them and a person connected with the other or between a person connected with one and a person connected with the other.

(3) If the transaction provides for the payment of any annuity or other annual payment, not being interest, being a payment chargeable to tax under Case III of Schedule D, the payment shall be treated for all the purposes of the Tax Acts as if it were a payment of annual interest.

(4) If the transaction is one by which the owner of any securities or other property carrying a right to income ("the owner") agrees to sell or transfer the property ("the relevant property"), and by the same or any collateral agreement—

(a) the purchaser or transferee ("the buyer"), or a person connected with him, agrees that at a later date he will sell or transfer the same or any other property to the owner or a person connected with him; or

(b) the owner or a person connected with him acquires an option which he subsequently exercises, to buy or acquire the same or any other property from the buyer or a person connected with the buyer;

then, without prejudice to the liability of any other person, the owner shall be chargeable to tax under Case VI of Schedule D on an amount equal to any income which arises from the relevant property at any time before the repayment of the loan or the termination of the credit.

(5) If under the transaction a person assigns, surrenders or otherwise agrees to waive or forego income arising from any property (without a sale or transfer of the property) then, without prejudice to the liability of any other person, he shall be chargeable to tax under Case VI of Schedule D on a sum equal to the amount of income assigned, surrendered, waived or foregone.

(6) If credit is given for the purchase price of any property, and the rights attaching to the property are such that, during the subsistence of the debt, the purchaser's rights to income from the property are suspended or restricted, he shall be treated for the purposes of subsection (5) above as if he had surrendered a right to income of an amount equivalent to the income which he has in effect foregone by obtaining the credit.

(7) The amount of any income payable subject to deduction of income tax shall be taken for the purposes of subsection (5) above as the amount before deduction of tax.

(8) References in this section to connected persons shall be construed in accordance with section 839.

787.—(1) Relief shall not be given to any person under any provision of the Tax Acts in respect of any payment of interest if a scheme has been effected or arrangements have been made (whether before or after the time when the payment is made) such that the sole or main benefit that might be expected to accrue to that person from the transaction under which the interest is paid was the obtaining of a reduction in tax liability by means of any such relief.

Restriction of relief for payments of interest.

(2) In this section "relief" means relief by way of deduction in computing profits or gains or deduction or set off against income or total profits.

(3) Where the relief is claimed by virtue of section 403(7) any question under this section as to what benefit might be expected to accrue from the transaction in question shall be determined by reference to the claimant company and the surrendering company taken together.

PART XVIII

DOUBLE TAXATION RELIEF

CHAPTER I

THE PRINCIPAL RELIEFS

Relief by
agreement with
other countries.

788.—(1) If Her Majesty by Order in Council declares that arrangements specified in the Order have been made with the government of any territory outside the United Kingdom with a view to affording relief from double taxation in relation to—

(a) income tax,

(b) corporation tax in respect of income or chargeable gains, and

(c) any taxes of a similar character to those taxes imposed by the laws of that territory,

and that it is expedient that those arrangements should have effect, then those arrangements shall have effect in accordance with subsection (3) below.

(2) Without prejudice to the generality of subsection (1) above, if it appears to Her Majesty to be appropriate, the arrangements specified in an Order in Council under this section may include provisions with respect to the exchange of information necessary for carrying out the domestic laws of the United Kingdom and the laws of the territory to which the arrangements relate concerning taxes covered by the arrangements including, in particular, provisions about the prevention of fiscal evasion with respect to those taxes; and where arrangements do include any such provisions, the declaration in the Order in Council shall state that fact.

(3) Subject to the provisions of this Part, the arrangements shall, notwithstanding anything in any enactment, have effect in relation to income tax and corporation tax in so far as they provide—

(a) for relief from income tax, or from corporation tax in respect of income or chargeable gains; or

(b) for charging the income arising from sources, or chargeable gains accruing on the disposal of assets, in the United Kingdom to persons not resident in the United Kingdom; or

(c) for determining the income or chargeable gains to be attributed—

(i) to persons not resident in the United Kingdom and their agencies, branches or establishments in the United Kingdom; or

(ii) to persons resident in the United Kingdom who have special relationships with persons not so resident; or

(d) for conferring on persons not resident in the United Kingdom the right to a tax credit under section 231 in respect of qualifying distributions made to them by companies which are so resident.

(4) The provisions of Chapter II of this Part shall apply where arrangements which have effect by virtue of this section provide that tax payable under the laws of the territory concerned shall be allowed as a credit against tax payable in the United Kingdom.

(5) For the purposes of this section and, subject to section 795(3), Chapter II of this Part in its application to relief under this section, any amount of tax which would have been payable under the law of a territory outside the United Kingdom but for a relief to which this subsection applies given under the law of that territory shall be treated as having been payable; and references in this section and that Chapter to double taxation, to tax payable or chargeable, or to tax not chargeable directly or by deduction shall be construed accordingly.

This subsection applies—

    (a) to any relief given with a view to promoting industrial, commercial, scientific, educational or other development in a territory outside the United Kingdom, being a relief with respect to which provision is made in the arrangements in question for double taxation relief; and

    (b) to any relief provided under and in accordance with the arrangements, where the latter expressly contemplate that the relief is to fall within this subsection.

(6) Except in the case of a claim for an allowance by way of credit in accordance with Chapter II of this Part, a claim for relief under subsection (3)(a) above shall be made to the Board.

(7) Where—

    (a) under any arrangements which have effect by virtue of this section, relief may be given, either in the United Kingdom or in the territory with the government of which the arrangements are made, in respect of any income or chargeable gains, and

    (b) it appears that the assessment to income tax or corporation tax made in respect of the income or chargeable gains is not made in respect of the full amount thereof, or is incorrect having regard to the credit, if any, which falls to be given under the arrangements,

any such assessments may be made as are necessary to ensure that the total amount of the income or chargeable gains is assessed, and the proper credit, if any, is given in respect thereof, and, where the income is, or the chargeable gains are, entrusted to any person in the United Kingdom for payment, any such assessment may be made on the recipient of the income or gains, and, in the case of an assessment in respect of income, may be assessed under Case VI of Schedule D.

(8) Any arrangements to which effect is given under this section may include provision for relief from tax for periods before the passing of this Act, or before the making of the arrangements, and provisions as to income or chargeable gains which is or are not subject to double taxation, and the preceding provisions of this section shall have effect accordingly.

(9) Any Order in Council made under this section revoking an earlier such Order in Council may contain such transitional provisions as appear to Her Majesty to be necessary or expedient.

(10) Before any Order in Council proposed to be made under this section is submitted to Her Majesty in Council, a draft of the Order shall be laid before the House of Commons, and the Order shall not be so submitted unless an Address is presented to Her Majesty by that House praying that the Order be made.

Arrangements made under old law.
1952 c.10.
1965 c. 25.

789.—(1) Notwithstanding section 793(2), any arrangements made in relation to the profits tax under section 347 of the Income Tax Act 1952 or any earlier enactment corresponding to that section shall, except in so far as arrangements made after the passing of the Finance Act 1965 provide otherwise, have effect in relation to corporation tax and income and gains chargeable to corporation tax as they are expressed to have effect in relation to the profits tax and profits chargeable to the profits tax, with the substitution of accounting periods for chargeable accounting periods (and not as they had effect in relation to income tax).

(2) In so far as any arrangements made before 30th March 1971 provide for the exemption of any income from surtax they shall have effect, unless otherwise modified by subsequent arrangements, as if they provided for that income to bear income tax at the basic rate and to be disregarded for the purpose of computing total income, except in so far as the computation affects the matters mentioned in section 835(5).

(3) Any reference in the Tax Acts (including this Part) to arrangements under or by virtue of section 788 includes a reference to arrangements having effect by virtue of this section.

Unilateral relief.

790.—(1) To the extent appearing from the following provisions of this section, relief from income tax and corporation tax in respect of income and chargeable gains shall be given in respect of tax payable under the law of any territory outside the United Kingdom by allowing that tax as a credit against income tax or corporation tax, notwithstanding that there are not for the time being in force any arrangements under section 788 providing for such relief.

(2) Relief under subsection (1) above is referred to in this Part as "unilateral relief".

(3) Unilateral relief shall be such relief as would fall to be given under Chapter II of this Part if arrangements with the government of the territory in question containing the provisions specified in subsections (4) to (10) below were in force by virtue of section 788, but subject to any particular provision made with respect to unilateral relief in that Chapter; and any expression in that Chapter which imports a reference to relief under arrangements for the time being having effect by virtue of that section shall be deemed to import also a reference to unilateral relief.

(4) Credit for tax paid under the law of the territory outside the United Kingdom and computed by reference to income arising or any chargeable gain accruing in that territory shall be allowed against any United Kingdom income tax or corporation tax computed by reference to that income or gain (profits from, or remuneration for, personal or professional services performed in that territory being deemed for this purpose to be income arising in that territory).

(5) Subsection (4) above shall have effect subject to the following modifications, that is to say—

(a) where the territory is the Isle of Man or any of the Channel Islands, the limitation to income or gains arising in the territory shall not apply;

(b) where arrangements with the government of the territory are for the time being in force by virtue of section 788, credit for tax paid under the law of the territory shall not be allowed by virtue of subsection (4) above in the case of any income or gains if any credit for that tax is allowable under those arrangements in respect of that income or those gains; and

(c) credit shall not be allowed by virtue of subsection (4) above for overseas tax on a dividend paid by a company resident in the territory unless—

> (i) the overseas tax is directly charged on the dividend, whether by charge to tax, deduction of tax at source or otherwise, and the whole of it represents tax which neither the company nor the recipient would have borne if the dividend had not been paid; or

> (ii) the dividend is paid to a company within subsection (6) below; or

> (iii) the dividend is paid to a company to which section 802(1) applies and is a dividend of the kind described in that subsection.

(6) Where a dividend paid by a company resident in the territory is paid to a company resident in the United Kingdom which either directly or indirectly controls, or is a subsidiary of a company which directly or indirectly controls—

(a) not less than 10 per cent. of the voting power in the company paying the dividend; or

(b) less than 10 per cent. of the voting power in the company paying the dividend if—

> (i) it has been reduced below that percentage on or after 1st April 1972; or

> (ii) it has been acquired on or after that date in exchange for voting power in another company in respect of which relief under this subsection by virtue of paragraph (a) above was due prior to the exchange;

> and the company receiving the dividend shows that the conditions specified in subsection (7) below are satisfied;

any tax in respect of its profits paid under the law of the territory by the company paying the dividend shall be taken into account in considering whether any, and if so what, credit is to be allowed in respect of the dividend.

In this subsection references to one company being a subsidiary of another are to be construed in accordance with section 792(2).

(7) The conditions referred to in subsection (6)(b) above are as follows—

Z

(a) that the reduction below the 10 per cent. limit (and any further reduction) or, as the case may be, the exchange (and any reduction thereafter) could not have been prevented by any reasonable endeavours on the part of the company receiving the dividend and was due to a cause or causes not reasonably foreseeable by it when control of the relevant voting power was acquired; and

(b) no reasonable endeavours on the part of that company could have restored or, as the case may be, increased the voting power to not less than 10 per cent.

(8) In subsection (7) above references to the company receiving the dividend include references—

(a) to any company of which it is a subsidiary within the meaning of section 792(2); and

(b) where prior to the reduction or exchange the voting power in question was controlled otherwise than directly by the company receiving the dividend, to each other company relevant for determining whether that voting power was controlled as required by subsection (6)(a) above.

(9) In subsection (7) above "the relevant voting power" means the voting power by virtue of which relief was due under subsection (6)(a) above prior to the reduction or exchange or, where control of the whole of that voting power was not acquired at the same time, that part of the voting power of which control was last acquired.

(10) In any case in which relief in respect of a dividend is due by virtue of subsection (6)(b) above, there shall be taken into account, as if it were tax payable under the law of the territory in which the company paying the dividend is resident, any tax that would be so taken into account under section 801 if the company paying the dividend and the company receiving it were related to each other within the meaning of section 801(5).

(11) Where—

(a) unilateral relief may by given in respect of any income or chargeable gain, and

(b) it appears that the assessment to income tax or corporation tax made in respect of the income or chargeable gain is not made in respect of the full amount thereof, or is incorrect having regard to the credit, if any, which falls to be given by way of unilateral relief,

any such assessments may be made as are necessary to ensure that the total amount of the income or chargeable gain is assessed, and the proper credit, if any, is given in respect thereof, and, where the income is, or the chargeable gain is, entrusted to any person in the United Kingdom for payment, any such assessment may be made on the recipient of the income or gain, and, in the case of an assessment in respect of income, may be assessed under Case VI of Schedule D.

(12) In this section and in Chapter II of this Part in its application to unilateral relief, references to tax payable or paid under the law of a territory outside the United Kingdom include only references—

(a) to taxes which are charged on income and which correspond to United Kingdom income tax, and

(b) to taxes which are charged on income or chargeable gains and which correspond to United Kingdom corporation tax;

but for this purpose tax under the law of any such territory shall not be treated as not corresponding to income tax or corporation tax by reason only that it is payable under the law of a province, state or other part of a country, or is levied by or on behalf of a municipality or other local body.

791. The Board may from time to time make regulations generally for carrying out the provisions of section 788 or any arrangements having effect thereunder, and may in particular by those regulations provide—

(a) for securing that relief from taxation imposed by the laws of the territory to which any such arrangements relate does not enure for the benefit of persons not entitled to such relief; and

(b) for authorising, in cases where tax deductible from any payment has, in order to comply with any such arrangements, not been deducted, and it is discovered that the arrangements did not apply to that payment, the recovery of the tax by assessment on the person entitled to the payment or by deduction from subsequent payments.

CHAPTER II

RULES GOVERNING RELIEF BY WAY OF CREDIT

General

792.—(1) In this Chapter, except where the context otherwise requires—

"arrangements" means any arrangements having effect by virtue of section 788;

"foreign tax" means, in relation to any territory, arrangements with the government of which have effect by virtue of section 788, any tax chargeable under the laws of that territory for which credit may be allowed under the arrangements;

"the United Kingdom taxes" means income tax and corporation tax;

"underlying tax" means, in relation to any dividend, tax which is not chargeable in respect of that dividend directly or by deduction; and

"unilateral relief" means relief under section 790.

(2) For the purposes of this Chapter one company is a subsidiary of another if the other company controls, directly or indirectly, not less than 50 per cent. of the voting power in the first company.

(3) Any reference in this Chapter to foreign tax shall be construed in relation to credit to be allowed under any arrangements as a reference only to tax chargeable under the laws of the territory with the government of which the arrangements were made.

PART XVIII
Reduction of
United Kingdom
taxes by amount
of credit due.

793.—(1) Subject to the provisions of this Chapter, where under any arrangements credit is to be allowed against any of the United Kingdom taxes chargeable in respect of any income or chargeable gain, the amount of the United Kingdom taxes so chargeable shall be reduced by the amount of the credit.

(2) Nothing in subsection (1) above authorises the allowance of credit against any United Kingdom tax against which credit is not allowable under the arrangements.

794.—(1) Subject to subsection (2) below, credit shall not be allowed under any arrangements against any of the United Kingdom taxes for any chargeable period unless the person in respect of whose income or chargeable gains the United Kingdom tax is chargeable is resident in the United Kingdom for that period.

(2) Credit may be allowed by way of unilateral relief—

(a) for tax paid under the law of the Isle of Man or any of the Channel Islands, if the person in question is, for the chargeable period in question, resident either in the United Kingdom or in the Isle of Man or any of the Channel Islands, as the case may be;

(b) for tax paid under the law of any territory and computed by reference to income from an office or employment the duties of which are performed wholly or mainly in that territory, against income tax chargeable under Schedule E and computed by reference to that income, if the person in question is for the year of assessment in question resident either in the United Kingdom or that territory; and

(c) for tax paid under the law of any territory in respect of interest on a loan where the following conditions are fulfilled, namely—

(i) that the person in question is a company which, for the chargeable period in question, carries on a banking business in the United Kingdom through a branch or agency;

(ii) that the loan was made by the company through the branch or agency in the United Kingdom;

(iii) that the territory under whose law the tax was paid is not one in which the company is liable to tax by reason of domicile, residence or place of management; and

(iv) that the amount of relief claimed does not exceed (or is by the claim expressly limited to) that which would have been available if the branch or agency had been a company resident in the United Kingdom and the loan had been made by it in the course of its banking business.

795.—(1) Where credit for foreign tax falls under any arrangements to be allowed in respect of any income and income tax is payable by reference to the amount received in the United Kingdom, the amount received shall be treated for the purposes of income tax as increased by the amount of the foreign tax in respect of the income, including in the case of a dividend any underlying tax which under the arrangements is to be taken into account in considering whether any and if so what credit is to be allowed in respect of the dividend.

(2) Where credit for foreign tax falls under any arrangements to be allowed in respect of any income or gain and subsection (1) above does not apply, then, in computing the amount of the income or gain for the purposes of income tax or corporation tax—

    (a) no deduction shall be made for foreign tax, whether in respect of the same or any other income or gain; and

    (b) the amount of the income shall, in the case of a dividend, be treated as increased by any underlying tax which, under the arrangements, is to be taken into account in considering whether any and if so what credit is to be allowed in respect of the dividend.

(3) The amount of any income or gain shall not be treated as increased under this section by reference to any foreign tax which, although not payable, falls to be taken into account for the purposes of section 788(5).

796.—(1) The amount of the credit for foreign tax which, under any arrangements, is to be allowed to a person against income tax for any year of assessment shall not exceed the difference between the amounts of income tax which would be borne by him for the year (no credit being allowed for foreign tax)—

Limits on credit: income tax.

    (a) if he were charged to tax on his total income for the year, computed in accordance with section 795; and

    (b) if he were charged to tax on the same income, computed in the same way, but excluding the income in respect of which the credit is to be allowed.

(2) Where credit for foreign tax is to be allowed in respect of income from more than one source, subsection (1) above shall be applied successively to the income from each source, but so that on each successive application, paragraph (a) shall apply to the total income exclusive of the income to which the subsection has already been applied.

(3) Without prejudice to subsections (1) and (2) above, the total credit for foreign tax to be allowed to a person against income tax for any year of assessment under all arrangements having effect by virtue of section 788 shall not exceed the total income tax payable by him for that year of assessment, less any income tax which he is entitled to charge against any other person.

797.—(1) The amount of the credit for foreign tax which under any arrangements is to be allowed against corporation tax in respect of any income or chargeable gain ("the relevant income or gain") shall not exceed the corporation tax attributable to the relevant income or gain, determined in accordance with subsections (2) and (3) below.

Limits on credit: corporation tax.

(2) Subject to subsection (3) below, the amount of corporation tax attributable to the relevant income or gain shall be treated as equal to such proportion of the amount of that income or gain as corresponds to the rate of corporation tax payable by the company (before any credit under this Part) on its income or chargeable gains for the accounting period in which the income arises or the gain accrues ("the relevant accounting period").

(3) Where in the relevant accounting period there is any deduction to be made for charges on income, expenses of management or other amounts which can be deducted from or set against or treated as reducing profits of more than one description—

(a) the company may for the purposes of this section allocate the deduction in such amounts and to such of its profits for that period as it thinks fit; and

(b) the amount of the relevant income or gain shall be treated for the purposes of subsection (2) above as reduced or, as the case may be, extinguished by so much (if any) of the deduction as is allocated to it.

(4) Where in accordance with section 239 any advance corporation tax falls to be set against the company's liability to corporation tax on its profits (within the meaning of that section) for the relevant accounting period—

(a) so far as that liability relates to the relevant income or gain, it shall be taken to be reduced by the amount of the credit for foreign tax attributable to that income or gain, as determined in accordance with subsections (2) and (3) above; and

(b) the amount of advance corporation tax which may be set against that liability, so far as it relates to the relevant income or gain, shall not exceed whichever is the lower of the limits specified in subsection (5) below;

and section 239(2) shall have effect in relation only to so much of the profits of the company chargeable to corporation tax for that period as does not include the relevant income or gain.

(5) In relation to an amount of income or gain in respect of which the company's liability to corporation tax is taken to be reduced as mentioned in paragraph (a) of subsection (4) above, the limits referred to in paragraph (b) of that subsection are—

(a) the limit which would apply under section 239(2) if that amount of income or gain were the company's only income or gain for the relevant accounting period; and

(b) the amount of corporation tax for which, after taking account of that reduction, the company is liable in respect of that amount of income or gain.

Interest on certain overseas loans.

798.—(1) This section applies in a case where—

(a) in any chargeable period the profits of any person ("the lender") which are brought into charge to income tax or corporation tax include an amount computed in accordance with section 795 in respect of interest ("foreign loan interest") on a loan made to a person resident outside the United Kingdom; and

(b) in determining the liability of the lender to income tax or corporation tax, expenditure related to the earning of the foreign loan interest is deductible in computing the profits referred to in paragraph (a) above; and

(c) the lender is entitled in accordance with this Chapter to credit for foreign tax chargeable on or by reference to the foreign loan interest;

and for the purpose only of determining whether the condition in paragraph (b) above is fulfilled in a case where the lender has in fact incurred no expenditure related to the earning of the foreign loan interest, it shall be assumed that he has incurred such expenditure.

(2) In subsection (1) above "interest", in relation to a loan, includes any introductory or other fee or charge which is payable in accordance with the terms on which the loan is made or is otherwise payable in connection with the making of the loan; and any reference in this section to foreign loan interest shall be construed accordingly.

(3) If in a case where this section applies the foreign tax referred to in subsection (1)(c) above is or includes an amount of spared tax, then for the purposes of income tax or corporation tax the amount which apart from this subsection would be the amount of the foreign loan interest shall be treated as increased by so much of the spared tax as does not exceed the permitted amount, as defined in subsection (4) below; but nothing in this subsection prejudices the operation of section 795 in relation to foreign tax which is not spared tax.

(4) In this section "spared tax" means foreign tax which although not payable falls to be taken into account for the purposes of credit by virtue of section 788(5); and the permitted amount, in relation to spared tax which is referable to the whole or any part of the foreign loan interest, is an amount which does not exceed—

(a) 15 per cent. of the interest to which the spared tax is referable, computed without regard to any increase under subsection (3) above; or

(b) if it is less, the amount of that spared tax for which, in accordance with any arrangements applicable to the case in question, credit falls to be given as mentioned in subsection (1)(c) above.

(5) If in a case where this section applies—

(a) the foreign tax referred to in subsection (1)(c) above is or includes an amount of tax which is not spared tax; and

(b) the amount of tax exceeds—

(i) the amount of the credit which, by virtue of this Chapter (but disregarding subsection (6) below), is allowed for that foreign tax against income tax or corporation tax; or

(ii) if it is less, 15 per cent. of the foreign loan interest, computed without regard to any increase or reduction under this section,

then, for the purposes of income tax or corporation tax, the amount which, apart from this subsection, would be the amount of the foreign loan interest shall be treated as reduced by a sum equal to the excess.

(6) Where this section applies, the amount of the credit for foreign tax referred to in subsection (1)(c) above which, in accordance with this Chapter, is to be allowed against income tax or corporation tax—

(a) shall be limited by treating the amount of the foreign loan interest (as increased or reduced under subsection (3) or (5) above) as reduced (or further reduced) for the purposes of this Chapter by an amount equal to so much of the lender's financial expenditure in relation to the loan concerned as is properly attributable to the period for which the interest is paid; and

(b) shall not exceed 15 per cent. of the foreign loan interest, computed without regard to paragraph (a) above or to any increase under subsection (3) above or any reduction under subsection (5) above.

(7) For the purposes of this section the lender's financial expenditure in relation to a loan is the aggregate of—

(a) the financial expenses (consisting of interest or similar sums) incurred by the lender in or in connection with the provision of the loan, so far as those expenses consist of payments which either are charges on income for the purposes of corporation tax or are deductible in computing profits of the lender which are brought into charge to income tax or corporation tax; and

(b) where the loan is financed by the issue of securities at a discount by the lender, so much of the amount of the discount as either constitutes such a charge as is mentioned in paragraph (a) above or is deductible as mentioned in that paragraph; and

(c) so much as it is just and reasonable to attribute to the loan of any interest or other return foregone by a person connected or associated with the lender in connection with the provision of funds to the lender, either interest free or in other circumstances more favourable to the lender than if the parties were at arm's length; and

(d) any other sum, whether paid by way of refund of tax or interest or by way of commission, which—

(i) is paid by the lender or a person connected or associated with him;

(ii) is paid directly or indirectly to the borrower or a person connected or associated with him;

(iii) is deductible as mentioned in paragraph (a) above;

(iv) would not, apart from this paragraph, be taken into account in determining the amount of the foreign loan interest; and

(v) it is reasonable to regard as referable to the loan or the foreign loan interest (or both).

(8) In a case where the amount of the lender's financial expenditure in relation to a loan is not readily ascertainable, that amount shall be taken, subject to subsection (9) below, to be such sum as it is just and reasonable to attribute to the financing of the loan, having regard, in particular, to any market rates of interest by reference to which the rate of interest on the loan is determined.

(9) The Board may by regulations supplement subsection (8) above—

(a) by specifying matters to be taken into account in determining such a just and reasonable attribution as is referred to in that subsection; and

(b) by making provision with respect to the determination of market rates of interest for the purposes of that subsection;

and any such regulations may make different provision for different cases.

(10) For the purposes of this section—

(a) section 839 applies; and

(b) subsection (10) of section 783 applies as it applies for the purposes of that section.

(11) Where the loan on which the foreign loan interest is payable was made pursuant to an agreement entered into before 1st April 1987, this section shall have effect subject to the following modifications in relation to interest payable before 1st April 1989—

(a) in subsection (1) in paragraph (a) the words "in a territory" shall be inserted after "resident" and the words following paragraph (c) shall be omitted;

(b) subsection (2) shall be omitted;

(c) in subsection (5) for paragraph (b) there shall be substituted—

"(b) that amount of tax exceeds the amount of the credit which, by virtue of this Chapter and in particular subsection (6) below, is allowed for that foreign tax against income tax or corporation tax;" and

(d) for subsections (6) to (10) there shall be substituted—

"(6) Where this section applies, the amount of the credit for foreign tax referred to in subsection (1)(c) above which, in accordance with this Chapter, is to be allowed against income tax or corporation tax shall not exceed 15 per cent. of the foreign loan interest, computed without regard to any increase under subsection (3) or any reduction under subsection (5) above.";

but subject to that, this section applies whether the loan was made before or after the passing of this Act.

Tax underlying dividends

799.—(1) Where in the case of any dividend arrangements provide for underlying tax to be taken into account in considering whether any and if so what credit is to be allowed against the United Kingdom taxes in respect of the dividend, the tax to be taken into account by virtue of that provision shall be so much of the foreign tax borne on the relevant profits by the body corporate paying the dividend as is properly attributable to the proportion of the relevant profits represented by the dividend.

Computation of underlying tax.

(2) Where under the foreign tax law the dividend has been increased for tax purposes by an amount to be set off against the recipient's own tax under that law or, to the extent that it exceeds his own tax thereunder,

PART XVIII

paid to him, then, from the amount of the underlying tax to be taken into account under subsection (1) above there is to be subtracted the amount of that increase.

(3) For the purposes of subsection (1) above the relevant profits, subject to subsection (4) below, are—

(a) if the dividend is paid for a specified period, the profits of that period;

(b) if the dividend is not paid for a specified period, but is paid out of specified profits, those profits; and

(c) if the dividend is paid neither for a specified period nor out of specified profits, the profits of the last period for which accounts of the body corporate were made up which ended before the dividend became payable.

(4) If, in a case falling under paragraph (a) or (c) of subsection (3) above, the total dividend exceeds the profits available for distribution of the period mentioned in that paragraph the relevant profits shall be the profits of that period plus so much of the profits available for distribution of preceding periods (other than profits previously distributed or previously treated as relevant profits for the purposes of this section or section 506 of the 1970 Act) as is equal to the excess; and for the purposes of this subsection the profits of the most recent preceding period shall first be taken into account, then the profits of the next most recent preceding period, and so on.

Dividends paid between related companies but not covered by arrangements.

800. Where—

(a) arrangements provide, in relation to dividends of some classes but not in relation to dividends of other classes, that underlying tax is to be taken into account in considering whether any, and if so what, credit is to be allowed against the United Kingdom taxes in respect of the dividends; and

(b) a dividend is paid which is not of a class in relation to which the arrangements so provide;

then, if the dividend is paid to a company which controls directly or indirectly, or is a subsidiary of a company which controls directly or indirectly, not less than 10 per cent. of the voting power in the company paying the dividend, credit shall be allowed as if the dividend were a dividend of a class in relation to which the arrangements so provide.

Dividends paid between related companies: relief for U.K. and third country taxes.

801.—(1) Where a company resident outside the United Kingdom ("the overseas company") pays a dividend to a company resident in the United Kingdom ("the United Kingdom company") and the overseas company is related to the United Kingdom company, then for the purpose of allowing credit under any arrangements against corporation tax in respect of the dividend, there shall be taken into account, as if it were tax payable under the law of the territory in which the overseas company is resident—

(a) any United Kingdom income tax or corporation tax payable by the overseas company in respect of its profits; and

(b) any tax which, under the law of any other territory, is payable by the overseas company in respect of its profits.

(2) Where the overseas company has received a dividend from a third company and the third company is related to the overseas company, then, subject to subsection (4) below, there shall be treated for the purposes of subsection (1) above as tax paid by the overseas company in respect of its profits any underlying tax payable by the third company, to the extent that it would be taken into account under this Part if the dividend had been paid by a company resident outside the United Kingdom to a company resident in the United Kingdom and arrangements had provided for underlying tax to be taken into account.

(3) Where the third company has received a dividend from a fourth company and the fourth company is related to the third company, then, subject to subsection (4) below, tax payable by the fourth company shall similarly be treated for the purposes of subsection (2) above as tax paid by the third company; and so on for successive companies each of which is related to the one before.

(4) Subsections (2) and (3) above are subject to the following limitations—

(a) no tax shall be taken into account in respect of a dividend paid by a company resident in the United Kingdom except United Kingdom corporation tax and any tax for which that company is entitled to credit under this Part; and

(b) no tax shall be taken into account in respect of a dividend paid by a company resident outside the United Kingdom to another such company unless it could have been taken into account under the other provisions of this Part had the other company been resident in the United Kingdom.

(5) For the purposes of this section a company is related to another company if that other company—

(a) controls directly or indirectly, or

(b) is a subsidiary of a company which controls directly or indirectly,

not less than 10 per cent. of the voting power in the first-mentioned company.

802.—(1) Subject to subsection (2) below, where—

U.K. insurance companies trading overseas.

(a) a company resident in the United Kingdom is charged to tax under Case I of Schedule D in respect of any insurance business carried on by it, and

(b) that business or any part of it is carried on through a branch or agency in a territory outside the United Kingdom,

then, in respect of dividends referable to that business which are paid to the company by companies resident in that territory, any tax payable by those companies in respect of their profits under the law of that or any other territory outside the United Kingdom, and any United Kingdom income tax or corporation tax so payable, shall, in considering whether any and if so what credit is to be allowed under any arrangements, be taken into account as tax so payable under the law of the first-mentioned territory is taken into account in a case falling within section 799.

PART XVIII

(2) Credit shall not be allowed to a company by virtue of subsection (1) above for any financial year in respect of a greater amount of dividends paid by companies resident in any overseas territory than is equal to any excess of—

   (a) the relevant fraction of the company's total income in that year from investments (including franked investment income and group income) so far as referable to the business referred to in subsection (1) above;

over

   (b) the amount of the dividends so referable which are paid to it in the year by companies resident in that territory and in respect of which credit may, apart from subsection (1) above, be allowed to it for underlying tax.

(3) For the purposes of subsection (2) above the relevant fraction, in relation to any overseas territory, is—

$$\frac{A}{B}$$

where—

   A is the company's local premium income in the financial year so far as referable to the business referred to in subsection (1) above;

   B is the company's total premium income in the financial year so far as referable to that business;

and premium income shall be deemed to be local premium income in so far as it consists of premiums under contracts entered into at or through a branch or agency in that territory by persons not resident in the United Kingdom.

Underlying tax reflecting interest on loans.

803.—(1) This section applies in a case where—

   (a) a bank or a company connected with a bank makes a claim for an allowance by way of credit in accordance with this Chapter; and

   (b) the claim relates to underlying tax on a dividend paid by the overseas company, within the meaning of section 801; and

   (c) that underlying tax is or includes tax payable under the law of a territory outside the United Kingdom on or by reference to interest on a loan made in the course of its business by that overseas company or by such third, fourth or successive company as is referred to in subsection (2) or (3) of that section; and

   (d) if the company which made the loan had been resident in the United Kingdom, then, in determining its liability to corporation tax, expenditure related to the earning of the interest on the loan would be deductible in computing the profits of the company brought into charge to tax.

(2) In a case where this section applies, the amount of the credit for that part of the foreign tax which consists of the tax referred to in subsection (1)(c) above shall not exceed an amount determined under subsection (3) below.

(3) The amount referred to in subsection (2) above is a sum equal to corporation tax, at the rate in force at the time the foreign tax referred to in paragraph (c) of subsection (1) above was chargeable, on so much of the interest on the loan as exceeds the amount of the lender's relevant expenditure which is properly attributable to the period for which that interest is paid.

(4) In subsection (3) above—

(a) "interest", subject to subsection (5) below, has the meaning assigned to it by section 798(2); and

(b) "the lender's relevant expenditure" means the amount which, if the company referred to in subsection (1)(d) above were resident in the United Kingdom (and liable to tax accordingly) would be its financial expenditure in relation to the loan, as determined in accordance with section 798(6) to (10).

(5) If, in accordance with subsection (6) or subsection (8) below, the amount of the dividend would be treated for the purposes of corporation tax as increased or reduced by any amount, then the amount which, apart from this subsection, would be the amount of the interest referred to in subsection (3) above shall be taken to be increased or reduced by the same amount as the dividend is so treated as increased or reduced.

(6) If, in a case where this section applies, the underlying tax is or includes an amount of spared tax, then, for the purposes of corporation tax, the amount which apart from this subsection would be the amount of the dividend shall be treated as increased by an amount equal to so much of that spared tax as does not exceed the permitted amount; but nothing in this subsection prejudices the operation of section 795 in relation to foreign tax which is not spared tax.

(7) In this section—

(a) "spared tax" has the same meaning as in section 798; and

(b) the permitted amount, in relation to spared tax which is referable to the whole or any part of the interest referred to in subsection (1)(c) above, is an amount which does not exceed—

(i) 15 per cent. of the interest to which that spared tax is referable; or

(ii) if it is less, the amount of that spared tax which under any arrangements is to be taken into account for the purpose of allowing credit against corporation tax in respect of the dividend concerned.

(8) If, in a case where this section applies—

(a) the underlying tax is or includes an amount of tax which is not spared tax, and

(b) that amount of tax exceeds 15 per cent. of the interest to which it is referable, then, for the purposes of corporation tax, the amount which would apart from this subsection be the amount of the dividend shall be treated as reduced by a sum equal to the excess.

(9) Where this section applies, the amount of the credit referred to in paragraph (a) of subsection (1) above which is referable to the underlying tax payable as mentioned in paragraph (c) of that subsection shall not exceed 15 per cent. of so much of the interest referred to in that paragraph as is included in the relevant profits of the company paying the dividend; and for the purposes of this subsection—

(a) "relevant profits" has the same meaning as, by virtue of section 799, it has for the purposes of the computation of underlying tax; and

(b) the amount of the interest shall be determined without making any deduction in respect of any foreign tax.

(10) In subsection (1) above "bank" means a company carrying on, in the United Kingdom or elsewhere—

(a) a banking business; or

(b) another business which includes the making of loans where the circumstances of the business are such that, in determining the liability of the company to corporation tax, expenditure related to the earning of the interest on those loans is deductible in computing the profits brought into charge to tax;

and section 839 applies for the purposes of subsection (1) above.

(11) Where the loan referred to in subsection (1)(c) was made pursuant to an agreement entered into before 1st April 1987, subsections (2) to (5) above shall not apply in relation to tax payable as mentioned in subsection (1)(c) above by reference to interest payable before 1st April 1989, but subject to that, this section applies whenever the loan referred to in subsection (1)(c) was made.

Miscellaneous rules

Relief against income tax in respect of income arising in years of commencement.

804.—(1) Subject to the provisions of this section, credit for overseas tax paid in respect of any income arising in the years of commencement shall be allowed under this Part against United Kingdom income tax chargeable for any year of assessment in respect of that income if it would have been so allowed but for the fact that credit for that overseas tax had been allowed against the United Kingdom income tax chargeable in respect of that income for a previous year of assessment.

(2) The amount of credit to be allowed in respect of any income by virtue of this section for any year of assessment shall not exceed the difference between—

(a) the total credit allowable against income tax in respect of that income under this Part (including this section) for all years of assessment for which credit is so allowable; and

(b) the amount of credit which was in fact so allowed in respect of that income for any earlier year or years of assessment.

(3) The total credit so allowable in respect of any income for all those years of assessment shall be taken to be the amount of the overseas tax charged on that income, adjusted where the number of the United Kingdom periods of assessment exceeds the number of foreign periods of assessment, in the proportion which the former number bears to the latter, a period for which part only of the income is charged to tax being counted not as one period but as a fraction equal to the proportion which that part of the income bears to the whole of the income.

(4) Where the same income is charged to different overseas taxes for different foreign periods of assessment, subsection (3) above, so far as it relates to the adjustment of overseas tax, shall be applied separately to each of the overseas taxes, and the total credit allowable shall be the aggregate of those taxes after the making of any adjustments in accordance with that subsection as so applied.

(5) Where credit against income tax for any year of assessment is allowed by virtue of subsection (1) above in respect of any income ("the original income") and subsequently by reason of the enactments relating to cessations, income arising in a non-basis period from the same source as the original income is not assessed to income tax, then if the amount of credit allowed against income tax in respect of the original income under this Part (including this section) for all years of assessment for which credit is so allowable exceeds the aggregate of the following amounts—

    (a) the amount of the credit against income tax which would have been allowed apart from subsection (1) above for all those years in respect of the original income; and

    (b) the amount of the overseas tax for which, under this Part, credit would have been allowable against income tax in respect of income arising in the non-basis period from the same source as the original income,

the person chargeable in respect of income (if any) from the same source in the year of assessment following the non-basis period shall be treated as having received in that year a payment chargeable under Case VI of Schedule D of an amount such that income tax thereon at the basic rate is equal to the excess.

(6) Any payment which a person is treated by virtue of subsection (5) above as having received shall not on that account constitute income of his for any of the purposes of the Income Tax Acts other than that subsection and in particular no part thereof shall constitute profits or gains brought into charge to income tax for the purposes of section 348.

(7) Any claim for relief by way of credit under subsection (1) above against income tax for any year of assessment shall be made within six years of the end of that year or, where there is more than one year of assessment in respect of which such relief may be given, within six years of the end of the later of them.

(8) In this section—

    "overseas tax" means tax under the law of a territory outside the United Kingdom;

PART XVIII

"non-basis period" means a period the income arising in which is, by reason only of the operation of the enactments relating to cessations, not chargeable to United Kingdom income tax for any year of assessment;

"United Kingdom period of assessment" and "foreign period of assessment", in relation to any income, mean respectively a year or other period for which under the relevant law the income falls to be charged to the relevant tax;

"years of commencement", in relation to income from any source, means the first three years of assessment for which income from that source falls to be assessed to income tax, and also, in the case of profits or gains chargeable to tax under Case I or II of Schedule D, the whole of any period falling partly within those years such that the profits or gains arising in the period fall to be assessed to income tax for a year of assessment later than those years;

references to the enactments relating to cessations are references to sections 63, 67 and 113; and

references to income arising in any year include, in relation to income the income tax on which is to be computed by reference to the amount of income received in the United Kingdom, references to income received in that year.

Elections against credit.

805. Credit shall not be allowed under any arrangements against the United Kingdom taxes chargeable in respect of any income or chargeable gains of any person if he elects that credit shall not be allowed in respect of that income or those gains.

Time limit for claims etc.

806.—(1) Subject to subsection (2) below and section 804(7), any claim for an allowance under any arrangements by way of credit for foreign tax in respect of any income or chargeable gain shall be made not later than six years from the end of the chargeable period for which the income or the gain falls to be charged to income tax or corporation tax, or would fall to be so charged if any income tax or corporation tax were chargeable in respect of the income or gain.

(2) Where the amount of any credit given under the arrangements is rendered excessive or insufficient by reason of any adjustment of the amount of any tax payable either in the United Kingdom or under the laws of any other territory, nothing in the Tax Acts limiting the time for the making of assessments or claims for relief shall apply to any assessment or claim to which the adjustment gives rise, being an assessment or claim made not later than six years from the time when all such assessments, adjustments and other determinations have been made, whether in the United Kingdom or elsewhere, as are material in determining whether any and if so what credit falls to be given.

CHAPTER III

MISCELLANEOUS PROVISIONS

Sale of securities with or without accrued interest.

807.—(1) In any case where—

(a) a person is treated under section 714(2) as receiving annual profits or gains on the day an interest period ends; and

(b) assuming that, in the chargeable period in which the day falls, he were to become entitled to any interest on the securities concerned, he would be liable in respect of the interest to tax chargeable under Case IV or V of Schedule D; and

(c) he is liable under the law of a territory outside the United Kingdom to tax in respect of interest payable on the securities at the end of the interest period or he would be so liable if he were entitled to that interest,

credit of an amount equal to the relevant proportion of the profits or gains shall be allowed against any United Kingdom income tax or corporation tax computed by reference to the profits or gains, and shall be treated as if it were allowed under section 790(4).

In this subsection the relevant proportion is the rate of tax to which the person is or would be liable as mentioned in paragraph (c) above.

(2) In any case where—

(a) a person is entitled to credit against United Kingdom tax under section 790(4) or any corresponding provision of arrangements under section 788; and

(b) the tax is computed by reference to income consisting of interest which falls due on securities at the end of an interest period and which is treated as reduced by virtue of section 714(5);

then the amount of that credit shall be a proportion of the amount it would be apart from this subsection, and the proportion is to be found by applying the formula—

$$\frac{I - R}{I}$$

where—

I is the amount of the interest; and

R is the amount by which it is treated as reduced.

(3) Where the person entitled to the credit is an individual, subsection (2) above does not apply unless the interest arises from securities to which the person either became or ceased to be entitled during the interest period.

(4) Where section 811(1) applies to any income and, if credit were allowable in respect of it the credit would be reduced by virtue of subsection (2) above, section 811(1) shall have effect in relation to the income as if the reference to any sum paid in respect of tax on it were a reference to the amount which would be the amount of the credit if it were allowable and subsection (2) above applied.

(5) Sections 710 and 711 shall apply for the interpretation of this section.

PART XVIII
Restriction on
deduction of
interest or
dividends from
trading income.

808. In the case of a person not resident in the United Kingdom who carries on in the United Kingdom a banking business, an insurance business or a business consisting wholly or partly in dealing in securities, receipts of interest or dividend which have been treated as tax-exempt under arrangements having effect by virtue of section 788 are not to be excluded from trading income or profits of the business so as to give rise to losses to be set off (under section 393 or 436) against income or profits.

In this section "securities" includes stocks and shares.

Relief in respect of
discretionary
trusts.

809.—(1) In any case where—

(a) a payment made by trustees falls to be treated as a net amount in accordance with section 687(2) and the income arising under the trust includes any taxed overseas income, and

(b) the trustees certify that—

(i) the income out of which the payment was made was or included taxed overseas income of an amount and from a source stated in the certificate, and

(ii) that amount arose to them not earlier than six years before the end of the year of assessment in which the payment was made;

then the person to whom the payment was made may claim that the payment, up to the amount so certified, shall be treated for the purposes of this Part as income received by him from that source and so received in the year in which the payment was made.

(2) In subsection (1) above "taxed overseas income", in relation to any trust, means income in respect of which the trustees are entitled to credit for overseas tax under this Part.

Postponement of
capital
allowances to
secure double
taxation relief.

810.—(1) Where—

(a) a person chargeable to tax under Schedule D in respect of a trade is liable to overseas tax in respect of any income arising from the trade, being overseas tax for which relief may be given by way of credit, repayment or set off under the preceding provisions of this Part, and

(b) the conditions specified in subsection (2) below are satisfied,

he may, in claiming the relief in respect of that income, claim a postponement under this section of the relevant capital allowances operating to reduce that income for the purposes of tax for any chargeable period.

(2) The conditions are—

(a) that the law under which the overseas tax is chargeable provides for deductions or allowances to be given corresponding to capital allowances, but on a different basis such that they operate to reduce the income in question (if at all) to a less extent than the capital allowances to which the claim relates, but are calculated to operate to a greater extent than the corresponding capital allowances to reduce income arising subsequently; and

(b) that the relief falling to be so given in respect of the income in question is less than it would be if the capital allowances to which the claim relates operated to reduce the income to the same extent only as the deductions or allowances so provided for.

(3) Where a person claims a postponement under this section of capital allowances for any chargeable period, then—

(a) for the purposes of making the assessment for that period, the amount of those allowances shall be reduced by such amount as may be necessary to secure that they operate to reduce the income only to the extent mentioned in subsection (2)(b) above (or such less amount as the claimant may require); and

(b) for the purpose of making the assessment for the following period that amount shall be added to the amount of the allowances for that period, and shall be deemed to be part of those allowances or, if there are no such allowances for that period, shall be deemed to be the allowances for that period.

(4) For the purposes of any claim under this section—

(a) there shall be taken into account such only of the relevant capital allowances, and the deductions or allowances operating to reduce the income in question for purposes of the overseas tax, as are calculated to give relief in respect of the same expenditure or the same assets; and

(b) no account shall be taken of expenditure incurred or treated for the purposes of Chapter I of Part III of the Finance Act 1971 as incurred on or after 27th October 1970.

1971 c. 68.

(5) In this section "overseas tax" means tax chargeable under the laws of any territory outside the United Kingdom, and "relevant capital allowances", in relation to any trade, means capital allowances falling to be made in taxing the trade.

(6) This section applies (with any necessary adaptations) in relation to a profession, employment, vocation or office, and in relation to the occupation of woodlands the profits or gains of which are assessable under Schedule D, as it applies in relation to a trade.

811.—(1) For the purposes of the Tax Acts, the amount of any income arising in any place outside the United Kingdom shall, subject to subsection (2) below, be treated as reduced by any sum which has been paid in respect of tax on that income in the place where the income has arisen (that is to say, tax payable under the law of a territory outside the United Kingdom).

Deduction for foreign tax where no credit allowable.

(2) Subsection (1) above—

(a) shall not apply to income the tax on which is to be computed by reference to the amount of income received in the United Kingdom; and

(b) shall not affect section 278(3); and

(c) shall not affect the liability to tax of an overseas life insurance company for any accounting period for which a charge to corporation tax under Case III of Schedule D arises under section 445 in respect of any of its income from the investments of its life assurance fund (excluding the pension fund and general annuity fund, if any) or for which such a charge would arise if there were such income;

and this section has effect subject to section 795(2).

Withdrawal of right to tax credit of certain non-resident companies connected with unitary states.

812.—(1) In any case where—

(a) a company has, or is an associated company of a company which has, a qualifying presence in a unitary state, and

(b) at any time when it or its associated company has such a qualifying presence, the company is entitled by virtue of arrangements having effect under section 788(1) to a tax credit in respect of qualifying distributions made to it by companies which are resident in the United Kingdom which is equal to one half of the tax credit to which an individual resident in the United Kingdom would be entitled in respect of such distributions,

then, notwithstanding anything to the contrary in the arrangements, the company shall not be entitled to claim under section 231(3) to have that tax credit set against the income tax chargeable on its income for the year of assessment in which the distribution is made or, where the credit exceeds that income tax, to have the excess paid to it.

(2) In this section and sections 813 and 814, "unitary state" means a province, state or other part of a territory outside the United Kingdom with the government of which the arrangements referred to in subsection (1) above have been made which, in taxing the income or profits of companies from sources within that province, state or other part, takes into account, or is entitled to take into account, income, receipts, deductions, outgoings or assets of such companies, or associated companies of such companies, arising, expended or situated, as the case may be, outside that territory and which has been prescribed under subsection (6) below as a unitary state for the purposes of this subsection.

(3) A company shall be treated as having a qualifying presence in a unitary state if it is a member of a group and, in any period for which members of the group make up their accounts ending after the relevant date, $7\frac{1}{2}$ per cent. or more in value of the property, payroll or sales of such members situated in, attributable to or derived from the territory outside the United Kingdom, of which that state is a province, state or other part, are situated in, attributable to or derived from that state.

(4) For the purposes of subsection (3) above—

(a) $7\frac{1}{2}$ per cent. or more in value of such property, payroll or sales as are referred to in that subsection shall be treated as being situated in, attributable to or derived from the state there referred to, unless, on making any claim under section 231(3), the claimant proves otherwise to the satisfaction of the Board; and

   (b) the value of the property, payroll or sales of a company shall be taken to be the value as shown in its accounts for the period in question and for this purpose the value of any property consisting of an interest in another member of the group or of any sales made to another such member shall be disregarded.

(5) Except where the context otherwise requires, in this section and sections 813 to 815—

   (a) "arrangements" means the arrangements referred to in subsection (1) above;

   (b) "group" and "member of a group" shall be construed in accordance with section 272(1) of the 1970 Act with the omission of the restriction in paragraph (a) of that subsection and the substitution of the words "51 per cent." for the words "75 per cent." wherever they occur;

   (c) section 839 applies;

   (d) section 416 applies with the substitution of the words "six years" for "one year" in subsection (1); and

   (e) "the relevant date" means the earliest of the following dates—

      (i) the date on which this section comes into force;

      (ii) the earliest date on which a distribution could have been made in relation to which the provisions of this section and sections 813 and 814 are applied by an order under this section;

      (iii) the earliest date on which a distribution could have been made in relation to which the provisions of section 54 of the Finance Act 1985 were applied by an order under that section.

1985 c. 54.

(6) The Treasury may by order prescribe those provinces, states or other parts of a territory outside the United Kingdom which are to be treated as unitary states for the purposes of subsection (2) above, but no province, state or other part of such a territory shall be so prescribed which only takes into account such income, receipts, deductions, outgoings or assets as are mentioned in that subsection—

   (a) if the associated company was incorporated under the law of the territory; or

   (b) for the purpose of granting relief in taxing dividends received by companies.

(7) The Treasury may by order prescribe that for subsections (3) and (4) above (or for those subsections as they have effect at any time) there shall be substituted either the following provisions—

      "(3) A company shall be treated as having a qualifying presence in a unitary state if it is subject to tax in such a state for any period ending after the relevant date for which that state charges tax.

      (4) For the purposes of subsection (3) above a company shall be regarded as subject to tax in a unitary state if it is liable there to a tax charged on its income or

profits by whatever name called and shall be treated as so charged unless it proves otherwise to the satisfaction of the Board.";

or the following provisions—

"(3) A company shall be treated as having a qualifying presence in a unitary state if it has its principal place of business in such a state at any time after the relevant date.

(4) For the purposes of subsection (3) above—

(a) a company shall be treated as having its principal place of business in a unitary state unless it proves otherwise to the satisfaction of the Board; and

(b) the principal place of business of a company shall include both the place where central management and control of the company is exercised and the place where the immediate day-to-day management of the company as a whole is exercised.".

(8) The provisions of this section and sections 813 to 815 shall come into force on such date as the Treasury may by order appoint and the Treasury may in the order prescribe that those provisions shall apply in relation to distributions made, in accounting periods ending after 5th April 1988, before the date on which the order is made.

(9) No order shall be made under this section unless a draft of it has been laid before and approved by a resolution of the House of Commons.

Recovery of tax credits incorrectly paid.

813.—(1) Where—

(a) section 812 applies so as to withdraw the entitlement of a company to claim to have a tax credit in respect of a qualifying distribution set against the income tax chargeable on its income and to have the excess of the credit over that income tax paid to it; and

(b) the company ("the recipient company") has either had that excess paid to it, or has received an additional amount in accordance with arrangements made under Regulation 2(1) of the Double Taxation Relief (Taxes on Income) (General) (Dividend) Regulations 1973;

S.I. 1973/317.

the recipient company shall be liable to a fine for the violation of the provisions of section 812 equal to twice the amount of the excess or the additional amount, as the case may be.

(2) Any fine payable under subsection (1) above—

(a) shall be payable to the Board;

(b) shall be treated as having become payable at the date when the excess or additional amount was paid to the recipient company; and

(c) may be recovered in accordance with subsections (3) to (7) below;

and any such fine is referred to below as "the recoverable amount".

(3) The recoverable amount may be assessed and recovered as if it were unpaid tax and section 30 of the Management Act (recovery of overpayment of tax etc.) shall apply accordingly.

(4) Any amount which may be assessed and recovered as if it were unpaid tax by virtue of this section shall carry interest at the rate of 9 per cent. per annum from the date when it was payable in accordance with subsection (1) above until the date it is paid.

(5) It is hereby declared that this section applies to a recoverable amount which is paid without the making of an assessment (but is paid after it is due) and that, where the recoverable amount is charged by any assessment (whether or not any part of it has been paid when the assessment is made), this section applies in relation to interest running before, as well as after, the making of the assessment.

(6) Where the recoverable amount is not paid by the recipient company within six months from the date on which it became payable—

   (a) the recoverable amount may at any time within six years from the date on which it became payable be assessed and recovered as if it were unpaid tax due from any person who—

      (i) is or was at any time prior to the expiration of that six year period connected with the recipient company, or

      (ii) would have been connected on the assumption that all the facts and circumstances relating to the recipient company at the time the excess or additional amount, as the case may be, was paid continued to apply for six years thereafter,

   and section 30 of the Management Act shall apply accordingly; and

   (b) as respects its accounting periods beginning with that in which the excess or additional amount referred to in subsection (1) above was paid and ending with that following that in which the recoverable amount is paid in accordance with the provisions of this section, the company which made the qualifying distribution in respect of which the recipient company received the excess or additional amount shall not be entitled—

      (i) to set any advance corporation tax paid by it against its liability to corporation tax for such periods in accordance with section 239; nor

      (ii) to surrender the benefit of the whole or any part of any amount of advance corporation tax to a subsidiary in accordance with section 240 in such periods.

(7) Where a recoverable amount is assessed and recovered from a person connected with the recipient company in accordance with subsection (6)(a) above, that person shall be liable for the interest payable in accordance with subsection (4) above, and until the interest is so paid, subsection (6)(b) above shall apply as if the words "the interest due in accordance with subsection (4) above is paid" were substituted for the words "the recoverable amount is paid in accordance with the provisions of this section".

(8) Interest payable under this section shall be paid without any deduction of income tax and shall not be allowed as a deduction in computing any income, profits or losses for any tax purposes.

(9) Where under the law in force in a territory outside the United Kingdom interest is payable subject to a deduction in respect of taxation and such deduction applies to an amount of interest paid in accordance with subsection (4) above, the reference to the rate of 9 per cent. per annum in that subsection shall be deemed to be a reference to such rate of interest as after such deduction shall be equal to the rate of 9 per cent. per annum.

Arrangements to avoid section 812.

814.—(1) In any case where arrangements are made, whether before or after the coming into force of this section, as a result of which interest is paid or a discount is allowed by or through a person who is resident in the United Kingdom, or carries on business in the United Kingdom through a branch or agency, and it is reasonable to suppose that, if such payment or allowance had not been made, a qualifying distribution would have been made by that person, or by another company resident in the United Kingdom to a company which has, or is an associated company of a company which has, a qualifying presence in a unitary state at the time when the payment or allowance is made, then—

(a) no person who receives that payment or allowance shall be entitled to relief from income tax or corporation tax thereon by virtue of arrangements having effect under section 788(1); and

(b) the payment or allowance shall not be allowed as a deduction in computing any income, profits or losses for any tax purposes.

(2) Without prejudice to the generality of subsection (1) above, where a payment or allowance is not of itself a payment or allowance to which that subsection applies, but is made in conjunction with other payments of whatever nature and taken together with those payments has substantially similar effect to a distribution, then, for the purposes of subsection (1) above it shall be treated as a payment or allowance within that subsection.

(3) Any company which has received such a payment of interest as is referred to in subsection (1) above, from which income tax has not been deducted by the person making the payment, and has a qualifying presence in a unitary state at the time of the payment, shall be treated for the purposes of section 813 as a company—

(a) from which the entitlement to claim payment of the excess of a tax credit over the income tax chargeable on its income has been withdrawn by section 812(1), and

(b) which has had paid to it such an excess in an amount equal to the income tax which should have been deducted from the payment of interest.

Power to inspect documents.

815. Where it appears to the Board that the provisions of sections 812 to 814 may apply to a company resident outside the United Kingdom ("the foreign parent"), the Board may, by notice given to the foreign parent or any associated company of the foreign parent, require that company within such time (not being less than 30 days) as may be specified in the notice to make available for inspection any books, accounts or other documents or records whatsoever of that company where in the opinion of the Board it is proper that they should inspect such documents for the purposes of ascertaining whether those provisions apply to the foreign parent or such associated company notwithstanding that in the opinion of the person to whom the notice is given those provisions do not apply to that company or any associated company of that company.

816.—(1) Where under the law in force in any territory outside the United Kingdom provision is made for the allowance, in respect of the payment of United Kingdom income tax or corporation tax, of relief from tax payable under that law, the obligation as to secrecy imposed by the Tax Acts upon persons employed in relation to Inland Revenue shall not prevent the disclosure to the authorised officer of the government of the territory in question of such facts as may be necessary to enable the proper relief to be given under that law.

Disclosure of information.

Section 790(12) shall apply for the interpretation of this subsection as it applies for the interpretation of that section.

(2) Where any arrangements have effect by virtue of section 788, the obligation as to secrecy imposed by any enactment shall not prevent the Board, or any authorised officer of the Board, from disclosing to any authorised officer of the government with which the arrangements are made such information as is required to be disclosed under the arrangements.

(3) Where a person beneficially entitled to income from any securities as defined by section 24 of the Management Act (information as to income from securities) is resident in a territory to which arrangements having effect under section 788 with respect to income tax or corporation tax relate, section 24(3) of that Act shall not exempt any bank from the duty of disclosing to the Board particulars relating to the income of that person.

(4) The obligation as to secrecy imposed by any enactments with regard to income tax or corporation tax shall not prevent the disclosure, to any authorised officer of any country to which a declaration made under section 514 of the 1970 Act (agreements about shipping etc.) relates, of such facts as may be necessary to enable relief to be duly given in accordance with the arrangements specified in the declaration.

PART XIX

SUPPLEMENTAL

Miscellaneous

Deductions not to be allowed in computing profits or gains.

817.—(1) In arriving at the amount of profits or gains for tax purposes—

(a) no other deductions shall be made than such as are expressly enumerated in the Tax Acts; and

(b) no deduction shall be made on account of any annuity or other annual payment (not being interest) to be paid out of such profits or gains in regard that a proportionate part of income tax is allowed to be deducted on making any such payment.

(2) In arriving at the amount of profits or gains from any property described in the Tax Acts, or from any office or employment, no deduction shall be made on account of diminution of capital employed, or of loss sustained, in any trade or in any profession, employment or vocation.

Arrangements for payments of interest less tax or of fixed net amount.

818.—(1) It is hereby declared that any provision made before or after the passing of this Act, whether orally or in writing, for the payment of interest "less tax", or using words to that effect, is to be construed, in relation to interest payable without deduction of tax, as if the words "less tax", or the equivalent words, were not included.

(2) In relation to interest on which the recipient is chargeable to tax under Case III of Schedule D, and which is payable without deduction of tax, any provision, made before or after the passing of this Act, whether orally or in writing, and however worded, for the payment of interest at such a rate ("the gross rate") as shall, after the deduction of income tax, be equal to a stated rate, shall be construed as if it were a provision requiring the payment of interest at the gross rate.

Old references to standard rate tax.

819.—(1) Where any provision, however worded, contained in an instrument (of whatever nature) made on or after 3rd September 1939 or in a will or codicil taking effect on or after that date provides for the payment, whether periodically or otherwise—

(a) of a stated amount free of income tax other than surtax; or

(b) of an amount which, after deduction of income tax at the standard rate, is equal to a stated amount;

it shall have effect as follows.

(2) If it is such a provision as is mentioned in subsection (1)(a) above it shall have effect as if it provided for the payment of the stated amount free of income tax other than such as exceeds the amount to which the person to whom the payment is made would be liable if all income tax were charged at the basic rate to the exclusion of any higher rate.

(3) If it is such a provision as is mentioned in subsection (1)(b) above it shall have effect as if it provided for the payment of an amount which after deduction of income tax at the basic rate is equal to the stated amount.

(4) Any instrument however worded conferring on any person a right to receive a dividend or interest the amount of which depends on the standard rate of income tax shall have effect as if instead of referring to the standard rate it referred to the basic rate.

(5) Any reference in a statutory instrument made under the Tax Acts to the standard rate of income tax shall have effect as if it were a reference to the basic rate.

820. In order to ensure the collection in due time of income tax which may be granted for any year commencing on 6th April, all such provisions contained in the Income Tax Acts as were in force on the preceding day shall have full force and effect with respect to tax which may be so granted, in the same manner as if that tax had been actually granted by Act of Parliament and those provisions had been applied thereto by the Act.

Application of Income Tax Acts from year to year.

821.—(1) Where, in any year of assessment, any half-yearly or quarterly payments have been made on account of any interest, dividends or other annual profits or gains, previously to the passing of the Act imposing income tax for that year, and tax has not been charged thereon or deducted therefrom or has not been charged thereon or deducted therefrom at the rate ultimately imposed for that year—

Under-deductions from payments made before passing of annual Act.

   (a) the amount not so charged or deducted shall be charged under Schedule D in respect of those payments, as profits or gains not charged by virtue of any other Schedule, under Case VI of Schedule D; and

   (b) the agents entrusted with the payment of the interest, dividends or other annual profits or gains shall furnish to the Board a list containing the names and addresses of the persons to whom payments have been made and the amount of those payments, upon a requisition made by the Board in that behalf.

(2) Any person liable to pay any rent, interest or annuity, or to make any other annual payment—

   (a) shall be authorised—

      (i) to make any deduction on account of income tax for any year of assessment which he has failed to make previously to the passing of the Act imposing the tax for that year, or

      (ii) to make up any deficiency in any such deduction which has been so made,

   on the occasion of the next payment of the rent, interest or annuity or making of the other annual payment after the passing of the Act so imposing the tax, in addition to any other deduction which he may be by law authorised to make; and

   (b) shall also be entitled, if there is no future payment from which the deduction may be made, to recover the sum which might have been deducted as if it were a debt due from the person as against whom the deduction could originally have been made if the Act imposing the tax for the year had been in force.

(3) Subsection (2) above shall apply with respect to—

(a) any payment for or in respect of copyright to which section 536 applies or of public lending right to which that section applies by virtue of section 537; and

(b) any royalty or other sum paid in respect of the user of a patent; and

(c) any rent, royalty or other payment which by section 119 or 120 is declared to be subject to deduction of tax under section 348 or 349 as if it were a royalty or other sum paid in respect of the user of a patent;

as it applies with respect to any rent, interest, annuity or other annual payment.

(4) In this section "interest" and "dividends" do not include any interest or dividend which is a distribution.

Over-deductions from interest on loan capital etc. made before passing of annual Act.

1968 c. 2.

822.—(1) If in any year of assessment ("the year") a resolution having statutory effect under the Provisional Collection of Taxes Act 1968 provides for the charging of income tax at a basic rate lower than that charged for the previous year, the following provisions of this section shall have effect with respect to deductions in respect of income tax by any body corporate, from payments of interest (not being a distribution) on any of its securities.

(2) Any deduction which was made before the expiration of one month from the passing of the resolution and which would, if the tax had been renewed at the rate imposed for the previous year, have been a legal deduction, shall be deemed to be a deduction rendered legal by section 2 of the Provisional Collection of Taxes Act 1968 and that section shall, subject to this section, apply accordingly.

(3) Any over-deduction to be made good under that section may be made good by a reduction of the amount of tax deducted from the next payment of like nature made on the security in question after the passing of the Act imposing the tax for the year.

(4) Any amount made good under section 2 of the Provisional Collection of Taxes Act 1968 shall—

(a) in the case of an over-deduction which is made good under subsection (3) above, enure to the benefit of the person entitled to the payment on the occasion of which the over-deduction is made good; and

(b) in any other case, enure to the benefit of the person entitled to the security in question at the date when the amount is made good,

irrespective, in either case, of whether or not he is the person who was entitled to the payment, or to the security at the date when the original deduction was made.

(5) Subsection (3) above shall not authorise the retention of any part of the amount over-deducted for more than one year from the passing of the Act imposing the tax for the year.

Adjustments of reliefs where given at different times.

823. Where under the provisions of the Income Tax Acts an individual—

  (a) is entitled to claim relief from income tax (other than relief in respect of life insurance premiums), by repayment or otherwise, in respect of—

       (i) any amount which is paid or borne by him out of his income or which is allowable or may be deducted from his income; or

       (ii) any reduction of an assessment relating to his income or any part of his income; or

       (iii) any adjustment or set-off with regard to a loss; and

  (b) claims that relief for any year of assessment,

any relief granted shall not extend so as to make the total income tax paid or payable by him for that year less than it would have been if the amount in respect of which relief is claimed had been deducted in computing his total income for that year and the amount of any other deductions or reliefs to which he is entitled for that year had been determined accordingly.

824.—(1) Subject to the provisions of this section, where—

  (a) income tax has been paid by or on behalf of an individual for a year of assessment for which he was resident in the United Kingdom; and

  (b) a repayment of that tax of not less than £25 is made by the Board or an inspector after the end of the 12 months following that year of assessment;

the repayment shall be increased under this section by an amount (a "repayment supplement") equal to interest on the amount repaid at the rate of 8.25 per cent. per annum for the period (if any) between the relevant time and the end of the tax month in which the order for the repayment is issued.

(2) Subsection (1) above shall with the necessary modifications apply to a payment of the whole or part of a tax credit as it applies to a repayment falling within that subsection of income tax paid in the year of assessment to which the tax credit relates.

(3) For the purposes of subsection (1) above—

  (a) if the repayment is of tax that was paid after the end of the 12 months following the year of assessment for which it was payable, the relevant time is the end of the year of assessment in which that tax was paid;

  (b) in any other case, the relevant time is the end of the 12 months mentioned in that subsection;

and, subject to subsection (5) below, where a repayment to which subsection (1) above applies is of tax paid in two or more years of assessment, the repayment shall as far as possible be treated for the purposes of this subsection as a repayment of tax paid in a later rather than an earlier year among those years.

PART XIX

(4) For the purposes of subsections (1) and (3) above, income tax deducted by virtue of regulations made under section 203 from a person's emoluments during any year of assessment shall (without prejudice to subsection (5) below) be treated as paid by him for that and no other year of assessment.

(5) Where in consequence of an assessment under Schedule E for any year of assessment there is made by the Board or an inspector a repayment of income tax of not less than £25, being an amount which takes account of tax overpaid or remaining unpaid for one or more earlier years of assessment, then—

(a) the repayment shall for the purposes of this subsection be attributable to such of the years in question, and in such proportions, as may be determined in accordance with regulations made under and for the purposes of this subsection by the Board; and

(b) subsections (1) and (3) above shall have effect in relation to so much of the repayment as is by virtue of paragraph (a) above attributed to any particular year of assessment as if in subsection (1) the words "of not less than £25" were omitted.

(6) The Treasury may by order from time to time increase or decrease the rate of interest by reference to which—

(a) repayment supplements are calculated under subsection (1) above; and

1975 c. 45.

(b) repayment supplements are calculated under section 47 of the Finance (No. 2) Act 1975.

(7) A repayment supplement shall not be payable under this section in respect of a repayment or payment made in consequence of an order or judgment of a court having power to allow interest on the repayment or payment, or in respect of a repayment of a post-war credit within the meaning of the Income Tax (Repayment of Post-War Credits) Act 1959.

1959 c. 28.

(8) A repayment supplement paid to any person under this section or under section 47 of the Finance (No. 2) Act 1975 shall not be income of that person for any tax purposes.

(9) Subsections (1) to (8) above shall apply in relation to a partnership, or a United Kingdom trust (as defined in section 231), or, in the case of a United Kingdom estate, the personal representatives of a deceased person as such (within the meaning of section 701) as they apply in relation to an individual.

(10) In this section—

"tax month" means the period beginning with the 6th day of any calendar month and ending with the 5th day of the following calendar month;

"United Kingdom estate" has the meaning given by section 701.

Repayment supplements: companies.

825.—(1) This section applies to the following payments made to a company in connection with any accounting period for which the company was resident in the United Kingdom ("the relevant accounting period"), that is to say—

(a) a repayment of corporation tax paid by the company for that accounting period (including advance corporation tax paid in respect of distributions made by the company in that accounting period and any sum paid in respect of that period on an assessment under section 430(7)(a)); or

(b) a repayment of income tax in respect of a payment received by the company in that accounting period on which the company bore income tax by deduction; or

(c) a payment of the whole or part of the tax credit comprised in any franked investment income received by the company in that accounting period.

(2) Subject to the following provisions of this section, where a payment of not less than £100 to which this section applies is made by the Board or an inspector after the end of the 12 months beginning with the material date, the payment shall be increased under this section by an amount (a "repayment supplement") equal to interest on the amount paid at the rate of 8.25 per cent. per annum for each complete tax month contained in the period (if any) beginning with the relevant date and ending at the end of the tax month in which the order for the payment is issued.

(3) For the purposes of subsection (2) above—

(a) if the payment is a repayment of corporation tax that was paid on or after the first anniversary of the material date, the relevant date is the anniversary of the material date that occurs next after the date on which that tax was paid;

(b) in any other case, the relevant date is the first anniversary of the material date;

and where a payment to which this section applies is a repayment of corporation tax paid by a company on different dates, the payment shall as far as possible be treated for the purposes of this subsection as a repayment of tax paid on a later rather than an earlier date among those dates.

(4) For the purposes of this section—

(a) a repayment of corporation tax made in consequence of a claim by a company under section 239(3) to have the whole or any part of an amount of surplus advance corporation tax arising in the case of any accounting period treated as if it were advance corporation tax paid in respect of distributions made by the company in any earlier accounting period shall be treated as a repayment of corporation tax paid for the accounting period in the case of which that amount of surplus advance corporation tax arose; and

(b) a repayment of income tax or corporation tax made on a claim under subsection (4) of section 419 shall be treated as if it were a repayment of corporation tax paid for the accounting period in which the repayment of, or of the part in question of, the loan or advance mentioned in that subsection was made.

(5) The Treasury may by order from time to time increase or decrease the rate of interest by reference to which repayment supplements are calculated under subsection (2) above.

(6) A repayment supplement shall not be payable under this section in respect of a payment made in consequence of an order or judgment of a court having power to allow interest on the payment.

(7) A repayment supplement paid under this section shall be disregarded for all purposes of income tax and corporation tax.

(8) In this section—

"tax month" means the period beginning with the 6th day of any calendar month and ending with the 5th day of the following calendar month;

"the material date" in relation to a payment to which this section applies, means the last date on which corporation tax on any of the profits of the company in question arising in the relevant accounting period could have been paid—

(a) in a case where section 10(1) applies, within the nine months there mentioned;

(b) in a case where section 478 applies, within the time limit imposed by subsection (2)(a) of that section, but subject to subsection (6) of that section.

(9) This section has effect subject to section 826(8).

Interest on tax overpaid.

826.—(1) In any case where—

(a) a repayment falls to be made of corporation tax paid by a company for an accounting period which ends after the appointed day; or

(b) a repayment of income tax falls to be made in respect of a payment received by a company in such an accounting period; or

(c) a payment falls to be made to a company of the whole or part of the tax credit comprised in any franked investment income received by the company in such an accounting period,

then, from the material date until that repayment or payment is made, the repayment or payment shall carry interest at the rate which, under section 89 of the Management Act, is for the time being the prescribed rate for the purposes of this section.

(2) In relation to corporation tax paid by a company for an accounting period, the material date for the purposes of this section is the date on which corporation tax was paid or, if it is later, the date on which corporation tax for that accounting period became (or, as the case may be, would have become) due and payable in accordance with section 10.

(3) In relation to a repayment of income tax falling within subsection (1)(b) above or a payment of the whole or part of a tax credit falling within subsection (1)(c) above, the material date is the date on which corporation tax became (or, as the case may be, would have become) due and payable for the accounting period in which the payment referred to in subsection (1)(b) above or, as the case may be, the franked investment income referred to in subsection (1)(c) above was received by the company.

(4) For the purposes of this section a repayment of tax made on a claim under section 419(4) shall be treated as if it were a repayment of corporation tax for the accounting period in which the repayment of, or of the part in question of, the loan or advance mentioned in section 419(4) was made but, in relation to such a repayment of tax, the material date for the purposes of this section is—

(a) the date on which the loan or advance (or part thereof) is repaid; or

(b) if it is later, the date on which the tax which is to be repaid was in fact paid.

(5) Interest paid under this section shall be paid without any deduction of income tax and shall not be brought into account in computing any profits or income.

(6) Where a repayment of corporation tax is a repayment of tax paid by a company on different dates, the repayment shall so far as possible be treated for the purposes of this section as a repayment of tax paid on a later rather than an earlier date among those dates.

(7) In any case where—

(a) there is in any accounting period of a company ("the later period") an amount of surplus advance corporation tax, as defined in section 239(3); and

(b) pursuant to a claim under section 239(3), the whole or any part of that amount is treated for the purposes of section 239 as discharging liability for an amount of corporation tax for an earlier accounting period ("the earlier period"); and

(c) a repayment falls to be made of corporation tax made for the earlier period,

then, in determining the amount of interest (if any) payable under this section on the repayment of corporation tax for the earlier period, no account shall be taken of any increase in the amount of the repayment resulting from section 239(3) except so far as concerns interest for any time after the date on which any corporation tax for the later period became due and payable (as mentioned in subsection (2) above).

(8) In consequence of the preceding provisions of this section, no repayment supplement (within the meaning of section 825) shall be paid in respect of any repayment of tax or payment of tax credit where the relevant accounting period (within the meaning of that section) ends after the appointed day.

(9) In this section "the appointed day" means such day or days, not being earlier than 31st March 1992, as the Treasury may by order appoint for the purposes of this section.

827.—(1) Where, under Chapter II of Part I of the Finance Act 1985 (value added tax), a person is liable to make a payment by way of— VAT penalties etc. 1985 c. 54.

(a) penalty under any of sections 13 to 17; or

(b) interest under section 18; or

(c) surcharge under section 19;

the payment shall not be allowed as a deduction in computing any income, profits or losses for any tax purposes.

1985 c. 54.

(2) A sum paid to any person by way of supplement under section 20 of the Finance Act 1985 (VAT repayment supplements) shall be disregarded for all purposes of corporation tax and income tax.

Orders and regulations made by the Treasury or the Board.

828.—(1) Subject to subsection (2) below, any power of the Treasury or the Board to make any order or regulations under this Act or under any other provision of the Tax Acts (including enactments passed after this Act) shall be exercisable by statutory instrument.

(2) Subsection (1) above shall not apply in relation to any power conferred by section 124(6) or 841(1)(b) or paragraph 15(4) of Schedule 3.

(3) Subject to subsection (4) below and to any other provision to the contrary, any statutory instrument containing any order or regulations made by the Treasury or the Board under this Act or under any other provision of the Tax Acts (including enactments passed after this Act) shall be subject to annulment in pursuance of a resolution of the House of Commons.

(4) Subsection (3) above shall not apply in relation to an order or regulations made under section 1(6), 257(11), 324, 376(5), 377(8), 658(3) or 791 or paragraph 7 of Schedule 14 or—

(a) if any other Parliamentary procedure is expressly provided;

(b) if the order in question is an order appointing a day for the purposes of any provision of the Tax Acts, being a day as from which the provision will have effect, with or without amendments, or will cease to have effect.

Application of Income Tax Acts to public departments and avoidance of exempting provisions.

829.—(1) Subject to subsections (2) and (3) below, all the provisions of the Income Tax Acts relating to the assessment, charge, deduction and payment of income tax shall apply in relation to public offices and departments of the Crown.

(2) Nothing in those provisions of the Income Tax Acts shall require the payment by any such office or department of any tax which would be ultimately borne by the Crown.

(3) Subsection (1) above shall not apply to public offices and departments of any country, state, province or colony within section 320(3)(b) or (c) and nothing in subsection (1) above shall exempt any government from taxation to which it is liable in connection with any

1925 c. 36.

office or department by virtue of section 25 of the Finance Act 1925 (liability in respect of trading operations of Dominion governments and others).

(4) No letters patent granted or to be granted by the Crown to any person, city, borough or town corporate of any liberty, privilege or exemption from subsidies, tolls, taxes, assessments or aids, and no statute which grants any salary, annuity or pension to any person free of any taxes, deductions or assessments, shall be construed or taken to exempt any person, city, borough or town corporate, or any inhabitant of any city, borough or town corporate, from income tax, and all non-obstantes in any such letters patent or statute made or to be made to the contrary effect shall be void.

830.—(1) The territorial sea of the United Kingdom shall for all purposes of income tax and corporation tax (including the following provisions of this section) be deemed to be part of the United Kingdom.

(2) In this section—

   (a) "exploration or exploitation activities" means activities carried on in connection with the exploration or exploitation of so much of the seabed and subsoil and their natural resources as is situated in the United Kingdom or a designated area;

   (b) "exploration or exploitation rights" means rights to assets to be produced by exploration or exploitation activities or to interests in or to the benefit of such assets; and

   (c) "designated area" means an area designated by Order in Council under section 1(7) of the Continental Shelf Act 1964.

1964 c. 29.

(3) Any profits or gains from exploration or exploitation activities carried on in a designated area or from exploration or exploitation rights shall be treated for the purposes of income tax or corporation tax as profits or gains from activities or property in the United Kingdom.

(4) Any profits or gains arising to any person not resident in the United Kingdom from exploration or exploitation activities or rights shall for the purposes of corporation tax be treated as profits or gains of a trade carried on by that person in the United Kingdom through a branch or agency.

(5) Any emoluments from an office or employment in respect of duties performed in a designated area in connection with exploration or exploitation activities shall be treated for the purposes of income tax as emoluments in respect of duties performed in the United Kingdom.

Interpretation

831.—(1) In this Act, except so far as the context otherwise requires—

Interpretation of this Act.

   (a) "the Corporation Tax Acts" means the enactments relating to the taxation of the income and chargeable gains of companies and of company distributions (including provisions relating also to income tax); and

   (b) "the Income Tax Acts" means the enactments relating to income tax, including any provisions of the Corporation Tax Acts which relate to income tax.

(2) In this Act "the Tax Acts", except so far as the context otherwise requires, means this Act and all other provisions of the Income Tax Acts and the Corporation Tax Acts.

(3) In this Act—

"the Management Act" means the Taxes Management Act 1970;   1970 c. 9

"the 1968 Act" means the Capital Allowances Act 1968;   1968 c. 3.

"the 1970 Act" means the Income and Corporation Taxes Act 1970; and   1970 c. 10.

"the 1979 Act" means the Capital Gains Tax Act 1979.   1979 c. 14.

PART XIX
1987 c. 42.
1978 c. 30.
1986 c. 9.

(4) Section 1 of the Family Law Reform Act 1987, the paragraph inserted in Schedule 1 to the Interpretation Act 1978 by paragraph 73 of Schedule 2 to that Act and section 1(3) of the Law Reform (Parent and Child) (Scotland) Act 1986 (legal equality of illegitimate children) shall be disregarded in construing references in this Act to a child or to children (however expressed).

(5) This Act, so far as it relates to capital gains tax, shall be construed as one with the 1979 Act.

(6) Any reference in this Act to a section, Part or Schedule is a reference to that section, Part or Schedule of or to this Act, unless the context otherwise requires.

Interpretation of
the Tax Acts.

832.—(1) In the Tax Acts, except in so far as the context otherwise requires—

"Act" includes an Act of the Parliament of Northern Ireland and a Measure of the Northern Ireland Assembly;

"additional rate", in relation to income tax for any year of assessment, means the rate of income tax determined by subtracting the basic rate for that year from the rate of tax which for that year is applicable to the second higher rate band;

"authorised unit trust" has the meaning given by section 468(6);

"basic rate", in relation to the charging of income tax for any year of assessment, means the rate of income tax determined in pursuance of section 1(2)(a), and any reference to the basic rate limit shall be construed in accordance with section 1(3);

"the Board" means the Commissioners of Inland Revenue;

"body of persons" means any body politic, corporate or collegiate, and any company, fraternity, fellowship and society of persons whether corporate or not corporate;

1986 c. 53.

"building society" means a building society within the meaning of the Building Societies Act 1986;

"capital allowance" means any allowance under the Capital Allowances Acts;

1971 c. 68.
1986 c. 41.

"the Capital Allowances Acts" means the 1968 Act, Chapter I of Part III of the Finance Act 1971 and Part III of Schedule 13 and Schedule 15 to the Finance Act 1986 (including enactments which under this Act or the 1970 Act are to be treated as contained in Part I of the 1968 Act);

"chargeable gain" has the same meaning as in the 1979 Act;

"chargeable period" means an accounting period of a company or a year of assessment;

"close company" has the meaning given by sections 414 and 415;

"collector" means any collector of taxes;

"company" means, subject to subsection (2) below, any body corporate or unincorporated association but does not include a partnership, a local authority or a local authority association;

"distribution" has the meaning given by Part VI with section 418;

"farm land" means land in the United Kingdom wholly or mainly occupied for the purposes of husbandry, but excluding any dwelling or domestic offices, and excluding market garden land, and "farming" shall be construed accordingly;

"franked investment income" shall be construed in accordance with section 238, but subject to section 247(1);

"franked payment" shall be construed in accordance with section 238, but subject to section 247(1);

"group income" has the meaning given by section 247(2);

"higher rate", in relation to the charging of income tax for any year of assessment, means any rate of income tax determined in pursuance of section 1(2)(b), and any reference to any higher rate band shall be construed in accordance with section 1(3);

"industrial assurance business" has the meaning given by section 1(2) of the Industrial Assurance Act 1923 or Article 3(1) of the Industrial Assurance (Northern Ireland) Order 1979; 1923 c. 8.
S.I. 1979/1574
(N.I. 13).

"inspector" means any inspector of taxes;

"interest" means both annual or yearly interest and interest other than annual or yearly interest;

"local authority" and "local authority association" have the meanings given by section 519;

"market garden land" means land in the United Kingdom occupied as a nursery or garden for the sale of the produce (other than land used for the growth of hops) and "market gardening" shall be construed accordingly;

"notice" means notice in writing;

"ordinary share capital", in relation to a company, means all the issued share capital (by whatever name called) of the company, other than capital the holders of which have a right to a dividend at a fixed rate but have no other right to share in the profits of the company;

"preference dividend" means a dividend payable on a preferred share or preferred stock at a fixed rate per cent. or, where a dividend is payable on a preferred share or preferred stock partly at a fixed rate per cent. and partly at a variable rate, such part of that dividend as is payable at a fixed rate per cent.;

"qualifying distribution" has the meaning given by section 14(2);

"qualifying policy" means a policy of insurance which is a qualifying policy for the purposes of Chapter I of Part VII;

"the rate of advance corporation tax" means the rate referred to in section 14(3);

"recognised clearing system" has the meaning given by section 124(6);

"surplus of franked investment income" has the meaning given by section 238;

"tax credit" means a tax credit under section 231;

"trade" includes every trade, manufacture, adventure or concern in the nature of trade;

"Ulster Savings Certificates" means savings certificates issued or treated as issued under section 15 of the Exchequer and Financial Provisions Act (Northern Ireland) 1950;

"unit holder" has the meaning given by section 468(6);

"unit trust scheme" has the meaning given by section 469;

"year of assessment" means, with reference to any income tax, the year for which such tax was granted by any Act granting income tax;

"the year 1988-89" means the year of assessment beginning on 6th April 1988, and any corresponding expression in which two years are similarly mentioned means the year of assessment beginning on 6th April in the first-mentioned of those two years;

and a source of income is within the charge to corporation tax or income tax if that tax is chargeable on the income arising from it, or would be so chargeable if there were any such income, and references to a person, or to income, being within the charge to tax, shall be similarly construed.

(2) The definition of "company" is subject to section 468, and does not apply in the following provisions of this Act, that is to say—

Chapter I of Part XVII;

sections 774 to 777;

section 839;

paragraph 15 of Schedule 3;

(and also does not apply where the context otherwise requires because some other definition of "company" applies).

(3) Except so far as the context otherwise requires, in the Tax Acts, and in any enactment passed after 12th March 1970 which by any express provision is to be construed as one with the Tax Acts, the Corporation Tax Acts or the Income Tax Acts, "tax", where neither income tax nor corporation tax is specified, means either of those taxes.

(4) Subsection (3) above is without prejudice to the provisions of section 9 which apply income tax law for certain purposes of corporation tax, and accordingly the employment of "income tax" rather than "tax" in any provision of the Tax Acts is not a conclusive indication that that provision is not applied to corporation tax by that section.

(5) In the Tax Acts any reference to a child, however expressed, shall be construed as including a reference to an adopted child.

This subsection does not apply for the purposes of paragraph 10 of Schedule 30.

833.—(1) In the Income Tax Acts references to profits or gains shall not include references to chargeable gains.

(2) References in the Income Tax Acts to the retail prices index are references to the general index of retail prices (for all items) published by the Department of Employment; and if that index is not published for a month which is relevant for the purposes of any provision of those Acts that provision shall be construed as referring to any substituted index or index figures published by that Department.

(3) For the purposes of any provision of the Income Tax Acts (other than section 550 or Schedule 2) requiring income of any description to be treated as the highest part of a person's income, his income shall be calculated without regard to—

    (a) any payment chargeable to tax by virtue of section 148; or

    (b) any amount included in his total income by virtue of section 547(1)(a); or

    (c) any chargeable sum as defined in paragraph 2 of Schedule 2.

(4) Subject to subsections (5) and (6) below, in the Income Tax Acts "earned income" means, in relation to any individual—

    (a) any income arising in respect of —

        (i) any remuneration from any office or employment held by the individual, or

        (ii) any pension, superannuation or other allowance, deferred pay or compensation for loss of office, given in respect of the past services of the individual or of the husband or parent of the individual in any office or employment, or given to the individual in respect of past services of any deceased person, whether the individual or husband or parent of the individual shall have contributed to such pension, superannuation allowance or deferred pay or not; and

    (b) any income from any property which is attached to or forms part of the emoluments of any office or employment held by the individual; and

    (c) any income which is charged under Schedule A, B or D and is immediately derived by the individual from the carrying on or exercise by him of his trade, profession or vocation, either as an individual or, in the case of a partnership, as a partner personally acting in the partnership.

In cases where the income of a wife is deemed to be income of the husband, any reference in this subsection to the individual includes either the husband or the wife.

(5) Without prejudice to the generality of the provisions of subsection (4) above, in the Income Tax Acts, except so far as is otherwise expressly provided, "earned income" also includes, in relation to any individual—

(a) any income arising in respect of Civil List pensions granted under the Civil List Act 1837 as amended by any subsequent enactment; and

(b) any annuity, pension or annual payment to which section 58(2) or 133 applies; and

(c) any payments chargeable to income tax under Schedule E by virtue of section 150, 151 or 617;

(d) any sum payable by way of annuity to an individual by virtue of a scheme under section 27 of the Agriculture Act 1967 (grants for relinquishing occupation of uncommercial agricultural units), unless the annuity was granted to the individual by reason of his having relinquished occupation before attaining the age of 55; and

(e) income which is earned income by virtue of section 529.

(6) The provisions of this section are without prejudice to any other provision of the Income Tax Acts directing income to be treated as earned income.

834.—(1) For the purposes of the Corporation Tax Acts, except in so far as the context otherwise requires—

"accounting date" means the date to which a company makes up its accounts and "period of account" means the period for which it does so;

"accounting period" shall be construed in accordance with section 12;

"allowable loss" does not include, for the purposes of corporation tax in respect of chargeable gains, a loss accruing to a company in such circumstances that if a gain accrued the company would be exempt from corporation tax in respect of it;

"branch or agency" means any factorship, agency, receivership, branch or management;

"charges on income" has the meaning given by section 338;

"the financial year 1988" means the financial year beginning with April 1988, and similarly with references embodying other dates;

"group relief" has the meaning given by section 402.

(2) Section 6(4) shall also apply for the purposes of the following provisions of this Act, that is to say—

Chapter II of Part X, except section 395;

sections 75 and 76;

section 490;

sections 768 and 769;

and also for sections 73 and 74 of the 1968 Act.

(3) For all the purposes of the Corporation Tax Acts dividends shall be treated as paid on the date when they become due and payable, except in so far as section 468(1) makes other provision as to amounts treated under that section as dividends.

(4) Except as otherwise provided by the Corporation Tax Acts, any apportionment to different periods which falls to be made under those Acts shall be made on a time basis according to the respective lengths of those periods.

835.—(1) In the Income Tax Acts "total income", in relation to any person, means the total income of that person from all sources estimated in accordance with the provisions of the Income Tax Acts.

(2) Any person who, on his own behalf or on behalf of another person, delivers a statement of the amount of his or that other person's total income shall observe the rules and directions contained in section 836.

(3) Where deductions reduce a person's total income and the order in which they are made or in which income of different descriptions is reduced thereby may affect his liability to income tax the deductions shall be made and treated as reducing income in accordance with subsections (4) and (5) below.

(4) Subject to any express provisions of the Income Tax Acts, any deductions allowable in computing a person's total income or to be made from a person's total income shall be treated as reducing income of different descriptions in the order which will result in the greatest reduction of his liability to income tax.

(5) Deductions from total income under Chapter I of Part VII shall be made after any other deductions and shall not affect the amount to be taken as a person's total income for the purposes of section 257(5) or 274 nor the amount determining whether a person is entitled to relief under section 263 or by how much relief under that section is reduced.

(6) In estimating the total income of any person—

    (a) any income which is chargeable with income tax by way of deduction at the basic rate in force for any year or which for the purposes of Schedule F comprises an amount equal to a tax credit calculated by reference to the rate of advance corporation tax in force for any year shall be deemed to be income of that year; and

    (b) any deductions which are allowable on account of sums payable under deduction of income tax at the basic rate in force for any year out of the property or profits of that person shall be allowed as deductions in respect of that year;

notwithstanding that the income or sums, as the case may be, accrued or will accrue in whole or in part before or after that year.

(7) Where an assessment has become final and conclusive for the purposes of income tax for any year of assessment—

    (a) that assessment shall also be final and conclusive in estimating total income; and

(b) no allowance or adjustment of liability, on the ground of diminution of income or loss, shall be taken into account in estimating total income unless that allowance or adjustment has previously been made on an application under the special provisions of the Income Tax Acts relating thereto.

(8) Subsection (7) above shall apply in relation to—

(a) any relief under section 353;

(b) any relief by reason of the operation of an election for the herd basis under Schedule 5; and

1971 c. 68.

(c) any allowance under Part I of the 1968 Act or Chapter I of Part III of the Finance Act 1971 to be given by way of discharge or repayment of tax and to be available or available primarily against a specified class of income (that is to say, any capital allowance to which section 71 of the 1968 Act applies, or as provided by section 532 of this Act, any capital allowance to which section 528(2) of this Act applies);

as it applies in relation to allowances or adjustments on the ground of diminution of income or loss.

Returns of total income.

836. The following rules and directions shall be observed in delivering returns of total income under section 835(2)—

First - Declaration of the amount of profits or gains returned, or for which the person in question has been or is liable to be assessed.

Second - Declaration of the amount of rents, interest, annuities or other annual payments, in respect of which the person in question is liable to allow the tax, with the names of the respective persons by whom such payments are to be made, distinguishing the amount of each payment.

Third - Declaration of the amount of annuities or other annual payments (not being interest) to be made out of the property or profits or gains assessed on the person in question, distinguishing each source.

Fourth - Statement of the amount of income derived according to the three preceding declarations.

Fifth - Statement of any tax which the person in question may be entitled to deduct, retain or charge against any other person.

"Annual value" of land.

837.—(1) For the purposes of, and subject to, the provisions of the Tax Acts which apply this section, the annual value of land shall be taken to be the rent which might reasonably be expected to be obtained on a letting from year to year if the tenant undertook to pay all usual tenant's rates and taxes, and if the landlord undertook to bear the costs of the repairs and insurance, and the other expenses, if any, necessary for maintaining the subject of the valuation in a state to command that rent.

1967 c. 9.

(2) Section 23 of the General Rate Act 1967 (adjustment of gross value by reference to provision of or payment for services etc.) shall apply for the purpose of subsection (1) above, and in relation to land in Scotland or Northern Ireland shall apply as if it extended to the whole of the United Kingdom.

(3) Where any question arises as to the annual value of land it shall be determined by the General Commissioners and those Commissioners shall hear and determine the question in like manner as an appeal.

838.—(1) For the purposes of the Tax Acts a body corporate shall be deemed to be—

(a) a "51 per cent. subsidiary" of another body corporate if and so long as more than 50 per cent. of its ordinary share capital is owned directly or indirectly by that other body corporate;

(b) a "75 per cent. subsidiary" of another body corporate if and so long as not less than 75 per cent. of its ordinary share capital is owned directly or indirectly by that other body corporate;

(c) a "90 per cent. subsidiary" of another body corporate if and so long as not less than 90 per cent. of its ordinary share capital is owned directly by that other body corporate.

(2) In subsection (1)(a) and (b) above "owned directly or indirectly" by a body corporate means owned, whether directly or through another body corporate or other bodies corporate or partly directly and partly through another body corporate or other bodies corporate.

(3) In this section references to ownership shall be construed as references to beneficial ownership.

(4) For the purposes of this section the amount of ordinary share capital of one body corporate owned by a second body corporate through another body corporate or other bodies corporate, or partly directly and partly through another body corporate or other bodies corporate, shall be determined in accordance with the following provisions of this section.

(5) Where, in the case of a number of bodies corporate, the first directly owns ordinary share capital of the second and the second directly owns ordinary share capital of the third, then for the purposes of this section, the first shall be deemed to own ordinary share capital of the third through the second, and, if the third directly owns ordinary share capital of a fourth, the first shall be deemed to own ordinary share capital of the fourth through the second and third, and the second shall be deemed to own ordinary share capital of the fourth through the third and so on.

(6) In this section—

(a) any number of bodies corporate of which the first directly owns ordinary share capital of the next and the next directly owns ordinary share capital of the next but one, and so on, and, if they are more than three, any three or more of them, are referred to as "a series";

(b) in any series—

(i) that body corporate which owns ordinary share capital of another through the remainder is referred to as the "first owner";

(ii) that other body corporate the ordinary share capital of which is so owned is referred to as "the last owned body corporate";

(iii) the remainder, if one only, is referred to as "an intermediary" and, if more than one, are referred to as "a chain of intermediaries";

(c) a body corporate in a series which directly owns ordinary share capital of another body corporate in the series is referred to as "an owner"; and

(d) any two bodies corporate in a series of which one owns ordinary share capital of the other directly, and not through one or more of the other bodies corporate in the series, are referred to as being directly related to one another.

(7) Where every owner in a series owns the whole of the ordinary share capital of the body corporate to which it is directly related, the first owner shall be deemed to own through the intermediary or chain of intermediaries the whole of the ordinary share capital of the last owned body corporate.

(8) Where one of the owners in a series owns a fraction of the ordinary share capital of the body corporate to which it is directly related, and every other owner in the series owns the whole of the ordinary share capital of the body corporate to which it is directly related, the first owner shall be deemed to own that fraction of the ordinary share capital of the last owned body corporate through the intermediary or chain of intermediaries.

(9) Where—

(a) each of two or more of the owners in a series owns a fraction, and every other owner in the series owns the whole, of the ordinary share capital of the body corporate to which it is directly related; or

(b) every owner in a series owns a fraction of the ordinary share capital of the body corporate to which it is directly related;

the first owner shall be deemed to own through the intermediary or chain of intermediaries such fraction of the ordinary share capital of the last owned body corporate as results from the multiplication of those fractions.

(10) Where the first owner in any series owns a fraction of the ordinary share capital of the last owned body corporate in that series through the intermediary or chain of intermediaries in that series, and also owns another fraction or other fractions of the ordinary share capital of the last owned body corporate, either—

(a) directly, or

(b) through an intermediary or intermediaries which is not a member or are not members of that series, or

(c) through a chain or chains of intermediaries of which one or some or all are not members of that series, or

(d) in a case where the series consists of more than three bodies corporate, through an intermediary or intermediaries which is a member or are members of the series, or through a chain or chains of intermediaries consisting of some but not all of the bodies corporate of which the chain of intermediaries in the series consists;

then, for the purpose of ascertaining the amount of the ordinary share capital of the last owned body corporate owned by the first owner, all those fractions shall be aggregated and the first owner shall be deemed to own the sum of those fractions.

839.—(1) For the purposes of, and subject to, the provisions of the Tax Acts which apply this section, any question whether a person is connected with another shall be determined in accordance with the following provisions of this section (any provision that one person is connected with another being taken to mean that they are connected with one another).

Connected persons.

(2) A person is connected with an individual if that person is the individual's wife or husband, or is a relative, or the wife or husband of a relative, of the individual or of the individual's wife or husband.

(3) A person, in his capacity as trustee of a settlement, is connected with any individual who in relation to the settlement is a settlor, with any person who is connected with such an individual and with a body corporate which, under section 681 is deemed to be connected with that settlement ("settlement" and "settlor" having for the purposes of this subsection the meanings given by subsection (4) of that section).

(4) Except in relation to acquisitions or disposals of partnership assets pursuant to bona fide commercial arrangements, a person is connected with any person with whom he is in partnership, and with the wife or husband or relative of any individual with whom he is in partnership.

(5) A company is connected with another company—

(a) if the same person has control of both, or a person has control of one and persons connected with him, or he and persons connected with him, have control of the other; or

(b) if a group of two or more persons has control of each company, and the groups either consist of the same persons or could be regarded as consisting of the same persons by treating (in one or more cases) a member of either group as replaced by a person with whom he is connected.

(6) A company is connected with another person if that person has control of it or if that person and persons connected with him together have control of it.

(7) Any two or more persons acting together to secure or exercise control of a company shall be treated in relation to that company as connected with one another and with any person acting on the directions of any of them to secure or exercise control of the company.

(8) In this section—

"company" includes any body corporate or unincorporated association, but does not include a partnership, and this section shall apply in relation to any unit trust scheme as if the scheme were a company and as if the rights of the unit holders were shares in the company;

"control" shall be construed in accordance with section 416; and

"relative" means brother, sister, ancestor or lineal descendant.

In relation to any period during which section 470(2) has effect the reference above to a unit trust scheme shall be construed as a reference to a unit trust scheme within the meaning of the Prevention of Fraud (Investments) Act 1958 or the Prevention of Fraud (Investments) Act (Northern Ireland) 1940.

Meaning of "control" in certain contexts.

840. For the purposes of, and subject to, the provisions of the Tax Acts which apply this section, "control", in relation to a body corporate, means the power of a person to secure—

(a) by means of the holding of shares or the possession of voting power in or in relation to that or any other body corporate; or

(b) by virtue of any powers conferred by the articles of association or other document regulating that or any other body corporate,

that the affairs of the first-mentioned body corporate are conducted in accordance with the wishes of that person, and, in relation to a partnership, means the right to a share of more than one-half of the assets, or of more than one-half of the income, of the partnership.

Recognised stock exchange and recognised investment exchanges.

841.—(1) In the Tax Acts "recognised stock exchange" means—

(a) the Stock Exchange; and

(b) any such stock exchange outside the United Kingdom as is for the time being designated for the purposes of this section as a recognised stock exchange by order made by the Board.

(2) An order made by the Board under this section—

(a) may designate a stock exchange by name, or by reference to any class or description of stock exchanges including a class or description framed by reference to any authority or approval given in a country outside the United Kingdom;

(b) may contain such transitional and other supplemental provisions as appear to the Board to be necessary or expedient;

(c) may be varied or revoked by a subsequent order so made.

(3) The Board may by regulations make provision securing that enactments in the Tax Acts containing references to the Stock Exchange have effect, for such purposes and subject to such modifications as may be prescribed by the regulations, in relation to all other recognised investment exchanges (within the meaning of the Financial Services Act 1986), or in relation to such of those exchanges as may be prescribed.

Investment trusts.

842.—(1) In the Tax Acts "investment trust" means, as respects any accounting period, a company which is not a close company and which is approved for the purposes of this section for that accounting period by the Board, and the Board shall not approve any company unless it is shown to their satisfaction—

(a) that the company's income is derived wholly or mainly from shares or securities; and

(b) subject to subsection (2) below, that no holding in a company, other than an investment trust or a company which would qualify as an investment trust but for paragraph (c) below, represents more than 15 per cent. by value of the investing company's investments; and

(c) that the shares or securities of the company are quoted on the Stock Exchange; and

(d) that the distribution as dividend of surpluses arising from the realisation of investments is prohibited by the company's memorandum or articles of association; and

(e) that the company does not retain in respect of any accounting period more than 15 per cent. of the income it derives from shares and securities.

(2) Subsection (1)(b) above shall not apply—

(a) to a holding in a company acquired before 6th April 1965 which on that date represented not more than 25 per cent. by value of the investing company's investments; or

(b) to a holding in a company which, when it was acquired, represented not more than 15 per cent. by value of the investing company's investments;

so long as no addition is made to the holding.

(3) For the purposes of subsection (2) above—

(a) "holding" means the shares or securities (whether of one class or more than one class) held in any one company; and

(b) an addition is made to a holding whenever the investing company acquires shares or securities of that one company, otherwise than by being allotted shares or securities without becoming liable to give any consideration, and if an addition is made to a holding that holding is acquired when the addition or latest addition is made to the holding; and

(c) where in connection with a scheme of reconstruction or amalgamation, a company issues shares or securities to persons holding shares or securities in a second company in respect of and in proportion to (or as nearly as may be in proportion to) their holdings in the second company, without those persons becoming liable to give any consideration, a holding of the shares or securities in the second company and a corresponding holding of the shares or securities so issued shall be regarded as the same holding.

(4) In this section "company" and "shares" shall be construed in accordance with sections 64, 93 and 155(1) of the 1979 Act.

Commencement, savings, repeals etc.

843.—(1) Except as otherwise provided by the following provisions of this section, this Act shall come into force in relation to tax for the year 1988-89 and subsequent years of assessment, and for companies' accounting periods ending after 5th April 1988.

(2) Except as otherwise provided by the following provisions of this section, such of the provisions of this Act as relate to capital gains tax (including the provisions of Part XVIII as applied to capital gains tax by section 10 of the 1979 Act) shall come into force in relation to that tax for the year 1988-89 and subsequent years of assessment.

Commencement.

(3) The following provisions of this Act, that is to say—

(a) so much of any provision as authorises the making of any Order in Council or regulations or other instrument;

(b) so much of any provision as relates to the making of a return, the furnishing of a certificate or the giving of any other information, including any such provision which imposes a duty on the Board or an officer of the Board as well as any such provision which imposes a duty on any other person;

(c) so much of any provision as imposes any penalty;

(d) except where the tax concerned is all tax for years of assessment before the year 1988-89 or accounting periods ending before 6th April 1988, so much of any other provision as confers any power or imposes any duty the exercise or performance of which operates or may operate in relation to tax for more than one chargeable period,

shall come into force for all purposes on 6th April 1988 to the exclusion of the corresponding enactments repealed by this Act.

(4) This section has effect except as otherwise provided by any other provision of this Act, and in particular except as provided by sections 96, 380 to 384, 393, 394, 400, 703 and 812.

Savings, transitional provisions, consequential amendments and repeals.
1978 c. 30.

844.—(1) Schedule 29, which makes amendments to other enactments consequential on the passing of this Act, shall have effect.

(2) Schedule 29, section 843 and this section are without prejudice to the provisions of the Interpretation Act 1978 as respects the effect of repeals.

(3) Schedule 30 which contains savings and transitional provisions shall have effect.

(4) The enactments mentioned in Schedule 31 are hereby repealed to the extent specified in the third column of that Schedule.

(5) Subject to subsection (6) below, section 843(3), Schedule 30 and to any other provision of this Act by which any provision is brought into force to the exclusion of the corresponding enactments repealed by this Act, those repeals shall come into force in accordance with subsections (1) and (2) of section 843.

(6) No provision mentioned in subsection (5) above shall be taken as bringing a repeal into force except to the extent that the repealed enactment is being superseded.

Short title.

845. This Act may be cited as the Income and Corporation Taxes Act 1988.

SCHEDULES

SCHEDULE 1

RESTRICTIONS ON SCHEDULE A DEDUCTIONS

Expenditure before 1964-65: deductions from rents

1.-(1) Except as provided by sub-paragraphs (2) and (3) below, no payment shall be deductible under sections 25 and 26 if made before the beginning of the year 1964-65.

(2) Where, by virtue of paragraph 1(2) of Schedule 2 to the 1970 Act, any amount fell to be treated as a payment in relation to premises made by a person in the year 1964-65 in respect of dilapidation attributable to that year, the amount shall be similarly treated for the purposes of sections 25 and 26.

(3) If the amount of any loss was treated, by virtue of paragraph 1(3) of that Schedule, as if it were a payment such as is mentioned in section 72(1) of the 1970 Act made by any person in respect of any premises in and in respect of any year, it shall be treated for the purposes of sections 25 and 26 as if it were a payment such as is mentioned in section 25(1) made by that person in respect of those premises in and in respect of that year.

(4) A deduction falling to be made by virtue of sub-paragraph (3) above shall be made notwithstanding anything in sections 392(3) and 396(1); and relief shall not be given under either of those sections in respect of the loss in so far as a deduction in respect of it is given under this paragraph.

Expenditure before 1964-65: deductions from other receipts

2.-(1) Subject to sub-paragraph (2) below, no payment shall be deductible under section 28 if made before the beginning of the year 1964-65.

(2) Sub-paragraph (1) above shall not prevent the deduction of a payment in so far as a loss in respect thereof was carried forward to the year 1964-65 by virtue of section 346 of the Income Tax Act 1952 (Case VI losses).

(3) Paragraph 1(4) above shall apply in the case of a deduction falling to made by virtue of sub-paragraph (2) above as it applies in the case of one falling to be made by virtue of paragraph 1(3) above.

Expenditure on sea walls before 1964-65

3.-(1) Section 30 shall not apply in relation to expenditure incurred before the beginning of the year 1964-65 except in accordance with sub-paragraphs (2) and (3) below.

(2) Subject to sub-paragraph (3) below, section 30 shall apply in relation to expenditure which, by virtue of paragraph 3(1) of Schedule 2 to the 1970 Act, was treated as if—

(a) it had been incurred in the year of assessment following that in which it was actually incurred, and

(b) in so far as it was incurred in repairing an embankment, it had been incurred in making it,

as if it had been incurred in that year and in making that embankment.

SCH. 1   (3) If, by virtue of the proviso to paragraph 3(1) of Schedule 2 to the 1970 Act, any expenditure fell to be treated for the purposes of sections 71 to 77 of that Act as if it were an amount paid by any person in and in respect of the year 1964-65 in respect of the maintenance of premises preserved or protected by an embankment, it shall be similarly treated for the purposes of sections 25 to 31.

PREMIUMS ETC. TAXABLE UNDER SCHEDULES A AND D: SPECIAL RELIEF FOR INDIVIDUALS

1. A claim for relief under this Schedule shall be made to the Board if the claimant is not resident in the United Kingdom.

2. The relief shall be computed in accordance with paragraphs 3 to 6 below, and in those paragraphs—

"chargeable sum" means an amount to which under section 34(1), (2), (3), (4) or (5), the claimant is treated as becoming entitled in the year of assessment, or in respect of which he is by virtue of section 34(6) or (7) or 35 or 36, chargeable to income tax for the year under Case VI of Schedule D;

"relevant period", in relation to any chargeable sum, means the period treated in computing the amount of the sum as being the duration of the lease in respect of which it arises or where it arises (by virtue of section 36) in connection with the sale of an estate or interest in land, means the period mentioned in subsection (1) of that section;

"yearly equivalent", in relation to any chargeable sum, means the amount which bears to that sum the same proportion as one bears to the number of years and fractions of years in the relevant period.

3. There shall be computed—

(a) the amount of the tax which, in respect of the chargeable sum or the aggregate of the chargeable sums, as the case may be, would be chargeable if—

(i) the relief were not given, and

(ii) that sum or aggregate were treated as the highest part of the claimant's total income, and

(iii) amounts deductible in computing the tax were so far as possible deducted from other sums from which they are deductible in the year rather than from that sum or aggregate, and

(b) the amount of the tax which, in respect of that sum or aggregate, would be chargeable if calculated in accordance with paragraph 4 below by reference to the yearly equivalent of that sum or, as the case may be, of each sum comprised in that aggregate,

and the relief shall consist of a reduction or repayment of tax equal to the difference between those amounts.

4.-(1) Where the relief is to be given in respect of one chargeable sum only, the tax shall be calculated for the purposes of paragraph 3(b) above as follows—

(a) from the yearly equivalent of that sum there shall be deducted such amounts as, following the principle set out in paragraph 3(a)(iii) above, are deductible from that sum;

(b) if any balance of the yearly equivalent remains, the tax in respect of the chargeable sum shall be calculated at the rate which, apart from the relief, would apply if the amount of the sum were reduced to the amount of that balance and were then treated as the highest part of the claimant's total income or, if two or more rates would then apply, at those rates in corresponding proportions;

    (c) if no such balance remains, the tax shall be calculated at the rate applicable to the highest part of the remainder of the claimant's total income for the year of assessment,

and, whether or not any such balance remains, the tax shall be arrived at by applying that rate, or those rates, to so much of the chargeable sum as remains after deducting such amounts as, following the principle set out in paragraph 3(a)(iii) above, are deductible from that sum.

(2) Where the relief is to be given in respect of two or more chargeable sums, the tax for each shall be calculated for the purposes of paragraph 3(b) above as provided by sub-paragraph (1) above, but so that—

    (a) the rate of tax on a sum arising in respect of any relevant period shall be calculated before the rate of tax on any sum arising in respect of a shorter relevant period, and

    (b) in calculating the rate of tax on a sum arising in respect of any relevant period and the deductions from that sum, an amount deducted in respect of a sum tax for which has already been calculated shall not again be deducted, and in calculating a rate of tax—

        (i) any chargeable sum tax for which has not already been calculated, or in respect of which no balance of the yearly equivalent remains, shall be disregarded, and

        (ii) as respects any other chargeable sum, the total income of the claimant shall be taken to include the sum, but on the assumption that the amount of it was only that of the balance remaining of the yearly equivalent.

(3) Where two or more chargeable sums arise in respect of relevant periods of equal duration they shall be treated for the purposes of this paragraph as a single chargeable sum of an amount equal to the aggregate of those sums and arising in respect of a relevant period of like duration.

5. A provision of paragraph 3 or 4 above requiring tax to be calculated as if an amount were treated as the highest part of the claimant's total income shall apply notwithstanding any provision of the Income Tax Acts directing other income to be treated as the highest part of his total income, but for the purposes of those paragraphs his total income shall be deemed—

    (a) not to include any amount in respect of which he is chargeable to tax under section 148, and

    (b) to include, in respect of any amount which would otherwise be included therein by virtue of section 547(1)(a), no greater amount than the appropriate fraction thereof within the meaning of section 550.

6. A provision of paragraph 3 or 4 above shall apply in relation to any part of the claimant's total income (as computed for the purposes of that provision) as respects which he would be entitled under Chapter I of Part VII to a deduction equal to that part as if that part were subject to a nil rate of tax.

SCHEDULE 3

MACHINERY FOR ASSESSMENT, CHARGE AND PAYMENT OF INCOME TAX UNDER SCHEDULE C AND, IN CERTAIN CASES, SCHEDULE D

PART I

PUBLIC REVENUE DIVIDENDS ETC. PAYABLE TO THE BANK OF ENGLAND OR THE BANK OF IRELAND OR ENTRUSTED FOR PAYMENT TO THE BANK OF ENGLAND, THE BANK OF IRELAND OR THE NATIONAL DEBT COMMISSIONERS

1. The Bank of England and the Bank of Ireland as respects the dividends and the profits attached thereto payable to them out of the public revenue of the United Kingdom, or payable out of any public revenue and entrusted to them for payment and distribution, and the National Debt Commissioners, as respects the dividends payable by them or of which they have the distribution, shall, when any payment becomes due, deliver to the Board true accounts, in books provided for the purpose, of—

    (a) the amounts of the dividends and profits attached thereto payable to the Bank, and

    (b) all dividends entrusted to the Bank or the National Debt Commissioners for payment to the persons entitled thereto, and

    (c) the amount of income tax chargeable thereon at the basic rate in force at the time of payment, without any other deduction than is allowed by the Income Tax Acts.

2.-(1) In the case of dividends and profits attached thereto payable to the Bank of England out of the public revenue of the United Kingdom, the Bank of England shall set apart the income tax in respect of the amount payable to them.

(2) In the case of dividends and profits attached thereto entrusted to the Bank of England for payment and distribution, dividends payable by the Bank of Ireland at its principal office in Belfast, and dividends payable by the National Debt Commissioners or of which the National Debt Commissioners have the distribution—

    (a) the Bank of England, the Bank of Ireland and the National Debt Commissioners respectively shall, before any payment is made by them, retain the amount of the income tax for the purposes of the Income Tax Acts, and

    (b) the retaining of the amount shall be deemed to be a payment of the income tax by the persons entitled to the dividends, and shall be allowed by them on the receipt of the residue thereof, and

    (c) the Bank of England, the Bank of Ireland and the National Debt Commissioners respectively shall be acquitted and discharged of a sum equal to the amount retained as though that sum had been actually paid.

(3) In relation to dividends payable to the Bank of Ireland out of the public revenue of the United Kingdom, and public revenue dividends which are entrusted to the Bank of Ireland for payment and distribution and are not payable by that Bank out of its principal office in Belfast, the following provisions shall have effect—

    (a) the money which, apart from this sub-paragraph, would be issuable to the Bank of Ireland under section 14 of the National Debt Act 1870, or otherwise payable to the Bank of Ireland for the purpose of dividends

Sch. 3

on securities of the United Kingdom government entered in the register of the Bank of Ireland in Dublin, shall be issued and paid to the Bank of England; and

(b) the Bank of England shall set apart and retain out of moneys so issued and paid to them the amount of the income tax on the dividends payable to the Bank of Ireland, and on the dividends on the securities of the United Kingdom government entered in the register of the Bank of Ireland in Dublin; and

(c) the Bank of England shall pay to the Bank of Ireland the residue of moneys so issued and paid to them, to be applied by the Bank of Ireland to the payment of the dividends; and

(d) the retaining of the amount shall be deemed to be a payment of the income tax by the persons entitled to the dividends, and shall be allowed by them on the receipt of the residue thereof, and the Bank of England and the Bank of Ireland shall be acquitted and discharged of a sum equal to the amount retained as though that sum had been actually paid.

3. Money set apart or retained under paragraph 2 above, and the amount of any tax charged on the trading profits of the Bank of England or the Bank of Ireland, shall be paid into the general account of the Board at the Bank of England or the Bank of Ireland.

4. No deduction of income tax under this Part of this Schedule shall be made from any dividends payable in respect of stock, securities or annuities standing in the name of the official custodian for charities, nor from any dividends in respect of which there is given to the Bank of England a certificate from the Charity Commissioners that the dividends are subject only to charitable trusts and are exempt from tax.

PART II

PUBLIC REVENUE DIVIDENDS PAYABLE BY PUBLIC OFFICES AND DEPARTMENTS

5. Where any payment is made of public revenue dividends payable by any public office or department of the Crown, the appropriate officer shall retain the income tax charged and pay the same into the general account of the Board at the Bank of England or the Bank of Ireland.

PART III

OTHER PUBLIC REVENUE DIVIDENDS, FOREIGN DIVIDENDS AND PROCEEDS OF COUPONS

6.-(1) The following persons are chargeable persons for the purposes of this Part of this Schedule—

(a) every person (other than the National Debt Commissioners or the Bank of England or the Bank of Ireland) who is entrusted with the payment of any dividends which are payable out of the public revenue of Northern Ireland, or which are payable to any persons in the United Kingdom out of any public revenue other than that of the United Kingdom or Northern Ireland;

(b) every person in the United Kingdom who is entrusted with the payment of any foreign dividends;

(c) every banker or other person in the United Kingdom who obtains payment of any dividends in such circumstances that the dividends are chargeable to tax under Schedule C, or in the case of foreign dividends, under Schedule D; and

(d) every banker in the United Kingdom who sells or otherwise realises coupons, and every dealer in coupons in the United Kingdom who purchases coupons, in such manner that the proceeds of the sale or realisation are chargeable to tax under Schedule C, or in the case of foreign dividends, under Schedule D.

(2) Every chargeable person shall deliver to the Board—

(a) on demand by the Board, true and perfect accounts of the amount of all such dividends or proceeds; and

(b) not later than 12 months after paying any dividends or effecting any other transaction in respect of which he is a chargeable person, and unless within that time he delivers an account with respect to the dividends or proceeds in question under sub-paragraph (a) above, a written statement specifying his name and address and describing those dividends or proceeds.

7. The Board shall have all necessary powers in relation to the examining, auditing, checking and clearing of the books and accounts of dividends or proceeds delivered under paragraph 6 above, and shall assess and charge the dividends or proceeds at the basic rate of tax in force at the time of payment, but reduced by the amount of the exemptions (if any) allowed by them, and shall give notice of the amount so assessed and charged to the chargeable person.

8. The chargeable person shall out of moneys in his hands pay the income tax on the dividends or proceeds on behalf of the persons entitled thereto, and shall be acquitted in respect of all such payments, and the provisions of the Income Tax Acts shall apply as in the case of dividends payable out of the public revenue of the United Kingdom and entrusted to the Bank of England for payment and distribution.

9. The chargeable person shall pay the income tax into the general account of the Board at the Bank of England or the Bank of Ireland within 30 days of the date of the issue of the notice of assessment, and in default of payment it shall be recovered from him in the same manner as other tax assessed and charged on him may be recovered.

10.-(1) Subject to sub-paragraph (2) below, a chargeable person who does all such things as are necessary to enable the tax to be assessed and paid shall receive as remuneration an allowance, to be calculated by reference to the amount of the dividends or proceeds paid from which tax has been deducted, and to be fixed by the Treasury at a rate not being less than 68p for every £1,000 of that amount.

(2) Sub-paragraph (1) above shall not apply to any person entrusted with the payment of dividends payable out of the public revenue of Northern Ireland.

11. Nothing in paragraphs 6 to 10 above shall impose on any banker the obligation to disclose any particulars relating to the affairs of any person on whose behalf he may be acting.

12. Where income tax in respect of the proceeds of the sale or realisation of any coupon has been accounted for under this Part of this Schedule by any banker or dealer, and the coupon has been subsequently paid in such manner that income tax has been deducted from the payment under any of the provisions of this Schedule, the tax so deducted shall be repaid.

A claim under this paragraph shall be made to the Board.

13.-(1) Without prejudice to the generality of paragraph 7 above, the Board may, by notice served on any chargeable person, require that person within such time as may be specified in the notice to make available at his premises for inspection by an officer authorised by the Board all such books and other documents in the possession or control of that person as the officer may reasonably require for the purpose of determining whether any accounts delivered by that person under paragraph 6 above are correct and complete.

(2) The Board may grant a certificate exempting any chargeable person from the provisions of sub-paragraph (1) above, and while the certificate is in force the powers conferred by that sub-paragraph shall not be exercisable in relation to that person; and any such certificate may be revoked at any time by the Board, and may contain such terms and conditions as they think proper.

14. In this Part of this Schedule—

"dividends" includes foreign dividends, and

"foreign dividends" has the meaning given by section 123.

PART IV

INTEREST PAYABLE OUT OF THE PUBLIC REVENUE OF THE REPUBLIC OF IRELAND ETC.

15.-(1) Any person who is entrusted with the payment of any interest, dividends or other annual payments which are payable to any persons in the United Kingdom out of the public revenue of the Republic of Ireland, or out of or in respect of the stocks, funds, shares or securities of any Republic of Ireland company, society, adventure or concern, shall be relieved from the obligation imposed on him under the preceding provisions of this Schedule to pay income tax thereon on behalf of the persons entitled thereto as regards any such interest, dividends or other annual payments in respect of which he furnishes to the Board, in such form and subject to such conditions as they may prescribe, a list containing—

(a) a full description of the interest, dividends or other annual payments, and

(b) the name and address of each person who is entitled thereto, and

(c) the amount thereof to which each such person is entitled.

(2) Any person entrusted with payment who, by virtue of sub-paragraph (1) above, is relieved from the obligation to pay income tax on interest, dividends or other annual payments, shall be entitled to the like remuneration to which, if he had paid tax thereon, he would have been entitled under paragraph 10 above.

(3) Any interest, dividends or other annual payments in respect of which the person entrusted with payment is relieved from the obligation to pay income tax by virtue of sub-paragraph (1) above, shall be assessable and chargeable under Case IV or V of Schedule D, as the case may be.

(4) The Board may make such regulations as may be necessary for the purposes of this paragraph.

(5) This paragraph shall apply to—

(a) any banker or other person in the United Kingdom who obtains payment of any such interest, dividends or other annual payments as is or are mentioned in sub-paragraph (1) above; and

(b) to any person who would, apart from this paragraph, be obliged to pay income tax in respect of the proceeds of the sale or other realisation of any coupon for any such interest, dividends or other annual payments,

as it applies to any person entrusted with the payment of any such interest, dividends or other annual payments, with the substitution in a case falling within paragraph (b) above, of references to the proceeds of the sale or other realisation for references to such interest, dividends or other annual payments.

In this sub-paragraph "coupon" has the same meaning as in section 123.

SCHEDULE 4

                     DEEP DISCOUNT SECURITIES

                          Interpretation

1.-(1) For the purposes of this Schedule—

   (a) "adjusted issue price", in relation to any security in a particular income period, is the aggregate of the issue price of the security and the income elements for all previous income periods;

   (b) "the amount payable on redemption" does not include any amount payable by way of interest;

   (c) "a deep discount", in relation to any redeemable security, means a discount which—

      (i) represents more than 15 per cent. of the amount payable on redemption of that security; or

      (ii) is 15 per cent. or less, but exceeds half Y per cent. of the amount so payable (where Y is the number of complete years between the date of issue of the security and the redemption date);

   (d) subject to sub-paragraph (2) below, "a deep discount security" means any redeemable security which has been issued by a company, after 13th March 1984, at a deep discount, other than—

      (i) a share in the company;

      (ii) a security in respect of which the amount payable on redemption is determined by reference to the movement of the retail prices index or any similar general index of prices which is published by, or by an agent of, the government of any territory outside the United Kingdom; or

      (iii) a security the whole or part of which, by virtue of section 209(2)(c), is a "distribution";

   (e) "a discount" means any amount by which the issue price of a redeemable security is less than the amount payable on redemption of that security;

   (f) "income period" means —

      (i) in the case of a security carrying a right to interest, any period to which a payment of interest which falls to be made in respect of the security is attributable; and

      (ii) in any other case, any year ending immediately before the anniversary of the issue of the security or any period of less than a year which begins on the issue or on such an anniversary and ends on the redemption date;

   (g) "the redemption date" in relation to any redeemable security, means the earliest date on which, under the terms on which the security is issued, the holder of the security will be entitled to require it to be redeemed by the company which issued it;

   (h) "yield to maturity", in relation to any security, means a rate (expressed as a percentage) such that if a sum equal to the issue price of the security were to be invested at that rate on the assumption that—

      (i) the rate would be applied on a compounding basis at the end of each income period; and

(ii) the amount of any interest attributable to an income period would be deducted after applying the rate,

the value of that sum at the redemption date would be equal to the amount payable on redemption of the security; and

(j) "chargeable security" has the meaning given by paragraph 2(5) below.

(2) Where securities which were issued on or before 13th March 1984 have been exchanged at any time after that date for new securities which would be deep discount securities but for this sub-paragraph, the new securities shall not be treated as deep discount securities if—

(a) the old securities would not have been deep discount securities if they had been issued after 13th March 1984;

(b) the date which is the redemption date in relation to the new securities is not later than the date which was the redemption date in relation to the old securities; and

(c) the amount payable on redemption of the new securities does not exceed the amount which would have been payable on redemption of the old securities.

(3) For the purposes of this Schedule, a security comprised in any letter of allotment or similar instrument shall be treated as issued unless the right to the security conferred by the letter or instrument remains provisional until accepted, and there has been no acceptance.

Charge to tax after acquisition of certain securities

2.-(1) This sub-paragraph applies to deep discount securities issued by a company on or after 19th March 1985 where one or both of the following applies—

(a) immediately before the issue the assets held by the company included relevant securities with a value equal to at least 75 per cent. of the value of all the assets held by it;

(b) the terms of issue of the deep discount securities are determined by the company by reference to (though not necessarily in such a way that they reflect) the terms of issue of relevant securities which are held by the company when the deep discount securities are issued or which it intends to acquire later.

(2) This sub-paragraph applies to deep discount securities issued by a company where—

(a) sub-paragraph (1) above would apply if the references to relevant securities included references to United Kingdom corporate bonds; and

(b) the company acquired those bonds on or after their issue (by another company) in circumstances where sub-paragraph (1) above would have applied if they had been deep discount securities.

(3) This sub-paragraph applies to deep discount securities of a particular kind issued by a company and in the case of which—

(a) neither of the preceding sub-paragraphs applies; and

(b) at any time in the first income period of the securities of that kind the assets held by the company include relevant securities with a value equal to at least 75 per cent. of the value of all the assets held by it.

(4) This sub-paragraph applies to deep discount securities issued by a company where either—

SCH. 4

(a) they are issued on a conversion to which section 82 of the 1979 Act applies of old securities; or

(b) they are issued by a company in exchange for old securities in circumstances in which section 85(3) of the 1979 Act applies or are treated as so issued by virtue of section 86(1) of that Act;

and in this sub-paragraph "old securities" means deep discount securities to which sub-paragraph (1), (2) or (3) above or this sub-paragraph applies, except that securities to which sub-paragraph (3) above applies are not old securities unless sub-paragraph (3)(b) has been fulfilled in their case by the time the conversion or exchange concerned takes place.

(5) In the following provisions of this Schedule "chargeable security" means a deep discount security to which any of the preceding sub-paragraphs applies.

(6) In this paragraph—

"relevant securities" means securities within the meaning of section 710, but excluding United Kingdom corporate bonds;

"terms of issue" includes terms relating to amounts payable on redemption or by way of interest, or to times of payment of such amounts; and

"value" in relation to assets means the price they might reasonably be expected to fetch on a sale in the open market.

(7) For the purposes of this paragraph—

(a) a company holds assets if it has a beneficial interest in them and acquires them if it acquires such an interest in them; and

(b) securities are of the same kind if they are treated as being of the same kind by the practice of a stock exchange, or would be so treated if dealt with on a stock exchange.

(8) In this paragraph "United Kingdom corporate bonds" means securities—

(a) issued by a company resident in the United Kingdom at the time of issue;

(b) the debt on which represents and has at all times represented a normal commercial loan, as defined in paragraph 1(5) of Schedule 18; and

(c) which are expressed in sterling and in respect of which no provision is made for conversion into, or redemption in, a currency other than sterling.

(9) For the purposes of sub-paragraph (8)(c) above—

(a) a security shall not be regarded as expressed in sterling if the amount of sterling falls to be determined by reference to the value at any time of any other currency or asset; and

(b) a provision for redemption in a currency other than sterling but at the rate of exchange prevailing at redemption shall be disregarded.

3.-(1) Where a person acquires a chargeable security, the chargeable amount shall be treated as income chargeable to tax under Case III or IV (as the case may be) of Schedule D on each of the following occasions—

(a) the end of each income period to fall within the period of ownership;

(b) the end of any income period which ends but does not begin in the period of ownership.

(2) In sub-paragraph (1) above "the chargeable amount" means—

(a) where paragraph (a) applies, an amount equal to the income element for the income period;

(b) where paragraph (b) applies, an amount equal to the income element for the part of the income period falling within the period of ownership.

(3) The income chargeable shall (notwithstanding anything in sections 64 to 67) be taken into account in computing tax charged for the year of assessment in which the occasion concerned occurs.

Charge to tax on disposal of securities

4.-(1) On the disposal by any person of any deep discount security—

(a) an amount which represents the accrued income attributable to the period between his acquisition and disposal of the security (the "period of ownership"), less any amount or amounts treated as income by virtue of paragraph 3 above, shall be treated as income chargeable to tax under Case III or, as may be, Case IV of Schedule D; and

(b) the tax shall (notwithstanding anything in sections 64 to 67 but subject to sub-paragraph (5) below) be computed on the income so arising from any disposal made in the year of assessment.

(2) The amount which represents the accrued income attributable to any period of ownership is the aggregate of the income elements for each income period or part of an income period in the period of ownership.

(3) In relation to any security, the income element for any income period shall be determined by applying the formula—

$$\frac{A \times B}{100} - C$$

where—

A is the adjusted issue price;

B is the yield to maturity; and

C is the amount of interest (if any) attributable to the income period.

(4) The income element for any period (the "short period") falling within an income period shall be determined by applying the formula—

$$\frac{P}{Y} \times I$$

where—

I is the income element for the income period in which the short period falls;

P is the number of days in the short period; and

Y is the number of days in that income period.

(5) Where—

(a) by virtue of sub-paragraph (1) above income tax is chargeable under Case IV of Schedule D, and

(b) the person making the disposal satisfies the Board, on a claim in that behalf, that he is not domiciled in the United Kingdom, or that, being a British subject or a citizen of the Republic of Ireland, he is not ordinarily resident in the United Kingdom,

SCH. 4   the tax shall be computed on the amounts, if any, received in the United Kingdom in the year of assessment in question in respect of the sum mentioned in sub-paragraph (1)(a) above (any such amounts being treated as income arising when they are received in the United Kingdom).

(6) For the purposes of sub-paragraph (5) above—

(a) there shall be treated as received in the United Kingdom all amounts paid, used or enjoyed in, or in any manner or form transmitted or brought to, the United Kingdom; and

(b) subsections (6) to (9) of section 65 shall apply as they apply for the purposes of subsection (5) of that section.

(7) Sections 348 to 350 and 123 shall not apply to so much of the proceeds of redemption of a deep discount security as represents income chargeable to tax under Case III or, as may be, Case IV of Schedule D.

Deduction of income element from total profits of company and allowance as charge on income

5.-(1) In computing the corporation tax chargeable for any accounting period of a company which has issued any deep discount security, the income element in respect of that security for any income period ending in or with that accounting period shall be allowed as a deduction against the total profits of the company for the accounting period as reduced by any relief other than group relief.

(2) The income element for any income period ending in or with an accounting period of a company which has issued a deep discount security shall be treated for the purposes of the Corporation Tax Acts, other than those of section 338(1), as a charge on income paid by the company in the accounting period.

(3) No income element in respect of any deep discount security shall be so allowed or treated unless—

(a) the cost of paying so much of the amount payable on redemption as represents the discount is ultimately borne by the company;

(b) the income element would not otherwise be deductible in computing the issuing company's profits or any description of those profits for purposes of corporation tax; and

(c) at least one of the conditions mentioned in sub-paragraph (4) below is satisfied.

(4) The conditions are—

(a) that the company exists wholly or mainly for the purpose of carrying on a trade;

(b) that the deep discount security was issued wholly and exclusively to raise money for purposes of a trade carried on by the company;

(c) that the company is an investment company.

(5) Where, on redemption of any deep discount security, any part of the amount payable on redemption is, by virtue of section 209(2)(d) and (e), a distribution of the company, sub-paragraphs (1) and (2) above shall not apply to any income element in respect of that security.

(6) Relief shall not be given under any provision of the Tax Acts in respect of any income element if (at any time) a scheme has been effected or arrangements have been made such that the sole or main benefit that might be expected to accrue to the company from the issue of the security in question is the obtaining of a reduction in tax liability by means of that relief.

(7) In sub-paragraph (6) above "relief" means relief by way of deduction in computing profits or gains or deduction or set-off against income or total profits; and where the relief is claimed by virtue of section 403(7) any question under this paragraph as to what benefit might be expected to accrue from the transaction in question shall be determined by reference to the claimant company and the surrendering company taken together.

6.-(1) Section 494 shall apply in relation to income elements in respect of deep discount securities and paragraph 5 above as it applies in relation to interest and section 338.

(2) In the application of section 494 to any deep discount security, subsection (2)(b) shall have effect as if the references to the rate at which interest was payable were references to the aggregate of the rate of interest payable and the amount of any income element in respect of the security for the period in question.

Disposals

7.-(1) Subject to sub-paragraphs (2) and (3) below, there is a disposal of a deep discount security for the purposes of this Schedule if there would be such a disposal for the purposes of the 1979 Act.

(2) Notwithstanding anything in section 49(1)(b) of that Act (no deemed disposal on death), where the assets of which a deceased person was competent to dispose include any deep discount security that security shall, for the purposes of this Schedule, be deemed to have been disposed of by the deceased immediately before his death.

(3) In any case where—

(a) there is a conversion of securities to which section 82 of the 1979 Act applies and those securities include deep discount securities; or

(b) securities including deep discount securities are exchanged (or by virtue of section 86(1) of that Act are treated as exchanged) for other securities in circumstances in which section 85(3) of that Act applies,

then the securities converted or exchanged shall (subject to sub-paragraph (4) below and notwithstanding section 78 of that Act) be treated for the purposes of the charge to tax under paragraph 4 above as having been disposed of immediately before the time of the conversion, or, as the case may be, the exchange, by the person who was the beneficial owner of the securities at that time.

(4) Where a person would (but for this sub-paragraph) be treated by sub-paragraph (3) above as having, for the purposes of paragraph 4 above, disposed of deep discount securities, other than chargeable securities, which are converted into, or exchanged for, other deep discount securities—

(a) he shall not be so treated—

(i) if the date which is the redemption date in relation to the new securities is not later than the date which was the redemption date in relation to the converted or exchanged securities; and

(ii) no consideration is given for the conversion or exchange other than the new securities; but

(b) the amount of the accrued income attributable to his period of ownership of the converted or exchanged securities (including any amount added by virtue of the previous operation of this paragraph) shall be added to the amount of the accrued income attributable to his period of ownership of the new securities.

8.-(1) Where any deep discount security is disposed of and acquired under a contract, the time at which the disposal and acquisition is made is the time at which the contract is made (and not, if different, the time at which the security is transferred).

(2) If the contract is conditional (and in particular if it is conditional on the exercise of an option) the time at which the disposal and acquisition is made is the time when the condition is satisfied.

Securities issued and owned by associated companies or group companies

9.-(1) Where a deep discount security issued by a company is at any time beneficially owned by another company which is—

    (a) an associated company (within the meaning of section 416) of the issuing company; or

    (b) a member of a group of companies of which the issuing company is also a member;

paragraph 5(1) and (2) above shall apply to any linked income element with the addition, after the words "the accounting period" of the words "in which the security is redeemed".

(2) In this paragraph "linked income element" means the income element in respect of the security in question for any income period in which the security is at any time beneficially owned by the other company.

(3) For the purposes of this paragraph, two companies shall be deemed to be members of a group of companies if one is a 51 per cent. subsidiary of the other or both are 51 per cent. subsidiaries of a third company.

Close companies

10.-(1) Where a deep discount security issued by a close company is at any time beneficially owned by—

    (a) a participator in the company;

    (b) an associate of such a participator; or

    (c) a company of which such a participator has control,

paragraph 5(1) and (2) above shall apply to any linked income element with the addition, after the words "the accounting period", of the words "in which the security is redeemed".

(2) In sub-paragraph (1) above "linked income element" means the income element in respect of the security in question for any income period in which the security is at any time beneficially owned by a person mentioned in that sub-paragraph.

(3) Any amount which a close company is allowed, by virtue of paragraph 5(1) above, to deduct from its total profits for any accounting period shall be treated for the purposes of section 423 as if it were interest paid by the company in that period.

(4) In this paragraph—

"associate" has the meaning given in section 417(3) and (4);

"control" shall be construed in accordance with section 416(2) to (6); and

"participator" means a person who is, in relation to a company, a participator for the purposes of Part XI (by virtue of section 417) other than a person who is a participator for those purposes by virtue only of his holding a deep discount security issued by the company.

(5) In determining whether a person who carries on a business of banking is a participator in a company for the purposes of this paragraph, there shall be disregarded any securities of the company acquired by him in the ordinary course of his business.

Early redemption

11.-(1) Where any deep discount security is redeemed before the redemption date by the company which issued it, paragraphs 4, 5, 7(1) and (2) and 8 to 10 above shall have effect subject to the provisions of this paragraph.

(2) The accrued income attributable to the period between the acquisition of the security by the person who, immediately before its redemption, was the beneficial owner of the security and its redemption shall be the amount paid to him on redemption of the security less the issue price of the security or, in a case where he did not acquire it on its issue, less the aggregate of—

  (a) the issue price; and

  (b) the accrued income attributable to the period beginning with the issue, and ending with his acquisition, of the security;

and, if in either case paragraph 3 above applies, less also an amount equal to the chargeable amount (within the meaning of that paragraph).

(3) The deduction allowed under paragraph 5(1) above in relation to the accounting period in which the deep discount security is redeemed shall be the amount paid by the company on redemption less the aggregate of—

  (a) the issue price of the security; and

  (b) the accrued income attributable to the period beginning with the issue of the security and ending with the last income period to end in or with the accounting period of the company which precedes that in which the security is redeemed.

(4) Where paragraph 9 or 10 above has applied to the deep discount security at any time, the amount mentioned in sub-paragraph (3)(b) above shall not include any linked income element (within the meaning of that paragraph).

(5) Where the aggregate mentioned in sub-paragraph (3) above exceeds the amount paid by the company on redemption of the security, the amount of the excess or, if it is less, the amount mentioned in paragraph (b) of that sub-paragraph shall be treated as income of the company—

  (a) arising in the accounting period in which the security is redeemed; and

  (b) chargeable to tax under Case VI of Schedule D.

(6) Where a resolution is passed, an order made or any other act takes place for the winding up of a company which has issued a deep discount security before the security is redeemed, this paragraph shall have effect in relation to any payment made in respect of the security in the course of the winding up as if the payment were made on redemption.

Identification of securities disposed of

12. The rules contained in section 88 of the Finance Act 1982 (identification, for the purposes of capital gains tax, of securities disposed of) shall apply for the purposes of this Schedule as they apply for the purposes of capital gains tax.

1982 c. 39.

Information

13.-(1) Every company which issues deep discount securities shall cause to be shown on the certificate of each such security the income element for each income period between the date of issue of the security and the redemption date.

2 B

SCH. 4   (2) Every company which issues a chargeable security to which paragraph 2(1), (2) or (4) above applies shall cause to be shown on the certificate of each such security the fact that tax is chargeable under paragraph 3 above.

Charities

14. A charity shall be exempt from income tax in respect of an amount which (apart from this paragraph) is chargeable to income tax by virtue of this Schedule if the amount is applicable and applied for charitable purposes.

In this paragraph "charity" has the same meaning as in section 506.

TREATMENT OF FARM ANIMALS ETC. FOR PURPOSES OF CASE I
OF SCHEDULE D

Farming: the general rule

1.-(1) Subject to the provisions of this Schedule, in computing profits or gains under Case I of Schedule D, animals kept by a farmer for the purposes of his farming shall be treated as trading stock.

(2) Animals forming part of production herds with respect to which an election under paragraph 2 below has effect shall not be so treated, but shall be treated instead in accordance with the rules set out in paragraph 3 below.

(3) An election under paragraph 2 below is referred to in this Schedule as "an election for the herd basis".

Farming: election for the herd basis

2.-(1) An election for the herd basis shall apply to all production herds of a particular class kept by the farmer making the election, including herds which he has ceased to keep before, or first begins to keep after, the making of the election.

(2) An election for the herd basis must be made in writing to the inspector, and must specify the class of herds to which it relates.

(3) Subject to paragraphs 6 and 12 below, an election for the herd basis made by any farmer shall be valid only if it is made not later than two years after the end of—

(a) the first chargeable period for which he is chargeable under Case I of Schedule D to tax in respect of the profits or gains of his farming, or is given relief under section 380 or 393(2) in respect of his farming, being profits or gains or relief the amount of which is computed by reference to the facts of a period during the whole or some part of which he kept a production herd of the class in question; or

(b) the first period for which an account is made up for his farming.

(4) An election for the herd basis made by any farmer shall be irrevocable and, subject to paragraph 6 below, shall have effect—

(a) in a case within sub-paragraph (3)(a) above, for the first chargeable period referred to in that sub-paragraph and all subsequent chargeable periods; and

(b) in a case within sub-paragraph (3)(b) above, for the first chargeable period for which the profits or gains or losses of his farming are computed by reference to the facts of the first period for which an account is made up for his farming.

3.-(1) Where an election for the herd basis has effect, the consequences for the purposes of computing profits or gains under Case I of Schedule D shall be as provided by this paragraph.

(2) The initial cost of the herd and, subject to the provisions of this paragraph as to replacements, the cost of any animal added to the herd shall not be deducted as an expense and the value of the herd shall not be brought into account.

(3) Where an animal which has theretofore been treated as part of the farmer's trading stock is added to the herd otherwise than by way of replacement, there shall be included as a trading receipt—

(a) in the case of an animal bred by the farmer, a sum equal to the cost of breeding it and rearing it to maturity; and

Sch. 5

(b) in any other case, a sum equal to the initial cost to the farmer of acquiring the animal, together with any cost incurred by him in rearing it to maturity.

(4) Where an animal (the "first animal") forming part of the herd dies, or ceases to form part of the herd, and is replaced in the herd by another animal (the "second animal")—

(a) any proceeds of sale of the first animal shall be included as a trading receipt; and

(b) the cost of the second animal, except in so far as that cost consists of such costs as are allowable apart from the provisions of this Schedule as deductions in computing profits or gains of farming under Case I of Schedule D, shall, subject to sub-paragraphs (5) and (6) below, be deducted as an expense.

(5) Where the second animal is of better quality than the first animal, the amount deducted shall not exceed the amount which it would have been necessary to expend in order to acquire an animal of the same quality as the first animal.

(6) Where the first animal was slaughtered by the order of any Ministry, government department or local or public authority under the law relating to diseases of animals, and the second animal is of worse quality, the amount included as a trading receipt shall not exceed the amount allowable as a deduction.

(7) Where the herd is sold as a whole, and another production herd of the same class is acquired, sub-paragraphs (1) to (6) above shall apply as though there had been sold from, and replaced in, the original herd a number of animals equal to the number in the original herd or in the newly acquired herd, whichever is the less.

(8) Subject to sub-paragraph (9) below, if (either all at once or over a period not exceeding 12 months) either—

(a) the whole of a herd is sold in circumstances in which sub-paragraph (7) above does not apply, or

(b) a part of a herd is sold on a substantial reduction being made in the number of animals in the herd,

any profit or loss arising from the transaction shall not be taken into account.

(9) Where within five years of the sale the seller acquires or begins to acquire another production herd of the class in question or, as the case may be, acquires or begins to acquire animals to replace the part of the herd in question—

(a) sub-paragraphs (4) to (7) above shall apply to the acquisition or replacement, except that, if the sale was one which the seller was compelled to effect by causes wholly beyond his control, the amount included as a trading receipt in respect of any animal sold which is replaced by an animal of worse quality shall not exceed the amount allowable as a deduction in respect of that animal of worse quality; and

(b) for the purpose of the application of those sub-paragraphs, the proceeds of sale of the animals comprised in the original herd or part of a herd shall be brought into account as if they had been respectively received at the times of the corresponding acquisitions.

(10) If an animal forming part of the herd is sold, and none of sub-paragraphs (4) to (9) above applies, any profit or loss arising from the transaction shall be included or deducted, as the case may be; and for the purposes of this sub-paragraph, that profit or loss shall be computed by comparing with the proceeds of sale—

(a) in the case of an animal bred by the farmer, the cost of breeding it and rearing it to maturity; and

(b) in any other case, a sum equal to the initial cost to the farmer of acquiring the animal (or in the case of an animal acquired otherwise than for valuable consideration, its market value when the farmer acquired it) together, in both cases, with any cost incurred by him in rearing it to maturity.

(11) Where the herd is sold as a whole, and another production herd of the same class is acquired, and the number of animals in the newly acquired herd is less than the number in the original herd, then, if the difference is not substantial, sub-paragraphs (8) and (9) above shall not apply, and sub-paragraph (10) above shall apply to a number of animals in the original herd equal to the difference.

(12) The preceding provisions of this paragraph shall apply in relation to the death or destruction of animals as they apply in relation to their sale, as if any insurance or compensation moneys received by reason of the death or destruction were proceeds of sale, and any reference in this paragraph to the proceeds of sale of an animal includes a reference to any proceeds of sale of its carcase or any part of its carcase.

Farming: provisions applicable to special cases

4. A farmer who, having kept a production herd of a particular class, ceases altogether to keep herds of that class for a period of at least five years shall, as respects production herds kept by him after the end of that period, be treated as if he had never kept any production herds of that class before the end of that period.

5.-(1) Where a farmer transfers to another person all or any of the animals which form part of a production herd otherwise than by way of sale or by way of sale but for a price other than that which they would have fetched if sold in the open market, and either—

(a) the transferor is a body of persons over whom the transferee has control or the transferee is a body of persons over whom the transferor has control or both the transferor and the transferee are bodies of persons and some other person has control over both of them; or

(b) it appears with respect to the transfer, or with respect to transactions of which the transfer is one that the sole or main benefit, or one of the main benefits, which (apart from the provisions of this paragraph) might have been expected to accrue to the parties or any of them was a benefit resulting from—

   (i) the obtaining of a right to make an election for the herd basis, or

   (ii) such an election having effect or ceasing to have effect, or

   (iii) such an election having a greater effect or a less effect;

the like consequences shall ensue, in relation to all persons concerned, for the purpose of computing profits or gains under Case I of Schedule D as would have ensued if the animals had been sold for the price which they would have fetched if sold in the open market.

(2) In this paragraph "body of persons" includes a partnership, and "control" has the meaning given by section 840.

6.-(1) Where the whole or a substantial part of a production herd kept by a farmer for the purposes of his farming is slaughtered by the order of any Ministry, government department or local or public authority under the law relating to the diseases of animals in such circumstances that compensation is payable in respect of it, an election for the herd basis thereupon made by the farmer in relation to that herd and any other production herds of the same class so kept by him shall, subject to sub-paragraph (2) below, be valid notwithstanding that it is not made within the time required by paragraph 2(3) above.

(2) An election for the herd basis made by virtue of sub-paragraph (1) above shall, subject to sub-paragraph (3) below, only be valid if made not later than two years after the end of the first chargeable period for which the tax chargeable on the farmer in respect of the profits or gains of his farming finally falls to be computed by reference to the facts of a period in which the compensation is relevant.

(3) If that first chargeable period is the second year of assessment within the meaning of section 62 and notice is given under subsection (2) of that section, then for the purposes of income tax (but not corporation tax), the election shall be valid if made not later than the giving of that notice.

(4) An election for the herd basis made by virtue of sub-paragraph (1) above shall, notwithstanding paragraph 2(4) above, have effect only for the chargeable period mentioned in sub-paragraph (2) above and subsequent chargeable periods except that for the purposes of income tax (but not corporation tax) the election shall have effect for earlier chargeable periods for the purposes of any claim under section 380 which is made by the farmer for relief in respect of his farming, if the relief falls to be computed wholly or partly by reference to the facts of a period in which the compensation is relevant.

(5) For the purposes of this paragraph, compensation shall be deemed to be relevant in any period if, but only if, it falls (or would but for an election under this paragraph fall) to be taken into account as a trading receipt in computing the profits or gains or losses of that or an earlier period.

Exclusion of working animals, and interpretation of preceding provisions

7. Nothing in this Schedule applies to any animals kept wholly or mainly for the work they do in connection with the carrying on of the farming.

8.-(1) In this Schedule "herd" includes a flock, and any other collection of animals however named.

(2) For the purposes of this Schedule, immature animals kept in a herd shall not be treated as forming part of the herd unless—

    (a) the land on which the herd is kept is such that animals which die or cease to form part of the herd cannot be replaced except by animals bred and reared on that land; and

    (b) the immature animals in question are bred in the herd, are maintained in the herd for the purpose of replacement, and are necessarily maintained for that purpose;

and references in this Schedule to herds shall be construed accordingly.

(3) References in this Schedule to an animal being added to a herd include references to an immature animal which is kept in the herd becoming a mature animal except that not more immature animals shall be treated as forming part of a herd than are required to prevent a fall in the numbers of the herd.

(4) Female animals shall be treated for the purposes of this Schedule as becoming mature when they produce their first young.

(5) In this Schedule "a production herd" means, in relation to a farmer, a herd of animals of the same species (irrespective of breed) kept by him wholly or mainly for the sake of the products which they produce for him to sell, being products obtainable from the living animal.

In this sub-paragraph "products obtainable from the living animal" means—

(a) the young of the animal, or

(b) any other product obtainable from the animal, not being a product obtainable only by slaughtering the animal itself.

(6) For the purposes of this Schedule, production herds kept by a farmer shall be deemed to be of the same class if, and only if, all the animals kept in the herds are of the same species (irrespective of breed) and the products produced for him to sell for the sake of which (either wholly or mainly) the herds are kept by him are of the same kinds in the case of all the herds; and elections for the herd basis shall be framed accordingly.

(7) Any reference in this Schedule to profits or gains chargeable to tax under Schedule D includes a reference to profits or gains which would be so chargeable if there were any such profits or gains for the chargeable period in question.

Application of preceding provisions to trades other than farming, creatures other than animals, and animals and creatures kept singly

9.-(1) The preceding provisions of this Schedule shall, with the necessary adaptations, apply in relation to trades other than farming, and trades consisting only in part of farming as they apply in relation to farming, and references to farmers shall be construed accordingly.

(2) Those provisions shall (both in relation to farming and in relation to other trades) apply in relation to living creatures other than animals as they apply in relation to animals.

(3) Laying birds shall be treated for the purposes of this Schedule as becoming mature when they first lay.

(4) The provisions of this Schedule shall (both in relation to farming and in relation to other trades) apply, with the necessary adaptations, in relation to animals or other creatures kept singly as they apply in relation to herds.

(5) Nothing in this Schedule shall apply in relation to any animal or other creature kept wholly or mainly for public exhibition or for racing or other competitive purposes.

Supplemental and saving

10. Where an election for the herd basis is made, every person carrying on any farming or other trade affected by the election shall, if required to do so by notice from the inspector, make and deliver to the inspector, within the time specified in the notice, such returns as to, and as to the products of, the animals or other creatures kept by him for the purposes of the trade as may be required by the notice.

11. Where an election for the herd basis has effect for any chargeable period after an assessment for that period has become final and conclusive, any such assessment or, on a claim therefor, repayment of tax shall be made as may be necessary to give effect to the election.

12. The validity of an election for the herd basis in force immediately before the commencement of this Schedule and made in pursuance of—

(a) section 35 of the Finance Act 1973 on or after 25th July 1973 and before 6th April 1976, or

1973 c. 51.

(b) section 48(6) to (9) of the Finance Act 1984,

1984 c. 43.

shall not be affected by the repeal of those sections by this Act.

SCHEDULE 6

TAXATION OF DIRECTORS AND OTHERS IN RESPECT OF CARS

PART I

TABLES OF FLAT RATE CASH EQUIVALENTS

TABLE A

Cars with an original market value up to £19,250 and having a cylinder capacity

Cylinder capacity of car in cubic centimetres	Age of car at end of relevant year of assessment	
	Under 4 years	4 years or more
1,400 or less	£580	£380
More than 1,400 but less than 2,000	£770	£520
More than 2,000	£1,210	£800

TABLE B

Cars with an original market value up to £19,250 and not having a cylinder capacity

Original market value of car	Age of car at end of relevant year of assessment	
	Under 4 years	4 years or more
Less than £6,000	£580	£380
£6,000 or more but less than £8,500	£770	£520
£8,500 or more but less than £19,250	£1,210	£800

TABLE C

Cars with an original market value of more than £19,250

Original market value of car	Age of car at end of relevant year of assessment	
	Under 4 years	4 years or more
More than £19,250 but not more than £29,000	£1,595	£1,070
More than £29,000	£2,530	£1,685

PART II

SUPPLEMENTARY PROVISIONS

Application of Tables A and B

1.—(1) In the case of cars with an original market value of £19,250 or less, Table A applies to those having an internal combustion engine with one or more reciprocating pistons, and Table B applies to other cars.

(2) A car's cylinder capacity is the cylinder capacity of its engine calculated as for the purposes of the Vehicles (Excise) Act 1971 or the Vehicles (Excise) Act (Northern Ireland) 1972.

1971 c. 10.
1972 c. 10 (N.I.).

Reduction for periods when car not available for use

2.—(1) If, for any part of the relevant year, the car was unavailable, the cash equivalent is to be reduced by an amount which bears to the full amount of the equivalent (ascertained under Part I of this Schedule) the same proportion as the number of days in the year on which the car was unavailable bears to 365.

(2) The car is to be treated as being unavailable on any day if—

(a) it was not made available to the employee until after that day, or it had ceased before that day to be available to him; or

(b) it was incapable of being used at all throughout a period of not less than 30 consecutive days of which that day was one.

Car used preponderantly for business purposes

3.—(1) The cash equivalent derived from Table A, B or C is to be reduced (or, where paragraph 2 above applies, further reduced) by half if it is shown to the inspector's satisfaction that the employee was required by the nature of his employment to make and made use of the car preponderantly for business travel, which means that such travel must have amounted to at least 18,000 miles in the relevant year.

(2) In relation to a car which for part of the year was unavailable in the sense of paragraph 2 above, the figure of 18,000 is proportionately reduced.

Reduction for employee paying for use of car

4. If in the relevant year the employee was required, as a condition of the car being available for his private use, to pay any amount of money (whether by way of deduction from his emoluments or otherwise) for that use, the cash equivalent—

(a) is to be reduced (or, if already reduced under the foregoing paragraphs, further reduced) by the amount so paid by the employee in or in respect of the year; or

(b) if that amount exceeds the equivalent shown in the applicable Table in Part I of this Schedule, is nil.

Cars with insubstantial business use and additional cars

5.—(1) The cash equivalent derived from Table A, B or C is to be increased by half if in the relevant year—

(a) the car was not used for the employee's business travel; or

(b) its use for such travel did not amount to more than 2,500 miles.

(2) In relation to a car which for part of the year was unavailable in the sense of paragraph 2 above, the figure of 2,500 is proportionately reduced.

(3) Without prejudice to sub-paragraph (1) above, if in any year a person is taxable under section 157 in respect of two or more cars which are made available concurrently, there shall be increased by half the cash equivalent derived from Table A, B or C in respect of each of those cars other than the one which in the period for which they are concurrently available is used to the greatest extent for the employee's business travel.

(4) In paragraphs 2 to 4 above references to the cash equivalent which is to be reduced shall be construed as references to the cash equivalent after any increase under this paragraph.

SCHEDULE 7

TAXATION OF BENEFIT FROM LOANS OBTAINED BY REASON OF EMPLOYMENT

PART I

MEANING OF "OBTAINED BY REASON OF EMPLOYMENT"

1.—(1) Subject to sub-paragraph (5) below, the benefit of a loan is obtained by reason of a person's employment if, in relation to that person, it is of a class described in sub-paragraphs (2), (3) or (4) below.

(2) A loan made by his employer.

(3) A loan made by a company—

  (a) over which his employer had control;

  (b) by which his employer (being a company) was controlled; or

  (c) which was controlled by a person by whom his employer (being a company) was controlled.

(4) A loan made in any case where—

  (a) his employer was, or had control over, or was controlled by, a close company; and

  (b) the loan was made by a person having a material interest in that close company or, that company being controlled by another company, in that other company.

(5) Sub-paragraph (2) above does not apply to a loan made by his employer, being an individual, and shown to have been made in the normal course of his domestic, family or personal relationships.

2. In paragraph 1 above—

  (a) references to a loan being made by any person include references to his assuming the rights and liabilities of the person who originally made the loan and to his arranging, guaranteeing or in any way facilitating the continuation of a loan already in existence;

  (b) "employer" includes a prospective employer; and

  (c) "company", except in the expression "close company", includes a partnership.

PART II

CALCULATION OF CASH EQUIVALENT OF LOAN BENEFIT

General

3.—(1) The cash equivalent for any year of the benefit obtained from a loan is—

  (a) the amount of interest (calculated in accordance with paragraph 4 or 5 below) which would have been payable for that year had interest at the official rate been payable on the loan, less

  (b) the amount of interest actually paid on the loan for that year.

(2) Where an assessment for any year in respect of a loan has been made or determined on the footing that the whole or part of the interest payable on the loan for that year was not in fact paid, but it is subsequently paid, then on a claim in that behalf, the cash equivalent for that year shall be recalculated so as to take that payment into account and the assessment shall be adjusted accordingly.

(3) All the loans between the same lender and borrower for which a cash equivalent falls to be ascertained and which are outstanding at any time, as to any amount, in any year are to be treated for the purposes of this Schedule as a single loan.

Normal method of calculation (averaging)

4. In the absence of a requirement or election that paragraph 5 below should apply, the amount of interest at the official rate payable on a loan for any year ("the relevant year") shall be ascertained as follows—

> (a) take half the aggregate of—
>
>> (i) the maximum amount of the loan outstanding on 5th April preceding the relevant year or, if it was made in that year, on the date on which it was made, and
>>
>> (ii) the maximum amount of the loan outstanding on 5th April in the relevant year or, if the loan was discharged in that year, the date of discharge;
>
> (b) multiply that figure by the number of whole months during which the loan was outstanding in that year, and divide by 12;
>
> (c) multiply the result by the official rate of interest in force during the period when the loan was outstanding in that year or, if the official rate changed during that period, the average rate during that period ascertained by reference to the number of days in the period and the number of days for which each rate was in force.

For the purposes of this paragraph, months begin on the sixth day of the calendar month.

Election for alternative method of calculation

5.—(1) For any year of assessment ("the relevant year") the alternative method of calculation set out in this paragraph applies if—

> (a) the inspector so requires, by notice given to the employee, for the purpose of any assessment to income tax (or the adjustment of any such assessment in consequence of an appeal); or
>
> (b) the employee so elects, by notice given to the inspector within the time allowed by sub-paragraph (2) below.

(2) An election by the employee must be made—

> (a) in a case where an assessment including the emoluments in question has been made on the basis of the normal method of calculation, within the time allowed for appealing against that assessment or such further time as the inspector may allow;
>
> (b) where no such assessment has been made, within six years after the end of the relevant year of assessment.

(3) The alternative method of calculating the amount of interest at the official rate payable on a loan for the relevant year is as follows—

> (a) take each period in the relevant year during which the official rate of interest remains the same;

SCH. 7

(b) for each such period take for each day in the period the maximum amount outstanding of the loan on that day, and add those amounts together;

(c) multiply that sum by the official rate in force during the period divided by 365; and

(d) add together the resulting figures for each period in the relevant year.

PART III

EXCEPTIONS WHERE INTEREST ELIGIBLE FOR RELIEF

6. Interest is eligible for relief for the purposes of this Part of this Schedule if it is eligible for relief under section 353 or would be eligible for such relief apart from subsection (2) of that section.

7. Section 160(1) does not apply to a loan in any year—

(a) for which interest is paid on the loan and the whole of that interest is eligible for relief, or

(b) for which no interest is paid on the loan but had interest been paid on it at the official rate the whole of that interest would have been eligible for relief.

8. Where for any year interest is paid on a loan and part of that interest is eligible for relief, the calculation of the cash equivalent under Part II of this Schedule is modified as follows—

(a) where paragraph 4 applies, the maximum amounts referred to in sub-paragraph (a)(i) and (ii) of that paragraph shall be proportionately reduced by reference to the proportion which so much of that interest paid for that year as is not eligible for relief bears to the whole of the interest so paid;

(b) where paragraph 5 applies, the maximum amounts referred to in sub-paragraph (3)(b) of that paragraph shall be proportionately reduced by reference to the proportion which so much of the interest paid on each such amount for the day in question as is not eligible for relief bears to the whole of the interest so paid; and

(c) the amount of interest eligible for relief shall be left out of account in ascertaining for the purposes of paragraph 3(1)(b) above the amount of interest paid for that year.

9.—(1) Where for any year—

(a) no interest is paid on a loan, but

(b) had interest been paid on it at the official rate part of that interest would have been eligible for relief,

then the calculation of the cash equivalent under Part II of this Schedule shall be modified as provided by paragraph 8(a) or (b) above with the substitution for the references to the amounts of interest paid or not eligible for relief of references to the amounts (ascertained in accordance with the following provisions of this paragraph) which would have been paid or would not have been eligible for relief.

(2) For the purposes of paragraph 8(a) above as applied by this paragraph, the whole amount of interest at the official rate which would have been paid for any year shall be taken to be the amount payable for that year calculated in accordance with paragraph 4 above (disregarding paragraph 8); and the amount of that interest which would not have been eligible for relief shall be ascertained—

   (a) by finding that amount on the assumption that the amount referred to in paragraph 4(a)(i) was the amount outstanding for the whole year;

   (b) by finding that amount on the assumption that the amount referred to in paragraph 4(a)(ii) was the amount outstanding for the whole year; and

   (c) by adding together the resulting figures and dividing by 2.

(3) For the purposes of paragraph 8(b) above as applied by this paragraph, the amount of interest which would have been paid and the amount of it which would not have been eligible for relief shall be ascertained on the assumption that interest at the official rate was paid daily throughout the year on the maximum amount outstanding on each day.

10.—(1) If—

   (a) a person has a loan on which no interest is paid and of which the benefit was obtained by reason of his or any other person's employment ("the employer's loan"); and

   (b) that person or his wife or her husband has another loan which was made later than, or at the same time as, the employer's loan and interest on which is, in whole or in part, eligible for relief;

then, for the purposes of determining whether, had interest been paid on the employer's loan at the official rate, the whole or any part of that interest would have been eligible for relief, sections 354(5) and (6), 355(1) to (4), 356 to 358 and 360 to 365 shall have effect as if the employer's loan were made after any other loan which falls within paragraph (b) above and which, in the context of the application of sections 354(1) to (4) and 355(5), relates to the same land, caravan or house boat as does the employer's loan.

(2) Where such a loan is made as is mentioned in paragraph (b) of sub-paragraph (1) above, sections 354(5) and (6), 355(1) to (4), 356 to 358 and 360 to 365 have effect in accordance with that sub-paragraph with respect to so much of the interest referred to therein as would be paid on and after the day on which the loan is made; and paragraph 9(3) above shall have effect for the purpose of determining how much of that interest would have been eligible for relief.

11.—(1) Where in any year a person has, alone or together with his wife or her husband, two or more loans—

   (a) on which no interest is paid, and

   (b) which, assuming the application of sections 354(1) to (4) and 355(5), would relate, in the context of those sections, to the same land, caravan or house boat,

then, for the purpose of determining whether, had interest been paid on any of those loans, it would, in whole or in part, have been eligible for relief, it shall be assumed in the first instance that those loans constitute a single loan (equal in amount to the aggregate of the actual loans) and to the extent that, had interest been paid on that single loan, it would have been eligible for relief, the relief shall then be attributed first to the earliest of the actual loans and, if all the relief is not thereby attributed, the balance shall be attributed to the next in time and so on with any of the balance remaining until the relief is wholly attributed.

(2) Nothing in sub-paragraph (1) above affects the operation of paragraph 10 above in relation to the priority which it gives to a loan falling within sub-paragraph (1)(b) of that paragraph, but any question which of two or more loans falling within sub-paragraph (1) above is the earlier shall be determined without regard to that paragraph.

12. References in paragraphs 10 and 11 above to a husband or wife do not include references to a separated husband or wife.

SCHEDULE 8

PROFIT-RELATED PAY SCHEMES: CONDITIONS FOR REGISTRATION

Form

1. The terms of the scheme must be set out in writing.

Employer and employment unit

2. The scheme must identify the scheme employer.

3. If the scheme employer does not pay the emoluments of all the employees to whom the scheme relates, the scheme must identify each of the persons who pays the emoluments of any of those employees.

4.—(1) The scheme must identify the undertaking to which the scheme relates and that undertaking must be one which is carried on with a view to profit.

(2) The references in sub-paragraph (1) above to an undertaking include references to part of an undertaking; and the provisions of a scheme identifying part of an undertaking must do so in such a way as to distinguish it, otherwise than by name only, from other parts of the undertaking.

Employees

5. The scheme must contain provisions by reference to which the employees to whom the scheme relates may be identified.

6. The scheme must contain provisions ensuring that no payments are made under it by reference to a profit period if the employees to whom the scheme relates constitute less than 80 per cent. of all the employees in the employment unit at the beginning of that profit period, but for this purpose any person who is at that time within paragraph 7 or 8 below shall not be counted.

7.—(1) The scheme must contain provisions ensuring that no payments are made under it to any person who is employed in the employment unit by a company and who has, or is an associate of a person who has, a material interest in the company.

(2) For the purposes of this paragraph a person shall be treated as having a material interest in a company—

(a) if he, either on his own or with any one or more of his associates, or if any associate of his with or without such other associates, is the beneficial owner of, or able (directly or through the medium of other companies or by any other indirect means) to control, more than 25 per cent. of the ordinary share capital of the company; or

(b) if, in the case of a close company, on an amount equal to the whole distributable income of the company falling to be apportioned under Chapter III of Part XI for the purpose of computing total income, more than 25 per cent. of that amount could be apportioned to him together with his associates (if any), or to any associate of his, or to any such associates taken together.

(3) In this paragraph—

"associate" has the same meaning as in section 417(3) and (4); and

"control" has the meaning given by section 840;

and the definition of "control" in section 840 applies (with the necessary modifications) in relation to a company which is an unincorporated association as it applies in relation to one that is not.

8. The persons within this paragraph are any of the following employees who are excluded by the scheme from receiving any payment of profit-related pay—

   (a) those who are not required under the terms of their employment to work in the employment unit for 20 hours or more a week;

   (b) those who have not been employed by a relevant employer for a minimum period (of not more than three years) specified in the scheme;

and for this purpose "relevant employer" means the scheme employer or any person who pays the emoluments of any of the employees to whom the scheme relates.

Profit periods

9. The scheme must identify the accounting period or periods by reference to which any profit-related pay is to be calculated.

10.—(1) Subject to sub-paragraphs (2) and (3) below, any such accounting period must be a period of 12 months.

(2) If the scheme is a replacement scheme, the first of two profit periods may be a period of less than 12 months, but the scheme may not provide for more than two profit periods.

(3) The scheme may make provision for a profit period to be abbreviated where registration of the scheme is cancelled with effect from a day after the beginning of the period; and a scheme making such provision may exclude the operation of all or any of the provisions of paragraph 13(4) and (5) or (as the case may be) paragraph 14(3)(b), (4) and (5) below in relation to the determination of the distributable pool for an abbreviated period.

(4) For the purposes of this paragraph, a scheme is a replacement scheme if—

   (a) it succeeds another scheme (or two or more other schemes) registration of which was cancelled under section 178(1)(a) on the ground of a change in the employment unit or in the circumstances relating to the scheme; and

   (b) that change occurred not more than three months before the beginning of the first (or only) profit period of the new scheme, and the Board are satisfied that it was not brought about with a view to the registration of the new scheme or in circumstances satisfying the conditions in section 177(1)(a), (b) and (c); and

   (c) not less than one half of the employees to whom the new scheme relates were employees to whom the previous scheme (or any of the previous schemes) related at the time of that change.

Distributable pool

11. The scheme must contain provisions by reference to which the aggregate sum that may be paid to employees in respect of a profit period ("the distributable pool") may be determined.

12. Except where the scheme is a replacement scheme (within the meaning of paragraph 10 above), the provisions for the determination of the distributable pool must employ either the method specified in paragraph 13 below ("method A") or the method specified in paragraph 14 below ("method B").

13.—(1) Method A is that the distributable pool is equal to a fixed percentage of the profits of the employment unit in the profit period.

(2) That percentage must be such that, on the assumption as to profits mentioned in sub-paragraph (3) below, it will produce a distributable pool equal to not less than 5 per cent. of the standard pay of the employment unit.

(3) The assumption referred to in sub-paragraph (2) above is that the profits in the profit period are the same as those in a base year specified in the scheme; and that base year must be a period of 12 months ending at a time within the period of two years immediately preceding the profit period, or the first of the profit periods, to which the scheme relates.

(4) Notwithstanding sub-paragraph (1) above, a scheme employing method A may include provision for disregarding profits in the profit period so far as they exceed 160 per cent. (or such greater percentage as may be specified in the scheme) of—

    (a) if the profit period is the first or only period to which the scheme relates, the profits for the base year referred to in sub-paragraph (3) above;

    (b) in any other case, the profits for the previous profit period.

(5) Notwithstanding sub-paragraph (1) above, a scheme employing method A may include provision to the effect that there shall be no distributable pool if the profits in the profit period are less than an amount specified in, or ascertainable by reference to, the scheme; but that amount must be less than the amount which would produce a distributable pool of 5 per cent. of the standard pay of the employment unit.

(6) The references in this paragraph to the standard pay of the employment unit are references to the amount which the scheme employer, at the time when he applies for registration of the scheme, reasonably estimates will be the annual equivalent of the pay, at the beginning of the profit period or first profit period, of the employees to whom the scheme will then relate; and for this purpose an estimate shall (in the absence of evidence to the contrary) be taken to be a reasonable one if it is based on the most recent information available to the employer as to the monthly or annual pay of the relevant employees.

14.—(1) Method B is that the distributable pool is—

    (a) if the profit period is the first or only profit period to which the scheme relates, a percentage of a notional pool of an amount specified in the scheme;

    (b) in any other case, a percentage of the distributable pool for the previous profit period.

(2) The amount of the notional pool referred to in sub-paragraph (1) above must not be less than 5 per cent. of the standard pay of the employment unit.

(3) The percentage referred to in sub-paragraph (1) above must be either—

    (a) that arrived at by expressing the profits in the profit period as a percentage of the profits in the preceding period of 12 months; or

    (b) the percentage mentioned in paragraph (a) above reduced (if it is more than 100) or increased (if it is less than 100) by a specified fraction of the difference between it and 100;

and the reference in paragraph (b) above to a specified fraction is a reference to a fraction of not more than one half specified in the scheme.

(4) Notwithstanding sub-paragraph (1) above, a scheme employing method B may include provision for disregarding profits in the profit period so far as they exceed 160 per cent. (or such greater percentage as may be specified in the scheme) of the profits in the preceding period of 12 months.

(5) Notwithstanding sub-paragraph (1) above, a scheme employing method B may include provision to the effect that there shall be no distributable pool if the profits in the profit period are less than an amount specified in, or ascertainable

by reference to, the scheme; but that amount must be less than the amount which would produce a distributable pool of 5 per cent. of the standard pay of the employment unit.

(6) Where by virtue of a provision of the kind described in sub-paragraph (5) above there is no distributable pool for a profit period, any comparison required in accordance with sub-paragraph (1)(b) to be made with the distributable pool for that period shall be made with what would have been the pool but for sub-paragraph (5).

(7) In this paragraph "standard pay of the employment unit" has the same meaning as it has in paragraph 13 above.

15. If the scheme is a replacement scheme (within the meaning of paragraph 10 above), it must provide for the distributable pool for a profit period to be equal to a specified percentage of the profits for the period.

Payment from distributable pool etc.

16. The scheme must provide for the whole of the distributable pool to be paid to employees in the employment unit.

17. The scheme must make provision as to when payments will be made to employees.

18.—(1) The provisions of the scheme must be such that employees participate in the scheme on similar terms.

(2) For the purposes of sub-paragraph (1) above, the fact that the payments to employees vary according to the levels of their remuneration, the length of their service or similar factors shall not be regarded as meaning that they do not participate on similar terms.

Ascertainment of profits

19.—(1) The scheme must provide for the preparation of a profit and loss account in respect of—

(a) each profit period of the employment unit; and

(b) any other period the profits for which must be ascertained for the purposes of this Chapter.

(2) The profit and loss account must give a true and fair view of the profit or loss of the employment unit for the period to which it relates.

(3) Subject to sub-paragraph (2) above, the requirements of Schedule 4 to the Companies Act 1985 shall apply (with any necessary modifications) to a profit and loss account prepared for the purposes of the scheme as they apply to a profit and loss account of a company for a financial year.

1985 c. 6.

(4) Notwithstanding the preceding provisions of this paragraph, a profit and loss account prepared for the purposes of the scheme must not make any deduction, in arriving at the profits or losses of the employment unit, for the remuneration of any person excluded from the scheme by virtue of paragraph 7 above.

(5) Notwithstanding the preceding provisions of this paragraph, if the scheme so provides in relation to any of the items listed in sub-paragraph (6) below, a profit and loss account prepared for the purposes of the scheme may, in arriving at the profits or losses of the employment unit—

(a) leave the item out of account notwithstanding that Schedule 4 to the Companies Act 1985 requires it to be taken into account; or

(b) take the item into account notwithstanding that Schedule 4 to the Companies Act 1985 requires it to be left out of account.

SCH. 8

(6) The items referred to in sub-paragraph (5) above are—

(a) interest receivable and similar income;

(b) interest payable and similar charges;

(c) goodwill;

(d) tax on profit or loss on ordinary activities (but not any penalty under the Taxes Acts);

(e) research and development costs;

(f) profit-related pay payable under the scheme;

(g) extraordinary income;

(h) extraordinary charges;

(j) extraordinary profit or loss;

(k) tax on extraordinary profit or loss.

1985 c. 6.

S.I. 1986/1032 (N.I. 6).

(7) References in this paragraph to Schedule 4 to the Companies Act 1985 shall be construed, in relation to Northern Ireland, as references to Schedule 4 to the Companies (Northern Ireland) Order 1986.

20.—(1) The scheme must provide that, in preparing a profit and loss account for the purposes of this Schedule, no changes may be made from the accounting policies used in preparing accounts for any earlier period relevant for those purposes, or in the methods of applying those policies, if the effect of the changes (either singly or taken together) would be that the amount of profits (or losses) differed by more than 5 per cent. from what would be that amount if no changes were made.

(2) Sub-paragraph (1) above has effect subject to paragraph 19(2) above.

SCHEDULE 9

APPROVED SHARE OPTION SCHEMES AND PROFIT SHARING SCHEMES

PART I

GENERAL

1.—(1) Subject to the provisions of this Schedule, on the application of a body corporate ("the grantor") which has established a share option scheme or a profit sharing scheme, the Board shall approve the scheme if they are satisfied that it fulfils such requirements of Part II and this Part as apply in relation to the scheme in question, and the requirements of Part III, IV or V of this Schedule; and in this Schedule—

> "the relevant requirements" means, in relation to any scheme, the requirements of this Schedule by reference to which the scheme is approved; and

> "savings-related share option scheme" means a scheme in relation to which the relevant requirements include the requirements of Part III of this Schedule.

(2) An application under sub-paragraph (1) above shall be made in writing and contain such particulars and be supported by such evidence as the Board may require.

(3) Where the grantor has control of another company or companies, the scheme may be expressed to extend to all or any of the companies of which it has control and in this Schedule a scheme which is expressed so to extend is referred to as a "group scheme".

(4) In relation to a group scheme the expression "participating company" means the grantor or any other company to which for the time being the scheme is expressed to extend.

2.—(1) The Board shall not approve a scheme under this Schedule if it appears to them that it contains features which are neither essential nor reasonably incidental to the purpose of providing for employees and directors benefits in the nature of rights to acquire shares or, in the case of a profit sharing scheme, in the nature of interests in shares.

(2) A profit sharing scheme shall not be approved under paragraph 1 above unless the Board are satisfied that, whether under the terms of the scheme or otherwise, every participant in the scheme is bound in contract with the grantor—

(a) to permit his shares to remain in the hands of the trustees throughout the period of retention; and

(b) not to assign, charge or otherwise dispose of his beneficial interest in his shares during that period; and

(c) if he directs the trustees to transfer the ownership of his shares to him at any time before the release date, to pay to the trustees before the transfer takes place a sum equal to income tax at the basic rate on the appropriate percentage of the locked-in value of the shares at the time of the direction; and

(d) not to direct the trustees to dispose of his shares at any time before the release date in any other way except by sale for the best consideration in money that can reasonably be obtained at the time of the sale or, in the case of redeemable shares in a workers' cooperative, by redemption.

(3) The Board must be satisfied in the case of a savings-related share option scheme or a profit sharing scheme—

(a) that there are no features of the scheme (other than any which are included to satisfy requirements of this Schedule) which have or would have the effect of discouraging any description of employees or former employees who fulfil the conditions in paragraph 26(1) or, as the case may be, 36(1) below from actually participating in the scheme; and

(b) where the grantor is a member of a group of companies, that the scheme does not and would not have the effect of conferring benefits wholly or mainly on directors of companies in the group or on those employees of companies in the group who are in receipt of the higher or highest levels of remuneration.

(4) For the purposes of sub-paragraph (3) above "a group of companies" means a company and any other companies of which it has control.

3.—(1) If, at any time after the Board have approved a share option scheme, any of the relevant requirements ceases to be satisfied or the grantor fails to provide information requested by the Board under paragraph 6 below, the Board may withdraw the approval with effect from that time or such later time as the Board may specify; but where rights obtained under a savings-related share option scheme before the withdrawal of approval from the scheme under this paragraph are exercised after the withdrawal, section 185(3) shall apply in respect of the exercise as if the scheme were still approved.

(2) If at any time after the Board have approved a profit sharing scheme—

(a) a participant is in breach of any of his obligations under paragraph 2(2)(a), (c) and (d) above; or

(b) there is, with respect to the operation of the scheme, any contravention of any of the relevant requirements, Schedule 10, the scheme itself or the terms of the trust referred to in paragraph 30(1)(c) below; or

(c) any shares of a class of which shares have been appropriated to the participants receive different treatment in any respect from the other shares of that class, in particular, different treatment in respect of—

(i) the dividend payable;

(ii) repayment;

(iii) the restrictions attaching to the shares; or

(iv) any offer of substituted or additional shares, securities or rights of any description in respect of the shares; or

(d) the Board cease to be satisfied that the scheme complies with the requirements of paragraph 2(3) above or paragraph 36 below; or

(e) the trustees, the grantor or, in the case of a group scheme, a company which is or has been a participating company fail or fails to furnish any information which they are or it is required to furnish under paragraph 6 below,

the Board may, subject to sub-paragraph (3) below, withdraw the approval with effect from that time or from such later time as the Board may specify.

(3) It shall not be a ground for withdrawal of approval of a profit sharing scheme that shares which have been newly issued receive, in respect of dividends payable with respect to a period beginning before the date on which the shares were issued, treatment which is less favourable than that accorded to shares issued before that date.

4. If an alteration is made in the scheme at any time after the Board have approved the scheme, the approval shall not have effect after the date of the alteration unless the Board have approved the alteration.

5. If aggrieved—

(a) in any case, by the failure of the Board to approve the scheme or to approve an alteration in the scheme or by the withdrawal of approval; or

(b) in the case of a savings-related share option scheme, by the failure of the Board to decide that a condition subject to which the approval has been given is satisfied; or

(c) in the case of a profit sharing scheme, by the failure of the Board to approve an alteration in the terms of the trust referred to in paragraph 30(1)(c) below;

the grantor may, by notice given to the Board within 30 days from the date on which it is notified of the Board's decision, require the matter to be determined by the Special Commissioners, and the Special Commissioners shall hear and determine the matter in like manner as an appeal.

6. The Board may by notice require any person to furnish them, within such time as the Board may direct (not being less than 30 days), with such information as the Board think necessary for the performance of their functions under the relevant provisions and as the person to whom the notice is addressed has or can reasonably obtain, including in particular information—

(a) to enable the Board to determine—

(i) whether to approve a scheme or withdraw an approval already given; or

(ii) the liability to tax, including capital gains tax, of any person who has participated in a scheme; and

(b) in relation to the administration of a scheme and any alteration of the terms of a scheme.

PART II

REQUIREMENTS GENERALLY APPLICABLE

7. The provisions of this Part apply in relation to all schemes unless otherwise stated.

8. The scheme must not provide for any person to be eligible to participate in it, that is to say, to obtain and exercise rights under it, or in the case of a profit sharing scheme to have shares appropriated to him, at any time when he has, or has within the preceding 12 months had, a material interest in a close company which is—

(a) a company shares in which, in the case of a profit sharing scheme, are to be appropriated or, in the case of a share option scheme, may be acquired pursuant to the exercise of rights obtained under the scheme; or

(b) a company which has control of such a company or is a member of a consortium which owns such a company.

In determining whether a company is a close company for the purposes of this paragraph, sections 414(1)(a) and 415 shall be disregarded.

9.—(1) A share option scheme must provide for directors and employees to obtain rights to acquire shares ("scheme shares") which satisfy the requirements of paragraphs 10 to 14 below.

(2) In the case of a profit sharing scheme, the shares to be acquired by the trustees as mentioned in paragraph 30 below ("scheme shares") must satisfy the requirements of paragraphs 10 to 12 and 14 below.

10. Scheme shares must form part of the ordinary share capital of—

(a) the grantor; or

(b) a company which has control of the grantor; or

(c) a company which either is, or has control of, a company which—

(i) is a member of a consortium owning either the grantor or a company having control of the grantor; and

(ii) beneficially owns not less than three-twentieths of the ordinary share capital of the company so owned.

11. Scheme shares must be—

(a) shares of a class quoted on a recognised stock exchange; or

(b) shares in a company which is not under the control of another company; or

(c) shares in a company which is under the control of a company (other than a company which is, or would if resident in the United Kingdom be, a close company), whose shares are quoted on a recognised stock exchange.

12.—(1) Scheme shares must be—

(a) fully paid up;

(b) not redeemable; and

(c) not subject to any restrictions other than restrictions which attach to all shares of the same class or a restriction authorised by sub-paragraph (2) below.

Sub-paragraph (b) above does not apply, in the case of a profit sharing scheme, in relation to shares in a workers' cooperative.

(2) Except as provided below, the shares may be subject to a restriction imposed by the company's articles of association—

(a) requiring all shares held by directors or employees of the company or of any other company of which it has control to be disposed of on ceasing to be so held; and

(b) requiring all shares acquired, in pursuance of rights or interests obtained by such directors or employees, by persons who are not (or have ceased to be) such directors or employees to be disposed of when they are acquired.

(3) A restriction is not authorised by sub-paragraph (2) above unless—

(a) any disposal required by the restriction will be by way of sale for a consideration in money on terms specified in the articles of association; and

(b) the articles also contain general provisions by virtue of which any person disposing of shares of the same class (whether or not held or acquired as mentioned in sub-paragraph (2) above) may be required to sell them on terms which are the same as those mentioned in paragraph (a) above.

(4) In the case of a profit sharing scheme, except in relation to redeemable shares in a workers' cooperative, nothing in sub-paragraph (2) above authorises a restriction which would require a person, before the release date, to dispose of his beneficial interest in shares the ownership of which has not been transferred to him.

13.—(1) In determining, in the case of a share option scheme, for the purposes of paragraph 12(1)(c) above whether scheme shares which are or are to be acquired by any person are subject to any restrictions, there shall be regarded as a restriction attaching to the shares any contract, agreement, arrangement or condition by which his freedom to dispose of the shares or of any interest in them or of the proceeds of their sale or to exercise any right conferred by them is restricted or by which such a disposal or exercise may result in any disadvantage to him or to a person connected with him.

(2) Sub-paragraph (1) does not apply to so much of any contract, agreement, arrangement or condition as contains provisions similar in purpose and effect to any of the provisions of the Model Rules set out in the Model Code for Securities Transactions by Directors of Listed Companies issued by the Stock Exchange in November 1984.

14.—(1) Except where scheme shares are shares in a company the ordinary share capital of which consists of shares of one class only, the majority of the issued shares of the same class either must be employee-control shares or must be held by persons other than—

(a) persons who acquired their shares in pursuance of a right conferred on them or an opportunity afforded to them as a director or employee of the grantor or any other company and not in pursuance of an offer to the public;

(b) trustees holding shares on behalf of persons who acquired their beneficial interests in the shares as mentioned in sub-paragraph (a) above; and

(c) in a case where the shares fall within sub-paragraph (c), but not within sub-paragraph (a), of paragraph 11 above, companies which have control of the company whose shares are in question or of which that company is an associated company.

(2) In its application to a profit sharing scheme, sub-paragraph (1) above shall have effect with the addition after the words "ordinary share capital of which" of the words "at the time of the acquisition of the shares by the trustees".

(3) For the purposes of this paragraph, shares in a company are employee-control shares if—

(a) the persons holding the shares are, by virtue of their holding, together able to control the company; and

(b) those persons are or have been employees or directors of the company or of another company which is under the control of the company.

15.—(1) Except in the case of a profit sharing scheme, the scheme may provide that if any company ("the acquiring company")—

(a) obtains control of a company whose shares are scheme shares as a result of making a general offer—

(i) to acquire the whole of the issued ordinary share capital of the company which is made on a condition such that if it is satisfied the person making the offer will have control of the company; or

(ii) to acquire all the shares in the company which are of the same class as the scheme shares;

(b) obtains control of a company whose shares are scheme shares in pursuance of a compromise or arrangement sanctioned by the court under section 425 of the Companies Act 1985 or Article 418 of the Companies (Northern Ireland) Order 1986; or

1985 c. 6.
S.I. 1986/1032
(N.I. 6).

(c) becomes bound or entitled to acquire shares in a company whose shares are scheme shares under sections 428 to 430 of that Act or Articles 421 to 423 of that Order,

any participant in the scheme may at any time within the appropriate period, by agreement with the acquiring company, release his rights under the scheme (in this paragraph referred to as "the old rights") in consideration of the grant to him of rights (in this paragraph referred to as "the new rights") which are equivalent to the old rights but relate to shares in a different company (whether the acquiring company itself or some other company falling within paragraph 10(b) or (c) above).

(2) In sub-paragraph (1) above "the appropriate period" means—

(a) in a case falling within paragraph (a), the period of six months beginning with the time when the person making the offer has obtained control of the company and any condition subject to which the offer is made is satisfied;

(b) in a case falling within paragraph (b), the period of six months beginning with the time when the court sanctions the compromise or arrangement; and

(c) in a case falling within paragraph (c), the period during which the acquiring company remains bound or entitled as mentioned in that paragraph.

(3) The new rights shall not be regarded for the purposes of this paragraph as equivalent to the old rights unless—

(a) the shares to which they relate satisfy the conditions specified, in relation to scheme shares, in paragraphs 10 to 14 above; and

(b) the new rights will be exercisable in the same manner as the old rights and subject to the provisions of the scheme as it had effect immediately before the release of the old rights; and

(c) the total market value, immediately before the release, of the shares which were subject to the participant's old rights is equal to the total market value, immediately after the grant, of the shares in respect of which the new rights are granted to the participant; and

(d) the total amount payable by the participant for the acquisition of shares in pursuance of the new rights is equal to the total amount that would have been payable for the acquisition of shares in pursuance of the old rights.

(4) Where any new rights are granted pursuant to a provision included in a scheme by virtue of this paragraph they shall be regarded—

(a) for the purposes of section 185 and this Schedule; and

(b) for the purposes of the subsequent application (by virtue of a condition complying with sub-paragraph (3)(b) above) of the provisions of the scheme,

as having been granted at the time when the corresponding old rights were granted.

(5) Where a scheme which was approved before 1st August 1987 is altered before 1st August 1989 so as to include such a provision as is mentioned above ("an exchange provision"), the scheme as altered may by virtue of this and the following sub-paragraphs apply that provision to rights obtained under the scheme before the date on which the alteration takes effect.

(6) If an exchange provision is applied as mentioned in sub-paragraph (5) above in a case where, on or after 17th March 1987 but before the date on which the alteration takes effect, an event has occurred by reason of which a person holding rights under the scheme would be able to take advantage of the exchange provision—

(a) the scheme may permit a person who held rights under the scheme immediately before that event to take advantage of the exchange provision; and

(b) in a case where rights then held would otherwise, by reason of the event, have ceased to be exercisable, the scheme may provide that the exchange provision shall apply as if the rights were still exercisable.

(7) The application of an exchange provision as mentioned in sub-paragraph (5) or (6) above shall not itself be regarded for the purposes of this Schedule as the acquisition of a right.

(8) Sub-paragraphs (5) and (6) above have effect subject to paragraph 4 above.

PART III

REQUIREMENTS APPLICABLE TO SAVINGS-RELATED SHARE OPTION SCHEMES

16.—(1) The scheme must provide for the scheme shares to be paid for with moneys not exceeding the amount of repayments made and any interest paid to them under a certified contractual savings scheme which has been approved by the Board for the purposes of this Schedule.

(2) Where the Board are satisfied that—

(a) a person has entered into a certified contractual savings scheme before 15th November 1980, and

(b) he has obtained rights under a scheme established before that date to acquire shares in a company of which he is an employee or director (or a company of which such a company has control) using repayments made under the certified contractual savings scheme;

then, repayments and interest paid under the certified contractual savings scheme shall be treated as repayments and interest paid, under a scheme approved by the Board for the purposes of this Schedule under sub-paragraph (1) above, and, accordingly, may be used for the purchase of shares under a savings-related share option scheme approved under this Schedule.

(3) The repayments and interest to which sub-paragraph (2) above applies shall not exceed the repayments and interest to which the participant would have been entitled if the terms of the scheme had corresponded to those of a certified contractual savings scheme approved by the Board under sub-paragraph (1) above.

17. Subject to paragraphs 18 to 21 below, the rights obtained under the scheme must not be capable of being exercised before the bonus date, that is to say, the date on which repayments under the certified contractual savings scheme are due; and for the purposes of this paragraph and paragraph 16 above—

(a) repayments under a certified contractual savings scheme may be taken as including or as not including a bonus;

(b) the time when repayments are due shall be, where repayments are taken as including the maximum bonus, the earliest date on which the maximum bonus is payable and, in any other case, the earliest date on which a bonus is payable under the scheme; and

(c) the question what is to be taken as so included must be required to be determined at the time when rights under the scheme are obtained.

18. The scheme must provide that if a person who has obtained rights under the scheme dies before the bonus date the rights must be exercised, if at all, within 12 months after the date of his death and if he dies within six months after the bonus date the rights may be exercised within 12 months after the bonus date.

19. The scheme must provide that if a person who has obtained rights under it ceases to hold the office or employment by virtue of which he is eligible to participate in the scheme by reason of—

1978 c. 44.

(a) injury or disability or redundancy within the meaning of the Employment Protection (Consolidation) Act 1978; or

(b) retirement on reaching pensionable age or any other age at which he is bound to retire in accordance with the terms of his contract of employment,

then the rights must be exercised, if at all, within six months of his so ceasing and, if he so ceases for any other reason within three years of obtaining the rights, they may not be exercised at all except pursuant to such a provision of the scheme as is mentioned in paragraph 21(1)(e) below; and in relation to the case where he so ceases for any other reason more than three years after obtaining the rights the scheme must either provide that the rights may not be exercised or that they must be exercised, if at all, within six months of his so ceasing.

20. The scheme must provide that where a person who has obtained rights under it continues to hold the office or employment by virtue of which he is eligible to participate in the scheme after the date on which he reaches pensionable age, he may exercise the rights within six months of that date.

21.—(1) The scheme may provide that—

(a) if any person obtains control of a company whose shares are scheme shares as a result of making a general offer falling within paragraph 15(a)(i) or (ii) above, rights obtained under the scheme to acquire shares in the company may be exercised within six months of the time when the person making the offer has obtained control of the company and any condition subject to which the offer is made has been satisfied;

1985 c. 6
S.I. 1986/1032
(N.I. 6).

(b) if under section 425 of the Companies Act 1985 or Article 418 of the Companies (Northern Ireland) Order 1986 (power to compromise with creditors and members) the court sanctions a compromise or arrangement proposed for the purposes of or in connection with a scheme for the reconstruction of a company whose shares are scheme shares or its amalgamation with any other company or companies, rights obtained under the share option scheme to acquire shares in the company may be exercised within six months of the court sanctioning the compromise or arrangement;

(c) if any person becomes bound or entitled, under sections 428 to 430 of that Act of 1985 or Articles 421 to 423 of that Order of 1986 (power to acquire shares of shareholders dissenting from schemes or contract approved by majority), to acquire shares in a company shares in which are scheme shares, rights obtained under the scheme to acquire shares in the company may be exercised at any time when that person remains so bound or entitled;

(d) if a company whose shares are scheme shares passes a resolution for voluntary winding up, rights obtained under a scheme to acquire shares in the company may be exercised within six months of the passing of the resolution; and

(e) if a person ceases to hold an office or employment by virtue of which he is eligible to participate in the scheme by reason only that—

　　(i) that office or employment is in a company of which the grantor ceases to have control; or

　　(ii) that office or employment relates to a business or part of a business which is transferred to a person who is neither an associated company of the grantor nor a company of which the grantor has control;

rights under the scheme held by that person may be exercised within six months of his so ceasing.

(2) For the purposes of this paragraph a person shall be deemed to have obtained control of a company if he and others acting in concert with him have together obtained control of it.

(3) Where a scheme which has been approved before 1st August 1986 has been or is altered before 1st August 1988 so as to include such a provision as is specified in sub-paragraph (1)(e) above, the scheme as altered may by virtue of this sub-paragraph apply that provision to rights obtained under the scheme before the date on which the alteration takes effect, and where that provision is so applied in relation to such rights—

(a) the scheme may permit a person having such rights to take advantage of the provision notwithstanding that under the scheme he would otherwise be unable to exercise those rights after he has ceased to hold the office or employment in question; and

(b) if, before the date on which the alteration takes effect, a person who held such rights on 18th March 1986 ceases, in either of the circumstances set out in sub-paragraph (1)(e) above, to hold an office or employment by virtue of which he was eligible to participate in the scheme, then, so far as concerns the rights so held, the scheme may permit him to take advantage of the provision in question as if the alteration had been made immediately before he ceased to hold that office or employment; and

(c) the application of the provision shall not itself be regarded as the acquisition of a right for the purposes of this Schedule.

This sub-paragraph has effect subject to paragraph 4 above.

22. Except as provided in paragraph 18 above, rights obtained by a person under the scheme must not be capable—

(a) of being transferred by him, or

(b) of being exercised later than six months after the bonus date.

23. No person shall be treated for the purposes of paragraph 19 or 21(1)(e) above as ceasing to hold an office or employment by virtue of which he is eligible to participate in the scheme until he ceases to hold an office or employment in the grantor or in any associated company or company of which the grantor has control.

24.—(1) The scheme must provide for a person's contributions under the certified contractual savings scheme to be of such amount as to secure as nearly as may be repayment of an amount equal to that for which shares may be acquired in pursuance of rights obtained under the scheme; and for this purpose the amount of repayment under the certified contractual savings scheme shall be determined as mentioned in paragraph 17 above.

(2) The scheme must not—

(a) permit the aggregate amount of a person's contributions under certified contractual savings schemes linked to savings-related share option schemes approved under this Schedule to exceed £100 monthly, nor

(b) impose a minimum on the amount of a person's contributions which exceeds £10 monthly.

(3) The Treasury may by order amend sub-paragraph (2) above by substituting for any amount for the time being specified in that sub-paragraph such amount as may be specified in the order.

25. The price at which scheme shares may be acquired by the exercise of a right obtained under the scheme—

(a) must be stated at the time the right is obtained, and

(b) must not be manifestly less than 90 per cent. of the market value of shares of the same class at that time or, if the Board and the grantor agree in writing, at such earlier time or times as may be provided in the agreement,

but the scheme may provide for such variation of the price as may be necessary to take account of any variation in the share capital of which the scheme shares form part.

26.—(1) Subject to paragraph 8 above, every person who—

(a) is a full-time employee or a full-time director of the grantor or, in the case of a group scheme, a participating company, and

(b) has been such an employee or director at all times during a qualifying period not exceeding five years, and

(c) is chargeable to tax in respect of his office or employment under Case I of Schedule E,

must be eligible to participate in the scheme, that is to say, to obtain and exercise rights under it, on similar terms, and those who do participate in the scheme must actually do so on similar terms.

(2) For the purposes of sub-paragraph (1) above, the fact that the rights to be obtained by the persons participating in a scheme vary according to the levels of their remuneration, the length of their service or similar factors shall not be regarded as meaning that they are not eligible to participate in the scheme on similar terms or do not actually do so.

(3) Except as provided by paragraph 19 above or pursuant to such a provision as is referred to in paragraph 21(1)(e) above, a person must not be eligible to participate in the scheme at any time unless he is at that time a director or employee of the grantor or, in the case of a group scheme, of a participating company.

REQUIREMENTS APPLICABLE TO OTHER SHARE OPTION SCHEMES

27.—(1) A person must not be eligible to obtain rights under the scheme at any time unless he is at that time a full-time director or qualifying employee of the grantor or, in the case of a group scheme, of a participating company, but the scheme may provide that a person may exercise rights under it after he has ceased to be a full-time director or qualifying employee.

(2) The scheme must not permit any person obtaining rights under it to transfer any of them but may provide that, if a person who has obtained rights under it dies before exercising them, they may be exercised after, but not more than one year after, the date of his death.

(3) Where the scheme contains the provision permitted by sub-paragraph (2) above and any rights are exercised—

(a) after the death of the person who obtained them; but

(b) before the expiry of the period of ten years beginning with his obtaining them;

subsection (3) of section 185 shall apply with the omission of the reference to subsection (5) of that section.

(4) In sub-paragraph (1) above "qualifying employee", in relation to a company, means an employee of the company (other than one who is a director of the company or, in the case of a group scheme, of a participating company) who is required, under the terms of his employment, to work for the company for at least 20 hours a week.

28.—(1) The scheme must provide that no person shall obtain rights under it which would, at the time they are obtained, cause the aggregate market value of the shares which he may acquire in pursuance of rights obtained under the scheme or under any other share option scheme, not being a savings-related share option scheme, approved under this Schedule and established by the grantor or by any associated company of the grantor (and not exercised) to exceed or further exceed the appropriate limit.

(2) The appropriate limit is the greater of—

(a) £100,000; or

(b) if there were relevant emoluments for the preceding year of assessment, four times the amount of the relevant emoluments for the current or preceding year of assessment (whichever of those years gives the greater amount); or

(c) if there were no relevant emoluments for the preceding year of assessment, four times the amount of the relevant emoluments for the period of 12 months beginning with the first day during the current year of assessment in respect of which there are relevant emoluments.

(3) For the purposes of sub-paragraph (1) above, the market value of shares shall be calculated as at the time when the rights in relation to those shares were obtained or, in a case where an agreement relating to them has been made under paragraph 29 below, such earlier time or times as may be provided in the agreement.

(4) For the purposes of sub-paragraph (2) above, the relevant emoluments are such of the emoluments of the office or employment by virtue of which the person in question is eligible to participate in the scheme as are liable to be paid under deduction of tax pursuant to section 203 after deducting amounts included by virtue of Chapter II of Part V.

29. The price at which scheme shares may be acquired by the exercise of a right obtained under the scheme—

(a) must be stated at the time the right is obtained, and

(b) must not be manifestly less than the market value of shares of the same class at that time or, if the Board and the grantor agree in writing, at such earlier time or times as may be provided in the agreement, but the scheme may provide for such variation of the price as may be necessary to take account of any variation in the share capital of which the scheme shares form part.

PART V

REQUIREMENTS APPLICABLE TO PROFIT SHARING SCHEMES

30.—(1) The scheme must provide for the establishment of a body of persons resident in the United Kingdom ("the trustees")—

(a) who, out of moneys paid to them by the grantor or, in the case of a group scheme, a participating company, are required by the scheme to acquire shares in respect of which the conditions in paragraphs 10 to 12 and 14 above are fulfilled; and

(b) who are under a duty to appropriate shares acquired by them to individuals who participate in the scheme, not being individuals who are ineligible by virtue of paragraph 8 or 35 of this Schedule; and

(c) whose functions with respect to shares held by them are regulated by a trust which is constituted under the law of a part of the United Kingdom and the terms of which are embodied in an instrument which complies with the provisions of paragraphs 31 to 34 below.

(2) If at any time after the Board have approved the scheme, an alteration is made in the terms of the trust referred to in sub-paragraph (1)(c) above, the approval shall not have effect after the date of the alteration unless the Board have approved the alteration.

(3) The scheme must provide that the total of the initial market values of the shares appropriated to any one participant in a year of assessment will not exceed the relevant amount.

(4) In this Part of this Schedule "initial market value", in relation to a participant's shares, means the market value of those shares determined—

(a) except where paragraph (b) below applies, on the date on which the shares were appropriated to him; and

(b) if the Board and the trustees agree in writing, on or by reference to such earlier date or dates as may be provided for in the agreement.

31. The trust instrument shall provide that, as soon as practicable after any shares have been appropriated to a participant, the trustees will give him notice of the appropriation—

(a) specifying the number and description of those shares; and

(b) stating their initial market value.

32.—(1) The trust instrument must contain a provision prohibiting the trustees from disposing of any shares, except as mentioned in paragraph 1(1)(a), (b) or (c) of Schedule 10, during the period of retention (whether by transfer to the participant or otherwise).

(2) The trust instrument must contain a provision prohibiting the trustees from disposing of any shares after the end of the period of retention and before the release date except—

    (a) pursuant to a direction given by or on behalf of the participant or any person in whom the beneficial interest in his shares is for the time being vested; and

    (b) by a transaction which would not involve a breach of the participant's obligations under paragraph 2(2)(c) or (d) above.

33. The trust instrument must contain a provision requiring the trustees—

    (a) subject to their obligations under paragraph 7 of Schedule 10 and to any such direction as is mentioned in paragraph 4(2) of that Schedule to pay over to the participant any money or money's worth received by them in respect of or by reference to any of his shares other than money's worth consisting of new shares within the meaning of paragraph 5 of that Schedule; and

    (b) to deal only pursuant to a direction given by or on behalf of the participant or any person in whom the beneficial interest in his shares is for the time being vested with any right conferred in respect of any of his shares to be allotted other shares, securities or rights of any description.

34. The trust instrument must impose an obligation on the trustees—

    (a) to maintain such records as may be necessary to enable the trustees to carry out their obligations under paragraph 7 of Schedule 10; and

    (b) where the participant becomes liable to income tax under Schedule E by reason of the occurrence of any event, to inform him of any facts relevant to determining that liability.

35.—(1) An individual shall not be eligible to have shares appropriated to him under the scheme at any time unless he is at that time or was within the preceding 18 months a director or employee of the grantor or, in the case of a group scheme, of a participating company.

(2) An individual shall not be eligible to have shares appropriated to him under the scheme at any time if in that year of assessment shares have been appropriated to him under another approved scheme established by the grantor or by—

    (a) a company which controls or is controlled by the grantor or which is controlled by a company which also controls the grantor, or

    (b) a company which is a member of a consortium owning the grantor or which is owned in part by the grantor as a member of a consortium.

36.—(1) Subject to paragraphs 8 and 35 above, every person who at any time—

    (a) is a full-time employee or a full-time director of the grantor or, in the case of a group scheme, a participating company, and

    (b) has been such an employee or director at all times during a qualifying period, not exceeding five years, ending at that time, and

    (c) is chargeable to tax in respect of his office or employment under Case I of Schedule E,

must then be eligible (subject to paragraphs 8 and 35 of this Schedule) to participate in the scheme on similar terms and those who do participate must actually do so on similar terms.

SCH. 9   (2) For the purposes of sub-paragraph (1) above, the fact that the number of shares to be appropriated to the participants in a scheme varies by reference to the levels of their remuneration, the length of their service or similar factors shall not be regarded as meaning that they are not eligible to participate in the scheme on similar terms or do not actually do so.

PART VI

MATERIAL INTEREST TEST

Interests under trusts

37.—(1) This paragraph applies in a case where—

(a) the individual ("the beneficiary") was one of the objects of a discretionary trust; and

(b) the property subject to the trust at any time consisted of or included any shares or obligations of the company.

(2) If neither the beneficiary nor any relevant associate of his had received any benefit under the discretionary trust before 14th November 1986, then, as respects any time before that date, the trustees of the settlement concerned shall not be regarded, by reason only of the matters referred to in sub-paragraph (1) above, as having been associates (as defined in section 417(3) and (4)) of the beneficiary.

(3) If, on or after 14th November 1986—

(a) the beneficiary ceases to be eligible to benefit under the discretionary trust by reason of—

(i) an irrevocable disclaimer or release executed by him under seal; or

(ii) the irrevocable exercise by the trustees of a power to exclude him from the objects of the trust; and

(b) immediately after he so ceases, no relevant associate of his is interested in the shares or obligations of the company which are subject to the trust; and

(c) during the period of 12 months ending with the date when the beneficiary so ceases, neither the beneficiary nor any relevant associate of his received any benefit under the trust,

the beneficiary shall not be regarded, by reason only of the matters referred to in sub-paragraph (1) above, as having been interested in the shares or obligations of the company as mentioned in section 417(3)(c) at any time during the period of 12 months referred to in paragraph (c) above.

(4) In sub-paragraphs (2) and (3) above "relevant associate" has the meaning given to "associate" by subsection (3) of section 417 but with the omission of paragraph (c) of that subsection.

(5) Sub-paragraph (3)(a)(i) above, in its application to Scotland, shall be construed as if the words "under seal" were omitted.

Options etc.

38.—(1) For the purposes of section 187(3)(a) a right to acquire shares (however arising) shall be taken to be a right to control them.

(2) Any reference in sub-paragraph (3) below to the shares attributed to an individual is a reference to the shares which, in accordance with section 187(3)(a), fall to be brought into account in his case to determine whether their number exceeds a particular percentage of the company's ordinary share capital.

(3) In any case where—

    (a) the shares attributed to an individual consist of or include shares which he or any other person has a right to acquire; and

    (b) the circumstances are such that, if that right were to be exercised, the shares acquired would be shares which were previously unissued and which the company is contractually bound to issue in the event of the exercise of the right;

then, in determining at any time prior to the exercise of that right whether the number of shares attributed to the individual exceeds a particular percentage of the ordinary share capital of the company, that ordinary share capital shall be taken to be increased by the number of unissued shares referred to in paragraph (b) above.

(4) This paragraph has effect as respects any time after 5th April 1987.

Shares held by trustees of approved profit sharing schemes

39. In applying section 187(3), as respects any time before or after the passing of this Act, there shall be disregarded—

    (a) the interest of the trustees of an approved profit sharing scheme in any shares which are held by them in accordance with the scheme and have not yet been appropriated to an individual; and

    (b) any rights exercisable by those trustees by virtue of that interest.

SCHEDULE 10

FURTHER PROVISIONS RELATING TO PROFIT SHARING SCHEMES

Limitations on contractual obligations of participants

1.—(1) Any obligation placed on the participant by virtue of paragraph 2(2) of Schedule 9 shall not prevent the participant from—

(a) directing the trustees to accept an offer for any of his shares ("the original shares") if the acceptance or agreement will result in a new holding being equated with the original shares for the purposes of capital gains tax; or

(b) directing the trustees to agree to a transaction affecting his shares or such of them as are of a particular class, if the transaction would be entered into pursuant to a compromise, arrangement or scheme applicable to or affecting—

   (i) all the ordinary share capital of the company in question or, as the case may be, all the shares of the class in question; or

   (ii) all the shares, or all the shares of the class in question, which are held by a class of shareholders identified otherwise than by reference to their employment or their participation in an approved scheme; or

(c) directing the trustees to accept an offer of cash, with or without other assets, for his shares if the offer forms part of a general offer which is made to holders of shares of the same class as his or of shares in the same company and which is made in the first instance on a condition such that if it is satisfied the person making the offer will have control of that company, within the meaning of section 416; or

(d) agreeing after the expiry of the period of retention to sell the beneficial interest in his shares to the trustees for the same consideration as, in accordance with sub-paragraph (d) of paragraph 2(2) of Schedule 9, would be required to be obtained for the shares themselves.

(2) No obligation placed on the participant by virtue of paragraph 2(2)(c) of Schedule 9 shall be construed as binding his personal representatives to pay any sum to the trustees.

(3) If, in breach of his obligation under paragraph 2(2)(b) of Schedule 9 a participant assigns, charges or otherwise disposes of the beneficial interest in any of his shares, then, as respects those shares, he shall be treated for the purposes of the relevant provisions as if at the time they were appropriated to him he was ineligible to participate in the scheme; and paragraph 6 below shall apply accordingly.

The period of retention

2. For the purposes of any of the relevant provisions, "the period of retention", in relation to any of a participant's shares, means the period beginning on the date on which they are appropriated to him and ending on the second anniversary of that date or, if it is earlier—

(a) the date on which the participant ceases to be a director or employee of the grantor or, in the case of a group scheme, a participating company by reason of injury or disability or on account of his being dismissed by reason of redundancy, within the meaning of the Employment Protection (Consolidation) Act 1978 or the Contracts of Employment and Redundancy Payments Act (Northern Ireland) 1965; or

1978 c. 44.
1965 c. 19 (N.I.).

(b) the date on which the participant reaches pensionable age; or

(c) the date of the participant's death;

(d) in a case where the participant's shares are redeemable shares in a workers' cooperative, the date on which the participant ceases to be employed by, or by a subsidiary of, the cooperative.

For the purposes of sub-paragraph (a) above, in the case of a group scheme, the participant shall not be treated as ceasing to be a director or employee of a participating company until such time as he is no longer a director or employee of any of the participating companies.

The appropriate percentage

3. Subject to paragraph 6(4) below, for the purposes of any of the relevant provisions charging an individual to income tax under Schedule E by reason of the occurrence of an event relating to any of his shares, any reference to "the appropriate percentage" in relation to those shares shall be determined according to the time of that event, as follows—

(a) if the event occurs before the fourth anniversary of the date on which the shares were appropriated to the participant and paragraph (c) below does not apply, the appropriate percentage is 100 per cent.;

(b) if the event occurs on or after the fourth anniversary and before the fifth anniversary of the date on which the shares were appropriated to the participant and paragraph (c) below does not apply, the appropriate percentage is 75 per cent.;

(c) if the participant—

(i) ceases to be a director or employee of the grantor or, in the case of a group scheme, a participating company as mentioned in paragraph 2(a) above, or

(ii) reaches pensionable age,

and the event occurs before the fifth anniversary of the date on which the shares were appropriated to him, the appropriate percentage is 50 per cent.

Capital receipts

4.—(1) Money or money's worth is not a capital receipt for the purposes of section 186(3) if or, as the case may be, to the extent that—

(a) it constitutes income in the hands of the recipient for the purposes of income tax; or

(b) it consists of the proceeds of a disposal falling within section 186(4); or

(c) it consists of new shares within the meaning of paragraph 5 below.

(2) If, pursuant to a direction given by or on behalf of the participant or any person in whom the beneficial interest in the participant's shares is for the time being vested, the trustees—

(a) dispose of some of the rights arising under a rights issue, as defined in section 186(8), and

(b) use the proceeds of that disposal to exercise other such rights,

the money or money's worth which constitutes the proceeds of that disposal is not a capital receipt for the purposes of section 186(3).

SCH. 10   (3) If, apart from this sub-paragraph, the amount or value of a capital receipt would exceed the sum which, immediately before the entitlement to the receipt arose, was the locked-in value of the shares to which the receipt is referable, section 186(3) shall have effect as if the amount or value of the receipt were equal to that locked-in value.

(4) Section 186(3) does not apply in relation to a capital receipt if the entitlement to it arises after the death of the participant to whose shares it is referable.

Company reconstructions

5.--(1) This paragraph applies where there occurs in relation to any of a participant's shares ("the original holding") a transaction which results in a new holding being equated with the original holding for the purposes of capital gains tax; and any such transaction is referred to below as a "company reconstruction".

(2) Where an issue of shares of any of the following descriptions (in respect of which a charge to income tax arises) is made as part of a company reconstruction, those shares shall be treated for the purposes of this paragraph as not forming part of the new holding, that is to say—

(a) redeemable shares or securities issued as mentioned in section 209(2)(c);

(b) share capital issued in circumstances such that section 210(1) applies; and

(c) share capital to which section 249 applies.

(3) In this paragraph—

"corresponding shares", in relation to any new shares, means those shares in respect of which the new shares are issued or which the new shares otherwise represent;

"new shares" means shares comprised in the new holding which were issued in respect of, or otherwise represent, shares comprised in the original holding; and

"original holding" has the meaning given by sub-paragraph (1) above.

(4) Subject to the following provisions of this paragraph, in relation to a profit sharing scheme, references in the relevant provisions to a participant's shares shall be construed, after the time of the company reconstruction, as being or, as the case may be, as including references to any new shares, and for the purposes of the relevant provisions—

(a) a company reconstruction shall be treated as not involving a disposal of shares comprised in the original holding;

(b) the date on which any new shares are to be treated as having been appropriated to the participant shall be that on which the corresponding shares were appropriated; and

(c) the conditions in paragraphs 10 to 12 and 14 of Schedule 9 shall be treated as fulfilled with respect to any new shares if they were (or were treated as) fulfilled with respect to the corresponding shares.

(5) In relation to shares comprised in the new holding, section 186(5) shall apply as if the references in that subsection to the initial market value of the shares were references to their locked-in value immediately after the company reconstruction, which shall be determined as follows—

(a) ascertain the aggregate amount of locked-in value immediately before the reconstruction of those shares comprised in the original holding which had at that time the same locked-in value; and

(b) distribute that amount *pro rata* among—

(i) such of those shares as remain in the new holding, and

(ii) any new shares in relation to which those shares are the corresponding shares, according to their market value immediately after the date of their reconstruction;

and section 186(5)(a) shall apply only to capital receipts after the date of the reconstruction.

(6) For the purposes of the relevant provisions if, as part of a company reconstruction, trustees become entitled to a capital receipt, their entitlement to the capital receipt shall be taken to arise before the new holding comes into being and, for the purposes of sub-paragraph (5) above, before the date on which the locked-in value of any shares comprised in the original holding falls to be ascertained.

(7) In the context of a new holding, any reference in this paragraph to shares includes securities and rights of any description which form part of the new holding for the purposes of Chapter II of Part IV of the 1979 Act.

Excess or unauthorised shares

6.—(1) This paragraph applies in any case where—

(a) the total amount of the initial market value of all the shares which are appropriated to an individual in any one year of assessment (whether under a single approved profit sharing scheme or under two or more such schemes) exceeds the relevant amount; or

(b) the trustees of an approved profit sharing scheme appropriate shares to an individual at a time when he is ineligible to participate in the scheme by virtue of paragraph 8 or 35 of Schedule 9.

(2) In this paragraph—

"excess shares" means any share which caused the relevant amount to be exceeded and any share appropriated after that amount was exceeded; and

"unauthorised shares" means any share appropriated as mentioned in sub-paragraph (1)(b) above.

(3) For the purposes of sub-paragraph (1)(a) above, if a number of shares is appropriated to an individual at the same time under two or more approved profit sharing schemes, the same proportion of the shares appropriated at that time under each scheme shall be regarded as being appropriated before the relevant amount is exceeded.

(4) For the purposes of any of the relevant provisions charging an individual to income tax under Schedule E by reason of the occurrence of an event relating to any of his shares—

(a) the appropriate percentage in relation to excess or unauthorised shares shall in every case be 100 per cent.; and

(b) without prejudice to section 187(8), the event shall be treated as relating to shares which are not excess or unauthorised shares before shares which are.

(5) Excess or unauthorised shares which have not been disposed of before the release date or, if it is earlier, the date of the death of the participant whose shares they are, shall be treated for the purposes of the relevant provisions as having been disposed of by the trustees immediately before the release date or, as the case may require, the date of the participant's death, for a consideration equal to their market value at that time.

(6) The locked-in value at any time of any excess or unauthorised shares shall be their market value at that time.

(7) Where there has been a company reconstruction to which paragraph 5 above applies, a new share (within the meaning of that paragraph) shall be treated as an excess or unauthorised share if the corresponding share (within the meaning of that paragraph) or, if there was more than one corresponding share, each of them was an excess or unauthorised share.

P.A.Y.E. deduction of tax

7.—(1) Subject to sub-paragraphs (4) and (5) below, where the trustees of an approved profit sharing scheme receive a sum of money which constitutes (or forms part of)—

(a) the proceeds of a disposal of shares falling within section 186(4), or

(b) a capital receipt,

in respect of which a participant in the scheme is chargeable to income tax under Schedule E in accordance with section 186, the trustees shall pay out of that sum of money to the company specified in sub-paragraph (3) below an amount equal to that on which income tax is so payable; and the company shall then pay over that amount to the participant but in so doing shall make a P.A.Y.E. deduction.

(2) Where a participant disposes of his beneficial interest in any of his shares to the trustees of the scheme and the trustees are deemed by virtue of section 186(9) to have disposed of the shares in question, this paragraph shall apply as if the consideration payable by the trustees to the participant on the disposal had been received by the trustees as the proceeds of disposal of shares falling within section 186(4).

(3) The company to which the payment mentioned in sub-paragraph (1) above is to be made is the company—

(a) of which the participant is an employee or director at the time the trustees receive the sum of money referred to in that sub-paragraph, and

(b) whose employees are at that time eligible (subject to the terms of the scheme and Schedule 9) to be participants in the approved profit sharing scheme concerned,

and if there is more than one company which falls within paragraphs (a) and (b) above, such one of those companies as the Board may direct.

(4) Where the trustees of an approved profit sharing scheme receive a sum of money to which sub-paragraph (1) above applies but—

(a) there is no company which falls within paragraphs (a) and (b) of sub-paragraph (3) above, or

(b) the Board is of opinion that it is impracticable for the company which falls within those paragraphs (or, as the case may be, any of them) to make a P.A.Y.E. deduction and accordingly direct that this sub-paragraph shall apply, then, in paying over to the participant the proceeds of the disposal or the capital receipt, the trustees shall make a P.A.Y.E. deduction in respect of an amount equal to that on which income tax is payable as mentioned in sub-paragraph (1) above as if the participant were a former employee of the trustees.

(5) Where the trustees of an approved profit sharing scheme receive a sum of money to which sub-paragraph (1) above applies and the Board direct that this sub-paragraph shall apply—

(a) the trustees shall make the payment mentioned in that sub-paragraph to the company specified in the Board's direction; and

(b) that company shall pay over that amount to the participant but in so doing shall make a P.A.Y.E. deduction, and for that purpose if the participant is not an employee of that company he shall be treated as a former employee;

but no such direction shall be given except with the consent of the trustees, the company or companies (if any) specified in sub-paragraph (3) above and the company specified in the direction.

(6) Where, in accordance with this paragraph any person is required to make a P.A.Y.E. deduction in respect of any amount, that amount shall be treated for the purposes of section 203 and any regulations made under that section as an amount of income payable to the recipient and assessable to income tax under Schedule E, and, accordingly, such deduction shall be made as is required by those regulations.

(7) Where, in connection with a transfer of a participant's shares to which sub-paragraph (c) of paragraph 2(2) of Schedule 9 applies, the trustees receive such a sum as is referred to in that sub-paragraph, that sum shall be treated for the purposes of the Income Tax Acts—

(a) as a sum deducted by the trustees pursuant to a requirement to make a P.A.Y.E. deduction under sub-paragraph (4) above; and

(b) as referable to the income tax to which, as a result of the transfer, the participant is chargeable by virtue of section 186(4).

(8) Unless the Board otherwise direct, in the application of this paragraph to a sum of money which constitutes or forms part of the proceeds of a disposal of, or a capital receipt referable to, excess or unauthorised shares (within the meaning of paragraph 6 above), the trustees shall determine the amount of the payment mentioned in sub-paragraph (1) above or, as the case may be, the amount of the P.A.Y.E. deduction to be made under sub-paragraph (4) above as if the shares were not excess or unauthorised shares.

SCHEDULE 11

RELIEF AS RESPECTS TAX ON PAYMENTS ON RETIREMENT OR REMOVAL FROM OFFICE OR EMPLOYMENT

PART I

GENERAL PROVISIONS

Preliminary

1. Relief shall be allowed in accordance with the following provisions of this Schedule in respect of tax chargeable by virtue of section 148, where a claim is made under section 188(6).

2.—(1) A person shall not be entitled to relief under this Schedule in so far as such relief, together with any personal relief allowed to him, would reduce the amount of income on which he is chargeable below the amount income tax on which he is entitled to charge against any other person, or to deduct, retain or satisfy out of any payment which he is liable to make to any other person.

(2) In sub-paragraph (1) above "personal relief" means relief under Chapter I of Part VII.

Relief by reduction of sums chargeable

3. In computing the charge to tax in respect of a payment chargeable to tax under section 148, being a payment made in respect of an office or employment in which the service of the holder includes foreign service, there shall be deducted from the payment a sum which bears to the amount which would be chargeable to tax apart from this paragraph the same proportion as the length of the foreign service bears to the length of the service before the relevant date.

Relief by reduction of tax

4.—(1) Subject to sub-paragraph (2) below, in the case of any payment in respect of which tax is chargeable under section 148, the following relief shall be allowed by way of deduction from the tax chargeable by virtue of that section, that is to say, there shall be ascertained—

    (a) the amount of tax which would be chargeable apart from this paragraph in respect of the income of the holder or past holder of the office or employment for the chargeable period of which the payment is treated as income;

    (b) the amount of tax which would have been so chargeable if the payment had not been made;

and the amount to be deducted shall be half the difference between the amount ascertained at (a) and the amount ascertained at (b).

(2) In the case of a payment which exceeds £50,000, this paragraph applies as if it were a payment of £50,000 exactly.

5.—(1) Subject to sub-paragraph (2) below, in the case of a payment which exceeds £50,000 and in respect of which tax is chargeable under section 148, the following relief shall be allowed by way of deduction from the tax chargeable by virtue of that section, that is to say, there shall be ascertained—

    (a) the amount of tax which would be chargeable apart from this paragraph and paragraph 4 above in respect of the income of the holder or past holder of the office or employment for the chargeable period of which the payment is treated as income; and

(b) the amount of tax which would have been so chargeable if the amount of the payment had been £50,000 exactly;

and the amount to be deducted shall be one-quarter of the difference between the amount ascertained at (a) and the amount ascertained at (b).

(2) In the case of a payment which exceeds £75,000, this paragraph applies as if it were a payment of £75,000 exactly.

(3) Any relief allowed by virtue of this paragraph shall be in addition to that allowed by virtue of paragraph 4 above.

6. Where tax is chargeable under section 148 in respect of two or more payments to or in respect of the same person in respect of the same office or employment and is so chargeable for the same chargeable period, those payments shall be treated for the purposes of paragraphs 4 and 5 above as a single payment of an amount equal to their aggregate amount.

7. Where tax is chargeable under section 148 in respect of two or more payments to or in respect of the same person in respect of different offices or employments and is so chargeable for the same chargeable period, paragraphs 4 to 6 above shall apply as if those payments were made in respect of the same office or employment.

Supplemental

8. Any reference in this Schedule to the emoluments of an office or employment is a reference to those emoluments exclusive of any payment chargeable to tax under section 148; and in calculating for any purpose of this Schedule the amount of such emoluments—

(a) there shall be included any balancing charge to which the holder of the office or employment is liable under section 33 of the 1968 Act or under Chapter I of Part III of the Finance Act 1971 ("the 1971 Act"), and

1971 c. 68.

(b) there shall be deducted any allowances under Chapter II of Part I of the 1968 Act or Chapter I of Part III of the 1971 Act, and any allowances for expenses under section 198 or 201, to which he is entitled,

and any such charges or allowances for a chargeable period shall, for the purpose of ascertaining the amount of the emoluments for any year of service, be treated as accruing from day to day, and shall be apportioned in respect of time accordingly.

9. In this Schedule "the relevant date" means, in relation to a payment not being a payment in commutation of annual or other periodical payments, the date of the termination or change in respect of which it is made and, in relation to a payment in commutation of annual or other periodical payments, the date of the termination or change in respect of which those payments would have been made.

10. In this Schedule, "foreign service", in relation to an office or employment, means—

(a) service before the year 1974-75 such that tax was not chargeable in respect of the emoluments of the office or employment—

(i) in the case of the year 1956-57 or any subsequent chargeable period, under Case I of Schedule E;

(ii) in the case of any preceding year of assessment, under Schedule E; or

(b) service after the year 1973-74 such that the emoluments from the office or employment were not chargeable under Case I of Schedule E (or would not have been so chargeable, had there been any) or that a deduction equal to their whole amount was or would have been allowable under paragraph 1 of Schedule 2 to the Finance Act 1974, paragraph 1 of Schedule 7 to the Finance Act 1977 or section 193(1) in charging them.

11. Any reference in this Schedule to the amount of tax to which a person is or would be chargeable is a reference to the amount of tax to which he is or would be chargeable either by assessment or by deduction.

PART II

PAYMENTS IN PURSUANCE OF PRE-10TH MARCH 1981 OBLIGATIONS

12. Where a payment is made in pursuance of an obligation incurred before 10th March 1981, the person chargeable to tax in respect of it may, by notice given to the inspector within six years after the year of assessment in which the payment is made, elect that Part I of this Schedule shall have effect in relation to the payment subject to the modifications contained in the following provisions of this Part, and those provisions shall have effect accordingly (and not otherwise).

13. The following paragraphs shall be inserted immediately before paragraph 3—

"2A. In computing the charge to tax in respect of a payment chargeable to tax under section 148, not being a payment of compensation for loss of office, there shall be deducted from the payment a sum equal to the amount (if any) by which the standard capital superannuation benefit for the office or employment in respect of which the payment is made exceeds £10,000.

2B.—(1) In this Schedule "the standard capital superannuation benefit", in relation to an office or employment, means a sum arrived at as follows, that is to say—

(a) there shall be ascertained the average for one year of the holder's emoluments from the office or employment for the last three years of his service before the relevant date (or for the whole period of his service if less than three years);

(b) one-twentieth of the amount ascertained at (a) shall be multiplied by the whole number of complete years of the service of the holder in the office or employment; and

(c) there shall be deducted from the product at (b) a sum equal to the amount, or, as the case may be, to the value at the relevant date, of any lump sum (not chargeable to tax) received or receivable by the holder in respect of the office or employment in pursuance of any such scheme or fund as was described in section 221(1) and (2) of the 1970 Act or is described in section 596.

(2) In sub-paragraph (1)(c) above the reference to a lump sum receivable by the holder includes a reference to a lump sum that would be receivable by him if he had exercised or refrained from exercising (with any necessary consent) any option or other right conferred on him by the rules of the scheme or fund.

2C. Where tax is chargeable under section 148 in respect of two or more payments to which paragraph 2A above applies, being payments made to or in respect of the same person in respect of the same office or employment or in respect of different offices or employments held under the same employer or under associated employers, then—

(a) paragraph 2A above shall apply as if those payments were a single payment of an amount equal to their aggregate amount and, where they are made in respect of different offices or employments, as if the standard capital superannuation benefit were an amount equal to the sum of the standard capital superannuation benefits for those offices or employments, and

(b) where the payments are treated as income of different chargeable periods, the relief to be granted under that paragraph in respect of a payment chargeable for any such period shall be the amount by which the relief computed in accordance with the preceding provision in respect of that payment and any payments chargeable for previous chargeable periods exceeds the relief in respect of the last mentioned payments;

and where the standard capital superannuation benefit for an office or employment in respect of which two or more of the payments are made is not the same in relation to each of those payments, it shall be treated for the purpose of this paragraph as equal to the higher or highest of those benefits."

14. In paragraph 3, after the words "from the payment" there shall be inserted the words "(in addition to any deduction allowed under the preceding provisions of this Schedule)".

15. In paragraph 4(1), for the words following sub-pargraph (b) there shall be substituted the following words—

"(c) the difference between the respective amounts of tax which would be so chargeable on the assumptions—

(i) that the appropriate fraction only of the payment (after deducting any relief applicable thereto under the preceding provisions of this Schedule) had been made, and

(ii) that no part of the payment had been made,

and disregarding, in each case, any other emoluments of the office or employment,

and the amount to be deducted shall be the difference between the amount ascertained at (a) and the sum of the amount ascertained at (b) and the appropriate multiple of the difference ascertained at (c)."

16. The following paragraphs shall be inserted after paragraph 5—

"5A.—(1) Where the income of the holder or past holder of the office or employment for the chargeable period of which the payment is treated as income includes income, income tax on which he is entitled to charge against any other person, or to deduct, retain or satisfy out of any payment which he is liable to make to any other person, the amounts referred to in sub-paragraphs (a) to (c) of paragraph 4 above shall be calculated as if that tax were not chargeable in respect of that income.

(2) Where for any year of assessment an individual claims relief under paragraph 4 above, and also under section 550 or Schedule 2, or under both that section and that Schedule, then, in computing the relief under paragraph 4 above, his income shall be deemed to include—

(a) in respect of any amount which would otherwise be included therein by virtue of section 547(1)(a), no greater amount than the appropriate fraction thereof within the meaning of section 550, and

(b) in respect of any chargeable sum within the meaning of Schedule 2 (including two or more sums treated for the purposes of paragraph 3 of that Schedule as one chargeable sum), no greater

SCH. 11

amount than the balance (if any) of the yearly equivalent thereof remaining after the making of any deduction required by that paragraph.

5B. In this Schedule "the appropriate fraction" (except in paragraph 5A(2)(a)) and "the appropriate multiple", in relation to any payment, mean respectively—

(a) where the payment is not a payment of compensation for loss of office, one-sixth and six, and

(b) where the payment is a payment of compensation for loss of office, one divided by the relevant number of years of unexpired service, and that number of years,

and for the purposes of this paragraph "the relevant number of years of unexpired service" means the number of complete years taken into account in calculating the amount of the payment, being years for which the holder of the office or employment would have been entitled (otherwise than by virtue of arrangements made in contemplation of his retirement or removal or of any relevant change in the functions or emoluments of the office or employment) to retain the office or employment or its full emoluments, and where the period so taken into account is less than one complete year or exceeds an exact number of years, it shall be treated for the purposes of this paragraph as one complete year or as the next higher number of complete years, as the case may be."

17. The following proviso shall be added at the end of paragraph 6—

"Provided that, where the appropriate fraction and the appropriate multiple are not the same for each of the payments, the calculations of relief under paragraph 4 above shall be made separately in relation to each payment or payments having a different appropriate fraction and multiple, and in any such calculation—

(a) any payment for which the appropriate multiple is lower shall be left out of account for all the purposes of that paragraph, and

(b) in ascertaining the difference at (c) of that paragraph it shall be assumed that the appropriate fraction only of any payment for which the appropriate multiple is higher had been made,

and the relief to be allowed shall be the sum of the reliefs so calculated in respect of the payments respectively."

18. The following words shall be added at the end of paragraph 7—

"and as if any emoluments of any of those offices or employments were emoluments of the same office or employment."

19. The following paragraph shall be inserted after paragraph 8—

"8A. In this Schedule "payment of compensation for loss of office" means a payment made—

(a) in pursuance of an order of a court in proceedings for wrongful dismissal or otherwise for breach of contract of employment, or by way of settlement of such proceedings or of a claim in respect of which such proceedings could have been brought, or

(b) by way of compensation for the extinguishment of any right the infringement of which would be actionable in such proceedings,

and any question whether, and to what extent, a payment is or is not a payment of compensation for loss of office shall be determined according to all the circumstances and not (or not exclusively) by reference to the terms on which it is expressed to be made."

SCHEDULE 12

FOREIGN EARNINGS

1. This Schedule shall have effect for the purpose of supplementing the provisions of section 193(1).

Emoluments eligible for relief

2.—(1) This paragraph has effect where a deduction falls to be allowed under section 193(1) in respect of the emoluments from an employment ("the relevant employment") for a year of assessment in which the duties of—

(a) the relevant employment; or

(b) any other employment or employments held by the person concerned which are associated with the relevant employment,

are not performed wholly outside the United Kingdom.

(2) The amount of the emoluments from the relevant employment in respect of which such a deduction is allowed for the year of assessment shall not exceed such proportion of the emoluments for that year from the relevant employment and the other employment or employments (if any) as is shown to be reasonable having regard to the nature of and time devoted to the duties performed outside and in the United Kingdom respectively and to all other relevant circumstances.

(3) For the purposes of this paragraph an employment is associated with another if they are with the same person or with persons associated with each other and—

(a) a company is associated with another company if one of them has control of the other within the meaning of section 416 or both of them are under the control within the meaning of that section of the same person or persons,

(b) an individual or partnership is associated with another person (whether or not a company) if one of them has control of the other within the meaning of section 840 or both are under the control within the meaning of that section of the same person or persons;

but paragraph (b) above shall not be construed as requiring an individual to be treated in any circumstances as under the control of another person.

Qualifying periods

3.—(1) For the purposes of section 193(1) a qualifying period is a period of consecutive days which either—

(a) consists entirely of days of absence from the United Kingdom; or

(b) consists partly of such days and partly of days included by virtue of sub-paragraph (2) below.

(2) Where, in the case of any person, a period consisting entirely of days of absence from the United Kingdom ("the relevant period") comes to an end and there have previously been one or more qualifying periods, the relevant period and the (or, if more than one, the last) qualifying period together with the intervening days between those periods shall be treated as a single qualifying period provided that—

(a) there are no more than 62 intervening days, and

(b) the number of days in the resulting period which are not days of absence from the United Kingdom does not exceed one-sixth of the total number of days in that period.

(3) For the purposes of section 193(1) the emoluments from an employment attributable to a qualifying period include any emoluments from that employment for a period of leave immediately following that period but not so as to make any emoluments for one year of assessment emoluments for another.

Supplementary

4. For the purposes of this Schedule a person shall not be regarded as absent from the United Kingdom on any day unless he is so absent at the end of it.

5. Notwithstanding section 132(4)(b), there shall be treated for the purposes of section 193(1) and this Schedule as performed outside the United Kingdom any duties which a person performs on a vessel or aircraft engaged on—

(a) a voyage or journey beginning or ending outside the United Kingdom (but exclusive of any part of it which begins and ends in the United Kingdom); or

(b) any part beginning or ending outside the United Kingdom of a voyage or journey which begins and ends in the United Kingdom;

and for the purposes of this paragraph any area designated under section 1(7) of the Continental Shelf Act 1964 shall be treated as part of the United Kingdom.

1964 c. 29.

6. Where an employment is in substance one the duties of which fall in the year of assessment to be performed in the United Kingdom, then, for the purposes of section 193(1), there shall be treated as so performed any duties performed outside the United Kingdom the performance of which is merely incidental to the performance of other duties in the United Kingdom.

7. In this Schedule references to an employment include references to an office.

Section 238(5),
241(4).

SCHEDULE 13

COLLECTION OF ADVANCE CORPORATION TAX

Duty to make returns

1.—(1) A company shall for each of its accounting periods make, in accordance with this Schedule, returns to the collector of the franked payments made and franked investment income received by it in that period and of the advance corporation tax (if any) payable by it in respect of those payments.

(2) A return shall be made for—

(a) each complete quarter falling within the accounting period, that is to say, each of the periods of three months ending with 31st March, 30th June, 30th September or 31st December which falls within that period:

(b) each part of the accounting period which is not a complete quarter and ends on the first (or only), or begins immediately after the last (or only), of those dates which falls within the accounting period;

(c) if none of those dates falls within the accounting period, the whole accounting period.

(3) A return for any period for which a return is required to be made under this paragraph ("a return period") shall be made within 14 days from the end of that period.

(4) Subject to paragraphs 4(2) and 7(3) below, no return need be made under this Schedule by a company for any period in which it has made no franked payments.

Contents of return

2.—(1) Subject to paragraph 7(2) below, the return made by a company for any return period shall show—

(a) the amount of the franked payments made by it in that period;

(b) the amount of franked investment income, if any, received by it in that period, and

(c) if any advance corporation tax is payable in respect of those payments, the amount thereof.

(2) The return shall specify whether any amount of franked payments is included under paragraph (a) of sub-paragraph (1) above in consequence of the giving of a notice under section 247(3) and, if so, the amount so included.

(3) For the purposes of paragraph (b) of sub-paragraph (1) above the amount of franked investment income received by a company in a return period shall be treated as including the excess, if any, of—

(a) any surplus of franked investment income carried forward to the accounting period for which the return is made; and

(b) any amount of franked investment income received by the company in that accounting period but before the beginning of the return period,

over the amount of any franked payments made by the company in that accounting period but before the beginning of the return period.

(4) For the purposes of paragraph (c) of sub-paragraph (1) above advance corporation tax shall be payable in respect of franked payments made in a return period if—

(a) the amount shown under paragraph (a) of that sub-paragraph exceeds the amount shown under paragraph (b) of that sub-paragraph, or

(b) no amount is shown under paragraph (b) of that sub-paragraph;

and the amount of that tax shall be calculated at the rate of advance corporation tax in force for the financial year in which the return period ends on an amount which, when that tax is added to it, is equal to that excess or, if no amount is shown under sub-paragraph (1)(b) above, to the amount shown under sub-paragraph (1)(a) above.

Payment of tax

3.—(1) Subject to paragraph 7(2) below, advance corporation tax in respect of franked payments required to be included in a return under this Schedule shall be due at the time by which the return for that period is to be made, and advance corporation tax so due shall be payable without the making of any assessment.

(2) Advance corporation tax which has become so due may be assessed on the company (whether or not it has been paid when the assessment is made) if that tax, or any part of it, is not paid on or before the due date.

(3) If it appears to the inspector that there is a franked payment which ought to have been and has not been included in a return, or if the inspector is dissatisfied with any return, he may make an assessment on the company to the best of his judgment; and any advance corporation tax due under an assessment made by virtue of this sub-paragraph shall be treated for the purposes of interest on unpaid tax as having been payable at the time when it would have been payable if a correct return had been made.

Receipt of franked investment income after payment of advance corporation tax

4.—(1) This paragraph shall have effect where—

(a) a return has been made of franked payments made in any return period falling within an accounting period and advance corporation tax has been paid in respect of those payments; and

(b) the company receives franked investment income after the end of the return period but before the end of the accounting period.

(2) The company shall make a return under paragraph 1 above for the return period in which the franked investment income is received whether or not it has made any franked payments in that period, and, subject to sub-paragraph (3) below, shall be entitled to repayment of any advance corporation tax paid (and not repaid) in respect of franked payments made in the accounting period in question.

(3) If no franked payments were made by the company in the return period for which a return is made by virtue of sub-paragraph (2) above the amount of the repayment shall not exceed the amount of the tax credit comprised in the franked investment income received; and in any other case the repayment shall not exceed the amount of the tax credit comprised in so much of that franked investment income, if any, as exceeds the amount of the franked payments made in that return period.

Claims for set-off in respect of franked investment income received by a company

5. Where under paragraph 2 or 4 above franked investment income received by a company falls to be taken into account in determining—

(a) whether advance corporation tax is payable or repayable; or

(b) the amount of such tax which is payable or repayable,

SCH. 13

the inclusion of that franked investment income in the appropriate return shall be treated as a claim by the company to have it so taken into account, and any such claim shall be supported by such evidence as the inspector may reasonably require.

6.—(1) Where a claim has been made under paragraph 5 above no proceedings for collecting tax which would fall to be discharged if the claim were allowed shall be instituted pending the final determination of the claim, but this sub-paragraph shall not affect the date when the tax is due.

(2) When the claim is finally determined any tax underpaid in consequence of sub-paragraph (1) above shall be paid.

(3) Where proceedings are instituted for collecting tax assessed, or interest on tax assessed, under any provision of this Schedule, effect shall not be given to any claim made after the institution of the proceedings so as to affect or delay the collection or recovery of the tax charged by the assessment or of interest thereon, until the claim has been finally determined.

(4) When the claim is finally determined any tax overpaid in consequence of sub-paragraph (3) above shall be repaid.

(5) References in this paragraph to proceedings for the collection of tax include references to proceedings by way of distraint or poinding for tax.

Qualifying distributions which are not payments and payments of uncertain nature

7.—(1) This paragraph applies to—

   (a) any qualifying distribution which is not a payment; and

   (b) any payment in respect of which the company making it would be liable to pay advance corporation tax if, but only if, it amounted to or involved a qualifying distribution and it is not in the circumstances clear whether or how far it does so.

(2) No amount shall be shown in respect of the qualifying distribution or payment under paragraph 2(1)(a) or (c) above and paragraph 3(1) above shall not apply to the payment of advance corporation tax in respect thereof.

(3) Particulars of the qualifying distribution or payment shall be given separately in the return for the return period in which it is made and if, apart from that distribution or payment, no franked payment is made in that period, a return containing those particulars shall be made for that period under paragraph 1 above.

(4) Any advance corporation tax payable in respect of the qualifying distribution or payment shall be assessed on the company and shall be so assessed without regard to any franked investment income received by the company but—

   (a) relief shall be given from the tax assessed (by discharge thereof) to the extent, if any, to which that tax exceeds the tax that would have been payable if the amount of the franked payment comprising the qualifying distribution or payment, calculated on the amount or value thereof shown in the assessment, had been included in the return under sub-paragraph (1)(a) of paragraph 2 above and the tax had been calculated in accordance with sub-paragraph (4) of that paragraph; and

   (b) for the purposes of the application of sub-paragraph (3) of that paragraph to any subsequent return period, the amount of that franked payment shall be taken to be the amount so calculated.

Items included in error

8. Where any item has been included in a return under this Schedule as a

franked payment made or as franked investment income received by a company but that item should have been included in a return or claim under Schedule 16, the inspector may make any such assessments, adjustments or set-offs as may be required for securing that the resulting liabilities to tax (including interest on unpaid tax) whether of the company or of any other person are the same as they would have been if the item had been included in the right return or claim.

Qualifying distribution made otherwise than in an accounting period

9. Where a company makes a qualifying distribution on a date which does not fall within an accounting period the company shall make a return of that distribution within 14 days from that date, and the advance corporation tax in respect thereof shall be due at the time by which the return is to be made, except where the distribution is not a payment in which case the advance corporation tax shall be assessed on the company.

Assessments and due date of tax

10.—(1) All the provisions of the Corporation Tax Acts as to the time within which an assessment may be made, so far as they refer or relate to the accounting period for which an assessment is made, or the accounting period to which an assessment relates, shall apply in relation to an assessment under this Schedule notwithstanding that, under this Schedule, the assessment may be said to relate to a quarter or other period which is not an accounting period; and the provisions of sections 36 and 39 of the Management Act as to the circumstances in which an assessment may be made out of time shall apply accordingly on the footing that any such assessment relates to the accounting period in which the quarter or other period ends or, in the case of an assessment under paragraph 9 above, to an accounting period ending on the date on which the distribution is made.

(2) Advance corporation tax assessed on a company under this Schedule shall be due within 14 days after the issue of the notice of assessment (unless due earlier under paragraph 3(1) or 9 above).

(3) Sub-paragraph (2) above has effect subject to any appeal against the assessment, but no such appeal shall affect the date when tax is due under paragraph 3(1) or 9 above.

(4) On the determination of an appeal against an assessment under this Schedule any tax overpaid shall be repaid.

(5) Any tax assessable under any one or more of the provisions of this Schedule may be included in one assessment if the tax so included is all due on the same date.

SCHEDULE 14

PROVISIONS ANCILLARY TO SECTION 266

PART I

MODIFICATION OF SECTION 266 IN CERTAIN CASES

Husband and wife

1.—(1) The references in section 266 to an individual's spouse shall include any person who was that individual's spouse at the time the insurance or contract was made, unless the marriage was dissolved before 6th April 1979.

(2) Where an election under section 287 is in force, the relief to which either the husband or the wife is entitled under section 266 in respect of an insurance or contract on the life of the other or made by the other shall not be affected by section 287(4), (5) or (6).

(3) Where throughout a year of assessment a woman is a married woman living with her husband, then—

  (a) if no election under section 283 is in force, section 274 and paragraph 6 below shall apply as if any relief to which the wife is entitled under section 266 were relief to which the husband is entitled; and

  (b) if such an election is in force, section 274 and paragraph 6 below shall apply separately to the amounts paid by each of them, but as if for the limit specified in that section there were substituted, in relation to each of them, a limit of £750 or one-twelfth of their total income, whichever is the greater, plus any amount by which the payments in respect of which relief can be given to the other fall short of the limit so substituted.

Premiums payable to friendly societies and industrial assurance companies

2.—(1) This paragraph applies to—

  (a) a policy issued in the course of an industrial assurance business; and

  (b) a policy issued by a registered friendly society in the course of tax exempt life or endowment business (as defined in section 466).

1976 c.40.

(2) Subject to paragraph 3(2) below, if a policy to which this paragraph applies was issued before the passing of the Finance Act 1976 (29th July 1976), section 266 shall have effect in relation to it as if subsections (2)(b), (3)(a), (b) and (d) were omitted; and if a policy to which this paragraph applies was issued after the passing of that Act, subsection (2)(b) of that section shall have effect in relation to it as if it permitted the insurance to be on the life of the individual's parent or grandparent or, subject to sub-paragraph (3) below, on the life of the individual's child or grandchild.

1976 c.40.

(3) Relief may be given in respect of premiums under a policy of insurance on the life of an individual's child or grandchild which was or is issued after the passing of the Finance Act 1976 (29th July 1976), as if subsection (3)(d) of section 266 were omitted, but may be given only if the annual amount of the premiums, together with that of any relevant premiums, does not exceed £52 if the policy was issued in respect of an insurance made before 25th March 1982 or £64 in any other case.

(4) For the purposes of sub-paragraph (3) above, a relevant premium, in relation to an insurance made at any time on the life of an individual's child or grandchild, is any premium under a policy of insurance on the same life, where the insurance is made at the same time or earlier, whether it is made by the individual or any other person.

(5) In this paragraph "child" includes a step-child and an illegitimate child whose parents have married each other after his birth, and "grandchild", "parent" and "grandparent" have corresponding meanings.

3.—(1) Where a policy is issued or a contract is made by a registered friendly society or a policy to which paragraph 2 above applies is issued by an industrial assurance company, section 266(4), (5) and (8) shall apply in relation to premiums payable under the policy or contract subject to the following provisions of this paragraph.

(2) References to the deductions authorised under section 266(5) shall be construed as including references to any amount retained by or refunded to the person paying the premium under any scheme made by the society or company in accordance with regulations made under this paragraph.

(3) The appropriate authority may make regulations authorising—

(a) the adoption by registered friendly societies and industrial assurance companies of any prescribed scheme for securing that in the case of policies or contracts to which the scheme applies amounts equal to 15 per cent. of the premiums payable are retained by or refunded to the person paying the premiums or that, in the case of such policies or contracts issued or made before 6th April 1979, the amounts expressed as the amounts of the premiums payable are treated as amounts arrived at by deducting 15 per cent. from the amounts payable and that the amounts of the capital sums assured or guaranteed are treated as correspondingly increased; or

(b) the adoption by any such society or company of any special scheme for that purpose which may, in such circumstances as may be prescribed, be approved by the appropriate authority.

(4) Increases treated as made in pursuance of regulations under this paragraph shall not be treated as variations of a policy or contract and shall be disregarded for the purposes of paragraph 2(3) above, sections 268(6), 460, 461(1) and 464 of, and paragraph 7 of Schedule 15 to, this Act and section 100 of the Stamp Act 1891 and the heading "Policy of Life Insurance" in Schedule 1 to that Act.

(5) The regulations may include such adaptations and modifications of the enactments relating to friendly societies or industrial assurance companies and such other incidental and supplementary provisions as appear to the appropriate authority necessary or expedient for the purpose of enabling such societies or companies to adopt the schemes authorised by the regulations.

(6) Subsections (4), (5) and (7) to (11) of section 6 of the Decimal Currency Act 1969 shall, with the necessary modifications, apply in relation to regulations made under this paragraph.

PART II

SUPPLEMENTARY PROVISIONS AS TO RELIEF UNDER SECTION 266

4.—(1) Where it appears to the Board that the relief (if any) to which a person is entitled under section 266 has been exceeded or might be exceeded unless the premiums payable by him under any policy or contract were paid in full, they may, by notice to that person and to the person to whom the payments are made, exclude the application of subsection (5) of that section in relation to any payments due or made after such date as may be specified in the notice and before such date as may be specified in a further notice to those persons.

(2) Where the application of section 266(5) is so excluded in relation to any payments, the relief (if any) to which the person by whom the payments are made is entitled under section 266 shall be given to him under paragraph 6 below.

5. Where a person is entitled to relief under section 266 in respect of a payment to which section 595 applies, section 266(5) shall not apply but the like relief shall be given to him under paragraph 6 below.

6.—(1) Where in any year of assessment the relief to which a person is entitled under section 266, otherwise than in accordance with subsections (6) and (7) of that section, has not been fully given in accordance with that section and the preceding provisions of this Schedule, he may claim relief for the difference, and relief for the difference shall then be given by a payment made by the Board or by discharge or repayment of tax or partly in one such manner and partly in another; and where relief so given to any person exceeds that to which he is entitled under section 266, he shall be liable to make good the excess and an inspector may make such assessments as may in his judgment be required for recovering the excess.

(2) The Management Act shall apply to any assessment under this paragraph as if it were an assessment to tax for the year of assessment in which the relief was given and as if—

(a) the assessment were among those specified in sections 55(1) (recovery of tax not postponed) and 86(2) (interest on overdue tax) of that Act; and

(b) the sum charged by the assessment were tax specified in paragraph 3 of the Table in section 86(4) of that Act (reckonable date).

7.—(1) The Board may make regulations for carrying into effect section 266(4), (5), (8) and (9) and the preceding provisions of this Schedule and paragraphs 9 and 10 of Schedule 15 ("the relevant provisions").

(2) Regulations under this paragraph may, without prejudice to the generality of sub-paragraph (1) above, provide—

(a) for the furnishing of such information by persons by whom premiums are payable as may be necessary for determining whether they are entitled to make deductions under section 266(5) and for excluding the operation of that subsection in relation to payments made by persons who fail to comply with the regulations;

(b) for rounding to a multiple of one penny any payment which, after a deduction authorised under section 266(5), is not such a multiple;

(c) for the manner in which claims for the recovery of any sum under section 266(5)(b) may be made;

(d) for the furnishing of such information by persons by or to whom premiums are payable as appears to the Board necessary for deciding such claims and for exercising their powers under paragraph 4 or 6 above; and

(e) for requiring persons to whom premiums are paid to make available for inspection by an officer authorised by the Board such books and other documents in their possession or under their control as may reasonably be required for the purposes of determining whether any information given by those persons for the purposes of the relevant provisions is correct and complete.

(3) The following provisions of the Management Act, that is to say—

(a) section 29(3)(c) (excessive relief);

(b) section 30 (recovery of tax repaid in consequence of fraud or negligence etc.);

(c) section 88 (interest); and

(d) section 95 (incorrect return or accounts);

shall apply in relation to the payment of a sum claimed under section 266(5)(b) to which the claimant was not entitled as if it had been income tax repaid as a relief which was not due.

8.—(1) A policy of life insurance issued in respect of an insurance made on or before 19th March 1968 shall be treated for the purposes of section 266(3)(b) as issued in respect of one made after that date if varied after that date so as to increase the benefits secured or to extend the term of the insurance.

(2) A variation effected before the end of the year 1968 shall be disregarded for the purposes of sub-paragraph (1) above if its only effect was to bring into conformity with paragraph 2 of Schedule 9 to the Finance Act 1968 (qualifying conditions for endowment policies, and now re-enacted as paragraph 2 of Schedule 15 to this Act) a policy previously conforming therewith except as respects the amount guaranteed on death, and no increase was made in the premiums payable under the policy.

(3) A policy which was issued in the course of industrial assurance business in respect of an insurance made after 13th March 1984 shall be treated for the purposes of section 266(3)(c) and this paragraph as issued in respect of an insurance made on or before that date if—

(a) the proposal form for the policy was completed on or before that date; and

(b) on or before 31st March 1984 the policy was prepared for issue by the company or society concerned; and

(c) on or before 31st March 1984 and in accordance with the normal business practice of the company or society a permanent record of the preparation of the policy was made in any book or by any other means kept or instituted by the company or society for the purpose.

(4) For the purposes of section 266(3)(c) a policy of life insurance which was issued in respect of an insurance made on or before 13th March 1984 shall be treated as issued in respect of an insurance made after that date if the policy is varied after that date so as to increase the benefits secured or to extend the term of the insurance.

(5) If a policy of life insurance which was issued as mentioned in sub-paragraph (4) above confers on the person to whom it was issued an option to have another policy substituted for it or to have any of its terms changed, then, for the purposes of that sub-paragraph and section 266(3)(c), any change in the terms of the policy which is made in pursuance of the option shall be deemed to be a variation of the policy.

(6) In any case where—

(a) one policy is replaced by another in such circumstances that the provisions of paragraph 20 of Schedule 15 apply; and

(b) the earlier policy was issued in respect of an insurance made on or before 13th March 1984; and

(c) the later policy confers on the life or lives assured thereby benefits which are substantially equivalent to those which would have been enjoyed by the life or lives assured under the earlier policy, if that policy had continued in force;

SCH. 14   then, for the purposes of section 266(3)(c), the insurance in respect of which the later policy is issued shall be deemed to have been made before 13th March 1984; and in this sub-paragraph "the earlier policy" and "the later policy" have the same meaning as in paragraph 20 of Schedule 15.

(7) In any case where—

(a) there is a substitution of policies falling within paragraph 25(1) or (3) of Schedule 15; and

(b) the old policy was issued in respect of an insurance made on or before 13th March 1984;

then, for the purposes of section 266(3)(c), the insurance in respect of which the new policy is issued shall be deemed to have been made before 13th March 1984; and in this sub-paragraph "the old policy" and "the new policy" have the same meaning as in paragraph 17 of Schedule 15.

Section 267.

SCHEDULE 15

QUALIFYING POLICIES

PART I

QUALIFYING CONDITIONS

General rules applicable to whole life and term assurances

1.—(1) Subject to the following provisions of this Part of this Schedule, if a policy secures a capital sum which is payable only on death, or one payable either on death or on earlier disability, it is a qualifying policy if—

    (a) it satisfies the conditions appropriate to it under sub-paragraphs (2) to (5) below, and

    (b) except to the extent permitted by sub-paragraph (7) below, it does not secure any other benefits.

(2) If the capital sum referred to in sub-paragraph (1) above is payable whenever the event in question happens, or if it happens at any time during the life of a specified person—

    (a) the premiums under the policy must be payable at yearly or shorter intervals, and either—

        (i) until the happening of the event or, as the case may require, until the happening of the event or the earlier death of the specified person, or

        (ii) until the time referred to in sub-paragraph (i) above or the earlier expiry of a specified period ending not earlier than ten years after the making of the insurance; and

    (b) the total premiums payable in any period of 12 months must not exceed—

        (i) twice the amount of the total premiums payable in any other such period, or

        (ii) one-eighth of the total premiums which would be payable if the policy were to continue in force for a period of ten years from the making of the insurance, or, in a case falling within sub-paragraph (ii) of paragraph (a) above, until the end of the period referred to in that sub-paragraph.

(3) If the capital sum referred to in sub-paragraph (1) above is payable only if the event in question happens before the expiry of a specified term ending more than ten years after the making of the insurance, or only if it happens both before the expiry of such a term and during the life of a specified person—

    (a) the premiums under the policy must be payable at yearly or shorter intervals, and either—

        (i) until the happening of the event or the earlier expiry of that term or, as the case may require, until the happening of the event or, if earlier, the expiry of the term or the death of the specified person, or

        (ii) as in sub-paragraph (i) above, but with the substitution for references to the term of references to a specified shorter period being one ending not earlier than ten years after the making of the insurance or, if sooner, the expiry of three-quarters of that term; and

(b) the total premiums payable in any period of 12 months must not exceed—

(i) twice the amount of the total premiums payable in any other such period, or

(ii) one-eighth of the total premiums which would be payable if the policy were to continue in force for the term referred to in sub-paragraph (i) of paragraph (a) above, or, as the case may require, for the shorter period referred to in sub-paragraph (ii) of that paragraph.

(4) If the capital sum referred to in sub-paragraph (1) above is payable only if the event in question happens before the expiry of a specified term ending not more than ten years after the making of the insurance, or only if it happens both before the expiry of such a term and during the life of a specified person, the policy must provide that any payment made by reason of its surrender during the period is not to exceed the total premiums previously paid under the policy.

(5) Except where—

(a) the capital sum referred to in sub-paragraph (1) above is payable only in the circumstances mentioned in sub-paragraph (3) or (4) above; and

(b) the policy does not provide for any payment on the surrender in whole or in part of the rights conferred by it; and

(c) the specified term mentioned in sub-paragraph (3) or, as the case may be, (4) above ends at or before the time when the person whose life is insured attains the age of 75 years;

the capital sum, so far as payable on death, must not be less than 75 per cent. of the total premiums that would be payable if the death occurred at the age of 75 years, the age being, if the sum is payable on the death of the first to die of two persons, that of the older of them, if on the death of the survivor of them, that of the younger of them, and in any other case, that of the person on whose death it is payable; and if the policy does not secure a capital sum in the event of death occurring before the age of 16 or some lower age, it must not provide for the payment in that event of an amount exceeding the total premiums previously paid under it.

(6) In determining for the purposes of sub-paragraph (5) above whether a capital sum is less than 75 per cent. of the total premiums, any amount included in the premiums by reason of their being payable otherwise than annually shall be disregarded, and if the policy is issued in the course of an industrial assurance business, 10 per cent. of the premiums payable under the policy shall be treated as so included.

(7) Notwithstanding sub-paragraph (1)(b) above, if a policy secures a capital sum payable only on death, it may also secure benefits (including benefits of a capital nature) to be provided in the event of a person's disability; and no policy is to be regarded for the purposes of that provision as securing other benefits by reason only of the fact that—

(a) it confers a right to participate in profits, or

(b) it provides for a payment on the surrender in whole or in part of the rights conferred by the policy, or

(c) it gives an option to receive payments by way of annuity, or

(d) it makes provision for the waiver of premiums by reason of a person's disability, or for the effecting of a further insurance or insurances without the production of evidence of insurability.

(8) In applying sub-paragraph (2) or (3) above to any policy—

(a) no account shall be taken of any provision for the waiver of premiums by reason of a person's disability, and

(b) if the term of the policy runs from a date earlier, but not more than three months earlier, than the making of the insurance, the insurance shall be treated as having been made on that date, and any premium paid in respect of the period before the making of the insurance, or in respect of that period and a subsequent period, as having been payable on that date.

(9) References in this paragraph to a capital sum payable on any event include references to any capital sum, or series of capital sums, payable by reason of that event but where what is so payable is either an amount consisting of one sum or an amount made up of two or more sums, the 75 per cent. mentioned in sub-paragraph (5) above shall be compared with the smaller or smallest amount so payable; and a policy secures a capital sum payable either on death or on disability notwithstanding that the amount payable may vary with the event.

(10) In relation to any policy issued in respect of an insurance made before 1st April 1976 this paragraph shall have effect—

(a) with the omission of sub-paragraphs (5) and (6) and in sub-paragraph (9) the words "but where what is so payable is either an amount consisting of one sum or an amount made up of two or more sums, the 75 per cent. mentioned in sub-paragraph (5) above shall be compared with the smaller or smallest amount so payable"; and

(b) with the substitution, for sub-paragraph (7)(b), of—

"(b) it carries a guaranteed surrender value;".

General rules applicable to endowment assurances

2.—(1) Subject to the following provisions of this Part of this Schedule, a policy which secures a capital sum payable either on survival for a specified term or on earlier death, or earlier death or disability, including a policy securing the sum on death only if occurring after the attainment of a specified age not exceeding 16, is a qualifying policy if it satisfies the following conditions—

(a) the term must be one ending not earlier than ten years after the making of the insurance;

(b) premiums must be payable under the policy at yearly or shorter intervals, and—

(i) until the happening of the event in question; or

(ii) until the happening of that event, or the earlier expiry of a specified period shorter than the term but also ending not earlier than ten years after the making of the insurance; or

(iii) if the policy is to lapse on the death of a specified person, until one of those times or the policy's earlier lapse;

(c) the total premiums payable under the policy in any period of 12 months must not exceed—

(i) twice the amount of the total premiums payable in any other such period, or

(ii) one-eighth of the total premiums which would be payable if the policy were to run for the specified term;

(d) the policy—

(i) must guarantee that the capital sum payable on death, or on death occurring after the attainment of a specified age not exceeding 16, will, whenever that event may happen, be equal to 75 per cent. at least of the total premiums which would be payable if the policy were to run for that term, disregarding any amounts included in those premiums by reason of their being payable otherwise than annually, except that if, at the beginning of that term, the age of the person concerned exceeds 55 years, the capital sum so guaranteed may, for each year of the excess, be less by 2 per cent. of that total than 75 per cent. thereof, the person concerned being, if the capital sum is payable on the death of the first to die of two persons, the older of them, if on the death of the survivor of them, the younger of them and in any other case the person on whose death it is payable; and

(ii) if it is a policy which does not secure a capital sum in the event of death before the attainment of a specified age not exceeding 16, must not provide for the payment in that event of an amount exceeding the total premiums previously paid thereunder; and

(e) the policy must not secure the provision (except by surrender in whole or in part of the rights conferred by the policy) at any time before the happening of the event in question of any benefit of a capital nature other than a payment falling within paragraph (d)(ii) above, or benefits attributable to a right to participate in profits or arising by reason of a person's disability.

(2) For the purposes of sub-paragraph (1)(d)(i) above, 10 per cent. of the premiums payable under any policy issued in the course of industrial assurance business shall be treated as attributable to the fact that they are not paid annually.

(3) Sub-paragraphs (8) and (9) of paragraph 1 above shall, with any necessary modifications, have effect for the purposes of this paragraph as they have effect for the purposes of that paragraph.

(4) In relation to any policy issued in respect of an insurance made before 1st April 1976 this paragraph shall have effect with the omission in sub-paragraph (1)(d)(i) of the words from "except that if" to the end, and in sub-paragraph (1)(e) of the words "in whole or in part of the rights conferred by the policy".

Special types of policy

(i) Friendly Society policies

3.—(1) Paragraphs 1 and 2 above do not apply to a policy issued by a registered friendly society in the course of tax exempt life or endowment business in respect of an insurance made or varied on or after 19th March 1985, but such a policy shall not be a qualifying policy unless—

(a) in the case of a policy for the assurance of a gross sum or annuity, the conditions in sub-paragraph (2) are fulfilled with respect to it; and

(b) in the case of a policy for the assurance of a gross sum, the conditions in sub-paragraphs (5) to (11) below are fulfilled with respect to it; and

(c) in the case of a policy issued by a new society, the contract for the insurance was made by a member of the society over the age of 18.

(2) The conditions referred to in sub-paragraph (1) above are as follows—

(a) subject to sub-paragraph (3) below, the period (the "term" of the policy) between—

(i) the making of the insurance or, where the contract provides for the term to begin on a date not more than three months earlier than the making of the insurance, that date, and

(ii) the time when the gross sum assured is payable (or, as the case may be, when the first instalment of the annuity is payable),

shall be not less than ten years, and must not, on any contingency other than the death, or retirement on grounds of ill health, of the person liable to pay the premiums or whose life is insured, become less than ten years;

(b) subject to sub-paragraph (4) below, the premiums payable under the policy shall be premiums of equal or rateable amounts payable at yearly or shorter intervals over the whole term of the policy of assurance, or over the whole term of the policy of assurance apart from any period after the person liable to pay the premiums or whose life is insured attains a specified age, being an age which he will attain at a time not less than ten years after the beginning of the term of the policy of assurance;

(c) until the expiration of three-quarters of the term of the policy of assurance, or of ten years from the beginning of the term, whichever is the shorter, the policy may not be surrendered to the friendly society for consideration exceeding the amount of the premiums paid, except that if a surrender value is prescribed by section 24 of the Industrial Assurance Act 1923 or section 3 of the Industrial Assurance and Friendly Societies Act 1929 or by Article 30 or 35 of and Schedule 7 to the Industrial Assurance (Northern Ireland) Order 1979, the limit on the consideration shall be either that value or the amount of the premiums paid whichever is the greater.

(3) Notwithstanding sub-paragraph (2)(a) above, the policy—

(a) may provide for a payment to a person of an age not exceeding 18 years at any time not less than five years from the beginning of the term of the policy if the premium or premiums payable in any period of 12 months in the term of the policy do not exceed £13;

(b) may provide for a payment at any time not less than five years from the beginning of the term of the policy, if it is one of a series of payments falling due at intervals of not less than five years, and the amount of any payment, other than the final payment, does not exceed four-fifths of the premiums paid in the interval before its payment.

For the purposes of paragraph (a) above, if the term begins on a date earlier than the making of the insurance, any premium paid in respect of a period before the making of the insurance, or in respect of that period and a subsequent period, shall be treated as having been payable on that date.

(4) Notwithstanding sub-paragraph (2)(b) above, the policy—

(a) may allow a payment at any time after the expiration of one-half of the term of the policy of assurance, or of ten years from the beginning of the term, whichever is the earlier, being a payment in commutation of the liability to pay premiums falling due after that time;

(b) may allow the person liable to pay the premiums to commute any liability for premiums where he ceases to reside in the United Kingdom or gives satisfactory proof of intention to emigrate;

(c) may allow any liability for premiums to be discharged in consideration of surrendering a sum which has become payable on the maturity of any other policy of assurance issued by the same friendly society to the

SCH. 15

person liable to pay the premiums, or to his parent, where that other policy of assurance is issued as part of the friendly society's tax exempt life or endowment business; and

(d) may make provision for the waiver of premiums by reason of a person's disability.

(5) Where the policy secures a capital sum which is payable only on death or only on death occurring after the attainment of a specified age not exceeding 16, that capital sum must be not less than 75 per cent. of the total premiums which would be payable if the death of the relevant beneficiary occurred at the age of 75.

(6) Where the policy secures a capital sum which is payable only on survival for a specified term, that capital sum must be not less than 75 per cent. of the total premiums which would be payable if the policy were to run for that term.

(7) Where the policy secures a capital sum which is payable on survival for a specified term or on earlier death, or on earlier death or disability (including a policy securing the sum on death only if occurring after the attainment of a specified age not exceeding 16), the capital sum payable on death, whenever that event occurs, must be not less than 75 per cent. of the total premiums which would be payable if the policy were to run for that term, except that if, at the beginning of that term, the age of the relevant beneficiary exceeds 55, that capital sum may, for each year of the excess, be less by 2 per cent. of that total than 75 per cent. thereof.

(8) For the purposes of sub-paragraphs (5) to (7) above—

(a) "the relevant beneficiary" means—

(i) if the capital sum concerned is payable on the death of the first to die of two persons, the older of them;

(ii) if that capital sum is payable on the death of the survivor of two persons, the younger of them; and

(iii) in any other case, the person on whose death that capital sum is payable; and

(b) in determining the total premiums payable in any circumstances—

(i) where those premiums are payable otherwise than annually, and the policy is issued by a new society, there shall be disregarded an amount equal to 10 per cent. of those premiums;

(ii) where the policy is issued by a society other than a new society, there shall be disregarded an amount equal to £10 for each year for which account is taken of those premiums; and

(iii) so much of any premium as is charged on the ground that an exceptional risk of death is involved shall be disregarded; and

(c) in determining the capital sum payable on any event, there shall be disregarded any provision of the policy under which, on the ground referred to in paragraph (b)(iii) above, any sum may become chargeable as a debt against that capital sum.

(9) If the policy does not secure a capital sum in the event of death occurring before the age of 16 or some lower age, it must not provide for the payment in that event of an amount exceeding the total premiums previously paid under it.

(10) References in this paragraph to a capital sum payable on any event include references to a capital sum or series of capital sums payable by reason of that event, but where what is so payable is either an amount consisting of one sum or an amount made up of two or more sums, any reference in sub-paragraphs (5) to (7) above to 75 per cent. of the total premiums payable in any circumstances

shall be compared with the smaller or smallest amount so payable; and for the purposes of those sub-paragraphs a policy secures a capital sum payable either on death or on disability notwithstanding that the amount may vary with the event.

(11) For the purposes of sub-paragraphs (5) to (7) and (10) above, in the case of a policy which provides for any such payments as are referred to in sub-paragraph (3) above ("interim payments"), the amount of the capital sum which is payable on any event shall be taken to be increased—

(a) in the case of a policy which secures such a capital sum as is referred to in sub-paragraph (5) above, by the total of the interim payments which would be payable if the death of the relevant beneficiary (within the meaning of that sub-paragraph) occurred at the age of 75; and

(b) in the case of a policy which secures such a capital sum as is referred to in sub-paragraph (6) or (7) above, by the total of the interim payments which would be payable if the policy were to run for the specified term referred to in that sub-paragraph.

4.—(1) The provisions of this paragraph have effect notwithstanding anything in paragraph 3 above.

(2) In determining whether a policy—

(a) which affords provision for sickness or other infirmity (whether bodily or mental), and

(b) which also affords assurance for a gross sum independent of sickness or other infirmity, and

(c) under which not less than 60 per cent. of the amount of the premiums is attributable to the provision referred to in paragraph (a) above,

is a qualifying policy, the conditions referred to in paragraph 3(1)(b) above shall be deemed to be fulfilled with respect to it.

(3) A policy shall cease to be a qualifying policy—

(a) if it falls within sub-paragraph (1) of paragraph 3 above and there is such a variation of its terms that any of the conditions referred to in that sub-paragraph ceases to be fulfilled; or

(b) if—

(i) for any purpose it falls within paragraph (1) of Schedule 1 to the Friendly Societies Act 1974 or paragraph 1 of Schedule 1 to the Friendly Societies Act (Northern Ireland) 1970,

1974 c. 46.
1970 c. 31 (N.I.).

(ii) it was issued by a new society, and

(iii) the rights conferred by it are surrendered in whole or in part.

5. Section 466 shall apply for the interpretation of paragraphs 3 and 4 above as it applies for the interpretation of sections 460 to 465.

6.—(1) A policy which was issued by any friendly society, or branch of a friendly society, in the course of tax exempt life or endowment business (as defined in section 466) in respect of insurances made before 19th March 1985 and which has not been varied on or after that date is a qualifying policy notwithstanding that it does not comply with the conditions specified in paragraph 1 or 2 above.

(2) Notwithstanding paragraphs 3 to 5 or sub-paragraph (1) above, if, on or after 19th March 1985, a person becomes in breach of the limits in section 464, the policy effected by that contract which causes those limits to be exceeded shall not be a qualifying policy; and in any case where—

SCH. 15   (a) the limits in that section are exceeded as a result of the aggregation of the sums assured or premiums payable under two or more contracts, and

(b) at a time immediately before one of those contracts was entered into (but not immediately after it was entered into) the sums assured by or, as the case may be, the premiums payable under the contract or contracts which were then in existence did not exceed the limits in that section,

only those policies effected by contracts made after that time shall be treated as causing the limits to be exceeded.

(ii) Industrial assurance policies

7.—(1) A policy issued in the course of an industrial assurance business, and not constituting a qualifying policy by virtue of paragraph 1 or 2 above, is nevertheless a qualifying policy if—

(a) the sums guaranteed by the policy, together with those guaranteed at the time the assurance is made by all other policies issued in the course of such a business to the same person and not constituting qualifying policies apart from this paragraph, do not exceed £1,000;

(b) it satisfies the conditions with respect to premiums specified in paragraph 1(2) above;

(c) except by reason of death or surrender, no capital sum other than one falling within paragraph (d) below can become payable under the policy earlier than ten years after the making of the assurance; and

(d) where the policy provides for the making of a series of payments during its term—

(i) the first such payment is due not earlier than five years after the making of the assurance, and the others, except the final payment, at intervals of not less than five years, and

(ii) the amount of any payment, other than the final payment, does not exceed four-fifths of the premiums paid in the interval before its payment; or

(e) the policy was issued before 6th April 1976, or was issued before 6th April 1979 and is in substantially the same form as policies so issued before 6th April 1976.

(2) For the purposes of this paragraph, the sums guaranteed by a policy do not include any bonuses, or in the case of a policy providing for a series of payments during its term, any of those payments except the first, or any sum payable on death during the term by reference to one or more of those payments except so far as that sum is referable to the first such payment.

8. Where a policy issued in respect of an insurance made after 1st April 1976 in the course of an industrial assurance business is not a qualifying policy by virtue of paragraph 1 or 2 above but is a policy with respect to which the conditions in paragraph 7(1)(b) and (c) above are satisfied, it shall be a qualifying policy whether or not the condition in paragraph 7(1)(a) above is satisfied with respect to it; but where that condition is not satisfied, relief under section 266 in respect of premiums paid under the policy shall be given only on such amount (if any) as would have been the amount of those premiums had that condition been satisfied.

(iii) Family income policies and mortgage protection policies

9.—(1) The following provisions apply to any policy which is not a qualifying policy apart from those provisions, and the benefits secured by which consist of or include the payment on or after a person's death of—

(a) one capital sum which does not vary according to the date of death, plus a series of capital sums payable if the death occurs during a specified period, or

(b) a capital sum, the amount of which is less if the death occurs in a later part of a specified period than if it occurs in an earlier part of that period.

(2) A policy falling within sub-paragraph (1)(a) above is a qualifying policy if—

(a) it would be one if it did not secure the series of capital sums there referred to, and the premiums payable under the policy were such as would be chargeable if that were in fact the case, and

(b) it would also be one if it secured only that series of sums, and the premiums thereunder were the balance of those actually so payable.

(3) A policy falling within sub-paragraph (1)(b) above is a qualifying policy if—

(a) it would be one if the amount of the capital sum there referred to were equal throughout the period to its smallest amount, and the premiums payable under the policy were such as would be chargeable if that were in fact the case, and

(b) it would also be one if it secured only that capital sum so far as it from time to time exceeds its smallest amount, and the premiums payable thereunder were the balance of those actually so payable.

Other special provisions

(i) Short-term assurances

10. A policy which secures a capital sum payable only on death or payable either on death or on earlier disability shall not be a qualifying policy if the capital sum is payable only if the event in question happens before the expiry of a specified term ending less than one year after the making of the insurance.

(ii) Personal accident insurance

11.—(1) A policy which evidences a contract of insurance to which sub-paragraph (3) below applies shall not be a qualifying policy unless it also evidences a contract falling within Class I or Class III in Schedule 1 to the Insurance Companies Act 1982.

(2) A policy which evidences a contract of insurance to which sub-paragraph (4) below applies shall not be a qualifying policy unless it also evidences a contract falling within section 83(2)(a) of the Insurance Companies Act 1974.

(3) This sub-paragraph applies to contracts of insurance issued in respect of insurances made on or after 25th March 1982 against risks of persons dying as a result of an accident or an accident of a specified class, not being contracts which—

(a) are expressed to be in effect for a period of not less than five years or without limit of time; and

(b) either are not expressed to be terminable by the insurer before the expiration of five years from their taking effect or are expressed to be so terminable before the expiration of that period only in special circumstances therein mentioned.

(4) This sub-paragraph applies to contracts of insurance issued in respect of insurances made before 25th March 1982 against risks of persons dying as a result of an accident or an accident of a specified class, not being contracts falling within section 83(2)(b) of the Insurance Companies Act 1974.

1974 c. 49.

(iii) Exceptional mortality risk

12. For the purpose of determining whether any policy is a qualifying policy, there shall be disregarded—

(a) so much of any premium thereunder as is charged on the grounds that an exceptional risk of death is involved; and

(b) any provision under which, on those grounds, any sum may become chargeable as a debt against the capital sum guaranteed by the policy on death.

(iv) Connected policies

13. Subject to paragraph 14 below, where the terms of any policy provide that it is to continue in force only so long as another policy does so, neither policy is a qualifying policy unless, if they had constituted together a single policy issued in respect of an insurance made at the time of the insurance in respect of which the first-mentioned policy was issued, that single policy would have been a qualifying policy.

14.—(1) A policy shall not be a qualifying policy if the policy is connected with another policy and the terms of either policy provide benefits which are greater than would reasonably be expected if any policy connected with it were disregarded.

(2) For the purposes of this paragraph a policy is connected with another policy if they are at any time simultaneously in force and either of them is issued with reference to the other, or with a view to enabling the other to be issued on particular terms or facilitating its being issued on those terms.

(3) In this paragraph "policy" means a policy effected in the course of long term business, as defined in section 1 of the Insurance Companies Act 1982, and includes any such policy issued outside the United Kingdom.

1982 c. 50.

(4) Where any person issues a policy—

(a) which by virtue of this paragraph is not a qualifying policy, or

(b) the issue of which causes another policy to cease by virtue of this paragraph to be a qualifying policy,

he shall within three months of issuing the policy give notice of that fact to the Board.

(5) The Board may, by notice, require any person who is, or appears to them to be, concerned in the issue of any such policy as is mentioned in sub-paragraph (4) above, to furnish them within such time (not being less than 30 days) as may be specified in the notice with such particulars as they think necessary for the purposes of this paragraph and as the person to whom the notice is addressed has or can reasonably obtain; but no solicitor shall be deemed for the purposes of this sub-paragraph to have been concerned in the issue of a policy by reason only that he has given professional advice to a client in connection with that policy.

(6) This paragraph shall apply to policies issued in respect of insurances made before 23rd August 1983 in accordance with sub-paragraphs (7) and (8) below.

(7) Where—

  (a) a policy is issued in respect of an insurance made before 23rd August 1983, and

  (b) a policy is issued in respect of an insurance made on or after that date which is connected with it within the meaning of this paragraph,

sub-paragraphs (1) to (6) above shall apply to the policy issued in respect of an insurance made before that date.

(8) Sub-paragraphs (1) to (7) above shall apply to policies issued in respect of insurances made before 23rd August 1983 (other than policies which, disregarding this paragraph, fall within sub-paragraph (7)) with the substitution—

  (a) in sub-paragraph (1) for the words "and the terms of either policy" of the words "the terms of which";

  (b) in sub-paragraph (3) for the words from "long term business" to "1982" of the words "ordinary long-term insurance business within the meaning of section 83(2) of the Insurance Companies Act 1974 (as enacted) or, in relation to a policy made after 25th March 1982, section 96(1) of the Insurance Companies Act 1982"; and

  (c) in sub-paragraphs (6) and (7) for the words "23rd August 1983" of the words "26th March 1980".

(9) In any case where payments made—

  (a) after 22nd August 1983, and

  (b) by way of premium or other consideration in respect of a policy issued in respect of an insurance made before that date,

exceed £5 in any period of 12 months, the policy shall be treated for the purposes of this paragraph as if it were issued in respect of an insurance made after 22nd August 1983; but nothing in this paragraph shall apply with respect to any premium paid in respect of it before that date.

(10) Sub-paragraphs (8) and (9) above do not apply in relation to policies issued in the course of industrial assurance business.

(v) *Premiums paid out of sums due under previous policies*

15.—(1) Where, in the case of a policy under which a single premium only is payable, liability for the payment of that premium is discharged in accordance with sub-paragraph (2) below, the policy is a qualifying policy notwithstanding anything in paragraph 1(2) or (3) or paragraph 2(1)(b) or (c) above; and where, in the case of any other policy, liability for the payment of the first premium thereunder, or of any part of that premium, is so discharged, the premium or part shall be disregarded for the purposes of paragraphs 1(2)(b) and (3)(b) and 2(1)(c) above.

(2) Liability for the payment of a premium is discharged in accordance with this sub-paragraph if it is discharged by the retention by the company with which the insurance is made of the whole or a part of any sum which has become payable on the maturity of, or on the surrender more than ten years after its issue of the rights conferred by, a policy—

  (a) previously issued by the company to the person making the insurance, or, if it is made by trustees, to them or any predecessors in office; or

(b) issued by the company when the person making the insurance was an infant, and securing a capital sum payable either on a specified date falling not more than one month after his attaining 25, or on the anniversary of the policy immediately following his attainment of that age,

being, unless it is a policy falling within paragraph (b) above and the premium in question is a first premium only, a policy which was itself a qualifying policy, or which would have been a qualifying policy had it been issued in respect of an insurance made after 19th March 1968.

(iv) Additional premiums under section 72(9) of the Finance Act 1984

16. In determining whether a policy is a qualifying policy, no account shall be taken of any amount recovered, as if it were an additional premium, in pursuance of section 72(9) of the Finance Act 1984.

(vii) Substitutions and variations

17.—(1) Subject to paragraph 19 below, where one policy ("the new policy") is issued in substitution for, or on the maturity of and in consequence of an option conferred by, another policy ("the old policy"), the question whether the new policy is a qualifying policy shall, to the extent provided by the rules in sub-paragraph (2) below, be determined by reference to both policies.

(2) The rules (for the purposes of which, the question whether the old policy was a qualifying policy shall be determined in accordance with this Part of this Schedule, whatever the date of the insurance in respect of which it was issued), are as follows—

(a) if the new policy would apart from this paragraph be a qualifying policy but the old policy was, the new policy is not a qualifying policy unless the person making the insurance in respect of which it is issued was an infant when the old policy was issued, and the old policy was one securing a capital sum payable either on a specified date falling not later than one month after his attaining 25 or on the anniversary of the policy immediately following his attainment of that age;

(b) if the new policy would apart from this paragraph be a qualifying policy, and the old policy was also a qualifying policy, the new policy is a qualifying policy unless—

(i) it takes effect before the expiry of ten years from the making of the insurance in respect of which the old policy was issued, and

(ii) subject to sub-paragraph (4) below, the highest total of premiums payable thereunder for any period of 12 months expiring before that time is less than one half of the highest total paid for any period of 12 months under the old policy, or under any related policy issued less than ten years before the issue of the new policy ("related policy" meaning any policy in relation to which the old policy was a new policy within the meaning of this paragraph, any policy in relation to which that policy was such a policy, and so on);

(c) if the new policy would not apart from this paragraph be a qualifying policy, and would fail to be so by reason only of paragraph 1(2) or (3) or 2(1)(a), (b) or (c) above, it is nevertheless a qualifying policy if the old policy was a qualifying policy and—

(i) the old policy was issued in respect of an insurance made more than ten years before the taking effect of the new policy, and, subject to sub-paragraph (4) below, the premiums payable for any period of 12 months under the new policy do not exceed the smallest total paid for any such period under the old policy; or

> > (ii) the old policy was issued outside the United Kingdom, and the circumstances are as specified in sub-paragraph (3) below.

(3) The circumstances are—

> (a) where the new policy referred to in sub-paragraph (2)(c) above is issued after 22nd February 1984, that the policy holder under the new policy became resident in the United Kingdom during the 12 months ending with the date of its issue;

> (b) where paragraph (a) above does not apply, that the person in respect of whom the new insurance is made became resident in the United Kingdom during the 12 months ending with the date of its issue;

> (c) that the issuing company certify that the new policy is in substitution for the old, and that the old was issued either by a branch or agency of theirs outside the United Kingdom or by a company outside the United Kingdom with whom they have arrangements for the issue of policies in substitution for ones held by persons coming to the United Kingdom; and

> (d) that the new policy confers on the holder benefits which are substantially equivalent to those which he would have enjoyed if the old policy had continued in force.

(4) Where the new policy is one issued on or after 1st April 1976 then, in determining under sub-paragraph (2) above whether that policy would or would not (apart from sub-paragraphs (1) to (3) above) be a qualifying policy, there shall be left out of account so much of the first premium payable thereunder as is accounted for by the value of the old policy.

18.—(1) Subject to paragraph 19 below and to the provisions of this paragraph, where the terms of a policy are varied, the question whether the policy after the variation is a qualifying policy shall be determined in accordance with the rules in paragraph 17 above, with references in those rules to the new policy and the old policy construed for that purpose as references respectively to the policy after the variation and the policy before the variation, and with any other necessary modifications.

(2) In applying any of those rules by virtue of this paragraph, the question whether a policy after a variation would be a qualifying policy apart from the rule shall be determined as if any reference in paragraphs 1 to 9, 12 and 13 above to the making of an insurance, or to a policy's term, were a reference to the taking effect of the variation or, as the case may be, to the term of the policy as from the variation.

(3) This paragraph does not apply by reason of—

> (a) any variation which, whether or not of a purely formal character, does not affect the terms of a policy in any significant respect, or

> (b) any variation effected before the end of the year 1968 for the sole purpose of converting into a qualifying policy any policy issued (but not one treated, by virtue of paragraph 8(1) and (2) of Schedule 14, as issued) in respect of an insurance made after 19th March 1968.

19.—(1) The following provisions of this paragraph shall have effect for determining for the purposes of this Schedule whether a policy has been varied or whether a policy which confers on the person to whom it is issued an option to have another policy substituted for it or to have any of its terms changed is a qualifying policy.

(2) If the policy is one issued in respect of an insurance made before 1st April 1976—

(a) any such option shall, until it is exercised, be disregarded in determining whether the policy is a qualifying policy; and

(b) any change in the terms of the policy which is made in pursuance of such an option shall be deemed to be a variation of the policy.

(3) If the policy is one issued in respect of an insurance made on or after 1st April 1976, the policy shall not be a qualifying policy unless it satisfies the conditions applicable to it under this Schedule before any such option is exercised and—

(a) each policy that might be substituted for it in pursuance of such an option would satisfy those conditions under the rules of paragraph 17 above; and

(b) the policy would continue to satisfy those conditions under the rules of that paragraph as applied by paragraph 18 above if each or any of the changes capable of being made in pursuance of such an option had been made and were treated as a variation;

and it shall not be treated as being varied by reason only of any change made in pursuance of such an option.

20.—(1) Where, as a result of a variation in the life or lives for the time being assured, a qualifying policy ("the earlier policy") is replaced by a new policy ("the later policy") which in accordance with the rules in paragraph 17 above is also a qualifying policy, then, subject to sub-paragraph (2) below, for the purposes of—

(a) sections 268 to 270 and 540 and 541; and

(b) any second or subsequent application of this paragraph;

the later policy and the earlier policy shall be treated as a single policy issued in respect of an insurance made at the time of the making of the insurance in respect of which the earlier policy was issued; and, accordingly, so long as the later policy continues to be a qualifying policy, the single policy shall also be treated as a qualifying policy for those purposes.

(2) Sub-paragraph (1) above does not apply unless—

(a) any sum which would otherwise become payable by the insurer on or in connection with the coming to an end of the earlier policy is retained by the insurer and applied in the discharge of some or all of the liability for any premium becoming due under the later policy; and

(b) no consideration in money or money's worth (other than the benefits for which provision is made by the later policy) is receivable by any person on or in connection with the coming to an end of the earlier policy or the coming into existence of the later policy.

(3) Any sum which is applied as mentioned in sub-paragraph (2)(a) above—

(a) shall be left out of account in determining, for the purposes of sections 268 to 270 and 540 and 541, the total amount which at any time has been paid by way of premiums under the single policy referred to in sub-paragraph (1) above; and

(b) shall not be regarded, in relation to that single policy, as a relevant capital payment, within the meaning of section 541.

(4) This paragraph applies where the later policy comes into existence on or after 25th March 1982.

CERTIFICATION OF QUALIFYING POLICIES

Policies issued in respect of insurances made on or after 1st April 1976 or varied on or after that date

21.—(1) A policy of life insurance issued in respect of an insurance made on or after 1st April 1976 or varied on or after that date (other than one to which paragraph 22(2)(c) below applies) shall not be a qualifying policy unless—

(a) it is certified by the Board as being a qualifying policy; or

(b) it conforms with a form which at the time the policy is issued or varied is either—

(i) a standard form certified by the Board as a standard form of qualifying policy; or

(ii) a form varying from a standard form so certified in no other respect than by making such additions thereto as are, at the time the policy is issued, certified by the Board as compatible with a qualifying policy when made to that standard form and satisfy any conditions subject to which they are so certified;

and any certificate issued in pursuance of paragraph (a) above shall be conclusive evidence that the policy is a qualifying policy.

(2) In issuing a certificate in pursuance of sub-paragraph (1) above the Board may disregard any provision of the policy, standard form or addition which appears to them insignificant.

(3) Where the Board refuse to certify a policy as being a qualifying policy, the person to whom it is issued may appeal to the General Commissioners or, if he so elects, to the Special Commissioners.

(4) Sub-paragraphs (1) to (3) above do not apply in relation to such a policy as is mentioned in paragraphs 3 to 6 above.

22.—(1) A body which issues or which, after 5th April 1979, has issued any policy of life insurance (other than one to which sub-paragraph (2)(c) below applies)—

(a) which is certified by the Board as being a qualifying policy; or

(b) which conforms with such a form as is mentioned in paragraph 21(1)(b) above, and is in the opinion of the body issuing it a qualifying policy,

shall, within three months of receipt of a request in writing by the policy holder, give to the policy holder a duly authenticated certificate to that effect, specifying in the certificate the name of the policy holder, the name of the person whose life is assured, the reference number or other means of identification allocated to the policy, the reference number of the relevant Inland Revenue certificate (if any), the capital sum or sums assured and the amounts and dates for payment of the premiums.

(2) Subject to sub-paragraph (3) below, where a policy of life insurance is varied after 5th April 1979, and, after the variation—

(a) it is certified by the Board as a qualifying policy, or

(b) it conforms with such a form as is referred to in sub-paragraph (1) above and is in the opinion of the body by whom it was issued a qualifying policy, or

(c) in the case of a policy issued in respect of an insurance made before 1st April 1976, it is in the opinion of the body by whom it was issued a qualifying policy,

that body shall, within three months of receipt of a request in writing by the policy holder, give to the policy holder a like certificate with respect to the policy as varied.

(3) Sub-paragraph (2) above shall not apply by reason of—

(a) any variation which, whether or not of a purely formal character, does not affect the terms of a policy in any significant respect; or

(b) any variation of a policy issued in respect of an insurance made on or before 19th March 1968, other than a variation by virtue of which the policy falls, under paragraph 8(1) and (2) of Schedule 14, to be treated as issued in respect of an insurance made after that date.

PART III

POLICIES ISSUED BY NON-RESIDENT COMPANIES

23. In this Part—

(a) any reference to a paragraph is a reference to that paragraph of this Schedule; and

(b) "the old policy" and "the new policy" have the same meanings as in paragraph 17.

24.—(1) This paragraph applies to a policy of life insurance—

(a) which is issued in respect of an insurance made after 17th November 1983; and

(b) which is so issued by a company resident outside the United Kingdom;

and in the following provisions of this paragraph such a policy is referred to as "a new non-resident policy" and the company by which it is issued is referred to as "the issuing company".

(2) Notwithstanding anything in paragraph 21—

(a) a new non-resident policy shall not be certified under sub-paragraph (1)(a) of that paragraph, and

(b) a new non-resident policy which conforms with such a form as is mentioned in sub-paragraph (1)(b) of that paragraph shall not be a qualifying policy,

until such time as the conditions in either sub-paragraph (3) or sub-paragraph (4) below are fulfilled with respect to it.

(3) The conditions first referred to in sub-paragraph (2) above are—

(a) that the issuing company is lawfully carrying on in the United Kingdom life assurance business (as defined in section 431(2)); and

(b) that the premiums under the policy are payable to a branch in the United Kingdom of the issuing company, being a branch through which the issuing company carries on its life assurance business; and

(c) the premiums under the policy form part of those business receipts of the issuing company which arise through that branch.

(4) The conditions secondly referred to in sub-paragraph (2) above are—

(a) that the policy holder is resident in the United Kingdom; and

(b) that the income of the issuing company from the investments of its life assurance fund is, by virtue of section 445, charged to corporation tax under Case III of Schedule D;

and expressions used in paragraph (b) above have the same meaning as in section 445(1).

25.—(1) In the application of paragraph 17 in any case where—

(a) the old policy was issued in respect of an insurance made after 17th November 1983 and could not be a qualifying policy by virtue of paragraph 24, and

(b) the new policy is not a new non-resident policy as defined in that paragraph,

the rules for the determination of the question whether the new policy is a qualifying policy shall apply with the modifications in sub-paragraph (2) below.

(2) The modifications are the following—

(a) if, apart from paragraph 24, the old policy and any related policy (within the meaning of paragraph 17(2)(b)) of which account falls to be taken would have been, or would have been capable of being certified as, a qualifying policy under paragraph 21, that policy shall be assumed to have been a qualifying policy for the purposes of paragraph 17(2); and

(b) if, apart from this paragraph, the new policy would be, or would be capable of being certified as, a qualifying policy, it shall not be such a policy or, as the case may be, be capable of being so certified unless the circumstances are as specified in paragraph 17(3); and

(c) in paragraph 17(3)(b) the words "either by a branch or agency of theirs outside the United Kingdom or" shall be omitted.

(3) In the application of paragraph 17 in any case where—

(a) the old policy is a qualifying policy which was issued in respect of an insurance made on or before 17th November 1983 but, if the insurance had been made after that date, the policy could not have been a qualifying policy by virtue of paragraph 24, and

(b) the new policy is issued after that date and is not a new non-resident policy, as defined in paragraph 24,

the rules for the determination of the question whether the new policy is a qualifying policy shall apply with the modification in sub-paragraph (2)(c) above.

26. If, in the case of a substitution of policies falling within paragraph 25(1) or (3), the new policy confers such an option as results in the application to it of paragraph 19(3), the new policy shall be treated for the purposes of paragraph 19(3) as having been issued in respect of an insurance made on the same day as that on which was made the insurance in respect of which the old policy was issued.

27.—(1) For the purposes of Part I and paragraphs 21 and 24, a policy of life insurance which was issued—

(a) in respect of an insurance made on or before 17th November 1983, and

(b) by a company resident outside the United Kingdom,

SCH. 15   shall be treated as issued in respect of an insurance made after that date if the policy is varied after that date so as to increase the benefits secured or to extend the term of the insurance.

(2) If a policy of life insurance which was issued as mentioned in sub-paragraph (1)(a) and (b) above confers on the person to whom it is issued an option to have another policy substituted for it or to have any of its terms changed, then for the purposes of that sub-paragraph any change in the terms of the policy which is made in pursuance of the option shall be deemed to be a variation of the policy.

SCHEDULE 16

COLLECTION OF INCOME TAX ON COMPANY PAYMENTS WHICH
ARE NOT DISTRIBUTIONS

Interpretation

1. In this Schedule "relevant payment" means any payment to which section 350(4)(a) applies.

Duty to make returns

2.—(1) A company shall for each of its accounting periods make, in accordance with this Schedule, returns to the collector of the relevant payments made by it in that period and of the income tax for which it is accountable in respect of those payments.

(2) A return shall be made for—

(a) each complete quarter falling within the accounting period, that is to say, each of the periods of three months ending with 31st March, 30th June, 30th September and 31st December which falls within that period;

(b) each part of the accounting period which is not a complete quarter and ends on the first (or only), or begins immediately after the last (or only), of those dates which falls within the accounting period;

(c) if none of those dates falls within the accounting period, the whole accounting period.

(3) A return for any period for which a return is required to be made under this paragraph shall be made within 14 days from the end of that period.

Contents of returns

3. The return made by a company for any period shall show—

(a) the amount of any relevant payments made by the company in that period; and

(b) the income tax in respect of those payments for which the company is accountable.

Payment of tax

4.—(1) Subject to sub-paragraph (4) below, income tax in respect of any payment required to be included in a return under this Schedule shall be due at the time by which the return is to be made, and income tax so due—

(a) shall be payable by the company without the making of any assessment; and

(b) may be assessed on the company (whether or not it has been paid when the assessment is made) if it, or any part of it, is not paid on or before the due date.

(2) If it appears to the inspector that there is a relevant payment which ought to have been and has not been included in a return, or if the inspector is dissatisfied with any return, he may make an assessment on the company to the best of his judgment; and any income tax due under an assessment made by virtue of this sub-paragraph shall be treated for the purposes of interest on unpaid tax as having been payable at the time when it would have been payable if a correct return had been made.

(3) Where a payment has been included in a return under Schedule 13 by virtue of paragraph 7(1)(b) of that Schedule and it becomes apparent that the payment is not a qualifying distribution but a relevant payment—

(a) sub-paragraph (1)(a) above shall not apply to that payment; and

(b) income tax shall be assessed in respect of it on the company.

Set-off of income tax borne on company income against tax payable

5.—(1) Where in any accounting period a company receives any payment on which it bears income tax by deduction the company may claim to have the income tax thereon set against any income tax which it is liable to pay under this Schedule in respect of payments made by it in that period.

(2) Any such claim shall be included in a return made under paragraph 2 above for the accounting period in question and (where necessary) income tax paid by the company under this Schedule for that accounting period and before the claim is allowed shall be repaid accordingly.

6.—(1) Where a claim has been made under paragraph 5 above no proceedings for collecting tax which would fall to be discharged if the claim were allowed shall be instituted pending the final determination of the claim, but this sub-paragraph shall not affect the date when the tax is due.

(2) When the claim is finally determined any tax underpaid in consequence of sub-paragraph (1) above shall be paid.

(3) Where proceedings are instituted for collecting tax assessed, or interest on tax assessed, under any provision of paragraph 4 above, effect shall not be given to any claim made after the institution of the proceedings so as to affect or delay the collection or recovery of the tax charged by the assessment or of interest thereon, until the claim has been finally determined.

(4) When the claim is finally determined any tax overpaid in consequence of sub-paragraph (3) above shall be repaid.

(5) References in this paragraph to proceedings for the collection of tax include references to proceedings by way of distraint or poinding for tax.

7. Income tax set against other tax under paragraph 5 above shall be treated as paid or repaid, as the case may be, and the same tax shall not be taken into account both under this Schedule and under section 7(2).

Items included in error

8. Where any item has been included in a return or claim under this Schedule as a relevant payment but should have been included in a return under Schedule 13, the inspector may make such assessments, adjustments or set-offs as may be required for securing that the resulting liabilities to tax (including interest on unpaid tax) whether of the company or of any other person are the same as they would have been if the item had been included in the right return.

Relevant payment made otherwise than in accounting period

9. Where a company makes a relevant payment on a date which does not fall within an accounting period the company shall make a return of that payment within 14 days from that date, and the income tax for which the company is accountable in respect of that payment shall be due at the time by which the return is to be made.

Assessments and due date of tax

10.—(1) All the provisions of the Income Tax Acts as to the time within which an assessment may be made, so far as they refer or relate to the year of assessment for which an assessment is made, or the year to which an assessment relates, shall apply in relation to any assessment under this Schedule notwithstanding that, under this Schedule, the assessment may be said to relate to a quarter or other period which is not a year of assessment, and the provisions of sections 36 and 37 of the Management Act as to the circumstances in which an assessment may be made out of time shall apply accordingly on the footing that any such assessment relates to the year of assessment in which the quarter or other period ends.

(2) Income tax assessed on a company under this Schedule shall be due within 14 days after the issue of the notice of assessment (unless due earlier under paragraph 4(1) or 9 above).

(3) Sub-paragraph (2) above has effect subject to any appeal against the assessment, but no such appeal shall affect the date when tax is due under paragraph 4(1) or 9 above.

(4) On the determination of an appeal against an assessment under this Schedule any tax overpaid shall be repaid.

(5) Any tax assessable under any one or more of the provisions of this Schedule may be included in one assessment if the tax so included is all due on the same date.

Saving

11. Nothing in paragraphs 1 to 10 above shall be taken to prejudice any powers conferred by the Income Tax Acts for the recovery of income tax by means of an assessment or otherwise; and any assessment in respect of tax payable under paragraph 9 above shall be treated for the purposes of the provisions mentioned in paragraph 10(1) above as relating to the year of assessment in which the payment is made.

SCHEDULE 17

DUAL RESIDENT INVESTING COMPANIES

PART I

DIVISION OF ACCOUNTING PERIODS COVERING 1st APRIL 1987

1.—(1) This Part of this Schedule has effect in the circumstances set out in section 404(3)(a).

(2) In this Part of this Schedule—

(a) "the straddling period" means the accounting period of the dual resident investing company which begins before and ends on or after 1st April 1987; and

(b) "dual resident investing company" has the same meaning as in section 404.

(3) It shall be assumed for the purposes of this Chapter (except section 404(3) to (6)) and Part II of this Schedule—

(a) that an accounting period of the company ends on 31st March 1987; and

(b) that a new accounting period begins on 1st April 1987, the new accounting period to end with the end of the straddling period.

(4) In this Part of this Schedule "the component accounting periods" means the two accounting periods referred to in sub-paragraph (3) above.

2. Subject to paragraph 5 below, for the purposes referred to in paragraph 1(3) above, the losses and other amounts of the straddling period of a dual resident investing company, excluding any such excess of charges on income as is referred to in section 403(7), shall be apportioned to the component accounting periods on a time basis according to their lengths.

3. If, in the straddling period of a dual resident investing company, the company has paid any amount by way of charges on income, then, for the purposes referred to in paragraph 1(3) above, the excess of that amount referred to in section 403(7) shall be apportioned to the component accounting periods—

(a) according to the dates on which, subject to paragraph 6 below, the interest or other payments giving rise to those charges were paid (or were treated as paid for the purposes of section 338); and

(b) in proportion to the amounts of interest or other payments paid (or treated as paid) on those dates.

PART II

EARLY PAYMENTS OF INTEREST ETC. AND CHARGES ON INCOME

Interpretation

4. In this Part of this Schedule—

(a) a "1986 accounting period" means an accounting period which begins or ends (or begins and ends) in the financial year 1986;

(b) a "post-1986 accounting period" means an accounting period which begins on or after 1st April 1987; and

(c) "dual resident investing company" has the same meaning as in section 404.

Early payment of interest etc.

5.—(1) If the conditions in sub-paragraph (2) or (3) below are fulfilled and if the Board so direct, this paragraph applies in relation to a 1986 accounting period of a dual resident investing company.

(2) The conditions in this sub-paragraph are applicable only if the company is carrying on a trade in the 1986 accounting period, and those conditions are—

(a) that in that accounting period the company has incurred a loss, computed as for the purposes of section 393(2), in carrying on that trade; and

(b) that in that period the company has made a payment falling within section 404(6)(a)(iii); and

(c) that the payment referred to in paragraph (b) above either did not fall due in that period or would not have fallen due in that period but for the making, on or after 5th December 1986, of arrangements varying the due date for payment.

(3) The conditions in this sub-paragraph are applicable only if the company is an investment company in the 1986 accounting period, and those conditions are—

(a) that for that accounting period the company has (apart from this paragraph) such an excess as is referred to in section 403(4); and

(b) that one or more of the sums which for that accounting period may be deducted as expenses of management under section 75(1) either did not fall due in that period or would not have fallen due in that period but for the making, on or after 5th December 1986, of arrangements varying the due date for payment.

(4) The Board shall not give a direction under this paragraph with respect to a 1986 accounting period of a dual resident investing company unless it appears to the Board that the sole or main benefit that might be expected to accrue from the early payment or, as the case may be, from the arrangements was that (apart from this paragraph) the company would, for that period, have an amount or, as the case may be, a larger amount available for surrender by way of group relief.

(5) If this paragraph applies in relation to a 1986 accounting period of a dual resident investing company which is carrying on a trade then, for the purposes of this Chapter and, where appropriate, any apportionment under paragraph 2 above—

(a) the loss (if any) of the company for that period shall be computed (as mentioned in section 403(1)) as if any payment falling within sub-paragraph (2)(b) above had not been made in that period; and

(b) the loss (if any) of the company for its first post-1986 accounting period shall be computed as if any such payment were made in that period.

(6) If this paragraph applies in relation to a 1986 accounting period of a dual resident investing company which is an investment company, then, for the purposes referred to in sub-paragraph (5) above—

(a) the amount which may be deducted as expenses of management for that period, as mentioned in section 403(4), shall be computed as if any sum falling within sub-paragraph (3)(b) above had not been disbursed; and

    (b) the amount which may be so deducted as expenses of management for the first of the company's post-1986 accounting periods shall be computed as if any such sum were disbursed in that period.

Early payment of charges on income

6.—(1) If, in the case of a dual resident investing company, either of the following conditions is fulfilled—

    (a) that any interest or other payment which is, or is treated as, a charge on income falls due in a post-1986 accounting period but is paid (or treated for the purposes of section 338 as paid) in a 1986 accounting period, or

    (b) that, on or after 5th December 1986, arrangements have been made such that any such interest or other payment which, but for the arrangements, would have fallen due in a post-1986 accounting period, fell due in a 1986 accounting period,

the interest or other payment shall, if the Board so direct, be treated for the purposes of this Chapter and, where appropriate, paragraph 3 above as paid in the post-1986 accounting period referred to in paragraph (a) or, as the case may be, paragraph (b) above.

(2) The Board shall not give a direction under this paragraph unless it appears to them that the sole or main benefit that might be expected to accrue from the early payment or, as the case may be, from the arrangements was that (apart from the direction) the interest or other payment would be attributed or apportioned to a 1986 accounting period rather than a post-1986 accounting period, so that, for the 1986 accounting period, the dual resident investing company would have an amount or, as the case may be, a larger amount available for surrender by way of group relief.

Appeals

7. Notice of the giving of a direction under paragraph 5 or 6 above shall be given to the dual resident investing company concerned; and any company to which such a notice is given may, by giving notice of appeal to the Board within 60 days of the date of the notice given to the company, appeal to the Special Commissioners against the direction on either or both of the following grounds—

    (a) that the conditions applicable to the company under paragraph 5(2) or (3) above are not fulfilled or, as the case may be, that neither of the conditions in paragraph 6(1) above is fulfilled;

    (b) that the sole or main benefit that might be expected to accrue from the early payment or, as the case may be, the arrangements was not that stated in paragraph 5(4) or, as the case may be, paragraph 6(2) above.

PART III

GENERAL

8.—(1) Parts I and II of this Schedule have effect in priority to section 409 and, accordingly, each of the component accounting periods resulting from the operation of Part I of this Schedule shall be regarded as a true accounting period for the purposes of that section.

(2) References in this Schedule to this Chapter do not include any provision of this Schedule.

GROUP RELIEF: EQUITY HOLDERS AND PROFITS OR ASSETS AVAILABLE FOR DISTRIBUTION

1.—(1) For the purposes of section 413(7) to (9) and this Schedule, an equity holder of a company is any person who—

(a) holds ordinary shares in the company, or

(b) is a loan creditor of the company in respect of a loan which is not a normal commercial loan,

and any reference in that section to profits or assets available for distribution to a company's equity holders does not include a reference to any profits or assets available for distribution to any equity holder otherwise than as an equity holder.

(2) For the purposes of sub-paragraph (1)(a) above "ordinary shares" means all shares other than fixed-rate preference shares.

(3) In this Schedule "fixed-rate preference shares" means shares which—

(a) are issued for consideration which is or includes new consideration; and

(b) do not carry any right either to conversion into shares or securities of any other description or to the acquisition of any additional shares or securities; and

(c) do not carry any right to dividends other than dividends which—

(i) are of a fixed amount or at a fixed rate per cent. of the nominal value of the shares, and

(ii) represent no more than a reasonable commercial return on the new consideration received by the company in respect of the issue of the shares; and

(d) on repayment do not carry any rights to an amount exceeding that new consideration except in so far as those rights are reasonably comparable with those general for fixed dividend shares listed in the Official List of the Stock Exchange.

(4) Subsection (7) of section 417 shall apply for the purposes of sub-paragraph (1)(b) above as it applies for the purposes of Part XI, but with the omission of the reference to subsection (9) of that section.

(5) In sub-paragraph (1)(b) above "normal commercial loan" means a loan of or including new consideration and—

(a) which does not carry any right either to conversion into shares or securities of any other description or to the acquisition of additional shares or securities; and

(b) which does not entitle that loan creditor to any amount by way of interest which depends to any extent on the results of the company's business or any part of it or on the value of any of the company's assets or which exceeds a reasonable commercial return on the new consideration lent; and

(c) in respect of which the loan creditor is entitled, on repayment, to an amount which either does not exceed the new consideration lent or is reasonably comparable with the amount generally repayable (in respect of an equal amount of new consideration) under the terms of issue of securities listed in the Official List of the Stock Exchange.

(6) Notwithstanding anything in sub-paragraphs (1) to (5) above but subject to sub-paragraph (7) below, where—

(a) any person has, directly or indirectly, provided new consideration for any shares or securities in the company, and

(b) that person, or any person connected with him, uses for the purposes of his trade assets which belong to the company and in respect of which there is made to the company—

(i) a first-year allowance within the meaning of Chapter I of Part III of the Finance Act 1971 ("the 1971 Act") in respect of expenditure incurred by the company on the provision of machinery or plant;

(ii) a writing-down allowance within the meaning of Chapter II of Part I of the 1968 Act or, as the case may be, Chapter I of Part III of the 1971 Act in respect of expenditure incurred by the company on the provision of machinery or plant; or

(iii) an allowance under section 91 of the 1968 Act in respect of expenditure incurred by the company on scientific research;

then, for the purposes of this Schedule, that person, and no other, shall be treated as being an equity holder in respect of those shares or securities and as being beneficially entitled to any distribution of profits or assets attributable to those shares or securities.

(7) In any case where sub-paragraph (6) above applies in relation to a bank in such circumstances that—

(a) the only new consideration provided by the bank as mentioned in paragraph (a) of that sub-paragraph is provided in the normal course of its banking business by way of a normal commercial loan as defined in sub-paragraph (5) above; and

(b) the cost to the company concerned of assets falling within paragraph (b) of that sub-paragraph which are used as mentioned in that paragraph by the bank or a person connected with the bank is less than the amount of that new consideration,

references in sub-paragraph (6) above, other than the reference in paragraph (a), to shares or securities in the company shall be construed as references to so much only of the loan referred to paragraph (a) above as is equal to the cost referred to in paragraph (b) above.

(8) In this paragraph "new consideration" has the same meaning as in section 254 and any question whether one person is connected with another shall be determined in accordance with section 839.

2.—(1) Subject to the following provisions of this Schedule, for the purposes of section 413(7) to (9) the percentage to which one company is beneficially entitled of any profits available for distribution to the equity holders of another company means the percentage to which the first company would be so entitled in the relevant accounting period on a distribution in money to those equity holders of—

(a) an amount of profits equal to the total profits of the other company which arise in that accounting period (whether or not any of those profits are in fact distributed); or

(b) if there are no profits of the other company in that accounting period, profits of £100;

and in the following provisions of this Schedule that distribution is referred to as "the profit distribution".

(2) For the purposes of the profit distribution, it shall be assumed that no payment is made by way of repayment of share capital or of the principal secured by any loan unless that payment is a distribution.

(3) Subject to sub-paragraph (2) above, where an equity holder is entitled as such to a payment of any description which, apart from this sub-paragraph, would not be treated as a distribution, it shall nevertheless be treated as an amount to which he is entitled on the profit distribution.

3.—(1) Subject to the following provisions of this Schedule, for the purposes of section 413(7) to (9) the percentage to which one company would be beneficially entitled of any assets of another company available for distribution to its equity holders on a winding-up means the percentage to which the first company would be so entitled if the other company were to be wound up and on that winding-up the value of the assets available for distribution to its equity holders (that is to say, after deducting any liabilities to other persons) were equal to—

(a) the excess, if any, of the total amount of the assets of the company, as shown in the balance sheet relating to its affairs as at the end of the relevant accounting period, over the total amount of those of its liabilities as so shown which are not liabilities to equity holders as such; or

(b) if there is no such excess or if the company's balance sheet is prepared to a date other than the end of the relevant accounting period, £100.

(2) In the following provisions of this Schedule a winding-up on the basis specified in sub-paragraph (1) above is referred to as "the notional winding-up".

(3) If, on the notional winding-up, an equity holder would be entitled as such to an amount of assets of any description which, apart from this sub-paragraph, would not be treated as a distribution of assets, it shall nevertheless be treated, subject to sub-paragraph (4) below, as an amount to which the equity holder is entitled on the distribution of assets on the notional winding up.

(4) If an amount ("the returned amount") which corresponds to the whole or any part of the new consideration provided by an equity holder of a company for any shares or securities in respect of which he is an equity holder is applied by the company, directly or indirectly, in the making of a loan to, or in the acquisition of any shares or securities in, the equity holder or any person connected with him, then, for the purposes of this Schedule—

(a) the total amount referred to in sub-paragraph (1)(a) above shall be taken to be reduced by a sum equal to the returned amount; and

(b) the amount of assets to which the equity holder is beneficially entitled on the notional winding-up shall be taken to be reduced by a sum equal to the returned amount.

(5) In sub-paragraph (4) above "new consideration" has the same meaning as in section 254 and any question whether one person is connected with another shall be determined in accordance with section 839.

4.—(1) This paragraph applies if any of the equity holders—

(a) to whom the profit distribution is made, or

(b) who is entitled to participate in the notional winding-up,

holds, as such an equity holder, any shares or securities which carry rights in respect of dividend or interest or assets on a winding-up which are wholly or partly limited by reference to a specified amount or amounts (whether the limitation takes the form of the capital by reference to which a distribution is calculated or operates by reference to an amount of profits or otherwise).

(2) Where this paragraph applies there shall be determined—

    (a) the percentage of profits to which, on the profit distribution, the first company referred to in paragraph 2(1) above would be entitled, and

    (b) the percentage of assets to which, on the notional winding-up, the first company referred to in paragraph 3(1) above would be entitled,

if, to the extent that they are limited as mentioned in sub-paragraph (1) above, the rights of every equity holder falling within that sub-paragraph (including the first company concerned if it is such an equity holder) had been waived.

    (3) If, on the profit distribution, the percentage of profits determined as mentioned in sub-paragraph (2)(a) above is less than the percentage of profits determined under paragraph 2(1) above without regard to that sub-paragraph, the lesser percentage shall be taken for the purposes of section 413(7) to (9) to be the percentage of profits to which, on the profit distribution, the first company referred to in paragraph 2(1) above would be entitled as mentioned in that paragraph.

    (4) If, on the notional winding-up, the percentage of assets determined as mentioned in sub-paragraph (2)(b) above is less than the percentage of assets determined under paragraph 3(1) above without regard to that sub-paragraph, the lesser percentage shall be taken for the purposes of section 413(7) to (9) to be the percentage to which, on the notional winding-up, the first company mentioned in paragraph 3(1) above would be entitled of any assets of the other company available for distribution to its equity holders on a winding-up.

    5.—(1) This paragraph applies if, at any time in the relevant accounting period, any of the equity holders—

    (a) to whom the profit distribution is made, or

    (b) who is entitled to participate in the notional winding-up,

holds, as such an equity holder, any shares or securities which carry rights in respect of dividend or interest or assets on a winding-up which are of such a nature (as, for example, if any shares will cease to carry a right to a dividend at a future time) that if the profit distribution or the notional winding-up were to take place in a different accounting period the percentage to which, in accordance with paragraphs 1 to 4 above, that equity holder would be entitled of profits on the profit distribution or of assets on the notional winding-up would be different from the percentage determined in the relevant accounting period.

    (2) Where this paragraph applies, there shall be determined—

    (a) the percentage of profits to which, on the profit distribution, the first company referred to in paragraph 2(1) above would be entitled, and

    (b) the percentage of assets to which, on the notional winding-up, the first company referred to in paragraph 3(1) above would be entitled,

if the rights of the equity holders in the relevant accounting period were the same as they would be in the different accounting period referred to in sub-paragraph (1) above.

    (3) If in the relevant accounting period an equity holder holds, as such, any shares or securities in respect of which arrangements exist by virtue of which, in that or any subsequent accounting period, the equity holder's entitlement to profits on the profit distribution or to assets on the notional winding-up could be different as compared with his entitlement if effect were not given to the arrangements, then for the purposes of this paragraph—

    (a) it shall be assumed that effect would be given to those arrangements in a later accounting period, and

(b) those shares or securities shall be treated as though any variation in the equity holder's entitlement to profits or assets resulting from giving effect to the arrangements were the result of the operation of such rights attaching to the shares or securities as are referred to in sub-paragraph (1) above.

In this sub-paragraph "arrangements" means arrangements of any kind whether in writing or not.

(4) Sub-paragraph (3) and (4) of paragraph 4 above shall apply for the purposes of this paragraph as they apply for the purposes of that paragraph and, accordingly, references therein to sub-paragraphs (2)(a) and (2)(b) of that paragraph shall be construed as references to sub-paragraphs (2)(a) and (2)(b) of this paragraph.

(5) In any case where paragraph 4 above applies as well as this paragraph, that paragraph shall be applied separately (in relation to the profit distribution and the notional winding-up)—

(a) on the basis specified in sub-paragraph (2) above, and

(b) without regard to that sub-paragraph,

and sub-paragraphs (3) and (4) of that paragraph shall apply accordingly in relation to the percentages so determined as if for the word "lesser" there were substituted the word "lowest".

6. For the purposes of section 413(7) to (9) and paragraphs 2 to 5 above—

(a) the percentage to which one company is beneficially entitled of any profits available for distribution to the equity holders of another company, and

(b) the percentage to which one company would be beneficially entitled of any assets of another company on a winding-up,

means the percentage to which the first company is, or would be, so entitled either directly or through another body corporate or other bodies corporate or partly directly and partly through another body corporate or other bodies corporate.

7.—(1) In this Schedule "the relevant accounting period" means—

(a) in a case falling within subsection (7) of section 413, the accounting period current at the time in question; and

(b) in a case falling within subsection (8) of that section, the accounting period in relation to which the share in the consortium falls to be determined.

(2) For the purposes of this Schedule, a loan to a company shall be treated as a security, whether or not it is a secured loan, and, if it is a secured loan, regardless of the nature of the security.

SCHEDULE 19

APPORTIONMENT OF INCOME OF CLOSE COMPANIES

PART I

DETERMINATION OF RELEVANT INCOME AND DISTRIBUTIONS

Relevant income

1.—(1) Subject to the provisions of this Part of this Schedule, the relevant income of a company for an accounting period is—

(a) in the case of a company which is a trading company or a member of a trading group, so much of its distributable income, other than trading income, for that period as can be distributed without prejudice to the requirements of the company's business;

(b) in the case of a company not within paragraph (a) above whose distributable income for that period consists of or includes estate or trading income—

(i) so much of the estate or trading income as can be distributed without prejudice to the requirements of the company's business so far as concerned with the activities or assets giving rise to estate or trading income; and

(ii) its distributable income, if any, other than estate or trading income;

(c) in the case of any other company, its distributable income for that period.

(2) In arriving at the relevant income for any accounting period—

(a) where under sub-paragraph (1) above regard is to be had to the requirements of a company's business, regard shall be had not only to the current requirements of the business but also to such other requirements as may be necessary or advisable for the maintenance and development of that business but, for this purpose, the provisions of paragraph 8 below shall apply;

(b) the amount of the estate or trading income shall be taken as the amount included in respect of it in the distributable income.

(3) In arriving at the relevant income for any accounting period of a company which is a trading company or a member of a trading group, regard shall be had not only to the current requirements of the company's business and to such requirements as may be necessary or advisable for the maintenance and development of that business as fall within sub-paragraph (2)(a) above, but also to any other requirements necessary or advisable for the acquisition of a trade or of a controlling interest in a trading company or in a company which is a member of a trading group by virtue of paragraph 7(2)(a) below; but, for this purpose, paragraph 9 below shall apply.

(4) For the purposes of sub-paragraph (3) above, the acquisition of a controlling interest in a company means the acquisition, whether on a single occasion or otherwise, of such ordinary share capital of that company as enables the acquiring company to exercise the greater part of the voting power in that company.

(5) For the purposes of sub-paragraph (3) above, the requirements of a company's business which are necessary or advisable for such an acquisition as is mentioned in that sub-paragraph include such requirements as are necessary or advisable for—

    (a) the redemption or repayment of any share or loan capital or debt (including any premium thereon) issued or incurred in or towards payment for that acquisition, or issued or incurred for the purpose of raising money to be applied in or towards payment therefor, or

    (b) meeting any obligation of the company in respect of that acquisition,

so far as any sum so expended or applied, or intended to be expended or applied, does not fall to be treated for the purposes of this Chapter as a distribution by the company.

Maximum amount of relevant income

2.—(1) Subject to paragraphs 10 and 12 below, the relevant income of a company shall in no case be taken to exceed the company's distributable investment income for the accounting period plus 50 per cent. of the estate or trading income for the period.

(2) In the application of sub-paragraph (1) above to a company which is a trading company or a member of a trading group, the trading income shall be disregarded; and in the application of that sub-paragraph to a trading company, the estate income—

    (a) if it is less than the appropriate fraction of the relevant maximum amount, shall be treated as reduced by one-half of the amount required to make it up to that fraction of the relevant maximum amount; or

    (b) if it is less than the appropriate fraction of the relevant minimum amount, shall be disregarded;

and in this sub-paragraph the appropriate fraction is—

$$\frac{A}{A + B}$$

where—

    A is the amount of the estate income, and

    B is the amount of the trading income.

(3) The relevant maximum and minimum amounts referred to above shall be determined as follows—

    (a) where the company has no associated company in the accounting period, those amounts are £75,000 and £25,000 respectively;

    (b) where the company has one or more associated companies in the accounting period—

        (i) the relevant maximum amount is—

$$\frac{£75,000}{1 + X}$$

        (ii) the relevant minimum amount is—

$$\frac{£25,000}{1 + X}$$

where X is the number of those associated companies.

SCH. 19   (4) In applying sub-paragraphs (2) and (3) above to any accounting period of a trading company, an associated company shall be disregarded if—

> (a) it was not a trading company, or has not carried on any trade, at any time in that accounting period; or
>
> (b) where it was an associated company during part only of that accounting period, it was not a trading company, or has not carried on any trade, at any time in that part of that accounting period;

and for the purposes of this paragraph a company is to be treated as an associated company of another at a given time if at that time one of the two has control of the other or both are under the control of the same person or persons.

(5) In determining how many associated companies a trading company has in an accounting period or whether a trading company has an associated company in an accounting period, an associated company shall be counted even if it was an associated company for part only of the accounting period, and two or more associated companies shall be counted even if they were associated companies for different parts of the accounting period.

(6) For an accounting period of less than 12 months the relevant maximum and minimum amounts determined in accordance with sub-paragraphs (1) to (5) above shall be proportionately reduced.

Distributions

3.—(1) For the purposes of this Chapter the distributions of a company for an accounting period shall, subject to sub-paragraphs (2) to (4) and paragraph 12 below, be taken to consist of—

> (a) any dividends which are declared in respect of the period and are paid during the period or within a reasonable time thereafter;
>
> (b) all distributions made in the period except dividends which, in relation to any previous period, would fall under paragraph (a) above; and
>
> (c) anything that would be a distribution but for section 213 or 219 (or both).

(2) Where a period of account is not an accounting period, dividends which, if it were an accounting period, would be treated under sub-paragraph (1)(a) above as distributions for that accounting period shall be apportioned to any accounting period or part of an accounting period falling within the period of account in proportion to the distributable income of each such period or part.

(3) For the purposes of determining whether there is any such excess as is referred to in section 424(1), no account shall be taken of a distribution which, in relation to the company making it, is a bonus distribution unless—

> (a) it is made to a person other than a close company, or
>
> (b) it is made to a close company and the share capital or security of which it consists is subsequently distributed, by that or any other close company, by a distribution falling within section 14(2)(b) to a person other than a close company.

(4) Where a bonus distribution has occurred and, by virtue of paragraph (a) or paragraph (b) of sub-paragraph (3) above, it falls to be taken into account for the purpose of determining whether there is any such excess as is referred to in section 424(1), no account shall be taken for that purpose of a qualifying distribution which consists of the repayment of the share capital or, as the case may be, the principal of the security, which constituted the bonus distribution.

(5) In sub-paragraphs (3) and (4) above "bonus distribution" means a distribution which in relation to the company making it is a distribution by virtue only of paragraph (c) of section 209(2).

Distributable income and estate or trading income

4.—(1) For the purposes of this Chapter, the distributable income of a company for an accounting period shall be the amount of its distributable profits for the period exclusive of the part attributable to chargeable gains; and for the purposes of this sub-paragraph—

(a) the distributable profits of a company for an accounting period shall be the aggregate of the following amounts, that is to say—

(i) the amount of any profits on which corporation tax falls finally to be borne, less the amount of that tax;

(ii) an amount equal to the qualifying distributions comprised in any franked investment income, other than franked investment income against which relief is given under section 242 or 243; and

(iii) an amount equal to any group income;

(b) the part of a company's distributable profits attributable to chargeable gains shall be taken to be the amount of the chargeable gains on which corporation tax is finally borne less the amount of that tax; and

(c) the amount on which corporation tax falls finally to be borne (but not the amount of that tax) shall be computed as if section 242 did not include subsection (5) or (6) of that section (and as if section 243 did not apply section 242(5));

and for the purposes of sub-paragraph (a)(ii) above relief under section 242 or 243 shall be treated as having been given first against franked investment income which is not trading income and secondly, so far as it cannot be so given, against franked investment income which is trading income.

(2) For the purposes of this Chapter, the distributable investment income of a company for an accounting period shall be the amount of the distributable income, exclusive of the part attributable to estate or trading income, and less whichever is the smaller of—

(a) 10 per cent. of the estate or trading income; and

(b) £1,000 or, if the company is a trading company or a member of a trading group, £3,000 or (in either case) if the accounting period is of less than 12 months, a proportionately reduced amount.

5.—(1) For the purposes of this Chapter, "estate or trading income" means estate income and trading income.

(2) For those purposes "estate income" means income which is chargeable to tax under Schedule A or Schedule B, and income (other than yearly or other interest) which is chargeable to tax under Schedule D, and which arises from the ownership or occupation of land (including any interest in or right over land) or from the letting furnished of any building or part of a building, but does not include trading income.

(3) For those purposes "trading income" means income which is not investment income for the purposes of paragraph 7(1) below; and, where the following conditions are satisfied with respect to a close company, that is to say—

(a) that its activities consist wholly or mainly of the carrying on of a trade; and

(b) that the trade consists wholly or mainly of one or more of the following, that is to say, life assurance business (within the meaning of section 431), insurance business of any other class, banking, money lending, financing of hire-purchase or similar transactions, or dealing in securities;

its income incidental to that trade shall also be trading income.

(4) For the purposes of sub-paragraph (3) above income of a company is incidental to its trade if, and only if—

(a) it is derived from investments (other than investments in a 51 per cent. subsidiary) or is interest on a debt; and

(b) any profit on the sale of the investments would be a trading receipt, and the debt, if proved to be a bad debt, would be allowed as a deduction in computing the company's trading income for the purposes of corporation tax.

6.—(1) The amount for part of an accounting period of any description of income referred to in paragraph 4 or 5 above shall be a proportionate part of the amount for the whole period.

(2) In determining the amount for any period of any description of income referred to in paragraph 4 or 5 above, any deduction from the company's profits for charges on income, expenses of management or other amounts which can be deducted from or set against or treated as reducing profits of more than one description shall be treated as made—

(a) first, from the company's income charged to corporation tax other than estate or trading income;

(b) secondly, so far as it cannot be made under paragraph (a) above, from the company's estate or trading income so charged;

(c) thirdly, so far as it cannot be made under paragraph (a) or (b) above, from the amount included in the company's profits in respect of chargeable gains.

(3) In the application of sub-paragraph (2) above to a company which is a trading company or a member of a trading group there shall be substituted for paragraph (b) the following paragraphs—

"(b) secondly, so far as it cannot be made under (a) above, from the company's estate income so charged;

(bb) thirdly, so far as it cannot be made under (a) or (b) above, from the company's trading income so charged;"

and in paragraph (c) for "thirdly" there shall be substituted "fourthly", and for "(a) or (b)" there shall be substituted "(a), (b) or (bb)".

Meaning of "trading company" and "member of a trading group"

7.—(1) For the purposes of this Chapter, a "trading company" is any company which exists wholly or mainly for the purpose of carrying on a trade, and any other company whose income does not consist wholly or mainly of investment income, that is to say, income which, if the company were an individual, would not be earned income; but for this purpose any amount which is apportioned to a company under section 423(1) shall be deemed to be income of the company and to be investment income.

(2) Subject to sub-paragraph (3) below, for the purposes of this Chapter, a company is to be treated as a member of a trading group if, but only if—

(a) it exists wholly or mainly for the purpose of co-ordinating the administration of a group of two or more companies each of which is under its control and exists wholly or mainly for the purpose of carrying on a trade; or

(b) it is under the control of another company resident in the United Kingdom and not itself under the control of a third company, and it exists wholly or mainly for the purpose of a trade or trades carried on by that other company or by a group which, consisting of that other company and a company or companies also under its control and resident in the United Kingdom, exists wholly or mainly for the purpose of carrying on that trade or trades.

(3) A company shall not be treated as a member of a trading group by reason only of any company having the control of another if that control is exercised through a company which is not resident in the United Kingdom or through a company whose control depends on a holding a profit on the sale of which would be treated as a trading receipt of the company.

Requirements of a company's business

8.—(1) For the purposes of paragraph 1(2) above there shall be regarded as income available for distribution and not as having been applied, or as being applicable, to the current requirements of a company's business, or to such other requirements as may be necessary or advisable for the maintenance and development of that business—

(a) any sum expended or applied, or intended to be expended or applied, out of the income of the company—

(i) in or towards payment for the business, undertaking or property which the company was formed to acquire or which was the first business, undertaking or property of a substantial character in fact acquired by the company, or

(ii) in redemption or repayment of any share or loan capital or debt (including any premium thereon) issued or incurred in or towards payment for any such business, undertaking or property, or issued or incurred for the purpose of raising money applied or to be applied in or towards payment therefor, or

(iii) in meeting any obligations of the company in respect of the acquisition of any such business, undertaking or property, or

(iv) in redemption or repayment of any share or loan capital or debt (including any premium thereon) issued or incurred otherwise than for adequate consideration; and

(b) any sum expended or applied, or intended to be expended or applied, in pursuance or in consequence of any fictitious or artificial transactions; and

(c) in the case of a company which is neither a trading company nor a member of a trading group, any sum expended or applied, or available to be expended or applied, out of the income of the company in or towards the redemption, repayment or discharge of any loan capital or debt (including any premium thereon) in respect of which any person is a loan creditor of the company; and

(d) in the case of a company which is neither a trading company nor a member of a trading group, any sum expended or applied, or available to be expended or applied, out of the income of the company in or towards the acquisition of an estate or interest in land or the construction or extension of a building, not being a construction or extension which constitutes an improvement or development of farm land or market garden land.

Sub-paragraph (d) above does not apply where the acquisition, construction or extension concerned was made in pursuance of a contract entered into before 24th March 1973.

(2) For the purposes of sub-paragraph (1)(a)(iv) above, share or loan capital or debt shall be deemed to be issued or incurred otherwise than for adequate consideration if—

(a) it is issued or incurred for consideration the value of which to the company is substantially less than the amount of the capital or debt (including any premium thereon); or

(b) it is issued or incurred in or towards, or for the purpose of raising money applied or to be applied in or towards, the redemption or repayment of any share or loan capital or debt which itself was issued or incurred for such consideration as is mentioned in paragraph (a) above or which represents, directly or indirectly, any share or loan capital or debt which itself was issued or incurred for such consideration.

(3) In relation to any loan capital or debt mentioned in sub-paragraph (1)(c) above which was issued or incurred by the company for money borrowed by it for the purpose of financing expenditure on any acquisition, construction or extension falling within sub-paragraph (1)(d) above, the expression "loan creditor" in sub-paragraph (1)(c) above shall be construed as if, in the definition of that expression in subsections (7) to (9) of section 417, subsection (9) were omitted.

(4) References in sub-paragraphs (1)(a) and (2)(b) above to the redemption or repayment of a company's share capital shall be construed as including references to the purchase by the company of its own shares.

(5) References in sub-paragraphs (1) to (4) above to money applied or to be applied for any purpose shall be deemed to include references to money applied or to be applied in or towards the replacement of that money.

9.—(1) Paragraph 1(3) above shall not apply to—

(a) the acquisition of a trade, or of an asset to be used in a trade, or of an interest in any such asset, which at the date of the acquisition or at any time within one year previously was owned by an associated company of the acquiring company; or

(b) the intended acquisition of a trade, or of such an asset or interest as is referred to in paragraph (a) above, which, at the end of the accounting period for which the acquiring company's relevant income is to be ascertained, is owned by a company which is then an associated company of the acquiring company;

and, where the trade, asset or interest was, or is, in part owned as mentioned above, paragraph 1(3) above shall not apply with respect to that part.

(2) Paragraph 1(3) above shall not apply to—

(a) the acquisition of shares which at the date of the acquisition or at any time within one year previously were owned by an associated company of the acquiring company or by a person who then had control of the acquiring company; or

(b) the intended acquisition of shares which at the end of the accounting period for which the acquiring company's relevant income is to be ascertained are owned by a company which is then an associated company of the acquiring company or by a person who has control of the acquiring company;

and where shares were, or are, in part owned as mentioned above, paragraph 1(3) above shall not apply with respect to that part.

(3) Paragraph 1(3) above shall not apply to—

(a) the acquisition of shares in a company which immediately before the acquisition or at any time within one year previously was an associated company of the acquiring company; or

(b) the intended acquisition of shares in a company which, at the end of the accounting period for which the acquiring company's relevant income is to be ascertained, is an associated company of the acquiring company.

(4) Section 416(1)—

(a) shall not apply for the purposes of paragraph (a) of sub-paragraphs (1), (2) and (3) above; and

(b) shall apply for the purposes of paragraph (b) of each of those sub-paragraphs with the omission of the words "or at any time within one year previously".

(5) For the purposes of paragraph (a) of sub-paragraphs (1), (2) and (3) above, another company is an associated company of the acquiring company if—

(a) the acquiring company controlled that other company or that other company controlled the acquiring company either at the date of the acquisition of the trade, asset or interest or at any time within one year previously; or

(b) a person who had control of the acquiring company at that date also controlled that other company either at that date or at any time within one year previously.

(6) In ascertaining for the purposes of sub-paragraphs (2) and (5) above or for the purposes of section 416(1) as it applies for the purposes of paragraph (b) of sub-paragraphs (1), (2) and (3) above, whether any person has control of a company—

(a) there shall be left out of account for the purposes of section 416(2)(c) the rights of another company as loan creditor in respect of a debt incurred or redeemable loan capital issued in connection with the acquisition from that company of any trade, any asset to be used in a trade, or any interest in any such asset;

(b) section 417(3)(a) shall have effect as if the reference to a partner of a participator were omitted;

(c) section 417(3)(a) and (b) shall have effect as if the expression "relative" did not have the meaning assigned to it by section 417(4) but meant husband or wife or, in the case of a director of the company, husband or wife or any child or remoter issue who is an infant; and

(d) section 417(3)(c) shall have effect as if the reference to any other person interested were a reference (and a reference only) to the trustees or to the personal representatives as defined in section 701.

(7) For the purposes of this paragraph the time of acquisition of a trade, asset or interest, or shares, acquired under a contract shall be—

SCH. 19

    (a) the time at which the contract is made, or

    (b) if it is conditional (and in particular if it is conditional on the exercise of an option), the time at which the condition is satisfied,

and not, if different, the time at which the trade, asset, interest or shares is or are conveyed or transferred.

(8) For the purposes of paragraph 1(3) above there shall be regarded as income available for distribution and not as having been applied, or as being applicable, to such requirements of a company's business as may be necessary or advisable for such an acquisition as is mentioned in paragraph 1(3) above any sum expended or applied, or intended to be expended or applied, as mentioned in paragraph 8(1)(a)(iv) or (b) above; and paragraph 8(2) and (5) above shall apply for the purposes of this sub-paragraph as they apply for the purposes of paragraph 8.

Cessations and liquidations

10.—(1) Where a close company ceases to carry on the trade, or the business of holding investments, in which its activities wholly or mainly consisted, the relevant income of the company for any accounting period in which that event occurs, or which ends in or within the 12 months ending with that event, shall be calculated as if—

    (a) paragraph 1(1)(a) and (b)(i) above referred respectively to the whole of the company's distributable income other than trading income and to the whole of the estate or trading income and not to so much thereof as can be distributed without prejudice to the requirements there mentioned, and paragraphs 1(2)(a) and 8 above were omitted;

    (b) in paragraph 2(1) above the words "50 per cent. of" were omitted.

(2) Where sub-paragraph (1) above applies for an accounting period and the company could not make distributions without prejudice to the claims of creditors (excluding those mentioned in sub-paragraph (3) below), the excess mentioned in section 424(1) shall be disregarded to the extent to which the company could not make distributions up to the amount of its relevant income without prejudice to those claims.

(3) Subject to sub-paragraph (4) below, the creditors to be excluded for the purposes of sub-paragraph (2) above are all participators and associates of participators, and all creditors in respect of debts originally created in favour of or due to a person who was then a participator or associate of a participator.

(4) A creditor is not to be excluded in respect of any debt which either—

    (a) arose in the ordinary course of the company's trade or the company's business of holding investments and also in the ordinary course of a trade or profession of the creditor or, as the case may be, of the participator or associate who was the original creditor; or

    (b) is a debt for remuneration chargeable to income tax under Schedule E; or

    (c) is a debt for any rent or other payment due for the use of tangible property or of copyright in a literary, dramatic, musical or artistic work within the meaning of the Copyright Act 1956 (or any corresponding right under the law of a country to which that Act does not extend), and not representing more than a reasonable commercial consideration for that use.

1956 c. 74.

(5) Where sub-paragraph (1) above applies for any accounting period, there shall be disregarded for the purposes of any apportionment made by virtue of section 424(2) so much of the relevant income of the company for that period as is equal to the amount which would be disregarded under sub-paragraph (2) above.

(6) Where a resolution is passed or an order is made for the winding up of a close company, or where any other act is done for a like purpose in the case of a winding up otherwise than under the Insolvency Act 1986, sub-paragraphs (1) to (5) above shall apply for any accounting period ending in or with the 12 months ending with the passing of the resolution or other event, or for any later accounting period, as they apply, in a case falling within sub-paragraph (1) above, for an accounting period in which a close company ceases to carry on a trade.

SCH. 19

1986 c. 45.

Legal restrictions on distributions

11.—(1) Subject to paragraph 12 below, where a company is subject to any restriction imposed by law as regards the making of distributions, the excess mentioned in section 424(1) shall be disregarded to the extent to which the company could not make distributions up to the amount of its relevant income without contravening that restriction.

(2) Except where paragraph 10(1) above applies, there shall be disregarded for the purposes of any apportionment made by virtue of section 424(2) so much of the relevant income of the company as is equal to any amount which would be disregarded under sub-paragraph (1) above.

Stock dividends

12.—(1) Where a company issues to a close company any relevant share capital, sub-paragraphs (2) and (3) below shall apply as regards that share capital, and in this paragraph—

"the relevant accounting period" means the accounting period of the close company in which the due date of issue falls;

"relevant share capital" means share capital to which section 249 applies; and

"appropriate amount in cash" has the meaning given by section 251(2).

(2) The relevant income of the close company for the relevant accounting period, as determined under paragraph 1 above, and the amount which, under paragraph 2 above (read, where appropriate, with paragraph 10 above) the relevant income of the close company for that period cannot exceed, shall each be increased by an amount equal to the appropriate amount in cash (or, if it would otherwise be nil, be treated as equal to the appropriate amount in cash).

(3) The amount, if any, which would otherwise be disregarded under paragraph 11(1) above shall be reduced by an amount equal to the appropriate amount in cash.

(4) Where a close company issues any relevant share capital in a case falling within section 249(4), (5) or (6) or sub-paragraph (1) above (read in each case with section 249(3)), the company shall be treated for the purposes of paragraph 3(1) and (2) above—

(a) as if a dividend of an amount equal to the appropriate amount in cash had been paid on the due date of issue; and

(b) where, in relation to that share capital, "the appropriate amount in cash" has the meaning given by section 251(2)(a), as if that dividend had been declared in respect of the accounting period (if any) in respect of which the relevant cash dividend (as defined in section 251(3)) was declared.

PART II

PROCEDURE

Notice of amount to be apportioned

13.—(1) Where in the case of any company the inspector proposes to apportion an amount under section 423 he shall serve on the company a notice showing the amount to be apportioned and, subject to any appeal under this paragraph and to paragraph 15 below, that notice shall be treated as conclusively establishing, both in relation to the company and for the purposes of any assessment under section 426, that an apportionment can be made in respect of that amount.

(2) After a notice under sub-paragraph (1) above has been served on the company it shall not be altered except on appeal or in accordance with paragraph 15 below.

(3) The company may by giving notice of appeal to the inspector within 30 days of the date of any notice under sub-paragraph (1) above appeal against that notice; and any notice under that sub-paragraph shall state the time within which notice of appeal may be given under this sub-paragraph.

(4) Subject to paragraph 18(2) below, any appeal under this paragraph shall be to the General Commissioners except that the company may elect (in accordance with section 46(1) of the Management Act) to bring the appeal before the Special Commissioners instead of the General Commissioners.

(5) The notice of appeal shall specify the grounds of appeal, but on the hearing of the appeal the Commissioners may allow the appellant to put forward any ground not specified in the notice, and take it into consideration if satisfied that the omission was not wilful or unreasonable.

(6) If a company fails or refuses, on being required to do so under paragraph 17 below, to furnish a statement of any amount which in the case of that company could be apportioned under section 423, or renders a statement with which the inspector is not satisfied, the inspector may make an estimate of that amount to the best of his judgment, and any relevant decision taken by the inspector under this sub-paragraph may be reviewed on appeal under this paragraph.

(7) Sections 113(1B) and (3) and 114(2) of the Management Act (supplementary provisions as to assessments and notices of assessment) shall apply to any notice under sub-paragraph (1) above as if the determination of the amount to be shown therein were the making of an assessment and the notice were a notice of assessment.

Notice of manner of apportionment

14.—(1) Where notice has been served on a company under paragraph 13 above showing an amount to be apportioned, the inspector shall serve on the company a notice showing the manner in which that amount is apportioned, (that is to say, the sum apportioned or sub-apportioned to each participator or, if the inspector thinks fit, to each class of share) and, subject to any appeal under this paragraph and to paragraph 15 below, that notice shall be treated, in relation to the company, as conclusively establishing the manner of apportionment.

(2) Paragraph 13(2) to (5) and (7) above shall apply also to a notice under this paragraph, but any appeal against such a notice by virtue of this sub-paragraph shall be to the Special Commissioners.

(3) The manner of apportionment shown in a notice under this paragraph may also be questioned on an appeal against any assessment made under section 426; and any relevant decision taken by the inspector under section 425(2) or (3) may be reviewed on an appeal under this paragraph or on an appeal against any such assessment.

Revision of apportionment

15.—(1) If the inspector discovers that the amount apportioned in the case of any company is or has become insufficient, he shall serve on the company a further notice under paragraph 13(1) above showing the further amount which ought in his opinion to be apportioned, and a further notice relating to that amount shall then be served under paragraph 14 above.

(2) Where the amount shown in a notice under sub-paragraph (1) of paragraph 13 above is excessive because the company's distributable income is smaller than it was taken to be for the purposes of that notice or because the company's distributions were greater than they were taken to be for those purposes, the inspector shall serve on the company a further notice under that sub-paragraph showing a reduced amount; and where such a notice is served—

(a) a further notice shall also be served under paragraph 14 above making such amendments in any previous notice under that paragraph as may be required to take account of the reduction in the amount apportioned; and

(b) there shall be made such adjustments by repayment or discharge of tax as may be required to secure that liabilities to tax under sections 426 to 430 are what they would have been if the notices originally served under paragraphs 13 and 14 above had been as amended by further notices served by virtue of this paragraph.

Protection by transmission of accounts

16.—(1) A close company may, at any time after the general meeting at which the accounts for any period of account are adopted, forward to the inspector a copy of those accounts, together with a copy of the report (if any) of the directors for that period and such further information (if any) as it may think fit, and may request the inspector to proceed under this paragraph in relation to any accounting period comprised in that period of account.

(2) Sub-paragraph (1) above shall not apply if the company is neither a trading company nor a member of a trading group and has no estate or trading income.

(3) Where the inspector receives a request made in accordance with sub-paragraph (1) above in relation to any accounting period, then, subject to sub-paragraph (4) below, he shall, within three months after receipt of the request, intimate to the company whether or not he proposes to make an apportionment in respect of the company for the accounting period under section 423.

(4) On receiving a request made in accordance with sub-paragraph (1) above the inspector may, not later than three months after the receipt of the request, call on the company to furnish him with such further particulars as he may reasonably require; and, if the inspector does so, the time for giving the intimation required by sub-paragraph (3) above shall not expire before three months after he has been furnished with those particulars.

(5) Where the inspector receives a request made in accordance with sub-paragraph (1) above in relation to any accounting period, and does not within the time limited by sub-paragraphs (3) and (4) above intimate his intention to make an apportionment in respect of the period, no such apportionment shall be made unless either—

(a) the information accompanying the request, and any further particulars furnished to the inspector in connection therewith, are not such as to make full and accurate disclosure of all facts and considerations which are material to be known to him, or

(b) within 12 months of the end of the period any of the provisions of paragraph 10 above have effect in relation to the company.

Information

17.—(1) The inspector may, by notice, require any company which is, or appears to him to be, a close company to furnish him within such time (not being less than 30 days) as may be specified in the notice with such particulars as he thinks necessary for the purposes of this Chapter.

(2) If for those purposes any person in whose name any shares are registered is so required by notice by the inspector, he shall state whether or not he is the beneficial owner of the shares and, if not the beneficial owner of the shares or any of them, shall furnish the name and address of the person or persons on whose behalf the shares are registered in his name.

(3) Sub-paragraph (2) above shall apply in relation to loan capital as it applies in relation to shares.

(4) The inspector may, for the purposes of this Chapter, by notice require—

(a) any company which appears to him to be a close company to furnish him with particulars of any bearer securities issued by the company, and the names and addresses of the persons to whom the securities were issued and the respective amounts issued to each person; and

(b) any person to whom securities were so issued, or to or through whom such securities were subsequently sold or transferred, to furnish him with such further information as he may require with a view to enabling him to ascertain the names and addresses of the persons beneficially interested in the securities.

In this sub-paragraph "securities" includes shares, stocks, bonds, debentures and debenture stock and also any promissory note or other instrument evidencing indebtedness to a loan creditor of the company.

(5) Any power which the inspector may exercise under this paragraph for the purposes of this Chapter may also be exercised for the purposes of sections 419 to 422.

Exercise of functions by the Board

18.—(1) Any functions conferred by this Chapter on the inspector may also be exercised by the Board; and references in this Chapter to the inspector shall be construed accordingly.

(2) Where by virtue of this paragraph a notice is served by the Board under paragraph 13(1) above any appeal under that paragraph shall be to the Special Commissioners.

SCHEDULE 20   Section 506.

CHARITIES: QUALIFYING INVESTMENTS AND LOANS

PART I

QUALIFYING INVESTMENTS

1. Investments specified in any of the following paragraphs of this Part of this Schedule are qualifying investments for the purposes of section 506.

2. Any investment falling within Part I, Part II, apart from paragraph 13 (mortgages etc.) or Part III of Schedule 1 to the Trustee Investments Act 1961.   1961 c. 62.

3. Any investment in a common investment fund established under section 22 of the Charities Act 1960 or section 25 of the Charities Act (Northern Ireland) 1964 or in any similar fund established for the exclusive benefit of charities by or under any enactment relating to any particular charities or class of charities.   1960 c. 58.
1964 c. 33 (N.I.).

4. Any interest in land, other than an interest held as security for a debt of any description.

5. Shares in, or securities of, a company which are quoted on a recognised stock exchange, or which are dealt in on the Unlisted Securities Market.

6. Units, or other shares of the investments subject to the trusts, of a unit trust scheme within the meaning of the Financial Services Act 1986.   1986 c. 60.

7.—(1) Deposits with an institution authorised under the Banking Act 1987 in respect of which interest is payable at a commercial rate.   1987 c. 22.

(2) A deposit mentioned in sub-paragraph (1) above is not a qualifying investment if it is made as part of an arrangement under which a loan is made by the authorised institution to some other person.

8. Certificates of deposit as defined in section 56(5).

9.—(1) Any loan or other investment as to which the Board are satisfied, on a claim made to them in that behalf, that the loan or other investment is made for the benefit of the charity and not for the avoidance of tax (whether by the charity or any other person).

(2) The reference in sub-paragraph (1) above to a loan includes a loan which is secured by a mortgage or charge of any kind over land.

PART II

QUALIFYING LOANS

10. For the purposes of section 506, a loan which is not made by way of investment is a qualifying loan if it consists of—

(a) a loan made to another charity for charitable purposes only; or

(b) a loan to a beneficiary of the charity which is made in the course of carrying out the purposes of the charity; or

(c) money placed on current account with an institution authorised under the Banking Act 1987 otherwise than as part of such an arrangement as is mentioned in paragraph 7(2) above; or   1987 c. 22.

SCH. 20

(d) any other loan as to which the Board are satisfied, on a claim made to them in that behalf, that the loan is made for the benefit of the charity and not for the avoidance of tax (whether by the charity or by some other person).

PART III

ATTRIBUTION OF EXCESS NON-QUALIFYING EXPENDITURE TO EARLIER CHARGEABLE PERIODS

11. This Part of this Schedule applies in the circumstances specified in subsection (6) of section 506 and in this Part—

(a) "the primary period" means the chargeable period of the charity concerned in which there is such an excess as is mentioned in that subsection;

(b) "unapplied non-qualifying expenditure" means so much of the excess referred to in that subsection as does not exceed the non-qualifying expenditure of the primary period; and

(c) "earlier period", in relation to an amount of unapplied non-qualifying expenditure, means any chargeable period of the charity concerned which ended not more than six years before the end of the primary period.

12.—(1) So much of the unapplied non-qualifying expenditure as is not shown by the charity to be the expenditure of non-taxable sums received by the charity in the primary period shall be treated in accordance with paragraph 13 below as non-qualifying expenditure of earlier periods.

(2) In sub-paragraph (1) above "non-taxable sums" means donations, legacies and other sums of a similar nature which, apart from section 505(1) of this Act and section 145 of the 1979 Act, are not within the charge to tax.

13.—(1) Where, in accordance with paragraph 12 above, an amount of unapplied non-qualifying expenditure ("the excess expenditure") falls to be treated as non-qualifying expenditure of earlier periods—

(a) it shall be attributed only to those earlier periods (if any) which, apart from the attribution, (but taking account of any previous operation of this paragraph) the relevant income and gains exceed the aggregate of the qualifying and non-qualifying expenditure incurred in that period; and

(b) the amount to be attributed to any such earlier period shall not be greater than the excess of that period referred to in paragraph (a) above.

(2) Where there is more than one earlier period to which the excess expenditure can be attributed in accordance with sub-paragraph (1) above, it shall be attributed to later periods in priority to earlier periods.

(3) In so far as any of the excess expenditure cannot be attributed to earlier periods in accordance with this paragraph, it shall be disregarded for the purposes of section 506(6) (and this Part of this Schedule).

14. All such adjustments shall be made, whether by way of the making of assessments or otherwise, as may be required in consequence of the provisions of this Part of this Schedule.

SCHEDULE 21

TAX RELIEF IN CONNECTION WITH SCHEMES FOR
RATIONALIZING INDUSTRY AND OTHER REDUNDANCY
SCHEMES

PART I

PRELIMINARY

1.—(1) In this Schedule—

"scheme" means a scheme which is for the time being certified or has at any
time been certified by the Secretary of State under section 568;

"payment" means a payment made under a scheme, being a payment made
to a person carrying on a trade to which the scheme relates and not
being a payment made by way of repayment of contributions;

"the person chargeable" means, in relation to any such payment, the person
liable to pay any tax which may fall to be paid by reason of the receipt
of the payment;

"damage" includes any loss, liability, expense or other burden, and
references to the amount of any damage are references to the sum which
would be fair compensation for that damage;

"contribution" includes part of a contribution, and "deductible
contribution" means a contribution allowed to be deducted under
section 568, any reduction under Part III of this Schedule being left out
of account; and

"asset" includes part of an asset.

(2) For the purposes of this Schedule, a sum received by any person by way of
repayment of contributions shall be deemed to be by way of repayment of the last
contribution paid by him, and, if the sum exceeds the amount of that
contribution, by way of repayment of the penultimate contribution so paid, and
so on.

PART II

RELIEF IN RESPECT OF CERTAIN PAYMENTS

2. The question whether any, and if so, what, relief is to be given shall be
determined separately in relation to each payment made under the scheme in
respect of the trade, but for the purpose of determining that question regard shall
be had, as provided by the following provisions of this Part of this Schedule, to
the sum ("the total payment") produced by adding the amount of the payment
to the amount of any payments previously so made.

3. No relief shall be given in respect of the payment unless the person
chargeable shows—

(a) the amount of the damage in respect of which the total payment has been
made; and

(b) how much of that amount is referable to damage in respect of which no
relief may be given under the Tax Acts.

4. No relief shall be given in respect of the payment unless the total payment, or
the amount of the damage in respect of which the total payment has been made,
whichever is the smaller, exceeds the aggregate amount of the deductible

contributions which have been paid in furtherance of the scheme in respect of the trade in question before the payment is made, exclusive of any contributions which have been repaid before the payment is made.

5. The amount of the reduction to be made in respect of the payment shall be arrived at by—

(a) ascertaining the sum which bears to the excess mentioned in paragraph 4 above the same proportion that the amount mentioned in paragraph 3(b) above bears to the amount mentioned in paragraph 3(a); and

(b) deducting from that sum the total amount of any reductions which have been or fall to be made under this Schedule in respect of payments previously made under the scheme in respect of the trade.

6.—(1) For the purposes of this Schedule, and subject to sub-paragraph (2) below, damage shall be deemed to be damage in respect of which relief may be given under the Tax Acts if and only if—

(a) the damage is attributable to any of the following events, that is to say, the demolition, destruction or putting out of use of any asset, or the disposition or termination of an interest in any asset, and, by reason of that event, an allowance falls to be made under Chapter I or Chapter II of Part I of the 1968 Act in taxing the trade; or

(b) the damage consists of any loss, liability, expense or other burden in respect of which an allowance may be made in computing the profits or gains of the trade for the purposes of the Tax Acts.

(2) Where an allowance under Chapter I of Part I of the 1968 Act in respect of any damage falls to be reduced in the proportion specified in section 3(4) of that Act, only a proportionately reduced amount of the damage shall be treated as being referable to damage in respect of which relief may be given under the Tax Acts.

(3) Where any event occurs which would give rise to an allowance under the Tax Acts in respect of any asset in taxing, or computing the profits or gains of, a trade but for any of the following matters, that is to say—

(a) that there are no profits or gains against which the allowance could be made, or

(b) that account is required to be taken of allowances previously made or deemed to have been made in respect of the asset; or

(c) that account is required to be taken of any sum which falls to be written off the expenditure incurred on the asset for the purpose of determining whether any and if so what allowance may be given by reason of the event; or

(d) that account is required to be taken of any sum falling to be taken into account as sale, insurance, salvage or compensation moneys, the like consequences shall ensue under this Schedule as if an allowance had fallen to be made by reason of that event.

(4) Where any damage is attributable to a permanent change in the purposes for which an asset is used, or the temporary or permanent putting out of use of an asset, the question whether the damage is damage in respect of which relief may be given under the Tax Acts shall be determined as if the damage had been attributable to a sale of the asset on the date upon which the change or putting out of use took place.

PART III

EXCLUSION OF RELIEF IN RESPECT OF CONTRIBUTIONS PAID AFTER RELIEF HAS BEEN GIVEN UNDER PART II

7. The provisions of this Part of this Schedule shall have effect where—

   (a) a contribution is paid under a scheme in respect of a trade; and

   (b) before the contribution is paid, payments have been made under the scheme to the person carrying on the trade; and

   (c) reductions have been made, under Part II of this Schedule, in the amounts which, by reason of those payments, are to be treated as trading receipts of the trade.

8. There shall be ascertained—

   (a) the total amount of those reductions; and

   (b) the sum by which that total would have been decreased if the contribution, and any previous contributions to which this Part of this Schedule applies, had been paid before any of the payments were made.

9. For the purpose of determining what deduction is to be made in respect of the contribution under section 568, the contribution shall be deemed to be reduced by the sum specified in paragraph 8(b) above, but—

   (a) for the purpose of the application of paragraph 8 above in relation to contributions subsequently paid under the scheme in respect of the trade, the total amount of the reductions referred to in that paragraph shall be treated as decreased by that sum; and

   (b) for the purpose of the application of paragraph 5 above in relation to payments subsequently made under the scheme in respect of the trade, the total amount of the reductions referred to in that paragraph shall be treated as decreased by that sum.

10. When two or more contributions are paid at the same time, the provisions of this Part of this Schedule shall have effect as if they were a single contribution.

SCHEDULE 22

REDUCTION OF PENSION FUND SURPLUSES

1.—(1) The Board may make regulations providing for this Schedule to apply, as from a prescribed date, in relation to any exempt approved scheme which is of a prescribed kind.

(2) The Board may make regulations providing for prescribed provisions of this Schedule to apply, as from a prescribed date, in prescribed circumstances, and subject to any prescribed omissions or modifications, in relation to any exempt approved scheme of another prescribed kind.

(3) In this Schedule "prescribed" means prescribed by regulations made by the Board.

2.—(1) The administrator of a scheme in relation to which this Schedule applies shall, in prescribed circumstances and at a prescribed time, either produce to the Board a written valuation such as is mentioned in sub-paragraph (2) below or give to the Board a certificate such as is mentioned in sub-paragraph (3) below.

(2) The valuation must be a valuation of the assets held for the purposes of the scheme and the liabilities of the scheme, must be determined in accordance with prescribed principles and fulfil prescribed requirements, and must be signed by a person with qualifications of a prescribed kind.

(3) The certificate must state whether or not the value of the assets (as determined in accordance with prescribed principles) exceeds the value of the liabilities (as so determined) by a percentage which is more than a prescribed maximum, must be in a prescribed form, and must be signed by a person with qualifications of a prescribed kind.

3.—(1) Subject to paragraph 4(4) below, where a valuation produced under paragraph 2 shows, or a certificate given under that paragraph states, that the value of the assets exceeds the value of the liabilities by a percentage which is more than the prescribed maximum, the administrator of the scheme shall within a prescribed period submit to the Board for their approval proposals which comply with sub-paragraph (2) below.

(2) The proposals must be proposals for reducing (or, subject to paragraph (b) below, eliminating) the excess in a way or ways set out in the proposals and falling within sub-paragraph (3) below; and they must be such as to secure that—

(a) by the end of a prescribed period the percentage (if any) by which the value of the assets exceeds the value of the liabilities is no more than the prescribed maximum; and

(b) if the way, or one of the ways, set out in the proposals falls within sub-paragraph (3)(a) below, there remains an excess which is of a level not less than the prescribed minimum.

(3) Subject to sub-paragraph (4) below, the permitted ways of reducing or eliminating the excess are—

(a) making payments to an employer;

(b) suspending for a period (of five years or less) set out in the proposals an employer's obligation to pay contributions under the scheme or reducing for such a period the amount of an employer's contributions under the scheme;

(c) suspending for a period (of five years or less) set out in the proposals the obligation of employees to pay contributions under the scheme or reducing for such a period the amount of employees' contributions under the scheme;

(d) improving existing benefits provided under the scheme;

(e) providing new benefits under the scheme;

(f) such other ways as may be prescribed.

(4) In prescribed circumstances sub-paragraph (3) above shall apply subject to such omissions or modifications as may be prescribed.

(5) Subject to paragraph 4(4) below, if the administrator of the scheme fails to submit proposals to the Board within the period mentioned in subparagraph (1) above, or if the proposals submitted to them within that period are not approved by the Board within a further prescribed period, paragraph 7 below shall apply.

4.—(1) Where a valuation has been produced under paragraph 2 above, the Board may serve on the administrator of the scheme a notice requiring him to furnish the Board, within a prescribed period, with such particulars relating to the valuation as may be specified in the notice.

(2) Where a certificate has been given under paragraph 2 above, the Board may serve on the administrator of the scheme a notice requiring him to produce to the Board, within a prescribed period, a written valuation such as is mentioned in paragraph 2(2) above.

(3) Where a valuation has been produced in compliance with a notice served under sub-paragraph (2) above, the Board may serve on the administrator of the scheme a further notice requiring him to furnish the Board, within a prescribed period, with such particulars relating to the valuation as may be specified in the notice.

(4) Where a notice is served on the administrator of a scheme under subparagraph (1) or (2) above, paragraph 3(1) and (5) above shall cease to apply.

5.—(1) Where particulars have been furnished under paragraph 4 above, or a valuation has been produced under that paragraph, the Board shall, within a prescribed period, serve on the administrator of the scheme a notice—

(a) stating that they accept the valuation produced under paragraph 2 or, as the case may be, 4 above; or

(b) stating that they do not accept the valuation so produced, and specifying their estimate of the value of the liabilities of the scheme at the relevant time and their estimate of the value of the assets held for the purposes of the scheme at that time.

(2) For the purposes of sub-paragraph (1)(b) above, the relevant time is the time specified in the valuation produced under paragraph 2 or 4 above as the time by reference to which the values of the assets and liabilities are determined.

(3) Where—

(a) in a case falling within sub-paragraph (1)(a) above, the valuation shows that the value of the assets exceeds the value of the liabilities by a percentage which is more than the prescribed maximum; or

(b) in a case falling within sub-paragraph (1)(b) above, the value of the assets as estimated by the Board exceeds the value of the liabilities as so estimated by a percentage which is more than the prescribed maximum;

the administrator of the scheme shall within a prescribed period submit to the Board for their approval proposals which comply with paragraph 3(2) to (4) above.

(4) If the administrator of the scheme fails to submit proposals to the Board within the period mentioned in sub-paragraph (3) above, or if proposals submitted to them within that period are not approved by the Board within a further prescribed period, paragraph 7 below shall apply.

6.—(1) Where proposals are submitted to the Board under paragraph 3(1) or 5(3) above and they approve them within the further prescribed period mentioned in paragraph 3(5) or 5(4) above, the administrator of the scheme shall carry out the proposals within the period mentioned in paragraph 3(2) above.

(2) If the administrator fails to carry out the proposals within that period, paragraph 7 below shall apply.

7.—(1) Where this paragraph applies the Board may specify a percentage equivalent to the fraction—

$$\frac{A}{B}$$

where—

A represents their estimate of the value of the liabilities of the scheme at the relevant time increased by a prescribed percentage; and

B represents their estimate of the value of the assets held for the purposes of the scheme at that time.

(2) For the purposes of this paragraph the relevant time is the time specified—

(a) in the valuation produced or certificate given under paragraph 2 above; or

(b) where a valuation has been produced under paragraph 4 above, in that valuation,

as the time by reference to which the values of the assets and liabilities are determined.

(3) Where a percentage has been so specified—

(a) section 592(2) shall apply only to that percentage of any income derived in the relevant period from the assets held for the purposes of the scheme;

(b) section 592(3) shall apply only to that percentage of any underwriting commissions applied in the relevant period for the purposes of the scheme;

(c) section 56 shall by virtue of subsection (3)(b) of that section not apply only to that percentage of any profits or gains arising to the scheme in the relevant period; and

(d) section 149B(1)(g) of the 1979 Act (capital gains tax exemption) shall apply only to that percentage of any gain accruing on the disposal in the relevant period of any of those assets.

(4) Sub-paragraphs (5) to (8) below shall apply where a percentage has been so specified, securities are transferred in the relevant period, and the transferor or transferee is such that, if he became entitled to any interest on them, exemption could be allowed under section 592(2).

(5) Section 715(1)(k) shall not apply.

(6) Where, in consequence of sub-paragraph (5) above, section 713(2)(a) or (3)(b) applies, the sum concerned shall be treated as reduced by an amount equal to the specified percentage of itself.

(7) Where, in consequence of sub-paragraph (5) above, section 713(2)(b) or (3)(a) applies, the relief concerned shall be treated as reduced by an amount equal to the specified percentage of itself.

(8) For the purposes of section 714(5), the amount of interest falling to be reduced by the amount of the allowance shall be treated as the amount found after applying section 592(2).

(9) In sub-paragraphs (4) to (8) above expressions which also appear in sections 710 to 728 have the same meanings as in those sections.

(10) In this paragraph "the relevant period" means the period begining at the relevant time and ending when it is proved to the satisfaction of the Board that the value of the assets (as determined in accordance with prescribed principles) exceeds the value of the liabilities (as so determined) by a percentage which is no more than the prescribed maximum.

8.—(1) The Board may make regulations providing that an appeal may be brought against a notice under paragraph 5(1)(b) above as if it were notice of the decision of the Board on a claim made by the administrator of the scheme concerned.

(2) Regulations under this paragraph may include—

(a) provision that bringing an appeal shall suspend the operation of paragraph 5(3) and (4) above; and

(b) other provisions consequential on the provision that an appeal may be brought (including provisions modifying this Schedule).

SCHEDULE 23

OCCUPATIONAL PENSION SCHEMES:

SCHEMES APPROVED BEFORE 23rd JULY 1987

Preliminary

1.—(1) This Schedule shall be deemed to have come into force on 17th March 1987 and, subject to sub-paragraphs (2) and (3) below, applies in relation to any retirement benefits scheme approved by the Board before the passing of the Finance (No.2) Act 1987 (23rd July 1987).

(2) The Board may by regulations provide that this Schedule, or any provision of it, shall not apply in relation to a scheme or to an employee—

    (a) in circumstances prescribed in the regulations;

    (b) in any case where in the opinion of the Board the facts are such that it would be appropriate for this Schedule, or the provision in question, not to apply.

(3) This Schedule shall not apply to a retirement benefits scheme if, before the end of 1987, the administrator of the scheme gave notice to the Board that it is not to apply.

(4) Where a notice is given to the Board under sub-paragraph (3) above, the scheme shall, with effect from 17th March 1987 or (if later) the date with effect from which it was approved, cease to be approved.

Accelerated accrual

2.—(1) This paragraph applies where an employee becomes a member of the scheme on or after 17th March 1987.

(2) Notwithstanding anything to the contrary in the rules of the scheme, they shall have effect as if they did not allow the provision for the employee of a pension exceeding one-thirtieth of his relevant annual remuneration for each year of service up to a maximum of 20.

3.—(1) This paragraph applies where an employee becomes a member of the scheme on or after 17th March 1987 and the scheme allows him to commute his pension or part of it for a lump sum or sums.

(2) If the employee's full pension (that is, the pension before any commutation) is equal to or less than a basic rate commutable pension, the rules of the scheme shall have effect (notwithstanding anything in them to the contrary) as if they did not allow him to obtain by way of commutation a lump sum or sums exceeding in all a basic rate lump sum.

(3) If the employee's full pension is greater than a basic rate commutable pension but less than a maximum rate commutable pension, the rules of the scheme shall have effect (notwithstanding anything in them to the contrary) as if they did not allow him to obtain by way of commutation a lump sum or sums exceeding in all the aggregate of—

    (a) a basic rate lump sum, and

    (b) an amount equal to the relevant percentage of the difference between a basic rate lump sum and a maximum rate lump sum.

(4) In this paragraph, as it applies in relation to an employee—

    (a) a "basic rate commutable pension" means a pension of one-sixtieth of his relevant annual remuneration for each year of service up to a maximum of 40;

(b) a "maximum rate commutable pension" means a pension of one-thirtieth of his relevant annual remuneration for each year of service up to a maximum of 20;

(c) a "basic rate lump sum" means a lump sum of three-eighths of his relevant annual remuneration for each year of service up to a maximum of 40;

(d) a "maximum rate lump sum" means a lump sum of such amount as may be determined by or under regulations made by the Board for the purposes of this paragraph and paragraph 4 below;

(e) "the relevant percentage" means the difference between a basic rate commutable pension and the employee's full pension expressed as a percentage of the difference between a basic rate commutable pension and a maximum rate commutable pension.

4.—(1) This paragraph applies where an employee becomes a member of the scheme on or after 17th March 1987 and the scheme provides a lump sum or sums for him otherwise than by commutation of his pension or part of it.

(2) If the employee's pension is equal to or less than a basic rate non-commutable pension, the rules of the scheme shall have effect (notwithstanding anything in them to the contrary) as if they did not allow the payment to him, otherwise than by way of commutation, of a lump sum or sums exceeding in all a basic rate lump sum.

(3) If the employee's pension is greater than a basic rate non-commutable pension but less than a maximum rate non-commutable pension the rules of the scheme shall have effect (notwithstanding anything in them to the contrary) as if they did not allow the payment to him, otherwise than by way of commutation, of a lump sum or sums exceeding in all the aggregate of—

(a) a basic rate lump sum, and

(b) an amount equal to the relevant percentage of the difference between a basic rate lump sum and a maximum rate lump sum.

(4) In this paragraph, as it applies in relation to an employee—

(a) a "basic rate non-commutable pension" means a pension of one-eightieth of his relevant annual remuneration for each year of service up to a maximum of 40,

(b) a "maximum rate non-commutable pension" means a pension of one-fortieth of his relevant annual remuneration for each year of service up to a maximum of 20,

(c) "basic rate lump sum" and "maximum rate lump sum" have the same meanings as in paragraph 3 above, and

(d) "the relevant percentage" means the difference between a basic rate non-commutable pension and the employee's actual pension expressed as a percentage of the difference between a basic rate non-commutable pension and a maximum rate non-commutable pension.

Final remuneration

5.—(1) This paragraph applies where an employee who is a member of the scheme retires on or after 17th March 1987.

(2) The rules of the scheme shall have effect as if they provided that in determining the employee's relevant annual remuneration for the purpose of calculating benefits, no account should be taken of anything excluded from the definition of "remuneration" in section 612(1).

(3) In the case of an employee—

(a) whose employer is a company and who at any time in the last ten years of his service is a controlling director of the company, or

(b) whose relevant annual remuneration for the purpose of calculating benefits, so far as the remuneration is ascertained by reference to years beginning on or after 6th April 1987, would (apart from this Schedule) exceed the permitted maximum,

the rules of the scheme shall have effect as if they provided that his relevant annual remuneration must not exceed his highest average annual remuneration for any period of three or more years ending within the period of ten years which ends with the date on which his service ends.

(4) In the case of an employee within paragraph (b) of sub-paragraph (3) above who retires before 6th April 1991, the rules of the scheme shall have effect as if they provided that his relevant annual remuneration must not exceed the higher of—

(a) the average annual remuneration referred to in that sub-paragraph, and

(b) his remuneration (within the meaning given by section 612(1)) assessable to income tax under Schedule E for the year of assessment 1986-87.

(5) For the purposes of this paragraph a person is a controlling director of a company if—

(a) he is a director (as defined in section 612), and

(b) he is within paragraph (b) of section 417(5),

in relation to the company.

Lump sums

6.—(1) This paragraph applies where an employee becomes a member of the scheme on or after 17th March 1987.

(2) If the rules of the scheme allow the employee to obtain, (by commutation of his pension or otherwise), a lump sum or sums calculated by reference to his relevant annual remuneration, they shall have effect as if they included a rule that in calculating a lump sum any excess of that remuneration over the permitted maximum should be disregarded.

Additional voluntary contributions

7.—(1) This paragraph applies where—

(a) the rules of the scheme make provision for the payment by employees of voluntary contributions, and

(b) on or after 8th April 1987 an employee enters into arrangements to pay such contributions.

(2) Notwithstanding anything in the rules of the scheme, they shall have effect as if they did not allow the payment to the employee of a lump sum in commutation of a pension if or to the extent that the pension is secured by the voluntary contributions.

8.—(1) This paragraph applies where an employee who is a member of the scheme ("the main scheme") is also a member of an approved scheme ("the voluntary scheme") which provides additional benefits to supplement those provided by the main scheme and to which no contributions are made by any employer of his.

(2) Any rules of the main scheme imposing a limit on the amount of a benefit provided for the employee shall have effect (notwithstanding anything in them to the contrary) as if they provided for the limit to be reduced by the amount of any like benefit provided for the employee by the voluntary scheme.

Supplementary

9. In this Schedule "relevant annual remuneration" means final remuneration or, if the scheme provides for benefits to be calculated by reference to some other annual remuneration, that other annual remuneration.

SCHEDULE 24

ASSUMPTIONS FOR CALCULATING CHARGEABLE PROFITS, CREDITABLE TAX AND CORRESPONDING UNITED KINGDOM TAX OF FOREIGN COMPANIES

General

1.—(1) The company shall be assumed to be resident in the United Kingdom.

(2) Nothing in sub-paragraph (1) above requires it to be assumed that there is any change in the place or places at which the company carries on its activities.

(3) For the avoidance of doubt, it is hereby declared that, if any sums forming part of the company's profits for an accounting period have been received by the company without any deduction of or charge to tax by virtue of section 47 or 48 the effect of the assumption in sub-paragraph (1) above is that those sums are to be brought within the charge to tax for the purposes of calculating the company's chargeable profits or corresponding United Kingdom tax.

(4) In any case where—

(a) it is at any time necessary for any purpose of Chapter IV of Part XVII to determine the chargeable profits of the company for an accounting period, and

(b) at that time no direction has been given under section 747(1) with respect to that or any earlier accounting period of the company,

it shall be assumed, for the purpose of any of the following provisions of this Schedule which refer to the first accounting period in respect of which a direction is given under that section, that such a direction has been given for that period (but not for any earlier period).

(5) Nothing in this Schedule affects any liability for, or the computation of, corporation tax in respect of a trade which is carried on by a company resident outside the United Kingdom through a branch or agency in the United Kingdom.

2.—(1) The company shall be assumed to have become resident in the United Kingdom (and, accordingly, within the charge to corporation tax) at the beginning of the first accounting period in respect of which a direction is given under section 747(1) and that United Kingdom residence shall be assumed to continue throughout subsequent accounting periods of the company (whether or not a direction is given in respect of all or any of them) until the company ceases to be controlled by persons resident in the United Kingdom.

(2) Except in so far as the following provisions of this Schedule otherwise provide, for the purposes of calculating a company's chargeable profits or corresponding United Kingdom tax for any accounting period which is not the first such period referred to in sub-paragraph (1) above (and, in particular, for the purpose of applying any relief which is relevant to two or more accounting periods), it shall be assumed that a calculation of chargeable profits or, as the case may be, corresponding United Kingdom tax has been made for every previous accounting period throughout which the company was, by virtue of sub-paragraph (1) above, assumed to have been resident in the United Kingdom.

3. The company shall be assumed not to be a close company.

4.—(1) Subject to sub-paragraph (2) below, where any relief under the Corporation Tax Acts is dependent upon the making of a claim or election, the company shall be assumed to have made that claim or election which would give the maximum amount of relief and to have made that claim or election within any time limit applicable to it.

(2) If, by notice given to the Board at any time not later than the expiry of the time for the making of an appeal under section 753 or within such longer period as the Board may in any particular case allow, the United Kingdom resident company which has or, as the case may be, any two or more United Kingdom resident companies which together have, a majority interest in the company so request, the company shall be assumed—

    (a) not to have made any claim or election specified in the notice; or

    (b) to have made a claim or election so specified, being different from one assumed by sub-paragraph (1) above but being one which (subject to compliance with any time limit) could have been made in the case of a company within the charge to corporation tax; or

    (c) to have disclaimed or required the postponement, in whole or in part, of an allowance if (subject to compliance with any time limit) a company within the charge to corporation tax could have disclaimed the allowance or, as the case may be, required such a postponement.

(3) For the purposes of this paragraph, a United Kingdom resident company has, or two or more United Kingdom resident companies together have, a majority interest in the company if on the apportionment of the company's chargeable profits for the relevant accounting period under section 747(3) more than half of the amount of those profits—

    (a) which are apportioned to all United Kingdom resident companies, and

    (b) which give rise to an assessment on any such companies under subsection (4)(a) of that section,

are apportioned to the United Kingdom resident company or companies concerned.

(4) In sub-paragraph (3) above "the relevant accounting period" means the accounting period or, as the case may be, the first accounting period in which the relief in question is or would be available in accordance with sub-paragraph (1) above.

Group relief etc.

5. The company shall be assumed to be neither a member of a group of companies nor a member of a consortium for the purposes of any provision of the Tax Acts.

6.—(1) In relation to section 247 it shall be assumed—

    (a) that the conditions for the making of an election under subsection (1) are not fulfilled with respect to dividends paid or received by the company; and

    (b) that the conditions for the making of an election under subsection (4) are not fulfilled with respect to payments made or received by the company.

(2) References in sub-paragraph (1) above to dividends or payments received by the company apply to any received by another person on behalf of or in trust for the company, but not to any received by the company on behalf of or in trust for another person.

7. The company shall be assumed not to be a subsidiary to which the benefit of any advance corporation tax may be surrendered under section 240.

Company reconstructions

8. Without prejudice to the operation of section 343 in a case where the company is the predecessor, within the meaning of that section, and a company resident in the United Kingdom is the successor, within the meaning of that section—

(a) the assumption that the company is resident in the United Kingdom shall not be regarded as requiring it also to be assumed that the company is within the charge to tax in respect of a trade for the purposes of that section, and

(b) except in so far as the company is actually within that charge (by carrying on the trade through a branch or agency in the United Kingdom), it shall accordingly be assumed that the company can never be the successor, within the meaning of that section, to another company (whether resident in the United Kingdom or not).

Losses in pre-direction accounting periods

9.—(1) Subject to sub-paragraph (2) below, this paragraph applies in any case where the company incurred a loss in a trade in an accounting period—

(a) which precedes the first accounting period in respect of which a direction is given under section 747(1) ("the starting period"); and

(b) which ended less than six years before the beginning of the starting period; and

(c) in which the company was not resident in the United Kingdom;

and in this paragraph any such accounting period is referred to as a "pre-direction period".

(2) This paragraph does not apply in any case where a declaration is made under paragraph 11(3) below specifying an accounting period of the company which begins before, or is the same as, the first pre-direction period in which the company incurred a loss as mentioned in sub-paragraph (1) above.

(3) If a claim is made for the purpose by the United Kingdom resident company or companies referred to in paragraph 4(2) above, the chargeable profits (if any) of the company for accounting periods beginning with that pre-direction period which is specified in the claim and in which a loss is incurred as mentioned in sub-paragraph (1) above shall be determined (in accordance with the provisions of this Schedule other than this paragraph) on the assumption that that pre-direction period was the first accounting period in respect of which a direction was given under section 747(1).

(4) A claim under sub-paragraph (3) above shall be made by notice given to the Board within 60 days of the date of the notice under subsection (1) or subsection (3) of section 753 relating to the starting period or within such longer period as the Board may in any particular case allow.

(5) For the purposes of a claim under sub-paragraph (3) above, it shall be assumed that Chapter IV of Part XVII was in force before the beginning of the first of the pre-direction periods.

(6) In determining for the purposes of this paragraph which accounting period of the company is the starting period, no account should be taken of the effect of any declaration under paragraph 11(3) below.

Capital allowances

10.—(1) Subject to paragraphs 11 and 12 below, if, in an accounting period falling before the beginning of the first accounting period in respect of which a direction is given under section 747(1), the company incurred any capital

SCH. 24

1971 c. 68.

expenditure on the provision of machinery or plant for the purposes of its trade, that machinery or plant shall be assumed, for the purposes of Chapter I of Part III of the Finance Act 1971, to have been provided for purposes wholly other than those of the trade and not to have been brought into use for the purposes of that trade until the beginning of that first accounting period, and paragraph 7 of Schedule 8 to that Act (expenditure treated as equivalent to market value at the time the machinery or plant is brought into use) shall apply accordingly.

(2) This paragraph shall be construed as one with Chapter I of Part III of the Finance Act 1971.

11.—(1) This paragraph applies in any case where it appears to the Board that the reason why no direction was given under section 747(1) in respect of an accounting period which precedes the starting period was that the effect of any allowance which would be assumed for that preceding period by virtue of this Schedule would be such that—

(a) the company would not have been considered to be subject in that accounting period to a lower level of taxation in the territory in which it was resident; or

(b) the company would have had no chargeable profits for that accounting period; or

(c) the chargeable profits of the company for that accounting period would not have exceeded £20,000 or such smaller amount as was appropriate in accordance with section 748(1)(d).

(2) In this paragraph "the starting period" means the first accounting period in respect of which a direction is given under section 747(1) and, in a case where a claim is made under sub-paragraph (3) of paragraph 9 above, no account shall be taken of the effect of that sub-paragraph in determining which accounting period is the starting period for the purposes of this paragraph.

(3) If, in a case where this paragraph applies, the Board so declare by notice given to every company to which, in accordance with section 753(1), notice of the making of the direction relating to the starting period is required to be given, the chargeable profits of that period and every subsequent accounting period and the corresponding United Kingdom tax for every subsequent accounting period shall be determined (in accordance with the provisions of this Schedule other than this paragraph) on the assumption that the accounting period specified in the declaration was the first accounting period in respect of which a direction was given and, accordingly, as if allowances had been assumed in respect of that accounting period and any subsequent accounting period which precedes the starting period.

(4) Nothing in sub-paragraph (3) above affects the operation of paragraph 9(3) above in a case where the accounting period specified in a claim under paragraph 9(3) above begins before the period specified in a declaration under sub-paragraph (3) above.

(5) Subject to sub-paragraph (6) below, the Board shall not make a declaration under sub-paragraph (3) above with respect to an accounting period which precedes the starting period unless the facts are such that—

(a) assuming the company to have been subject in that period to a lower level of taxation in the territory in which it was resident, and

(b) assuming the company to have had in that period chargeable profits of such an amount that the condition in section 748(1)(d) would not be fulfilled,

a direction could have been given in respect of that period under section 747(1).

(6) In its application to a company falling within section 749(3), sub-paragraph (5) above shall have effect with the omission of paragraph (a).

(7) In this paragraph "allowance" means an allowance under Chapter I of Part I of the 1968 Act or Chapter I of Part III of the Finance Act 1971.

Unremittable overseas income

12. For the purposes of the application of section 584 to the company's income it shall be assumed—

(a) that any reference in paragraph (a) or paragraph (b) of subsection (1) of that section to the United Kingdom is a reference to both the United Kingdom and the territory in which the company is in fact resident; and

(b) that a notice under subsection (2) of that section (expressing a wish to be assessed in accordance with that subsection) may be given on behalf of the company by the United Kingdom resident company or companies referred to in paragraph 4(2) above.

SCHEDULE 25 Section 748.

CASES EXCLUDED FROM DIRECTION-MAKING POWERS

PART I

ACCEPTABLE DISTRIBUTION POLICY

1. The provisions of this Part of this Schedule have effect for the purposes of paragraph (a) of subsection (1) of section 748.

2.—(1) Subject to sub-paragraph (2) below, a controlled foreign company pursues an acceptable distribution policy in respect of a particular accounting period if, and only if—

    (a) a dividend which is not paid out of specified profits is paid for that accounting period or for some other period which, in whole or in part, falls within that accounting period; and

    (b) the dividend is paid during, or not more than eighteen months after the expiry of, the period for which it is paid or at such later time as the Board may, in any particular case, allow; and

    (c) the dividend is paid at a time when the company is not resident in the United Kingdom (whether or not it is at that time a controlled foreign company); and

    (d) the proportion of the dividend or, if there is more than one, of the aggregate of those dividends which is paid to persons resident in the United Kingdom represents at least 50 per cent. of the company's available profits for the accounting period referred to in paragraph (a) above or, where sub-paragraph (4) or (5) below applies, of the appropriate portion of those profits;

and for the purposes of this sub-paragraph a dividend which is not paid for a specified period shall be treated as paid for the period or periods the profits of which are, in relation to the dividend, the relevant profits for the purposes of section 799.

(2) In the case of a controlled foreign company which is not a trading company, sub-paragraph (1) above shall have effect with the substitution of 90 per cent. for 50 per cent.

(3) For the purposes of this Part of this Schedule, a dividend represents those profits of the controlled foreign company in question which in relation to that dividend are the relevant profits for the purposes of section 799 and, accordingly, where those profits are the profits of a period which falls partly within and partly outside an accounting period of that company, the necessary apportionment shall be made to determine what proportion of those profits is attributable to that accounting period.

(4) This sub-paragraph applies where—

    (a) throughout the accounting period in question all the issued shares of the controlled foreign company are of a single class, and

    (b) at the end of that accounting period some of those shares are held by persons resident outside the United Kingdom, and

    (c) at no time during that accounting period does any person have an interest in the company other than an interest derived from the issued shares of the company;

SCH. 25

and in a case where this sub-paragraph applies the appropriate portion for the purposes of sub-paragraph (1)(d) above is the fraction of which the denominator is the total number of the issued shares of the company at the end of the accounting period in question and, subject to sub-paragraph (8) below, the numerator is the number of those issued shares by virtue of which persons resident in the United Kingdom have interests in the company at that time.

(5) This sub-paragraph applies where—

(a) throughout the accounting period in question there are only two classes of issued shares of the controlled foreign company and, of those classes, one ("non-voting shares") consists of non-voting fixed-rate preference shares and the other ("voting shares") consists of shares which carry the right to vote in all circumstances at general meetings of the company; and

(b) at the end of that accounting period some of the issued shares of the company are held by persons resident outside the United Kingdom; and

(c) at no time during that accounting period does any person have an interest in the company other than an interest derived from non-voting or voting shares;

and in a case where this sub-paragraph applies the appropriate portion of the profits referred to in sub-paragraph (1)(d) above is the amount determined in accordance with sub-paragraph (6) below.

(6) The amount referred to in sub-paragraph (5) above is that given by the formula—

$$\frac{P \times Q}{R} + \frac{(X - P) \times Y}{Z}$$

where—

P is the amount of any dividend falling within (a) and (b) of sub-paragraph (1) above which is paid in respect of the non-voting shares or, if there is more than one such dividend, of the aggregate of them;

Q is, subject to sub-paragraph (8) below, the number of the non-voting shares by virtue of which persons resident in the United Kingdom have interests in the company at the end of the accounting period in question;

R is the total number at that time of the issued non-voting shares;

X is the available profits for the accounting period in question;

Y is, subject to sub-paragraph (8) below, the number of voting shares by virtue of which persons resident in the United Kingdom have interests in the company at the end of that accounting period; and

Z is the total number at that time of the issued voting shares.

(7) For the purposes of sub-paragraph (5)(a) above, non-voting fixed-rate preference shares are shares—

(a) which are fixed-rate preference shares as defined in paragraph 1 of Schedule 18; and

(b) which either carry no right to vote at a general meeting of the company or carry such a right which is contingent upon the non-payment of a dividend on the shares and which has not in fact become exercisable at any time prior to the payment of a dividend for the accounting period in question.

(8) In any case where the immediate interests held by persons resident in the United Kingdom who have indirect interests in a controlled foreign company at the end of a particular accounting period do not reflect the proportion of the shares or, as the case may be, shares of a particular class in the company by virtue of which they have those interests (as in the case where they hold, directly or indirectly, part of the shares in a company which itself holds, directly or indirectly, some or all of the shares in the controlled foreign company) the number of those shares shall be treated as reduced for the purposes of sub-paragraph (4) or (6) above, as the case may be, to such number as may be appropriate having regard to—

(a) the immediate interests held by the persons resident in the United Kingdom; and

(b) any intermediate shareholdings between those interests and the shares in the controlled foreign company.

(9) The definition of "profits" in section 747(6)(b) does not apply to any reference in this paragraph to specified profits or to relevant profits for the purposes of section 799.

3.—(1) Subject to sub-paragraphs (2) and (5) below, for the purposes of this Part of this Schedule, the available profits of a controlled foreign company for any accounting period shall be ascertained by—

(a) determining what would be the relevant profits of that period for the purposes of section 799 if a dividend were paid for that period; and

(b) deducting so much of those relevant profits as consists of an excess of capital profits over capital losses.

(2) If, for any accounting period of the controlled foreign company which is of less than 12 months duration, the available profits, as ascertained under sub-paragraph (1) above, are less than the chargeable profits (determined on the additional assumptions in section 750(3)(a)) then, if the Board so declare, for the purposes of this Part of this Schedule the available profits for the accounting period shall be those chargeable profits.

(3) The definition of "profits" in section 747(6)(b) does not apply to the reference in sub-paragraph (1)(a) above to relevant profits for the purposes of section 799.

(4) In sub-paragraph (1)(b) above "capital profits" means gains—

(a) which accrue on the disposal of assets; and

(b) which, if the company were within the charge to corporation tax in respect of the activities giving rise to those disposals, would not be taken into account as receipts in computing the company's income or profits or gains or losses for the purposes of the Income Tax Acts;

and the expression "capital losses" shall be construed accordingly.

(5) In any case where—

(a) a controlled foreign company pays a dividend for any period out of specified profits, and

(b) those profits represent dividends received by the company, directly or indirectly, from another controlled foreign company,

so much of those specified profits as is equal to the dividend referred to in paragraph (a) above shall be left out of account in determining, for the purposes of this Part of this Schedule, the available profits of the controlled foreign company referred to in that paragraph for any accounting period.

4.—(1) For the purposes of this Part of this Schedule, where—

SCH. 25

    (a) a controlled foreign company pays a dividend ("the initial dividend") to another company which is also not resident in the United Kingdom, and

    (b) that other company or another company which is related to it pays a dividend ("the subsequent dividend") to a United Kingdom resident, and

    (c) the subsequent dividend is paid at a time when the company paying it is not resident in the United Kingdom; and

    (d) the subsequent dividend is paid out of profits which are derived, directly or indirectly, from the whole or part of the initial dividend,

so much of the initial dividend as is represented by the subsequent dividend shall be regarded as paid to the United Kingdom resident.

(2) For the purposes of this paragraph, one company is related to another if the other—

    (a) controls directly or indirectly, or

    (b) is a subsidiary of a company which controls directly or indirectly,

at least 10 per cent. of the voting power in the first-mentioned company; and where one company is so related to another and that other is so related to a third company, the first company is for the purposes of this paragraph related to the third, and so on where there is a chain of companies, each of which is related to the next.

PART II

EXEMPT ACTIVITIES

5.—(1) The provisions of this Part of this Schedule have effect for the purposes of paragraph (b) of subsection (1) of section 748.

(2) In the case of a controlled foreign company—

    (a) which is, by virtue of section 749(3), presumed to be resident in a territory in which it is subject to a lower level of taxation, and

    (b) the business affairs of which are, throughout the accounting period in question, effectively managed in a territory outside the United Kingdom other than one in which companies are liable to tax by reason of domicile, residence or place of management,

references in the following provisions of this Part of this Schedule to the territory in which that company is resident shall be construed as references to the territory falling within paragraph (b) above, or, if there is more than one, to that one of them which may be notified to the Board by the United Kingdom resident company or companies referred to in paragraph 4(2) of Schedule 24.

6.—(1) Throughout an accounting period a controlled foreign company is engaged in exempt activities if, and only if, each of the following conditions is fulfilled—

    (a) that, throughout that accounting period, the company has a business establishment in the territory in which it is resident; and

    (b) that, throughout that accounting period, its business affairs in that territory are effectively managed there; and

    (c) that any of sub-paragraphs (2) to (4) below applies to the company.

(2) This sub-paragraph applies to a company if—

(a) at no time during the accounting period in question does the main business of the company consist of either—

    (i) investment business, or

    (ii) dealing in goods for delivery to or from the United Kingdom or to or from connected or associated persons; and

(b) in the case of a company which is mainly engaged in wholesale, distributive or financial business in that accounting period, less than 50 per cent. of its gross trading receipts from that business is derived directly or indirectly from connected or associated persons.

(3) This sub-paragraph applies to a company which is a holding company if at least 90 per cent. of its gross income during the accounting period in question is derived directly from companies which it controls and which, throughout that period—

(a) are resident in the territory in which the holding company is resident; and

(b) are not themselves holding companies, but otherwise are, in terms of this Schedule, engaged in exempt activities;

and a holding company to which this sub-paragraph applies is in this Part of this Schedule referred to as a "local holding company".

(4) This sub-paragraph applies to a company which is a holding company, but not a local holding company, if at least 90 per cent. of its gross income during the accounting period in question is derived directly from companies which it controls and which, throughout that period—

(a) are local holding companies; or

(b) are not themselves holding companies (whether local or not), but otherwise are, in terms of this Schedule, engaged in exempt activities.

(5) Any reference in sub-paragraph (3) or (4) above to a company which a holding company controls includes a reference to a trading company in which the holding company holds the maximum amount of ordinary share capital which is permitted under the law of the territory—

(a) in which the trading company is resident; and

(b) from whose laws the trading company derives its status as a company.

(6) The following provisions of this Part of this Schedule have effect in relation to sub-paragraphs (1) to (4) above.

7.—(1) For the purposes of paragraph 6(1)(a) above, a "business establishment", in relation to a controlled foreign company, means premises—

(a) which are, or are intended to be, occupied and used with a reasonable degree of permanence; and

(b) from which the company's business in the territory in which it is resident is wholly or mainly carried on.

(2) For the purposes of sub-paragraph (1) above the following shall be regarded as premises—

(a) an office, shop, factory or other building or part of a building; or

(b) a mine, an oil or gas well, a quarry or any other place of extraction of natural resources; or

(c) a building site or the site of a construction or installation project;

SCH. 25   but such a site as is referred to in paragraph (c) above shall not be regarded as premises unless the building work or the project, as the case may be, has a duration of at least twelve months.

8.—(1) Subject to sub-paragraph (4) below, the condition in paragraph 6(1)(b) above shall not be regarded as fulfilled unless—

    (a) the number of persons employed by the company in the territory in which it is resident is adequate to deal with the volume of the company's business; and

    (b) any services provided by the company for persons resident outside that territory are not in fact performed in the United Kingdom.

(2) For the purposes of sub-paragraph (1)(a) above, persons who are engaged wholly or mainly in the business of the company and whose remuneration is paid by a person connected with, and resident in the same territory as, the company shall be treated as employed by the company.

(3) In the case of a holding company, sub-paragraph (2) above shall apply with the omission of the words "wholly or mainly".

(4) For the purposes of sub-paragraph (1)(b) above, no account shall be taken of services—

    (a) provided through a branch or agency of the controlled foreign company if the profits or gains of the business carried on through the branch or agency are within the charge to tax in the United Kingdom; or

    (b) provided through any other person whose profits or gains from the provision of the services are within the charge to tax in the United Kingdom and who provides the services for a consideration which is, or which is not dissimilar from what might reasonably be expected to be, determined under a contract entered into at arm's length; or

    (c) which are no more than incidental to services provided outside the United Kingdom.

9.—(1) Subject to sub-paragraph (3) below, for the purposes of paragraph 6(2)(a)(i) above, each of the following activities constitutes investment business—

    (a) the holding of securities, patents or copyrights;

    (b) dealing in securities, other than in the capacity of a broker;

    (c) the leasing of any description of property or rights; and

    (d) the investment in any manner of funds which would otherwise be available, directly or indirectly, for investment by or on behalf of any person (whether resident in the United Kingdom or not) who has, or is connected or associated with a person who has, control, either alone or together with other persons, of the controlled foreign company in question.

(2) In sub-paragraph (1)(b) above "broker" includes any person offering to sell securities to, or purchase securities from, members of the public generally.

(3) For the purposes of paragraph 6(2) above, in the case of a company which is mainly engaged in banking or any similar business falling within paragraph 11(1)(c) below, nothing in sub-paragraph (1) above shall require the main business of the company to be regarded as investment business.

10. Goods which are actually delivered into the territory in which the controlled foreign company is resident shall not be taken into account for the purposes of paragraph 6(2)(a)(ii) above.

11.—(1) For the purposes of paragraph 6(2)(b) above, each of the following activities constitutes wholesale, distributive or financial business—

    (a) dealing in any description of goods wholesale rather than retail;

    (b) the business of shipping or air transport, that is to say, the business carried on by an owner of ships or the business carried on by an owner of aircraft ("owner" including, for this purpose, any charterer);

    (c) banking or any similar business involving the receipt of deposits, loans or both and the making of loans or investments;

    (d) the administration of trusts;

    (e) dealing in securities in the capacity of a broker, as defined in paragraph 9(2) above;

    (f) dealing in commodity or financial futures; and

    (g) insurance business which is long-term business or general business, as defined in section 1 of the Insurance Companies Act 1982.

(2) In a case where the gross trading receipts of a company include an amount in respect of the proceeds of sale of any description of property or rights, the cost to the company of the purchase of that property or those rights shall be a deduction in calculating the company's gross trading receipts for the purposes of paragraph 6(2)(b) above.

(3) In the case of a controlled foreign company engaged in a banking or other business falling within sub-paragraph (1)(c) above—

    (a) no payment of interest received from a company resident in the United Kingdom shall be regarded for the purposes of paragraph 6(2)(b) above as a receipt derived directly or indirectly from connected or associated persons, but

    (b) it shall be conclusively presumed that the condition in paragraph 6(2)(b) above is not fulfilled if, at any time during the accounting period in question, the amount by which the aggregate value of the capital interests in the company held directly or indirectly by—

        (i) the persons who have control of the company, and

        (ii) any person connected or associated with those persons,

    exceeds the value of the company's fixed assets is 15 per cent. or more of the amount by which the company's outstanding capital exceeds that value.

(4) For the purposes of this paragraph, in relation to a controlled foreign company—

    (a) "capital interest" means an interest in the issued share capital or reserves of the company or in a loan to or deposit with the company or the liability of a guarantor under a guarantee given to or for the benefit of the company;

    (b) except in the case of the liability of a guarantor, the value of a capital interest is its value as shown in the company's accounts;

    (c) in the case of the liability of a guarantor, the value shall be taken to be the market value of the benefit which the controlled foreign company derives from the provision of the guarantee;

    (d) the value of the company's fixed assets means the value, as shown in the company's accounts, of the plant, premises and trade investments employed in the company's business; and

(e) "outstanding capital" means the total value of all the capital interests in the company, less the value, as shown in the company's accounts, of any advances made by the company to persons resident outside the United Kingdom and falling within paragraph (i) or paragraph (ii) of sub-paragraph (3)(b) above.

(5) For the purposes of sub-paragraph (4) above—

(a) "trade investments", in relation to a controlled foreign company, means securities any profit on the sale of which would not be brought into account as a trading receipt in computing the chargeable profits of an accounting period in which that profit arose; and

(b) the reference in paragraph (e) to advances made to a person by the controlled foreign company includes, in the case of a company which is a person resident outside the United Kingdom and falling within paragraph (i) or paragraph (ii) of sub-paragraph (3)(b) above, any securities of that company which are held by the controlled foreign company but are not trade investments, as defined in paragraph (a) above;

and in this sub-paragraph "securities" includes stocks and shares.

(6) In the application of paragraph 6(2)(b) above in the case of a controlled foreign company engaged in insurance business of any kind—

(a) the reference to gross trading receipts which are derived directly or indirectly from connected or associated persons is a reference to those which, subject to sub-paragraph (7) below, are attributable, directly or indirectly, to liabilities undertaken in relation to any of those persons or their property;

(b) the only receipts to be taken into account are commissions and premiums received under insurance contracts;

(c) so much of any such commission or premium as is returned is not to be taken into account; and

(d) when a liability under an insurance contract is reinsured, in whole or in part, the amount of the premium which is attributable, directly or indirectly, to that liability shall be treated as reduced by so much of the premium under the reinsurance contract as is attributable to that liability.

(7) In determining, in relation to a controlled foreign company to which sub-paragraph (6) above applies, the gross trading receipts referred to in paragraph (a) of that sub-paragraph, there shall be left out of account any receipts under a local reinsurance contract which are attributable to liabilities which—

(a) are undertaken under an insurance contract made in the territory in which the company is resident; and

(b) are not reinsured under any contract other than a local reinsurance contract; and

(c) relate either to persons who are resident in that territory and are neither connected nor associated with the company or to property which is situated there and belongs to persons who are not so connected or associated;

and in paragraph (a) above "insurance contract" does not include a reinsurance contract.

(8) In sub-paragraph (7) above "local reinsurance contract" means a reinsurance contract—

(a) which is made in the territory in which the controlled foreign company is resident; and

(b) the parties to which are companies which are resident in that territory.

(9) For the purposes of sub-paragraphs (7) and (8) above, any question as to the territory in which a company is resident shall be determined in accordance with section 749 and, where appropriate, paragraph 5(2) above; and, for the purpose of the application of those provisions in accordance with this sub-paragraph, the company shall be assumed to be a controlled foreign company.

12.—(1) Subject to sub-paragraph (2) below, in paragraphs 6 and 8(3) above and sub-paragraphs (4) and (5) below "holding company" means—

(a) a company the business of which consists wholly or mainly in the holding of shares or securities of companies which are either local holding companies and its 90 per cent. subsidiaries or trading companies and either its 51 per cent. subsidiaries or companies falling within paragraph 6(5) above; or

(b) a company which would fall within paragraph (a) above if there were disregarded so much of its business as consists in the holding of property or rights of any description for use wholly or mainly by companies which it controls and which are resident in the territory in which it is resident.

(2) In determining whether a company is a holding company for the purposes of paragraph 6(3) above (and, accordingly, whether the company is or may be a local holding company), sub-paragraph (1) above shall have effect with the omission from paragraph (a) thereof of the words "either local holding companies and its 90 per cent. subsidiaries or".

(3) In its application for the purposes of this paragraph, section 838 shall have effect with the omission of—

(a) in subsection (1)(a), the words "or indirectly"; and

(b) subsection (2).

(4) For the purposes of sub-paragraph (3) or (4), as the case may be, of paragraph 6 above, as it applies in relation to a holding company part of whose business consists of activities other than the holding of shares or securities or the holding of property or rights as mentioned in paragraph (a) or (b) of sub-paragraph (1) above, the company's gross income during any accounting period shall be determined as follows—

(a) there shall be left out of account so much of what would otherwise be the company's gross income as is derived from any activity which, if it were the business in which the company is mainly engaged, would be such that paragraph 6(2) above would apply to the company; and

(b) to the extent that the receipts of the company from any other activity include receipts from the proceeds of sale of any description of property or rights, the cost to the company of the purchase of that property or those rights shall (to the extent that the cost does not exceed the receipts) be a deduction in calculating the company's gross income, and no other deduction shall be made in respect of that activity.

(5) For the purposes of sub-paragraphs (3) and (4) of paragraph 6 above, so much of the income of a holding company as—

(a) is derived directly from another company which it controls and which is not a holding company but otherwise is, in terms of this Schedule, engaged in exempt activities, and

(b) was or could have been paid out of any non-trading income of that other company which is derived directly or indirectly from a third company connected or associated with it,

shall be treated, in relation to the holding company, as if it were not derived directly from companies which it controls.

(6) The reference in sub-paragraph (5) above to the non-trading income of a company is a reference to so much of its income as, if the company were carrying on its trade in the United Kingdom, would not be within the charge to corporation tax under Case I of Schedule D.

PART III

THE PUBLIC QUOTATION CONDITION

13.—(1) The provisions of this Part of this Schedule have effect for the purposes of section 748(1)(c).

(2) Subject to paragraph 14 below, a controlled foreign company fulfils the public quotation condition with respect to a particular accounting period if—

(a) shares in the company carrying not less than 35 per cent. of the voting power in the company (and not being shares entitled to a fixed rate of dividend, whether with or without a further right to participate in profits) have been allotted unconditionally to, or acquired unconditionally by, the public and, throughout that accounting period, are beneficially held by the public; and

(b) within the period of 12 months ending at the end of the accounting period, any such shares have been the subject of dealings on a recognised stock exchange situated in the territory in which the company is resident; and

(c) within that period of 12 months the shares have been quoted in the official list of such a recognised stock exchange.

14.—(1) The condition in paragraph 13(2) above is not fulfilled with respect to an accounting period of a controlled foreign company if at any time in that period the total percentage of the voting power in the company possessed by all of the company's principal members exceeds 85 per cent.

(2) For the purposes of paragraph 13(2) above shares in a controlled foreign company shall be deemed to be beneficially held by the public if they are held by any person other than—

(a) a person connected or associated with the company; or

(b) a principal member of the company;

and a corresponding construction shall be given to the reference to shares which have been allotted unconditionally to, or acquired unconditionally by, the public.

15.—(1) References in this Part of this Schedule to shares held by any person include references to any shares the rights or powers attached to which could, for the purposes of section 416, be attributed to that person under subsection (5) of that section.

(2) For the purposes of this Part of this Schedule—

(a) a person is a principal member of a controlled foreign company if he possesses a percentage of the voting power in the company of more than 5 per cent. and—

(i) where there are more than five such persons, if he is one of the five persons who possess the greatest percentages, or

(ii) if, because two or more persons possess equal percentages of the voting power in the company, there are no such five persons, he is one of six or more persons (so as to include those two or more who possess the equal percentages) who possess the greatest percentages; and

(b) a principal member's holding consists of the shares which carry the voting power possessed by him.

(3) In arriving at the voting power which a person possesses, there shall be attributed to him any voting power which, for the purposes of section 416, would be attributed to him under subsection (5) or (6) of that section.

(4) In this Part of this Schedule "shares" include "stock".

PART IV

REDUCTIONS IN UNITED KINGDOM TAX AND DIVERSION OF PROFITS

16.—(1) The provisions of this Part of this Schedule have effect for the purposes of section 748(3).

(2) Any reference in paragraphs 17 and 18 below to a transaction—

(a) is a reference to a transaction reflected in the profits arising in an accounting period of a controlled foreign company; and

(b) includes a reference to two or more such transactions taken together.

17.—(1) A transaction achieves a reduction in United Kingdom tax if, had the transaction not been effected, any person—

(a) would have been liable for any such tax or for a greater amount of any such tax; or

(b) would not have been entitled to a relief from or repayment of any such tax or would have been entitled to a smaller relief from or repayment of any such tax.

(2) In this Part of this Schedule and section 748(3) "United Kingdom tax" means income tax, corporation tax or capital gains tax.

18. It is the main purpose or one of the main purposes of a transaction to achieve a reduction in United Kingdom tax if this is the purpose or one of the main purposes—

(a) of the controlled foreign company concerned; or

(b) of a person who has an interest in that company at any time during the accounting period concerned.

19.—(1) The existence of a controlled foreign company achieves a reduction in United Kingdom tax by a diversion of profits from the United Kingdom in an accounting period if it is reasonable to suppose that, had neither the company nor any company related to it been in existence—

(a) the whole or a substantial part of the receipts which are reflected in the controlled foreign company's profits in that accounting period would have been received by a company or individual resident in the United Kingdom; and

(b) that company or individual or any other person resident in the United Kingdom either—

(i) would have been liable for any United Kingdom tax or for a greater amount of any such tax; or

     (ii) would not have been entitled to a relief from or repayment of any such tax or would have been entitled to a smaller relief from or repayment of any such tax.

 (2) For the purposes of sub-paragraph (1) above, a company is related to a controlled foreign company if—

  (a) it is resident outside the United Kingdom; and

  (b) it is connected or associated with the controlled foreign company; and

  (c) in relation to any company or companies resident in the United Kingdom, it fulfils or could fulfil, directly or indirectly, substantially the same functions as the controlled foreign company.

 (3) Any reference in sub-paragraph (1) above to a company resident in the United Kingdom includes a reference to such a company which, if the controlled foreign company in question were not in existence, it is reasonable to suppose would have been established.

SCHEDULE 26

RELIEFS AGAINST LIABILITY FOR TAX IN RESPECT OF CHARGEABLE PROFITS

Trading losses and group relief etc.

1.—(1) In any case where—

  (a) an amount of chargeable profits is apportioned to a company resident in the United Kingdom, and

  (b) the company is entitled, or would on the making of a claim be entitled, in computing its profits for the appropriate accounting period, to a deduction in respect of any relevant allowance, and

  (c) for the appropriate accounting period the company has no profits against which a deduction could be made in respect of that allowance or, as the case may be, the amount of that allowance exceeds the profits against which a deduction falls to be made in respect of it,

then, on the making of a claim, a sum equal to corporation tax at the appropriate rate on so much of the relevant allowance or, as the case may be, of the excess of it referred to in paragraph (c) above as is specified in the claim shall be set off against the company's liability to tax under section 747(4)(a) in respect of the chargeable profits apportioned to it.

(2) In this paragraph—

  (a) "the appropriate accounting period" means the accounting period for which, by virtue of section 754(2), the company is regarded as assessed to corporation tax in respect of the chargeable profits concerned; and

  (b) "the appropriate rate" means the rate of corporation tax applicable to profits of the appropriate accounting period or, if there is more than one such rate, the average rate over the whole accounting period.

(3) In this paragraph "relevant allowance" means—

  (a) any loss to which section 393(2) applies;

  (b) any charge on income to which section 338(1) applies;

  (c) any expenses of management to which section 75(1) applies;

  (d) so much of any allowance to which section 74 of the 1968 Act applies as falls within subsection (3) of that section; and

  (e) any amount available to the company by way of group relief.

(4) In any case where, for the appropriate accounting period, an amount would have been available to the company by way of group relief if a claim had been made under section 412, such a claim may be made for the purposes of this paragraph at any time before the end of the accounting period following that in which the assessment under section 747(4)(a) is made, notwithstanding that the period of two years referred to in section 412(1)(c) has expired.

(5) Where, by virtue of sub-paragraph (1) above, a sum is set off against a liability to tax, so much of the relevant allowance as gives rise to the amount set off shall be regarded for the purposes of the Tax Acts as having been allowed as a deduction against the company's profits in accordance with the appropriate provisions of those Acts.

(6) In its application to a claim under this paragraph, section 43 of the Management Act (time limit for making claims) shall have effect as if, in subsection (2)—

2 F

SCH. 26

(a) any reference to an assessment to income tax were a reference to an assessment under section 747(4)(a); and

(b) any reference to a year of assessment were a reference to an accounting period.

Advance corporation tax

2.—(1) In any case where—

(a) an amount of chargeable profits is apportioned to a company resident in the United Kingdom, and

(b) the company has an amount of advance corporation tax which, apart from this paragraph, would, in relation to the appropriate accounting period, be surplus advance corporation tax for the purposes of section 239(3),

then, on the making of a claim, so much of that advance corporation tax as is specified in the claim and does not exceed the relevant maximum shall be set against the company's liability to tax under section 747(4)(a) in respect of the chargeable profits apportioned to it, to the extent that that liability has not or could not have been relieved by virtue of paragraph 1 above.

(2) So much of any advance corporation tax as, by virtue of this paragraph, is set against the company's liability to tax under section 747(4)(a) in respect of chargeable profits shall be regarded for the purposes of the Tax Acts as not being surplus advance corporation tax within the meaning of section 239.

(3) In this paragraph "the appropriate accounting period" has the same meaning as in paragraph 1 above and "the relevant maximum", in relation to the liability to tax referred to in sub-paragraph (1) above, is the amount of advance corporation tax that would have been payable (apart from section 241) in respect of a distribution made at the end of the appropriate accounting period of an amount which, together with the advance corporation tax in respect of it, is equal to—

(a) that amount of the chargeable profits apportioned to the company on which it is chargeable to corporation tax for that accounting period,

less

(b) any amount which, for that accounting period, is to be regarded, by virtue of paragraph 1(5) above, as having been allowed as a deduction against the company's profits.

Gains on disposal of shares in controlled foreign companies

3.—(1) This paragraph applies in any case where—

(a) a direction has been given under subsection (1) of section 747 in respect of an accounting period of a controlled foreign company ("the direction period"); and

(b) the company's chargeable profits for the direction period have been apportioned among the persons in subsection (3) of that section; and

(c) a company resident in the United Kingdom ("the claimant company") disposes of—

(i) shares in the controlled foreign company, or

(ii) shares in another company which, in whole or in part, give rise to the claimant company's interest in the controlled foreign company, being, in either case, shares acquired before the end of the direction period; and

(d) by virtue of the apportionment referred to in paragraph (b) above, a sum is, under section 747(4)(a), assessed on and recoverable from the claimant company as if it were an amount of corporation tax; and

(e) the claimant company makes a claim for relief under this paragraph;

and in this paragraph the disposal mentioned in paragraph (c) above is referred to as "the relevant disposal".

(2) Subject to the following provisions of this paragraph, in the computation under Chapter II of Part II of the 1979 Act of the gain accruing on the relevant disposal, the appropriate fraction of the sum referred to in sub-paragraph (1)(d) above shall be allowable as a deduction; but to the extent that any sum has been allowed as a deduction under this sub-paragraph it shall not again be allowed as a deduction on any claim under this paragraph (whether made by the claimant company or another company).

(3) In relation to the relevant disposal, the appropriate fraction is—

$$\frac{A}{B}$$

where—

A is the average market value in the direction period of the shares disposed of, and

B is the average market value in that period of the interest in the controlled foreign company which, in the case of the claimant company, was taken into account in the apportionment referred to in sub-paragraph (1)(b) above.

(4) Where, before the relevant disposal—

(a) a dividend is paid by the controlled foreign company, and

(b) the profits out of which the dividend is paid are those from which the chargeable profits referred to in sub-paragraph (1)(b) above are derived, and

(c) at least one of the two conditions in sub-paragraph (5) below is fulfilled,

this paragraph does not apply in relation to a sum assessed and recoverable in respect of so much of the chargeable profits as corresponds to the profits which the dividend represents.

(5) The conditions referred to in sub-paragraph (4) above are—

(a) that the effect of the payment of the dividend is such that the value of the shares disposed of by the relevant disposal is less after the payment than it was before it; and

(b) that, in respect of a dividend paid or payable on the shares disposed of by the relevant disposal, the claimant company is, by virtue of paragraph 4(2) below, entitled under Part XVIII to relief (by way of underlying tax) by reference to sums which include the sum referred to in sub-paragraph (1)(d) above.

(6) A claim for relief under this paragraph shall be made before the expiry of the period of three months beginning—

(a) at the end of the accounting period in which the relevant disposal occurs; or

(b) if it is later, on the date on which the assessment to tax for which the claimant company is liable by virtue of section 747(4)(a) becomes final and conclusive.

(7) In identifying for the purposes of this paragraph shares in a company with shares of the same class which are disposed of by the relevant disposal, shares acquired at an earlier time shall be deemed to be disposed of before shares acquired at a later time.

Dividends from the controlled foreign company

4.—(1) This paragraph applies in any case where—

(a) a direction has been given under subsection (1) of section 747 in respect of an accounting period of a controlled foreign company, and

(b) the company's chargeable profits for that period have been apportioned among the persons referred to in subsection (3) of that section, and

(c) the controlled foreign company pays a dividend in whole or in part out of the total profits from which (in accordance with subsection (6)(a) of that section) those chargeable profits are derived.

(2) Subject to paragraphs 5 and 6 below, where this paragraph applies, the aggregate of the sums assessed on and recoverable from companies resident in the United Kingdom in accordance with section 747(4)(a) in respect of the chargeable profits referred to in sub-paragraph (1)(b) above shall be treated for the purposes of Part XVIII as if it were an amount of tax paid in respect of the profits concerned under the law of the territory in which the controlled foreign company was resident and, accordingly, as underlying tax for the purposes of Chapter II of that Part.

(3) In the following provisions of this paragraph and in paragraphs 5 and 6 below, the aggregate of the sums which, under sub-paragraph (2) above, fall to be treated as underlying tax is referred to as the "gross attributed tax".

(4) If, in the case of a person who receives the dividend, section 796 or section 797 has the effect of reducing the amount which (apart from that section) would have been the amount of the credit for foreign tax which is to be allowed to that person, then, for the purposes of sub-paragraph (5) below, the amount of that reduction shall be determined and so much of it as does not exceed the amount of the foreign tax, exclusive of underlying tax, for which credit is to be allowed in respect of the dividend is in that sub-paragraph referred to as "the wasted relief".

(5) Except for the purpose of determining the amount of the wasted relief, the gross attributed tax shall be treated as reduced by the aggregate of the wasted relief arising in the case of all the persons falling within sub-paragraph (4) above and, on the making of a claim by any of the companies referred to in sub-paragraph (2) above—

(a) the amount of tax assessed on and recoverable from the company in accordance with section 747(4)(a) in respect of the chargeable profits referred to in sub-paragraph (1) (b) above shall, where appropriate, be reduced; and

(b) all such adjustments (whether by repayment of tax or otherwise) shall be made as are appropriate to give effect to any reduction under paragraph (a) above.

5.—(1) In so far as any provision of—

(a) arrangements having effect by virtue of section 788, or

(b) section 790,

makes relief which is related to foreign dividends received by a company resident in the United Kingdom conditional upon that company either having a particular degree of control of the company paying the dividend or being a subsidiary of another company which has that degree of control, that condition shall be treated as fulfilled in considering whether any such company is by virtue of paragraph 4(2) above entitled to relief under Part XVIII in respect of any of the gross attributed tax.

(2) Notwithstanding anything in paragraph 4(2) above, in section 795(2)(b) the expression "underlying tax" does not include gross attributed tax.

(3) In a case where the controlled foreign company pays a dividend otherwise than out of specified profits and, on the apportionment referred to in paragraph 4(1) above, less than the whole of the chargeable profits of the controlled foreign company concerned is apportioned to companies which are resident in the United Kingdom and liable for tax thereon as mentioned in section 747(4)(a)—

(a) the gross attributed tax shall be regarded as attributable to a corresponding proportion of the profits in question, and in this sub-paragraph the profits making up that proportion are referred to as "taxed profits";

(b) so much of the dividend as is received by, or by a successor in title of, any such company shall be regarded as paid primarily out of taxed profits; and

(c) so much of the dividend as is received by any other person shall be regarded as paid primarily out of profits which are not taxed profits.

(4) The reference in sub-paragraph (3)(b) above to a successor in title of a company resident in the United Kingdom is a reference to a person who is such a successor in respect of the whole or any part of that interest in the controlled foreign company by virtue of which an amount of its chargeable profits was apportioned to that company.

6.—(1) In any case where—

(a) on a claim for relief under paragraph 3 above, the whole or any part of any sum has been allowed as a deduction on a disposal of shares in any company; and

(b) that sum forms part of the gross attributed tax in relation to a dividend paid by that company; and

(c) a person receiving the dividend in respect of the shares referred to in paragraph (a) above ("the primary dividend") or any other relevant dividend is, by virtue of paragraph 4(2) above, entitled under Part XVIII to relief (by way of underlying tax) by reference to the whole or any part of the gross attributed tax;

the amount which, apart from this paragraph, would be available by way of any such relief to the person referred to in paragraph (c) above shall be reduced or, as the case may be, extinguished by deducting therefrom the amount allowed by way of relief as mentioned in paragraph (a) above.

(2) For the purposes of sub-paragraph (1)(c) above, in relation to the primary dividend, another dividend is a relevant dividend if—

(a) it is a dividend in respect of shares in a company which is resident outside the United Kingdom; and

(b) it represents profits which, directly or indirectly, consist of or include the primary dividend.

SCHEDULE 27

DISTRIBUTING FUNDS

PART I

THE DISTRIBUTION TEST

Requirements as to distributions

1.—(1) For the purposes of this Chapter, an offshore fund pursues a full distribution policy with respect to an account period if—

    (a) a distribution is made for that account period or for some other period which, in whole or in part, falls within that account period; and

    (b) subject to Part II of this Schedule, the amount of the distribution which is paid to the holders of material and other interests in the fund—

        (i) represents at least 85 per cent. of the income of the fund for that period, and

        (ii) is not less than 85 per cent. of the fund's United Kingdom equivalent profits for that period; and

    (c) the distribution is made during that account period or not more than six months, or such longer period as the Board may in any particular case allow, after the expiry of it; and

    (d) the form of the distribution is such that, if any sum forming part of it were received in the United Kingdom by a person resident there and did not form part of the profits of a trade, profession or vocation, that sum would fall to be chargeable to tax under Case IV or V of Schedule D;

and any reference in this sub-paragraph to a distribution made for an account period includes a reference to any two or more distributions so made or, in the case of paragraph (b), the aggregate of them.

(2) Subject to sub-paragraph (3) below, with respect to any account period for which—

    (a) there is no income of the fund, and

    (b) there are no United Kingdom equivalent profits of the fund,

the fund shall be treated as pursuing a full distribution policy notwithstanding that no distribution is made as mentioned in sub-paragraph (1) above.

(3) For the purposes of this Chapter, an offshore fund shall be regarded as not pursuing a full distribution policy with respect to an account period for which the fund does not make up accounts.

(4) For the purposes of this paragraph—

    (a) where a period for which an offshore fund makes up accounts includes the whole or part of two or more account periods of the fund, then, subject to paragraph (c) below, income shown in those accounts shall be apportioned between those account periods on a time basis according to the number of days in each period which are comprised in the period for which the accounts are made up;

    (b) where a distribution is made for a period which includes the whole or part of two or more account periods of the fund, then, subject to sub-paragraph (5) below, the distribution shall be apportioned between those account periods on a time basis according to the number of days in each period which are comprised in the period for which the distribution is made;

(c) where a distribution is made out of specified income but is not made for a specified period, that income shall be attributed to the account period of the fund in which it in fact arose and the distribution shall be treated as made for that account period; and

(d) where a distribution is made neither for a specified period nor out of specified income, then, subject to sub-paragraph (5) below, it shall be treated as made for the last account period of the fund which ended before the distribution was made.

(5) If, apart from this sub-paragraph, the amount of a distribution made, or treated by virtue of sub-paragraph (4) above as made, for an account period would exceed the income of that period, then, for the purposes of this paragraph—

(a) if the amount of the distribution was determined by apportionment under sub-paragraph (4)(b) above, the excess shall be re-apportioned, as may be just and reasonable, to any other account period which, in whole or in part, falls within the period for which the distribution was made or, if there is more than one such period, between those periods; and

(b) subject to paragraph (a) above, the excess shall be treated as an additional distribution or series of additional distributions made for preceding account periods in respect of which the distribution or, as the case may be, the aggregate distributions would otherwise be less than the income of the period, applying the excess to later account periods before earlier ones, until it is exhausted.

(6) In any case where—

(a) for a period which is or includes an account period, an offshore fund is subject to any restriction as regards the making of distributions, being a restriction imposed by the law of any territory outside the United Kingdom; and

(b) the fund is subject to that restriction by reason of an excess of losses over profits (applying the concepts of "profits" and "losses" in the sense in which and to the extent to which they are relevant for the purposes of the law in question);

then in determining for the purposes of the preceding provisions of this paragraph the amount of the fund's income for that account period, there shall be allowed as a deduction any amount which, apart from this sub-paragraph, would form part of the income of the fund for that account period and which cannot be distributed by virtue of the restriction.

Funds operating equalisation arrangements

2.—(1) In the case of an offshore fund which throughout any account period operates equalisation arrangements, on any occasion in that period when there is a disposal to which this sub-paragraph applies, the fund shall be treated for the purposes of this Part of this Schedule as making a distribution of an amount equal to so much of the consideration for the disposal as, in accordance with this paragraph, represents income accrued to the date of the disposal.

(2) Sub-paragraph (1) above applies to a disposal—

(a) which is a disposal of a material interest in the offshore fund concerned; and

(b) which is a disposal to which this Chapter applies (whether by virtue of section 758(3) or otherwise) or is one to which this Chapter would apply if subsections (5) and (6) of that section applied generally and not only for the purpose of determining whether, by virtue of subsection (3) of that section, there is a disposal to which this Chapter applies; and

(c) which is not a disposal with respect to which the conditions in subsection (4) of that section are fulfilled; and

(d) which is a disposal to the fund itself or to the persons concerned in the management of the fund ("the managers") in their capacity as such.

(3) On a disposal to which sub-paragraph (1) above applies, the part of the consideration which represents income accrued to the date of the disposal is, subject to sub-paragraph (4) and paragraph 4(4) below, the amount which would be credited to the equalisation account of the offshore fund concerned in respect of accrued income if, on the date of the disposal, the material interest which is disposed of were acquired by another person by way of initial purchase.

(4) If, after the beginning of the period by reference to which the accrued income referred to in sub-paragraph (3) above is calculated, the material interest disposed of by a disposal to which sub-paragraph (1) above applies was acquired by way of initial purchase (whether or not by the person making the disposal)—

(a) there shall be deducted from the amount which, in accordance with sub-paragraph (3) above, would represent income accrued to the date of the disposal, the amount which on that acquisition was credited to the equalisation account of the fund in respect of accrued income; and

(b) if in that period there has been more than one such acquisition of that material interest by way of initial purchase, the deduction to be made under this sub-paragraph shall be the amount so credited to the equalisation account on the latest such acquisition prior to the disposal in question.

(5) Where, by virtue of this paragraph, an offshore fund is treated for the purposes of this Part of this Schedule as making a distribution on the occasion of a disposal, the distribution shall be treated for those purposes—

(a) as complying with paragraph 1(1)(d) above; and

(b) as made out of the income of the fund for the account period in which the disposal occurs; and

(c) as paid, immediately before the disposal, to the person who was then the holder of the interest disposed of.

(6) In any case where—

(a) a distribution in respect of an interest in an offshore fund is made to the managers of the fund, and

(b) their holding of that interest is in their capacity as such, and

(c) at the time of the distribution, the fund is operating equalisation arrangements,

the distribution shall not be taken into account for the purposes of paragraph 1(1) above except to the extent that the distribution is properly referable to that part of the period for which the distribution is made during which that interest has been held by the managers of the fund in their capacity as such.

(7) Subsection (2) of section 758 applies for the purposes of this paragraph as it applies for the purposes of that section.

Income taxable under Case IV or Case V of Schedule D

3.—(1) Sub-paragraph (2) below applies if any sums which form part of the income of an offshore fund falling within section 759(1)(b) or (c) are of such a nature that—

(a) the holders of interests in the fund who are either companies resident in the United Kingdom or individuals domiciled and resident there—

(i) are chargeable to tax under Case IV or Case V of Schedule D in respect of such of those sums as are referable to their interests; or

(ii) if any of that income is derived from assets within the United Kingdom, would be so chargeable had the assets been outside the United Kingdom; and

(b) the holders of interests who are not such companies or individuals would be chargeable as mentioned in sub-paragraph (i) or (ii) above if they were resident in the United Kingdom or, in the case of individuals, if they were domiciled and both resident and ordinarily resident there.

(2) To the extent that sums falling within sub-paragraph (1) above do not actually form part of a distribution complying with paragraphs 1(1)(c) and (d) above, they shall be treated for the purposes of this Part of this Schedule—

(a) as a distribution complying with those paragraphs and made out of the income of which they form part; and

(b) as paid to the holders of the interests to which they are referable.

Commodity income

4.—(1) To the extent that the income of an offshore fund for any account period includes profits from dealing in commodities, one half of those profits shall be left out of account in determining for the purposes of paragraphs 1(1)(b) and 5 below—

(a) the income of the fund for that period; and

(b) the fund's United Kingdom equivalent profits for that period;

but in any account period in which an offshore fund incurs a loss in dealing in commodities the amount of that loss shall not be varied by virtue of this paragraph.

(2) In this paragraph "dealing in commodities" shall be construed as follows—

(a) "commodities" does not include currency, securities, debts or other assets of a financial nature but, subject to that, means tangible assets which are dealt with on a commodity exchange in any part of the world; and

(b) "dealing" includes dealing by way of futures contracts and traded options.

(3) Where the income of an offshore fund for any account period consists of profits from dealing in commodities and other income, then—

(a) in determining whether the condition in paragraph 1(1)(b) above is fulfilled with respect to that account period, the expenditure of the fund shall be apportioned in such manner as is just and reasonable between the profits from dealing in commodities and the other income; and

SCH. 27

(b) in determining whether, and to what extent, any expenditure is deductible under section 416 in computing the fund's United Kingdom equivalent profits for that period, so much of the business of the fund as does not consist of dealing in commodities shall be treated as a business carried on by a separate company.

(4) Where there is a disposal to which paragraph 2(1) above applies, then, to the extent that any amount which was or would be credited to the equalisation account in respect of accrued income, as mentioned in sub-paragraph (3) or (4) of that paragraph, represents profits from dealing in commodities, one half of that accrued income shall be left out of account in determining under those sub-paragraphs the part of the consideration for the disposal which represents income accrued to the date of the disposal.

United Kingdom equivalent profits

5.—(1) Any reference in this Schedule to the United Kingdom equivalent profits of an offshore fund for an account period is a reference to the amount which, on the assumptions in sub-paragraph (3) below, would be the total profits of the fund for that period on which, after allowing for any deductions available against those profits, corporation tax would be chargeable.

(2) In this paragraph the expression "profits" does not include chargeable gains.

(3) The assumptions referred to in sub-paragraph (1) above are—

(a) that the offshore fund is a company which, in the account period in question, but not in any other account period, is resident in the United Kingdom; and

(b) that the account period is an accounting period of that company; and

(c) that any dividends or distributions which, by virtue of section 208, should be left out of account in computing income for corporation tax purposes are nevertheless to be brought into account in that computation in like manner as if they were dividends or distributions of a company resident outside the United Kingdom.

(4) Without prejudice to any deductions available apart from this sub-paragraph, the deductions referred to in sub-paragraph (1) above include—

(a) a deduction equal to any amount which, by virtue of paragraph 1(6) above, is allowed as a deduction in determining the income of the fund for the account period in question; and

(b) a deduction equal to any amount of tax (paid under the law of a territory outside the United Kingdom) which was taken into account as a deduction in determining the income of the fund for the account period in question but which, because it is referable to capital rather than income, does not fall to be taken into account by virtue of section 811.

(5) For the avoidance of doubt it is hereby declared that, if any sums forming part of the offshore fund's income for any period have been received by the fund without any deduction of or charge to tax by virtue of section 47 or 48, the effect of the assumption in sub-paragraph (3)(a) above is that those sums are to be brought into account in determining the total profits referred to in sub-paragraph (1) above.

MODIFICATIONS OF CONDITIONS FOR CERTIFICATION IN CERTAIN CASES

Exclusion of investments in distributing offshore funds

6.—(1) In any case where—

(a) in an account period of an offshore fund (in this Part of this Schedule referred to as the "primary fund"), the assets of the fund consist of or include interests in another offshore fund; and

(b) those interests (together with other interests which the primary fund may have) are such that, by virtue of subsection (3)(a) or, if the other fund concerned is a company, subsection (3)(b) or (c) of section 760, the primary fund could not, apart from this paragraph, be certified as a distributing fund in respect of that account period; and

(c) without regard to the provisions of this paragraph, that other fund could be certified as a distributing fund in respect of its account period or, as the case may be, each of its account periods which comprises the whole or any part of the account period of the primary fund;

then, in determining whether anything in section 760(3)(a) to (c) prevents the primary fund being certified as mentioned in paragraph (b) above, the interests of the primary fund in that other fund shall be left out of account except for the purposes of determining the total value of the assets of the primary fund.

(2) In this Part of this Schedule an offshore fund falling within sub-paragraph (1)(c) above is referred to as a "qualifying fund".

(3) In a case falling within sub-paragraph (1) above—

(a) section 760(3)(a) to (c) shall have effect in relation to the primary fund with the modification in paragraph 7 below (in addition to that provided for by sub-paragraph (1) above); and

(b) Part I of this Schedule shall have effect in relation to the primary fund with the modification in paragraph 8 below.

7. The modification referred to in paragraph 6(3)(a) above is that, in any case where—

(a) at any time in the account period referred to in paragraph 6(1) above, the assets of the primary fund include an interest in an offshore fund or in any company (whether an offshore fund or not); and

(b) that interest falls to be taken into account in determining whether anything in section 760(3)(a) to (c) prevents the primary fund being certified as a distributing fund in respect of that account period; and

(c) at any time in that account period the assets of the qualifying fund include an interest in the offshore fund or company referred to in paragraph (a) above;

for the purposes of the application in relation to the primary fund of section 760(3)(a) to (c), at any time when the assets of the qualifying fund include the interest referred to in paragraph (c) above, the primary fund's share of that interest shall be treated as an additional asset of the primary fund.

8.—(1) The modification referred to in paragraph 6(3)(b) above is that, in determining whether the condition in paragraph 1(1)(b)(ii) above is fulfilled with respect to the account period of the primary fund referred to in paragraph 6(1) above, the United Kingdom equivalent profits of the primary fund for that period shall be treated as increased by the primary fund's share of the excess income (if any) of the qualifying fund which is attributable to that period.

(2) For the purposes of this paragraph, the excess income of the qualifying fund for any account period of that fund is the amount (if any) by which its United Kingdom equivalent profits for that account period exceed the amount of the distributions made for that period, as determined for the purposes of the application of paragraph 1(1) above to the qualifying fund.

(3) If an account period of the qualifying fund coincides with an account period of the primary fund, then the excess income (if any) of the qualifying fund for that period is the excess income which is attributable to that period of the primary fund.

(4) In a case where sub-paragraph (3) above does not apply, the excess income of the qualifying fund which is attributable to an account period of the primary fund is the appropriate fraction of the excess income (if any) of the qualifying fund for any of its account periods which comprises the whole or any part of the account period of the primary fund and, if there is more than one such account period of the qualifying fund, the aggregate of the excess income (if any) of each of them.

(5) For the purposes of sub-paragraph (4) above, the appropriate fraction is—

$$\frac{A}{B}$$

where—

A is the number of days in the account period of the primary fund which are also days in an account period of the qualifying fund; and

B is the number of days in that account period of the qualifying fund or, as the case may be, in each of those account periods of that fund which comprises the whole or any part of the account period of the primary fund.

9.—(1) The references in paragraphs 7 and 8(1) above to the primary fund's share of—

(a) an interest forming part of the assets of the qualifying fund, or

(b) the excess income (as defined in paragraph 8 above) of the qualifying fund,

shall be construed as references to the fraction specified in sub-paragraph (2) below of that interest or excess income.

(2) In relation to any account period of the primary fund, the fraction referred to in sub-paragraph (1) above is—

$$\frac{C}{D}$$

where—

C is the average value of the primary fund's holding of interests in the qualifying fund during that period; and

D is the average value of all the interests in the qualifying fund held by any persons during that period.

Offshore funds investing in trading companies

10.—(1) In any case where the assets of an offshore fund for the time being include an interest in a trading company, as defined in sub-paragraph (2) below, the provisions of section 760(3) have effect subject to the modifications in sub-paragraphs (3) and (4) below.

(2) In this paragraph "trading company" means a company whose business consists wholly of the carrying on of a trade or trades and does not to any extent consist of—

    (a) dealing in commodities, as defined in paragraph 4(2) above, or dealing, as so defined, in currency, securities, debts or other assets of a financial nature; or

    (b) banking or money-lending.

(3) In the application of section 760(3)(b) to so much of the assets of an offshore fund as for the time being consists of interests in a single trading company, for the words "10 per cent." there shall be substituted the words "20 per cent.".

(4) In the application of section 760(3)(c) to an offshore fund the assets of which for the time being include any issued share capital of a trading company or any class of that share capital, for the words "more than 10 per cent." there shall be substituted the words "50 per cent. or more".

Offshore funds with wholly-owned subsidiaries

11.—(1) In relation to an offshore fund which has a wholly-owned subsidiary which is a company the provisions of section 760(3) and Part I of this Schedule shall have effect subject to the modifications in sub-paragraph (3) below.

(2) Subject to sub-paragraph (3) below, for the purposes of this paragraph, a company is a wholly-owned subsidiary of an offshore fund if and so long as the whole of the issued share capital of the company is—

    (a) in the case of an offshore fund falling within section 759(1)(a), directly and beneficially owned by the fund; and

    (b) in the case of an offshore fund falling within section 759(1)(b), directly owned by the trustees of the fund for the benefit of the fund; and

    (c) in the case of an offshore fund falling within section 759(1)(c), owned in a manner which, as near as may be, corresponds either to paragraph (a) or paragraph (b) above.

(3) In the case of a company which has only one class of issued share capital, the reference in sub-paragraph (2) above to the whole of the issued share capital shall be construed as a reference to at least 95 per cent. of that share capital.

(4) The modifications referred to in sub-paragraph (1) above are that, for the purposes of section 760(3) and Part I of this Schedule—

    (a) that percentage of the receipts, expenditure, assets and liabilities of the subsidiary which is equal to the percentage of the issued share capital of the company concerned which is owned as mentioned in sub-paragraph (2) above shall be regarded as the receipts, expenditure, assets and liabilities of the fund; and

    (b) there shall be left out of account the interest of the fund in the subsidiary and any distributions or other payments made by the subsidiary to the fund or by the fund to the subsidiary.

Offshore funds with interests in dealing and management companies

12.—(1) Section 760(3)(c) shall not apply to so much of the assets of an offshore fund as consists of issued share capital of a company which is either—

(a) a wholly-owned subsidiary of the fund which falls within sub-paragraph (2) below; or

(b) a subsidiary management company of the fund, as defined in sub-paragraph (3) below.

(2) A company which is a wholly-owned subsidiary of an offshore fund is one to which sub-paragraph (1)(a) above applies if—

(a) the business of the company consists wholly of dealing in material interests in the offshore fund for the purposes of and in connection with the management and administration of the business of the fund; and

(b) the company is not entitled to any distribution in respect of any material interest for the time being held by it;

and paragraph 11(2) above shall apply to determine whether a company is, for the purposes of this paragraph, a wholly-owned subsidiary of an offshore fund.

(3) A company in which an offshore fund has an interest is for the purposes of sub-paragraph (1)(b) above a subsidiary management company of the fund if—

(a) the company carries on no business other than providing services falling within sub-paragraph (4) below either for the fund alone or for the fund and for any other offshore fund which has an interest in the company; and

(b) the company's remuneration for the services which it provides to the fund is not greater than it would be if it were determined at arm's length between the fund and a company in which the fund has no interest.

(4) The services referred to in sub-paragraph (3) above are—

(a) holding property (of any description) which is occupied or used in connection with the management or administration of the fund; and

(b) providing administrative, management and advisory services to the fund.

(5) In determining, in accordance with sub-paragraph (3) above, whether a company in which an offshore fund has an interest is a subsidiary management company of that fund—

(a) every business carried on by a wholly-owned subsidiary of the company shall be treated as carried on by the company; and

(b) no account shall be taken of so much of the company's business as consists of holding its interests in a wholly-owned subsidiary; and

(c) any reference in sub-paragraph (3)(b) above to the company shall be taken to include a reference to a wholly-owned subsidiary of the company.

(6) Any reference in sub-paragraph (5) above to a wholly-owned subsidiary of a company is a reference to another company the whole of the issued share capital of which is for the time being directly and beneficially owned by the first company.

Disregard of certain investments forming less than 5 per cent. of a fund

13.—(1) In any case where—

(a) in any account period of an offshore fund, the assets of the fund include a holding of issued share capital (or any class of issued share capital) of a company; and

(b) that holding is such that by virtue of section 760(3)(c) the fund could not (apart from this paragraph) be certified as a distributing fund in respect of that account period;

then, if the condition in sub-paragraph (3) below is fulfilled, that holding shall be disregarded for the purposes of section 760(3)(c).

(2) In this paragraph any holding falling within sub-paragraph (1) above is referred to as an "excess holding".

(3) The condition referred to in sub-paragraph (1) above is that at no time in the account period in question does that portion of the fund which consists of—

(a) excess holdings, and

(b) interests in other offshore funds which are not qualifying funds,

exceed 5 per cent. by value of all the assets of the fund.

Power of Board to disregard certain breaches of conditions

14. If, in the case of any account period of an offshore fund ending after the passing of the Finance (No. 2) Act 1987 (23rd July 1987), it appears to the Board that there has been a failure to comply with any of the conditions in paragraphs (a) to (c) of section 760(3) (as modified, where appropriate, by the preceding provisions of this Part of this Schedule) but the Board are satisfied— 1987 c. 51.

(a) that the failure occurred inadvertently; and

(b) that the failure was remedied without unreasonable delay,

the Board may disregard the failure in determining whether to certify the fund as a distributing fund in respect of that account period.

PART III

CERTIFICATION PROCEDURE

Application for certification

15.—(1) The Board shall, in such manner as they think appropriate, certify an offshore fund as a distributing fund in respect of an account period if—

(a) an application in respect of that period is made under this paragraph; and

(b) the application is accompanied by the accounts of the fund for, or for a period which includes, the account period to which the application relates; and

(c) there is furnished to the Board such information as they may reasonably require for the purpose of determining whether the fund should be so certified; and

(d) they are satisfied that nothing in section 760(2) or (3) prevents the fund being so certified.

(2) An application under this paragraph shall be made to the Board by the fund or by a trustee or officer thereof on behalf of the fund and may be so made—

(a) before the expiry of the period of six months beginning at the end of the account period to which the application relates; or

(b) at such later time as the Board may in any particular case allow.

(3) In any case where, on an application under this paragraph, the Board determine that the offshore fund concerned should not be certified as a distributing fund in respect of the account period to which the application relates, they shall give notice of that fact to the fund.

(4) If at any time it appears to the Board that the accounts accompanying an application under this paragraph in respect of any account period of an offshore fund or any information furnished to the Board in connection with such an application is or are not such as to make full and accurate disclosure of all facts and considerations relevant to the application, they shall give notice to the fund accordingly, specifying the period concerned.

(5) Where a notice is given by the Board under sub-paragraph (4) above, any certification by them in respect of the account period in question shall be void.

Appeals

16.—(1) An appeal to the Special Commissioners—

(a) against such a determination as is referred to in paragraph 15(3) above, or

(b) against a notification under paragraph 15(4) above,

may be made by the offshore fund or by a trustee or officer thereof on behalf of the fund, and shall be so made by notice specifying the grounds of appeal and given to the Board within 90 days of the date of the notice under paragraph 15(3) or (4), as the case may be.

(2) The jurisdiction of the Special Commissioners on an appeal under this paragraph shall include jurisdiction to review any decision of the Board which is relevant to a ground of the appeal.

PART IV

SUPPLEMENTARY

Assessment: effect of non-certification

17. No appeal may be brought against an assessment to tax on the ground that an offshore fund should have been certified as a distributing fund in respect of an account period of the fund.

18.—(1) Without prejudice to paragraph 17 above, in any case where no application has been made under paragraph 15 above in respect of an account period of an offshore fund, any person who is assessed to tax for which he would not be liable if the offshore fund were certified as a distributing fund in respect of that period may by notice in writing require the Board to take action under this paragraph with a view to determining whether the fund should be so certified.

(2) Subject to sub-paragraphs (3) and (5) below, if the Board receive a notice under sub-paragraph (1) above, they shall by notice invite the offshore fund concerned to make an application under paragraph 15 above in respect of the period in question.

(3) Where sub-paragraph (2) above applies, the Board shall not be required to give notice under that sub-paragraph before the expiry of the account period to which the notice is to relate nor if an application under paragraph 15 above has already been made; but where notice is given under that sub-paragraph, an application under paragraph 15 above shall not be out of time under paragraph 15(2)(a) above if it is made within 90 days of the date of that notice.

(4) If an offshore fund to which notice is given under sub-paragraph (2) above does not, within the time allowed by sub-paragraph (3) above or, as the case may be, paragraph 15(2)(a) above, make an application under paragraph 15 above in respect of the account period in question, the Board shall proceed to determine the question of certification in respect of that period as if such an application had been made.

(5) Where the Board receive more than one notice under sub-paragraph (1) above with respect to the same account period of the same offshore fund, their obligations under sub-paragraphs (2) and (4) above shall be taken to be fulfilled with respect to each of those notices if they are fulfilled with respect to any one of them.

(6) Notwithstanding anything in sub-paragraph (5) above, for the purpose of a determination under sub-paragraph (4) above with respect to an account period of an offshore fund, the Board shall have regard to accounts and other information furnished by all persons who have given notice under sub-paragraph (1) above with respect to that account period; and paragraph 15 above shall apply as if accounts and information so furnished had been furnished in compliance with sub-paragraph (1) of that paragraph.

(7) Without prejudice to sub-paragraph (5) above, in any case where—

(a) at a time after the Board have made a determination under sub-paragraph (4) above that an offshore fund should not be certified as a distributing fund in respect of an account period, notice is given under sub-paragraph (1) above with respect to that period; and

(b) the person giving that notice furnishes the Board with accounts or information which had not been furnished to the Board at the time of the earlier determination;

the Board shall reconsider their previous determination in the light of the new accounts or information and, if they consider it appropriate, may determine to certify the fund accordingly.

(8) Where any person has given notice to the Board under sub-paragraph (1) above with respect to an account period of an offshore fund and no application has been made under paragraph 15 above with respect to that period—

(a) the Board shall notify that person of their determination with respect to certification under sub-paragraph (4) above; and

(b) paragraph 16 above shall not apply in relation to that determination.

Postponement of tax pending determination of question as to certification

19.—(1) In any case where—

(a) an application has been made under paragraph 15 above with respect to an account period of an offshore fund and that application has not been finally determined; or

(b) paragraph (a) above does not apply but notice has been given under paragraph 18(1) above in respect of an account period of an offshore fund and the Board have not yet given notice of their decision as to certification under paragraph 18(4) above;

any person who has been assessed to tax and considers that, if the offshore fund were to be certified as a distributing fund in respect of the account period in question, he would be overcharged to tax by the assessment may, by notice given to the inspector within 30 days after the date of the issue of the notice of assessment, apply to the General Commissioners for a determination of the amount of tax the payment of which should be postponed pending the determination of the question whether the fund should be so certified.

(2) A notice of application under sub-paragraph (1) above shall state the amount in which the applicant believes that he is over-charged to tax and his grounds for that belief.

(3) Subsections (3A) onwards of section 55 of the Management Act (recovery of tax not postponed) shall apply with any necessary modifications in relation to an application under sub-paragraph (1) above as if it were an application under subsection (3) of that section and as if the determination of the question as to certification (whether by the Board or on appeal) were the determination of an appeal.

Information as to decisions on certification etc.

20. No obligation as to secrecy imposed by statute or otherwise shall preclude the Board or an inspector from disclosing to any person appearing to have an interest in the matter—

(a) any determination of the Board or (on appeal) the Special Commissioners whether an offshore fund should or should not be certified as a distributing fund in respect of any account period; or

(b) the content and effect of any notice given by the Board under paragraph 15(4) above.

SCHEDULE 28

COMPUTATION OF OFFSHORE INCOME GAINS

PART I

DISPOSALS OF INTERESTS IN NON-QUALIFYING FUNDS

Interpretation

1. In this Part of this Schedule "material disposal" means a disposal to which this Chapter applies, otherwise than by virtue of section 758.

Calculation of unindexed gain

2.—(1) Where there is a material disposal, there shall first be determined for the purposes of this Part of this Schedule the amount (if any) which, in accordance with the provisions of this paragraph, is the unindexed gain accruing to the person making the disposal.

(2) Subject to section 757(3) to (6) and paragraph 3 below, the unindexed gain accruing on a material disposal is the amount which would be the gain on that disposal for the purposes of the 1979 Act if it were computed—

    (a) without regard to any charge to income tax or corporation tax by virtue of section 761; and

    (b) without regard to any indexation allowance on the disposal under Chapter III of Part III of the Finance Act 1982.

1982 c. 39.

3.—(1) If the amount of any chargeable gain or allowable loss which (apart from section 763) would accrue on the material disposal would fall to be determined in a way which, in whole or in part, would take account of the indexation allowance on an earlier disposal to which paragraph 2 of Schedule 13 to the Finance Act 1982 (disposals on a no gain/no loss basis) applies, the unindexed gain on the material disposal shall be computed as if—

    (a) no indexation allowance had been available on any such earlier disposal; and

    (b) subject to that, neither a gain nor a loss had accrued to the person making such an earlier disposal.

(2) If the material disposal forms part of a transfer to which section 123 of the 1979 Act (roll-over relief on transfer of business) applies, the unindexed gain accruing on the disposal shall be computed without regard to any deduction which falls to be made under that section in computing a chargeable gain.

(3) If the material disposal is made otherwise than under a bargain at arm's length and a claim for relief is made in respect of that disposal under section 79 of the Finance Act 1980 (relief for gifts), that section shall not affect the computation of the unindexed gain accruing on the disposal.

1980 c. 48.

(4) Where, in the case of an insurance company carrying on life assurance business, a profit arising from general annuity business and attributable to a material disposal falls (or would but for the reference to offshore income gains in section 437(2) fall) to be taken into account in the computation under section 436, the unindexed gain, if any, accruing to the company on the disposal shall be computed as if section 31(1) of the 1979 Act (exclusion of certain sums in computing chargeable gain) did not apply.

(5) Notwithstanding section 29 of the 1979 Act (losses determined in like manner as gains) if, apart from this sub-paragraph, the effect of any computation under the preceding provisions of this Part of this Schedule would be to produce

SCH. 28   a loss, the unindexed gain on the material disposal shall be treated as nil; and accordingly for the purposes of this Part of this Schedule no loss shall be treated as accruing on a material disposal.

(6) Section 431 has effect in relation to sub-paragraph (4) above as if it were included in Chapter I of Part XII.

Gains since 1st January 1984

4.—(1) This paragraph applies where—

(a) the interest in the offshore fund which is disposed of by the person making a material disposal was acquired by him before 1st January 1984; or

(b) he is treated by virtue of any provision of sub-paragraphs (3) and (4) below as having acquired the interest before that date.

(2) Where this paragraph applies, there shall be determined for the purposes of this Part of this Schedule the amount which would have been the gain on the material disposal—

(a) on the assumption that, on 1st January 1984, the interest was disposed of and immediately reacquired for a consideration equal to its market value at that time; and

(b) subject to that, on the basis that the gain is computed in like manner as, under paragraphs 2 and 3 above, the unindexed gain on the material disposal is determined;

and that amount is in paragraph 5 below referred to as the "post-1983 gain" on the material disposal.

(3) Where the person making the material disposal acquired the interest disposed of—

(a) on or after 1st January 1984, and

1982 c. 39.

(b) in such circumstances that, by virtue of any enactment other than section 86(5) of or Schedule 13 to the Finance Act 1982 (indexation provisions), he and the person from whom he acquired it ("the previous owner") fell to be treated for the purposes of the 1979 Act as if his acquisition were for a consideration of such an amount as would secure that, on the disposal under which he acquired it, neither a gain nor a loss accrued to the previous owner,

the previous owner's acquisition of the interest shall be treated as his acquisition of it.

(4) If the previous owner acquired the interest disposed of on or after 1st January 1984 and in circumstances similar to those referred to in sub-paragraph (3) above, his predecessor's acquisition of the interest shall be treated for the purposes of this paragraph as the previous owner's acquisition, and so on back through previous acquisitions in similar circumstances until the first such acquisition before 1st January 1984 or, as the case may be, until an acquisition on a material disposal on or after that date.

The offshore income gain

5.—(1) Subject to sub-paragraph (2) below, a material disposal gives rise to an offshore income gain of an amount equal to the unindexed gain on that disposal.

(2) In any case where—

(a) paragraph 4 above applies, and

(b) the post-1983 gain on the material disposal is less than the unindexed gain on the disposal,

the offshore income gain to which the disposal gives rise is an amount equal to the post-1983 gain.

PART II

DISPOSALS INVOLVING AN EQUALISATION ELEMENT

6.—(1) Subject to paragraph 7 below, a disposal to which this Chapter applies by virtue of section 758(3) gives rise to an offshore income gain of an amount equal to the equalisation element relevant to the asset disposed of.

(2) Subject to sub-paragraphs (4) to (6) below, the equalisation element relevant to the asset disposed of by a disposal falling within sub-paragraph (1) above is the amount which would be credited to the equalisation account of the offshore fund concerned in respect of accrued income if, on the date of the disposal, the asset which is disposed of were acquired by another person by way of initial purchase.

(3) In the following provisions of this Part of this Schedule, a disposal falling within sub-paragraph (1) above is referred to as a "disposal involving an equalisation element".

(4) Where the asset disposed of by a disposal involving an equalisation element was acquired by the person making the disposal after the beginning of the period by reference to which the accrued income referred to in sub-paragraph (2) above is calculated, the amount which, apart from this sub-paragraph, would be the equalisation element relevant to that asset shall be reduced by the following amount, that is to say—

(a) if that acquisition took place on or after 1st January 1984, the amount which, on that acquisition, was credited to the equalisation account of the offshore fund concerned in respect of accrued income or, as the case may be, would have been so credited if that acquisition had been an acquisition by way of initial purchase; and

(b) in any other case, the amount which would have been credited to that account in respect of accrued income if that acquisition had been an acquisition by way of initial purchase taking place on 1st January 1984.

(5) In any case where—

(a) the asset disposed of by a disposal involving an equalisation element was acquired by the person making the disposal at or before the beginning of the period by reference to which the accrued income referred to in sub-paragraph (2) above is calculated, and

(b) that period began before 1st January 1984 and ends after that date,

the amount which, apart from this sub-paragraph, would be the equalisation element relevant to that asset shall be reduced by the amount which would have been credited to the equalisation account of the offshore fund concerned in respect of accrued income if the acquisition referred to in paragraph (a) above had been an acquisition by way of initial purchase taking place on 1st January 1984.

(6) Where there is a disposal involving an equalisation element, then, to the extent that any amount which was or would be credited to the equalisation account of the offshore fund in respect of accrued income, as mentioned in any of sub-paragraphs (2) to (5) above, represents profits from dealing in commodities, within the meaning of paragraph 4 of Schedule 27, one half of that accrued income shall be left out of account in determining under those sub-paragraphs the equalisation element relevant to the asset disposed of by that disposal.

7.—(1) For the purposes of this Part of this Schedule, there shall be determined, in accordance with paragraph 8 below, the Part I gain (if any) on any disposal involving an equalisation element.

(2) Notwithstanding anything in paragraph 6 above—

(a) if there is no Part I gain on a disposal involving an equalisation element. that disposal shall not give rise to an offshore income gain; and

(b) if, apart from this paragraph, the offshore income gain on a disposal involving an equalisation element would exceed the Part I gain on that disposal, the offshore income gain to which that disposal gives rise shall be reduced to an amount equal to that Part I gain.

8.—(1) On a disposal involving an equalisation element, the Part I gain is the amount (if any) which, by virtue of Part I of this Schedule (as modified by sub-paragraphs (2) to (5) below), would be the offshore income gain on that disposal if it were a material disposal within the meaning of that Part.

(2) For the purposes only of the application of Part I of this Schedule to determine the Part I gain (if any) on a disposal involving an equalisation element, subsections (5) and (6) of section 758 shall have effect as if, in subsection (5), the words "by virtue of subsection (3) above" were omitted.

1982 c. 39.

(3) If a disposal involving an equalisation element is one which, by virtue of any enactment other than section 86(5)(b) of or Schedule 13 to the Finance Act 1982. is treated for the purposes of the 1979 Act as one on which neither a gain nor a loss accrues to the person making the disposal, then, for the purpose only of determining the Part I gain (if any) on the disposal, that enactment shall be deemed not to apply to it (but without prejudice to the application of that enactment to any earlier disposal).

1983 c. 28.

(4) In any case where a disposal involving an equalisation element is made by a company which has made an election under Schedule 6 to the Finance Act 1983 (indexation: election for pooling) and the asset disposed of consists of or includes securities which, by virtue of paragraph 3(3) of that Schedule, are to be treated for the purposes of the 1979 Act as a single asset or part of a single asset, then, for the purpose only of determining the Part I gain (if any) on the disposal—

(a) the reference in paragraph 2(2)(b) above to an indexation allowance under Chapter III of Part III of the Finance Act 1982 shall be construed as including a reference to an indexation allowance under Schedule 6 to the Finance Act 1983; and

(b) if some of the securities comprised in the asset disposed of were acquired by the company making the disposal before 1st January 1984 and some were not, paragraph 4(2) above shall not apply and paragraph 5 above shall have effect with the omission of sub-paragraph (2) (together with the reference to it in sub-paragraph (1)).

(5) The reference in sub-paragraph (4)(b) above to securities acquired before 1st January 1984 includes a reference to securities which, by virtue of any provision of paragraph 4 above, are treated as so acquired.

SCHEDULE 29

CONSEQUENTIAL AMENDMENTS

THE CAPITAL ALLOWANCES ACTS

1. The Capital Allowances Act 1968 and Part III of the Finance Act 1971 shall apply in relation to a trade, profession or vocation chargeable in accordance with section 65(3) as they apply to one chargeable to tax under Case I or II of Schedule D. 1968 c. 3.

1971 c. 68.

2. No allowance shall be made under Chapter I of Part III of the Finance Act 1971 in respect of any expenditure incurred by a Member of the House of Commons in or in connection with the provision or use of residential or overnight accommodation to enable him to perform his duties as such a Member in or about the Palace of Westminster or his constituency.

TAXES MANAGEMENT ACT 1970 c.9

3. The Taxes Management Act 1970 shall have effect subject to the amendments made by paragraphs 4 to 10 below.

4. The following subsections shall be inserted in section 8 after subsection (3)—

"(3A) A notice given to trustees under this section may require a return of the income arising to them to include particulars of the manner in which the income has been applied, including particulars as to the exercise of any discretion and of the persons in whose favour it has been exercised.

In this subsection "trustees" and "income" have the same meaning as in section 686 of the principal Act.

(3B) A notice given to a person under this section may require him to include in the return of his income particulars of premiums paid by him or his wife living with him under policies of life insurance or contracts for deferred annuities and of deductions made from the premiums payable."

5. In section 16(1)(c) and (2)(b) after "copyright" there shall be inserted "or public lending right".

6. The following section shall be inserted after section 16—

"Agency workers. 16A.—(1) Where—

(a) any services which an individual renders or is under an obligation to render under a contract are treated under section 134(1) of the principal Act as the duties of an office or employment held by him; or

(b) any remuneration receivable under or in consequence of arrangements to which subsection (6) of that section applies is treated under that subsection as emoluments of an office or employment held by an individual,

section 15 above shall apply as if that individual were employed—

(i) in a case within paragraph (a) above, by the persons or each of the persons from whom he receives any remuneration under or in consequence of the contract; and

(ii) in a case within paragraph (b) above, by the other party to the arrangements,

and section 16 above shall not apply to any payments made to that individual under or in consequence of that contract or those arrangements.

(2) In subsection (1) above "remuneration", in relation to an individual, does not include anything in respect of which he would not have been chargeable to tax under Schedule E if it had been receivable in connection with an office or employment held by him but, subject to that, includes every form of payment and all perquisites, benefits and profits whatsoever."

7.—(1) In subsection (1) of section 18 after the words "income tax" there shall be inserted the words "other than interest to which subsection (4) below applies".

(2) In subsection (2) and (3) of that section for the words "this section" there shall be substituted the words "subsection (1) above".

(3) The following subsection shall be inserted at the end of that section—

"(4) Where interest on any securities issued subject to the condition that interest is payable without deduction of tax is paid without deduction of tax—

(a) any person by whom such interest is paid,

(b) any person who receives, on behalf of any other person who is a registered or inscribed holder of such securities, any interest paid without deduction of tax, and

(c) any person who has acted as intermediary in the purchase of any securities on which the interest is payable without deduction of tax,

shall, on being so required by the Board, furnish to the Board—

(i) the names and addresses of the persons to whom such interest has been paid, or on whose behalf such interest has been received, or on whose behalf such securities have been purchased, and

(ii) the amount of the interest so paid or received, or the amount of the securities so purchased."

8.—(1) In subsection (1) of section 55 (recovery of tax not postponed) the following paragraph shall be added after paragraph (f)—

"(g) a notice under subsection (1) or subsection (3) of section 753 of the principal Act where, before the appeal is determined, the appellant is assessed to tax under section 747(4)(a) of that Act by reference to an amount of chargeable profits specified in that notice".

(2) The following subsection shall be inserted in that section after subsection (6)—

"(6A) Where an appeal is brought against an assessment to tax under section 747(4)(a) of the principal Act as well as against a notice under section 753(1) or (3) of that Act—

(a) an application under subsection (3) above may relate to matters arising on both appeals and, in determining the amount of tax the payment of which should be postponed, the Commissioners shall consider the matters so arising together; and

(b) if the Commissioners have determined the amount of tax the payment of which should be postponed solely in relation to one of the appeals, the bringing of the other appeal shall be taken to be a change of circumstances falling within subsection (4) above; and

(c) any reference in this section to the determination of the appeal shall be construed as a reference to the determination of the two appeals, but the determination of one before the other shall be taken to be a change of circumstances falling within subsection (4) above."

9. The following Table shall be substituted for the Table in section 98—

"TABLE

1.	2.

Part III of this Act, except sections 16 and 24(2).
Section 51 of this Act.
In the principal Act—
  section 181(1);
  regulations under section 202;
  section 217;
  section 226(3) and (4);
  section 234(7)(b), (8) and (9);
  section 250(6) and (7);
  section 272(7);
  section 310(4) and (5);
  regulations under section 333;
  regulations under section 476(1);
  section 481(5)(k);
  section 482(3);
  regulations under section 482(11);
  section 483;
  regulations under section 555(7);
  section 561(8);
  section 588(7);
  regulations under section 602;
  section 605(1), (2), (3)(b) and (4);
  regulations under section 612(3);
  regulations under section 639;
  section 652;
  section 669;
  section 680;
  section 700(4);
  section 708;
  section 728;
  section 729(11);
  section 730(8);
  section 737(8);
  section 745(1);
	In the principal Act—
	  section 38(5);
	  section 41(2);
	  section 42;
	  section 124(3);
	  section 136(6);
	  section 139(5) or (6);
	  section 148(7);
	  section 180(1);
	  regulations under section 202;
	  regulations under section 203;
	  section 216;
	  section 226(1) and (2);
	  section 234(5), (6) and (7)(a);
	  section 250(1) to (5);
	  section 310(1), (2) and (3);
	  section 313(5);
	  regulations under section 333;
	  section 350(1);
	  section 375(5);
	  regulations under section 476(1);
	  regulations under section 482(11);
	  section 552;
	  regulations under section 555(7);
	  regulations under section 566(1) or (2);
	  section 577(4);
	  section 588(6);
	  regulations under section 602;
	  section 605(3)(a);
	  regulations under section 612(3);
	  regulations under section 639;
	  section 772(6);
	  Schedule 3, paragraph 6;
	  Schedule 13;

SCH. 29

1.	2.

section 755;
section 768(9);
section 772(1) and (3);
section 774(5);
section 778;
section 815;
Schedule 3, paragraph 13(1);
Schedule 5, paragraph 10;
Schedule 9, paragraphs 6 and 25;
Schedule 15, paragraph 14(5);
Schedule 19, paragraph 17;
Schedule 22, paragraph 4.
Section 32 of the Finance Act 1973.
Paragraph 2 of Schedule 15 to the Finance Act 1973.
Regulations under section 149D of the Capital Gains Tax Act 1979.
Paragraph 6(9) of Schedule 1 to the Capital Gains Tax Act 1979.
Section 67(4) of, and paragraph 4(3) of Schedule 12 to, the Finance Act 1980.
Section 84 of the Finance Act 1981.
Paragraph 15(1) of Schedule 14 to the Finance Act 1984.
Paragraph 6(1) of Schedule 22 to the Finance Act 1985.
	regulations under paragraph 7 of Schedule 14;
	Schedule 15, paragraph 14(4);
	Schedule 16;
	Schedule 22, paragraph 2.
	Regulations under section 149D of the Capital Gains Tax Act 1979.
	Section 67(2) of, and paragraph 4(1) of Schedule 12 to, the Finance Act 1980.
	Regulations 16 and 17 of the Income Tax (Interest Relief) Regulations 1982.
	Paragraph 15(3) of Schedule 14 to the Finance Act 1984.
	Paragraph 10 of Schedule 16 to the Finance Act 1986.

The references in this Table to regulations under section 602 have effect only for the purpose of giving effect to any provision mentioned in paragraphs (a) and (b) of subsection (2) of that section."

10.—(1) The Taxes Management Act 1970, as amended by the Finance (No.2) Act 1987, shall have effect, after the day appointed under section 95 of the 1987 Act for the purposes of the provision in question, subject to the following amendments.

(2) In section 11(8) for "286" there shall be substituted "419".

(3) In section 30(2A) and (3A) for "87 of the Finance (No.2) Act 1987" there shall be substituted "826 of the principal Act".

(4) In section 87A—

(a) in subsection (1) for "243(4)" there shall be substituted "10";

(b) in subsection (3) for the words from "266" to "Taxes Act" there shall be substituted "346(2) or 347(1) of the principal Act, section 267(3C) or 278(5) of the Income and Corporation Taxes Act 1970";

(c) in subsection (4), in paragraph (a) for "85 of the Finance Act 1972" there shall be substituted "239 of the principal Act", and in paragraph (b) for "85" there shall be substituted "239"; and

(d) in subsection (5) for the words from "subsection" to "1972" there shall be substituted "section 252(5) of the principal Act".

(5) In section 89 for "87 of the Finance (No.2) Act 1987" there shall be substituted "826 of the principal Act".

(6) In section 91(2A) for "90 of the Finance (No.2) Act 1987" there shall be substituted "10 of the principal Act".

(7) In section 94(8) for the words from "subsection (3)" to "1972" there shall be substituted "section 239(3) of the principal Act";

(8) In section 109—

(a) in subsection (3) for "286" and "(4)" there shall be substituted "419" and "(3)";

(b) in subsection (3A) for "(5)" and "286" (twice) there shall be substituted "(4)" and "419".

THE FRIENDLY SOCIETIES ACT (NORTHERN IRELAND) 1970 c.31 (N.I.)

11. In section 1 of the Friendly Societies Act (Northern Ireland) 1970 at the end of subsection (3) there shall be added the following—

"but nothing in this subsection shall apply with respect to—

(a) policies issued in respect of insurances made on or after 19th March 1985; or

(b) policies issued in respect of insurances made before that date which are varied on or after that date."

THE FINANCE ACT 1973 c.51

12. In section 38 of the Finance Act 1973 the following shall be substituted for subsection (4)—

'(4) Gains accruing to a person not resident in the United Kingdom on the disposal of exploration or exploitation rights or of exploration or exploitation assets shall, for the purposes of capital gains tax or corporation tax on chargeable gains, be treated as gains accruing on the disposal of assets used for the purposes of a trade carried on by that person in the United Kingdom through a branch or agency.

This subsection shall have effect in relation to gains accruing on disposals before 13th March 1984 with the omission of the words "exploration or exploitation assets".'

FRIENDLY SOCIETIES ACT 1974 c.46

13. In section 7 of the Friendly Societies Act 1974 at the end of subsection (3) there shall be added the following—

"but nothing in this subsection shall apply with respect to—

(a) policies issued in respect of insurances made on or after 19th March 1985; or

(b) policies issued in respect of insurances made before that date which are varied on or after that date."

THE SOCIAL SECURITY ACTS

14. In section 9(1) of the Social Security Act 1975 and the Social Security (Northern Ireland) Act 1975 (Class IV contributions) the reference to profits or gains chargeable to income tax under Case I or II of Schedule D shall be taken to include a reference to profits or gains consisting of a payment of enterprise allowance (within the meaning of section 127 of this Act) chargeable to income tax under Case VI of Schedule D.

CAPITAL GAINS TAX ACT 1979 c.14

15. In the Capital Gains Tax Act 1979—

(a) for "the Taxes Act", in each place where it occurs except sections 1, 31 and 34(4)(a), the definition of "the Taxes Act" in section 155(1) and paragraph 6(8) of Schedule 1 and any provision mentioned in paragraph (b) below, there shall be substituted "the Taxes Act 1988";

(b) in sections 16, 26, 29A, 32, 35, 75, 84, 87, 98, 107 and 136(10), paragraphs 4 and 5 of Schedule 5 and paragraphs 12 and 21 of Schedule 6 for "the Taxes Act" there shall be substituted "the Taxes Act 1970";

and in addition the 1979 Act shall have effect subject to the amendments specified in relation thereto in paragraphs 16 to 28 and 32 below.

16. In section 18 (residence etc.) the following subsections shall be inserted after subsection (4)—

"(5) A period during which a member of a visiting force to whom section 323(1) of the Taxes Act 1988 applies is in the United Kingdom by reason solely of his being a member of that force shall not be treated for the purposes of capital gains tax either as a period of residence in the United Kingdom or as creating a change in his residence or domicile.

This subsection shall be construed as one with subsection (2) of section 323 and subsections (4) to (8) of that section shall apply accordingly.

(6) An Agent-General who is resident in the United Kingdom shall be entitled to the same immunity from capital gains tax as that to which the head of a mission so resident is entitled under the Diplomatic Privileges Act 1964.

(7) Any person having or exercising any employment to which section 320(2) of the Taxes Act 1988 applies (not being a person employed in any trade, business or other undertaking carried on for the purposes of profit) shall be entitled to the same immunity from capital gains tax as that to which a member of the staff of a mission is entitled under the Diplomatic Privileges Act 1964.

(8) Subsections (6) and (7) above shall be construed as one with section 320 of the Taxes Act 1988."

17. In section 31 (consideration chargeable to tax on income) the following subsection shall be inserted after subsection (3)—

"(4) The reference in subsection (1) above to computing income or profits or gains or losses shall not be taken as applying to a computation of a company's income for the purposes of subsection (2) of section 76 of the Taxes Act 1988."

18. The following section shall be inserted after section 32—

"Expenditure: amounts to be included as consideration.

32A.—(1) Section 32(1)(a) above applies as if the relevant amount as defined in the following provisions of this section in the cases there specified had formed part of the consideration given by the person making the disposal for his acquisition of the assets in question.

(2) Where an amount is chargeable to tax by virtue of section 162(5) of the Taxes Act 1988 in respect of shares or an interest in shares, then—

(a) on a disposal of the shares or interest, where that is the event giving rise to the charge; or

(b) in any case, on the first disposal of the shares or interest after the event,

the relevant amount is a sum equal to the amount so chargeable.

(3) If a gain chargeable to tax under section 135(1) or (6) of the Taxes Act 1988 is realised by the exercise of a right to acquire shares, the relevant amount is a sum equal to the amount of the gain so chargeable to tax.

(4) Where an amount is chargeable to tax under section 138 of the Taxes Act 1988 on a person acquiring any shares or interest in shares, then on the first disposal (whether by him or another person) of the shares after his acquisition, the relevant amount is an amount equal to the amount so chargeable.

(5) Where an amount was chargeable to tax under section 185(6) of the Taxes Act 1988 in respect of shares acquired in exercise of any such right as is mentioned in section 185(1) of that Act, the relevant sum in relation to those shares is an amount equal to the amount so chargeable.

(6) Subsections (2), (3), (4) and (5) above shall be construed as one with sections 162, 135, 138 and 185 of the Taxes Act 1988 respectively."

19. In section 33 (exclusion of certain expenditure) the following subsection shall be added after subsection (2)—

"(3) No account shall be taken of any relief under Chapter II of Part IV of the Finance Act 1981 or under Schedule 5 to the Finance Act 1983, in so far as it is not withdrawn and relates to shares issued before 19th March 1986, in determining whether any sums are excluded by virtue of subsection (1) or (2) above from the sums allowable as a deduction in the computation of gains or losses for the purposes of this Act."

20. The following section shall be inserted after section 33—

"Transfer of certain securities.

33A.—(1) Where there is a transfer of securities within the meaning of section 710 of the Taxes Act 1988 (accrued income scheme)—

(a) if section 713(2)(a) or (3)(a) of that Act applies, section 31 above shall be disregarded in computing for capital gains tax purposes the gain accruing on the disposal concerned;

(b) if section 713(2)(b) or (3)(b) of that Act applies, section 33 above shall be disregarded in computing for capital gains tax purposes the gain accruing to the transferee if he disposes of the securities;

but subsections (2) and (3) below shall apply.

(2) Where the securities are transferred with accrued interest (within the meaning of section 711 of that Act)—

   (a) if section 713(2)(a) of that Act applies, an amount equal to the accrued amount (determined under that section) shall be excluded from the consideration mentioned in subsection (8) below;

   (b) if section 713(2)(b) of that Act applies, an amount equal to that amount shall be excluded from the sums mentioned in subsection (9) below.

(3) Where the securities are transferred without accrued interest (within the meaning of section 711 of that Act)—

   (a) if section 713(3)(a) of that Act applies, an amount equal to the rebate amount (determined under that section) shall be added to the consideration mentioned in subsection (8) below;

   (b) if section 713(3)(b) of that Act applies, an amount equal to that amount shall be added to the sums mentioned in subsection (9) below.

(4) Where section 716 of that Act applies—

   (a) if subsection (2) or (3) of that section applies, section 31 above shall be disregarded in computing for capital gains tax purposes the gain accruing on the disposal concerned, but the relevant amount shall be excluded from the consideration mentioned in subsection (8) below; and

   (b) if subsection (4) of that section applies and the securities were transferred as mentioned in subsection (1) of that section after 18th March 1986, section 33 above shall be disregarded in computing for capital gains tax purposes the gain accruing on the disposal concerned, but the relevant amount shall be excluded from the sums mentioned in subsection (9) below.

(5) In subsection (4) above "the relevant amount" means an amount equal to—

   (a) if paragraphs (b) and (c) below do not apply, the amount of the unrealised interest in question;

   (b) if section 719 of the Taxes Act 1988 applies—

        (i) in a case falling within subsection (4)(a) above, amount A (within the meaning of section 719);

        (ii) in a case falling within subsection (4)(b) above, amount C (within the meaning of section 719);

   (c) if the unrealised interest is subject to the provisions of regulations under section 476(1) of that Act and would not on being paid (to whatever person) be a gross payment within the meaning of those regulations, the grossed up equivalent of the unrealised interest (calculated in accordance with section 726 of that Act).

Paragraphs (a), (b) and (c) above shall be construed as one with sections 716, 719 and 726 respectively.

(6) In relation to any securities which by virtue of subsection (7) below are treated for the purposes of this sub-paragraph as having been transferred, subsections (2) and (3) above shall have effect as if for "applies" (in each place where it occurs) there were substituted "would apply if the disposal were a transfer".

(7) Where there is a disposal of securities for capital gains tax purposes which is not a transfer for the purposes of section 710 of the Taxes Act 1988 but, if it were such a transfer, one or more of the following paragraphs would apply, namely, paragraphs (a) and (b) of section 713(2) and paragraphs (a) and (b) of section 713(3) of that Act, the securities shall be treated—

    (a) for the purposes of subsection (6) above, as transferred on the day of the disposal, and

    (b) for the purposes of subsections (2) and (3) above, as transferred with accrued interest if, had the disposal been a transfer for the purposes of section 710, it would have been a transfer with accrued interest and as transferred without accrued interest if, had the disposal been such a transfer, it would have been a transfer without accrued interest.

(8) The consideration is the consideration for the disposal of the securities transferred which is taken into account in the computation for capital gains tax purposes of the gain accruing on the disposal.

(9) The sums are the sums allowable to the transferee as a deduction from the consideration in the computation for capital gains tax purposes of the gain accruing to him if he disposes of the securities.

(10) Where on a conversion or exchange of securities a person is treated as entitled to a sum under subsection (2)(a) of section 713 of the Taxes Act 1988 an amount equal to the accrued amount (determined under that section) shall, for capital gains tax purposes, be treated as follows—

    (a) to the extent that it does not exceed the amount of any consideration which the person receives (or is deemed to receive) or becomes entitled to receive on the conversion or exchange (other than his new holding), it shall be treated as reducing that consideration; and

    (b) to the extent that it does exceed that amount, it shall be treated as consideration which the person gives on the conversion or exchange;

and where on a conversion or exchange of securities a person is treated as entitled to relief under subsection (3)(a) of that section an amount equal to the rebate amount (determined under that section) shall, for capital gains tax purposes, be treated as consideration which the person receives on the conversion or exchange.

(11) In subsection (10) above "conversion" means conversion within the meaning of section 82 below and "exchange" means an exchange which by virtue of Chapter II of Part IV of this Act does not involve a disposal."

21. In section 101 the following subsection shall be inserted after subsection (8)—

"(8A) Section 356(3)(b) and (5) of the Taxes Act 1988 shall apply for the purposes of subsection (8) above only in relation to residence on or after 6th April 1983 in living accommodation which is job-related within the meaning of that section."

22. The following section shall be inserted after section 123—

"Harbour authorities.   123A.—(1) For the purposes of this Act any asset transferred on the transfer of the trade shall be deemed to be for a consideration such that no gain or loss accrues to the transferor on its transfer; and for the purposes of Schedule 5 to this Act the transferee shall be treated as if the acquisition by the transferor of any asset so transferred had been the transferee's acquisition thereof.

(2) This section applies only where the trade transferred is transferred from any body corporate other than a limited liability company to a harbour authority by or under a certified harbour reorganisation scheme (within the meaning of section 518 of the Taxes Act 1988) which provides also for the dissolution of the transferor."

23. The following section shall be inserted after section 132—

"Deep discount securities.   132A.—(1) Subject to subsections (2) and (3) below, in computing for the purposes of capital gains tax, the gain accruing on the disposal by any person of any deep discount securities (within the meaning of Schedule 4 to the Taxes Act 1988)—

(a) section 31 above shall not apply but the consideration for the disposal shall be treated as reduced by the amount mentioned in paragraph 4(1)(a) of that Schedule (including any amount mentioned in paragraph 3 of that Schedule); and

(b) where that amount exceeds the consideration for the disposal, the amount of the excess shall be treated as expenditure within section 32(1)(b) above incurred by that person on the security immediately before the disposal.

(2) Subsection (3) below applies where—

(a) there is a conversion of securities to which section 82 above applies and those securities include deep discount securities; or

(b) securities including deep discount securities are exchanged (or by virtue of section 86(1) above are treated as exchanged) for other securities in circumstances in which section 85(3) above applies.

(3) Where this subsection applies—

(a) subsection (1) and section 31 above shall not apply but any sum payable to the beneficial owner of the deep discount securities by way of consideration for their disposal (in addition to his new holding) shall be treated for the purpose of capital gains tax as reduced by the amount of the accrued income on which he is chargeable to income tax by virtue of paragraph 7(3) of Schedule 4 to the Taxes Act 1988 or, in a case where paragraph 3 of that Schedule applies, on which he would be so chargeable if that paragraph did not apply; and

    (b) where that amount exceeds any such sum, the excess shall be treated as expenditure within section 32(1)(b) above incurred by him on the security immediately before the time of the conversion or exchange.

(4) Where a disposal of a deep discount security is to be treated for the purposes of capital gains tax as one on which neither a gain nor a loss accrues to the person making the disposal, the consideration for which the person acquiring the security would, apart from this subsection, be treated for those purposes as having acquired the security shall be increased by the amount mentioned in paragraph 4(1)(a) of Schedule 4 to the Taxes Act 1988 (including any amount mentioned in paragraph 3 of that Schedule).".

24. The following section shall be inserted after section 142—

"Disposal of assets in premiums trust fund etc.

142A.—(1) Subject to subsection (4) below, for the year 1972-73 and subsequent years of assessment the chargeable gains or allowable losses accruing on the disposal of assets forming part of a premiums trust fund shall be taken to be those allocated to the corresponding underwriting year.

(2) The amount of the gains or losses so allocated at the end of any accounting period shall be such proportion of the difference mentioned in subsection (3) below as is allocated to the underwriting year under the rules or practice of Lloyd's.

(3) That difference is the difference between the valuations at the beginning and at the end of the accounting period of the assets forming part of the fund, the value at the beginning of the period of assets acquired during the period being taken as the cost of acquisition and the value at the end of the period of assets disposed of during the period being taken as the consideration for the disposal.

(4) Subsections (1) to (3) above do not apply to the computation of chargeable gains or allowable losses on the disposal of gilt-edged securities as defined in Schedule 2 to this Act or of qualifying corporate bonds as defined in section 64 of the Finance Act 1984.

(5) The Board may, by regulations made by statutory instrument which shall be subject to annulment in pursuance of a resolution of the House of Commons, provide—

    (a) for the assessment and collection of tax charged in accordance with this section;

    (b) for modifying the provisions of this section in relation to syndicates continuing for more than two years after the end of an underwriting year;

    (c) for giving relief from capital gains tax in cases of an underwriter dying while carrying on his business, and

    (d) for giving credit for foreign tax."

2 G

25. The following section shall be inserted after section 144—

"Profit sharing and share option schemes

Approved profit
sharing and
share option
schemes.

144A.—(1) Notwithstanding anything in a profit sharing scheme approved under Schedule 9 of the Taxes Act 1988 or in paragraph 2(2) of that Schedule or in the trust instrument relating to that scheme, for the purposes of capital gains tax a person who is a participant in relation to that scheme shall be treated as absolutely entitled to his shares as against the trustees of the scheme.

(2) For the purposes of capital gains tax—

(a) no deduction shall be made from the consideration for the disposal of any shares by reason only that an amount determined under section 186 or 187 of or Schedule 9 or 10 to the Taxes Act 1988 is chargeable to income tax under section 186(3) or (4) of that Act;

(b) any charge to income tax by virtue of section 186(3) of that Act shall be disregarded in determining whether a distribution is a capital distribution within the meaning of section 72(5)(b) above;

(c) nothing in any provision of section 186 or 187 of or Schedule 9 or 10 to that Act with respect to—

(i) the order in which any of a participant's shares are to be treated as disposed of for the purposes of those provisions as they have effect in relation to profit sharing schemes, or

(ii) the shares in relation to which an event is to be treated as occurring for any such purpose,

shall affect the rules applicable to the computation of a gain accruing on a part disposal of a holding of shares or other securities which were acquired at different times; and

(d) a gain accruing on an appropriation of shares to which section 186(11) applies shall not be a chargeable gain.

(3) In subsection (2) above "participant" and "the trust instrument" have the meanings given by section 187 of the Taxes Act 1988.

(4) Where a right to acquire shares in a body corporate is released in consideration of the grant of a right to acquire shares in another body corporate in accordance with a provision included in a scheme pursuant to paragraph 15 of Schedule 9 to the Taxes Act 1988, the transaction shall not be treated for the purposes of this Act as involving any disposal of the first-mentioned right but for those purposes the other right shall be treated as the same asset acquired as the first-mentioned right was acquired.

This subsection does not apply in relation to a savings-related share option scheme, within the meaning of section 187 of that Act, unless the first-mentioned right was acquired as mentioned in section 185(1) of that Act."

26. The following sections shall be inserted after section 149—

"Building societies and life policies.

149A.—(1) If in the course of or as part of an amalgamation of two or more building societies or a transfer of engagements from one building society to another, there is a disposal of an asset by one society to another, both shall be treated for the purposes of corporation tax on chargeable gains as if the asset were acquired from the one making the disposal for a consideration of such amount as would secure that on the disposal neither a gain nor a loss would accrue to the one making the disposal.

In this subsection "building society" means a building society within the meaning of the Building Societies Act 1986.

(2) Where any investments or other assets are or have been, in accordance with a policy issued in the course of life assurance business carried on by an insurance company, transferred to the policy holder on or after 6th April 1967, the policy holder's acquisition of the assets and the disposal of them to him shall be deemed to be, for the purposes of this Act, for a consideration equal to the market value of the assets.

In this subsection "life assurance business" and "insurance company" have the same meaning as in Chapter I of Part XII of the Taxes Act 1988.

Miscellaneous exemptions.

149B.—(1) The following gains shall not be chargeable gains—

(a) gains accruing on the disposal of stock—

(i) transferred to accounts in the books of the Bank of England in the name of the Treasury or the National Debt Commissioners in pursuance of any Act of Parliament; or

(ii) belonging to the Crown, in whatever name it may stand in the books of the Bank of England;

(b) any gain accruing to a person from his acquisition and disposal of assets held by him as part of a fund mentioned in section 613(4) of the Taxes Act 1988 (Parliamentary pension funds) or of which income is exempt from income tax under section 614(1) of that Act (social security supplementary schemes);

(c) any gain accruing to a person from his acquisition and disposal of assets held by him as part of a fund mentioned in section 614(4) or paragraph (b), (c), (d), (f) or (g) of section 615(2) of the Taxes Act 1988 (India etc. pension funds) or as part of a fund to which subsection (3) of that section applies (pension funds for overseas employees);

(d) any gain accruing to a person from his acquisition and disposal of assets held by him as part of any fund maintained for the purpose mentioned in subsection (5)(b) of section 620 or subsection (5) of section 621 of the Taxes Act 1988 under a scheme for the time being approved under that subsection;

(e) any gain accruing on the disposal by the trustees of any settled property held on trusts in accordance with directions which are valid and effective under section 9 of the Superannuation and Trust Funds (Validation) Act 1927 (trust funds for the reduction of the National Debt);

(f) any gain accruing to a consular officer or employee, within the meaning of section 322 of the Taxes Act 1988, of any foreign state to which that section applies on the disposal of assets which at the time of the disposal were situated outside the United Kingdom;

(g) any gain accruing to a person from his disposal of investments if, or to such extent as the Board are satisfied that, those investments were held by him or on his behalf for the purposes of a scheme which at the time of the disposal is an exempt approved scheme;

(h) any gain accruing to a person on his disposal of investments held by him for the purposes of an approved personal pension scheme;

(j) any gain accruing to a unit holder on his disposal of units in an authorised unit trust which is also an approved personal pension scheme or is one to which section 592(10) of the Taxes Act 1988 applies.

In this subsection "exempt approved scheme" and "approved personal pension scheme" have the same meanings as in Part XIV of the Taxes Act 1988.

(2) Where a claim is made in that behalf, a gain which accrues to a person on the disposal of investments shall not be a chargeable gain for the purposes of capital gains tax if, or to such extent as the Board are satisfied that, those investments were held by him or on his behalf for the purposes of a fund to which section 608 of the Taxes Act 1988 applies.

A claim under this subsection shall not be allowed unless the Board are satisfied that the terms on which benefits are payable from the fund have not been altered since 5th April 1980.

(3) A local authority, and a local authority association, within the meaning of section 519 of the Taxes Act 1988, shall be exempt from capital gains tax.

(4) Any terminal bonus, or interest or other sum, payable under a certified contractual savings scheme—

(a) in respect of money raised under section 12 of the National Loans Act 1968; or

(b) in respect of shares in a building society,

shall be disregarded for all purposes of the enactments relating to capital gains tax.

This subsection shall be construed as one with section 326 of the Taxes Act 1988.

(5) A signatory to the Operating Agreement made pursuant to the Convention on the International Maritime Satellite Organisation which came into force on 16th July 1979, other than a signatory designated for the purposes of the Agreement by the United Kingdom in accordance with the Convention, shall be exempt from capital gains tax in respect of any payment received by that signatory from the Organisation in accordance with the Agreement.

(6) The following shall, on a claim made in that behalf to the Board, be exempt from tax in respect of all chargeable gains—

(a) the Trustees of the British Museum and the Trustees of the British Museum (Natural History); and

(b) an Association within the meaning of section 508 of the Taxes Act 1988 (scientific research organisations).

(7) The Historic Buildings and Monuments Commission for England, the Trustees of the National Heritage Memorial Fund, the United Kingdom Atomic Energy Authority and the National Radiological Protection Board shall be exempt from tax in respect of chargeable gains; and for the purposes of this subsection gains accruing from investments or deposits held for the purposes of any pension scheme provided and maintained by the United Kingdom Atomic Energy Authority shall be treated as if those gains and investments and deposits belonged to the Authority.

(8) There shall be exempt from tax any chargeable gains accruing to the issue department of the Reserve Bank of India constituted under an Act of the Indian legislature called the Reserve Bank of India Act 1934, or to the issue department of the State Bank of Pakistan constituted under certain orders made under section 9 of the Indian Independence Act 1947.

(9) Any disposal and acquisition made in pursuance of an arrangement mentioned in subsection (1) or (2) of section 129 of the Taxes Act 1988 (stock lending) shall, subject to regulations under subsection (4) of that section, be disregarded for the purposes of capital gains tax.

Business expansion schemes. 149C.—(1) In this section "relief" means relief under Chapter III of Part VII of the Taxes Act 1988, Schedule 5 to the Finance Act 1983 ("the 1983 Act") or Chapter II of Part IV of the Finance Act 1981 ("the 1981 Act") and "eligible shares" has the meaning given by section 289(4) of the Taxes Act 1988.

(2) A gain or loss which accrues to an individual on the disposal of any shares issued after 18th March 1986 in respect of which relief has been given and not withdrawn shall not be a chargeable gain or allowable loss for the purposes of capital gains tax.

(3) The sums allowable as deductions from the consideration in the computation for the purposes of capital gains tax of the gain or loss accruing to an individual on the disposal of shares issued before 19th March 1986 in respect of which any relief has been given and not withdrawn shall be determined without regard to that relief, except that where those sums exceed the consideration they shall be reduced by an amount equal to—

(a) the amount of that relief; or

(b) the excess,

whichever is the less, but the foregoing provisions of this subsection shall not apply to a disposal falling within section 44(1) above.

(4) Sections 88 and 89 of the Finance Act 1982 (identification of securities disposed of) shall not apply to shares in respect of which any relief has been given and not withdrawn; and any question—

(a) as to which of any such shares issued to a person at different times a disposal relates; or

(b) whether a disposal relates to such shares or to other shares;

shall for the purposes of capital gains tax be determined as for the purposes of section 299 of the Taxes Act 1988, or section 57 of the Finance Act 1981 if the relief has only been given under that Act.

(5) Where an individual holds shares which form part of the ordinary share capital of a company and the relief has been given (and not withdrawn) in respect of some but not others, then, if there is within the meaning of section 77 above a reorganisation affecting those shares, section 78 shall apply separately to the shares in respect of which the relief has been given (and not withdrawn) and to the other shares (so that shares of each kind are treated as a separate holding of original shares and identified with a separate new holding):

(6) Where section 44 above has applied to any eligible shares disposed of by an individual to his or her spouse ("the transferee"), subsection (2) above shall apply in relation to the subsequent disposal of the shares by the transferee to a third party.

(7) Where section 85 or 86 above would, but for this subsection, apply in relation to eligible shares in respect of which an individual has been given relief, that section shall apply only if the relief is withdrawn.

(8) Sections 78 to 81 above shall not apply in relation to any shares in respect of which relief (other than relief under the 1981 Act) has been given and which form part of a company's ordinary share capital if—

(a) there is, by virtue of any such allotment for payment as is mentioned in section 77(2)(a) above, a reorganisation occurring after 18th March 1986 affecting those shares; and

(b) immediately following the reorganisation, the relief has not been withdrawn in respect of those shares or relief has been given in respect of the allotted shares and not withdrawn.

(9) Where relief is reduced by virtue of subsection (2) of section 305 of the Taxes Act 1988—

(a) the sums allowable as deductions from the consideration in the computation, for the purposes of capital gains tax, of the gain or loss accruing to an individual on the disposal, after 18th March 1986, of any of the allotted shares or debentures shall be taken to include the amount of the reduction apportioned between the allotted shares or (as the case may be) debentures in such a way as appears to the inspector, or on appeal to the Commissioners concerned, to be just and reasonable; and

(b) the sums so allowable on the disposal (in circumstances in which subsections (2) to (7) above do not apply) of any of the shares referred to in section 305(2)(a) shall be taken to be reduced by the amount mentioned in paragraph (a) above, similarly apportioned between those shares.

(10) There shall be made all such adjustments of capital gains tax, whether by way of assessment or by way of discharge or repayment of tax, as may be required in consequence of the relief being given or withdrawn.

Personal equity plans.

149D.—(1) The Treasury may make regulations providing that an individual who invests under a plan shall be entitled to relief from capital gains tax in respect of the investments.

(2) Subsections (2) to (5) of section 333 of the Taxes Act 1988 (personal equity plans) shall apply in relation to regulations under subsection (1) above as they apply in relation to regulations under subsection (1) of that section but with the substitution for any reference to income tax of a reference to capital gains tax.

(3) Regulations under this section shall be made by statutory instrument which shall be subject to annulment in pursuance of a resolution of the House of Commons.".

27. In section 155 (interpretation) after subsection (1) there shall be inserted—

"(1A) In this Act "retail prices index" shall have the same meaning as in the Income Tax Acts and, accordingly, any reference in this Act to the retail prices index shall be construed in accordance with section 833(2) of the Taxes Act 1988.".

28. In section 157 (savings) after subsection (1) there shall be inserted—

"(1A) No letters patent granted or to be granted by the Crown to any person, city, borough or town corporate of any liberty, privilege, or exemption from subsidies, tolls, taxes, assessments or aids, and no statute which grants any salary, annuity or pension to any person free of any taxes, deductions or assessments, shall be construed or taken to exempt any person, city, borough or town corporate, or any inhabitant of the same, from tax chargeable in pursuance of this Act."

FINANCE ACT 1982 c.39

29. In section 134(1) after second "Act" there shall be inserted "or in Chapter V of Part XII of the Taxes Act 1988".

ADMINISTRATION OF JUSTICE ACT 1985 c.61

30. In paragraph 36(3) of Schedule 2 to the Administration of Justice Act 1985 for all the words preceding "any reference" there shall be substituted the words "(3) In sections 745(3) and 778(3) of, and paragraph 14(5) of Schedule 15 to, the Income and Corporation Taxes Act 1988".

LAW REFORM (MISCELLANEOUS PROVISIONS) (SCOTLAND) ACT 1985 c.73

31. In Schedule 1 to the Law Reform (Miscellaneous Provisions) (Scotland) Act 1985 for the heading preceding paragraph 41 there shall be substituted the following—

"Income and Corporation Taxes Act 1988";

and in paragraph 41 for "30(5)" there shall be substituted the words "745(3) and 778(3) of, and paragraph 14(5) of Schedule 15 to, the Income and Corporation Taxes Act 1988".

TRANSLATION OF REFERENCES TO ENACTMENTS REPEALED AND RE-ENACTED

32. In the enactments specified in Column 1 of the following Table for the words set out or referred to in Column 2 there shall be substituted the words set out in the corresponding entry in Column 3.

Enactment amended	Words to be omitted	Words to be substituted
In the Finance Act 1952 c. 33		
Section 74(4)	52 of the Finance Act 1974	519 of the Income and Corporation Taxes Act 1988
In the Finance Act 1956 c. 54		
Section 26(2)	226(13) of the Income and Corporation Taxes Act 1970	620(9) of the Income and Corporation Taxes Act 1988
In the Trustee Investments Act 1961 c. 62		
Schedule 1, Part II, Paragraph 10A	from "section 358" to the end	subsection (1) of section 468 of the Income and Corporation Taxes Act 1988, in relation to which that subsection does not, by virtue of subsection (5) of that section, apply.
In the Finance Act (Northern Ireland) 1967 c. 20 (N.I.)		
Section 6(3)	52 of the Finance Act 1974	519 of the Income and Corporation Taxes Act 1988
In the Provisional Collection of Taxes Act 1968 c. 2		
Section		
1(1A)(a)	343 of the Income and Corporation Taxes Act 1970	476 of the Income and Corporation Taxes Act 1988
1(1A)(b)	27 of the Finance Act 1984	479 of that Act
5(1)(c)	from "243(6)" to "1972"	8(5) of the Income and Corporation Taxes Act 1988
5(2)	from "the said" to "1972"	sections 8(5) and 822 of the 1988 Act (over-deductions from preference dividends before passing of annual Act)
In the Capital Allowances Act 1968 c.3		
Section		
12(3)	154 or 251(1)	113 or 337(1)
15(3)	178 (three times)	394
26(7)	463	706
33(2)(b)	Part III of the Finance Act 1976	Part V of the principal Act
34(3)	Part III of the Finance Act 1976	Part V of the principal Act
34(4)	Part III of the Finance Act 1976	Part V of the principal Act
47(4)	189(2)	198(2)
48(1)	154 or 251(1)	113 or 337(1)
48(6)(a)	154	113
60(10)	134 (twice)	87
60(10)	(5)	(7)

Enactment amended	Words to be omitted	Words to be substituted
60(11)	115	60
67(3)	154 or 251(1)	113 or 337(1)
67(3)	252(2)	343(2)
69	111	54
70(5)	169	383
72(2)	115	60
78(1)(a)	533	839
79(1)	154 or 251(1)	113 or 337(1)
79(4)	154	113
80(3)(b)	171 or 177(1)	385 or 393(1)
82(1)	52 or 53	348 or 349(1)
82(2)	411(1)(c)	577(1)(c)
85(1A)	533	839
85(4)	111	54
90	130	74
91(3)	115	60
100(2)	250(5)	9(5)
100(5)	1970	1988
Schedule		
2, para. 8(1)(c)	78(1) or 306(1) of the principal Act	32(1) of the principal Act or section 306(1) of the Income and Corporation Taxes Act 1970
7, para.1(1)(a)	533	839
para.4(3)	63 of the Finance (No.2) Act 1987	404 of the principal Act
In the Finance Act 1969 c. 32		
Section 58(1)(a)	204 of the Income and Corporation Taxes Act 1970	203 of the Income and Corporation Taxes Act 1988
In the Taxes Management Act 1970 c. 9		
Section		
6(1)(c)	463	706
8(8)	457 or 458	683 or 684
8(9)	86 of the Finance Act 1972	231 of the principal Act
9(4)	155	114
11(6)	85(4) of the Finance Act 1972	239(4) of the principal Act
12(5)	137(4)	100(2)

Enactment amended	Words to be omitted	Words to be substituted
15(7)(a)	from "section 196" to "1977"	sections 141, 142, 143, 145 or 154 to 165 of the principal Act
15(11)(b)	Part II of the Finance Act 1976	Part V of the principal Act
19(2)	80 to 82	34 to 36
27(2)	454(3)	681(4)
29(2)	Schedule 16 to the Finance Act 1972	sections 426 to 430 of the principal Act
29(8)	39(3)	284(4)
30	47 or 48 (twice)	824 or 825 of the principal Act or section 47
31	all of subsection (3)	(3) The appeal shall be to the Special Commissioners if the assessment is made—
		(a) by the Board; or
		(b) under section 350, 426, 445, 740, 743(1) or 747(4)(a) of the principal Act; or
		(c) under section 38 of the Finance Act 1973 or section 830 of the principal Act and is not an assessment to tax under Schedule E;
		or if the appeal involves any question as to the application of Part XV or XVI of the principal Act.
35(2)(b)	187	148
42(3)(a)	27	278
42(3)(c)	section 218	subsection (5) of section 614
42(3)(c)	that section	section 615(3) of that Act
47B	Schedule 5 to the Finance Act 1983	Chapter III of Part VII of the principal Act
47B	paragraph 5A(5) of that Schedule	section 294(5) of that Act
55(1)(b)	204	203
55(1)(c)	Schedule 20 to the Finance Act 1972	Schedule 16 to the principal Act
55(1)(e)	Schedule 14 to the Finance Act 1972	Schedule 13 to the principal Act
55(1)(g)	88 of the Finance Act 1984	753 of the principal Act
55(1)(g)	82(4)(a)	747(4)(a)
58(3)(b)	from "sections" to "that Act or"	section 102, 113(5), 263(5) and (6), 343(10) or 783(9) of the principal Act, or paragraph 22 of Schedule 7 to the Income and Corporation Taxes Act 1970, or
63(3) (as substituted by Schedule 4 to the Debtors (Scotland) Act 1987 c.18)	204	203
71(1)	Part XI	
78(1)	89	sections 6 to 12 and Parts VIII and XI 43

Enactment amended	Words to be omitted	Words to be substituted
78(4)	VII of Part II of the Finance Act 1984	V of Part XVII of the principal Act
78(5)	533	839
86(2)(b)	204	203
86(2)(d)	14 to the Finance Act 1972	13 to the principal Act
86(4)	5 (three times)	3
86(4)	4(3)	5(4)
86(4)	14 to the Finance Act 1972	13 to the principal Act
86(4)	243(4)	10(1)
86(4)	344	478
87	14 (four times)	13
87	20 (four times)	16
87	the Finance Act 1972	the principal Act
88(2)	14 or 20 to the Finance Act 1972	13 or 16 to the principal Act
88(5)(b)	4(2)	5(2)
88(5)(c)	4(3)	5(4)
91(3)(c)	204	203
93(1)	39(3)	284(4)
93(3)	204	203
94(2)	240(5) or 246(3)	7(2) or 11(3)
95(1)(a)	39(3)	284(4)
109(4)	286(5)	419(4)
109(1)–(3),(5)	section 286	sections 419 and 420
118(1)	526(5)	832(1)
118(1)	354	468
118(1)	1970	1988
Schedule		
2, para.2(2), in column 1 of the Table	II of Part I	I of Part VII
	65(4)	351(5)
	3	2
para.2(2), in column 2 of the Table	158(1)	121(1), (2)
	315(3)	441(3)
	331	459
	332	460
	338	467
	339	484
	384	527
	389	534

Enactment amended	Words to be omitted	Words to be substituted
3, para.3,5	391	536
para.5B	392	538
para.8	204 (three times)	203
para.8	65 of the Finance Act 1976	159 of the principal Act
	section 286	sections 419 and 420
last para.	15 of Schedule 16 to the Finance Act 1972	13 of Schedule 19 to the principal Act
	from "11" to "to the principal Act"	102, 113(5), 263(5) and (6), 343(10) and 783(9) of the principal Act, to paragraph 22 of Schedule 7 to the Income and Corporation Taxes Act 1970

In the Income and Corporation Taxes Act 1970 c. 10

Section

267(3)	Chapter VI of Part XII of this Act	section 468 of the Taxes Act 1988
267(3)	that Chapter	section 842 of that Act
267(4)	137(4) of this Act	100(2) of the Taxes Act 1988
272(1)(d)	532 of this Act	838 of the Taxes Act 1988
272(2)(c)	340 of this Act	486 of the Taxes Act 1988
272(5)	V of Part XII of this Act	VI of Part XII of the Taxes Act 1988
273(2)(c)	Chapter VI of Part XII of this Act	section 842 of the Taxes Act 1988
273(2)(d)	63 of the Finance (No.2) Act 1987	404 of the Taxes Act 1988
276(1A)(b)	63 of the Finance (No.2) Act 1987	404 of the Taxes Act 1988
278(3A)(a)	262(2) of this Act	409(2) of the Taxes Act 1988
281(6)	533 of this Act	839 of the Taxes Act 1988
306	304(5) above	130 of the Taxes Act 1988
306	304(3) above (twice)	75(4) of the Taxes Act 1988
306	304 above	75 of the Taxes Act 1988
540(2)	1979	1979 and any reference in this Act to the Taxes Act 1988 is a reference to the Income and Corporation Taxes Act 1988.

In the Finance Act 1970 c. 24

Section

29(6)	The words from "and the Board" to the end	and any other payment or part of a payment which is to be treated as mineral royalties by virtue of regulations made under section 122(5) of the Income and Corporation Taxes Act 1988

Enactment amended	Words to be omitted	Words to be substituted
Schedule 6, para.7(2)	29 of this Act	122 of the Income and Corporation Taxes Act 1988

In the Friendly Societies Act (Northern Ireland) 1970 c. 31 (N.I.)

Enactment amended	Words to be omitted	Words to be substituted
Section		
1(5)	(2) and (3) respectively of section 337 of the Income and Corporation Taxes Act 1970	(1) and (2) respectively of section 466 of the Income and Corporation Taxes Act 1988
82(4)	226(13) of the Income and Corporation Taxes Act 1970	620(9) of the Income and Corporation Taxes Act 1988

In the Finance Act 1971 c. 68

Enactment amended	Words to be omitted	Words to be substituted
Section		
21	the whole of subsection (6)	(6) Part II of Schedule 3 to this Act shall have effect.
40(2)(a), 43(3)	533	839
44(5), (6)	VIII of the Taxes Act or Chapter II of Part III of the Finance Act 1976 (Schedule E) (twice)	Schedule E
44(6)	63 of the Finance (No. 2) Act 1987	404 of the Taxes Act
44(6)	533 of the Taxes Act	839 of that Act
44(7)	533	839
47(1)	the whole of paragraph (ii)	(ii) the provisions of this Chapter as applied by this subsection shall have effect subject to section 198(2) of the Taxes Act (offices and employments with duties abroad).
47(2)	from beginning to "shall each"	Section 306 of the Income and Corporation Taxes Act 1970 (capital allowances for machinery and plant used by investment or life assurance companies) shall
69(2)	1970	1988
Schedule		
3, para.8(1), (5)	the Taxes Act	the Income and Corporation Taxes Act 1970
para.8(3)	the words from "sub-paragraphs" to "this Schedule"	section 598(2) to (4) of the Taxes Act
para.8(4)	1970	1970 or Chapter I of Part XIV of the Taxes Act
8, para.3	533 (three times)	839
para.8(4), 8A(11)	169(4)(d), 174(6) and 259(2)	383(5)(d), 388(7) and 403(3)
para.13	533 of the Taxes Act	839 of that Act
para.13	63 of the Finance (No.2) Act 1987	404 of the Taxes Act

Enactment amended	Words to be omitted	Words to be substituted
In the Finance Act 1972 c. 41		
Section		
68(10)	533	839
69(1)(c)(i)	533	839
69(4)	80	34
134(2)	1970	1988
In the Finance Act 1973 c. 51		
Section		
32(1)(b)	30 above	395 of the Taxes Act 1988
32(1)(c)	31 above	116 of that Act
32(1)(c)	85(5) of the Finance Act 1972	239(5) of that Act
32(1)(d)	92 of the Finance Act 1972	240 of that Act
32(2)	from beginning of paragraph (a) to end of paragraph (d)	(a) section 410(1) or (2) of or paragraph 5(3) of Schedule 18 to the Taxes Act 1988;
		(b) section 395(1)(c) of that Act;
		(c) section 116(1) of that Act;
		(d) paragraph 5(3) of Schedule 18 to or section 240(11) of that Act.
32(3)	258 of the Income and Corporation Taxes Act 1970	402 of the Taxes Act 1988
38(2)(d)	237(5) of the Taxes Act	254(1) of the Taxes Act 1988
38(3)	from beginning to "such rights"	Any gains accruing on the disposal of exploration or exploitation rights
38(3B)	533 of the Taxes Act	839 of the Taxes Act 1988
38(5)	the Taxes Act	the Taxes Act 1970
59	all of subsection (2)	(2) In this Act—
		(a) "the Taxes Act 1970" means the Income and Corporation Taxes Act 1970; and
		(b) "the Taxes Act 1988" means the Income and Corporation Taxes Act 1988.
Schedule		
15, para.2,4	this Act	this Act or section 830 of the Taxes Act 1988
15, para.6	533 of the Taxes Act	839 of the Taxes Act 1988

Enactment amended	Words to be omitted	Words to be substituted

In the Friendly Societies Act 1974 c. 46

Section		
7(5)	(2) and (3) respectively of section 337 of the Income and Corporation Taxes Act 1970	(1) and (2) respectively of section 466 of the Income and Corporation Taxes Act 1988
93(4)	226(13) of the Income and Corporation Taxes Act 1970	620(9) of the Income and Corporation Taxes Act 1988

In the Social Security Act 1975 c. 14 and in the Social Security (Northern Ireland) Act 1975 c. 15

Schedule		
2, para.1		
para.3(1)	1970 (three times)	1988
para.3(1)(a)	1970	1988
para.3(1)(b)	section 168	sections 380 and 381
para.3(1)(c)	169	383
para.3(1)(d)	171	385
para.3(2)(a)	section 174	sections 388 and 389
para.3(2)(b)	II of Part I of the Act of 1970	I of Part VII of the Act of 1988
para.3(2)(c)	226 and 227	619 and 620
para.3(2)(d)	section 75 of the Finance Act 1972	section 353 of the Act of 1988
para.3(2)(d)	173 of the Act of 1970	387 of the Act of 1988
para.3(2)(e)	53	350
para.3(2)(f)	175	390
	the whole paragraph	(f) section 617(5) of the Act of 1988 (relief for Class 4 contributions)
para.3(4)(a)	52 or 53 of the Act of 1970	348 or 349(1) of the Act of 1988
para.3(4)(b)	75 of the Finance Act 1972	353 of that Act
para.4(1)	IV of Part I of the Act of 1970	II of Part VII of the Act of 1988
para.4(1)	38	283
para.4(3)	23 of the Finance Act 1971	287 of that Act
para.4(3)	37 (twice)	279
para.4(3)	1970	1988
para.4(3)	38	283
para.4(3)	23 of the Finance Act 1971	287 of that Act
para.5(2)	Chapter VI of Part VI of the Act of 1970	sections 111 to 115 of the Act of 1988
para.5(2)	152	111
para.6(b)	114 of the Act of 1970	59 of the Act of 1988

Enactment amended	Words to be omitted	Words to be substituted
In the Oil Taxation Act 1975 c. 22		
Section		
3(2)	412	579
3(2)	13 of this Act	492 of the Taxes Act
5(7)	533	839
5(8)	532	838
6(4)(b)	532	838
21(2)	1970	1988
Schedule		
3, para.1(2)	533	839
para.2A(2)(b)	533	839
para.5(5)	534	840
4, para.2(2)	533	839
para.4(8)	533	839
para.7(2)	533	839
In the Finance (No.2) Act 1975 c. 45		
Section		
47(11)	110(1) of the Finance Act 1972	231(5) of the Income and Corporation Taxes Act 1988
47(11)	432(4) of the Taxes Act	701(4) of that Act
47(12)	432(8) of the Taxes Act	701(9) of the Income and Corporation Taxes Act 1988
58(10)	323 of the Taxes Act	431 of the Income and Corporation Taxes Act 1988
In the Finance Act 1976 c. 40		
Section		
41(1)	section 168 of the Taxes Act	sections 380 and 381 of the Income and Corporation Taxes Act 1988
41(2)	section 168	sections 380 and 381
41(2)	533 of the Taxes Act	839 of the Income and Corporation Taxes Act 1988
41(6)	section 168	sections 380 and 381
131(2)	from beginning to "such a security"	A security issued by the Inter-American Development Bank
In the Finance Act 1978 c. 42		
Section		
37(4)	section 84(1), (2) and (3) of the Taxes Act	subsections (1) to (4) and (6) of section 38 of the Income and Corporation Taxes Act 1988
37(6)(a)	533 of the Taxes Act	839 of the Income and Corporation Taxes Act 1988

In the Capital Gains Tax Act 1979 c. 14

Enactment amended Section	Words to be omitted	Words to be substituted
1(2)	Taxes Act	Taxes Act 1970 and Part VIII of the Taxes Act 1988
10(4)	518	816
14(2)	(4) to (7) of section 122	(6) to (9) of section 65
14(2)	(3) of the said section 122	(5) of that section
15(5)(d)	246(2)(b)	11(2)(b)
31(2)	the Taxes Act which under that Act	the Taxes Act 1970 or the Taxes Act 1988 which under either of those Acts
34(4)(a)	the Taxes Act which under that Act	the Taxes Act 1970 or the Taxes Act 1988 which under either of those Acts
34(4)(b)	76	30
34(4)(c)	141	91
45(4)	40	285
45(4)	41	286
60(c)	153(1), (2)	112(1), (2)
63(3)	454 (twice)	681
63(3)	(3)	(4)
74(1)	paragraph 5 of Schedule 16 to the Finance Act 1972	section 426 of the Taxes Act 1988
74(2)	sub-paragraph (6) of the said paragraph 5	section 427(4) of the Taxes Act 1988
74(2)	sub-paragraph (2)(b) of that paragraph	section 426(2)(b) of that Act
74(5)	formed part of the said paragraph 5	were included in sections 426 to 428 of the Taxes Act 1988
85(1)	526(5)	832(1)
89(1)	34 of the Finance (No.2) Act 1975	249 of the Taxes Act 1988
89(1)	the said section 34 (twice)	that section
89(1)(b)	3(1) of Schedule 8	12(1) of Schedule 19
89(1)	paragraph 1 of the said Schedule 8	section 251(2) of the Taxes Act 1988
90(1)	34 of the Finance (No.2) Act 1975	249 of the Taxes Act 1988
90(3)	paragraph 1 of Schedule 8 to the Finance (No.2) Act 1975	section 251(2) to (4) of the Taxes Act 1988
92(b)	358	468(6)
92(c)	359	842
101(8)(a)	paragraph 4A of Schedule 1 to the Finance Act 1974	section 356 of the Taxes Act 1988
119(4)	140(2)	98(2)
124(8)	11 of Schedule 16 to the Finance Act 1972	7 of Schedule 19 to the Taxes Act 1988
126(7)	11 of Schedule 16 to the Finance Act 1972	7 of Schedule 19 to the Taxes Act 1988

Enactment amended	*Words to be omitted*	*Words to be substituted*
136(10)(b)	11 of Schedule 16 to the Finance Act 1972	7 of Schedule 19 to the Taxes Act 1988
137(9)	535	841
145	Subject to	Subject to section 505(3) of the Taxes Act 1988 and
149(7)	303(1)	417(1)
152(2)	535	841
155(1)	282 and 283	414 and 415
155(1)	302	416
155(1)	432(4)	701(4)
155(1)	the definition of "the Taxes Act"	"the Taxes Act 1970" and "the Taxes Act 1988" mean the Income and Corporation Taxes Act 1970 and Income and Corporation Taxes Act 1988 respectively;
155(1)	137(4)	100(2)
155(2)	42(1)(2)	282(1) and (2)
Schedule 1, para.6(7)	454(3)	681(4)
para.6	the whole of sub-paragraph (8)	(8) The schemes and funds referred to in sub-paragraph (7)(b)(ii) above are funds to which section 615(3) of the Taxes Act 1988 applies, schemes and funds approved under section 620 or 621 of that Act, sponsored superannuation schemes as defined in section 624 of that Act and exempt approved schemes and statutory schemes as defined in Chapter I of Part XIV of that Act.
3, para.5	80 (three times)	34
para.5(3)	82	36
para.5(4)	(3) or subsection (4)	(4) or (5)
para.5(5)	Part III	section 348 or 349
para.6(1)	83(2)	37(4)
para.6(2)	81	35
para.6(3)	82(2)(b)	36(2)(b)
para.7	80(2)	34(2) and (3)
para.9(2)	492	785

In the European Parliament (Pay and Pensions) Act 1979 c. 50

Section 8(1)	subsections (1A) and (1B) of section 229 of the Income and Corporation Taxes Act 1970	section 629(2) and (3) of the Income and Corporation Taxes Act 1988

Enactment amended	Words to be omitted	Words to be substituted
In the Finance Act 1980 c.48		
Section		
64(9)(b)	154(2) or 155(1) of the Taxes Act	113(2) or 114(1) of the Taxes Act 1988
65(5), 66(5)	154(2), 155(1) or 252(2) of the Taxes Act	113(2), 114(1) or 343(2) of the Taxes Act 1988
70(3)	the said Act of 1971	the Finance Act 1971
73(6)	533 of the Taxes Act	839 of the Taxes Act 1988
107(7)	Part II of the said Act of 1975	Chapter V of Part XII of the Taxes Act 1988
108(9)(b)	Part II of that Act	Chapter V of Part XII of the Taxes Act 1988
118	the whole of subsection (3)	(3) The trustees of the National Heritage Memorial Fund shall be treated for the purposes of section 49(2) of the Finance Act 1974 and section 99 above as a body of persons established for charitable purposes only.
122(2)	1970	1970 and "the Taxes Act 1988" means the Income and Corporation Taxes Act 1988
Schedule		
17, para.13(3)	533 of the Taxes Act	839 of the Taxes Act 1988
para.16(3)	532 of the Taxes Act	838 of the Taxes Act 1988
para.19(2)	533 of the Taxes Act	839 of the Taxes Act 1988
18, para.9	paragraph 2(1)(a) above	section 213(3)(a) of the Taxes Act 1988
para.23(1)	paragraph 13 above	section 214(2) of the Taxes Act 1988
para.23(1)	paragraph 1 above	section 213(2) of that Act
In the Finance Act 1981 c. 35		
Section		
83(7)	454(3)	681(4)
84(2)	(4) of section 481	(5) of section 745
84(2)	481(1)	745(1)
139(2)	1970	1988
In the Housing (Northern Ireland) Order 1981 (S.I. No.156 N.I.3)		
Article		
146(3)	341 (three times)	488
146(3)	1970 (three times)	1988

Enactment amended	*Words to be omitted*	*Words to be substituted*
In the Iron and Steel Act 1982 c. 25		
Section		
13(3)	252(3) of the Income and Corporation Taxes Act 1970	343(3) of the Income and Corporation Taxes Act 1988
13(4)	265(1) of the Income and Corporation Taxes Act 1970	345(1) of the Income and Corporation Taxes Act 1988
In the Finance Act 1982 c. 39		
Section		
27	this Act (three times)	this Act or the Taxes Act 1988
70(1)	38(4) of the Finance Act 1973	830(4) of the Taxes Act 1988
70(12)	533 of the Taxes Act	839 of the Taxes Act 1988
72(5)	137(4) of the Taxes Act	100(2) of the Taxes Act 1988
88(9)(a)	Chapter IV of Part II of the Finance Act 1985	section 710 of the Taxes Act 1988
88(9)(b)	section 36 of the Finance Act 1984	Schedule 4 to that Act
88(9)(c)	VII of Part II of that Act	V of Part XVII of the Taxes Act 1988
147(1)	532(1)(b) of the Taxes Act	838 of the Taxes Act 1988
147(2), (3)	the Taxes Act	the Taxes Act 1970
157	the whole of subsection (2)	(2) In this Act—
		(a) "the Taxes Act 1970" means the Income and Corporation Taxes Act 1970; and
		(b) "the Taxes Act 1988" means the Income and Corporation Taxes Act 1988".
Schedule		
11, para.4(3)	154(2), section 155(1) or section 255(2) of the Taxes Act	113(2), 114(1) or 243(2) of the Taxes Act 1988
para.4(4)	533 of the Taxes Act	839 of the Taxes Act 1988
12, para. 3(3)(b)	341 of the Taxes Act	488 of the Taxes Act 1988
para. 3(3)(e)	Chapter III of Part XI of the Taxes Act	Part XI of the Taxes Act 1988
para. 3(3)	533 of the Taxes Act	839 of the Taxes Act 1988
13, para.3(3)(a)	the Taxes Act	the Taxes Act 1970
21, para.3(2)	463 of the Taxes Act	706 of the Taxes Act 1988
In the Finance Act 1983 c. 28		
Section		
46(3)	Commission	Historic Buildings and Monuments Commission

Enactment amended	Words to be omitted	Words to be substituted
Schedule		
6, para.1(2)	the whole of paragraph (aa) as inserted by paragraph 11(2) of the Finance Act 1984	nor (ab) deep discount securities (within the meaning of Schedule 4 to the Income and Corporation Taxes Act 1988); nor
para.1(2)(c)	VII of Part II of the Finance Act 1984	V of Part XVII of the Income and Corporation Taxes Act 1988
8, para. 11(2)	533 of the Taxes Act	839 of the Income and Corporation Taxes Act 1988
In the Oil Taxation Act 1983 c. 56		
Section		
15(4)	533	839
Schedule		
2, para.11(2)	and section 17 of the principal Act	of the principal Act and section 500 of the Taxes Act
2, para.11(3)(a)	302	416
2, para.12(1)	and section 17 of the principal Act	of the principal Act and section 500 of the Taxes Act
In the Telecommunications Act 1984 c. 12		
Section		
62(7)	subsection (10) of section 48 of the Finance Act 1981	section 400(9) of the Income and Corporation Taxes Act 1988
72(3)(b)	paragraph (a) of the proviso to section 21(3) of the Finance Act 1970	section 592(5) of the Income and Corporation Taxes Act 1988
72(3)	II of Part II of the said Act of 1970	I of Part XIV of that Act
72(4)	"416" and "1970"	"581" and "1988"
In the Finance Act 1984 c. 43		
Section		
50(1)	income tax, corporation tax, or capital gains tax	capital gains tax or corporation tax on chargeable gains
60(1)	252 of the Taxes Act	343 of the Taxes Act 1988
79(10)	Part II of the Oil Taxation Act 1975	Chapter V of Part XII of the Taxes Act 1988
113(8)	532 of the Taxes Act	838 of the Taxes Act 1988
115(2)	534 of the Taxes Act	840 of the Taxes Act 1988
115(7)	532 of the Taxes Act	838 of the Taxes Act 1988
128	1970	1970; and "the Taxes Act 1988" means the Income and Corporation Taxes Act 1988

Enactment amended	*Words to be omitted*	*Words to be substituted*
Schedule		
14, para.1(1)	VII of Part II of this Act	V of Part XVII of the Taxes Act 1988
para.7(6)(b)	45 of the Finance Act 1981	740 of the Taxes Act 1988
para.8(6)	45 of the Finance Act 1981	740 of the Taxes Act 1988
para.12(7)	45 of the Finance Act 1981	740 of the Taxes Act 1988
para.15(2)	(5) of section 481 of the Taxes Act	(6) of section 745 of the Taxes Act 1988

In the Inheritance Tax Act 1984 c. 51

Section		
6(3)(e)	415 of the Taxes Act	326 of the Taxes Act 1988
12(2)(a)	II of Part II of the Finance Act 1970	I of Part XIV of the Taxes Act 1988
12(2)(c)	II of Part I of the Finance (No. 2) Act 1987	IV of Part XIV of the Taxes Act 1988
13(4)(b)	the Finance Act 1978	Schedule 9 to the Taxes Act 1988
21(3)	230 of the Taxes Act	657 of the Taxes Act 1988
72(4)	Finance Act 1978	Taxes Act 1988
86(3)	Finance Act 1978	Taxes Act 1988
91(2)(c)	Part XV of the Taxes Act	Part XVI of the Taxes Act 1988
94(2)(a)	239 of the Taxes Act	208 of the Taxes Act 1988
94(3)	258 of the Taxes Act or of section 92 of the Finance Act 1972	240 or 402 of the Taxes Act 1988
96	234(3) of the Taxes Act	210(4) of the Taxes Act 1988
97	the Taxes Act (twice)	the Taxes Act 1970
102(1)	Chapter III of Part XI of the Taxes Act	Chapter I of Part XI of the Taxes Act 1988
151(1)	218 of the Taxes Act	615(3) of the Taxes Act 1988
151(1)	226 or 226A	620 or 621
151(1)	II of Part II of the Finance Act 1970	I of Part XIV of that Act
151(1)	226(11) of the Taxes Act	624 of that Act
151(1A)	II of Part I of the Finance (No.2) Act 1987	IV of Part XIV of the Taxes Act 1988
152(a)	II of Part I of the Finance (No.2) Act 1987	IV of Part XIV of the Taxes Act 1988
152(b)	226 or 226A of the Taxes Act	620 or 621 of the Taxes Act 1988
152(b)	the commencement of that Act	6th April 1970
174(1)(a)	VII of Part II of the Finance Act 1984	V of Part VII of the Taxes Act 1988
174(1)(a)	92(3)	757(3)
174(1)(b)	1 of Schedule 9 to the Finance Act 1984	4 of Schedule 4 to that Act
174(1)(b)	2(2)	7(2)
178(1)	358 of the Taxes Act	468 of the Taxes Act 1988
204(5)	from "478" to "1981"	739 or 740 of the Taxes Act 1988

Enactment amended	Words to be omitted	Words to be substituted
272	52 of the Finance Act 1974	519 of the Taxes Act 1988
272	the definition of the Taxes Act	"the Taxes Act 1970" means the Income and Corporation Taxes Act 1970; "the Taxes Act 1988" means the Income and Corporation Taxes Act 1988;

In the Finance Act 1985 c. 54

Section

56(1)(c)	enactment	enactment (including any contained in the Taxes Act)
56(8)	Chapter I of Part XIV	sections 520 to 533
57(7)	533	839
68(7)	Taxes Act	Income and Corporation Taxes Act 1970
71(6)	the Taxes Act	the Income and Corporation Taxes Act 1970
72(1)	this subsection	section 128 of the Taxes Act
80(5)(b)	13 of the Oil Taxation Act 1975	492 of the Taxes Act
98(2)	1970	1988

Schedule

17, para.3(2), 5(4)(a),6(d)	533	839
19, para.16(3)	from "Part I" to "1983"	Chapter III of Part VIII of the Taxes Act
para.22	Schedule 16 to the Finance Act 1973	section 457 of the Taxes Act
para.23	paragraph 6(2) of the said Schedule 16	section 142A of the Capital Gains Tax Act 1979
20, para.1(2)	302	416
para.8(5)	532(1)	838(1)

In the Companies Act 1985 c. 6

Section

209(3)(b)	444 of the Income and Corporation Taxes Act 1970	670 of the Income and Corporation Taxes Act 1988
266(4)	359 (twice)	842
266(4)	1970	1988

In the Trustee Savings Bank Act 1985 c. 58

Schedule 2

para.4(2)	Taxes Act (twice)	the Income and Corporation Taxes Act 1970
6(1)	137	100
(4)	177	393
(8)	29 of the Finance Act 1973	410(1) to (6) of the Taxes Act
7(2)	26 of the Finance Act 1982	369 of the Taxes Act
9(1)	1970	1988

Enactment amended	*Words to be omitted*	*Words to be substituted*
In the Bankruptcy (Scotland) Act 1985 c. 66		
Schedule 3 Part I		
para.1(1)	204 of the Income and Corporation Taxes Act 1970	203 of the Income and Corporation Taxes Act 1988
para.1(2)	69 of the Finance (No.2) Act 1975	559 of the Income and Corporation Taxes Act 1988
In the Housing Associations Act 1985 c. 69		
Section		
62(2)	341	488
62(2)	1970	1988
In the Airports Act 1986 c. 31		
Section		
77(2)	1970 Act	Income and Corporation Taxes Act 1970
77(4)	48(10) of the Finance Act 1981	400(9) of the 1988 Act
77(5)	261(2) of the 1970 Act	408(2) of the 1988 Act
77(5)	262(1) of the 1970 Act	409(1) of that Act
77(5)	262(2)	409(2)
77(6)	1970 (twice)	1988
77(6)	258 to 264	Chapter IV of Part X
In the Finance Act 1986 c. 41		
Section		
24(4)	Finance Act 1978	Taxes Act 1988
58(4)	497 of the Taxes Act	788 or 789 of the Taxes Act 1988
69(6)	535 of the Taxes Act	841 of the Taxes Act 1988
78(9)	126 of the Finance Act 1984	324 of the Taxes Act 1988
114(2)	1970	1970 and "the Taxes Act 1988" means the Income and Corporation Taxes Act 1988
Schedule		
13, para.17	134 of the Taxes Act	87 of the Taxes Act 1988
para.17	(5) of the said section 134	(7) of that section
15, para.10(1)	533 of the Taxes Act	839 of the Taxes Act 1988
para.10(4)	80 of the Taxes Act	34 of the Taxes Act 1988
16, para.8(5)	from "154(2)" to first "Act"	113(2), 114(1) or 343(2) of the Taxes Act 1988
para.8(8)	533 of the Taxes Act	839 of the Taxes Act 1988

Enactment amended	Words to be omitted	Words to be substituted
In the Gas Act 1986 c. 44		
Section 63(9)	533 of the Income and Corporation Taxes Act 1970	839 of the Income and Corporation Taxes Act 1988
In the Insolvency Act 1986 c. 45		
Schedule 6, para. 1	204 of the Income and Corporation Taxes Act 1970	203 of the Income and Corporation Taxes Act 1988
para. 2	69 of the Finance (No. 2) Act 1975	559 of the Income and Corporation Taxes Act 1988
In the Social Security Act 1986 c. 50		
Section		
23(5)	204	203
23(5)	1970	1988
84(1)	365 (twice)	315
84(1)	1970	1988
Schedule 6, para.1(2)	365	315
para.1(2)	1970	1988
In the Building Societies Act 1986 c. 53		
Schedule 8, para.7	Schedule 8 to the Finance Act 1986	section 333 of the Income and Corporation Taxes Act 1988
In the Financial Services Act 1986 c. 60		
Schedule 15, para.14(5)	332	460(1) or 461(1)
para.14(5)	1970	1988
In the Companies (Northern Ireland) Order 1986 (S.I.No.1032 N.I.6)		
Article 217(3)(b)	444 of the Income and Corporation Taxes Act 1970	670 of the Income and Corporation Taxes Act 1988
274(4)	359 (twice)	842
274(4)	1970	1988

Enactment amended	Words to be omitted	Words to be substituted
In the Social Security (Northern Ireland) Order 1986 (S.I.No.1888 N.I.18)		
Article		
2(1)	365 (twice)	315
2(1)	1970	1988
24(5)	204	203
24(5)	1970	1988
Schedule		
6, para.1(2)	365	315
1(2)	1970	1988
In the Finance Act 1987 c. 16		
Section		
62(5)	258	413(3)
72	1970	1988
Schedule		
10, para.8(4)	533	839
para.8(4)	302	416
13, para.11(2)	533	839
14, para.10(2)	532	838
In the Debtors (Scotland) Act 1987 c. 18		
Section		
53(6)	65(1A)	351(2)
53(6)	1970	1988
63(9)	65(1A)	351(2)
63(9)	1970	1988
In the Abolition of Domestic Rates Etc. (Scotland) Act 1987 c. 47		
Section 3(5)	the whole of paragraph (b)	(b) "retail prices index" has the meaning given by section 833 of the Income and Corporation Taxes Act 1988
In the Finance (No.2) Act 1987 c. 51		
Section		
84(1)	247 of the Taxes Act	12 of the Income and Corporation Taxes Act 1988

SCHEDULE 30

TRANSITIONAL PROVISIONS AND SAVINGS

Corporation tax payment dates

1.—(1) In this paragraph, an "old company" means a company to which section 244 of the 1970 Act applied in respect of the last accounting period ending before 17th March 1987.

(2) In relation to an old company—

    (a) "the company's section 244 interval" means the interval after the end of an accounting period of the company which, in accordance with section 244 of the 1970 Act, was the period within which corporation tax assessed for that period was required to be paid; and

    (b) "the period of reduction" means the number of whole days which are comprised in a period equal to one-third of the difference between nine months and the company's section 244 interval.

(3) Subject to sub-paragraph (6) below, with respect to the first accounting period of an old company beginning on or after 17th March 1987, section 243(4) of the 1970 Act and section 10(1) of this Act (time for payment of corporation tax) shall have effect as if for the reference to nine months there were substituted a reference to a period which is equal to the company's section 244 interval less the period of reduction.

(4) Subject to sub-paragraph (6) below, with respect to any accounting period of an old company which begins—

    (a) after the accounting period referred to in sub-paragraph (3) above, but

    (b) before the second anniversary of the beginning of that period,

section 10(1) of this Act shall have effect as if for the reference to nine months there were substituted a reference to a period equal to the previous payment interval less the period of reduction.

(5) In relation to any accounting period of an old company falling within sub-paragraph (4) above, "the previous payment interval" means the interval after the end of the immediately preceding accounting period within which corporation tax for that preceding period is required to be paid by virtue of section 243(4) of the 1970 Act or section 10(1) of this Act, as modified by this paragraph.

(6) If the accounting period referred to in sub-paragraph (3) above or any accounting period falling within sub-paragraph (4) above is less than 12 months, the sub-paragraph in question shall have effect in relation to that accounting period as if for the reference in that sub-paragraph to the period of reduction there were substituted a reference to the number of whole days comprised in a period which bears to the period of reduction the same proportion as that accounting period bears to 12 months.

(7) With respect to any accounting period of an old company which falls within sub-paragraph (3) or (4) above, section 86(4) of the Management Act (interest on overdue tax) shall have effect as if, in paragraph 5(a) of the Table (the reckonable date in relation to corporation tax), the reference to the nine months mentioned in section 243(4) of the 1970 Act or section 10(1) of this Act were a reference to the period which, under sub-paragraphs (3) to (6) above, is substituted for those nine months.

(8) In section 88(5)(e) of the Management Act (the date when corporation tax ought to have been paid) for the words from "where section 244(1)" to "the interval" there shall be substituted "in the case of an accounting period in respect

of which section 10(1) of the principal Act applies as modified by sub-paragraph 1(3) or (4) of Schedule 30 to that Act, at the end of the period which, under that sub-paragraph, is substituted for the period of nine months".

(9) With respect to any accounting period of an old company which falls within sub-paragraph (3) or (4) above, section 825 shall have effect as if, in subsection (8) in paragraph (a) of the definition of "the material date", the reference to the nine months mentioned in section 10(1) were a reference to the period which, under sub-paragraphs (1) to (8) above is substituted for those nine months.

Duration of leases

2.—(1) Subject to sub-paragraph (2) and paragraph 3 below, section 38 has effect—

    (a) as respects a lease granted after 12th June 1969; and

    (b) so far as it relates to section 34(5), as respects a variation or waiver the contract for which is entered into after that date.

(2) So far as relates to relief under—

    (a) section 385 or 393; or

    (b) section 380(1) as applied by subsection (2) of that section; or

    (c) section 25(1);

given by setting a loss against, or making a deduction from, income of—

        (i) the year 1988-89 or any subsequent year of assessment, or

        (ii) a company's accounting period ending after 5th April 1988,

section 38 shall be deemed to have had effect as from the passing of the Finance Act 1963, and as respects leases granted at any time.

(3) Notwithstanding section 31 or any other enactment governing the order in which reliefs are given, in applying sub-paragraph (2) above it shall be assumed that all relief which could not be affected by the operation of that sub-paragraph was given (for all years of assessment and accounting periods before or after the passing of this Act) before relief which could be affected by the operation of that sub-paragraph.

(4) All such adjustments shall be made, whether by way of assessment or discharge of repayment of tax, as are required to give effect to section 38 with this paragraph.

3.—(1) Sections 24 and 38 shall have effect subject to the modifications set out in sub-paragraphs (2) to (4) below in relation to any lease granted after 12th June 1969 and before 25th August 1971 and, so far as section 38 relates to section 34(5), in relation to any variation or waiver the contract for which was entered into between those dates, except to the extent that section 38 affects the computation of the profits or gains or losses of a trade, profession or vocation or relates to relief under—

    (a) section 25(1);

    (b) section 385 or 393;

    (c) subsection (1) of section 380 as applied by subsection (2) of that section; or

    (d) section 779(5).

(2) In section 24, in subsection (1), in the definition of "premium", the words from "or to" to "landlord", and subsections (3) and (4) shall be omitted.

(3) In subsection (1) of section 38 the following paragraph shall be inserted before paragraph (a)—

> "(aa) where the terms of the lease include provision for the determination of the lease by notice given by the landlord, the lease shall not be treated as granted for a term longer than one ending at the earliest date on which it could be determined by notice so given;";

and sub-paragraph (ii) of paragraph (a) and paragraph (c) shall be omitted.

(4) In subsection (2) of that section for the words "Subsection (1)" there shall be substituted the words "Subsection (1)(a)", and subsection (4) of that section shall be omitted.

4.—(1) Where section 38 does not have effect, the following provisions of this paragraph shall apply in ascertaining the duration of a lease for the purposes of sections 34 to 36.

(2) Subject to sub-paragraph (4) below, where the terms of the lease include provision for the determination of the lease by notice given either by the landlord or by the tenant, the lease shall not be treated as granted for a term longer than one ending at the earliest date on which it could be determined by notice.

(3) Subject to sub-paragraph (4) below, where any of the terms of the lease (whether relating to forfeiture or to any other matter) or any other circumstances render it unlikely that the lease will continue beyond a date falling before the expiration of the term of the lease, the lease shall not be treated as having been granted for a term longer than one ending on that date.

(4) Where the duration of a lease falls to be ascertained after the date on which the lease has for any reason come to an end, the duration shall be taken to have extended from its commencement to that date, and where the duration falls to be ascertained at a time when the lease is subsisting the preceding provisions of this paragraph shall be applied in accordance with circumstances prevailing at that time.

(5) In relation to Scotland, "term" in this paragraph, where referring to the duration of a lease, means "period".

(6) This paragraph shall be construed as one with Part II.

Repeal of section 136 of the Income Tax Act 1952: allowance of annual value of land as a business expense

5.—(1) This paragraph has effect for allowing deductions by reference to those which would have fallen to be made if section 136 of the Income Tax Act 1952 had applied for the years 1963-64 and 1964-65.

(2) Subject to the provisions of this paragraph, an allowance under this paragraph shall be made to the person ("the occupier") carrying on a trade where land which was occupied by him at any time before the end of the year 1962-63 for the purposes of the trade permanently ceases to be occupied by him for those purposes.

(3) The amount of the allowance shall be the excess of—

> (a) the aggregate of any deductions in respect of the annual value of the land which, by virtue of section 136, would have been made in computing the profits or gains of the trade for the years 1963-64 and 1964-65 but for section 29(1) of the Finance Act 1963 and the repeal by that Act of section 136;

over

> (b) the aggregate of any deductions relating to the land made in computing the profits or gains of the trade for those years, being—

(i) deductions permitted by section 29(2) of the Finance Act 1963, so far as made in respect of the period in respect of which the deductions mentioned in paragraph (a) above would have been made; or

(ii) deductions in respect of rent from which an amount representing tax was deducted under section 173 of the Income Tax Act 1952, so far as made in respect of that period.

(4) The allowance shall be made by—

(a) treating the amount of it as rent paid for the land by the occupier (in addition to any actual rent), becoming due from day to day during the period defined in sub-paragraph (5) below; and

(b) allowing deductions accordingly in computing the profits or gains of the trade chargeable under Case I of Schedule D for any chargeable period the profits or gains for which fall to be computed by reference to a period including the period defined in sub-paragraph (5) below or any part thereof.

(5) The period referred to in sub-paragraph (4) above is that ending when the land permanently ceases to be occupied by the occupier for the purposes of the trade, and of a duration, equal to the aggregate of—

(a) the number of months and fractions of months during which the land was occupied by him for the purposes of the trade in so much of the period by reference to which the profits or gains of the trade for the year 1963-64 fell to be computed as fell before the beginning of that year; and

(b) the number of months and fractions of months during which the land was so occupied in so much of the period by reference to which the profits or gains of the trade for the year 1964-65 fell to be computed as fell before the beginning of the year 1963-64.

(6) No allowance shall be made under this paragraph where the date on which the land permanently ceases to be occupied by the occupier for the purposes of the trade—

(a) falls within a chargeable period in which he permanently ceases to carry on the trade; or

(b) where the occupier is not a company, falls within a year of assessment and also within a period by reference to which the profits or gains of the trade for that year of assessment fall to be computed.

(7) Where, by reason of a change in the persons carrying on the trade, the trade falls to be treated for any of the purposes of the Income Tax Acts as permanently discontinued, a person engaged in carrying on the trade immediately before the change occurred who continues to be so engaged immediately after it occurred shall be treated for the purposes of this paragraph as not having been in occupation of the land at any time before it occurred.

(8) Where there has been a change in the persons carrying on the trade, but by virtue of section 113 of this Act or section 17(1) of the Finance Act 1954 (company reconstructions before introduction of corporation tax), the trade does not by reason of the change fall to be treated for any of the purposes of the Income Tax Acts as permanently discontinued, this paragraph (including this sub-paragraph) shall apply as if any occupation of the land before the change occurred by the persons carrying on the trade immediately before it occurred were occupation by the persons carrying on the trade immediately after it occurred.

(9) Where section 343(1) applies, then for the purposes of this paragraph any occupation of land for the purposes of the trade by the predecessor shall be treated as having been the occupation of the successor.

Subsection (6) of that section shall apply to this sub-paragraph as it applies to subsections (2) to (5) of that section, and in this paragraph "predecessor" and "successor" have the same meaning as in that section.

(10) Where section 518 has effect, then for the purposes of this paragraph any occupation of land for the purposes of the trade by the transferor shall be treated as having been the occupation of the transferee.

This sub-paragraph shall be construed as one with section 518.

(11) Sub-paragraphs (1) to (10) above shall apply in relation to a profession or vocation as they apply in relation to a trade, but as if the reference in sub-paragraph (4) to Case I of Schedule D were a reference to Case II of that Schedule.

(12) For the purposes of this paragraph, any occupation of land by the London Transport Board which was by virtue of paragraph 6 of Schedule 3 to the Finance Act 1970 immediately before the commencement of this Act treated as occupation by another body, shall continue to be so treated by virtue of this sub-paragraph.

Loss relief etc.

6.—(1) The substitution of this Act for the corresponding enactments repealed by this Act shall not alter the effect of any provision enacted before this Act (whether or not there is a corresponding provision in this Act) so far as it determines whether and to what extent—

    (a) losses or expenditure incurred in, or other amounts referable to, a chargeable period earlier than those to which this Act applies may be taken into account for any tax purposes in a chargeable period to which this Act applies; or

    (b) losses or expenditure incurred in, or other amounts referable to, a chargeable period to which this Act applies may be taken into account for any tax purposes in a chargeable period earlier than those to which this Act applies.

(2) Without prejudice to sub-paragraph (1) above, the repeals made by this Act shall not affect the following enactments (which are not re-enacted)—

    (a) section 27(4) of the Finance Act 1952 (restrictions on removal of six year time limit on carry forward of trading losses);

    (b) section 29(3) of the Finance Act 1953 (Isles of Scilly);

    (c) section 17 of, and Schedule 3 to, the Finance Act 1954 (company reconstructions before corporation tax) so far as in force by virtue of the saving in Part IV of Schedule 22 to the Finance Act 1965, and section 80(8) of the Finance Act 1965 (which amends Schedule 3 to the Finance Act 1954);

    (d) section 82(4) of the Finance Act 1965 (losses allowable against chargeable gains);

    (e) section 85 of the Finance Act 1965 (carry forward of surplus of franked investment income: dividends paid out of pre-1966-67 profits) and the enactments amending that section;

    (f) paragraph 25 of Schedule 15 to the Finance Act 1965 (continuity of elections for purposes of corporation tax);

    (g) paragraph 7 of Schedule 16 to the Finance Act 1965 (overseas trade corporations);

in so far as those enactments may be relevant to tax for any chargeable period to which this Act applies.

7.—(1) This paragraph shall apply with respect to claims for group relief in respect of any amount which is attributable—

(a) to writing-down allowances, within the meaning of Chapter II of Part I of the 1968 Act, or, as the case may require, Chapter I of Part III of the Finance Act 1971, in respect of expenditure incurred by the surrendering company on the provision of machinery or plant; or

(b) to initial allowances under section 56 of the 1968 Act (expenditure in connection with mines etc.) in respect of expenditure incurred by the surrendering company and falling within section 52(1) of that Act of 1971 (works in a development area or in Northern Ireland); or

(c) to allowances under section 91 of the 1968 Act in respect of expenditure incurred by the surrendering company on scientific research;

where the expenditure is incurred under a contract entered into by the surrendering company before 6th March 1973.

(2) Notwithstanding anything in section 410(1) to (6) or 413(7) to (10) or in Schedule 18 but subject to sub-paragraph (5) below, group relief may be claimed in respect of any such amount as is referred to in sub-paragraph (1) above if—

(a) immediately before 6th March 1973—

(i) the surrendering company and the company claiming relief were members of a group of companies, and

(ii) throughout the period beginning on that date and ending at the end of the accounting period in respect of which the claim is made, there is no reduction in the rights of the parent company with respect to the matters specified in section 413(7)(a) and (b); or

(b) immediately before 6th March 1973 the company claiming relief was a member of a consortium and, throughout the period beginning on that date and ending at the end of the accounting period in respect of which the claim is made, there is—

(i) no variation in the percentage of the ordinary share capital of the company owned by the consortium which is beneficially owned by that member, and

(ii) no reduction in the rights of that member (in respect of the company owned by the consortium) with respect to the matters specified in section 413(7)(a) and (b);

and in either case no such arrangements as are specified in section 410(1) or (2) have come into existence after 5th March 1973 with respect to any of the companies concerned and no variation is made in any such arrangements which are in existence on that date with respect to any of those companies.

(3) For the purposes of sub-paragraph (2)(a) above, "the parent company" means the company of which another member of the group referred to in that sub-paragraph was, immediately before 6th March 1973, a 75 per cent subsidiary, and the rights of the parent company referred to in that paragraph are—

(a) if the parent company is either the surrendering company or the company claiming relief, its rights in the other company; and

(b) in any other case, its rights in both the surrendering company and the company claiming relief.

(4) For the purposes of this paragraph an amount which the claimant company claims by way of group relief shall be treated as attributable to an allowance falling within any of paragraphs (a) to (c) of sub-paragraph (1) above to the extent that that amount would not have been available for surrender by the surrendering company if no such allowance had been available to the surrendering company in respect of the expenditure concerned.

(5) Sub-paragraph (2) above shall not apply if, during the period referred to in that sub-paragraph—

(a) there is a major change in the nature or conduct of a trade or business carried on by the relevant company; or

(b) the relevant company sets up and commences a trade or business which it did not carry on immediately before 6th March 1973.

(6) In sub-paragraph (5) above—

"a major change in the nature or conduct of a trade or business" has the same meaning as in section 245(1); and

"the relevant company" means, if the machinery or plant to which the allowance relates was brought into use on or before 6th March 1978, the company claiming group relief and in any other case either that company or the company which if sub-paragraph (5) did not apply would be the surrendering company.

(7) This paragraph shall be construed as if it were contained in Chapter IV of Part X.

Capital allowances

8. Without prejudice to paragraphs 6 and 7 above, where a person is, immediately before the commencement of this Act, entitled to a capital allowance by virtue of any enactment repealed by this Act, he shall not cease to be so entitled by reason only of that repeal, notwithstanding that the enactment in question is not re-enacted by this Act; and accordingly the provisions of this Act shall apply, with any necessary modifications, so far as may be necessary to give effect to any such entitlement.

Social security benefits

9.—(1) In relation to any period before regulations containing the first schemes under section 20 of the Social Security Act 1986 and Article 21 of the Social Security (Northern Ireland) Order 1986 providing for income support come into force—

1986 c. 50.
S.I. 1986/1888 (N.I.18).

(a) the repeal by this Act of sections 27 and 28 of the Finance Act 1981 shall not have effect;

1981 c. 35.

(b) sections 151 and 152 of this Act shall not have effect;

(c) section 204 of this Act shall have effect with the substitution for paragraph (b) of the following paragraph—

"(b) he has claimed a payment of supplementary allowance under the Supplementary Benefits Act 1976 or the Supplementary Benefits (Northern Ireland) Order 1977 in respect of a period including that time and his right to the allowance is subject to any condition contained in section 5 of the said Act of 1976 or, in Northern Ireland, Article 7 of the said Order (requirements as to registration and availability for employment)"

and with the addition at the end of the following—

"(2) Any reference in this section to section 5 of the Supplementary Benefits Act 1976 or to Article 7 of the Supplementary Benefits (Northern Ireland) Order 1977 includes a reference to that section or Article as amended by any other enactment including an enactment passed or made after the passing of this Act"; and

(d) section 617(2) of this Act shall have effect with the substitution for paragraph (a) of the following paragraphs—

"(a) payments of benefit under the Supplementary Benefits Act 1976 or the Supplementary Benefits (Northern Ireland) Order 1977 other than payments of supplementary allowance which are taxable by virtue of section 27 of the Finance Act 1981;

(aa) payments by way of an allowance under section 70 of the Social Security Act 1975 or section 70 of the Social Security (Northern Ireland) Act 1975;".

1986 c. 50.

S.I. 1986/1888 (N.I.18).

(2) In relation to any period before regulations containing the first schemes under section 20 of the Social Security Act 1986 and Article 21 of the Social Security (Northern Ireland) Order 1986 providing for family credit come into force, section 617(2) of this Act shall have effect with the addition after paragraph (b) of the following paragraph—

"(bb) payments in respect of family income supplement under the Family Income Supplements Act 1970 or the Family Income Supplements Act (Northern Ireland) 1970;".

Children's settlements: irrevocable dispositions made before 22nd April 1936

10.—(1) Sub-paragraph (2) below applies to any disposition which—

(a) was made, directly or indirectly, by any person ("the settlor") after 5th April 1914 and before 22nd April 1936, and

(b) immediately before 22nd April 1936, was an irrevocable settlement within the meaning of Chapter II of Part XV.

(2) Subject to the provisions of this paragraph, any income which, by virtue or in consequence of any disposition to which this sub-paragraph applies, is payable to or applicable for the benefit of a child of the settlor for some period less than the life of the child, shall, if and so long as the child is an infant and unmarried, be deemed for all purposes of the Income Tax Acts to be the income of the settlor, if living and not to be the income of any other person.

(3) Sub-paragraph (2) above shall not apply as regards any income—

(a) which is derived from capital which, at the end of the period during which that income is payable to or applicable for the benefit of the child, is required by the disposition to be held on trust absolutely for, or to be transferred to, the child; or

(b) which is payable to or applicable for the benefit of a child during the whole period of the life of the settlor.

(4) Income shall not be deemed, for the purposes of this paragraph, to be payable to or applicable for the benefit of a child for some period less than its life by reason only that the disposition contains a provision for the payment to some other person of the income in the event of the bankruptcy of the child, or of an assignment thereof, or a charge thereon, being executed by the child.

(5) In this paragraph, unless the context otherwise requires—

"child" includes a step-child or an illegitimate child, and

"disposition" includes any trust, covenant, agreement or arrangement.

(6) Sections 661 and 662 shall apply as if this paragraph were contained in Chapter I of Part XV, and this paragraph, notwithstanding that it is referred to in Chapter II of that Part, shall not be construed as one with that Chapter.

Pre-1959 settlements

11.—(1) Where, in the case of any settlement made before 16th April 1958, any sums payable by the settlor or by the wife or husband of the settlor would, by virtue only of section 671(3), fall to be treated as the income of the settlor and not as the income of any other person, the sums shall not be so treated if—

(a) no power by reason of which they would fall to be so treated has been exercised after 15th April 1958, or is or can become exercisable after 5th April 1959, or such later date as the Board may in any particular case allow, and

(b) neither the settlor nor the wife or husband of the settlor has received or is entitled to any consideration or benefit in connection with the fulfilment of the condition set out in paragraph (a) above,

or if the settlement was entered into in connection with any judicial separation or any agreement between spouses to live separate and apart, or with the dissolution or annulment of a marriage.

(2) Where, in the case of any settlement made before 16th April 1958, any income arising under the settlement would, by virtue only of section 672(3), fall to be treated as the income of the settlor and not as the income of any other person, the income shall not be so treated if—

(a) no power by reason of which it would fall to be so treated has been exercised after 15th April 1958 or is or can become exercisable after 5th April 1959, or such later date as the Board may in any particular case allow; and

(b) neither the settlor nor the wife or husband of the settlor has received or is entitled to any consideration or benefit in connection with the fulfilment of the condition set out in paragraph (a) above.

12. Where, in the case of any settlement made before 9th July 1958, any income arising under the settlement would, by virtue only of section 674, fall to be treated as the income of the settlor and not as the income of any other person, it shall not be so treated if—

(a) no power by reason of which it would fall to be so treated has been exercised after 8th July 1958, or is or can become exercisable after 5th April 1959, or such later date as the Board may in any particular case allow; and

(b) neither the settlor nor the wife or husband of the settlor has received or is entitled to any consideration or benefit in connection with the fulfilment of the condition set out in paragraph (a) above.

General powers of amendment in Acts relating to overseas countries

13. Where under any Act passed before this Act and relating to a country or territory outside the United Kingdom there is a power to affect Acts passed or in force before a particular time, or instruments made or having effect under such Acts, and the power would but for the passing of this Act have included power to change the law which is reproduced in, or is made or has effect under, this Act, then that power shall include power to make such provision as will secure the like change in the law reproduced in, or made or having effect under, this Act notwithstanding that it is not an Act passed or in force before that time.

Double taxation agreements

1979 c.47.   14. The repeal by this Act of section 16 of the Finance (No.2) Act 1979 shall not prejudice the effect of any Order in Council which gives effect to arrangements contained in the Convention mentioned in that section and is made under section 497 of the 1970 Act.

Securities

1985 c. 54.   15. The repeal by this Act of Schedule 22 to the Finance Act 1985 shall not affect the continued operation of paragraph 6 of that Schedule in relation to the holding of securities by any person at any time during the year (within the meaning of that Schedule).

Building societies

16. Any enactment relating to building societies contained in this Act which re-enacts an enactment which was an existing enactment for the purposes of section 121 of the Building Societies Act 1986 shall continue to be an existing enactment for those purposes.

1986 c. 53.

Pension business

17. Any reference to pension business in any enactment (other than an enactment repealed by this Act) which immediately before the commencement of this Act was such a reference by virtue of paragraph 11(3) of Part III of Schedule 5 to the Finance Act 1970 shall not be affected by the repeal by this Act of that paragraph and accordingly the business in question shall continue to be known as pension business.

1970 c. 24.

Stock relief

1981 c. 35.   18. Schedule 9 to the Finance Act 1981 shall continue to have effect in relation to any relief to which paragraph 9 or 17(1) of that Schedule applied immediately before the commencement of this Act notwithstanding the repeal by this Act of that Schedule.

Schedule E emoluments

1974 c. 30.   19. The repeal by this Act of section 21 of the Finance Act 1974 shall not affect the taxation of emoluments which if that section had been in force before 1973-74 would have fallen within Case I or Case II of Schedule E, and, accordingly, any such emoluments shall not be chargeable under Case III of Schedule E.

Unitary states

20. The repeal by this Act of section 54 of and Schedule 13 to the Finance Act 1985 shall not prevent the Treasury making an order under subsection (7) of section 54 exercising the powers conferred on the Treasury by that subsection in relation to distributions made in chargeable periods ending before 6th April 1988 and, accordingly, subsections (7) and (8) of section 54 shall continue to have effect in later chargeable periods for that purpose.

Continuity and construction of references to old and new law

21.—(1) The continuity of the operation of the Tax Acts and of the law relating to chargeable gains shall not be affected by the substitution of this Act for the enactments repealed by this Act and earlier enactments repealed by and corresponding to any of those enactments ("the repealed enactments").

(2) Any reference, whether express or implied, in any enactment, instrument or document (including this Act and any Act amended by this Act) to, or to things done or falling to be done under or for the purposes of, any provision of this Act shall, if and so far as the nature of the reference permits, be construed as including, in relation to the times, years or periods, circumstances or purposes in relation to which the corresponding provision in the repealed enactments has or had effect, a reference to, or as the case may be to things done or falling to be done under or for the purposes of, that corresponding provision.

(3) Any reference, whether express or implied, in any enactment, instrument or document (including the repealed enactments and enactments, instruments and documents passed or made after the passing of this Act) to, or to things done or falling to be done under or for the purposes of, any of the repealed enactments shall, if and so far as the nature of the reference permits, be construed as including, in relation to the times, years or periods, circumstances or purposes in relation to which the corresponding provision in this Act has effect, a reference to, or as the case may be to things done or falling to be done under or for the purposes of, that corresponding provision.

(4) Any reference to Case VIII of Schedule D, whether a specific reference or one imported by more general words, in any enactment, instrument or document shall, in relation to the chargeable periods to which section 843(1) applies, be construed as a reference to Schedule A, and for the purposes of sub-paragraph (2) above, Schedule A in this Act shall be treated as corresponding to Case VIII of Schedule D in the repealed enactments, and any provision of this Act or of any Act passed after 12th March 1970 and before this Act referring to Schedule A shall be construed accordingly.

SCHEDULE 31

REPEALS

Chapter	Short title	Extent of repeal
1965 c. 25.	Finance Act 1965	Section 84. Schedule 20.
1969 c. 32.	Finance Act 1969	In section 52(1) the words from "or through" to the end.
1970 c. 9.	Taxes Management Act 1970	In section 88(5)(e) the words from "or" to the end. In section 118(1)(a) the words from "as" to "Act". In Schedule 2, in paragraph 2(2), the words "section 311".
1970 c. 10.	Income and Corporation Taxes Act 1970	Sections 1 to 237. Section 238(1) to (3). Sections 239 to 266. Section 277. Sections 282 to 305. Sections 307 to 341A. Sections 343 to 535. Schedules 1 to 13. In Schedule 14, paragraphs 1 to 10 and 12 to 27. In Schedule 15, in Part II of the Table in paragraph 11 the entry relating to the Finance Act 1969. Schedule 16.
1970 c. 24.	Finance Act 1970.	Sections 11 to 14. Section 16. Sections 19 to 26. Section 29(1), (2), (3)(a), (4) and (8). In Schedule 3, paragraphs 2 to 7. In Schedule 4, paragraphs 6, 8, 9(6) and 11. Schedule 5.
1970 c. 54.	Income and Corporation Taxes (No.2) Act 1970	The whole Act.
1971 c. 68.	Finance Act 1971	Sections 13 to 20. Section 21(1) to (5). Sections 22 to 28. Sections 32 to 36. Section 39. Section 50(8). Section 54. Schedule 2. Schedule 3, except paragraph 8. Schedule 4. In Schedule 6, Parts I and III.

Chapter	Short title	Extent of repeal
		Schedule 7. In Schedule 8, paragraph 16(3) to (9). In Schedule 9, paragraph 4.
1972 c. 41.	Finance Act 1972	Sections 62 to 66. Section 67(2)(c). Sections 70 to 77. Sections 79 to 95. Sections 97 to 110. Section 111(2). Section 124. Schedules 9 to 23. In Schedule 24, paragraphs 15 to 33.
1973 c. 51.	Finance Act 1973	Sections 10 to 31. In section 32, subsection (5) and in subsection (6) the words from "sections" to "1972". Sections 33 to 36. In section 38, in subsection (1) the words "income tax" and "and corporation tax" and subsection (6). Sections 39 and 40. Section 43. Sections 52 and 53. In section 54(1) the words "income tax, corporation tax or". Schedules 8 to 14. In Schedule 15, paragraphs 1 and 3. Schedule 16. In Schedule 21, paragraphs 6 to 9.
1974 c. 30.	Finance Act 1974	Sections 7 to 16. Sections 18 to 23. Sections 25 to 28. Section 30. Sections 36 and 37. In section 52 the words "the Income Tax Acts, the Corporation Tax Acts and". Schedules 1 and 2. In Schedule 12, paragraphs 7 to 12.
1974 c. 39.	Consumer Credit Act 1974	In Schedule 4, paragraph 29.
1974 c. 44	Housing Act 1974	Section 120.
1974 c. 46.	Friendly Societies Act 1974	Section 64. In Schedule 9, paragraph 23.

Chapter	Short title	Extent of repeal
1974 c. 49.	Insurance Companies Act 1974	In Schedule 1, the entry relating to the Income and Corporation Taxes Act 1970.
1975 c. 7.	Finance Act 1975	Sections 5 to 12. Sections 16 and 17. Schedules 1 and 2. In Schedule 12, paragraphs 16 and 19.
1975 c. 18.	Social Security (Consequential Provisions) Act 1975	In Schedule 2, paragraphs 38 and 39.
1975 c. 22.	Oil Taxation Act 1975	Sections 13 to 20. Schedule 9.
1975 c. 45.	Finance (No. 2) Act 1975	Sections 25 to 43. Section 44(1) to (3) and (6). Section 46(6). In section 47, in subsection (1) the words "income tax or" and subsections (3), (5) to (7), (9) and (10). Section 48. Sections 50 to 53. Sections 68 to 71. Schedule 8. Schedules 12 and 13.
1976 c. 40.	Finance Act 1976	Sections 24 to 38. Sections 44 to 50. Sections 60 to 71. Section 72(1) to (12). Schedules 4, 7 and 8. In Schedule 9, paragraphs 3, 4, 8, 9 and 12 to 16.
1976 c. 71.	Supplementary Benefits Act 1976	In Schedule 7, paragraph 16.
1977 c. 36.	Finance Act 1977	Sections 17 to 39. Sections 45 to 48. Schedules 7 and 8.
1977 c. 49.	National Health Service Act 1977	In Schedule 15, paragraph 57.
1977 c. 53.	Finance (Income Tax Reliefs) Act 1977	The whole Act.
1978 c. 23.	Judicature (Northern Ireland) Act 1978	In Schedule 5, the entry relating to the Income and Corporation Taxes Act 1970.
1978 c. 29.	National Health Service (Scotland) Act 1978	In Schedule 16, paragraph 37.
1978 c. 42.	Finance Act 1978	Sections 13 to 28. Section 29(1), (2) and (4). Sections 30 to 36. Sections 41 to 43. Sections 53 to 61. Schedules 2 to 5. Schedule 9.

Chapter	Short title	Extent of repeal
1978 c. 44.	Employment Protection (Consolidation) Act 1978	In Schedule 16, paragraphs 9 and 14.
1979 c. 14.	Capital Gains Tax Act 1979	Section 155(5). In Schedule 7, paragraph 5; in paragraph 8, in Part I of the Table, the entries relating to sections 265, 352 and 526 of the 1970 Act, the Finance Act 1972, section 29 of the Finance Act 1970, section 67 of the Finance Act 1976 and section 45 of the Finance Act 1977, and paragraph 3 in Part II of the Table; and in paragraph 9 the entries relating to sections 186, 246, 265, 266, 305, 352, 359, 360, 474, 488 and 489 of the 1970 Act, the Finance Act 1972, the Finance Act 1973, sections 26 and 30 of the Finance Act 1974, section 42 of and Schedule 8 to the Finance (No. 2) Act 1975, section 67 of the Finance Act 1976 and the Finance Act 1978 (except section 64(5)).
1979 c. 25.	Finance Act 1979	The whole Act.
1979 c. 34.	Credit Unions Act 1979	Section 25.
1979 c. 47.	Finance (No.2) Act 1979	Sections 5 to 13. Sections 15 and 16. In section 17(1) the words "income tax, corporation tax and". Schedules 1 and 2.
1980 c. 48.	Finance Act 1980	Sections 18 to 56. Section 57(1), (2)(b), (3) and (4). Sections 59 and 60. Section 61(1). Section 63. Section 70(1), (2), (4), (5) and (6). Section 88(7). Section 109(11). Section 118(1) and (2). Section 119. Section 121. Schedules 8 to 11. In Schedule 18, paragraphs 1 to 8, 13, 14 and 17 to 22 and, in paragraph 23, in sub-paragraph (1) the definitions of "control"

Chapter	Short title	Extent of repeal
		and "distributing company", in the definition of "group" the words "except in paragraph 7(2)(c)" and from "and" to the end, and all the subsequent definitions except that of "shares", and sub-paragraphs (2) and (4).
1981 c. 35.	Finance Act 1981	Sections 19 to 37. Section 38(1) and (2). Sections 39 to 72. Section 120. Section 138. Schedules 9 to 12.
1981 c. 61.	British Nationality Act 1981	In Schedule 7, the entry relating to the Income and Corporation Taxes Act 1970.
1981 c. 64.	New Towns Act 1981	In Schedule 12, paragraph 16.
1982 c. 39.	Finance Act 1982	Sections 20 to 26. Sections 28 to 67. Section 78. Section 80(4). Section 136. Section 137(4) and (5). Section 138. In section 157(5) the words from "or" to "of that Act". Schedules 7 to 10. In Schedule 21, paragraph 3(1).
1982 c. 50.	Insurance Companies Act 1982	In Schedule 5, paragraphs 10, 17, 24, 25 and 28(b).
1982 c. 52.	Industrial Development Act 1982	In Schedule 2, paragraphs 16 and 18.
1982 c. 53.	Administration of Justice Act 1982	Sections 46(2)(e) and 74.
1983 c. 21.	Pilotage Act 1983	In Schedule 3, paragraph 10.
1983 c. 28.	Finance Act 1983	Sections 10 to 28. Section 46(1), (2) and (3)(a) and (b). Schedules 4 and 5.
1983 c. 49.	Finance (No. 2) Act 1983	Sections 1 to 5. Schedule 1.
1983 c. 56.	Oil Taxation Act 1983	Section 11.
1984 c. 12.	Telecommunications Act 1984	In Schedule 4, paragraph 62.
1984 c. 28.	County Courts Act 1984	In Schedule 2, paragraph 37.
1984 c. 43.	Finance Act 1984	Sections 17 to 43. In section 44, in subsection (1) the words from "256" to "relief) and" and subsection (3).

Chapter	Short title	Extent of repeal
		Sections 45 to 49. Section 50(10)(a) and (c). Sections 51 to 55. In section 56, subsections (1) and (2) and in subsection (4) the words from the beginning to "assessment and". Section 72. In section 73, subsections (1) to (3), (5) and (6). Sections 74 to 77. In section 79, in subsection (5) the words from "and in relation" to the end. Sections 82 to 100. Section 126(3)(a). Schedules 7 to 10. In Schedule 11, paragraphs 1(2)(a) to (e) and (j), 2 and 3 and in paragraph 7 the words "income tax, corporation tax or". In Schedule 13, paragraph 5. In Schedule 14, paragraph 15(4). Schedules 15 to 20.
1984 c. 48.	Health and Social Security Act 1984	In Schedule 4, paragraph 2.
1984 c. 51.	Inheritance Tax Act 1984	In Schedule 8, paragraphs 8, 17, 18, 21 and 22.
1984 c. 62.	Friendly Societies Act 1984	Section 2(4), (5)(a) and (b) and (6).
1985 c. 54.	Finance Act 1985	Sections 34 to 49. Sections 51 to 54. Section 60. Sections 64 and 65. In section 72, in subsection (1), paragraph (b) and "and" immediately preceding it, and subsection (7). Sections 73 to 77. Schedules 9 to 13. In Schedule 14, paragraph 16. Schedule 18. Schedules 22 and 23. In Schedule 25, paragraphs 7, 8 and 9.
1985 c. 58.	Trustee Savings Bank Act 1985	In Schedule 2, paragraphs 6(3) and (5) to (7) and 7(1), and in paragraph 9 the definition of "exempt investment".
1985 c. 71.	Housing (Consequential Provisions) Act 1985	In Schedule 2, paragraphs 18(2) and (3), 28, 31 and 54(2).

Chapter	Short title	Extent of repeal
1985 c. 73.	Law Reform (Miscellaneous Provisions) (Scotland) Act 1985	In Schedule 1, paragraph 38.
1986 c. 39.	Patents, Designs and Marks Act 1986	In Schedule 2, paragraph 1(2)(c).
1986 c. 41.	Finance Act 1986	Sections 16 to 23. Section 24(1) to (3). Sections 25 to 32. Sections 34 to 54. Section 56(7)(a) and (b). Sections 61 to 63. Schedules 7 and 8. In Schedule 9, paragraphs 1 to 21 and 23. Schedules 10, 11 and 12. In Schedules 13, paragraphs 2(5)(a) and (b) and 26 and 27. In Schedule 16, paragraph 10(7). Schedule 17. In Schedule 18, paragraphs 1 to 6, in paragraph 9(1), paragraph (a) and in paragraph (c) the words "section 477 or" and paragraph 9(2).
1986 c. 45.	Insolvency Act 1986	In Schedule 14 the entries relating to the Income and Corporation Taxes Act 1970, the Finance Act 1972, the Finance Act 1981 and the Finance Act 1983.
1986 c. 50.	Social Security Act 1986	In Schedule 10, paragraphs 71 and 101.
1986 c. 53.	Building Societies Act 1986	In Schedule 18, paragraphs 7 and 15.
1987 c. 16.	Finance Act 1987	Sections 20 to 39. Section 40(1) and (2). Sections 41 to 46. Section 70(1). Section 71. Schedules 3 to 6. In Schedule 11, paragraphs 6 and 7. Schedule 15, except paragraph 12.
1987 c. 22.	Banking Act 1987	In Schedule 6, paragraphs 13, 16 and 24.
1987 c. 45.	Parliamentary and other Pensions Act 1987	In Schedule 3, paragraphs 2 and 5.
1987 c. 51.	Finance (No. 2) Act 1987	Sections 1 to 63. Section 64(2). Sections 65 to 68. Sections 70 and 71.

Chapter	Short title	Extent of repeal
		In section 73(1) the words "income tax, corporation tax or".
		Sections 74 to 77.
		Section 87.
		In section 88, subsections (5) and (6) and the words following paragraph (c) in subsection (7).
		Section 90.
		Sections 92 and 93.
		Schedules 1 to 5.
		In Schedule 6, paragraphs 1, 3, 6 and 8.

Arms Control and Disarmament (Privileges and Immunities) Act 1988

1988 CHAPTER 2

An Act to provide for conferring privileges and immunities on observers, inspectors and auxiliary personnel exercising functions under international agreements or arrangements for furthering arms control or disarmament.   [9th February 1988]

BE IT ENACTED by the Queen's most Excellent Majesty, by and with the advice and consent of the Lords Spiritual and Temporal, and Commons, in this present Parliament assembled, and by the authority of the same, as follows:—

1.—(1) The Diplomatic Privileges Act 1964 shall have effect as if in Schedule 1 to that Act—

Privileges and immunities for observers, inspectors etc. 1964 c. 81.

(a) references to a diplomatic agent included references to any person designated by a State other than the United Kingdom as an observer or inspector under the Stockholm Document; and

(b) references to the members of the administrative and technical staff, or of the service staff, of a mission included references to persons designated as aforesaid as auxiliary personnel for an inspection carried out under that document and performing administrative and technical or, as the case may be, domestic services.

(2) Her Majesty may by Order in Council confer such privileges and immunities (not exceeding those conferred by the said Act of 1964) as appear to Her Majesty to be required for giving effect to any provision of an international agreement or arrangement superseding the Stockholm Document or otherwise making provision for furthering arms control or disarmament; but no such Order shall be made unless a draft of it has been laid before and approved by a resolution of each House of Parliament.

(3) If in any proceedings any question arises whether or not any person is entitled to any privilege or immunity by virtue of this Act a certificate issued by or under the authority of the Secretary of State stating any fact relating to that question shall be conclusive evidence of that fact.

(4) In this section "the Stockholm Document" means the document dated 19th September 1986 and concluded at the Stockholm Conference on confidence and security building measures and disarmament in Europe.

Short title and extent.

2.—(1) This Act may be cited as the Arms Control and Disarmament (Privileges and Immunities) Act 1988.

(2) This Act extends to Northern Ireland.

(3) Her Majesty may by Order in Council provide for this Act to extend, with such modifications as may be specified in the Order, to any of the Channel Islands, the Isle of Man or any colony.

INDEX

TO THE

PUBLIC GENERAL ACTS

AND

GENERAL SYNOD MEASURES 1988

A

B

C

CHAPTER IV

MORAL RIGHTS

Right to be identified as author or director

Chapter III

Exceptions to Rights of Design Right Owners

Infringement of copyright

Availability of licences of right

Crown use of designs

General

Chapter IV

Jurisdiction of the Comptroller and the Court

Jurisdiction of the comptroller

Jurisdiction of the court

Chapter V

Miscellaneous and General

Miscellaneous

Extent of operation of this Part

Interpretation

Part IV

Registered Designs

Amendments of the Registered Designs Act 1949

PART I

CONSTITUTION AND ADMINISTRATION OF THE COURT

§ 1. Number of judges of Court, II, p. 1783.
  2. Composition of Court, II, p. 1784.
  3. Exchequer causes, II, p. 1784.
  4. Power of judges to act in cases relating to rates and taxes, II, p. 1784.

PART II

GENERAL POWERS OF THE COURT IN RELATION TO PROCEDURE

  5. Power to regulate procedure etc. by act of sederunt, II, p. 1785.
  6. Allocation of business etc. by act of sederunt, II, p. 1786.
  7. Fees on remit to accountants etc., II, p. 1786.
  8. Rules Council, II, p. 1787.

PART III

ORDINARY ACTIONS

Proof

  9. Allowing of proof by Lord Ordinary, II, p. 1787.
  10. Evidence on commission in Outer House, II, p. 1787.
  11. Jury actions, II, p. 1788.

Trial by jury

  12. Summoning of jury, II, p. 1788.
  13. Selection of jury, II, p. 1788.
  14. Application of view by jury, II, p. 1788.
  15. Illness or death of juror during trial, II, p. 1788.
  16. Trial to proceed despite objection to opinion and direction of judge, II, p. 1789.
  17. Return of verdict, II, p. 1789.

Judgment

  18. Lord Ordinary's judgment final in Outer House, II, p. 1789.

PART IV

OTHER CAUSES

Consistorial causes

  19. Lord Advocate as party to action for nullity of marriage or divorce, II, p. 1789.
  20. Orders with respect to children, II, p. 1789.

Exchequer causes

  21. Exchequer causes to have precedence, II, p. 1790.
  22. Lord Advocate to sue and be sued on behalf of the Crown, II, p. 1790.
  23. Lord Advocate may be heard last, II, p. 1790.
  24. Appeal to House of Lords, II, p. 1790.

E

B

G

H

PART I

RENTED ACCOMMODATION

CHAPTER I

ASSURED TENANCIES

Meaning of assured tenancy etc.

1 and Sch. 1.   Assured tenancies, IV, pp. 2915, 3025.
2.   Letting of a dwelling-house together with other land, IV, p. 2917.
3.   Tenant sharing accommodation with persons other than landlord, IV, p. 2917.
4.   Certain sublettings not to exclude any part of sublessor's premises from assured tenancy, IV, p. 2918.

Security of tenure

5.   Security of tenure, IV, p. 2918.
6.   Fixing of terms of statutory periodic tenancy, IV, p. 2919.
7 and Sch. 1.   Orders for possession, IV, pp. 2921, 3030.
8.   Notice of proceedings for possessions, IV, p. 2921.
9.   Extended discretion of court in possession claims, IV, p. 2922.
10.   Special provisions applicable to shared accommodation, IV, p. 2923.
11.   Payment of removal expenses in certain cases, IV, p. 2924.
12.   Compensation for misrepresentation of concealment, IV, p. 2924.

Rent and other terms

13.   Increases of rent under assured periodic tenancies, IV, p. 2924.
14.   Determination of rent by rent assessment committee, IV, p. 2925.
15.   Limited prohibition on assignment etc. without consent, IV, p. 2927.
16.   Access for repairs, IV, p. 2927.

Miscellaneous

17.   Succession to assured periodic tenancy by spouse, IV, p. 2927.
18.   Provisions as to reversions on assured tenancies, IV, p. 2928.
19.   Restriction on levy of distress for rent, IV, p. 2929.

CHAPTER II

ASSURED SHORTHOLD TENANCIES

20.   Assured shorthold tenancies, IV, p. 2929.
21.   Recovery of possession on expiry or termination of assured shorthold tenancy, IV, p. 2930.
22.   Reference of excessive rents to rent assessment committee, IV, p. 2931.
23.   Termination of rent assessment committee's functions, IV, p. 2932.

CHAPTER III

ASSURED AGRICULTURAL OCCUPANCIES

24 and Sch. 3.   Assured agricultural occupancies, IV, pp. 2932, 3036.
25.   Security of tenure, IV, p. 2932.
26.   Rehousing of agricultural workers etc., IV, p. 2933.

CHAPTER IV

PROTECTION FROM EVICTION

27.   Damages for unlawful eviction, IV, p. 2933.
28.   The measure of damages, IV, p. 2935.
29.   Offences of harassment, IV, p. 2936.
30.   Variation of scope of 1977 ss. 3 and 4, IV, p. 2937.

Part IV

Change of Landlord: Secure Tenants

Preliminary

I

PART I

THE CHARGE TO TAX

Income tax

Corporation tax

Small companies' rate

Advance corporation tax

The six Schedules

PART II

PROVISIONS RELATING TO THE SCHEDULE A CHARGE AND THE ASSOCIATED SCHEDULE D CHARGES

General

Deductions and other allowances

Premiums, leases at undervalue etc.

Supplemental: Schedules A and D

CHAPTER III

PROFIT-RELATED PAY

Preliminary

The relief

Registration

Administration

Supplementary

CHAPTER IV

OTHER EXEMPTIONS AND RELIEFS

Share option and profit sharing schemes

Retirement benefits etc.

Foreign emoluments and earnings, pensions and certain travel facilities

Other expenses, subscriptions etc.

C

L

> § 1.   Open register, II, p. 1041.
>   2 and Sch.   Repeals, II, pp. 1042, 1043.
>   3.   Short title, commencement and extent, II, p. 1042.

> § 1.   Qualified duty to consent to assigning, underletting etc. of premises, II, p. 1501.
>   2.   Duty to pass on applications, II, p. 1502.
>   3.   Qualified duty to approve consent by another, II, p. 1502.
>   4.   Breach of duty, II, p. 1503.
>   5.   Interpretation, II, p. 1503.
>   6.   Application to Crown, II, p. 1504.
>   7.   Short title, commencement and extent, II, p. 1504.

PART I

PRELIMINARY

> § 1.   Purpose of this Act, II, p. 1713.
>   2.   Interpretation, II, p. 1713.

PART II

LEGAL AID BOARD AND LEGAL AID

> 3 and Sch. 1.   The Legal Aid Board, II, pp. 1714, 1747.
>   4.   Powers of the Board, II, p. 1715.
>   5.   Duties of the Board, II, p. 1716.
>   6.   Board to have separate legal aid fund, II, p. 1717.
>   7.   Accounts and audit, II, p. 1718.

PART III

ADVICE AND ASSISTANCE

> 8.   Scope of this Part, II, p. 1718.
>   9.   Availability of, and payment for, advice and assistance, II, p. 1719.

P

PARLIAMENT—

Orders, regulations etc., subject to annulment on resolution of either House of Parliament, Under—

Housing Scotland Act (c. 43, ss. 3(4), 40 (adding s.23A(6) to 1984 c.58), 41(3), 53(2), 56(8), sch. 1 para. 10(4)) ... ... III, pp. 2520, 2542, 2549, 2551, 2565

Immigration Act (c. 14, ss. 5(3), 9(3)) ... ... II, pp. 1319, 1321

Legal Aid Act (c. 34, s. 36(2)(*a*)) ... ... II, p. 1741

Local Government Act (c. 9, ss. 15(2)(3), 20(5))... ... ... II, pp. 1148, 1155

Local Government Finance Act (c. 41, s. 143(3)) ... ... III, p. 2406

Malicious Communications Act (c. 27, s. 2(*b*)) ... ... II, p. 1506

Merchant Shipping Act (c. 12, ss. 11(4)(*b*), 53(1)) ... ... II, pp. 1203, 1243

Norfolk and Suffolk Broads Act (c. 4, s. 24(2) ... ... II, p. 1063

Public Utility Transfers and Water Charges Act (c. 15, ss. 5(5), s. 6(4)) ... ... II, p. 1331

Road Traffic Act (c. 52, s. 195(3)) ... ... IV, p. 3260

Road Traffic (Consequential Provisions) Act (c. 54, sch 4, para. 3(3)) ... ... IV, p. 3400

Road Traffic Offenders Act (c. 53, ss. 13(6), 88(3)) ... ... IV, pp. 3273, 3316

Scotch Whisky Act (c. 22, ss. 3(4), 4(*b*)) ... ... II, pp. 1488, 1489

Social Security Act (c. 7, ss. 13(7), 17(*b*), 18(8)) ... ... II, pp. 1109, 1112, 1113

Church of England (Legal Aid and Miscellaneous Provisions) Measure (No. 1, s. 4(6)) IV, p. 3407

Resolution of each House of Parliament required for approval of Orders, regulations etc., Under—

Arms Control and Disarmament (Privileges and Immunities) Act (c. 2, s. 1(2)) ... I, p. 1039

Copyright, Designs and Patents Act (c. 48, ss. 7(4), 66(4)) ... ... IV, pp. 2649, 2670

Road Traffic Act (c. 52, s. 195(5)) ... ... IV, p. 3260

Orders, regulations, reports, statements, drafts etc. to be laid before and approved by resolution of the House of Commons, Under—

Local Government Finance Act (c. 41, ss. 104(8), 106(4)) ... ... III, pp. 2386, 2387

PROTECTION OF ANIMALS (AMENDMENT) ACT 1988: c. 29 ... ... II, p. 1513

§ 1. Disqualification orders on first conviction of cruelty, II, p. 1513.
2. Offences relating to animal fights, II, p. 1513.
3 and Sch. 3. Short title, repeals, commencement and extent, II, pp. 1514, 1515.
Schedule. II, p. 1515.

PROTECTION AGAINST CRUEL TETHERING ACT 1988: c. 31 ... ... II, p. 1522

§ 1. Offence of cruel tethering, II, p. 1522.
2. Short title and commencement, II, p. 1522.

PUBLIC PROSECUTOR. Consent of

Director of Public Prosecutions to institution of proceedings required Under—

Coroners Act (c. 13, s. 17(3)) ... ... II, p. 1301

Merchant Shipping Act (c. 12, ss. 30(8)(*a*), 31(5)(*a*), 32 (substituting s. 27(7)(*a*) to 1970 c. 36)) ... ... II, pp. 1217, 1218, 1220

PUBLIC UTILITY TRANSFERS AND WATER CHARGES ACT 1988: c. 15 ... ... II, p. 1325

Public utility transfers

§ 1. Power to act in relation to proposals for privatisation etc., II, p. 1325.

Water charges

2. Charges by statutory water companies, II, p. 1327.
3. Provisions regulating the charges of all water undertakers, II, p. 1327.
4. Metering trials schemes, II, p. 1328.
5 and Sch. 1. Provisions relating to meters etc., II, pp. 1330, 1333.

Supplemental

6 and Schs. 2, 3. Consequential amendments and repeals, II, pp. 1331, 1339, 1340.
7. Interpretation, II, p. 1332.
8. Short title, commencement and extent, II, p. 1332.
Schedule 1—Provisions relating to meters etc., II, p. 1333.
Schedule 2—Consequential amendments, II, p. 1339.
Schedule 3—Repeals, II, p. 1340.

R

RATE SUPPORT GRANTS ACT 1988: c. 51 ... ... IV, p. 3114

§ 1 and Sch. 1. Total expenditure: 1985-86 to 1988-89, IV, pp. 3114, 3120.
2 and Sch. 1. Multipliers: 1985-86, IV, pp. 3115, 3120.

PART I

TRIAL

Introductory

Trial

Verdict

After conviction

PART II

SENTENCE

Introductory

24. Short title, commencement and extent, IV, p. 2637.
Schedule 1.—Electoral Procedure, IV, p. 2638.
Schedule 2.—Appointment of headteachers, deputies and assistants, IV, p. 2639.
Schedule 3.—Delegation Orders, IV, p. 2641.
Schedule 4.—Minor and Consequential Amendments, IV, p. 2643.

SCOTCH WHISKY ACT 1988: C. 22 ... ... II, p. 1487.

1. Prohibition of production in Scotland of whisky other than Scotch whisky, II, p. 1487.
2. Restrictions on sale of spirits as Scotch whisky, II, p. 1488.
3. Interpretation, orders and consequential amendments, II, p. 1488.
4. Corresponding provision for Northern Ireland, II, p. 1489.
5. Citation, commencement and extent, II, p. 1489.

SEARCH, Powers of, Under—
Copyright, Designs and Patents, Act (c. 48, ss. 109, 200) ... ... IV, pp. 2691, 2737.
Criminal Justice Act (c. 33, s. 142(1)(*c*)) ... ... II, p. 1625.
Education Reform Act (c. 40, s. 215(2)(*a*)) ... ... III, p. 2242.
Finance Act (c. 39, s. 10) ... ... III, p. 1862.

SEIZURE, Powers of, Under—
Copyright, Designs and Patents, Act (c. 48, ss. 100(1)-(5), 196(1)-(4) ... ...
... ... IV, pp. 2686, 2687, 2734, 2735.
Criminal Justice Act (c. 33, ss. 69 (substituting s. 43(1) of 1973 c. 62), 77(10)(11). 142(2). 147 (adding
s. 54(1)(*b*) to 1984 c. 60)) ... ... II, pp. 1573, 1582, 1625, 1628.
Education Reform Act (c. 40, s. 215(2)(*d*) (5)) ... ... III, pp. 2242,2243.
Road Traffic Act (c. 52, s. 176(4)(6)) ... ... IV, p. 3249.

SERVICE BY POST, Under—
Employment Act (c. 19, s. 14(1)) ... ... II, p. 1386.
Housing Act (c. 50, s. 91(2)) ... ... IV, p. 2988.
Housing (Scotland) Act (c. 43, s. 54(*c*)) ... ... III, p. 2549.
Regional Development Grants (Termination) Act (c. 11, s. 1(3)) ... ... II, p. 1191.
Road Traffic Act (c. 52, s. 164(10)) ... ... IV, p. 3242.
Road Traffic Offenders Act (c. 53, ss. 7(*b*), 27(3)) ... ... IV, pp. 3270.
School Boards (Scotland) Act (c. 47, s. 13(3)(*b*)) ... ... IV, p. 2630.

SHERIFF COURT, Jurisdiction Under—
Access to Medical Reports Act (c. 28, s. 8(1) (2)) ... ... II, pp. 1510, 1511.
Copyright, Designs and Patents Act (c. 48, ss. 115(2), 205(2), 232(2)) IV, pp. 2695, 2739, 2750.
Criminal Justice Act (c. 33, s. 142(1)) ... ... II, p. 1625.

SOCIAL SECURITY ACT 1988 C. 7 ... ... II, p. 1101.

Attendance allowance

§ 1. Attendance allowance. II, p. 1101.

Industrial injuries

2 and Sch. 1. Introduction of retirement allowance and other provisions relating to industrial injuries
benefit. II, pp. 1102, 1115.

Family credit

3. Family credit. II, p. 1104.

Young persons

4. Income support and child benefit. II, p. 1104.
5. Annual review of child benefit. II, p. 1106.

Short-term benefits

6. Contribution conditions for short-term benefits. II, p. 1106.
7. Unemployment benefit and occupational pension. II, p. 1106.

Emergency payments

8. Emergency payments by local authorities and other bodies. II, p. 1107.

Earnings factors etc.

9 and Sch. 2. Earnings factors and transfer values. II, pp. 1107, 1115.
10. Increase and reduction of benefit by reference to earnings. II, p. 1107.

T

W